VOLUME 1

GATES ON EVIDENCE
Zambian Theory and Practice

GATES ON EVIDENCE

Zambian theory and Practice

By

Reagan Blankfein Gates, PG Dip Business Management (USW), LL. M (UNISA), LL. B (UNZA), AHCZ

Founding and Managing Partner
Reagan Blankfein Gates Legal Practitioners

Formerly Assistant Senior Research Advocate
Judiciary of Zambia

Formerly Lecturer of International Investment, Contract and Company Law
Cavendish University Zambia

Formerly Lecturer of Pension Law (UG), Insurance Law (PG), Legal Aspects of International Finance (PG)
ZCAS University

First edition published 2023
by Thankerton Publishing Limited
Plot No 30107, Off Manchinchi Road, Olympia Park Lusaka, Zambia

Thankerton Publishing is an imprint of Thankerton Publishing Limited. It has as its objectives, the furtherance of learning, scholarship and edification and enabling authors to bring their work to the masses by leveraging its publication capabilities.

First edition published by Thankerton Publishing Limited 2022

National Archives of Zambia Cataloguing in Publication Data
A catalogue record for this book is available from the National Archives of Zambia

Reagan Blankfein Gates, author.

Gates on Evidence: Zambian Theory and Practice / Reagan Blankfein Gates — First edition.
Evidence (Law)—Zambia.

Typeset in Palatino Linotype by Mwanida Banda: bmwanida@gmail.com

Printed by Amazon Kindle Direct Publishing, USA.

For further information on this and other works by this author and updates generally, visit our homepage: http://thankertonpublishing.com.

In memory of my late daughter
Olivia Kaitlyn Gates
who died during her birth on 4 September 2020

CONTENTS SUMMARY

DETAILED CONTENTS

FOREWORD

By the Hon. Mr. Chief Justice Ernest L. Sakala (Rtd)

At its most elementary characterisation, the practice of law in general and mastering the rules of evidence (and their skillful deployment prior to and during trial) in particular, encompasses conducting research to find pertinent rules of law and then applying those same rules to the specific set of facts and circumstances for which counsel has been hired by the layperson. However, in the Zambian Law of Evidence which is primarily premised on English common law, the legal rules applicable to different sets of circumstances are derived from and premised on numerous sources, including the Constitution, statutory law, the common law and writings of jurists, among others. This complicates what is already an extensive branch of the law which encompasses civil and criminal law on the one hand, and adjectival law on the other.

This book, *Gates on Evidence: Zambian Theory and Practice* introduces first-time readers in the law of evidence, law lecturers, would-be practitioners, legal practitioners as well as magistrates and judges of the Superior Courts, and I dare say, policy-makers to not only what the law has been and is, but also where it should be headed in keeping with contemporary trends in the commonwealth and civil jurisdictions as well as other international fora.

The book also seeks to demystify this somewhat enigmatic branch of the law by employing a pithy style complete with decided cases from this jurisdiction and cases from other jurisdictions which still continue to influence the development of Zambian jurisprudence. Finally, the text illustrates how the different pieces come together and can be used in practice by students, litigants, practitioners and judges as the case may be.

I must conclude this foreword by pointing out that the author has vast work history from several law firms and the public sector where he worked previously. He has experience in corporate, commercial, criminal and civil litigation. From 2013 to 2016 he worked in, the Judiciary of Zambia as a Senior Research Advocate. Some of his duties included drafting opinions on rulings and judgments, conducting general and specific research into legal questions arising from cases before the court, statutory interpretation and general case management. In the end, he established his own law practice, Reagan Blankfein Gates Legal Practitioners in 2018 where he currently serves as Managing Partner.

I, therefore warmly welcome *Gates Evidence: Zambian Theory and Practice* and unreservedly recommend it to all who seek an easy-to-read but detailed text that arguably leaves no stone unturned and caters to the needs of students, lecturers, legal practitioners and judges alike. I do not doubt that it will be a valuable resource to those interested in appreciating the minutiaeof the theory and practice of the law of evidence within the Zambian context.

The Hon. Chief Justice Ernest L. Sakala (Rtd)
Lusaka, July 2022

PREFACE

The law of evidence is at the core of the practice of law leading to litigation. It, therefore, cannot be emphasised enough that a thorough understanding of the subject specifically the rules of admissibility, weight and relevance ought to underpin any practice. It is a truism that cases are won or lost because of a profound appreciation of evidence or lack thereof and the skilful and well-timed deployment thereof and not so much the substantive law or facts that may inform a cause. For an advocate who seeks to make a success of his litigation practice, a working knowledge of the rules and law of evidence is a *sine qua non* to this goal.

Unlike most branches of law, the law of evidence is experienced in real-time during trial and its sometimes-fatal consequences are brought to bear at once. This is because at trial, evidential questions or disputations will arise without warning and without any preparation for them, indeed, *ex improviso,* and must be addressed and determined as and when they arise and not later. Thus, when there is an attempt to introduce objectionable evidence, this must be objected to immediately. Failure to do so at the precise moment when the attempt is made may mean that fatal evidence which would otherwise not have been admissible is admitted. In the same analogy, objections that are raised during trial must be dealt with whether well-founded or not. Courts will listen to the objection in real time and ask counsel on the other side to respond before making a ruling. A failure to effectively deal with evidential issues which arise, as said in the preface to the first edition of *Murphy on Evidence* or more correctly, *A Practical Approach to Evidence*, 'ex improviso, [and] which no human ingenuity could foresee,' may also prove fatal. Whether counsel has the wherewithal to deal with evidentiary issues at trial is a skill that requires to be developed, fined tune and deployed so frequently that it becomes second nature. It must equip counsel with the instinct to immediately detect what is right, that is, what is admissible, relevant and has weight while at the same time, that which is inadmissible irrelevant and lacking in weight based on the common law and statutory rules of the law of evidence as circumscribed by rules of practice and where relevant, substantive law. The significance of the foregoing should not be lost on students, lecturers, legal practitioners and judges.

I would be remiss in my duties if I did not take the time to pay tribute to those that mustered the courage and took on the unenviable task of, prior to this work, authoring texts in the law of evidence from a Zambian vantage point. Professors Hatchard and Ndulo' s text, *The Law of Evidence in Zambia: Cases and Materials* was the first text of its kind to address the subject from a Zambian perspective. This text remains in print today and in many respects continues to be relevant. It stands atop the hill of knowledge as a pioneering work in the sphere law relating to Zambian evidence and explains the rules of evidence by employing the case method. It is without question a ground-breaking piece. It is a text I have relied on in writing this text to continue the journey started by those pioneering learned authors. My learned Colleague, Brian J Mwanza has written and published *Passing the Bar Made Easy: Evidence and Procedure* and deserves commendation for producing a work specifically geared at examination preparation for bar students. It is a text I recommend for this purpose. In the year 2022, my other learned colleague, Bright Chilufya Kaluba, published his work entitled *Evidence Law Practice and Procedure in Zambia.* The significance of this achievement cannot be overemphasised. Given the complexity of the subject, through its rather wide-ranging nature, and practical eminence, Mr. Kaluba has accomplished several things: (i) he has, in so far as authorship in this esoteric branch of the law is concerned, singlehandedly brought scholarship in the Zambian Law of Evidence into the 21st Century, when in the years following the publication by Hatchard and Ndulo, no other text had been published by a Zambian author for well over 37 years; (ii) he has skilfully managed to meld the rules of evidence with the general rules of practice in a manner that makes his text a 'one-stop shop' for the application of rules of evidence within the context of the rules of court much as that other text, by erstwhile Judge Dr Patrick Matibini, SC entitled *Zambian Civil Procedure,* does from a civil procedure perspective; and (iii) he has managed to deploy our most recent jurisprudence not only from our superior courts but from selected commonwealth jurisdictions. In that sense, his work is a *tour de force* in the rarefied field of the Zambian law of evidence. It too is a text to which I have made several references principally because of the last point here made and as such, is deserving of a space in your library.

This first edition of *Gates on Evidence: Zambian Theory and Practice* is an attempt not only to add to the body of knowledge in this respect but also to present this rather complex subject in terms of the theories that underpin and inform the considerations of practice in our courts by whatever name called. To this end, I have endeavoured to supply students, lecturers, legal practitioners, and judges with that which I hope will be considered a repository of the Zambian law of evidence at present and in future. The structure of the text has been designed to help the reader to grasp the core concepts of the subject with ease and serenity. The information is presented in a logical structure with an accessible explanation of concepts in a clear and precise format tinged with the necessary level of detail and background where this is called for. Though the text may go further than most in several respects, and appear dense, it still manages to lay an excellent foundation for learning the law of evidence within the Zambian context irrespective of the reader's motivation for its study. In saying the preceding, Iam alive to the fact that the needs of students and lecturers on the one hand and candidates for the Legal Practitioners Qualifying Examinations Course (offered by the Zambia Institute of Advanced Legal Education (ZIALE)), practitioners and judges on the other, may be varied. Even so, this work, it is hoped, will sit in the middle of the needs of the various sets of audiences at whom it is aimed. A great effort has been made to present the work not only in terms of the thoughts of the author and those of other scholars, but also through the interpretation of the law of evidence as can be evidenced through judicial pronouncements by our courts or put another way, by reference to the *ipsissma verba* of judges. Therefore, the book brings the practical realities of substantive law as taught at university and procedural law as inculcated at ZIALE by including, among other things, cases, extracts from other jurists and contemporary discussion.

While every effort has been made to acknowledge sources in keeping with good academic practice, I apologise if I inadvertently left unacknowledged any sources used in this publication and will gladly take any required measures at the first opportunity.

The law, it is hoped, is as stated on 30 June 2022, though it has been possible to include changes to the law brought about by the enactment of the Children's Code, Act No 12 of 2022. Finally, I take full responsibility for any errors and omissions.

RBG
Lusaka, July 2022

ACKNOWLEDGEMENTS

This book has been under 'construction' for the better part of the last 4 years. During that time, I have become indebted to so many people directly or indirectly. Having started writing the text less than a year after setting up my law practice it became clear to me that this text would demand more than any works I had done previously. The team at Reagan Blankfein Gates Legal Practitioners (RBGLP), past and present have been helpful in this regard by working on instructions that would have been mine to work on otherwise, and in that regard gave me time to dedicate to this project. In this regard I would like to thank Annalise, Melody, Mwima, David, Mary, Tafwakose, Musendeka, Emmanuel, Precious, Martha, Jethro, Andrew, Brighton, Elizabeth, Chileshe, Chansa, Theresa, Bodwell, Hastings and Sinikiwe. I could not ask for a better team. Iam incredibly thankful to Chabala Chilufya our erstwhile office manager at RBGLP who took on, under extreme pressure and my time-bound demands, the unenviable task of type source material on which this work was based. I am further thankful to the erstwhile Chief Justice of Zambia, Mr. Justice Ernest L. Sakala for accepting to write the foreword to this text, Dr. Munyonzwe Hamalengwa for reviewing the entire text and giving helpful suggestions a good number, of which have been taken on board to strengthen the text and for having saved me from some rather obvious and glaring errors. I recognise Diana Musunga Mwewa's comments on chapter one and her helpful suggestions in that regard. The indefatigable and inimitable Mwanida Banda took on the uninviting task of having to typeset this work as she has done with my other previous projects. I am grateful for her attendance to the task in a limited space of time. Jehaph James Nkhata was a great help in ensuring that I did not lose the manuscript in its digital format. I acknowledge without reserve, the moral support I have received from fellow advocates and authors, Brian J Mwanza and Joseph Chirwa in word and deed. I am further grateful to the team at Thankerton Publishing for ensuring that this work saw the light of day. I am also indebted to the many works, including various law reports from several jurisdictions and electronic sites with case summaries, that I have had to rely on and which have been accordingly acknowledged, and some of which have been included in the select bibliography towards the end of this text. Finally, and as always, I am sincerely grateful to Mushota my wife for her support and patience during the subsistence of this project.

LAW REPORT ABBREVIATIONS

ACSR	Australian Corporations and Securities Report
All ER Rep	All England Reports Reprint
All ER (D)	All England Reports
All ER	All England Reports
ALR	Administrative Law Reports
App Cas	Appeal Cases
B & Ad	Barnwell & Adolphus' King's Bench Reports
B & CR	Reports of Bankruptcy & Companies Winding up Cases
BCC	British Company Law and Practice
BCLC	Butterworths Company Law Cases
Ch app	Law Reports Chancery appeals
Ch/D	Law Reports Chancery Division
CLR	Commonwealth Law Reports
Com Cas	Commercial Cases
Comp Cas Mad	Company Cases Madras (India)
Con LR	Construction Law Reports (UK)
CP Law	Reports Common Pleas
CPD	Law Reports Common Pleas Division
DLR	Directors Law Reports
DLR(2d)	Dominion Law Reports Second Series
Dr & Sm	Drewly and Smale's Vice-Chancellor's Reports
EB & E	Ellis, Blackburn & Ellis' Queen's Bench Reports
ER	English Reports
Eq	Equity Cases
Eq Cas Abr	Equity Cases Abridged
EWCA	England and Wales Court of Appeal
EWHC	High Court of England and Wales Reports
Ex Law	Reports Exchequer Division
F	Federal Reporter (USA); Fraser's Court of Session Cases
Fam	Family Law Reports
HCA	Hong Kong Court of Appeal
H Ct of Australia	High Court of Australia
H & M	Henning and Munford's Reports
HK	Ndola High Court Registry (Zambia)
HP	Lusaka High Court, Principal Registry (Zambia)
HPC	High Court for Zambia, Commercial Division
Hare	Hare Law Reports
IRLB	Industrial Relations Law Bulletin
IRLR	Irish Law Reports
JBL	Journal of Business Law
Jur	Juridical Review
KB/D	Kings Bench Division
LSG	Law Society Gazette
LJPC	Law Journal Privy Council
LJQB	Law Journal Queens Bench

LR	Law Reports
LR app Cas	Law Reports appeal Cases
LR Eq	Law Reports Equity
Lloyd's	Lloyd's Law Reports
LS Gaz	Law Society Gazette
Macq	Macqueen's Scotch Appeal Cases
Meg	Megone's Companies Act Cases
NE	North Eastern Reporter
NI/NILR	Northern Ireland Law Reports
NIJB	Northern Ireland Judgments Bulletin
NLJ	New Law Journal
NZCA	New Zealand Court of Appeal
NZLR	New Zealand Law Report
PCC	Palmer's Company Cases
P. Wms	Peere Williams' Reports
QB/D	Queens Bench
QdR/QR	Queensland Reports
Qd Sup Ct	Queensland Supreme Court
R	The Reports in all the Courts
SCLR	Scottish Civil Law Reports
SE	South Eastern Reporter (United States)
SJ	Solicitor's Journal
SLR	Scottish Law Reports
SLT	Scottish Law Reports
SN	Session Notes
Sol Jo	Solicitor's Journal and Reporter
TC	Tax Cases (United Kingdom)
The Times	The Times Reports
TLR	Times Law Reports
UKSC	United Kingdom Supreme Court
VLR	Victorian Law Report
WLR	Weekly Law Reports
WN	Weekly Notes
WR	Weekly Reporter
CAZ	Zambian Court of Appeal (Neutral Citation)
ZMHC	Zambian High Court (Neutral Citation)
ZMSC	Zambian Supreme Court (Neutral Citation)
ZR	Zambia Law Report

TABLE OF CASES

B

C

E

F

G

H

I

J

K

L

M

N

O

P

S

T

U

Z

1

INTRODUCTION

1.1 Introduction

The concept of evidence and its functions is not confined to the courtroom or legal proceedings in general. Be that as it may, '[m]ost lawyers and students think of evidence as a collection of rules governing what facts may be proved in court, what materials may be placed before the court to prove those facts and the form in which those materials should be placed before court. What they may have in mind is not evidence but the law of evidence itself.'[1] It may thus come as a surprise to many a law student and advocates that evidence is simply information that gives the basis for the belief that a particular set of facts is either true or false. Different kinds of people, among them, journalists, historians and, yes, scientists, may seek information relating to the same set of facts for different purposes without the involvement of legal proceedings or trial as an end. The journalist, for his story, the historian to prove a historic linkage to his thesis, and the scientist, to prove the link between the occurrence of a disease and the chemicals to which victims are exposed. None of these preceding scenarios involve proving that a set of facts is accurate in a legal proceeding but they all involve the search for evidence nonetheless. Be that as it may, each of the foregoing persons mentioned will use different methods and procedures depending on the goal of their inquiry at the end of which the truthfulness of a certain set of facts will be proved or disproved.

In what Cohen[2] calls the principle of "universal cognitive competence", there exists the '[…] belief that the truth of facts, whose existence is in question may be established by drawing […inferences] from information that the inquirer has collected for that purpose.'[3] While the foregoing suggests that the concept of evidence is not confined to legal proceedings by whatever name called, it goes too far in implying that there can be absolute certitude as regards the truthfulness of the facts in question. Such is an all too impossible endeavour in an imperfect world. It is never the purpose of the law in general or evidence in particular to seek ultimate truth. It therefore follows that the existence or lack thereof of a fact or facts is predicated on the determination made by the inquirer as set out in the relevant procedure to his inquiry. If this be so, it can be said that the fact(s) has (have) been proved. Thus, for example, in civil proceedings, the matter is said to have been proved on a balance of probability

[1] Murphy P, *Murphy on Evidence* (9th edn OUP 2005) 1.

[2] LJ Cohen, "Freedom of Proof" in WL Twining (ed), Facts in Law (1983) 1, 10; see also JD Jackson, "Theories of Truth Finding in Criminal Procedure: An Evolutionary Approach" (1988) 10 *Cardozo LR* 475.

[3] Dennis I, *The Law of Evidence*(5th edn Sweet & Maxwell 2013) 4.

(or which side has the preponderance of evidence) and in criminal matters, that it has been proved beyond reasonable doubt.[4] However, as Dennis[5] has noted:

> [p]roof is a term with a variable meaning. In legal discourse it may refer to the outcome of the process of evaluating evidence and drawing inferences from it, or it may be used more widely to refer to the process itself and/ or to the evidence which is being evaluated. It is usually clear from the context which meaning is intended.

We must hasten to add that not all issues involving the determination of the truth of facts that are disputed, reach trial. Even in a criminal matter in which a complaint is made to the police, it behooves the police and investigative officers to determine whether the facts before them are such as would form a basis for taking the matter to trial for prosecution of the suspect. If the police determine that there is insufficient evidence to charge a suspect with a crime, they will end the investigation on account of want of evidence. Should the matter reach trial, the law of evidence will then come into its own, even though as we have already seen, and will become apparent later in this text, the law of evidence also carries significance in the pretrial stages of any case.

This chapter provides a brief introduction to the law of evidence in Zambia. We will briefly discuss the following:

(i) Historical development;
(ii) Sources of the law of evidence in Zambia;
(iii) Definition of evidence;
(iv) Terminology;
(v) Characteristics of the law of evidence; and
(vi) Functions of a judge at trial

1.2 Historical development

1.2.1 General

A historical analysis of the development of the law of evidence is important to help the reader put the subject in context. At trial, counsel must be at his sharpest. His grasp of authorities and their skillful deployment, at its purest and his ability to respond in real time, at its swiftest. This is because an authority or set of authorities that may have been decided in a different context from that in *casu*; a different factual matrix; and under different circumstances and law, may be used as authority by opposing counsel to persuade the court to decide in favour of the client whose counsel has adverted to such authorities. A knowledge of the historical development of the law of evidence will assist counsel to counter by arguing for example, that the cited authority or set of authorities was or were now bad law and a relic of history or that the context, factual matrix and circumstances under which the said authority or set of

---

[4] See *Woolmington v DPP* [1935] UKHL 1; [1935] AC 462; 25 Cr App R 72.

[5] Dennis I, *The Law of Evidence*.

authorities was or were decided are markedly different from the case before court.

1.2.2 *Civil cases*

We must go back some 3 centuries to the 18th century to consider the modern development of the modern law of evidence in England. A leading work of that time, Gilbert's *Law of Evidence* shows two ways in which evidence was considered which are strikingly different from the trend today.

The first is that there existed a large body of rules which, unlike today, excluded classes of witnesses and not classes of evidence. While today a witness may give evidence by oath or affirmation, only witnesses who would give evidence on oath were permitted to do so.[6] The oath was a guarantor of truth, and as such, could not be made optional if only to protect society and the court system from lies and paganism or atheism.[7] Nor would those with an interest in the outcome of the case, however trifling, nor a past criminal conviction. A rather curious consequence of this rule was that litigants were barred from testifying in their own cause.

The second, is that there was an emphasis placed on written rather than oral testimony. The rationale for this is quite clear as man was then, and more so now, subject to the treachery of memory and under such circumstances, it was more reliable to look to written evidence rather than oral evidence as the former was less prone to fallibility. The foregoing has attempted to briefly discuss the origin of the law and evidentiary procedure in civil matters. We now turn to evidence in criminal matters.

1.2.3 *Criminal cases*

Allen, Taylor and Nairns[8] note that the position was different in criminal matters[9] which were, according to Professor Glanville Williams,[10] done by jury dating back to the 13th century. Citing John Langbein, Allen *et al*[11] argue that in the early parts of the 18th century anything resembling the adversarial trial we are so accustomed to today was entirely non-existent. Langbein notes: '[...] adversary procedure cannot be defended as part of our historic common law bequest. The criminal lawyer and the complex procedures that have grown up to serve him are historical upstarts.'[12] By adversarial system is meant a system of trial in which the following are present:

---

[6] It was thought at the time that only witnesses with a religious affiliation could be considered responsible members of society and as such credible witnesses. The system could not fathom a witness without a religious or theist inclinations to give credible evidence without professing faith in a higher authority who punished wrong doers or liars. Without accountability to a deity and fear of retribution for false testimony, the theory may have gone, how could one be trusted to tell the truth?

[7] See the comment by Taylor, 1872, Vol II, para 1248.

[8] Allen C Taylor Chris and Nairns J, *Practical Guide to Evidence* (5th edn Routledge 2016).

[9] For a more detailed description see generally, Williams G, *The Proof of Guilt: A Study of the English Criminal Trial* (2nd edn Stevens & Sons London).

[10] Williams G, *The Proof of Guilt.*

[11] Allen C Taylor Chris and Nairns J, *Practical Guide to Evidence.*

[12] Langbein, 1978 at 316.

1.2.3.1 *A Neutral judge who acts as an umpire*[13]

The judge's role is simply to ensure that procedural rules are adhered to, evidence followed, all the while reminding him or herself of the law applicable to the issues, and of the evidence tendered during trial. As argued by counsel in *Priscillar Mwenya Kamanga v Attorney-General, Peter Ng'andu Magande*[14] 'the judge's neutrality and impartiality [are] cardinal in our adversarial system. The judge [is], therefore, not expected to descend into the dust of the conflict.' In *Mumba and Others v The People,*[15] the Supreme Court of Zambia said the following:

> We wish, in passing, to comment on the active participation of the trial court in this case. Whereas, a court may occasionally ask one or two question on matters of clarification, it is very undesirable for it to take active role in examining a witness. This may compromise the court's neutral position in the eyes of the parties i.e., possible bias on the part of the court may not be ruled out.[16]

The position in England & Wales is not any different from that obtaining in this jurisdiction as shown in *R v Sharp*[17] wherein it was held that a judge may ask questions to clarify matters that the judge has not fully appreciated. Further, it has been shown in *R v MM*[18] *by* the EWCA that it is permissible for a Judge to pose questions to a witness, irrespective, for purposes of resolving any ambiguity arising during testimony.

---

[13] A judge must, according to *Porter v Magill* [2002] 1 All ER 465, be a "a fair minded and informed observer."

[14] [2008] 2 ZR 7 (SC).

[15] SCZ Appeal No 92 of 1995 (unreported).

[16] See further, the rather interesting and amusing case of *Gerrison Zulu v Zambia Electricity Supply Corporation Limited* [2005] ZR 39 (SC) where it was observed *inter alia* that '[a]lthough a trial Judge has the Judicial discretion to ask questions during the trial, he should not use his discretion to insert himself into the substantive questioning during the trial. The trial Judge should ask questions only to clear a point.' Further, that '[t]he learned Judge in this case went beyond the normal intervention. The discretion to ask questions must be enlightened by intelligence and learning, controlled by sound principles of law, of firm courage combined with calmness of mind, freedom from partiality, not swayed by sympathy, nor warped by prejudice nor moved by any kind of influence, save alone the overwhelming passion to do what is just. and finally that '[t]he Judge part when evidence is being given is to listen to it; asking question, only when it is necessary to clear a point, to see to it that the advocates behave themselves; and keep to the rules laid down by law' to exclude irrelevancies and discourage repetitions; to make sure by wise intervention that he follows the points made by the advocates; and assess their worth; and at the end make up his mind where the truth lies;' see further, *R v Oliva* [1965] 3 All ER 116; *R vRoberts* [1984] 80 Cr App R 89; As to recusal of judge if it appears that he/she may not be seen as impartial because of his previous association with the dispute or any of the disputants, see *Metropolitan Properties Co (FGC) Ltd v Lannon and Others* [1968] 3 All ER 304; *Mwenya v The People* [1973] ZR 261 (HC); *William Harrington v Dora Siliya and The Attorney General* (SCZ Judgment No 14 of 2011).

[17] [1993] 3 All ER 225.

[18] [2011] EWCA Crim 1291 at 35.

1.2.3.2 *The litigants themselves are responsible for producing the proof and the quality of the proof upon which the court will determine the case at hand*

On this, Lord Denning's dictum in *Jones v National Coal Board*[19] is instructive: '[a] judge is not allowed in a civil dispute to call a witness whom he thinks might throw light on the facts. He must rest content with the witnesses called by the parties.'[20] This facet of the adversarial system presents constraints on freedom of proof. This is because it invariably permits parties to not bring before the court matters or evidence that may be adverse to their cause. This may, but usually includes matters passing between parties and their attorneys which may not be adduced as evidence under the guise of attorney-client privilege.[21] As Lord Wilberforce has noted in *Air Canada v Secretary of State for Trade,*[22] '[i]t often happens, from the imperfection of evidence, or the withholding of it, sometimes by the party in whose favour it would tell if presented, that an adjudication has to be made which is not, and is known not to be, the whole truth of the matter.'

1.2.3.3 *An intricate set of rules exists to manage not only the trial in general but the actions of counsel in particular*

The goal of any trial is to ensure not only that justice is done but that it is seen to be done. To ensure that this is so, an intricate set of rules discussed throughout this text has been developed to manage the trial and counsel with this goal in mind.

1.2.3.4 *Issues between the disputants are determined by each party having their day in court*

A trial is a confrontation between two sides in which, as we have said under point 1, the judge acts as umpire. It is in this sense that any party be it the defendant (in civil matters) or the accused (in criminal matters) has a constitutional right to confront his accuser and the evidence against him (that is to say, the right to cross examine prosecution witnesses and test prosecution evidence). To do so, he must have adequate notice of the allegations against him.[23] He has the right to counsel of his own choosing.

---

[19] [1975] 2 All E R 155.

[20] Quoted by counsel in *Priscillar Mwenya Kamanga v Attorney-General, Peter N'gandu Magande* [2008] 2 ZR 7 (SC); See *Bozy Simutenda v Attorney-General and Mathews Kakungu Siame* (2019/CCZ/001); Even so, it is important to produce all the relevant evidence at trial as appellate courts will only admit fresh evidence under very limited circumstances upon demonstrating to the appellate court that the fresh evidence could not be found despite it being searched for with due diligence, that said evidence is credible, that it will have significance on the final determination of the matter: *Ernest Chiombe v Sampa Kasongo Mulilo Chiombe* (CAZ Appeal No 12 of 2016); *Zambia Revenue Authority v Hitech Trading Company Limited* (SCZ Judgment No. 40 of 2000) [2000] ZMSC 67.

[21] Discussed in more detail in chapter 14.

[22] [1983] 2 AC 394 at 438.

[23] See *A v United Kingdom* (2009) 49 EHRR 29; *Secretary of the Home Department v AF* (No 3) [2009] UKHL 28; [2009] 3 All ER 643.

The foregoing speaks to what may be termed procedural justice. This was exemplified in the case of *Woolmington v DPP.*[24] Reginald Woolmington was a 21-year-old farm labourer from Castleton, Dorset. He married 17-year-old Violet in August 1934. She gave birth to his child in October. Shortly after, the couple fell out. On 22 November 1934, Violet left the matrimonial home to live with her mother. On 10 December, Reginald stole a double-barrelled shotgun and cartridges from his employer and sawed off the barrel. He then cycled to his mother-in-law's house where he shot and killed Violet. He was arrested on 23 January 1935 and was charged with murder.

Woolmington's defence was that he did not intend to kill and thus lacked the necessary mens rea. Specifically, he claimed that he had wanted to win her back and planned to scare her by threatening to kill himself if she refused. He had attempted to show her the gun which discharged accidentally, killing her instantly.

At the Bristol Assizes, Judge Swift ruled that the case was so strong against him that the burden of proof was on him to show that the shooting was accidental. The jury deliberated for 69 minutes. On February 14, 1935 he was convicted (and automatically sentenced to death).

On appeal to the Court of Criminal Appeal, his defence team argued that the judge had mis-directed the jury. Lord Justice Avory refused leave to appeal, relying on a passage of Foster's *Crown Law* (1762):

> In every charge of murder, the fact of killing being first proved, all the circumstances of accident, necessity, or infirmity are to be satisfactorily proved by the prisoner, unless they arise out of the evidence produced against him; for the law presumeth the fact to have been founded in malice, until the contrary appeareth. And very right it is, that the law should so presume. The defendant in this instance standeth upon just the same foot that every other defendant doth: the matters tending to justify, excuse, or alleviate, must appear in evidence before he can avail himself of them.

The Attorney-General[25] then gave a *fiat*[26] to allow an appeal to the highest court, the House of Lords. The issue brought to that court was whether the statement of law in Foster's *Crown Law* was correct when it said that if a death occurred, it is presumed to be murder unless proved otherwise. Stating the judgment for a unanimous Court, Viscount Sankey gave his now famous "Golden thread" speech:

---

[24] [1935] AC 462 *per* Lord Sankey, adopted in *Murono v The People* [2004] ZR 207 where the Supreme Court restated the principle as follows: '[i]n criminal cases, the rule is that the legal burden of proving every element of the offence charged and consequently, the guilt of the accused lies from beginning to end on the prosecution. The standard of proof is high; It was observed in *Lambert* [2001] UKHL 37, [2002] 2 AC 545 at 82 *per* Lord Hope of Craighead that '[i]t is generally accepted that Woolmington changed the law as to the burden of proof in the case of common law defences such as self-defence and non-insane automatism;' see also *Kalaluka Musole v The People* (1963-1964) ZR and NRLR 173; *The People v Kamwandi* [1972] ZR 131.

[25] Sir Thomas Inskip.

[26] Intervention on paper.

> Throughout the web of the English Criminal Law one golden thread is always to be seen that it is the duty of the prosecution to prove the [accused's] guilt subject to [...] the defence of insanity and subject also to any statutory exception. If, at the end of and on the whole of the case, there is a reasonable doubt, created by the evidence given by either the prosecution or the [accused] ... the prosecution has not made out the case and the [accused] is entitled to an acquittal. No matter what the charge or where the trial, the principle that the prosecution must prove the guilt of the [accused's] is part of the common law of England and no attempt to whittle it down can be entertained.[27]

The case for civil matters is for one to set out their case from the outset. Order VI r 1 of the HCR[28] requires that a writ of summons be accompanied not only by a statement of claim but a list and description of documents, list of witnesses and letter of demand acknowledged by the defendant or affidavit of service attesting to the service of the letter of demand which shall set out the claim and circumstances surrounding the claim. A Writ of Summons without the said documents will not be accepted. Similarly, Order XI r 1(b) of the HCR[29] requires that a memorandum of appearance be accompanied by a defence and counter claim (if any), together with a list of documents to be relied on by the defendant at trial and list of witnesses to be called by the defendant at trial. With specific reference to criminal proceedings in the Subordinate Courts, there is no requirement for pretrial pleadings in criminal matters which results in ambushes and elongation of criminal cases. In the High Court, however, there is a requirement for depositions which may loosely be said to amount to pretrial proceedings. Be that as it may, that an accused person should know the charge he has to answer to enable him confront his accuser, is a fundamental facet of due process. It has been said in *Robert Ndecho and Another v R*[30] that:

> [i]t would be a denial of natural justice that [the accused] should be burdened with the fear that during the course of his trial he might have to defend himself against other offences disclosed by the evidence of which he had received no notice and no particulars. Such a departure from the basic principle of English common law will have to receive express legislative sanction before this court will countenance it.

Having one's 'day in court' through the device of confrontation thus requires, among other things, the filing of pleadings as required by rules of court; that the witness be present in court in person,[31] that he gives oral testimony

---

[27] [1935] AC 462 at 481. Professor Sir John Smith QC, a leading Criminal Lawyer is quoted as saying of this decision: "Never, in my opinion, has the House of Lords done a more noble deed in the field of criminal law than on that day." - 38 NILQ 224; Brian Block, Hostettler J, *Famous Cases: Nine Trials That Changed the Law* (Waterside Press, 2002) 51.

[28] As amended by SI No 58 of 2020 (High Court Amendment Rules, 2020).

[29] As amended by SI No 58 of 2020 (High Court Amendment Rules, 2020).

[30] 18 E.A. App R Vol viii 171.

[31] Which includes appearing by video conference.

through examination in chief, that the testimony be rigorously tested via cross-examination to determine not only the reliability of the evidence but the witness's credibility.[32]

We will return to the issue of adversarialism in the next chapter. Going back to the 13th into the 17th century, professor Williams[33] tells the story of a biased jury against the accused person, wherein the accusations were made by the grand jury which jury also sat to determine the fate of the accused at trial. In 1352 the British Parliament passed legislation to allow an accused person to challenge any of the jurors that had indicted him from sitting on the jury setting the stage for the removal of jurors who might be prejudiced against the accused person at trial.

While initially the jury was constituted of judges and witnesses, it soon became apparent that the knowledge that these juries possessed was flawed, punctuated by gossip, and enveloped by prejudice. Curiously, the solution was to call witnesses on behalf of the prosecution but still none for the accused persons.[34] In instances where the prosecution was unrepresented, and this was not unheard of, the judge had latitude to provide advice and comment throughout the subsistence of the trial; to informally control the jury[35] which, by the way, never retired to consider the verdict but openly discussed in court allowing the judge to give guidance where he deemed it proper. The accused was confined to his prison cell until the date of trial making it impossible for him to gather any witnesses in support of his case.

After 1640 those accused of felonies deserving capital punishment upon their guilt being proved were grudgingly permitted the right to call witnesses. This can be seen from the fact that such witnesses could not give evidence on oath which was predicated on the notion, as we have already seen above, that witnesses that contradicted prosecution witnesses were lying.

Professor Williams[36] opines thus:

> [....] There were no rules of evidence, and the early state trials show men being condemned on the written accusations of witnesses with whom they were not confronted.
>
> Not only hearsay evidence but evidence of the accused's bad character was freely admitted to prove his guilt, and the witnesses against him were frequently perjured-as was sometimes shown by later official investigations, which however came too late to save the wretched defendant from his face. The evidence of accomplices, taken after they had been tortured in prison, or while they were under

---

[32] *Kafuti Vilongo v The People* [1977] ZR 423.

[33] Williams G, *The Proof of Guilt.*

[34] A report is made on *Throckmorton's case* 1554 1 St. Tr. 869 at 885 where, when the accused asked a friend who was present at his trial to contradict the evidence for the prosecution, one commissioner shockingly retorted: "Go your ways, Fitzwilliams, the court hath nothing to do with you. Peradventure you would not be so ready in a good cause."

[35] Normally a body of twelve people sworn to reach a verdict in a legal case based on the evidence submitted at trial. The Jury system does not exist in Zambia.

[36] Williams G, *The Proof of Guilt* 6.

> postponed sentence of death, and so subject to the greatest temptation to say whatever might be required of them, whether true or not, was admitted without reservation or caution of any kind.

Nor could an accused person initially cross-examine witnesses on anything including legal points. The accused had no access to counsel while he had to face off against eminent members of the bar representing the prosecution. He had no advance knowledge of the evidence against him nor was he given access to law texts or other authority nor did he have the benefit of notes to refer to.[37] By mid-1730 however, counsel was permitted to appear before court on behalf of some accused persons.[38]

1.2.4 *Changes brought about in the 19th Century*

From 1836, counsel who represented felony accused clients were, with the backing of statutory authority, permitted to directly address the jury on their client's behalf doing away with their participation being down to the discretion of the judge.[39]

It may come as a surprise to many that this intolerable situation was vociferously defended by eminent men of the bench. The 1836 reform for full representation of the accused by counsel of their choosing was resisted by 12 of the 15 judges of the time.[40] Chief Justice Coke went so far as to claim in *Thomas*[41] that'the Jesuits have much slandered our common law in the case of trials of offenders for their lives...first, the testimonies and proofs of the offence ought to be clear and manifest, as there can be no defence of it; secondly, the court ought to be instead of counsel for the prisoner.' Of course, this language and the behaviour it was calculated to defend was shocking for a Chief Justice to support and was only meant to perpetuate an incredibly unfair heavy-handed system if only to retain, for the justices of that time, the perceived influence

[37] Here again, the scandalous proceedings in *Throckmorton's case* 1554 1 St. Tr. 869 give us a window not only into the tragedy that were early trials but also of a rare accused person who had a treason charge decided in his favour. Defending himself as a lay person, he referred to certain statutes on a question of the law and asked the judges to refer to them to which the judges retorted: 'there should be no books brought at his desire; 'the judges,' so the report goes, 'knew the law with such sufficiency that it was unnecessary to refer to any books in question.' Thanks to his retentive memory and quick wit which enabled him to recite statutes from memory as well as decided cases he had heard in parliamentary debates, prosecution's counsel grumbled under his breath: "If I had thought you had been so well furnished with Book Cases I would have been better provided for you." Others were not so gifted and their fate was a foregone conclusion even before the trial commenced.

[38] Initially, they were only permitted to examine and cross examine witnesses.

[39] Allen C Taylor Chris and Nairns J *Practical Guide to Evidence;* on the variety in the mode of trial see Anon, 1833, pp 276-77; Cottu, 1822, pp 88-90; Williams G, *The Proof of Guilt* 8.

[40] See *A century of Law Reform* (London 1901) 50 cited in Williams G, *The Proof of Guilt 8;* Allen C Taylor Chris and Nairns J *Practical Guide to Evidence* posit that '[t]he intervention of counsel in criminal trials may have been accepted initially because judges were aware of the imperfections which existed in criminal procedure [....]

[41] (1613) 2 Bulstrode 147, 80 ER 1022; Co. *Inst.* iii 29, 137.

they had on the system as it stood then. It was, as Carlos Ghosn[42] said of his motivations for fleeing Japan on 31 December 2019 where he was facing criminal charges[43] for Beirut, Lebanon,[44] "a rigged system where guilt [was] presumed, and discrimination [against the accused was] rampant and basic human rights [which we now take for granted in criminal trials] were denied." However, it reflected the attitudes of that time precisely incarnated in the following lines quoted in professor William's work:[45]

> For lest the sturdy criminal false witnesses should bring
> His witnesses were not allowed to swear to anything,
> And lest the wily advocate the Court should overreach
> His advocate was not allowed the privilege of speech
> Yet, such was the humanity and wisdom of the law
> That if in the indictment there appeared to be a flaw,
> The Court assigned him Counsellors to argue on the doubt,
> Provided he himself had first contrived to point it out.
> Yet lest their mildness should by some be craftily abused,
> To show him the indictment they most steadfastly refused,
> But still that he might understand the nature of the charge,
> The same was, in the Latin tongue, read out to him at large![46]

Before the advent of the 19th century, a viewpoint was held by many that case/ common law was a system of reasoning deduced from legal maxims. As a corollary then, court decisions were evidence of such maxims. To that end, it was thought that compared to the rigidity and slow nature of statutory law as promulgated by parliament, the common law had, inherently built into it, flexibility which rendered itself to being used as a tool for reform. While we talk of binding precedent today, there was little scope for this before the 19th century because the three established common law courts each developed its own system and when married with an inadequate case reporting system, one is not left wondering why this was so. Even so, given that there had been established a long line of similar decisions on certain matters in the law, it was accepted that such could indeed form binding precedent. A change thus occurred which also affected the law of evidence, that is to say, no longer was common law considered to be in a constant flexible state of development and simply a system of reasoning but that court decisions shaped the material of

[42] Carlos Ghosn, KBE is a Brazilian-born businessman who also has French and Lebanese nationality. As of January 2020, and this writing, he was an internationally wanted fugitive from the Japanese criminal Justice system. Ghosn has served as the CEO of Michelin North America, chairman and CEO of Renault, chairman of AvtoVAZ, chairman and CEO of Nissan, and chairman of Mitsubishi Motors. Ghosn was also chairman and CEO of the Renault–Nissan–Mitsubishi Alliance, a strategic partnership among those automotive manufacturers through a complex cross-shareholding agreement.

[43] For what prosecutors and former colleagues termed a 'pervasive culture of financial misconduct and raiding of corporate resources for personal gain.

[44] A country with no extradition treaty with Japan.

[45] Williams G, *The Proof of Guilt* 10.

[46] See Thayer, *Preliminary Treatise on Evidence* (London) Chaps. 2-5; Stephen, *History of the Criminal Law* i 221, 225-8, 254 *et seq.*, 284, 326, 331-7, 358, 382; Holdsworth, *History of English Law* ix 216-7, 232 *et seq.*

the law.[47] To bring certitude to the system of evidence, courts had to come up with a rule-based system encased in each decision they made as it related to the law of evidence as we will see later in this text.

There were a few differences between the developments in civil evidence and criminal evidence. As regards civil evidence, the goal of achieving certitude was attained by a detailed rule-based system of exclusions aided by an institutional framework[48] that permitted for a unified approach to civil appeals.[49] The same could not be said of criminal evidence for which judges were hampered in their efforts to develop a detailed unified approach due to want of an appeal framework available in civil evidence until 1907 when the English Court of Criminal Appeals was established. This coming into being of the Court of Criminal Appeals enabled the criminal evidence to develop in the same manner as its civil counterpart. The modern English law of criminal evidence is predicated on three pillars namely statute law, common law and discretionary powers.

The 19th century also witnessed the gradual removal of religious based restrictions relating to the competence of witnesses we discussed earlier. The Common Procedure Act 1854 provided for affirmations as an acceptable alternative to taking religious oaths. An amendment to the Act saw the foregoing extended to criminal proceedings in 1861. The Evidence Further Amendment Act 1869 permitted those refused to take an oath other than for religious reasons to do so by way of affirmation.

Also removed during the 19th century were witness disqualifications based criminal convictions[50] or having a financial interest in *casu*. The Evidence Amendment Act 1851[51] provided that parties, unless otherwise stated, were competent witnesses in civil trial. The Criminal Evidence Act 1898 provided that an accused person was competent to give evidence in all criminal matters. As this is a text mainly targeted at a Zambian audience, it is only proper to turn to sources of the Zambian law of evidence, which we now do.

1.3 Sources of the law of evidence in Zambia

The law of evidence in Zambia must be seen within the context of the country's legal-political history in general phased out as follows:

(i) the rule by the British South African country (a commercial company chartered to act as an agent of the British government;
(ii) the direct rule by the British government; and
(iii) the reign of the federation of the two Rhodesias (Northern and Southern Rhodesia) and Nyasaland.

---

[47] See Simpson, 1981; Sugarman, 1986, pp 26-61; Best, 1870, pp 146-47; Twining, 2006, 45-75.

[48] Evans, 1987, 64; Allen, 1964, pp 219-21.

[49] There remains very little use for this system in England following the abolition of trial by jury in civil cases. Though it can be deduced from the design of the central sitting area for justices and counsel at the Supreme Court building at Lusaka that this was the idea, there clearly has never been any use for the jury system in the Zambian jurisdiction where the judge/magistrate has always been both the trier of fact and law.

[50] Lord Denman's Act 1843 which also made substantial changes permitting interested persons to testify.

[51] Also known as Lord Brougham's Act.

While no attempt is made to delve into the detailed historic issues relating to the law of evidence in Zambia, it is perchance, good to note that the law of evidence in this jurisdiction, like England, is premised on legislation; case law (local and foreign); discretion of the courts; and customary law.[52]

1.3.1 *Legislation*

While in no way a starting point, legislation is none the less an indispensable part of the law of evidence. Large parts of the law of evidence are governed by statutory law including the Constitution,[53] the Evidence Act, 1968[54] the Evidence (Bankers' Books) Act, 1964[55] among others. We consider a few pertinent statutes which in themselves do not constitute an exhaustive list simply because almost every statute in this jurisdiction invariably contains provisions relating to the taking of evidence. It is quite impossible due to time and space in a work of this kind to consider each and every statute in this context. The best approach is to be on the lookout for such provisions whenever one is dealing with a matter relating to a specific statute.

1.3.1.1 *The Constitution*[56]

The Constitution is the Supreme law of the land.'[...] any other written law, (including, *inter alia,* the Evidence Act, 1967[57]) customary law and customary practice that is inconsistent with its provisions is void to the extent of the inconsistency.'[58] It follows that the law and procedure relating to evidence in Zambia ought to be consistent with, is premised on, and draws its validity

[52] We will not, in this work concern ourselves with this source as 'the application of customary law is restricted to cases arising solely out of customary law disputes and these are heard in local courts. In any event, in customary procedure, all evidence, including hearsay, is admissible as the issue for the court is always one of the weight to be attached to a particular item of evidence.' – Hatchard J and Ndulo M, *The Law of Evidence in Zambia: Cases and Materials*(SAIPR 2013) 2.

[53] Act No 2 of 2016.

[54] Chapter 43 of the Laws of Zambia as amended by Act No 3 of 1968.

[55] Chapter 44 of the Laws of Zambia.

[56] Act No 2 of 2016.

[57] Chapter 43 of the Laws of Zambia.

[58] Article 1(1) of Act No 2 of 2016; See *Bank of Zambia v Caroline Anderson and Andrew W. Anderson* (SCZ Judgment No 13 of 1993); *Attorney-General v Mooka Mubiana* (SCZ Judgment No 38 of 1993); *Yonnah Shimonde and Freight and Liners and Meridien BIAO Bank (Z) Ltd* (SCZ Judgment No 7 of 1999); In *Christine Mulundika v Mulundika and 7 Others v People* (SCZ Judgment 25 of 1995) [1996] ZMSC 26, the appellant challenged the constitutionality of certain provisions of the Public Order Act Cap 104, especially section 5(4). The H challenge followed on the fundamental freedoms and rights guaranteed by arts 20 and 21 of the Constitution. A subsidiary challenge related to the exemption of certain office-holders from the need to obtain a permit. It was held (by a majority, Chaila JS dissenting) inter alia that s 5(4) of the Public Order Act Chapter 104 contravened Articles 20 and 21 of the Constitution and was null and void; As to which court(s) now has (have) jurisdiction over constitutional matters, see Article 128(1) of the Constitution as amended by Act No 2 of 2016, see *The People v The Director of Public Prosecutions Ex-parte Rajan Mathani* (SCZ Selected Judgment No 21 of 2019) which explains the delineation between the role of the High Court (Bill of Rights actions); The Constitutional Court (All requiring its interpretation as envisaged under Article 128 of the Constitution, and not reserved for the High Court); The Supreme Court: All appeals relating to Bill of Right actions commenced in the High Court, and all constitutional matters that are not the kind envisaged under Article 128 of the Constitution.

from the constitution as does the legislative authority with which parliament is clothed.[59] Part III of the Constitution guarantees fundamental freedoms which a court cannot, in the consideration of evidence, ignore. For example, Article 18(7) provides that '[a] person who is tried for a criminal offence shall not be compelled to give evidence at the trial.'[60]We will return to Article 18(7) several times over the course of this text. Discussing the issue of confession evidence in *Chola and Others v The People*,[61] Ngulube DCJ as he then was opined as follows:

> The presumption of innocence and the rule against an accused being compelled to incriminate himself have resulted in the requirement that the prosecution must prove beyond reasonable doubt that a confession was made freely and voluntarily. The danger which the system of criminal justice guards against by this requirement is that even the innocent could be forced to make unreliable self-incriminating statements which have been induced. A demonstration which amounts to a confession must equally be proved to have been given freely and voluntarily after due caution.

1.3.1.2 *The Evidence Act, 1967*[62]

This is supposed to be the centrepiece of legislation relating to evidence in Zambia but is woefully inadequate. It is only 9 sections long and offers nothing much in terms of defining terms.[63] This inadequacy has led to frustration by counsel and attempts to persuade the courts to supplement the provisions of the Act in rather ingenious and dexterous ways. Such a scenario arose in *Kabwe Transport Company Ltd v Press Transport (1975) Limited.*[64] This was an appeal from a judgment of a judge of the High Court. The facts of this case were that the plaintiff's driver was driving on the Lusaka-Kabwe Road. The driver was driving an articulated vehicle consisting of one mechanical horse and three trailers. In the opposite direction the defendant's driver was driving a truck towing a trailer behind it. There was a collision as a result of which two persons in the plaintiff's vehicle were killed but two persons in the defendant's vehicle survived.The case arose out of a claim by the plaintiff against the defendant for negligent driving as a result of which damage was caused. The relevant parts of the judgment appear *obiter* in the judgment of Gardner JS, as he then was:

[59] See generally, Articles 62(2), 63(1) and 66.

[60] See *Simutenda v The People* (SCZ Judgment No 40 of 1975); *Davis Chiyengwa Mangoma v The People* (SCZ Appeal No 217 of 2015).

[61] [1988 – 1989] ZR 163.

[62] Chapter 43 of the Laws of Zambia. We will discuss the Act later in the text.

[63] Only four terms are defined under s 2: "business" includes any public transport, public utility or similar undertaking carried on by a local authority and the activities of the General Post Office; "document" includes any device by means of which information is recorded or stored, and books, maps, plans and drawings; "proceedings" includes arbitration and references, and "court" shall be construed accordingly; "statement" includes any representation of fact, whether made in words or otherwise.

[64] [1984] ZR 43 (SC).

> A further point on a matter of law has been raised by Mr. Jearey, that is whether it is improper in the courts of this country for evidence of previous criminal convictions to be produced. Mr. Jearey has referred us to the case of *Hollington v F. Hewthorn & Company Limited*[65], in which it was held that a certificate of a conviction cannot be tendered in evidence in civil proceedings. The *ratio decidendi* of that case was that the criminal proceedings were not relevant and that they were *"res alios inter acta."* The case of *Siwingwa v Phiri,*[66] which was decided in this country by a High Court judge resulted in a ruling that the Civil Evidence Act 1968 applied in this country by virtue of s 10 of the High Court Act,[67] which provides that the practice and procedure at present prevailing in the courts of England and Wales shall apply in this country. Mr. Jearey argued that that provision can be called in aid in default of any legislation in Zambia. There is in fact in Zambia an Evidence Act, Cap [43], in which there is no provision for the calling of evidence in criminal proceedings to assist a decision in civil proceedings. This Court has been asked to decide whether the provisions of section 10 of the High Court Act enables courts in this country to decide that there is an absence of legislation when, in this specific instance, there is a definite act dealing with evidence. We have no hesitation in finding that, where there is a specific act dealing with a matter of law, such as evidence, in this country, there is no default of legislation as envisaged by section 10 of the High Court Act. The result, therefore, is that there is no provision for convictions in criminal trial to be referred to and taken note of in a civil trial [....][68]

We will return to the foregoing later in this text in our discussion on judgments as evidence of facts on which they were predicated.

1.3.1.3 The Evidence (Bankers' Books) Act, 1964[69]

In terms of s 3 of the Evidence (Bankers' Books) Act,[70] 'a copy of any entry in a banker's book shall in all legal proceedings be received as *prima facie* evidence of such entry, and of the matters, transactions and accounts therein recorded.' It was held in *Joseph Knox Simwanza v The People,*[71] that on a proper reading of the Act the object of the Act was to oblige bankers to produce documents which they would otherwise not have been obliged to produce under the law relating to the relationship between the banker and his customer [....]' The Court was '[...] satisfied that the absence of a search warrant [did] not make documents from the bank inadmissible by statute.'

---

[65] [1943] 2 All ER 35.

[66] [1979] ZR 145.

[67] Chapter 27 of the Laws of Zambia.

[68] *Siwingwa v Phiri* [1979] ZR 145 disapproved; an analysis of the two decisions all things considered is given in chapter 24.

[69] Chapter 44 of the Laws of Zambia.

[70] Chapter 44 of the Laws of Zambia.

[71] [1985] ZR 15 (SC).

1.3.1.4 *The Electronic Communications and Transactions Act*[72]

The preamble to this Act provides that it is an Act meant to do the following:

> [...] provide a safe and effective environment for electronic transactions; promote secure electronic signatures; facilitate electronic filing of documents by public authorities; provide for the use, security, facilitation and regulation of electronic communications and transactions; promote legal certainty and confidence, and encourage investment and innovation in relation to electronic transactions; regulate the National Public Key Infrastructure; repeal and replace the Electronic Communications and Transactions Act, 2009; and provide for matters connected with, or incidental, to the foregoing.

Of special interest is s 96, which provides that despite any other written law, evidence which is obtained by means of an interception effected in contravention of [the] Act, is not admissible in any criminal proceedings except with the leave of the court, and in granting or refusing such leave, the court shall have regard, among other things, to the circumstances in which it was obtained, the potential effect of its admission or exclusion on issues of national security and the unfairness to the accused person that may be occasioned by its admission or exclusion.

1.3.1.5 *The Children's Code*[73]

The relevant part of this Act is s 78 for our purposes which provides for competency, that is to say, whether the witness in question, specifically, a child of tender years, is competent to give sworn/unsworn testimony at trial. Same is discussed later in this text under para 1.8.2.2(ii) *et seq.*

1.3.1.6 *The Authentication of Documents Act*[74]

The relevance of the Act to the law of evidence can be deduced from the name itself. In terms of s 2, "authentication", when applied to a document, means the verification of any signature thereon.[75] The term "document" means, according to s 2, any deed, contract, power of attorney, affidavit, or other writing, but does not include an affidavit sworn before a Commissioner of the High Court. The section and its ambit of application has been discussed in the recent Court of Appeal decision in *Johanes Kenneth Siogopi (T/A Nam Transport Co. A*

[72] No 4 of 2021.

[73] Chapter 53 as amended by Act No 3 of 2011.

[74] Chapter 75 of the Laws of Zambia; see also The Electronic Communications and Transactions Act, 2009 (repealed) (General) Regulations, 2011 for similar provisions; ss 2 and 8; *OTK Limited v Amanita Zambiana Limited, Diego Gan-Maria Casilli, Amanita Premium Oils Limited, Amanita Milling Limited* 2005/HPC/0199; Shuko Willie Chunga v Hildah Nukwase Mwanza Chunga and 2 Others 2022/HPF/D/053.

[75] *Lumus Agricultural Services Company (Z) Ltd v Gwembe Valley Development Company Ltd (In receivership)* [1999] ZR 1; see also *Johannes Kenneth Siogopi (T/A Nam Transport Co. A Partnership) v The Director of Public Prosecutions Appeal* No 196/2020.

Partnership) v The Director of Public Prosecutions.[76] The question that fell to be determined was whether the documents produced by the appellant namely, (i) An extract from the Registrar of Business Names from the Republic of Tanzania; (ii) A Motor vehicle Registration Cards for the Truck and Trailer [in question]; and (iii) A Bill of Lading, required authentication within the context of s 2. According to the Court, when such a question arises, a judge of first instance needs to consider the documents before him in light of the definition given under s 2 in order to determine whether the documents in question come within the purview of s 2.

(i) How documents executed outside Zambia are to be authenticated

In terms of s 3, [a]ny document executed outside Zambia shall be deemed to be sufficiently authenticated for the purpose of use in Zambia if-(a) in the case of a document executed in Great Britain or Ireland it be duly authenticated by a notary public under his signature and seal of office; (b) in the case of a document executed in any part of Her Britannic Majesty's dominions outside the United Kingdom it be duly authenticated by the signature and seal of office of the mayor of any town or of a notary public or of the permanent head of any Government Department in any such part of Her Britannic Majesty's dominions; (c) in the case of document executed in any of Her Britannic Majesty's territories or protectorates in Africa it be duly authenticated by the signature and seal of office of any notary, magistrate, permanent head of a Government Department, Resident Commissioner or Assistant Commissioner in or of any such territory or protectorate; (d) in the case of a document executed in any place outside Her Britannic Majesty's dominions (hereinafter referred to as a "foreign place") it be duly authenticated by the signature and seal of office-(i) of a British Consul-General, Consul or Vice-Consul in such foreign place; or (ii) of any Secretary of State, Under-Secretary of State, Governor, Colonial Secretary, or of any other person in such foreign place who shall be shown by the certificate of a Consul or Vice-Consul of such foreign place in Zambia to be duly authorised under the law of such foreign place to authenticate such document.

The interpretation of s 3 has been considered in several Zambian authorities. In *Lumus Agricultural Services Company (Z) Ltd v Gwembe Valley Development Company Ltd (In receivership)*[77] the Supreme stated as follows:[78]

> It is quite clear from section 3 that if a document executed outside Zambia is authenticated as provided, then it shall be deemed or presumed to be valid for use in this country and if it is not authenticated then the converse is true that it is deemed not to be valid and cannot be used in the country.

---

[76] Appeal No 196/2020; Following *Lumus Agricultural Services Company (Z) Ltd v Gwembe Valley Development Company Ltd (In receivership)*[1999] ZR 1.

[77] [1999] ZR 1 (SC); See *Zalawi Haulage Limited v Goldman Insurance Limited* (Appeal 45 of 2019); [2019] ZMCA 239 (16 December 2019).

[78] [1999] ZR 1 (SC) at 8.

It has been said by the Court of Appeal in *Johanes Kenneth Siogopi (T/A Nam Transport Co. A Partnership) v The Director of Public Prosecutions*[79]that '...executing a document implies signing it appropriately and the listed documents in the definition are validated by the signatures of parties thereto or their deponents.'

In *Anuj Kumar Rathi Krishnan v The People*[80] it was observed thus:

> This section demonstrates the need for a document executed outside Zambia to be notarised for it to be valid for use in Zambia...since the said documents were deposed to outside Zambia, they should have been authenticated in accordance with section 3 of The Authentication of Documents Act,[81] for purpose of validating them, for use in Zambia. In view of the fact that the documents were not so authenticated, the trial Court erred at law in admitting them in evidence.

The case of *Steak Ranches International BV v Steak Ranches Ltd*[82] as discussed here below relates to an interlocutory application by the defendant to dismiss the action by the plaintiff on a preliminary point of law. It is made pursuant to Orders 14A R 1 and 33 rule 7, RSC. By the said application, the defendant sought an order to dismiss the action in question upon the determination of the following points of law, namely:

1 Authentication issue
   (a) Whether or not the Franchise agreement was executed in South Africa;
   (b) Whether it was authenticated for use in Zambia and
   (c) If the Franchise Agreement was not authenticated then whether the Franchise Agreement can be used before the Court in Zambia
2 *Conveniens* Forum issue
   (a) Whether or not the dispute between the parties should be heard in South Africa due to the fact that the governing law of the Franchise Agreement as stated in clause u is South African law for the enforcement of any alleged right.

In deciding against the defendant, Mutuna J (as he then was) observed as follows:

> The effect of the principles highlighted in the foregoing authorities is that a document executed outside Zambia needs to be authenticated in accordance with Section 3 of the Act if it is to be valid for use in Zambia. However, the facts of the *Lumus*[83] and *Rhati*[84] cases indicate

[79] Appeal No 196/2020.
[80] HPA/11/2010 (Unreported).
[81] Chapter 75 of the Laws of Zambia.
[82] (HP 183 of 2011), [2012] ZMHC 25.
[83] [1999] ZR 1 (SC).
[84] HPA/11/2010 (Unreported).

> that the persons challenging the use of the documents executed outside the country were strangers or third parties to the documents. In the former case the First Appellant who challenged the use of a notice of appointment of receivers executed outside Zambia was not a party to the document. The same was the case in the *Rhati*[85] case, in which the appellant challenged the validity of documents to which he was not a party and which emanated from the United Kingdom. In this matter the defendant who is challenging the use of the agreement is a party to the agreement. To this extent the two cases, of *Lumus*[86] and *Rhati*[87] are distinguished from this matter. Further in, my considered view, where the party challenging a document executed outside Zambia is a party to the document and he does not, as is the case in this matter, dispute that he executed the document or the validity of the signatures thereon, there is no need for such a document to be authenticated in accordance with Section 3 of the Act to make it valid for use in Zambia. My finding is arrived at by revisiting the definition and indeed purpose of authentication of document as highlighted in Section 2 of the Act and *Black's Law Dictionary*, which is for purposes of validating or proving that the document is genuine. The parties to this matter have both confirmed that they executed the agreement and have not disputed this fact nor the genuiness of the agreement and as such it is to be taken as a genuine document which does not need authentication. In making the foregoing finding I have also revisited the other holding by the Court in the *Lumus*[88] case at page 9 which states that; "We agree with the decision that an instrument which is not attested or registered is valid between the parties but ineffective against other persons..."

In *African Alliance Pioneer Master Fund v Vehicle Insurance Ltd*,[89] the Supreme Court, as in other cases considered under this head, took time to consider the implications of s 3 and further, the ramifications emanating from the use of documents in want of authentication contrary to s 3.

As a final point, the Zambian Court of Appeal has noted in *Zalawi Haulage Limited v Goldman Insurance Limited*,[90] '[...] that there exist exceptions to the authentication rule. The exception is to the effect that the document which is not attested is valid and binding between the parties but is ineffective against

---

[85] HPA/11/2010 (Unreported).

[86] [1999] ZR 1 (SC).

[87] HPA/11/2010 (Unreported).

[88] [1999] ZR 1 (SC).

[89] (SCZ Appeal No 21 of 2011); *Rainbow Tourism Group (Z) Ltd v Savoy Hotel Ltd and Another* (Selected Judgment No 13 of 2017).

[90] (Appeal 45 of 2019), [2019] ZMCA 239 (16 December 2019) at J 12.

other persons.[91] Further, that '[t]he authentication rule is designed to prevent mischief. It is not there to aid or enable mischief.'[92]

(ii) Authentication by magistrate in Her Britannic Majesty's dominions

According to s 4, [n]otwithstanding anything in the last preceding section contained, it shall be sufficient authentication of a document executed in any part of Her Britannic Majesty's dominions for use in Zambia which affects or relates to property not exceeding in value or amount four hundred kwacha if there be appended to or endorsed on such document a statement signed by a magistrate of the part of Her Britannic Majesty's dominions in which such document is executed-(a) that the person executing such document is a person known to him; or (b) that two other persons known to him have severally testified before him that the person executing such document is a person known to each of them.

(iii) Saving as to affidavit sworn before a Commissioner of the High Court

It is provided in s 5 that [a]n affidavit sworn before and attested by a Commissioner of the High Court beyond the confines of Zambia shall require no further authentication and may be used in all cases and matters in which affidavits are admissible as freely as if it had been duly made and sworn to within Zambia.

1.3.1.7 The Penal Code[93]

The relevant provisions are to be found in s 57(1) which provides as follows:

> Any person who - Offences in respect of seditious practices
> (a) does or attempts to do, or makes any preparation to do, or conspires with any person to do, any act with a seditious intention;
> (b) utters any seditious words;
> (c) prints, publishes, sells, offers for sale, distributes or reproduces any seditious publication;
> (d) imports any seditious publication, unless he has no reason to believe that it is seditious;

[91] *Lumus Agricultural Services Company Limited and Others vs Gwembe Valley Development Company Limited (In receivership)* (SCZ No 1 of 1999); *Anuj Kumar Rathi Krishnan v The People* HPA/ 11/ 2010; *African Alliance Pioneer Master Fund v Vehicle Finance* Appeal No 21 of 2011; *Steak Ranches v Steak Ranches* Appeal No 219/2012; *National and Grindlays Bank Limited v Vallabhji and Others* [1966] 2 ALL ER 62 6; AS to there being no need for authentication of a power of attorney where execution occurs in this jurisdiction and the addresses of the donor and donee happen to be in Zambia, see *Samuel Chitungu v Ansom Enterprises Ltd* (2015/HP/0815).

[92] At J 14.

[93] Chapter 87 of the Laws of Zambia.

> is guilty of an offence and is liable for a first offence to imprisonment for seven years or to a fine not exceeding six thousand penalty units or to both; and any seditious publication shall be forfeited.

In terms of s 57(2), '[a]ny person who, without lawful excuse, has in his possession any seditious publication is guilty of an offence and is liable for a first offence to imprisonment for two years or to a fine not exceeding three thousand penalty units or to both, and for a subsequent offence to imprisonment for five years; and such publication shall be forfeited.

In terms of s 59, '[n]o person shall be convicted of an offence under section fifty-seven on the uncorroborated testimony of one witness.'

1.3.1.8 *The Criminal Procedure Code*[94]

Part V of the Criminal Procedure Code[95] provides for the mode of taking and recording evidence in inquiries and trials in the following terms:

(i) Evidence to be taken in presence of accused

In terms of s 191, '[e]xcept as otherwise expressly provided, all evidence taken in any inquiry or trial under this Code shall be taken in the presence of the accused, or, when his personal attendance has been dispensed with, in the presence of his advocate (if any).

(ii) Reports by medical officers in public service

By s 191A(1), [t]he contents of any document purporting to be a report under the hand of a medical officer employed in the public service upon any matter relevant to the issue in any criminal proceedings shall be admitted in evidence in such proceedings to prove the matters stated therein: Provided that-(i) the court in which any such report is adduced in evidence may, in its discretion, cause the medical officer to be summoned to give oral evidence in such proceedings or may cause written interrogatories approved by the court to be submitted to him for reply, and such interrogatories and any reply thereto purporting to be a reply from such person shall likewise be admissible in evidence in such proceedings;(ii) at the request of the accused, made not less than seven days before the trial, such witness shall be summoned to give oral evidence.

According to s 191A(2), [t]he court may presume that the signature on any such report is genuine and that the person signing it held the office and qualifications which he professed to hold as appearing in the report at the time when he signed it.

---

[94] Chapter 88 of the Laws of Zambia.

[95] Chapter 88 of the Laws of Zambia; see reference in *Anuj Kumar Rathi Krishna v The People* (SCZ Judgment No 19 of 2011).

By s 191A(3), [n]othing in this section contained shall be deemed to affect any provision of any written law under which any certificate or other document is made admissible in evidence, and the provisions of this section shall be deemed to be additional to, and not in substitution of, any such provision.

It is provided under s 191A(4), that for the purposes of this section, the expression "medical officer" shall mean a medical practitioner registered as such under the Medical and Allied Professions Act.

(iii) Evidence of analyst

According to s 192(1), [w]henever any fact ascertained by any examination or process requiring chemical or bacteriological skill is or may become relevant to the issue in any criminal proceedings, a document purporting to be an affidavit relating to any such examination or process shall, if purporting to have been made by any person qualified to carry out such examination or process, who has ascertained any such fact by means of any such examination or process, be admissible in evidence in such proceedings to prove the matters stated therein: Provided that-

(i) the court in which any such document is adduced in evidence may, in its discretion, cause such person to be summoned to give oral evidence in such proceedings or may cause written interrogatories to be submitted to him for reply, and such interrogatories and any reply thereto purporting to be a reply from such person shall likewise be admissible in evidence in such proceedings;

(ii) at the request of the accused, made not less than seven days before the trial, such witness shall be summoned to give oral evidence.

By s 192(2), it is provided that [n]othing in this section contained shall be deemed to affect any provision of any written law under which any certificate or other document is made admissible in evidence, and the provisions of this section shall be deemed to be additional to, and not in substitution of, any such provision.

(iv) Evidence of photographic process

According to s 193, [w]here any photograph is or may become relevant to the issue in any criminal proceedings, a document purporting to be an affidavit made by the person who processed such photograph shall be admissible in evidence in any such proceedings as proof of such processing: Provided that the court in which any such document is produced may, if it thinks fit, summon such person to give evidence orally.

Evidence of plans, theft of postal matters and goods in transit on railways: It is provided under 194(1) that [i]n any criminal proceedings, a certificate purporting to be signed by a police officer or any other person authorised under rules made in that behalf by the Chief Justice, by statutory instrument, and certifying that a plan or drawing exhibited thereto is a plan or drawing made by him of the place or object specified in the certificate and that the plan or drawing is correctly drawn to a scale so specified and clearly indicates, where applicable, the direction of North in relation to the places or objects depicted thereon, shall be evidence of the relative positions of the things shown on the plan or drawing.

According to s 194(2), [i]n any proceedings for an offence consisting of the stealing of goods in the possession of the Zambia Railways, or receiving or retaining goods so stolen knowing them to have been stolen, or for the theft of postal matter under the Penal Code, or for an offence under the Postal Services Act, a statutory declaration made by any person-(a) that he despatched or received or failed to receive any goods or postal packet or that any goods or postal packet when despatched or received by him were in a particular state or condition; or (b) that a vessel, vehicle or aircraft was at any time employed by or under the Postmaster-General for the transmission of postal packets under contract; shall be admissible as evidence of the facts stated in the declaration.

By s 194(3), [n]othing in this section shall be deemed to make a certificate or statutory declaration admissible as evidence in proceedings for an offence except in a case where and to the extent to which oral evidence to the like effect would have been admissible in those proceeding.

Finally, in terms of s 194(4), [n]othing in this section shall be deemed to make a certificate or any plan or drawings exhibited thereto or a statutory declaration admissible as evidence in proceedings for any offence-(a) unless a copy thereof has, not less than seven days before the hearing or trial, been served on the person charged with the offence; or (b) if that person, not later than three days before the hearing or trial or within such further time as the court may in special circumstances allow, serves notice in writing on the prosecutor requiring the attendance at the trial of the person who signed the certificate or the person by whom the declaration was made, as the case may be; or (c) if the court before whom the said proceedings are brought requires the attendance at the trial of the person who signed the certificate or the person by whom the declaration was made, as the case may be.

(v) Interpretation of evidence to accused or his advocate

According to s 195(1), [w]henever any evidence is given in a language not understood by the accused, and he is present in person, it shall be interpreted to him in open court in a language understood by him. By s 195(2), [i]f he appears by advocate, and the evidence is given in a language other than the English language, and not understood by the advocate, it shall be interpreted to such advocate in the English language. Finally, according to s 195(3), [w]hen documents are put in for the purpose of formal proof, it shall be in the discretion of the court to cause to be interpreted as much thereof as appears necessary.

(vi) Remarks respecting demeanour of witness

In terms of s 196, [a] magistrate shall record the sex and approximate age of each witness, and may also record such remarks (if any) as he thinks material respecting the demeanour of any witness whilst under examination.

1.3.1.9 The Subordinate Courts Act[96]

(i) Summoning witnesses

According to s 41, in any suit or matter, and at any stage thereof, a Subordinate Court, either of its own motion or on the application of any party, may summon any person within Zambia to attend to give evidence, or to produce any document in his possession or power, and may examine such person as a witness, and require him to produce any document in his possession or power, subject to just exceptions.

(ii) Compelling Attendance-Penalty on non-attendance

In terms of s 42, [i]f the person summoned as in the last preceding section provided, having reasonable notice of the time and place at which he is required to attend, after tender of his reasonable travelling expenses to and from the Subordinate Court, fails to attend accordingly, and does not excuse his failure to the satisfaction of the court, he shall, independently of any other liability, be guilty of a contempt of court, and may be proceeded against by warrant to compel his attendance.

(iii) Refusal to be sworn or to give evidence

It is provided under s 43, [i]f, in any suit or matter, any person, whether appearing in obedience to a summons or brought up under warrant, being required to give evidence, refuses to take an oath, or to answer any question

[96] Chapter 28 of the Laws of Zambia; As regards original jurisdiction as respects civil matters, see ss 3,11 and 20 of Cap 28; see as regards original jurisdiction in criminal matters, schedule 5 to s 11 of the Criminal Procedure Code Chapter 88 of the Laws of Zambia which provides for matters triable by the High Court, which by implication means all matters not listed there, are reserved for trial by the Subordinate Courts except in matters where the court is required to conduct a preliminary inquiry; As to power of the Subordinate Court after conducting such an inquiry see *The People v Petrol Zambwela*, 17th December, 2002; [2002] ZMHC: The accused appeared before the Subordinate Court of the First Class for the Kalomo District on a charge of murder contrary to section 200 of the Penal Code, Cap. 87 of the Laws of Zambia. The matter was before the Magistrate for a Preliminary Inquiry as the case is triable by the High Court. The prosecutor applied for the withdrawal of the case. The learned magistrate in allowing the application invoked the provisions of Section 88 (b) of the Criminal Procedure Code, Chapter 88 of the Laws of Zambia and acquitted the accused. The matter was reviewed through the monthly returns. It was held that s 280 of the Criminal Procedure Code Chapter 88 of the Laws of Zambia empowers a Subordinate Court to discharge an accused person if at the close of the inquiry the evidence is insufficient to commit the accused for trial. There is no provision for an acquittal before a Subordinate Court; This portion of our discussion does not cover procedural issues that touch on evidence. They are discussed elsewhere in this text. Where not specifically dealt with, readers are referred to, Rules of Court applicable in this jurisdiction, and texts such as Matibini P, *Zambian Civil Procedure;* Kaluba BC, *Evidence Law,* in so far as it touches on procedural matters relating to the law of evidence; *Rules of Court;*and specialised texts of that sought.

lawfully put to him, or to produce any document in his possession or power, and does not excuse his refusal to the satisfaction of a Subordinate Court, he shall, independently of any other liability, be guilty of a contempt of court, and the court may, by warrant, commit him to prison, without hard labour, there to remain for not more than one month, unless he, in the meantime, consents to take an oath, or to answer duly, or to produce any such document, as the case may be; and he shall also be liable to a fine not exceeding seven hundred and fifty penalty units.

(iv) Bystander may be required to give evidence

In terms of s 44, [a]ny person present in court, whether a party or not in a cause or matter, may be compelled by a Subordinate Court to give evidence, or produce any document in his possession or in his power, in the same manner and subject to the same rules as if he had been summoned to attend and give evidence, or to produce such document, and may be punished in like manner for any refusal to obey the order of the court.

(v) Prisoner may be brought up by warrant to give evidence

By s 45, [a] magistrate may issue a warrant under his hand to bring up any person confined as a prisoner under any sentence or otherwise, to be examined as a witness in any suit or matter depending in any Subordinate Court, and the gaoler, or person in whose custody such prisoner shall be, shall obey such warrant, by bringing such prisoner in custody and delivering him to an officer of the court.

(vi) Allowances to witnesses

According to s 46, [i]t shall be lawful for the presiding magistrate, in civil as well as criminal proceedings, to order and allow to all persons required to attend, or examined, as witnesses, such sum or sums of money as shall seem fit, as well as for defraying the reasonable expenses of such witnesses as for allowing them a reasonable compensation for their trouble and loss of time. But it shall not be lawful, in any criminal proceeding, for any person to refuse to attend as a witness or to give evidence, when so required by process of the court, on the ground that his expenses have not been first paid or provided for.

(vii) How allowances are defrayed

In terms of s 47, [a]ll sums of money allowed under the provisions of the last preceding section shall be paid, in civil proceedings, by the party on whose behalf the witness is called, and shall be recoverable as ordinary costs of suit, if a Subordinate Court shall so order, and, in criminal proceedings, they shall, where not ordered to be paid by the party convicted or the prosecution, be paid out of the general revenues of the Republic.

(viii) Inspection

It is provided in s 48, that [i]n any cause or matter, a Subordinate Court may make such order for the inspection by the court, the parties or witnesses of any real or personal property, the inspection of which may be material to the determination of the matter in dispute, and may give such directions with regard to such inspection as to the court may seem fit.

(ix) Witnesses as to African customary law

In terms of s 49, [a] Subordinate Court may, in any cause or matter in which questions of African customary law may be material to the issue, call as witnesses thereto chiefs or other persons whom the court considers to have special knowledge of African customary law.

(x) A person not entitled to inspection or copy of record of evidence

According to s 50, [a] person shall not be entitled, as of right, at any time or for any purpose, to inspection or a copy of the record of evidence given in any case before any Subordinate Court, or to a copy of the notes of such court, save as may be expressly provided by any rules of court.

(xi) Evidence before Subordinate Courts, recording of

By s 51(1), [i]n every case heard before a Subordinate Court, and at every stage thereof, the presiding magistrate shall, save as hereinafter provided, take down in writing the oral evidence given before the court: Provided that, should the presiding magistrate, in any case, find himself temporarily incapacitated from taking down such evidence, it shall be lawful for the magistrate to direct that such evidence shall be taken down by the clerk of the court or officer performing his duties in court.

According to s 51(2), [b]efore any clerk of the court or other officer shall take down in writing any oral evidence as aforesaid, an oath shall be tendered to and taken by such clerk of the court or officer for the accurate and faithful recording of such oral evidence, according to the true purport and meaning thereof; and such oath shall be in such terms as to such presiding magistrate may seem apt and sufficient: Provided always that a clerk of the court or officer performing his duties in court, who shall once have duly taken such oath, shall not again be required to take such oath in respect of the same or of any subsequent case.

By s 51(3), [a]fter taking such oath as aforesaid, the clerk of the court or other officer shall take down in writing such oral evidence in manner as aforesaid, under the supervision and control of the presiding magistrate, who may, at any time before appending his signature to such writing, amend anything therein which he may consider requires to be amended; and, before so appending his signature, such magistrate shall peruse and examine such writing, and satisfy himself that it is, in substance, an accurate and faithful record of the oral evidence given.

In terms of s 51(4), [n]otwithstanding the foregoing provisions of this section, the Chief Justice may authorise that the oral evidence given before a specified Subordinate Court, either generally or in a particular case, may be recorded in shorthand or by any other system of verbatim reporting and afterwards transcribed into longhand. Any such authority given by the Chief Justice shall be subject to the following conditions:(a) no person shall be employed for the purpose of so recording or transcribing unless the magistrate is satisfied that such person is competent, reliable and suitable for the purpose; (b) before any person so records and transcribes, or so records or transcribes, he shall take an oath for the faithful and accurate recording and transcription, or recording or transcription, according to the true purport and meaning of the evidence. Such oath shall be in such terms as the Chief Justice may direct.

(xii) Perjury

According to s 52(1), [a] Subordinate Court of the first or second class, if it appears to it that a person has been guilty of perjury in any proceeding before it, may-(a) after calling upon such person to show cause why he should not be punished as for a contempt of court, commit him to prison for any term not exceeding six months, with or without hard labour, or fine him any sum not exceeding one thousand five hundred penalty units, or impose both such penalties upon him, in each such case as for a contempt of court; or (b)after preliminary inquiry, commit him for trial upon information for perjury, and bind any person by recognizance to give evidence at such trial.

In terms of s 52(2), [o]n imposing any penalty as for a contempt of court under this section, a Subordinate Court shall, forthwith, send a copy of the proceedings to the High Court. The High Court may, thereupon, without hearing any argument, vary or set aside the order of the Subordinate Court.

In terms of s 52(3), [e]xcept where the order of the Subordinate Court is set aside by the High Court, any penalty imposed under this section shall be a bar to any other criminal proceedings in respect of the same offence.

1.3.1.10 The High Court Act[97]

The High Court Act provides for matters relating to evidence in PART VII, that is, ss 27 to 38 as follows:

[97] Chapter 27 of the Laws of Zambia; As regards original jurisdiction with respect to civil matters, see also Articles 133 and 134 of the Constitution as amended by Act No 2 of 2016; As regards original jurisdiction with respect to criminal matters, see schedule 5 to s 11 of the Criminal Procedure Code Chapter 88 with respect to matters triable by the High Court. This portion of our discussion, like the one before it, does not cover procedural issues that touch on evidence. They are discussed elsewhere in this text. Where not specifically dealt with, readers are referred to, Rules of Court applicable in this jurisdiction, and texts such as Matibini P, *Zambian Civil Procedure;* Kaluba BC, *Evidence Law,* and specialised texts of that sought.

(i) Summoning and compelling attendance of witnesses

According to s 27(1), [i]n any suit or matter, and at any stage thereof, the Court, either of its own motion or on the application of any party, may summon any person within the jurisdiction to give evidence, or to produce any document in his possession or power, and may examine such person as a witness and require him to produce any document in his possession or power, subject to just exceptions.

By s 27(2), [i]f any person summoned as in subsection (1) provided, having reasonable notice of the time and place at which he is required to attend and after tender of his reasonable travelling expenses to and from the Court, fails to attend accordingly and does not excuse his failure to the satisfaction of the Court, he shall, independently of any other liability, be guilty of a contempt of court, and may be punished therefor, and may be proceeded against by warrant to compel his attendance.

According to s 27(3), [n]othing in this section contained shall be construed so as to make it lawful in any criminal proceeding for any person to refuse or fail to attend as a witness or to give evidence on the ground that his expenses have not first been paid or provided for.

(ii) Refusal to be sworn or to give evidence

It is provided in s 28 that [i]f, in any suit or matter, any person, whether appearing in obedience to a summons or brought up under warrant, being required to give evidence, refuses to take an oath or make an affirmation in lieu thereof, or to answer any question lawfully put to him, or to produce any document in his possession or power, and does not excuse his refusal to the satisfaction of the Court, he shall independently of any other liability, be guilty of a contempt of court, and the Court may, by warrant, commit him to prison, there to remain until he consents to take the oath or make an affirmation, or to answer duly, or to produce any such document, as the case may be.

(iii) Evidence of bystander

According to s 29, [a]ny person present in court, whether a party or not in a cause or matter, may be compelled by the Court to give evidence or to produce any document in his possession or power, in the same manner and subject to the same rules as if he had been duly summoned to attend and give evidence or to produce such document, and may be dealt with under the provisions of section twenty-eight for any refusal to obey the order of the Court.

(iv) Evidence of prisoners

In terms of s 30, [a] Judge may issue a warrant under his hand to bring up any person confined as a prisoner under any sentence or otherwise, to be examined as a witness in any cause or matter depending in the Court, and the gaoler or person in whose charge such prisoner may be shall obey such warrant by bringing up such prisoner in custody and delivering him to an officer of the Court: Provided that this section shall not apply in any case to which section sixty-four of the Prisons Act applies.[98]

(v) Allowances to witnesses

According to s 31(1), [i]t shall be lawful for the Court, in civil as well as criminal proceedings, to order and to allow to all persons required to attend or be examined as witnesses such sum of money as the Chief Justice may, by rule made with the concurrence of the Minister responsible for finance, prescribe, as well for defraying the reasonable expenses of such persons as for allowing them a reasonable compensation for their trouble and loss of time.

In terms of s 31(2), [a]ll sums of money allowed under the provisions of this section shall be payable, in civil proceedings, by the party on whose behalf the witness is called, and shall be recoverable as ordinary costs of suit unless the Court shall otherwise order, and in criminal proceedings they shall, where not ordered to be paid by the person convicted or the prosecutor, be paid out of the general revenues of the Republic.

(vi) Commissioners of the Court

It is provided in s 32(1), that a Judge may, in respect of any proceedings in the Court, appoint any person or persons to be a Commissioner or Commissioners for taking affidavits and declarations and receiving production of documents, or for taking and receiving the evidence of witnesses on interrogatories or otherwise. According to s 32(2), [a]ny order of the Court or of a Judge for the attendance and examination of witnesses or the production of documents before any Commissioner appointed under the provisions of this section and within the jurisdiction of the Court shall be enforced in the same manner as an order to attend and be examined or produce documents before the Court.

(vii) Inspection

By s 33, [i]n any cause or matter, the Court may make such order for inspection by the Court, the parties or witnesses of any real or personal property the inspection of which may be material to the determination of the matter in dispute, and may give such directions with regard to such inspection as to the Court may seem fit.

(viii) Evidence of African customary law and assessors thereof

According to s 34(1), [t]he Court may, in any cause or matter in which questions of African customary law may be material to the issue- (a) call as witnesses thereto chiefs or other persons whom the Court considers to have special knowledge of African customary law; (b) call any such chiefs or persons to its

[98] Chapter 97 of the Laws of Zambia.

assistance as assessors of African customary law; (c) consult, if it shall think fit and, to such extent as to it seems proper, give effect to any book or publication which the Court shall consider to be an authority on African customary law.

It is provided in s 34(2), that [i]t shall be the duty of assessors called under the provisions of subsection (1) to advise the Court on all matters of African customary law which may arise in the cause or matter concerned, and to tender their opinions to the Court on such cause or matter generally, but in reaching its decision the Court shall not be bound to conform to such opinions.

By s 34(3), [a]ssessors called under the provisions of subsection (1) shall be paid such fees and allowances as the Chief Justice may, by rule made with the concurrence of the Minister responsible for finance, determine, and such fees and allowances shall be paid out of the general revenues of the Republic unless the Court, in any particular civil cause or matter, orders that they shall be costs in the proceedings concerned.

(ix) Record of evidence, etc

In terms of s 35(1), it is provided that [s]ave as hereinafter in this section provided, no person shall be entitled as of right at any time or for any purpose to inspection or a copy of a record of evidence given in any case before the Court, or to a copy of the notes of the Court, save as may be expressly provided by rules of court. By s 35(2), any party to any cause or matter before the Court shall, on payment of such fee as may be prescribed by rules of court, be entitled to a copy of the record of evidence given in such cause or matter. In terms of s 35(3), [t]he Director of Public Prosecutions shall, without payment of fee, be entitled to the record of evidence given in any criminal proceedings before the Court.

(x) Oaths, etc

According to s 36(1), [w]henever an oath is required to be taken under the provisions of this or any other law, or in order to comply with any such law, the following provisions shall apply: (a) The person taking the oath shall hold, if a Christian, a copy of the Gospels of the Four Evangelists or of the New Testament, or, if a Jew, a copy of the Old Testament, in his uplifted right hand, or, if he be physically incapable of so doing, he may hold such copy otherwise, or, if necessary such copy may be held before him by the officer administering the oath, and shall say or repeat after such officer the words "I swear by Almighty God that . . ." followed by the words of the oath prescribed by law or by the practice of the court, as the case may be: Provided that if any person desires to take the oath in the form and manner in which an oath is usually administered in Scotland, he shall be permitted to do so. (b) If the person taking the oath is neither a Christian nor a Jew, he may take the oath in any manner which he declares to be, or accepts as, binding on his conscience or which is lawful according to any law, and in particular he may do so by raising his right hand and saying or repeating after the officer administering the oath the words "I swear by Almighty God that . . ." followed by the words of the oath prescribed by law or by the practice of the court, as the case may be: Provided that if the person taking the oath is physically incapable of raising his right hand, he may say or repeat the words of the oath without raising his right hand. (c) If any person shall express any objection to taking an oath or desires to make an affirmation in lieu thereof, he may make such affirmation without being further questioned as to the grounds of such objection or desire, or otherwise, and in such case there shall be substituted for the words "I swear by Almighty God" aforesaid the words "I do solemnly and sincerely affirm" and such consequential variations of form as may be necessary shall thereupon be made.

In terms of s 36(2), [n]otwithstanding any other provision contained in this section, any person may be required to make an affirmation in the form specified in paragraph (c) of subsection (1) if it is not reasonably practicable to administer an oath to him in the manner appropriate to his religious belief, and for the purposes of this subsection "reasonably practicable" means reasonably practicable without inconvenience or delay.

By s 36(3), [w]here any oath has been duly administered and taken, the fact that the person to whom such oath was administered had, at the time of taking such oath, no religious belief, or had a religious belief other than that to which the oath taken normally applies, shall not for any purpose affect the validity of such oath.

It is provided in s 36(4), that [f]or the purposes of [s 36], "officer" means any person duly authorised by law to administer oaths, and shall include any Assistant Registrar, Deputy Assistant Registrar and official interpreter administering an oath in the presence of a Judge or the Registrar or other person authorised by any law to administer oaths.

(xi) Recording of proceedings

According to s 37, [t]he proceedings in any cause or matter before the Court shall be taken down and recorded in such manner as may be prescribed by rules of court.

(xii) Perjury

By s 38(1), [t]he Court, if it appears to it that a person has been guilty of perjury in any proceeding before it, may, after calling upon such person to show cause why he should not be punished as for a contempt of court, commit him to prison for any term not exceeding six months, with or without hard labour, or fine him any sum not exceeding one hundred penalty units, or impose both such penalties upon him, in each such case as for a contempt of court. According to s 38(2), [a]ny penalty imposed under this section shall be a bar to any other criminal proceedings in respect of the same offence.

1.3.1.11 *The Constitutional Court Act*[99]

Matters relating to evidence under theConstitutional Court Act[100] are provided for under Part III of the Act, that is ss 13 through 22 in the following terms:

(i) Summoning and compelling attendance of witnesses

In terms of s 13(1), [t]he Court may, in any suit or matter in which the Court is exercising original jurisdiction— (a) summon a person to give evidence or produce a document in that person's possession or power; and (b) examine a person as a witness and require the person to produce any document in that person's possession or power. (2) The Court may, at any stage of a suit or matter, exercise the power in subsection (1) on its own motion or on the application of a party to the suit or matter. (3) A person who is summoned and given reasonable notice of the time and place at which that person is required to attend, in accordance with subsection (1), but fails to attend without reasonable excuse commits contempt of court and may be proceeded against by warrant to compel that person's attendance.

(ii) Refusal to be sworn or to give evidence

According to s 14(1), [a] person who appears before the Court in obedience to a summons or under warrant and being required to give evidence refuses to— (a) take an oath; (b) answer a question lawfully put to that person; or (c) produce a document in that person's possession or power; commits contempt of court and may, by warrant, be committed to prison by the Court.

In terms of s 14(2), [a] person committed to prison under subsection (1) shall remain in prison until that person consents to take the necessary oath, answer the question or produce the document required under that subsection. (3) A person's liability under subsection (1) does not affect any other liability that may attach to that person for a contravention of that subsection.

(iii) Evidence of bystander

By s 15, [a] person who is present in Court, whether as a party in a matter or not, may be compelled by the Court to give evidence or to produce a document in that person's possession or power, in the same manner and subject to the same rules as if that person had been duly summoned to attend and give evidence or to produce that document, and may be dealt with under the provisions of section fourteen for any refusal to obey the order of the Court.

---

[99] Chapter 27 of the Laws of Zambia; As to original jurisdiction in civil (constitutional) matters, see also Article 120(2) of the Constitution as amended by Act No 2 of 2016; Like the preceding two portions, this portion of our discussion, does not cover procedural issues that touch on evidence. They are discussed elsewhere in this text. Where not specifically dealt with, readers are referred to, Rules of Court applicable in this jurisdiction, and texts such as Matibini P, *Zambian Civil Procedure;* Kaluba BK, *Evidence Law,* and specialised texts of that sought.

[100] Chapter 27 of the Laws of Zambia; this portion does not cover procedural issues that touch on evidence. They are discussed elsewhere in this text. In any case, a more detailed approach is taken in texts such as Matibini P, *Zambian Civil Procedure* and specialised texts of that sought.

(iv) Evidence of prisoner

In terms of s 16, [a] judge may issue a warrant under the judge's hand to bring up a person confined as a prisoner under a sentence or otherwise, to be examined as a witness in any matter pending in the Court, and the jailer or person in whose charge that prisoner is shall obey the warrant by bringing up the prisoner in custody and delivering that prisoner to an officer of the Court.

(v) Allowances to witnesses

In terms of s 17(1), [t]he Court may order, and allow to be paid to a person required to attend or be examined, as a witness, such sum of money as the Chief Justice may, with the approval of the Minister responsible for finance, prescribe for defraying the reasonable expenses of that person. According to s 17(2), [a] sum of money allowed under subsection (1) shall be paid by the party on whose behalf the witness is called, and shall be recoverable as ordinary costs of the hearing unless the Court orders otherwise.

(vi) Inspection

By s 18, [t]he Court may, in any matter, make an order for inspection by the Court, the parties or witnesses, of any real or personal property, the inspection of which may be material to the determination of the matter in dispute, and may give such directions with regard to that inspection as the Court considers necessary.

(vii) Evidence of Zambian customary law and assessors

It is provided under s 19(1) that the Court may, in any matter in which a question of Zambian customary law is material to the matter— (a) call as a witness a person whom the Court considers to have special knowledge of Zambian customary law; (b) call a chief or person, to the Court's assistance, as an assessor of Zambian customary law; or (c) consult and, to the extent necessary, give effect to any book or publication which the Court considers to be an authority on Zambian customary law. In terms of s 19(2), [a]n assessor called as a witness under subsection (1) shall advise the Court on all matters of Zambian customary law, which may arise in the matter concerned, and tender the assessor's opinion to the Court on the matter generally, but in reaching its decision the Court is not bound by the assessor's opinion. (3) An assessor called under subsection (1) shall be paid such fees and allowances as the Chief Justice may prescribe, with the approval of the Minister responsible for finance. (4) The fees and allowances under subsection (3) shall be paid out of the Consolidated Fund unless the Court orders otherwise. (5) An assessor called under this section shall take an oath prescribed in the rules.

(viii) Record of evidence, etc

According to s 20(1), [a] party to a matter before the Court is, on payment of such fee as may be prescribed by the rules, entitled to a copy of the record of evidence given in that matter. (2) Despite subsection (1), a person is not entitled, as of right at any time or for any purpose, to inspect a copy of a record of evidence given in a matter before the Court, or to a copy of the notes of the Court, except where expressly provided by the rules.

(ix) Recording of proceedings

In terms of s 21, [t]he proceedings in a matter before the Court shall be taken down and recorded in a manner prescribed by the rules.

(x) Perjury

By s 22(1), [w]here it appears to the Court that a person has committed perjury in any proceeding before the Court, the Court may call that person to show cause why the person should not be convicted for perjury. By s 22(2), [w]here a person fails to show cause why the person should not be convicted for perjury, the Court shall convict the person. According to s 22(3), [a] person convicted under subsection (2) is liable to a fine not exceeding fifty thousand penalty units or imprisonment for a term not exceeding six months, or to both. It is provided in s 22(4), [a] penalty imposed under this section is a bar to any other criminal proceedings in respect of the same offence.

1.3.1.12 The Employment Code[101]

The relevant parts with respect to the law of evidence under the Employment Code (ECA)[102] is that relating to the termination and expiration of the contract of employment. According to s 52(5), '[a]n employer shall bear the burden of proof that the termination of a contract of employment was fair and for a valid reason.'

1.3.1.13 The Road Traffic Act[103]

In terms of s 229(1) of the Road Traffic Act,

> [i]n any proceedings for an offence against this Act, a certificate in the prescribed form purporting to be signed by a road traffic inspector or by a police officer of or above the rank of Inspector and certifying that a person specified in the certificate stated to the road traffic inspector or to the police officer—
>
> (a) that a particular motor vehicle was being driven by, or belonged to, that person on a particular occasion;

[101] Act No 3 of 2019.

[102] Act No 3 of 2019.

[103] No 11 of 2002.

> (b) that a particular motor vehicle belonged on a particular occasion to a firm in which that person stated that the person was at the time of the statement a partner; or
> (c) that a particular motor vehicle belonged on a particular occasion to a corporation of which that person stated that the person was at the time of the statement a director, officer or employee;
>
> shall be admissible as evidence for the purposes of determining by whom the vehicle was being driven, or to whom it belonged, as the case may be, on that occasion.

According to s 229(2),

> Nothing in this section shall be deemed to make a certificate admissible as evidence in proceedings for any offence—
> (a) unless a copy of the certificate has not less than seven days before the hearing or trial been served on the person charged with the offence; or
> (b) if that person, not later than three days before hearing or trial, or within such further time as the court may in special circumstances allow, serves notice on the prosecutor requiring the attendance at the trial of the person who signed the certificate.

1.3.1.14 The Cyber Security and Cyber Crimes Act[104]

It is provided under PART X which covers the matter of electronic evidence in s 73 as follows: According to s 73(1) in any legal proceedings, the rules of evidence shall not be applied so as to deny the admissibility of a data message in evidence— (a) on the mere grounds that it is constituted by a data message; or (b) if it is the best evidence that the person adducing it could reasonably be expected to obtain, on the grounds that it is not in its original form. In terms of s 73(2) information in the form of a data message shall be given due evidential weight. By s 73(3), in assessing the evidential weight of a data message, regard shall be had to—(a) the reliability of the manner in which the integrity of the data message was generated, stored or communicated; (b) the reliability of the manner in which the integrity of the data message was maintained; (c) the manner in which its originator was identified; and (d) any other relevant factor.

1.3.1.15 The Children's Code[105] *- A further consideration*

(i) General

Assented to on 9 August 2022, the Children's Code (CCA, 2022) is representative of perhaps the most ambitious and detailed single piece of legislation relating to

[104] No 2 of 2021.

[105] Act No 12 of 2022.

children that the Zambian Parliament has enacted. In its preamble, it provides that it is:

> An Act to reform and consolidate the law relating to children; provide for parental responsibility, custody, maintenance, guardianship, foster care, adoption, care and protection of children; provide for the grant of legal aid to, and establish procedures for the treatment of, children in conflict with the law; provide for the making of social welfare reports in respect of a child in conflict with the law; establish diversion and alternative correctional programmes and promote the rehabilitation of a child in conflict with the law through programmes to facilitate restorative justice and compliance with laws; provide for the protection of a child victim and child witness in investigative and judicial processes; provide for the probation of a child in conflict with the law and provision of probation services; provide for the development of treatment programmes, early intervention services and programmes to combat crime and prevent further offending; limit the negative effects of confinement by minimising the impact of a finding of guilty on the family of a child in conflict with the law and facilitate the reintegration of the child in conflict with the law into society; provide for the establishment of child approved centres and child reformatory centres; provide for the regulation of child care facilities; provide for child safeguarding [....]

Further to the forgoing the Act domesticates the following International Conventions: (i) the Convention on the Rights of the Child; (ii) the African Charter on the Rights, and Welfare of the Child; (iii) the Convention on Protection of Children and Cooperation in Respect of Inter-Country Adoption; and (iv) the Convention on the Civil Aspects of International Child Abduction

In terms of s 297 the following is provided:

> (1) The Legitimacy Act, 1929, the Juveniles Act, 1956, the Adoption Act, 1956, and the Affiliation and Maintenance of Children Act, 1995 are repealed.
> (2) Despite subsection (1), all orders and warrants made or issued under the repealed Acts shall remain in force and be enforced in accordance with the terms of the orders or warrants as if made or issued under this Act.
> (3) Despite subsection (1), any registration or approval issued under the repealed Acts shall be valid until the 31st of December being a date after the commencement of this Act, after which the holder of the registration or approval shall apply for registration or approval in accordance with the provisions of this Act.

According to s 298:

> (1) [a] reference in a written law or document to a juvenile court shall be construed as a reference to the juvenile court under this Act.
> (2) For the avoidance of doubt, a person who was an officer or employee of the Social Welfare Department and Child

Development Department before the commencement of this Act shall continue to be an officer or employee of the Social Welfare Department and Child Development Department.

(3) The service of the persons referred to in subsection (2) shall be treated as continuous service.

(4) Nothing in this Act affects the rights and liabilities of any person employed in the Social Welfare Department and Child Development Department before the coming into operation of this Act.

(ii) Evidence of a child

The question of how evidence of a child may be received is to be found in s 78 of the CCA, 2022 which is discussed in detail below.

We will return to a more detailed discussion of s 78 of CCA, 2022 in later chapters.

As the foregoing brief but by no means exhaustive foray into legislation relevant to the law of evidence in Zambia demonstrates, there are several statutes dealing with specific areas of the law of evidence but none that comprehensively deal with the subject. All efforts to craft and enact a comprehensive Evidence Act have, as at the writing of this work, failed.

1.3.1.16 Various individual provisions in individual statutes

While not possible to specifically name and state individual provisions in individual statutes that speak to the matter of evidence and same shall be received or rejected, what is important to remember is that statutes will ordinarily provide for this facet of adjectival law. It is therefore important for counsel to have working knowledge of this very important aspect depending on which statute or statutes apply to the particular cause he is instructed to prosecute or defend. It would folly not to do so, and courts are unlikely to take kindly to such gaps in knowledge of counsel properly so called.

1.3.2 The common law

As noted earlier, Zambia's legal history is tied to its political and social development. To that end, Zambia, as a former British protectorate is a common law jurisdiction. The gap created by the lack of a comprehensive statute or statutes on the law of evidence in Zambia has meant that courts have relied heavily on common law cases, generally those from England. Though the said cases are not binding but of persuasive value, the alacrity with which they are cited and the readiness by which our courts accept them has raised them to the aura of being authoritative expositions of the law as we know it in this jurisdiction. As a result of the practice to refer not only to English decisions but also, decisions of other commonwealth and foreign countries, the law of evidence in this jurisdiction has been coloured and greatly influenced by

English, commonwealth and foreign decisions where no local authorities[106] exist. One reason for this appears to be what was provided in s 2 of the English Law (Extent of Application) Act[107] and substantially remains the case following the latest amendment[108] to that section discussed below:

> 2. Subject to the provisions of the Constitution of Zambia and to any other written law-
> (a) the common law; and
> (b) the doctrines of equity; and
> (c) the statutes which were in force in England on the 17th August, 1911 (being the commencement of the Northern Rhodesia Order in Council, 1911); and
> (d) any statutes of later date than that mentioned in paragraph (c) in force in England, now applied to the Republic, or which hereafter shall be applied thereto by any Act or otherwise; and[109]
> (e) the Supreme Court Practice Rules of England in force until 1999:[110]
> shall be in force in the Republic.
>
> Provided that the Civil Court Practice 1999 (The Green Book) of England or any other civil court practice rules issued after 1999 in England shall not apply to Zambia except in matrimonial causes.

Concerning the foregoing, as it stood then, but in words that still ring true today, Hatchard and Ndulo[111] opine as follows:

> For a statute of such fundamental significance, Chapter 11 is uncomfortably vague. There is doubt about the significance of the 1911 date, about precisely whish pre-1911 English statutes are applicable, about what the doctrine of equity means and most of all there is doubt about whether it embraces the law as developed in the common law jurisdictions other than England. It is possible to argue that the law referred to can include only English common law. The History of the enactment supports this view although past history is increasingly of questionable significance in the circumstances of Zambia. The title of the Act, as well as the side notes to it which refer to English law, supports the view that it refers to exclusively to England, although these are not necessarily determinate of the issue. This construction is also favoured by preliminary definition in the Interpretation and

[106] Here too, it is debatable if there are actually local authorities properly so called, as these local authorities seem to only, in the majority of cases to regurgitate points of law already espoused in English and other foreign decisions.

[107] Chapter 2 of the Laws of Zambia.

[108] See Act No 6 of 2011.

[109] The word "and" was inserted by way of amendment through Act No 14 of 2002.

[110] Paragraph (e) was inserted by way of amendment through Act No 14 of 2002.

[111] Hatchard J and Ndulo M, *The Law of Evidence* 1.

> General Provisions Act[112] [...] although again there is room for dispute on this point.

The confusion wrought by s 2 of the English Law (Extent of Application) Act[113] particularly after legislative changes[114] made in 2002 by Parliament, has been demonstrated in the *Ruth Kumbi v Robinson Kaleb Zulu*[115] debacle. The case of *Ruth Kumbi*[116] was a motion to move the Zambian Supreme Court to restore a matter to the active cause list pursuant to Rule 70(1) of the Supreme Court Rules. Commenting on s 2 of the English Law (Extent of Application) Act[117] the Court opined as follows:

> [...] before section 2 of the English Law (Extent of Application Amendment) Act, Chapter 11 was amended by Act No 14 of 2002, the Rules of the Supreme Court only filled gaps in our own practice and procedure, with the insertion of (e) in section 2 of the English law (Extent of Application Amendment) Act, Chapter 11, the whole of 1999 edition of the White Book has been incorporated in our Rules and procedures. Now by statue, the Zambian Courts are bound to *follow all the rules and procedure followed in England as stated in the 1999 edition of the White Book. The entire provisions of the rules of the Supreme Court as expounded in the White Book, 1999 edition, including the decided case, are now Zambian law by statute and as such binding on the Zambian Courts* (emphasis added).[118]

This clearly was neither Parliament's nor the Supreme Court's finest hour in so far as developing our jurisprudence was concerned. The consequences were far reaching. Advocates almost overnight threw out local rules which included the bulk of the High Court and Supreme Court rules in the dustbin of legal history. How the Supreme Court could not have foreseen the consequences of interpreting the law this way defies logic. It surely could not have been Parliament's expressed intention to, in one sweep, get rid of our rules and replace them with the Rules of the Supreme Court, RSC, 1965 (The White Book) 1999 Edition in its entirety. A purposive interpretation could surely have led the Supreme Court to conclude that a literal interpretation of the Act as amended would lead to the absurdity of constricting Parliament's power to legislate in this space rendering s 2 as amended, unconstitutional. It ought to have been clear to both Parliament and ultimately the Supreme Court that we were a jurisdiction which still needed to develop our own rules to, as a very sovereign nation is wont to do, supplant foreign laws and rules, a vestige of

[112] Chapter 2 of the Laws of Zambia.

[113] Chapter 2 of the Laws of Zambia.

[114] See Act No 14 of 2002.

[115] (SCZ Judgment No 19 of 2009).

[116] (SCZ Judgment No 19 of 2009); *The People v The Principal Resident Magistrate Ex Parte Faustine Kabwe and Aaron Chungu* (SCZ Judgment No 17 of 2009).

[117] Chapter 2 of the Laws of Zambia.

[118] Emphasis added.

our colonial past. The way to do that was not to entrench the use of foreign rules and thereby perpetuate the disinclination to be innovative and as such, to continue depending on foreign laws and rules, but to reinforce what had always been the goal in this jurisdiction as can be deduced from s 10[119] of the High Court Act:

> The jurisdiction vested in the Court shall, as regards practice and procedure, be exercised in the manner provided by this Act and the Criminal Procedure Code, or by any other written law, or by such rules, order or directions of the Court as may be made under this Act, or the said Code, or such written law, *and in default thereof in substantial conformity with the law and practice for the time being observed in England in the High Court of Justice* (emphasis added).[120]

Clearly, and with the greatest respect, the Supreme Court might have omitted to consider the catastrophic implications of its holding but in its defence, it may have had very little leeway (but which leeway, it is submitted with respect, it ought to have exploited creatively) as elaborated in the 2011 English Law (Extent of Application) Act Parliamentary Committee Report:[121]

> Section 2 of the English Law (Extent of Application) Act, Chapter 11 of the Laws of Zambia, provides for the application of English laws in Zambian matrimonial causes and the Supreme Court Practice Rules of England (The White Book). The White Book provides for practice and procedure in civil matters. The enactment of the English Law Extent of Application (Amendment) Act No 14 of 2002 meant that the Supreme Court Practice Rules of England in force until 1999 had the force of law in Zambia, subject to the provisions of the Constitution of Zambia and any other written law. It was notable that the White Book consisted of two volumes: one containing procedure and the other containing English statutes that underpinned and reinforced the procedure set out in the first volume. Therefore, the effect of the application of the White book to Zambia in its entirety was that not only English practice and procedure but also English statutes were imported into the Zambian laws. This state of affairs had since been confirmed in terms of judicial interpretation by the Supreme Court of Zambia. Further, following enactment by the Zambian Parliament of the Matrimonial Causes Act No 20 of 2007, it became necessary to amend the English Law (Extent of Application) Act so that the Zambian courts could apply the Matrimonial Causes Act, No 20 of 2007. In a nutshell, the wholesale application of the White Book to Zambia had the effect of creating uncertainty in the applicability of English statutes and procedures set out in the White Book and casting doubt over the sovereign power

[119] Prior to its amendment by Act No 7 of 2011.

[120] Emphasis added.

[121] Report of the Committee on Legal Affairs, Governance, Human Rights and Gender Matters on The English Law (Extent of Application) (Amendment) Bill, NAB 7 of 2011 For the Fifth Session of the Tenth National Assembly Appointed on 24 February, 2011.

> of the Zambian state, through its Parliament, to decide on individual laws to include in the country's statute book, which laws should be tailored for the peculiarities of the Zambian situation and not the more advanced English situation. The above notwithstanding, there is need for the Zambian courts to continue to have access to English practice and procedure, albeit in a restricted manner in that they may fall back on the White Book only to the extent that the Zambian High Court Rules do not have a provision to deal with a particular aspect of a matter before the courts. As the law currently stands, the application of the White Book to Zambia had rendered the Zambian High Court Rules redundant as, in practice, the White Book had been applied whether or not there was a gap in the Zambian Rules.

Thankfully, the law was again amended to reflect the foregoing concerns rendering *Ruth Kumbi*[122] bad law and ending this debacle that threatened to derail the development of local jurisprudence.

Section 2 of English Law (Extent of Application) (Amendment) Act[123] was amended by the deletion of the *Ruth Kumbi*[124] linked s 2[125] and the substitution 'therefor' of the following:

> Subject to the provisions of the Constitution and to any other written law-
> (a) the common law;
> (b) the doctrines of equity;
> (c) the statutes which were in force in England on 17th August, 1911, being the commencement of the Northern Rhodesia Order in Council 1911; and
> (d) any statutes of a later date than that mentioned in paragraph
> (c) in force in England, now applied to the Republic, or which shall apply to the Republic by an Act of Parliament, or otherwise;
>
> shall be in force in the Republic.

Section 10 of the High Court Act[126] now reads as follows:

> (1) The jurisdiction vested in the Court shall, as regards practice and procedure, be exercised in the manner provided by this Act, the Criminal Procedure Code, the Matrimonial Causes Act, 2007, or any other written law, or by such rules, orders or directions of the Court as may be made under this Act, the Criminal Procedure Code, the Matrimonial Causes Act, 2007, or such written law, and *in default thereof in substantial conformity with the Supreme Court Practice, 1999 (White Book) of England and subject to subsection (2),*

[122] (SCZ Judgment No 19 of 2009).

[123] No 6 of 2011.

[124] (SCZ Judgment No 19 of 2009).

[125] Under Act No 14 of 2002.

[126] As amended by Act No 7 of 2011.

the law and practice applicable in England in the High Court of Justice up to 31st December, 1999 (emphasis added).[127]

(2) The Civil Court Practices, 1999 (Green Book) of England and any civil court practice rules issued in England after 31st December, 1999, shall not apply to Zambia.

For the avoidance of doubt, Parliament further amended the Supreme Court Act in 2011[128] by the deletion of the old s 8 therein and the substitution therefor of the following new section:

> (1) Subject to subsection (2), the jurisdiction vested in the Court shall, as regards practice and procedure, be exercised in the manner provided by this Act and rules of Court.
>
> (2) Notwithstanding subsection (1), where this Act or rules of court do not make provision for any particular point of practice and procedure,[129] the practice and procedure of the Court shall be-
>
> (a) in relation to criminal matters, as nearly as may be in accordance with the law and practice observed in the Court of Criminal Appeal in England; and
>
> (b) subject to subsection (3), in relation to civil matters, as nearly as may be in accordance with the Supreme Court Practice, 1999 (White Book) of England and the law and practice in the Court of Appeal in England in force up to 31st December, 1999
>
> (3) The Civil Court Practice, 1999 (Green Book) of England and any civil practice rules in England after 31st December, 1999, shall not apply to Zambia.

1.3.3 *Customary law*[130]

This [part of our discussion focuses on] the legal system of Zambia as inherited at independence in 1964, to enable the reader [appreciate the legal setting that impacts the law of evidence in this jurisdiction]. Zambia is said to be a dual legal system because the two systems of statutory and customary laws and courts exist side by side. The Dualism of the Legal System Zambia has a dual legal system. She practices both customary laws of the indigenous peoples of Zambia and the received English Law inherited from the British by virtue of colonization. The customary laws of the indigenous peoples of Zambia comprise their traditions and customs received by oral transmission from their ancestors. Many of the indigenous ethnic groups were kingdoms that existed separately and independently in the pre-colonial era. The distinctions in their customary laws are still evident but this research shows a trend of "copying" from each

[127] Emphasis added.

[128] The Supreme Court (Amendment) Act No 8 of 2011.

[129] Emphasis added.

[130] This part of the chapter, unless expressly stated, is excerpted from Zambia Law Development Commission, *Report to the Minister of Justice on the Restatement of Customary Law Project* found at https://zldc.org.zm/index.php/reports/download-file... retrieved on 4/5/22.

other, which is giving rise to a slow, but definite [harmonisation] of common principles of customary laws in [this jurisdiction]. The similarity in principles of customary laws shown [within this part of our discussion] also arises from the fact that the differences are not so much due to ethnicity as to the lineage systems prevailing [....] Development of [...] customary laws also ensure their continued relevance, and therefore, their preservation and relevance to the development of the country. Otherwise, customary law could be retarded. Zambia's received law comprises enactments of the colonial legislature known as Ordinances by virtue of s 4(1) of the Zambia Independence Order Act of 1964. These include the Applied Acts of the Legislature of the Federation of Rhodesia and Nyasaland, by virtue of s 2 of the Interpretation and General Provisions Act.[131] Statutes in force in England up to 17 August 1912 are also applicable in Zambia. Statutes in force in England after 17 August 1911 apply to Zambia if specifically made applicable by an enactment of the Zambian Parliament. Thus, Zambian Courts also apply other British law and practice for the time being in force in England. They continued to apply to Zambia at independence and still do. 1 Countries, which formed the Federation of Rhodesia and Nyasaland, are the present Zambia, then Northern Rhodesia, Zimbabwe, then Southern Rhodesia, and Malawi, then Nyasaland; the names they acquired at independence. 17 August 1911 is the date when the Northern Rhodesia Order-in-Council commenced. Section 20 of the English Law (Extent of Application) Act.[132] These were intended to apply to Europeans only in civil and criminal matters, and for both Europeans and Africans in public law. The indigenous customary law was left to apply to Africans as this primarily (regulated and still) regulates personal matters. The rationale seems to have been that application of the British personal law to Africans would result in great injustice. The exception of the application of British personal law to Africans thus continued even after independence, culminating into the current Article 23(4)(c) & (d) of the [...] Constitution.[133] There is great need to re-examine this clause that has resulted in excepting the constitutional prohibition of discrimination [from applying to] customary law and personal law where the most inhuman and degrading practices are permitted.[134] Usually placed in the category of received law, probably for reasons of its British oriented jurisprudence and pattern, are statutes enacted by the Zambian Parliament. However, these are increasingly reflecting Zambian needs. They are placed here only because they are written, unlike the indigenous customary laws. With the received enactments came [as discussed above] [...] the English common law, which developed from English customary laws applied by the kings' court justices as they went on circuits hearing cases. As these customary laws varied from locality to locality, and were unwritten, they were developed into a uniform law of common application to the whole kingdom for the purpose of certainty and consistency.

[131] Chapter 2 of the Laws of Zambia.

[132] Chapter 11 of the Laws of Zambia.

[133] See also Articles 1 and 7; *Rosemary Chibwe v Austin Chibwe* (SCZ 38 of 2000), [2000] ZMSC 59.

[134] See *Rosemary Chibwe v Austin Chibwe* (SCZ 38 of 2000), [2000] ZMSC 59.

The common law was further refined by the rules of equity. These developed with the recognition that the application of common law sometimes causes undue injustice because of the application of the precedent rule (stare decisis). These rules of equity were thus developed to enhance equity and fairness. If there is conflict between the rules of law and equity, equity prevails. Thus, a dual legal system resulted, where on one hand, received law is administer, and on the other, customary law. As earlier mentioned, the policy to preserve customary law was in recognition of the fact that the general application of English law to indigenous people, particularly in the civil matters of marriage, succession, property, and family, might generally cause some injustice. The co-existence of the two legal systems thus necessitated a dual judicial court system in the Native courts and the Higher Courts. Since independence in 1964, all courts under the adjudicature have jurisdiction on all disputes under statutory law and customary law. Matters governed by Customary Law commence in local courts which replaced Native Courts in 1966, and appeals lie to the Subordinate Court[135] and from there, to the High Court[136] [the Court of Appeal or the Constitutional Court, as the case may be] and to the Supreme Court, [which together with the Constitutional Court is] the highest Court of Zambia. There is strict adherence to [...] Zambian Statutes by the Judiciary. British Law, which is not of direct application to Zambia, is resorted to only to fill a vacuum left by local law. International law is taken judicial notice of but cannot be observed or enforced unless or until it has been domesticated through an Act of the Zambian Parliament. Since independence, all statutory laws apply to all people who reside in Zambia, except in areas of personal laws and customary laws excepted by the [...] Constitution in Article [1(1), 7 and] 23(4)(c) and (d) as earlier mentioned for those who have not chosen received laws to apply to them. However, the issue of choice is non-existent because even Zambians who would have been thought to have made that choice cannot do so in these areas of the law where other members of the family still generally have influence. For example, most Zambians who choose to marry under the Marriage Act[137] still fulfil customary law requirements prior to registration of their marriages to have them recognised by their parents and relatives. There is hardly any room for real choice. Consequently, the effect of this provision is to place all Zambian under customary law governance in matters of personal law. The result is that in so far as this aspect of the law is concerned, the Bill of Rights[138] in law is administered in local and traditional courts. While customary law has been recognised as a system of laws applicable in the country, the handling of the undesirable practices of customary laws has posed a challenge that has not

[135] See s 58(2) of the Subordinate Courts Act Chapter 28 of the Laws of Zambia.

[136] See *Ann P Nkhoma v Smart Nkhoma* [2004] ZMHC 1; see s 8 of the Subordinate Courts Act Chapter 28 of the Laws of Zambia; ss 5, 10, 34 and 38 of the High Court Act Chapter 27 of the Laws of Zambia; s 19 of the Constitutional Court Act No 8 of 2016.

[137] Chapter 50 of the Laws of Zambia.

[138] Part III of The Constitution.

been, to date, confronted. The colonial manner of attempting to mitigate on these practices has continued. Part of the problem is that customary law is the basis of our identity as a people, and disapproval of some of it has been feared as likely to be seen as denial of that identity. Some of the existing provisions like s 16 of the Subordinates Court Act[139] provide that the application of customary law shall not be repugnant to justice and morality or by necessary implication contrary to any written law. Section 12(1)(a) of the Local Courts Act[140] provides that local courts shall only administer African customary law in so far as it is not repugnant to equity, morality, and good conscience.[141] This attempt to mitigate the undesirable effects of customary laws has not been effective because it depends on the sitting justice choosing to exercise the discretion given to apply these undefined standards.

1.3.4 Judicial discretion

In general, judicial discretion is the power reposed in the courts to make decisions based on their preference. This ability to exercise preferences is a facet of Montesquieu's separation of powers doctrine and speaks to the supposed independence of the judiciary. Where suitable, generally and in this case with specific reference to the law of evidence, judicial discretion permits a judge to determine a legal question or matter within a range of possible choices. So, for example, a judge has the discretion to exclude evidence as hearsay. He may, where appropriate, and where the defence raises an objection in a criminal matter to evidence of a confession as having been obtained by torture,[142] stay proceedings to conduct a *voire dire*[143] to establish whether the confession was freely given or was premised on police pre-trial impropriety.[144]

Discretion must, however, be exercised judiciously. It must be within the confines of the constitution or relevant statute or binding precedent. Failure to follow the law as provided is tantamount to abuse of discretion and deemed to undermine the rule of law. The court's actions may be deemed *ultra-vires* and

---

[139] Chapter 28 of the Laws of Zambia.

[140] Chapter 29 of the Laws of Zambia.

[141] See also s 12; *Kaniki v Jairus* [1967] ZR 71 (HC); *Rosemary Chibwe v Austin Chibwe* (SCZ 38 of 2000), [2000] ZMSC 59.

[142] On the routine use of (and acceptance of evidence which was a product of) torture by the Crown in the Court of Star Chamber, during the 16th and 17th century, and its subsequent abolition in 1640 by the Long Parliament after the English civil war, See Holdsworth W, *A History of English Law* Vol. 5 (3rd edn Methuen 1945) 194-195 which was cited by Lord Bingham in *A v Secretary of State for the Home Department* [2005] UKHL 71 at para. 12; [2005] 3 WLR 1249; [2006] 1 All ER 575, HL (also known as the *Belmarsh 9* case) wherein it was held that 'the principles of common law, standing alone, compelled the exclusion of evidence obtained by torture by a third party as unreliable, unfair, offensive to ordinary standards of humanity and decency, and incompatible with the principles that should animate a tribunal seeking to administer justice.'- Uglow S, *Evidence: Text and Materials*15.

[143] See discussion below.

[144] See *R v Horseferry Road Magistrates' Court Ex p. Bennett* [1994] 1 AC 42 HL; *Nalishwa v The People* [1972] ZR 26; *Chigowe v The People* [1977] ZR 21; *Patrick Sakala v The People* [1980] ZR 205 (SC); *Chinyama and Others v The People* [1977] ZR 426; *Petrol v The People* [1973] ZR 145 (CAZ).

subject to challenge and reversal on appeal or/and by way of judicial review where the court is a Magistrates' Court, and the abuse of discretion complained against is in a civil matter or criminal matters '[where] the judge is satisfied that there is a case fit for further investigation at full inter-partes hearing of a substantive application for judicial Review'[145] for as shown in *The People v The Director of Public Prosecutions ex-parte Dr. Rajan Mahtani,*[146] '[it is] within the province of judicial review to interrogate any processes and decisions relating to criminal investigations without arresting said investigations.' As held by Siavwapa J in *The People v The Director of Public Prosecutions ex-parte Dr. Rajan Mahtani,*[147] (in rejecting the idea that criminal proceedings were not amenable to judicial review thereby distinguishing *C and S Investments Limited, Ace Car Hire Limited, Sunday Maluba v The Attorney General*[148] wherein the Supreme Court held that 'civil proceedings cannot be used to arrest criminal investigations'[149]), '[...] criminal matters are not shielded from the long arm of judicial review where decisions are made that fall within the ambit of judicial review.' Judicial review is not applicable to criminal matters in the Magistrates' Court where procedure in dealing unsatisfactory decisions by the Magistrates' Court an appeal, is already provided for in the Criminal Procedure Code.[150] As the then US Chief Justice John Marshall opined in *Osborn v Bank of the United States:*[151]

> Judicial power, as contradistinguished from the power of the laws, has no existence. Courts are the mere instruments of the law, and can will nothing. When they are said to exercise a discretion, it is a mere legal discretion, a discretion to be exercised in discerning the course prescribed by law; and, when that is discerned, it is the duty of the court to follow it. Judicial power is never exercised for the purpose of giving effect to the will of the judge, always for the purpose of giving effect to the will of the legislature; or, in other words, to the will of the law.

We will return to this issue later but for now, we must turn to the definition of evidence.

---

[145] *R v Secretary of State for the Home Department, ex parte Rukshanda Begum* [1990] COD 107; *R v Inland Revenue Commissioners, ex-parte National Federation of Self-employed and Small Business Ltd* [1982] AC 617 at 642 on when leave for judicial review should be granted.

[146] 2015/HP/0942.

[147] 2015/HP/0942.

[148] [2004] ZR 216.

[149] As opposed to criminal proceedings.

[150] Chapter 88 of the Laws of Zambia; For an explanation of whether A Magistrate Court is subject to judicial review, see *The People v The Director of Public Prosecutions ex-parte Dr. Rajan Mahtani* 2015/HP/0942 but see when not in *The People v The Principal Resident Magistrate Ex Parte Faustine Kabwe and Aaron Chungu* (SCZ Judgment No 17 of 2009) a case which was concerned with whether a case to answer/no case to answer stage ruling by a magistrate could be appealed against or amenable to judicial review. In the case of C and S Investments Limited, *Ace Car Hire Limited, Sunday Maluba v The Attorney General* [2004] ZR 216 it was held that 'civil proceedings cannot be used to arrest criminal proceedings.'

[151] 22 U.S. 738 (1824).

1.4 Definition of evidence

Though one would be hard pressed to find any statute that defines the term evidence,[152] many writers of textbooks on the law of evidence have sought to start by defining what evidence, the law of evidence or the rules of evidence is(are). As early as 1870 WM Best[153] defined evidence as 'any matter of fact, the effect, tendency, or design of which is to produce in the mind a persuasion, affirmative or disaffirmative, of the existence of some other matter of fact.'[154]. Writing in 1898, James Bradley Thayer[155] considered the law of evidence to be 'a set of rules and principles affecting judicial investigations into questions of fact;'[156] John Henry Wigmore[157] said the following regarding evidence:

> What we are concerned with is the process of presenting evidence for the purpose of demonstrating an asserted fact. In this process, then, the term Evidence represents: any knowable fact or group of facts, not a legal or a logical principle, considered with a view to its being offered before a legal tribunal for the purpose of producing a persuasion, positive or negative, on the part of the tribunal as to the truth of a proposition, not of law or logic, on which the determination of the tribunal, as to the truth of a proposition, not of law or of logic, on which the determination of the tribunal is to be asked.[158]

Evidence has similarly been defined by GD Nokes[159] as 'that which makes evident a fact to a judicial tribunal'; by Murphy[160] '[...] in general terms as any

[152] For example, neither the Evidence Act Chapter 43 nor the Evidence (Bankers' Books) Act Chapter 44 of the Laws of Zambia nor The Plea Negotiations and Agreements Act No 20 of 2010 nor The Interpretation and General Provisions Act, Chapter 2 of the Laws of Zambia on the one hand nor the Constitution, on the other, define the term despite many references to it.

[153] Best WM, *Principles of the Law of Evidence* (5th edn H Sweet 1870); Cf Bentham J 'Anarchical Fallacies', in Wadron, J (ed) *Nonsense Upon Stilts: Bentham, Burke and Marx on the Rights of Man*, 1987, London: Methuen, Article II.

[154] Best, 1870, p 10. Cf Bentham, 1838-43, Vol 6, 208.

[155] Better known as JB Thayer (January 15, 1831 – February 14, 1902), Thayer was an American legal theorist and educator who took interest in the historical evolution of law. He was, from 1873 to 1883, Royall professor of law at Harvard. He then served as Weld professor of law also at Harvard from 1883-1893. His works included *The Origin and Scope of the American Doctrine of Constitutional Law* (1893); Cases on Evidence (1892); *Cases on Constitutional Law* (1895); *The Development of Trial by Jury* (1896); *A Preliminary Treatise on Evidence at Common Law* (1898), and a Short life of John Marshall (1901); and edited the 12th edition of Kent's *Commentaries and the Letters of Chauncey Write* (1877), and *A Westward of Journey with Mr. Emerson* (1884).

[156] Thayer JB, *A Preliminary Treatise on Evidence at the Common Law* (Little Brown Books 1898) 263.

[157] Better known as JH Wigmore (1863-1943), Wigmore was professor of Law and Dean of Northwestern Law School (1901 to 1929) and expert in the law of evidence. He is best known for his *Treatise on the Anglo-American System of Evidence in Trials at Common Law* (1904) and the Wigmorian Analysis, a graphical method for analysis of legal evidence in trials. His other works included *Treatise on Evidence* (1st edn, 1909-15; 3rd edn, 1940) and *The Principles of Judicial Proof* (1913, 1931; later *The Science of Judicial Proof*, 1937). He required his students, as a starting point, to learn the science of evidence (for which he developed the Wigmorean method, a thorough yet cumbrous system of for a meticulous analysis of evidence to be presented at trial) before turning to the law of evidence, a facet lost to the despotism of contemporary practice-predicated undergraduate and postgraduate ZIALE like syllabi and examinations.

[158] (Wigmore, 1983, Vol I, section 1).

[159] Nokes GD, *An Introduction to the Law of Evidence* (4th edn Sweet & Maxwell 1967) 1.

[160] Murphy P, *Murphy on Evidence* 9th edn (OUP, 2005) 2.

material which has the potential to change the state of a fact-finder's belief with respect to any factual proposition which is to be decided and which is in dispute';[161] by Keane[162] as 'information by which facts tend to be proved'; by Dennis,[163] as '[...] information that provides grounds for belief that a particular fact or set of facts is true'; and by Tapper[164] as 'something which may satisfy an inquirer of [a] fact's existence.'

While the foregoing definitions are helpful as a starting point to appreciate what the substance of the law of evidence is, they are inadequate in helping the reader to appreciate the profound, varied and sometimes confusing rules at the centre of this fascinating subject. A legal practitioner or advocate will need to appreciate the law of evidence in so far as it relates to trial at three levels:[165]

(i) What facts, figures, data, statistics, material or information will be required to support or refute an assertion at trial;
(ii) Demonstrating by way of disputation the relevance of one's witnesses' testimony or challenge the testimony of the opposing side's witness for want of relevance; and
(iii) Determining whether a certain item which may be deemed relevant is admissible or it ought to be excluded on the basis of exclusionary rule of evidence.

1.5 Terminology

To comprehend the length, breadth and depth of the law of evidence, a good place to start is to understand the various terms that are used throughout the study of the subject. In this part of the chapter, we discuss the following:

(i) basic terms;
(ii) terminology relating to admissibility, relevance and weight;
(iii) terminology relating to merits of evidence;
(iv) terminology relating to the form of evidence;
(v) terminology relating to facts:
(a) Facts to be proved;
(b) Facts in issue;
(c) Facts forming part of the res gestae;
(d) Facts relevant to facts in issue
(vi) Standards of comparison

1.5.1 Basic terms

It is nearly impossible to talk about evidence or the rules of evidence without mentioning the basic terms of 'parties'; 'admission of evidence' and 'tribunal of law and fact.' Naturally, our discussion begins with these terms below.

---

[161] See a more formal definition in Achinstein P, *The Nature of Explanation* (1983) cited by Murphy P, *Murphy on Evidence* (9th edn OUP 2005) 2.

[162] Keane A, *The Modern Law of Evidence* 6th edn (OUP, 2006) 1.

[163] Dennis I, *The Law of Evidence* 3.

[164] Tapper C, *Cross and Tapper on Evidence* 11th edn (OUP, 2007) 1.

[165] See Allen C, *Practical Guide to Evidence* 4th edn (Routledge, 2008).

1.5.1.1 *Parties*

Within the context of a trial, parties are persons natural or juridical generally referred to as plaintiff[166] and/or defendant. The plaintiff is the person who brings a lawsuit to court by filing a writ[167]/originating summons[168]/originating notice of motion/petition[169] against the defendant. The defendant is a person against whom the lawsuit is brought. Depending on the mode of commencement or jurisdiction, the plaintiff may also be termed a Claimant;[170] or Petitioner. The defendant may also be referred to as the respondent.[171] '[...] the court may in any cause or matter determine the issues and questions in dispute so far as they affect the rights and interests of the persons who are parties to the case or matter.'[172] Irrespective, a party who seeks to place evidence before a court of law in a trial is said to tender/offer evidence before that court. He is referred to as the proponent of the evidence tendered. The party who is against the evidence tendered presumably to the detriment of his case, is referred to as the opponent. The opponent is at liberty, within the context of evidentiary rules, to object to the tendering of evidence for any number of reasons. The Court will then have to be persuaded to admit or exclude the evidence in question.

1.5.1.2 *Admission or exclusion of evidence*

Admission of evidence refers to a scenario where the court permits a party to place evidence before it. The court may on its own motion refuse to admit the evidence but do not count on it during trial. As an advocate, one is expected to have a working knowledge of the rules of evidence and be quick to his/ her feet to object. As he does this, the advocate must persuade the court using legal reasoning predicated on rules of evidence both statutory or/ and binding precedent that the evidence being adduced/introduced/presented/tendered ought to be excluded. Of course, the court will allow for a response from the proponent's counsel and then a reply from opposing counsel before the court makes a ruling to 'sustain' or 'overrule' the objection.

1.5.1.3 *Tribunal of law and fact*

In Zambia the functions of tribunal of law and tribunal of fact in both criminal and civil matters are merged in either the magistrate or the judge presiding over the trial in question.[173] Zambia does not provide for a jury system where

[166] Generally, a person who has a cause of action against another, called the defendant and brings same in a court of law.

[167] Order VI R1&2 of the High Court Rules, Chapter 27 of the Laws of Zambia.

[168] Order 30 matter under the High Court Rules; First stage of Judicial Review under Order 53 of the Rules of the Supreme Court, RSC, 1965, White Book (1999) edition.

[169] In matrimonial causes, petition for winding-up and election petitions and constitutional matters.

[170] As in England and Wales.

[171] One who responds to the plaintiff's claim.

[172] Order 15 r. 6(1), RSC.

[173] See discussion of this under *voir dire* below.

these roles are divided between the magistrate/judge being a trier of law and the jury being a trier of fact. We will revisit this issue later in the text.

1.5.2 *Terminology relating to relevance, weight and admissibility: a distinction of concepts*

The concepts of *relevance*, *weight* and *admissibility* are indispensable to an appreciation of the law of evidence. It would be almost impossible to successfully prosecute or defend a case against one's client without counsel having a working knowledge of the same. While the three concepts are strictly speaking distinguishable, the job of understanding them has not been made any easier by court decisions that have appeared to blur the distinctions between them and merged one concept with the other.[174]

Starting with the concept of *relevance*, if we imagine James as having been charged with theft, any item that goes to show during trial that James committed the offence with which he is charged or disproves that he committed the offence with which he is charged is relevant to James' case. The former is relevant in so far as the prosecution is concerned and the latter in so far as James' defence is concerned. It follows that an item of evidence that neither proves nor disproves the case against James is *irrelevant*.

What then is the relationship between *relevance/irrelevance* and *admissibility/ inadmissibility*? It has been said by Thayer[175] that '(1) ...without exception, nothing which is not supposed to be, logically relevant is admissible; and (2) ... subject to many exceptions and qualifications, whatever is logically relevant is admissible [....]'[176] It follows that an item of evidence that is *irrelevant* to both sides of the case is rationally inadmissible.[177] Even so, the foregoing is a general rule. *Relevance* is not synonymous with *admissibility* for an item that may be *relevant* may, depending on the factual matrix and unique circumstances of a case *vis-*

---

[174] See comments of Lord Simon of Glaisdale in *DPP v Kilbourne* [1973] AC 729 where he said the following in parts relevant to our discussion: '[y]our lordships have been concerned with four concepts in the law of evidence: (i) relevance (ii) admissibility (iii) corroboration (iv) weight. The first two terms are frequently, and in many circumstances legitimately, used interchangeably; *but I think it makes for clarity if they are kept separate* [...]' (emphasis added).

[175] Thayer JB, *A Preliminary Treatise on Evidence at the Common Law* 226.

[176] It was observed in *Hollington v F Hewthorn & Co Ltd* [1943] KB 587 at 594 CA that 'nowadays it is relevance [...] that is the main consideration, and, generally speaking, all evidence that is relevant to an issue is admissible, while all that is irrelevant is excluded.' Rule 402 of the American Federal Rules of Evidence similarly provides: 'All relevant evidence is admissible, except as otherwise provided by the Constitution of the United States, by Act of Congress, by these rules, or by other rules prescribed by the Supreme Court pursuant to statutory authority. Evidence which is not relevant is not admissible.'

[177] Be that as it may, the EWCA has held in *Sammon* [2011] EWCA Crim 1199 that where irrelevant evidence has been admitted in favour of the prosecution, the EWCA will not find the conviction to be unsafe unless it can be sufficiently shown to the court that the evidence in question is prejudicial to the accused; It has, for example, been held in *Makin v Attorney-General for New South Wales* [1894] AC 57 that 'it is undoubtedly not competent for the prosecution to adduce evidence tending to show that the accused has been guilty of criminal acts other than those covered by the indictment, for the purpose of leading to the conclusion that the accused is a person likely from his criminal conduct or character to have committed the offence for which he is being tried.'

à-vis exclusionary rules of evidence,[178] yet be deemed to be *inadmissible.*[179] It is also the case that in exceptional situations, irrelevant evidence is admissible to lay a foundation for some other evidence deemed relevant such as inability to locate a relevant document in order to lay a foundation for tributary evidence of the lost document.[180] For this reason, where the question of *admissibility* arises, and it will from time to time in any trial, it is for the judge to determine as *admissibility* is a question of law.[181] In so doing, the judge will, given that *relevance*[182] is a conditional predicate for *admissibility*, and the most important predicate at that, also be deciding the question of *relevance.*[183] The foregoing is demonstrated in Lord Herschell LC'S opinion in *Makin v Attorney General for New South Wales*[184] wherein he stated as follows:

> It is undoubtedly not competent for the prosecution to adduce evidence tending to show that the accused has been guilty of criminal acts other than those covered in the indictment, for the purpose of leading to the conclusion that the accused is a person likely from his criminal conduct or character to have committed the offence for which he is being tried. On the other hand, the mere fact that the evidence adduced tends to show the commission of other crimes does not render it inadmissible if it is relevant to an issue before the [court] and it may be so relevant if it bears upon the question whether the acts alleged to constitute the crime charged in the indictment were

[178] Some rules based on public policy and estoppel (the latter amenable to a waiver) for example, proscribe proof of certain facts all together. Other rules such as the rule relating to *similar fact evidence* only prohibit the proof of certain facts for certain matters. *The rule against hearsay* makes inadmissible an otherwise relevant fact of statements made by a person other than the one giving oral testimony nor is opinion evidence generally admissible it being the province of the court to form such opinion as it deems consequential, and not the witnesses. It has been said in *Chiluba v The People* [1976] ZR 272 that the opinion of an expert even though a strong guide to court should not substitute for the Court's opinion which opinion is what counts.' Similarly, in *Chuba v The People* [1976] ZR 272 (SC), the Supreme Court in laying down the correct procedure for admitting expert evidence held *inter alia*, that, '[....] the evidence of a handwriting expert is an opinion only and the matter is one on which the court has to make a finding. It is for this reason that in addition to his opinion, the expert should place before the court all the materials used by him in arriving at his opinion so that the court may weigh their relative significance.' Additionally, this principle of law was outlined in the earlier case of *Sithole v The State Lotteries Board* [1975] ZR 106 where counsel submitted that an expert's opinion is not to be accepted blindly by the court and that the function of the expert is to give the court the benefit of his special training and skill, and assist the court in coming to a conclusion. Be that as it may, it was held in *R v Silverlock* [1894] 2 QB 766 that a court must only receive what is termed expert opinion evidence if the witness has satisfied the court that she or he is skilled, qualified and experienced in the area of evidence he is volunteering an opinion. The general rule as regards *extrinsic evidence* is that a document is conclusive and exclusive as to its contents or as evidence of the terms therein: *Holmes Ltd v Buildwell Construction Co Ltd* [1973] ZR 97 which also discusses exceptions to the general rule.

[179] Or as Lord Simon of Glaisdale has opined in *DPP v Kilbourne* [1973] AC 729, '[...] some relevant evidence is inadmissible and some admissible evidence is irrelevant' and later, that '[a]ll relevant evidence is prima facie admissible.'

[180] *DPP v Kilbourne* [1973] AC 729.

[181] See *Kashiba v The People* [1971] ZR 95 where it was held that it was the duty of the trial court to determine the admissibility of an incriminating statement; Counsel will be expected to argue their respective points of view and persuade the Court to decide in their client's favour.

[182] See *Sims* [1946] 1 KB 531; *Harris v Director of Public Prosecutions* [1952] AC 694, 710.

[183] Dennis I, *The Law of Evidence.*

[184] [1894] AC 57, 65.

> designed or accidental, or to rebut a defence which would otherwise be open to the accused.

Clearly some evidence, no matter how relevant to a fact in issue, is inadmissible.[185] The first part of what Lord Herschell says, relates not to exclusion of evidence on grounds of irrelevancy but rather, the fact that the logical probative value[186] of the evidence is far outweighed by its prejudice to the accused. As regards the second part of Lord Herschell's opinion, one finds this to be a scenario in which the logically probative consequence to be bigger[187] than the prejudice admitting such evidence would cause to the accused. For that reason, at the risk of sounding tautological, it is admissible and unlikely, in contradistinction to the former scenario, to endanger the constitutionally guaranteed concept of a fair trial.[188]

Turning to the concept of weight, 'the extent to which a piece of evidence makes the case of one of the parties more likely to be true is not a matter of *relevance* but of *weight*.'[189] We ought to remember that the question of the *weight* to be attached to evidence adduced is one of fact to be decided by a judge/ magistrate (where, as in this jurisdiction, no jury system exists, but for the jury where, as in the United States (and in England and Wales, in criminal matters), one does).

In terms of s 5 of the Evidence Act:[190]

> (1) In estimating the weight, if any, to be attached to a statement admissible as evidence by virtue of this Act, regard shall be had to all the circumstances from which any inference can reasonably be drawn as to the accuracy or otherwise of the statement, and in particular to the question whether or not the person who supplied the information contained or recorded in the statement did so contemporaneously with the occurrence or existence of the facts stated, and to the question whether or not that person, or any person concerned with making or keeping the record containing the statement, had any incentive to conceal or misrepresent the facts.

---

[185] In the same vein, *per* Lord Simons in *Kilbourne*, '[n]ot all admissible evidence is universally relevant. Admissible evidence may be relevant to one count of an indictment and not to another. It may be admissible against one accused (or party) but not another. It may be admissible to rebut a defence but inadmissible to reinforce the case for the prosecution.' By way of illustration, see summing up of Scrutton J in *Rex v Smith* reported in *Notable British Trials Series* 276-78 wherein the jury [trier of fact] was directed to consider the drowning of other newly wedded and well-insured wives of the accused for the purpose only of rebutting a defence of accidental death by drowning, but not otherwise for the purpose only of rebutting a defence of accidental death by drowning, but not otherwise for the purpose of positive proof of the murder charged.

[186] 'Logically probative or disprobative evidence is that which makes the matter requiring proof more or less probable:' *per* Lord Simon in *DPP v Kilbourne* [1973] AC 729.

[187] See also, *Rex v Christie* [1914] AC 545, 560, 599 *per* Lord Moulton.

[188] Article 18(1).

[189] Allen C, *Practical Guide to Evidence* (4th edn Routledge 2008).

[190] Chapter 43 of the Laws of Zambia, As amended by No. 3 of 1968.

(2) For the purpose of any rule of law or practice requiring evidence to be corroborated or regulating the manner in which uncorroborated evidence is to be treated, a statement rendered admissible as evidence by this Act shall not be treated as corroboration of evidence given by the maker of the statement.

1.5.2.1 Relevance

(i) General considerations

According to Stephens,[191] 'the term 'relevant' means that 'any two facts to which it applied are so related to each other that according to the common course of events one either taken by itself or in connection with other facts proves or renders probable the past, present, or future existence or non-existence of the other.' Lord Simon's definition in *DPP v Kilbourne*[192] is shorter but deserving of further elaboration. He opines that '[e]vidence is relevant if it is logically probative or disprobative of some matter which requires proof.' We saw earlier that the law of evidence does not seek ultimate truth for the simple reason that it is impossible to do so in an imperfect world. It follows therefore that Lord Simon's words cannot be understood to mean that evidence has to be conclusive. One is however left wondering what in essence determines that which, to quote Lord Simons, 'is logically probative or disprobative.'[193] While there is a tacit reference to, as Thayer[194] has opined, logic and general experience, one will be hard pressed to find a rule of law on which to predicate his argument to persuade the court that a particular kind of item being offered as evidence is relevant (i.e., '[...] logically probative or disprobative').

Be that as it may, the fact that the concept of relevance relates to evidence which makes the matter requiring proof more or less probable,[195] must not be lost to counsel at trial. It behooves counsel to argue persuasively and to convince the court that the disputed item is one which, as has been shown by Lord Steyn in *R v A (No 2),*[196] so far as advancing (or overcoming) the proposition in issue is concerned, contains some predisposition to logic and collective sense. There is a line of authorities[197] which supports this philosophy. Therefore, when your opponent objects to a certain item being admitted into evidence, he almost certainly is saying it is *irrelevant.* Your job as counsel is to convince the court otherwise. As we have seen in our brief discussion of the concept of relevance above, *relevance* is not always synonymous with *admissibility.* The general rule as set out in *Kilbourne*[198] is that admitted evidence *ought* to be relevant evidence

[191] Stephen JF, *A Digest of the Law of Evidence* (3rd edn Macmillan 1877) 4.

[192] [1973] AC 729, 756 *per* Lord Simon.

[193] According to Lord Simon, the term 'logically probative (or logically disprobative)' is not one of which self-expresses '[...] the element of experience which is so significant of its operation in law, and possibly elsewhere.'

[194] Thayer JB, *A Preliminary Treatise on Evidence at the Common Law* 265.

[195] Stephen JF *A Digest of the Law of Evidence.*

[196] [2001] UKHL 25; [2001] 2 Cr. App. R. 351 HL; [2002] AC 45, para 31.

[197] *R v Turner* [1975] QB 834, 841; *R v Sandhu* [1997] Crim LR 288; *R v Byrne* [2002] 2 Cr App R 311.

[198] [1973] AC 729.

or it is not evidence at all. Still as a line of cases,[199] aspects of which must now be considered as historical relics, demonstrate, so far as the matter of logical relevance goes, rather than what was termed 'abstract legal theory' in *R v Guney*,[200] it is the facts of a particular situation that will give a court sufficient predication for a court's ruling for or against relevancy of a particular item at trial.

(ii) Could there be a concept of legal relevance as opposed to logical relevance?[201]

Whether there ought to be a concept of *legal relevance* as opposed to *logical relevance* is a question that has exercised the minds of jurists[202] since the 19th century and in recent times the courts. JB Thayer, for example, was of the view that the set of principles that guided judicial investigations into questions relating to fact had, save as an aid in the selection of factual material on which said reasoning was anchored, nothing to do with the process of reasoning. In essence, that the law provided no assessment of relevance, only a tacit reference to logic and general experience.[203] The principles of logic and experience, Thayer contended, were apparent and recognised.

Wigmore, while accepting that the origin of the concept of relevance was logic and shared sense, contended that instances where the bearing of particular facts on particular issues had been ruled upon by courts were legion. Therefore, or so Wigmore's contention went, '[...] the united logic of a great many judges and lawyers furnished evidence of the sense common to a great many individuals, and so acquired the authority of law. It was therefore proper, he argued, to talk of legal relevance.'[204]

We will now embark on a consideration of a few cases[205] in which the above issues have arisen and the opinions of the courts on the matter of legal relevance both in civil and criminal cases have been traversed. In *DPP v Camplin*[206] it was held that when considering the defence of provocation, the issues of age and sex ought to be considered relevant. This is a specific rule which of course is in the company of many others.[207] We must note however that judges routinely reject evidence of scant weight for want of relevance. As exemplified in *R v*

---

[199] See *R v Batt* [1994] Crim LR 592; *R v Wright* [1994] Crim LR 55; *R v Grant* [1996] 1 Cr App R 73; *R v Halpin* [1996] Crim LR 112; *R v Bracewell* [1978] 68 Cr App R 44; *R v Sawoniuk* [2000] 2 Cr App R 220; *R v Phillips* [2003] 2 Cr App R 521.

[200] [1998] 2 Cr App R 705.

[201] See generally, Allen C, *Practical Guide to Evidence* 14-22.

[202] The most prominent of which were two Americans namely JB Thayer (1831-1902) and JH Wigmore (1863-1943).

[203] Thayer JB, *A Preliminary Treatise on Evidence at the Common Law* 265.

[204] Wigmore 1983 Vol 1 section 12 as paraphrased in Taylor AC, *Practical Guide to Evidence* 14.

[205] See additional analysis in Taylor AC, *Practical Guide to Evidence* 14.

[206] [1978] AC 705 but see *R v Guney* [1998] 2 Cr App R 242, 265.

[207] See for example, *Hansard*, HL Deb, 23 March 1999, col 1216 relating to what is now ss 41-43 of the Youth Justice and Criminal Evidence Act 1999 (inapplicable in this jurisdiction) where the UK Parliament stipulated the statutory framework for determining the relevance of a complainant's previous sexual history where the accused is on trial for rape.

Byrne,[208] this is accomplished by eroding the boundary between *relevance* and *weight* through the use of the concept known as 'sufficient relevance.' There are good and compelling reasons for this approach, the most potent of which is that the field of judicial inquiry must be kept within reasonable confines. This is to prevent confusion and erroneous decisions from creeping into the judicial arena. Additionally, courts must strike a balance between the veritable fact of limits to life and the cost of unnecessarily prolonging a trial if only to allow all manner of evidence conceived by the mind and contrived by the heart of man or specifically, the litigants to be considered and a determination to be made as to their relevance or lack thereof and their admissibility or inadmissibility.

In *Hollingworth v Head*,[209] the plaintiff sold a quantity of guano to the defendant. When he sued the defendant for the price, the defendant alleged that he was entitled, by the terms of the contract, to refuse payment. He alleged that the guano, which had been sold under the name of 'Rival guano', was of a new kind and that in order to persuade him to place an order, the plaintiff had sold it at £7 per tonne on the condition that if it was not equal to Peruvian guano, the price of which was £14 per tonne, the defendant was not to pay for it. The plaintiff denied that this had been a condition of the contract. The question arose whether, in order to prove the existence of the condition, the defendant could cross examine the plaintiff about sales of Rival guano to other customers on the same condition, and whether evidence could be called as part of the defendant's case to this effect. The Court of Common Pleas held that such evidence and cross-examination were inadmissible as not being relevant to the issue between the parties.[210]

A closer examination of the judges' decisions considered in *Hollingworth v Head*,[211] appear to support the conclusion that the central concern of the court in deciding as it did was not so much the question of relevance (which in any case was deemed too remote) but the '[...] need to save time and ensure that the [court] was not distracted from the point in issue.'[212]

In *Vernon v Bosley*,[213] Lord Hoffmann seems to have accepted that a notion of legal evidence happened which, in some cases would, as he saw it, comprise an eligible party's right to cherry-pick how to present his case by allusion to other public or private comforts.

According to some,[214] the question of whether legal relevance as opposed to logical relevance in terms of strictness ought to be recognised is a dead one

---

[208] [2002] 2 Cr App R 311.

[209] [1986] AC 41. This summary is extracted from Allen C, *Practical Guide to Evidence* 15.

[210] Per Wiles J: 'I do not see how the fact that a man has once or more in his life acted in a particular way makes it probable that he so acted on a given occasion.' See further *R v Blastland* [1986] AC 41 (which appeared to limit the concept of relevance in law) but see *R v Greenwood* [2004] EWCA Crim 1338.

[211] [1986] AC 41. This summary is extracted from Allen C, *Practical Guide to Evidence* 15.

[212] Allen C, *Practical Guide to Evidence* 15.

[213] [1994] *The Times, 8 April,* but see decision *in Jones v University of Warwick* [2003] 3 All ER 760.

[214] Allen C Taylor Chris and Nairns J, *Practical Guide to Evidence.*

in civil matters due to the Civil Procedure Rules in England.[215] The debate in criminal matters however, is alive and well. Be that as it may, Allen *etal*[216] contend, the development of the concept faces several challenges including impossibility of definition; impossibility of developing a consistent body of case law owing to each case being decided on its own facts. They add that the danger that such a concept would exclude logically relevant evidence for want of precedent is real and that even if this challenge was overcome, we would still have to contend with what they term 'a large number of cumbersome rules and exceptions.'[217] Citing James,[218] Trautman[219] and Weyrauch,[220] they conclude that placing '[...] the concept of relevance within a complex body of case law would make it even more difficult that it already is to adapt the law to changing circumstances.'[221]

(iii) Evidence with 'direct' relevance *vs* evidence relevant to 'collateral facts'

It has been contended that while a party with evidence with a direct relevance to a disputed central question has an absolute right to tender such evidence, the same cannot be said of a party that has evidence relevant to collateral facts.[222] While we need not revisit the definition of what relevance is, we must make the point that *collateral facts* are those facts that relate to some secondary issue which itself touches on the problem of whether a fact in issue will be proven or not. A party with *collateral facts* faces two challenges to having his evidence admitted its relevance to collateral facts not being an issue. Firstly, he ought to argue to the satisfaction of the court that the collateral facts that he wishes/intends to prove will, when so proved afford a sensible inference to be drawn as regards the matter in dispute. Secondly, as has been shown in *Managers of the Metropolitan Asylum District v Hill and Others*[223] (which demonstrates how difficult it may be to apply the distinction in practice) he must, to the satisfaction of the court, prove that the evidence relating to the collateral facts in question will to a reasonable degree, be conclusive steering clear of any difficulties or indeterminate debate of exactly the matching kind as that which has to be determined on the central dispute.

[215] See Rule 32.1 inapplicable to Zambia but which nevertheless clothes a court in its civil jurisdiction the power to control matters by way of directions relating to issues on which it requires evidence, the kind of evidence required to decide the issues in question and the manner in which such evidence is to be adduced. As a matter of interest, order 3(2) of our High Court Rules provides as follows: '[s]ubject to any particular rules, the Court or a Judge may, in all causes and matters, *make any interlocutory order which it or he considers necessary for doing justice, whether such order has been expressly asked by the person entitled to the benefit of the order or not.'* (emphasis added).

[216] Allen C Taylor Chris and Nairns J, *Practical Guide to Evidence.*

[217] Allen C Taylor Chris and Nairns J, *Practical Guide to Evidence* 18.

[218] James, 'Relevancy, probability and the law' (1941) 29 *California LR* 689.

[219] Trautman, 'Logical or legal relevancy – a conflict in theory' (1952) 5 *Vanderbilt LR* 385.

[220] Twining, *Rethinking Evidence: Exploratory Essays*, 2nd edn 2006 41-45; 61-65.

[221] Allen C Taylor Chris and Nairns J, *Practical Guide to Evidence* 18.

[222] Allen C, *Practical Guide to Evidence.*

[223] [1882] 47 LT 29, 35 *per* Lord Watson.

There are two justifications already traversed above which give sufficient predication for the foregoing approach:

(i) Collateral issues have the tendency to confuse courts before which they are brought; and

(ii) The inquiry that the court is asked to make during trial ought to be kept within reasonable confines to enable the court, according to Lord O'Hagan in *Managers of the Metropolitan Asylum District v Hill and Others,*[224] to ensure 'promptitude, precision and satisfaction in the administration of justice.'[225]

The court may have to deal with the question of whether the facts are directly relevant to facts in issue or simply collateral. The question is important because it will determine whether the person who seeks to tender the evidence relating to such facts has an absolute right to do so or has to satisfy the court, where the facts are deemed to be collateral, that the collateral facts that he intends to prove will afford a sensible inference to be drawn as regards the matter in dispute and secondly, that the evidence relating to the collateral facts in question will be reasonably conclusive steering clear of any complications or indeterminate debate of exactly the equivalent kind as that which has to be determined on the pivotal dispute. Such a scenario arose in the recent case of *R v Funderburk.*[226] The accused had been charged with sexual offences relating to having sexual intercourse with a girl aged 13. The girl's testimony which included a detailed account of her sexual encounters with the accused included the assertion that she lost her virginity due to the first of several acts of intercourse with the accused. The accused's defence was that he never had intercourse with the complainant and that her testimony was a product of fantasy or/and her sexual experiences with other men despite her tender age. In order to substantiate this theory, the defence wished to call P with whom the girl, it was alleged, had conversations about her previous sexual experiences, to give evidence to this effect. The trial judge refused to permit either the evidence of P or the defence to cross-examine the complainant on the subject of the conversation in question. He ruled that whether or not the girl was a virgin at the material time was irrelevant to the charge of unlawful sexual intercourse. While accepting the need to keep criminal trials within certain bounds and to avoid confusing the court with matters on the periphery, the court held that the cross-examination on previous inconsistent statements should have been allowed. Further, that had the girl denied making such statements to P, P should have been called to rebut the girl's evidence. Said the court, '[...] where the disputed issue is a sexual one between two persons in private the difference between questions going to credit (collateral facts) and questions going to the issue is reduced to vanishing point.' The Court was of the view that the challenge to the girl's claim of loss of virginity was sufficiently closely related to the subject matter

[224] [1882] 47 LT 29.

[225] [1882] 47 LT 29 at 31.

[226] [1990] 1 WLR 587, [1990] 2 All ER 482 CA (Crim Div). Cf *R v Neal* [1998] Crim LR 737; See also *Nagrecha* [1997] 2 Cr. App. R. 401 CA *per* Lord Rose LJ at 410.

of the indictment. According to the Court, had the court below (jury) known, that the girl was not a virgin as she had claimed in her evidence, they would have reappraised her testimony as to credibility. Therefore, said the court, justice required that evidence be called to demonstrate the challenge to the girl's testimony.

1.5.2.2 *Admissibility*

(i) General

Evidence is deemed admissible if it may be legally offered[227] at trial. In addition to conforming with the exclusionary rule relating to relevance, admissibility connotes amenability with all manner of exclusionary rules within the confines of the law of evidence. It follows that while all admissible evidence is relevant not all relevant evidence is necessarily admissible.[228] The simple fact for the foregoing is that the law of evidence is predicated on many rules that have to be adhered to for purposes of consistency, fairness and timeous disposal of cases at the least cost possible without confusing the court with remote matters which are not central to the resolution to the facts in issue.[229] Such rules already alluded to above forbid the admission of certain facts whether same are in issue or/and they are relevant to the facts in issue. They relate to, among others, public policy, similar facts, estoppel, hearsay and opinion/expert evidence. It is important to repeat here, albeit briefly, that the rules of evidence necessitate the distinction already discussed above, between relevance and admissibility. ''Relevancy' signifies [...] something which renders the existence of a fact probable or improbable. 'Admissibility' signifies compliance with all the exclusionary rules, including that prohibiting the receipt of irrelevant evidence.'[230]

(ii) Admissibility of evidence under the Evidence Act 1967

(a) Admissibility of documentary evidence as to facts in issue

The admissibility of documentary evidence as to facts in issue is provided for under s 3 of the Evidence Act 1967 in the following terms:

> (1) In any civil proceedings where direct oral evidence of a fact would be admissible, any statement made by a person in a document and tending to establish that fact shall, on production of the original document, be admissible as evidence of that fact if the following conditions are satisfied, that is to say:

---

[227] Or adduced.

[228] As shown in *DPP v Kilbourne* [1973] AC 729, in exceptional situations, irrelevant evidence is admissible to lay a foundation for some other evidence deemed relevant such as inability to locate a relevant document in order to lay a foundation for tributary evidence of the lost document.

[229] Or to repeat Lord O'Hagan's words in *Managers of the Metropolitan Asylum District v Hill and Others* [1882] 47 LT 29 at 31, to ensure 'promptitude, precision and satisfaction in the administration of justice.'

[230] Cross R and Wilkins N, *An Outline of the Law of Evidence* (4th edn Butterworths 1975) 184.

(a) if the maker of the statement either-
  (i) had personal knowledge of the matters dealt with by the statement; or
  (ii) where the document in question is or forms part of a record purporting to be a continuous record, made the statement (in so far as the matters dealt with thereby are not within his personal knowledge) in the performance of a duty to record information supplied to him by a person who had, or might reasonably be supposed to have, personal knowledge of those matters; and

(b) if the maker of the statement is called as a witness in the proceedings:
Provided that the condition that the maker of the statement shall be called as a witness need not be satisfied if he is dead, or unfit by reason of his bodily or mental condition to attend as a witness, or if he is outside Zambia and it is not reasonably practicable to secure his attendance, or if all reasonable efforts to find him have been made without success.

(2) In any civil proceedings, the court may, at any stage of the proceedings, if having regard to all the circumstances of the case it is satisfied that undue delay or expense would otherwise be caused, order that such a statement as is mentioned in subsection (1) shall be admissible as evidence or may, without any such order having been made, admit such a statement in evidence-
  (a) notwithstanding that the maker of the statement is available but is not called as a witness;
  (b) notwithstanding that the original document is not produced, if in lieu thereof there is produced a copy of the original document or of the material part thereof certified to be a true copy in such manner as may be specified in the order or as the court may approve, as the case may be.

(3) For the purposes of this section, a statement in a document shall not be deemed to have been made by a person unless the document or the material part thereof was written, made or produced by him with his own hand, or was signed or initialed by him or otherwise recognised by him in writing as one for the accuracy of which he is responsible.

(4) For the purposes of deciding whether or not a statement is admissible as evidence by virtue of the foregoing provisions, the court may draw any reasonable inference from the form or contents of the documents in which the statement is contained, or from any other circumstances, and may, in deciding whether or not a person is fit to attend as a witness, act on a certificate purporting to be the certificate of a medical practitioner, and, where the proceedings are with the aid of assessors, the court may in its discretion reject the statement notwithstanding that the

> requirements of this section are satisfied with respect thereto, if for any reason it appears to it to be inexpedient in the interests of justice that the statement should be admitted.

In *Lufeyo Matatiyo Kalala v The Attorney-General,*[231] the appellant (the plaintiff) sued the Attorney-General (the defendant) for damages for assault, torture and false imprisonment. During the course of the plaintiff's evidence, he sought to produce two medical report forms which he received when he was medically examined on the day of his release from police custody. There was no objection to the production of these forms and the documents were admitted in evidence without comment. It was held as follows: (i) The only way a document may be received in evidence other than by production by its maker is [in s 3 of] the Evidence Act.[232] (ii) Before the court can exercise its discretion to admit a statement without the maker being called as a witness, it must be satisfied that undue delay or expense would otherwise be caused.[233]

(b) Admissibility of certain trade or business or professional records in criminal proceedings

The admissibility of certain trade or business or professional records in criminal proceedings is provided for under s 4 of the Evidence Act, 1967[234] in the following terms:

> (1) In any criminal proceedings where direct oral evidence of a fact would be admissible, any statement contained in a document and tending to establish that fact shall, on production of the document, be admissible as evidence of that fact if-
>
> (a) the document is, or forms part of, a record relating to any trade or business or profession and compiled, in the course of that trade or business or profession, from information supplied (whether directly or indirectly) by persons who have, or may reasonably be supposed to have, personal knowledge of the matters dealt with in the information they supply; and
>
> (b) the person who supplied the information recorded in the statement in question is dead, or outside of Zambia, or unfit by reason of his bodily or mental condition to attend as a witness, or cannot with reasonable diligence be identified or found, or cannot reasonably be expected (having regard to the time which has elapsed since he supplied the information and to all the circumstances) to have any recollection of the matters dealt with in the information he supplied.

231 [1977] ZR 310 (SC).

232 Chapter 43 of the Laws of Zambia.

233 See *Stanbic Bank Plc v Savenda Management Services* (CAZ Appeal No 16/2017).

234 As amended by Act No 3 of 1968.

> (2) For the purpose of deciding whether or not a statement is admissible as evidence by virtue of this section, the court may draw any reasonable inference from the form or content of the document in which the statement is contained, and may, in deciding whether or not a person is fit to attend as a witness, act on a certificate purporting to be a certificate of a fully registered medical practitioner.

In *Muvuma Kambanja Situna v The People,*[235] the appellant was convicted of one count of aggravated robbery and two counts of attempted murder. The trial court considered that the appellant had been properly identified at the parade by the single identifying witness despite allegations by the defence that the parade was improperly conducted and the inherent danger of an honest mistake in the circumstances. Hearsay evidence was admitted supporting the conviction. It was held inter alia that hearsay evidence which does not fall within the exceptions to the rule and which does not come within s 4 of the Evidence Act,[236] is inadmissible as evidence of the truth of that which is alleged.

(iii) Evidence may be admissible for one purpose but irrelevant for another

It is also worth pointing out that the fact that evidence is admissible for one purpose does not mean it will, without more, also be relevant for some other purpose. The foregoing notwithstanding the overall admissibility of the evidence in question is not affected by its admissibility status as regards the 'other purpose.' To illustrate s 159 of the Penal Code[237] provides as follows:

> (1) Any male person who has carnal knowledge of a female person who is to that person's knowledge his grandmother, mother, sister, daughter, grand-daughter, aunt or niece commits a felony and is liable, upon conviction, for a term of not less than twenty years and may be liable to imprisonment for life.
> (2) Any female person who has carnal knowledge of a male person who is to that person's knowledge her grand-father, father, brother, son, grand-son, uncle or nephew commits a felony and is liable, upon conviction, for a term of not less than twenty years and may be liable to imprisonment for life.
> (3) For the purposes of this section, it is immaterial that carnal knowledge was had with consent of the other person.
> (4) Any person who attempts to commit incest commits a felony and is liable to imprisonment for a term of not less than ten years and not exceeding twenty-five years.

---

[235] [1982] ZR 115 (SC); *Re The People* (SCZ Judgment No 28 of 1982).

[236] Chapter 43 of the Laws of Zambia.

[237] Chapter 87 of the Laws of Zambia.

Where the accused are charged under s 159(1)(2), '[...] a sister's informal extra-judicial admission of incest is evidence against her, but it is inadmissible hearsay as far as her co-accused brother is concerned.'[238] Further, any evidence to show that the incestuous act was consensual will be irrelevant to the facts in issue, and as such inadmissible under s 159(3).

Further to the foregoing, we must stress that remotely relevant evidence or evidence that is liable to be manufactured or likely to lead to conjecture or unnecessary expenditure of time[239] is inadmissible. As Willes J opined in *Hollingham v Head:*[240] '[i]t may often be difficult to decide upon the admissibility of evidence, where it is offered for the purpose of establishing probability, but to be admissible it must at least afford a reasonable inference as to the principal matter in dispute.' Similarly, in *Holcombe v Hewson*[241] the plaintiff took out an action for breach of a publican's contract to purchase beer from him. The defendant asserted that the plaintiff had supplied bad beer. The plaintiff sought to adduce evidence that he had supplied other publicans with good beer. This was deemed inadmissible. Lord Ellenborough quipped that the plaintiff 'might deal well with one and not with others.'

The basis for excluding evidence that may be manufactured with ease is the common law rule that a party to a proceeding may not adduce evidence on the basis that he has, on a previous occasion, uttered statements consistent with his current testimony before court. According to the oft quoted words of Eyre CB:[242] '[t]he presumption is that no man will declare anything against himself unless it were true, but that every man, if he were in a difficulty, or in view of one, would make declarations for himself.'

Agassiz v London Tramway Co,[243] is authority for excluding evidence that has the tendency to produce peripheral issues. A passenger on a train claimed damages for injuries caused by a collision, alleged to be due to the negligence of the driver. She said that she heard another passenger tell the conductor that the driver ought to be reported, only to be met by the disconcertingly frank reply, "He has already been reported, for he has been off the lines five or six times today-he is a new driver." The evidence was rejected because it would have given rise to many collateral issues as to whether the driver had been reported, and whether he had been off the points five or six times or was a new driver.[244]

---

[238] Cross R and Wilkins N, *An Outline of the Law of Evidence* 184.

[239] See *DPP v Kilbourne* [1973] AC 729.

[240] [1858] 27 LJCP 241.

[241] [1810] 2 Camp 391.

[242] 24 State Tr. 1093.

[243] [1872] 21 WR 199.

[244] Cross R and Wilkins N, *An Outline of the Law of Evidence* 184.

1.5.2.3 Weight

(i) The Evidence Act, 1967[245]

The weight to be attached to evidence is provided for in s 5 of the Evidence Act, 1967[246] as follows:

> (1) In estimating the weight, if any, to be attached to a statement admissible as evidence by virtue of this Act, regard shall be had to all the circumstances from which any inference can reasonably be drawn as to the accuracy or otherwise of the statement, and in particular to the question whether or not the person who supplied the information contained or recorded in the statement did so contemporaneously with the occurrence or existence of the facts stated, and to the question whether or not that person, or any person concerned with making or keeping the record containing the statement, had any incentive to conceal or misrepresent the facts.
>
> (2) For the purpose of any rule of law or practice requiring evidence to be corroborated or regulating the manner in which uncorroborated evidence is to be treated, a statement rendered admissible as evidence by this Act shall not be treated as corroboration of evidence given by the maker of the statement.

(ii) The common law

(a) The English position

According to Lord Simmons,[247] '[w]eight of evidence is the degree of probability (both intrinsically and inferentially) which is attached to it by the tribunal of fact once it is established to be relevant and admissible in law.' The foregoing definition presupposes that any consideration of the weight of evidence can only begin after a judge admits the evidence on account of its relevance to the facts in issue. In other words, inadmissible and irrelevant evidence has no weight worth considering nor does evidence that a factfinder (that is to say judge or magistrate) finds incredible or unreliable. Determining that evidence is relevant is indicating that the evidence in question is capable of 'affecting the probability of a fact in issue in the estimation of a rational factfinder, on the assumption that the factfinder could find the evidence to be credible and reliable. In this sense the relevance of evidence is its potential weight as tending to prove one or more facts in issue.'[248] Deciding on weight is a process that a factfinder can engage in only after deciding that evidence in question is credible and reliability. There are several factors that may affect the weight attached to evidence. 'Obvious instances are provided by the age, reliability or

[245] Chapter 43 of the Laws of Zambia.

[246] As amended by No 3 of 1968.

[247] In *DPP v Kilbourne* [1973] AC 729.

[248] Dennis I, *The Law of Evidence* 111.

demeanour of a witness, the proximity in time of certain facts to those under investigation and the number of possible explanations of a particular event.'[249] It is a process that entails 'estimating the degree to which the evidence does affect the probability of a fact in issue [....]'[250] The higher the risk of unreliability of the evidence, the lower the weight that will be attached to the evidence in question.

(b) The Zambian judicial take on weight *vis-à-vis* admissibility

The concepts discussed above as explored and clarified under English common law have found application in this jurisdiction as can be deduced from a discussion regarding decisions that now follows.

Nsofu v The People,[251] is authority that touches on weight to be attached to evidence that is predicated on corroboration. Corroboration must not be equated with independent proof; it is not evidence which needs to be conclusive in itself. This is because corroboration is independent evidence which tends to confirm that the witness is telling the truth specifically, that the offence was not only committed but that it was the accused who committed it. Thus, where the evidence of a witness requires to be corroborated it is nonetheless the evidence of the witness on which the conviction is based. Under those circumstances, the corroborative evidence will serve only to satisfy the court that it is safe to rely on the evidence of the witness in question. In essence then the reliability and/ or persuasiveness of evidence requiring corroboration is increased if it is so corroborated and reduced, if the opposite is the case.

In *Happy Mbewe v The People,*[252] the appellant was charged with inflicting grievous bodily harm. At the close of the prosecution case, he, was put on his defence. He called one witness who had been present in court throughout the trial. In the interests of justice, the court disallowed his testimony and convicted the appellant, sentencing him to fifteen months imprisonment with hard labour. He appealed against both conviction and sentence. It was held: as follows: (i) There is no rule of law that witnesses must remain outside until called to give evidence; and indeed, if a judge in his discretion, so rules, he cannot refuse to hear the testimony of a witness who has remained in court throughout. (ii) The evidence is admissible, but the court in considering the evidence at the end of the trial, will have to determine what weight to attach to that evidence. (iii) It is a serious misdirection, prejudicial to the appellant and fatal to the prosecution case to disallow the witnesses' evidence.

In *Jackson Sakala v The People,*[253] the Supreme Court adopted its holding in *Donald Fumbelo v The People*[254] and *Joseph Mulenga and Another v The People,*[255] that

[249] Cross R and Wilkins N, *An Outline of the Law of Evidence* 184.

[250] Dennis I, The Law of Evidence 112.

[251] [1973] ZR 287 (SC); followed in *Machipisha Kombe v The People* [2009] ZR 282.

[252] [1983] ZR 59 (HC); *Moore Lambeth County Court Registrar* [1969] 1 WLR 141.

[253] Appeal No 60/2021 at J 13 para 5.11.

[254] (Appeal No 476 of 2013) followed in *Passmore Kwechele v The People* CAZ Appeal No 140 of 2018.

[255] [2008] 2 ZR 1 (SC).

an accused person must cross examine witnesses whose testimony contradicts his version on a particular issue. When he raises his own version for the first time during his defence, it raises a very strong presumption that the version is an afterthought. Hence less weight will be attached to such version and in a contest for credibility against other witnesses, the accused is likely to be disbelieved.

In *Wamulume Miyutu & Another v People,*[256] the Supreme Court relying on the decision *Maketo v The People*[257] in which it was held that 'an extra-curial confession made by one accused person incriminating other co-accused [was] evidence against himself and not the other persons unless those other persons or any of them [adopted] the confession and [made] it their own,' attached no weight to an ex-curia statement in which one accused person incriminated another and excluded same, holding that it had been improperly admitted by the trial court.

1.5.3 Methodological terms frequently used in the law of evidence

Throughout this text, we will come across methodological terms that are frequently used in the law of evidence. This portion of the chapter therefore deals with the most important ones with which we need to be familiar. They include the following:

- (i) Terminology relating to merits of evidence
- (ii) Terminology relating to the form of evidence
- (iii) Terminology relating to facts which relate to the following:
    - (a) Facts to be proved
    - (b) Facts in issue
    - (c) Facts forming part of the *res gestae*
    - (d) Facts relevant to facts in issue
- (iv) Standards of comparison

We will now consider each briefly in turn.

1.5.4 Terminology relating to merits of evidence

By terminology relating to merits of evidence is meant the qualities which at any given time, evidence may be said to retain. They include the following:

1.5.4.1 Direct evidence

Direct evidence is that class of evidence which by its very nature, necessitates no mental process in order for the court to draw the conclusion the proponent of the evidence seeks.It 'consists only of matters directly perceived by a witness and objects or documents produced for inspection by the court with a view to

[256] (Appeal No 23 of 2016), [2017] ZMSC 39.

[257] [1979] ZR 23 (SC).

assessing their physical qualities.'[258] Direct evidence is highly dependent on the credibility of the proponent of the evidence. The proponent may be adducing falsities; he may be biased against the accused for example or simply mistaken as to what he really perceived. 'The requirement of personal knowledge and forensic testing mean that the court can estimate how much reliance to place on the witness before it, given the four possible testimonial infirmities to which all witnesses are subject: defective memory, ambiguity of narration and insincerity'.[259] For that reason, '[...] direct [...] evidence may fail to prove the fact in issue [...] because the credibility of the witness is destroyed.'[260] The material utensils deployed in the assessment of witness credibility during trial include the oath, the witness' demeanour and cross-examination. As may be readily discernible then from the preceding then, it is not always possible to prove facts in issue by way of direct evidence. As has been said in *United States v Nelson,*[261] '[...] under some conditions circumstantial evidence may be equally or more reliable than direct evidence.'[262] We turn to a brief discussion of circumstantial evidence next.

1.5.4.2 Circumstantial evidence

Circumstantial evidence is that type of evidence from which a preferred conclusion may be drawn.[263] Regarding the significance of circumstantial evidence at trial, Pollock CB has, by way of analogy of a cord, opined in *Exall:*[264]

> One strand of the cord might be insufficient to sustain the weight, but three stranded together may be quite of sufficient strength. Thus, it may be in circumstantial evidence – there may be a combination of circumstances, no one of which would raise a reasonable conviction, or more than a mere suspicion; but the whole, taken together, may create a strong conclusion of guilt, that is, with as much certainty as human affairs can require or admit of.

---

[258] Peter Murphy, *Murphy on Evidence* 20. If this be so, then any evidence outside this definition is circumstantial evidence.

[259] Dennis I, *The Law of Evidence* 671.

[260] *United States v Nelson* [1969] 419 F. 2d 1237.

[261] [1969] 419 F. 2d 1237.

[262] See also *R v Onufrejczyk* [1955] 1 QB 388; *DPP v Nieser* [1958] 3 WLR 757, 766; *Fanwell v R* [1959][1959] 1 R & N 81; *Nkumbula v R* [1961] R & N 589; *David Zulu v The People* [1977] ZR 151 (SCZ); *Patrick Sakala v The People* [1980] ZR 205 (SC); *Naweji v The People* [1981] (unreported).

[263] Peter Murphy, *Murphy on Evidence* 20 cites Schum (D. Schum, The Evidential Foundations of Probabilistic Reasoning (1994), 18-19,81-83) whom he says 'contends convincingly that even the direct perception of a witness is ultimately circumstantial. He argues that testimony by a witness, W, of his direct perception of an occurrence (O) is in fact merely potential evidence (E*) of O, and is actual evidence (E) only that W believes that O occurred. Consequently, W's testimony becomes evidence (E) of O only subject to the jury's views as to (1) whether W actually believes that O occurred; (2) whether W's belief was founded on objective sensory evidence; and (3) the quality of that sensory evidence. On the other hand, it could be argued that these are simply factors the jury must take into account in deciding whether to accept W's testimony, which would not do violence to the definition of direct evidence offered in the text.'

[264] [1866] 4 F & F 922 at 929.

In the discussion that follows, we analyse circumstantial evidence through the eyes of case law, Wigmore's analysis of circumstantial evidence, the general law and then the types of circumstantial evidence.

(i) The Wigmorean approach to the concept of circumstantial evidence[265]

JH Wigmore[266] whom we have already encountered in this text embarked on an extensive and quite clearly, and by all accounts, exhaustive examination of the use of circumstantial evidence. His is arguably the most fêted analysis of the subject by any jurist before and since as regards the use of circumstantial evidence to prove a range of facts. He convincingly demonstrated how circumstantial evidence can thus be employed in any given case. There were things that direct evidence was incapable of proving and circumstances in which circumstantial evidence was 'more reliable than direct evidence.'[267] He said among these were the state of a person's mind i.e., to say one's consciousness; knowledge, belief, motive and intent. Therefore, said Wigmore, a person's knowledge and/or belief could be proved by statements attributable to the person in question or those made to him. As regards intent, the same could be proved by evidence of the accused's actions. Therefore, a person's belief and knowledge, he contended, forms the basis upon which the court will draw an inference (which must be the only reasonable inference[268]) as does 'the evidence of what he did about what he intended to do or what his motive was for what he did.'

Wigmore further highlighted instances in which circumstantial evidence could be employed to prove the physical commission of the offence with which the accused was charged. They included, according to him, evidence of the following:

(a) Planning and preparation preceding the commission of the crime; and
(b) Avoidance of detection by evidence of any, some and/or all of the following:
    (i) Destruction of evidence;
    (ii) Flight from the scene of the crime; and
    (iii) Other incriminating action(s) taken after the commission of the offence with which the accused is charged.

Though advances in forensic science and psychology have made Wigmore's analysis antiquated, and the demands of modern litigation practice deemed his approach too impractical to be useful, one must look with admiration at how Wigmore, with very little of the technological and scientific advancements today, did, with single minded determination, move the subject of evidence

[265] See generally, *The Principles of Judicial Proof* 1913 Part I.

[266] (1863-1943) in *The Principles of Judicial Proof* 1913 Part I.

[267] See also *R v Onufrejczyk* [1955] 1 QB 388; *DPP v Nieser* [1958] 3 WLR 757, 766; *Fanwell v R*[1959] 1 R & N 81; *Nkumbula v R* [1961] R & N 589; *David Zulu v The People* [1977] ZR 151 (SCZ); *Patrick Sakala v The People* [1980] ZR 205 (SC); *Naweji v The People* [1981] (unreported).

[268] See *Naweji v The People* [1981] (unreported).

forward. Quite apart from its historical value, it is a tribute to the 'universality and utility of'[269] circumstantial evidence.

(ii) A general case-based outline to the concept of circumstantial evidence

Unlike direct evidence which does not require a mental process upon which the court will draw the conclusion the proponent of such evidence seeks, circumstantial evidence must, as a starting point, be subjected to two tests: firstly, that the court (in its role as trier of fact) accepts this class of evidence and secondly, that the court draws the sort of inference from the evidence tendered that the proponent seeks. As held in *David Zulu v The People*,[270] circumstantial evidence '[...] is not direct proof of a matter at issue but rather is proof of facts not in issue but relevant to the fact in issue and from which an inference of the fact in issue may be drawn.'[271] As discussed above and as conventional wisdom has shown, it is not always possible to prove certain facts in issue using direct evidence alone. Under such situations, barring evidence that is too speculative or remote, circumstantial evidence may be the only way to prove facts in issue. This was the case in *Joseph Mutapa Tobo v The People*[272] wherein the Court observed as follows: 'We are satisfied [...] that, even if the confession was excluded the circumstantial evidence adequately connected the appellant with the commission of the offence.' In fact, '[...] since under some conditions circumstantial evidence may be equally or more reliable than direct evidence, it would be wholly irrational to impose an absolute bar upon the use of circumstantial evidence to prove any fact, including a fact from which another fact is to be inferred.'[273]

An example here may help. If there has been a homicide of which the victim is Chomba to which no direct witness is present but Chisanga on his way home notices Kangwa running away from the scene of the homicide, carrying a blood stained knife within the vicinity of the homicide, that is, where the dead body of the victim was found, provided that Chisanga is deemed a credible witness at trial, the court may draw the inference that Kangwa killed Chomba and that at the time Kangwa perceived him as running from the scene of the crime, he was so running to avoid arrest. The foregoing illustration is indicative of the fact that where the required evidence is obvious and compelling, circumstantial evidence is '[...] equally or more reliable than direct evidence.'[274] A similar inference could be drawn regarding robbery of a store where the accused is

[269] Murphy P, *Murphy on Evidence* 20.

[270] [1977] ZR 151 (SC).

[271] This, it was said was a peculiar weakness of circumstantial evidence but see *United States v Nelson* [1969] 419 F. 2d 1237.

[272] [1991] SJ (SC).

[273] *United States v Nelson* [1969] 419 F. 2d 1237.

[274] *United States v Nelson* [1969] 419 F. 2d 1237.

seen running in the vicinity at about the same time as the robbery is reported to have been committed, with a stash of cash in his hands, away from the store. A line of cases illustrates the preceding. We discuss a few below.

In *R v Onufrejczyk*,[275] it was held that on a charge of murder, the fact of death was provable by circumstantial evidence the fact that neither the body or a trace thereof had been found and notwithstanding the fact that no confession had been obtained from the accused person. In *DPP v Nieser*[276] Diplock J opined as follows:

> It may, we think, be misleading to speak of the 'doctrine' of recent possession in cases of receiving. It is a convenient way of referring compendiously to the inferences of fact which, in the absence of any satisfactory explanation by the accused, may be drawn as matters of common sense from other facts, including, in particular, the fact that the accused has in his possession property which it is proved had been unlawfully obtained shortly before he was found to be in possession of it.

The learned judge then followed the foregoing by outlining instances in which the property was stolen, received or possessed by the possessor with no guilty knowledge. He then added:

> But the inference appropriate to the particular facts proved is not a presumption of law; it is merely an inference of fact drawn by applying common sense to the proved facts, and there is no 'doctrine' that in a receiving case where recent possession on the part of an accused is proved he is presumed, in the absence of evidence to the contrary to have known the true facts of the way in which the goods were obtained.

The foregoing was quoted with approval in *Fanwell v R*.[277] F and M found in possession of clothes that had recently been stolen. Evidence adduced at trial proved that the two had on the material night gone to a mutual friend's house with the clothes in question. On the day following, F sold a shirt while M was found putting on clothing from those stolen the night before from a room in the mining compound broken into on the material night. The rest of the clothing were found in F's room who accused M of the theft. Both accused persons were convicted of the crime. Explaining the meaning of the foregoing in *Fanwell*, Clayden FJ who delivered the judgment of the court opined that the statement of the law in *Nieser* were matters relating to general principles applicable to inferences in the criminal law. Further, that it was not mandatory

[275] [1955] 1 QB 388.

[276] [1958] 3 WLR 757, 766, approved in *Fanwell v R* [1959].

[277] [1959] R & N.

to draw an inference of guilt from circumstantial evidence. For an inference of guilt to be drawn from such evidence, the judge said, it must be the only reasonable inference.[278] By way of illustration therefore,

> [...] if a person is in possession of property recently stolen and gives no explanation the proper inference from all the circumstances of the case may be that he was the thief, or broke in to steal and stole, or was a receiver, or even, despite no explanation, cannot be said beyond reasonable doubt to be guilty. And if explanation is given, because guilt is a matter of inference, there cannot be conviction if the explanation might reasonably be true, for then guilt is not the only reasonable inference.

In *Nkumbula v R*[279] a case of causing death by dangerous driving where there was no expert evidence to show the cause of death of the victim, the court took the view that this was not fatal to the prosecution's case. In *Patrick Sakala v The People,*[280] the appellant was convicted of murder of a boy aged four years, the child of one Rute with whom the appellant had been travelling together for about two hours. The appellant proposed love to Rute and on her refusal, he assaulted her so severely that she was rendered unconscious for about eight hours. On regaining consciousness, she found that her suitcase had disappeared and the child was dead. There was no dispute as to the appellant's identity nor was the assault challenged. The crucial issue was whether the appellant caused the child's death. On appeal the appellant denied killing the child and argued that there was no direct evidence connecting him with the offence. In dismissing the appeal, the court was 'satisfied that the circumstantial evidence was so cogent and compelling that on no rational hypothesis other than murder [could] the facts in this case be accounted for.' The court then concluded as follows:

> We are agreed that the circumstantial evidence implicating the appellant with the crime charged is overwhelming. He had the opportunity and the motive. It seems probable to us that having beaten up the child's mother and left her for dead the appellant must have decided to take the child's life in an effort to the eliminate the chances of his being later identified by the child [....]

In the celebrated case of *David Zulu v The People,*[281] the appellant was convicted of the murder of a woman in the course of a sexual assault; the injuries found

[278] For a demonstration of this principle at play, see *Naweji v The People* [1981] (unreported), where the Supreme Court rejected the test of 'strong circumstantial evidence' as a basis for conviction. The proper test, according to the Court was '[...] not whether there is strong circumstantial evidence, but whether the inference of guilt is the only one reasonably possible.' The Court's answer as to whether this had been so in the court below, was in the negative.

[279] [1961] R & N 589.

[280] [1980].

[281] [1977] ZR 151 (SCZ); See also *R v Onufrejczyk* [1955] 1 QB 388; *DPP v Nieser* [1958] 3 WLR 757, 766; *Fanwell v R* [1959]; *Nkumbula v R* [1961] R & N 589; *Patrick Sakala v The People* [1980] ZR 205 (SC); *Naweji v The People* [1981] (unreported).

on the body suggested that she had struggled with her assailant. The evidence established that the appellant and the deceased had been drinking beer together at a bar and were seen leaving the bar together at about midnight; between 0600 and 0700 hours the next day the deceased's partially undressed body was found. The appellant was traced and when arrested was found to have scratches on the neck and chest. He explained in evidence that the scratches were caused by flying pieces of iron at his place of work, an explanation which was not rebutted. The trial court without any evidence to support the finding said that the appellant had protective clothing at work and therefore that the flying particles of iron could not penetrate such clothing; the trial court consequently inferred that the scratches on the appellant were sustained during the struggle with the deceased. It was held as follows:

(i) It is a weakness peculiar to circumstantial evidence that by its very nature it is not direct proof of a matter at issue but rather is proof of facts not in issue but relevant to the fact in issue and from which an inference of the fact in issue may be drawn.

(ii) It is incumbent on a trial judge that he should guard against drawing; wrong inferences from the circumstantial evidence at his disposal before he can feel safe to convict. The judge must be satisfied that the circumstantial evidence has taken the case out of the realm of conjecture so that it attains such a degree of cogency which can permit only an inference of guilt.

(iii) The appellant's explanation was a logical one and was not rebutted, and it was therefore an unwarranted inference that the scratches on the appellant's body were caused in the course of committing the offence at issue.

David Zulu[282] was followed in *Mwanaute v The People*[283] where the Court observed as follows: as follows:

> Applying the above principles [from *David Zulu v The People*[284]] to the facts of this case, we are satisfied that the learned trial judge was on firm ground when he drew the inference of guilt on the basis of the circumstantial evidence before him. The totality of this circumstantial evidence which is that the appellant was the last person seen with the child before the child wound up dead in the bus, takes this case out of conjecture.

---

[282] [1977] ZR 151 (SCZ); See also *R v Onufrejczyk* [1955] 1 QB 388; *DPP v Nieser* [1958] 3 WLR 757, 766; *Fanwell v R* [1959]; *Nkumbula v R* [1961] R & N 589; *Patrick Sakala v The People* [1980] ZR 205 (SC); *Naweji v The People* [1981] (unreported).

[283] (Appeal No 200/2011).

[284] [1977] ZR 151 (SCZ).

(iii) Should *direct evidence* and *circumstantial evidence* be treated differently?

The question of whether *direct evidence* and *circumstantial evidence* must be treated differently is an important one not least because as shown in*United States v Nelson:*[285]

> [E]ither direct or circumstantial evidence may fail to prove the fact in issue – direct evidence because the credibility of the witness is destroyed; circumstantial evidence for that reason, or because the inference from the proven circumstances to the fact in issue is too speculative or remote. Whether such a failure has occurred is an appropriate inquiry in any case – be the evidence direct, circumstantial, or both. But since under some conditions circumstantial evidence may be equally or more reliable than direct evidence, it would be wholly irrational to impose an absolute bar upon the use of circumstantial evidence to prove any fact, including a fact from which another fact is to be inferred.

In rejecting the attempt to reduce the significance of circumstantial evidence, Heward CJ, in *PL Taylor and Others v R*,[286] observed that '[…] circumstantial evidence is very often the best. It is evidence of surrounding circumstances which, by underlying coincidences, is capable of proving a proposition with the accuracy of mathematics.' However, as held in *David Zulu v The People*,[287]circumstantial evidence '[…] is not direct proof of a matter at issue but rather is proof of facts not in issue but relevant to the fact in issue and from which an inference of the fact in issue may be drawn.' It is submitted that this holding is the only difference that is worth considering between direct evidence and circumstantial evidence. The holding in *David Zulu*[288] that the fact that circumstantial evidence 'is not direct proof of a matter'[289] is a particular weakness of the circumstantial evidence should now be considered, it is submitted with great respect, to be a concept unfit for purpose for our times. It follows that but for the exception expressed in *David Zulu*[290] relating to the 'difference implicit in the necessity for the drawing of an inference,'[291] there really is no need to treat, (as the various authorities we have considered thus far have shown) circumstantial evidence differently from direct evidence. On this point, two English decisions should be of considerable persuasive value to our courts.

---

[285] [1969] 419 F. 2d 1237.

[286] 21 Cr App R 20.

[287] [1977] ZR 151 (SCZ).

[288] [1977] ZR 151 (SCZ).

[289] *Nyambe v The People* (SCZ Judgment No 5 of 2011).

[290] [1977] ZR 151 (SCZ).

[291] Murphy P, *Murphy on Evidence* 20.

In *R v Hodge*[292] for example, Baron Alderson opined that in a situation where the evidence against the accused was entirely circumstantial, the guilt of the accused could be proved and so held if the [court] was satisfied 'not only that the circumstances were consistent with his having committed the act, but they must also be satisfied that the facts were such as to be inconsistent with any other rational conclusion than that the prisoner was the guilty person.' The foregoing is similar to the Zambian Supreme Court's guidance in *Naweji v The People*,[293] where the Court rejected the test of 'strong circumstantial evidence' as a basis for conviction. The proper test, according to the Court was '[…] not whether there is strong circumstantial evidence, but whether the inference of guilt is the only one reasonably possible.' It would follow from the foregoing that if the court finds that the inference of guilt is not the only reasonably possible, and that there is an alternative reasonable explanation pointing to the innocence of the accused person, the court must logically, acquit the accused. The preceding is so because the suggestion that the court should satisfy itself that the evidence 'is the only one reasonably possible' to the exclusion of all reasonable/rational accounts other than the accused's guilt, logically follows from the age-old general rule that the prosecution carries the burden to prove the guilt of the accused beyond reasonable doubt.[294] In *McGreevy v DPP*,[295] Lord Morris of Borth-y-Gestopined as follows:

> I think this is consistent with the view that Hodge's Case […] was reported not because it laid down a new rule of law, but because it was thought to furnish a helpful example of one way in which a [judge could direct himself] in a case where the evidence was circumstantial [….]
>
> I see no advantage in seeking for the purposes of a summing-up to classify evidence into direct and circumstantial, with the result that, if the case for the prosecution depends (as to the commission of the act) entirely on circumstantial evidence (a term which would need to be defined) the judge [comes] under an obligation to comply with a special requirement when summing up.

(iv) Restating the law of circumstantial evidence as discussed in *David Zulu v The People*[296]

The law of circumstantial evidence as held in *David Zulu*[297] has been that conviction based on circumstantial evidence was only to be done if the evidence before court was one that would lead to no other inference than the guilt of

---

[292] [1838] 2 Lewin 227, 228.

[293] [1981] (unreported).

[294] See *Woolmington v DPP* [1935] UKHL 1; [1935] AC 462; 25 Cr App R 72 where the presumption of the accused was first articulated in the commonwealth. For a Zambian take, see *Murono v The People* [2004] ZR 207.

[295] [1973] 1 WLR 276.

[296] [1977] ZR 151 (SCZ).

[297] [1977] ZR 151 (SCZ).

the accused.[298] In 2015, two cases came before the Supreme Court in which a restatement of the law as regards circumstantial evidence in this jurisdiction was made. The first was *Saidi Banda v The People*[299] and the second, *Mucheleta v The People.*[300]

In *Saidi Banda vThe People,*[301] the appellant was convicted of the murder of a business associate evidence that was wholly circumstantial. The Supreme Court seized the occasion to reaffirm the law on circumstantial evidence. In so doing, the Court proposed a systematic approach to drawing an inference in the following terms:

> It is unnecessary for us, in the present case, to give any further elaborations on how circumstantial evidence should and has been applied by our courts. We, however, wish to restate the law as regards circumstantial evidence by adding that this form of evidence, notwithstanding to weakness as we alluded to in the *David Zulu case,* is in many instances probably as good, if not even better than, direct evidence. We are sympathetic to the observation by Lord Heward, Chief Justice of England in *P.L. Taylor and Other v R,*[302] where at page 21 he states:
>
> > It has been said that the evidence against the applicants is circumstantial; so, it is, but circumstantial evidence is very often the best. It is evidence of surrounding circumstances which, by undersigned coincidences, is capable of proving a proposition with the accuracy of mathematics.
>
> Where the prosecution's case depends wholly or in part on circumstantial evidence, the court is, in effect, being called upon to reason in a staged approach. The court must first find that the prosecution evidence has established certain basic facts. Those facts do not have to be proved beyond reasonable doubt. Taken by themselves, those facts cannot, therefore, prove the guilt of the accused person. The court should then infer or conclude from a combination of those established facts that a further fact or facts exist. The court must then be satisfied that those

---

[298] Malila M, *The Contours of a Developing Jurisprudence of the Zambian Supreme Court: Reflections on my first five years as judge* (2014 - 2019).

[299] [Selected Judgment No 3 of 2015].

[300] [SCZ Appeal No 124/2015].

[301] [Selected Judgment No 3 of 2015]; Case is also [in]famous for the castigation of counsel for ignorance and unfamiliarity with legal issues in the case, in the following terms: "The learned senior counsel's incoherent discourse on extraneous arguments in his submissions have, in our view, reduced to insignificance the main issue that may have been sought to be highlighted under that ground of appeal. These kinds of arguments have the overall effect of impoverishing our jurisprudence. We do not want to say that this ground of appeal is bogus, but we can say it has failed." Four years later, in his book *The Contours of a Developing Jurisprudence of the Zambian Supreme Court* [...],Justice Malila SC regretted having used 'immoderate and perhaps overly critical language' in some of his judgments for lawyers he had 'perceived as careless or incompetent' and in this particular case, admitted that he had been 'rather harsh in [his] language against counsel's submission;' See application in *Ezious Munkombwe and Others v The People* (CAZ Appeals Nos 7,8 and 9 of 2017); *Kangwa Esther Rozaria v The People* (CAZ Appeal No 171 of 2017).

[302] 21 Cr App R 20; see *Makas Mazuba v The People* SCZ Appeal No 116/2021.

> further facts implicate the accused in a manner that points to nothing else but his guilt.
>
> Drawing conclusions from one set of established facts to find that another fact or facts are proved, clearly involves a logical and rational process of reasoning. It is not a matter of casting any onus on the accused, but a conclusion of guilt a court is entitled to draw from the weight of circumstantial evidence adduced before it.

Mucheleta v The People[303] was an appeal against the judgment of the High Court in which the appellant was convicted of spousal murder. The couple had for years endured a matrimonial union that was not the happiest of marriages. They quarrelled regularly and the appellant not infrequently assaulted the deceased physically. On the fateful day, the appellant locked out his wife. She had gone out drinking till very late in the night, out of the house. Her lifeless body was discovered outside the family home by a passer-by in the morning. It was lying in a pool of blood with a blue cell phone next to it. It had a deep cut on the left side of its head and part of the ear was cut off. The appellant had behaved suspiciously throughout the night, walking to the pit latrine on a number of times in the course of the night under the guise of going to relieve himself. On the third such trip to the pit latrine he was seen wearing a T-shirt but came back without it. There was a suggestion that his soiled T-shirt had been thrown into the pit latrine. Like the case was in *Saidi Banda*,[304] the evidence against the appellant was immensely circumstantial and, in some instances, the oral testimony accepted by the High Court was in the class of the kind that ought to have been corroborated but for reasons that could only be described as curious, was not so corroborated. The Court guided as follows:

> We have no trepidation in stating that we have serious reservations as to whether the learned trial judge entertained, as she ought to have, caution regarding the evidence that was tendered before her with regard to both it being circumstantial and it being given by witnesses who were related to the deceased person, and therefore with a possible interest of their own to serve. The learned judge was duty bound to consider the peculiar nature of circumstantial evidence and to employ a reasoned approach in coming to the conclusion that the inculpatory facts as presented by the prosecution witnesses were incompatible with the innocence of the appellant and incapable of explanation upon any other hypothesis than that of the appellant's guilt.
>
> Where, as here the prosecution's case rested entirely on circumstantial evidence, the trial court was expected to reason in a staged approach. The court should have first found that the prosecution evidence did establish basic facts. Those basic facts did not have to be proved beyond reasonable doubt. Therefore, taken by themselves, those facts could not prove the guilt of the appellant. Next, the court should have inferred or concluded from a combination

[303] (SCZ Appeal No 124/2015).

[304] (SCZ Selected Judgment No 3 of 2015).

of those established facts that a further fact or facts existed. The court should them have been satisfied that those further facts implicated the appellant in a manner that points to nothing else but his guilt.

A perusal of the judgment of the lower court shows that the learned trial judge employed no such logical and rational process of reasoning, although she referred to our caution in *David Zulu v The People*[305]

It is quite clear to us that the learned judge glossed over significant guidelines as to how circumstantial evidence is to be treated. The conclusions of the learned judge in the critical part of her judgment [...] are evidently not borne out of any evaluation of the evidence of witnesses, particularly the conflicting testimonies on the issue of the cell phone.

The learned judge made inferential deductions which are obtuse, skewed and incomprehensible. What is more, the conclusions on the guilt of the appellant are destitute of any logical analysis of the circumstantial evidence tendered, nor did the learned trial judge make any effort to address her mind to the question of whether the prosecution witnesses, who were related to the deceased, could be witnesses whose evidence required to be treated with caution and circumspection. The learned judge did not even entertain the thought that Prosecution Witness No 3 was a minor whose evidence required to be received after a *voire dire* was administered and recorded.

On the aggregate of these circumstances, we are inclined to accept the common position taken by the appellant's learned counsel and the Acting Director of Public Prosecutions that the conviction of the appellant in the circumstances of the case as described, was unsafe.

(v) Typical examples of circumstantial evidence[306]

We must begin this brief discussion by stating that there are certain classes of evidence whose ubiquity has led to them being referred to as presumptions of fact. While we will delve into these later, it is worth mentioning that particular examples arise as regards marriage, legitimacy, death, negligence and facts forming part of the *res gestae*.

(vi) Evidence concerning motive, plan or opportunity

When it comes to determining the guilt of the accused in so far as committing the offence with which he is charged is concerned, one cannot discount the relevance of motive. Motive is the principal factor behind what individuals may or may not do. Investigators into any crime will seek, as a starting point, to find out what the motive for any crime be it homicide, robbery etc., might have been. It has, however, been shown in *R v Ellwood*[307] that 'there is a great difference between absence of proved motive and proved absence of motive.'[308] Be that as it may, the significance of a pre-conceived plan in proving the guilt

[305] [1977] ZR 15.

[306] See generally, Hatchard J and Ndulo M, *The Law of Evidence* 8-9.

[307] [1908] 1 Cr App R 181.

[308] *Per* Channel J.

of the accused on the basis of evidence while to be carefully sought or treated due to the fact that '[e]very person who is charged with a criminal offence-shall be presumed to be innocent until he is proved or has pleaded guilty[... .]',[309] cannot be discounted. By way of example then, the fact that the accused bought a gun with which the deceased is alleged to have been killed carries such weight as to require an explanation from the accused without which he may, together with other facts, be convicted.

Regarding opportunity, a plethora of authorities including *Woolf v Woolf*[310] show that presence at the scene of the crime is normally essential, unless the accused can establish a credible *alibi*.[311] The law on *alibi* has been clearly stated in *Katebe v The People*[312] where it was held as follows:

> Where a defence of *alibi* is set up and there is some evidence of such an alibi it is for the Prosecution to negative it; that there is no onus on the accused person to establish his *alibi*. Further that [it is] dereliction of duty for an investigating officer not to mane proper investigation of an alleged *alibi*.

Bwalya v The People[313] offers the following qualification or clarification to the rule in Katebe:

> Simply to say 'I was in Kabwe at the time' does not place a duty on the police to investigate; this is tantamount to saying that every time an accused says 'I was not there' he puts forward an alibi which it is the duty of the police to investigate. If the appellant had given the names or addresses of the people in Kabwe in whose company he alleged to have been on the day in question it would have been the duty of the police to investigate; but the appellant not having done so there was no dereliction of duty on the part of the police.

Katebe v People[314] was distinguished and as such deemed to be of little assistance to the defence because there was no evidence of such alibi which would have necessitated the Police taking the necessary steps to investigate the *alibi* and the investigating officer could not be said to have committed a dereliction of his duty. The accused's statement to the Police where he said [...] he had been at Kanchele Village was, according to the court, a wild statement not warranting any investigation by the Police. The Court found that the prosecution had proved its case beyond reasonable doubt against both accused and in consequence convicted them as charged.

---

[309] Article 18(2)(a) of the Constitution as amended by Act No 2 of 2016.

[310] [1931] P 134.

[311] See *The People v Martin Minganja ("Mamado Goloko")* HR/053/2014 (unreported); *The Attorney-General v Valentine Shula Musakanya* [1981] ZR 1 (SCZ); *Katebe v The People* [1975] ZR 13 (SCZ); *Woolf v Woolf* [1931] P 134.

[312] [1980] ZR 249 (HC); *Nzala v The People* [1976] ZR 221 (SC).

[313] [1975] ZR 125.

[314] [1980] ZR 249 (HC).

(vii) Evidence establishing the fact of an individual's habits

Even though the admissibility of evidence establishing the fact of an individual's habits may be challenged partly due to rules relating to evidence of similar facts which we will look at later in this text, it has been held in *Joy v Phillips, Mills & Co*[315] that:

> Wherever an inquiry has to be made into the cause of the death of a person and, there being no direct evidence, recourse must be had to circumstantial evidence, any evidence as to the habits and ordinary doings of the deceased which may contribute to the circumstances by throwing light upon the probable cause of death is admissible, even in the case of a prosecution for murder.

(viii) Evidence of business practices

The practice alleged must be so firmly established as to lead to the inference, the drawing of which the proponent of the evidence in question seeks from the court to be so drawn as a matter of logic.[316]

1.5.4.3 Hearsay evidence

As the term suggests, 'hearsay' means that the witness giving testimony is saying what he heard and asserting that what the person who said what the present witness is asserting was/is true. For example, if A steals a copy of this book from a book shop but B who observed A's theft is not called as a witness to testify to this fact or more accurately, to what he perceived, and C testifies that he was told by B that A stole a copy of this book and asserts that B's statement is true, this is hearsay evidence and is inadmissible 'as evidence of any fact asserted.'[317] The surest way to steer clear of the rule against hearsay is to call the witness who perceived the relevant act/fact for himself. However, since the general rule against hearsay applies only when the object of making an out-of-court statement by someone other than its maker is to establish what was said as being true, this strict general rule can be evaded by the prosecution not making the object of C's testimony the establishment for the truthfulness of what B told him but rather, that the statement was made by B.[318] As the Privy Council said in *Subramaniam v Public Prosecutor:*[319]

> Evidence of a statement made to a witness by a person who is not himself called as a witness may or may not be hearsay. It is hearsay and inadmissible when the object of the evidence is to establish the

[315] [1916] KB 849.

[316] See *Trotter v Mclean* [1879] 13 Ch D 574.

[317] *R v Sharp* [1988] 86 Cr App R 274, 278.

[318] See *Subramanian v The Public Prosecutor* [1956] 1 WLR 965; *R v Willis* [1960] 1 All ER 331; *Mutambo v The People* [1965] ZR 15; *Ratten v The Queen* [1972] AC 378.

[319] [1956] 1 WLR 965.

> truth[320] of what is contained in the statement.[321] It is not hearsay and is admissible when it is proposed to establish by the evidence, not the truth of the statement, but the fact that it was made.[322]

There are of course several exceptions brought about by legislation and case law over the years to which we must pay attention. We will of course discuss these in greater detail later in the text. For now, we outline some below with reference to cases in which they were considered.

1. Dying declarations[323]
2. Declarations against interest[324]
3. Declarations in public documents[325]
4. *Res gestae*[326]
5. Documentary evidence[327]

1.5.4.4 Original evidence

A useful distinction in the law of evidence has to do with evidence which is termed 'original' and that which is not, that is to say evidence which comes before court in some derivative or second-hand fashion. By way of example, this distinction finds itself in the differentiation between what is termed primary evidence and secondary evidence as regards proving the contents of a document. Primary evidence involves the production of the original document or alternatively admission by the opponent whatever his designation,[328] of the contents of the document in question. Secondary evidence means a copy of the

---

[320] *Keith Akekelwa Mukata v The People* (CAZ Appeal No 10 of 2018).

[321] *Muvuma Kambanja Situna v The People* [1982] ZR 115 (SC): Hearsay evidence which does not fall within the exceptions to the rule and which does not come within s 4 of the Evidence Act, Chapter 43 of the Laws of Zambia, is inadmissible as evidence of the truth of that which is alleged.

[322] Quoted with approval by Lord Parker CJ in *R v Willis* [1960] 1 All ER 331; see also Mutambo and 5 Others v The People [1965] ZR 15 (CA); *Times Newspaper Zambia Limited v Kapwepwe* [1973] ZR 292.

[323] *R v Woodcock* [1789] 1 Leach 500; *R v Osman* 15 Cox, CC 1; *R v Peel* 2 F & F 21; *R v Gloster* 16 Cox CC 471; *R v Perry* [1909] 2 KB 697.

[324] See *Donnelly v United States* 228 US 243, 33 S Ct 449, 57 L Ed 820 (1913); *Scolari v United States* 406 F 2d 563 (9th Cir), cert denied, 395 US 981, 89 S Ct 2140, 23 L Ed 2d 769 (1969); *United States v Harris* 403 US 573, 584, 91 S Ct 2075, 29 L Ed 2d 723 (1971); *Chambers v Mississippi* 410 US 284, 299, 93 S Ct 1038, 35 L Ed 297 (1973); *United States v Goodlow* [1974] 500 F. 2d 954.

[325] See *Sturla v Freccia* 5 App Cas 643; *Higham v Ridgeway* [1808] 10 East, 109; *Irish Society v Bishop of Derry* [1846] 12 C1 & F 641; *Price v Earl of Torrington* 1 Salk 285; *Doe v Turford* 3 B & Ad 890; 37 RR 581; *Smith v Blakey* LR 2 QB 326; *Mellow v Walmesley* [1905] 2 Ch 164; *Duke of Newcastle v Hundred of Broxtowe* 4B & Ad 273; *Thomas v Jenkins* 6 Ad & E 525, 45 RR 560; *Rowe v Brenton* 8 B & C 737; *Mercer v Denne* [1905] 2 Ch 538.

[326] See *Thompson v Trevanion* [1693] Skin 402; 14 Digest (Repl) 450, 4367; *Keefe v State* (50 Ariz 293); *People v Poland* 22 ILL 2d 175 at 181; *R v Bedingfield* [1879] 14 Cox CC 341; *O'Leary v R* [1946] 73 CLR 402; *Subramanian v The Public Prosecutor* [1956] 1 WLR 965; *Ratten v The Queen* [1972] AC 378; *The People v John Ng'uni* [1977]; *DPP v Christie* [1914] AC 545; 24 Cox CC; *Teper v R* [1952] AC 480; [1952] All ER 447; Taylor 1961 (3) SA 614; *The Schwalbe* [1861] Lush 239; 1 Digest (Repl) 234, 1247.

[327] See the Evidence Act chapter 43 of the Laws of Zambia (discussed above); *Lungu v The People* [1968] ZR 24; *R v Gillespie and Simpson* (1967) 51 Cr App R 172; *Hollington v F Hewthorn & Company Limited* [1943] KB 587; *Kabwe Transport Co v Press Transport* [1984] ZR 43 (which disapproved *Simwinga v Phiri* [1979] ZR 145 as regards application of Cap 43).

[328] Plaintiff or defendant; applicant or respondent; Petitioner or respondent; appellant or respondent as the case may be.

document in question or oral testimony as to the contents of the document. The case of *George Bienga v The People*[329] is illustrative. It was held therein as follows:

(i) The secondary evidence of the original document is admissible provided it can be established that the original is lost or cannot be produced. Secondary evidence may either be in the form of a copy of the original or by oral evidence.
(ii) When the original document is in the possession of a stranger, the proper course for the party desiring to prove the contents of the documents is to serve the stranger with a witness summons to produce the original.
(iii) Before secondary evidence of a lost document can be admitted, the court must be satisfied that the document cannot be found and an adequate search has been made.
(iv) It is difficult to lay down any general rule as to the degree of diligence necessary in searching for the original document to entitle the party to give secondary evidence of the contents. If document be of considerable value, or if there be reason to suspect that the party not producing it has a strong interest which he would induce him to withhold it, a very strict examination would be required; but if a document is useless, and the party could not have an interest in keeping it back, a much less strict search would be necessary.

1.5.4.5 *Prima facie (presumptive) evidence vs conclusive evidence*

Prima facie or presumptive evidence is that class of evidence which is declared to be sufficient evidence of a fact unless and until evidence rebutting the presumption is adduced by an opponent. Where the latter scenario arises, the court will have to weigh all the evidence before it in order to determine whether the fact in question has been proved. Such declarations are usually made in pieces of legislation.

For example, s 9(1) of the Road Traffic Act[330] provides that '[a]ny extract from a register or other records kept in terms of this Act or any regulation made under it shall, if it purports to be certified to be a true extract by the officer having custody or control of such register or records, be received in any court on production by any person and without further proof as prima-facie evidence of the facts therein stated.' However, evidence can be adduced which contradicts this presumption by contending that the said 'extract' is not 'from a register or other records' and that if it is, it has not been 'kept in terms of the Act or any regulation made under it' and as such cannot be accepted in court without more. Further, that if the foregoing test has been met, that it does not purport to nor has been certified 'to be a true extract by the officer having custody or control of such register or records.' Further, in terms of s 9(2), '[t]he registration document of any motor vehicle or trailer shall be received in

[329] [1978] ZR 32.

[330] No 11 of 2002.

any court on production by any person and without further proof as *prima-facie* evidence of the facts stated in the registration document.' However, where evidence is adduced to show that such registration was procured by fraud, the court will have to, despite the provisions of s 9(2), have to weigh the evidence adduced on the strength of s 9(2), and that which seeks to rebut this presumption.[331]

To be noted also is s 3 of the Evidence (Bankers' Books) Act[332] which provides as follows: '[s]ubject to the provisions of this Act, a copy of any entry in a banker's book shall in all legal proceedings be received as *prima facie* evidence of such entry, and of the matters, transactions and accounts therein recorded.' However, as shown in *Joseph Knox Simwanza v The People*[333] even where such is the case, same is rebuttable in a proper case where the circumstances and factual matrix make it just to rebut the presumption.

1.5.5 Terminology relating to the form of evidence

Evidence that falls in any one of the classes we have just discussed will only be received by the court if it is in any one of the following forms:

(a) Oral evidence
(b) Documentary evidence
(c) Real evidence

We will now discuss each in turn.

1.5.5.1 Oral evidence

Oral evidence consists of anything that any witness gives on a witness stand in court. Invariably, such evidence must be given on oath or affirmation in court. Where however a witness is unable to attend court e.g., a patient who cannot leave the hospital, his oral evidence may be taken out of court. It is also possible for oral evidence to be given via video link[334] or where permissible, by affidavit[335] or witness statements.[336] The foregoing have the same significance as oral evidence given on a witness stand in court.

1.5.5.2 Documentary evidence[337]

The term documentary evidence must be understood to refer to any document by whatever name called, which may include but is not limited to '...paper,

[331] See similar presumptions under ss 11(10); 22 of the Road Traffic No 11 of 2002; 34. Under s 34 of SI 38 of 2010, '[a] voter's card completed under these Regulations shall be admissible as prima facie evidence of the matters contained therein in any proceedings under these Regulations. When voter's card deemed to be cancelled.'; *Laurie v Raglan Building Co* [1941] 3 All ER 332 *per* Lord Greene, MR.

[332] Chapter 44 of the Laws of Zambia.

[333] [1985] ZR 15 (SC).

[334] This appears to be provided for in the case of child witnesses under s 78 of the Children's Code, 2022.

[335] See Order 5 rr 11-20 of the High Court Rules (HCR), Chapter 27 of the Laws of Zambia on rules relating to affidavits.

[336] As is required under Order 53 of the HCR in commercial matters.

[337] See Order 5 rr 3-10 of the HCR.

stone, marble, clay [...] metal'[338] which is produced in court for the court's inspection as direct or hearsay evidence relating to its contents. According to Darling J in *R v Daye*,[339] 'any written thing capable of being evidence is properly described as a document and that it is immaterial on what the writing may be inscribed.' Darling J, guarded himself 'against being supposed to assent to the argument that a thing is not a document unless it be a paper writing.' He added that '[...] it is a document no matter upon what material it be, provided it is in writing or printing and capable of being evidence.' According to s 2 of the Evidence Act,[340] '"document" includes any device by means of which information is recorded or stored, and books, maps, plans and drawings.' Clearly, the definitions of what amounts to documentary evidence have had built in the them the flexibility to be aware of the changes that may come about with time. In recent times, digital platforms and more advanced devices, computer storage, recordings and other retrieval systems have made it fitting for a recalibration of the outmoded understanding[341] of the term documentary evidence[342] as have film, tape, videotape, microfilm, microfiche, among others.[343]

1.5.5.3 Real evidence

Real evidence denotes material from which the court can on its own by using its own senses and without more, draw inferences or conclusions. It therefore follows that any material objects made available for the court's inspection including human or animal characteristics and a witness's demeanour during oral testimony are part and parcel of what is termed real evidence. Irrespective, 'what is important in each case is the visual, aural or other sensory impression which the evidence, by its own characteristics, produces on the court, and on which the court may act to find proved any fact which seems to follow from it.'[344]

1.5.6 Terminology relating to facts to be proved

1.5.6.1 General

The goal of evidence is to, so far as this is possible, establish the probability of the facts on which a party predicates his case. To that end, the court must not concern itself with what are termed supernumerary facts or those facts which are unhelpful or unrelated to the purpose for which evidence is sort

[338] See *R v Daye* [1908] KB 333, 340.

[339] [1908] KB 333, 340.

[340] Chapter 43 of the Laws of Zambia.

[341] See this view in *Glyn v Western Feature Film Co* [1915] 85 LJ Ch 261.

[342] See *Grant v Southwestern & County Properties Ltd* [1975] Ch 185; *Senior v Holdsworth, ex parte Independent Television News Ltd* [1976] QB 23.

[343] However, see *Kajala v Noble* [1982] 75 Cr App R 149 in which it was shown that the rule requiring proof by primary evidence was 'limited and confined to written documents in the strictest sense of the term, and has no relevance to tapes or film.'

[344] Murphy P, *Murphy on Evidence* 23.

in a particular case, and which, in any case, are unhelpful to the court, and may in fact, simply prejudice the court against a party. The court should rather concern itself with evidence that is confined to proving facts of that goal. The following are facts which a party may be at liberty to prove at trial:

(i) Facts in issue
(ii) Facts forming part of the *res gestae*
(iii) Facts relevant to facts in issue
(iv) Standards of comparison

We discuss the foregoing in turn.

1.5.6.2 Facts in issue

Also referred to as ultimate facts, facts in issue are that class of facts which a party, irrespective, must prove at trial in order to succeed in his claim or defence. The foregoing entails that those facts in issue will, in a criminal case be used by the prosecution to get a conviction (or acquittal for the accused) and in a civil matter, that a party (plaintiff) is entitled to his claim (or his defence where the party is the defendant in the cause). To determine what these facts are, one must look to the substantive law (tort, contract, the criminal law etc.,) germane to the cause of action/charge on the one hand, and the defence, on the other. How many those facts are, is predicated on the nature of the case before court. In so far as procedure goes, the facts in issue will be deduced from a statement of claim or where a matter is commenced by originating summons or originating notice of motion, in the accompanying affidavit in support of such originating process (in civil matters) or a charge/indictment (in criminal matters). It is therefore no concern of the law of evidence what the exact nature of the facts ought to be. We must follow the foregoing with concrete examples that illustrate how what we have said actually works in practice in civil matters on the one hand and criminal matters, on the other.

1.5.6.3 Facts in issue in civil cases

As alluded to already, as far as civil matters are concerned, the facts in issue are those facts which, having regard to the statement of claim or related procedural documentation as the case may be, and the relevant substantive law, are '... necessary to the success of any claim or defence at issue.' It follows that the party whose job it is to prove a fact in issue as an indispensable measure of their claim or defence, bears the legal burden of proof. Two examples relating to a claim in contract on the one hand, and tort on the other demonstrate this.

In a classic action for breach of contract, the following will ordinarily be the facts in issue:

(a) That there was a binding contract (oral or written);
(b) That due performance by both parties of their obligations as set out in the terms of the contract was a conditional precedent;
(c) That there has been a breach of said terms and conditions of the contract in question;

(d) That as a result of such breach, the plaintiff has suffered loss for which he seeks relief under the law; and where there is a defence to the claim,
(e) Such facts as are raised in an affirmative defence beyond bare denials and may include the following:
   (i) Misrepresentation;
   (ii) Mistake;
   (iii) Illegality;
   (iv) Duress;
   (v) Undue influence;
   (vi) Lack of capacity; and
   (vii) Discharge by performance etc.

In a classic action for the tort of negligence, the facts in issue will ordinarily be as follows:
(i) That the defendant owed a duty of care to the plaintiff;
(ii) That the defendant breached this duty;
(iii) That as a result of this breach the plaintiff has suffered loss and damage; and
(iv) That the plaintiff is entitled to recover at law

The facts in issue gleaned from a statement of claim are here, as in the former example above, raised in an affirmative defence which ought to, as shown in *China Henan International Economic Technical Cooperation v Mwange Contractors Limited*[345] go over and above bare denials. It is incumbent upon the defendant to deny all claims made in the statement of claim as he wishes to contest, for example, 'he may deny that he did the alleged act, or that he did it negligently, or that it caused the alleged damage.'[346] This is so because it behooves the plaintiff to prove that a causal link exists between a set of circumstances likely to bring about an accident and the accident itself.[347] The defendant must, where he alleges contributory negligence for example, specifically plead this with particulars clearly set out in his defence[348] as should any defence by him, that the plaintiff is wholly responsible for the complaint of injury made in that plaintiff's statement of claim. Though the defendant may also, as shown in *Southport Corporation v Esso Petroleum Co Ltd,*[349] give evidence of inevitable accident, though not having specifically pleaded it, he is well advised to specifically plead this with particulars precisely set out in his defence. The foregoing is also true when what the defendant seeks to do, in so far as facts in issue are concerned, is to not only traverse the plaintiff's entire case but to raise a case of his own against the plaintiff or facts that may ambush the plaintiff in

[345] (SCZ Judgment No 7 of 2002).
[346] Jacob JIH and Goldrein IS (Ed), *Bullen & Leake & Jacob's Precedents of Pleadings* (13th ed Thomson Sweet & Maxwell) 1318.
[347] See *Machen v Lancs & Yorkshire Ry* [1918] 88 LJKB 371; *Jones v Gt. Western Ry* [1930] 47 TLR at 41; *The Liesbosch* [1933] AC 449 at 460.
[348] See *Fookes v Slaytor* [1978] 1 WLR 1293.
[349] [1956] AC 218 at 231.

the same cause.[350] Finally, as shown in *Letang v Ottawa Ry,*[351] under the maxim *volenti non fit injuria,* the defendant is entitled to a decision in his favour if he can prove that 'the plaintiff voluntarily and freely with full knowledge of the nature of the risk he ran impliedly agreed to incur it.'

The importance of the defence going beyond bare denials is demonstrated in Order 53 r 2 of the High Court Rules,[352] which govern commercial matters states:

> The defence shall specifically traverse allegation of fact made in the statement of claim or counter-claim as the case may be. A general or bare denial of such allegation or a general statement of non-admission of them shall not be a traverse thereof. A defence that fails to meet requirements of this direction shall be deemed to have admitted the allegations not traversed and in an appropriate case the plaintiff may be entitled to enter Judgment on Admission.

The effect and interpretation of the foregoing came up in the case of *China Henan International Economic Technical Cooperation v Mwange Contractors Limited.*[353] This wasan appeal against the ruling of the High court, in which that court entered Judgment on admission at a scheduling conference on the grounds that the defence which was filed by the appellant did not rebut in full the allegations contained in the statement of claim. In agreeing with the court below, the Supreme Court showed that the statement of claim which was filed by the respondent was very detailed. It explained the facts on which the plaintiff relied and claims damages for breach of contract. The defence filed by the appellant, however, contained but three paragraphs as follows:

1. The defendant admits paragraphs 1 and 2.
2. The contents of paragraphs 3,4,5,6,7,8,9 and 10 are denied and the defendant shall put the plaintiff to strict proof thereof.
3. SAVE as hereinafter expressly admitted the defendant denies each and every allegation contained in the statement of claim as though seriatim.

The preceding was a rather bizarre exercise in concision gone wrong. It barely countered the claims by the plaintiff, it was bereft of any facts in issue or/and raised no further facts in issue for the Court to consider which could entitle the defendant to a successful defence. According to the Supreme Court, this defence clearly fell far short of the standard required in [civil] commercial cases. It did not traverse specific allegations of fact contained in the statement of claim. It was a general statement of non-admission, containing bare denials.

[350] Jacob JIH and Goldrein IS (Ed), *Bullen & Leake & Jacob's Precedents of Pleadings;* see also *Davie v New Merton Board Mills* [1956] 1 All ER 379; *Bill v Roe* [1968] 1 WLR 925.

[351] [1926] AC 725 at 731; see also, *Merrington v Ironbridge Metal Works* [1952] 3 All ER 1101; *Imperial Chemical Industries Ltd v Shatwell* [1965] AC 656; *Burnett v British Waterways Board* [1973] 1 WLR 700 CA.

[352] Chapter 27 of the Laws of Zambia.

[353] (SCZ Judgment No 7 of 2002).

1.5.6.4 Facts in issue in criminal cases

Key to deducing the facts in issue in a criminal matter is a reference to the essential elements of the offence as it appears in the charge or summons. Unlike civil matters, where the accused pleads not guilty, all the facts necessary to prove the commission of the offence by the accused come into play as facts in issue whose legal burden to prove, as established in *Woolmington v DPP*,[354] lies on the prosecution.[355] As in trials in the High Court, summary trials as are normally held in the magistrates/subordinate courts demand of the prosecution the duty to direct whatever evidence they have only to those elements deemed essential as evidenced in the indictment. 'The facts in issue in a criminal case will be the commission by the accused of the *actus reus*, the presence of any necessary *mens rea*, and any defence, going beyond a mere denial of the prosecution case, which the defence must or may raise.'[356] By way of illustration, if the accused person is charged with theft by servant contrary to section 272 and 278 of the Penal Code,[357] the prosecution must, in order to secure a conviction, prove all the ingredients of the offence. As regards the offence of theft by servant therefore, the prosecution will have to prove beyond reasonable doubt the following:

- All the elements of the offence of theft.
- That at the time of the offence, the accused was employed by the complainant.
- That, the property which is the subject of the charge is actually property of the complainant.

Quite apart from the foregoing, the prosecution has to prove that the theft such as the accused is charged with fits the definition set out in s 265 of the Penal Code.[358] Further, the prosecution must adduce evidence that the accused did not have any bonafide claim of right to the property which is the subject of the charge. This is because s 8 of the Penal Code[359] provides thus: '[a] person is not criminally responsible in respect of an offence relating to property, if the act done or omitted to be done by him with respect to the property was done in the exercise of an honest claim of right and without intention to defraud.'

Veering away from the foregoing is a sojourn into the irrelevant which will only lead to (in the face of a robust focused defence using the foregoing

[354] [1935] UKHL 1; [1935] AC 462; 25 Cr App R 72; see also *Sims* [1946] KB 531 *per* Lord Goddard CJ at 539.

[355] Thus, as shown in *Saluwena v The People* [1965] ZR 4, '[i]f the accused's case is reasonably possible although not probable, then a reasonable doubt exists and the prosecution cannot be said to have discharged its burden of proof.' Be that as it may, in certain instances where the accused pleads as a defence, insanity or provocation, the legal burden to prove the facts in issue that arise as a result of these defences, lies on the accused. It behooves the prosecution to rebut such evidence as may be put before the court in support of the aforementioned defences, if they are to succeed in discharging their overall burden as set out in *Woolmington* and *Sims*, to prove the accused's guilt.

[356] Murphy P, *Murphy on Evidence* 24.

[357] Chapter 87 of the laws of Zambia.

[358] Chapter 87 of the laws of Zambia.

[359] Chapter 87 of the Laws of Zambia.

provisions of the law in favour of their client) the accused being entitled to his defence and acquittal if not at case or no case to answer stage, then at the conclusion of trial. As shown in *The People v Japau*,[360] '[a] submission of no case to answer may properly be upheld if an essential element of the alleged offence has not been proved,[361] or when the prosecution evidence has been so discredited by cross-examination, or is so manifestly unreliable, that no reasonable tribunal could safely convict on it.'[362]

We must conclude this part by referring to what are termed collateral or secondary facts in issue. They affect not only the admissibility of evidence but the credibility of witnesses. It is therefore permissible to call evidence to show or tending to show that secondary evidence relating to the authenticity of the contents of a document in question may be adduced because, after due search, the original cannot be found or that a confession is admissible for want of oppression. It is also permissible, as regards, the matter of credibility of witnesses, to call evidence to show that the witness in question '[…] is likely to be a witness with an interest of his own to serve or to be a witness with some bias;'[363] This is because, as shown in *Simon Malambo Choka v The People*,[364] '[a] witness with a possible interest of his own to serve should be treated as if he were an accomplice to the extent that his evidence requires corroboration.' Further, according to the holding in *Phiri and Others v The People*,[365] there must be something more than a belief in the truth of his evidence based simply on his demeanour and the plausibility of his evidence, and that "something more" must satisfy the court that the danger that the accused is being falsely implicated has been excluded and that it is safe to rely on the evidence of the suspect witness. The foregoing holdings are based on the earlier case of *Machobane v The People*.[366] The appellant was convicted in the High Court of the offence of stock theft. The material evidence was based on the testimony of the appellant's brother in whose kraal were found cattle which belonged to the complainant. The appellant appealed against conviction and sentence. It was held in parts relevant to our discussion that,

> [w]hile a conviction on the uncorroborated evidence of an accomplice is competent as a strict matter of law, the danger of such conviction is a rule of practice which has become virtually equivalent to a rule of

---

360 [1967] ZR 95 (HC); see also, *The People v Winter Makowela & Another* [1979] ZR 290.

361 See *Godfrey Chimfwembe v The People* (SCZ/9/145/2013).

362 See ss 206 or ss 291 of the Criminal Procedure Code Chapter 88 of the Laws of Zambia; *The People v Winter Makowela & Another* [1979] ZR 290; *The People v Mukemu* [1972] ZR 290; *Mwewa Murono v The People* 2004 ZR 207 (SC).

363 *Simon Malambo Choka v The People* [1978] ZR 243 (SCZ).

364 [1978] ZR 243 (SCZ).

365 SCZ Judgment No 1 of 1978.

366 [1972] ZR 101 (CA).

> law, and an accused should not be convicted on the uncorroborated testimony of a witness with a possible interest unless there are some special and compelling grounds.

Aside from the foregoing, it is also permissible to call evidence to show that the witness concerned is mentally unstable due to a mental illness rendering his testimony unreliable.

1.5.6.5 Facts relevant to facts in issue

We have already considered the subject of *relevance* above. We looked at and discussed the definition of *relevance* given by Lord Simon of Glaisdale in *DPP v Kilbourne*[367] wherein he said in part: 'evidence is *relevant* if it is logically probative or disprobative of some matter which requires proof.' Further, that 'it is sufficient to say [...] relevant evidence is evidence which makes the matter which requires proof more or less probable.'[368] It is thus worth repeating here that based on Lord Kilbourne's definition, relevant evidence is that which has probative value to assist the court in determining facts in issue. Far from being a legal concept, relevance is concerned with logic, that is, it styles the connection between a piece of evidence on the one hand, and a fact in issue on the other, the proof of which evidence is directed at. In short if the evidence proves or disproves a fact in issue it is relevant, if it cannot do either, it is irrelevant. It also ought to be repeated that while all admissible evidence (even that which is immaterial) is relevant, not all relevant evidence is admissible not only thanks to the many rules of evidence we have encountered thus far but will come across later in the text.

If as we have said above, relevance is a concept steeped in logic, it must plausible follow that its determination must, as shown in *Randall*,[369] follow the course of common sense. However, while the identification of relevant facts is easy, the same cannot be said about the narrative relating to the same facts in the abstract. Two examples properly illustrate the foregoing:

(i) Presumption of continuance

We must state from the outset that this is not a legal presumption but one grounded in logic. Even so, it is true that several facts and set of circumstances may, in the absence of an intervening event, continue unchanged (much like

[367] [1973] AC 729 at 756.

[368] See further definitions also discussed above including the more complex definition of relevance in Stephen's Digest and the simpler definition to be found in American Federal Rule of Evidence 401 where relevant evidence is simply defined as [...] evidence having any tendency to make the existence of any fact that is of consequence to the determination of the action more probable or less probable than it would be without the evidence.'

[369] [2004] 1 All ER 67 per Lord Steyn.

Newton's first law of motion, if you will). When such is the case, evidence that a fact existed at some time other than the time in issue is deemed relevant to prove the existence of such a fact at the time in issue.[370]

(ii) Admission of evidence of habit/routine practice

(a) General

The rule relating to admissibility of evidence of habit or routine practice entails that evidence of habit of an individual or a company or indeed any organisation may be admitted to prove that the person, company or organisation as the case may be did behave in a particular manner at the time in issue. The American Rule of Evidence 406, provides as follows on this matter: 'Evidence of the habit of a person or the routine practice of an organisation, whether corroborated or not and regardless of the presence of eyewitnesses, is relevant to prove that the conduct of the person or organisation on a particular occasion was in conformity with the habit or routine practice.' However, whatever the conduct/behaviour or routine for which this evidence sought, it is incumbent upon the defendant to show a consistent pattern of conduct, if he/it has to persuade the court that the conduct in issue is routine or habitual.

(b) The American Rule of Evidence Rule 406: habit/routine practice[371]

Evidence of a person's habit or an organisation's routine practice may be admitted to prove that on a particular occasion the person or organisation acted in accordance with the habit or routine practice. The court may admit this evidence regardless of whether it is corroborated or whether there was an eyewitness.

In an oft-quoted paragraph, McCormick,[372] describes habit in terms effectively contrasting it with character:

> Character and habit are close akin. Character is a generalised description of one's disposition, or of one's disposition in respect to a general trait, such as honesty, temperance, or peacefulness. 'Habit,' in modern usage, both lay and psychological, is more specific. It describes one's regular response to a repeated specific situation. If we

[370] See *Brown v Wren Brothers* [1851] 1 QB 390 (where evidence to prove that a partnership existed at some earlier time was admissible to support the inference that the partnership had continued to exist); *Attorney-General v Bradlaugh* (1885) 14 QBD 667 (where evidence that a person had held certain theological views before the time the court was concerned with was admitted to draw the inference that that the person had continued to hold such views at the time in issue); *Beresford v St Albans Justices* (1905) 22 TLR 1 (where evidence of the speed the person was driving at minutes before was admitted to draw the inference of what speed he had been driving at, at the time in issue); *Woolf v Woolf* [1913] P 134 (where it was held that sharing the same bedroom by a couple not married to each other was relevant to the allegation that they had committed adultery and the existence at the said time of an adulterous relationship).

[371] This portion is excerpted wholly from LII Federal Rules of Evidence Rule 406. Habit; Routine Practice https://www.law.cornell.edu/rules/fre/rule_406 retrieved on 19/04/22. Any changes made are for spelling, stylistic, structural reasons and referencing consistency with the rest of the text only.

[372] §162 at 340.

> speak of character for care, we think of the person's tendency to act prudently in all the varying situations of life, in business, family life, in handling automobiles and in walking across the street. A habit, on the other hand, is the person's regular practice of meeting a particular kind of situation with a specific type of conduct, such as the habit of going down a particular stairway two stairs at a time, or of giving the hand-signal for a left turn, or of alighting from railway cars while they are moving. The doing of the habitual acts may become semi-automatic.

Equivalent behaviour on the part of a group is designated "routine practice of an organisation" in the rule.

Agreement is general that habit evidence is highly persuasive as proof of conduct on a particular occasion [...]:[373]

> Character may be thought of as the sum of one's habits though doubtless it is more than this. But unquestionably the uniformity of one's response to habit is far greater than the consistency with which one's conduct conforms to character or disposition. Even though character comes in only exceptionally as evidence of an act, surely any sensible man in investigating whether X did a particular act would be greatly helped in his inquiry by evidence as to whether he was in the habit of doing it.

When disagreement has appeared, its focus has been upon the question what constitutes habit, and the reason for this is readily apparent. The extent to which instances must be multiplied and consistency of [behaviour] maintained in order to rise to the status of habit inevitably gives rise to differences of opinion.[374] While adequacy of sampling and uniformity of response are key factors, precise standards for measuring their sufficiency for evidence purposes cannot be formulated.

The rule is consistent with prevailing views. Much evidence is excluded simply because of failure to achieve the status of habit. Thus, evidence of intemperate "habits" is generally excluded when offered as proof of drunkenness in accident cases,[375] and evidence of other assaults is inadmissible to prove the instant one in a civil assault action.[376] In *Levin v United States*,[377] testimony as to the religious "habits" of the accused, offered as tending to prove that he was at home observing the Sabbath rather than out obtaining money through larceny by trick, was held properly excluded:

---

[373] McCormick §162 at 341.

[374] Lewan, Rationale of Habit Evidence, 16 Syracuse L.Rev. 39, 49 (1964).

[375] Annot., 46 A.L.R.2d 103.

[376] Annot., 66 A.L.R.2d 806.

[377] 119 U.S.App.D.C. 156, 338 F.2d 265 (1964).

> It seems apparent to us that an individual's religious practices would not be the type of activities which would lend themselves to the characterisation of 'invariable regularity.'[378] Certainly the very volitional basis of the activity raises serious questions as to its invariable nature, and hence its probative value.[379]

These rulings are not inconsistent with the trend towards admitting evidence of business transactions between one of the parties and a third person as tending to prove that he made the same bargain or proposal in the litigated situation.[380] Nor are they inconsistent with such cases as *Whittemore v Lockheed Aircraft Corp.*[381] upholding the admission of evidence that plaintiff's intestate had on four other occasions flown planes from defendant's factory for delivery to his employer airline, offered to prove that he was piloting rather than a guest on a plane which crashed and killed all on board while en route for delivery.

A considerable body of authority has required that evidence of the routine practice of an organisation be corroborated as a condition precedent to its admission in evidence.[382] This requirement is specifically rejected by the rule on the ground that it relates to the sufficiency of the evidence rather than admissibility.[383] The rule also rejects the requirement of the absence of eyewitnesses, sometimes encountered with respect to admitting habit evidence to prove freedom from contributory negligence in wrongful death cases.[384] The omission of the requirement from the California Evidence Code is said to have effected its elimination.[385]

> The language of Rule 406 has been amended as part of the restyling of the Evidence Rules to make them more easily understood and to make style and terminology consistent throughout the rules. These changes are intended to be stylistic only. There is no intent to change any result in any ruling on evidence admissibility.[386]

[378] 1 Wigmore 520.

[379] *Id.* at 272.

[380] Slough, Relevancy Unraveled, 6 Kan.L.Rev. 38–41 (1957).

[381] 65 Cal App 2d 737, 151 P 2d 670 (1944).

[382] 5 Kan.L.Rev. 404, 449 (1957).

[383] A similar position is taken in New Jersey Rule 49.

[384] For comment critical of the requirements see Frank, J., in *Cereste v. New York, N.H. & H.R. Co.*, 231 F.2d 50 (2d Cir. 1956), cert. denied 351 U.S. 951, 76 S.Ct. 848, 100 L.Ed 1475, 10 Vand.L.Rev. 447 (1957); McCormick §162, p. 342.

[385] Comment, Cal.Ev.Code §1105.

[386] Committee Notes on Rules—2011 Amendment.

1.5.6.6 *Facts forming part of the res gestae*[387]

Res gestae[388] refers to '[t]he events, circumstances, remarks, etc. which relate to a particular case, especially as constituting admissible evidence in a court of law.'[389] According to Lord Tomlin in *Homes v Newman*[390] *res gestae* is 'a phrase adopted to provide a respectable legal cloak for a variety of cases to which no formula of precision can be applied.' It may simply be roughly translated as 'the transaction' or 'the story.' While serving as a helpful starting point, none of the definitions or translations hereinbefore mentioned tell us anything about the rules of evidence relating to the facts pertaining to or establishing a measure of the transaction or the story. It is perchance worth mentioning that despite its status as a long-standing concept in the law of evidence, *res gestae* has always exercised the minds of advocates, judges and writers alike primarily because as we show later in this text, 'its precise doctrinal significance at common law has remained persistently unclear.'[391]

The inclusionary common law concept of *res gestae* entails that where a fact or statement of fact or opinion is so closely related in terms of time or place or set of circumstances with an act, an event or a state of affairs in issue 'that it can be said to form a part of the same transaction as the act or event in issue, [it] is itself admissible in evidence.'[392] In *The People v John Nguni,*[393] the accused was charged with manslaughter of one Knife Rive. The accused and the deceased were in the house of one William Phiri, where drinks were being sold. Esther Mawila, the wife of William Phiri was also present in the house. As a result of some remarks made by the deceased to Esther Mawila, the accused became annoyed, caught hold of the deceased and pushed hint outside the house. Some three minutes thereafter, the deceased came back and fell outside the doorway of the house crying "Look what John Ng'uni has done to me." The deceased bore a wound on the left forearm which was bleeding profusely. He died the following morning. The accused was arrested and was charged with the offence. The prosecution was unable to adduce direct evidence of the wounding and relied upon the alleged utterance by the deceased. It was submitted by the State that the alleged utterance by the deceased should be admitted as it formed part of the *res gestae*. It was held that evidence of a statement made by a person who is not called as a witness may be admitted as part of the *res gestae* and can be treated as an exception to the hearsay rule

[387] See analysis of the concept in the following cases: *Thompson v Trevanion* [1693] Skin 402; 14 Digest (Repl) 450, 4367; *Keefe v State* (50 Ariz 293); *People v Poland* 22 ILL 2d 175 at 181; *R v Bedingfield* [1879] 14 Cox CC 341; *O'Leary v R* [1946] 73 CLR 402; *Subramaniam v The Public Prosecutor* [1956] 1 WLR 965; *Ratten v The Queen* [1972] AC 378; *The People v John Ng'uni* [1977] ZR 376 (HC); *DPP v Christie* [1914] AC 545; 24 Cox CC; *Teper v R* [1952] AC 480; [1952] All ER 447; *R v Taylor* 1961 (3) SA 614; *The Schwalbe* [1861] Lush 239; 1 Digest (Repl) 234, 1247.

[388] Origin Latin, literally 'things done.'

[389] Meaning of *res gestae* in English Law www.lexico.com retrieved on 10/3/2020.

[390] [1931] 2 Ch 112, Ch D at 120.

[391] Dennis I, *The Law of Evidence* 736.

[392] Keane A & Mckeown P, *The Modern Law of Evidence* (9th edn OUP 2012) 355.

[393] [1977] ZR 376 (HC); see also *Keefe v State* (50 Ariz 293) *per* Lockwood J.

provided it is made in such conditions of involvement or pressure as to exclude the possibility of concoction or distortion to the advantage of the maker or to the disadvantage of the accused.[394]

There is another specific species of *res gestae* which relates to dying declarations which as seen already is exemplified in the celebrated case of *The People v John Nguni.*[395] 'The rationale for this is that it has been generally accepted that a dying person would not want to die with a lie on their lips, either in anticipation of meeting their maker or to die with a free conscience.'[396] A traditional authority is the 18th century case of *R v Woodcock.*[397] The accused was charged with and tried for the murder of his wife. Saying nothing about her impending death, she made a statement to a magistrate on oath. The Court took the view that she knew that she was going to die and as such held as follows:

> [...] The general principle on which the species of evidence is admitted s, that they are declarations made in extremity, when the party is at the point of death, and when every hope of this world is gone; when every motive to falsehood is silenced, and the mind is induced by the most powerful considerations to speak the truth; a situation so solemn and so awful is considered by law as creating an obligation equal to that which is imposed by a positive oath administered in a court of justice [....]

Thus, in *R v Mumenga,*[398] where the prosecution sought to put in evidence a statement by the deceased made to the District Commissioner as the victim lay dying in the hospital was ruled as being admissible as the deceased had made it '[...] under a settled hopeless expectation of death [...] and when the deceased had abandoned all hope of living, for he said to the recording magistrate 'Iam dying.''[399] However, in *The People v Pelete Banda,*[400] it was held *inter alia* that for the court to accept a dying declaration as such, the maker of the statement ought to have believed on reasonable grounds that he was in imminent danger of death or serious bodily harm. Additionally, that it was not a question of what the attacker intended but whether he had a reasonable apprehension that he was in danger of death or serious bodily harm.

The devil is, however, in the detail as the exception was much more limited than the phraseology would seem to imply. For example, it was held in *R v Madobi*[401] that the rule was inapplicable to a community in Papua

---

394 *Chisoni Banda v The People* (SCZ Judgment No 8 of 1991).

395 [1977] ZR 376 (HC); see also *Keefe v State* (50 Ariz 293) *per* Lockwood J.

396 Mwanza BJ, *Passing The Bar Made Easy: Evidence and Procedure* (Brian J Mwanza, 2020).

397 (1789) 1 Leach 500 at 502-504, *per* Eyre CB.

398 (1954) 5 NRLR 280.

399 But see *Waugh v R* [1950] AC 203 for a different decision on this point based on the circumstances and facts of that particular case.

400 [1977] ZR 363 (HC).

401 [1963] 6 FLR 1.

New Guinea where the future life was believed to be spent in comfort on a neighbouring island. The case of *R v Mead*[402] is authority for the position that dying declarations are only admissible where the charge in question related to murder or manslaughter and the circumstances of the death are the subject of the declaration.

There has been a decision in a recent case that has extended the concept of *res gestae* in this jurisdiction. It had always been the assumption that for a spontaneous statement made by a deceased to qualify as *res gestae*, there must not be passage of time between the happening of the event and the time the statement is made as demonstrated in *John Nguni*[403] where the deceased made the statement almost immediately, he was stabbed. However, the Supreme Court of Zambia has clarified this issue in *Samuel Mwamba Mutambalilo v The People.*[404] On the 17 September 2013 at Mkushi in the Central Province of the Republic of Zambia the appellant murdered Stanley Fwalanga (the deceased). Suffice to state that although the deceased died on the 17 September 2013, the incident which is in contention happened in May 2013. It was during the month of May 2013 when Oswald Siwila a general worker at Dausea Farm was awakened by a knock around midnight. When he opened the door, he found the deceased outside and since he was new in the area, he did not know the deceased. Oswald Siwila observed that the deceased was burnt from the neck up to the waist. He said the deceased told him that he had been burnt by the appellant whom he referred to as 'Bashi Mwaba.' According to Oswald Siwila, the deceased who was shivering said he needed clothes and fire to warm himself. Oswald Siwila then gave the deceased clothes and sat him by the fire so that the deceased could warm himself. The witness then went to wake up his neighbour Reagan Chilekwa, a member of the neighbourhood watch, who recognised the deceased. Fred Fwalanga and his wife were informed around 01:00 hours of the serious condition the deceased was in. The deceased told his relatives that he owed the appellant a sum of ZMW10.00 and when he failed to pay him, he poured hot water on him and that this happened at the appellant's house. The following morning the deceased was rushed to the hospital where doctors confirmed that the burns were a result of the hot water which had been poured on him. Meanwhile, the matter was reported to Mkushi Police Station and although the deceased was in a critical condition, he was able to talk and he informed Sergeant Nyirongo who interviewed him that. the appellant burnt him with hot water. The deceased was immediately admitted at Mkushi General Hospital. Interestingly, a statement was only recorded from him in hospital on the 4 September, 2013, four months after the incidence. The statement was produced and admitted in evidence without any objection from the defence. The following is the statement recorded by the police:

[402] [1824] 2 B & C 605.

[403] [1977] ZR 376 (HC).

[404] No 47/2015.

> I do recall very well on the 27th May, 2013 at around 18:00 hours, as I was coming from my grandmother going home, I passed through the home of M/Samuel Matambalilo whom I owed some money. When I reached there M/Samuel Matambalilo started asking me as to when I [was going to repay] him the money I [owed] him and I told him that I paid the money to his son when he was out. He started complaining that we the people of that area [...] were not good. He was saying these words whilst drinking home brewed beer. Then he went into the grass thatched kitchen whilst complaining without me knowing what he went to do. I just felt hot water being poured on me and I looked as to see who poured water on me. [At this precise moment] I [...] saw M/Samuel Matambalilo holding a pot. Then I had to undress the T-Shirt of which even my skin started peeling off. That is how I left the T-Shirt in his yard and started struggling to go home. When I reached the main road, I failed to move and just slept on the road. After sometime [,] I just [felt] people lifting me and when I opened [my] eyes I saw M/Samuel was among the people who lifted me and took me in the bush. [A]fter sometime in the bush, I [forced myself to move until I reached a certain Farm belonging to a certain white man and found two Security Guards whom I requested to spend a night with and asked them if they could inform my relatives]. On 28/05/2013 at around 02:00 hours [...] my relatives [...] came and picked me and took me to the Police and later took me to the Clinic. [I was] later [...] to Mkushi District Hospita1.

That the appellant was apprehended and charged with the offence of assault occasioning actual bodily harm. Trial could not proceed as the deceased passed away before he could testify. The issue in the above case was whether the statement made by qualified as *res gestae*, considering that it was made 6 hours after the event. In answering the question, the Court opined that the factor to consider was not the time that had passed between the incidence and the making of the statement, but whether going by what had transpired between the event and the making of the statement, the deceased had an opportunity for reasoned reflection which would have motivated him to concoct or distort the story surrounding the event. The Supreme Court relied on the case of *R v Andrews*[405] where a man was attacked and robbed by two men. The man named his attackers to the police, referring to the co-accused O'Neill by name and to the appellant, Donald Andrews as "Donald" or "Donavan". The victim died before trial. The House of Lords held that the evidence was rightly admitted as part of *res gestae*. Consequently, the Court upheld the decision of the High Court because, as already mentioned, the primary consideration was not whether time had passed but whether, during that time, the deceased had an opportunity to fabricate a story to his advantage and to the disadvantage of the accused person.

---

[405] [1987] 1 All ER 513.

The rationale for accepting such kind of evidence has been shown in *R Christie*[406] and *Adelaide Chemical and Fertilizer Co Ltd v Carlyle*[407] to be, among other things, the fact that in its absence, understanding the true nature of the transaction in question may, without such evidence shedding such light as only it can, appear to the court to be not only incomprehensible and indecipherable but also worthless. Evidence under the doctrine *res gestae* is thus received as an exception to the common law rule of hearsay[408] as evidence of things asserted by a party other than the witness on the stand.[409]

Right from the start, the exception and the limitations discussed above were attacked and panned. Uglow[410] contends that the exception as limited by its application to instances of manslaughter or murder as held in *R v Mead*[411] was, never mind the rather curious decision in *R v Madobi*[412] on the subject, as colourful an anachronism of the common law of hearsay as one could ever get. He adds as follows:[413]

> [...] its justification was assaulted on all sides, not least on the basis that a victim of a serious assault, believing that they are about to die, is likely to be in a highly emotional and probably confused state, a state, moreover, where theological concerns have less significance than in previous centuries. Indeed, it has been suggested that motives such as a desire to protect relatives or close friends or to pay off old scores may be as significant.

It is worth mentioning before moving on that the expansion of *res gestae* under the Criminal Justice Acts of 1995 and 2003 in England & Wales has seen the significance of this exception diminished in those jurisdictions. Not so in this jurisdiction where the lack of statutory innovation has left the system in dire straits making it harken back to the days of old with reliance of local authorities which themselves were derived from English authorities which have long been overtaken by contemporary statutory provisions. That bus is yet to arrive at, let alone leave the station.

Sir Rupert Cross[414] has categorised the cases in which hearsay evidence has been admitted under the concept of *res gestae* as follows:[415]

---

406 [1914] AC 545, HL at 553 *per* Lord Atkinson.

407 [1940] 64 CLR 514 (High Court of Australia) at 531.

408 See basis as elucidated by Lockwood J in the American case of *Keefe v State* (50 Ariz 293); *R v Andrews* [1978] AC 281 *per* Lord Ackner.

409 But see dicta to the contrary *per* Lord Atkinson in *R v Christie* [1914] AC 545, HL at 553 and *per* Dixon J in *Adelaide Chemical and Fertilizer Co Ltd Carlyle* [1940] 64 CLR 514 (High Court of Australia) at 531.

410 Uglow S, *Evidence: Cases and Materials* (2nd edn Sweet & Maxwell, 1997).

411 [1824] 2 B & C 605.

412 [1963] 6 FLR 1.

413 Uglow S, *Evidence: Cases and Materials* at 614.

414 Tapper C, *Cross and Tapper on Evidence* 567-77; RN Gooderson, "*Res Gesta* in Criminal Cases" [1956] CLJ 199 and [1957] CLJ 55.

415 As paraphrased in Keane A & Mckeown P, *The Modern Law of Evidence* 355.

(i) Statements by participants in or observers of events or, as they would more accurately be described in the light of subsequent developments, statements by persons emotionally overpowered by an event;
(ii) Statements accompanying the maker's performance of an act;
(iii) Statements relating to a physical sensation; and
(iv) Statements relating to a mental state

1.5.7 *Principles of evaluation*

There will inevitably come a time during trial at which the court will have to evaluate the conduct of a party against an already set objective canon. For this to happen, it will have to be shown/proved to the court what the objective test at the material time is or was. We may think here of the standard of the reasonable man[416] required in the tort of negligence. This standard, demands that evidence be given as to how a reasonable man faced with similar circumstances as the defendant/accused may have acted. Once established, this aspect will, become relevant to the assessment of how the defendant in question acted. While it is not expected that a man on the clapham bus will behave as a lawyer, doctor or electrician will,[417] unless he is one, it must be remembered that in circumstances where the defendant professes to be a member of a profession, he must, in dealing with others, exhibit a degree of skill or care expected of members of that profession. If the preceding is the case, and because this will fall outside the usual experience of common men and the court, 'the [objective] standard may be proved' as shown in *Chapman v Walton*,[418] 'by expert evidence of the conduct in such circumstances [....]'[419] Expert evidence may also be proved as regards matters relating to what is accepted practice of men of commerce, as exemplified in *Noble v Kennoway*[420] where it was held on the basis of expert evidence that an underwriter under an obligation to inform himself with respect to the practice of the trade he in regardless of whether such practice is established or not.[421]

1.6 Characteristics of the law of evidence

It is perhaps important to deal with the characteristics of the law of evidence at this point before going further in the text to get a sense of the length, breadth and depth and how it interacts with other parts of the law.

---

[416] Described by Sir Richard Henn Collins MR in *McQuire v Western Morning News* [1903] 2 KB 100 at 109 as "the man on a Clapham Omnibus." The phrase is generally attributed to Lord Bowen whom, as junior counsel, first coined the phrase in the *Tichborne Claimant case* in 1871; see also Room R (ed.), *Brewer's Dictionary of Phrase and Fable* (15th edn 1996) 761.

[417] Rogers WVM, *Winfield & Jolowicz Tort* (18th edn Sweet & Maxwell 2010).

[418] (1833) 10 Bing 57.

[419] Murphy P, *Murphy on Evidence* 31.

[420] [1780] 2 Doug KB 510; *Fleet v Murton* [1871] QB 126.

[421] https://onlinelibrary.wiley.com/doi/pdf/10.1111/j.1468-2230.1969.tb01239.x retrieved on 6/4/21.

1.6.1 *The law of evidence originated, beginning in the 17th c. rulings of English common law judges*

Rulings of 17th c. English common law judges have broadly been imported into this jurisdiction as such. As noted earlier in the text, there has been, unlike the situation is in England, very little statutory intervention in this area to date. Be that as it may, both aspects attendant to the development of the law of evidence have lent themselves to two concepts unique to the system of adversarial procedure which is at the centre of the conduct of trials in Zambia namely: (a) party autonomy on the one hand and (b) orality of evidence on the other. We discuss these concepts in turn below:

1.6.1.1 Party autonomy

The concept of party autonomy under the law of evidence necessary means that the parties return the independence to decide to commence and or defend the matter in court. It is for the parties to conduct a thorough investigation, to collate the evidence and decide what facts to bring to court. The parties will also have the liberty to decide which witnesses and how many of those witnesses are going to testify before court. In this entire process, the court will, but for seeking clarification and ensuring that the trial is conducted in accordance with the law and procedural rules, be a silent observer or umpire listening to the evidence and arguments presented by the parties and ruling on questions of law and fact raised during trial.

It is also the case that the parties may compromise in civil matters or where the matter is criminal in nature, have the accused plead guilty to the same or lesser charge thereby obviating the need for a trial. In fact, according to XXXI Rule 4(1) of the High Court (Amendment) Rules,[422] all matters are subject to referral to mediation, again lessening the number of cases that actually end up going to trial. It therefore would seem that despite what it is meant to do, the adversarial system of litigation does not in many cases live up to its intended purpose, that is, '[...] a free-raging official enquiry into the truth of disputed or uncertain facts.'[423] Rather, '[it] is more of a process in which, if the matter ever gets to trial, two or more parties present competing versions of a past or present reality and invite the adjudicator to choose between them.'

1.6.1.2 Orality of evidence

The principle of orality is synonymous with the concept of testimony which in common legal parlance is applied to the evidence that a witness gives under oath or affirmation as the case may be. Sworn or affirmed statements such as those hereinbefore described are offered to the court as being true because the witness says so or simply as evidence of facts stated. While, as we have

[422] SI No 72 of 2018.

[423] Dennis I, *The Law of Evidence* 15.

already noted testimony is synonymous with orality, the rules of evidence coupled with those of both the criminal law and civil procedure have, by way of statute or common law permitted for the use of written sworn evidence to be admitted into evidence by way of what are referred to as affidavit evidence with regard to, as already discussed elsewhere in this text, chamber matters whether these be substantive as are all matters referenced under Order XXX, HCR or interlocutory,[424] or judicial review proceedings.

The foundational significance of orality to adversarial adjudication generally less so in civil matters than criminal proceedings was concisely stated in the High Court ofAustralia decision of Butera *v Director of Public Prosecutions for The State of Victoria:*[425]

> The adducing of oral evidence from witnesses in criminal trials underlies the rules of procedure which the law ordains for their conduct. A witness who gives evidence orally demonstrates, for good or ill, more about his or her credibility than a witness whose evidence is given in documentary form. Oral evidence is public; written evidence may not be. Oral evidence gives to the trial the atmosphere which, though intangible, is often critical to the jury's estimate of the witnesses. By generally restricting the jury to consideration of testimonial evidence in its oral form, it is thought that the jury's discussion of the case in the jury room will be more open, the exchange of views among jurors will be easier, and the legitimate merging of opinions will more easily occur than if the evidence were given in writing or the jurors were each armed with a written transcript of the evidence.

Orality as a principle simply means that evidence relating to disputed facts ought to be given by witnesses called to court and put on the witness stand to testify to such facts as are disputed based on their knowledge of the facts in question. Only in such a way will, or so the argument goes, the court be able to make a determination based on not only the demeanour of the witness, but the usual reliability of evidence given under oath which is then tested under cross-examination.[426] In addition, oral testimony ensures 'maximum participation in decision-making in the sense that parties can confront their accusers and challenge the evidence against them'[427] through the device of cross-examination. To that end, Article 18(2)(e) provides that

> [e]very person who is charged with a criminal offence-shall be afforded facilities to examine in person or by his legal representative the witness called by the prosecution before the court, and to obtain attendance and carry out the examination of witnesses to testify on his behalf before the court on the same conditions as those applying to witnesses called by the prosecution.

[424] See *Sun Country Limited v Charles Kearney and Another* SCZ Appeal No 7 of 2017.

[425] (1987) 164 CLR 180 at 189 para 15; Coram: Mason C.J., Brennan, Deane, Dawson and Gaudron JJ.

[426] See however, s 78 in the Children's Act, 2022 that provides for a different approach in proceedings relating to children.

[427] Dennis I, *The Law of Evidence* 15.

The technique is not fool proof and is liable to generating inaccurate findings by the court where the witness in question lacks credibility or/and reliability. This concern and others like it led the common law to develop rules and techniques aimed at guaranteeing not only the credibility of testimony but its reliability too. We outline five of those rules below:

- A witness could only speak to matters within his personal knowledge, thus excluding hearsay evidence.
- A witness was (and still is generally) required to be sworn in (or to affirm) that the testimony he was going to give was the truth, the whole truth and nothing but the truth with the consequence that if he lied on oath, he would be liable to being prosecuted for the offence of perjury. This is now subject to s 212[428] of the Criminal Procedure Code[429] which permits the giving of unsworn evidence[430] in criminal matters which because it is not subject to cross-examination does not carry the same weight as that which is tested under cross-examination.
- The witness was (and to a large extent still is more so in criminal proceedings and less so in civil ones) to give testimony orally to enable the court to determine his demeanour and factor this into the equation when determining the weight to be attached to that witness's testimony.
- The witness was (and still is) liable to cross-examination to test the veracity of his testimony thus testing his credibility or the reliability of his testimony
- In certain situations, it was permissible to introduce into evidence collateral facts as respect's a witness's bias, bad character and disability.

1.6.1.3 *Strict rules of evidence*

In defining the nature of civil and criminal proceedings,[431] the rules of evidence which have been developed according to the common law and statutory prescription are referred to as 'strict rules of evidence.' According to Butler Sloss P in *Re T*,[432] 'the strict rules of evidence applicable in a criminal trial, which is adversarial in nature, are to be contrasted with the partly inquisitorial approach of the court dealing with children's cases in which the rules of evidence are considerably relaxed.'

1.6.1.4 *The law of evidence while far-reaching lacks certainty as to its parameters*

The law of evidence is a species of adjectival law. However, while the law of evidence is concerned with the collection of evidence before trial, its presentation

[428] Part VI: Procedure in Trials Before Subordinate Courts.

[429] Chapter 88 of the Laws of Zambia.

[430] See on this issue, s 78 in respect of the Children's Act, 2022.

[431] See below, distinction of the law of evidence as regards criminal law proceedings on the one hand and civil proceedings on the other.

[432] [2004] 2 FLR 838.

during trial and evaluation for purposes of making a determination after trial, one cannot say for certain where the law of evidence starts and ends in certain respects e.g., as respects other parts of adjectival law namely procedural law. By way of illustration Article 18(5) of the Constitution provides for the concept of double jeopardy.[433] Article 18(6) provides for the effect of a pardon and Article 18(7) bars the conviction of anyone charged with a criminal offence unless 'that offence is defined and the penalty is prescribed in a written law.'[434] Whether one classifies an issue arising out of the foregoing as evidential rather than procedural will largely be a matter of test and not any defined boundaries as such.

1.6.1.5 *The law of evidence is untidy and complex*

The law of evidence does not provide us with clearly defined rules each with specific delineatory scope. What we find upon examination of the subject is its multifaceted structure with an interplay between specific rules and amorphous rules punctuated by flexible approaches to their application. It invites the use of discretionary powers by courts which may be strictly and quite liberally applied and thus generating an inconsistent and inscrutable mosaic for parties, advocates and judges alike.

1.7 Distinguishing civil and criminal proceedings

In trying to appreciate the multifaceted nature of the law of evidence one must understand the distinction that exists in its application to civil proceedings as opposed to proceedings of a criminal nature. As has already been highlighted and will be discussed in greater detail later in the text, there are differences in how the law of evidence is deployed as respects the following:

- (i) Admissibility of hearsay evidence;
- (ii) Judicial discretion; and
- (iii) Standard of proof, among others.

It will become readily discernible later, that compared to its application to civil cases and procedure, there is a more extensive application of the law

[433] In criminal matters a plea of *autrefois convict* and *autrefois acquit* corresponds to estoppel: s 138 of the Criminal procedure Code Chapter 88 of the laws of Zambia in line with Article 18(5) provides as follows: '[a] person who has been once tried by a court of competent jurisdiction for an offence, and convicted or acquitted of such offence, shall, while such conviction or acquittal remains in force, not be liable to be tried again on the same facts for the same offence'; Accordingly, s 20 of the Penal Code, Chapter 87 of the Laws of Zambia provides as follows: 'A person cannot be punished twice either under the provisions of this Code or under the provisions of any other law for the same act or omission, except in the case where the act or omission is such that by means thereof he causes the death of another person, in which case he may be convicted of the offence of which he is guilty by reason of causing such death, notwithstanding that he has already been convicted of some other offence constituted by the act or omission.'

[434] Provided that nothing in this clause shall prevent a court of record from punishing any person for contempt of itself notwithstanding that the act or omission constituting the contempt is not defined in a written law and the penalty therefore is not so prescribed.

of evidence and more evidentiary issues in criminal cases and procedure. 'Traditional common law rules, refined by the courts over three centuries, have been combined with a substantial amount of statute-based law to create an extensive and complex legal regime.'[435] That the foregoing is the case can be discerned from the fact that as shown in *Wildman v DPP*.[436] '[i]n criminal proceedings, the formal rules of evidence can be relaxed in relation to preliminary issues such as the extension of custody limits, so long as the issue is determined fairly.'[437]

The foregoing notwithstanding, an examination of the civil process in so far as the application of the law of evidence is concerned, shows that this too is a montage of different strands brought on by the existence of statutory provisions enacted to regulate rules of evidence in the individual statutes' spheres of influence. It goes without saying that other differences are apparent in the application of the rules of evidence in different courts. For example, the strictness and rigour with which the law of evidence and its rules is applied in the High Court's many civil divisions[438] is not matched by the relaxed rules to be found in its industrial relations division.[439]

Nor is there uniformity between the evidentiary rules that apply to usual civil courts such as the subordinate court, High Court, Court of Appeal, Constitutional Court and Supreme Court on the one hand and the Local Court on the other, nor one between the civil courts hereinbefore mentioned and different tribunals such as the Lands Tribunal,[440] Tax Appeals Tribunal,[441] Competition and Consumer Protection Tribunal[442] among others whose enabling statutes confer, as will be discernible from their names, specific relevant jurisdiction.[443] In each case, as regards application of the rules of evidence, the relevant statute may provide for such application thereby permitting their use or in the alternative, grant the relevant tribunal power to determine that tribunal's own

---

435 Dennis I, *The Law of Evidence* 17.

436 [2001] Crim LR 565.

437 Taken from Tapper C, Cross & Tapper on Evidence at 12; see the extension of this application to the questions relating to the determination of facts deemed relevant to disclosure of evidence to the defence: R v Law (1996) The Times, 15 August.

438 Which include among others, commercial, Probate, family.

439 This is a historical matter. Before the amendment of the constitution in 2016, the Industrial Relations Court was a stand-alone Court with its own Statutes and Rules. After the enactment, that Court became a division of the High Court but in the absence of new rules, has continued to use the same relaxed rules of procedure and relaxed approach to the application of the rules of evidence in labour disputes that come before it.

440 Created under the Lands Tribunal Act No 39 of 2010.

441 Created under the Tax Appeals Tribunal Act No 1 of 2015.

442 Created under s 67 of the Competition and Consumer Protection Act No 24 of 2010; See also, Competition and Consumer Protection (Tribunal) Rules, 2012 (SI No 37 of 2012).

443 See for example s 4 of the Lands Tribunal; s 5 of the Tax Appeals Tribunal; s 68 of the CCPC Tribunal.

procedure.[444] There appears to be no variation of style and detail in this area as the provisions relating to procedure are crafted similarly. The difference is only with regard to jurisdiction of individual tribunals as the statutes creating them may specify.

1.7.1 Where there is no specified procedure

The foregoing discussion presupposes statutory provisions that relate to jurisdiction and procedure as regards evidentiary matters. However, there are instances in which no statutory provisions are available. In that regard, the principal of natural justice[445] will hold sway in any trial or enquiry. The following cases exemplify this:

In *R v Deputy Industrial Injuries Commissioner Ex p. Moore,*[446] the applicant was employed as a crane driver. Every few minutes while at work, she had to lean forward in the cab of the crane for the purpose of seeing that the lift of the crane was correctly positioned for the load which was to be lifted. On one such occasion the movement caused a sharp pain in her back which disappeared when she straightened her back, but the pain later returned and three days afterwards she was found to have a prolapsed intervertebral disc. Her claim for industrial injury benefit was rejected by the insurance officer and, on appeal, by the local appeal tribunal. On appeal to the deputy industrial injuries commissioner, an oral hearing took place, during which unsworn evidence was given by a consultant orthopaedic surgeon who said that he thought that the prolapsed intervertebral disc was due to the tearing of a ligament when the applicant leant forward in the usual course of her work, and by a senior medical officer of the Ministry of Pensions and National Insurance who was of the opinion that there was probably a pre-existing degenerative condition of the applicant's back and that it was most unlikely that a normal ligament would be torn by the mere act of bending forward. Medical opinions which had been given in two other cases were referred to and the two medical witnesses were asked whether they agreed with them, and were cross-examined at some length

---

[444] See for example s 9 of the Tax Appeals Tribunal Act which provides as follows: **9**(1) The Tribunal may —*(a)* order the parties or either of them to produce to the Tribunal such information as the Tribunal considers necessary for purposes of the proceedings; or *(b)* take any other course which may lead to the just, speedy and inexpensive settlement of any matter before the Tribunal. (2) The Tribunal may summon witnesses, call for the production and inspection of any book, document, record or other thing, and examine witnesses. (3) A summons for the attendance of a witness or for the production of any book, document, record or other thing shall be signed by the Registrar and served in the same manner as a *subpoena* for the attendance of a witness at a civil trial in the High Court. (4) A person giving evidence or summoned to give evidence or to produce any book, document, record or other thing before the Tribunal shall be entitled to the same privileges and immunities as if the person were summoned to attend or were giving evidence in a civil proceeding before the High Court. (5) A person summoned under this section, other than a public officer or a person with an interest in the proceedings for which the person is summoned, may on the order of the Tribunal be paid from moneys appropriated by Parliament such allowances as may be prescribed; see also similarly worded provisions in ss 71 and 72 of the CCPC, 2010 as regards evidentiary matters before the CCPC Tribunal; and s 11 as regards evidentiary matters before the Lands Tribunal.

[445] Or in keeping with recent trends as shown *R (on the application of Smith) v Parole Board* [2005] UKHL 1; [2005] 1 All ER 755 HL, 'fairness.'

[446] [1965] 1 All ER; [1965] 1QB 465.

on them. The senior medical officer of the ministry expressed his agreement with those opinions. The deputy commissioner regarded the medical evidence in the previous cases as part of the evidence before him and dismissed the applicant's appeal, saying that the weight of the medical evidence was against the applicant. On appeal by the applicant from an order of the Queen's Bench Divisional Court dismissing a motion for an order of certiorari to bring up and quash the deputy commissioner's decision on the ground, *inter alia*, that he wrongly admitted as evidence the medical opinions in the previous cases, It was held that the applicant had not shown that there was an error of law on the face of the record by reason of the admission of inadmissible evidence and the appeal must be dismissed, since—(i) even if the rules of evidence applicable to court proceedings had to the applied, the medical opinions given in the previous cases had been put to the medical witnesses who had been invited to comment on them and who had been cross-examined on them and, accordingly, having been adopted by one medical witness, they became part of his evidence; and (ii) the National Insurance (Industrial Injuries) Act, 1946, and the regulations made thereunder contained no express provision relating to the procedure to be adopted on an appeal to a deputy commissioner while reg 26(1) (b)a of the National Insurance (Industrial Injuries) (Determination of Claims and Questions) Regulations, 1948, gave him discretion to determine 81 his own procedure, provided he observed the rules of natural justice, and he could take into account any material which had some probative value.[447]

In *Bushell v Secretary of State for the Environment,*[448] the House considered planning procedures adopted on the construction of two new stretches of motorway, and in particular as to whether the Secretary of State had acted unlawfully in refusing to allow objectors to the scheme to cross-examine the Department's witnesses. It held: He had not acted unlawfully (Lord Edmund-Davies's dissenting). Lord Diplock said:

> What is fair procedure is to be judged not in the light of constitutional fictions as to the relationship between the minister and the other servants of the Crown who serve in the government department of which he is the head, but in the light of the practical realities as to the way in which administrative decisions involving forming judgments based on technical considerations are reached. To treat the minister in his decision-making capacity as someone separate and distinct from the department of government of which he is the political head and for whose actions he alone in constitutional theory is accountable to Parliament is to ignore not only practical realities but also Parliament's intention. Ministers come and go; departments,

[447] Editor's notes: As to the hearing of appeals by industrial injuries commissioners, see 27 Halsbury's Laws (3rd Edn) 865, 866, para 1513; As to the purpose and application of the law of evidence to a quasi-judicial tribunal, see 15 Halsbury's Laws (3rd Edn) 261, 262, para 475; For the National Insurance (Industrial Injuries) Determination of Claims and Questions) Regulations, 1948, reg 26, see 15 Halsbury's Statutory Instruments (1st Re-issue) 320.

[448] [1981] AC 75: summary taken from https://swarb.co.uk/bushell-v-secretary-of-state-for-the-environment-hl-7-feb-1980/ retrieved on 16/04/22.

> though their names may change from time to time, remain. Discretion in making administrative decisions is conferred upon a minister not as an individual but as the holder of an office in which he will have available to him in arriving at his decision the collective knowledge, experience and expertise of all those who serve the Crown in the department of which, for the time being, he is the political head. The collective knowledge, technical as well as factual, of the civil servants in the department and their collective expertise is to be treated as the minister's own knowledge, his own expertise.

Further, that:

> The subject matter of [a local inquiry] is the objections to the proposed scheme that have been received by the minister from local authorities and from private persons in the vicinity of the proposed stretch of motorway whose interests may be adversely affected, and in consequence of which he is required [...] to hold the inquiry. The purpose of the inquiry is to provide the minister with as much information about those objections as will ensure that in reaching his decision he will have weighed the harm to local interests and private persons who may be adversely affected by the scheme against the public benefit which the scheme is likely to achieve and will not have failed to take into consideration any matters which he ought to have taken into consideration.

Lord Edmund-Davies (dissenting) spoke of the well-established basic principle that a defendant should have an opportunity of testing the evidence against him unless there are good and cogent reasons why that is either impossible or undesirable. He said:

> The general law may, I think, be summarised in this way: (a) In holding an administrative inquiry (such as that presently being considered) the inspector was performing quasi-judicial duties. (b) He must therefore discharge them in accordance with the rules of natural justice (c) Natural justice requires that objectors (no less than departmental representatives) be allowed to cross-examine witnesses called for the other side on all relevant matters, be they matters of fact or matters of expert opinion. (d) In the exercise of jurisdiction outside the field of criminal law, the only restrictions on cross-examination are those general and well-defined exclusionary rules which govern the admissibility of relevant evidence [...] beyond those restrictions there is no discretion on the civil side to exclude cross-examination on relevant matters.

In *Mahon v Air New Zealand,*[449] following an air disaster in which a civil aircraft owned by the defendant airline crashed in Antarctica killing the 257

[449] [1984] 3 All ER 201; [1983] NZLR 662; [1984] AC 808.

passengers and crew on board, the appellant, a judge of the New Zealand High Court, was appointed to be a royal commission to inquire into the cause and circumstances of the disaster. After a lengthy inquiry the judge produced a detailed report in which he found that the single, dominant and effective cause of the crash was the act of the airline in changing the computer flight track of the aircraft to fly directly at an Antarctic volcano, Mt Erebus, without telling the aircrew, who had been briefed on a flight path that would have taken the aircraft well to the west of Mt Erebus, and that that mistake was directly attributable to incompetent administrative procedures within the airline. The judge also found that the chief executive of the airline, certain of its executive pilots and members of the airline's navigation section had engaged in 'a pre-determined plan of deception [as] part of an attempt to conceal a series of disastrous administrative blunders' and that their evidence amounted to an 'orchestrated litany of lies'. In particular, the judge found that there had been a deliberate destruction, on the orders of the airline's chief executive, of all documents disclosing the mistake in changing the aircraft's flight track and that there had been a deliberate concealment from the relevant authorities of a change in the flight path used by the airline on Antarctic flights. The judge accordingly ordered the airline to pay $NZ150,000.00 by way of contribution to the cost of the inquiry. The airline applied for judicial review of the costs order in the royal commission report. The application was removed into the Court of Appeal, which held that the order should be set aside because the judge had acted contrary to natural justice and in excess of his jurisdiction in finding that members of the airline's management had conspired to commit perjury at the inquiry. The judge appealed to the Privy Council against the setting aside of the costs order. It was held as follows: (1) A tribunal making a finding in the exercise of an investigative jurisdiction (such as a royal commission) was required to base its decision on evidence that had some probative value, in the sense that there had to be some material that tended logically to show the existence of facts consistent with the finding and that the reasoning supporting the finding, if disclosed, was not logically self-contradictory.[450] (2) A tribunal exercising an investigative jurisdiction was also required to listen fairly to any relevant evidence conflicting with, and any rational argument against, a proposed finding that a person represented at the inquiry whose interests (including his career and reputation) might be affected wished to place before the inquiry. Accordingly, a person represented at the inquiry who would be adversely affected by a decision to make a finding was entitled to be informed that there was a risk of the finding being made and to be given the opportunity to adduce additional material of probative value which might deter the tribunal from making that finding.[451] (3) Since the judge's findings that there had been a deliberate destruction of documents and concealment of the change in flight path had been made in the absence of any probative evidence and without giving the persons affected by those findings the opportunity to rebut

[450] Dictum of Diplock LJ in *R v Deputy Industrial Injuries Comr, ex p Moore* [1965] 1 All ER at 94 applied.

[451] Dictum of Diplock LJ in *R v Deputy Industrial Injuries Comr, ex p Moore* [1965] 1 All ER at 95 applied.

them, and since those findings formed the basis of the judge's conclusion that members of the airline's management had conspired to commit perjury, which in turn was a major influence in inducing the judge to make the costs order, it followed that the costs order had been made in breach of the rules of natural justice and had rightly been set aside. The judge's appeal would accordingly be dismissed.[452]

It has been shown in *R v Commissioner for Racial Equality Ex p. Cottrell & Rothon (a firm)*[453] that the concept of natural justice is one to be applied with elasticity and not rigidity. Thus, in *Lanford v General Medical Council*,[454] the appellant, a registered medical practitioner, was charged by the Professional Conduct Committee of the General Medical Council with using obscene and indecent language and behaving improperly to two female patients in the course of professional consultations and examinations. The incidents were said to have taken place about six days apart. In one case the appellant allegedly used obscene language and indecently assaulted the patient when conducting an internal inspection to check the position of a coil. In the other case the appellant allegedly used obscene language and behaved improperly towards the patient when she consulted him about an infected toe. The language and acts complained of had no relevance to the medical examination itself. There was a striking similarity in what the appellant allegedly said to both patients but not in what he did to them. The legal assessor directed the committee on corroboration by stating that the evidence of each patient was capable of amounting to corroboration of the other's account if they gave independent evidence of separate incidents involving the appellant, the circumstances were such as to exclude any danger of a jointly fabricated account and there was such a striking similarity or similarities in each account as to be probative. The committee found the appellant guilty of serious professional misconduct and ordered that his name be erased from the register. The appellant appealed to the Privy Council, contending (1) that the legal assessor had misdirected the committee on the question of corroboration since he should have warned them against treating one incident as corroboration of the other because the admitted similarity in what the appellant allegedly said to each patient could not properly be relied on by the prosecution where there was no striking similarity in what he allegedly did to them and (2) that the complaints on which the charge was based ought to have been heard separately. It was held as follows: (1) Similar fact evidence was admissible if its similarities were either unique, in which event its probative value would approach that of a fingerprint, or striking, when the probative value would vary depending on how striking the similarity was. Since the evidence of what the appellant said before and after his examination of the patients tended, if believed, to prove that the relevant physical contact when examining them was indecent and improper the evidence of what he allegedly said in one case was capable of corroborating the evidence of indecency in the other, provided a striking similarity was found between the

[452] Editor's notes: For the right to be heard before a tribunal reaches a decision, see 1 Halsbury's Laws (4th edn) paras 74–76, and for cases on the subject, see 1(1) Digest (Reissue) 200–201, 1172–1176.

[453] [1980] 3 All ER 265.

[454] [1989] 2 All ER 921; [1990] AC 13.

two cases.[455] (2) Since there was a striking similarity between the two complaints it was eminently proper and in the interests of justice for the two complaints to be heard together. It followed therefore that the appeal would be dismissed. *Per curiam:* (1) The onus and standard of proof in disciplinary proceedings before the Professional Conduct Committee of the General Medical Council and the relevant legal principles were those applicable to a criminal trial. (2) Where a charge of professional misconduct is founded on two or more separate incidents, those incidents should each be made the subject of a separate charge of professional misconduct instead of being listed as particulars of one offence of professional misconduct. Such a practice should be followed even when the prosecutor intends to have the charges heard together, as he may properly do in many cases.[456]

1.8 Functions of the judge at trial

1.8.1 General

In so far as courtroom drama goes, the judge, unless restrained by law, exercises almost unquestioned and wide-ranging authority. This is more so in a non-jury jurisdiction such as Zambia whether the trial concerned in civil or criminal. In civil proceedings for example, the judge determines questions of admissibility of evidence, amendments, if any, to pleadings, among other matters. The judge is also responsible for controlling proceedings in his/her court. Be that as it may, a plaintiff[457] is free to terminate proceedings by filing a notice of discontinuance which serves to notify both the court presiding over such a case and the defendant[458] therein of the said discontinuance. The same wide-ranging authority is exercised by a magistrate or judge as the case may be, in criminal matters, as shown in *Broad v R*[459] as respects discontinuance through amendment of indictment, evidence, acceptance of a plea of guilty as same will be of no effect unless the presiding magistrate consents to said discontinuance. Having said that, we ought to be alive to the overriding power that the Director of Public Prosecutions is clothed with under the Criminal Procedure Code[460] to stop a prosecution by way of entering of what is termed a nolle prosequi.[461] In s 81(1) of that Act it is provided as follows:

455 *Boardman v DPP* [1974] 3 All ER 887 applied.

456 Editor's notes: For serious professional misconduct by a medical practitioner, see 30 Halsbury's Laws (4th edn) paras 123, 125, and for cases on the subject, see 33 Digest (Reissue) 294–297, 2360–2368.For the admissibility of evidence of similar offences and acts of the accused, see 11 Halsbury's Laws (4th edn) paras 375–381, and for cases on the subject, see 14(2) Digest (Reissue) 509–521, 4167–4248.

457 Or petitioner/ applicant/appellant as the case may be.

458 Or respondent.

459 (1979) 68 Cr App R 281.

460 Chapter 88 of the Laws of Zambia.

461 *Nolle prosequi* [ˌnälēpräsəˌkwē], abbreviated nol or nolle pros, is legal Latin meaning "to be unwilling to pursue;" a formal notice of abandonment by a plaintiff or prosecutor of all or part of a suit or action. In Commonwealth and US common law, it is used for prosecutors' declarations that they are voluntarily ending a criminal case before trial or before a verdict is rendered; it is a kind of motion to dismiss and contrasts with an involuntary dismissal.

> In any criminal case and at any stage thereof before verdict or judgment, as the case may be, the Director of Public Prosecutions may enter a nolle prosequi, either by stating in court, or by informing the court in writing, that the People[462] intend that the proceedings shall not continue, and, thereupon, the accused shall stand discharged in respect of the charge for which the nolle prosequi is entered, and, if he has been committed to prison, shall be released, or, if he is on bail, his recognizances shall be treated as being discharged; but such discharge of an accused person shall not operate as a bar to any subsequent proceedings against him on account of the same facts.

Section 81(1) restricts the entry of *nolle prosequi* to "any stage thereof before verdict or judgment." A question arose in the case of *R v Grafton (John Peter)*[463] as to whether the DPP could justifiably and without prejudice, invoke the power [under s 81(1)] to discontinue the case after the court had received part of the prosecution's evidence. The EWCA held that this was permissible to do at common law as the power to discontinue could be exercised even at this late stage. *R v Canterbury Justices Ex p. Klisiak,*[464] is authority for the fact that the prosecution can discontinue proceedings in the magistrates' courts at any time as long as this is before "[...] verdict or judgment." The Court also held the view that if such was the case, the court would not, as ordinarily should be the case with the entry of a *nolle,* order a discharge, but rather an acquittal.[465] This position finds support in s 201 of the Criminal Procedure Code[466] which provides as follows: 'If a complainant, at any time before a final order is passed in any case under this Part, satisfies the court that there are sufficient grounds for permitting him to withdraw his complaint, the court may permit him to withdraw the same, and shall, thereupon, acquit the accused.'

It will be apparent from the foregoing that the judge's role in an adversarial system such as ours is to be neutral and to act as an umpire.[467] As argued by counsel in *Priscillar Mwenya Kamanga v Attorney-General, Peter N'gandu Magande*[468] 'the judge's neutrality and impartiality is cardinal in our adversarial system. The judge [is], therefore, not expected to descend into the dust of the conflict.' In *Mumba and Others v The People,*[469] the Supreme Court of Zambia said the following said regarding the participation of a judge in a trial: '[w]hereas, a court may occasionally ask one or two question on matters of clarification, it is very undesirable for it to take active role in examining a witness.' The reason for this is very simple, for a court to take an active role in the trial, said the

[462] That is to say the Prosecution.

[463] [1992] 3 WLR 532; [1992] 4 All ER 609.

[464] [1981] 2 All ER 129.

[465] See Okotie (unreported November 12, 1998, CA) which is authority for the point that the Court has no jurisdiction to tell the prosecution what to do except in very exceptional situations.

[466] Chapter 88 of the Laws of Zambia.

[467] A judge must, according to *Porter v Magill* [2002] 1 All ER 465, be a "a fair minded and informed observer."

[468] [2008] 2 ZR 7 (SC); *Jones v National Coal Board* [1957] 2 ALL ER 155; *Re Enock and Zaretzky, Bock and Co* [1910] 1 KB 327; *Porter v Magill* [2002] 1 ALL ER 465.

[469] SCZ Appeal No 92 of 1995 (unreported).

Supreme Court, '[...] may compromise the court's neutral position in the eyes of the parties i.e., possible bias on the part of the court may not be ruled out.'

The litigants themselves are responsible for producing the proof and the quality of the proof upon which the Court will determine the case at hand.[470] On this, Lord Denning's dictum in *Jones v National Coal Board*[471]" is instructive: '[a] judge is not allowed in a civil dispute to call a witness whom he thinks might throw light on the facts. He must rest content with the witnesses called by the parties.'[472] As a result, as shown above and as will be shown in the following chapters of this text, an intricate set of rules exists to manage not only the trial in general but the actions of counsel in particular. As such in a criminal case the magistrate or judge will preside over a trial in a manner that ensures fairness ensuring that the rules on procedure and evidence are followed. Thus, as already shown above, in criminal matters, the admission of evidence, taking of plea and the question of indictments all come within the judge's sphere of control.

1.8.2 Classification of a judge's functions

In a non-jury jurisdiction such as Zambia, a judge's functions fall into the following:

(i) Admissibility of evidence
(ii) Control over questions to be considered by the judge as a trier of fact
(iii) Control of issues to be considered by the judge at law

We consider the above in turn.

1.8.2.1 Admissibility of evidence

It is the sole responsibility of the parties in a case to produce such evidence as they feel the court ought to have through oral testimony, documentary evidence or such pleadings as the case in question demands. How much of this is produced is largely dependent on the facts available, the experience and skill of counsel, where parties are in fact represented. Admissibility relates to whether the evidence that any party to a case seeks to bring before court meets the test of relevance, weight and fairness. As a primary question of fact, it is for the judge and the judge alone to decide whether the foregoing conditions for admissibility have been met 'and normally the question whether an item of evidence is admissible is a wholly different question to that which needs to be decided in the action itself.'[473] Be that as it may 'it may replicate the very

---

[470] See *Jones v National Coal Board* [1957] 2 ALL ER 155; *Re Enock and Zaretzky, Bock and Co* [1910] 1 KB 327 quoted in *Priscillar Mwenya Kamanga v Attorney-General, Peter N'gandu Magande* [2008] 2 ZR 7 (SC).

[471] [1975] 2 All E R 155.

[472] Quoted by counsel in *Priscillar Mwenya Kamanga v Attorney-General, Peter N'gandu Magande* [2008] 2 ZR 7 (SC).

[473] Uglow S, *Evidence: Text and Materials* 2nd edn (Thomson Sweet & Maxwell) 50-1.

question that the judge later needs to decide.'[474] This was amply demonstrated by Lord Denman CJ as he then was, in *Doe d. Jenkins v Davies*:[475]

> There are conditions precedent which are required to be fulfilled before evidence is admissible for the [court]. Thus, an oath, or its equivalent, and competence, are conditions precedent to admitting viva voce evidence; and the apprehension of immediate death to admitting evidence of dying declarations; a search to secondary evidence of lost writings; and stamps to certain written instruments; and so is consanguinity or affinity in the declarations of deceased relatives. The judge alone has to decide on their credibility. If counter-evidence is offered, he must receive it before he decides [....]

In doing all the things outlined by Denman CJ, the Judge/Magistrate can ask for no one's opinion though he may ask counsel to address him on any point for which he seek to make a determination in so far as that relates to 'the fact on a condition precedent.'[476] Where the issue is one that the judge/magistrate will have to decide at the end of the trial, the court ought to make a *prima facie*[477] determination as to whether the evidence can be admitted having met the level of sufficiency required or that it should be rejected as being inadmissible on the premise that the objections to its admission are on *terra firma*. Even if the Court pivots towards accepting the evidence in question *prima facie*, it will still need to hear the foundation of the defence to decide the core question regarding which it has made a *prima facie* decision. The case of *Stowe v Querner*[478] exemplifies this. The plaintiff brought an action against an insurance company on an insurance policy. It was countered by the defendant that said policy had never been executed. The plaintiff sought to introduce secondary evidence of the contents of the original insurance policy which had, according to the plaintiff, allegedly been lost. The judge admitted the secondary evidence but still left the question as to whether the defence claim had never existed to the jury. Of course, within the context of the no such thing would happen. As such the judge would have to decide the defence claim himself at the end of trial in his judgment. We now turn to the discussion relating to the *voire dire* which mainly happens in criminal proceedings but is not unheard of in civil cases as regards admissibility of evidence.

---

474 Uglow S, *Evidence: Text and Materials* 51.

475 (1847) 10 QB 314 at 323.

476 Uglow S, *Evidence: Text and Materials* 51.

477 As said in *The People v The Principal Resident Magistrate Ex Parte Faustine Kabwe and Aaron Chungu* (SCZ Judgment No 17 of 2009), by Sakala CJ as he then was, the expression *"prima facie"* is from Latin. According to various English Dictionaries, among many others, the expression means: on its first appearance; by first instance; at first sight; at first view; on its face; the first flush; and from a first impression.

478 (1870) LR 5 Ex. 155.

1.8.2.2 *Voire dire*

(i) A general analysis

The term *voire dire*[479] comes from the Anglo-Norman language.[480] The term *voir* (or *voire*), in the foregoing amalgamation, originates from Old French and descends from the Latin term *verum*,[481] itself linked to the contemporary French word *voire*, ("indeed"), but not to the more common word *voir* ("to see"), which arises from the Latin term *vidēre*. The great jurist William Blackstone referred to it as *veritatem dicere*,[482] which was translated by John Winter Jones[483] as "[t]o speak the truth." The contemporary interpretation is now premised on the false etymology to mean "to see [them] say". In contemporary Canadian legal French, the expression is presently used as *le voir-dire*.

Historically, a challenge to the standing and remaining of a particular juror on the jury would attract trial by other members of the jury. In those circumstances, the challenged juror would take an oath of *voir dire*, meaning "to tell the truth."[484] However, when the function of trying challenges to jurors was transferred to the judge, the foregoing process was discontinued by default.

In Australia, the rule about *voire dire* is in s 189 of the Evidence Act 1995 which provides as follows: "[o]n a *voir[e] dire*, parties can call witnesses, cross-examine opponent's witnesses and make submissions- as they might in the trial proper."[485] The High Court of Australia has held in *Jago v The District Court of NSW and others*[486] that the *voire dire* is an unsuitable forum for the trial judge to rebuke counsel or for counsel to make submissions as to the conduct of the court to the trial judge.[487]

In Zambia and other commonwealth jurisdictions[488] which we have considered above, *voire dire* refers to a "trial within a trial." It is essentially a hearing to determine the admissibility of evidence, or the competency of a witness or juror (as the case may be).[489] It is triggered, particularly in criminal trials, by disputes relating to admissibility of evidence where there is an objection to certain types of evidence being produced. By way of example

---

479 (Pronounced /ˈvwɑːr dɪər/; often /vɔɪr daɪər/).

480 *American Heritage Dictionary of the English Language* 5th edn (Houghton Mifflin Harcourt 2019) Retrieved 13 May, 2020.

481 "that which is true."

482 Blackstone W, *Blackstone's Commentaries on the Laws of England. Book 3*, Ch. 23. p.394: *'A juror may himself be examined on oath of voir dire, veritatem dicere ....'*

483 Jones, J. (1823). *A Translation of All the Greek, Latin, Italian, and French Quotations which Occur in Blackstone's Commentaries on the Laws of England, And Also in the Notes of the Editions by Christian, Archbold, and Williams.* Vol. III. p. 197.

484 Blackstone's Commentaries, vol. 3 p. 364.

485 Jill Hunter et al, *The Trial* (The Federal Press, 2015) 55.

486 (1989) HCA 46.

487 Moles, Robert N, Sangha Bibi (3 May 2007). "*Jago v The District Court of NSW and others* (1989) HCA 46."

488 Which include the United Kingdom (except Scotland), Cyprus, Hong Kong, Ireland, Australia, New Zealand, Papua New Guinea and Canada.

489 Duhaime L, "*Voir Dire* definition". *Duhaime's Legal Dictionary*. Duhaime.org. Retrieved 13 May 2020.

where, as is usually the case, a police officer whose was the arresting or/ and the investigation officer before trial, does during his oral evidence tell the court that he interviewed the accused who voluntarily confessed,[490] and thereby seeks to introduce the confession document into evidence, the defence may object to the production of such a confession document to the crime with which the accused is charged citing involuntariness. While '[t]he argument as to admissibility often involves points of law and can be disposed of on the basis of depositions and submissions of counsel',[491] ordinarily, when such an objection is raised, the judge will be compelled to conduct a factual inquiry to probe into whether there are grounds to admit into evidence the confession (or indeed any other evidence) whose admissibility is now objected to by the defence. Such a hearing will of course happen in open court and not in chambers. As shown in *Lawrence*[492] the accused, his legal advisors and the prosecution should all be present. For the foregoing reasons, in jurisdictions where the jury system is used, to avoid bias, the jury may be removed from the court for the *voire dire*. Of course, no such move is necessary in our jurisdiction where the judge is both trier of fact and interpreter of the law.

The absence of a jury in our legal system entails that the judge will remain present even when the subject the *voire dire* relates to is the admissibility of a confession. This presents challenges of its own. The judge's presence during the, *voire dire*, for lack of an alternative given the constraints of the system means that there is a chance that, and some will argue this is a certainty, the hearing of incriminating evidence by the presiding judge prejudices the accused especially where he rules against the accused in the *voire dire*.[493] Be that as it may, it has been held in the Canadian case of *Erven v The Queen*[494] that evidence on a *voire dire* cannot impact the trial itself even in circumstances where the judge has ruled against the accused in the *voire dire*. This is because the assumption is that the judge will ordinarily ignore what he or she heard during *voire dire*.

(ii) *Voire dire* and juveniles

The foregoing shows that the court has little choice but to conduct "a trial within a trial" where the question of admissibility relates to a confession irrespective of forum in our court system.[495] Similarly, the court is statutorily mandated[496] to conduct a "trial within a trial" where the issue concerns the admissibility of evidence of a child of tender years whose competence to testify

---

[490] See ch 19 below; for a brief but lucid discussion of confessions see Hatchard J and Ndulo M, *The Law of Evidence* 272-4; *The King v Voisin* [1918] 1 KB 531; *R v Kahyata* [1964] Z&NR 86; *Zondo v R* [1964] Z&NRR 97; *Chileshe v The People* [1972] ZR 48; *Muwowo v The People* [1965] ZR 91; *R v Thompson* [1893] 2 QB 12 among others.

[491] Uglow S, *Evidence: Text and Materials* 51.

[492] [1933] AC 699.

[493] But see *Erven v The Queen* [1979] 1 SCR 926.

[494] [1979] 1 SCR 926.

[495] *Liverpool Juvenile Court Ex p. R* [1987] 2 All ER 668.

[496] See s 122 of the Juveniles Act chapter 53 as amended by Act No 3 of 2011.

is in question.[497] By way of illustration, s 78(1)(2) of the Children's Code[498, 499] provides as follows:

In terms of s 78(1),

> [w]here, in any criminal or civil proceedings against a person, a child is called as a witness, the juvenile court or Children's Court shall receive the evidence, on oath, of the child if, in the opinion of the juvenile court or Children's Court, the child possesses sufficient intelligence to justify the reception of the child's evidence, on oath, and understands the duty of speaking the truth.

The foregoing relates to competency, that is to say, whether the witness in question, say a child of tender years, is competent to give sworn testimony at trial. By virtue of s 78(1), (which is the exact replica of the former s 122 in the now repealed Juveniles Act[500]) the judge is, ('[w]here, in any criminal or civil proceedings against any person, a child below the age of fourteen is called as a witness,') called upon to receive the evidence, on oath, of the child.' However, this must only be so if 'in the opinion of the court, the child is possessed of sufficient intelligence to justify the reception of the child's evidence, on oath, and understands the duty of speaking the truth.' For the court to form such an opinion, it must 'conduct a factual inquiry to determine the question of the child's competence to testify through a '*voire dire.*' At the end of such a 'trial within a trial,' the court may conclude that '[...] the child is not possessed of sufficient intelligence to justify the reception of the child's evidence, on oath, and does not understand the duty of speaking the truth.'[501] In that case, under the former s 122 of the Juveniles Act,[502] the court was mandated not to receive the child's evidence. This is no longer the case under the Children's Code.[503] In place of the proviso that proscribed the receipt of sworn (or unsworn) evidence from a child [...] not possessed of sufficient intelligence to justify the reception of the child's evidence, on oath,' in circumstances where such a child 'does not' in addition, 'understand the duty of speaking the truth,'[504] is s 78(2) of the Children's Code which provides as follows:

---

[497] See the position of the Supreme Court on this matter in *Mucheleta v The People* [SCZ Appeal No 124/2015] where the point that evidence by a juvenile/minor was one to be subjected to a *voire dire* before it could be accepted; *The People v Thomas Manroe* (HPA/50/2010); *Ackson Mwape v The People* (SCZ Appeal No 132 of 2010); *Philip Mungala v The People* (SCZ Appeal No 003 of 2019).

[498] Act No 12 of 2022.

[499] Which replaces S 122 in particular and The Juveniles Act, Chapter 53 as amended by Act No 3 of 2011; A brief history relating to this provision is given in Kaluba BC, Evidence Law at 523-524 and the cases cited thereunder: s 120(1) of the Juveniles Ordinance, Chapter 8 of the Laws of Zambia (Repealed); *The People v Banda* [1972] ZR 307 (HC); *Mwelwa v the People v Humphrey Chikumbi* (HKSE/02/2010); *Mazabuka v The People* [1973] ZR 1 (CA).

[500] Chapter 53 of the Laws of Zambia (Repealed).

[501] See *Mucheleta v The People* [SCZ Appeal No 124/2015].

[502] Chapter 53 of the Laws of Zambia (Repealed).

[503] Act No 12 of 2022.

[504] See *Mucheleta v The People* [SCZ Appeal No 124/2015].

> [i]f, in the opinion of the juvenile court or Children's Court, the child does not possess sufficient intelligence to justify the reception of the child's evidence, on oath, and does not understand the duty of speaking the truth, the child may give—
> (a) unsworn evidence that may be received as evidence in a juvenile court or Children's Court; or
> (b) evidence through a child welfare inspector responsible for the child's case.

The use of the permissive "may" as regards the court's options in instances where it determines that sworn evidence may not be received from a child of tender yers appears to permit it to consider the circumstances, facts and nature of offence before it may allow the receipt of such evidence in unsworn format or through a child welfare inspector responsible for the child's case.' While the allowing of receipt of unsworn evidence is a departure from s 122 of the now repealed Juveniles Act,[505] it is more in keeping with contemporary treatment for child witnesses who are considered as belonging to the vulnerable class of witnesses that requires a variation of the strictures of the law of evidence by statutory injunction.

But there is more. If the court decides in favour of the child because in the court's opinion, the child 'is possessed of sufficient intelligence to justify the reception of the child's evidence, on oath, and does understand the duty of speaking the truth' and as such deems such testimony admissible, this may yet not make the 'accused [...] liable to be convicted of the offence unless that evidence is corroborated[506] by some other material evidence in support thereof implicating the accused.' Specifically, s 78(9) of the Children's Code,[507] provides as follows: '[a] juvenile court or Children's Court may, having regard to the nature and circumstances of the offence in question, require evidence presented before the juvenile court or Children's Court to be corroborated by some other material evidence.' Bear in mind though that as noted already, this presents the challenge of the 'trial within a trial' disclosing information which the court presiding over the *voire dire* may consider when, at the end of the trial and for purposes of rendering a verdict, thus prejudicing the accused.

In *Hampshire*[508] the prosecution's witness was a child who was a victim of a sexual assault whom the judge examined in circumstances similar to those envisaged under s 122 of the Children's Code[509] and formed the opinion, that the child was 'possessed of sufficient intelligence [...] and [did] understand the duty of speaking the truth' and as such competent to testify on oath. On appeal Auld J made the following observations '[...] In our judgment, [...] a judge who considers it necessary to investigate a child's competence to give evidence in addition to or without the benefit of an earlier view of a videotaped interview

[505] Chapter 53 of the Laws of Zambia (repealed).

[506] See *Mucheleta v The People* [SCZ Appeal No 124/2015].

[507] Act No 12 of 2022.

[508] [1995] 2 All ER 1019, *per* Auld J.

[509] Act No 12 of 2022.

[...] should do so in open court in the presence of the accused because it is part of the trial [....] In addition to the foregoing and because we have a none jury system, the Judge's function encompasses that which would only be the preserve of the jury in a jury system which is to say his is also '[...] to assess the child's evidence, including its weight, from the evidence he or she gives on the facts of the case after the child has been found competent to give it. The exercise of determining competence is not a necessary aid to that function [....]'

A point worth mentioning is the need to record proceedings during the *voire dire*. In *Makhanganya v R*,[510] Forbes FJ explained why it was essential that not only should the *voire dire* be conducted and the record show this but also that the record show in addition the actual questions put to the juvenile and the answers received, and the conclusions reached by the court.[511] Forbes FJ concluded his judgment with the following passage: '[u]nless a *voire dire* is carried out as I have indicated, trial court cannot be satisfied that a child is fit to be sworn, or even to give evidence unsworn, and unless a *voire dire* is recorded an appellate court cannot be satisfied that the trial court has appreciated and carried out its duty.'This decision was followed in *Sakala v The People*,[512] a decision that shows the fatal consequences of not properly conducting a *voire dire* by the trial court.[513] The applicant applied for leave to appeal against conviction and sentence. It was held that it is essential with regard to a juvenile of tender years that the trial court not only conduct a *voire dire* but also record the questions and answers and the trial court's conclusion to enable the appellate court to be satisfied that the trial court has carried out its duty. Baron JP (as he then was) opined as follows:[514]

> In the present case the record does not enable this court to satisfy itself that the trial court has appreciated and carried out its duty. Indeed, it appears on the face of the record that the magistrate did not satisfy himself that the juvenile was possessed of sufficient intelligence to justify the reception of his evidence. In the absence of a proper *voire dire* the court must discount the evidence of the juvenile and we are, therefore, with the greatest regret, left with no alternative but to grant this application; we will treat the hearing as the hearing of the appeal and allow the appeal and set aside the conviction and sentence.

The foregoing authorities, and other discussed in this text which were decided on the basis of s 122 of the now repealed Juveniles Act[515] must now be seen within the context of s 78(1)(2) of the the Children's Code.[516] It is perchance

[510] [1963] R and N 698.

[511] See *Chibwe v The People* [1972] ZR 239 (CA); *The People v Thomas Manroe* (HPA/50/2010); *Levy Ndalunga v The People* (SCZ Appeal No 003 of 2019).

[512] [1972] ZR 35 (CA).

[513] *Goba v the People* [1966] ZR 113 (CA); *Semani v The People* [1973] ZR 203 (CA).

[514] [1972] ZR 35 (CA) at 36, lines 1-5.

[515] Chapter 53 of the Laws of Zambia.

[516] Act No 12 of 2022.

worth remembering that in terms of s 65,[517] the Magistrates'/Subordinate Court '... sitting for the purposes of hearing a charge against a child or for any other purpose relating to a child shall constitute itself as a juvenile court.' It follows therefore that as shown in, *In Liverpool Juvenile Court Ex p. R*,[518] a *voire dire* is expected and ought to be conducted even if the issue arises at trial being conducted in the Subordinate Court or where such Court constitutes itself into a Juvenile Court as per s 63 of the Juveniles Act.[519] The burden of proving that evidence now impugned meets the test of admissibility lies on the party who seeks to adduce such evidence.[520] It is also worth mentioning that in proceedings relating to the criminal law, the prosecution bears the legal burden of proof.[521] Interestingly, the burden borne by the defence in criminal matters is similar to that in civil cases which is on a balance or preponderance of probabilities.

(iii) Cognitively impaired witnesses

When addressing the question of defective intellect, the law does not take a blanket approach nor indeed place such evidence in a special category. This is because such things as cognitive impairment borne of a temporal ailment or indeed inebriation would only incapacitate the witness concerned for a limited time period. As such, that would only call for an adjournment and nothing more as such a witness, will again be competent once he recuperates from the ailment or attains sobriety. Additionally, a witness may be cognitively impaired but still have his evidence admitted, as we soon show. The foregoing scenarios are different from a permanent or sustained cognitive impairment which, as we show below, will justify non-receipt of the particular witness's evidence following a *voire dire*.

At common law a witness deemed to be cognitively impaired was competent to give evidence as long as such witnesses could give a coherent account and could comprehend the landscape, seriousness and solemnity of an oath. While it was once thought that any and all persons with defective intellect were neither competent nor compellable, the law must now be seen to be that set out in *R v Samuel Hill*.[522] Evidence of a lunatic, under confinement in a lunatic asylum, is admissible as a witness, if the Judge considers him competent in point of understanding, and to be aware of the nature and sanction of an oath. The lunatic may be examined and cross-examined, and witnesses called on either side in order to determine the question of competency; but when admitted, it is for the jury to determine whether his testimony is affected by his

[517] Chapter 53 of the Laws of Zambia.

[518] [1987] 2 All ER 668.

[519] Chapter 53 of the Laws of Zambia.

[520] See *R v Yacoob* (1981) 72 Cr App R 313, *per* Watkins LJ; Ewing [1983] 2 AII ER 645 at 652-653 *per* O'Connor LJ.

[521] See *Woolmington v DPP* [1935] AC 462; *Miller v Minister of Pensions* [1947] 2 ALL ER 272; *Sucha Singh and Another v State of Punjab* [2003] 7 SCC 643 all quoted by Justice AMB Bobo in *The People v Martin Minganja ("Mamado Goloko") John Siame* HR/053/2014 (unreported).

[522] 169 ER 495;*R v Dunning* [1965] Crim LR 372; *R v Lee* [1988] Crim LR 525).

insanity, and what degree of weight is to be attached to it. It logically follows therefore that the competence of witnesses deemed cognitively impaired to give evidence ought to and is generally evaluated in ways similar to other categories of witnesses.[523]

As in other cases where a warning is necessary, the magistrate or judge before whom a cognitively impaired person appears, ought to warn himself of the danger present in acting on the uncorroborated evidence of a person whose cognitive impairment affects his or her ability to give coherent, lucid responses and on the whole, reliable evidence.[524] However, as noted elsewhere in this text, as a matter of law, corroboration is not obligatory to sustain a conviction. In any case, as has been observed in *Bromley v R*:[525] the rules of practice requiring the giving of a warning owe their existence, as Lord Hailsham acknowledges in *R vSpencer*,[526] 'partly to the inherent dangers involved, and partly to the fact that the danger is not necessarily obvious to a lay mind.'[527] If the danger is equally obvious to the lay mind, a failure to warn of its existence is much less likely to result in a miscarriage of justice and thus much less likely to provide a ground for quashing a conviction than if the court has a special knowledge of the danger. If the danger is so obvious that the [court is] fully alive to it without a warning, no warning need be given. As Barwick CJ said in *Kelleher v Queen*:[528] 'The rule of practice as to the warning to be given to the jury is related to the reasons which have prompted it. In my opinion, it does not require a warning where those reasons have no play.'

According to the Magistrates Handbook:[529]

> If a witness who has been sworn appears, while attempting to give evidence, to be of unsound mind or too incoherent or incapable of communication to make sense, the court may rule the witness incompetent. In such cases the court should conduct a *voire dire* in the usual way and make an appropriate ruling. If the court rules that the witness is incompetent the magistrate must then note on the record that any evidence already given by the witness will be ignored for the purpose of the trial. If the incompetency appears to be temporary the court may adjourn the taking of his evidence until the incapacity is over.

'It is obvious from the foregoing passage that the trial court will only conduct a *voire dire* when it becomes apparent that there is something unusual with the

---

[523] See *R v Hill* (1851) 165 ER 495; *R v Dunning* [1965] Crim LR 372; *R v Lee* [1988] Crim LR 525.

[524] *Bromley v R* (1986) 161 CLR 315; [1986] HCA 49.

[525] (1986) 161 CLR 315; [1986] HCA 49 para 6 *per* Gibbs CJ.

[526] (1986) 3 WLR 348 at 353.

[527] See also *per* Lord Ackner at 359 and *per* Lord Diplock in *Hester* at 325.

[528] (1974) 131 CLR 534 at 543.

[529] Swarbrick EJ, *Magistrates Handbook* (6th edn....) at 642.

witness before it.'[530] Such a *voire dire* relates not to the circumstances in which the offence was committed, rather, the competence of the witness in question to testify.[531] Nor is the *voire dire* conducted to determine whether the evidence given is credible for credibility is an issue that can only be determined after the assessment of all the evidence presented before court.[532]

(iv) *Voire dire* and the admissibility of confessions in criminal cases

(a) Introduction

In criminal proceedings, a judge will usually be confronted with the need to determine whether a confession by an accused person was voluntarily given and as such meets the test of admissibility. The usual case is for such a confession and incriminating statement to be made to a police officer through whom the prosecution will attempt to adduce such a confession at trial. Recall that Article 18(7) of the Constitution provides that '[a] person who is tried for a criminal offence shall not be compelled to give evidence at the trial.' This is meant to be a bulwark against self-incrimination.[533] The concept of confession runs against this constitutional bulwark. As Muna Ndulo[534] notes:

> The issue of confessions is tied up with the accused's right against self-incrimination. The foundation underlying the privilege is the respect a government must accord to the dignity and integrity of its citizens and the fact that confessions are often unreliable. It is desirable that a government seeking to punish ana individual produce the evidence against him by its own independent labours, rather than from the accused's own mouth.

In *Zondo v R*[535] it was observed[536] as follows:

> The basis upon which evidence of an incriminating statement is excluded in the absence of proof of the condition of admissibility is not that the law presumes the statement to be untrue in the absence of such proof, but because of the danger which induced confessions or admissions present to the innocent and the due administration of justice. The danger has been aptly pointed out by the American Authority on evidence.

[530] *Mike Nedic Miloslav v The People* (SCZ Judgment No 26 of 2014) at J24; see *The People v Aaron Shamapepe* (CAZ Appeal No 64 of 2018) *per* Muchenga DJP at J4-J5; *Spittle v Walton* [1871] LR 11 Eq 420.

[531] *The People v Aaron Shamapepe* (CAZ Appeal No 64 of 2018).

[532] *The People v Aaron Shamapepe* (CAZ Appeal No 64 of 2018).

[533] See a Canadian take in the leading case of *R v Henry* [2005] 3 SCR 609 but see *R v Nedelcu* 2012 SCC 59.

[534] Ndulo, M "Confessions – Tainted Evidence?" 1973 *Zambia Law Journal* 101 quoted in Hatchard J and Ndulo M, *The Law of Evidence in Zambia: Cases and Materials* 272-74.

[535] [1964] SJNR 102.

[536] Charles J, as he then was.

According to Professor Wigmore,[537]

> The real objection [to confessions] is that any system of administration which permits the prosecution to trust habitually to compulsory self-disclosure as a source of proof must itself suffer morally thereby. The inclination develops to rely mainly upon such evidence, and to be satisfied with an incomplete investigation of the other sources [...] ultimately the innocent are jeopardised by the encroachment of a bad system.

Given the foregoing misgivings about confession evidence, it is necessary to consider the circumstances and conditions under which courts in this jurisdiction will admit confession evidence.

(b) Judges' rules[538]

One cannot have a complete discussion regarding admissibility of evidence as respects confessions without reference to what are termed Judges' Rules. Formerly prepared for police in England & Wales, the Rules and their successor are a set of guiding principle about police and inquisitorial procedures and the admissibility of the resulting confessions as evidence in court. They have become an integral part of evidentiary legal practice in much of the commonwealth including this jurisdiction, with variations being made over time, as we show below.[539]

Originally issued in 1912 by the judges of the King's Bench, they were intended to give English police forces guidance on the procedures that they should follow in detaining and questioning suspects.[540] The issuance of the Rules was a response to what had been seen as a divergence that had developed in police questioning and interrogation procedures that had resulted among diverse police departments. The Rules also replaced, among others, informal procedural guidance in this area by Sir Howard Vincent[541] in the *Police Code and Manual of Criminal Law.*

It must be remembered that far from being rules of law, the Rules were meant only as a guide to the police setting out inacceptable that if brought to the attention of the Court would almost certainly lead to a judge conducting *voire dire* and ultimately exercising his discretion to exclude evidence on the basis that the conditions for admissibility had not been met for want of

537 Evidence, vol 4, section 2250.

538 It was held in *Charles Lukongolo and Others v The People*[1986] ZR 115 (SC), that '[t]he Judges' Rules applicable in Zambia are the 1930 rules set out in paragraph 1118 of the 35th Edition of Archbold.

539 In England and Wales for example, the rules have been superseded by Code C made pursuant to the Police and Criminal Evidence Act 1984.

540 T. E. St. Johnston (1966). "Judges' Rules and Police Interrogation in England Today". *Journal of Criminal Law and Criminology*. 57(1). Retrieved on 24 May 2020.

541 Colonel Sir Charles Edward Howard Vincent KCMG CB DL (31 May 1849 – 7 April 1908), known as Howard Vincent or C. E. Howard Vincent, was a British soldier, barrister, police official and Conservative Party politician who sat in the House of Commons from 1885 to 1908.

voluntariness in confessions by the accused for example.[542] Lawrence J (as he then was) observed as follows in *R v Voisin*[543] that:

> In 1912 the judges, at the request of the Home Secretary, drew up some rules as guidance for police officers. These rules have not the force of law; they are administrative directions the observance of which the police authorities should enforce upon their subordinates as tending to the fair administration of justice. It is important that they should do so, for statements obtained from prisoners, contrary to the spirit of these rules, may be rejected as evidence by the judge presiding at the trial.[544]

The Rules:

- Permitted the police to question any person with a view to finding out whether, or by whom, an offence had been committed.
- Mandated the police to give a warn and caution when they had evidence to suspect that a person had committed an offence.
- Obligated additional thoughtfulness once a person was charged and proscribed questioning after charging save in extraordinary circumstances.
- Mandated that a record of interrogation to be kept.
- Gave guidance on the best way to record a formal written statement.

While the rules were not, as shown in *R v Voisin,*[545] meant to modify the law relating to the admissibility of evidence, they invariably became a code of best practice. If followed, or so the argument went, statements given to the police by a suspect who later becomes the accused would be admitted in evidence by a court. Included in the Rules was administrative guidance on a suspect's access to counsel of their own choosing, or legal aid if the suspect could not afford one, and the interrogation, *inter alia,* of children.[546]

(v) Applicable principles in Zambia: the case of *Shamwana and 7 Others v The People*[547]

The case of *Shamwana and 7 Others v The People*[548] is arguably the most celebrated decision in the criminal law in this jurisdiction not only because of the serious

---

[542] T. E. St. Johnston (1966). "Judges' Rules and Police Interrogation in England Today".

[543] [1918] 1 KB 531.

[544] See *Shabadine Peart v. The QueenJudgment of the Lords of the Judicial Committee of the Privy Council.* BAILII. 14 February 2006. [2006] UKPC 5 on the status of the Judges' Rules in Jamaica.

[545] [1918] 1 KB 531.

[546] Recall that five further rules were added to the original four Rules in 1918, and the rules were further explained in 1934 in a Home Office Circular 536053/23. Reissued in 1964 as *Practice Note (Judge's Rules)* [1964] 1 WLR 152, the Rules were replaced in England and Wales in 1986 by Code C made pursuant to the Police and Criminal Evidence Act 1984 (PACE), a guideline that mainly preserves the requirements set out in the Rules. For Zambian readers of this text, it will be noted that Zambian Courts as we show later, still use the pre 1964 Judges' Rules.

[547] [1985] ZR 41 (SC).

[548] [1985] ZR 41 (SC).

charges that were brought against the accused persons but because of the principles it espoused that continue to shape criminal procedure and the adjectival law of evidence with which we are interested in this text. Largely because of its length, most people including students, legal practitioners and judges are unlikely to ever read the case in its entirety. Nonetheless, for those that can find the time, it is worth a shot. Under this head, we only focus on the pronouncements and earlier authorities used by the Supreme Court in that case as regards confessions, admissibility, and the (pre-1964) Judges' Rules. It was held in *Charles Lukongolo and Others v The People,*[549] that '[t]he Judges' Rules applicable in Zambia are the 1930 rules set out in paragraph 1118 of the 35th Edition of Archbold.' First the brief facts:

> Seven of the appellants were convicted of treason while one was convicted of misprision of treason. Originally, all of them were charged with one count of treason alleging that they prepared to overthrow the lawful Government. At the close of the prosecution case the trial court ruled that some of the overt acts had not been made out; the court amended the particulars of one of the remaining overt acts; it placed one of the accused on his defence on the lesser charge of misprision. On appeal, numerous grounds were argued alleging, inter alia, that the charge was bad for duplicity because two or more conspiracy overt acts were laid and because the evidence disclosed two different subplots for executing the coup plot; that the charge was bad for duplicity because while the court used the word "prepared", one overt act used the word "endeavoured". It was also argued that certain overt acts were bad for uncertainty; the conspiracy overt act was bad for uncertainty because detailed particulars of the acts of omissions of each accused were not given, the overt act alleging that one of the appellants was in command of "the said illegal army stationed at Chilanga", was bad for uncertainty because the illegal army was first mentioned in an overt act not alleged against the particular accused. Other complaints were directed against the amendments to the information effected at the close of the prosecution case. It was also argued that the trial was unfair; that the evidence of an accomplice who testified after bargaining with the prosecution should have been excluded; that certain, documents were wrongly admitted and in any case their contents were hearsay evidence. Other misdirections were alleged concerning the admission of confessions and interrogation notes; and the talking of judicial notice of another court's case record. The learned trial judge made use of evidence tendered ostensibly in support of overt acts not made out; and he also relied in certain respects on the uncorroborated evidence of a co-accused. A key accomplice witness told certain lies but a, final finding was made in the ruling on no case submissions that he was credible. There were a number of accomplice witnesses and the question arose whether there was corroboration for their evidence and whether they could mutually corroborate each other. On appeal, held *inter alia:*

[549] [1986] ZR 115 (SC).

- On a charge of treason, no evidence is admissible of any distinct or independent overt act not laid in the indictment unless it amounts to a direct proof of the overt acts that are laid; the evidence of distinct overt acts of the appellants in45 furtherance of the coup plot afforded direct proof of the overt act of conspiracy to overthrow the Government and was properly admitted;
- Although statement made in breach of the Judges' Rules is admissible the breach raises rebuttable presumption of involuntariness and unfairness. Where a breach of the Judges' Rules has been admitted or established, it is for the prosecution to advance an explanation acceptable to the court for such breach.[550]

Regarding the matter of admissibility, confessions and the Judges' Rules, the Court took time to review authorities on the issue as follows:

We begin with an examination of the principles applicable to the admissibility of confessions and the exercise of the trial court's discretion. The classic formulation of the principle applicable to the admissibility of confessions appears in Lord Summer's speech in *Ibrahim v R*,[551] where he stated, at page 609:

> It has long been established as a positive rule of English criminal law that no statement by an accused is admissible in evidence against him unless it is shown by the prosecution to have been voluntary statement in the sense that it has not been obtained from him either by fear of prejudice or hope of advantage exercised or held out by person in authority.

This formulation was expressly approved by the House of Lords in *Commissioner of Customs and Excise v Hare and Power* (49).[552]

In *Muwowo v The People*,[553] the Court of Appeal said (per Charles, J.) at page 95:

> "An incriminating statement made by an accused to person in authority is not admissible in evidence unless it is proved beyond reasonable doubt to have been made by him voluntarily. In that context the words 'made voluntarily' do not mean 'volunteered' but made in the exercise of free choice to speak or to be silent."

In *Zeka Chinyama and Others v The People*,[554] we said, at page 430, lines 11 to 18:

[550] *Chilufya v The People* [1975] ZR 138 explained.

[551] [1914] AC 599, 609.

[552] (1967) 61 Cr App.

[553] [1965] ZR 91, See also *Zondo v R* [1964] SJNR 102.

[554] [1977] ZR 426.

> In practice, when dealing with an objection to the admission of an alleged confession the trial court will first satisfy itself that it was freely and voluntarily made; if so satisfied, the court in a proper case must then consider whether the confession should in the exercise of its discretion be excluded, notwithstanding that it was voluntary and therefore strictly speaking admissible, because in all the circumstances the strict application of the rules as to admissibility would operate unfairly against the accused.

We continued at page 431, lines 37 to 46 and page 432, lines 1 to 11: largely

> The precise position of the Judges' Rules is important. Their breach does not render evidence, and in particular a confession, automatically inadmissible; they are rules of practice indicating what conduct on the part of police officers the court will regard as unfair or improper. Since in practice most cases in which the issue of the court's discretion arises involve alleged improprieties by police officers, the issue has come to be associated with breaches of the Judges' Rules, and no other impropriety is alleged here; but for completeness it should be said that the principle of fair conduct underlying the Judges' Rules are principles in their own right independently of those rules, and that unfair or improper conduct on the part of people other than the police officers can equally lead to the exclusion of evidence in the exercise of the discretion of the court. The circumstances, then, in which the discretion to exclude confession made to a police officer falls to be considered are when such confession has been held to have been voluntarily made but there has been a breach of the Judges' Rules or other unfair conduct surrounding the making of the confession, either on the part of the police officer or some other person, which might indicate to a judge that there is danger of unfairness. The test as to whether the discretion should be exercised is whether the application of the strict rules of admissibility would operate unfairly against the accused."

And at page 431, lines 41 to 47, and page 432, line 1 we said:

> The circumstances in which the reception of evidence would operate unfairly against an accused will depend on the facts of the particular case and do not lend themselves to precise definition. But the dicta in *Callis v Gunn*[555] and *R v Payen*,[556] would seem to suggest the following as a general principle: that the discretion ought to be exercised in favour of the accused where, but for the unfair or improper conduct

[555] [1963] 2 All ER 677.

[556] [1963] 1 All ER 848.

> complained of, the accused might not voluntarily have provided the evidence in question or the opportunity to obtain it.

The case of *Chilufya v The People*,[557] has been referred to in support of the proposition that confessionary evidence should be excluded in the absence of a warn and caution. We would like to stress that, that case was not intended to be a departure from the already well-established practice. That this was so is plain from what we said, at page 139, lines 26 to 32:

> Judges' Rules are not rules of law; they are rules of practice drawn up for the guidance of police officers and a statement made in breach of such rules is not ipso facto inadmissible if it is a voluntary statement although the court has a discretion to disallow it.

In that case, unlike in the present one, no warn and caution was ever administered at all. Our courts do not usually take kindly to any deliberate non-compliance with the Judges' Rules and, in the absence of good reasons or what are called "exceptional circumstances", they tend to exercise their discretion in favour of exclusion. It was for that reason that we said in lines 35 to 38 of the same page:

> As a general rule in this country, however, a confession made to a person in authority, such as a police officer, in the absence of any warning, is prima facie inadmissible. It is only in very exceptional circumstances that such a conference will be admissible.

In *Chulu v The People*,[558] the High Court held to the effect that, although the breach of the Judges' Rules does not automatically invalidate anything done in pursuance thereof, it does raise a rebuttable presumption of involuntariness and unfairness. Thus, both *Chilufya*[559] and *Chulu*,[560] were designed to serve as a strong reminder to the police to ensure the observance of the Judges' Rules, particularly those that require the giving of the usual warn and caution to a defendant or a suspect so as to inform or remind him of his right to exercise a free choice to speak or to be silent (see *Muwowo* (above)). By "special circumstances" (or good reasons) was meant such circumstances or reasons as would persuade the trial court to exercise its discretion in favour of admission of confessionary evidence, such as where the defendant or suspect made a spontaneous confession before the police could administer the usual warn and caution; or where the breach had not induced the accused to make a confession which he would not otherwise have made. The exercise of a trial court's discretion whether

[557] [1975] ZR 138.

[558] [1969] ZR 128.

[559] [1975] ZR 138.

[560] [1969] ZR 128.

to exclude or admit confessionary evidence will always depend on the facts of each particular ease. Where a breach of the Judges' Rules has been admitted or established, it is for the prosecution to advance an explanation acceptable to the court for such breach.

In any event, recent trends in England indicate that certain inroads have been made into the extent of the judge's exercise of his residual discretion to exclude evidence admissible in law, including confessions obtained breach of the Judges' Rules simpliciter. Many English authorities on the subject have emerged in recent times, notable among them are *R v Sang*,[561] and *R v Rennie*.[562]

In paragraph 22-39 of Phipson, headed "Breach of the Judges' Rules" is to be found the following:

> Prior to *R v Sang*[563] it was commonly thought that the court had discretion to exclude confessions when there had been breach of the Judges' Rules simpliciter. Indeed, in *R v Henry* Lord Diplock referred to 'the discretion that had long been exercised in England under the Judges' Rules to refuse to admit confessions by the accused even though strictly they may be admissible.' However, *R v Prayer*,[564] shows that there has been in recent years a tendency in the Court of Appeal to treat a breach of the Judges. Rules as only a guide to whether the confession was in fact voluntary. In *R v Houghton*[565], for instance, the Court of Appeal found that there had been a flagrant disregard of paragraph (d) of the principles at the beginning of the Judges' Rules, but upheld the judge's exercise of his discretion to admit the evidence of a confession by the accused. The judge had said that he was satisfied that the confession had been made voluntarily. The Court of Appeal found no ground for holding that the discretion had been exercised wrongly. The Court also said that the irregularities on the part of the police had no bearing upon the confession by the accused.

In the recent case of *R v Cockley*,[566] the Court of Appeal, discussing the exercise of the trial court's discretion, said in the last paragraph at page 664:

> The trial judge has of course a discretion to exclude admissible evidence if in his judgment its prejudicial effect would be disproportionate to its probative value. But such a discretion is to be exercised to promote, not to defeat, the course of justice.

---

[561] [1979] 2 All ER 1222.

[562] [1982] 1 WLR 64, [1982] 1 All ER 424.

[563] [1979] 2 All ER 1222.

[564] [1972] 56 Cr App R 151.

[565] [1979] 69 Cr App R 197.

[566] (1964) 148 JPR 663.

All this is reinforced by paragraph 15-25 of Archbold which says that:

> Even when the voluntary nature of a defendant's incriminating assertions has been established or (admitted) judges are still invited to exercise their discretion and exclude them on the ground of some breach of the Judges' Rules [...] Judges rarely accede to these invitations and this approach is fortified if not actually confirmed by the *obita dicta* of the House of Lords in *R v Sang*.[567]

Further, the following appears in paragraph 22-31 (3) of Phipson:

> There may be circumstances where a confession, induced by a breach of the Rules, is obtained by improper or unfair means though it is 'voluntary' and therefore admissible in law. See however, the judgment of the Court of Appeal in *R v Rennie*[568] which would seem to indicate that a confession which is admissible in law should not lightly be rejected.

The effect of the *obita dicta* in *R v Sang*[569] on the Judges' Rules may be summarised in the following propositions:

(1) breach of the Judges' Rules does not by itself confer upon a judge a discretion to reject a subsequent confession admissible in law;

(2) the discretion does, however, arise if the breach has induced the accused to make a confession which he would not otherwise have made, because the breach will be improper if not unfair; and

(3) if the breach is such that the confession which it induces is not voluntary, the judge has no discretion, and must exclude the confession as inadmissible in law.[570]

A point has arisen as to when the trial court should consider and exercise its discretion either in favour or against exclusion of evidence of a confession obtained in breach of the Judges' Rules or by means of some other impropriety emanating from an unfair or improper conduct on the part of the police or someone else. It has been submitted by the appellants that it is universal practice to deal with both voluntariness (in the case of an alleged confession) and the exercise of the court's discretion, together and that, where breach of the Judges' Rules is in issue, a trial-within-a trial should be held.

The answer to the first part of the question is to be found in the case of *Chinyama and Others*[571] and is reflected also in *Njobvu and Another v The People*.[572] The position is that, where any challenge is made as to

---

567 [1979] 2 All ER 1222.

568 [1982] 1 WLR 64, [1982] 1 All ER 424.

569 [1979] 2 All ER 1222.

570 See paragraph 22-40 of *Phipson' s Manual on The Law of Evidence.*

571 [1977] ZR 426.

572 [1978] ZR 372, 377.

the admissibility of evidence of a confession, it is the duty of the judge to hold a trial-within-a-trial on the *voire dire* in order to determine whether the accused's confession was made freely and voluntarily, if he so determines, he must then consider, in a proper case, whether the confession, notwithstanding that it was voluntary and, therefore, admissible as a matter of law, should in the exercise of his discretion, be excluded on the ground that the strict application of the rules as to admissibility would operate unfairly against the accused; for instance, where, but for the unfair or improper conduct complained of, either on the part of a police officer or of some other person, the accused would not otherwise have made the confession.

Where the impropriety alleged is a breach of the Judges' Rules, and the breach is not in dispute, then the breach becomes part of the general issues and the trial judge need not decide, at that stage, the question of exercising his discretion in the matter unless the circumstances of the case so warrant or there is a request to that effect, in which case, he may invoke his discretion without the necessity of holding a trial-within-a- trial.

The critical question, however, is as to what should happen where the impropriety alleged is a breach of the Judges' Rules and there is dispute about it: should a trial-within-a-trial be held in those circumstances?

In *Chinyama and Others*,[573] we said at page 436, lines 1 to 2: "As this court made clear in *Tapisha v The People*,[574] trial-within-a-trial is only held to determine the issue of voluntariness."

Headnote (i) in *Tapish*[575] at page 223, lines 1 to 5, says this: "(i) Where any question arises as to the voluntariness of statement or any part of it, including the signature, then because voluntariness is, as a matter of law, a condition precedent to the admissibility of the statement, this issue must be decided as preliminary one by means of a trial-within-a-trial."[576] This clearly indicates that the holding of trial-within-a-trial can only take place when it becomes necessary to determine the issue of the voluntariness of a confession or any part of it, on the ground that voluntariness is, as a matter of law, a condition precedent to the admissibility of confession.

As the exercise of the court's discretion in favour of an accused necessarily leads to the exclusion of a confession, it is arguable that, where the production of an alleged confession is challenged on the ground of breach of the Judges' Rules, the procedure adopted when the question is whether the confession is admissible in law should apply. Paragraph 22-09 of Phipson says that: "[a]lthough the authorities considered below related to the procedure when the question is whether the confession is admissible in law, the same procedure clearly applies when the Judges' discretion is invoked. Frequently, both questions are raised on the same issue. "

573 [1977] ZR 426.

574 [1973] ZR 222.

575 [1973] ZR 222.

576 See also page 225, lines 9 to 17 and page 226, lines 37 to 46 of the judgment.

The learned authors of *Archbold* provide more substance in paragraph 15-77 (6)(iii):

> It is still common for defending counsel to obtain 'a trial-within-a-trial' in the absence of the jury in order that the judge should determine whether there had been a breach of the Judges' Rules, [...] and to submit that if there had been (or may have been) a breach the judge had a discretion to exclude evidence of any confession or admission which followed the breach, whether or not the breach was instrumental in inducing the accused to confess. So, for at any rate as the Judges' Rules are concerned, it had certainly been assumed by the Court of Appeal prior to *R v Sang*[577] that the judges had such discretion, though in *R v Prayer*,[578] the Court of Appeal appeared to be leaning to the view that the question whether there had been a breach of the rules was only relevant to the question whether the subsequent confession was voluntary as a matter of law.

This then puts it beyond doubt that it is competent for a trial court to hold a trial-within-a-trial when there is a challenge based on a disputed breach of the Judges' Rules in order to determine the issue.

It is important to note that, when a judge has ruled at a trial-within-a-trial to the effect that a statement made by the accused, whether oral or written, was made voluntarily and is, therefore, admissible in evidence as a matter of law, if further evidence relevant to the issue of admissibility of the exercise of the court's discretion emerges later in the trial, the judge is entitled to reconsider his earlier ruling. If, however, no such further evidence emerges, the need to reconsider his ruling already made does not arise. In *R v Watson*,[579] the court held that nothing had emerged after the trial-within-the-trial which should have caused the trial judge to have reconsidered his ruling.

(vi) The discretion to admit confessions extracted in breach of the judges' rules: case law

In *Chilufya v The People*,[580] the appellant was convicted on one count of store breaking. The trial magistrate made a number of serious misdirections which adversely affected his finding as to the appellant's guilt. (i) The alleged confession to an investigating officer was in breach of the Judges' Rules in that there was no warning administered to the appellant. (ii) When a police officer was about to give evidence as to an alleged confession the magistrate did not inquire whether there was any objection to the admission of that evidence. (iii) The property was not conclusively proved to have been in the appellant's possession. It was held as follows: (i) Judges' Rules are not rules

[577] [1979] 2 All ER 1222.

[578] [1972] 56 Cr App R 151 at 160.

[579] [1980] 2 All ER 293.

[580] [1975] ZR 138 (SC).

of law: they are rules of practice drawn up for the guidance of police officers and a statement made in breach of such rules is not ipso facto inadmissible if it is a voluntary statement although the court has a discretion to disallow it. (ii) As a general rule in this country, a confession made by a defendant to a person in authority, such as a police officer, in the absence of any warning, is prima facie inadmissible. It is only in very exceptional circumstances that such a confession will be admissible. (iii) The doctrine of recent possession applies only when the property the subject of the charge is conclusively shown to have been in the accused's possession.

In *Zeka Chinyama and Others v The People*,[581] the appellants were convicted of murder. The prosecution case was based largely upon alleged confessions. The appeal of the third appellant was allowed at the conclusion of the hearing for reasons not connected with the subject of this report. It was argued on behalf of the first and second appellants that on the facts, and in spite of the findings that the confessions were freely and voluntarily made, the trial judge should have exercised his discretion in favour of the appellants and excluded the statements. It was held as follows: (i) When dealing with an objection to the admission of an alleged confession the trial court must first satisfy itself that it was freely and voluntarily made; if so satisfied, the court in a proper case must then consider whether the confession should in the exercise of its discretion be excluded, notwithstanding that it was voluntary and therefore strictly speaking admissible, on the ground that in all the circumstances the strict application of the rules as to admissibility would operate unfairly against the accused. (ii) The court is not required in every case to make a decision whether or not in the exercise of its discretion to exclude a confession; 20 where every circumstance which might conceivably be regarded as indicating unfairness has been considered in the very decision that the confession was voluntary the question of the exercise of the court's discretion does not arise.[582] (iii) The question of the discretion to exclude a confession made to a police officer falls to be considered when such confession has been held to have been voluntarily made, but there has been a breach of the Judges' Rules or other unfair conduct surrounding the making of the confession, either on the part of a police officer or of some other person, which might indicate to a judge that there is danger of unfairness. (iv) The circumstances in which the reception of evidence would operate unfairly against an accused will depend on the facts of the particular case and do not lend themselves to precise definition. The discretion ought to be exercised in favour of the accused where, but for the unfair or improper conduct complained of, the accused might not voluntarily have provided the evidence in question or the opportunity to obtain it. (v) The court must be satisfied on a balance of probability that its discretion to exclude evidence ought to be exercised. *Per curium:* Zambia still operates under the pre-1964 English Judges' Rules. The common practice of questioning persons in custody without administering the usual caution, which is a clear breach

[581] [1977]ZR 426.

[582] Dictum of Clayden FJ, in *Mbopeleghe v R* 1960 R & N 508 cited with approval.

of rule 3, could well lead to a court in its discretion excluding a statement subsequently given voluntarily after a proper caution.

(vii) Basis for admissibility of confession evidence

In *George Musongo v The People,*[583] the applicant, an accountant employed by the National Hotels Corporation, was convicted of theft by public servant. It was alleged that he had on certain specified dates received amounts of cash from two receptionists in the hotel which he checked against their receipt books, but that he was unable to account for sum of ZMW811.81. The shortage was discovered by an internal auditor in the course of a routine examination of the books of the hotel. The auditor questioned the two receptionists and the applicant and in the course of this questioning the applicant admitted that he had used the money; the auditor then asked him to reduce his confession to writing which the applicant did. The main ground of appeal was that the trial magistrate misdirected himself in failing to exercise his discretion to exclude the applicant's confession to the auditor since it was made without any warning that the applicant was not obliged to make it. It was held as follows: (i) As a police officer trying to discover the perpetrator of a crime is entitled to put questions to any person, whether suspected or not, from whom he considers useful information can be obtained, there can be no objection whatsoever to any other person in similar circumstances doing likewise notwithstanding the fact that such person is, or is not, a person in authority. (ii) The Judges' Rules were formulated for the guidance of police officers, they put police officers on guard with regard to what type of conduct on their part will, or will not, be regarded by judges as improper or unfair *vis-a-vis* a person suspected of' having committed a crime. (iii) However, the principles of fair conduct underlying the Judges'' Rules are principles in their own right independently of those rules, and unfair or improper conduct on the part of people other than police officers can equally lead to the exclusion of' evidence in the discretion of a court.[584] (iv) In all cases the issue must always be whether the accused was so unfairly or improperly treated in all the circumstances that the evidence ought to be rejected. (v) Whereas failure on the part of a police officer to administer a caution constitutes an impropriety in respect of which a trial court may exercise its discretion in favour of the accused, similar failure on the part of any other person in authority (or indeed anybody else) does not necessarily amount to an impropriety as it cannot reasonably be expected that a person, other than a police officer, should of necessity appreciate the niceties of what should, and should not, be done in such circumstances.

In *Sipalo Cibozu and Chibozu v The People,*[585] the appellants, father and son respectively were convicted of the murder of the deceased, the first appellant's sister and the second appellant's aunt. The only evidence against them was

[583] [1978] ZR 266 (SC).

[584] Dictum in *Chinyama v The People* (SCZ Judgment No 27 of 1976) cited with approval.

[585] [1981] ZR 28 (SC).

that of two incriminating statements made by both appellants to a village headman. However, the statements were extracted from the appellants without any "warn and caution" having been administered and admitted in evidence without the appellants being asked whether they had any objection to their admission. The second statements, made to the sole police investigating officer a detective, sergeant, were admitted by the learned trial judge after a trial within a trial in which the appellants contested the voluntariness of the statements. A post-mortem report under the hand of a Government Medical Officer who was not called as a witness, was produced in evidence under the provisions of s. 191A of the Criminal Procedure Code. On appeal, it was held as follows: (i) The village headman is in law a person in authority; therefore a "warn and caution" was supposed to be administered before extracting the statements from the appellants. (ii) The appellants were supposed to have been asked whether they had any objective to their admission, and if so, a trial within trial be instituted to determine the voluntariness of their admission. (iii) An inference of the first appellant's guilt cannot safely be drawn simply from an allegation made in his presence in the absence of material particular. (iv) The failure by the learned trial judge to observe the inconsistency in the prosecution evidence constitutes a serious misdirections (v) The failure by the learned judge to notice or explore the discrepancy in the second appellant's statement lends force to the appellant's contention that they were forced to sign already prepared statements. (vi) Medical reports usually require explanation not only of the terms used but also of the conclusions to be drawn from the facts and opinions stated in the report. It is therefore highly desirable for the person who carried out the examination in question and prepared the report to give verbal evidence. (vii)Information relating to the severity of injuries sustained by the victim is essential to a proper consideration of the question of sentence and may in some cases be essential on the question of verdict.

In *Boniface Chanda Chola, Christopher Nyamande and Nelson Sichula v The People*,[586] the appellants were charged with murder committed in the course of robbery involving a car. Two witnesses called for the prosecution were soldiers who admitted they had stolen guns that had passed to the appellants but there was no evidence that the guns were used in the offence. Although the guns were later retrieved by the soldiers they were not handed to the police and the matter was not reported. Another witness had been recruited to drive the vehicle after it had been stolen. There was also evidence that shortly before the robbery the three accused and the driver stayed at another witness's house which witness was called by the prosecution. Shortly after the offence the three appellants visited the two soldiers and one of the soldiers asked the appellants if they had committed the offence. The first appellant admitted doing so, the other two appellants remained silent. There was also evidence that during the course of police investigations two appellants led police officers to the scene where photographs were taken. This was disputed by the appellants who said the taking of the photographs had been forcibly stage-managed. The trial

[586] [1988 – 1989] ZR 163 (SC); see *R v Thompson* (1893) 2 QB; *Li Shu-ling v R* [1989] AC 145 - 281 at 270.

judge found that the driver of the car and the soldiers were not accomplices, their evidence was capable of corroborating other witnesses, and convicted the appellants. The appellants appealed. The appellants argued that the admissions by one of them in the presence of all could not be construed as an admission when they remained silent in the face of the admission. The appellants disputed the admissibility of the photographs and said they did not represent any truth or actual re-enactment of the events in which they denied any participation. Further, the appellants contended that even if the witnesses were not accomplices, they were witnesses who had possible interests of their own to serve and that their evidence should have been approached on the same footing as for accomplices. It was held as follows: (1) Mere silence in the face of an accusation cannot amount to an acknowledgement of the truth of someone else's admission. The evidence has to show some positive conduct, action or demeanour as to accept the truth of the admission. (2) The leading by an accused of the police to a place they already know and where no real evidence or fresh evidence is uncovered cannot be regarded as a reliable and solid foundation on which to draw an inference of guilt. (3) In the case where the witnesses are not necessarily accomplices, the critical consideration is not whether the witnesses did in fact have interests or purposes of their own to serve, but whether they were witnesses who, because of the category into which they fell or because of the particular circumstances of the case, may have had a motive to give false evidence. Where it is reasonable to recognize this possibility, the danger of false implication is present and it must be excluded before a conviction can be held to be safe. Once this is a reasonable possibility, the evidence falls to be approached on the same footing as for accomplices.

In *Major Isaac Masonga v The People,*[587] the appellant was charged before a court martial with the following charges: 1st charge: committing a civil offence contrary to section 73 of the Defence Act. That is to say, communication of classified matters to unauthorized persons contrary to section 5(1) of the State Securities Act; 2nd charge: making a false accusation contrary to section 70 (a) of the Defence Act, in that he made a false accusation against the Air Commander (Lt. General C.E.A. Singogo) to the effect that the Air Commander (Lt. General C.E.A Singogo) hated him and Kaonde people in general, because of the former Air Commander (Lt. General Kayumba RTD), whom he (the accused) claimed to be his uncle; 3rd charge: making a false statement in a complaint contrary to section 70(b) of the Defence Act, in that he made a false statement in a complaint to the effect that the Air Commander (Lt. General C.E.A. Singogo) confessed at a meeting with Mrs. Masonga to hating Mrs. Masonga and Major Masonga because they are Kaonde's by tribe a statement which was meant to impugn the character of the Air Commander (Lt. General C.E.A. Singogo); 4th charge: making a false statement in a complaint contrary to section 70(b) of the Defence Act, whilst suppressing material facts, made a false statement in a compliant to the effect, that the Zambia Air Force Command blocked him from taking up an employment contract at the institute of Humanitarian Law, Sanremo, Italy,

[587] (SCZ Judgment No 24 of 2009).

(242) which action he alleged was preceded by the missing of his personnel file by the Zambia Air Force. The last charge was dropped on 3rd March, 2009 at the hearing of this appeal. The appellant was acquitted. It was held as follows: (1) The notion of "equality of arms" is an essential feature of a fair trial and is the expression of the balance that must exist between prosecution and defence and also respect for the principal of advisory proceedings. (2) It is trite law and a constitutional duty for the prosecution to guarantee a fair trial and a fair trial starts with investigations. Any shortcomings in the investigations may seriously jeopardize the right to a fair proceeding, and thereby also prejudice the accused person's rights to be presumed innocent. (3) It is a well-established principal at law that a suspect who has to be interviewed by a person in authority has to be warned and cautioned before he makes any statement which may be produced in Court against him. (4) Every suspect has a fundamental right not to give evidence against himself unless he freely decides to do so. (5) Any fair or improper conduct by persons, other than police officers extracting evidence can lead to exclusion of evidence by the discretion of the Court. (6) The Courts have a mandatory duty not only to guarantee a fair trial, but also to ensure that even the investigations are conducted in accordance with well-established principals of fair trial for all suspects regardless of their social status. (7) It is cardinal that the Courts, which include the Court Martial: have a constitutional duty to administer justice and to be seen to guarantee all procedural protection to all persons and to ensure that all those persons who appear before them have no legitimate reasons to be intimidated.

(viii) Production of confession evidence at trial: guidelines

In *Daka v The People,*[588] the appellant was convicted in a Subordinate Court of the Third Class of receiving stolen property contrary to s 286(1) of the Penal Code.[589] He appealed against conviction and sentence. It was held as follows: (i) A confession is not properly admissible unless the accused is given the opportunity to object to its production in evidence. (ii) The practice of asking the accused to admit his signature on a document being put in evidence is wrong and the accused should not be asked anything unless he later chooses to give evidence. (iii) When a statement by an accused person is put into evidence, if it is in the vernacular, an English translation must be provided to, or made by, the court.

In *Charles Nalumino v The People,*[590] the appellant was convicted of communicating classified matters to unauthorised persons contrary to s 15(1) of the State Security Act.[591] The conviction was based solely on the evidence of a disputed confession about which no enquiry as to objection was made to counsel for the defence. Furthermore, the trial judge did not believe the defence evidence of beatings because there were no external injuries. It was held as

[588] [1972] ZR 70 (HC).

[589] Chapter 87 of the Laws of Zambia.

[590] [1986] ZR 102 (SC).

[591] Chapter 110 of the Laws of Zambia.

follows: held: (i) It is immaterial whether or not an accused is represented by counsel, the court must in all cases ask the defence whether they wish to object to the admission in evidence of a confession. (ii) It is not in all cases that an assault wild be followed by manifestations of external injuries. Lack of such injuries is not a ground for disregarding medical evidence supportive of an appellant's allegation of assault.

It has been said in *Mwiya and Ikweti v The People*[592] that when the accused in a criminal case denies making a confession or statement attributed to him, but raises no question as to the voluntariness of that confession or statement, the trial court need not hold a trial within a trial before admitting the confession or statement into evidence.[593]

In *Kangachepe Mbao Zonde and Others v The Queen*,[594] the appellants were sentenced to death by the High Court. The main ground of appeal was that there had been a breach of the Judges' Rules in the obtaining of statements from the accused and the statements should accordingly not have been admitted in evidence. It was held as follows: (a) The Judges' Rules are administrative directions enforced by the police authorities as tending to the fair administration of justice. (b) In deciding whether a statement made by an accused person to the police is admissible, the test which a court must apply is not whether the Judges' Rules have been infringed, but whether the prosecution has affirmatively established that the statement was made freely and voluntarily. (c) In this case the statements were properly admitted.[595]

It has been held in *Mwiya and Ikweti v The People*[596] that when the accused in a criminal case denies making a confession or statement attributed to him, but raises no question as to the voluntariness of that confession or statement, the trial court need not hold a trial within a trial before admitting the confession or statement into evidence.

It has been held in *Chisoni Banda v The People*,[597] that in a prosecution for possession of an instrument of housebreaking contrary to s 275(c), Penal Code,[598] the prosecution must prove that the defendant possessed a certain implement at night and that this implement is a housebreaking implement; if the trial magistrate is "sure" of these elements, the accused then bears the burden of proving lawful excuse for the possession.[599]

In *Edward Kunda v The People*,[600] the appellant was found by the police on the roof of a store and in possession of some stolen property. He made a statement to the police admitting the charge of having broken into the store. The trial magistrate did not ask the appellant whether he had any objection to

---

592 [1968] ZR 53 (CA).

593 See also *Steve Mushoke v The People* (SCZ Judgment No 31 of 2014).

594 [1963-1964] Z and NRLR 97; *The People v Obino* [1968] ZR 40 (HC).

595 [1963-1964] Z and NRLR 97 (CA); but see *Chigowe v The People* (SCZ Judgment No 10 of 1977).

596 [1968] ZR 53 CA overruling *Aleck Lukere v The Queen* [1963-1964] Z and NRLR 57; see also *Nyambe and Others v The People* (CAZ Judgment No 173 of 1968).

597 [1968] ZR 6 (CA).

598 Chapter 87 of the Laws of Zambia.

599 *R v Patterson* [1962] 1 All ER 340. *The People v Chanda* [1972] ZR 116 (HC).

600 [1971] ZR 99 (CA).

the admission of evidence of the confession being given. It was held that the question of the voluntariness of a confession applies to both written and verbal confession.

In *Island Nkhuwa v The People,*[601] the appellant was charged on two counts of stealing four gallons of Government diesel on two occasions. When evidence was given of the confession it was alleged that it was extorted by force. The trial magistrate did not hold a trial within trial and convicted the accused. It was held as follows: (i) Where a confession is put in evidence by the prosecution and the defence raise the question of involuntariness, the practice of the courts is to have a trial within a trial and this applies whether or not the confession is verbal or in writing. (ii) If a statement is wrongly admitted in evidence, that error may subsequently be rectified where the defendant gives evidence and his story is tested as to the involuntariness of the statement.

In *The People v Chanda,*[602] the accused were charged with murder contrary to s 177 of the Penal Code.[603] At the conclusion of trial, it was held as follows: (i) Where it is shown that an accused person has at first denied a crime and then after a considerable period in police custody suddenly comes forward with a confession, these circumstances in themselves raise a prima facie reasonable suspicion of involuntariness which requires cogent evidence to remove. (ii) A judge has a discretion to exclude a confession even though freely and voluntarily made and otherwise admissible, if he considers that it was taken in circumstances unfair to the accused. (iii) Evidence discovered in consequence of an involuntary confession is admissible.

In *Daniel Mubita Situmbeko v The People,*[604] the accused was charged in the Subordinate Court with stock theft and the matter came before a Class II Magistrate. The prosecutor applied for and was granted several adjournments for the express purpose of ascertaining whether the accused had any previous convictions. Finally, the prosecutor informed the court that the record of previous convictions of the accused did not reveal a conviction for stock theft and the trial proceeded. During the course of the trial the prosecution sought to lead evidence of a confession alleged to have been made by the accused. Objection was taken and a trial within a trial was held during the course of which the disputed statement was received in evidence. On review -It was held as follows: (i) It is a serious irregularity and fatal to the prosecution case to inform the court of the previous convictions of an accused person before the commencement of the trial. (ii)[605] If after verdict it transpires that an accused person has a previous conviction for stock theft so that the provisions of section 275(b) of the Penal Code[606] apply, a magistrate who does not have the jurisdiction to impose the minimum sentence of seven years can commit the accused to the High Court for sentence in terms of s 217 of the Criminal

[601] [1971] ZR 134 (HC).

[602] [1972] ZR 116 (HC); *Nyambe and Others v The People* (CAZ Judgment No 173 of 1968).

[603] Chapter 87 of the Laws of Zambia.

[604] [1977] ZR 133 (HC).

[605] Editor's note: As to (ii) compare *People v Chilembe* [1975] ZR 40 in which the opposite view was taken.

[606] Chapter 87 of the Laws of Zambia.

Procedure Code.[607] (iii) A statement to which objection has been taken can be admitted in evidence only after a ruling by the court at the end of the trial within a trial.

In *Nalishwa v The People,*[608] the appellant was convicted of murder. The evidence against appellant was that he was seen talking to the deceased shortly before her death, confessed and when formally charged made reply by admitting charge. Appellant appealed against conviction on grounds that confession was inadmissible. It was held as follows: (i) Where two confessions are made and the first is held not to have been freely and voluntarily made, the second will be equally inadmissible, even though there has been no fresh inducement, unless it is shown that the previous inducement has ceased to operate on accused's mind. (ii) Principles of fair conduct are principles in their own right independent of the Judges' Rules. Where there has been any impropriety it is incumbent on the trial judge to consider whether the case is proper one for the exercise of his discretion to exclude evidence the admission of which would operate unfairly against the accused and failure so to consider is serious misdirection.

In *Kafuti Vilongo v The People,*[609] the appellant, a juvenile, appealed against a finding of guilty on a charge of arson. In the main, the evidence against him consisted of circumstantial evidence and a confession. The alleged confession was objected to on the grounds that it was recorded in a language which the appellant did not understand or understood only a little. It was also argued that the appellant could have been seared and when he came to give evidence the appellant said that he had been beaten by the police and forced to sign a statement. It was held as follows: (i) The objection to the production of the confection statement on the grounds that the appellant did not understand or use the language in which it was recorded does not raise a triable issue to be dealt with by the procedure of trial within a trial; it is a matter to be dealt with as one of the general issues. (ii) The objection that the appellant could have been scared is not sufficient; it must be alleged that he was actually put in fear which induced the making of the confession statement. (iii) Once the appellant said in evidence that he had been beaten by the police and forced to sign a statement, the allegation should have been dealt with by the trial court in its judgment.

It has been held in *Patrick Kunda and Robertson Muleba Chisenga v The People,*[610] that in a trial within a trial held to determine whether to admit statements allegedly made by the appellants, the learned commissioner ruled that he did not believe the appellants without setting out in detail the reasons for his ruling. He admitted the statements in evidence. It was held as follows: (i) The result of such brevity is that there is no judgment on the trial within the trial and the appellants are deprived of their opportunity to appeal against it. (ii)

[607] Chapter 88 of the Laws of Zambia.

[608] [1972] ZR 26 (CA); *Chongwe v The People* [1977] ZR 21 (SC); *see also R v Smith* [1959] 2 All ER 193.

[609] [1977] ZR 423 (SC).

[610] [1980] ZR 105 (SC).

It would be unsafe to allow the admission of statements to stand, the appeal would be dealt with on the basis that the statements have been excluded.

In *Webster Kayi Lumbwe v The People*,[611] the accused appealed against his conviction on a charge of espionage contrary to section 3(c) of the State Security Act.[612] He was alleged to have passed classified information to the CIA: an action prejudicial to the safety or interests of the Republic of Zambia and intended to be directly or indirectly useful to a foreign power. He was given the minimum mandatory sentence of twenty years imprisonment with hard labour. Grounds of Appeal were inter alia that his confession was wrongly admitted and that the trial court misdirected itself in finding the charge of espionage proved after choosing to believe the prosecution witnesses. It was held as follows: (i) An appeal court will not interfere with a trial court finding of fact, on the issue of credibility unless it is clearly shown that the finding was erroneous. (ii) When an objection to the admissibility of a confession was withdrawn in order to enable the defence to cross - examine on it, an appellant cannot complain about its admission unless he can point to an irregularity or impropriety rendering its admission unsatisfactory. (iii) No appeal lies against a mandatory minimum sentence.

It has been shown in *Joseph Mutapa Tobo v The People,*[613] that in determining whether a confession statement was made voluntarily the Court should not have sight of it in order to satisfy itself that, taking into account the detail in the statement, the accused made it. It is also incorrect to ignore the fact that the person making the statement was tortured before the police became involved in the investigation. While the real value of the evidence of a medical expert consists of logical inferences which he draws from what he himself observes, it can also be accepted that when doctors examine a patient in the course of their duties, they make notes and any doctor would be able to make an opinion based on those notes. There is nothing wrong or unacceptable about a doctor taking into account what a patient has told him or other doctors have recorded about a patient in coming to his opinion.

Finally, in the earlier case of *Wilfred Kashiba v The People,*[614] the applicant was convicted of store-breaking. The evidence of the arresting officer contained an allegedly free and voluntary statement of the accused but the magistrate did not inform the accused of his rights before the statement was admitted. The applicant applied to the Court of Appeal for leave to appeal. It was held as follows:

(i) It is the duty of the trial court in all cases, even if the question is not raised by the defence, to satisfy itself as to the admissibility of an incriminating statement. The court must satisfy itself, before evidence as to the content of the statement, that it was freely and voluntarily made, and where an accused is unrepresented, the court must take

[611] [1986] ZR 93 (SC).

[612] Chapter 110 of the Laws of Zambia.

[613] [1990 – 1992] ZR 140 (SC).

[614] [1971] ZR 95 (CA); Quoted with approval in *Miyutu & Another v People* (Appeal 23 of 2016) [2017] ZMSC 39.

particular care that the accused is made fully aware of his rights and, if necessary, to test the evidence on this issue.

(ii) Whether or not an accused is represented, the record should state whether the allegedly free and voluntary character of a statement was challenged, the subsequent proceedings on the issue and the ruling of the court. These steps are not mere formalities; failure to take them is a serious irregularity which will lead to the setting aside of the conviction unless the appellate court is satisfied that, on the remainder of the evidence, the trial court must inevitably have come to the same conclusion.

(ix) Exclusion of evidence extracted unfairly from the accused: case law

In *Chileshe v The People,*[615] the accused was convicted of the offence of office breaking contrary to s 273(1) of the Penal Code,[616] in the Subordinate Court of the First Class at Mufulira which conviction was supported solely by the accused's confession admitted in evidence. It was held as follows: (i) The 1964 revised Judges' Rules have not been applied in Zambia and the pre-1964 Judges' Rules are still applicable. (ii) Under the pre-1964 Judges' Rules applicable in Zambia a person in custody whether he has been charged or not must be cautioned before any interrogation takes place. (iii) If a court is satisfied that the statement was made voluntarily but, in a manner, unfair to the accused, the court has discretion to exclude such statement under the pre-1964 Judges' Rules.

In *Banda v The People,*[617] [d]uring [the appellant's] trial on a murder charge a statement, in which he confessed to the offence, was admitted in evidence against the appellant. There was a discrepancy between the police officer who took down the statement and a civilian witness as to whether the required warn and caution statement had actually been administered. In admitting the statement, the trial Court had relied heavily on a statement from the bar by the appellant's counsel during the trial that his initial instructions had been that the statement was free and voluntary. On appeal the Court held that the failure to administer the warn and caution created a rebuttable presumption of involuntariness and, as there was a discrepancy between the prosecution witnesses as to whether this had happened, it had not been rebutted. It was further held that the statement should be excluded as the stance taken by the appellant's counsel at the trial had amounted to actual prejudice to the appellant. The appellant's challenge to the admission of the statement could not have received fair consideration when defending counsel made damaging statements, contrary to his duty to the client. The statement was excluded but, as there was sufficient other evidence to convict the appellant, the appeal was dismissed.

---

[615] [1972] ZR 48 (HC); *The People v Chanda* [1972] ZR 116 (HC).

[616] Chapter 87 of the Laws of Zambia.

[617] [1990 – 1992] ZR 70 (SC) 20.

(x) *Voire dire* proceedings

As is already apparent at this point in this chapter, a *voire dire* is a trial-within-a trial. This means the proceedings there under will be similar to any trial including the trial proper to which the *voire dire* relates. Steve Uglow[618] postulates that two issues invariably arise as regards *voire dire* proceedings:

(i) Where the [accused] testifies, what questions can be put by the prosecution in cross-examination?

(ii) The [accused's] evidence may well be relevant (and incriminating)[619] to the issues in the trial proper. What use can the prosecution make of this testimony later in the trial?

Recall that facts in issue are that class of facts which a party, irrespective, must prove at trial in order to succeed in his claim or defence. As respects *voire dire*, the fact in issue is whether the conditions of admissibility were met or not. Revisiting confessions again, it would follow that the fact in issue is not so much the truthfulness or falsity of the confession in question but whether said confession was obtained voluntarily or by oppression from the police through the device of torture for example. Thus, questions that are not relevant in so far as the fact in issue is concerned may not be asked or relied upon in a *voire dire*. The *People*[620] cannot therefore ask the accused whether the confession now impugned is true as this is not relevant to the fact in issue which is whether the confession was obtained voluntarily or under oppression. Nor can the *People* rely on the truthfulness of the confession in question. The foregoing is ably demonstrated by the Privy Council[621] and in particular Lord Edmund-Davies[622] in the English case of *Wong Kam-ming v The Queen*[623] which dealt with Criminal evidence – Admissions and confessions – Answers and statements to police – Issue as to admissibility – Whether on *voire dire* prosecution entitled to cross-examine accused as to truth of confession – Whether prosecution entitled on trial of general issue to adduce evidence of and cross-examine accused as to evidence given on *voire dire*.

An indictment charged the appellant and five other men with murder at a massage parlour. The only evidence implicating the appellant was a signed statement he had given to the police in which he admitted that he had been present at the material time at the parlour, that at one stage he had had a knife in his hand and that he had 'chopped' someone at the parlour. At the commencement of the trial counsel for the appellant challenged the admissibility of the statement on the ground that it was not made voluntarily. The trial judge dealt with that issue of admissibility on the *voire dire* on which the appellant gave evidence as to the circumstances in which the statement

[618] Uglow S, *Evidence: Text and Materials* 56.

[619] See Article 18(7) of the Constitution as amended by Act No 2 of 2016.

[620] Which is the designation in court documents for the prosecution in criminal trials in Zambia.

[621] Lord Diplock, Lord Hailsham of St Marylebone, Lord Salmon, Lord Edmund-Davies and Lord Keith of Kinkel 17, 18, 19 October, 20 December 1978.

[622] See below.

[623] [1979] 1 All ER 939.

was made, and was then cross-examined on the contents of the statement to establish their truth. Shorthand-writers took down the cross-examination. The trial judge ruled that the statement was inadmissible. When trial of the general issue was resumed the Crown sought to establish the appellant's presence at the parlour by calling the shorthand-writers to produce extracts from the transcript of the cross-examination on the *voire dire*. The judge allowed the Crown to adduce that evidence in support of its case, and also allowed the Crown to cross-examine the appellant on his evidence-in-chief on the general issue by reference to the extracts from his cross-examination on the *voire dire*. In his summing-up the trial judge told the jury that the answers in cross-examination on the *voire dire* indicated that the appellant was present at the parlour. The appellant was convicted of murder. His appeal against conviction was dismissed by the Court of Appeal of Hong Kong. He appealed to the Judicial Committee of the Privy Council contending that, on the *voire dire*, cross-examination as to the truth of his statement ought not to have been permitted, but that, if it was permissible, the Crown was not entitled at the trial of the general issue to adduce evidence of his testimony on the *voire dire* or to cross-examine him on that evidence. It was held that the appeal would be allowed, and the conviction quashed, for the following reasons: (i) (Lord Hailsham of St Marylebone dissenting) On a *voire dire* as to the admissibility of an extra-judicial statement by an accused the prosecution was not entitled to cross-examine the accused as to the truth of the statement, for the sole issue on the *voire dire* was whether the statement had been made voluntarily, and whether it was true was not relevant to that issue. It followed that the Crown's cross-examination of the appellant on the *voire dire* was a substantial irregularity in the trial.[624] (ii) Furthermore, whether the accused's statement was excluded or admitted on the *voire dire*, the Crown was not entitled as part of its case on the general issue to adduce evidence of the testimony given by the accused on the *voire dire*. Accordingly, the calling of the shorthand-writers to give evidence of what the appellant had said on the *voire dire*, and his cross-examination on the general issue were also substantial irregularities in the trial.[625] *Per Curiam:* Where a statement is admitted as voluntary on the *voire dire* and the accused in giving evidence on the general issue gives evidence as to the reliability of the admissions in the statement, and in so doing departs materially from his testimony on the *voire dire*, cross-examination on the discrepancies between his testimony on the *voire dire* and his evidence on the general issue is permissible, for then his statements in evidence on the *voire dire* stand on the same basis as, for example, evidence given by the accused in a previous trial where the jury have disagreed.

For ease of reference and because of the significance of the case, we reproduce the headnote relating to the appeal and Lord Edmund-Davies's speech in *Wong Kam-ming v The Queen:*[626]

---

[624] *R v Hammond* [1941] 3 All ER 318 overruled.

[625] *R v Treacy* [1944] 2 All ER 229 applied.

[626] [1979] 1 All ER 939 at 939-943.

This was an appeal in forma pauperis, by special leave of the Judicial Committee granted on 1 March 1978, by Wong Kam-ming against the judgment of the Court of Appeal of Hong Kong (Briggs CJ and Huggins JA, McMullin J dissenting) dated 12 July 1977 whereby the appellant's appeal against his conviction by the Supreme Court of Hong Kong (before Commissioner Garcia and a jury) on 1 October 1976 for murder and on two counts of wounding with intent to do grievous bodily harm was dismissed. The facts are set out in the majority judgment of the Board.

LORD EDMUND-DAVIES. This is an appeal by special leave granted by this Board from a judgment of the Court of Appeal of Hong Kong, dismissing the appeal of Wong Kam-ming against his conviction in October 1976 of murder by the Supreme Court (Commissioner Garcia and a jury). The indictment charged the appellant and five other males on counts of murdering one man and of maliciously wounding two others. The case for the Crown was that the accused men were part of a gang who went to a massage parlour in Kowloon and there fatally attacked the manager and wounded others in retaliation for an earlier attack on one of their number. Four of the accused were acquitted on all charges, while the other two (including the present appellant) were convicted on each.

When the trial opened, the only evidence implicating the appellant consisted of a signed statement which he had given to the police. In this he admitted being one of those present in the massage parlour, that at one stage he had a knife in his hand and that he had 'chopped' one of those present. Defending counsel having intimated to the court that he challenged the admissibility of this statement on the ground that it was not voluntary, before the Crown opened its case the judge (in the absence of the jury) proceeded to deal with the issue of admissibility on the *voire dire*. After two police witnesses had testified to its making, the appellant gave evidence that he was never cautioned, that he was questioned at length while in custody, that he was grabbed by the shirt and shaken, that an inducement was offered that if he confessed his 'sworn brother' would not be arrested and that he had been forced to copy out and sign a statement drafted by the police. Under cross-examination he was asked a series of questions based on the detailed contents of the statement, and directed at establishing its truth. At this stage it is sufficient to say that, at the conclusion of the *voire dire*, the trial judge excluded the statement.

This ruling placed the Crown in dire difficulty, for it is common ground that without it they could not establish even that the appellant was present in the massage parlour at any material time. Finding themselves in that situation, they resorted to a course of action which none of their Lordships had hitherto ever heard of. Prosecuting counsel indicated to the trial judge (in the absence of the jury) that he proposed to establish, by reference to what had transpired in the *voire dire*, that the appellant had, 'in circumstances where there is no question of involuntariness, admitted he was present and involved in the incident with which we are concerned'. As authority for submitting that he should be allowed to prove such admission by calling the shorthand-writer present during the *voire dire* he cited *R v Wright*[627] to which reference must later be made. Defending counsel's objection was overruled, the trial judge holding that *R v Wright*[628] was good law, and expressly refusing to exercise in favour of the appellant any discretion he might have to exclude the proffered new evidence. Two shorthand-writers were then called to produce extracts from their transcripts of what the appellant had said during the *voire dire*, and this despite a renewed objection by defending counsel.

A submission of 'No case' was likewise overruled, the trial judge saying:

> The main point here is presence at the scene at the relevant time.' Defending counsel thereupon called the appellant. Following his evidence-in-chief, he was closely cross-examined by reference to the shorthand transcript of what he had said on the *voire dire*, prosecuting counsel repeatedly pointing out discrepancies and observing at one stage: 'That is extraordinarily different from the evidence you have given this time.

And in the course of summing-up the judge told the jury that the appellant—

> [...] in certain proceedings held on 25th and 26th August this year gave answers to certain questions put to him in cross-examination by [Crown counsel], and such answers indicate that he was present in the premises of the music parloura on the night of 28th December 1975. A copy of those questions and answers is also in your hands.'

Following on these proceedings which, it will be seen, had taken several unusual turns, the jury, as already indicated, convicted the appellant on all three charges, and he was sentenced to death on the murder charge. The conduct of the trial has been attacked in several respects, and these were conveniently summarised by counsel for the appellant in framing the following questions: 1. During the cross-examination of an accused in the *voire dire* as to the admissibility of his challenged statement, may questions be put as to its truth? 2. If 'Yes', has the court a discretion to exclude such cross-examination, and (if so) was it properly exercised in the present case? 3. Where, although the confession is held inadmissible, the answers to questions 1 and 2 are nevertheless in favour of the Crown, is the prosecution permitted, on resumption of the trial of the main issue, to adduce evidence of what the accused said during the *voire dire*? 4. If 'Yes', is there a discretion to exclude such evidence, and (if so) was it properly exercised here? 5.

---

[627] [1969] SASR 256.

[628] [1969] SASR 256.

Even though it be held that the answer to question 3 is 'No', may the accused nevertheless be cross-examined on what he said during the *voire dire*? Their Lordships proceed to consider these questions.

Questions 1 and 2: relevance of truth of extra-judicial statements

In *R v Hammond*[629] prosecuting counsel was held entitled to ask the accused, when cross-examining him during the *voire dire*, whether a police statement which the accused alleged had been extorted by gross maltreatment was in fact true, and elicited the answer that it was. Upholding the propriety of putting the question, Humphreys J said in the Court of Criminal Appeal:

> In our view, [the question] clearly was not inadmissible. It was a perfectly natural question to put to a person, and it was relevant to the issue of whether the story which he was then telling of being attacked and ill-used by the police was true or false [...] it surely must be admissible, and in our view, it is admissible, because it went to the credit of the person who was giving evidence. If a man says, "I was forced to tell the story. I was made to say this, that and the other", it must be relevant to know whether he was made to tell the truth, or whether he was made to say a number of things which were untrue. In other words, in our view, the contents of the statement which he admittedly made and signed were relevant to the question of how he came to make and sign that statement, and, therefore, the questions which were put were properly put.

Although much criticised, that decision has frequently been followed in England and Wales and in many other jurisdictions, though it would serve little purpose to refer to more than a few of the many decisions cited by learned counsel. Mention must, however, be made to *DeClercq v R*, a majority decision of the Supreme Court of Canada following *R v Hammond*,[630] where Martland J said:

> [...] it does not follow that the truth or falsity of the statement must be irrelevant [...] An accused person, who alleged that he had been forced to admit responsibility for a crime committed by another, could properly testify that the statement obtained from him was false. Similarly, where the Judge conducting the *voire dire* was in some doubt on the evidence as to whether the accused had willingly made a statement, or whether, as he contended, he had done so because of pressure exerted by a person in authority, the admitted truth or the alleged falsity of the statement could be a relevant factor in deciding whether or not he would accept the evidence of the accused regarding such pressure.

[629] [1941] 3 All ER 318 at 321.

[630] 70 DLR (2d) 530 at 537.

Their Lordships were told by learned counsel that in England and Wales it has become common practice for prosecuting counsel to ask the accused in the *voire dire* whether his challenged statement was in fact true. It is difficult to understand why this practice is permitted, and impossible to justify it by claiming that in some unspecified way it goes to 'credit'. As McMullin J said in his dissenting judgment in the instant case:

> […] I cannot see that the answer to this question has any material relevance even to the issue of credibility. Where the answer to the question "Is this confession the truth?" is "No" the inquiry is no further advanced. The credibility of the defendant in relation to the alleged improprieties can scarcely be enhanced or impaired by an answer which favours his own interests in opposing the admission of the statement. On its own, demeanour apart, it is neutral.

The cogency of these observations may be respectfully contrasted with those of Huggins JA who said, in delivering the majority judgment:

> Although questions may be put to the defendant as to the truth of his extrajudicial confession that does not make the truth or falsehood of that confession relevant to the issue of voluntariness: what is relevant—because it goes to the credibility of the defendant—is that the defendant asserts that the extrajudicial confession is true or false.

But the basis of this assertion is unclear. If the accused denies the truth of the confession or some self-incriminating admission contained in it, the question whether his denial is itself true or false cannot be ascertained until after the *voire dire* is over and the accused's guilt or innocence has been determined by the jury, an issue which the judge has no jurisdiction to decide. If, on the other hand, the accused made a self-incriminating admission that the statement is true, then, as one critic has expressed it, 'If the confession is true, this presumably shows that the accused tends to tell the truth, which suggests that he is telling the truth in saying the police were violent'.[631]

The sole object of the *voire dire* was to determine the voluntariness of the alleged confession in accordance with principles long established by such cases as *Ibrahim v R*. This was emphasised by this Board in *Chan Wai-Keung v R*, while the startling consequences of adopting the Hammond approach were well illustrated in the Canadian case of *R v Hnedish*,[632] where Hall CJ said:

'Having regard to all the implications involved in accepting the full impact of the Hammond decision which can, I think, be summarized by saying that regardless of how much physical or mental torture or abuse has been inflicted on an accused to coerce him into telling what

[631] Heydon: Cases and Materials on Evidence (1975) at 181.

[632] (1958) 26 WWR 685 at 688.

is true, the confession is admitted because it is in fact true regardless of how it is obtained, I cannot believe that the Hammond decision does reflect the final judicial reasoning of the English courts … I do not see how under the guise of "credibility" the court can transmute what is initially an inquiry as to the "admissibility" of the confession into an inquisition of an accused. That would be repugnant to our accepted standards and principles of justice; it would invite and encourage brutality in the handling of persons suspected of having committed offences.'

It is right to point out that learned counsel for the Crown did not seek to submit that the prosecution could in every case properly cross-examine the accused during the *voire dire* regarding the truth of his challenged statement. Indeed, he went so far as to concede that in many cases it would be wrong to do anything of the sort. But he was unable to formulate an acceptable test of its propriety, and their Lordships have been driven to the conclusion that none exists. In other words, in their Lordships' view, *R v Hammond* was wrongly decided, and any decisions in Hong Kong which purported to follow it should be treated as overruled. The answer to question 1 is therefore 'No', and it follows that question 2 does not fall to be considered.

Questions 3 and 4

Their Lordships turn to questions 3 and 4. As part of its case on the main issue, may the prosecution lead evidence regarding the testimony given by the accused on the *voire dire*? As already related, the trial judge originally thought that this question required a negative answer, but he was led to change his mind by the decision in R v Wright, where the Supreme Court of South Australia held that the Crown was entitled to lead such evidence, subject to the discretion of the trial judge to disallow it. But the weight of judicial authority is against such a conclusion. The earliest relevant decision appears to be that of the Federal Supreme Court of Southern Rhodesia in *Chitambala v R*[633] where Clayden ACJ said:

'In any criminal trial the accused has the right to elect not to give evidence at the conclusion of the Crown case. To regard evidence given by him on the question of admissibility as evidence in the trial itself would mean either that he must be deprived of that right if he wishes properly to contest the admissibility of a statement, or that, to preserve that right, he must abandon another right in a fair trial, the right to prevent inadmissible statements being led in evidence against him … To me it seems clear that deprivation of rights in this manner, and the changing of a trial of admissibility into a full investigation of the merits, cannot be part of a fair criminal trial.'

This decision was followed in *Hong Kong in Li Kim-hung v R* and in *Ng Chun-kwan v R*. In the latter McMullin J (who dissented in the instant case) said, in giving the judgment of the Full Court.[634]

[633] [1961] R & N 166 at 169.

[634] [1974] Hong Kong LR 319 at 328.

> [...] what the accused says on the *voire dire* may not be used as substantive evidence against him or his co-accused [...] In this respect evidence on the *voire dire* is distinguishable from an extra-judicial confession and the basis for the distinction lies in the accused's right to remain silent upon the trial of the general issue even though he has elected to give evidence on the *voire dire*.

Yet in the instant appeal counsel for the Crown felt constrained to submit that, even were the trial judge to exclude a confession on the ground that torture had been used to extort it, any damaging statements made by the accused on the *voire dire* could nevertheless properly be adduced as part of the prosecution's case. Boldness could go no further.

Fortunately for justice, their Lordships have concluded that, where the confession has been excluded, the argument against ever admitting such evidence as part of the Crown case must prevail. But what if the confession is held admissible? In such circumstances, it is unlikely that the prosecution will need to do more than rely on the confession itself. Nevertheless, in principle should they be prevented from proving in addition any admission made by the accused on the *voire dire*? This question has exercised their Lordships a great deal, but even in the circumstances predicated it is preferable to maintain a clear distinction between the issue of voluntariness, which is alone relevant to the *voire dire*, and the issue of guilt falling to be decided in the main trial. To blur this distinction can lead, as has already been shown, to unfortunate consequences, and their Lordships have therefore concluded that the same exclusion of evidence regarding the *voire dire* proceedings from the main trial must be observed, regardless of whether the challenged confession be excluded or admitted.

It follows that question 3 must be answered in the negative, and question 4 accordingly does not arise.

Question 5

Question 5 remains for consideration by their Lordships. Notwithstanding the answer to question 3, in the event of the accused giving evidence in the main trial, may he be cross-examined in respect of statements made by him during that *voire dire*? In the instant case the majority of the court held that he could, and McMullin J (who dissented) had earlier been of the same view, having said in *Ng Chun-kwan v R*:[635]

'The only way in which evidence of an admission made by the accused on the *voire dire* may be adduced in evidence is by way of rebuttal if he gives evidence on the general issue and if that evidence is inconsistent with what he has said on the *voire dire* ... we cannot see any warrant for the contention ... that everything which transpires in the course of a *voire dire* is to be regarded as having acquired an indefeasible immunity from all further resort for any purpose whatsoever.'

[635] [1974] Hong Kong LR 319 at 328.

The problem is best approached in stages. In *R v Treacy*,[636] where the accused's answers under police interrogation were held inadmissible, it was held that he could not be cross-examined to elicit that he had in fact given those answers, Humphrey J saying:

'In our view, a statement made by a prisoner under arrest is either admissible or it is not admissible. If it is admissible, the proper course for the prosecution is to prove it ... If it is not admissible, nothing more ought to be heard of it, and it is a complete mistake to think that a document can be made admissible in evidence which is otherwise inadmissible simply because it is put to a person in cross-examination.'

In their Lordships' judgment, *R v Treacy*[637] was undoubtedly correct in prohibiting cross-examination as to the contents of confessions which the court has ruled inadmissible. But what if during the *voire dire* the accused has made self-incriminating statements not strictly related to the confession itself but which nevertheless have relevance to the issue of guilt or innocence of the charge preferred? May the accused be cross-examined so as to elicit those matters? In the light of their Lordships' earlier conclusion that the Crown may not adduce as part of its case evidence of what the accused said during a *voire dire* culminating in the exclusion of an impugned confession, can a different approach here be permitted from that condemned in R v Treacy[638]?

Subject to what was said to be the court's discretion to exclude it in proper circumstances, counsel for the Crown submitted that it can be, citing in support s 13 of the Hong Kong Evidence Ordinance, which was based on the familiar provision in s 4 of the Criminal Procedure Act 1865 of the United Kingdom, relating to the confrontation of a witness with his previous inconsistent statements. But these statutory provisions have no relevance if the earlier statements cannot be put in evidence. And, having already concluded that the *voire dire* statements of the accused are not admissible during the presentation of the prosecution's case, their Lordships find it impossible in principle to distinguish between such cross-examination of the accused on the basis of the *voire dire* as was permitted in the instant case by the trial judge and upheld by the majority of the Court of Appeal and that cross-examination based on the contents of an excluded confession which, it is common ground, was rightly condemned in *R v Treacy*.[639]

But what if the *voire dire* resulted in the impugned confession being admitted, and the accused later elects to give evidence? If he then testifies to matters relating, for example, to the reliability of the confession (as opposed to its voluntariness, which *ex hypothesi*, is no longer in issue) and in so doing gives answers which are markedly different from his testimony given during the *voire dire*, may he be cross-examined so as to establish that at the earlier stage of the trial he had told a different story? Great injustice could well result from the

[636] [1944] 2 All ER 229 at 236.

[637] [1944] 2 All ER 229 at 236.

[638] ([1944] 2 All ER 229 at 236).

[639] ([1944] 2 All ER 229 at 236).

exclusion of such cross-examination, and their Lordships can see no justification in legal principle or on any other ground which renders it impermissible. As has already been observed, an accused seeking to challenge the admissibility of a confession may for all practical purposes be obliged to testify in the *voire dire* if his challenge is to have any chance of succeeding, and his evidence is then (or certainly should be) restricted strictly to the issue of admissibility of the confession. But the situation is quite different where, the confession having been admitted despite his challenge, the accused later elects to give evidence during the main trial and, in doing so, departs materially from the testimony he gave in the *voire dire*. Having so chosen to testify, why should the discrepancies not be elicited and demonstrated by cross-examination? In their Lordships' view, his earlier statements made in the *voire dire* provide as acceptable a basis for this cross-examination to that end as any other earlier statements made by him, including, of course, his confession which, though challenged, had been ruled admissible. Indeed, for such purposes and in such circumstances, his *voire dire* statements stand on no different basis than, for example, the sworn testimony given by an accused in a previous trial where the jury had disagreed.

No doubt the trial judge has a discretion and, indeed, a duty to ensure that the right of the prosecution to cross-examine or rebut is not used in a manner unfair or oppressive to the accused, and no doubt the judge is under an obligation to see to it that any statutory provisions bearing on the situation (such as those earlier referred to) are strictly complied with. But, subject thereto, their Lordships hold that cross-examination in the circumstances predicated which is directed to testing the credibility of the accused by establishing the inconsistencies in his evidence is wholly permissible.

In the instant case, however, the challenged confession was excluded. It therefore follows that in the judgment of their Lordships no less than three substantial irregularities occurred in the trial: (1) in the *voire dire* the accused was cross-examined with a view to establishing that his extra-judicial statement was true; (2) in the trial proper, the Crown was permitted to call as part of its case evidence regarding answers given by the accused during the *voire dire*; and (3) the accused was permitted to be cross-examined so as to demonstrate that what he had said in chief was inconsistent with his statement in the *voire dire*.

As a result, evidence was wrongly placed before the jury that the appellant was one of those present in the massage parlour at the material time and that he had then been in possession of a weapon. But for that evidence, it is common ground that the submission of 'No case' made by defending counsel must have succeeded.

It follows that their Lordships will humbly advise Her Majesty that this appeal should be allowed and the conviction quashed.

According to Uglow,[640] *Wong Kam-ming*[641] is persuasive authority for the following propositions:

(i) During cross-examination on the voir dire, the accused may not be asked questions as to the truth of the challenged statement,

(ii) Whether or not the judge has admitted the statement, the prosecution may not lead evidence of what the accused said on the voir dire as part of the crown case,

(iii) Where the judge has excluded the statement and the accused subsequently gives evidence in the trial, the accused may not be cross-examined as to discrepancies between present evidence and what was said on the voir dire,

(iv) Where the judge has admitted the statement and the accused subsequently gives evidence in the trial, the accused may be cross-examined by prosecuting counsel as to discrepancies between present evidence and what was said on the voir dire-the defendant's statements on oath on the voir dire are not to be differentiated by any other earlier statements made [by] the accused.

It would follow from the foregoing that as shown in *R v Brophy*[642] which would appear to be in line with Article 18(7) of Part III of the Constitution, incriminating statements made by the accused in a *voir dire* are inadmissible in the main trial by either the prosecution or the defence.

In *R v Brophy*,[643] the respondent was charged on an indictment containing 49 counts, including 12 counts of murder arising from an explosion and fire in which 12 people died, 36 counts of causing explosions or possessing explosives or firearms on various occasions between September 1976 and February 1978 and one count (count 49) of belonging to a proscribed organisation, i.e. the IRA, between specified dates in 1976 and 1978 contrary to s 19(1)(a) of the Northern Ireland (Emergency Provisions) Act 1973. The respondent pleaded not guilty to all the charges. There was no evidence to connect him with the crimes except a number of verbal and written statements which he had made or was alleged by the Crown to have made to the police after his arrest. The respondent challenged the admissibility of the statements under s 8(2)a of the Northern Ireland (Emergency Provisions) Act 1978 (which consolidated the 1973 Act)[644] on the ground that he had been induced to make them by being subjected

[640] Uglow S, *Evidence: Text and Materials*58.

[641] [1979] 1 All ER 939.

[642] [1981] 2 All ER 705.

[643] [1981] 2 All ER 705.

[644] Section 8(2) provided: 'If, in any such proceedings where the prosecution proposes to give in evidence a statement made by the accused, prima facie evidence is adduced that the accused was subjected to torture or to inhuman or degrading treatment in order to induce him to make the statement, the court shall, unless the prosecution satisfies it that the statement was not so obtained—(a) exclude the statement, or (b) if the statement has been received in evidence, either—(i) continue the trial disregarding the statement; or (ii) direct that the trial shall be restarted before a differently constituted court (before which the statement in question shall be inadmissible).'

to torture or to inhuman or degrading treatment while in custody. The trial judge, sitting without a jury, dealt with the issue of admissibility on a *voire dire* at which the respondent gave evidence challenging the admissibility of the statements. In his evidence-in-chief in answer to questions from his counsel the respondent stated that he had been a member of the IRA during the greater part of the period charged in count 49. After the *voire dire* the judge ruled that he was not satisfied that the statements had not been induced by torture or inhuman or degrading treatment and excluded evidence of them from the substantive trial. When the substantive trial resumed the Crown proposed to call the shorthand writer who had recorded the evidence at the *voire dire* to prove the respondent's statement on the *voire dire* that he had been a member of the IRA. The objection of counsel for the respondent to the admission of this evidence was overruled by the judge who admitted it on the ground that it was not strictly relevant to the central question in dispute on the *voire dire*, i.e. the admissibility of the respondent's statements to the police, and because it had been freely given during the respondent's examination-in-chief. Since the first 48 counts were unsupported by any evidence the respondent was acquitted on those counts but on count 49 he was convicted. The respondent appealed to the Court of Appeal in Northern Ireland which allowed his appeal on the ground that the respondent's evidence at the *voire dire* as to his membership of the IRA could be regarded as relevant to the issue on the *voire dire* and accordingly was inadmissible at the substantive trial. The Crown appealed.

It was held as follows: Where evidence was given on a *voire dire* by an accused person in answer to questions by his counsel, and without objection by counsel for the Crown, his evidence was to be treated as relevant to the issue at the *voire dire* unless it was clearly and obviously irrelevant, and the accused was to be given the benefit of any reasonable doubt as to relevancy. The respondent's statement that he had been a member of the IRA was relevant to the issue at the *voire dire* whether he had been subjected to inhuman or degrading treatment, for by showing that he had been a member of the IRA for several years up to a few months before the date of the murders charged and that the police knew or suspected this, he could then ask the court to infer that not only would they be more hostile to him but also that they would have expected him to have received instruction how to avoid succumbing to the normal techniques of interrogation which did not involve ill-treatment. Although it had not been proved that the police did know of his membership of the IRA it was reasonable to assume that if he had been a member of the IRA for six years the police would probably have been aware of that fact. It followed therefore that, since the respondent's evidence as to his IRA membership was relevant to the issue at the *voire dire*, it was not admissible in the substantive trial and the appeal would be dismissed.

Per Curiam:

(1) At a trial before a judge sitting without a jury, it is not normally necessary at the substantive trial to go through the formal step of proving the evidence given by the accused at the *voire dire* because

the judge has himself heard the evidence given at the *voire dire* and is himself the sole judge of fact at the substantive trial.

(2) If, at the *voire dire*, the accused, whether in answer to questions from his own counsel or not, goes out of his way to boast of having committed the crimes with which he is charged, or if he uses the witness box as a platform for a political speech, his evidence so far as it relates to those matters will almost certainly be irrelevant to the issue at the *voire dire*, and different considerations will apply to its admissibility at the substantive trial.

(3) The right of the accused to give evidence at the *voire dire* without affecting his right to remain silent at the substantive trial is absolute and is not to be made conditional on an exercise of judicial discretion.[645]

Lord Fraser opined[646] that '[t]he right of the accused to give evidence at the *voir dire* without affecting his right to remain silent at the substantive trial is [...] absolute and is not to be made conditional on an exercise of judicial discretion.' In saying so, his lordship was rejecting the idea that since statements made at a voir dire even those that are incriminating are made voluntarily they ought to be admissible and as such could be used in examination in chief by the defence or cross-examination by the prosecution. It would follow that the prosecution faces significant constraints in using any part of the *voire dire* evidence in the substantive trial.

1.8.2.3 *Control over questions to be considered by the judge as a trier of fact: judicial discretion to exclude evidence*

A judge[647] has wide ranging authority not only to exclude evidence but the discretion to exclude evidence which would ordinarily be admissible. While this typically arises out of the court's inherent power to supervise trials and ensure fairness, its fundamental basis is a constitutional one.[648] Article 18(7) of the Constitution provides for example that '[a] person who is tried for a criminal offence shall not be compelled to give evidence at the trial.' In fact, in *David Dumina v The People*[649] the Supreme Court held that '[...] a court must not hold the fact that an accused remains silent against him.'[650] The common law presented judges with a rather odd scenario where while they had the

[645] Dictum of Lord Hailsham in *Wong Kam-ming v The Queen* [1979] 1 All ER at 946–947 applied.

[646] *R v Brophy* [1981] 2 All ER 710d-e.

[647] Or Magistrate as the case may be.

[648] See Article 18 of the Constitution.

[649] [1988 – 1989] ZR 199 (SC).

[650] But See, for academic interests only, *Lt. Gen. Geojago Robert Chaswe Musengule, Amon Sibande v The People* HPA/16/2009 on how, as argued by counsel, but rejected both in this case and on appeal in *Lt. General Geojago Robert Musengule and Amon Sibande v The People* [SCZ Selected Judgment No 19 of 2017], this may be a legal fiction in the light of the provisions of Part VI of the ACC Act, as the Act requires a satisfactory explanation from a person charged with an offence under Part IV; see also for academic reasons only similar arguments by counsel, which were ultimately rejected in *The People v Austin Chisanga Liato* [Selected Judgment No 21 of 2010] regarding a similar provision, s 71(1)&(2) and s 78 of the Forfeiture of Proceeds of Crime Act No 19 of 2010.

power to exclude admissible evidence, they had no power to include otherwise inadmissible evidence irrespective of public policy or administration of justice considerations that would have arisen. Be that as it may, Article 118(a)(b) and (e) of the Constitution,[651] provides as follows: '[i]n exercising judicial authority, the courts shall be guided by the following principles: (a) justice shall be done to all, without discrimination; (b) justice shall not be delayed; (e) justice shall be administered without undue regard to procedural technicalities.' The foregoing provisions of the Constitution entail that Courts will have to be fair by not delaying justice unnecessarily. Further and of particular interest is Article 118(e) which within the context of our present discussion appears to permit a judge to 'admit otherwise inadmissible [...] evidence if the court is satisfied that it is in the interests of justice to do so.'[652] This Constitutional position overrides the common law in the restrictions placed on judges as regards issues of admissibility. Nevertheless, the Zambian Constitutional Court has observed as follows as regards Article 118(e) in particular in *Henry M Kapoko and The People:*[653]

> The approach we have taken is in our view broad enough to accommodate a range of legal questions and problems. While the facts and law in each case will vary [,] the principle laid out by this Court on the meaning and application of Article 118(2)(e) remains constant. The court's word is clear. Article 118(2)(e) is not intended to do away with existing principles, laws and procedures, even where the same constitute technicalities. It is intended to avoid a situation where a manifest injustice would be done by paying unjustifiable regard to a technicality.

Judicial discretion to exclude evidence must therefore be seen within the context of the following:

(i) That the evidence in question is relevant;
(ii) Said relevant evidence possesses sufficient probative value necessitating its admission considering the time and trouble this will cause; and
(iii) Evidence in question does not come under any exclusionary rules under the law of evidence.

As already shown, the judge is clothed with the power to do justice under the Constitution. He also can invoke common law precedent. The space of a judge's discretion to exclude evidence at common law[654] is exemplified in *R v Sang*.[655] The two accused were jointly charged with conspiring with others to utter forged United States banknotes, and with unlawful possession of them. At the arraignment they pleaded not guilty to both counts. Before counsel for

[651] As amended by Act No 2 of 2016.

[652] Uglow S, *Evidence: Text and Materials* 60.

[653] 2016/CC/0023.

[654] This would be in instances where the evidence in question would prejudice the accused to such an extent that this outweighs any probative value such evidence may hold.

[655] *R v Sang, R v Mangan* [1979] 2 All ER 46.

the Crown opened the case for the prosecution, counsel for one of the accused asked the court to hold a trial within a trial in order that it might consider whether the involvement of the accused in the offences charged arose out of the activities of an agent provocateur. He said that he hoped at such a trial to establish, by cross-examination of a police officer, and by evidence-in-chief from an alleged police informer, that his client had been incited by the police through the officer and the informer to commit the offences and that they would not have been committed but for the police inspired activities of the officer and the informer. Counsel then hoped to persuade the judge to rule, in the exercise of his discretion, that the Crown should not be allowed to lead any evidence of the commission of the offences thus incited, and to direct that a verdict of not guilty be returned. The Crown contended that, even if it were established that the facts were as alleged, the judge had no discretion to exclude the evidence and that to hold otherwise would be to reintroduce into English law the defence of entrapment, which had no place in the legal system. Without hearing the evidence, the judge ruled that he did not possess the discretion to exclude the evidence and thereby prevent the prosecution proceeding with the charges. The accused then retracted their please, pleaded guilty and were each sentenced to a term of imprisonment.

On appeal against the judge's ruling, it was held that a judge at a criminal trial had no discretion to exclude evidence tendered by the prosecution because it had been obtained illegally, unfairly, by trick or by other misrepresentation, except where the actions of the prosecution amounted to an abuse of the process of the court and were oppressive. In the accused's case, where the evidence would be immediately probative of the offences charged and there was no suggestion that the actions of the prosecution amounted to an abuse of the process of the court, the judge had no discretion to exclude the evidence and it followed that the appeal would be dismissed.[656]

1.8.2.4 Control over issues before court

Though issues relating to any matter brought before and to be decided by the court are set out in a statement of claim or indictment as the case may be, it is for the Magistrate/judge who has the sole responsibility of deciding whether there is sufficient evidence to ultimately convince him to go to trial. When preliminary

[656] *Kuruma Son of Kaniu v R* [1955] 1 All ER 236; *Sneddon v Stevenson* [1967] 2 All ER 1277 applied; *Brannan v Peek* [1947] 2 All ER 572; *Noor Mohamed v R* [1949] 1 All ER 365; *Harris v Director of Public Prosecutions* [1952] 2 All ER 1044; dictum of Lord Goddard CJ in *Kuruma Son of Kaniu v R* [1955] 1 All ER at 239 and dictum of Lord Widgery CJ in *R v Mealey, R v Sheridan* (1974) 60 Cr App R at 63–64 explained; *R v Christie* [1914–15] All ER Rep 63; *R v McEvilly, R v Lee* (1974) 60 Cr App R 150 considered; *Jeffrey v Black* [1978] 1 All ER 555; *R v Payne* [1963] 1 All ER 848; *King v R* [1968] 2 All ER 610 doubted; *R v Ameer, R v Lucas* [1977] Crim LR 104 disapproved; For official collaboration in crime, see 11 Halsbury's Laws (4th Edn) para 47, and for cases on the subject, see 14(1) Digest (Reissue) 98, 651–653; for submissions on the admissibility of evidence, see 11 Halsbury's Laws (4th Edn) para 283; for the court's discretion to admit or reject evidence wrongfully obtained, see 17 ibid para 12, and for a case on the subject, see 14(2) Digest (Reissue) 469, 3913.

issues are raised orally or by formal application say by way of Order 14A,[657] the Court[658] has the sole responsibility '[…] upon the application of a party or of its own motion determine any question of law or construction of any document arising in any cause or matter at any stage of the proceedings where it appears to the Court that (a) such question is suitable for determination without a full trial of the action, and (b) such determination will finally determine (subject only to any possible appeal) the entire cause or matter or any claim or issue therein.'[659] Further, '[u]pon such determination the Court may dismiss the cause or matter or make such order or judgment as it thinks just.'[660] Additionally, '[t]he Court shall not determine any question under this Order unless the parties have either - (a) had an opportunity of being heard on the question, or (b) consented to an order or judgment on such determination.'[661] Only the judge will have to decide whether there is sufficient evidence to decide in favour of the plaintiff or that sufficient evidence has been presented to defeat the plaintiff's claim.

1.8.2.5 Withdrawal of issues[662]

The ability to withdraw either specific issues or the whole case from the jury is a facet of jury systems to which our jurisdiction does not subscribe. We therefore

---

[657] Of the Rules of the Supreme Court, 1965, RSC, (The White Book) (1999) Edition; see also Order III Rule 2 of the HCR: *Bellamano v Ligure Lombarda Ltd* (SCZ Judgment No 54 of 1976); Practice Direction No 15 of 1971; According to 14A/2/3, RSC, the requirements for employing the procedure under Order 14A are as follows:

(a) the defendant must have given notice of intention to defend: See procedure to be followed as set out in *Indeni Petroleum Refinery Co Limited v Kafco Oil Limited and 3 Others* (Selected Judgment No 29 of 2017); *Hakainde Hichilema and 5 Others v The Government of the Republic of Zambia* (SCZ Appeal No 28 of 2017): Order III Rule 2 of the HCR is unsuitable for issues in limine that seek to have the court render a final order or to terminate whole matters before court, as this ought to properly be brought on the strength of Order 14A and 33, RSC; *Sam Chisulo v Mazzonite Ltd* (CAZ Appeal No 67 of 2019); *The Law Association of Zambia v The President of the Republic of Zambia, The Attorney General and the National Assembly* (Petition No 189 of 2019); applied in *Huazhu Lin and Tu Rui Lin Trading Company Ltd v Butembo Investment Ltd* (2018/HP/0564).

(b) the question of law or construction is suitable for determination without a full trial of the action (para. 1 (i)(a));

(c) such determination will be final as to the entire cause or matter or any claim or issue therein (para. 1 (i)(h)); and

(d) the parties had an opportunity of being heard on the question of law or have consented to an order or judgment being made on such determination (para. 1 (3)). See the somewhat unsatisfactory decision of the Supreme Court on this point in *African Banking Corporation v Mubende Country Lodge Limited* Appeal No 116/2016.

[658] Court is used here instead of 'judge' as according to O 14A r 4, 'the jurisdiction of the Court under this Order may be exercised by a master.'

[659] O14 r 1.

[660] O14 r 2.

[661] O14A r 3.

[662] This is exemplified in such English cases as *Metropolitan Railway Co. v Jackson* [1877] 3 AC 193 at 196 *per* Lord Cairns L.C.; *R v Acott (Brian Gordon)* [1977] 1 All ER 706 at 713b-d, *per* Lord Steyn; [1977] WLR 306.

will not delve much into this.[663] Be that as it may, suffice it to say that in our system the Court is judge (trier of law) and jury (trier of fact). Therefore, only the judge decides whether adequate evidence has been offered on an issue in the particular case and also whether he has been persuaded by the evidence to decide one way or the other in the judgment that he eventually renders.

1.8.2.6 Case to answer/no case to answer

At the end of the plaintiff's or prosecution's case the defence may submit that the prosecution or the plaintiff has not produced evidence of sufficient quality or/and quantity to warrant finding in the prosecution's or defendant's favour (i.e., justifying finding that the accused or defendant has a case to answer and ought to be put on his defence).

(i) Civil matters

A submission of no case to answer is almost never made in civil cases in this jurisdiction. The very nature of civil proceedings makes this submission by defence counsel procedurally unlikely. Recall that Order 3 r 2 of the High Court Rules[664] provides that '[s]ubject to any particular rules, the Court or a Judge may, in all causes and matters, *make any interlocutory order which it or he considers necessary for doing justice,* whether such order has been expressly asked [for] by the person entitled to the benefit of the order or not' (emphasis added). It would appear that on the strength of that Order, such a submission may actually be made. If in theory the submission of "no case to answer" was indeed made, it would take the defendant electing the fact that the Judge is not expected to express an opinion before he hears the entire evidence as trier of fact and law would prevent him from expressing an opinion midstream. Only a defendant electing not to call any evidence would in theory compel the

[663]Nor will we discuss the concept of summing up or directing the jury wherein after the parties have presented their respective cases, the judge will sum up the case for the jury. Those that seek to read up on the matter may consider decisions in *R vMcVey* [1988] Crim LR 127; *McGreevy v DPP* [1973] 1 All ER 503; *Wilson* [1991] Crim LR 838; *DPP v Stonehouse* [1977] 2 All ER 909 at 927f-928c, *per* Lord Salmon; *R vWang* [2005] 1 All ER 782. We will also not delve into specific functions of the jury (which though a mainstay of the American legal system is now generally confined to criminal trials in England and Wales with a few exceptions in civil matters) as such delineation of functions between judge and jury do not exist in this country. Here again, one may, for academic and juristic interest, consider the following authorities on the issue: *R v Gilks* [1972] 3 All ER 280; *Brutus v Cozen* [1972] 2 All ER.: 1297, *per* Lord Reid; *DPP v Stonehouse* [1977] 2 All ER 909, *per* Lord Diplock; Lord Justice Auld, *A Review of the Criminal Courts of England and Wales* (2001), Ch.5, para.99ff; T. Arnold, *Symbols of Government* (Harbinger, 1962), pp 144-145; P. Devlin: *Trial by Jury* (Stevens, 1956) where he said as paraphrased in Uglow S, *Evidence: Text and Materials* at 69: '[t]rial by jury' was 'a paradigm of English Criminal law, 'described as a bulwark against oppression, a safeguard of [...] liberties since the common sense of the ordinary person prevails when all else fails.' However, even this bulwark against oppression could not be a reliable source of fairness or/and impartiality. For example, '[a]fter the trial of the Quakers, Penn and Mead, in 1670, for 'conspiratorial gathering' the jury were fined and imprisoned until eventually released by the Chief Justice who declared 'the right of juries to give their verdict by their conscience.' – Harman, H and Griffith, J *"Justice Deserted"* (NCCL 1979) 11 cited in Uglow S, *Evidence: Text and Materials* 8.

[664] Chapter 27 of the Laws of Zambia. Similar wording is to be found under Order III r 2 of the Rules of the Subordinate Court Act Chapter 28 of the Laws of Zambia.

judge to rule on a submission of "no case to answer".[665] The foregoing, it would appear, is yet to be tested in this jurisdiction.

(ii) Criminal matters

The general practice in criminal matters is for the defence to submit, at the close of the prosecution's case, that the prosecution has not produced sufficient evidence on an essential component of the offence to warrant the finding of a case to answer and as such to put the accused on his defence. The question of what amounts to sufficient evidence has been considered in the case of *R v Galbraith*[666] wherein Lord Lane CJ (as he then was) opined as follows:

> How then should the judge approach a submission of 'no case'?
>
> (1) If there is no evidence that the crime alleged has been committed by the [accused], there is no difficulty. The judge will of course stop the case.
>
> (2) The difficulty arises where there is some evidence but it is of a tenuous character, for example, because of inherent weakness or vagueness or because it is inconsistent with other evidence. (a) Where the judge comes to the conclusion that the prosecution evidence, taken at its highest, is such that a [judge] properly directed could not properly convict upon it, it is his duty, upon a submission being made, to stop the case. (b) Where, however, the prosecution evidence is such that its strength or weakness depends on the view to be taken of a witness's reliability, or other matters which are generally speaking within the province of the [judge] and where on one possible view of the facts there is evidence upon which a [tribunal] could properly come to the conclusion that the defendant is guilty, then the judge should [find the accused with a case to answer and put him on his defence to enable the judge hear his side of the story before he can render a judgment].

In the Practice Direction[667] Lord Parker, CJ specified that a submission of no case to answer may suitably be upheld (a)When there has been no evidence to prove the essential element of the alleged offence; and (b)When evidence adduced by the prosecution has been so discredited that no reasonable tribunal could safely convict on it.

In his comments on the issue, R. Pattenden[668] notes as follows:

> The object of a submission of no case on a trial on indictment is two-fold. To avoid the risk of a perverse [...] verdict and to protect the

[665] See *Alexander v Rayson* [1935] 1 A ll ER R 185; *Benjamin Ltd v Kythira Investments Ltd* [2003] EWCA Civ 1794 but see *Mullan v Birmingham City Council* [2000] C.P. Rep. 61 which shows that whether a defendant is put to election or not is within a judge's discretion.

[666] [1981] 2 All ER 1060 at 1062e; see also *R v Daley* [1993] 4 All ER 86 at 94g-j, *per* Lord Muskill.

[667] [1962] 1 All ER 448.

[668] Pattenden, R. "The Submission of No Case-Some Recent Developments" [1982] Crim.L.R. 558 at 564-5.

> accused against a prosecutor who has failed to make out a prima facie case and hopes to make good the deficiency by cross-examining the witness for the defence. The accused needs this sort of protection as much in a case where the prosecution evidence is so unsound that no reasonable [tribunal] could believe the evidence against him as in a case where the prosecution has not mustered sufficient evidence, even if all the evidence is believed, for a lawful conviction [....]

1.8.2.7 *Before the subordinate/magistrates' court*

Whether a submission of no case to answer is made or not, it is incumbent on the court of its own motion to make a determination whether a *prima facie* case against the accused is made out. Section 206 of the Criminal Procedure Code[669] provides that '[i]f at the close of the evidence in support of the charge, it appears to the court that a case is not made out against the accused person sufficiently to require him to make a defence, the court shall dismiss the case, and shall forthwith acquit him.' According to Evans J (as he then was) in the *People v Japau*[670] there is a case to answer if the prosecution evidence is such that a reasonable tribunal might convict upon it if no explanation were offered by the defence. A submission of no case to answer may properly be upheld if an essential element of the alleged offence has not been proved, or when the prosecution evidence has been so discredited by cross-examination, or is so manifestly unreliable, that no reasonable tribunal could safely convict on it.

Section 206 of the Criminal Procedure Code[671] was considered and construed in *Hahuti v The People*.[672] The appellant was convicted of stock theft. The ox was stolen sometime in October 1972. It was next seen being sold by the appellant in May, 1973. Recent possession could not support such a case. A period of eight months could not be said to be recent possession as the ox could have changed hands during that period. The appellant was put on his defence and he gave evidence stating when he was in possession of the ox thus filling the gap in the prosecution evidence. After reviewing a number of cases, Doyle CJ (as he then was) observed as follows at 156 (lines 18-24):

> A man against whom there is no prima facie case at the close of the case for the prosecution is entitled to an acquittal. An error on the part of the trial court in thinking that there is prima facie case cannot alter that position. In my opinion section 206 of the CPC is mandatory, and means that if it appears to a court properly directed that the case is not made out, the accused is entitled to an acquittal. The appellant in this case should have been acquitted at the close of the prosecution case.

669 Chapter 88 of the Laws of Zambia.
670 [1967] ZR 95 (HC).
671 Chapter 88 of the Laws of Zambia.
672 [1974] ZR 154 (HC).

1.8.2.8 *Before the High Court*

The law pertaining to a case to answer or no case to answer stage in criminal proceedings before the High Court is set out in s 291 of the Criminal Procedure Code.[673] A common mistake[674] at this stage is for counsel to invoke s 206 of Criminal Procedure Code[675] in conjunction with the authority of *The People v Japau.*[676] However, s 206, as already shown, is only applicable to criminal proceedings before the subordinate/magistrates' court. Section 291(1) of the Criminal Procedure Code[677] which applies to High Court criminal proceedings provides as follows:

> When the evidence of the witnesses for the prosecution has been concluded, and the statement or evidence (if any) of the accused person before the committing court has been given in evidence, the court, if it considers that there is no evidence that the accused or any one of several accused committed the offence shall, after hearing, if necessary, any arguments which the advocate for the prosecution or the defence may desire to submit, record a finding.

Concerning the foregoing, it has been held in *Mwewa Murono v The People*[678] as follows:

> The finding that a judge has to record under s 291(1) [...] is the same as that under s 206 [....] The judge on considering that there is no evidence that the accused or any one of several accused committed the offence must acquit the accused. The finding must show that there is no evidence that the accused committed the offence followed by an order acquitting the accused.

Section 291(1) is explicit in its requirement that the prosecution must make a case against the accused sufficiently requiring the accused person or persons to make a defence. Failure to so do is a necessary predicate to the court dismissing the prosecution's case and acquitting the accused proximately. The crucial question to invite is whether in the event that the accused elected to remain muted and offered no explanation in view of the evidence so far adduced, an unflappable tribunal, appropriately guiding itself, could convict him. If the answer is yes, then there is a *prima facie* case. If no, there is no case to answer. The prosecution at this point does not need to prove the case beyond reasonable doubt.[679] Consider similar observations by Matibini J (as he then was) in *The People v Paulo Pupilo:*[680]

[673] Chapter 88 of the Laws of Zambia.

[674] This was pointed out in *Shamwana and 7 Others v The People* (1985) ZR 41 (SC).

[675] Chapter 88 of the Laws of Zambia.

[676] [1967] ZR 95.

[677] Chapter 88 of the Laws of Zambia.

[678] [2004] ZR 207.

[679] See *The People v Japau* [1967] ZR 95.

[680] HP/226/2010) [2012] ZMHC 54.

A practical question that however arises is simply this: What is the test to be applied to determine whether or not there is "no case to answer." The answer is to be found in the case of *The People v Japau.*[681] In the *Japau* case (supra), Evans J, observed at page 96, that the test to apply is well known, and was succinctly stated by Lord Parker CJ in the Practice Note.[682] In the Practice Note, Lord Parker observed that those who sat in the Divisional Court had the distinct impression that justices were being persuaded all too often to uphold a submission of no case. In the result, the Queen's Bench Division thought that as matter of practice, justices should be guided by the following considerations. A submission that there is no case to answer may properly be made and upheld:

(a) When there has been no evidence to prove an essential element in the alleged offence; and
(b) When the evidence adduced by the prosecution has been so discredited as a result of cross-examination, or is so manifestly unreliable that no reasonable tribunal could safely convict on it.

Thus, Lord Parker CJ, observed that apart from these two situations referred to above, a tribunal should not in general be called on to reach a decision as to conviction or acquittal until the whole of the evidence which either side wishes to tender has been placed before it. If, however, Lord Parker CJ; went on, a submission is made that there is no case to answer, the decision should depend not so much on whether the adjudicating tribunal (if compelled to do so) would at that stage convict or acquit, but on whether the evidence is such that a reasonable tribunal might convict on the evidence so far laid before it, there is a case to answer.

In the case of *Regina v Galbraith*[683]the Court of Appeal discussed the approach judges should take when there is a submission of no case to answer. Lord Lane CJ, guidance at page 1043 D, was stated in these words: If there is no evidence that the crime has been committed, by the defendant there is no difficulty. The judge will of course stop the case. The difficulty arises where there is some evidence, but it is of a tenuous character, for example because of inherent weaknesses or vagueness or because it is inconsistent with other evidence.

Lord Lane CJ continued: where the judge comes to the conclusion that the prosecution evidence taken at its highest is such a jury properly directed could not properly convict upon it, it is his duty, upon a submission being made to stop the case. Where however the prosecution evidence is such that its strength or weakness depends on the view to be taken of the witnesses' reliability or other matters which are generally speaking within the possible view of the facts, there is evidence upon which a jury could properly come to the conclusion that the defendant is guilty, then the judge should allow the matter to be tried by the jury.

---

[681] [1967] ZR 95.

[682] [1962] 1 ALL ER 446.

[683] [1981] 1WLR 1039.

> Lane CJ, opined that the second of the two schools of thought is to be preferred. That is, a judge should stop a case only if there is no evidence upon which a jury properly directed could properly convict.[684] It is instructive to note that in Zambia we do not have the jury system. Questions of fact and law are decided by the judge. Whether submission of no case is made or not, it is incumbent on the Court of its own motion to make a determination whether a prima facie case against the accused is made out.[685]

1.8.2.9 *Are decisions at case to answer/no case to answer stage appealable or reviewable? the case of The People v the Principal Resident Magistrate*[686] *Ex Parte Faustine Kabwe and Aaron Chungu*[687]

A successful submission of no case to answer terminates proceedings against the accused and automatically leads to his acquittal. An unsuccessful submission means that he is put on his defence. The question of whether the magistrate is obliged to give reasons for finding that there is a case or that there is indeed no case to answer as the case may be, and whether the decision at this stage is subject to review or/and appeal was considered in the case of *The People v The Principal Resident Magistrate Ex Parte Faustine Kabwe and Aaron Chungu.*[688]

> **SAKALA CJ: delivered the judgment of the Court.**
>
> According to the Notice and Memorandum of Appeal, this is an appeal against the Ruling of the High Court dated 27th April, 2009 refusing the application by Messrs. Faustin Mwenya Kabwe and Aaron Chungu, (the applicants in the Court below) for leave to apply for judicial review. For convenience, we shall continue referring to them as the applicants.
>
> The brief fact, which were common cause, leading to this appeal are that the applicants are currently on trial in a criminal matter before the Subordinate Court of the Principal Resident Magistrate, Holden at Lusaka, on several counts of corruption. In that trial, the prosecution closed its case. By a Ruling dated 15th April, 2009, the Principal Resident Magistrate ruled that the applicants had a case to answer and put them on their defence.
>
> Aggrieved by the Ruling, the applicants applied to the High Court for leave to apply for judicial review, seeking the relief in the form of an order for mandamus to compel the Principal Resident Magistrate to give his reasons for finding that the applicants had a case to answer. The application, which was supported by an affidavit verifying the facts; set out the relief sought, the grounds the law, the interim relief, and miscellaneous issues which the applicants indicated that the Court should be aware of.

---

[684] See *Murono v The People* [2004] ZR 207 at 212 *per* Munthali Ag, JS.

[685] See *Murono v The People* [2004] ZR 207 at 212 *per* Munthali Ag, JS.

[686] Now rechristened as *Chief Resident Magistrate.*

[687] SCZ Judgment No 17 of 2009.

[688] SCZ Judgment No 17 of 2009.

The trial judge considered Order 53/14/28 of the Rules of the Supreme Court, White Book, and the authorities cited on behalf of the applicants, in particular the case of *R v Civil Service Appeal Board, Expart Cunningham.*[689] The trial judge noted the principle that a Tribunal is required to give reasons for its decisions; but observed that in the case before him, he was dealing with the Court of the Principal Resident Magistrate; that that Court is governed by the provisions of the Criminal Procedure Code;[690] and that these provisions provided for an appeal against all decisions of all the Courts that are lower than the Supreme Court of Zambia. The trial judge pointed out that should the applicants be convicted of the criminal offences they are charged; and then decided to appeal against the conviction, the manner in which the Principal Resident Magistrate arrived at his decision on finding the applicants with a case to answer would be the subject of an appeal. The Court concluded that the decisions of the Principal Resident Magistrate are subject to appeal under the provisions of the Criminal Procedure Code; and that therefore judicial review cannot lie against that Court. Leave to apply for judicial review was refused; hence this appeal to this Court.

The Memorandum of Appeal set out only one ground of appeal. Namely, that the Court below misdirected itself on a point of law only when it held that the decisions of the Court of the Principal Resident Magistrate are subject to appeal under the provisions of the Criminal Procedure Code,[691] hence review is not available. On behalf of the applicants, Mr. Sangwa filed very detailed written heads of arguments based on this ground. The heads of arguments set out the facts of the case, and procedural clarification before delving into the ground of the appeal itself.

We have already set out the facts of the case in this judgment. But before summarizing the heads of arguments; it is pertinent to comment on what Mr. Sangwa has set out as procedural clarification in the heads of arguments. According to Mr. Sangwa, there is need to clarify the procedure on how an application of this nature can be prosecuted before the Supreme Court. He cited the case of *Chitala (Secretary General of the Zambia Democratic Congress) v The Attorney General,*[692] where this Court said:

> Under the Supreme Court of Zambia Act, this is an appeal against the decision of a High Court judge refusing to grant leave to bring judicial review proceedings. Under the Rules of the Supreme Court of England which apply to supply a *cassus omissus* in our own rules of practice, and procedure, this would be a renewal of the application for leave to the appellate Court.

[689] [1991] 4 ALL ER 310.

[690] Chapter 88 of the Laws of Zambia.

[691] Chapter 88 of the Laws of Zambia.

[692] [1995–1997] ZR 91.

Mr. Sangwa pointed out that having made this observation in the Chitala case; this Court said no more as to whether in view of the above observation, we have to follow our own Rules of the Supreme Court or the Rules of the Supreme Court of England [and Wales].

According to counsel, there is a difference between an appeal against the Court's decision to grant leave to apply for judicial review and a renewal of the application for leave to apply for judicial review before the Supreme Court, one it has been refused by the High Court.

He explained that an appeal entails a review of the decision of the Court below; whereas in the case of a renewal of an application for leave to apply for judicial review before the Supreme Court, the decision of the Court below is not up for consideration; as a renewal it is a fresh application in which the Supreme Court is expected to make its own judgment uninfluenced by what may or may not have been said in the High Court. According to Mr. Sangwa; the position has been complicated further by the decision of this Court in the case of *Mung'omba and Others v Machungwa and Others*.[693] He pointed out that under our own Supreme Court Rules; this is an appeal and in the case of Chitala, this Court proceeded on the premises that it was an appeal and reviewed the decision of the Court below, and dealt with the substantive application for judicial review.

We have considered the issue of procedural clarification as raised by Mr. Sangwa in his written heads of arguments. In our view, there is nothing that requires clarification in terms of procedure on who an application of this nature must be prosecuted before the Supreme Court. The Chitala case settled the procedure; while the *Mung'omba case*,[694] explained in detail as to when a party can invoke Order 53 of the Supreme Court Rules.

Under the Rules of the Supreme Court of Zambia; this is an appeal against the decision of a High Court judge refusing to grant leave to bring judicial review proceedings, (see *Chitala* case).[695] The applicants themselves in the present case brought these proceedings to this Court styled as an appeal against a High Court judge's decision refusing to grant leave to apply for judicial review.

The record is described as "Record of Appeal". The Notice reads "Notice of Appeal". This Notice of appeal reads: '[t]ake Notice that Faustin Mwenya Kabwe, and Aaron Chungu, being dissatisfied with the Ruling of Honourable Mr. Justice E. M. Hamaundu given at Lusaka on the 27th day of April, 2009, intends to appeal against the entire ruling.'

And the Memorandum of Appeal reads:

"MEMORANDUM OF APPEAL PURSUANT TO RULE 58 OF THE RULES OF THE SUPREME COURT OF ZAMBIA"

The appellants above-named, appeals to the Supreme Court against the ruling herein dated the 27th day of April, 2009, on the ground

[693] [2003] ZR 17.

[694] [2003] ZR 17.

[695] [1995–1997] ZR 91.

that the Court below misdirected itself on a point of law when it held that the decisions of the Court of the Principal Resident Magistrate are subject to appeal under the provisions of the Criminal Procedure Code, hence judicial review is not available.

Quite clearly, the applicants brought these proceedings to this Court by way of appeal following what we said in *Chitala* case.[696] If they had followed what we said in *Mung'omba* case,[697] then they would have come to this Court by way of a renewal of an application for leave. But for the benefit of the trial Courts and the legal practice in Zambia, we would like to indicate that by virtue of the English Law (Extent of Application) (Amendment) Act No 14 of 2002, the Supreme Court Practice Rules of England in force until 1999, now apply to Zambia. This means that part of our procedure and practice. For purposes of the proceedings before us, we are satisfied that the applicants fully understood the procedure to be followed in the prosecution of their case before this Court. The case of *Chitala*,[698] made it absolutely clear that the Rules of the Supreme Court of England would, "apply to supply *cassus omissus*[699] in our own rules of practice and procedure", at that time when there was a *cassus omissus* in our rules. The *Mung'omba* case[700] which was last latest on the point only affirmed the position in *Chitala*[701] as it existed then when the Court held:

> 1. There is no rule under the High Court in which judicial review proceedings can be instituted and conducted. Thus, by virtue of section 10 of the High Court Act Chapter 27 of the laws of Zambia, the High Court is guided to the procedure and practice to be adopted.
> 2. The practice and procedure in England is provided for in Order 53 of the Rules of the Supreme Court (RSC).
> 3. Order 53 is comprehensive. It provides for the basis of judicial review: the parties; how to seek the remedies, and what remedies, are available.

[...] although the matter was argued both as an appeal, and as a renewal of an application for leave, we shall only consider the heads of arguments in so far as they relate to the appeal. The gist of the written heads of arguments on the only ground of appeal is that, as correctly noted by the trial judge, there is no provision for interlocutory appeals against decisions of the Subordinate Court made pursuant to the provisions of s 206 of the Criminal Procedure Code; and that the right to appeal to the High Court against the decision of the Subordinate Court arises only following upon a conviction of an accused person pursuant to the provisions of section 321 of the Criminal Procedure

[696] [1995–1997] ZR 91.

[697] [2003] ZR 17.

[698] [1995–1997] ZR 91.

[699] The term *Cassus omissus* refers to a situation omitted from or not provided for by statute or regulation and therefore governed by the common law.

[700] [2003] ZR 17.

[701] [1995–1997] ZR 91.

Code.[702] It was contended that at the time of an appeal against conviction, the decision of the Court under the provisions of s 206 of the Criminal Procedure Code will have become moot, as the accused will have already given his defence, and will have been convicted on the totality of what has been said by both the prosecution and the defence.

It was also contended that the Principal Resident Magistrate's exercise of the powers under section 206 of the Criminal Procedure Code is subject to judicial review. It was pointed out that to qualify for judicial review the decision must meet certain conditions explained by Lord Diplock in the case of *Council of Civil Service Unions v Minister for the Civil Service*.[703] It was argued that the Ruling of 15th April, 2009, by the Principal Resident Magistrate had an impact on the applicants, and has to be reviewed by this Court as stated in the cases of *Chitala*[704] and *the Attorney-General v Shamwama and Others*.[705] It was submitted that on basis of the documents in support of the application, leave ought to have been granted, and should still be granted; that the application is neither frivolous nor vexatious or hopeless; that the issue is whether it was appropriate for the Magistrate to deliver a Ruling in the exercise of his powers under section 306 of the Criminal Procedure Code without providing reasons for the Ruling.

It was pointed out that the reason advanced for the application for leave to apply for judicial review is procedural impropriety in that rules of natural justice were not observed; that as a remedy the applicants are seeking an order of mandamus to compel the Principal Resident Magistrate to give his reasons to justify the finding that the applicants have a case to answer. In his brief oral submissions, Mr. Sangwa indicated that if this Court treated this case on as appeal in the conventional sense, then the order of mandamus should be granted; but should this Court treats this as a renewal of an application then leave should be granted and the case remitted to the High Court before a different judge to be determined on merit and that in the interim, the granting of the leave should operate as a stay of proceedings in the Subordinate Court, until after the matter has been determined by the High Court.

On behalf of the State, Mr. Sichinga, the Solicitor General, also filed written heads of arguments in response. He pointed out that the State supported the whole Ruling, and opposed the ground of appeal advanced by the applicants. The summary of the Solicitor General's written heads of arguments is that the trail Court was on firm ground when he held that the decisions of the Court of the Principal Resident Magistrate are subject to appeal pursuant to the provisions of the Criminal Procedure Code; and that it is trite law that judicial review lies against any inferior Court, but that it is only in rare situations that judicial review will lie against a decision of the Magistrate Court,

[702] Chapter 88 of the Laws of Zambia.

[703] [1985] AC 374.

[704] [1995–1997] ZR 91.

[705] [1981] ZR 12.

because the proper remedy is an appeal as opposed to judicial review. The case of *R v Wandsworth County Court, Ex parte Siva Subramaniam,*[706] was cited in support of this proposition.

It was contended by the Solicitor-General that at the stage of the proceedings, a finding of a case to answer, and putting the applicants on their defence is in fact not a finding of guilty to the charges; that there is no legal requirement under section 206 of the Criminal Procedure Code that the Court must give reasons in acquitting the accused person, but that it must merely appear to the Court that a case has not been made against the accused person; and that the converse as also true that where the Court finds an accused with a case to answer, it must merely appear to the Court that a case has been made out. In his oral submissions, the Solicitor General pointed out that the issue for consideration by this Court is whether or not the trial judge was right in refusing to grant leave on a true construction of section 206 of the Criminal Procedure Code. He submitted that there was no procedural impropriety; but that the Court acted within the confines of section 206 of the Criminal Procedure Code. In his short reply, Mr. Sangwa pointed out that the applicants' cry was simply one of procedural fairness; asking for the Court to point out the prosecution evidence that justifies a finding of a case to answer to enable them address that evidence in their defence.

We have very carefully considered the facts of this appeal, the judgment of the trial Court, and the arguments by both learned Counsel. On 15th April, 2009, the Principal Resident Magistrate, at the close of the prosecution case in a criminal trial found the applicants and other with a case to answer, and put each one of them on defence. In putting the applicants and others on their defence, the Principal Resident Magistrate concluded as follows in his Ruling:

> Taking into account all the foregoing, I am satisfied that the prosecution has made out a prima facie case on each one of the counts herein, in respect of each one of the accused persons in this case requiring the accused persons to be put on their defence. Now therefore, I have found each of the accused persons in this case with a case to answer in respect of the respective charges against each one of them, and accordingly put each one of them on defence.

Dissatisfied with this Ruling, the two applicants applied to the High Court for leave to apply for judicial review seeking for an order of mandamus to compel the Principal Resident Magistrate to give reasons for his Ruling of putting the applicants and others on their defence. The High Court judge dismissed the application. In dismissing the application, the High Court judge, among other matters had this to say:

[706] [2003] WLF 475.

> In summary, therefore, the decisions of the Court of the Principal Resident Magistrate are subject to appeal under the provisions of the Criminal Procedure Code. Therefore, judicial review cannot lie against that Court in the circumstances of this case. Leave to apply for judicial review is not granted.

The applicants appealed against the Ruling of the High Court to this Court. In Zambia, the procedure to be followed in criminal matters is set out in the Criminal Procedure Code.[707] S 206 of the [Criminal Procedure] Code[708] reads:

> If, at the close of the evidence in support of the charge, it appears to the Court that a case is not made against the accused person sufficient to require him to make a defence, the Court shall dismiss the case, and shall forthwith acquit him.

The use of the phrase "if [...] it appears to the Court" in the section is not without any significance. The learned Principal Resident Magistrate in his Ruling was "[...] satisfied that the prosecution has made out a prima facie case on each one of the counts [....]" The expression "*prima facie* is from Latin. According to various English Dictionaries, among many others, the expression means: on its first appearance; by first instance; at first sight; at first view; on its face; the first flush; and from a fresh impression.

We agree with the submission by the Solicitor General that there is no requirement under s 206 of the Code that the Court must give reasons for acquitting an accused person; that it must merely appear to the Court. The converse, therefore, must also be true that where the Court finds an accused with a case to answer, it must merely appear to the Court that a case has been made out against the accused.

In our considered view, a finding of a case to answer is based on the Courts feeling or impressions and appearance of the evidence. But above all, the finding or a prima face case is not a final verdict. In the case of *Harrison v Department of Security*,[709] the Court stated:

"Magistrates are not obliged to give reasons for rejecting a submission of no case to answer".

We agree with this proposition of the law because a finding of a case to answer is not a final verdict. However, a finding of no case to answer is a final verdict and therefore a Magistrate would be required and obliged to give reasons. However, the most important issue in the present appeal is one of procedure. We have said before that there can be no interlocutory appeals in criminal matters. Mr. Sangwa agrees with this position in his written heads of arguments. His complaint is that at the time of an appeal against conviction, the decision of the

[707] Chapter 88 of the Laws of Zambia.

[708] Chapter 88 of the Laws of Zambia.

[709] [1997] C.O.D. 220 D.C, also cited in Archbold page 407, 1999 edn.

> Court under s 206 of the Criminal Procedure Code[710] will have become moot. We sympathize with Mr. Sangwa; but as for now that is the law. The issues raised in this purported appeal are only relevant at the end of the criminal trial should there be a conviction.
>
> We are, therefore, satisfied that the trial judge did not misdirect himself on a point of law; when he held that the decisions of the Court of the Principal Resident Magistrate are subject to appeal under the provisions of the Criminal Procedure Code. This appeal was definitely misconceived. It is, accordingly, dismissed with costs to the State in this Court and in the Court below to be taxed in default of agreement. For avoidance of doubt, we direct that the criminal trial in the Subordinate Court must proceed.

In summary, the case of *the People v the Principal Resident Magistrate Ex Parte Faustine Kabwe And Aaron Chungu*[711] is authority for the following propositions:

1. There is no provision for interlocutory appeal against decisions of the Subordinate Courts made pursuant to the provisions of s 206 of the Criminal Procedure Code;[712] and that the right to appeal to the High Court against the decision of the Subordinate Court arises, and following upon a conviction of an accused person pursuant to the provisions of s 321 of the Criminal Procedure Code.[713]
2. There is no requirement under s 206 of the Criminal Procedure Code[714] that the Court must give reasons[715] for acquitting an accused person; that it must merely appear to the Court. The converse, therefore, must also be true that where the Court finds an accused with a case to answer, it must merely appear to the Court that a case has been made out against the accused.
3. A finding of a case to answer is based on the Court's feeling or impressions, and appearance of the evidence. Above all, the finding of *prima facie* case is not a final verdict.
4. Magistrates are not obliged to give reasons for rejecting a submission of no case to answer.

1.9 Mode of taking and recording evidence in criminal inquiries and trials

Part V of the Criminal Procedure Code[716] provides for the mode of taking and recording evidence in inquiries and trials.

---

[710] Chapter 88 of the Laws of Zambia.

[711] SCZ Judgment No 17 of 2009.

[712] Chapter 88 of the Laws of Zambia.

[713] Chapter 88 of the Laws of Zambia.

[714] Chapter 88 of the Laws of Zambia.

[715] But see Bayles, *Procedural Justice* (1990), Ch 4; For a discussion on why reasons ought to be given for administrative decisions, see Galligan DJ, *Due Process and Fair Procedures* (1996) 429-437.

[716] Chapter 88 of the Laws of Zambia.

1.9.1 *Evidence to be taken in presence of accused*

In terms of s 191, except as otherwise expressly provided, all evidence taken in any inquiry or trial under this Code shall be taken in the presence of the accused, or, when his personal attendance has been dispensed with, in the presence of his advocate (if any).[717]

1.9.2 *Reports by medical officers in public service*

In terms of s 191A(1), [t]he contents of any document purporting to be a report under the hand of a medical officer employed in the public service upon any matter relevant to the issue in any criminal proceedings shall be admitted in evidence in such proceedings to prove the matters stated therein: Provided that- (i) the court in which any such report is adduced in evidence may, in its discretion, cause the medical officer to be summoned to give oral evidence in such proceedings or may cause written interrogatories approved by the court to be submitted to him for reply, and such interrogatories and any reply thereto purporting to be a reply from such person shall likewise be admissible in evidence in such proceedings; (ii) at the request of the accused, made not less than seven days before the trial, such witness shall be summoned to give oral evidence.

According to s 191A(2), [t]he court may presume that the signature on any such report is genuine and that the person signing it held the office and qualifications which he professed to hold as appearing in the report at the time when he signed it. By s 191A(3), [n]othing in [s 191A shall be deemed to affect any provision of any written law under which any certificate or other document is made admissible in evidence, and the provisions of this section shall be deemed to be additional to, and not in substitution of, any such provision. It is provided in s 191A(4) that [f]or the purposes of this section, the expression "medical officer" shall mean a medical practitioner registered as such under the Health Professions Act.[718]

1.9.3 *Evidence of analyst*

According to s 192(1), whenever any fact ascertained by any examination or process requiring chemical or bacteriological skill is or may become relevant to the issue in any criminal proceedings, a document purporting to be an affidavit relating to any such examination or process shall, if purporting to have been made by any person qualified to carry out such examination or process, who has ascertained any such fact by means of any such examination or process, be admissible in evidence in such proceedings to prove the matters stated therein: Provided that-(i) the court in which any such document is adduced in evidence may, in its discretion, cause such person to be summoned to give oral evidence

[717] No 33 of 1972.

[718] No 24 of 2009 Which under s 78 repealed the Medical and Allied Professions Act Chapter 297 of the Laws of Zambia.

in such proceedings or may cause written interrogatories to be submitted to him for reply, and such interrogatories and any reply thereto purporting to be a reply from such person shall likewise be admissible in evidence in such proceedings; (ii) at the request of the accused, made not less than seven days before the trial, such witness shall be summoned to give oral evidence.

By s 192(2), [n]othing in [s 192] shall be deemed to affect any provision of any written law under which any certificate or other document is made admissible in evidence, and the provisions of this section shall be deemed to be additional to, and not in substitution of, any such provision.[719]

1.9.4 *Evidence of photographic process*

In terms of s 193, [w]here any photograph is or may become relevant to the issue in any criminal proceedings, a document purporting to be an affidavit made by the person who processed such photograph shall be admissible in evidence in any such proceedings as proof of such processing: Provided that the court in which any such document is produced may, if it thinks fit, summon such person to give evidence orally.[720]

1.9.5 *Evidence of plans, theft of postal matters and goods in transit on railways*

According to s 194(1), [i]n any criminal proceedings, a certificate purporting to be signed by a police officer or any other person authorised under rules made in that behalf by the Chief Justice, by statutory instrument, and certifying that a plan or drawing exhibited thereto is a plan or drawing made by him of the place or object specified in the certificate and that the plan or drawing is correctly drawn to a scale so specified and clearly indicates, where applicable, the direction of North in relation to the places or objects depicted thereon, shall be evidence of the relative positions of the things shown on the plan or drawing.

By s 194(2), in any proceedings for an offence consisting of the stealing of goods in the possession of the Zambia Railways, or receiving or retaining goods so stolen knowing them to have been stolen, or for the theft of postal matter under the Penal Code, or for an offence under the Postal Services Act,[721] a statutory declaration made by any person- (a) that he despatched or received or failed to receive any goods or postal packet or that any goods or postal packet when despatched or received by him were in a particular state or condition; or (b) that a vessel, vehicle or aircraft was at any time employed by or under the Postmaster-General for the transmission of postal packets under contract; shall be admissible as evidence of the facts stated in the declaration.

In terms of s 194(3), nothing in this section shall be deemed to make a certificate or statutory declaration admissible as evidence in proceedings for

[719] No 1 of 1936 as amended by No 11 of 1963.

[720] No 50 of 1957.

[721] Chapter 470 of the Laws of Zambia.

an offence except in a case where and to the extent to which oral evidence to the like effect would have been admissible in those proceedings.

It is provided in s 194(4) that [n]othing in [s 194] shall be deemed to make a certificate or any plan or drawings exhibited thereto or a statutory declaration admissible as evidence in proceedings for any offence-(a) unless a copy thereof has, not less than seven days before the hearing or trial, been served on the person charged with the offence; or (b) if that person, not later than three days before the hearing or trial or within such further time as the court may in special circumstances allow, serves notice in writing on the prosecutor requiring the attendance at the trial of the person who signed the certificate or the person by whom the declaration was made, as the case may be; or (c) if the court before whom the said proceedings are brought requires the attendance at the trial of the person who signed the certificate or the person by whom the declaration was made, as the case may be.[722]

1.9.6 Interpretation of evidence to accused or his advocate

In terms of s 195(1), [w]henever any evidence is given in a language not understood by the accused, and he is present in person, it shall be interpreted to him in open court in a language understood by him. By s 195(2), [i]f he appears by advocate, and the evidence is given in a language other than the English language, and not understood by the advocate, it shall be interpreted to such advocate in the English language. According to s 195(3), [w]hen documents are put in for the purpose of formal proof, it shall be in the discretion of the court to cause to be interpreted as much thereof as appears necessary.

1.9.7 Remarks respecting demeanour of witness

In terms of s 196, [a] magistrate shall record the sex and approximate age of each witness, and may also record such remarks (if any) as he thinks material respecting the demeanour of any witness whilst under examination.

[722] No 16 of 1959.

2

THE OBJECTIVES OF THE LAW OF EVIDENCE

`The rules of evidence, as discussed elsewhere in this text, are a species of what is termed adjectival/procedural law. By their existence, or so the theory goes, a fair and consistent application of fundamental justice[1] is almost certainly guaranteed in all matters that come before a court of competent jurisdiction.[2] Together with what any legal practitioner worth his salt will readily identify as rules of court,[3] the rules of evidence encompass the guidelines by which a court perceives and regulates what transpires in civil, criminal or administrative suits and any other proceedings over which a court has jurisdiction. This in and of itself presents challenges to both a practitioner whose legal training is mainly a diet of substantive law and the judge, who is called upon to rule on different rules of evidence. It most certainly will, as we see later, confuse a litigant who may see his case won or lost purely on evidentiary or procedural grounds. By definition, and in contrast, substantive law is composed of a set of laws that governs the behaviour of members of the public. While adjectival or procedural law is concerned with procedures for making, administering, and enforcing substantive law, substantive law has as its premise, the definition of rights and responsibilities in civil law, criminal law, administrative law, tort, among others and the consequences that follow once the rules underlying substantive law are breached or contravened, as the case may be. It may, unlike adjectival law of which the rules of evidence are a species, be codified or be predicated on judicial precedent.

The familiar areas of substantive law, among them contract, tort and the criminal law present the student of law with a visible and appreciable prescription of how to do things within the context of the relevant law and the consequences, as we have already said above, of the breaking the rules attendant to such laws. Therefore, where a party breaches the terms of a contract, he is liable to pay damages under the law of contract, as would a negligent defendant

[1] Or of 'due process' in the United States legal system.

[2] Though as we will see in this chapter, this, for one or more reasons, is not always achieved.

[3] See the Subordinate Court Rules (SCR), chapter 28 of the Laws of Zambia; the High Court Rules (HCR), Chapter 27 of the Laws of Zambia; Supreme Court Rules (SCR); Supreme Court Rules (SCR), Chapter 25 of the Laws of Zambia; the Rules of the Supreme Court, RSC, 1965, White Book (1999) edition.

in a suit for the tort of negligence. Under the criminal law, '[a]ny person who of malice aforethought causes the death of another person by an unlawful act or omission is guilty of murder.'[4] According to s 201(2):[5]

> (1) A person convicted of murder shall be sentenced to life imprisonment or, where there are extenuating circumstances, a sentence other than life imprisonment.;
> (b) insertion of the following new subsection immediately after subsection (1):
> (2) An extenuating circumstance referred to under subsection (1) shall not apply to murder committed in the course of aggravated robbery with a firearm under section 294.

It follows that while the foregoing substantive rules will underpin contested trials, they play no overt role seeing as all concerned will ordinarily know what the rule is unless the rule concerned is one that raises constitutional rules and is liable to be struck down.[6]

It therefore behooves a legal practitioner to solve the problem of establishing facts. For example, as regards an alleged breach of contract, what are the facts of the breach as alleged? Could the plaintiff be to blame? Was the contract simply frustrated? Could it be deemed to be illegal? Was the contract vitiated by mistake, misrepresentation, fraud, undue influence or duress? Where the claim is in the tort of negligence resulting in an accident and injury for example, the facts to be established would include the following: what really happened? Was the defendant negligent? Was he the cause of the injury birthing the suit of negligence? Was there contributory negligence? If the scenario presented to the legal practitioner is a prosecution for murder contrary to s 200 of the Penal Code[7] quoted above, did the accused intentionally kill the victim? Could there be another person guilty of this crime? Was he sane at the time? Where was he at the material time? Was the homicide committed in self defence? Where there extenuating circumstances? Should the charge be reduced to manslaughter?

To establish such facts as the legal practitioner seeks, and the court will be called upon to determine, we must look to the law of evidence and not the substantive law on which the suit in question is premised. This is because only the law of evidence is concerned with the establishing of facts. Further, as regards the nature of the suit, the two opposing sides to such suit will present different stories of the same event to the Court which the court will, as said

[4] Section 200 of The Penal Code, chapter 87 of the Laws of Zambia.

[5] Section 201 of The Penal Code, chapter 87 of the Laws of Zambia as amended by Act No 23 of 2022; In *Kanyanga v The People* SCZ Appeal No 237 of 2011, the Supreme Court guided that s 201 should be read with Garner B A, Black's Law Dictionary [...], which defines extenuation as: 'Mitigating circumstance, means a fact or situation that does not justify or excuse a wrongful act or offence, but J10 that reduces the culpability and this may reduce punishment. A fact or situation that does not bear on the question of a defendant's guilt, but that is considered by the court in imposing punishment and especially in lessening severity of a sentence.'

[6] See article 1(1) of the Constitution.

[7] Chapter 87 of the Laws of Zambia.

above, need to determine by deciding what the facts are. To do so, the court will have to call upon the rules of evidence in aid. This is because the rules of evidence or the law within which they find their operational plane have as their core function, the regulation of the 'process of proof of facts for the purposes of legal proceedings.'[8]

Thus, questions as regards what evidence is admitted; what evidence is relevant; what weight to place upon any particular piece of evidence; what witnesses may indeed testify; and how the testimony will be presented to the court, are all in the province of the law of evidence. 'This process and its accompanying rules do not lay down any substantive law and are equally applicable whether the court is dealing with a personal injury claim, unfair dismissal or a criminal case.'[9] While the rules of evidence, being adjectival in nature, will not in and of themselves, decide the rights, obligations and/or wrongs of parties to a suit (which only substantive law is capable of doing), they will 'attach themselves to and qualify the operation of'[10] [...] substantive rules. This they do by controlling 'the flow and nature of the information which can be presented to the court.'[11]

The foregoing notwithstanding, it ought to be remembered that rules of evidence may nevertheless be decisive in the determination of a matter. 'Procedural rights, especially in relation to the rules of evidence, are often seen to take precedence over the justice of the decision itself and over more pragmatic aims such as the determination of truth or law enforcement.'[12] For example, if a key piece of evidence is deemed inadmissible in a criminal prosecution e.g., a confession for want of voluntariness, an accused who may have been convicted, may, without anything more, and because of that crucial decision be acquitted. J. Frank[13] illustrates the foregoing as follows:

> [Substantive] rules, it is said, state what a man may or may not lawfully do out of court, before any litigation occurs. The orthodox theory holds that, from those rules, grow 'substantive legal rights ', such as the right not to have others trespass on one's land or the right to have a contract performed [....]
>
> But if one of a man's 'substantive' rights has been invaded, or threatened with invasion, and he does bring a law-suit, the suit is supposed to be governed by another kind of rules, rules of 'procedure', which relate to what must be done in court. Those conduct-in-court rules cover such subjects as the way a suit must be commenced, the way in which a party must state ('plead') his claim or defence, the sort of evidence the courts will receive or reject. These 'procedural' rules are customarily designated as 'adjective', or 'remedial', or 'dependent'

[8] Dennis I, *The Law of Evidence* 27.

[9] Uglow S, *Evidence: Text and Materials* 1.

[10] Uglow S, *Evidence: Text and Materials* 1.

[11] Uglow S, *Evidence: Text and Materials* 1.

[12] Uglow S, *Evidence: Text and Materials* 17; Frank J, *Courts on Trial* (Princeton, 1973) 103-104; Lord Woolf, Access to Justice: Interim Report (Lord Chancellor's Dept. June 1995), Ch.3.

[13] Frank J, *Courts on Trial* (Princeton, 1973) 103-104.

> or subordinate'. These labels indicate that these rules are really subordinate, are mere 'machinery', used in vindicating the rights given by the 'substantive' rules, rules which supposedly pre-exist and are independent of what any court may do about them.
>
> That notion of the 'subordinate' character of 'procedure' may easily mislead. For the failure of a lawyer to comply with a procedural rule [...] may spell a litigant's defeat in a law-suit, completely frustrating his 'substantive' right. Such a defeat, for 'procedural' errors, is fully as disastrous to him as if the court held that he had no such right.

To further demonstrate the somewhat dubious distinction that is painstakingly made in extant literature between adjectival/procedural law on the one hand, and substantive law on the other, Frank postulates that an accurate description of what a party faces when a matter comes to trial is to state that '[i]f certain facts are 'proved', in accordance with the requirements and within the limits allowed by procedural rules, then a favourable decision should result.'[14] The opposite is also true: no favourable result would emanate from facts whose proof is not in harmony with the necessities and within the parameters permitted by procedural rules. He concludes that the distinction made between substantive and procedural rules though useful in certain instances, 'is artificial' in this respect: '[a]ll the rules, including the 'substantive' may be looked at as 'procedural' in the sense that they are all merely weapons in the courtroom fight'[15] in an adversarial type trial.

The foregoing has been demonstrated in two leading two leading Zambian Supreme Court decisions:[16]

In *Chikuta v Chipata Rural Council*[17] the appellant was the secretary of the Chipata Rural Council, and a specified officer as defined in the Local Government Officers Act. On 28 August, 1972, the appellant was convicted on two counts of forgery and uttering, contrary to ss 347 and 352 of the Penal Code.[18] He was sentenced to six months' imprisonment with hard labour on each count and the whole of those sentences was suspended. Prior to this he had been suspended from duty by the respondent. On 1September, 1972, the Council met for the purpose of determining whether or not the appellant should be dismissed. The then chairman of the Council gave his view of the appellant's behaviour, which was clearly very favourable to the appellant. A vote was taken and, by 34 votes to 1, the Council resolved to remove the appellant's suspension from duty and to reinstate him in the Council's service. Subsequently, there was correspondence with the Minister and on 3 May, 1973, the Council reaffirmed its resolution that the appellant be reinstated. There was further correspondence with the Minister and on 5 October, 1972

[14] Frank J, *Courts on Trial* (Princeton, 1973) 104.

[15] Frank J, *Courts on Trial* 104.

[16] Though these decisions and any like them should be read within the context of Article 118(1)(e) of the Constitution.

[17] [1974] ZR 241.

[18] Chapter 87 of the Laws of Zambia.

the Council, by resolution, reversed its previous resolutions and dismissed the appellant from his employment with effect from the date of his conviction. The appellant brought this matter before the High Court by means of an originating summons seeking a declaration that he was still employed by the Council. The High Court refused to make the declaration sought by the appellant. It was held *inter alia* that (i) there is no case in the High Court where there is a choice between commencing an action by a writ of summons or by an originating summons. The procedure by way of an originating summons only applies to those matters referred to in Order 6 r 2, of the High Court Rules[19] and to those matters which may be disposed of in chambers (ii) where any matter is brought to the High Court by means of an originating summons when it should have been commenced by writ, the court has no jurisdiction to mate any declarations.

Another important case in this space is that of *New Plast Industries v The Commissioner of Lands and The Attorney-General.*[20] This was an appeal against a ruling of the High Court on a preliminary issue, namely, that the Lands and Deeds Registry Act[21] provides for a procedure under s 97 for appealing against a decision of the Lands and Deeds Registry. After the ruling of the court dismissing the whole action on a preliminary issue, the appellant applied to the court to review its judgment pursuant to order 39(1) of the High Court Rules before the summons could be uplifted and without hearing the appellant. The court dismissed the application on the ground that the application for Judicial Review was irregular. It was held *inter alia*: that it was not entirely correct that the mode of commencement of any action largely depends on the reliefs sought. The correct position is that the mode of commencement of any action is generally provided by the relevant statute.

This seeming precedence of procedural rules in trial settings as seen above and demonstrated in *Chikuta*[22] and *New Plast Industries*[23] is not without its critics especially as it relates to criminal procedure.[24] The criticism is placed on a familiar plane: simply put, it is that the formality of the trial and the ability of procedural rules to torpedo a case means that no priority is given to the discovery of truth and the justice of the decision in question. Cross[25] for example, questions the logic behind the presumption of innocence such as is provided for under Article 18(2)(a) of our Constitution when the very fact that a person has been charged with an offence and made to appear in court to answer such charges means he is more likely to be presumed as having committed the offence than not, because let's face it, you really would eliminate all those not suspected to have committed the offence before you take the case to court wouldn't you? In some instances, such as a charge of murder or

[19] Chapter 27 of the Laws of Zambia.

[20] SCZ Judgment No 8 of 2001.

[21] Chapter 185 of the Laws of Zambia.

[22] [1974] ZR 241.

[23] SCZ Judgment No 8 of 2001.

[24] See Mark R, *Minority Verdict* (Dimbleby Lecture BBC, 1973).

[25] Cross R, "The Right to Silence and the Presumption of Innocence-sacred Cows or Safeguards of Liberty" (1970) 11 J.S.P.T.L. 66.

aggravated robbery, no bail is granted.[26] What does that do to the presumption of innocence? The debate rages on but is unsuited to a work of this sort.

Even so, there is symbolic value to our adversarial and procedural type of trial, and to argue against its structure and imperfections, of which there are many,[27] is to blindly ignore this important facet of adjudication as we soon show. It is in the rules of procedure and those of evidence as applied at trial that we discern the distinction between the trial 'as a logical function and the trial as a symbol.'[28] Outwardly then, the trial retains its objectives or aims which are to find the truth but at the same time makes application of the truth so found, to legal rules.[29] Despite its weaknesses, the courtroom is a safer place to find the truth out than say a police station. It is in the courtroom that the constitutional and fundamental rights of the accused are of foremost importance no matter how egregious the offence with which he is charged and, however, weak his defence or even where none apparently exists. The trial must demonstrate that society is fair and just. This in fact is a veritable goal in a court of law and specifically in criminal trials where justice must not only be done but must be seen to be done, and where the dignity of the court must not be offended or justice tainted with illegality. The preceding is exemplified in the infamous *Scottsboro case*.[30] This was a case that involved an allegation of rape of two white girls by nine black teenagers on the Southern Railroad from Chattanooga to Memphis on March 25, 1931. As Arnold[31] observes in his comments on that case, '[…] the cultural value of the ideal of a fair trial is advanced as much by its failure as it is by its success. Any violation of the symbol of a ceremonial trial rouses persons who would be left unmoved by an ordinary non-ceremonial injustice.'

In chapter one, we sought to demonstrate and indeed went some length to establish aspects that are key to the study of the law of evidence. We showed that these aspects contexualise, among other things, the flexible philosophies that permeate the application of the rules of evidence. It is important to, within the context of our discussion in this chapter, revisit and reiterate the positions taken thus far and as discussed under chapter 1. It must be remembered, that the objectives to be analysed here will find themselves discussed in the chapters that follow as they form the main premise of this text.

2.2 Dispute resolution and the contested trial

As a starting point, it is useful to recall that the principles of evidence find their most useful premise in the theatre of the contested trial which has, at

[26] See s 123(1)(iv) of the Criminal Procedure Code, Chapter 88 of the Laws of Zambia.

[27] Arnold T, The Symbols of Government (Harbinger, 1962), 141-143.

[28] Uglow S, *Evidence: Text and Materials* 20.

[29] Uglow S, *Evidence: Text and Materials.*

[30] *Powell v Alabama*, 1932, 287 U.S. 45; *Norris v Alabama* (1935), 294 U.S. 587, 595–596; *www.pbs.org/wgbh/amex/scottsboro/;* Horne G, *Powell v Alabama: The Scottsboro Boys and American Justice* (1997); Linder DO,*"The Trials of 'The Scottsboro Boys'". Famous Trials. University of Missouri–Kansas City, 1999); Douglas OL,* "Without Fear or Favor: Judge James Edwin Horton and the Trial of the 'Scottsville Boys'", *Vol. 68 UMKC Law Review 549, 550.*

[31] Arnold T, The Symbols of Government (Harbinger, 1962), 141-143.

its core aim, the resolution of disputes. Be that as it may, the contested trial or adjudication, may be an instrument for the implementation of law. Under this guise, the form of the dispute rather than its substance is a more important consideration.[32] H.L.A Hart[33] has in fact gone so far as to postulate that public official led adjudication of questions that relate not only to rights but obligations, accountabilities and station basically define legal systems in virtually all jurisdictions be they of a common law, civil or Roman Dutch persuasion.

While the final decision will be given by the adjudicator, parties to the legal proceedings play a useful role by the presentation of what have been termed "proofs"[34] designed to persuade the adjudicator to determine the matter in favour of one of the parties. Essentially, unlike alternative means of dispute resolution like that of the Inuit where concepts of "facts", "truth" or "evidence" are of no consequence to resolving disputes,[35] contested trials are binary, zero-sum constructs where there has to be a winner and a loser. It follows that the adjudicator has his work cut out. He has no choice but to determine the dispute rationally, that is, by using reason as regards facts of law and fact deemed relevant to the dispute within a prescribed framework. It has thus been held *inter alia* in *The Attorney-General v Marcus Kampumba Achiume*[36] that 'an unbalanced evaluation of the evidence where only the flaws of one side but not of the other are considered is a misdirection entitling [the appellate court] to interfere.'[37] J. Dewey[38] has observed the differences between normal everyday human behaviour and that which is expected and required in contested trials. As regards everyday human behaviour where people may respect differences of opinion, Dewey notes as follows: '[h]uman conduct, broadly viewed, falls into two sorts [....] Sometimes human beings act with a minimum of foresight, without examination of what they are doing and of probable consequences. They act not upon deliberation but from routine, instinct, the direct pressure of appetite, or a blind 'hunch' [....]'[39]

It is of course unlikely that a judge who, in adjudicating upon a matter, does so 'with a minimum of foresight, without examination of what they are doing and of probable consequences' of their actions will last very long in their job. Further, they are unlikely to achieve what is termed by Twinning[40] as 'Bentham's rectitude of decision'[41] which is achieved by the accurate application of substantive law to the true facts of the dispute premised on the deployment of rules of evidence in totality. He argues that 'rectitude of decision is seen as the primary end of adjudication, as a necessary means to enforcement of law and vindication of rights (expletive justice); expletive justice is an important, if not necessarily an overriding, social value; the concept of 'rectitude of decision' leads directly to such notions as truth, facts, relevance, evidence, and inference and to a number of assumptions about the possibility of knowledge (or at least of warranted conclusions of fact) and about valid reasoning.'[42] Nor would an adjudicator properly so called and qualified to preside over court proceedings be expected to 'act not upon deliberation but from routine, instinct, the direct pressure of appetite, or a blind 'hunch'.[43]

As regards adjudication and adjudicators as finders of fact and law, Dewey[44] observes as follows:

> In the other sort of case, action follows upon a decision, and the decision is the outcome of inquiry, comparison of alternatives, weighing of facts; deliberation or thinking has intervened. Considerations which have weight in reaching the conclusion as to what is to be done, or which are employed to justify it when it is questioned, are called 'reasons.' If they are stated in sufficiently general terms they are 'principles.' When the operation is formulated in a compact way, the decision is called a conclusion, and the considerations which led up to it are called the premises. Decisions of the of the first type may be reasonable: that is, they may be adapted to good results; those of the second type are reasoned or rational, increasingly so in the degree of care and thoroughness with which inquiry has been conducted and the order in which connections have been established between the considerations dealt with.

Courts are expected and required to arrive at a decision no matter the nature of the evidence presented and disputations advanced by the parties. This is the case even where the case is difficult, the evidence evenly balanced or downright borderline and the best that can be accomplished are declarations of likelihoods. In keeping with Dewey's proposition, magistrates and judges alike must, based on the evidence presented before them,[45] and arguments from counsel, work towards 'proof of a proposition.'[46] The magistrate or judge must '[...] sieve the evidence or attempt to analyse, access or apply judicial reasoning logic to [...]'[47] his ruling, order or judgment as the case may be. His, is a public announcement of the decision[48] he has arrived at, which, if it has to be deemed rectitudinous, must be reasoned, that is, complete with justifications for deciding one way and not the other, for the plaintiff and not the defendant or vice versa. As has been observed by DSA Idid:[49]

> The decision must show the parties that the judge actively wrestled with their claims and arguments and made a scholarly decision based on his or her own reason and logic [...] The [...] opinions of the parties in a case should not be copied verbatim and adapted to the judgment of the court. It is not just acceptable for a judge to mention in his judgment that he agrees with the submissions of a party and he has nothing to add. A judge should tower above the parties and their counsel by applying some level of judicial reasoning logic in evaluating a case [....]

At the risk of being tautological, we cannot overemphasise the point enough, nor should the point be lost on those whom it behooves to know such as judges,

[43] Dewey J, "Logical Method and Law" 17.

[44] Dewey J, "Logical Method and Law" 17.

and advocates, that the need to predicate judicial decisions on reason and logic is the premise on which the rules of evidence are chiselled into shape and hewn into useful implements that aid the courts in properly applying substantive law to the facts of each case and its evaluation. The use of reason and logic also implies that simply based on the facts and evidence presented before a court of law, a magistrate or judge will, at least as far as the evidence presented before him by both sides is concerned, know, through rational inquiry, what happened at the material time as regards the case before him which he is called upon to determine.

Zambian Courts, like all common law jurisdictions, 'place considerable emphasis on the discovery of "truth" in a positivist, cognitive sense of establishing precisely what happened.'[50] The preceding is achieved by evaluating assertions put forward by parties to a trial which are capable of being proved or disproved on the basis of evidence in support or rigorous testing through cross-examination as regards oral testimony or indeed contradictory documentation to that presented by the other side.[51] In the final analysis, when a judge makes a decision either way, and thereby towers 'above the parties and their counsel by applying some level of judicial reasoning logic in evaluating a case',[52] he does so within the confines of the strength of the evidence presented and counsel's arguments in support of such evidence.

It is often said that no one can read another's mind, that in fact, as Brown CJ said as quoted by Mr. Justice Frankfurter in *Leland v State of Oregon,*[53] 'even the devil himself knoweth not the mind of man.' That, in a court trial setting ordinarily presents problems for a magistrate or judge. This is because in an adversarial system the Judge or magistrate can only work with that which is presented to him, and nothing more, even if that means that some crucial evidence has been concealed. In *Benson Nguila v The Queen*[54] the appellant was jointly charged with another accused with the crime of arson. It was contended that the other accused's plea of guilty was equivocal (in that he claimed to have been compelled to commit the offence), that he should have been acquitted, and that as the appellant was jointly charged with him, he also should be acquitted. It was also contended that the appellant was entitled to succeed since the prosecution had failed to tender in evidence at the trial a statement which amounted to a simple denial of the charge. It was held *inter alia* that the prosecution has discretion as to what evidence it calls, although it

[50] Uglow S, *Evidence: Text and Materials* 5.

[51] See *William Muzala Chipango & Others v The People* [1978] ZR 304 where the Supreme Court observed as follows: [...] 'it is sufficient to stress that quite apart from the misdirection concerning the proper approach to witnesses, the conflicts and inconsistencies in their evidence were so serious that convictions based on their evidence could not in any event stand.' As to what ought to happen when there are fundamental flaws in the evidence characterised by inconsistencies, see *Kafuti Vilongo v The People* [1977] ZR 423; But see effect of minor inconsistencies in *Madubula v The People* [1993-1994] ZR 91.

[52] Idid DSA, *A Practical Guide for Courts and Tribunals* (Lexis Nexis, 2011) 49.

[53] 343 U.S. 790, 803 (1952) (dissenting opinion).

[54] [1963-1964] Z and NRLR 14.

will normally put in evidence any documentary evidence relevant to the case.[55] Further, in *Abel Banda v The People*[56] it was held that '[a] prosecutor is under no duty to place before court all the evidence known to him, however, where he knows of a credible witness whose evidence supports the accused's innocence, he should inform the defence about him.'

There is the added burden that '[t]he human understanding is not composed of dry light, but is subject to influence from the will and the emotions, a fact that creates fanciful knowledge; man prefers to believe what he wants to be true.'[57] In this sense, recreating and appreciating the truth about a set of facts presented by two sides to a matter, parties with diametrically opposed objectives, is nothing short of a herculean task for the adjudicator. Nevertheless, we must acknowledge that given the constraints placed on the court in recreating and appreciating the truth regarding past events, the aim should not be, and is never the search for ultimate truth, but merely an account of possibilities. This perpetual intestinal struggle between the search for ultimate truth through rational inquiry and the limits and challenges the adversarial system places on the adjudicator to reconstruct and find the truth is ably described in the following observation by Blackburn:[58]

> As well as the norm of truth or hitting the target, there are norms of right procedure. These govern whether you have done your stuff properly: taken the right observations, made the right inferences,hedged in the right places, weighed the evidence carefully and, in short, made yourself immune to procedural criticism. It may not follow that you arrive at the truth. The evidence may be poor, or misleading, or the interpretation which everyone supposes reasonable may be based on insufficient science or general misunderstanding. A trial may be fairly conducted, yet unhappily arrive at the wrong verdict. Still, there is nothing better that we can do. We act under the conviction that our best procedures, although they may let us down, markedly increase the chance that we get things right. Provided there was nothing better which we should have done then we may be immune from charges of irrationality, negligence or carelessness. Our procedures accord with

---

[55] Lord Wilberforce has observed in *Air Canada v Secretary of State for Trade* (No 2) [1983] 2 AC 394; [1983] 2 WLR 494; [1983] 1 All ER 910, HL,'[i]t often happens, from the imperfection of evidence, or the withholding of it, sometimes by the party in whose favour it would tell if presented, that an adjudication has to be made which is not, and is known not to be, the whole truth of the matter.'

[56] [1986] ZR 105; See also *Kalebu Banda v The People* [1977] ZR 169 where the Supreme Court held as follows: 'The first question is whether the failure to obtain evidence was a dereliction of duty on the part of the Police which prejudiced the accused when evidence has not been obtained in circumstances where there was a duty to do so – and a fortiori when it was obtained and not laid before the Court and possible prejudice has resulted, then an assumption favourable to the accused must be made.' Further, that the said presumption/assumption 'will not necessarily be fatal to the prosecution case; "favourable" means "in favour of", not "conclusive". The extent of the presumption will depend on the nature of the evidence in question and the circumstances of the case, it; is an item of evidence presumed to exist, but its probative value will depend on the facts. The presumption is simply notional evidence to be considered along with all the other evidence in the case.'

[57] Francis Bacon, *The New Organon*, XLIX, 44.

[58] Blackburn S, *Truth* (Penguin, 2005) 29-30

reason, and it is only bad luck that might stop us hitting the truth.

2.2.1 *Common law jurisdictions and the adversarial trial*

In both civil and criminal cases, the Zambian trial is predicated on the adversarial system. Of its origin, it has been said: 'of the actual conduct of a trial we know almost nothing before the sixteenth century, not nearly enough until the eighteenth. How the jury informed itself or was informed, how rules of evidence emerged, when and in what detail directions were given by the judges, these are things we do not know.'[59]

There was, we are told,[60] an attempt in the formative years to whittle away at the adversarial trial especially during the absolutist monarchies of the Tudors and the Stuarts who introduced inquisitorial courts the most (in)famous of which was the Star Chamber, known for trials without juries, ostensibly anonymous allegations, interrogation of the accused by judges under oath or in many instances, through the device of torture. The popular and political response during the seventeenth century was to demarcate instances under which the Crown could restrict a person's freedom in addition to inflicting punishment. Coke CJ is said to have said for example that '[n]o free man shall be taken or imprisoned ruined or disseised or outlawed or exiled or in any way ruined, nor will we go or send against him, except by the lawful judgment of his peers or by the law of the land.' This was done through what we now term as the common law trial. The adversarial system was the device through which the trial was facilitated.

The foregoing was predicated on two principles, the first pronounced by Coke CJ in *Dr. Bonham's case*[61] that a man could not be judge in his own cause *(nemo iudex in suam causam),* and the second being that both sides of the argument should be heard *(audi auterum partem).* Of the two principles, it is the *nemo iudex* principle that forever immortalised the concept of court neutrality in trials. The second principle would find its acceptance in the case of *The King v University of Cambridge.*[62] In 1723, the Court of King's Bench issued mandamus to the University of Cambridge requiring the restoration to one Dr Bentley of the degrees of Bachelor of Arts and Bachelor and Doctor of Divinity of which he had been deprived by the University without a hearing. Dr Bentley had been served with a summons to appear before a University Court in an action for debt. He said the process was illegal, that he would not obey it and that the Vice-Chancellor was not his judge. He was then accused of contempt and without further notice, deprived of his degrees by the 'congregation' of the University. Fortescue J said: '[t]he laws of God and man both give the party an opportunity to make his defence, if he has any. I remember to have heard it observed by a very learned man upon such an occasion, that even God

[59] Milsom S, *Historical Foundations of the Common Law* (Butterworths, 1981), Ch 14.

[60] Radcliffe and Cross, *The English Legal System* (5th edn Butterworths, 1971) 107; Holdsworth, *History of English Law* (Vol. V, Methuen, 1936-72) 155 ff.

[61] [1610] 8 Co.Rep. 113b.

[62] [1723], 1 St Tr 557.

himself did not pass sentence upon Adam, before he was called upon to make his defence.' Lord Kenyon CJ[63] would say in *R v Gaskin*:[64] '[i]t is to be found at the head of our criminal law, that every man ought to have an opportunity of being heard before he is condemned.'

For ease of reference, we will use as a basis for our discussion, the criminal trial. A trial within the adversarial setting may be thought of as constituting three parts, i.e., the presentation of evidence; the making of arguments by the parties *in prosé* or through their counsel; and of course, the decision of the court. All three aspects will happen 'within a trial which is separated, geographically, chronologically and formally, from all the previous events such as the police investigation, the review of the evidence by the prosecution, or any preliminary hearings before judges or magistrates.'[65] It follows, therefore, that the decision rendered is, and ought to be, in theory, as well as in practice, premised solely on the evidence presented in court and is isolated from any extraneous material including public opinion, news articles, the judge's own biases etc.

It is in the foregoing that the rules of evidence find their most portent application. As already highlighted in chapter 1, common law judges take a formally passive approach to trials letting the prosecution and defence or plaintiff and defendant as the case may be, to take the lead. This approach to the discovery of truth thus invites limitations. It is unlikely that parties will call as their witnesses, those that will damage their case. It is therefore always the case that only witnesses who will advance a party's cause will be called to testify. Through cross-examination, the parties deploy vociferous attacks against the credibility and reliability of the other side's testimony or/and submissions. Through a multifaceted coordinated approach of objections and contentious argumentation, they object to testimony that may be hearsay or new issues that may be raised in re-examination. They may ask the court to rule on relevance, on admissibility, on weight and related matters, if only to derail the other side and persuade the court to ultimately decide in their favour. In this contested trial, the court is aided to reconstruct the past events birthing the trial through the rules of evidence and procedure.

> But we would be right to be very skeptical about such aims-more often than not contested trials conclude with no more than a partial and incomplete account. That very account is distorted by arguments about technical points of law, sometimes substantive but often evidential. To the participant or the outsider, these do not appear to be about "the real issue". Yet the outcome frequently depends on the outcome of that argument. Even when the "real" issue is centre stage, the role of the modern trial lawyer is about presenting the most plausible account of events [....].[66]

Partly due to the nature of the adversarial system, as described above, courts

[63] The Latin phrase *'audi alteram partem'* is ascribed to Kenyon CJ.

[64] [1799] 8 Term Rep 209.

[65] Uglow S, *Evidence: Text and Materials* 6.

[66] Uglow S, *Evidence: Text and Materials* 5.

have always sought to exercise wide-ranging control over the evidence that can be deemed admissible at trial.

2.2.2 *Civil law jurisdictions and the investigative or inquisitorial trial*

The civil law jurisdictions of continental Europe such as those of France and Germany take an inquisitorial/investigative-judge-supervised approach to criminal proceedings which ultimately leads to trial, which trial is a review of the investigative process. Partly because of the inquisitorial nature of the trials in civil jurisdictions, the focus is not so much on formal rules but on finding out the truth. Nor is the trial date as pivotal as is a common law 'day in court' trial. In France, a major civil law jurisdiction, a *juge d'instruction* may conduct several hearings during which time relevant witness statements are recorded and interrogation of the accused may occur. It is on the basis of these documents that the trial, which is merely the final stage of the judicial process presided over by a professional judge, will be conducted. All questions by counsel are to be asked through the presiding judge and not directly.[67]

Proponents and supporters of the civil jurisdiction inquisitorial method see it as a more desirable approach compared to the common law alternative which does not empower judges to investigate matters thereby clothing them, as does the civil jurisdiction approach in theory, with supervisory power over the entire judicial process. J. Hodgson[68] argues for example, that the adversarial system is inherently unfair, and favours the powerful and rich who can afford to hire as many lawyers as they like, over the poor, and accentuates cultural differences. Whether this criticism is merited is a question that may be better answered in a work focused on a comparative study of the common law and civil jurisdiction trials.[69] It is worth remembering though, that while in France the trial judge will have before him a dossier, complete with witness statements and interrogations of the accused/defendant(s), a common law judge will know nothing about the case before trial. He will, unlike his French counterpart, not have been involved in any pre-trial investigation nor will he have taken witness statements, interviewed the accused or the like.

In theory at least, the intention of the supervisory role that the judge is allowed to take up in civil jurisdictions such as France is more of an indication of the desire to seek out information deemed relevant than an indication of an effective system superior to the common law approach. It has been shown for example that in France, judicial supervision has led to case overload[70] as a consequence of magistrates and prosecutors being less than thorough in their

[67] See the reforms in Italy's new Code of Criminal Procedure as discussed in Zander M, "From Inquisitorial to Adversarial-the Italian Experiment" (1991) 141 NLJ 678.

[68] Hodgson J, "Constructing the Pre-trial Role of the Defence in French Criminal Procedure" (2002) 6 I.J.E.P.1.

[69] For an analysis of the French Criminal Investigations see, Cooper J, "Criminal Investigations in France" (1991) 141 NLJ 381.

[70] A problem just as common in common law jurisdictions like Zambia.

scrutinisation of even straight forward cases.[71] The lack of a defence set up such as is the case in common law jurisdictions means that there is no impetus for stressed magistrates and prosecutors to be insightful in their investigation of cases. Despite the highlighted differences, from a historical point of view, both systems have something to commend them. While the civil jurisdictions thought it wise to give the supervisory role of cases to an official of the State, the common law jurisdictions' choice was that of an adversarial approach to trial with an emphasis on formal rules, meant that only the most relevant evidence was deemed admissible and thus of consequence, at trial. In both systems, but more so in the civil trial, '[t]here is an importance of dialogue between the accused, the lawyer and the State.'[72]

2.2.3 The inconsequence of "facts", "truth" or "evidence" among the inuit[73]

Among the Inuit, concepts of "facts", "truth" or "evidence" as is common place in the common law and civil law jurisdictions, are of no consequence to resolving disputes.[74] The apparently irrational techniques they deploy to resolve disputes are summarised by Mansell,Meteyard and Thompson[75] as follows:

> […] the Inuit used what at first sight seems a ludicrous method of dispute resolution: dispute resolution by so-called 'song-duel'. Boxing and head-butting contests were other means of resolving disputes not involving homicide. Clearly, in both boxing and head-butting competitions the facts which led to the dispute were completely irrelevant. Like trial by battle, there was no concern with issues of justice but only with a resolution, whatever that might be. He who won acquired vindication and esteem; he who lost, lost standing in the eyes of the community. Song-duels were altogether more subtle in their operation (they could hardly be less!) because of the participation of the community. While there was a plethora of forms a song-duel could take, depending upon local
>
> custom, a typical song-duel occurred in a public gathering with each of the disputants (or his representative) singing in turn a song of contempt and abuse directed at the opponent. Like the boxing or buffeting contest, the song need have no relevance to the dispute in hand or its facts. Rather, it was concerned to score points through ridicule, and it was said that singing skill may equal or outrank gross physical prowess. It also seems that the choice of the song-duel as a means of resolution was chosen, not surprisingly, by those who were clearly physically weaker than the adversary.
>
> The singing was highly stylised with traditional patterns of

[71] See for example, Hodgson j, "The Police, the Prosecutor and the *Juge d'instruction"* (2001) 41 Brit J Criminal 342.

[72] Uglow S, *Evidence: Text and Materials* 6.

[73] Uglow S, *Evidence: Text and Materials* 56.

[74] Uglow S, *Evidence: Text and Materials* 56.

[75] Mansell W, Meteyard B and Thompson A, *A Critical Introduction to Law* (3rd edn Cavendish, 2004) 47-48.

composition and it has been suggested that the Inuit's best songs of abuse did have quite highly developed property rights attached to them! Indeed, the better known and more predictable the song, the greater the ability of the audience to participate, appreciate and empathise. Such empathy was generally expressed by violent but friendly digs in the ribs of the good singer. The winner was the man who could win over the audience or simply silence his opponent.

There are a number of features of the song-duels which are relevant to our consideration of law. Unlike the Elk Soldier Chiefs who lay down a ruling, in the song-duel, it was the community that decided victor and vanquished. Even more significantly, the winner of the song-duel won the dispute even though neither the case itself nor the facts of the case are ever alluded to. The rights and wrongs of the social dispute were determined not by a discussion of the merits of the case

but by talking about something else which *can* be decided!

The great advantage of this process is that a social dispute, to which there is simply no ready or obvious solution that would be accepted as correct by both parties, is *translated* into a form which is amenable to decision. The social problem is not faced but rather sidestepped. Just as a contest of physical violence, such as trial by battle, or boxing, *does* provide a solution of sorts, so does the song-duel, but in a more subtle way.

Admittedly, at first sight this bizarre process for resolving disputes seems to be of little relevance to our way of dealing with them, but several points need to be made. The most obvious is that in our experience most law students on first visiting the courts, and particularly the courts hearing appeals, are immediately impressed (as often are the litigants themselves) by the fact that the court does not seem to be hearing argument 'about the real issue'. Rather, what they experience is a debate over what seems to be a technical point of law. It is, of course, just such legal points that determine cases.

A second obvious point is that just as the Inuit has, or often may have, a nominee to sing his song, so of course does the litigant in a Rule of Law jurisdiction have his or her barrister or legal representative to sing his or her song for him or her. Significantly, although one of the principles of justice in such societies is that all are equal before the law, it is well known and understood that all legal representation is not of the same quality or competence. A true generalisation is that the more one can afford to pay one's advocate the greater will be the prospect of success in the court. The better the payment, an Inuit may say, the better the song. Anyone whose instinct is to question this proposition need only consider why some barristers or advocates are able to command fees greatly in excess of others. And, to read autobiographies or biographies of great legal figures is to read of people (certainly in the common law jurisdictions) who gained fame, wealth and prestige through winning cases against prediction.

Although one might consider that any analogy between Inuit song-duels and Western courts is fundamentally flawed and misplaced because the result of the song-duel seems much more arbitrary than court decisions, this almost certainly underestimates the Inuit. There is little doubt that an Inuit with a very strong social case is in a strong position to sing a powerful song to which the community will be sympathetic. If the merits of the case were overwhelming the wrongdoer would hardly welcome a song-duel.

We have suggested that the sidestepping of the issue renders the dispute resolvable, but the sidestepping, or the translation itself, may also to an extent defuse the issues. It is easier to be detached from the social issue while fully participating in the song-duel. In writing about the duels, Hoebel (1967, p 96) noted that: 'In spite of the nastiness of the insults hurled it is good form for neither party to show anger or passion. And it is expected that the participants will remain the best of friends thereafter.'

As long as the issue which resolves the dispute is not the social issue itself, a losing litigant is always able to blame his loss on a badly sung song (or an incompetent advocate) rather than being forced to accept the very real humiliation that his own case lacked justification.

Finally, the participation of the community is also significant. Not only does the participation have the effect of controlling the formalised conflict (in the pressure upon the participants to retain self-control) but it also exerts group pressure on the participants not to irrevocably disrupt the community. They are under pressure to abide by the community rules and, in many song-duels, winner and loser, in spite of the decision, are expected to be reconciled and as a token of this to exchange presents. Thus, the community strength is reasserted by reintegrating the parties in conflict back into the community. The song-duel then serves a function beyond the interests of the parties in that it reasserts the unity of the community.

In summary, then, it is impossible not to see the advantages of sidestepping the issues in a dispute. Although there is an obvious 'downside' to the method in that underlying social issues *may* remain, as we saw in the Nuer world, this process (if accepted by the litigants) does turn an irresolvable dispute into one which may be resolved. It may defuse the issue, and through the participation of the community it may allow the reintegration of the parties.

2.3 The rationalist approach to adjudication: further analysis

The rationalist approach to adjudication is, as noted above, a theoretical model crafted by Twinning[76] based on Bentham's work on judicial evidence.[77] In it, Twinning reasons that the essential precept of the Rationalist Tradition lies in

[76] Twinning W, *Rethinking Evidence: Exploratory Essays* (NWUP).

[77] Bentham J, *Rationale of Judicial Evidence*, J.S. Mill (ed) (Hunter and Clarke, 1827), vol. 2 425-434; vol.4 5-12, 428; Twinning WL, *Theories of Evidence: Bentham and Wigmore* (SUP, 1985) Ch.2; Postema, Bentham and Wigmore (Clarendon Press, 1986) Chs 10 onwards.

the orthodox culmination of adjectival law [or procedural law of which the law or/and rules of evidence are a species] which is the attainment of correctness of verdict in adjudication. 'In respect of questions of fact, that involve the pursuit of truth about particular past events through rational means. Rectitude of decision is given a high, but not overriding, priority as a means to securing justice under the law.'[78] To that end, at the core of the archetypal Rationalist premise which Twinning promotes is an instrumentalist philosophy premised on the fact that the quest for truth through the device of reason is but a means, and an indispensable one at that, to the application of utilitarian/substantive law. What then becomes apparent from Twinning's model is the fact that for there to be rectitude/correctness of decision, it is necessary for facts to be 'determined through the accurate evaluation of relevant and reliable evidence by a competent and impartial adjudicator applying the specified burden and standard of proof.'[79] To add, the trial must be presided over by '[...] a fair and impartial [judge], *ex vi termini* ("by definition"), a [judge] free from bias or prejudice, and, above all, from coercion and intimidation.'[80] Finally, there must be guaranteed, 'adequate safeguards against corruption and mistake and adequate provision for review and appeal.'[81] The comments by Ngulube DCJ as he then was in *The Attorney-General v Marcus Kampumba Achiume*[82] are demonstrative of the foregoing:

> I think that basically the position in this case was that the learned trial judge was faced with two conflicting versions of the same event. Each side had its fair share of flaws or weaknesses in the evidence, and in resolving the conflict the learned trial judge pointed out the weaknesses in the defendant's case only. If I apprehend correctly, Mr. Kinariwala's submission is in effect that an unbalanced evaluation of the evidence where only the flaws of one side but not of the other are considered is a misdirection entitling this court to interfere. I find that there is a great deal of substance and fierce in this submission. It is, in my view, from a reading of the judgment below that, in highlighting, weaknesses in the defendant's case, the learned trial judge had glossed over, even turned a blind eye to the weaknesses in the plaintiff's case, with the result that the full significance of certain aspects of the evidence was apparently not appreciated. I would agree that the case of *Peters v Sunday Post Ltd*[83] to that effect, which Mr. Kinariwala cited in his list of authorities, is in point.

If the foregoing be the case, it logically follows that in order for the aims of adjudication to be achieved then the adjudicator must have, available to him, evidence that is not only relevant and reliable but the kind that is presented

[78] Twinning W, *Rethinking Evidence* 78-79.

[79] Dennis I, *The Law of Evidence* 29.

[80] *Weems et al. v. State*, Id., at 214 per John C. Anderson CJ.

[81] Dennis I, *The Law of Evidence* 29.

[82] [1983] ZR 1 (SC).

[83] (1958) EA 424.

in a manner that will enable the adjudicator to discover the truth through the equable application of rules of evidence and other procedural rules that among other things clearly set out the burdens of and standards of proof. Only through these means can an adjudicator conceive and deliver a rational, well-reasoned judgment.[84]

The foregoing does not, however, end the philosophical underpinnings of the concept of rectitude of decision. Bentham[85] postulated that the best way to attain rectitude of decision in any judicial proceedings was to predicate it on what he termed a "Natural System of Procedure." He was in essence advocating for a system that was bereft of technical rules, chief among these, those rules that sought to exclude certain classes of evidence or particularised the weight to be attached to one piece of evidence in contradistinction to other types of evidence. The better approach, Bentham argued, was to abolish all constraints so long as the evidence in question was probative in so far as the issues of fact in *casu* were concerned. This would invariably only leave the factfinder to decide matters of reliability. He maintained that as a rider, the adjudicator must be given free rein in evaluating the evidence. Rather than being prescriptive as regards what evidence could be admissible or be deemed relevant or what weight could be attached to evidence by a factfinder, the law's core concern ought to-be, or so Bentham argued-the enhancement of factfinding. This could be done in several ways related to refining the factfinder's appreciation of aspects that influence, among other facets of evidence, weight on the one hand and relevance on the other. It would also include training the factfinder in what reasoning should be deployed in the assessment of evidence.

The utilitarian model as postulated by Bentham was, however, not sacrosanct and where in the cost-benefit analysis, it appeared that the benefit of attaining rectitude of decision was outstripped by the cost, then it would be advisable, said Bentham, to exclude the evidence in question. This was a rather significant concession. This we say because the utilitarian principle of attaining rectitude of decision namely by a "Natural System of Procedure" is a concept that permits no restrictions on proof. However, in the context of this climbdown was contained a realisation that it was necessary to place constraints on his theory which could only find its full application in an ideal world of unlimited time and competing values. It is from this vantage point that the relevance having rules of evidence, which is, 'to articulate and justify the constraints on the principle of free proof which the rationalist model of adjudication might otherwise logically adopt.'[86]

It is helpful to note that rules of evidence may, in terms of importance, be divided into 'epistemic' rules and those of a 'non-epistemic' nature. The

[84] See *Samuel Sooli v The People* [1981] ZR 298; *Stephen Manda v The People* [1980] ZR 116; by way of illustration, in in the case of *Ticky v The People* [1968] ZR 21,it was held that it is the magistrate's duty to consider in his judgment each defence made and it must be evident from his judgment that he did so.

[85] Bentham J, *Rationale of Judicial Evidence*.

[86] Dennis I, *The Law of Evidence* 30.

former which may include rules relating to 'identification evidence' and those relating to 'expert opinion evidence'[87] are chiefly concerned with truth finding, hence correctness[88] of decision. The latter class of rules, which include rules relating to the examination of witnesses *vis-à-vis,* integrity of police in the investigation of offences, and those that relate to vulnerable and suspect witnesses, are concerned, not with truth finding but rather, values which may have a bearing on evidential matters during trial. Thus, when arguments regarding admissibility, relevance and/or weight arise at trial, it is recourse to the foregoing rules that determines whether a piece of evidence ought to be admitted, deemed relevant or of such sufficient weight as to have a bearing on the decision of the court on an interlocutory application or in the court's final judgment.

2.3.1 *Matters that place constraints on freedom of proof*

It is abundantly clear from a consideration of epistemic and non-epistemic concepts regarding the rules of evidence that one will have to navigate the competing goals of these diametrically opposed objectives. In this part therefore, we discuss how such competing aims may be determined.

2.3.1.1 The need to lessen expense and delay in adjudication

Part of the criticism laid at the door of our system of adjudication is the extremely long time it takes for matters to be resolved and the expense to which disputants are put partly because of the nature of the rules of court, partly because of the level of competence of counsel, and partly because to this day, most courts still write in free long hand thereby egregiously and infuriatingly slowing down the proceedings punctuating it with a stop start, 'slow down', 'watch the court's hand', 'you are too fast' or exclamations of 'Court of record!' from judges/magistrates frustrated by the slowness of writing in contradistinction to the fast pace of oral interactions between counsel and witnesses and even between counsel and the presiding judge. The use of real time reporters has only started making its way through the court system in recent times. Still a good number of judges would rather take down submissions in long hand even when real time court reporters are present resulting in duplication of work, slow progress and redundancy of the reporters who must still be paid for their work.

Zambian trials are not the stuff that Hollywood legal dramas are made of. They are slow, they are boring and generally lack drama and have normalised a glacial approach to adjudication. As Thurman Arnold[89] has observed, '[...] all the machinery surrounding the ideal of a fair trial has its social cost in delays, technicalities and injustices in the judicial process.' The lack of technology and sometimes lack of proficiency both at the bar and on the bench has in

[87] As this class of evidence runs the risk of being unreliable.

[88] Or rectitude of decision.

[89] Arnold T, The Symbols of Government (Harbinger, 1962), 141-143.

certain cases, not helped. It therefore follows that anything that would hasten the conclusion of court proceedings is latched onto.[90] The reasons for this are simple. It is not profitable nor is it practicable for the courts nor the parties to hear all manner of evidence without restraint as this would be too costly to justify the outcome however thorough and fair the trial may turn out. From a rationalist approach and for both epistemic and non-epistemic reasons, if the evidence is useless to proving facts in issue, it is, and should be inadmissible not only because of its cost but because as noted in chapter 1, it tends to distract the factfinder and confuse issues. Thus, some common law evidentiary rules including that to exclude statements made out of court which are consistent with the witness's present testimony must thus be seen within the light of cost-reduction and nothing else.

2.3.1.2 *Fairness within the context of procedural rules*

While it is a given that the rules of evidence are multifaceted, it is also important to realise the reason for which they exist or the purpose they ultimately serve. Rules of evidence lend credence to principles that are the basis of a fair trial as we know it. The right to a fair trial is so fundamental as to render proceedings illegitimate when it is ignored. To illustrate, Article 18(9) of the Constitution[91] provides that '[a]ny court or other adjudicating authority prescribed by law for determination of the existence or extent of any civil right or obligation shall be established by law and shall be independent and impartial; and where proceedings for such a determination are instituted by any person before such a court or other adjudicating authority, *the case shall be given a fair hearing within a reasonable time.*' Therefore, evidence that has been obtained by inhuman and degrading treatment;[92] breaches to individual liberty;[93] privacy; or offends our notion of what constitutes just and fair proceedings[94] will not be permitted to constitute the record on which the court will render a decision. The foregoing takes a serious tone when it comes to the protection of rights in criminal trials.[95] In *Joshua Mapushi v The Queen*[96] it was held, *inter alia*, that:

> […] An accused person has the right to be tried in a manner and form prescribed by law and the accepted practice of the criminal courts or the purpose of ensuring a fair trial and all that it involves. Consequently, if that right is infringed by disregarding the manner and form in any particular and the accused is convicted, he has prima facie suffered an injustice and that injustice becomes substantial.

---

[90] Recently, SI No 58 of 2020 was issued for this very reason.

[91] The Constitution (Amendment) Act No 2 of 2016.

[92] Contrary to Article 15.

[93] Contrary to Articles 11, 12, 13,14,16, 17, 19, 20, 21, 22, 23, 24 of the Zambian Constitution.

[94] Contrary to Article 18.

[95] See article 18 discussed below.

[96] [1963-1964] Z and NRLR 90.

In *Patel v Attorney General,*[97] Skinner CJ, as he then was, sitting as a puisne judge held *inter alia*, '[…] The manifest object of [Article 18] is to ensure that every accused person is accorded a fair trial. The provisions of the section including those guaranteeing the right to Counsel are designed to ensure that the accused has a fair trial […]'[98]

What is patent from the foregoing constitutional provisions and the holding in *R v Mapushi*[99] is the premium placed on the right to a fair trial especially in criminal proceedings where liberty or life is at stake. The concept of fairness informs rules of evidence and in the application of these rules backed by constitutional provisions, a trial finds its legitimacy. Non-observance of these constitutional injunctions is grounds for appeal to an appellate court of competent jurisdiction which is in keeping with the rationalist approach to adjudication that there be adequate provision for review[100] and appeal.'[101]

The concept of *fairness* is synonymous with *justice* and equality before the law for all, irrespective of station in life. The concept of justice may be applied to substantive rules in question. It may be gainsaid that any substantive rule is likely to be tainted with economic, political or social overtones. Thus, in a jurisprudential naturalist approach to law, simply because a law has been passed does not make it just. Further, the concept of justice may be applied to the outcome of a trial.[102] Thus, when the verdict is said to be unjust/unfair, it is because it runs against the weight of evidence more than anything else. When what is criticised is the punishment, what is meant is that the sentence may be too light or too grave for the offence committed, depending on one's vantage point, that is whether one is the offender or the victim (or the victim's family[103] in the event of a homicide for example). These are issues, the scope of which, go beyond the aims of this text and are better discussed in a text dedicated to that particular subject matter. For obvious reasons, it is the justice of the procedure that we are most concerned with and that will inform what we discuss going forward in this chapter and those that follow.

As already noted in this text, procedural fairness in the court room entails that in an adversarial type of adjudication, 'truth is more likely to emerge from confrontation mediated through identifiable procedures that are compatible with generally accepted standards of fairness.'[104] It is rather telling that the adversarial system does allow for 'truth…to emerge.' As we earlier said, this is the best that can be hoped for. The reasons, as previously discussed in this text are simple. Procedural fairness is important in so far as epistemic and non-epistemic reasons are concerned. As regards the epistemic reasons, it

---

[97] [1969] ZR 97.

[98] See further, *People v Henry Kunda* [1977] ZR 223.

[99] [1963-1964] Z and NRLR 90.

[100] See Order 39 of the HCR.

[101] Dennis I, *The Law of Evidence* 29.

[102] For an illuminating analysis see Hatchard J and Ndulo M, *Readings in Criminal Law & Criminology in Zambia*(Multimedia Publication/James Currey 1994) Ch 9.

[103] See a critique of the case of.

[104] Dennis I, *The Law of Evidence* 13.

can be contended that procedural fairness promotes Twinning's rectitude of decision by enabling all parties to 'locate, produce and test all the relevant and worthwhile evidence on the facts in dispute'[105] a facet which has been described as 'particularly important in an adversary system of adjudication where litigants have to rely on their own efforts to find and present evidence.'[106] There are of course constraints on this discussed elsewhere in this text to this apparent advantage of an adversarial trial including the liberty of parties to leave out issues from the court record of evidence that they deem adverse to their cause. As Lord Wilberforce has noted in *Air Canada v Secretary of State for Trade,*[107] '[i]t often happens, from the imperfection of evidence, or the withholding of it, sometimes by the party in whose favour it would tell if presented, that an adjudication has to be made which is not, and is known not to be, the whole truth of the matter.' Further, encased in the concept of procedural fairness is the concept of "equality of arms" which is deemed to be essential under Article 6 of the European Convention on Human Rights (ECHR).[108] The fact is though that no parties may be considered equal which is why it becomes necessary for each to have counsel of their own choosing. This too presents problems in that the quality of counsel that will be chosen will generally depend on the resources available to the party concerned. And even if it assumed that counsel hired on both sides are of equal ability, the very fact that information passing between counsel and clients is privileged means that, part of the evidence that may lead to the discovery of the whole truth is not available to the court hence compromising the ability of the adjudicator to discover the complete truth.

As regards the non-epistemic importance of procedural fairness, all that can be said at this point is that parties that have been given the opportunity to be part of the adjudication process and have participated in it fully are more likely to accept the resulting court decision as a legitimate resolution of their dispute irrespective.[109] More so, the public will be more accepting of a decision where it is shown that the parties concerned were treated fairly and that from the tenor of its procedural rulings and its final judgment, the court applied its mind to the evidence before it based on the governing procedural

[105] Dennis I, *The Law of Evidence* 32.

[106] Zuckerman AAS, "Privilege and Public Interest" in Tapper C (ed), *Crime Proof and Punishment* (Butterworths, 1981) 248.

[107] [1983] 2 AC 394 at 438.

[108] See *X v Federal Republic of Germany (1151/61) (1962) 7 Collection of Decisions of the European Commission of Human Rights 118.*

[109] See Bayles, *Procedural Justice* (1990) 127-135; Tyler T, *Why People Obey the Law* (1990).

and substantive law concerned.[110] *The Minister of Home Affairs, The Attorney General v Lee Habasonda*[111] was an appeal against a "purported" judgment of the High Court declaring s 13(1)(a) of the Societies Act,[112] as flawed, since it gave the Minister of Home Affairs unfettered and uncontrolled subjective discretion. The parties to the action relied on affidavit evidence. In addition to the affidavit evidence, the parties filed detailed written skeleton arguments. In the "purported" judgment, the trial judge reproduced the skeleton arguments, verbatim from the first page to the last page, including the expressions, "My Lord", "We submit," and "We pray". The judgment of the trial judge ran into 49 pages, 48 of those pages consisted of verbatim reproduction or recitals of the originating notice of motion, the affidavits and the skeleton arguments. On behalf of the Court Sakala CJ, as he then was observed as follows:

> On a consideration of the pleadings on record and the issues raised, it is our view that this is not a case where we should rewrite the judgment on behalf of the trial judge. We must, however, stress for the benefit of the trial courts that every judgment must reveal a review of the evidence, where applicable, a summary of the arguments and submissions, if made, findings of fact, the reasoning of the court on the facts and the application of the law and authorities, if any, to the facts. Finally, a judgment must show the conclusion. A judgment which only contains verbatim reproduction and recitals is no judgment. In addition, a court should not feel compelled or obliged and moved by any decided cases without giving reasons for accepting those authorities. In other words, a court must reveal its mind to the evidence before it and no just simply accept any decided case.

However, a fair trial in and of itself does not guarantee the court arriving at the correct conclusion. This is why there must be an accessible system of appeal.[113] This was the scenario in *Nyampala Safaris (Z) Limited and Others v Zambia*

[110] Summers RS, "Evaluating and Improving Legal Processes: A Plea for Process Values" (1974) 60 Cornell L.R. 1; See Malila M, *The Contours of a Developing Jurisprudence of the Zambian Supreme Court*; H.L. HO, the Duty to Give Reasons (2000), 20 *Legal Stud* 42; s 169(1) of the Criminal Procedure Code Chapter 88 of the Laws of Zambia; Order XXXVI, HCR, Chapter 27 of the Laws of Zambia; *Mbomena v The People* [1967] ZR 89 (CA): The judge's approach should take into account the facts and law in so far as the same relate to the evidence and in all cases, the defences that the accused has mounted; *Ticky v The People* [1968] ZR 89 (CA): The magistrate must remind himself in his judgment of the burden and degree of proof; *Muvuma Kambanja Situna v The People* [1982] ZR 115 (SC): The judgment of the trial court must show on its face that adequate consideration has been given to all relevant material that has been placed before it, otherwise an acquittal may result where it is not merited; *Wilson Masauso Zulu v Avondale Housing Project Ltd* [1982]ZR 172 (SC): The trial court has a duty to adjudicate upon every aspect of the suit between the parties so that every matter in controversy is determined in finality; For instances when a court may review its own final judgment (or Ruling for that matter), and the question of new evidence on appeal, see analysis in Kaluba BC, *Evidence Law* at 602 to 606 and cases and rules of court cited thereunder.

[111] (SCZ Judgment No 23 of 2007); ; see *Zambian Breweries Plc v Lameck Sakala* SCZ Appeal No 173 of 2009 where it was held that '[e]very judgment must reveal a review of the evidence, where applicable, a summary of the arguments and submissions, if made, the findings of fact, the reasoning of the court on the facts and the application of the law and authorities, if any, to the facts.'

[112] Chapter 119 of the Law of Zambia.

Wildlife Authority and Others[114] wherein the Supreme Court held that the High Court arrived at the correct conclusion of refusing to grant the application for Judicial Review but for wrong reasons and in the process varied the High Court judgment accordingly.

(i) The role of appellate courts in practice[115]

One might imagine from reading the relevant parts of the Subordinate Courts Act,[116] High Court Act,[117] the Court of Appeal Act,[118] the Supreme Court Act[119] and by extension, the case of *Nyampala Safaris*[120] above,that appellate courts have, procedurally speaking, wide-ranging powers of review of decisions of courts below. The reality is, however, very different.[121] This is so because where there has been a substantial breach of the constitutional right to a fair trial which is inclusive of pre-trial conduct by the police, the trial court itself can use its discretion to either halt the trial as an abuse of process as was done in *R v Loosely*[122] or simply exclude the offending type of evidence for want of admissibility. It has in fact been held *inter alia* in *Alubisho v The People*[123] that with the exception of prescribed minimum or mandatory sentences a trial court has a discretion to select a sentence that seems appropriate in the circumstances of each individual case.

An appellate court does not normally have such wide-ranging and unfettered discretion as is imagined by many, which sometimes may include those in legal practice, to interfere with the lower Court's decision. Thus, it has been held in *Imusho v The People*[124] that '[a]n appellate court will not interfere with a finding of fact if there was reasonable ground for it, but such finding will be set aside if it was made on a view of the facts which could not reasonably be entertained.'[125] We illustrate this using the example of how appellate courts have dealt with the matter of sentencing in this country. It ought to be remembered that the discretion to impose sentences except for those already prescribed by statute lies with the trial court and not the appellate court. Hilbery J in the case of *R v Ball*[126] observed that'[i]n deciding the appropriate sentence, a court should always be guided by certain considerations. The first and foremost is the public interest. The criminal law is publicly enforced, not only with the object of punishing crime, but also in the hope of preventing it.'

The role of the appellate court therefore is only to guide lower courts on how to employ the powers granted to them in sentencing matters, and not to substitute its sentence for its own. Thus, in *Nevers Sekwila Mumba v Muhabi Lungu*,[127] the Supreme Court stated as follows: 'This Court will [...] affirm or overrule the trial Court on any valid legal point presented by the record, regardless of whether that point was considered or even rejected.'[128] This

---

[114] [2004] ZR 49 (SCZ).

[124] [1972] ZR 77 (CA).

[126] [1951] 35 Criminal Appeal Reports 164 at 165.

[127] SCJ No 55 of 2014.

[128] *Imusho v The People* [1972] ZR 77 (CA).

holding is similar to that in the Kenyan decision of *Okeno v Republic*[129] in which the role of the first appellate Court was given as follows:

> An appellant on first appeal is entitled to expect the evidence as a whole to be submitted to a fresh and exhaustive examination[130] and to the appellate Court's own decision on the evidence. The first appellate Court must itself weigh conflicting evidence and draw its own conclusion.[131] It is not the function of a first appellate Court merely to scrutinize the evidence to see if there was some evidence to support the lower Court's findings and conclusions; it must make its own findings and draw its own conclusions. Only then can it decide whether the magistrate's findings should be supported. In doing so, it should make allowance for the fact that the trial court has had the advantage of hearing and seeing the witnesses.[132]

The case of *Stephen James Hardy v The People*[133] illustrates the preceding points. The appellant was charged in the Subordinate Court of the First Class with five counts of theft by public servant contrary to ss 243 and 248 of the Penal Code.[134] He pleaded guilty to all counts and asked that three similar offences be taken into consideration. He was sentenced to six months' imprisonment on each count, to run consecutively, that is, a total of two and a half years. He appealed against sentence. It was held as follows: (i) Even if it could be said that the magistrate erred in his assessment of the appellant's position, there was not such an error as to entitle an appellate court to interfere; the appellate court will not interfere unless the sentence is manifestly excessive or wrong in principle. (ii) The appellate court will not interfere with the sentence if the magistrate was influenced by proper considerations in arriving at the sentence even if there was some misdirection from which no injustice resulted. (iii) It is not the correct approach simply to add together the sentences for the individual offences regarded individually; the court must look at the whole course of conduct and impose a sentence commensurate with that.

The restrictions placed on the powers of the court to review and amend sentences in *Stephen James Hardy*[135] and *Alubisho v The People*[136] do not mean that appellate courts are powerless to deal with appeals, even those, within the context of our discussion, that deal with sentencing. The common law system of appeal, such as the one used in this jurisdiction, is not one that deals with the rightness of the decision appealed against but rather, a review of the process employed in arriving at the decision now impugned.[137] In *Jutronich, Schutte and*

[129] [1972] EA 32.

[130] *Pandya v Republic* (1957) EA 336.

[131] *Shantilal M. Ruwala v Republic* [1957] EA 570.

[132] See *Peters v Sunday Post*, [1958] EA 424.

[133] [1971] ZR 64 (HC).

[134] Chapter 87 of the Laws of Zambia.

[135] [1971] ZR 64 (HC).

[136] [1976] ZR 11.

[137] See *Nyampala Safaris (Z) Limited and Others v Zambia Wildlife Authority and Others* [2004] ZR 49 (SCZ).

Lukin v The People[138] Blagden CJ outlined three instances[139] in which an appellate court could amend a sentence, specifically, that, in dealing with appeals against sentence the appellate court should ask itself these three questions:

(1) Is the sentence wrong in principle?

Comment:

As shown in *The People v Berejena*[140] an appellate court should and ought to act under this scenario only where there has been a blatant disregard of the principles of sentencing. The case of The *People and Kayombwe*[141] also illustrates the fact that it is permissible for the appellate court to act under principle (1) where the court below passes a particular sentence e.g., a fine where the circumstances of the convict are such that he will be unable to pay such a fine. In *Kayombwe*,[142] the High Court substituted the fine with a suspended sentence.

(2) Is the sentence so manifestly excessive [or so totally inadequate][143] as to induce a state of shock?[144]

Comment:

Under scenario (2), the appellate court not only has authority to reduce a manifestly excessive sentence, but to reduce one that is deemed to be totally inadequate. In *Kalunga v The People,*[145] the appellant pleaded guilty to five charges of theft by servant and was convicted on those pleas in the subordinate court. The magistrate in sentencing the appellant drew attention to the fact that although the appellant was a first offender, he had stolen five times and that the amount involved was large. He sentenced him to eighteen months' imprisonment with hard labour on each count, the sentences to run concurrently. On appeal the High Court judge set aside this sentence on the ground that it was wrong in principle because there was no basis for making the sentences run concurrently. He then proceeded to impose considerably enhanced sentences but suspended portions of them so that the period during which the appellant would actually be in prison was two years and three months instead of eighteen months. It was held *inter alia*, that,

[138] [1965] ZR 9 (CA) at 10.

[139] Applied with approval in *Alubisho v The People* [1976] ZR 11; *Sachingongov The People* SCZ Judgment No 8 of 1981; *Kaambo v The People* [1976] ZR 122.

[140] [1984] ZR 19.

[141] [1978] ZR 294.

[142] [1978] ZR 294.

[143] Words in parenthesis added in *Alubisho v The People* [1976] ZR 11.

[144] See *Gideon Hammond Millard v The People* [1998] SJ 34 (SC): '[a]n appellate court should not lightly interfere with the discretion of the trial court on question of sentence but that for the appellate court to decide to interfere with the sentence, it must come to it witha sense of shock;' *Chola and Another v The People* [1975] ZR 242 (SC); *Kenneth Mtonga and Victor Kaonga v The People* (SCZ Judgment No 5 of 2000); *Paul Zulu v The People* HPA/50/2010.

[145] [1975] ZR 72; *Jamu v The People* SCZ Judgment No 21 0f 1980.

> It is not proper to enhance a sentence simply because the appellate court, had it tried the case, would have imposed a somewhat greater sentence. Just as an appellate court will not interfere with a sentence as being too high unless that sentence comes to the court with a sense of shock, equally it will not interfere with a sentence as being too low unless it is of the opinion that it is totally inadequate to meet the circumstances of the particular offence.[146]

A rare case in which the appellate court was compelled to interfere with the sentence of the lower court is *The People v Mulwanda.*[147]The accused was convicted of six counts of corrupt practices involving large bribes which the accused was found to have accepted as a senior civil servant. The prosecution case was based on evidence of witnesses who had been detained under s 33(6) of the Preservation of Public Security Regulations. The trial magistrate imposed a fine of K1,000.00 on each count and also imposed sentences of imprisonment in lieu. It was held inter alia that the sentence was too lenient. A custodial sentence would have been appropriate and accordingly, in addition to the fines, a sentence of fifteen months' imprisonment with hard labour was to be imposed on each count to run concurrently.

Doyle CJ gave his reasons for interfering with the lower court's sentence in the following terms:

> I fully appreciate the fact that the convict has suffered by this but that cannot completely offset that this was a very serious offence. I think that it would come with a sense of shock to the whole of the public were a custodial sentence not imposed. Here was a man, admittedly without previous convictions, as would be expected in a high civil servant. He had twenty-two years' loyal service, but despite that, when the crux came, he took large bribes. It is impossible for this court to fail to intervene where the courts regularly sentence junior civil servants and junior men in positions outside Government to jail for offences of less serious import but in this case a person in high position is allowed to escape with what is in effect mere financial restoration to the status quo. I am astonished that such a light sentence was passed in such a case. I fully appreciate the matters which have been raised on behalf of the convict, but I cannot think that I would be doing my duty if I allowed this case to pass without altering the sentence. I have given great thought to the matter. Had this case been properly dealt with, a more substantial sentence would have been passed. He was charged with six counts which means that the maximum sentence could have been twelve years' imprisonment on those six counts. That of course would be excessive but I have no doubt that two years would not have been an excessive sentence. Having heard everything said on his behalf, I am unable to refrain from reviewing this matter

[146] See application in *Banda v The People* [1981] ZR 26; *Massissani v The People* SCZ Judgment No 47 of 1977.

[147] [1974] ZR 46 (HC).

> and altering the sentence. I would like to point out one thing. The learned magistrate in imposing these fines of K1,000 on each count also imposed sentences of imprisonment in lieu. He made the fines consecutive but the imprisonment concurrent. I doubt if this is a proper order. However, as the fine has been paid I do not propose to interfere. I propose to retain the sentences of fines which have been paid. I propose further to add to these fines a custodial sentence and I impose a sentence of fifteen months' imprisonment with hard labour on each count concurrent. Because of the long trial and because of the fact that the prisoner has been perhaps lulled into a sense of false security, because of an inadequate sentence, I consider that I am justified in imposing a somewhat smaller sentence than would ordinarily have been imposed at trial.

(3) Are there exceptional circumstances which would render it an injustice if the sentence was not reduced?

Comment:

Neither Blagden CJ in *Jutronich, Schutte and Lukin v The People*[148] nor Silungwe CJ in *Alubisho v The People*[149] elaborated on what may fit what Blagden CJ termed, and Silungwe CJ[150] accepted as 'exceptional circumstances', nor have cases that have followed these decisions provided an (in)exhaustive list of what those circumstances may be. There is therefore little authority for the exceptional circumstances anticipated, though Hatchard and Ndulo[151] have suggest, based on *Zulu v The People,*[152] that the said circumstances 'would cover both facts arising from the commission of the offence and also matters affecting the accused and his family.'

Therefore, 'only if one or other of these questions can be answered in the affirmative should the appellate court interfere.'[153] The appellate court ought not to interfere with the decision of the court below if the decision appealed against is one which, considering the factual matrix and set of circumstances of the case which the court below had to deal with, is one which could rationally have been reached by any equable tribunal.[154] Finally, there is some guidance when the appeal in question attacks certain findings of fact by the court of first instance or that below. In *Nkhata and Four Others v The Attorney General*[155] it was held that a trial judge sitting alone without a jury can only be reversed on fact when it is positively demonstrated to the appellate court that:

---

[148] [1965] ZR 9 (CA) at 10.

[149] [1976] ZR 11.

[150] Who wrote the judgment of the Court.

[151] Hatchard J and Ndulo M, *Readings in Criminal Law & Criminology in Zambia* 113.

[152] [1974] ZR 58.

[153] [1965] ZR 9 (CA) at 10.

[154] See for example, *Massissaniv The People* SCZ Judgment No 47 of 1977.

[155] [1966] ZR 174; see also *Attorney-General v Peter M. Ndhlovu* [1986] ZR 12; In *Eagle Charalambous Transport Limited v Gideon Phiri* [1994] ZR 52 the Supreme Court reversed the findings of fact as it was clear from the quotation that the learned Commissioner did not give a balanced evaluation of the evidence before him.

(a) by reason of some non-direction or misdirection or otherwise the judge erred in accepting the evidence which he did accept; or
(b) in assessing and evaluating the evidence the judge has taken into account some matter which he ought not to have taken into account, or failed to take into account some matter which he ought to have taken into account; or
(c) it unmistakably appears from the evidence itself, or from the unsatisfactory reasons given by the judge for accepting it, that he cannot have taken proper advantage of his having seen and heard the witnesses; or
(d) in so far as the judge has relied on manner and demeanour, there are other circumstances which indicate that the evidence of the witnesses which he accepted, is not credible, as for instance, where those witnesses have on some collateral matter deliberately given an untrue answer.

In the case of *Zulu v Avondale Housing Project Ltd*[156] the Supreme Court held as follows:

> [...] before this court can reverse findings of fact made by a trial judge, we would have to be satisfied that the findings in question were either perverse or made in the absence of any relevant evidence or upon a misapprehension of the facts or that they were findings which, on a proper view of the evidence, no trial court acting correctly could reasonably make.

(ii) Avoidance of error

'To err is human [...]' goes the old refrain. Adjudication (never mind the procedural, evidentiary and substantive rules (and laws) that govern it) is a human led process and as such, not immune to error. It is not a cloistered virtue. The risk always exists that even when the law, be it evidentiary, procedural or substantive, is followed to the letter, errors will be made in judgment. As has been said by Blackburn,[157]

> [t]he evidence may be poor, or misleading, or the interpretation which everyone supposes reasonable may be based on insufficient science or general misunderstanding. A trial may be fairly conducted, yet unhappily arrive at the wrong verdict. Still, there is nothing better that we can do. We act under the conviction that our best procedures, although they may let us down, markedly increase the chance that we get things right.

When the adjudicator premises, thanks to the nature of the adversarial trial, his/her decision on poor or misleading evidence or an incorrect interpretation

[156] [1982] ZR 172; quoted in *Attorney-General v Marcus Kampumba Achiume* [1983] ZR 1; see also *Watt v Thomas* [1947] 1 All ER 582; *Benmax v Austin Motor Co. Ltd* [1955] 1 All ER 326.

[157] Blackburn S, *Truth* (Penguin, 2005) 29-30.

of the facts within the context of the law or indeed the wrong interpretation of the relevant law with respect to the evidence before him, a wrong decision will be arrived at. The same will be true if, due to incompetence or carelessness, a court conducts an unfair trial. The result may be a wrong acquittal, a wrong conviction or a wrong judgment. When this happens, a miscarriage of justice has occurred. It is under those circumstances that one of the objectives of the rules of evidence comes to the fore, namely, to ensure that there is allocation of error, the aim of which is to minimise the miscarriage of justice.[158] Some[159] have argued that this is the foundation principle of the law of evidence. When the necessity to avoid erroneous convictions, acquittals and/or judgments is achieved through the employment of rules of admissibility and usage of evidence, the freedom of proof is constrained in as much the same way as it is constrained when the evidence presented is insufficient or erroneous.

(iii) Quest for other ideals

There are always competing claims to be dealt with under the rules of evidence that may lay claim to protection. So, quite apart from the quest for truth, which appears to be the overwhelming goal of the adversarial trial, which goal falls, as stated above, into the epistemic basket, other non-epistemic ideals may make substantial entitlements to protection. It goes without saying that in so far as a potent device for allocating priorities among these competing claims is concerned, it is the law of evidence that must be our first port of call. As would become readily discernible, however, this is no easy task and while questions may be asked as to what value to place on the quest for truth in adversarial trials or how the many claims for fairness, free proof, human rights and competing interests may be determined in terms of constraints on proof, no easy answers can be offered under our model of adjudication whose core concern is rectitude of decision. Nor can we argue that the overriding principle is free proof in all instances. To say so would be to imply that facets considered integral to the proper administration of justice, facets that have received constitutional backing e.g., the right not to incriminate oneself; the right to counsel; and as such, the right not to disclose any matters passing between counsel and the accused, would fall by the wayside in order to achieve free proof. This is not a position society would be willing to accept. Be that as it may, there are at least three conceivable methods to the subject of settling rival objectives:[160]

> The first is some reasonably comprehensive version of Benthamite

[158] This is the basis for the concepts of the burden and standard of proof discussed in chapter 3 below. The higher the burden, the lower the chances that a wrong conclusion will be drawn. As such, in criminal cases, the burden of proof must be beyond reasonable (but not all shadow) of doubt. The goal is to minimise, so far as this is possible, the risk of an erroneous convictions; for a consideration of the concept of miscarriage of justice, see *Wang v Health Professionals Council of Zambia* (2012/HK/339) [2013] ZMHC 24; *Patel v The People* (1969) ZR 132 (HC); *Joseph Knox Simwanza v The People* (1985) ZR 15 (SC); *Kafirsam v The People* [1968] ZR 147 (HC); *Denis Simon Salima Bwalya v The People* [1979] ZR 1 (SC); *Joseph Nkole v The People* [1977] ZR 351 (SC); *Mutale v The People* [1973] ZR 25 (CAZ); s 68(5) of The Health Professions Act No 24, 2009; s 80(5) of The Accountants Act No 13 of 2008, among others.

[159] Stein A, *Foundations of Evidence Law*, 2005; Laudan, *Truth, Error and Criminal Law*, (2006).

[160] Dennis I, *The Law of Evidence* 36.

utilitarianism. This would begin by conceding a high value to rectitude of decision, essentially for the reasons given by Bentham; that because the law raises expectations and enables people to regulate their conduct, it is necessary to satisfy such expectations and maintain security and stability by correct application of the law.[161] It would then be necessary to consider the precise mix of rules and discretion required to maximise accuracy of factfinding.[162] Finally this approach would acknowledge the existence of other social goals such as the security of the state, or police propriety, and the need to establish how those goals might be furthered or hindered by particular rules of evidence. A complex calculation of overall gains and losses to utility would be required where such goals conflicted with rectitude.

2.4 Fundamental rights and the law of evidence

An alternate approach to the utilitarian paradigm discussed above may be to resolve aims and goals predicated on the human rights plane. Once this approach is accepted, a shift in focus from municipal wellbeing to the defence of individual cloistered interests occurs. As Maher[163] notes, 'law as a means of subjecting human conduct to the governance of rules necessarily adopts a specific conception of moral personality, one which respects the autonomy of those subject to the legal order.' As we will see from the discussion that follows on the bill of rights and the law of evidence, individual human rights are placed on a higher plane than other rights. Dworkin[164] argues against the leading philosophy of Anglo-American acceptable positivism as offered by Hart[165] and utilitarianism by propositioning that rights of the individual against the state occur separately from the inscribed law, functioning as "trumps" against the comforts or widely held desires of the mainstream. These rights, as our discussion on the bill of rights elsewhere in this text shows, can be derogated from by constitutional means. However, constitutional protections must, and a *fiotori*, are almost always premised on international instruments and best practice.

Also, to be considered, are Lord Kenyon CJ's[166] words in *R v Gaskin*:[167] '[i] t is to be found at the head of our criminal law, that every man ought to have an opportunity of being heard before he is condemned.' This concept known by the Latin phrase *'audi alteram partem'* is linked to the rule of law, and by necessary implication, adjudicative justice, in terms of the liberal theory of dispositive justice, must pattern its decisions on the respect for the autonomy

[161] Bentham J, *Treatise on Judicial Evidence,* E. Dumont (ed) (London: 1825) 2.

[162] Galligan DJ *"More Scepticism About Scepticism"* (1988) 8 OJLS 249, 256-257.

[163] Maher G, "Natural Justice as Fairness" in DN McCormick and PBH Birks (eds), *The Legal Mind: Essays for Tony Honore* (1986) 103, 114.

[164] See Dworkin RM, *Taking Rights Seriously* (Gerald Duckworth & Co Ltd, 1977).

[165] Hart HLA, *The Concept of Law* (1961).

[166] The Latin phrase *'audi alteram partem'* is ascribed to Kenyon CJ.

[167] [1799] 8 Term Rep 209.

of the individual. 'The idea [...] is that the best justification of natural justice lies in the moral requirement of respect for the autonomy of the party affected by a decision; this leads to using a procedure which gives him a role in it and can thus explain to him the basis on which the application of the rule or policy to him is justified.'[168]

Finally, the right to individual autonomy is given impetus in the right against wrongful conviction. Therefore, where an appellate court finds that on the facts, it is unsafe to convict, it will quash or vary the conviction. Be that as it may, as many cases and some statutory provisions show, where the appellate court considers that the point of the appeal may be decided by the appellate court or ought to have been decided in favour of the appellant by the court below, the appellate court will not quash the decision/conviction/ judgment if it considers that no miscarriage of justice has or actually occurred.[169] The reasons for considering a conviction by the court below to be safe are varied and inexhaustive. They will largely depend on the factual matrix and circumstances of each particular case. This is exemplified in the case of *Musonda v The People.*[170] On 6th August, 1968, in the subordinate court of the first class for the Luanshya District, the appellant was convicted of careless driving, failing to render assistance, and failing to report an accident. He was fined a total of K55, and it was ordered that he be disqualified from driving for two years. He appealed against conviction and sentence. The State did not support the conviction and in fact drew the attention of the Court to the case of *Dahl v R.*[171] After consideration of the facts and submissions by both sides, Whelan, J, as he then was, held as follows:

> In view of the fact that the vital issue in this case was one of identity and there was a possibility of mistaken identity because at least two prosecution witnesses had seen accused at the police station shortly before the identification parade, which might have influenced their identification of him, and also the fact that the State did not disclose in evidence to the trial court that there had been an identity parade and the outcome of it, I consider that it would be unsafe to allow this conviction to stand and the appeal against conviction on all three counts is allowed. The convictions are quashed and the fines imposed

[168] Maher G, "Natural Justice as Fairness"; Dworkin RM, "Principle, Policy, Procedure" in C. Tapper (ed.), *Crime Proof and Punishment* (Butterworths, 1981) 193 wherein it is contended that the principles lie not only in the promotion of factually correct decisions but in the fact that what is termed "due process" is a touchstone for the respect of the autonomy of the individual and his rights in the web of adjudicative justice.

[169] See *Wang v Health Professionals Council of Zambia* (2012/HK/339) [2013] ZMHC 24; *Patel v The People* [1969] ZR 132 (HC); *Joseph Knox Simwanza v The People* (1985) ZR 15 (SC); *Kafirsam v The People* [1968] ZR 147 (HC); *Denis Simon Salima Bwalya v The People* [1979] ZR 1 (SC); *Joseph Nkole v The People* [1977] ZR 351 (SC); *Mutale v The People* [1973] ZR 25 (CAZ); s 68(5) of The Health Professions Act No 24, 2009; s 80(5) of The Accountants Act No 13 of 2008, among others; for comparison see RCCJ Report, Ch 10 paras 27-34; Criminal Appeal Act 1995, though no change of substance to the 'miscarriage of justice' concept was intended.

[170] [1968] ZR 98 (HC).

[171] 5 NRLR 159.

in respect of each of them and the order relating to disqualification are set aside.

The importance of the right against wrongful conviction is best demonstrated where a wrongful conviction may result in capital punishment[172] for offences such as aggravated robbery. In *Nkumbula v the people*[173] it was held, among other things, that it is unsafe to uphold a conviction on a charge of armed aggravated robbery where there is no direct evidence of the use of firearms. The appellant's conviction was substituted with aggravated robbery under s 294(1) of the Penal Code.[174]

2.5 The Bill of rights

The relevant parts of article 18[175] provide as follows:

18 (1) If any person is charged with a criminal offence, then, unless the charge is withdrawn, the case shall be afforded a fair hearing within a reasonable time by an independent and impartial court established by law.

(2) Every person who is charged with a criminal offence-

(a) shall be presumed to be innocent until he is proved or has pleaded guilty;

(b) shall be informed as soon as reasonably practicable, in a language that he understands and in detail, of the nature of the offence charged;

(c) shall be given adequate time and facilities for the preparation of his defence;

(d) shall unless legal aid is granted to him in accordance with the law enacted by Parliament for such purpose be permitted to defend himself before the court in person, or at his own expense, by a legal representative of his own choice;

(e) shall be afforded facilities to examine in person or by his legal representative the witnesses called by the prosecution before the court, and to obtain the attendance and carry out the examination of witnesses to testify on his behalf before the court on the same conditions as those applying to witnesses called by the prosecution; and

(f) shall be permitted to have without payment the assistance of an interpreter if he cannot understand

---

[172] For a brief discussion as to whether life imprisonment as provided for under Act No 23 of 2022 is equivalent to capital punishment, see Muskan Bangani, "Life Imprisonment-An Alternative To Capital Punishment" written by Muskaan Bangani of Mody University of Science and Technology, Lakshmangarh, Rajasthan and curated by Naman Jain of Bennett University, Greater Noida https://leggerhythms.org/life-imprisonment-an-alternative-to-capital 25/7/20 punishment/#:~:text=Furthermore%2C%20various%20legal%20researchers%20have%20also%20stated%20 that,such%20criminal%2C%20who%20has%20committed%20a%20barbaric%20crime Retrieved on 04/01/23.

[173] [1983] ZR 103 at 104, applied in the High Court case of *The People v Ackim Manda and Malie Simbeye* [1992] SJ (HC).

[174] Chapter 87 of the Laws of Zambia.

[175] Provisions to secure protection of law.

the language used at the trial of the charge;
and except with his own consent the trial shall not take place in his absence unless he so conducts himself as to render the continuance of the proceedings in his presence impracticable and the court has ordered him to be removed and the trial to proceed in his absence.

(3) When a person is tried for any criminal offence, the accused person or any person authorised by him in that behalf shall, if he so requires and subject to payment of such reasonable fee as may be prescribed by law, be given within a reasonable time after judgment a copy for the use of the accused person of any record of the proceedings made by or on behalf of the court.

(4) A person shall not be held to be guilty of a criminal offence on account of any act or omission that did not, at the time it took place, constitute such an offence, and a penalty shall not be imposed for any criminal offence that is severer in degree or description than the maximum penalty that might have been imposed for that offence at the time it was committed.

(5) A person who shows that he has been tried by a competent court for a criminal offence and either convicted or acquitted shall not again be tried for that offence or for any other criminal offence of which he could have been convicted at the trial for that offence, except upon the order of a superior court in the course of appeal or review proceedings relating to the conviction or acquittal. In *Moses Sachigogo v The People*[176] the accused was tried by the Subordinate Court of the First Class in Kitwe and convicted of two offences: (1) obtaining goods by false pretences and (2) impersonating a public officer. He was sentenced to a total of two years' imprisonment. The appellant appealed to set aside the conviction and sentence on the ground that prior to his conviction by the court below he had been prosecuted before the senior resident magistrate who had acquitted him of the charges. It was found that this plea was taken by the accused in court below and even though there was evidence of his trial before the senior resident magistrate the issue was not properly tried and determined. It was held that the procedure applicable in High Court under s. 249 of the Criminal Procedure Code[177] when autrefois acquit is pleaded is applicable in the subordinate court when the same is pleaded. Failure to observe the procedure renders the proceedings a nullity.

(6) A person shall not be tried for a criminal offence if he shows that he has been pardoned for that offence.

(7) A person who is tried for a criminal offence shall not be compelled to give evidence at the trial.

(8) A person shall not be convicted of a criminal offence unless

[176] [1971] ZR 139 (HC).

[177] Chapter 88 of the Laws of Zambia.

> that offence is defined and the penalty is prescribed in a written law:
>
> Provided that nothing in this clause shall prevent a court of record from punishing any person for contempt of itself notwithstanding that the act or omission constituting the contempt is not defined in a written law and the penalty therefore is not so prescribed.

2.6 The quest for attaining legitimacy of adjudication

Adjudicative decisions must be seen to be and are in facts supposed to be legitimate. This thesis is based on the fact that an adjudicative process that achieves the objectives of dispute resolution and implementation of the law in theory is useless if it is not accepted and respected as authoritative by the parties and public for want of legitimacy. By legitimacy is meant that the decision is not only factually correct but also morally authoritative and expressive of the rule of law. Be that as it may, it is important to realise that the legitimacy of a particular decision will depend on the nature of the dispute concerned. To that end, we will proceed by exploring the concept of legitimacy of decision through the eyes of criminal proceedings and thereafter civil proceedings.

2.6.1 *Criminal proceedings*

Criminal proceedings are primarily concerned with the application of the criminal law. According to Hart,[178] '[t]he aim of making an act criminal is to announce to society that these acts are not to be done and to secure that fewer of them are done.'[179] Further, Wechsler has opined as follows:

> Whatever views one holds about the penal law, no one will question its importance to society. This is the law on which men place their ultimate reliance for protection against all the deepest injuries that human conduct can inflict on individuals and institutions. By the same token, penal law governs the strongest force that we permit official agencies to bring to bear on individuals. Its promise as an instrument of safety is matched only by its power to destroy. Nowhere in the entire legal field is more at stake for the community or the individual.

At the centre of the foregoing is the law's aim to accord to each person not only the freedom to think as they will and speak as they think but to act as they deem fit but at the same time respecting the right of others to have, accorded to them, respect, dignity and autonomy.[180] The foregoing is reflected in the fact that without a blameworthy state of mind, there can be no liability for a criminal offence. This is to say in other words that one's autonomy, or freedom to act as he chooses is not to be infringed upon unless it can be shown that in

---

[178] Hart, HLA, *Punishment and Responsibility* (OUP 1968), 6.

[179] 'Punishment-the chief distinguishing characteristic of the criminal law-involves the imposition of both a legal sanction, such as imprisonment or a fine, and a moral sanction in the form of the stigma of conviction' –Dennis, *The Law of Evidence* 54 citing N. Walker, *Punishment Danger and Stigma* (Blackwell, 1980), Ch 7.

[180] See *Pretty v UK* (2002) 35 EHRR 1 at 65: "the very essence of the [ECHR] is respect for human dignity and human freedom."

so acting, he abused such freedom. It has been argued,[181] following from the foregoing that 'criminal laws should comply with our basic principles of justice such as the harm principle[182] [as noted already] the autonomy principle,[183] the culpability principle,[184] and the equality principle.[185]' It may perhaps be added that by necessary implication, the concept of distributive justice in so far as the criminal law is concerned, should only be applied to those who break the law and are liable, as a consequence, to be penalised.[186]

To achieve the foregoing, it is important that a criminal trial, which by its very nature is the means by which the People (represented by the prosecution) apply the criminal law, be a public one.[187] The insistence on a criminal trial being public is linked to the purpose which the criminal trial serves which, as Hay[188] gaudily shows in discussing the employment of criminal courts in the 18th century, is that as a philosophical podium, it serves as a means of communication with the public by the state. A trial that is not open to public scrutiny and is not freely reportable provides space for the ugliest parts of our nature to come forth. It breeds corruption, conceals incompetence, condones abuses, infringes on the rights of the accused and is unlikely to observe the principle of autonomy and equality before the law. More likely than not, it will render even the court itself hopelessly inadequate to counter the power of the state and the conviction of the accused a foregone conclusion. 'Innocent until proven guilty'[189] as constitutionally guaranteed[190] will become 'guilty until proven innocent,'[191] the burden dangerously shifting to the accused, with no

[181] Baker, DJ, *Glanville Williams Textbook of Criminal Law* (Sweet & Maxwell, 2012); Said dignity and human freedom extends to victims of the offence in question and witnesses to the offence at trial as shown in *Doorson v The Netherlands* [1996] 22 EHRR 330 and *HM Advocates v Murtagh* [2009] UKPC 36.

[182] Baker DJ, "A Critical Evaluation of the Historical and Contemporary Justifications for Criminalizing Begging," (2009) 73(3) *J. Crim. L.* 212.

[183] Schneewind JB, *The Invention of Autonomy*, (CUP, 1998).

[184] Perkin RM, "A Rationale of *Mens Rea*," (1993) 52 *Harvard Law Review* 905.

[185] Blackstone WT, "On the Meaning and Justification of The Equality Principle," (1967) 77(4) *Ethics* 239.

[186] Hart, HLA, *Punishment and Responsibility* (OUP 1968) Ch I and VIII, esp. 8-13, 207-209; Williams G, *Textbook of Criminal Law*, 2nd edn(Steven & Sons, 1983).

[187] See among others, Twinning WL, *Theories of Evidence: Bentham and Wigmore* (1985) Ch. 2; Duff A, *Trials and Punishments* (1986) 148; Pattenden R, *Judicial Discretion and Criminal Litigation* (Clarendon Press, 1990), Ch.5; Duff etal, "Introduction: Towards a Normative Theory of the Criminal Trial" in Duff (eds), *The Trial on Trial* (2004), Vol.1 p 1; Dubber MM, "The Criminal Trial and the Legitimation of Punishment", 85 in Duff (eds), *The Trial on Trial* (2004).

[188] Hay D, "Property, Authority and the Criminal Law" in Hay (eds), *Albion's Fatal Tree* (Pantheon Books, 1975) 28.

[189] Recall that the burden of proof in criminal trials is always on the prosecution: *Woolmington v DPP*[1935] UKHL 1; [1935] AC 462; 25 Cr App R 72; In *Kalaluka Musole v The People* [1963–1964] & NRLR 173 (CA), the CAZ held, *inter alia*, that it is always for the prosecution to prove that the accused actually had the intent necessary to constitute the crime, and that that proof may emerge from evidence or statements made by the accused about his own state of mind or may be made by way of inference from the totality of the circumstances; In *Maseka v The People* [1972] ZR 9 the High Court was of the view that an explanation which might reasonably be true entitles an accused to an acquittal even if the Court does not believe it, and that *an accused is not required to satisfy the Court as to his innocence but simply to raise a reasonable doubt as to his guilt* (emphasis added).

[190] See Article 18(2)(a).

[191] Recall that Article 18(2)(a) of the Constitution provides that '[e]very person who is charged with a criminal offence- shall be presumed to be innocent until he is proved or has pleaded guilty.'

safeguards against self-incrimination.[192] In this way, constitutional norms will be desecrated; justice will be tainted, the dignity of the court offended and the legitimacy of the final outcome deemed highly questionable.

That the prosecution must satisfy the burden placed upon them since the decision in *Woolmington,*[193] a requirement now codified under Article 18(2)(a) of the Constitution has significant consequences for the criminal justice system in general and the evidentiary rules that relate to the criminal trial in particular, cannot be overemphasised. In the event that the accused pleads not guilty, he invites the prosecution as representatives of the people, to prove their case against him. He dares them to satisfy the high burden of proof, i.e., beyond reasonable doubt, and justify their claim not only that an offence has been committed against the people, but also, that the accused committed the offence with which he is charged, and as such, ought to be condemned and consequently punished. In this way, the Zambian common law-based trial serves a justificatory and demonstrative function. The Court is invited to consider the evidence from the prosecution and possibly, from the accused, if at the end of the prosecution's case, the accused is found with a case to answer[194] and elects not to remain silent in accordance with the constitutional injunction under Article 18(7).[195] Following the end of the trial, the court is called upon to render a verdict. It is in the verdict that we see whether 'the factual demonstration has or has not been made out.'[196] Further, as Duff[197] has opined, 'to indict someone for a criminal offence is to offer a particular criticism of his conduct; to try him is to seek to determine the justice of that criticism;

[192] Recall that Article 18(7) of the Constitution provides that '[a] person who is tried for a criminal offence shall not be compelled to give evidence at the trial.'

[193] [1935] UKHL 1; [1935] AC 462; 25 Cr App R 72; *Moonga v The People* [1969] ZR 63.

[194] See s 206 of the Criminal Procedure Code considered in *The People v Japau*[1967] ZR 95; s 291 of the Criminal Procedure Code Chapter 87 of the Laws of Zambia considered in *Mwewa Murono v The People* [2004] ZR 207.

[195] Which must not be held against the accused according to *David Dimuna v The People* [1988 – 1989] ZR 199 (SC); but see arguments by counsel in *L.T. Gen. Geojago Robert Chaswe Musengule, Amon Sibande v The People* HPA /16/2009 that the constitutional right to remain silent was a legal fiction in the light of the provisions of Part VI of the ACC Act No 42 of 1996 (repealed and replaced by Act No 38 of 2010 which itself was repealed and replaced by Act No 3 of 2012) as the Act required a satisfactory explanation from a person charged with an offence under Part IV; Similar provisions were considered in the Corrupt Practices Act, No 10 of 1980 (repealed and replaced by Act No 42 of 1996): *In re Thomas Mumba v The People* [1984] ZR 38; but see rejection of this reasoning which used as its basis the Supreme Court's observation in *Zyambo v The people* [1977] ZR 153 that s 319 of the Penal Code Chapter 87 of the Laws of Zambia does not impose any greater obligation on an accused person than to give an explanation which might reasonably be true, when he has satisfied the Court that the case has not been proved beyond reasonable doubt and has discharged the obligation imposed on him by the section. Similarly, said the Court, s 49(2) of the Anti-Corruption Commission Act No 42 of 1996 required a satisfactory explanation from a person charged with an offence under Part IV of the ACC Act No 42 of 1996 where it was alleged that he/she solicited, accepted or obtained or agreed to accept or attempted to receive or obtain any payment. In the absence of such an explanation, the presumption was that the said payment was solicited, accepted or obtained or agreed to be accepted, or obtained corruptly. The Court therefore found that that s 49(2) under Part IV of the ACC Act No 42 of 1996 which required an explanation from the accused person was not in contravention of Article 18(2) of the Constitution. This reasoning was upheld on appeal in *Lt. General Geojago Robert Musengule and Amon Sibande v The People* [SCZ Selected Judgment No 19 of 2017] and *In re Thomas Mumba v The People* [1984] ZR 38 distinguished which cases are further discussed in chapter 2.

[196] Dennis I, *The Law of Evidence* 53.

[197] Duff A, *Trials and Punishments* (1986) 39.

to convict him is to blame him publicly for that offence.' Thus, where a guilty verdict is handed down, another purpose is served by the criminal trial: it is a moral condemnation of the accused.

Apart from the foregoing, we have to be alive to another function served by a verdict in criminal proceedings. It is the outward demonstration not only of the norms of the criminal law but a communication to the wider public of the constraints that society itself has placed on individual autonomy, of behaviour that is unacceptable, and the consequences of contravening the provisions of the law relating to the kind of behaviour for which the accused was charged, tried and found guilty and for which he must be sentenced, as an example to the rest of society in general and would-be-offenders in particular.

What then is the significance of the preceding perspectives discussed to the aims of the rules of evidence? Irrespective of the decision arrived at or verdict handed down, we cannot escape the fact that such a factual decision is premised on 'the probative value of the evidence' deemed admissible and as such adduced at trial. The factual verdict must also be seen within the context of a moral lense. A guilty verdict leads to a sentence, which is society's chosen method of punishing convicts. It must therefore logically follow that only those for whom the evidence shows are guilty of the offence must be convicted. It would indeed taint justice, offend the dignity of the court and undermine the criminal law if those adjudged to be guilty were not convicted, or where they were convicted, were not punished.[198] It would also weaken society's willingness to accept and respect verdicts handed down as to the accused's guilt when in fact a careful analysis of the evidence ought to logically have led to an acquittal.[199]

However, while a factual guilty verdict may, as discussed above, serve the dual purpose of firstly, expressing society's dim view of the convict's actions, and secondly a condemnatory or moral one, the verdict itself may be flawed.[200] It may, for example, have relied on evidence obtained by torture, a practice that is deemed inhuman and degrading, and itself criminal under national law[201] and international law,[202] to get rather reliable evidence which led to a factually correct decision. In *A v Secretary of State for the Home Department*[203] the House of Lords confirmed the inadmissibility of evidence obtained by torture, as a matter of law. Lord Bingham was categorical, holding that 'the principles of common law, standing alone, compelled the exclusion of evidence obtained by torture by a third party as unreliable, unfair, offensive to ordinary standards of humanity and decency, and incompatible with the principles that should

[198] See Zuckerman AAS, "Illegally Obtained Evidence: Discretion as a Guardian of Legitimacy" [1987] C.L.P. 55, 56.

[199] See *L.T. Gen. Geojago Robert Chaswe Musengule, Amon Sibande v The People* HPA /16/2009 and the cases referred to therein.

[200] Holdsworth W, *A History of English Law* Vol. 5 (3rd edn Methuen 1945) 194-195.

[201] See Article 15 of the Zambian Constitution which provides that '[a] person shall not be subjected to torture, or to inhuman or degrading punishment or other like treatment.'; See *inter alia* Articles 3, 6 of the ECHR.

[202] See for example Articles 3 and 6 of the ECHR.

[203] [2005] UKHL 71 at para. 12; [2005] 3 WLR 1249; [2006] 1 All ER 575, HL.

animate a tribunal seeking to administer justice.'[204] In *Jalloh v Germany*,[205] it was held *inter alia* premised on arts. 3 and 6 of the ECHR that '[i]t cannot be excluded that on the facts of a particular case the use of evidence obtained by intentional acts of ill -treatment not amounting to torture will render the trial against the victim unfair, irrespective of the seriousness of the offence allegedly committed, the weight attached to the evidence and the opportunities which the victim had to challenge its admission and use at his trial.'

There are good and compelling reasons for this binary approach as expressed in the foregoing authorities especially within the context of the criminal law and rules of evidence. As shown in *A v Secretary of State for the Home Department*,[206] and discussed above, were the criminal law to permit for evidence obtained by a flawed process that ignores the autonomy and dignity of the individual, it would fail to convince society that the criminal process, which is predicated on this self-contradictory plane, is capable of expressing values held by society as regards certain acts based on a higher moral ground, when it itself is so fundamentally flawed as to be based on, and driven by, the violation of the very same values it is supposed to exemplify on behalf of society in the condemnation of the convict.[207] To guard against loss of public confidence in the criminal process in general and the criminal law in particular, verdicts must be satisfactory. To do so, the state in general and courts in particular ensure that verdicts veer away from this apparent contradiction by aiming to project not only rules but proof rules by putting both on the same footing.[208] It has been observed thus, that 'serious breaches of due process, serious failures to address the [accused] as a responsible citizen, undermine the legitimacy of the trial as a process that calls citizens to account to answer charges of wrongdoing, and thus also undermine the legitimacy of the verdict as a judgment that is to emerge from such a process.'[209] As has been shown in many criminal trials that have ended in acquittals in the High Court, the investigative process cannot be divorced from the actual trial. Both are two sides of the same coin of the proper administration of justice.[210] Of due process. Baron J's take in the case of *The People v Chrison Mwambona*[211] is illustrative of the preceding. It shows that the determination as to the guilt or lack thereof of the accused will have within it, a discussion of the conduct of the proceedings not only from the commencement of trial, but from the commencement of the investigative process. There in, Baron J, as he then was, observed as follows:

> [...] if certain police officers should conceive their function to be only to secure convictions, they will not achieve their object by the kind of

[204] Uglow S, *Evidence: Text and Materials* 15.

[205] App No 54810/00, 44 Eur HR Rep 32 [2007] para 106.

[206] [2005] UKHL 71 at para. 12; [2005] 3 WLR 1249; [2006] 1 All ER 575, HL.

[207] See Zuckerman AAS, "Illegally Obtained Evidence: Discretion as a Guardian of Legitimacy" 55.

[208] Duff etal, "Introduction: Towards a Normative Theory of the Criminal Trial."

[209] Duff etal, "Introduction: Towards a Normative Theory of the Criminal Trial" 25.

[210] See Zuckerman AAS, "Illegally Obtained Evidence: Discretion as a Guardian of Legitimacy."

[211] [1971] ZR 168 (HC).

> conduct I have seen in this case. Casual and slip-shod investigations, or investigation which ignores lines of inquiry which might exculpate the accused (whether raised by the accused himself or emerging during interviews with other witnesses), far from advancing the prosecution case, can serve only to cast doubt on it and on the bona fides of the officers concerned [...] *it is not the function of the police to secure convictions. Their duty, once an offence is suspected to have been committed, is to investigate the matter as fully as possible and to pursue every line of inquiry which may help to throw light on it, irrespective of whether any particular line appears prejudicial or favourable to the suspect. In short, it is the function of the police to seek out as much evidence as they can and to lay it all before the court* (emphasis added).

Before turning to civil proceedings, it is perchance worth recapitulating a few points. We have noted that rather than factual accuracy of decisions being at the core of adjudication, it is the pursuit of truth that is more important and which in fact fundamental to the adjudicative process and on which a legitimate verdict is handed down. As exemplified in *Wilson Masauso Zulu v Avondale Housing Project Limited,*[212] (a civil case) 'the trial court has a duty to adjudicate upon every aspect of the suit between the parties so that every matter in controversy is determined in finality.[213] A decision which, because of uncertainty or want of finality leaves the doors open for further litigation over the same issues between the same parties can and should be avoided.'[214] To be deemed legitimate, a verdict must be factually accurate and must have been proven, on the evidence on record, beyond reasonable doubt. But as we have seen, a verdict that is factually accurate may still be flawed having been obtained by torture for example and thus lack the moral or expressive authority required and expected of a verdict and lead to illegitimacy and lack of acceptance by the parties and the larger public.

2.6.2 *Civil proceedings*

There are, as has been demonstrated in this text thus far, several differences between the civil process and the criminal process discussed above. Unlike the criminal process, the civil process does not have as its core aim, castigation or culpability for the party found liable for breach of contract or for a tort for example. It follows that the fundamental aim of the civil process is redress. For example, the grant of damages in a breach of contract verdict is to bring the innocent party to the position he would have been in had the breach not been committed. So is the goal of a favourable decision in a tort process. It is meant

[212] [1982] ZR 175.

[213] *Zambia Telecommunications Company Ltd (Zamtel) v Aaron Mweene Mulwanda and Paul Ngandwe* (SCZ Judgment No 7 of 2012).

[214] See similar principle albeit in a criminal context, in Jackson JD, "Managing Uncertainty and Finality: The function of the Criminal Trial in Legal Inquiry" in Duff (eds), *The Trial on Trial* (2004), Vol. 1, 121 wherein truth-finding, the rules of court and those of evidence are explained within the context of finality of decision.

to bring the victim of the tort, at least so far as money can, to the position he would have been in, had the tort not been committed. The aim then, unlike that in the criminal process, is neither justificatory nor meant to be a behavioural guide for the parties, even though it may be, at some level be argued that this is what is achieved as a precedent set in one case by a superior court will be used in similar cases in future. The principal concerns of the civil process may include, but are not limited, to the following:[215]

(i) Defining rights and obligations;
(ii) The implementation of rights and obligations;
(iii) Defining questions of status;
(iv) Determining capacity;
(v) Assigning risk etc.

The foregoing may be said to be premised on the following core concerns:[216]

(i) Redressing grievances;
(ii) Conferring benefits;
(iii) Lawful activity regulation; and
(iv) Effecting private arrangements.

It is in the civil process, within the context of procedural and evidentiary rules, that we see the confluence of the effect of social, economic and political considerations nay the ubiquitous question of individual autonomy, fundamental freedoms and the essence of self-determination for all juristic and non-juristic persons on the determination of disputes.[217] For that reason, the Supreme Court has given the following guidance as regards what sort of judgments the lower courts must render in *Sun Country Limited and Others v Savory and Another*:[218]

> 1. Every judgment must reveal a review of the evidence, where applicable, a summary of the arguments and submissions, if made, findings of fact, the reasoning of the court on the facts and the application of the law and authorities, if any, to the facts. Finally, a judgment must show the conclusion. A judgment which only contains verbatim reproduction and recitals is no judgment. In addition, a court should not feel compelled or obliged and moved by any decided cases without giving reasons for accepting those authorities. In other words, a court must reveal its mind to the evidence before it and not just simply accept any decided case. The learned trial Judge revealed his reasoning when he found from the evidence that was before him, that the relationship between

[215] Dworkin RM, *Law's Empire* (1986), Ch 8; See also Stein and Shand, Legal Values (1974), Chs 5 and 6; Genn H, *Judging Civil Justice* (CUP, 2010) Ch 1.

[216] Summers R and Howard C, *Law, its Nature, Function and Limits* 2nd edn (1972).

[217] Dworkin RM, Law's Empire (1986), Ch 8. See also Stein and Shand, Legal Values (1974), Chs 5 and 6; Genn H, *Judging Civil Justice* (CUP, 2010) Ch 1.

[218] (Appeal No 122/2006) [2017] ZMSC 81 (9 August 2017).

the parties had broken irretrievably because they had lost trust and confidence in each other and could not work together. It was from this evidence that the trial Judge deduced that it was just and equitable to wind up the Company.[219]

2. A judgment should be thorough, exhaustive, and clear on issues. There are seven essential elements of a judgment, namely: an introductory structure, setting forth the nature of the case and identifying the parties; the facts; the law relevant to the issues; the application of the law to the facts; the remedy; and the order.[220]

It must be added that, as we have already pointed out above, the civil process does not have as its goal, the punishment and/or condemnation of the 'guilty' party. Thus, a judgment in a civil case will stand upon the exhaustion of the appeal process if it is factually correct unless it can be shown that a judgment was procured by fraud as was the case in *Jonathan Van Blerk v Attorney General, Lusaka City Council, Legacy Holdings Limited & 3 others*[221] or under such exceptional circumstances as leave the court with no option but to reopen the case in question.

It is therefore worth repeating at this juncture that as was said in *Wilson Masauso Zulu v Avondale Housing Project Limited*,[222] 'the trial court has a duty to adjudicate upon every aspect of the suit between the parties so that every matter in controversy is determined [with] finality.' Ensuring that every matter in controversy is determined with finality may also entail, as shown in *The Attorney General v Aboubacar Tall and Zambia Airways Corporation Ltd*,[223] a court in a proper case, joining another party to the proceedings when both the plaintiff and the defendant have closed their cases and before judgment has been delivered by invoking order 14 r 5, HCR.[224] It therefore becomes apparent that the restoration of equipoise and congruence between disputants on the one hand and the application of state policy through the device of the civil law on the other, are front and centre of the aims of the civil process.[225] It is therefore quite difficult to see how the goal of truth finding which, as highlighted in this text, is quite limited given that the parties will only present to court that which is favourable to their case, can be of prime importance.

---

[219] *Minister of Home Affairs, Attorney General v Lee Habasonda* [2007] ZR 207 followed.

[220] *Zambia Telecommunications Company Limited v Aaron Mulwanda and Paul Ngandwe* [2012] 1 ZR 405 followed.

[221] SCZ/8/03/2020: The Supreme Court held that the concept of finality of litigation envisaged in s 14(1) of the Lands Acquisition Act Chapter 189 of the Laws of Zambia could not override a challenge on a claim of fraud as a means to vitiate a judgment obtained under the said section because fraud unravels all without exception.

[222] [1982] ZR 175.

[223] (SCZ Appeal No 77 of 1994).

[224] See *Hotelier Limited Ody's Works Limited v Finsbury Investments Limited* 2011/HP/260 where Order 14 r 5 HCR and Order 15 of the Rules of the Supreme Court, 1965, the White Book (1999) edition (The White Book) where considered; s 13 of the High Court Act, Chapter 27 of the laws of Zambia which together Order 14 r 5 HCR and Order 15 RSC, according to the Court in *Aboubacar Tall*, are intended to avoid a multiplicity of actions.

[225] Dennis I, *The Law of Evidence*; Weinstein J, "Some Difficulties in Devising Rules for Determining Truth in Judicial Trials" (1966) 66 Col. L.R. 223, 241 onwards.

Courts have to be resigned to the fact that as observed in *Air Canada v Secretary of State for Trade*,[226] '[i]t often happens, from the imperfection of evidence, or the withholding of it, sometimes by the party in whose favour it would tell if presented, that an adjudication has to be made which is not, and is known not to be, the whole truth of the matter; yet, if the decision has been in accordance with the available evidence and with the law, justice will have been fairly done.'[227] It is therefore the case that common law courts in general and Zambian courts in particular, do not actively seek to find out any matters which, if they were, would lead to the finding of the ultimate truth even when the means to do so are available. They confine themselves to the evidence presented by the parties. This is premised on the theory that the public interest only demands the fair adjudication and settlement of the dispute in question. It is this fair adjudication and fair settlement of disputes based solely on the evidence presented to the court by the disputants/parties that lends legitimacy to any decision rendered by the court in question.

[226] [1983] 2 AC 394.

[227] *Per* Lord Wilberforce at 438.

3

THE BURDEN AND STANDARD OF PROOF

1.1 Introduction

The adversarial system of adjudication means that disputes are and will, when they arise, be by necessary implication, resolved through the device of the contested trial. Accordingly, whether the nature of the contested trial is civil or criminal, there will, at the very least, be present in the contest, one issue of fact that the contending parties will see differently and which ought to be decided by the court. In civil cases for example, the mere fact that the plaintiff raises issues of fact in his statement of claim[1] does not stop the defendant from raising a counter claim quite apart from a defence to the plaintiff's own claims. It follows that under such circumstances, both the statement of claim and the counter claim will be determined as part of the same proceedings. The title of this chapter behooves us to discuss the following general questions:

- (i) What is proof?
- (ii) What is the burden of proof?
- (iii) Who bears the burden of proof which is to say who bears the burden of adducing evidence to prove the issue(s) in question?
- (iv) What is the standard of proof?
- (v) What standard of proof is expected and required to determine the sufficiency of evidence in so far as the threshold to discharge the burden of proof is concerned?

At the end of this chapter we should be in a position to appreciate which party, in either civil or criminal proceedings, has the obligation to prove facts in issue and why. As regards criminal proceedings, we must be able to explain why, in instances where a party bears the burden of proving a fact or set of facts in issue, a court ought to and does require that such a party puts forward appropriate evidence to create a *prima facie* case. Further to the foregoing, we should be in a position to show the extent or degree to which the party who bears the burden of proving a fact or set of facts in issue must persuade the court before it can regard that fact or set of facts to have been proved legally under the following scenarios:

- (a) Criminal proceedings:
  - (i) Where the prosecution is party called upon to prove a fact or a set of facts in issue; and

[1] Which by procedure always accompanies a Writ of Summons.

(ii) Where the accused is such a party and is relying on that fact or set of facts in his defence

(b) Civil proceedings:

(i) Where the party in question is a party in civil proceedings.

3.2 The evidential concept of proof

To speak of proof is to, in everyday ordinary life, ask for substantiation of any claim by whatever name called or however described conceived by the mind of man and contrived by his heart. The demand for proof in a legal sense at least is therefore quite simply a demand for evidence for an assertion made. Quite apart from assisting those that demand for proof for an assertion made to come to a decision based on the evidence provided, once the correctness of an assertion is demonstrated and/or the information or evidence provided deemed sufficient, proof can be said '[...] to establish a fact [or its refutation or to produce belief [or the lack thereof] in the certainty of something [....][2] in the mind of a fact-finder. For a lawyer, it is evidence that determines the Ruling or Judgment of the Court. It has been noted that,

> In a court, the range of assertions that can be made is wide – from a simple factual issue of identification of a criminal to the proper interpretation of a contractual term to a qualitative judgment as to what may be in the best interests of a child. The court needs to reach an authoritative determination of each of these issues, establishing the truth.[3]

The premise of the judicial process which must be viewed as inclusive of the pre-trial stage of investigation in the criminal law by the police or other investigative agencies[4] for example and trial proper, is society's fervent belief that through the employment of the rules of evidence and a rational application of decision techniques born of everyday human experience once weaved into human ability to recreate the past, predicated on a judge's training and wisdom, it is possible "to hold for true or real with assurance and on (what is held to be) an adequate objective foundation" in a lexical sense at least. Regardless, and as admirable as these aims are, the idea that through permitted legal procedure and the careful and correct employment of rules of evidence a court can, as it were, reconstruct the past and thereby determine what transpired including the circumstances the event in question occurred in at a certain time and location is one which is, as we saw in chapter two, fraught with intractable difficulties. Uglow[5] identifies two difficulties. We discuss them below seriatim:

The first difficulty is what he refers to as 'the realistic point.'[6] According to him courts are presided over by magistrates or judges who employ practical reasoning to the craft of the legal process. Judges and magistrates therefore realise that their time for acquiring information is very limited indeed. One can hardly argue against this proposition. By way of illustration, the Judiciary 2020

Annual Report[7] gives the following statistics in case load by court:[8]

3.2.1 *The Small Claims Court*

The Small Claims Court had 1,606 cases that were brought forward from 2019, 3,077 cases were filed in the year under review and 3,130 cases were disposed of leaving 1,553 cases pending at the end of 2020.

3.2.2 *The Local Courts*

The Local courts had 31,557 civil cases that were brought forward from 2019. 134,260 cases were filed, 120,268 cases were disposed of and 45,549 cases were pending at the end of 2020.

3.2.3 *The Subordinate Courts*

Criminal and Civil Cases During the period under review, the Subordinate Courts received a total of 37,685 cases; 24,909 of the cases were criminal cases and 12,776 were civil cases. A total of 12,797 criminal cases and 10,957 civil cases were brought forward from 2019; bringing the total number of cases that were before the Courts to 61,439. The Courts disposed of 24,929 criminal cases and 12,352 civil cases. 12,777 criminal cases and 11,381 civil cases were pending at the end of 2020.

3.2.4 *The High Court*

3.2.4.1 *Criminal Cases*

During the year under review, the High Court had a total number of 4,410 criminal cases out of which 1,790 were brought forward from the previous year and 2,620 were filed in the year under review. The court disposed of a total of 2,317 cases leaving 2,093 criminal cases pending at the end of the year.

3.2.4.2 *Civil Cases*

A total of 6,579 civil cases were brought forward from 2019 across all divisions of the High Court. 5,317 cases were filed in 2020 out of which 3,248 were filed at the General List, 1,048 at the Commercial Court Division and 1,021 at the Industrial Relations Division. The Court disposed of a total of 6,770 cases: 5,245, 895 and 630 at the General List, Commercial Division and Industrial Relations Division, respectively. A total of 5,126 civil cases were pending at the end of 2020.

3.2.5 *The Court of Appeal*

[7] At the time of writing, the 2021 Report had not been presented to the National Assembly and as such, was unavailable for use. It would seem however that very little has changed.

[8] Excerpted from Judiciary 2020 Annual Report at 11 – 16. The structure in this text starts with the lowest court and ends with the Highest Courts as opposed to the report which starts with the Highest courts and ends with the lowest courts.

The Court of Appeal had 10 gazetted sessions, out of which 9 were conducted. Only 1 was not held due to the COVID-19 pandemic. In terms of the Court's case load, 396 were brought forward from 2019, of which 320 were civil and 76 criminal. The cases filed in 2020 were 478; that is 275 civil and 203 criminal. The total number of cases before the Court of Appeal in the year under review was 874. The Court disposed of 90 civil cases and 69 criminal cases, totalling 159 cases disposed of. Pending at the end of 2020 were 505 civil cases and 210 criminal cases, bringing the total number pending to 715.

3.2.6 *The Constitutional Court*

The Court had a total of 43 cases, 18 of which were brought forward from 2019 while 25 were filed in 2020. The number of cases disposed of was 22, and a balance of 21 cases was recorded at the end of 2020.

3.2.7 *The Supreme Court*

There was a total of 298 criminal cases before the Court, 87 of which were brought forward from 2019 while 211 were filed in the year 2020 itself. Of the 298 criminal cases, the Court disposed of 210, leaving a balance of 88 cases at the end of the year in question. In terms of civil cases, 58 were brought forward from 2019 while 15 were filed during the year under review, bringing the total number of civil cases before the Court to 73. Out of that number, 72 cases were disposed of, and 1 case was pending at the close of 2020.

3.2.8 *A practical approach*

A practical approach therefore compels courts to focus not on issues on the periphery which in any case may wind up confusing the court and waste its time, but on core issues that need to be determined which entails only calling for evidence on those issues only and deciding one way or the other within the context of the best evidence before them, even when such evidence is not all the evidence available nor the ultimate truth.[9] The court focuses on the issues that it needs to decide, listens only to relevant data about those issues and settles on the " best truth " even if that truth is not perfect due to constraints brought about by the adversarial system of adjudication practiced in this jurisdiction. As noted earlier from Lord Wilberforce in *Air Canada v Secretary of State for Trade,*[10] '[i]t often happens, from the imperfection of evidence, or the withholding of it, sometimes by the party in whose favour it would tell if presented, that an adjudication has to be made which is not, and is known not to be, the whole truth of the matter.' One ought to remember that it is not an exact science. Lawyers and judges alike can therefore only dream, and it is a pipeline dream, of a day when the legal process will stand toe to toe with pure science in terms of certitude as regards standards of enquiry and empirical evidence. Between now and then (if that day ever comes), lawyers and courts can only hope to

[10] [1983] 2 AC 394 at 438.

do their best in the circumstances. Even so, which must be said with a dash of frustration, 'moral certainty does not compare with scientific certainty.'[11]

A second challenge that Uglow[12] identifies relates to what he terms '[...] a philosophical issue about the possibility of knowing with certainty what happened and how people acted.' As opposed to the certitude that science and mathematics offer through formulae, extrapolations, and hypotheses, he charges that 'the inferential, common-sense logic of the courtroom requires that we must test, as best we can, the strength and validity of our assumptions and the interferences that are drawn from them.' Following from this we are then left to ask as Uglow[13] does, how strong the inference must be for it to be regarded as correct, and further, how confident we must be in the conclusions we draw from the lack of certainty in a scientific sense brought about, as expressed by Lord Wilberforce in *Air Canada v Secretary of State for Trade,*[14] by constraints to proof because of the nature of our adversarial system of trial wherein the litigants themselves are responsible for producing the proof and the quality of the proof upon which the Court will determine the case at hand, a position supported byLord Denning in his dictum in *Jones v National Coal Board.*[15] He discoursed that '[a] judge is not allowed in a civil dispute to call a witness whom he thinks might throw light on the facts. He must rest content with the witnesses called by the parties.'[16]

The neutral judge in an adversarial trial is subjected to conflicting versions relating to the same matter by the plaintiff/defendant or prosecution/defence. He it is that must turn what may be termed the probable into the possible. He alone must determine the case before him. He alone must give a verdict, that is, in civil matters, a finding for one party; and in criminal cases, a verdict of guilty or not guilty, as the case may be. To return to our themes already discussed in chapter 2 of this text, for there to be rectitude/correctness of decision, it is necessary for facts to be 'determined through the accurate evaluation of relevant and reliable evidence by a competent and impartial adjudicator applying the specified burden and standard of proof.'[17]

More important, the trial must be presided over by '[...] a fair and impartial [judge], *ex vi termini* ("by definition"), a [judge] free from bias or prejudice, and, above all, from coercion and intimidation.'[18] It logically follows then that in order for the aims of adjudication to be achieved, the adjudicator must have, available to him, evidence that is not only relevant but reliable. The evidence must be the kind that is presented in a style that will enable the adjudicator to discover the truth through the unflappable application of rules of evidence and

[11] Uglow S, *Evidence: Text and Materials*76.

[12] Uglow S, *Evidence: Text and Materials* 76.

[13] Uglow S, *Evidence: Text and Materials.*

[14] [1983] 2 AC 394 at 438.

[15] [1975] 2 All E R 155.

[16] Quoted by counsel in *Priscillar Mwenya Kamanga v Attorney-General, Peter N'gandu Magande* [2008] 2 ZR 7 (SC).

[17] Dennis I, *The Law of Evidence* 29.

[18] *Weems et al. v. State*, Id., at 214 *per* John C. Anderson CJ.

other procedural rules that *inter alia,* clearly set out the burdens and standards of proof. Only through these means can an adjudicator conceive of and deliver a rational, well-reasoned judgment.[19] The court must therefore direct its mind to the resolution and characterisation of what is fanciful and fictitious on the one hand and what is factual and demonstrable on the other.[20] It therefore follows that '[t]he mere production of evidence is not proof and at the end of a trial, the trier of fact must decide whether the facts in issue have been satisfactorily established.'

This, as may be apparent from the preceding, encompasses a two-stage process (which we will delve into further still below) predicated on cognitive perception.

3.3 Burden and standard of proof

3.3.1 General observations

3.3.1.1 Burden of proof

The term burden of proof, which is also known as "the onus of proof" is drawn from the basic general proposition that in legal proceedings, 'he who asserts must prove.' It follows that a party who/which makes a positive assertion must prove that assertion. It is not for the defendant/accused to disprove the positive assertion. It has been observed in by Baron JP *Maseka*[21] that:

> An explanation which might reasonably be true entitles an accused to an acquittal even if the court does not believe it; an accused is not required to satisfy the court as to his innocence, but simply to raise a reasonable doubt as to his guilt. A fortiori, such a doubt is present if there exists an explanation which might reasonably be true; for the court to be in doubt does not imply a belief in the honesty generally of the accused nor in the truth of the particular explanation in question. An accused who is shown to have told untruths in material respects is in no different position from any other witness; the weight to be attached to the remainder of his evidence is reduced, but it is not rendered worthless.

The observations of Ngulube DCJ as he then was, in the case of *Mohamed v the Attorney General*[22] are pertinent:

> An unqualified proposition that a plaintiff should succeed automatically whenever a defence has failed is unacceptable to me. A plaintiff must prove his case and if he fails to do so, the mere failure of

[19] See *Samuel Sooli v The People* [1981] ZR 298; *Stephen Manda v The People* [1980] ZR 116; by way of illustration, in in the case of *Ticky v The People* [1968] ZR 21,it was held that it is the magistrate's duty to consider in his judgment each defence made and it must be evident from his judgment that he did so.

[20] Mansell W, Meteyard B and Thompson A, *A Critical Introduction to Law* (3rd edn Cavendish, 2004).

[21] 1972 ZR 9 at 13.

[22] [1982] ZR 49.

> the opponent's defence does not entitle him to judgment. I would not accept the proposition that even if a plaintiff's case has collapsed of its inanition or for some reason or other, judgment should nevertheless be given to him on the ground that [a] defence set up by the opponent has also collapsed. Quite clearly a defendant in such circumstances would not even need a defence.

In other words, and in a general sense, it behooves the party who puts into motion the legal mechanism to resolve a legal matter to validate the accuracy of any avowals by satisfying the factfinder that the assertions in question are true. From the foregoing is drawn the refrain that in civil actions, the plaintiff bears the burden of proof while in criminal cases, the prosecution bears such a burden. The position as regards the burden of proof in criminal cases is a constitutional one. Article 18(2)(a) provides that '[e]very person who is charged with a criminal offence - shall be presumed to be innocent until he is proved or has pleaded guilty.' The presumption of innocence cannot be derogated from and must be automatically assumed. Therefore, even where an accused person is charged with the offence of murder contrary to s 200[23] of the Penal Code,[24] a non-bailable offence that carries, in the absence of extenuating circumstances,[25] a life sentence,[26] he must be presumed innocent 'until he is proved or has pleaded guilty.' Before going further in this discussion, it is perchance vital that we refer to Article 18(7) of the Constitution which provides that '[n]o person who is tried for a criminal offence shall be compelled to give evidence at the trial.' The significance of this constitutional injunction is that it elevates the common law position described in *Woolmington*[27] to a fundamental right. Thus,

> [...] it is the duty of the prosecution to prove the [accused's] guilt subject to [...] the defence of insanity and subject also to any statutory exception.[28] If, at the end of and on the whole of the case, there is a reasonable doubt, created by the evidence given by either the prosecution or the prisoner... the prosecution has not made out the case and the prisoner is entitled to an acquittal. No matter what the charge or where the trial, the principle that the prosecution must prove the guilt of the [accused] is part of [Zambian law] and no attempt to

[23] Section 200 of the Penal Code Chapter 87 of the Laws of Zambia provides as follows: 'Any person who of malice aforethought causes the death of another person by an unlawful act or omission is guilty of murder.'

[24] Chapter 87 of the Laws of Zambia.

[25] See for example, the recent case of *Abedinegal Kipeshi and Best Kayakula v The People* [Selected Judgment No 35 of 2017] (the *Kikondo* case) which appended the law as expressed in previous cases as regards extenuating circumstances in the case of homicide because of suspicion of witchcraft.

[26] According to 201(1) as amended by s 14 of Act No 23 of 2022, (1) A person convicted of murder shall be sentenced to life imprisonment or, where there are extenuating circumstances, a sentence other than life imprisonment.; (b) insertion of the following new subsection immediately after subsection (1): (2) An extenuating circumstance referred to under subsection (1) shall not apply to murder committed in the course of aggravated robbery with a firearm under section 294.; and (c) renumbering of subsection (2) as subsection (3).

[27] [1935] AC 462.

[28] These exceptions are discussed below.

> whittle it down can be entertained.[29]

Therefore, the prosecution will have to show not only that a murder has been committed but that the accused did 'of malice aforethought [cause] the death of [the victim] by an unlawful act or omission' and not somebody else or that some other event caused the victim's death. This has been demonstrated in the recent decision in *Makas Mazuba v The People*[30] where the Supreme Court stated the following: '[w]e have time and again stressed that the quality of evidence that the prosecution adduces at trial, invariably determines whether the burden of proof which is incumbent upon the prosecution to prove the accused guilty beyond reasonable doubt, has been discharged.' In this sense, the prosecution is said to bear the legal burden of proof to prove all the elements of the charge as set out in the law. We can illustrate this using the offence of aggravated robbery. Section 294(1) of the Penal Code[31] provides as follows:

> Any person who, being armed with any offensive weapon or instrument, or being together with one person or more, steals anything, and, or immediately after the time of stealing it, uses or threatens to use actual violence to any person or property to obtain or retain the thing stolen or to prevent or overcome resistance to its being stolen or retained, is guilty of the felony of aggravated robbery [....]

The Supreme Court has thus guided in *The People v Chimbala,*[32] that '[i]t is necessary, under a charge of aggravated robbery, to prove that the taking and force used or threatened contemporaneously with the taking, was accompanied by an intent to deprive the owner permanently of the thing taken.' Further, in *Mugala v The People*[33] it was held that in a case of aggravated robbery '[i]t is necessary for the prosecution to show that the violence was used in order to obtain or retain the thing stolen.' In this and other criminal proceedings the importance of the presumption of innocence is such that in circumstances where, as in *Mushemi Mushemi v The People,*[34] there is conflicting evidence, the court will have to show why it believes one witness over another. The applicant was convicted on two counts of producing a document false in a material particular contrary to s 6 of the Exchange Control Act: the falsity alleged being the representation that he would be a member of the presidential delegation to the Far East and further a representation that the members of the Central Committee and other officials would require a group imprest. In deciding the case, the learned magistrate refused to admit certain defence evidence and, in a judgment, glossing over the evidence he discounted the testimony of several

---

[29] [1935] AC 462 at 481.

[30] SCZ Appeal No 116/2021 at J29.

[31] Chapter 87 of the Laws of Zambia.

[32] [1973] ZR 118.

[33] [1975] ZR 282.

[34] [1982] ZR 71 (SC).

prosecution and defence witnesses reducing the issue to one of credibility of the applicant. On an application for leave to appeal. It was held as follows: (i) [a] conviction which is based on finding of fact which is in direct conflict with the overwhelming balance of the evidence, that evidence having been glossed over, cannot be upheld. (ii) [t]he credibility of a witness cannot be assessed in isolation from the rest of the witnesses whose evidence is in substantial conflict with that of the witness. The judgment of the trial court faced with such conflicting evidence should show on the face of it why a witness who has been seriously contradicted by others is believed in preference to those others.

It has been held in *Dorothy Mutale and Richard Phiri v The People,*[35] that where two or more inferences are possible [...] the court will adopt the one that is more favourable or less favourable to an accused if there is nothing to exclude that inference. Where there are lingering doubts, the court is required to resolve such doubts in favour of the accused. Thus, in *Saluwema v The People*[36] it was held that '[i]f the accused's case is 'reasonably possible' although not probable, then a reasonable doubt exists, and the prosecution cannot be said to have discharged its burden of proof.'

Commenting on why the presumption is a cornerstone of the criminal trial, Fitzjames Stephen,[37] observes as follows:

> If it be asked why an accused person is presumed to be innocent, I think the true answer is, not that the presumption is probably true, but that society in the present day is so much stronger than the individual, and is capable of inflicting so very much more harm on the individual than the individual as a rule can inflict upon society, that it can afford to be generous. It is, however, a question of degree, varying according to time and place, how far this generosity can or ought to be carried [....]

An important point to consider, the foregoing notwithstanding, is the fact that the need to discharge the burden of proof is removed where the accused person pleads guilty to the charge he is facing. Even so, it behooves the court to ensure not only that the accused committed the offence to which he is pleading guilty but also that the accused person appreciates each and every ingredient of the crime and the consequences of making such a plea. A failure to do so renders the

[35] [1997] SJ 51 (SC); see *Wanausi v The People* [1976] ZR 103.

[36] [1965] ZR 4 (CA).

[37] Fitzjames Stephen, *History of the Criminal Law*, Vol. 1 354.

plea in question invalid.[38] In *The People v John Kapalu Kanguya,*[39] the accused was charged with driving a motor vehicle whilst under the influence of intoxicating liquor or drugs contrary to s 198 of the Roads and Road Traffic Act.[40] When being charged he said "I understand the charge, I plead guilty", thereafter the court recorded a plea of guilty. The facts were read out and he admitted them to be correct. He was sentenced to six months' imprisonment with hard labour and fined K10. The sentence was suspended for twelve months. It was held *inter alia*: (i) The plea was equivocal, the accused being unrepresented, the magistrate before accepting a plea of guilty should have satisfied himself that the accused admitted each and every ingredient of the offence with which he was charged; and (ii) Admitting the facts does not validate an equivocal or imperfect plea.

To ensure that this is the case, the court ought to engage the accused through a series of questions, and ought to satisfy itself that the guilty plea is unequivocal.[41]

What options does the court which finds itself in a scenario where the charge or information as framed appears to be at variance with the evidence and as such unable to assist the court in properly adjudicating on the case, but after an accused person has already taken plea? This issue arose in the *cause célèbre Shamwana and 7 Others v People,*[42] where it was observed that under such circumstances, the court, under s 273 of the Criminal Procedure Code,[43] has power to amend of its own motion the particulars of an overt act in line with the evidence given. To properly do so, however, the amendment must not alter the substance of the allegation but merely correct such things as a misdescription. Where such an amendment is made and an adjournment offered to enable the prosecution to recall witnesses, no injustice can be said to have been made.

Similarly, in civil cases, the plaintiff is put to strict proof. If for example the claim is premised on negligence by the defendant which matters will usually

---

[38] *Like Silishebo v The People* (SCZ Appeal No 24 of 1981).

[39] [1979] ZR 288 (HC); see also *Chipendeka v The People* [1969] ZR 82 (HC); *Ezara Moyo v The People* [1981] ZR 173 (SC); *Gift Mulonda v The People* [2004] ZR 135 (SC); *The People v Mwaiba Kakuya* [1990] SJ (HC); as to consequences on appeal of unequivocal or otherwise non-existent or defective guilty pleas, see Boniface Chanda Chola, *Christopher Nyamande and Nelson Sichula v The People* [1988 – 1989] ZR 163 (SC); As to the court's discretion to permit the accused to change his plea at any time before sentence is passed, see *Tito Manyika Tepula v The People* [1981] ZR 304 (SC): A trial judge has a discretion to allow an accused person to retract his plea of guilty at any time before sentence is passed on him; *Gideon Hammond Millard v The People* [1998] SJ 34 (SC); as to what may be good and sufficient grounds allowing the court to exercise such a discretion see *R v Durham Quarter Sessions, Ex p Virgo* [1952] All ER 466; *R v Cole* (1965) 2 QB 388; As to the positives of a guilty plea see *Moses Mwiba v The People* [1971] ZR 131: It's a sign of contrition; *William v The People* [1972] ZR 5 (HC): Saves the court time; *Benua v The People* [1976] ZR 13 (SC): [a] plea of guilty must be taken into account in considering a sentence unless there are circumstances such as a man being caught red-handed when he has no alternative. Failure to take into account a plea of guilty is an error in principle; *Michael Coetzee v The People* [1995] SJ (SC): it is mitigatory in so far as sentencing is concerned; as to the obligation of the court when a plea of not guilty is entered, see on appeal, *Noah Kambobe v The People* (SCZ Judgment No 13 of 2002): a sentence of thirty-two years imprisonment and formula adopted was not only wrong in principle but also produced a truly shocking sentence, and this, after a guilty plea to a charge of manslaughter.

[40] Chapter 766 repealed by the Road Traffic Act No 11 of 2002.

[41] *The People v John Kapalu Kanguya* [1979] ZR 288 (HC).

[42] [1985] ZR 41.

[43] Chapter 88 of the Laws of Zambia.

have been set out in a writ and statement of claim and related mandatory case commencement documentation filed into court, the plaintiff will be required to prove not only that the defendant in *casu* had a duty of care[44] towards him, but that the defendant also caused the material injuries forming the basis of the suit in breach of that duty.

While the foregoing explanation may seem to imply a very simple scenario to the issue of the burden of proof, the reality is that the legal process irrespective of nature, that is whether it be criminal or civil, is rarely confronted with just one single simple issue. We must therefore point out even at this early stage that the concept of the burden of proof as it relates to a specific issue need not be and is not automatically on the plaintiff or the prosecution. Returning to the example of a murder charge, at trial the accused might raise one, two or several defences against the charge including self-defence, provocation, *alibi* (for which he bears no legal burden to prove but only a duty to adduce sufficient evidence to raise each particular defence) and/or diminished responsibility. In the case of diminished responsibility, the burden of proof will lie, not with the prosecution, but the accused who raises the positive assertion. Similarly, in civil matters, such as ones relating to negligence as alluded to in the preceding paragraph, the defendant may, as part of his defence, assert that the plaintiff was contributorily negligent. Here again, the burden of proof is on the defendant to prove his assertion of contributory negligence and not for the plaintiff to disprove it. The preceding leave us with the next question which is what standard must be met in terms of proof for a court to convict in a criminal matter or decide for one party in a civil one, as the case may be?

3.3.1.2 Standard of proof

The term standard of proof also referred to as the "quantum of proof" relates to '[...] the level of certainty and the degree of evidence necessary to establish proof in a criminal or civil proceeding.[45] It ought to be remembered therefore that 'what is provable must be expressed in terms of what is probable. In a criminal trial when an individual's liberty is at stake, proof of guilt requires that a [judge] is "sure " or "is satisfied" beyond reasonable doubt'[46] which is why the standard of proof must be beyond reasonable doubt. The standard of proof in civil matters is a tard lower and less rigorous. It is on a "balance

[44] The neighbour principle elucidated in *Donoghue v Stevenson* [1932] UKHL 100, a House of Lord's momentous decision relating to Scots delict law and English tort law which became the basis for the modern law of negligence, establishing general principles of the duty of care. Lord Atkin's neighbour principle, that people must take reasonable care not to injure others who could foreseeably be affected by their action or inaction, was a response to a question a lawyer posed: Castle R, "Lord Atkin and the neighbour test: origins of the principles of negligence in *Donoghue v Stevenson*". *Ecclesiastical Law Journal*. **7** (33): 210 214. doi:10.1017/s0956618x00005214. The genesis of the principle in relation to law is attributable to Buller, F (1817) [1768], *An Introduction to the Law relative to Trials at Nisi Prius. R Pheney and S Sweet. p. 24b.* cited in *Castle, Richard (2003). "Lord Atkin and the neighbour test: origins of the principles of negligence in Donoghue v Stevenson." Ecclesiastical Law Journal.* 7 *(33): 210–214.* doi:10.1017/s0956618x00005214 in the following terms: "Of Injuries arising from Negligence or Folly. Every man ought to take reasonable care that he does not injure his neighbour; therefore, wherever a man receives any hurt through the default of another, though the same were not wilful, yet if it be occasioned by negligence or folly, the law gives him an action to recover damages for the injury so sustained."

[45] https://www.merriam-webster.com/legal/standard%20of%20proof retrieved on 18/12/22.

[46] Uglow S, *Evidence: Text and Materials* 51.

of probabilities" or a preponderance of probabilities.[47] Being cognisant of the fact that law is not an exact science, judges must so far as is practicable, steer clear of attaching scientific or mathematical precision to express the concept of standard of proof.

Eggleston,[48] has expressed his view of what the concept of standard of proof means in the following terms:

> The word 'probable,' from which the term 'probability' is derived, originally meant ' provable ' or 'capable of being tested'. In the course of time, however, it acquired the secondary meaning of 'likely to happen,' so that when we speak of an event as being ' probable ', we mean that we think the chances of its happening are at least better than even. We also mean that it is less than certain [....]
>
> While we ordinarily use the term 'probability theory 'as if it were a single thing, there are in fact several theories of probability [...] In 'classical' probability theory, probability is the ratio of favourable outcomes to all possible outcomes, where all outcomes have an equal likelihood of happening ; the probability of throwing a six with a 'fair ' die is one-sixth, since the die has six faces, and if the die is fair, each face has an equal chance of being uppermost.
>
> For the statistician, probability refers to the frequency of occurrences of an event which happens a number of times. Thus, if a statistician is asked to estimate the probability of a person living to a certain age, he will refer to life tables that tell him what proportion of people of the same age as the subject have, in past experience, survived to the specified age.
>
> There is a third concept of probability which is often referred to as a 'degree of belief 'but which I would prefer to call a 'degree of likelihood 'or 'degree of persuasion.' This is often called 'subjective probability 'or 'psychological probability'. While probabilities of the first and second kind can be given mathematical equivalents, any attempt to put a figure on subjective probabilities is likely to meet with the criticism that it is incapable of quantification ... the kind of probabilities that lawyers are mainly concerned with are of the subjective kind. They sometimes relate to the past and sometimes to the future, but except in rare cases they are not susceptible of verification. By contrast, if the assumptions of classical probability theory are accepted [...] the conclusions follow from the premises; and for probabilities based on frequency, past experience offers a measure of frequency that can be applied to the case in hand [....]

As far as the advocate is concerned, the *standard of proof* is simply the portrayal of a certain level of 'probability that a specific fact or state of affairs exists.'[49] The difference in standard of proof required in criminal matters on the one hand and civil matters on the other, speaks to 'the relative position of the parties

[47] 'Clear and convincing proof is a more demanding standard of proof and is used in certain civil actions (as a civil fraud suit):' https://www.merriam-webster.com/legal/standard%20of%20proof retrieved on 18/12/22.

[48] Eggleston R, *Evidence, Proof and Probability* 2nd edn (Weidenfeld, 1983) at 8-9.

[49] Uglow S, *Evidence: Text and Materials* 77.

and the possible outcome of the proceedings.'[50] Put another way, in criminal matters, the accused is prosecuted by the state and the eventual outcome of a guilty verdict, quite apart from the fact the trial is of unequal parties, is the loss of his liberty or more seriously as in cases of murder and treason in this jurisdiction, the loss of his life. It therefore makes sense that the standard of proof be stricter and higher than that in civil matters which is usually a contest between relative equals[51] and the consequence of an adverse decision being the payment of damages only.

It has been shown in *In Re Samuel Winship*[52] that because an accused person has more to lose, should he be convicted, than does a defendant, should the decision not go his way, the higher standard of proof placed upon the prosecution ensures, so far as this is possible, that the margin of error as regards wrong conviction is reduced in his favour. This is in keeping with the observations made by Lord Woolf CJ in *R v B*:[53]

> At the heart of our criminal justice system is the principle that while it is important that justice is done to the prosecution and justice is done to the victim, in the final analysis the fact remains that it is even more important that an injustice is not done to [an accused person]. It is central to the way we administer justice in this country that although it may mean that some guilty people go unpunished, it is more important that the innocent are not wrongly convicted.

There is a history to the foregoing. Sir William Blackstone[54] noted in his eighteenth-century treatise *Commentaries on the Laws of England*[55] that '[...] the law holds that it is better that ten guilty persons escape than that one innocent suffer.' Further, that,

> [o]f great importance to the public is the preservation of this personal liberty; for if once it were left in the power of any the highest magistrate to imprison arbitrarily whomever he or his officers thought proper, (as in France it is daily practiced by the crown,) there would soon be an end of all other rights and immunities. Some have thought that unjust attacks, even upon life or property, at the arbitrary will of the magistrate, are less dangerous to the commonwealth than such as

[55] The *Commentaries on the Laws of England* are an influential 18th-century treatise on the common law of England by Sir William Blackstone, originally published by the Clarendon Press at Oxford, 1765–1770. The work is divided into four volumes, on the rights of persons, the rights of things, of private wrongs and of public wrongs. The *Commentaries* were long regarded as the leading work on the development of English law and played a role in the development of the American legal system. They were in fact the first methodical treatise on the common law suitable for a lay readership since at least the Middle Ages. The common law of England has relied on precedent more than statute and codifications and has been far less amenable than the civil law, developed from the Roman law, to the needs of a treatise. The *Commentaries* were influential largely because they were in fact readable, and because they met a need. The *Commentaries* are often quoted as the definitive pre-Revolutionary source of common law by United States courts. Opinions of the Supreme Court of the United States quote from Blackstone's work whenever they wish to engage in historical discussion that goes back that far, or farther (for example, when discussing the intent of the Framers of the Constitution). The book was famously used as the key in Benedict Arnold's book cipher, which he used to communicate secretly with his conspirator John André during their plot to betray the Continental Army during the American Revolution.

> are made upon the personal liberty of the subject. To bereave a man of life, or by violence to confiscate his estate, without accusation or trial, would be so gross and notorious an act of despotism, as must at once convey the alarm of tyranny throughout the whole kingdom; but confinement of the person, by secretly hurrying him to jail, where his sufferings are unknown or forgotten, is a less public, a less striking, and therefore a more dangerous engine of arbitrary government.

Be that as it may, there has been refinement of Sir Blackstone's refrain in atleast two leading cases from England[56] and India[57] as we see below.

3.3.1.3 *Why it is important to know which party bears the burden of proof*

There are several compelling reasons that attach to knowledge regarding which party bears the burden of proof.[58] Conventionally, the party with the burden of proof on the initial fact in issue has the right to calling evidence on the said fact in issue. It follows therefore that knowing which party bears the burden of proof helps the factfinder answer the procedural question of who has the right to call evidence at trial first.

Further to the foregoing, the importance of knowing which party has the burden of proof is put in sharp focus in criminal matters when the defence makes a submission of no case to answer. It has been held in held in *Mwewa Murono v The People*[59] as follows:

> The finding that a judge has to record under s 291(1)[60] [...] is the same as that under s 206[61] [....] The judge on considering that there is no evidence that the accused or any one of several accused committed the offence must acquit the accused. The finding must show that there is no evidence that the accused committed the offence followed by an order acquitting the accused.

It can be added from the foregoing that in order for the factfinder to rule on the submission he will have to know the allocation of the burden of proof. As shown in *Murono*[62] and *Japau*,[63] if the party bearing the burden of proof, in this case, the prosecution, fails to adduce sufficient evidence to satisfy a reasonable factfinder to the necessary degree, the submission of no case to answer by the defence will succeed. The opposite is also true.

In addition to the preceding, the allocation of the burden of proof and the standard of proof required thereof is important at the end of trial in helping the factfinder determine the case one way or the other. At this stage, the factfinder is called upon to decide by whom and to what extend the factfinder has to be persuaded that the facts as presented are true. It is especially so when the factfinder is left unsure either because the witnesses provided contradictory evidence or the case is borderline that the rules that relate to the burden and standard of proof aid him to determine the case one way or the other. Courts

[60] Criminal Procedure Code Chapter 88 of the Laws of Zambia.

have had occasion to pronounce themselves on this matter.

The principle as to what the phrase *"beyond reasonable doubt"* indicates or the gradation to which the prosecution must demonstrate the satisfaction of the standard was stated by Lord Denning in the case of *Miller v Minister of Pensions*[64] in the following terms:

> .... [t]hat degree is well settled. It need not reach certainty, but it must carry a high degree of probability. Proof beyond reasonable doubt does not mean proof beyond a shadow of doubt. The law would fail to protect the community if it permitted fanciful possibilities to deflect the course of justice. If the evidence is so strong against a man as to leave only a remote possibility in his favour which can be dismissed with the sentence 'of course, it is possible but not in the least probable,' the case is proved beyond reasonable doubt....(emphasis added by Court).
>
> It is true that under our existing jurisprudence in criminal matter, we have to proceed with presumption of innocence, but at the same, that presumption is to be judged on the basis of conceptions of a reasonable prudent man. Smelling doubts for the sake of giving benefit of doubt is not the law of the land.

Further, in the Indian case of *Sucha Singh and Another v State of Punjab*[65] the Supreme Court of India opined as follows:

> [...] Exaggerated devotion to the rule of benefit of doubt must not nurture fanciful doubts or lingering suspicion and thereby destroy social defence. Justice cannot be made sterile on the plea that it is better to let a hundred guilty escape than punish an innocent. Letting the guilty escape is not doing justice according to law [....] Prosecution is not required to meet any and every hypothesis put forward by the accused. A reasonable doubt is not an imaginary, trivial or merely possible doubt based upon reason and common sense. It must grow out of the evidence in the case. If a case is proved perfectly, it is argued that it is artificial; if a case has some flaws inevitable because human beings are prone to err, it is argued that it is too imperfect. One wonders whether in the meticulous hypersensitivity to eliminate a rare innocent from being punished, many guilty persons must be allowed to escape. Proof beyond reasonable doubt is a guideline, not a fetish.

It is difficult, despite the fact that the foregoing authorities are only of persuasive value, to find fault with the conclusions reached therein.

Further still, and this requires additional elaboration, the rules regarding the burden of proof but more especially those relating to standard of proof are necessary in the allocation of risk of adjudicatory error. The foregoing is premised on the idea that decisions in any legal proceedings are predicated

---

[64] [1947] 2 ALL ER 272.

[65] [2003] 7 SCC 643.

not on mathematical precision but, if you will, a probabilistic approach to truth finding. Thus, the question as to who ought to bear the risk of an error being made by the factfinder is of supreme importance. The question in and of itself exercises the mind into interrogating the historical, public policy, psychological, scientific, and social values or otherwise that ought to be attached to diverse classes of trials. We will return to this theme later under the allocation of, and the burden of proof, on the one hand, and the standard of proof in criminal matters in general with specific reference to the constitutional presumption of innocence, on the other. Recall that Article 18(2)(a) of the Zambian Constitution provides that '[e]very person who is charged with a criminal offence - shall be presumed to be innocent until he is proved or has pleaded guilty.'

Lastly, the rules regarding burden of proof and standard of proof and their correct application are matters that an appellate court will review in deciding whether the appeal succeeds or not. An incorrect application or a misdirection by the court below will be grounds for quelling a conviction and consequently, the sentence inspired by such a conviction, in a criminal appeal.

3.3.2 *Different classes of burden*

The law of evidence recognises several classes of burden. The most significant dissimilarity is one to be found between the burden of proof on the one hand and the burden of adducing evidence on the other. Also known, according to Lord Denning,[66] as the "legal burden", the concept which we have already discussed above has been said by Glanville Williams[67] to be the "persuasive burden;" in *DPP v Morgan*[68] as the "probative" burden; by Lord Bridge[69] as the "fixed burden of proof." Of course, the *numero uno* in so far as illustrations of burden of proof go, is Lord Sankey's golden thread in *Woolmington v DPP*[70] which is the 'principle that the prosecution must prove the guilt of the [accused]' or put another way, that the burden of proof in criminal cases is on the prosecution to prove the elements of the offence with which the accused is charged beyond reasonable doubt. In what has led some[71] to describe the burden of proof as "the risk of non-persuasion," if the prosecution succeeds in discharging their burden to the requisite standard in criminal matters, the factfinder will have no choice but to convict and return with a verdict of guilty. Failure by the prosecution in discharging their burden compels the factfinder to acquit the accused. It is conceivably important to note that such legal burdens as hereinbefore described are set by the law, and as Lord Sankey noted in

---

[66] Denning A T, "Presumptions and Burdens" (1945) 61 L.Q.R. 379.

[67] Williams G, *Criminal Law The General Part* (2nd edn Stevens & Sons, 1961) Ch 23; *Lambert* [2001] UKHL 37; [2002] 2 AC 545 at 547 *per* Lord Hope of Craighead.

[68] [1976] AC 182 HL.

[69] Bridge N (later Lord Bridge), *"Presumptions and Burdens"* (1949) 12 M.L.R. 273, 274.

[70] [1935] AC 462 *per* Lord Sankey, adopted in *Murono v The People* [2004] ZR 207 where the Supreme Court restated the principle as follows: '[i]n criminal cases, the rule is that the legal burden of proving every element of the offence charged and consequently, the guilt of the accused lies from beginning to end on the prosecution. The standard of proof is high.'

[71] Wigmore, Vol. IX (Chadbourn rev., 1981), para. 2485.

Woolmington,[72] 'do not shift throughout the progression of trial.'[73] Next, we turn to the "evidential burden."

What is termed the "evidential burden" in contradistinction to the "legal burden" discussed above is simply the mandatory burden a party has to adduce evidence. The evidence should be of such sufficiency as to raise an issue fit for the court's consideration. We must again return to the *Woolmington*[74] principle on the burden of proof and the fact that the prosecution will bear such a burden throughout the trial. Within the context of the evidential burden, the prosecution would have to adduce the necessary evidence of such sufficiency as to satisfy an equable tribunal properly directing its mind that the elements of the charge/offence have been proved beyond reasonable doubt thus proving the elements of the charge/offence. The Supreme Court has stated in *Murono v The People*[75] that '[i]n criminal cases, the rule is that the legal burden of proving every element of the offence charged and consequently, the guilt of the accused lies from beginning to end on the prosecution.' Further, that '[t]he standard of proof is high.'[76] It can thus be said from the foregoing that the prosecution bears the evidential burden for making out a *prima facie* case for the accused to answer which if he did not by offering an alternative to the prosecution's case, the court would convict him on the charge.

We may at this juncture wonder how the issue of who may have an evidential burden on a specific issue in question is determined by the court. The answer to such a question lies in the way a similar question regarding the legal burden is determined. If, as discussed above, the prosecution bears the legal burden in criminal matters, as per Lord Sankey's golden thread in *Woolmington*,[77]it must logically follow that he who bears the legal burden must ordinarily also bear the evidential burden to adduce sufficient evidence on the particular issue in question through oral testimony, documentary evidence or/ and real evidence. It is the case though that where a presumption becomes part of the factual matrix and circumstances of a particular case, 'it may have the effect of relieving a party of the obligation to adduce evidence on a point, other than evidence of the fact forming the foundation of the presumption.'[78] The concept concerning who bears the evidential burden discussed above is a

[72] [1935] AC 462 *per* Lord Sankey, adopted in *Murono v The People* [2004] ZR 207 where the Supreme Court restated the principle as follows: '[i]n criminal cases, the rule is that the legal burden of proving every element of the offence charged and consequently, the guilt of the accused lies from beginning to end on the prosecution. The standard of proof is high.'

[73] See for example, *DPP v Morgan* [1975] 2 AII ER 347, *per* Lord Cross; see further, the ground breaking decisions, discussed later in this text, on the Zambian jurisprudential front, in *People v Austin Chisanga Liato* [Selected Judgment No 21 of 2015] and *Lt Gen Geojago Robert Musengule and Amon Sibanda v The People* [SCZ Selected Judgment No 19 of 2017].

[74] [1935] AC 462.

[75] [2004] ZR 207 adopted in *Murono v The People* [2004] ZR 207.

[76] This is with reference to the requirement that the charge must be proved beyond reasonable doubt but see *Miller v Minister of Pensions* [1947] 2 ALL ER 272; *Sucha Singh and Another v State of Punjab* [2003] 7 SCC 643.

[77] [1935] AC 462.

[78] Dennis I, *The Law of Evidence* 442.

general rule with exceptions which may include the use of judicial evidence,[79] judicial notice[80] and presumptions.[81] In this sense, procedures of evidence and the employment of judicial notice and presumptions may be said to be alternatives to the concept of "proof."

We must now move the discussion forward on the relationship of the burden of proof and the evidential burden in so far as the general rule discussed above is concerned. There are of course situations in which though a party may bear the evidential burden, he will not at the same time, as is generally supposed, bear the legal burden of proof.[82] For example, where the accused is charged with murder, he may seek to show to the court that even though there indeed was a homicide, this was committed due to provocation or that it was done in self-defence. He may do this, as implied in the preceding statement, by raising this defence, and producing evidence to substantiate the defence(s). He may also predicate his story on what the evidence that the prosecution itself may have placed before court in their quest to discharge their burden if only to raise a reasonable doubt in the mind of the factfinder as to whether he killed as a result of provocation or self-defence.

A principle that is readily distillable from *Mancini v DPP*[83] is that where sufficient evidence appears to exist for a general defence to the offence/charge to raise a reasonable doubt, but no such defence is raised by the accused, the

---

[79] Which include the following:

1. Direct evidence
2. Circumstantial evidence
3. Real evidence
4. Primary and secondary evidence
5. Documentary Evidence
6. Hearsay Evidence
7. Best Evidence
8. Opinion evidence

[80] Where a party asks the court to take judicial notice of a fact, the court will not demand for evidence of the existence of such a fact to be adduced. In *Mwape v The People* [1976] wherein Silungwe CJ as he was then opined that '[a] court [...] will, for instance, take judicial notice of matters of common knowledge which are so notorious that to lead evidence in order to establish their existence may be unnecessary and could, as Phipson puts it in his Manual of the Law of Evidence, 10th edn at p 21 be 'an insult to the intelligence to require evidence'; see further *Clinton v Lyons & Co Ltd* [1912] 3 KB 198.

[81] There are several presumptions including (i) conclusive/irrebuttable presumptions e.g., s 14(3) of the Penal Code provides '[a] male person under the age of twelve years is presumed to be incapable of having carnal knowledge.' This presumption, no matter the evidence, oral, real or documentary available to prove the charge of rape against a 12 year old is irrebuttable; (ii) presumptions of fact whose effect is to compel the court to determine that because fact A is true then fact B which by common sense should go hand in hand with fact should also be true: *Attorney-General v Bradlaugh* (1885) 14 QBD 667. This identifies more with circumstantial evidence than it does with presumptions; (iii) Rebuttable presumptions or evidential presumptions as they are called in English law are that class of presumptions the essence of which is that where a particular fact is proved/admitted then by necessary implication it is not necessary to prove other presumed facts: *Chard v Chard* [1955]; (iv) Other presumptions include that of innocence according to Article 18(2) of the Constitution, and that of sanity under s 11 of the Penal Code chapter 87 of the Laws of Zambia. We will discuss these further, later in the text.

[82] *Hill v Baxter* [1958] 1 QB 277 at 284-5, where though the accused *bore the evidential burden to produce sufficient evidence to raise the* defence of automatism to compel the court into determining that a material issue fit for consideration had been raised, the prosecution nevertheless bore the legal burden of disproving the said defence.

[83] [1942] AC 1 HL; see generally, Doran S, [1991] Crim. L.R. 878.

court ought to direct its mind to this fact.[84] In the event that the evidential burden in the scenario above is not discharged, all the prosecution will have to do is to prove the elements of the offence/charge to the requisite standard. However, where the evidential burden has been successfully discharged thereby increasing the legal scope of the prosecution's legal burden as a consequence, the prosecution has its work cut out. Not only does it have to prove the elements of the offence/charge but also the fact that the accused was indeed not provoked nor did he act in self-defence when he killed the victim.

There are further important distinctions worthy of note as regards the concepts of the legal burden on the one hand and the evidential burden on the other. By convention and practice, evaluation of the question of whether the evidential burden has been discharged is limited to the favourable evidence as regards the issue in question. The court does not ask itself whether, on comparison with evidence against the burden being discharged, it should decide that the burden has been proved, but rather, whether the evidence placed before it to discharge the burden is of such sufficiency as to raise a question for the contemplation of the court. The preceding is in contradistinction to the process the court takes when deciding whether a legal burden has been discharged. Here the court takes into consideration all the evidence made available to it which includes not only the evidence in support of drawing the conclusion that the evidential burden has been discharged but also any that is averse to such a conclusion.

Further to the foregoing, it has been shown in *Jayasena v R*[85] that the discharge of an evidential burden need not be conflated with a decision, as would be in the discharge of a legal burden, proving any fact in issue. In *R v Hunt (Richard Selwyn)*[86] the court demurred to the stubbornness on leaving the burden during a prosecution on the accused. This was because according to the court, 'the discharge of an evidential burden proves nothing – it merely raises an issue.' It follows that the only significance to be attached to the discharge of an evidential burden is that the question relating to the evidential burden was validly raised with sufficient predication for the possible existence of a material fact as to justify a finding in favour of the party that bears the evidential burden. To that end, it has been suggested by Lord Bingham that it is rather erroneous to call the evidential burden "an evidential burden of proof."[87] According to his Lordship, 'it is a burden of raising, on the evidence in the case, an issue as to the matter in question fit for consideration by the tribunal of fact. If an issue is properly raised, it is for the prosecutor to prove, beyond reasonable doubt, that the ground of exoneration does not avail the [accused].' In the earlier case of *Jayasena v R*,[88] Lord Devlin reasoned that 'it is misleading to call it a burden

[84] It must be noted that the principle in Mancini was made within the context of a judge directing a jury, a concept that is strange and foreign to our legal system.

[85] [1970] AC 618 at 624 PC *per* Lord Devlin.

[86] [1987] AC 352 at 358 HL *per* Lord Ackner.

[87] *Sheldrake v DPP* [2004] UKHL 43; [2005] 1 All ER 237.

[88] [1970] AC 618.

of proof, whether described as legal or evidential or by any other objective, when it can be discharged by production of evidence that falls short of proof.' According to some,[89] '[t]he issue here is whether a party with the evidential burden has a duty to raise the issue as part of its case or, more broadly, whether the issue exists on the facts of the case, and it is immaterial that the issue was not raised by a specific party.'

We said earlier that one of the distinguishing characteristics between the evidential burden and the legal burden is what the factfinder will look at in determining the question before him either way. We must take this discussion further in our comparison of the two burdens but this time with specific focus on the legal burden. Unlike the evidential burden, the discharge of the legal burden goes over and beyond simple specific questions but involves the factfinder taking, as we said before, all the evidence before him in order to make a determination. It thus falls to reason that the legal burden is only discharged later in the trial when the factfinder is called upon to make a determination as to whether the facts whose possible reality is in issue, exist or not. In our legal system, a judge makes determinations as regards both the discharge of the evidential as well as the legal burden of proof. For the former, as and when it arises and for the latter, when the judge has to consider what verdict to issue at the close of trial.[90]

3.3.3 *The distinction between the evidential burden and the legal burden: judicial interpretation*

The distinction between the evidential burden and the legal burden is well settled and requires no further elaboration. We demonstrate the foregoing by looking at a few cases where the matter has arisen and been considered.

The case of *Hill v Baxter*[91]is authority for the position stated earlier that the evidential burden on the one hand and the legal burden on the other, need not rest on the same party. They may, as usually happens in criminal matters, rest on dissimilar parties, that is the accused and the prosecution respectively. In *Hill v Baxter*[92], the accused bore the evidential burden to present evidence of such sufficiency as to advance the issue of automatism for the court's consideration. Be that as it may, the prosecution bore the legal burden of refuting the said defence. Lord Devlin observed as follows:

> I am satisfied that even in a case in which liability depended upon full proof of mens rea, it would not be open to the defence to rely upon automatism without providing some evidence of it. If it amounted to insanity in the legal sense, it is well established that the burden of proof would start with and remain throughout upon the defence. But

[89] Singh C and Ramjohn M, *Unlocking Evidence* (3rd edn Routledge, 2016) 29; see also, *R v Gill* (1963) 47 Cr App R 166; *Bullard v R* [1957] AC 635; *AG's Reference (No 4 of 2002)* [2004] 3 WLR 976; *DPP v Sheldrake* [2004] QB 487.

[90] See Williams G, "The Evidential Burden: Some Common Misapprehensions" (1977) 127 NLJ 156.

[91] [1958] 1 QB 277 at 284-5 *per* Devlin J.

[92] [1958] 1 QB 277 at 284-5 *per* Devlin J.

> there is also recognized in the criminal law a lighter burden which the accused discharges by producing some evidence, but which does not relieve the prosecution from having to prove in the end all the facts necessary to establish guilt ... It would be quite unreasonable to allow the defence to submit at the end of the prosecution's case that the Crown had not proved affirmatively and beyond a reasonable doubt that the accused was at the time of the crime sober, or not sleepwalking or not in a trance or black-out. Iam satisfied that such matters ought not to be considered at all until the defence has produced at least prima facie evidence [....]
>
> By the end of the prosecution case, they will have adduced evidence relating to all definitional elements of the offence. But by that stage there is no requirement to disprove all possible defence, normally they will have to adduce some evidence relating to it. If they persuade the judge that they have produced enough evidence, at the end of the case the prosecution normally must satisfy the court that not only did the defendant commit the offence but also, they had no viable defence.

Further, *Hill v Baxter*[93] is authority for the proposition, according to Lord Devlin, that as regards the concept of burden of proof, the evidential burden is the lighter version and the legal burden, by necessary implication, heavier version. The former is discharged by the accused by adducing some evidence of such sufficiency as to raise a question for the contemplation of the court. Discharging the evidential burden thus has the consequence of widening the prosecution's burden. The prosecution is thereby called upon to 'prove in the end all the facts necessary to establish guilt [....]'

In *Jayasena v R*,[94] Lord Devlin put it as follows:

> Their Lordships do not understand what is meant by the phrase 'evidential burden of proof'. They understand, of course, that in trial by jury a party may be required to adduce some evidence in support of his case, whether on the general issue or on a particular issue, before that issue is left to the jury. How much evidence has to be adduced depends upon the nature of the requirement. It may be such evidence as, if believed and left uncontradicted and unexplained, could be accepted by the jury as proof. It is doubtless permissible to describe the requirement as a burden, and it may be convenient to call it an evidential burden. But it is confusing to call it a burden of proof. Further, it is misleading to call it a burden of proof, whether described as legal or evidential or by any other adjective, when it can be discharged by the production of evidence that falls short of proof. The essence of the appellant's case is that he has not got to provide any sort of proof that he was acting in private defence. So, it is a misnomer

[93] [1958] 1 QB 277 at 284-5 *per* Devlin J.

[94] [1970] AC 618 PC.

> to call whatever it is that he has to provide a burden of proof [....][95]

In *R v Edwards*[96] the appellant was charged on indictment with selling by retail intoxicating liquor without holding a justices' licence authorising the sale, contrary to s 160(1)(a) a of the Licensing Act 1964. At the trial the prosecution proved that the appellant had sold intoxicating liquor on the occasion in question but did not adduce any evidence that he was not in possession of a justices' licence. The appellant was convicted and appealed, contending that, since the clerk to the licensing justices was required by s 30(1) of the 1964 Act to keep a register giving particulars of justices' licences granted in the district, the question whether a licence had been granted to him was not one peculiarly within his own knowledge and accordingly the onus was on the prosecution to prove that no licence had been granted to him.

It was held that where an enactment made the doing of a particular act an offence, save in specified circumstances, or by persons of specified classes or with special qualifications or with the permission or licence of specified authorities, and, on its true construction, the effect of the enactment was to prohibit the doing of the act in question subject to a proviso, exception, excuse or qualification, there was no need for the prosecution to establish a *prima facie* case that the proviso etc., did not apply. In those circumstances, whether or not the matter was peculiarly within the knowledge of the accused, it was sufficient for the prosecution to prove the act in question and the burden, in the sense of the legal or persuasive burden, then lay on the accused to prove that the proviso etc applied. It followed that the onus lay on the appellant to prove that a justices' licence had been granted to him. The appeal would therefore be dismissed.[97]

In *R v Hunt*[98] the [accused] was found to be in possession of a powder containing morphine mixed with two other substances which were not controlled drugs. He was charged with unlawfully possessing a controlled drug, namely morphine, contrary to s 5(2) of the Misuse of Drugs Act 1971. Under para 3a of Sch 1 to the Misuse of Drugs Regulations 1973 any preparation of morphine containing not more than 0·2% of morphine compounded with other ingredients was excepted from the prohibition on possession of controlled drugs contained in s 5 of the 1971 Act. At the trial the prosecution did not adduce evidence as to the proportion of morphine in the powder. The [accused] submitted that there was no case to answer because the prosecution had failed to show that the powder was not within the exception contained in para 3, but following an adverse ruling by the judge he changed his plea to guilty and was sentenced to three months' imprisonment. The defendant

[95] Cited in *Regina v Daniel* CACD (Times 08-Apr-02, Bailii, [2002] EWCA Crim 959, [2003] 1 Cr App R 99); *Lynch v Director of Public Prosecutions Admn (*Bailii), [2001] EWHC Admin 882); *Sheldrake v Director of Public Prosecutions;* Attorney General's Reference No 4 of 2002 HL (House of Lords, Bailii, [2004] UKHL 43, [2005] 1 AC 264, Times 14-Oct-04, [2005] 1 All ER 237, [2004] 3 WLR 976.

[96] [1975] QB 27 CA.

[97] *Applying R v Scott* (1921) 86 JP 69; *R v Oliver* [1943] 2 All ER 800; Explaining *R v Stone* (1801) 1 East 639; dictum of Bayley J in *R v Turner* (1816) 5 M & S at 211.

[98] [1987] AC 352 HL; (1986) 84 Cr App R 163; [1986] 3 WLR 1115; [1987] AC 352; [1987] 1 All ER 1.

appealed against his conviction to the Court of Appeal, contending that the burden lay on the prosecution to prove that he did not fall within the exception contained in para 3. The Court of Appeal dismissed the appeal, holding that the burden of proof was on the defendant to show that he did fall within the exception. The [accused] appealed to the House of Lords, contending that if the defendant raised a statutory defence, then provided there was evidence to support the defence the burden was on the prosecution to negative the defence.

It was held that there was no rule of law that the burden of proving a statutory defence lay on the [accused] only where the statute specifically so provided, since a statute could place the burden of proof on the defendant by necessary implication and without doing so expressly. Each case turned on the construction of the particular legislation but the court should be very slow to infer from the statute that Parliament intended to impose an onerous duty on the defendant to prove his innocence in a criminal case. The occasions on which a statute would be construed as imposing a burden of proof on the defendant were generally limited to offences arising under enactments which prohibited the doing of an act save in specified circumstances or by persons of specified classes or within specified qualifications or with the licence or permission of specified authorities. On the true construction of para 3 of Sch 1 to the 1973 regulations the offence was possession of morphine in a prohibited form and therefore the burden lay on the prosecution to prove not only that the powder contained morphine but also that it was not morphine in the form permitted by para 3 of Sch 1. It followed that the Court of Appeal had been wrong to hold that the burden of proof in relation to para 3 lay on the defendant. The appeal would accordingly be allowed.[99]

In *R v Lambert*,[100] the [accused], L, was arrested in possession of a bag containing over £140,000 worth of cocaine. He was charged with an offence of possession of a controlled drug with intent to supply contrary to s 5a of the Misuse of Drugs Act 1971. At his trial, which took place in April 1999, L relied on the defence provided by s 28(2)b and (3)(b) of the 1971 Act, asserting that he had not believed or suspected, or had reason to suspect, that the bag had contained cocaine or any controlled drug. The judge directed the jury, in accordance with the accepted view of the law at the time, that the prosecution had to prove only that L had knowingly had the bag in his possession and that it had contained a controlled drug, and that thereafter the burden was cast upon L to bring himself within s 28 and to prove, on the balance of probabilities, that he had not known that the bag had contained a controlled drug. In short, the judge directed the jury that s 28 imposed a legal rather than a merely evidential burden upon the [accused]. L was convicted, and his appeal was dismissed by the Court of Appeal. On his appeal to the House of Lords, which was heard after the implementation of the Human Rights Act 1998 on 2 October 2000, L

---

[99] *Woolmington v DPP* [1935] All ER Rep 1; *R v Edwards* [1974] 2 All ER 1085 considered; Decision of Court of Appeal [1986] 1 All ER 184 reversed; Editor's Notes: For the burden of proof in criminal proceedings, see 11 Halsbury's Laws (4th edn) paras 354–357, and for cases on the subject, see 14(2) Digest (Reissue) 474–477, 3918–3948; For the possession of controlled drugs, see 11 Halsbury's Laws (4th edn) para 1092 and 30 ibid para 750, and for cases on the subject, see 15 Digest (Reissue) 1068–1071, 9154–9169; For the Misuse of Drugs Act 1971, s 5, see 41 Halsbury's Statutes (3rd edn) 884.

[100] [2001] 3 All ER 577; [2001] UKHL 37; [2002] 2 AC 545 HL.

contended, inter alia, that the judge's direction that the accused had a legal burden to establish the s 28 defence violated the presumption of innocence in art 6(2)c of the European Convention for the Protection of Human Rights and Fundamental Freedoms 1950 (as set out in Sch 1 to the 1998 Act). The issue therefore arose whether an appellant could rely on the 1998 Act at a time when it was in force in respect of a conviction at a date when it was not in force. In contending that that question should be answered in the affirmative, L relied on s 6(1)d of the 1998 Act which rendered it unlawful for a public authority—a term which included a court and the House of Lords in its judicial capacity—to act in a way that was incompatible with convention rights. Alternatively, he relied on the combined effect of ss 7e and 22f of the 1998 Act. Under s 7(1)(b), a person who claimed that a public authority had acted in a way which was made unlawful by s 6(1) could rely on the convention right concerned in any legal proceedings. S 22(4) provided that s 7(1)(b) applied to proceedings brought by or at the instigation of a public authority whenever the act in question had taken place, but that otherwise that subsection did not apply to an act taking place before the coming into force of that section. By virtue of s 7(6), 'legal proceedings' in sub-s (1)(b) included proceedings brought by or at the instigation of a public authority and an appeal against a decision of a court or tribunal.

It was held that where a person appealed subsequent to the implementation of the 1998 Act against a conviction before the implementation of that Act, he could not (Lord Steyn dissenting) rely on an alleged breach of his convention rights by the trial court. S 7(6) distinguished between proceedings brought by a public authority and an appeal against a decision of a court, whereas s 22(4) extended the application of s 7(1)(b) only where proceedings were brought by a public authority. That indicated that an appeal by an unsuccessful defendant was not to be treated as a proceeding brought by or at the instigation of a public authority within the meaning of s 22(4). Moreover, it would be surprising if s 6(1), which, unlike s 7(1)(b), had no express provision extending its effect, produced a contrary result so as to be applicable to acts which had taken place before convention rights became part of domestic law. It followed in the instant case that L could not rely on the 1998 Act to challenge the judge's direction to the jury on the nature of the burden imposed upon him by s 28 of the 1971 Act. In any event (Lord Steyn concurring), even if the trial judge had given a direction that the burden on L was only an evidential burden, the jury would have reached the same result. Accordingly, the appeal would be dismissed. *Per* curiam: (1) Although, on its ordinary meaning, s 28 of the 1971 Act imposes a legal burden upon the accused, it is to be read as imposing only an evidential burden in cases where the accused is entitled to rely on art 6(2) of the convention. Such a reading, in contrast to the ordinary meaning of s 28, is compatible with art 6(2). (2) Where a person, who has been charged with an offence of possessing a controlled drug contrary to s 5 of the 1971 Act, claims that he was unaware that the bag he was carrying contained a controlled drug, the prosecution does not have to prove that the accused knew that the bag contained such a drug, let alone a particular controlled drug. It is left to the accused to raise the issue of lack of knowledge as a defence.[101]

3.3.4 *A tactical or provisional burden?*

The question whether there is a third concept described by some as a tactical or as said in *DPP v Morgan,*[102] a "provisional burden" is of great academic and practical interest. While there exists in the literature the equation of the evidential burden to a tactical equation, this is a gross mischaracterisation of the concept which as Dennis[103] has ably demonstrated, is 'a confusing tendency to conflate' the two concepts. He adds that the concept of a tactical burden need not and should not be 'be regarded as a term of art in the same way as the legal and evidential burdens' are. Further, that 'it is merely a useful explanatory term to describe a straightforward idea.' Thus, 'when a party has discharged an evidential burden and raised an issue for the court to consider, there arises a tactical onus on the other party to respond with some rebutting evidence. There is no legal obligation to adduce (further) evidence on the issue, but the party against whom the evidence has been adduced increases the risk of losing on the issue if nothing is done to challenge the evidence.' We will shortly return to this issue below.

We now turn again to Lord Sankey's "golden thread" in *Woolmington*[104] which is to the effect that the prosecution bears the burden of proving any facts in issue beyond reasonable doubt. In a murder charge the facts are invariably that the accused with *mens rea* killed the victim. Both the legal as well as the evidential burden to prove the elements of the charge including the *actus reus* are on the prosecution to prove. The accused bears no burden. Even if, as the case was in *Woolmington,*[105] his defence is that the killing was an accident, he does not have to nor will he be called upon to prove that the killing was indeed an accident.

The reasons for the foregoing in the grand scheme of things are clear: defences such as provocation, accidental homicide or indeed self-defence are merely a denial of intention. They do not speak to any new issues, for which the prosecution bears the burden of proof,[106] being raised by the accused in criminal proceedings. Accordingly, in *Woolmington,*[107] it was not for the accused to prove that he had no intention to fire the gun that killed his wife but rather for the prosecution to prove beyond reasonable doubt that the accused not only had the *mens rea* (the intention or "guilty mind") to, but did indeed fire (*actus reus*) the gun that killed his wife.

Herein lies the issue of what is termed a tactical burden. It must be remembered that the answer to the question whether the prosecution has discharged its burden cannot be known until a verdict is rendered. Consequently, it may

[101] *R v McNamara* (1988) 87 Cr App R 246 approved; Decision of the Court of Appeal [2001] 1 All ER 1014 affirmed on different grounds.

[102] [1976] AC 182.

[103] Dennis I, *The Law of Evidence* 444.

[104] [1935] AC 462.

[105] [1935] AC 462.

[106] *Woomington v DPP* [1935] AC 462.

[107] [1935] AC 462.

well be that at the close of its case, the prosecution may have discharged their legal burden, i.e., in the case of a murder charge, that the accused intended to, and indeed killed the victim. The prosecution indeed has a right to rely on the foregoing inference. The accused thus has a choice to make. He may (though he need not to), testify. He may also choose not to testify but if he were to elect to remain silent,[108] which procedurally and constitutionally he has the right to do,[109] he is taking a huge gamble, indeed a huge risk.[110] Remember that he will have been put on his defence which implies that without an explanation from him, the court would be inclined to convict him. In fact, under s 212[111] of the Criminal Procedure Code[112] '[i]f the accused person says that he does not mean to give or adduce evidence or make an unsworn statement,[113] and the court considers that there is evidence that he committed the offence, the advocate for the prosecution may then sum up the case against the accused person, and the court shall then call upon the accused person personally or by his advocate to address the court on his own behalf.' Be that as it may, electing to be silent does not automatically mean that the accused will be convicted simply because he has been put on his defence or 'found with a case to answer.'

In *Dickson Sembauke Changwe and Ifellow Hamuchanje v The People*,[114] it was observed that the fact that the appellants elected to remain silent, was not a factor to be held against them. Further, that '[t]he prosecution have to prove their case and an accused who remains silent is, nonetheless, entitled to have any defence, which he sought to introduce during cross-examination or otherwise duly considered.' From the foregoing, it becomes abundantly clear why the accused ought to, for tactical reasons (for he bears the "tactical burden"), give his side of the story by giving oral testimony if only to add a reservation in the [court's] mind as to whether the gunfire was premeditated or inadvertent.

In *David Dimuna v The People*,[115] the accused was found with a case to answer.[116] In the course of the trial, when the learned trial judge found that there was a case to answer and put the appellant on his defence, he explained the courses open to the appellant and said 'you may elect also to remain silent but you have to understand that is an unwise course to take because at this point in time I have evidence from the prosecution and I do not have anything from your side.' In responding to counsel's criticism of the foregoing, the Supreme Court opined *inter alia:*

> There is nothing improper in a judge commenting on the fact that an appellant has remained silent. Whilst a court must not hold the fact that an accused remains silent against him, there is no impropriety in a comment that only the prosecution evidence was available to the court. It is no more than a statement of fact and does not suggest that remaining silent is an indication of guilt.

Even so, in *Chimbini v The People*,[117] the appellant was convicted of robbery. The

[115] [1988 – 1989] ZR 199 (SC).

[116] Which may exist on the basis of even one element being established: *The People v Kombe Joseph Champako* (HN/59/2011).

[117] [1973] ZR 191 (CA).

case against the appellant rested entirely on the evidence of the complainant who said that she had known him before and that she recognised him as one of her assailants. The appellant when called upon to make his defence elected to remain silent. The Supreme Court observed as follows:

> There is no evidence as to what, if anything, the appellant said when he was first apprehended by the complainant's husband; the evidence of the arresting officer is that when charged the appellant denied the charge. In court the appellant, when called upon to make his defence, elected to remain silent. Where the evidence against an accused person is purely circumstantial and his guilt entirely a matter of inference, it is trite that the inference of guilt may not be drawn unless it is the only inference which can reasonably be drawn from the facts. In such cases the fact that an accused person has elected not to give evidence on oath may, in certain circumstances, tend to support the case against him, but will certainly not do so unless the inference was one which could properly be drawn in the first place. Where, however, as in the present case, there is direct evidence by a complainant that she identified as her assailant a man whom she had known before, and this evidence, if accepted, establishes the guilt of the accused, the fact that he chooses to remain silent may properly be taken into account. This fact is part of the totality of the evidence which the court must consider in coming to the conclusion that it is satisfied beyond reasonable doubt as to the guilt of the accused.
>
> The magistrate on the whole of the evidence in this case, including the fact that the appellant elected to remain silent, was entitled to accept the complainant's identification and was entitled to convict; he did not misdirect himself and there is no basis on which this court can interfere. The appeal against conviction must be dismissed.

3.3.5 *Allocation of the burden and standard of proof*

3.3.5.1 *General considerations*

The allocation of the burden of proof, also known as the probative or persuasive burden is determined by rules of substantive law. It is, to all intents and purposes, the allocation of risk. The implication of the foregoing is as may have become apparent already, that in the absence of evidence or inability to satisfy the factfinder, the party bearing the burden will lose. The preceding is demonstrated in the case of *Khalid Mohamed v The Attorney General*[118] wherein Ngulube DCJ as he was then, opined as follows:

> An unqualified proposition that a plaintiff should succeed automatically whenever a defence has failed is unacceptable to me. A plaintiff must prove his case and if he fails to do so the mere failure of the opponent's defence does not entitle him to judgment. I would not accept the proposition that even if a plaintiff's case has collapsed of its inanition

[118] [1982] ZR 49 (SC).

> or for some reason or other, judgment should nevertheless be given to him on the ground that [the] defence set up by the opponent has also collapsed. Quite clearly a defendant in such circumstances would not even need defence.

Ngulube DCJ was simply repeating the oft cited common law principle, albeit in more animated diction that "he who asserts must prove." Thus, a party who makes a positive assertion bears the burden of proof. This was exemplified in *Wakelin v London and South Western Railway.*[119] The complainant's husband was killed on a railway level crossing. While admitting to the fact that the victim had been run over by one of their trains and neglecting certain warnings, they elected to call no evidence. Instead, they submitted that there was no case to answer as it had not been shown whether the victim died because of the train company's fault or as a result of throwing himself against the train. Lord Halsbury LC held *inter alia:*

> My Lords, it is incumbent upon the plaintiff in this case to establish by proof that the husband's death had been caused by some negligence of the defendants ... That is the fact to be proved. If the fact is not proved, the plaintiff fails, and if in the absence of direct proof, the circumstances which are established are equally consistent with the allegation of the plaintiff as with the denial of the defendant, the plaintiff fails for the very simple reason that the plaintiff is bound to establish the affirmative of the proposition [....]

As in *Khalid Muhammad,*[120] the plaintiff in *Wakelin*[121] had the burden to prove not only that the husband had died, a fact which was proved at trial, but also that his death on the railway was as a result or a consequence of the accused company's negligence. In other words, the complainant's proving of the death of her husband placed no burden on the accused company to disprove the negligence asserted by the complainant through the prosecution. Therefore, the allocation of burdens serves several aims including the following:

(i) specifying which party has the right to call witnesses first to adduce evidence;
(ii) determining which party can make "no case to answer" submissions; and
(iii) subsidence of uncertainties for the factfinder.

3.3.5.2 *Allocation of the burden and standard of proof in criminal matters*

The starting point hereunder is reference to the fundamental right expressed under Article 18(2)(a) of the Constitution which provides that '[e]very person who is charged with a criminal offence - shall be *presumed* to be innocent until he is proved or has pleaded guilty.' As already explained

[119] [1887] 12 AC 41.
[120] [1982] ZR 49 (SC).
[121] [1887] 12 AC 41.

elsewhere in this text, the implication of this constitutional injunction is that it elevates the common law concept of presumption of innocence implied in the *Woolmington*[122] decision to a constitutionally guaranteed right. Thus, as already shown, '[…] it is the duty of the prosecution to prove the [accused's] guilt subject to [...] the defence of insanity and subject also to any statutory exception [….] No matter what the charge or where the trial, the principle that the prosecution must prove the guilt of the [accused] is part of [Zambian law] and no attempt to whittle it down can be entertained.'[123]

As discussed earlier in this text, the concept of burden of proof is important for several reasons including providing a rule for decision making when the judge becomes uncertain as to which way he should decide an issue; the calling of witnesses; who should submit at "no case to answer" stage; and the allocation of risk for wrong decisions. The last point is worthy of further elaboration. As a general point, recall that Sir William Blackstone[124] noted in his eighteenth-century treatise *Commentaries on the Laws of England*[125] that '[…] the law holds that it is better that ten guilty persons escape than that one innocent suffer.' It is thus deemed to be better to acquit a guilty party than to convict an innocent one. The concept of burden of proof and the rules thereof are thus designed to minimise the risk of wrong conviction. It logically follows that the prosecution ought to overcome the essential constitutional constraints under Article 18(2)(a) that the accused will, unless he pleads guilty[126] or is adjudged to be at the end of his trial, be presumed innocent by proving his guilt beyond reasonable doubt. However, both Lord Blackstone's rule and the constitutional presumption of innocence ought to be understood within the context of judicial interpretation of the standard of proof in criminal cases which should be *"beyond reasonable doubt."* According toLord Denning in the case of *Miller v Minister of Pensions,*[127] '[….] It is true that under our existing jurisprudence in criminal matter, we have to proceed with presumption of innocence, but at the same, that presumption is to be judged on the basis of conceptions of a reasonable prudent man. Smelling doubts for the sake of giving benefit of doubt is not the law of the land.' Further, in the Indian case of *Sucha Singh and Another v State of Punjab*[128] the Supreme Court of India held in part that '[j]ustice cannot be made sterile on the plea that it is better to let a hundred guilty escape than punish an innocent. Letting the guilty escape is not doing justice according to law [....] Proof beyond reasonable doubt is a guideline, not a fetish.'

[122] [1935] AC 462.

[123] See also *Murono v The People* [2004] ZR 207 where the Supreme Court restated the principle in *Woolmington* as follows: '[i]n criminal cases, the rule is that the legal burden of proving every element of the offence charged and consequently, the guilt of the accused lies from beginning to end on the prosecution. The standard of proof is high.'

[124] Blackstone, William, *Commentaries on the Laws of England*, facsimile edition with introductions by Stanley N. Katz. (Univ. Chicago, 1979). 4 vols.

[125] The *Commentaries on the Laws of England* are an influential 18th-century treatise on the common law of England by Sir William Blackstone, originally published by the Clarendon Press at Oxford, 1765–1770.

[126] See procedure for a plea of not guilty, a refusal to plead and a plea of guilty in ss 276-280 of the Criminal Procedure Code Chapter 88 of the Laws of Zambia.

[127] [1947] 2 ALL ER 272.

[128] [2003] 7 SCC 643.

A supplementary point is illustrated by AJ Ashworth[129] who contends that the presumption of innocence speaks to the political and moral values regarding the individual (including liberty, privacy, dignity and a good reputation) in liberal civilised societies which as is illustrated in Article 18(2)(a) of the Constitution is, in theory at least, a fundamental right in the Bill of Rights or Part III of the Constitution. The institution of criminal proceedings against an individual runs counter, and in fact invades the individual's space to enjoy liberty, privacy, dignity and a good reputation. If a question be asked then of why the concept of the presumption of innocence is important, the answer is that there must be justification by the state for invading the individual's rights by proving that he has abused his freedoms and thereby committed an offence against society as a whole: *The People*. This is important because the individual is faced with the prospect of, during his trial, deprivation of such trial and negative publicity; and afterwards, should he be convicted, stigma of conviction, negative publicity and chastisement. Should the significance of the presumption of innocence be affected by the gravity or notoriety of the offence in question? This question arose in the South African Constitutional Court decision of *State v Coetzee*[130] wherein Sachs J opined as follows:

> There is a paradox at the heart of all criminal procedure in that the more serious the crime and the greater the public interest in securing convictions of the guilty, the more important do constitutional protections of the accused become. The starting point of any balancing enquiry where constitutional rights are concerned must be that the public interest in ensuring that innocent people are not convicted and subjected to ignominy and heavy sentences massively outweighs the public interest in ensuring that a particular criminal is brought to book. Hence the presumption of innocence, which serves not only to protect a particular individual on trial, but to maintain public confidence in the enduring integrity and security of the legal system. Reference to the prevalence and severity of a certain crime therefore does not add anything new or special to the balancing exercise. The perniciousness of the offence is one of the givens, against which the presumption of innocence is pitted from the beginning, not a new element to be put into the scales as part of a justificatory balancing exercise. If this were not so, the ubiquity and ugliness argument could be used in relation to murder, rape, car-jacking, housebreaking, drug-smuggling, corruption . . . the list is unfortunately almost endless, and nothing would be left of the presumption of innocence, save, perhaps, for its relic status as a doughty defender of rights in the most trivial of cases.

There are additional practical points to be made as regards the constitutional

[129] Ashworth, "Four Threats to the presumption of Innocence" (2006) 10 E. & P. 241; see also, Stumer, *The Presumption of Innocence* (Hart Publishing, 2010); Hock LH, "The Presumption of Innocence as Human Right" in Roberts P and Hunter J (eds), Criminal Evidence and Human Rights (2012), 259.

[130] [1997] 2 LRC 593 followed by Steyn J in *R v Lambert* [2001] UKHL 37; [2002] 2 AC 545 at 34.

presumption of innocence in criminal matters.[131] The following have been suggested:

(i) A criminal prosecution is essentially a contest between the state and a private individual.[132] It is quite clear that this is not a contest of equals not only because of the power of the state but its resource availability in so far as investigation and prosecution of a case compared to the accused. For this reason, it is considered appropriate that the state, and not the accused bears the burden of not only obtaining but discharging such burden beyond reasonable doubt.

(ii) For the second reason, we have to go back to *Woolmington.*[133] Recall that at the Bristol Assizes, Judge Swift ruled that the case was so strong against Reginald Woolmington, the accused, that *the burden of proof was on him to show that the shooting was accidental.*[134] He was convicted (and automatically sentenced to death). In the EWCA, Lord Justice Avory refusal to grant leave to appeal, was predicated on a passage of Foster's *Crown Law* (1762) which read in part, *'[i]n every charge of murder, the fact of killing being first proved [...] the law presumeth the fact to have been founded in malice, until the contrary appeareth.'*[135] Of course, this was overturned in the House of Lords as exemplified in Lord Sankey's golden thread speech for which the *Woolmington case* is so famous for. More on this later. For now, it must be observed that had the House of Lords followed the lower courts, the burden of proving one's innocence would be on the accused. In other words, he would be presumed guilty until proven innocent. Under those circumstances, as the case was with Reginald Woolmington, the factfinder would be put in a position where he would convict every time the accused was vague as respects decisive facts relating to his guilt or innocence.

(iii) If the accused was presumed guilty until the contrary was proven, he would be facing a monumental, and sometimes (where the treachery of memory holds sway due to the passage of time or loss of relevant documents), an impossible task to prove his innocence. As has been argued by some,[136] '[...] placing the burden of proof on a defendant [or accused] will often deprive him of a fair opportunity to answer the allegations against him.'

3.3.5.3 *The significance of Woolmington's case*[137]

[131] See generally Roberts P, "Taking the Burden of Proof Seriously" [1995] Crim. L.R. 783 cited in Dennis I, The Law of Evidence 446-445.

[132] Under the UK's Corporate Manslaughter and Corporate Homicide Act 2007, companies and organisations may be tried, and where appropriate, be found guilty of corporate manslaughter as a resulting from serious management failures that lead to a gross breach of a duty of care.

[133] [1935] AC 462.

[134] Emphasis added.

[135] Emphasis added.

[136] Roberts P, "Taking the Burden of Proof Seriously" [1995] Crim. L.R. 783, 786.

[137] [1935] AC 462.

The importance of the Woolmington case cannot, as has already been made apparent from references made to it in this text thus far, be overemphasised. Two points, however, stand out as regards the case's significance:

(i) *Woolmington*[138] overturned a long held and respected position of the law known as Foster's doctrine[139] on the presumption of malice. *Woolmington*[140] did not restrict the requirement that the burden of proof be on the prosecution to only murder cases but to 'the web of English criminal law' or put another way, all criminal matters.

(ii) The *Woolmington* decision had another, perhaps, unintended consequence. It changed, according to Lord Hope of Craighead in *R v Lambert*,[141] 'the law as to burden of proof in the case of common law defences such as self-defence and non-insane automatism.' Thus, a slew of cases decided that the prosecution not only had the burden to prove the *mens rea* but also any and all defences raised against the charge with which he was faced. Thus, in *Mancini v DPP*,[142] the prosecution had to prove that the accused did not act under provocation; in *R v Gill*,[143] that the accused did not act under duress; in *Bratty v Attorney General for Northern Ireland*,[144] that the accused did not act in a state of sane automatism; and in *R v Lobell*,[145] that the accused did not act in self-defence.

3.3.5.4 *The exceptions to the general to the general rule in Woolmington*[146]

While most people would readily understand the general rule 'that the prosecution must prove the guilt of the [accused],' what is generally lost in interpretation are the exceptions highlighted by Lord Sankey's golden thread speech. They include the following:

(i) The defence of insanity; and
(ii) Statutory exceptions;
  (a) Express statutory exceptions; and
  (b) Implied statutory exception

(i) The defence of insanity

When in his speech in *Woolmington*,[147] Lord Sankey opined *inter alia* that 'it is the duty of the prosecution to prove the [accused's] guilt', he subjected or conditioned the foregoing on two exceptions the first of which was the defence

138 [1935] AC 462.
139 Foster's *Crown Law* (1762).
140 [1935] AC 462.
141 [2001] UKHL 37; [2002] 2 AC 545 at 82.
142 [1942] AC 1 HL.
143 [1963] 1 WLR 841 CCA.
144 [1963] AC 386 HL; It is to be remembered that a plea of insanity puts the burden of proof on the accused.
145 [1957] 1 QB 547 CCA.
146 [1935] AC 462.
147 [1935] AC 462.

of insanity. The implication thus was that where a defence of insanity was raised, the burden of proof lay, not on the prosecution, but exceptionally, on the accused. The basis for this reasoning appears to have been Lord Sankey's disinclination to overrule the *McNaghten*[148] rules given their quasi legislative status since they were adumbrated in *McNaghten's Case.*[149] The case ushered in the conventional test for insanity in the English criminal proceedings which is to ask whether the accused was at the material time so cerebrally troubled that he should be adjudged not to know or to have known the "nature and quality" of his action(s) or whether he is or was capable of realising that what he was doing or did was wrong. Beyond this supposition which is gleaned from Lord Sankey's own statements in *Woolmington*[150] for his reliance on *McNaghten's Case*[151] being that it was 'quite exceptional',there are no reasons, in fact, no good reasons to be found for the exclusion of the defence of insanity from the general rule as regards the burden of proof in criminal cases.[152] This though is quite problematic as *McNaghten's Case*[153] was decided in an era, prior to *Woolmington.*[154] As we mentioned earlier, this was an era fraught with decidedly disturbing procedural and evidentiary norms which would be anathema to any civilised society's criminal justice system today. The accused, as alluded to in *Jayasena v R,*[155] bore the burden of proof relating to any and all common law defences.

A few other points merit mention before we move on from the present discussion. The first is that the standard of proof demanded of the accused as shown in cases such as R *v Oliver Smith*[156] and *R v Carr-Briant*[157] dealing with the defence of insanity or *R v Dunbar*[158] regarding the defence of diminished responsibility, is on the balance of probabilities. As discussed earlier, where the preceding defences are raised, the prosecution is duty bound to adduce evidence as the case may be, that the accused in a murder charge was in fact sane or could not be said to have had diminished responsibility because he was in fact insane at the material time, subject of the criminal proceedings, as they relate specifically to the murder charge. If the prosecution have raised the issue as hereinbefore explained, they will, as a matter of procedure, bear the burden of proving the said issue beyond reasonable doubt. The issue is no different if what is raised by the prosecution[159] is the accused's fitness to plead. As shown

[148] *M'Naghten* (1843) 10 Cl. & Fin. 200.

[149] *M'Naghten* (1843) 10 Cl. & Fin. 200.

[150] [1935] AC 462.

[151] *M'Naghten* (1843) 10 Cl. & Fin. 200.

[152] According to the decision in *R v Lambert Ali and Jordan* [2001] 1 Cr App R 205.

[153] *M'Naghten* (1843) 10 Cl. & Fin. 200.

[154] [1935] AC 462.

[155] [1970] AC 618 at 623 *per* Lord Devlin; see additional analysis in Best WM, *A Treatise on the Principles of the Law of Evidence* (S. Sweet, 1849); See also the 1972 Criminal Review Committee's 11th Report para 140 wherein the rule regarding insanity is described as being anomalous.

[156] (1911) 6 Cr App R 19 at 20 CCA.

[157] [1943] KB 607 CCA.

[158] [1958] 1 QB 1.

[159] The issue may be raised by the prosecution or the defence.

in *R v Robertson,*[160] the prosecution will under such circumstances bear the burden of proof. The standard of proof ought to be beyond reasonable doubt.

(ii) Statutory exceptions

Excluded from Lord Sankey's golden thread in *Woolmington*[161] as regards the burden of proof in criminal matters are, '[…] any statutory exceptions.'[162] It has been suggested,[163] the foregoing notwithstanding, that the decision in *Woolmington*[164] being as it was, insistent on the fundamental nature of the burden of proof ought to have affected the methods and procedures related to enactment and construction of statutory offences. Further, that it ought to have, by necessary implication, stymied the tendency by Parliament to expressly reverse the onus. Finally, that it ought to have shaped judicial determinations regarding the question whether the legislature had reversed the onus impliedly. However, the discussion that follows shows a trend in the opposite direction on the preceding matters. According to Lord Ackner in *R v Hunt,*[165] the legislature may, if it deems it necessary, impose a burden of proof on the accused 'either expressly or by necessary implication.' There are generally two classes of statutory exceptions namely (a) express statutory exceptions and (b) implied statutory exception. We discuss each in turn.

(a) Express statutory exceptions

It goes without saying that the existence of a number of statutes in this jurisdiction which expressly impose the burden of proof on the accused rather than the prosecution is ordinarily expected given the decision in *Woolmington.*[166] Statutes that provide for special defences abound and include those specifically providing for the defence of diminished responsibility against a charge of murder. Further, as two recent decisions[167] discussed below demonstrate, they also include statutes that reverse the burden of proof and those that lower the standard of proof.

In *People v Austin Chisanga Liato,*[168] the Supreme Court had occasion to interpret provisions of the Forfeiture of Proceeds of Crime Act,[169] primarily as regards the burden of proof on the one hand and the standard of proof on the other, in cases concerning forfeiture of proceeds of crime under the Forfeiture

---

[160] [1968] 1 WLR 1767 CA.

[161] [1935] AC 462.

[162] In *R v Hunt* [1987] AC 352 HL, Lord Ackner rejected the idea that Lord Sankey's reference to 'any statutory exceptions' was limited to express statutory exceptions only.

[163] Dennis I, *The Law of Evidence.*

[164] [1935] AC 462.

[165] [1987] AC 352 HL.

[166] [1935] AC 462.

[167] *People v AustinChisanga Liato* Selected Judgment No 21 of 2015; *Lt Gen Geojago Robert Musengule and Amon Sibanda v The People* [SCZ Selected Judgment No 19 of 2017].

[168] Selected Judgment No 21 of 2015.

[169] No 19 of 2010.

of Proceeds of Crime Act.[170] The respondent was alleged to have possessed and concealed ZMW2,100,000.00 in Bank notes at his farm in two metal trunks, which were in turn buried in the earth and covered with concrete slabs. The money was assumed to be proceeds of crime. The respondent was convicted by the Magistrates Court on one count of possession of property suspected to be proceeds of crime contrary to s 71(1) of the Forfeiture of Proceeds of Crime Act.[171] Upon his conviction, he was sentenced to 24 months imprisonment with hard labour. Following his conviction, the respondent appealed to the High Court. The High court reversed the judgment of the Magistrates Court and acquitted him. The prosecution wholly dissatisfied with this reversal appealed to the Supreme Court. The Court was called upon to determine the following questions:

(i) Whether a predicate offence needed to be established first before a conviction for the offence of possessing property suspected of being proceeds of crime contrary to s 71(1) of the Forfeiture of Proceeds of Crime Act could be made.
(ii) What constituted 'reasonable suspicion' for tenacities of demonstrating the ingredients of the offence under s 71(1) of the Forfeiture of Proceeds of Crime Act.
(iii) What the necessary standard of proof was to establish reasonable suspicion under s 71(1) of the Act for purposes of securing a conviction.
(iv) Whether s 71(2) of the Forfeiture of Proceeds of Crime Act shifts the burden to prove the offence under s 71(1) from the prosecution to the accused person.

The justices held that in order to secure a conviction under s 71(1) of the Forfeiture of Proceeds of Crime Act,[172] no predicate offence required to be proved. As regards the definition of 'reasonable suspicion' under s 71(1) of the Act, the Court was of the opinion that *the term denoted a state of conjecture or surmise, where proof is lacking.*[173]

As regards the standard of proof, the Court took the view that proof beyond reasonable doubt (as intimated in *Woolmington*[174]) for reasonable suspicion was neither contemplated nor intended under s 71(1) of the Act. Section 78 of the Act provides that 'save as otherwise provided in this Act, any question of fact to be decided by the Court proceedings under that Act is to be decided on the balance of probabilities.' According to the Court, this lowered the standard of proof in proving the offence envisaged in s 71 from that beyond reasonable doubt as held in criminal in *Woolmington v DPP*[175] to merely *a balance of probabilities.*[176]

As regards the burden of proof, the Court rejected the notion that s 71(2)

[170] No 19 of 2010.
[171] No 19 of 2010.
[172] No 19 of 2010.
[173] Emphasis added.
[174] [1935] AC 462, 481.
[175] [1935] AC 462, 481.
[176] Emphasis added.

imposed a duty on the accused to prove any ingredient of the offence under s 71(1) or put another way, that the provision placed the burden of proving the offence on the accused. All the provision did, said the Court, was afford the accused an opportunity to explain the absence of reasonable grounds for the suspicion that the property he was found in possession of under s 71(1) were proceeds of crime.

The case of *Lt Gen Geojago Robert Musengule and Amon Sibanda v The People*[177] was an appeal against a judgment of the High Court rendered in its appellate jurisdiction. The High Court upheld the Magistrates Court's decision convicting the appellants and sentencing them as a consequence, on numerous counts of abuse of authority of office and corrupt practices by a public officer contrary to germane provisions of the Anti-Corruption Commission Act.[178]

One contention centred on whether s 49(2) of the Anti-Corruption Commission Act[179] was in conflict with Article 18(7) of the Constitution, which provides that a person who is tried for a criminal offence shall not be compelled to give evidence at the trial. S 49(2) of the Anti-Corruption Commission Act[180] was couched as follows:

> Where, in any proceedings for an offence under Part IV, it is proved that any person solicited, accepted or obtained or agreed to accept or attempted to receive or obtain any payment in any of the circumstances set out in the relevant section under which he is charged, then such payment shall, in the absence of a satisfactory explanation, be presumed to have been solicited, accepted or obtained or agreed to be accepted, received or obtained corruptly.

Rejecting the argument that under s 49(2) of the Anti-Corruption Commission Act,[181] if an accused person elected to remain silent or elected not to give a satisfactory explanation, the trial court was entitled to presume that any payment received by him was corruptly solicited, accepted, received or obtained and would convict him accordingly,[182] the Supreme Court opined as follows:

> Despite that ringing phrase of Viscount Sanky LC in the landmark case of *Woolmington v DPP*,[183] regarding that 'golden thread of English criminal law', there are numerous developments that we can point to confirming that the presumption of innocence is not cast in stone, and it gives way in appropriate circumstances to a 'presumption of culpability', for lack of a better expression. It is an elementary point

[177] [SCZ Selected Judgment No. 19 of 2017].

[178] Chapter 91 of the Laws of Zambia which Act was repealed and replaced by the Anti-Corruption Act No 38 of 2010, which was in turn repealed by the Anti-Corruption Act No 3 of 2012.

[179] Chapter 91 of the Laws of Zambia (repealed).

[180] Chapter 91 of the Laws of Zambia (repealed).

[181] Chapter 91 of the Laws of Zambia which Act (repealed).

[182] Anchored on counsel's interpretation of *Re Thomas Mumba* [1984] ZR 38.

[183] [1935] AC 462, 481.

that parliament has never been averse to creating statutory exceptions that cast the burden on the accused person to disprove his culpability. For example, our penal code has given recognition to the principle of recent possession. In circumstances where a person is found to be in possession of goods reasonably suspected to have been stolen, he or she will be expected to offer an explanation. In other words, there will be a presumption that the goods were stolen by that person unless he proves his innocence.[184]

More recently, in *The People v Austin Chisanga Liato*,[185] we interpreted s 71(2) of the Forfeiture of Proceeds of Crime Act[186] *as reversing, to a certain extent, the burden of proof in matters involving forfeiture of proceeds of crime.*[187]

Bearing in mind the supremacy of the Constitution, it goes without saying that any subsidiary legislation, be it the Penal Code, the Anti-Corruption Act or the Forfeiture of Proceeds of Crime Act, that provides for any shift in the evidentiary burden, must still accord with Article 1.8 of the Constitution, or it will be void for being inconsistent with the Constitution.

We have examined the provisions of Article 18(2), which guarantees the presumption of innocence. We agree that the provision entails that an accused person cannot be called upon to incriminate him or herself by volunteering evidence favourable to the prosecution's case on demand. The prosecution must prove the allegations. The requirement under s 49(2) of the Anti-Corruption Commission Act may indeed appear to contravene Article 18(2) of the Constitution, as the learned counsel for the second appellant perceives it. That perception is, however, illusory when one considers the provisions of Article 18(12) of the Constitution which reads: Nothing contained or done under the authority of any law shall be held to be inconsistent with or in contravention of paragraph (a) of Clause 2 to the extent that it is shown that the law in question imposes upon any person charged with a criminal offence the burden of proving particular facts.

We must add that the shifting of the evidential burden and the burden of proof in some cases is not a phenomenon peculiar to Zambia. The essence of the presumption of innocence is that the prosecution bears the burden of proving that the accused person is guilty, failure of which would warrant an acquittal. The question therefore is: does the burden of proof shift onto the accused person if he is required to give an explanation? In our considered view, merely being called upon to offer an explanation does not amount to being requested to prove that one is innocent. To begin with, the requirement for the accused to give an explanation under s 49(2) emanates from the fact that there is already proof that he had solicited, obtained, or accepted a payment, which creates a presumption that he did so corruptly. The section therefore, creates a presumption that, if he fails to give a

[184] The case of *Zonde & Others v The People* [1980) ZR 337] was deemed instructive.

[185] [Selected Judgment No 21 of 2015].

[186] No 19 of 2010.

[187] (Emphasis added).

> satisfactory answer, then he must have received, solicited, obtained, or accepted the payment corruptly. In the face of such an allegation, the accused has the right and not an obligation to explain his position. The accused person thus still maintains his right to remain silent. At this stage the prosecution has not established that the accused person is guilty; the burden to prove so still remains on it to prove beyond reasonable doubt. Therefore, the accused person still is presumed innocent until such a burden has been discharged by the prosecution. In *Kenious Sialuzi v The People,*[188] we said that the appellant's silence did not change the burden of proof cast on the prosecution to prove his guilt beyond all reasonable doubt because there was no burden of proof cast on him to prove any particular fact. But if he does elect to remain silent, which he is entitled to do, the court will not speculate as to possible explanations for the event in question. The court's duty is to draw the proper inference from whatever evidence it has before it [....]
>
> Counsel relied heavily on the High Court case of *Re Thomas Mumba,* in which the court found [s]ection 53 of the Corrupt Practices Act No. 14 of 1980 to have been unconstitutional. This compelled the accused person who elected to give evidence before court to do so on oath. The constitutional provision which was held to have been contravened gave the accused person who, in the first place, has the right to be silent but has opted to give evidence but is compelled to give that evidence on oath.
>
> We do not find the case of *Re Thomas Mumba* to be of any assistance to the second appellant's argument. Being of that persuasion, we hold that Ground One has no merit and we dismiss it.

(b) Implied statutory exception

It has generally been accepted that express statutory provisions may, as shown in *thePeople v Austin Chisanga Liato*[189] and *Lt Gen Geojago Robert Musengule and Amon Sibanda v The People*[190] reverse the burden of proof. What has, however, proved polemical has been the conclusion that the exceptions in *Woolmington*[191] were not limited to express provisions but should be logically be taken to include implied statutory exceptions. The effect of the foregoing is to whittle away at the general principle that the prosecution ought to prove the guilt of the accused and not the other way round.

The earliest expression of acceptance of the position that Lord Sankey's 'statutory exceptions' went beyond those statutes that expressly cast the burden of proof on the accused to encompass those that did so impliedly occurred in the case of *R v Turner.*[192] The accused was charged with being in possession of pheasants without the presents particularly difficult problems of

[188] [2006] ZR 87.

[189] Selected Judgment No 21 of 2015.

[190] [SCZ Selected Judgment No. 19 of 2017].

[191] [1935] AC 462, 481.

[192] (1816) 5 M & S 206, as adapted in Uglow S, *Evidence* 85-86.

construction when what might be regarded as a matter of defence appears in a clause creating the offence rather than in some subsequent proviso from which it may more readily be inferred that it was intended to provide for a separate defence which a defendant must set up and prove if he wishes to avail himself of it. Bayley J observed as follows:

> My Lords, I am, of course, well aware of the body of distinguished academic opinion that urges wherever a burden of proof is placed on a defendant by statue the burden should be an evidential burden and not a persuasive burden, and that has the support of the distinguished signatories to the 11th Report of the Criminal Law Revision Committee [...] My Lords, such a fundamental change is, in my view, a matter for Parliament and not a decision of your Lordships' House [...]

Rather than looking at the curious problem presented in the foregoing as chipping away at the *Woolmington*[193] principle as regards the presumption of innocence, what becomes glaringly clear is that the Court chose to frame this as a matter of statutory interpretation. Allied to the preceding where practical considerations as they relate to the accused and the challenge of discharging his burden of proof. By way of example, the prosecution may have available to them forensic evidence relating to the murder of the victim based on their own analysis but which the accused will not have the same level of access to. Where ambiguity resulted from circumstances, facts and specific statutory provisions as regards the matter of whether the particular Act in question had impliedly reversed the burden of proof by implication, such ambiguity should be resolved, said the House of Lords, as usually is the case in criminal cases, in favour of the accused.

The latter case of *R v Hunt*[194] flatly rejected the assertion that Lord Sankey's reference to "any statutory exception" was confined to express statutory exceptions. Lord Ackner observed that Parliament had legislative authority to impose a burden of proof on the accused "expressly or by necessary implication."

Further to the preceding, the House of Lords vetoed the suggestion that any burden on the accused should be construed as an evidential one and not legal one. In his speech in support of said rejection, Lord Griffiths opined as follows:

> My Lords, I am, of course well aware of the body of distinguished opinion that urges that wherever a burden of proof is placed upon a defendant by statute the burden should be an evidential burden and not a persuasive burden, and that it has the support of the 11th Report of the Criminal Law Revision Committee, Evidence (General) 1972 (Cmnd 4991). *My Lords, such a fundamental change is, in my view, a*

[193] [1935] AC 462, 481.

[194] [1987] AC 352.

> *matter for Parliament and not a decision for your Lordships' House.*[195]

Applying the foregoing to the scenario in this jurisdiction as demonstrated in *Liato*[196] and *Musengule,*[197] where there is a statutory exception as regards the presumption of innocence or burden of proof, the burden imposed on the accused is a legal one and not an evidential one unless the contrary can be demonstrated. In *Musengule,*[198] the Supreme Court held the view that the fact thatParliament had never 'been averse to creating statutory exceptions that cast the burden on the accused person to disprove his culpability' to be an elementary one.' The example given was that which came up for consideration in the case of *Zonde and Others v The People,*[199] where the Supreme Court held that '[t]he doctrine of recent possession applies to a person *in the absence of any explanation*[200] that might be true when found in possession of the complainant's property barely a few hours after the complainant had suffered an aggravated robbery.'[201] Put another way, the burden of proof is placed on the accused to prove his innocence which is a roundabout way of saying that the accused is presumed guilty until he can prove otherwise by way of a satisfactory explanation.

While the foregoing examples illustrate cases of express provisions relating to reversal of the burden and by necessary implication, the presumption of innocence, they are also important as regards the concept of implied reversal, polemical as this may be. The point to be made though is that the likely space for construing statutes as having impliedly reversed the burden of proof and thereby undermine the presumption of innocence under Article 18(2)(a) of the Constitution is fairly vast if one considers the draftsperson's inclination

---

[195] Emphasis added.

[196] Selected Judgment No 21 of 2015.

[197] *Regina v Edwards* ([1975] 1 QB 27); *Regina v Hunt (Richard)* HL ([1987] 1 AC 352, [1987] 1 All ER 1.

[198] [SCZ Selected Judgment No 19 of 2017].

[199] (1980) ZR 337.

[200] Emphasis added.

[201] In *George Nswana v The People* [1988 – 1989] ZR 174 (SC), the appellant was found in possession of a car two days after it was stolen. The correct car number was etched on its windows and appeared on the licence disc but the vehicle carried a false number plate. When the applicant was apprehended, he produced a blue book which bore a false name of the purported owner. At his trial he said he was in possession of the car as a driver of his employer who had asked him to drive it. In an earlier explanation to the police, he said he had borrowed the car from the person he said in evidence was his employer. The trial magistrate found that as a prudent driver the applicant must have noticed the suspicious features surrounding the car and, that coupled with recent possession and that the applicant's explanation was not true, convicted him. In the Supreme Court he argued that the telling of lies does not necessarily indicate guilt and the magistrate's finding that the applicant did not obtain possession from another person should be rejected. It was held inter alia, that the inference of guilt based on recent possession, particularly where no explanation is offered which might reasonably be true, rests on the absence of any reasonable likelihood that the goods might have changed hands in the meantime and the consequent high degree of probability that the person in recent possession himself obtained them and committed the offence. Where suspicious features surround the case that indicate that the applicant cannot reasonably claim to have been in innocent possession, the question remains whether the applicant, not being in innocent possession, was the thief or a guilty receiver or retainer.

to employ terms such as 'excuse, proviso, exemption or qualification.'[202] As demonstrated in *Zonde,*[203] *Liato*[204] and *Musengule,*[205] however, courts are more likely to follow the *Hunt*[206] principle where there is a clearly expressed legislative intent to place the burden of proof on the accused even though this be by implication.

A case that may be of interest to our courts in view of s 42[207] of the Forest Act[208] is that of *R (Grundy and Co Excavations Ltd) v Halstead MagistratesCourt.*[209] The casewas concerned with the felling of trees in want of a licence contrary to s 17 of the UK Forestry Act 1967. On the instruction of the owner of the land in question who desired to make a hard standing, Grundy's employees cut down 86 trees. A felling licence under s 9(1) of the Act had not been obtained. Grundy's defence was that he was not aware that a licence was required. The trial judge held that the only burden of proof on the prosecutor was to prove that the accused felled the trees and that it was then for the accused to prove on the balance of probability either that he had a licence or that a licence was not required because the Act provided for a number of exceptions.[210] The Divisional Court, however, construed the Act as placing the legal burden on the accused. It is worth noting, before moving on that as regards statutory exceptions to the *Woolmington*[211] doctrine, '[t]t is [...] clear that, while the general principles are those set out in *Edwards,*[212] each case depends upon the construction of the particular statute. The question in each case will be whether the provision concerned is an 'exception, exemption, proviso, excuse or qualification.'

3.3.5.5 *Reverse onus vis-à-vis human rights and the presumption of innocence*[213]

(i) Reverse onus and the Constitution

In this jurisdiction the presumption of innocence in criminal matters is a constitutional and thus, by necessary implication, a fundamental right not

[202] *Per* Lord Clark in *R (Grundy and Co Excavations Ltd) v Halstead Magistrates Court* [2003] EWHC 272 (Admin), [2003] 1 PLR 89.

[203] (1980) ZR 337.

[204] Selected Judgment No 21 of 2015.

[205] [SCZ Selected Judgment No 19 of 2017].

[206] [1987] AC 352.

[207] Which provides as follows: 'Except as otherwise provided in this Act, any person who cuts, or takes or otherwise deals with any forest produce or does any other act the doing of which requires a licence, without a licence, commits an offence.'

[208] Act No 7 of 1999.

[209] [2003] EWHC 272 (Admin); *R v Edwards* ([1975] 1 QB 27); *R v Hunt* (Richard) HL ([1987] 1 AC 352, (1986) 84 Cr App R 163, [1986] 3 WLR 1115, [1987] AC 352, [1987] 1 All ER 1.

[210] Emphasis added.

[211] [1935] AC 462, 481.

[212] *R v Edwards* ([1975] 1 QB 27) where it was held that '[o]n a charge of selling intoxicating liquor without a justices' licence, it is not for the prosecutor to prove that the defendant had no licence but for the defendant to prove that he had (https://swarb.co.uk/grundy-and-co-excavations-ltd-and-another-regina-on-the-application-of-v-halton-division-magistrates-court-admn-24-feb-2003/).

[213] See generally, Dennis I, "Reverse Onus and the Presumption of Innocence" [2005] Crim.L.R. 901 at 937; Padfield N, "The Burden of Proof Unresolved" [2005] Cambridge L.J.17.

to be easily derogated from except as permitted under the Bill of Rights.[214] Specifically, Article 18(2)(a) of the Constitution provides that '[e]very person who is charged with a criminal offence - shall be *presumed* to be innocent until he is proved or has pleaded guilty.' Thus, the debate regarding reverse onus and its constitutionality has centred on the fundamental nature of the right to be presumed innocent, and to place the burden of proving otherwise on the prosecution. Put another way, the accused is ordinarily treated as not having committed the offence with which he is charge or any offence for that matter, and should be treated as such unless and until the prosecution has adduced evidence of such sufficiency as to satisfy an autonomous and unbiassed tribunal that the accused is guilty of the offence with which he is charged or, as the case may be, the accused pleads guilty. What this leads to is encapsulated in the words of Chomba J in *The People v Chimbala:*[215]

> '[I]t is incumbent upon the prosecution to prove accused's guilt beyond reasonable doubt. If on considering all the evidence adduced for and against the charge I remain in reasonable doubt as to the accused's guilt I shall be duty bound to resolve such doubt in the favour of the accused and therefore to acquit him.'

The only exemption to the foregoing relates to strict liability offences. This is because in those sorts of cases, the prosecution is required only to prove the *actus reus* without the need to prove that the accused formed the intention to act as he did or short of that, to produce the result that are now subject of the criminal proceedings. While this may look at first glance to a reversal of the burden of proof, it most certainly is not. It is only an acknowledgement by the criminal law that there is no need for the prosecution to prove what ordinarily is an indispensable part of the offence in question.

(i) Reversal of the burden: When the defendant has to prove some defence

There are instances, some of which we have considered elsewhere in this text, where the burden of proof is reversed for the accused to prove a defence raised. The question of whether this infringes the constitutional nay human rights presumption of innocence arose in *Salabiaku v France*.[216] A Zairian national living in Paris, went to the airport to collect, as he said, a parcel of foodstuffs sent from Africa. He could not find this, but was shown a locked trunk, which he was advised to leave alone. He however took possession of it, went through the green customs channel and was detained. The trunk contained cannabis. He was charged with two offences, a criminal offence of illegally importing narcotics and a 'customs offence' of smuggling prohibited goods. At trial and

---

[214] Part III of the Constitution; see derogation under Article 18(12) considered in *Lt. General Geojago Robert Musengule and Amon Sibande v The People* [SCZ Selected Judgment No 19 of 2017].

[215] [1973] ZR 118 (HC).

[216] (1988) 13 EHRR 379, 10519/83, [1988] ECHR 19; summary excepted from https://swarb.co.uk/salabiaku-v-france-echr-7-oct1988/#:~:text=Salabiaku%20v%20France%3A%20ECHR%207%20Oct%201988%20A, through%20the%20green%20customs%20channel%20and%20was%20detained; *R v Lambert* [2001] 3 All ER 577.

on appeal he was acquitted of the former but convicted of smuggling, an offence relating to any act of smuggling or undeclared import: a person in possession of contraband goods 'shall be deemed liable for the offence.' The accused may exculpate himself by establishing force majeure resulting 'from an event responsibility for which is not attributable to him and which it was absolutely impossible for him to avoid'. The 'almost irrebuttable presumption' [...] was said to be incompatible with article 6.[217] It was held that Contracting States may apply the criminal law to an act where it is not carried out in the normal exercise of one of the rights protected under the Convention, and accordingly, to define the constituent elements in the resulting offence. Further, that Contracting States may penalise a simple or objective fact as such, irrespective of whether it results from criminal intent or from negligence. Examples of such offences may be found in the laws of the Contracting States. However, the Applicant was not convicted for mere possession of unlawfully imported prohibited goods. Article 392(1) of the Customs Code does not appear under the heading 'classification of customs offences' but under that of 'criminal liability'. Under this provision a conclusion is drawn from a simple fact, which in itself does not necessarily constitute a petty or a more serious offence, that the 'criminal liability' for the unlawful importation of the goods, whether they are prohibited or not, or the failure to declare them, lies with the person in whose possession they are found. It infers therefrom a legal presumption on the basis of which (the French Courts) found the Applicant guilty of smuggling prohibited goods [...] This shift from the idea of accountability in criminal law to the notion of guilt shows the very relative nature of such a distinction. It raises a question with regard to Article 6.2 of the Convention. The Convention does not prohibit presumptions of fact in principle, but does require certain limits as regards criminal law. If 6.2 merely laid down a guarantee to be respected by the courts in the conduct of legal proceedings, its requirements would in practice overlap with the duty of impartiality imposed in paragraph 1. Above all, the national legislature would be free to strip the trial court of any genuine power of assessment and deprive the presumption of innocence of its substance, if the words 'according to law' were construed exclusively with reference of domestic law. Such a situation could not be reconciled with the object and purpose of Article 6, which, by protecting the right to a fair trial and in particular the right to be presumed innocent, is intended to enshrine the fundamental principle of the rule of law. Article 6.2 does not therefore regard presumptions of fact or of law provided for in the criminal law with indifference. It requires States to confine them within reasonable limits which take into account the importance of what is at stake and maintain the rights of the defence.

We saw earlier from a consideration of *Liato*[218] and *Musengule*[219] that there are several statutes that expressly or by implication, reverse the burden of proof. They include from our discussion above, s 49(2) of the Anti-Corruption

[217] Of the European Convention on Human Rights (ECHR).

[218] [Selected Judgment No 21 of 2015].

[219] [SCZ Selected Judgment No 19 of 2017].

Commission Act,[220] s 71(2) of the Forfeiture of Proceeds of Crime Act[221] which was construed by the Supreme Court in *Liato*[222] as reversing, to a certain extent, the burden of proof in matters involving forfeiture of proceeds of crime,[223] s 42 of the Forest Act, [224] and s 3(1) (among others) of the Penal Code.[225] In *Liato*[226] and *Musengule*[227] the Supreme Court was called upon to pronounce itself on how provisions in Forfeiture of Proceeds of Crime Act[228] and those in the Anti-Corruption Commission Act[229] which on their face appeared to fall foul of Article 18(2)(a) could not be deemed unconstitutional for failure to comply with the requirement that the accused had to be presumed innocent, and by extension, though not forming the thrust of the appellant's argument, that the provisions in fact contrary to Article 18(7), compelled the accused to give evidence potentially incriminating him. What counsel did was to play a high stakes game. It is a game that compelled the Court to dig dip.

In *Musengule*,[230] the Supreme Court was at pains to explain that contrary to what appeared to be common belief, the Zambian Parliament had in fact shown guarded alacrity in creating statutory exceptions to the general rule regarding burden of proof. The Court adverted to the Penal Code's 'recognition of the principle of recent possession.' According to the Court, '[i]n circumstances where a person is found to be in possession of goods reasonably suspected to have been stolen, he or she will be expected to offer an explanation' [...] to 'proves his innocence.'[231] This explanation, as may be patent, is in no way satisfactory as regards the question whether the particular provision in the Penal Code[232] runs afoul of Articles 18(2)(a) and by extension Article 18(7). Nor was the Court's interpretation of s 71(2) of the Forfeiture of Proceeds of Crime Act[233] as 'reversing, to a certain extent, the burden of proof in matters involving forfeiture of proceeds of crime'[234] in *The People v Austin Chisanga Liato*.[235] The Court admitted as much when it stated that 'any subsidiary legislation, be it the Penal Code, the Anti-Corruption Act or the Forfeiture of Proceeds of Crime Act, that provides for any shift in the evidentiary burden, must still accord

[220] Chapter 91 of the Laws of Zambia (repealed) which itself, repealed The Corrupt Practices Act No 14 of 1980.

[221] No 19 of 2010; For a concise lucid historical analysis see J Chirwa, "The Tyranny of Good Intentions and Death of Presumption of Innocence," *The Mast on Saturday*, May 7, 2022.

[222] [Selected Judgment No 21 of 2015].

[223] (Emphasis added).

[224] No 7 of 1999.

[225] Chapter 87 of the Laws of Zambia.

[226] [Selected Judgment No 21 of 2015].

[227] [SCZ Selected Judgment No 19 of 2017].

[228] No 19 of 2010.

[229] Chapter 91 of the Laws of Zambia (repealed) which itself, repealed The Corrupt Practices Act No 14 of 1980.

[230] [SCZ Selected Judgment No 19 of 2017].

[231] The case of *Zonde & Others v The People* [1980) ZR 337] was deemed instructive.

[232] Chapter 87 of the Laws of Zambia.

[233] No 19 of 2010.

[234] (Emphasis added).

[235] [Selected Judgment No 21 of 2015].

with Article 18 of the Constitution, or it will be void for being inconsistent with the Constitution.' Be that as it may, this statement is problematic. With the deepest respect, there quite honestly is no problem with the evidentiary burden shifting during trial. Further, it does not appear that Lord Sankey's golden thread sought to include in the burden that lies on the prosecution to prove the charges against an accused person, what the Supreme Court here was talking about: the evidential burden. It is doubtful that Lord Sankey could, in his *dicta*, have meant that statutory exceptions meant evidential burden exceptions in addition to legal burden exceptions. This is so, it is submitted with respect, because he did not set a general rule imposing the evidential burden to which statutory provisions could make exceptions by reversing same, on the prosecution. Thus, a statute imposing an evidential burden is nothing special. It is only confirmation by codification of what the common law has provided in various court decisions.

It must be submitted with the deepest respect, that the Court then went further to draw the conclusion that was as half-hearted an admission as one would ever get before construing s 49(2) of the Anti-Corruption Commission Act as not contravening Article 18(2) which places the presumption of innocence on a fundamental right footing in keeping with Lord Sankey's golden thread in *Woolmington*. 'We agree', the Court noted, 'that the provision entails that an accused person cannot be called upon to incriminate him or herself by volunteering evidence favourable to the prosecution's case on demand. The prosecution must prove the allegations.' The Court then went on to acknowledge by equivocating on whether s 49(2) of the Anti-Corruption Commission Act contravenes Article 18(2) of the Constitution 'as the learned counsel for the second appellant perceives it.' The Court found itself caught between declaring s 49(2) of the Anti-Corruption Commission Act unconstitutional (which it really is if one considers it solely within the context of Article 18(2)(a)) on the one hand and acquitting the accused, on the other, the latter of which it seemed disinclined to do. It appeared that this would be a step too far. To extricate itself from this potentially embarrassing situation, the Court sought solace and found it in the dreaded Constitutional claw back clause found in Article 18(12) of the Constitution which reads: '[n]othing contained or done under the authority of any law shall be held to be inconsistent with or in contravention of paragraph (a) of Clause 2 to the extent that it is shown that the law in question imposes upon any person charged with a criminal offence the burden of proving particular facts.' This claw back clause presents one of the most dangerous threats to the presumption of innocence which the Constitution itself supposedly guarantees. It empowers Parliament to, without more, enact any legislation to reverse any burden on the prosecution to prove a charge. In theory, it has the potential to take us back to the heretical pre-*Woolmington* era when the legal burden to prove one's innocence lay on the accused. It must be added for the avoidance of doubt, that the phrase 'the burden of proving particular facts' must be taken to apply to the legal burden rather than the evidential burden being reversed. This distinction is important in view of what the Court said next:

> The essence of the presumption of innocence is that the prosecution bears the burden of proving that the accused person is guilty, failure of which would warrant an acquittal. The question therefore is: does the burden of proof shift onto the accused person if he is required to give an explanation? In our considered view, merely being called upon to offer an explanation does not amount to being requested to prove that one is innocent. To begin with, the requirement for the accused to give an explanation under s 49(2) emanates from the fact that there is already proof that he had solicited, obtained, or accepted a payment, which creates a presumption that he did so corruptly. The section therefore, creates a presumption that, if he fails to give a satisfactory answer, then he must have received, solicited, obtained, or accepted the payment corruptly. In the face of such an allegation, the accused has the right and not an obligation to explain his position. The accused person thus still maintains his right to remain silent. At this stage the prosecution has not established that the accused person is guilty; the burden to prove so still remains on it to prove beyond reasonable doubt. Therefore, the accused person still is presumed innocent until such a burden has been discharged by the prosecution.

Again, in making reference to both the shift in the burden of proof and the evidential burden, the Court was conflating two different issues which could find no support in either s 49 of the Anti-Corruption Commission Act, s 71(2) of the Forfeiture of Proceeds of Crime Act; the concept of recent possession in the Penal Code[236] or indeed Article 18(12) of the Constitution. As noted above, which is not explained in the Court's judgment, the "evidential burden" unlike the "legal burden" is simply the mandatory burden a party has to adduce evidence. All that is required is that it be sufficient as to raise an issue fit for the court's contemplation. It follows that as regards the evidential burden; the prosecution will be duty bound to present sufficient evidence if only to placate a fair-minded tribunal that the elements of the charge/offence have been proved beyond reasonable doubt.[237] It can thus be said from the foregoing that the prosecution bears the evidential burden for making out a *prima facie* case for the accused to answer which if he did not by offering an alternative to the prosecution's case, the court would convict him of the charge. However, this is not the same thing as saying that what the relevant provisions in the statutes that Supreme Court considered, and Article 18(12) of the Constitution provide for is a reversal of not only the burden of proof, which they do, but the evidential burden which they do not.

It is easy to, as was said by Lord Devlin in *Jayasena v R*,[238] conflate the discharge of an evidential burden with a decision, as would be in the discharge

[236] Chapter 87 of the Laws of Zambia.

[237] *Murono v The People* [2004] ZR 207; This is with reference to the requirement that the charge must be proved beyond reasonable doubt but see *Miller v Minister of Pensions* [1947] 2 ALL ER 272; *Sucha Singh and Another v State of Punjab* [2003] 7 SCC 643.

[238] [1970] AC 618 at 624 PC *per* Lord Devlin.

of a legal burden, proving any fact in issue. With deep respect, this appears to have been the error that the Supreme Court fell into if only to extricate itself from what are apparently unconstitutional provisions salvageable only with reference to the dark ages and frankly, not-fit-for-purpose, claw back clauses scheme drafting employed in our Bill of Rights. Article 18(12) makes a mockery of Article 18(7). It ought to have been clearly explained what the difference between the concept of legal burden and evidential burden was and is. While logic entails that Lord Sankey's golden thread in *Woolmington,*[239]means that generally he who bears the legal burden must normally also bear the evidential burden to adduce sufficient evidence on the particular issue in question, there are exceptions to this. For example, where a presumption becomes an integral part of the facts in issue relating to a particular case, 'it may, as Dennis[240] has pointed out, 'have the effect of relieving a party of the obligation to adduce evidence on a point, other than evidence of the fact forming the foundation of the presumption.'For example,in *Hill v Baxter*,[241] the accused bore the evidential burden to produce sufficient evidence to raise the defence of automatism to compel the court into determining that a material issue fit for consideration had been raised, the prosecution nevertheless bore the legal burden of disproving the said defence.Thus, the general rule relating to the evidential burden is fraught with exceptions among them, the use of judicial evidence,[242] judicial notice[243] and presumptions.[244]

---

[239] [1935] AC 462.

[240] Dennis I, *The Law of Evidence* 442.

[241] [1958] 1 QB 277 at 284-5.

[242] Which include the following:

1. Direct evidence
2. Circumstantial evidence
3. Real evidence
4. Primary and secondary evidence
5. Documentary Evidence
6. Hearsay Evidence
7. Best Evidence
8. Opinion evidence

[243] Where a party asks the court to take judicial notice of a fact, the court will not demand for evidence of the existence of such a fact to be adduced. In *Mwape v The People* [1976] wherein Silungwe CJ as he was then opined that '[a] court [...] will, for instance, take judicial notice of matters of common knowledge which are so notorious that to lead evidence in order to establish their existence may be unnecessary and could, as Phipson puts it in his Manual of the Law of Evidence, 10th edn at p 21 be 'an insult to the intelligence to require evidence'; see further *Clinton v Lyons & Co Ltd* [1912] 3 KB 198.

[244] There are several presumptions including (i) conclusive/irrebuttable presumptions e.g., at s 14(3) of the Penal Code provides '[a] male person under the age of twelve years is presumed to be incapable of having carnal knowledge.' This presumption, no matter the evidence, oral, real or documentary available to prove the charge of rape against a 12-year-old is irrebuttable; (ii) presumptions of fact whose effect is to compel the court to determine that because fact A is true then fact B which by common sense should go hand in hand with fact should also be true: *Attorney General v Bradlaugh* (1885) 14 QBD 667. This identifies more with circumstantial evidence than it does with presumptions; (iii) Rebuttable presumptions or evidential presumptions as they are called in English law are that class of presumptions the essence of which is that where a particular fact is proved/admitted then by necessary implication it is not necessary to prove other presumed facts: *Chard v Chard* [1955]; (iv) Other presumptions include that of innocence according to Article 18(2) of the Constitution, and that of sanity under s 11 of the Penal Code chapter 87 of the Laws of Zambia. We will discuss these further, later in the text.

Distillable from *Mancini v DPP*[245] is the principle that where sufficient evidence appears to exist for a general defence to the offence/charge to raise a reasonable doubt, but no such defence is raised by the accused, the court ought to direct its mind to this fact.[246] In the event that the evidential burden in the scenario above is not discharged, all the prosecution will have to do is to prove the elements of the offence/charge to the requisite standard. However, where the evidential burden has been successfully discharged thereby increasing the legal scope of the prosecution's legal burden as a consequence, the prosecution has its work cut out. Not only does it have to prove the elements of the offence/charge but also the fact that the accused was indeed not provoked nor did he act in self-defence when he killed the victim.

In *R v Hunt (Richard Selwyn),*[247] the Court took the view that 'the discharge of an evidential burden proves nothing – it merely raises an issue.' Thus, the only significance to be attached to the discharge of an evidential burden is that the question relating to the evidential burden was validly raised with sufficient predication for the possible existence of a material fact as to justify a finding in favour of the party that bears the said evidential burden. Hence, Lord Bingham suggested, it is rather erroneous to call the evidential burden "an evidential burden of proof."[248] Further, that 'it is a burden of raising, on the evidence in the case, an issue as to the matter in question fit for consideration by the tribunal of fact. If an issue is properly raised, it is for the prosecutor to prove, beyond reasonable doubt, that the ground of exoneration does not avail the [accused].' The distinguishing characteristics between the evidential burden and the legal burden, as noted earlier, relate to what the factfinder will look at in determining the question before him either way. In our legal system, a judge makes determinations as regards both the discharge of the evidential as well as the legal burden of proof, for the former, as and when it arises and for the latter, when the judge has to consider what verdict to issue at the close of trial.[249]

The constitutional presumption of innocence is in theory and until parliament legislates in accordance with the claw back clause in Article 18(12) of the Constitution, as it has done with the statutes discussed in *Liato*[250] and *Musengule,*[251] a given, and a fundamental right at that. The Court's explanation of what the presumption of innocence entails in the said authorities, while quite clear and in keeping with the law as we know it, is only blunted by the answer it gave to its own question in *Musengule*[252] on whetherthe burden of proof shift onto the accused person if he is required to give an explanation.

---

[245] [1942] AC 1 HL; see generally, Doran S, [1991] Crim. L.R. 878.

[246] It must be noted that the principle in Mancini was made within the context of a judge directing a jury, a concept that is strange and foreign to our legal system.

[247] [1987] AC 352 at 358 HL *per* Lord Ackner.

[248] *Sheldrake v DPP* [2004] UKHL 43; [2005] 1 All ER 237.

[249] See Williams G, "The Evidential Burden: Some Common Misapprehensions" (1977) 127 NLJ 156.

[250] S 49(2) of Chapter 91 of the Laws of Zambia (repealed).

[251] S 71(2) of the Forfeiture of Proceeds of Crime Act No 19 of 2010.

[252] [1935] AC 462.

Firstly, the Court says 'merely being called upon to offer an explanation does not amount to being requested to prove that one is innocent.' It, however, appears to contradict itself by saying that 'the requirement for the accused to give an explanation under s 49(2)' of the Anti-Corruption Commission Act, 'emanates from the fact that *there is already proof*[253] that he had solicited, obtained, or accepted a payment, which creates a presumption that he did so corruptly.' If as the Court reasoned, s 49(2) of the Anti-Corruption Commission Act 'creates a presumption that, if the accused fails to give a satisfactory answer, then he must have received, solicited, obtained, or accepted the payment corruptly' how can it be said that this does not run counter to Article 18(2)(a) of the Constitution which plainly provides that '[a] person who is tried for a criminal offence shall not be compelled to give evidence at the trial'?

With the deepest respect, to say, as the Supreme Court opined that '[i]n the face of such an allegation, the accused has the *right and not an obligation to explain*[254] his position is legal legerdemain and semantics more than anything else. It is quite a stretch. Clearly, no matter how conceived by the mind of man or contrived by his heart, the accused cannot under the circumstances in question be said to 'still [maintain] his right to remain silent.' Tactically,[255] he has to offer an explanation because the law compels him to. As the Court itself noted, 'the requirement for the accused to give an explanation under s 49(2) of the Anti-Corruption Commission Act, 'emanates from the fact that *there is already proof*[256] that [the accused] solicited, obtained, or accepted a payment, which *creates a presumption*[257] that he did so corruptly.' To offer no 'explanation' under those circumstances is to lend credence to the assertion that the accused 'solicited, obtained, or accepted a payment, which *creates a presumption*[258] that he did so corruptly.' Therefore, though at this stage 'the prosecution has not established that the accused person is guilty' and 'the burden to prove so still remains on' the prosecution 'to prove' the charge 'beyond reasonable doubt,' if the accused has offered no explanation as required under s 49(2) of the Anti-Corruption Commission Act, it is difficult to see how, as the Supreme Court opined, 'the accused person' can, to all intents and purposes be '[...] presumed innocent' in the sense expected under Article 18(7) and Lord Sankey's golden thread in *Woolmington*,[259] the holding in *Kenious Sialuzi v The People*,[260] to which the Court adverted, notwithstanding.

A few more cases and the observations therein merit our attention:

[253] Empasis added.

[254] Empasis added.

[255] See discussion on the concept of a tactical burden above.

[256] Empasis added.

[257] Empasis added.

[258] Empasis added.

[259] [1935] AC 462.

[260] [2006] ZR 87.

In *R v Lambert*[261] the accused was charged with possession of cocaine with intent to supply contrary to s 28 of the UK Misuse of Drugs Act 1971[262] which provides as follows: "[…] it shall be a defence for the accused to prove that he neither knew of nor suspected nor had reason to suspect the existence of some fact alleged by the prosecution [….]" This *prima facie* appeared to place the legal burden of proof on the accused and to run counter to the provisions of the ECHR under Art. 6 which provides as follows:

> 1. In the determination of his civil rights and obligations or of any criminal charge against him, everyone is entitled to a fair and public hearing within a reasonable time by an independent and impartial tribunal established by law. Judgment shall be pronounced publicly but the press and public may be excluded from all or part of the trial in the interest of morals, public order or national security in a democratic society, where the interests of juveniles or the protection of the private life of the parties so require, or the extent strictly necessary in the opinion of the court in special circumstances where publicity would prejudice the interests of justice.
> 2. Everyone charged with a criminal offence shall be presumed innocent until proven guilty according to law.
> 3. Everyone charged with a criminal offence has the following minimum rights:
>   (a) to be informed promptly, in a language which he understands and in detail, of the nature and cause of the accusation against him;
>   (b) to have adequate time and the facilities for the preparation of his defence;
>   (c) to defend himself in person or through legal assistance of his own choosing or, if he has not sufficient means to pay for legal assistance, to be given it free when the interests of justice so require;
>   (d) to examine or have examined witnesses against him and to obtain the attendance and examination of witnesses on his behalf under the same conditions as witnesses against him;
>   (e) to have the free assistance of an interpreter if he cannot understand or speak the language used in court.

Lord Steyn opined as follows:

> […] It is nevertheless right to say that in a constitutional democracy limited inroad on the presumption of innocence may be justified. The approach to be adopted was stated by the European Court of Human

[261] [2001] 3 AII ER 577; see earlier case of *AG of Hong Kong v Lee Kwong-Kut* [1993] AC 951; *R v Johnstone* [2003] 3 All ER 884; *Sheldrake v DPP* [2005] 1 All ER 237; *Attorney-General's Reference (No 4 of 2002)* 1 All ER 237.

[262] See similar provisions in the Narcotic Drugs and Psychotropic Substances Act, Chapter 96 of the Laws of Zambia.

Rights in *Salabiaku v France*.[263]

Presumptions of fact or of law operate in every legal system. Clearly, the Convention does not prohibit such presumptions in principle. It does, however, require the contracting states to remain within certain limits in this respect as regards criminal law… Article 6(2) does not therefore regard presumptions of fact or of law provided for in the criminal law with indifference. It requires states to confine them within reasonable limits which take into account the importance of what is at stake and maintain the rights of the defence.

This test depends upon the circumstances of the individual case. It follows that a legislative interference with the presumption of innocence requires justification and must not be greater than is necessary. The principle of proportionality must be observed.

[…] In the present case the defence under [s] 28 is one directly bearing on the moral blameworthiness of the accused. It is this factor alone which could justify a maximum sentence of life imprisonment. In my view there is an inroad on the presumption even if an issue under section 28 is in strict law regarded as a pure defence.

It is now necessary to consider the question of justification for the legislative interference with the presumption of innocence. I am satisfied that there is an objective justification for some interference with the burden of proof in prosecutions under section 5 of the 1971 Act. The basis for this justification is that sophisticated drug smugglers, dealers and couriers typically secrete drugs in some container, thereby enabling the person in possession of the container to say that he was unaware of the contents. Such defences are commonplace and they pose real difficulties for the police and prosecuting authorities.

That is, however, not the end of the matter. The burden is on the state to show that the legislative means adopted were not greater than necessary. Where there is objective justification for some inroad on the presumption of innocence the legislature has a choice. The first is to impose a legal burden of proof on the accused. If such a burden is created the matter in question must be taken as proved against the accused unless he satisfies the jury on a balance of probability to the contrary … The second is to impose an evidential burden only on the accused. If this technique is adopted the matter must be taken as proved against the accused unless there is sufficient evidence to raise an issue on the matter but, if there is sufficient evidence, then the prosecution [has] the burden of satisfying the jury as to the matter beyond reasonable doubt in the ordinary way … It is important to bear in mind that it is not enough for the defence merely to allege the fact in question: the court decides whether there is a real issue on the matter … A transfer of a legal burden amounts to a far more drastic interference with the presumption of innocence than the creation of an evidential burden on the accused. The former requires the accused to establish his innocence. It necessarily involves the risk that, if the jury are faithful to the judge's direction, they may convict where the accused has not discharged the legal burden resting on him but left

[263] (1988) 13 EHRR 379, 10519/83, [1988] ECHR 19.

> them unsure on the point. This risk is not present if only an evidential burden is created.

The case of *R v Johnstone*[264] was one which was concerned with pirated recordings of acts by famous artists. Section 92(5) of the Trade Marks Act 1994, provided the accused with a defence in that he could '[...] show that he believed on reasonable grounds that the use of the sign in the manner in which it was used, or was to be used, was not an infringement of the registered trade mark [...]' Lord Nicholls opined as follows:

> In evaluating these factors, the court's role is one of review. Parliament, not the court, is charged with the primary responsibility for deciding, as a matter of policy, what should be the constituent elements of a criminal offence. I echo the words of Lord Woolf in *AG of Hong Kong v Lee Kwong-kut*.[265]
>
> In order to maintain the balance between the individual and the society as a whole, rigid and inflexible standards should not be imposed on the legislature's attempts to resolve the difficult and intransigent problems with which society is faced when seeking to deal with serious crime.
>
> The court will reach a different conclusion from the legislature only when it is apparent the legislature has attached insufficient importance to the fundamental right of an individual to be presumed innocent until proven guilty.
>
> I turn to s 92(1) Counterfeiting is fraudulent trading. It is a serious contemporary problem. Counterfeiting has adverse economic effects on genuine trade. It also has adverse effects on consumers, in terms of quality of goods and, sometimes, on the health or safety of consumers. The Commission of the European Communities has noted the scale of this 'widespread phenomenon with a global impact '. Urgent steps are needed to combat counterfeiting and piracy ... Protection of consumers and honest manufacturers and traders from counterfeiting is an important policy consideration. (2) The offences created by s 92 have rightly been described as offences of 'near absolute liability '. The prosecution is not required to prove intent to infringe a registered trade mark. (3) The offences attract a serious level of punishment: a maximum penalty on indictment of an unlimited fine or imprisonment for up to ten years or both, together with the possibility of confiscation and deprivation orders. (4) Those who trade in brand products are aware of the need to be on guard against counterfeit goods. They are aware of the need to deal with reputable suppliers and keep records and of the risks they take if they do not. (5) The s 92(5) defence relates to facts within the accused person's own knowledge: his state of mind, and the reasons why he held the belief in question. His sources of supply are known to him. (6) Conversely, by and large it is to be expected that those who supply traders with counterfeit products,

[264] [2003] 3 All ER 884.

[265] [1993] AC 951.

> if traceable at all by outside investigators, are unlikely to be co-operative. So, in practice, if the prosecution must prove that a trader acted dishonestly, fewer investigations will be undertaken and fewer prosecutions will take place.
>
> In my view factors (4) and (6) constitute compelling reasons why the s 92(5) defence should place a persuasive burden on the accused person [....]

In *Sheldrake v DPP*,[266] the accused faced the charge of being driving under the influence of excessive alcohol. It was contended that the defence under s 5(2) of the UK Road Traffic Act 1988 which imposed the burden of proof as regarding there being no likelihood of the accused being in charge of the vehicle while under the influence of alcohol contravened the presumption of innocence guaranteed by Art 6(2) of the ECHR. Lord Bingham observed as follows:

> It may not be very profitable to debate whether section 5(2) infringes the presumption of innocence. It may be assumed that it does. Plainly the provision is directed to a legitimate object: the prevention of death, injury and damage caused by unfit drivers. Does the provision meet the tests of acceptability identified in the Strasbourg jurisprudence? In my view, it plainly does. I do not regard the burden placed on the defendant as beyond reasonable limits or in any way arbitrary. It is not objectionable to criminalise a defendant's conduct in these circumstances without requiring a prosecutor to prove criminal intent. The defendant has a full opportunity to show that there was no likelihood of his driving, a matter so closely conditioned by his own knowledge and state of mind at the material time as to make it much more appropriate for him to prove on the balance of probability that he would not have been likely to drive than for the prosecutor to prove, beyond reasonable doubt, that he would. I do not think the imposition of a legal burden went beyond what was necessary. If a driver tries and fails to establish a defence under section 5(2), I would not regard the resulting conviction as unfair, as the House held that it might or would be in *R v Lambert*.[267] I find no reason to conclude that the conviction of Mr. Sheldrake was tainted by any hint of unfairness.

In *Attorney-General's Reference (No 4 of 2002)*,[268] the majority felt that the s 11(2)[269] could be *readdown* to impose merely an evidential burden. In his dissent,

[266] [2005] 1 AII ER 237.

[267] [2002] 2 AC 545.

[268] [2005] 1 AII ER 237.

[269] According to Uglow, '[t]he House of Lords has found the provisions of s 11 of the Terrorism Act 2000 more difficult to interpret. This section makes it an offence to belong to a proscribed organisation but provides a defence under s 11(2) for the accused to show that the organisation was not proscribed when he joined and that he had not taken part in the activities of the organisation since it was proscribed. It was clear that Parliament had intended this to impose a legal burden on the defendant, since s.118 of the Act lists a number of sections which are to be understood as imposing an evidential burden only, and s 11(2) is not among those listed.' – Uglow S, *Evidence: Text and Materials*, 92-3.

however, Lord Carswell opined as follows:

> [...] (a) It is not easy to determine what is to be proved and by whom in respect of the date when the defendant joined the organisation. If he raises the issue, it would hardly be appropriate for the prosecution to have to prove that he became a member before the date on which it was proscribed. The only sensible answer must be that the defendant has to establish this fact, but it would be a strange procedure if the onus then reverted to the prosecution to prove that he had taken part in the activities of the organisation.

It has been noted perhaps correctly that '[t]he balancing test for reversing the burden of proof is assessing the justification and the proportionality.'[270] As the foregoing authorities demonstrate, however, this is a herculean test fraught with many dangers of incorrect interpretation and dubious legislative schemes that may or may not contravene Article 18(7) of the Constitution. There indeed appears to be no clarity as regards the construction of statutes which may appear to impose the burden of proof on the accused.

3.3.5.6 *Allocation of the burden and standard of proof in civil matters*

(i) General

The general rule[271] as regards the burden of proof in civil cases is 'he who asserts must prove.'[272] Thus, in an action for the tort of negligence the plaintiff bears the burden of proof as regards (i) demonstrating the presence of the breach (ii) demonstrating the breach of the duty of care; and (iii) demonstrating the scope of the wounds and impairment. Lord Reid has accurately observed as follows in *Bonnington Castings Ltd v Wardlaw*:[273]

> It would seem obvious in principle that a plaintiff must prove not only the negligence or breach of duty but also that such fault caused or materially contributed to his injury, and there is ample authority for that proposition. I can find neither reason nor authority for the rule being different when there is a breach of a statutory duty [...] In my judgment the employee must in all cases prove his case by the ordinary standard of proof in civil actions: he must make it appear that at least on a balance of probability the breach of duty caused or materially contributed to his injury.

---

[270] Uglow S, *Evidence: Text and Materials* 93.

[271] According to Lord Nicholls in *Re H (Minors)* [1996] AC 563 AT 586 HL, "[g]enerally, although there are exceptions, a plaintiff or applicant must establish the existence of all the preconditions and other facts entitling him to the order he seeks."

[272] It must be pointed out though that the concept of burden of proof in civil cases is not nearly as decisive as that under criminal matters. This though is a general rule with exceptions: *Rhesa Shipping Co SA v Edmunds* [1985] 2 All ER 712 *per* Lord Brandon at 718; *Stephens v Cannon* [2005] EWCA Civ 222.

[273] [1956] A.C. 613, *per* Lord Reid.

In *Zambia Railways Ltd v Pauline S. Mundia and Another,*[274] Silomba JS a he then was, in reading the judgment of the Court, observed as follows:

> In the appeal before us, we are dealing with a civil case and not a criminal case. The standard of proof in a civil case is not as rigorous as the one obtaining in a criminal case. Simply stated, the proof required is on a balance of probability "as opposed to beyond all reasonable doubt in a criminal case". The old adage is true that he who assents a claim in a civil trial must prove on a balance of probability that the other party is liable. In these proceedings, the respondents alleged negligence against the appellant as the cause of the accident. It was, therefore, their duty to prove that the appellant was negligent for their claim for damages to succeed on a balance of probability.

Put another way, the burden of proving an assertion lies on the party who makes the assertion in question. While this ordinarily be construed to mean that only the party who makes a positive assertion bears the burden of proving it, there is nothing to stop a party who makes a negative assertion from proving said assertion. In *Soward v Leggatt,*[275] the plaintiff who was the defendant's landlord claimed in his suit that the defendant had not correctly refurbished and preserved the premises which were subject of the proceedings. In his pleadings, the defendant made a positive assertion to the effect that he had done so. Lord Abinger C.B. opined as follows:

> Looking at these things according to common sense, we should consider what the substantive fact to be made out, and on whom it lies to make it out. It is not so much the form of the issue which ought to be considered, as the substance and effect of it. In many cases, a party, by a little difference in the drawing of his pleadings might make it either affirmative or negative, as he pleased.

What is clear from the preceding is the fact that even though the defendant had in his pleadings made a positive assertion which ordinarily placed the burden of proof on him, the burden of proof, proof of a negative assertion made by the plaintiff, was on the plaintiff.

It follows therefore that when the court is asked to take action on a particular issue, the party who moves the court to so do bears the obligation to show why the action he seeks the court to take ought to be taken. This he can do by presenting evidence of such sufficiency in the face of cross-examination and evidence countering his as to lead the court to decide in his favour. Thus,

---

[274] [2008] 1 ZR 287 (SC); see also *Joseph Manjata v Alfred Chikwaba* (2014/HP/1706); *Elias Tembo v Florence Chiwala Salati and 2 Others* (SCZ Appeal No 200 of 2016).

[275] (1836) 7 C&P 613 at 615 *per* Lord Abinger CB; In *Abrath v North Eastern Railway* (1883) 11 QBD 440 CA which was a suit for malicious prosecution, the plaintiff bore the burden of proving on the one hand, the fact of prosecution and on the other, what may be termed want of reasonable and probable cause for the prosecution. See specifically, the comments of Bowen J at 457-458.

where the cause of action is breach of contract for example, the plaintiff will bear the burden of proving not only the reality of the contract in question but also that the same was breached by the defendant for which the plaintiff must be rewarded damages the extent of which the plaintiff will bear the burden of proving.[276] In the absence of such evidence, the party who or which bears the burden to prove the assertion will lose. This, even where the other party offers nothing in response. In *Khalid Mohamed*[277] the Supreme Court rejected the proposition that there should be automatic success for the plaintiff where a defence fails. The Court insisted that 'a plaintiff must prove his case and if he fails to do so the mere failure of the opponent's defence does not entitle him to judgment.'[278] The Court went so far as to demonstrate that in circumstances where the plaintiff's evidence failed of its own lethargy[279] 'a defendant in such circumstances would not even need a defence.'[280] Thus, a party who makes a positive assertion bears the burden of proof.

This was exemplified in *Wakelin v London and South Western Railway.*[281] The complainant's husband was killed on a railway level crossing. While admitting to the fact that the victim had been run over by one of their trains and neglecting certain warnings, they elected to call no evidence. Instead, they submitted that there was no case to answer as it had not been shown whether the victim died because of the train company's fault or as a result of throwing himself against the train. Lord Halsbury LC held that in this situation, the burden of proving that the death of the spouse was caused by some kind of carelessness on the part of the defendants is squarely on the shoulders of the plaintiff. That is the reality that has to be shown. If the fact is not proven, then the plaintiff loses, and if in the absence of direct proof, the circumstances that are established are equally consistent with the allegation of the plaintiff as with the denial of the defendant, then the plaintiff loses for the very simple reason that the plaintiff is bound to establish the affirmative of the proposition.

In *Wakelin*[282] the plaintiff bore the burden to prove (i) that the husband had died, which she did at trial and (ii) that his death on the railway was a consequence of the accused company's negligence.

The foregoing notwithstanding, it ought to be remembered that in practice the defendant in the tort action of negligence may, where the defence in

---

[276] It has however been shown in *Joseph Constantine Steamship Line Ltd v Imperial Smelting Corp Ltd* [1941] 2 All ER 165 at 179-180, *per* Viscount Maugham, that the defendant may indeed bear the burden of proving a particular issue in an action for breach of contract e.g., an assertion alluding to the fact that there was want of disclosure by the plaintiff. A ship on charter was destroyed in an explosion, the cause of which was unknown. The claimant charterers claimed damages from the owner for failure to load. The owners' defence was that the charter party had been frustrated by the explosion. The House of Lords decided that, where the defendant establishes a frustrating event, the burden rested on the claimant charterers to show that event had occurred and the contract had been broken as a result of the owners' fault: Uglow, *The Law of Evidence* 98; but see *Munro, Brice & Co v War Risks Association* [1918] 2KB 78.

[277] [1982] ZR 49 (SC).

[278] *Per* Ngulube CJ, as he then was.

[279] Or 'inanition.'

[280] *Per* Ngulube CJ, as he then was.

[281] [1887] 12 AC 41.

[282] [1887] 12 AC 41.

question goes beyond sheer rejection bear the burden of proof. This is true where questions of *volenti non fit injuria*[283] or contributory negligence arises. Under such circumstances, the burden of proof is on the defendant in the cause and not the plaintiff. The burden of proving those issues rests upon the defendant.

A rather interesting case that demonstrates how the burden of proof may be borne by a different party depending on the issue in question is the contract dispute in *the Glendarroch.*[284] A ship was lost when it struck a rock and the plaintiff sued for non-delivery of the sacks of cement it was carrying. The contract expressly provided that the shipowners were not liable in respect of loss caused by "perils of the sea", provided that the owners were not negligent. If the plaintiff proved the contract and breach, the burden was on the owners to show that it was as a result of "peril of the sea." However, once it had been shown that the ship had sunk because of a "peril of the sea," it was for the plaintiff to show negligence, if they were to rely upon the proviso.

(ii) Termination and expiration of contract of employment under the Employment Code (ECA, 2019)[285]

According to s 52(5) of the ECA, 2019, '[a]n employer shall bear the burden of proof that the termination of a contract of employment was fair and for a valid reason.'

(iii) A higher standard than a mere balance of probabilities?

The question whether all matters falling under the realm of civil proceedings ought to be confined within the strictures of one rigid standard - 'balance of probabilities' or 'the preponderance of evidence' is one that has been considered in discussions and cases centering around the question standard of proof. While a lower standard than that expected in criminal matters is all that is generally required in civil matters, it is evident that in order to succeed, he who asserts must prove by offering evidence that is far superior and more in keeping with the facts of the case so as to persuade the court that his version of events is deserving of attention by the court and a determination in his favour. To paraphrase Ngulube CJ, as he then was, in *Mohamed v the Attorney General:*[286]

[283] *Volenti non fit iniuria (or injuria)* is Latin for "to a willing person, injury is not done." It is a common law doctrine which provides that one cannot bring an action in tort or delict if that person conscientiously places himself in a position where they may be harmed doing so in the knowledge that a degree of harm may indeed be the consequence of their action(s). However, the defence is only available if it is specifically pleaded: *Henry Mwamba v Metal Fabricators of Zambia* 2005/HN/279; but see decision in *Kalunga (Suing as Administratrix of the estate of the Late Emmanuel Bwalya) v Konkola Copper* [2004] ZR 40 Mines where it was held *inter alia*; 'the duty of care by employees has developed to the extent that there is virtually no room for volenti non fit injuria to apply in cases of negligence where there is common law or statutory duty of care by an employer to his employee except where such doctrine has been pleaded.'

[284] [1894] P. 226; Summary excerpted from Uglow *S, Evidence* 100.

[285] Act No 3 of 2019.

[286] [1982] ZR 49; *Galaunia Farms v National Milling Company Ltd and Another* (SCZ Judgment No 1 of 2004), [2016] ZMSC 212; *Hanif Mohamed Bhura v Yusuf Ibrahim Issa Ismail* (SCZ Appeal No 146 of 2014), [2016] ZMSC 8.

Within the realm of legal proceedings, there exists an unwarranted notion, deemed intolerable by many, that proclaims a plaintiff's automatic triumph in the event of a failed defense. Such a proposition, devoid of qualification, runs counter to the principles of justice. The burden of proof rests squarely upon the plaintiff, and should they fail to discharge this obligation, the mere collapse of the opponent's defense does not grant them an entitlement to judgment. Thus, the proposition that, even if a plaintiff's case crumbles into oblivion or encounters any other reason for dissolution, they should still be bestowed with judgment on the grounds that the defenses raised by their adversary have also faltered ought to be vehemently rejetced. The simple reason fro this position is that such a stance is unmistakably flawed, as it renders the defendant's need for a defense entirely redundant in such circumstances.

Even so, Lord Denning, as he then was appears to have suggested in two cases, that there were circumstances and proper cases in which a standard higher than a mere balance of probability was merited. In *Bater v Bater*,[287] the wife petitioned for divorce, alleging cruelty. It was held that it had not been a misdirection for the petitioner to have to prove her case beyond reasonable doubt: 'A high standard of proof' was required because of the importance of such a case to the parties and the community. Although it was a misdirection for a judge in matrimonial proceedings to say that the criminal standard of proof applied to allegations of cruelty it was correct to say that they had to be proved beyond reasonable doubt. *Per* Denning LJ:

> The difference of opinion which has been evoked about the standard of proof in recent cases may well turn out to be more a matter of words than anything else. It is of course true that by our law a higher standard of proof is required in criminal cases than in civil cases. But this is subject to the qualification that there is no absolute standard in either case. In criminal cases the charge must be proved beyond reasonable doubt, but there may be degrees of proof within that standard. As Best CJ and many other great judges have said, 'in proportion as the crime is enormous, so ought the proof to be clear'. So also in civil cases, the case may be proved by a preponderance of probability, but there may be degrees of probability within that standard. The degree depends on the subject-matter. A civil court, when considering a charge of fraud, will naturally require for itself a higher degree of probability than that which it would require when asking if negligence is established. It does not adopt so high a degree as a criminal court, even when it is considering a charge of a criminal nature; but still, it does require a degree of probability which is commensurate with the occasion. Likewise, a divorce court should require a degree of probability which is proportionate to the subject-matter.

It has been shown in *Hornal v Newburger*[288] that in a civil action where fraud or other matter which is or may be a crime is alleged against a party or against persons not parties to the action, the standard of proof to be applied

[287] (1951) P 35, summary taken from https://swarb.co.uk/bater-v-bater-CA-1951/ retrieved on 22/04/2022.

[288] (1957) 1 QB 247.

is that applicable in civil actions generally, namely, proof on the balance of probability, and not the higher standard of proof beyond all reasonable doubt required in criminal matters. However, there is no absolute standard of proof, and no great gulf between proof in criminal matters on the one hand, and proof in civil matters, on the other. The preceding is so because in all cases the degree of probability must be commensurate with the occasion and proportionate to the subject-matter. The elements of gravity of an issue are part of the range of circumstances which have to be weighed when deciding as to the balance of probability. The plaintiff in an action for damages for breach of warranty or, alternatively, for fraudulent misrepresentation, alleged that the director of the defendant company had in the course of negotiations for the purchase of a used capstan lathe stated that it had been reconditioned by a reputable firm of toolmakers. The defendants denied that the statement had been made. If it had been made the director must have known it to be untrue. The county court judge found that the statement had been made, but held on the claim for breach of warranty that it had not been made contractually. On the claim based on fraud he said that he was satisfied on the balance of probability that the statement had been made, and that, that was the correct standard to apply; but that he would not have been so satisfied if the criminal standard of proof was to be applied. He gave judgment for the defendants on the ground that the plaintiff had not shown that he had suffered damage by relying on the fraudulent misrepresentation; but he ordered that the plaintiff should pay only one-fourth of the defendants' costs. On appeal by the plaintiff and cross-appeal by the defendants, it was held, that the judge had applied the correct standard of proof but that on the facts the plaintiff had suffered damage and was entitled to Judgment.[289]

A plethora of authorities have held certain instances beyond those considered in the preceding authorities to come within the province of a higher burden than a mere burden of proof. These have included contempt of court proceedings;[290] fraud in election petitions[291] (including presidential petitions[292]); fraud in other civil matters;[293] professional misconduct;[294] child protection proceedings;[295] and matrimonial causes.[296] In the stated cases, a common thread is that the misconduct alleged is of such a nature that to satisfy the court of its occurrence,

[289] Dicta of Lord Sumner in *Lek v Mathews* (1927) 29 Ll.L.Rep. 141, 164, and of Denning LJ in *Bater v Bater* [1951] P 35, 36-37; 66 TLR (Pt. 2) 589; [1950] 2 All E.R. 458 applied; *Thurtell v Beaumont* (1823) 1 Bing 339 disapproved; *Preston-Jones v Preston-Jones* [1951] AC 391; [1951] 1 TLR 8; [1951] 1 All ER 124 distinguished.

[290] *Re Brambelvale Ltd* (1970) Ch 128.

[291] *Akashambatwa Mbikusita Lewanika and Others v Jacob Titus Chiluba* (SCZ Judgment No 14 of 1998); *Michael Mabenga v Sikota Wina and Others* (2003) ZR 11; *Nkandu Luo Another v Mwamba Another* Appeal 10 of 2016 2018 ZMCC 254.

[292] *Akashambatwa Mbikusita Lewanika and Others v Jacob Titus Chiluba*(SCZ Judgment No 14 of 1998).

[293] *Sithole v State Lotteries Board* [1975] ZR 106 (SC): If a party alleges fraud the extent of the onus on the party alleging is greater than a simple balance of probabilities; *RR Sambo, NN Sambo and Lusaka Urban District Council v Pikani Mwanza* (SCZ Judgment No 16 of 2016).

[294] In *Re A Solicitor* (1993) QB 69.

[295] In *Re H (Minors)* (1996) AC 563.

[296] *Preston Jones v Preston Jones* (1951) AC 391.

the plaintiff ought to show more than a mere preponderance of evidence. He ought to go further to prove, quite beyond a mere balance of probabilities, that the party in question had a blameworthy state of mind as to be deemed culpable. However, such proof as is asked for, and expected is short of proof beyond reasonable doubt which is reserved for criminal proceedings.[297]

3.3.5.7 *Standard of proof in criminal matters*

As we have stated elsewhere in this text, it behooves the party bearing the burden of proof at the close of a criminal trial to prove his assertions beyond reasonable doubt. In *Miller v Ministry of Pensions*[298] a case we have already encountered in this text, Denning J noted that the standard of proof in criminal matters which is that the case has to be proved beyond reasonable doubt before an accused person could be found guilty was well settled. He, however, went on to show that to prove beyond reasonable doubt was not to prove with certitude that the accused did indeed commit the offence with which he had been charged, but rather, that 'it must carry a high degree of probability.' It was not the same thing, he opined, as 'proof beyond the shadow of a doubt.' How could it be? we may ask. The answer is as follows: The adjudicator is asked to recreate and appreciate the truth about a set of facts that happened in the past presented by two contending sides led by counsel with different stories and objectives in favour of their respective clients. The adversarial system by its very nature, as we noted earlier thus places enormous constraints to the extent that one cannot hope to achieve the ultimate truth or expect a matter to be proved beyond a shadow of the doubt. The best that can be hoped for and achieved is merely an account of possibilities achieved through rational inquiry and the limits and challenges the adversarial system places on the adjudicator to reconstruct and find the truth. Blackburn[299] has put it thus:

> As well as the norm of truth or hitting the target, there are norms of right procedure. These govern whether you have done your stuff properly: taken the right observations, made the right inferences,hedged in the right places, weighed the evidence carefully and, in short, made yourself immune to procedural criticism. It may not follow that you arrive at the truth. The evidence may be poor, or misleading, or the interpretation which everyone supposes reasonable may be based on insufficient science or general misunderstanding. A trial may be fairly conducted, yet unhappily arrive at the wrong verdict. Still, there is nothing better that we can do. We act under the conviction that our

[297] See however, the rather curious Indian Supreme Court decision in *Shri Kirpal Singh v Shri VV Giri* (1970) AIR 2097 which equated the standard of proof in corruption and fraudulent activities in election petitions to proof beyond reasonable doubt; see also *Dingwall v J Wharton (Shipping) Ltd* Lloyd's Law Rep 213 at 216, where Lord Tucker opined as follows: 'Iam quite unable to accede to the proposition that there is some intermediate onus between that which is required in criminal cases and the balance of probability which is sufficient in timeous civil actions.'

[298] [1947] 2 AII ER 372 at 373-374.

[299] Blackburn S, *Truth: A Guide for the Perplexed* (Penguin, 2005) 29-30.

> best procedures, although they may let us down, markedly increase the chance that we get things right. Provided there was nothing better which we should have done then we may be immune from charges of irrationality, negligence or carelessness. Our procedures accord with reason, and it is only bad luck that might stop us hitting the truth.

The foregoing is in keeping with Lord Denning's observation that if the standard of proof was loftier than beyond reasonable doubt as to require proof of ultimate truth beyond a shadow of doubt, the law would be admitting 'fanciful possibilities' with the consequence of deflecting justice and thereby fail to protect society for whose protection it is created. It thus followed that '[i]f the evidence is so strong against a man as to leave only a remote possibility in his favour which can be dismissed with the sentence 'of course it is possible, but not in the least probable, the case is proved beyond reasonable doubt [....]' However, '[...] nothing short of that will suffice.'[300]

Regarding the standard of proof placed on the accused or the defence, in a criminal matter, Lord Denning held that the 'case must be decided according to the preponderance of probability.' He added: '[t]hat degree is well settled. It must carry a reasonable degree of probability, but not so high as is required in a criminal case. If the evidence is such that the tribunal can say: 'We think it more probable than not', the burden is discharged, but, if the probabilities are equal, it is not [....]'

The second aspect of the standard of proof which we have also already encountered in this text saw its genesis in *R v Summers*[301] which is that at the close of the criminal trial, the party on whom the legal burden of proof lies ought to convince the trier of fact of the truthfulness of his statements. It has been suggested by some[302] that this concept or aspect was introduced to counter the difficulties brought about by the concept of proving an assertion 'beyond reasonable doubt' as demonstrated in *Miller*.[303] Expressing his misgivings about 'reasonable doubt' Lord Goddard CJ observed as follows in *R v Hepworth:*[304]

> [...] it is very difficult to tell a jury what is a reasonable doubt. To tell a jury that it must not be a fanciful doubt is something that is without real guidance. To tell them that a reasonable doubt is such a doubt as to cause them to hesitate in their own affairs never seems to me to convey any particular standard ... It may be that in some cases the word 'satisfied' is enough. Then, it is said that the jury in a civil case has to be satisfied and, therefore, one is only laying down the same standard of proof as in a civil case. I confess that I have had some difficulty in understanding how there is or there can be two standards; therefore, one would be on safe ground if one said in a criminal case to

---

300 *Miller v Ministry of Pensions* [1947] 2 All ER 372 at 373-374.

301 [1952] 1 All ER 1059, CA.

302 See generally Dennis, I *The Law of Evidence* 482-483.

303 *Miller v Ministry of Pensions* [1947] 2 All ER 372.

304 [1955] 2 All E.R. 918 at 919-920.

> a jury: 'You must be satisfied beyond reasonable doubt' and one could also say : ' You, the jury, must be completely satisfied ', or better still : ' You must feel sure of the prisoner's guilt '. But I desire to repeat what I said in *R v Kritz*: 'It is not the formula that matters: it is the effect of the summing up. If the jury are made to understand that they have to be satisfied and must not return a verdict against a defendant unless they feel sure, and that the onus is all the time on the prosecution and not on the defence, that is enough.'[305]

Accordingly, the England and Wales revision to the 2010 Crown Court Bench Book advises judges to veer away from using the term 'reasonable doubt' in directing juries but instead to only state that the jury must convict only when it is 'sure' of the guilt of the accused. Thus, where the court believes that the accused is 'probably guilty' or 'likely to be guilty,' the court is admitting of not being 'sure.' Under such circumstances, it must acquit the accused. As a general point, Sir William Blackstone[306] noted that '[…] the law holds that it is better that ten guilty persons escape than that one innocent suffer.'[307] It is thus deemed to be better to acquit a guilty party than to convict an innocent one. The concept of burden of proof and the rules thereof are thus designed to minimise the risk of wrong conviction. According toLord Denning in the case of *Miller v Minister of Pensions,*[308] '[….] It is true that under our existing jurisprudence in criminal matter, we have to proceed with presumption of innocence, but at the same, that presumption is to be judged on the basis of conceptions of a reasonable prudent man. Smelling doubts for the sake of giving benefit of doubt is not the law of the land.' Further, in the Indian case of *Sucha Singh and Another v State of Punjab*[309] the Supreme Court of India held in part that '[j]ustice cannot be made sterile on the plea that it is better to let a hundred guilty escape than punish an innocent. Letting the guilty escape is not doing justice according to law [….] Proof beyond reasonable doubt is a guideline, not a fetish.' However, when the court is unsure, acquitting an accused person is not to accommodate fanciful objections as Lord Denning feared in *Miller*[310] or advocating the sterility of law as apprehended in *Sucha Singh*, (cases which must be taken to have stood only against 'speculative doubts' being 'insufficient to justify not convicting'[311])

[305] For further insight into the difficulties wrought by the expression 'reasonable doubt' see especially within the context of a jury system but bearing principles that may apply to a non-jury system such as our, Yap Chuan Ching (1976) 63 Cr App R 7 at 9-10, per Lawton L.J; Stephens [2002] EWCA Crim 1529; Carr-Briant [1943] 2 AII E.R. 156 at 158, PER Humphreys J; C. Wells, " The Impact of Feminist Thinking on Criminal Law and Justice " [2004] Crim LR (Anniversary Edition) 88; Doheny [1997]1 Cr App R 369 at 372-375, *per* Phillips LJ; M., Redmayne, " Science, Evidence and Logic " [1996] 59 MLR 747; Adams [1996] 2 Cr. App. R. 467 at 481, *per* Rose LJ; M. Redmayne, "Appeals to Reason ", [2002] 65 MLR 19.

[306] Blackstone, William, *Commentaries on the Laws of England*, facsimile edition with introductions by Stanley N. Katz. (Univ. Chicago, 1979). 4 vols.

[307] The *Commentaries on the Laws of England* are an influential 18th-century treatise on the common law of England by Sir William Blackstone, originally published by the Clarendon Press at Oxford, 1765–1770.

[308] [1947] 2 ALL ER 272.

[309] [2003] 7 SCC 643.

[310] *Miller* [1947] 2AII ER 372.

[311] Dennis I, *The law of Evidence* 482.

but acknowledging that there is a price to be paid within the constraints of the adversarial system which when compared to wrongfully convicting an innocent person is not nearly as egregiously immoral and harmful.

3.3.5.8 Standard of proof in civil matters

Also known as the preponderance of probabilities, the standard of proof in civil matters as well as where the assertion is made by the accused who as a result of such assertion will bear the burden of proof in criminal matters, is on a balance of probabilities. As Denning J opined in parts relevant to this discussion but also in trying to distinguish the standard of proof in civil matters from that in criminal matters:

> the [...] degree of cogency [...] required to discharge a burden in a civil case [...] is well settled. It must carry a reasonable degree of probability, but not so high as is required in a criminal case. If the evidence is such that the tribunal can say: 'We think it more probable than not', the burden is discharged, but, if the probabilities are equal, it is not [....]

It follows from the foregoing that discharging the burden of proof on the preponderance of probabilities is not an exact science or a mathematical exercise into determining the exact quantity of evidence adduced by one party as against another. What it is, is whether the party bearing the burden has absolutely shown that his assertion is more likely than not. As shown in *Miller*,[312] such a burden as is required in civil matters, is not discharged by a mere claim that a party's version of events when compared to that of his opponent(s), is more likely. Lord Brandon said as much, if not more in *Rhesa Shipping Co SA v Edmunds*[313] when he observed as follows:

> [...] the legal concept of proof of a case on a balance of probabilities must be applied with common sense. It requires a judge of first instance, before he finds that a particular event occurred, to be satisfied on the evidence that it is more likely to have occurred than not. If such a judge concludes [...] that the occurrence of an event is extremely improbable, a finding by him that it is nevertheless more likely to have occurred than not, does not accord with common sense. This is especially so when it is open to the judge to say simply that the party on whom the burden of proving that the event occurred lies has therefore failed to discharge such burden.

Be that as it may, the nature and complexion of the cases that courts may grapple that may come under the guise of 'civil matters' requiring proof on

---

[312] *Miller* [1947] 2AII ER 372.

[313] [1985] 2 AII ER 712 at 718F.

balance of probabilities rather than beyond reasonable doubt has compelled many courts to not be held captive but to, while adhering to the standard of proof in civil matters, in each case consider not only the seriousness of the allegations on a case-by-case basis but the nature of proceedings before them. In this way the civil standard has flexibility built into it allowing the courts room for manoeuvre depending on the nature of the allegations and type of proceedings. Thus, it has been said in *Re Dellow's Will Trust*,[314] that '[t]he more serious the allegation the more cogent is the evidence required to overcome the unlikelihood of what is alleged and thus to prove it.' In the earlier case of *Hornal Neuberger Products Ltd*,[315] '[t]he Court of Appeal held that in civil proceedings, proof of an allegation of crime need only be on the basis of the balance of probabilities.'[316] According to Lord Nicholls in *Re H (Minors)*,[317] '[t]his approach also provides a means by which the balance of probability standard can accommodate one's instinctive feeling that even in civil proceedings a court should be more sure before finding serious allegations proved than when deciding less serious or trivial matters.' Elsewhere, that, '[w]here allegations of crime are made in civil proceedings, the standard of proof is the preponderance of probabilities.' However, where the seriousness of the allegation may require that different contemplations be reflected on. In *Re Dellow's Will Trusts*,[318] where the question was whether a wife had killed her husband prior to ending her own life Ungoed-Thomas J observed as follows:

> It seems to me that in civil cases it is not so much that a different standard of proof is required in different circumstances varying according to the gravity of the issue, but [...] the gravity of the issue becomes part of the circumstances which the court has to take into consideration in deciding whether or not the burden of proof has been discharged. The more serious the allegation the more cogent is the evidence required to overcome the unlikelihood of what is alleged and thus to prove it...

The case of *Comet Products UK Ltd v Hawkex Plastic Ltd*[319] is authority for the position that the standard of proof in contempt of court matters, irrespective, is that beyond reasonable doubt as is required to be attained in criminal matters.

---

[314] *Re Dellow's Will Trusts* [1964] 1 AII ER 771, *per* Ungoed-Thomas J.

[315] [1956] 3 AII ER 970, *per* Denning LJ at 973: '[t]he more serious the allegation the higher the degree of probability that is required: but it need not, in a civil case, reach the very high standard required by the criminal law.'

[316] *Per* Lord Nicholls in *Re H (Minors)* [1996] 1 AII ER 1at 16-17.

[317] [1996] 1 AII ER 1at 16-17 approving the judgment of Morris LJ who said in *Hornal v Neuberger Products Ltd* [1956] 3 AII ER 970; [1957] 1 QB 247 at 266 that '[...] though no court [...] would give less attention to issues lacking gravity than to those marked by it, the very element of gravity becomes a part of a whole range of circumstances which have to be weighed in the scale when deciding as to the balance of probabilities; Stein, A. "An Essay on Uncertainty and Fact Finding in Civil Litigation, with Special Reference to Contract Cases" (1948) 48 U of Toronto L.J. 299.

[318] [1964] 1 AII ER 771.

[319] [1971] 1 AII ER 1141.

In *Comet Products*,[320] which was a passing off case, the plaintiffs[321] applied to the court for the committal of the defendants for contempt of court. The query that fell to be determined by the court was whether the defendants could be cross-examined. Lord Denning M.R. observed as follows:

> [...] A criminal contempt is one which takes place in the face of the court, or which prejudices a fair trial and so forth. A civil contempt is different. A typical case is disobedience to an order made by the court in a civil action [...] Although this is a civil contempt, it partakes of the nature of a criminal charge. The defendant is liable to be punished for it. He may be sent to prison. The rules as to criminal charges have always been applied to such a proceeding [...] we ourselves in this court, in *Re Bramblevale Ltd*,[322] said that it must be proved with the same degree of satisfaction as in criminal charge. It follows that the accused is not bound to give evidence unless he chooses to do so [....][323]

3.4 Burden and standard of proof of foundation facts for the admissibility of evidence: *Voire Dire*[324]

Whether or not evidence is admissible is dependent on the existence of certain facts which form the basis for the admissibility of the evidence in question. They form what has been termed foundation facts. A good way to illustrate the foregoing is to refer to confession evidence. Where an accused person is said to have confessed to the commission of an offence with which he is charged, there may be an objection as to the admissibility of such evidence based on the argument that the said confession was not obtained voluntarily but rather by oppression or the saying or doing of anything that may render the evidence obtained under such circumstances unreliable. In this scenario, the presence of foundation facts may be uncertain. This creates a situation in which the court will be compelled to conduct a *voire dire* to determine whether the foundation facts, now in dispute as regards the confession, have been prove. We will demonstrate this in terms of the *voire dire* in criminal matters and the *voire dire* in civil proceedings.

3.4.1 *Criminal matters*

As we have already shown, when it becomes necessary to conduct a trial within a trial or a *voire dire* the question centres on proving that conditions as regards admissibility have been met. The burden of proving this beyond reasonable

[320] [1971] 1 AII ER 1141.

[321] Or Claimants.

[322] [1969] 3 All ER 1062.

[323] See also *Savenda Management Services Limited v Stanbic Bank Zambia Limited & Another* (Appeal No 37/2017) [2018] ZMSC 349 (23 November 2018) (*The Chifire Contempt Case*); For a criticism of this decision see Phiri C "A Curious Decision by Zambia's Highest Court: Six Years Imprisonment for Civil Contempt?": https://doi.org/10.1163/17087384-12340046; For additional analysis of the issue of proof in civil cases, see, Miller C, "Proof of Civil Contempt" [1996] 112 LQR 539; Redmayne M," Standards of proof in Civil Litigation" (1999) 62 Mod. 167.

[324] See generally, Dennis I, *The Law of Evidence* 487-489; Uglow, *Evidence: Texts and Materials* 119-121.

doubt lies on the party who wishes to adduce the evidence in question. The burden of proving that the conditions of admissibility have been met must lie on the party wishing to adduce the evidence. In *R v Yacoob,*[325] where the issue to be determine in a *voire dire* related to the competence and compellability of the prosecution's witness as to whether she was married to the accused, Watkins LJ opined thus:

> "[a]s to the burden of proof in this context, it is for the prosecution, once the issue of competence of one of its witnesses is raised, to prove that that person is competent to testify... The burden will be discharged if the trial judge is satisfied beyond a reasonable doubt upon admissible and sufficient evidence of competence."

The case of *R v Ewing*[326] was concerned with the comparison of handwriting by an expert in accordance with s 8 of the England & Wales Criminal Procedure Act 1865. It was a requirement under the said section for the judge to satisfy himself that the handwriting in question was that of the accused before expert comparison could be permitted. Regarding the question whether the standard ought to be on a balance of probabilities (as in civil matters) or beyond reasonable doubt (as in criminal matters generally), O'Connor LJ held as follows:

> '[...] any writing proved to the satisfaction of the judge to be genuine, 'do not say anything about the standard of proof is to be governed by common law [....] It follows that when the section is applied in criminal cases, the criminal standard should be used. Were it otherwise, the situation created would be unacceptable, where conviction depends on proof that disputed handwriting is that of the accused person and where that proof depends on comparison of the disputed writing with samples alleged to be genuine writings of the accused; we cannot see how this case can be said to be proved beyond reasonable doubt, if the [prosecution] only has to satisfy the judge on a balance of probabilities, that the allegedly genuine samples were in fact genuine. The [judge] may be satisfied beyond reasonable doubt that the crucial handwriting is by the same hand as the allegedly genuine writings, but if there is a reasonable doubt about the fact the disputed writing was that of the accused and the case is not proved [....][327]

3.4.2 *Civil matters*

In civil matters, when issues relate to admissibility prerequisites to be satisfied regarding evidence proffered by the defence or of evidence proffered in such proceedings irrespective, the standard is one predicated on the preponderance of probabilities. In *Mattey and Queeley,*[328] the defence wanted to place reliance

[325] (1981) 72 Cr App R 313.

[326] [1983] 2 AII ER 645 at 652-653.

[327] See however decision in *R v Angeli* [1978] 3 All ER 950 where this was not followed; See further, *Blyth v Blyth* [1966] 1 All ER 524.

[328] [1995] Crim LR 308.

on the inscribed accounts of witnesses who at the time were resident in France making it impossible for them to be present for the trial, an assertion the defence had the burden of proving on a balance of probabilities.[329] To do so required that there be provided to the court corroborative evidence that at the same time met the threshold of admissibility. It followed that more was required than statements that were before court to satisfy the judge on the preponderance of probabilities.

[329] This would now come under the provisions of s 116 of the UK Criminal Justice Act 2003.

4

WITNESSES

4.1 Introduction

A witness is a person who gives evidence. Specifically, he or she, as the case may be, testifies in a suit or cause or trial before a court or a properly constituted judicial or quasi-judicial tribunal on the premise that he/she has personal knowledge of the facts about which he is called to give testimony. The importance of oral testimony by a witness in our adversarial system cannot be overemphasised. The early common law's concern with oral testimony can be seen in the many classes of persons who were disqualified from giving oral testimony as witnesses if only because they were deemed to be undependable. By the late 18th century, the class of persons deemed incompetent and as such disqualified from lawfully being called to give evidence included the following:[1]

(i) Convicted felons;
(ii) Parties to cases;
(iii) Non-Christians;
(iv) Spouses to parties to a matter; and
(v) All manner of interested parties to the outcome of a particular matter.

As we saw in chapter 1, having one's 'day in court' through the device of confrontation as is the mainstay of the adversarial trial, requires, among other things, the presence of a witness in court in person;[2] that such witness gives oral testimony through examination in chief; and that the testimony is scrupulously tested via cross-examination to determine not only the reliability of the evidence but also, the witness's credibility.[3]

The orality principle which we encountered in chapter 1 means, as we saw earlier, that to disputed facts evidence is and must be given by witnesses before court and put on the witness stand based on their knowledge of the facts in question. Only in such a way will the court be able to make a determination based not only on the demeanour of the witness but the usual reliability of evidence given under oath which, as already noted, is then tested under cross-

[1] For an attack on the early common law rules of competency, see Bentham J *Rationale of Judicial Evidence* (JS Mill (ed))(London, 1827), Vol. 5, p 743: "In principle" he said, "there is but one mode of searching out the truth [...] Be the dispute what it may, - see everything that is to be seen; hear everybody who is likely to know anything about the matter: hear every body, but most attentively of all, and first of all, those who are likely to know most about it, the parties."

[2] Which includes appearing by video conference.

[3] *Kafuti Vilongo v The People* [1977] ZR 423.

examination. In addition, oral testimony ensures 'maximum participation in decision-making in the sense that parties can confront their accusers and challenge the evidence against them' through the device of cross-examination. This chapter will therefore focus on the following:

(i) Authority to call witnesses;
(ii) Classes of witnesses and their competence and compellability; and
(iii) Oaths and affirmations

4.2 Authority to call witnesses

The concept of party autonomy under the law of evidence necessary means that the parties retain the independence to decide to commence and or defend the matter in court. It is for the parties to conduct a thorough investigation, to collate the evidence and decide what facts to bring to court. The parties will also have the liberty to decide which witnesses and how many of those witnesses are going to testify before court and in what order they will do so.[4] The magistrate's/judge's role is simply to ensure that procedural rules are adhered to, evidence followed, and all the while reminding him or herself of the law applicable to the issues, and of the evidence tendered during trial, and where absolutely necessary, to seek clarification. The judge is a silent observer or umpire listening to the evidence and arguments presented by the parties and ruling on questions of law and fact raised during trial.[5] He is not, as shown in *Priscillar Mwenya Kamanga v Attorney-General, Peter N'gandu Magande*[6] 'not expected to descend into the dust of the conflict.'[7] Lord Denning's dictum in *Jones v National Coal Board*[8]" is instructive: '[a] judge is not allowed in a civil dispute to call a witness whom he thinks might throw light on the facts. He must rest content with the witnesses called by the parties.'[9]

4.2.1 *Civil matters*[10]

4.2.1.1 General

The general law as regards the role of the magistrate/judge is well settled. Even so, a regards civil proceedings, the rules of procedure may permit the court to, among other things, require that the number of witnesses to appear is indicated beforehand and limited to that during the course of the trial. In this regard, Order VI Rule 1 of the High Court Rules (HCR) requires that a

---

[4] *Bozy Simutanda v Attorney-General and Mathews Kakungu Siame* (2019/CCZ/001).

[5] A judge must, according to *Porter v Magill* [2002] 1 All ER 465, be a "a fair minded and informed observer."

[6] [2008] 2 ZR 7 (SC).

[7] See further, *Mumba and Others v The People* SCZ Appeal No 92 of 1995 (unreported); See *Gerrison Zulu v Zambia Electricity Supply Corporation Limited* [2005] ZR 39 (SC); *R v Oliva* [1965] 3 All ER 116; *R v Roberts* [1984] 80 Cr App R 89.

[8] [1975] 2 All E R 155.

[9] Quoted by counsel in *Priscillar Mwenya Kamanga v Attorney-General, Peter N'gandu Magande* [2008] 2 ZR 7 (SC).

[10] A more detailed analysis is offered in Kaluba BK, *Evidence Law: Practice and Procedure in Zambia* (Chribwa Publishers, 2022) Ch V 149-228 and in cases cited and reproduced thereunder.

writ of summons be accompanied by statement of claim, list and description of documents, list of witnesses and letter of demand. Similarly, under Order XI Rule 1(b), HCR, a memorandum of appearance must be accompanied by a defence, list of documents and list of witnesses. The foregoing power may also extend to matters such as the expert witnesses to be called; the form of evidence to be given as regards certain facts in issue. Under Order 53 of the HCR, cross-examination is done based on readily filed witness statements without prior oral examination in chief. In matters that have been commenced by originating summons, the court may, at any stage, in accordance with Order 28 r 8, RSC, and as exemplified in *African Banking Corporation (Z) Limited (t/a Bank ABC) v Plinth Technical Works Limited and Others,*[11]order that the proceedings be continued as though same were commenced by writ. It has been held in *Thorne v Mulenga and Others*[12] that the court may under such circumstances also order that any affidavits filed into court stand as pleadings and accordingly give further directions as to the conduct of the matter. It has further been shown in *Kanjala Hills Lodge Limited and Another v Stanbic Bank Limited*[13] that the judge can, where he considers it necessary, and having regard to affidavit evidence presented by the parties at the hearing of a matter commenced by writ, hear evidence *viva voice.*

We have elsewhere in this text discussed substantive provisions relating to evidence under the High Court Act.[14] Procedurally, the receipt of evidence in civil matters is regulated, among other rules of practice such as those in the RSC, and Order V, HCR divided under three parts: (i) Exclusion of evidence; (ii) Documentary evidence; and (iii) Affidavit evidence. We discuss each below in turn:

4.2.1.2 Exclusion of witnesses

(i) Ordering witnesses out of court

In terms of Order V Rule 1, on the application of either party, or on its own motion, the Court may order witnesses on both sides to be kept out of court; but this rule does not extend to the parties themselves or to their professional representatives, although intended to be called as witnesses.

(ii) Preventing communication with witnesses

According to Order V Rule 2, the Court may, during any trial, take such means as it considers necessary and proper for preventing communication with witnesses who are within the Court House or its precincts awaiting examination.

[11] SCZ Judgment No 28 of 2015 (Unreported); see also *Thorne v Mulenga and Others* [2010] 1 ZR 221 at 240 *per* Kajimanga J.

[12] [2010] 1 ZR 221 at 240 *per* Kajimanga J.

[13] (2012) 2 ZR 285 at 296 *per* Muyovwe JS.

[14] Chapter 27 of the Laws of Zambia; There are similar provisions under the Subordinate Courts Rules, Chapter 28 of the Laws of Zambia; The Court of Appeal Rules, Act No 7 of 2017; The Constitutional Court Rules, Act and the Supreme Court Rules, Act Chapter 25 of the Laws of Zambia.

4.2.1.3 Documentary evidence

(i) Entries in books of account

According to Order V Rule 3, [e]ntries in books of account, kept in the course of business with such a reasonable degree of regularity as shall be satisfactory to the Court or a Judge, shall be admissible in evidence whenever they refer to a matter into which the Court or a Judge has to inquire, but shall not alone be sufficient evidence to charge any person with liability.

(ii) Government Gazettes

It is provided under Order V Rule 4, that [t]he Government Gazette in Zambia and any Government Gazette of any Commonwealth Country may be proved by the bare production of the Government Gazette.

(iii) Proof of Proclamations, etc

By Order V Rule 5, [a]ll Proclamations, Acts of State, whether legislative or executive, nominations, appointments, and other official communications of the Government, appearing in any Gazette referred to in the last preceding rule may be proved by the production of such Gazette, and shall be *prima facie* proof of any fact of a public nature which they were intended to notify.

(iv) Books of science, maps, charts, etc

In terms of Order V Rule 6, [o]n matters of public history, literature, science or art, the Court or a Judge may refer, if it or he shall think fit, for the purposes of evidence, to such published books, maps or charts as the Court or a Judge shall consider to be of authority on the subject to which they relate.

(v) Foreign law

In terms of Order V Rule 7, [b]ooks printed or published under the authority of the government of a foreign country and purporting to contain the statutes, code or other written law of such country, and also printed and published books of reports of the decisions of the courts of such country, and books proved to be commonly admitted in such courts as evidence of the law of such country, shall be admissible as evidence of the law of such country.

(vi) Public maps

By Order V Rule 8, [a]ll maps made under the authority of any government or of any public municipal body, and not made for the purpose of any litigated question, shall prima facie be deemed to be correct, and shall be admitted in evidence without further proof.

(vii) Examined or certified copies of documents admissible in evidence

It is provided under Order V Rule 9 that [w]henever any book or other document is of such a public nature as to be admissible in evidence on its mere production from the proper custody, and no Act or statute exists which renders its contents provable by means of a copy, any copy thereof or extract therefrom shall be admissible in evidence, if it purports to be signed and certified as a true copy or extract by the officer to whose custody the original is entrusted.

(viii) Production of documents without giving evidence

In terms of Order V Rule 10, [a]ny person, whether a party or not, in a cause or matter may be summoned to produce a document, without being summoned to give evidence; and, if he [causes] such document to be produced, the Court or a Judge may dispense with his personal attendance.

4.2.1.4 Affidavits

(i) Affidavits to be filed

In terms of s 11, [b]efore an affidavit is used in any proceeding for any purpose, the original shall be filed in the Court, and the original or an office copy shall alone be recognised for any purpose by the Court or a Judge.

(ii) Not to be sworn before certain persons

According to Rule 12, [a]n affidavit shall not be admitted which is proved to have been sworn before a person on whose behalf the same is offered, or before his Advocate, or before a partner or clerk of his Advocate.

(iii) Defective in form

In terms of Rule 13, [t]he Court or a Judge may permit an affidavit to be used notwithstanding it is defective in form according to these Rules, if the Court or a Judge is satisfied that it has been sworn before a person duly authorised.

(iv) Amendment and re-swearing

By Rule 14, [a] defective or erroneous affidavit may be amended and re-sworn, by leave of the Court or a Judge, on such terms as to time, costs or otherwise as seem reasonable.

(v) No extraneous matter

It is provided in Rule 15, that [a]n affidavit shall not contain extraneous matter by way of objection or prayer or legal argument or conclusion.

(vi) Contents of affidavits

According to Rule 16, [e]very affidavit shall contain only a statement of facts and circumstances to which the witness deposes, either of his own personal knowledge or from information which he believes to be true.[15]

(vii) Grounds of belief to be stated

In terms of Rule 17, [w]hen a witness deposes to his belief in any matter of fact, and his belief is derived from any source other than his own personal knowledge, he shall set forth explicitly the facts and circumstances forming the ground of his belief.

(viii) Informant to be named

It is provided under Rule 18, that [w]hen the belief of a witness is derived from information received from another person, the name of his informant shall be stated, and reasonable particulars shall be given respecting the informant, and the time, place and circumstances of the information.

(ix) Copies of exhibits

By Rule 19, [w]here any document referred to in an affidavit and exhibited thereto is a handwritten document other than a statement of account, book of account or extract therefrom, there shall also be exhibited therewith a typewritten or printed copy thereof certified in such affidavit to be a true and correct copy of the original.[16]

---

[15] It has, based on this rule, been held in, among others, *Philip Mutantika and Malyata Sheal S v Kenneth Chipungu* (SCZ Judgment No 13 of 2014); and *African Alliance Master Fund v Vehicle Finance Insurance* (2017/HP/ARB/007), that an affidavit that contains or advances legal arguments is liable to be expunged for offending the rules of evidence; It has further been shown in *Nkumbula and Another v Attorney General* (1979) ZR 267 at 272; *Kambarange Mpundu Kaunda v The People* [1992] ZMSC 62 (19 March 1992); (1992) SJ 1 (SC), that affidavits are inappropriate means for producing evidence where the matter in question in general or the facts in issue are controversial ones.; see also additional instances where the use of affidavit evidence may be appropriate: *Construction sales and Services Ltd and Others v Standard Bank Ltd* (SCZ Judgment No 4 of 1992); It is also to be noted that where the core source of evidence is an affidavit such as an application for judicial review as was the case in *Chilufya v Attorney General* (2003) ZR 53; A party cannot be heard, as has been demonstrated in *New Plast Industries v The Commissioner of Lands and the Attorney-General* (SCZ Judgment No 8 of 2001), to say they were not afforded an opportunity to give their evidence orally; as to exparte or interparte hearings relating affidavit evidence see, *Miles Emmanuel Sampa and Others v Inonge Wina and Another* (SCZ/8/294/2014); *Benjamin Yoram Mwila v Victor John Bradury* (SCZ Judgment No 18 of 2013); *Vas Sales Agencies Ltd and Finsbury Investment Ltd and 2 Others* (SCZ Judgment No 2 of 1999); as to advocates swearing affidavits in contentious matters, see *Chikuta v Chipata Rural District Council* [1983] ZR 26 (SC); *Shell and BP Zambia Ltd v Cornidaris and Others* [1974] ZR 281; but see *Post Newspapers Ltd v Rupiah Bwezani Banda* (SCZ Judgment No 25 of 2009); *Kalusha Bwalya v Chardore Properties Ltd and Another* (2009/HPC/0294); Order V Rules 15-18 of SCR, Chapter 28 of the Laws of Zambia; Order V of HCR, Rules 15-18, Chapter 27 of the Laws of Zambia for limited instances, mainly procedural, in which counsel may swear an affidavit.

[16] Reference to affidavits includes a reference to exhibits or copies of those exhibits: Order 14 of the SCR, Cap 28 and Order 14 of the HCR, Cap 27; Order VI Rule 10, [12] and 13 of the Constitutional Court Act No 8 of 2016: *Bozy Simutanda v Attorney General and Mathews Kakungu Siame* (2019/CCZ/001); Order 28 Rule 1A (9), RSC.

(x) Rules in taking affidavits

According to Rule 20, [t]he following rules shall be observed by Commissioners and others before whom affidavits are taken:

(a) Every affidavit taken in a cause or matter shall be headed in the Court and in the cause or matter.

(b) It shall state the full name, trade or profession, residence and nationality of the witness

(c) It shall be in the first person and divided into convenient paragraphs, numbered consecutively.

(d) Any erasure, interlineation or alteration made before the affidavit is sworn shall be attested by the Commissioner, who shall affix his signature or initials in the margin immediately opposite to the interlineation, alteration or erasure.

(e) Where an affidavit proposed to be sworn is illegible or difficult to read, or is, in the judgment of the Commissioner, so written as to facilitate fraudulent alteration, he may refuse to swear the witness, and require the affidavit to be re-written in an unobjectionable manner.

(f) The affidavit shall be signed by the witness (or, if he cannot write, marked by him with his mark in the presence of the Commissioner).

(g) The jurat[17] shall be written, without interlineation, alteration or erasure (unless the same be initialed by the Commissioner), immediately at the foot of the affidavit, and towards the left side of the paper, and shall be signed by the Commissioner:[18]

   (i) It shall state the date of the swearing and the place where it is sworn.

   (ii) It shall state that the affidavit was sworn before the Commissioner or other officer taking the same.

   (iii) Where the witness is illiterate or blind, it shall state the fact, and that the affidavit was read over (or translated into his own language in the case of a witness not having sufficient knowledge of English), and that the witness appeared to understand it.

   (iv) Where the witness makes a mark instead of signing, the jurat shall state that fact, and that the mark was made in the presence of the Commissioner.

   (v) Where two or more persons join in making an affidavit, their several names shall be written in the jurat, and it shall appear by the jurat that each of them has been sworn to the truth of the several matters stated by him in the affidavit.

---

[17] That non-compliance with this requirement is fatal can be seen in, among others, *Genesis Finance Ltd v Longreach Commodities Ltd & Another* (2012/HPC/0144); *Indo-Zambia Bank Ltd v Amazon Carriers and Another* (2014/HPC/0141).

[18] That an affidavit that has not been commissioned will be expunged from the record has been demonstrated in *Annet Soko v Donhood Investments Ltd and Martha Mushipe* (2014/HPC/0323).

(h) [t]he Commissioner shall not allow an affidavit, when sworn, to be altered in any manner without being re-sworn.

(i) If the jurat has been added and signed, the Commissioner shall add a new jurat on the affidavit being re-sworn; and, in the new jurat, he shall mention the alteration.

(j) The Commissioner may refuse to allow the affidavit to be re-sworn, and may require a fresh affidavit.

(k) The Commissioner may take, without oath, the declaration of any person affirming that the taking of any oath whatsoever is, according to his religious belief, unlawful, or who, by reason of immature age or want of religious belief, ought not, in the opinion of the Commissioner, to be admitted to make a sworn affidavit. The Commissioner shall record in the attestation the reason of such declaration being taken without oath.

(l) Every certificate on an exhibit referred to in an affidavit signed by the Commissioner before whom the affidavit is sworn shall be marked with the short title of the cause or matter.

At this point we must briefly explain the foregoing provisions as regards the matter of affidavit evidence[19] in civil cases as it relates to chamber matters whether these be substantive as are all matters referenced under Order XXX, HCR or interlocutory.

While neither the substantive provisions nor court rules attach a definite definition of an affidavit, the same has been defined as '[…] a written statement made in proceedings verified by an oath or affirmation.'[20] A judicial definition can be found in the Nigerian decision of *Josien Holdings Ltd and Others v Lornmead Ltd and Another* wherein an affidavit was defined as a statement of fact which the affiant or deponent verily swears (or affirms) to the best of his knowledge and belief to be true. Thus, as noted in *African Banking Corporation v Mattaniah Investments and Four Others*,[21]

> […] an affidavit may only contain such facts as the deponent is able of his own knowledge to prove. In exceptional circumstances, an affidavit can contain information of beliefs that the deponent is able to prove but not of his personal knowledge. In the latter case, the deponent is not only supposed to disclose the source of the information but must as well state the facts that form the basis on which the statement made is to be believed.

Whether an affidavit is admissible will be dependent on the nature of the proceedings in question and the stage of such proceedings. It will further be noted from the rules considered above that the validity of an affidavit is

---

[19] Reference to affidavits includes a reference to exhibits or copies of those exhibits: Order 14 of the SCR, Cap 28 and Order 14 of the HCR, Cap 27; Order VI Rule 12 of the Constitutional Court Act No 8 of 2016; Order 28 Rule 1A (9), RSC.

[20] Atkins Court Forms 2nd edn vol 18 (Butterworths, 1996) 390.

[21] CAZ Application No 73 of 2019.

determined by its compliance with the statutory provisions in various statutes,[22] rules of court and such practice directions as may have been issued in this regard.[23] Once filed, the affidavit ought to be normally served on the otherside unless it is an affidavit which is filed for the benefit of the court only or an affidavit filed in support of an application that may ordinarily be granted ex-parte. Finally, where the ultimate purpose of an affidavit is to have it employed at trial, it ought to be sufficiently proved based on the rules of admissibility, relevance and weight, as a document.[24]

4.2.1.5 Objections to evidence

(i) When to be made

It is provided under Rule 21 that [i]n every case, and at every stage thereof, any objection to the reception of evidence by a party affected thereby shall be made at the time the evidence is offered: Provided that the Court may, in its discretion, on appeal, entertain any objection to evidence received in a subordinate court, though not objected to at the time it was offered.

(ii) Where question objected to

According to Rule22, [w]here a question proposed to be put to a witness is objected to, the Court or a Judge, unless the objection appears frivolous, shall, if required by either party, take a note of the question and objection, and mention on the notes whether the question was allowed to be put or not and, if put, the answer to it.

(iii) Marking of rejected documents

By Rule 23, [w]here a document is produced and tendered in evidence and rejected by the Court or a Judge, the document shall be marked as having been so tendered and rejected.

4.2.1.6 Taking of evidence and marking of rejected documents

(i) Evidence of witnesses, how taken

In terms of Rule 24, [i]n the absence of any agreement between the parties, and subject to these Rules, the witnesses at the trial or any suit shall be examined viva voce and in open court; but the Court may at any time, for sufficient

---

[22] See for example, s 2 of The Interpretation and General Provisions Act; The Official Oaths Act, Chapter 5 of the Laws of Zambia; see further, Order V, HCR, Chapter 27 of the Laws of Zambia; Order V SCR, Chapter 28 of the Laws of Zambia.

[23] However, as has been held in *Sun Country Ltd v Charles Kearney and Roslyn Kearney* (SCZ Appeal No 7 of 2017), the court may, even in the face of defects in an affidavit still permit it to be used, provided that is satisfied that it was sworn before a duly authorised person: Order V Rule 14 of the Subordinate Court Rules, Chapter 28 of the Laws of Zambia; Order V Rule 14 of both the High Court Rules, Chapter 27 of the Laws of Zambia.

[24] *Habib Bank Ltd v Opomulero* (2002) 15 NWLR (Pt 690) at 315.

reason, order that any particular fact or facts may be proved by affidavit, or that the affidavit of any witness may be read at the hearing or trial, on such conditions as the Court may think reasonable; or that any witness whose attendance in court ought, for some sufficient cause, to be dispensed with be examined by interrogatories or otherwise before an officer of the Court or other person: Provided that, where it appears to the Court that the other party bona fide desires the production of a witness for cross-examination, and that such witness can be produced, an order shall not be made authorising the evidence of such witness to be given by affidavit.

(ii) Admission of affidavits

According to Rule 25, [i]n any suit, the Court may, in its discretion, if the interests of justice appear absolutely so to require (for reasons to be recorded in the minutes of the proceedings), admit an affidavit in evidence, although it is shown that the party against whom the affidavit is offered in evidence has had no opportunity of cross-examining the person making the affidavit.

(iii) Evidence on commission

According to Rule 26, [t]he Court or a Judge may, in any suite where it shall appear necessary for the purpose of justice, make any order for the examination, before any officer of the Court or other person, and at any place, of any witness or person, and may order any deposition so taken to be filed in the Court, and may empower any party to any such suit to give such deposition in evidence therein on such terms, if any, as the Court or a Judge may direct.

(iv) How to be taken

In terms of Rule 27, [e]vidence on commission, when not directed to be taken upon interrogatories previously settled, shall be taken, as nearly as may be, as evidence at the hearing of a suit, and then the notes of the evidence shall be read over to the witness and be signed by him. If the witness refuses, the officer of the Court or other person shall add a note of his refusal, and the statement may be used as if he had signed it.

(v) Evidence before suit instituted

By Rule 28, [e]vidence may be taken in like manner, on the application of any person, before suit instituted, where it is shown to the satisfaction of the Court or a Judge on oath that the person applying has good reason to apprehend that a suit will be instituted against him in the Court, and that some person within the jurisdiction at the time of the application can give material evidence respecting the subject of the apprehended suit, but that he is about to leave the jurisdiction, or that, from some other cause, the person applying will lose the benefit of his evidence if it be not at once taken; and the evidence so taken may be used at the hearing, subject to just exceptions: Provided always that the Court or a Judge may impose any terms or conditions with reference to the examination of such witness, and the admission of his evidence, as to the Court or a Judge may seem reasonable.

(vi) Facilities for proving deed, etc

It is provided under Rule 29 that [a]ny party desiring to give in evidence any deed or other instrument which shows upon the face of it that it has been duly executed may deliver to the opposite party, not less than four clear days before the return day, a notice in writing specifying the date and nature of and the parties to such deed or instrument, and requiring the opposite party to admit that the same was executed as it purports to have been, saving all just exceptions as to its admissibility, validity and contents; and if, at or before the hearing of the suit, the party so notified shall neglect or refuse to give such admission, the Court or a Judge may adjourn the hearing in order to enable the party tendering such deed or instrument to obtain proof of the due execution thereof, and, upon production of such proof, the Court or a Judge may order the costs of such proof to be paid by the party so neglecting or refusing, whether he be the successful party or not.

(vii) Commission or letter of request

According to Rule 30, [w]here the Court or a Judge to which or to whom application is made for the issue of a commission for the examination of a person residing at a place not within Zambia is satisfied that the evidence of such person is necessary, the Court may issue such commission or a letter of request.

(viii) Not to issue until sum deposited in court to cover cost thereof

In terms of Rule 31, [t]he Court shall not issue any commission or letter of request abroad for the taking of evidence, unless and until the person applying for the issue of such commission or letter of request shall have paid into court by way of deposit, or shall have given approved security for, such sum as the Court or a Judge shall consider sufficient to cover the expenses incurred, or likely to be incurred, in connection with and in consequence of the grant of any such application.

4.2.2 *Criminal matters*

4.2.2.1 *The prosecution's authority*

The authority by the prosecution to call witnesses in criminal matters is extensive. Be that as it may, such autonomy as the prosecution enjoys to call witnesses and the discretion to pick and choose which witnesses will give oral testimony at trial is premised on and circumscribed by the duty to act fairly. The foregoing limitation is predicated on the significant role which public prosecutors play in any common law criminal justice system including ours. Rather than being deemed as proponents of a cause, which at first glance they appear to be, in representing society to prove charges against the accused, their effective role is premised on the duty to act with the prosecutor's overall obligation "of fairness as a minister of justice."[25]

The prosecutors' role's significance can be deduced from the fact that they counsel investigative arms, determine on the basis of evidence whether a criminal prosecution must be instituted and having decided to institute formal criminal proceedings before a court of law, to prosecute the accused, and aid courts in sentencing the accused once he or she is convicted of the offence with which he is charged. It is in the foregoing actions expected of a prosecutor which includes the proper exercise of discretion in deciding which witnesses to call in order to aid in proving the prosecution's case, that prosecutors are said to 'uphold the rule of law and deliver justice for and on behalf of their communities.'[26]

To the foregoing reasons as to why the prosecution or prosecutor must act fairly must be added a far more fundamental essential predicate. Perhaps more than anyone else in a criminal prosecution which threatens the liberty or even life of the accused but in addition, the victim(s) of the offence, friends, family and society at large, the prosecutor has a central role. His actions, including how and whom he decides to invite as witnesses invariably affects other aspects of criminal proceedings and the behaviour of stakeholders such as defence counsel, the police and the justices that preside over criminal cases in fulfilling their duties and exercising, with specific reference to the courts, the powers with which they are clothed. Thus, not only should prosecutors or the prosecution exercise the highest ethical standards in their autonomy to call witnesses, they must do this not to secure a conviction at any cost but go about their work in interests of justice. In the *Sugarman's case*[27] Lord Hewart CJ, observed as follows:

> It cannot be too often made plain that the business of counsel for the [prosecution] is fairly and impartially to exhibit all the facts to the jury. The [prosecution] has no interest in procuring a conviction. Its only interest is that the right person should be convicted, that the truth should be known, and that justice should be done.

Thus, as held in *Kasumu v The People*,[28] '[i]t is no part of the prosecution's function to place technical obstacles in the way of the introduction of relevant evidence; it is the function of the court to arrive at the truth and it is the function of the prosecution to assist the court to do so.' It therefore falls to reason that

[25] *R v Russell-Jones* [1995] 1 Cr App R 538 at 544 *per* Kennedy LJ; *R v Olivia* [1965] 3 All ER 116 at 122 per Lord Parker.

[26] Crown Prosecution Service, Ethical Principles for the Public Prosecutor: Statement of https://www.cps.gov.uk/legal-guidance/ethical-principles-public-prosecutor-statement retrieved on 11/2/2021.

[27] 25 Cr App R 109.

[28] [1978] ZR 252; cited and quoted with approval in *Mushemi v The People* [1982] ZR 71.

uppermost in the prosecutor's mind ought to be a consideration of not only the rights and views, as well as the legitimate interests, privacy but concerns of witnesses and victims alike in circumstances where their interests, personal or otherwise might be affected. In addition, the prosecution must ensure that both the witnesses he chooses to call in aid of his case and the victims of the offence with which the accused is charged, are made aware of their rights so far as this is practicable within the context of the accused's rights on the one hand and the prosecutor's obligation to 'prosecute firmly and fairly and not beyond what is indicated by the evidence.'[29] In *Benson Nguila v The Queen,*[30] the appellant was jointly charged with another accused with the crime of arson. It was contended that the other accused's plea of guilty was equivocal (in that he claimed to have been compelled to commit the offence), that he should have been acquitted, and that as the appellant was jointly charged with him, he also should be acquitted. It was also contended that the appeal was entitled to succeed since the prosecution had failed to tender in evidence at the trial a statement which amounted to a simple denial of the charge. It was held *inter alia* that the prosecution has a discretion as to what evidence it calls, although it will normally put in evidence any documentary evidence relevant to the case.

Further to the foregoing, the autonomy and discretion that the prosecution or prosecutors enjoy to call witnesses is also circumscribed by the requirement placed upon them by the laws of Zambia beginning with the Constitution which in Part III guarantees fundamental freedoms; the Criminal Procedure Code[31] which provides mandatory procedure for all trial participants; practice directions if any and such directions as the court may provide during criminal proceedings. It has thus been held in *Brown and Brown*[32] as follows:

> (1) The prosecution have a discretion in deciding which witnesses it will rely on for the purpose of establishing a prima facie case … [at] … committal proceedings … and will serve their statements accordingly. It must normally disclose any potentially material statement not served.
>
> (2) Counsel for the prosecution must have at court all witnesses whose statements have been served, whether as part of the depositions or as additional evidence, upon whom he intends to rely, unless any such witness is conditionally bound or the defence agree that he need not attend because, for example, his evidence can be admitted.
>
> (3) Counsel for the prosecution enjoys a discretion whether to call or to tender a particular witness whom he has required to attend. Further, counsel may refuse even to tender a witness, notwithstanding that the witness's statement has been included in the depositions, if he decides that the witness is unworthy

[29] Crown Prosecution Service, Ethical Principles for the Public Prosecutor: Statement of https://www.cps.gov.uk/legal-guidance/ethical-principles-public-prosecutor-statement retrieved on 11/2/2021.

[30] (1963-1964) Z & NRLR 14.

[31] Chapter 88 of the Laws of Zambia.

[32] [1997] 1 Cr App R 112 at 113-114.

of belief.[33] Our adversarial system requires counsel for the prosecution to present a case against the defendant. He must always act in the interests of justice and to promote a fair trial, and his discretion must be exercised with these objects in mind. He should not refuse to call a witness merely because his evidence does not fit in exactly with the case he is seeking to prove. But he need not call a witness whose evidence is inconsistent with, or contrary to, the case he is prosecuting since such witnesses' evidence will be unworthy of belief if his case be correct.

(4) Counsel for the prosecution ought normally to call, or offer to call, all the witnesses who give direct evidence of the primary facts of the case unless the prosecutor regards the witness's evidence as unworthy of belief.

(5) It is for counsel for the prosecution to decide which witnesses give direct evidence of the primary facts of the case. He may reasonably take the view that what a particular witness has to say is, at best, marginal.

(6) Counsel for the prosecution is also the primary judge of whether or not a witness to the material events is unworthy of belief.

(7) Counsel for the prosecution, properly exercising his discretion, is not obliged to offer a witness upon whom the Crown does not rely merely in order to give the defence material with which to attack the credit of other witnesses on whom the Crown does rely. The law does not insist that the prosecution are obliged to call a witness for no purpose other than to assist the defence in its endeavours to destroy the Crown's case. Such a course would merely serve to confuse a jury. The Crown's obligation is to make such witnesses available to the defence so that the defence can call them if they choose to do so. The jury will then be clear that evidence is led by the party who wishes to rely upon it and can be tested by cross-examination by the other party, if that party wishes to challenge the evidence ".

Prosecutors must also be alive to Supreme Court decisions or indeed any superior court decisions that may have an impact on any matter pertaining to their conduct of trial, particularly, the constraints placed upon them in using their discretion to call witnesses. 'Prosecutors are subject to the same duties to the court and to others with whom they have dealings, and they must uphold the same professional standards of conduct and ethics.'[34] There are a few authorities worth considering as regards both the former and latter point.

It has been held in *Abel Banda v The People*[35] that a prosecutor is not required to bring all evidence before Court, but has a duty to bring to notice of the Court or the defence any credible witness whose evidence is inconsistent

[33] See *R v Cairns* [2002] EWCA Crim 2838, [2003] 1 Cr App R 38.

[34] Crown Prosecution Service, Ethical Principles for the Public Prosecutor: Statement of https://www.cps.gov.uk/legal-guidance/ethical-principles-public-prosecutor-statement retrieved on 11/2/2021.

[35] [1986] ZR 105 (SC).

with accused's guilt. Thus, in Charles *Lukolongo and Others v The People*[36] the appellants were each charged and convicted of two counts of murder and one count of aggravated robbery. There was evidence that the appellant had been questioned by the police while in custody but before being warned and cautioned. On appeal it was argued that the Judges' Rules at present in force in Zambia required that persons in custody should be warned before being questioned and their answers were therefore inadmissible. It was further argued that footprints which were seen by the police should have been compared with the shoes of the accused persons; that the identification parade was unfair because the suspects were the only ones not wearing shoes; and that the articles found after improper questioning should not have been admitted in evidence. It was held in part that 'Where evidence available only to the police is not placed before the court, the court must presume that, had the evidence been produced, it would have been favourable to the accused. This presumption can only be displaced lay strong evidence.'

In *R v Harris,*[37] Lord Hewart expressed the view that that appeared to suggest that the prosecution had no discretion in which witnesses they called specifically, that the prosecution was 'bound to call all the material witnesses before the court even though they give inconsistent accounts, in order that the whole of the facts may be before the [court].' The error in this reasoning is clear when one notes that the prosecution's case is to prove the charges against the accused within the context of their duty to be fair. In fact, the dictum by Lord Hewart must be deemed to be just that and of no contemporary legal standing in the face of the Privy Council's decision in *Adel Mohammed el Dabbah v Attorney-General for Palestine*[38] which held that the prosecution in a criminal case has a discretion as to what witnesses they wish to call. It is consistent with that discretion that it should be a general practice of prosecuting counsel, if he finds no sufficient reason to the contrary, to tender for cross-examination by the defence, witnesses whose names are on the back of the information but who have not been called to give evidence for the prosecution. Even so, it remains a matter for the discretion of the prosecutor.[39] In *Dallison v Caffery*[40] Lord Denning, MR opined as follows:

> The duty of a prosecution counsel or solicitor, as I have always understood it, is this: if he knows of a credible witness who can speak to material facts which tend to show the prisoner to be innocent, he must either call that witness or make his statement available to the defence. It would be highly reprehensible to conceal from the court the evidence which such a witness can give. If the prosecuting counsel or solicitor knows, not of credible witness, but a witness who he does not accept as credible, he should tell the defence about him so that they can call him if they wish.

---

[36] [1986] ZR 115 (SC).

[37] [1927] 2 KB 587 at 590.

[38] [1944] AC 156.

[39] See further, para 1373 of the 35th edn of Archbold.

[40] [1964]2 All ER 610 at 618.

Diplock LJ for his part took the view that it was erroneous to posit that a prosecutor had a duty to call all evidence known to him in the following terms:[41]

> This contention seems to me to be based on the erroneous proposition that it is the duty of the prosecutor to place before the court all the evidence known to him; whether or not it is probative of the guilt of the accused person. A prosecutor is under no such duty. His duty is to prosecute, not to defend. If he happens to have information from a credible witness which is inconsistent with the guilt of the accused, or although not inconsistent with his guilt is helpful to the accused, the prosecutor should make such witness available to the defence.

In *Boy Otto v The People*,[42] the appellant was arrested by the police on a charge of being in recent possession of a stolen vehicle. While in custody the police took several statements from him. In one of the statements, he had named the person from whom he said he had borrowed the vehicle, which was his defence. Before the trial magistrate this statement was not produced and the only evidence adduced by the police was a statement by the appellant denying the charge. The magistrate convicted the appellant of the offence. It was held on appeal as follows: (i) In cases of recent possession, the fact that the person found in possession gives an explanation is a matter which is so crucial that it ought to be produced before the court to enable it to make a conclusion; (ii) It is the duty of the police to produce before court all the statements taken from an accused whether favourable or against him; (iii) In the instant case since all the statements were not produced before the trial magistrate he was misled and did not take the steps as he would have done.

However, given that prosecutors have a duty to act fairly, such discretion ought to be exercised in a manner that is fair to the accused and which does not mislead him, by the prosecution preventing the full facts from emerging. If the former were the case, it would form the basis for an appeal. In line with the duty to act fairly, and as noted above, the prosecution will ordinarily, as a general rule of practice, tender for cross-examination by the defence, a witness called by the prosecution whom the prosecution does not seek to examine. Additionally, the prosecution will put into evidence relevant documentary evidence. Be that as it may, the prosecution must, as is in the nature of our adversarial system, retain the freedom or autonomy over the conduct of its case including the discretion as to what witnesses they call in aid of that case.[43] To re-emphasise the point, it is to be noted that the prosecution has discretion as to which witnesses they will call in aid of their case, and what evidence such witnesses will adduce within the context of their duty to act fairly and in accordance with the rule of law.

---

[41] *Dallison v Caffery* [1964] 2 All ER 610 at 622.

[42] [1970] ZR 65 (CA).

[43] *Dallison v Caffery* [1964]2 All ER 610.

4.2.2.2 *The defence and the obligation to call witnesses*

Under Article 18(7) of the Constitution, '[a] person who is tried for a criminal offence shall not be compelled to give evidence at the trial.' The foregoing fundamental right to 'plead the 18th' or remain silent if an accused so wishes has no claw back clause. It logically follows that there is, unlike in the case of the prosecution, no obligation placed on the accused or his defence counsel to call any particular person(s) as a witness(es) in aid of the accused's case. He cannot be compelled even when put on his defence to do so simply because 'he who alleges must prove' and the prosecution bears that burden. As a practical matter though, to successfully discharge some evidential burden, the accused may tactically find it prudent to have himself testify. Indeed, where necessity is laid upon him, he must call an apposite witness to testify accordingly. A failure to testify under such circumstances may well lead to negative consequences, the accused's right not to testify, notwithstanding. In *Dickson Sembauke Changwe and Ifellow Hamuchanje v The People*,[44] it was observed that the fact that the appellants elected to remain silent, was not a factor to be held against them. The question whether the court must make comments on an accused electing to remain silent or not calling any witnesses at all when called upon to do so arose in *David Dimuna v The People*.[45] The Supreme Court took the view that for a judge to note that the accused elected to remain silent and that only the prosecution evidence was available to the court' was 'no more than a statement of fact and' that this did 'not suggest that remaining silent is an indication of guilt.'Even so, in *Chimbini v The People*,[46] the Supreme Court observed as follows:

> Where the evidence against an accused person is purely circumstantial and his guilt entirely a matter of inference, it is trite that the inference of guilt may not be drawn unless it is the only inference which can reasonably be drawn from the facts. In such cases the fact that an accused person has elected not to give evidence on oath may, in certain circumstances, tend to support the case against him, but will certainly not do so unless the inference was one which could properly be drawn in the first place.

However, in *R v Weller*,[47] the EWCA underscored the need for judges to be wary and slow in making comments on an accused's election to remain silent. To say, for example that if the accused's story was truthful at all, he would have called witnesses to support his case was deemed inappropriate.

---

[44] [1988 – 1989] ZR 144 (SC).

[45] [1988 – 1989] ZR 199 (SC).

[46] [1973] ZR 191 (CA).

[47] [1994] Crim LR 856.

4.2.2.3 *The role of the judge*

What then is the role of the judge in all this? It generally is that he must be an umpire and as such a neutral observer. The adversarial system compels him to remember that it is the parties to the criminal proceedings, i.e., the prosecution and defence that have the right to call witnesses. In exceptional circumstances where something arises that could not have been reasonably anticipated and the interests of justice call for it in terms of Article 118(2)(e) of the Constitution which enjoins courts to administer justice 'without undue regard to procedural technicalities,' a judge may exercise his discretion to call a witness at any time during trial to speak to the issue that has arisen or as the Supreme Court guided albeit in a slightly different context, in *Mumba and Others v The People*,[48] '[...] a court may occasionally ask one or two question on matters of clarification [....]' This procedure must, however, be considered exceptional and is to be employed sparingly, for if it were not, it would run counter to the principles of conducting a trial in our adversarial process which are premised on party autonomy and may be deemed to be meddling in the adversarial process in so far as the judge's role is concerned.

A judge ought to be wary of being adjudged to have abandoned his neutrality by 'descending into the dust of conflict.'[49] A judge must, according to *Porter v Magill*,[50] be a 'a fair minded and informed observer.'[51] As noted elsewhere in this text, the judge's role is simply to ensure that procedural rules are adhered to, evidence followed, all the while reminding him or herself of the law applicable to the issues, and of the evidence tendered during trial. In view of the foregoing, the Supreme Court's dictum in *Mumba and Others v The People*,[52] is instructive: '[...] it is very undesirable for [a judge] to take an active role in examining a witness. This may compromise the court's neutral position in the eyes of the parties i.e., possible bias on the part of the court may not be ruled out.' It would appear that the Court of Appeal (or the Supreme Court itself, where leave to appeal is granted by the Court of Appeal), would interfere with a judge's refusal to exercise the discretion to call a witness even if he should or ought to have done so.

4.3 Classes of witnesses and their competence and compellability

A discussion concerning classes of witnesses and their competency and compellability must ordinarily begin with the noting that the general rule with respect to this subject is to the effect that everyone is deemed competent to testify and as such is compellable to testify, and during such testimony be it by witness statement, affidavit evidence or as is the cornerstone of our adversarial

[48] SCZ Appeal No 92 of 1995 (unreported).

[49] See Counsel's arguments on this point in *Priscillar Mwenya Kamanga v Attorney-General, Peter N'gandu Magande* [2008] 2 ZR 7 (SC).

[50] *Porter v Magill* [2002] 1 All ER 465.

[51] See further, *Gerrison Zulu v Zambia Electricity Supply Corporation Limited* [2005] ZR 39 (SC); *R v Oliva* [1965] 3 All ER 116; *R v Roberts* [1984] 80 Cr App R 89.

[52] SCZ Appeal No 92 of 1995 (unreported).

system, orally, is legally obligated to tell the truth with the warning that lying constitutes the offence of perjury for which they may be tried, convicted and sent to jail. In fact, by way of illustration, s 52[53] of the Subordinate Court Act[54] provides as follows on the matter of perjury:

> (1) A Subordinate Court of the first or second class, if it appears to it that a person has been guilty of perjury in any proceeding before it, may-
> (a) after calling upon such person to show cause why he should not be punished as for a contempt of court, commit him to prison for any term not exceeding six months, with or without hard labour, or fine him any sum not exceeding one thousand five hundred penalty units, or impose both such penalties upon him, in each such case as for a contempt of court; or
> (b) after preliminary inquiry, commit him for trial upon information for perjury, and bind any person by recognizance to give evidence at such trial.
>
> (2) On imposing any penalty as for a contempt of court under this section, a Subordinate Court shall, forthwith, send a copy of the proceedings to the High Court. The High Court may, thereupon, without hearing any argument, vary or set aside the order of the Subordinate Court.
>
> (3) Except where the order of the Subordinate Court is set aside by the High Court, any penalty imposed under this section shall be a bar to any other criminal proceedings in respect of the same offence.

4.3.1 Competence

The term competence refers to a person's ability to testify in court proceedings. There is a legal assumption that any person is ordinarily competent unless barred from doing so for want of such competence premised on a disability such as insanity or want of age. In both cases but more so the latter which may require a *voire dire* to determine, it is because a basic requirement of competence is the ability by the would-be witness to have a sufficient appreciation of the seriousness of the occasion and the significance of telling the truth that is considered cardinal. While witnesses may give sworn testimony or unsworn testimony, the former is not permitted for persons such as young ones who lack a sufficient appreciation of the gravity of the occasion the importance attached to telling the truth. However, where the preceding is the case, as we have shown elsewhere in this text, it is still possible for such children to give evidence in terms of s 78 of the Children's Code[55] which as seen elsewhere in this text provides that '[i]f, in the opinion of the juvenile court or Children's

[53] As amended by Act No 13 of 1994.

[54] Chapter 28 of the Laws of Zambia.

[55] Act No 12 of 2022.

Court, the child does not possess sufficient intelligence to justify the reception of the child's evidence, on oath, and does not understand the duty of speaking the truth, the child may give— (a) unsworn evidence that may be received as evidence in a juvenile court or Children's Court; or (b) evidence through a child welfare inspector responsible for the child's case.'

4.3.2 *Compellability*

Any person deemed competent may be compelled to testify during court proceedings.[56] Should a person be unwilling to so testify he will be compelled to so appear and give testimony through a *subpoena* which is a writ issued mainly by a court, to compel oral testimony by a reluctant witness or where required, production of evidence documentary or otherwise under a penalty of contempt of court for failure to adhere to or comply with such *subpoena*. The two commonly used classes of subpoenas[57] are as follows:

(i) *Subpoena ad testificandum:* A *subpoena ad testificandum* is a court summons ordering the person to which it is addressed to appear before court and give oral testimony during court proceedings. The use of a writ to compel attendance to testify in court proceedings has its origins in the ecclesiastical courts of the Middle Ages, particularly in England following which it was adopted throughout England and continental Europe. Failure to comply with the court order ordinarily leads to punishment for contempt of court. The writ in its current form and its formalised use by our courts was imported into this jurisdiction by British colonialists. It cannot, however, be gainsaid that the import of the practice was new. This is because being summoned to a hearing in the local courts was employed and enforced in pre-colonial Zambia with varying consequences from chiefdom to chiefdom.

(ii) *Subpoena duces tecum:*[58] A *subpoena duces tecum* otherwise known as a 'subpoena for production of evidence,' is a summons of court which orders the person to whom it is directed to not only appear before court but to do so and produce relevant documents or other

[56] With respect to the power of the court to compel witness attendance see ss 143-148 of the Criminal Procedure Code chapter 88 of the Laws of Zambia.

[57] Something akin to this is to be found under ss 143-145 of the Criminal Procedure Code Chapter 88 of the Laws of Zambia which provides as follows: '[i]f it is made to appear that material evidence can be given by, or is in the possession of, any person, it shall be lawful for a court having cognizance of any criminal cause or matter to issue a summons to such person requiring his attendance before such court, or requiring him to bring and produce to such court, for the purpose of evidence, all documents and writings in his possession or power, which may be specified or otherwise sufficiently described in the summons.' In terms of s 144, '[i]f, without sufficient excuse, a witness does not appear in obedience to the summons, the court, on proof of the proper service of the summons a reasonable time before, may issue a warrant to bring him before the court at such time and place as shall be therein specified. According to s 145, '[i]f the court is satisfied that any person will not attend as a witness unless compelled to do so, it may at once issue a warrant for the arrest and production of such person before the court at a time and place to be therein specified. Warrant for witness in first instance.'

[58] Pronounced in English /səˈpiːnə ˌdjuːsiːz ˈtiːkəm/ *sə-PEE-nə DEW-seez TEE-kəm.*

palpable evidence for use during court proceedings.[59] Failure to comply with a *subpoena duces tecum* puts the person concerned at the risk of being adjudged to be in contempt of court and liable to conviction and imprisonment or a fine[60] as the case may be. While similar in form and intent to the *Subpoena ad testificandum*, the *subpoena duces tecum* specifically instructs the person to whom it is addressed to bring in documentary or any tangible evidence that is relevant to the proceedings such as emails, financial statements, annual reports, photographs, hand books, papers, or like evidence for the court. A subpoena must comply with the requirement for personal service.

4.3.1 *The accused as the prosecution's witness*

At common law, the accused is not a competent witness for the prosecution.[61] This is so even if the accused wishes to testify for the prosecution. It has been shown in *R v Grant*[62] that where there are co-accused persons in any criminal proceedings, one of them may not be called to give evidence against the other co-accused persons in aid of the prosecution's case. There are, however, at least four ways of getting around this impediment. All of them involve the prosecution using a person whom, as regards the criminal proceedings in question, is not liable to be convicted or one who is no longer liable (i.e., to say a co-accused whose charges have been dropped) to be convicted of an offence:[63]

(i) Where in terms of s 81 of the Criminal Procedure Code[64] the Director of Public Prosecutions enters a *nolle prosequi*. That section provides as follows:

> (1) In any criminal case and at any stage thereof before verdict or judgment, as the case may be, the Director of Public Prosecutions may enter a nolle prosequi, either by stating in court, or by informing the court in writing, that the People intend that the proceedings shall not continue, and, thereupon, the accused shall stand discharged in respect of the charge for which the nolle prosequi is entered, and, if he has been committed to prison, shall be released, or, if he is on bail, his recognizances shall be treated as being discharged; but such discharge of an accused person shall not operate as a bar to any subsequent proceedings against him on account of the same facts.
>
> (2) If the accused shall not be before the court when such *nolle prosequi* is entered, the Registrar or clerk of such court shall

[59] *Perry v Gibson* (1834), 1 Ad and El 48; Order 38 Rule 1(6), RSC; *Hickman v Berens* (1895) 2 Ch 638 but see *Pioneer Concrete Gold Coast Pty Ltd v Cassidy* (No 2) (1969) Qd R 290; *R v Secretary of State for India, Ex parte Ezekiel* (1941) 2 KB 169, [1941] 2 All ER 546; *George Bienga v The People* [1978] ZR 32 (HC).

[60] See for example, s 148 of the Criminal Procedure Code Chapter 88 of the Laws of Zambia.

[61] See *R v Rhodes* [1899] 1 QB 77.

[62] [1944] 2 All ER 311; see also *R v Payne* (1872) L.R. 1 C.C.R. 349; *R v Sharrock* (1948) 32 Cr. App. R. 124.

[63] For examples of where this happened, see *The People v Japau* [1967] ZR 95 (HC); *Shamwana and 7 Others v The People* [1985] ZR 41 (SC).

[64] Chapter 88 of the Laws of Zambia.

> forthwith cause notice in writing of the entry of such nolle prosequi to be given to the keeper of the prison in which such accused may be detained, and also, if the accused person has been committed for trial, to the subordinate court by which he was so committed, and such subordinate court shall forthwith cause a similar notice in writing to be given to any witnesses bound over to prosecute and give evidence and to their sureties (if any), and also to the accused and his sureties, in case he shall have been admitted to bail.[65]

In *Director of Public Prosecutions v Mbayo Mutwala Augustino*,[66] the respondent was charged with aggravated robbery. When the matter came before the High Court the state advocate appearing for the prosecution informed the trial judge that the relevant police docket was missing and untraceable and asked for an adjournment; the judge granted an adjournment of two days only. On the adjourned hearing the state advocate informed the judge that in terms of ss 81 and 82 of the Criminal Procedure Code[67] he was entering a *nolle prosequi.* The judge asked on what grounds the state wished to enter a *nolle prosequi* and an exchange ensued which was set out in detail in the judgment of the Court of first instance, after which the judge ruled that the position of the state amounted to offering no evidence and he consequently acquitted the respondent. The Director of Public Prosecutions appealed. Chomba JS, as he then was, opined as follows:

> This power is exercised in accordance with the provisions of s 81(1) of the Criminal Procedure Code,[68] of the Laws, by entering a *nolle prosequi.* This section in effect states that once a nolle prosequi has been entered the accused in respect of whom it is entered shall stand discharged. On a proper construction this section gives no power to the court to require reasons to be furnished as to why the Director of Public Prosecutions proposes to enter a nolle prosequi nor may a court refuse the exercise of that power by the Director of Public Prosecutions. This legal position is underlined by Clause (6) of Article 58[69] .., which expressly states that the powers of the Director of Public Prosecutions as stipulated by that Article are not subject to the direction or control of any other person or authority.

(ii) The prosecution applies for and is granted an order for separate trials for the co-accused persons one of which it intends to use as a witness

[65] As amended by No 28 of 1940, No 5 of 1962; SI No 63 of 1964 and SI No 152 of 1965.

[66] [1977] ZR 287 (SC).

[67] Chapter 88 of the Laws of Zambia.

[68] Chapter 88 of the Laws of Zambia.

[69] Now Article 180(7).

in the trial in which is no longer jointly charged with other persons in accordance with s 135(3) of the Criminal Procedure Code[70] which provides as follows:[71]

> Where, before trial, or at any stage of a trial, the court is of opinion that a person accused may be embarrassed in his defence by reason of being charged with more than one offence in the same charge or information, or that for any other reason it is desirable to direct that any person should be tried separately for any one or more offences charged in a charge or information, the court may order a separate trial of any count or counts of such charge or information.

(iii) Where one of the co-accused persons is acquitted for want of evidence against him by the prosecution at case to answer/no case to answer stage.[72]

(iv) Where, as in *Shamwana and 7 Others v The People*,[73] a co-accused person bargains with the prosecution, gets concessions and as such, has charges dropped against him, or pleads guilty to one of the charges or a lesser charge even if later, as in *R v McEwan*,[74] it is determined that he equivocated in pleading guilty at committal stage[75] or the trial itself.

A few observations must be made predicated on case authority as regards point (iv). As a general rule set out in *R v Weekes*,[76] it is preferable to ensure that no impression that the erstwhile co-accused has a continuing interest for manufacturing evidence to suit the prosecution's goal of conviction is created. In order that this be the case, it is preferable that the-would-be prosecution witness be sentenced before he/she can give evidence on behalf of the prosecution. It has, however, been noted in *R v Palmer*[77] that this is an issue that the court will ultimately have to deal with by employing its discretion. The same position has been taken in cases such as *R v Pipe*[78] and *R v Turner*[79] as regards cases where criminal proceedings are subsisting against a co-accused at the time he is called to give evidence against another co-accused person. In *R v Pipe*,[80] the accused had against him a subsisting prosecution for theft. An accomplice who was to be tried separately was called to testify against the

[70] Chapter 88 of the Laws of Zambia.

[71] See *The People v Mwaiba Kakuya* [1990] SJ (HC).

[72] *The People v Japau* [1967] ZR 95 (HC); *Mwewa Murono v The People* [2004] ZR 207; see also, *The People v Winter Makowela & Another* [1979] ZR 290; ss 206 & 291 of the Criminal Procedure Code Chapter 88 of the Laws of Zambia.

[73] [1985] ZR 41 (SC).

[74] [2011] EWCA Crim 1026.

[75] See *R v Palmer* [1994] 99 Cr App R 83 CA.

[76] [1982] 74 Cr App R 161 at 166 *per* Boreham J.

[77] [1994] 99 Cr App R 83 CA.

[78] [1996] 51 Cr App R 17.

[79] [1975] 61 Cr App R 67.

[80] [1996] 51 Cr App R 17.

accused. It was observed that as a general rule, unless the prosecution had agreed to discontinue the case against an accomplice, he ought not to be called to testify. In *R v Turner*,[81] Lawton LJ took the view that continuing inducements in favour of an accomplice should not be a bar against his testimony but that this was a matter for the court's discretion.[82] The situation is different when what the co-accused does is to, when giving evidence in chief[83] or under cross-examination[84] in his defence, consciously or inadvertently incriminates a co-accused person on oath. Where this happens, such evidence is treated as being part and parcel of the case record and is not to be excluded but rather taken into consideration by the court. Humphreys J has opined as follows in *R v Rudd*:[85]

> [...] while a statement made in the absence of the accused person by one of his [co-accused] cannot be evidence against him, if the [co-accused] goes into the witness box and gives evidence in the course of a joint trial, then what he says becomes evidence for all the purposes of the case including the purpose of being evidence against a [co-accused].

Under s 243 of the Criminal Procedure Code[86] which relates to committal proceedings, it is provided as follows:

> If, after receipt of the authenticated copy of the depositions and statement as aforesaid and before the trial before the High Court, the Director of Public Prosecutions shall be of opinion that there is, in any case committed for trial, any material or necessary witness for the prosecution or the defence who has not been bound over to give evidence on the trial of the case, the Director of Public Prosecutions may require the Subordinate Court which committed the accused person for trial to take the depositions of such witness and compel his attendance either by summons or by warrant as herein before provided.[87]

4.3.2 *The accused as a defence witness*

As seen elsewhere in this text, the accused was not always a competent witness. This changed with the coming into force of the Evidence Act 1898[88] in England.

[81] [1975] 61 Cr App R 67.

[82] See support for this position in.

[83] *R v Rudd* [1948] 32 Cr App R 138 CCA.

[84] *R v Paul* [1920] 2 KB 183.

[85] [1948] 32 Cr App R 138 CCA at 140.

[86] Chapter 88 of the Laws of Zambia.

[87] No 28 of 1940 as amended by SI No 63 of 1964.

[88] The Act has since been amended by the Police and Criminal Evidence Act 1984, Criminal Justice and Public Order Act 1994 and the Youth Justice and Criminal Evidence Act 1999. It is to be noted that said Act and the amendments hereof are inapplicable to Zambia.

4.3.2.1 *The accused's competence and compellability*

An accused person is competent to give testimony in criminal proceedings. This follows the general rule that all person irrespective of age are competent to testify and give evidence in criminal proceedings. Thus, as regards procedure as pertaining to what stage an accused person may be give evidence, s 149 of the Criminal Procedure Code provides that '[w]here the person charged is called by the defence as a witness to the facts of the case or to make a statement without being sworn he shall be heard immediately after the close of the evidence for the prosecution.'

(i) The accused's right to silence: a historical perspective

As noted earlier, it goes without saying that the adversarial system, the common law favoured system of a contested trial would be incomplete in its current form without the principle of orality which is a necessary predicate to adjudication at common law. We also stated that this central role that oral testimony also gave rise to strict rules as regards the class of persons who were permitted to testify at trial. Convicted felons, non-Christians, spouses to those on trial, parties to the proceedings, and any person or entity with a possible interest to serve were all precluded from giving testimony. They were incompetent – they could not lawfully be called to give evidence. They were, as a consequence, deemed non-compellable – they could not be lawfully be obliged to give evidence. The foregoing did not sit well with Jeremy Bentham who would sarcastically state as follows:[89] 'in principle there is but one mode of searching out the truth [...] Be the dispute what it may, - see everything that is to be seen; hear everybody who is likely to know anything about the matter: hear every body, but most attentively of all, and first of all, those who are likely to know most about it, the parties.'

It is attacks such as the preceding one that would lead to several reforms that not only dismantled common law restrictions on competence and compellability but culminated into the Criminal Evidence Act 1898 which made the accused person as noted earlier, a competent and compellable witness for the defence. Yet, as welcome as this change was to the criminal law, there had always been entertained, and for good reason, trepidation that making the accused competent and compellable, even though this was just for the defence, was a roundabout way of exerting pressure on them to give evidence. It was imagined that cross-examination by prosecution would only lead some if not all accused persons to unwittingly incriminate themselves.

The existence of the (ii) proviso to s 157 of the Criminal Procedure Code[90] states that, 'the failure of any person charged with an offence or of the wife or husband, as the case may be, of the person so charged, to give evidence shall

[89] Bentham J, *Rationale of Judicial Evidence* (JS Mill (ed) (London, 1827), Vol 5 743.

[90] Chapter 88 of the Laws of Zambia.

not be made the subject of any comment by the prosecution' owes its origin to Proviso (b) (now repealed) to s 1 of the Criminal Evidence Act 1898. The idea which, based on the retention of the proviso in our own Criminal Procedure Code,[91] continues to be premised on the philosophical and historical reasoning behind that proviso, is as follows: to pacify those that were opposed to the reform that led to making the accused not only competent but compellable ensuring that the 1898 Act, as does our Criminal Procedure Code,[92] retained a proviso to guard against pressuring the accused into testifying and potentially incriminating himself. Thus, 'the failure of any [accused person], to give evidence [was] not… made the subject of any comment by the prosecution.' As we show below, refusal to testify could generally not, nor does it currently, except in a few specified situations inclusive of statutory requirements, be a basis for the prosecution to invite the court to draw inferences which are adverse to the accused's innocence.

Even so, it would appear that the 1898 Act was not fool proof as regards the injunction against adverse comments. The accused's protection from comment turned out to be a circumscribed one. As it turned out, two issues that eventually led to considerable but irreconcilable case law by different courts were left to be interpreted by the courts. The 1898 Act did not, for some curious reason, address itself to the question whether the court could of its own volition make adverse comments on the accused's failure to testify in the witness box by electing to be silent (or, as in this jurisdiction, pleading the 18th as it were). Nor did the 1898 Act deal with the question of whether a co-accused person was permitted to make adverse comments against a fellow co-accused. As we show later, the Supreme Court has held in *Dickson Sembauke Changwe and Ifellow Hamuchanje v The People*[93] that the accused has every right to remain silent and that this should not be held against him. However, and more important, it has stated in *David Dimuna v The People*[94] that judges can take note of the fact that the accused elected to remain silent and that only the prosecution evidence was available to the court.

There is a historical perspective to comments such as those to be found in *David Dimuna.*[95] As noted earlier, tremendous case law developed with specific reference to the extent to which courts could comment on the accused's decision not to speak in his own defence. We discuss some of the notable ones below.

Our first port of call is *R v Rhodes*[96] where Lord Russell of Killowen CJ, as he was then, took the view that the court was not proscribed by the Criminal Evidence Act 1898 from making comments (including adverse ones) on the evidence in the case. Further, that, '[t]he nature and degree of such comment must rest entirely in the discretion of the judge who tries the case; and it is

---

[91] Chapter 88 of the Laws of Zambia.

[92] Chapter 88 of the Laws of Zambia.

[93] [1988 – 1989] ZR 144 (SC).

[94] [1988 – 1989] ZR 199 (SC).

[95] [1988 – 1989] ZR 199 (SC).

[96] [1899] 1 QB 77 AT 83.

impossible to lay down any rule as to the cases in which he ought or ought not to comment on the failure of the prisoner to give evidence, or as to what those comments should be.' The implication was that judge's discretion to comment on an accused's refusal to testify in his own defence even when this was adverse to his innocence was unfettered. At a time of their own choosing: when and however they chose to do so, they were unconstrained and as such, it would be held later in *R v Voisin*,[97] that such exercise of discretion could not be reviewed on appeal.

It would be half a century before this position was reversed. The question of whether the discretion to comment on an accused's refusal to testify was absolute and unfettered came up and was considered by the Privy Council in *Waugh v R*.[98] The accused had been charged with murder. The prosecution presented weak evidence on the said charge. However, the judge in summing up adversely commented not less than nine times on the accused's refusal to testify. He twice suggested that the jury was at liberty to treat the failure to testify as evidence suggestive of guilt. The accused was accordingly found guilty of the offence and accordingly convicted. It was held that the judge's comments were tantamount to a wrongful exercise of discretion. The Privy Council quashed the conviction. The Privy Council noted that care needed to be exercised by a judge in commenting on an accused's failure to give evidence. The judge had a duty to be careful in commenting on a failure to give evidence. On the facts, the judge's his frequent observations and propositions that quiet was suggestive of guilt was a grave exodus from justice.[99]

The case of *Waugh v R*[100] was a watershed moment regarding the extent and context within which judges could adversely comment on an accused's choice not to give evidence in his defence when called upon to do so. Further, it threw, by the wayside, the positions taken in *R v Rhodes*[101] and *R v Voisin*,[102] which were to the effect that judges' adverse comments on the accused's freedom to remain silent were unfettered and unreviewable on appeal. To that extent, and to the extent that *Waugh v R*[103] recognised the right for an accused person not to incriminate himself, it was in keeping with what has now become a fundamental right in this jurisdiction in Article 18(2), which assures any accused person the presumption of innocence. As the Supreme Court noted in *Lt Gen Geojago Robert Musengule and Amon Sibanda v The People*,[104] the provision in Article 18(2) entails that an accused person cannot be called upon to incriminate him or herself by volunteering evidence favourable to the prosecution's case on demand. It can

---

97 [1918] 1 KB 531 CCA; See also, *R v Bernard* (1908) 1 Cr App R 218.

98 [1950] AC 203.

99 For the Zambian position which agrees with these observations, see *David Dimuna v The People* [1988 – 1989] ZR 199 (SC).

100 [1950] AC 203.

101 [1899] 1 QB 77 AT 83.

102 [1918] 1 KB 531 CCA; See also, *R v Bernard* (1908) 1 Cr App R 218.

103 [1950] AC 203.

104 [SCZ Selected Judgment No 19 of 2017].

thus be gainsaid that the (ii) proviso to s 157 of the Criminal Procedure Code[105] states that, 'the failure of any person charged with an offence [...] to give evidence shall not be made the subject of any comment by the prosecution' draws inspiration from Article 18(2)(a) and 18(7) of the Constitution. On the basis of the foregoing, for a court to make adverse comments which imply that an accused's failure to give evidence in his defence when called upon to do so infers that he or she is guilty of the offence charged is unconstitutional and out of touch with a judge's responsibility to be an umpire and fair referee. If it were done, *Waugh v R*[106] shows that this would be a basis for appeal and review by a superior court. Thus, the constitutional injunction is more important and decisive in how judges use their discretion in the foregoing circumstances. On this score, common-sense inferences suggesting an accused's guilt, no matter how logical, ought not be resorted to.

That *Waugh v R*[107] was now the gold standard for when and in what manner judges could comment on an accused's failure to give evidence in his own defence when called upon to do so can be seen from the positions taken in later cases in England and as we have seen already, in a few Supreme Court decisions in this jurisdiction.[108] Lord Parker CJ, as he was then, sought in *R v Bathurst*,[109] as did others after him, to clarify what effect an accused's failure to testify in his defence could have on evidence although he did so *obiter*, his comments have become persuasive rules for trial judges on suitable formulae when it comes to commenting on an accused's failure to testify in his own defence:

> [...] the accepted form of comment is to inform the jury that, of course, the accused is not bound to give evidence, that he can sit back and see if the prosecution have proved their case, and that, while the jury had been deprived of the opportunity of hearing his story tested in cross-examination, the one thing they must do is to assume that he is guilty because he has not gone into the witness box.

That the accused is not bound to say anything and cannot be compelled to do so is, as a general rule, trite.[110] He need not prove anything and cannot, by constitutional guarantee be forced to incriminate himself.[111] He is after all, presumed innocent.[112] However, Lord Parker's comment in *R v Bathurst*,[113] implies that in the event that an accused person fails to give evidence in his

---

[105] Chapter 88 of the Laws of Zambia.

[106] [1950] AC 203.

[107] [1950] AC 203.

[108] *Dickson Sembauke Changwe and Ifellow Hamuchanje v The People* [1988 – 1989] ZR 144 (SC); *David Dimuna v The People* [1988 – 1989] ZR 199 (SC); *Chimbini v The People* [1973] ZR 191 (CA).

[109] [1968] 2 QB 99 CA.

[110] Article 18(7).

[111] Article 18(7).

[112] Article 18(2)(a).

[113] [1968] 2 QB 99 CA.

own defence, an idea seemingly supported by Lawton LJ in *R v Sparrow*,[114] the accused person's case is weakened and in such a scenario, said Lawton LJ, a judge was entitled to make a more strident observation or comment, even going beyond *Bathurst*[115] in the interest of justice especially where, as in *Sparrow*, [116] a strong *prima facie* case has been made by the prosecution and the accused has been put on his defence indicating to him that without hearing from him the court would likely convict him. In *R v Mutch*,[117] Lawton LJ went so far as to illustrate the differences in cases that required no strong comment and those that did. In the former scenario the Lord Justice observed that a strong adverse comment would not be appropriate in cases where a simple denial was all that was required with respect to the prosecution's case. However, in cases of 'confession and avoidance,' where the accused sought to offer 'to give an innocent explanation of *prima facie* incriminating prosecution evidence,'[118] a stronger comment may be necessary. Conventional wisdom would be that if the explanation required was one that only he could give and under the circumstances was within his personal knowledge, his decision not to give evidence when called upon to do so in terms of, among others, ss 158, 208, 228 of the Criminal Procedure Code,[119] the accused's 'failure to support it from the witness box yields an inference that he may be afraid that it will not stand up to cross-examination.'[120]

Further to the foregoing, there appears to have been a sort of disharmony that was created in the many decisions that were made concerning the matter of whether an inference of guilt could not be made at all in any case where the accused failed to testify in his own defence when called upon to do so. While Lawton LJ appears to have scoffed at the idea of their being a general duty placed upon a judge not to draw an inference of guilt in any and all cases where there was a failure to testify by the accused person in *R v Harris*,[121] this was not supported in cases such as *R v Taylor*[122] and *R v Fullerton*[123] which supported the approach suggested in *Bathurst*[124] also referred to as the Judicial Studies Specimen direction referenced above.

In 1994, in a bid to clarify the position of the common law as regards an accused person's right to remain silent, the EWCA in *R v Martinez Tobon*,[125] abridged the necessary principles in the following terms:

---

[114] (1987) 84 Cr App R 75 CA; see further *R v Squire* [1990] Crim LR 341.

[115] [1968] 2 QB 99 CA.

[116] (1987) 84 Cr App R 75 CA.

[117] [1973] 1 All ER 178 at 181.

[118] Dennis I, *The Law of Evidence* 532.

[119] Chapter 88 of the Laws of Zambia.

[120] Dennis I, *The Law of Evidence* 532.

[121] (1987) 84 Cr App R 75 CA

[122] [1993] Crim. L.R. 223 CA.

[123] [1994] Crim. L.R. 63 CA.

[124] [1968] 2 QB 99 CA.

[125] (1994) 98 Cr App R 375 CA.

(1) The judge should give the jury a direction along the lines of the Judicial Studies Board specimen direction based on *R v Bathurst*[126]
(2) The essentials of that direction are that the defendant is under no obligation to testify and the jury should not assume he is guilty because he has not given evidence.
(3) Provided those essentials are complied with, the judge may think it appropriate to make a stronger comment where the defence case involves alleged facts which (a) are at variance with prosecution evidence or additional to it and exculpatory, and (b) must, if true, be within the knowledge of the defendant.
(4) The nature and strength of such comment must be a matter for the discretion of the judge and will depend upon the circumstances of the individual case. However, it must not be such as to contradict or nullify the essentials of the conventional direction".

(ii) Failure to testify: a contemporary common law view

As noted earlier, for the accused to be deemed competent he must be capable of meeting intellectual qualities that will ensure that he gives coherent and intelligible testimony. This ordinarily rules out the mentally handicapped[127] or children that do not appreciate the solemnity of a trial or indeed the importance of telling the ruth. In the latter case, children are only excluded from giving sworn evidence in terms of s 78(1) of the Children's Code.[128] However, as shown elsewhere in this text, in terms of s 78(2):

> [i]f, in the opinion of the juvenile court or Children's Court, the child does not possess sufficient intelligence to justify the reception of the child's evidence, on oath, and does not understand the duty of speaking the truth, the child may give—
> (a) unsworn evidence that may be received as evidence in a juvenile court or Children's Court; or
> (b) evidence through a child welfare inspector responsible for the child's case.

The test of competence, within the context of our current discussion must be understood within the context of s 157 of the Criminal Procedure Code[129] which provides as follows that '[e]very person charged with an offence [...] shall be a competent witness for the defence at every stage of the proceedings, whether the person so charged is charged solely or jointly with any other person.' The reference to 'every stage of the proceedings' must be taken to include committal, trial, trial within a trial (*voire dire*) or indeed the sentencing stage

[126] [1968] 1 AII ER 1175 at 1175 [1968] 2 QB 99 at 107.

[127] See procedure for mentally handicapped accused persons under ss 160-167A of the Criminal Procedure Code Chapter 88 of the Laws of Zambia.

[128] Act No 12 of 2022.

[129] Chapter 88 of the Laws of Zambia.

of the criminal proceedings. The foregoing entails that the prosecution may, as discussed earlier, not call an accused person as a witness to give testimony against himself or indeed a co-accused unless they use the procedures open to them by which a co-accused person they seek to use as a prosecution witness ceases to be a co-accused person.

Further to the preceding, attention must be drawn to the provisos to s 157. The first one provides that 'a person so charged shall not be called as a witness in pursuance of this section, except upon his own application.' What then is to be made of the expression 'except upon his own application'? This is reference to the fact that the accused person has the freedom to choose whether he will testify or not.

The (ii) proviso states that, 'the failure of any person charged with an offence or of the wife or husband, as the case may be, of the person so charged, to give evidence shall not be made the subject of any comment by the prosecution.' Further, according to the (iv) proviso, 'nothing in [s 157] shall make a husband compellable to disclose any communication made to him by his wife during the marriage, or a wife compellable to disclose any communication made to her by her husband during the marriage.' Be that as it may, in terms of proviso (v) of s 157, 'a person charged and being a witness in pursuance of [s 157] may be asked any question in cross-examination, notwithstanding that it would tend to criminate him as to the offence charged'[130] irrespective of whether he has elected to testify willingly or not. The point to remember is that once he elects to enter the witness box[131] to testify, he is treated just like any other witness for the defence by the prosecution. However, in terms of the proviso (vi) to s 157, no question to show commission of offence for which accused is not charged can be asked by the prosecution in the following terms:]

> A person charged and called as a witness, in pursuance of this section, shall not be asked, and, if asked, shall not be required to answer, any question tending to show that he has committed or been convicted of, or been charged with any offence other than that wherewith he is then charged, or is of bad character, unless-
>
> (a) the proof that he has committed or been convicted of such other offence is admissible evidence to show that he is guilty of the offence wherewith he is then charged; or
>
> (b) he has, personally or by his advocate, asked questions of the witnesses for the prosecution with a view to establishing his own good character, or has given evidence of his own good character, or the nature or conduct of the defence is such as to involve imputations on the character of the complainant or the witnesses for the prosecution; or
>
> (c) he has given evidence against any other person charged with the same offence.

[130] Similar to s 101 of the Criminal Justice Act 2003 of the UK.

[131] Proviso (vii) to s 157 provides that 'every person called as a witness in pursuance of this section shall, unless otherwise ordered by the court, give his evidence from the witness box or other place from which the other witnesses have given their evidence.'

In terms of proviso (viii) to s 157, 'nothing in [the] section shall affect the provisions of section two hundred and twenty-eight or any right of the person charged to make a statement without being sworn.' As to when an accused person may be called to give testimony, s 158 of the Criminal Procedure Code[132] provides that '[w]here the person charged is called by the defence as a witness to the facts of the case or to make a statement without being sworn, he shall be heard immediately after the close of the evidence for the prosecution.'[133]

In view of the foregoing, and in addition, an accused person is well advised to note the provisions in ss 206 and 291 of the Criminal Procedure Code.[134] If within the context of those sections, the prosecution has made its case, satisfying the court that there is a case to answer owing to proof of an essential element of the charge being proved as explained in *Murono*[135] and *Japau*,[136] the court will put the accused on his defence.[137] In essence, the court is saying that an essential element of the alleged offence has been proved; and the prosecution evidence has not been so discredited by cross-examination and may, without hearing from the accused be reliable enough that a reasonable tribunal could safely convict on it.

In the case of *Regina v Galbraith*[138] the applicant was convicted on an indictment charging that he fought and made an affray. He was convicted and sentenced to four years imprisonment. He applied for leave to appeal against conviction on the ground that the Judge wrongly rejected a submission at the end of the prosecution case that the case against him should be withdrawn from the jury. The applicant made a self-exculpatory statement to the police to the effect that at the material time when the affray was in progress, he had not been in the bar at all but downstairs in the lavatory. There were two witnesses who testified that the applicant was in the bar together with two others standing by the fight watching with knives out in a threatening way. Lord Lane CJ opined as follows:[139]

> (1) If there is no evidence that the crime has been committed by the defendant, there is no difficulty. The judge will of course stop the case.
>
> (2) The difficulty arises where there is some evidence, but it is of a tenuous character, for example because of inherent weakness or vagueness or because it is inconsistent with other evidence:

[132] Chapter 88 of the Laws of Zambia.

[133] No 6 of 1972.

[134] Chapter 88 of the Laws of Zambia.

[135] [2004] ZR 207.

[136] [1967] ZR 95 (HC); see also, *The People v Winter Makowela & Another* [1979] ZR 290.

[137] The test to apply is well known and was succinctly stated by Parker LCJ, in the Practice Note published in (1962) 1 All ER 448; *Bhatt v R* (1957) EACA 332: there is a case to answer if the prosecution evidence is such that a reasonable tribunal might convict upon it if no explanation were offered by the defence – *The People v Japau* [1967] ZR 95 (HC).

[138] (1981) 1 WLR 1039.

[139] (1981) 1 WLR 1039 at 1043 (B-D).

> (a) Where the judge comes to the conclusion that the prosecution evidence taken at its highest, is such that a jury properly directed could not properly convict upon it, it is his duty, upon a submission being made, to stop the case.
>
> (b) Where however the prosecution evidence is such that its strength or weakness depends on the view to be taken of the witnesses' reliability, or other matters which are generally speaking within the province of the jury and where on one possible view of the facts there is evidence upon which a jury could properly come to the conclusion that the defendant is guilty, then the judge should allow the matter to be tried by the jury. It follows that we think the second of the two schools of thought is to be preferred.

While making the accused a competent witness for and in his own defence, proviso (i) to s 157 of the Criminal Procedure Code[140] does not go further to make him a compellable witness even for the defence. He cannot be called as a witness in his own defence 'except upon his own application.' The fact that the accused cannot be compelled to give evidence as a witness, in other words, his right to remain silent, 'to plead the 18th' as it were, is not without its attendant perils. While the Supreme Court has said in *Dickson Sembauke Changwe and Ifellow Hamuchanje v The People,*[141] that the fact that the accused elects to remain silent should not be held against him, it has stated in *David Dimuna v The People*[142] that judges can take note of the fact that the accused elected to remain silent and that only the prosecution evidence was available to the court. More telling, however, is the Supreme Court's position in *Chimbini v The People,*[143] that in situations where the evidence is purely circumstantial, and it is possible to draw the inference of guilt if it is the only inference that can be drawn, '[…] the fact that an accused person has elected not to give evidence on oath may, in certain circumstances, tends to support the case against him […]' Though qualified, this points to there being in existence a movement towards '*de facto* compellability for all accused persons.'[144]

In any case, as we have seen elsewhere in this text, there are statutory requirements that, as the Supreme Court has held in *The People v Austin Chisanga Liato*[145] as regards s 71(1)(2) of the Forfeiture of Proceeds of Crime Act;[146] *Lt Gen Geojago Robert Musengule and Amon Sibanda v The People*[147] as regards

140 Chapter 88 of the Laws of Zambia.

141 [1988 – 1989] ZR 144 (SC).

142 [1988 – 1989] ZR 199 (SC).

143 [1973] ZR 191 (CA).

144 Dennis I, *The Law of Evidence* 530.

145 Selected Judgment No 21 of 2015.

146 No 19 of 2010.

147 [SCZ Selected Judgment No. 19 of 2017].

the interplay between s 49(2) of the Anti-Corruption Commission Act[148] and Article 18(7) of the Constitution; and *Zonde and Others v The People,*[149] where the Supreme Court held that '[t]he doctrine of recent possession applies to a person *in the absence of any explanation*[150] that might be true when found in possession of the complainant's property barely a few hours after the complainant had suffered an aggravated robbery,'[151] appear to place the burden of proof on the accused to prove his innocence. To decide against giving evidence in one's defence under such circumstances and in the face of judicial authority to so do under certain circumstances will quite clearly demand good and compelling reasons, for such a decision to not work against the accused person.

In England and Wales, s 35 of the Criminal Justice and Public Order Act 1994 headlined "Effect of accused's silence at trial," provides as follows:[152]

> (1) At the trial of any person [. . .] for an offence, subsections (2) and (3) below apply unless—
> (a) the accused's guilt is not in issue; or
> (b) it appears to the court that the physical or mental condition of the accused makes it undesirable for him to give evidence; but subsection (2) below does not apply if, at the conclusion of the evidence for the prosecution, his legal representative informs the court that the accused will give evidence or, where he is unrepresented, the court ascertains from him that he will give evidence.
>
> (2) Where this subsection applies, the court shall, at the conclusion of the evidence for the prosecution, satisfy itself (in the case of

---

148 Chapter 91 of the Laws of Zambia (repealed).

149 (1980) ZR 337.

150 Emphasis added.

151 In *George Nswana v The People* [1988 – 1989] ZR 174 (SC), the appellant was found in possession of a car two days after it was stolen. The correct car number was etched on its windows and appeared on the licence disc but the vehicle carried a false number plate. When the applicant was apprehended, he produced a blue book which bore a false name of the purported owner. At his trial he said he was in possession of the car as a driver of his employer who had asked him to drive it. In an earlier explanation to the police, he said he had borrowed the car from the person he said in evidence was his employer. The trial magistrate found that as a prudent driver the applicant must have noticed the suspicious features surrounding the car and, that coupled with recent possession and that the applicant's explanation was not true, convicted him. In the Supreme Court he argued that the telling of lies does not necessarily indicate guilt and the magistrate's finding that the applicant did not obtain possession from another person should be rejected. It was held *inter alia,* that the inference of guilt based on recent possession, particularly where no explanation is offered which might reasonably be true, rests on the absence of any reasonable likelihood that the goods might have changed hands in the meantime and the consequent high degree of probability that the person in recent possession himself obtained them and committed the offence. Where suspicious features surround the case that indicate that the applicant cannot reasonably claim to have been in innocent possession, the question remains whether the applicant, not being in innocent possession, was the thief or a guilty receiver or retainer.

152 For a detailed analysis of s 35 of the Criminal Justice and Public Order Act 1994 see generally, Dennis I, *The Law of Evidence* 533-541.

proceedings on indictment [with a jury][153] , in the presence of the jury) that the accused is aware that the stage has been reached at which evidence can be given for the defence and that he can, if he wishes, give evidence and that, if he chooses not to give evidence, or having been sworn, without good cause refuses to answer any question, it will be permissible for the court or jury to draw such inferences as appear proper from his failure to give evidence or his refusal, without good cause, to answer any question.

(3) Where this subsection applies, the court or jury, in determining whether the accused is guilty of the offence charged, may draw such inferences as appear proper from the failure of the accused to give evidence or his refusal, without good cause, to answer any question.

(4) This section does not render the accused compellable to give evidence on his own behalf, and he shall accordingly not be guilty of contempt of court by reason of a failure to do so.

(5) For the purposes of this section a person who, having been sworn, refuses to answer any question shall be taken to do so without good cause unless—

(a) he is entitled to refuse to answer the question by virtue of any enactment, whenever passed or made, or on the ground of privilege; or

(b) the court in the exercise of its general discretion excuses him from answering it.

(6) [154]

(7) This section applies—

(a) in relation to proceedings on indictment for an offence, only if the person charged with the offence is arraigned on or after the commencement of this section;

(b) in relation to proceedings in a magistrates' court, only if the time when the court begins to receive evidence in the proceedings falls after the commencement of this section.

What is apparent from the provisions in s 35[155] are the curbs it places on the right of an accused person to remain silence when called upon to give testimony in his defence. The practical implications of s 35 would appear to be that it compels the accused to give evidence even when he does not desire to do so. Thus, some jurists[156] have seen it fit to analyse s 35 within the context of witnesses. Contrary to the position that still holds true today in Zambia pursuant to the relevant proviso under s 157 of the Criminal Procedure Code,[157] s 35 permits a judge/

[153] Words in s. 35(2) inserted (24.7.2006 for E.W. and 8.1.2007 for N.I., otherwise prosp.) by Criminal Justice Act 2003 (c. 44), ss. 331, 336, Sch. 36 para. 63; S.I. 2006/1835, art. 2(h) (subject to art. 3); S.I. 2006/3422, art. 2(c)(i).

[154] S 35(6) repealed (30.9.1998) by 1998 c. 37, ss. 35(b), 120(1)(2), Sch. 9 para. 2, Sch. 10 (with Sch. 9); S.I. 1998/2327, art. 2(1)(z)(aa)(3)(v).

[155] Of the Criminal Justice and Public Order Act 1994.

[156] Dennis I, *The Law of Evidence*.

[157] Chapter 88 of the Laws of Zambia.

magistrate, as the case may be, to draw adverse inferences in the event that an accused person fails to testify the following conditions having been satisfied: if certain conditions are satisfied such as, mental lucidity;[158] that the accused is aware of his right to testify and the consequences in terms of s 35 of refusing to do so; and that the prosecution has made out a *prima facie* case leading the court to find the accused with a case to answer. In other words, the court has drawn a provisional conclusion which is to the effect that 'the prosecution evidence is sufficiently credible, reliable and probative to incriminate the accused.'[159] There is no need at this stage for the court to have to reach the conclusion on whether the prosecution have discharged their legal burden as required in criminal cases. However, it has been observed in *R v Cowan,*[160] that that the inference drawn from an accused's failure to testify when called upon to do so might be 'a further evidential factor in support of the prosecution case.'

In *R v Cowan*[161] where the interpretation of s 35 arose, it was held that the said section was of general application and not only applicable to exceptional cases. Even so, 'a judge retains a discretion as to the direction to be given to a jury on the proper inferences to be drawn from a failure to testify, and in an appropriate case a judge should direct the jury that it would not be proper to draw any adverse inference.'[162] Futher, the following were highlighted as essential elements in the event that an accused person failed to give evidence in his own defence. They are modified to fit our non-jury system. Be that as it may, they are at this point in our jurisprudence, of academic interest but where appropriate, persuasive should the law go in the direction that English law has gone on the silence of the accused person:

> (1) The judge will have [to remember] that the burden of proof remains upon the prosecution throughout and what the required standard is.
> (2) It is necessary for the judge to make clear [to the accused] that he is entitled to remain silent. That is his right and his choice. The right of silence remains.
> (3) An inference from failure to give evidence cannot on its own prove guilt.
> (4) Therefore, the [judge] must be satisfied that the prosecution have established a case to answer before drawing any inferences from silence. Of course, the judge must have thought so or the question whether the defendant was to give evidence would not have arisen. But the [judge] may not believe the witnesses whose evidence the judge considered sufficient to raise a prima facie case. [The judge] must find there to be a case to answer on the

[158] See *R v Friend* [1997] 2 Cr App R 231 *per* Otton LJ.

[159] Dennis I, *The Law of Evidence* 536.

[160] [1996] QB 373 at 379.

[161] [1996] QB 373 CA.

[162] Dennis I, The Law of Evidence 534-535.

prosecution evidence before drawing an adverse inference from the defendant's silence.

(5) If, despite any evidence relied upon to explain his silence or in the absence of any such evidence, the [judge] conclude[s] the silence can only sensibly be attributed to the [accused's] having no answer or none that would stand up to cross-examination, he/she may draw an adverse inference.

The foregoing, especially the reference to the [judge] being satisfied that the prosecution has made out a case to answer before drawing any inference from silence, must be seen within the context of showing the interplay between ss 35 and 38(3); the latter of which provides that '[a] person shall not have the proceedings against him transferred to the Crown Court for trial, have a case to answer or be convicted of an offence solely on an inference drawn from such a failure or refusal as is mentioned in [s]...35(3) [....]' Section 38(3) seeks to prevent the conviction of an accused person solely on the basis that he elected to remain silent when called upon to give evidence in his defence. The observation in *R v Cowan*[163] that an accused's failure to testify when called upon to do so might be 'a further evidential factor in support of the prosecution case' may lend itself to the suggestion that the accused's said failure may be a further piece of evidence that resolves any feelings that the court may have as regards the accused's guilt. The preceding is demonstrated in *Murray v DPP*[164] which was a case in which the accused was charged with attempted murder and possession of a firearm with intent to endanger life. Though the evidence was merely circumstantial, it was cogent enough as to show that the accused had been involved with the attack of the victim, and therefore took the charge against the accused out of the real of conjecture. The accused elected to remain silent. Surprised, the judge, given the accused's reticence to assert his innocence on oath, expressed a common-sense inference that the accused was guilty. The accused's appeal was dismissed with the House of Lords observing that an adverse reference, more than being made with specific reference to specific facts, could be extended to what it termed a general inference of guilt of the accused person of the offence with which he is charged. On the one hand, Lord Mustill opined as follows:

> If the defendant does not go on oath to say that the witnesses who have spoken to his actions are untruthful or unreliable, or that an inference which appears on its face to be plausible is in reality unsound for reasons within his knowledge, the factfinder may suspect that the defendant does not tell his story because he has no story to tell, or none that will stand up to scrutiny; and this suspicion may be sufficient to convert a provable prosecution case into one which is

[163] [1996] QB 373 at 379.

[164] (1993) 97 Cr App R 151.

> actually proved [...] So also, if the defendant seeks to outflank the case for the prosecution by means of a ' positive ' defence – as for example where he replies in relation to a charge of murder that although he did kill the deceased he acted under provocation. If he does not give evidence in support of this allegation there will in very many cases be a legitimate inference that the defence is untrue.[165]

Lord Slynn,[166] on the other hand, held that a failure to answer 'parts of the prosecution case [that] had so little evidential value that they called for no answer' suggesting that a judge could not employ inferential reasoning unless the prosecution had made out a pellucid and strong case on the face of it, and that in the circumstances, the accused was possessed of such knowledge as only would enable him to deny the charge or to offer an explanation.[167]

Despite the preceding, it appears that there is no clarification as regards instances where it would be inappropriate to draw adverse inferences in terms of s 35. It is debatable to what extent the decision to draw adverse inferences ought to be predicated solely on the strength of the prosecution case as made out. Still to be resolved is the issue of what would be deemed a genuine justification for failure by an accused person in the face of the provisions in s 35 to testify in his own defence when called upon to do so at the end of the prosecution case, and the court having found him with a case to answer. It has been held in *R v Becouarn*[168] that the failure by an accused person to testify on the basis that he may be cross-examined on previous convictions was not a good basis for avoiding the drawing of an adverse inference.[169]

4.4 The accused's spouse as a witness

4.4.1 *A brief historical analysis*

As with almost anything legal in this jurisdiction, we must turn to the development of the law as respects a spouse' competence and compellability in England. At common law, the spouse of an accused person was not a competent witness and as such not compellable. In *Hoskyn v Commissioner of Police for the Metropolis,*[170] the accused had married the complainant only two days before he was to face trial for assaulting her. The House considered whether she

[165] (1993) 97 Cr App R 151 at 155.

[166] *Murray v DPP* (1993) 97 Cr App R 151 at 160.

[167] *Murray v DPP* (1993) 97 Cr App R 151 at 160-161; *R v Birchall* [1999] Crim LR 311 CA.

[168] [2005] UKHL 55; [2006] 1 Cr App R 2.

[169] See further, *R v Napper* [1996] Crim. L.R. 591 CA; *R v Bowden* [1999] 2 Cr App R 176; *R v Hamidi and Cherazi* [2010] EWCA Crim 66; *R v Barry* [2010] EWCA Crim 195; On the interplay between s 35 and Art. 6 of the ECHR see *Murray v United Kingdom* (1996) 22 EHRR 29; *Condron v United Kingdom* (2000) 31 EHRR 1; however, compare this to proviso (vi) to s 157 of the Criminal Procedure Code Chapter 88 of the Laws of Zambia.

[170] [1978] HL; [1979] AC 474.

was compellable as a witness against him as his wife. Lord Edmund-Davies observed in his speech that the House of Lord's disinclination to approve propositions by Avory J in *R v Lapworth*[171] which were to the effect that '[...] a wife was always a competent witness on a charge against her husband of having assaulted her' was rooted in the past. As he saw it, the

> [...] reluctance to accept [Lord Avory's] view [derived] seemingly from harking-back to the strong opposition at common law to one spouse ever testifying against the other, and opposition based on a variety of reasons such as the unity of person, the fear of consequent discord and dissension, and the natural repugnance created by such a prospect.

Lord Edmund-Davies' observations came after those of Lord Wilberforce who had quoted three Lords on appeal from an earlier case of *Leach v R*:[172] Earl Loreburn LC made reference to 'a fundamental and old principle [...] that you ought not to compel a wife to give evidence against her husband in matters of a criminal kind.' Lord Halsbury opined as follows:

> [...] since the foundations of the common law it has been recognised that [i.e., To compel a wife to give evidence against her husband] is contrary to the course of the law [....] If you want to alter the law which has lasted for centuries and which is almost ingrained in the English Constitution, in the sense that everybody would say, '[t]o call a wife against her husband is a thing that cannot be heard of [....]'

Lord Atkinson observed in his speech as regards the position of the law on this subject: '[t]he principle that a wife is not to be compelled to give evidence against her husband is deep seated in the common law of this country [...]. Thus, Lord Wilberforce further observed as follows, taking aim at the attempt to distinguish an earlier decision of the House of Lords in *Leach v R*[173] as attempted in *R v Lapworth*:[174]

> I respect the view of these experienced judges [Earl Loreburn LC; Lord Halsbury; and Lord Atkinson] as to the practice, but against this they give no weight to such authority as can be found which I have cited, which, in the view of one respected author, led him to think that the 'better opinion' is against compellability. Nor do they examine in any depth, or indeed at all, the fundamental question which I think to be this: a wife is in principle not a competent witness on a criminal charge against her husband. This is because of the identity of interest

[171] [1931] 1 KB 117.
[172] [1912] AC 305.
[173] [1912] AC 305.
[174] [1931] 1 KB 117.

> between husband and wife and because to allow her to give evidence would give rise to discord and to perjury and would be, to ordinary people, repugnant. Limited exceptions have been engrafted on this rule, of which the most important, and that now relevant, relates to cases of personal violence by the husband against her. This requires that, as she normally is the only witness and because otherwise a crime would go without sanction, she be permitted to give evidence against him. But does this permission, in the interest of the wife, carry the matter any further, or do the general considerations, arising from the fact of marriage and her stats as a wife, continue to apply so as to negative compulsion? That argument was in just this form put to the House of Lords and in general form answered in the affirmative. It was not faced in *R v Lapworth*[175] at all.
>
> My Lords, after careful consideration I have reached the conclusion that *R v Lapworth*[176] was wrongly decided and must be overruled, that the general principles stated in *Leach v R*[177] apply and that the wife should be held non-compellable.

It is worth remembering that though the above 20th century cases demonstrate the evolution of the law with respect to the competence and compellability of a spouse, as early as 1861 in *R v Lord Audley,*[178] an exception to disqualifying a spouse had been judicially recognised which was that in cases which were as a result of one spouse being violent against another, there should be no argument against her testifying against the husband as a prosecution witness. Lord Wilberforce has noted in *Hoskyn v Commissioner of Police for the Metropolis,*[179] that '[t]his requires that, as she normally is the only witness and because otherwise a crime would go without sanction, she be permitted to give evidence against him.' Even so, *Hoskyn*[180] only made the wife competent but not compellable.

The common law position of a spouse being incompetent as a witness saw changes following the enactment of the Evidence (Further Amendment) Act 1853 which made a spouse a competent witness in civil matters. It would take another 45 years or so for the position to change as highlighted in the preceding authorities. The year 1898 saw the enactment of The Criminal Evidence Act 1898. Section 1 of that Act made a spouse a competent and compellable witness for the defence but not for the prosecution.[181] Section 4(1) of the same Act provided that '[t]he wife or husband of a person charged with an offence under

175 [1931] 1 KB 117.

176 [1931] 1 KB 117.

177 [1912] AC 305.

178 [1631] 1 KB 117.

179 [1978] HL; [1979] AC 474.

180 [1978] HL; [1979] AC 474.

181 This is exemplified in *R v Deacon* [1973] 2 All ER 1145.

any enactment mentioned in the schedule to this Act may be called as a witness either for the prosecution or defence and without the consent of the person charged.' This section was interpreted in *Leach v R*[182] which may have led the EWCA to interpret the case as one simply focused on statutory interpretation in *R v Lapworth.*[183] In answering the question whether the wife of one charged under a scheduled Act (in this case the Punishment of Incest Act 1908) was a compellable witness, the EWCA opined as follows: '[...] at common law the wife was a competent witness where personal injuries to herself were involved, but in such cases she was also at common law a compellable witness; the effect of making her a competent witness by statute must be the same.' On appeal to House of Lords, the Lordships attention was drawn to the three exceptions to the rule relating to a spouse's incompetence namely, treason, violence and abduction. As noted elsewhere in this text, the House of Lords rejected the EWCA's analogy as exemplified in the speeches of Earl Loreburn LC; Lord Halsbury; and Lord Atkinson quoted partly above.

From the preceding, it is only logical to conclude that there were of course exceptions to the incompetence and non-compellability of a spouse premised as discussed in the common law authorities considered above especially as respects cases of violence against and abduction of the spouse on the one hand, and treason on the other, who was the sole witness to the offence against the accused spouse. The decision in *Hoskyn v Commissioner of Police for the Metropolis,*[184] which made the spouse competent but not compellable did not help with what was seen by some, as an unsatisfactory state of the law. This would lead to legislative changes in England to deal with the challenge. Amazingly, none of the changes that have been made in England on this score have been made in Zambia. The law has remained stark in the past and appears to be ruled from the graves of those that enacted and/or interpreted it at the material time.

Noteworthy changes were wrought into English statutory law by s 80[185] of the Police and Criminal Evidence Act 1984 (PACE) on this matter. Of particular interest are s 80(1)-(4) which provide as follows:

> (1) In any proceedings the wife or husband of the accused shall be competent to give evidence—
>
> (a) subject to subsection (4) below, for the prosecution; and
>
> (b) on behalf of the accused or any person jointly charged with the accused.

[182] [1912] AC 305.

[183] [1931] 1 KB 117.

[184] [1978] HL; [1979] AC 474.

[185] Which is headlined 'Competence and compellability of accused's spouse or civil partner.'

(2) In any proceedings the spouse or civil partner[186] of a person charged in the proceedings shall, subject to subsection (4) below, be compellable to give evidence on behalf of that person.

(2A) In any proceedings the spouse or civil partner of a person charged in the proceedings shall, subject to subsection (4) below, be compellable—

(a) to give evidence on behalf of any other person charged in the proceedings but only in respect of any specified offence with which that other person is charged; or

(b) to give evidence for the prosecution but only in respect of any specified offence with which any person is charged in the proceedings.

(3) In relation to the spouse or civil partner of a person charged in any proceedings, an offence is a specified offence for the purposes of subsection (2A) above if—

(a) it involves an assault on, or injury or a threat of injury to, the spouse or civil partner or a person who was at the material time under the age of 16;

(b) it is a sexual offence alleged to have been committed in respect of a person who was at the material time under that age; or

(c) it consists of attempting or conspiring to commit, or of aiding, abetting, counselling, procuring or inciting the commission of, an offence falling within paragraph (a) or (b) above.

(4) No person who is charged in any proceedings shall be compellable by virtue of subsection (2) or (2A) above to give evidence in the proceedings.

(4A) References in this section to a person charged in any proceedings do not include a person who is not, or is no longer, liable to be convicted of any offence in the proceedings (whether as a result of pleading guilty or for any other reason).

A brief discussion of the above is perhaps merited. The first point to note is that s 80(1) of PACE has been replaced by s 53(1) of the Youth Justice and Criminal Evidence Act 1999 (YJCEA) which provides essentially to the same effect that the spouse of an accused person is competent to give evidence for all parties concerned (prosecution & defence). However, we must be alive to the provisions of s 80(4) which provides that '[n]o person who is charged in any proceedings shall be compellable by virtue of [s 80(2) or s 80(2A)] above to give evidence in the proceedings.' It falls to reason that where spouses are jointly charged in the same proceedings neither will be competent for the prosecution whether they are charged jointly for the same offence or for different offence.

[186] Reference to a Civil Partner is meant to include civil unions as they relate to same sex unions which are of course illegal in Zambia.

Carrying the discussion further, it is clear that the primary law with respect to the English statutory law of spousal compellability is provided for under s 80(2) and s 80(3) wherein it is provided that the spouse or civil partner of an accused person is a compellable witness in any case on behalf of the accused but this does not apply in a case where both the husband and wife or their civil partner, as the case may be, are charged in the same proceedings.[187] The foregoing is demonstrated in *R v Pitt*.[188] On 21 October 1981 in the Crown Court at Chelmsford before his Honour Judge Taylor and a jury, the appellant, Ian Barry Pitt, was convicted on one count of assault occasioning actual bodily harm and for that offence, and for breach of a suspended sentence and of a community service order, was sentenced in all to 18 months' imprisonment. He appealed with leave of the single judge against the conviction on the ground that the trial judge wrongly allowed the appellant's wife, who gave evidence for the Crown against the appellant, to be treated as a hostile witness. Peter Pain J opined as follows:

> Up to the point where she goes into the witness box, the wife has a choice: she may refuse to give evidence or waive her right of refusal. The waiver is effective only if made with full knowledge of her right to refuse. If she waives her right of refusal, she becomes an ordinary witness. She is by analogy in the same position as a witness who waives privilege, which would entitle him to refuse to answer questions on a certain topic.
>
> In our view, in these circumstances, once the wife has started on her evidence, she must complete it. It is not open to her to retreat behind the barrier of non-compellability if she is asked questions that she does not wish to answer. Justice should not allow her to give evidence which might assist, or injure, her husband and then to escape from normal investigation.
>
> It follows that if the nature of her evidence justifies it, an application may be made to treat her as a hostile witness.

However, as has been repeatedly shown elsewhere in this text, not even s 80(2) and s 80(3) of PACE resolve the issue of a spouse's compellability as a prosecution witness or when he or she is jointly charged with the accused.[189] Additionally, like s 53(1) of the Youth Justice and Criminal Evidence Act 1999, s 80(2) and s 80(3) of PACE are subject to the provisions of s 80(4) of PACE in cases where both the husband and wife or their civil partner, as the case may be, are charged in the same proceedings.[190]

What then is the position of a divorced spouse or civil partner? The combined effect of the amended provisions in s 53(1) of the YJCEA 1999 and s 80(5) is

---

[187] See PACE s 80(4) and (4A), as substituted by Youth Justice and Criminal Evidence Act 1999; see *R v Pitt* [1982] 3 All ER 63 at 66b-d, *per* Peter Pain J.

[188] [1982] 3 All ER 63.

[189] For arguments for and against spousal compellability see Dennis I, *The Law of Evidence* 543-544.

[190] See *RL* [2008] EWCA Crim 973; [2008] 2 Cr App R 18.

that a divorced spouse is as competent and as compellable as any witness. Such erstwhile spouse or civil partner is to be treated as though they were never married to or were never in any civil partnership with the accused for purposes of criminal proceedings. For ease of reference, s 80(5)(5A) of PACE provides as follows:

> (5) In any proceedings a person who has been but is no longer married to the accused shall be competent and compellable to give evidence as if that person and the accused had never been married.
>
> (5A) In any proceedings a person who has been but is no longer the civil partner of the accused shall be compellable to give evidence as if that person and the accused had never been civil partners.

To demonstrate, in *R v Khan*,[191] the witness, a woman who had undergone a Muslim marriage ceremony with the accused which, on account him being already married to another woman under English law, was adjudged bigamous and void ab initio, was held not to be a wife under s 80 of PACE.

It is safe to conclude that the end of a marital or civil union, as the case may be, seems to do away with interests inherent in preserving confidence and stability in a union or/and are far outweighed by the greater interest of permitting parties to proceedings relevant access to all necessary evidence and which in the Zambian context is to be found under Article 18(2)(e)(f) of the Constitution and provides as follows:

> (e) shall be afforded facilities to examine in person or by his legal representative the witnesses called by the prosecution before the court, and to obtain the attendance and carry out the examination of witnesses to testify on his behalf before the court on the same conditions as those applying to witnesses called by the prosecution; and
>
> (f) shall be permitted to have without payment the assistance of an interpreter if he cannot understand the language used at the trial of the charge;
>
> and except with his own consent the trial shall not take place in his absence unless he so conducts himself as to render the continuance of the proceedings in his presence impracticable and the court has ordered him to be removed and the trial to proceed in his absence.

The question of whether the principle of non-compellability could be applied to those who simply cohabited came up in *R v Pearce*.[192] The EWCA rejected an attempt to extent the principle to cohabitees even when such had lived

---

[191] (1986) 84 Cr App R 44; as to application to long term partners see *R v Pearce* [2001] EWCA Crim 2834; [2002] 1 Cr App R 39 but see dissenting view *per* Kennedy LJ AT 39.

[192] [2001] EWCA Crim 2834; [2002] 1 Cr App R 39.

together and had children saying that the interests of the family against those of the community and that in this case and that given the factual matrix and the circumstances of the case, the latter held sway.

Another issue worthy of consideration is the effect of the removal of judicial immunity to protection from prosecution for rape of one's wife by the House of Lords in *R v R*.[193] The [accused] married his wife (complainant) in August 1984. After the marriage did not work, she moved out in October 1989 and took her son to live with her parents. At the time of the incident in November 1989, they were separated but not legally divorced. The [accused] broke in to her parents' home and attempted to have sexual intercourse with the complainant who did not consent. The [accused] was charged with attempted rape under s1(1) of the Sexual Offences (Amendment) Act 1976 and with assault occasioning actual bodily harm under s 47 Offences Against the Person Act 1861. The [accused] appealed his conviction on the issues of attempted rape and consent against s1(1) of the Sexual Offences (Amendment) Act 1976. He argued on the grounds of the marital rape exemption that existed under the common law of England and the principle that a husband could not rape his wife, as the contract of marriage gave irrevocable consent. The court upheld his conviction for attempted rape. There was no marital rape exception under English law and this was a 'common law fiction' that existed. The concept of irrevocable consent of a wife to her husband was classed as [an] unacceptable concept in modern times; each is seen as equal partners in a marriage. The relationship between the parties to rape does not matter; rape is rape. The word 'unlawful' that is included in the definition of rape under the Sexual Offences (Amendment) Act 1976 was said to include marital rape.

Though it seems from a reading of the subs-s 3(a)(b) and sub-s (7) of the Protection of Children Act 1978[194] or Part 1 of the Sexual Offences Act 2003 that a wife is not compellable as a witness for the prosecution in a case of rape of her person by her husband owing to the fact that the rape of an adult is not included in subs (3)(b), this is a debate for academic interest only since it is unlikely that the prosecution will put a victim of rape who is unwilling to testify against her husband in the witness box in aid of their case. What seems logical, though, based on sub 3(a) which provides that a wife is a compellable witness in any case against her husband relating to assaulting her and combined conventional legal wisdom, the wife ought to be a compellable witness in a rape charge against her husband in which she is the victim.

---

[193] [1992] 1 AC 599; summary with minor modifications taken from All Answers ltd, '*R v R* [1992] 1 AC 599' (Lawteacher.net, February 2021) <https://www.lawteacher.net/cases/r-v-r-1992.php?vref=1> accessed 28 February 2021.

[194] For a Zambian take see the Children's Code, Act No 12 of 2022.

4.4.2 *Competence and compellability of a spouse in Zambia*

4.4.2.1 *Statutory law*

The starting point when it comes to the question of spousal competence and compellability in this jurisdiction is s 151 of the Criminal Procedure Code[195] which provides as follows:

> (1) In any inquiry or trial, the wife or husband of the person charged shall be a competent witness for the prosecution or defence without the consent of such person -
> (a) in any case where the wife or husband of a person charged may, under any law in force for the time being, be called as a witness without the consent of such person;
> (b) in any case where such person is charged with an offence under Chapter XV[196] of the Penal Code or with bigamy;
> (c) in any case where such person is charged in respect of an act or omission affecting the person or property of the wife or husband of such person or the children of either of them.
>
> (2) For the purpose of this section -
> (a) 'wife' and 'husband' include the parties to a customary marriage;
> (b) 'customary marriage' includes a union which is regarded as marriage by the community in which the parties live."

The above section appears to have been derived from s 4 of the Criminal Evidence Act 1898, which we have already encountered elsewhere in this text, and as such, is similarly worded. The position of spouse as regards her competence to testify against an accused spouse under the circumstances envisaged in s 151 of the Criminal Procedure Code[197] has been described as follows:[198]

> The general rule is that the accused's spouse is an incompetent witness for the prosecution. It is subject to important exceptions under [s 151 of the Criminal Procedure Code] in these cases, the accused's spouse is a competent though not compellable witness for the Crown [....]

---

[195] Chapter 88 of the Laws of Zambia.

[196] OFFENCES AGAINST MORALITY: ss 132-164A; See *Brenda Tembo Mukakulwa v The People* (HPA/13/2018).

[197] Chapter 88 of the Laws of Zambia.

[198] Cross on Evidence, 3rd edn at 147-148.

Phipson on Evidence[199] puts it this way:

> Amongst witnesses, whether in civil or criminal proceedings, the wives or husbands of the parties were at Common Law early considered incompetent to testify, either for or against each other, by reason of their unity of person and interest. Even at Common Law, however, an exception was always made, from necessity, in cases of personal violence or forcible marriage, and perhaps also, from public policy in those of treason. By statute, also this general incompetency has been gradually removed, both in civil cases and to a very large extent in criminal trials, by a series of Acts culminating in the Criminal Evidence Act, 1898, and the Theft Act, 1968, s. 30.

And further that[200]

> In criminal proceedings the accused; the wife or husband of as the accused (except in certain cases); any person jointly indicted and jointly tried with the accused, and the wife or husband of such person; are incompetent as witnesses for the prosecution. To render co-defendants or their spouses competent to be called by the prosecution, such co-defendants must have been acquitted, or have obtained a nolle prosequi, or have pleaded guilty, or must be tried separately.

In *The People v Mushaikwa,*[201] the accused was charged with murder. The prosecution sought a ruling from the court as to whether the accused's wife, who was the only eye witness, was a competent witness for the prosecution. The prosecution alleged that the accused had consented to his wife giving evidence. A preliminary issue as to whether the accused's spouse was a competent and compellable witness for the prosecution, regard being had to the provisions of s 151 of the Criminal Procedure Code[202] was raised. It was held as follows:

(i) The case did not fall within s 151 of the Criminal Procedure Code[203] and therefore the question had to be decided according to common law rules.

(ii) At common law the wife of an accused person is not a competent witness for the prosecution save in cases of forcible marriage and possibly treason on both of which occasions the spouse is competent and compellable.

(iii) Generally, all competent witnesses are compellable; but in the case of the spouse of an accused person although the spouse may be rendered by statute a competent witness in certain cases the spouse is not compellable in these instances.

---

199 11th edn, para 1474 under the heading "Husband and Wife."

200 Para 1478 (Incompetency in Criminal Proceedings - Witnesses for the prosecution).

201 [1973] ZR 161 (HC).

202 Chapter 88 of the Laws of Zambia.

203 Chapter 88 of the Laws of Zambia.

(iv) In these instances, the court has a duty to inform the spouse that he/she has the right to refuse to give evidence.
(v) Failure by the court to give such warning renders the evidence given by the spouse totally inadmissible.

4.4.2.2 *The common law position as respects a spouse's competence and compellability*

The common law position as respects a spouse's competence and compellability is invariably derived from English common law. Therefore, in coming to a decision on the preliminary issue raised as regards the wife's competence to testify against her accused husband in *The People v Mushaikwa,*[204] Silungwe CJ, as he then was, borrowed heavily from English and common law jurisdiction authorities. Among the cases that were cited in that case were *R v Mount.*[205] Three men were convicted of shop-breaking. The wife of one of them had given evidence for the Crown, and this necessitated the quashing of all three convictions. Shop breaking was not among the offences mentioned in the schedule to the Act of 1898, and it did not fall within any of the other exceptions to the rule. The general rule rendered the accused's spouse incompetent to testify to matters occurring before as well as during the marriage, and the matters occurring after a judicial separation.[206]

In *The People v Mushaikwa,*[207] the accused had been the subject of a medical examination at Chainama Hills Hospital, Lusaka for the purpose of ascertaining his mental condition. He was charged with the murder of his brother Kansisiyo Moyo Mushaikwa on 18 January, 1972, an offence contrary to s 200 of the Penal Code[208] The case is now ready for trial. On the *issue in limine* raised by the prosecution which was to the effect that the accused's wife, who was the main and only eye witness, was a competent witness for the prosecution with the accused's consent which was supported by the defence, and that such consent has already been obtained, the Court made reference to the East African decision in *Abdulrahman Bin Mohamed and Another v R,*[209] where in delivering the judgment of the Court of Appeal, Sir Ronald Sinclair, P., said as follows:

> Under the Common Law of England which was applied to Zanzibar by Art 24 of the Zanzibar Order-in-Council, 1924, subject to certain exceptions which are not applicable in the present case, the husband or wife of the person charged is not a competent witness for the prosecution. S 147 of the Criminal Procedure Decree (Cap 8), provides

[204] [1973] ZR 161 (HC).

[205] (1934) 24 Cr App R 135.

[206] The general incompetence of the accused's divorced spouse recognised in *R v Algar* (1954) 1 QB 279 was confined, it was said, to matters occurring during [. . .] the marriage.

[207] [1973] ZR 161 (HC); *Nalumino Nalumangwe and Another v The People* [1986] ZR 28 (SC): Evidence of [a spouse] is not admissible against him on a criminal charge.

[208] Chapter 87 of the Laws of Zambia.

[209] (1963) EALR 188.

> that in any inquiry or trial the wife or husband of the person charged shall be a competent witness for the prosecution or the defence with the consent of such person in certain cases specified in the section. The charge of murder in the present case does not fall within the cases specified in the section. If, therefore, Fatuma was the wife of a marriage such as is contemplated by the relevant law in force in Zanzibar she was not a competent witness for the prosecution as against her husband.[210]

Following the preceding, Silungwe CJ opined that '[a]t common law the wife of this accused is not a competent witness for the prosecution and consequently no degree of consent by the accused can turn the other spouse into a competent witness.' He went on to find that the accused's spouse was not a competent witness for the prosecution. He, however, clarified as follows:

> The short effect of my ruling on this point generally is that the accused's spouse is a competent witness for the prosecution only -
> (a) in the common law cases of forcible marriage and possibly treason on the ground that the public interest in the safety of the State outweighs whatever public interests are promoted by preventing one spouse from testifying against the other.[211] . . . and
> (b) in all cases set out under s 151 of the C.P.C.

Further that,

> When questions of competence and compellability of a witness arise, it must in the first place be decided by the trial court whether or not the particular person is a competent witness. If it is held that the witness is incompetent it becomes unnecessary to consider the question of-compellability. I am, nevertheless, going to consider it here in the hope that it would serve as a guide to magistrates once they have found a witness to be competent to give evidence either for the prosecution or defence [....][212]

Is a competent witness in the form of a spouse also a compellable witness in this jurisdiction? The question was also raised and dealt with in *Mushaikwa.*[213] The position in this jurisdiction is that all witnesses competent to give evidence are in general compellable to do so.[214] It was, however, observed that there are exceptions to this general rule when the intended witness belongs to a certain class of persons among them, a fact we have already encountered in this text,

[210] (1963) EALR 188 at 189.

[211] See *Director of Public Prosecutions v Blady* (1912) 2 KB 89 *per* Lush J; personal violence is already covered by s 151(1)(c) of the Criminal Procedure Code Chapter 88 of the Laws of Zambia.

[212] For example, under s 151 and s 157 of the Criminal Procedure Code Chapter 88 of the Laws of Zambia.

[213] [1973] ZR 161 (HC).

[214] Citing *R v Lapworth* (1931) 1 KB 117.

children, persons of defective intellect, the head of state, diplomats of foreign states and the accused's spouse.

To be noted too is the observation *per* Cram J in *R v Kwalira and Another*[215] cited and quoted in *Mushaikwa:*[216] a distinction could be drawn between "competent" which must mean that the witness must obey a *subpoena*, and "compellable" which could mean "must give evidence", and it is distinctly arguable that, being one person, so long as the husband (wife) remains uncompellable, the wife (husband) must too, except with express words in the relevant statute. The accused's spouse, although rendered competent by statute to give evidence for the prosecution in certain criminal proceedings, is not thereby made compellable to give such evidence.[217] In *R v Acaster,*[218] Darling, J, took the view that the proper course to take where a spouse was called as a witness would be to warn such spouse that she could not be obliged to give evidence when called as a witness by either the prosecution or her husband in any case in which she is not a compellable witness.[219] In *Guza v R*[220] which approved the position taken by Darling J in *R v Acaster,*[221] Cram, J, observed as follows:

> Further, the appellant's wife, although a competent witness, was not compellable. Although the right to speak or keep silent was at her election, the appellant had, nonetheless, the right to have the election put to the witness. Failure to inform the witness of her right could and did result in damning evidence being given. No warning was given to this woman. This was a serious irregularity and, of course, it is impossible to say what choice this woman might have made had her legal rights been put to her, as should have been done by the learned magistrate, who, throughout was in control of the admissibility of evidence. The result of this irregularity is to exclude the important evidence of possession of this woman and to throw the record open to the appellate court which is compelled to come to its own conclusion.

Therefore, the common law position when it comes to the competence and compellability of a spouse in this jurisdiction is encapsulated in the words of Silungwe CJ, as he then was, expressed in the following terms:

> The position, as I see it, is that in those cases in which the accused's spouse is competent to give evidence for the prosecution (or the defence) such spouse is not a compellable witness except on charges of personal violence against that spouse (and possibly of treason) when

[215] (1962) A.L.R. Mal. 2 (1961-63) 242.

[216] [1973] ZR 161 (HC).

[217] *Leach v R* (1912) AC 305.

[218] (1912) 106 LT 384.

[219] Followed by Cram J, in *R v Kwalire and Another* (1962) A.L.R. Mal. 2 (1961-63) 242 at 243 and 244; *Guza v R* (1962) A.L.R. Mal. 136.

[220] (1962) A.L.R. Mal. 136 at 142.

[221] (1912) 106 LT 384.

the spouse is both competent and compellable. Where the accused's spouse is called to give evidence, he or she ought to be warned by the judge or the trial court that he or she has the right to refuse to give evidence.[222] Failure to do so is a serious irregularity that must, on appeal, result in the exclusion of his or her evidence.

4.5 Children as witnesses

4.5.1 *A general and historical perspective*

At common law no unsworn evidence could be given in any court proceedings. It was thought at the time, as appears to be thought by those religiously inclined that swearing on the Bible, the Quran or indeed any other religious text based on one's religious persuasion added certainty to the witness' testimony in that he was made self-aware of the punishment that would follow from his deity or circular authorities if he perjured himself. The offence of perjury has existed in the law since the early years of the 17th century. It was therefore argued, and for good reason, that no person takes the witness stand before appreciating the solemnity of the occasion and the implication of taking an oath to tell the truth.

While the matter was a clear cut one for those of majority age, the same could not be said when those called to be witnesses were young people. Unlike old people, young people or children are more likely not to appreciate the importance of telling the truth. The courts have said as much in a number of cases. Atkin J observed in *R v Dossi*[223] that children '[...] are possibly more under the influence of third persons – sometimes their parents – than are adults, and they are apt to allow their imaginations to run away with them and to invent untrue stories.' In *DPP v Hester,*[224] Lord Morris of Borth-Y-Gest opined *inter alia* that '[s]ometimes it may be that owing to immaturity or perhaps to lively imaginative gifts there is no appreciation of the gulf that separates truth from falsehood.' Lord Hailsham of St Marylebone in somewhat hilarious terms says of children's testimony in *DPP v Kilbourne:*[225] '[w]hen a small boy relates a sexual incident implicating a given man he may be indulging in fantasy.'

Be that as it may, leaving children's testimony out completely was likely to cause problems that would include unsuccessful prosecutions of accused persons' where the child was the only witness to an offence or the most important witness in the prosecution's case. To that end, efforts were made to permit children to testify via unsworn testimony.

The first approach consisted of the creation of an inferior class of testimony. In 1933, it became permissible for children to give unsworn evidence albeit unsworn in criminal proceedings on condition that (i) that the child appreciated the solemn duty to speak the truth and (ii) that the child in question was of intelligence as would be sufficient to validate receipt of his testimony by the

[222] *R v Kwalire and Another* (1962) A.L.R. Mal. 2 (1961-63) 242 at 243-244.

[223] (1918) 13 Cr.App.R 158 at 161.

[224] [1972] 3 All ER 1056.

[225] [1973] 1 All ER 440.

court. However, unsworn evidence was then, as it is now, inferior evidence in that it could only stand if corroborated, a feature that unfortunately appears to persist in our legal system to this day. Unlike sworn evidence, no accused person could be convicted on the unsworn evidence of a child or indeed anyone else.[226]

The second approach was taken in a in case that has lent its name to the said stratagem. In *R v Hayes*,[227] the EWCA recognised that world had moved on from a more devout approach to life of a bygone era and as such, belief in a god or God was not to be a determining factor in whether a person (including a child as envisaged under s 78(1) of the Children's Code[228] as regards criminal matters in this jurisdiction) could give evidence on oath.[229] The facts of the case[230] were as follows:

> Two boys aged 11 and 13 were questioned by the trial judge on their knowledge of God and on the religious instruction they received at school. Both claimed to be ignorant of the existence of God and to have received no religious instruction. Both, however, claimed also to be aware of the importance of telling the truth, particularly when they were in court. Upholding the judge's decision to allow them to give sworn testimony the Court of Appeal took a policy decision to secularise the common law test. It was sufficient appreciation of the solemnity of the occasion, and should understand that the duty of speaking the truth in court involved a higher duty than in everyday life. If these conditions were satisfied, it was not necessary that the child should be aware of the religious significance of an oath.

The significance of *R v Hayes*,[231] lies not only in its secularisation of the common law test for competence thus abandoning the requirement for the child to be conscious of the religious significance of the oath he was about to take, but also the fact that it also simplified the giving of evidence by young children. It further almost blurred the distinction between the tests for sworn and unsworn testimony of children to almost a waning point.[232] In the face of this decision, it was only logical to ask whether there should be actual corroboration as respects unsworn evidence and for the judge to warn himself in the face of unsworn evidence. It is a question that was relevant when it came to the proviso (b) to s 122 of the now repealed Juveniles Act[233] which required corroboration for the evidence of a child who gave sworn testimony without which no conviction would occur in criminal matters.

[226] A provision that until recently was part of the law in s 122 of the now repealed Juveniles Act Chapter 53 of the Laws of Zambia.

[227] (1977) 64 Cr App R 194 CA; [1977] 1 WLR 234.

[228] Act No 12 of 2022 applicable to criminal matters considered in the section that follows.

[229] See proviso (a) to s 122 of the Juveniles Act Chapter 53 of the Laws of Zambia.

[230] As summarised in Dennis I, *The Law of Evidence* 547-548.

[231] (1977) 64 Cr App R 194 CA; [1977] 1 WLR 234,

[232] Which is what is attempted under s 78 of the Children's Code, Act No 12 of 2022.

[233] Chapter 53 of the Laws of Zambia as amended by Act No 3 of 2011, itself now repealed and replaced by s 78 of the Children's Code, Act No 12 of 2022.

What then is the minimum age of competence? In the earlier case of *R v Wallwork*[234] it had been said by dicta that no testimony from children as young as five or six should be received into evidence. This was discarded by the EWCA in *R v Z*[235] which held that this was a matter within the purview of the judge's discretion.

4.5.2 *Competence of children as witnesses in criminal matters*

4.5.2.1 *The general law*

The law of competency as it relates to children is captured in s 78 of the Children's Code[236] which provides as follows:

In terms of s 78(1),

> [w]here, in any criminal or civil proceedings against a person, a child is called as a witness, the juvenile court or Children's Court shall receive the evidence, on oath, of the child if, in the opinion of the juvenile court or Children's Court, the child possesses sufficient intelligence to justify the reception of the child's evidence, on oath, and understands the duty of speaking the truth.

According to s 78(2),

> [i]f, in the opinion of the juvenile court or Children's Court, the child does not possess sufficient intelligence to justify the reception of the child's evidence, on oath, and does not understand the duty of speaking the truth, the child may give—
> (a) unsworn evidence that may be received as evidence in a juvenile court or Children's Court; or
> (b) evidence through a child welfare inspector responsible for the child's case.

It is perhaps important that we begin this discussion with what a child is in terms of s 2 of the Children's Code.[237] According to that section, '"child" has the meaning assigned to the word in the Constitution.' The relevant Constitutional provision in this regard is Article 266 which provides as follows: '"child" means a person who has attained, or is below, the age of eighteen years.' The foregoing marks a departure from the previous position which tied the age of a child within the context the law of evidence in terms of s 122 of the now

[234] (1958) 42 Cr App R 153 CCA.

[235] [1990] 2 QB 355 CA.

[236] Act No 12 of 2022; by way of comparison see s 53(3) of the YJCEA 1999 of the UK which provides as follows: "A person is not competent to give evidence in criminal proceedings if it appears to the court that he is not a person who is able to – (a) understand questions put to him as a witness and (a) give answers to them which can be understood"; S 53(1) of the YJCEA. Chapter 53 of the Laws of Zambia as amended by Act No 3 of 2011.

[237] Act No 12 of 2022.

repealed Juveniles Act[238] to "below the age of 14". This was a rather armophous and uncertain definition which presumably excluded any evidence from someone who had attained the age 14. The Constitutionally tied age is not only for children below the age of 18 but includes those that have attained the age oif 18.

By virtue of the preceding provision, the judge is, '[w]here, in any criminal or civil proceedings against any person, a child is called as a witness,' called upon, in fact mandated to receive the evidence, on oath, of the child.' However, this must only be so if 'in the opinion of the court, the child is possessed of sufficient intelligence to justify the reception of the child's evidence, on oath, and understands the duty of speaking the truth.' For the court to form such an opinion, it must 'conduct a factual inquiry to determine the question of the child's competence to testify through a *'voire dire.'* At the end of such a 'trial within a trial,' the court may come to the conclusion that '[...] the child is not possessed of sufficient intelligence to justify the reception of the child's evidence, on oath, and does not understand the duty of speaking the truth.'[239] In that case the court is mandated not to receive the child's evidence.

It ought to be emphasised here and now that in terms of s 78(1) of the Children's Code[240] a child who 'has attained, or is below, the age of eighteen' may give sworn testimony both in criminal cases with which we are concerned here and civil matters without being subjected to the requirements of s 78.[241] It follows that unlike the previous position where a child under 14 could not give unsworn testimony in terms of s 122(b) of the now repealed Juveniles Act,[242] now the court is permitted to receive unsworn evidence from a child who has attained or is below the age of eighteen in terms of s 78(2)(a) that may not be received under the requirements of s 78(1). If same may not be received in terms provided for under s 78(2)(a), it may, in terms of s 78(2)(b) be received '[...] through a child welfare inspector responsible for the child's case.' The English position appears to, as exemplified by in *R v Barker,*[243] on a similar provision in England,[244] require no formal requirement for the child to appreciate the importance of speaking the truth, give unsworn testimony which, thanks to it not being open to cross-examination, is considered an inferior form of testimony. The question of whether an appeal may succeed solely on the basis only that a child gave unsworn testimony would now seem redundant in the face of s 78(2) of the Children's Code, as would any authorities

[238] Chapter 53 of the Laws of Zambia (repealed).

[239] See *Mucheleta v The People* [SCZ Appeal No 124/2015].

[240] Act No 12 of 2022.

[241] *Darius Sinyinza v The People* (SCZ Judgment No 2 of 2009): The correct procedure to be adopted in the conduct of a voire dire is to be found in section [78 of the Children's Code, Act No 12 of 2022]. The Court must first decide that the proposing witness is a child of tender years; if he is not, the section does not apply, and the only manner in which the witness's evidence can be received is on oath.

[242] Chapter 53 of thew Laws of Zambia (repealed); *Partford Mwale v The People* CAZ Appeal No 8 of 2016; *Richard Daka v The People* SCZ Judgment No. 33 of 2013.

[243] [2010] EWCA Crim 4.

[244] S 53(1) of the YJCEA.

on the point.[245] There has to be more to the appeal. This is because if this is not the only evidence, despite the default, the accused may still be convicted on other evidence. There is the usual reminder by judges and counsel alike that the witness is under oath especially during cross-examination. This is a warning that should the witness tell lies, he will be guilty of perjury which is an indictable offence punishable by the court.

What if the evidence given by a child who has attained or is below the age of eighteen is a lie? While it is difficult to imagine that a child closer to the age of eighteen or who has attained the age of eighteen may not readily appreciate the solemnity of the occasion, and as such when he lies, he may, as Atkin J observed in *R v Dossi*[246] be '[...] under the influence of third persons – sometimes his] parents – than are adults, [permitting his] imaginations to run away with [him] and to invent untrue stories,' the likelihood of this happening appears to rise the younger the child is, that is, the further away he is from the age of eighteen. In the latter circumstances more than the former, it may also be, as shown in *DPP v Hester*,[247] '[...] that owing to immaturity or perhaps to lively imaginative gifts there is no appreciation of the gulf that separates truth from falsehood.' "if competent, as defined by the statutory criteria, in the context of credibility in the forensic process, the child witness starts off on the basis of equality with every witness." These positions appear to have been doubted in *R v Barker*[248] where the EWCA opined as follows as regards credibility of a child witness: 'if competent, as defined by the statutory criteria, in the context of credibility in the forensic process, the child witness starts off on the basis of equality with every witness.' It has been said further in *R v Barker*[249] that competence is not synonymous credibility. Thus, so far as this relates to s 78, it should fall to reason that if the judge upon conducting a *voire dire* is of the view that the child in question is competent in terms of s 78 of the Children's Code,[250] he ultimately will have to make a determination as regards the truthfulness and accuracy of the child's evidence. In *R v Barker*, the EWCA refused to reverse the conviction for rape of a child aged just under three at the time of the offence and four and a half at the time of trial. Despite her tender years, the Court took the view that she made for a 'compelling as well as a competent witness.' The position taken was to the effect that it was open to the court essentially properly directing its mind to 'reach a safe conclusion on the evidence of a single competent witness whatever her age or disability.'[251]

Under such circumstances, a child giving unsworn evidence may strictly speaking not be held to have perjured himself and be punished for it. Section

[245] But see *Partford Mwale v The People* CAZ Appeal No 8 of 2016; *Richard Daka v The People* SCZ Judgment No 33 of 2013.

[246] (1918) 13 Cr App R 158 at 161.

[247] [1972] 3 All ER 1056.

[248] [2010] EWCA Crim 4.

[249] [2010] EWCA Crim 4.

[250] Act No 12 of 2022.

[251] Dennis I, *The Law of Evidence* 552.

78 appears to have removed the specific requirement under s 122 of the repealed Juveniles Act for corroboration for a conviction to stand, even where the evidence by the child was sworn. The preceding speaks to weight. What the former s 122 did, sadly and honestly, was that it put the sworn evidence of a child deemed competent to give sworn evidence on the same footing as any unsworn evidence whether of a child or indeed any other witness.[252] In reality, there appeared to be no difference in the weight attached to the sworn evidence of a child and the unsworn evidence of another child who has attained or is below the age of eighteen. Be that as it may, the nature and effect of the sworn evidence of a child was considered in *Chisha v The People*.[253] The case against the applicant rested solely on the evidence of a boy aged fourteen years. The trial judge conducted a perfectly, proper *voire dire*, at the end of which he was satisfied that the boy was able to give evidence on oath. The issue was whether the sworn evidence of a child is to be treated like the sworn evidence by any other witness. Silungwe CJ, as he was then, delivered the judgment of the Court. He observed that the main issue in the case was whether the sworn evidence of a child is to be treated like the sworn evidence by any other witness. He drew the conclusion that it was well established as a matter of law that sworn evidence of a child in criminal cases does not require corroboration, but that the Court should warn itself that there is a risk in acting on the uncorroborated evidence of young boys and girls.[254]

Section 122 of the repealed Juveniles Act[255] was in need of review given common law developments in this area of the law elsewhere in the commonwealth. It may be worth our while to state at this juncture that while the 'Hayes test' is a common law staple when it comes to competence, the test of competence of a child under s 78 of the Children's Code 'directs the court to assess the child's intellectual capacities, notably the child's moral sense.'[256]

It ordinarily ought to follow that if the court decides in favour of the child because in the court's opinion, the child 'is possessed of sufficient intelligence to justify the reception of the child's evidence, on oath, and does understand the duty of speaking the truth' and as such deems such testimony admissible, this, in terms of s 78 of the Children's Code,-may make the 'accused [...] liable to be convicted of the offence' without 'that evidence' being 'corroborated[257] by some other material evidence in support thereof implicating the accused.' This is because in terms of s 78(9), '[a] juvenile court or Children's Court may, having regard to the nature and circumstances of the offence in question,

---

[252] Compare s 291(2) of the Criminal Procedure Code Chapter 88 of the Laws of Zambia.

[253] [1980] ZR 36; approved in *The People v Thomas Monroe* (HPA/50/2010); *Christopher Nonde Lushinga v The People* (SCZ Judgment No 15 of 2011); *Partford Mwale v The People* (CAZ Appeal No 8 of 2016).

[254] *Per* Lord Goddard in *R v Campbell* [1956] 2 All ER 212; See this being done by Matibini J in *The People v Inonge Anayawa Lubinda Sinjambi* HT/23/2010.

[255] Chapter 53 of the Laws of Zambia.

[256] Dennis I, *The Law of Evidence* 552.

[257] Thus the decision in *Mucheleta v The People* [SCZ Appeal No 124/2015] and other like it decided in the era of s 122 of the now repealed Juveniles Act must now be seen within the context of s 78 of the Children's Code Act No 12 of 2022.

require evidence presented before the juvenile court or Children's Court to be corroborated by some other material evidence.' Thus, corroboration is no longer a mandatory requirement when the sworn evidence of the child is involved. The Court ought to consider each case on its own facts. However, as shown in *Richard Daka v The People*,[258] it is not enough for the trial court to simply state that the child possesses sufficient intelligence to give evidence on oath without specifically stating that the child understands the importance of telling the truth. Where that occurs, the requirements of the law under s 78(1) of the Children's Code[259] are not satisfied rendering the *voire dire* defective. Bear in mind though that as noted already, this presents the challenge of the 'trial within a trial' disclosing information which the court presiding over the *voire dire* may take into account when, at the end of the trial and for purposes of rendering a verdict, thus prejudicing the accused. *The People v Banda*[260] was a matter that came before the High Court for confirmation of the order made by a magistrate of the third class detaining the accused during the President's pleasure. It was held *inter alia* that it is the duty of the court when faced with a child witness to inquire as to the age of the child and if necessary, assess its age, to investigate whether it understands the meaning of an oath and if it does not understand the meaning of an oath to investigate whether the child understands the difference between truth and falsehood and the need to speak the truth. The court should always show these inquiries and the conclusions reached.

The process envisaged under s 78(1) of the Children's Code[261] presupposes, as is ordinarily expected in civil and criminal proceedings, that the party calling the young child bears the burden of satisfying the court on the balance of probabilities, of the child's competent to testify and give evidence in the proceedings in question. Be that as it may, though, it is for the court to ask the child any questions it deems necessary in order to enable it determine the question of competence in the presence of the parties to the proceedings. In this process, as alluded to elsewhere in this text, the court may entertain expert opinion on whether the child is competent to give evidence. However, the expert's opinion is only meant to aid the court in coming to its decision and not to displace the court's own opinion as regards the competence of the child in question.

Throughout the entirety of the procedure envisaged under s 78,[262] it must not be lost on any court conducting a *voire dire* that only a witness, and in this

[258] (SCZ Appeal 333 of 2013) [2014] ZMSC 28; *Goba v The People* [1966] ZR 113; *Mwabona v The People* (1973) ZR 28; *Bernard Chisha v The People* [1980] ZR 36; *Patrick Sakala v The People* [1980] ZR 205; *Emmanuel Phiri v The People* [1982] ZR 77; *Dorothy Mutale & Another v The People* [1997] ZR 51; *Joseph Mwamba v The People* [2007] SCJ [...] 103; *Machipisha Kombe v The People* [2009] ZR 282.

[259] Act No 12 of 2022.

[260] [1972] ZR 307 (HC).

[261] Act No 12 of 2022; by way of comparison see s 53(3) of the YJCEA 1999 of the UK which provides as follows: "A person is not competent to give evidence in criminal proceedings if it appears to the court that he is not a person who is able to – (a) understand questions put to him as a witness and (a) give answers to them which can be understood.'

[262] Act No 12 of 2022.

case, a child witnesses who has a sufficient understanding of the seriousness of the juncture and of the special obligation to tell the truth as it relates to taking an oath or affirmation should be sworn in or 'affirmed in.' There of course is a presumption that the foregoing is appreciated by a child witness or any witness for that matter if he can give intelligible testimony. However, like any proper presumption, it may be rebutted by evidence that satisfies the court that the contrary is true. If the rebuttal is successful by showing that the witness does not appreciate the seriousness of the occasion or importance of telling the truth due to want of maturity or cannot give intelligible testimony at the very minimum, such a witness ought not be sworn in, irrespective, to ensure the integrity of the proceedings, fairness of the trial process, and more important, to avoid offending the dignity of the court and the tainting justice.

In so far as the issue of a child's competency arises, the judge will deal with the same as a question relating to admissibility of evidence. In so doing, the court and counsel ought to be alive to the rather strict and protyective requirements wrought into the system by the Children's Code.[263]

In terms of s 78(3), [a] child required to give evidence in a juvenile court or Children's Court shall be prepared to testify by a child welfare inspector or any other authorised officer.

By s 78(4), [a] child that is giving evidence in a court shall—(a) be questioned in an environment that is child friendly; (b) be questioned in camera; (c) be questioned in a manner that is proportional to the child's age and maturity of the child; (d) not interact or be in the same room with a person the child is testifying against; and (e) not be questioned more than twice.

It is provided in s 78(5) that [s]ubject to subsection (4)(d), a person the child is testifying against or that person's legal practitioner shall cross examine a child witness through—(a) a child welfare inspector, an authorised officer or a child's next friend, acting as an intermediary; or (b) the use of a video link.

According to s 78(6), [t]he juvenile court or Children's Court shall— (a) permit recorded pre-trial interviews with a child to be presented as evidence in lieu of a live testimony by a child; or (b) request a report from a child welfare inspector or other authorised officer who has interviewed a child to be used as evidence.

In terms of s 78(8), [a]child witness shall be protected from threats, intimidation, reprisal or any other form of victimisation prior to and when giving evidence before a juvenile court or Children's Court.

Under such circumstances as are envisaged in s 78(3)-(8), the judge may, under s 78(1) and (2) of the Children's Code,[264] make a determination from viewing the recording or via video conference facilities in terms of s 78(5) (b) of the Children's Code.[265] If the judge cannot make up his/her mind from recorded evidence of a child about his competence, he is to go through the

[263] Act No 12 of 2022.

[264] Act No 12 of 2022.

[265] Act No 12 of 2022.

same steps stipulated under s 78(1) and (2)[266] to determine the issue of the child's competence. As said before, this may be accomplished by the judge simply asking general questions of the child in front of the accused person and in some instances especially ones where the witness has a mental disability, the judge may call in aid, expert opinion. Even so, as indicated earlier, the ultimate decision as to the competence of the witness is the judge's to make and upon it whether such evidence as the child witness is intended to give is admissible.

In *R v Barker*,[267] the EWCA observed that the test of competency entails a decision by the trial judge that is witness-specific, and that the clear words of s 53 of the UK YCEA 1999 which in our jurisdiction would appear to straddle the common law and the statutory provisions in s 122 of the Juveniles Act and ss 160-167 of the Criminal Procedure Code,[268] should not be annotated or re-explained:

> These statutory provisions are not limited to the evidence of children. They apply to individuals of unsound mind. They apply to the infirm. The question in each case is whether the individual witness, or, as in this case, the individual child, is competent to give evidence in the particular trial. The question is entirely witness or child specific. There are no presumptions or preconceptions. The witness need not understand the special importance that the truth should be told in court, and the witness need not understand every single question or give a readily understood answer to every question. Many competent adult witnesses would fail such a competency test. Dealing with it broadly and fairly, provided the witness can understand the questions put to him and can also provide understandable answers, he or she is competent. If the witness cannot understand the questions or his answers to questions which he understands cannot themselves be understood he is not. The questions come, of course, from both sides. If the child is called as a witness by the prosecution, he or she must have the ability to understand the questions put to him by the defence as well as the prosecution and to provide answers to them which are understandable. The provisions of the statute are clear and unequivocal, and do not require reinterpretation.

4.5.2.2 A child's competence and s 78(1 and (2) in the eyes of Zambian case law

A plethora of Zambian authorities relating to the interpretation and application of the provisions of what once was s 122 of the Juveniles Act[269] which has now been repealed and replaced and expanded by s 78 of the Children's Code[270] show the strictness with which said provisions, in so far as they remain

[266] Act No 12 of 2022.

[267] [2010] EWCA Crim 4; see also *R v Macpherson* [2005] EWCA Crim 3605; [2006] 1 Cr App R 30; *R v Malicki* [2009] EWCA Crim 365.

[268] Chapter 88 of the Laws of Zambia.

[269] Chapter 53 of the Laws of Zambia (repealed).

[270] Act No 12 of 2022.

relevant under the new statutory regime, must be followed by the trial Court if any conviction and sentence based on a child's evidence, sworn or unsworn is to hold. We consider a few below.[271] In *The People v Inonge Anayawa Lubinda Sinjambi,*[272] the accused were charged with the offence of murder contrary to section 200 of the Penal Code. Particulars of the offence were that the accused jointly and whilst acting together murdered the deceased. Matibini J, as he then was outlined the following useful point:

> 1. Where a confession is proved, it is the best evidence that can be proved.
> 2. A1 was a principal actor in the commission of the murder and therefore on the basis of the confession, the Court was satisfied beyond reasonable doubt that A1 was guilty of the offence of murder.
> 3. It is well established as a matter of law that sworn evidence of a child in criminal cases does not require corroboration. But the Court should warn itself that there is a risk in acting on the uncorroborated evidence of young boys and girls.
> 4. By reason of immaturity of mind of a child, whether the evidence is sworn[273] or unsworn,[274] falls within the category of what may conveniently called "suspect witness," whose evidence must as a necessity be treated as suspect.
> 5. A conviction which is founded on suspect evidence[275] cannot be regarded as safe unless such evidence is supported to such an extent as satisfies the giver of facts that the danger therein placing reliance upon suspect evidence has been excluded.
> 6. It is competent for a Court to convict on the basis of circumstantial evidence.

Sakala v The People[276] is an example of the sad consequences that may follow if the trial court fails to adhere to the procedure under s 78(1)(2) of the Children's Code[277] (formerly s 122).[278] This was an application for leave to appeal against conviction and sentence. While the court was of the view that the application lacked merit, it was however forced to admit that the Court below had made a fatal error. The principal witness for the prosecution, without whose evidence prosecution counsel conceded the conviction could not stand, was an 11-year-old boy. It appeared from the record that the learned Magistrate conducted a

[271] All these authorities must now be seen within the context of s 78 of the Children's Code, Act No 12 of 2022.

[272] HT/23/2010.

[273] Section 78(1) of the Children's Code.

[274] Section 78(2)(a) of the Children's Code.

[275] Christopher Allen uses the term 'hazardous evidence' and generalises the application of the term to all kinds of evidence because as he sees it, '[...] all evidence emerges as a result of some kind of selection; [...] too much has to be taken on trust;' [and that] a third reason for the hazardous nature of evidence is that [it is] presented through the medium of language': Allen C, *Practical Guide to Evidence* 241-242.

[276] [1972] ZR 35 (CA).

[277] Act No 12 of 2022.

[278] As explained in *The People v Banda* [1972] ZR 307 (HC).

voire dire as required by s 120 of the Juveniles Ordinance.[279] The record on this point simply read as follows: 'Juvenile of tender years does not know the oath but knows what to tell the truth is. Not sworn. Makes unsworn evidence.'

This matter had been considered by the Federal Supreme Court in the case of *Makhanganya v R*,[280] where Forbes FJ, explained why it was essential that not only should the *voire dire* be conducted and the record show this but also that the record show in addition the actual questions put to the juvenile and the answers received, and the conclusions reached by the court. Forbes FJ concluded as follows: '[u]nless a *voire dire* is carried out as I have indicated, trial court cannot be satisfied that a child is fit to be sworn, or even to give evidence unsworn, and unless a voire dire is recorded an appellate court cannot be satisfied that the trial court has appreciated and carried out its duty.'

In *Sakala v The People*,[281] the record did not enable the High Court to, on appeal, satisfy itself that the trial court had appreciated and carried out its duty. Indeed, it appeared on the face of the record that the magistrate did not satisfy himself that the juvenile *was possessed of sufficient intelligence to justify the reception of his evidence*.[282] In the absence of a proper *voire dire*, Baron JP opined, the court ought to have discounted the evidence of the juvenile. The High Court noted that it was with the greatest regret that it was left with no alternative but to grant the application treating the hearing before it as the hearing of the appeal and allowed the appeal and set aside the conviction and sentence.

In *Zulu v The People*,[283] the appellant was convicted of the defilement of a twelve-year-old girl. The first ground of appeal was that the *voire dire* conducted by the magistrate did not satisfy the provisions of s 78(1)(2) of the Children's Code.[284] The Court made mention of the fact that the section and procedure to be followed by a trial court had not only been considered in *Makhanganya v R*[285] a case referred to by the Supreme Court in *Sakala v The People*,[286] but observed that the subject still caused confusion - partly perhaps because Forbes, FJ, in *Makhanganya v R*[287] did not deal with one of the requirements which the section specifies. The Court proposed therefore, for the assistance of magistrates, to set out the correct procedure to be followed under s 78(1)(2) of the Children's[288] as follows:[289]

[279] Now the Juveniles Act Chapter 53 of the Laws of Zambia.

[280] 1963 R & N 698.

[281] [1972] ZR 35 (CA).

[282] Emphasis added.

[283] [1973] ZR 326 (SC).

[284] Chapter 53 of the Laws of Zambia.

[285] (1963) R & N 698.

[286] [1972] ZR 35 (CA).

[287] (1963) R & N 698; see *Richard Daka v The People* SCZ Judgment No 33 of 2013.

[288] Chapter 53 of the Laws of Zambia.

[289] Chapter 53 of the Laws of Zambia.

> Thus, the steps are: First, the court must conclude that the proposing witness is a child of tender years; if he is not, the section does not apply, and the only manner in which the witness' evidence can be received is on oath. Second, having concluded that the witness is a child of tender years the court must inquire whether the child understands the nature of an oath; if he does, he is sworn in the ordinary way, and his evidence is received on the same basis as that of an adult witness. Third, if the court is not satisfied that the child understands the nature of an oath, it must then satisfy itself (a) that he is possessed of sufficient intelligence to justify the reception of his evidence and (b) that he understands the duty of speaking the truth; if the court is satisfied on both these matters then the child's evidence may be received although not on oath, and in that event, in addition to any other cautionary rules relating to corroboration (for instance, because the offence charged is a sexual one) there arises the statutory requirement of corroboration contained in the proviso to s 78(1) of the Children's Code. But if the court is not satisfied on either of the foregoing points the child's evidence may not be received at all.
>
> We stress again, as we did in *Sakala's case*,[290] that not only must the record show that a voire dire has been conducted, but also the questions asked, the answers received and the conclusions reached by the court.

The Court went on:

> In the present case the magistrate appears to have confused the requirements and the tests. The prosecutrix, in answer to the court, said "I know the need for telling the truth. If I tell lies, God will punish me." The magistrate then recorded this conclusion: "Satisfied that the witness of tender years knows the need of telling the truth. She can therefore be sworn on the Bible." This is not the test for the swearing of a witness; a witness cannot be sworn sinless the court is satisfied he understands the nature of an oath. Nor could the magistrate have received the prosecutrix's evidence unsworn unless he was satisfied not only that she understood the need to tell the truth but also that she was possessed of sufficient intelligence to justify the reception of her evidence; there is nothing in the record to suggest that the magistrate directed his mind to the child's intelligence.

The Supreme Court ordered a retrial in terms of s 15(2) of the Supreme Court of Zambia Act,[291] which reads: '[t]he Court shall, if it allows an appeal against the conviction, either quash the conviction and direct a judgment and verdict of acquittal to be entered or, if the interests of justice so require, order a new trial.' The Supreme Court noted that the discretion contained in s 15(2) should certainly not be exercised where the result would be to give the prosecution a second bite at the cherry on the merits. The Court adverted to Winn LJ, said in

[290] *Sakala v The People* [1972] ZR 35.

[291] Chapter 25 of the Laws of Zambia.

Royal v Prescott - Clarke[292] who opined as follows on the matter:

> [. . .] where there is no question of the prosecution being given a further opportunity to go out and scout about for evidence to strengthen their case, but it is merely a matter of their going to look in a newspaper, and if they find there what they need, bringing the newspaper to the court, in all ordinary circumstances and in the absence of any conduct on the part of the prosecution which might be properly described as misconduct or election not to call other evidence and in the absence of any grave potential prejudice to the accused, there is only one way in which the discretion can properly be exercised.[293]

As the Court saw it, where a *voire dire* has been inadequate the fault lies with the court. There was no question of the prosecution being given a second bite al the cherry, or the opportunity to scout about for evidence to strengthen their case; and there was no prejudice to the appellant. The Court was satisfied that it had the power, in a proper case, to order a retrial where the appeal had been allowed only because of a defective *voire dire.*

In *Chewe v The People,*[294] the appellant was convicted of defilement. The complainant was a girl who gave her age as thirteen and there was nothing on the record to suggest that a *voire dire* was conducted. The Director of Legal Aid submitted that on the authority of *Sakala v The People*[295] the failure to conduct a *voire dire* was fatal. Quoting s 122(1) of the Juveniles Act,[296] Baron DCJ noted that the first decision to be made in terms of s 122(1) is whether the proposing witness is a child of tender years; if he is not then s 122(1) does not apply and the witness' evidence cannot be received save on oath. *It was observed that* there was no definition in the Juveniles Act[297] nor, indeed, anywhere else of a "child of tender years." However, according to Lord Goddard CJ in *R v Campbell,*[298] '[w]hether a child is of tender years is for the good sense of the court.' The DCJ, however, pointed out that '[i]t would unquestionably be far more satisfactory if the legislature were to lay down a specific age below which the provisions of s 122(1) of the Juveniles Act[299] were to be applied; in the absence of such legislation the decision must be made by the court in each case.' Returning to the case, he concluded on behalf of the court as follows:

> In the present case the record is completely silent on the point and we must assume, on the basis of the standard presumption that procedural matters of this kind have been correctly carried out, that

[292] [1966] 2 All ER 366.
[293] [1966] 2 All ER 366 at 369.
[294] [1974] ZR 18 (SC).
[295] [1972] ZR 35.
[296] Now s 78(1) of the Children's Code.
[297] Chapter 53 of the Laws of Zambia.
[298] [1956] 2 All ER 272.
[299] Chapter 53 of the Laws of Zambia.

> the court was satisfied that this child was not a child of tender years. The child was duly sworn on the Bible in Nyanja [...] The appeal was dismissed.

A question that has always existed in view of the provisions such as those under s 78(1)(2) of the Children's Code[300] is whether a child of tender years, that is, a child who has attained or is under the age of eighteen and whom the court deems capable of giving sworn evidence in terms of s 78(1) can corroborate another child of tender years. In *Christopher Nonde Lushinga v The People,*[301] the appellant was convicted on two counts of a defilement of child contrary to s 138(1) of the Penal Code.[302] On committal to the High Court for sentence, the appellant was sentenced to 25 years imprisonment on each count, ordered to run concurrently. The appellant appealed against both conviction and sentence. It was held inter alia that two children of tender years giving their unsworn evidence cannot as a matter of law corroborate one another.

4.5.3 *Competence of children as witnesses in civil matters*

The position of child witnesses in civil cases is the same as that relating to criminal matters as captured under s 78(1)(2) of the Children's Code.[303] This is so because s 78(1) refers to 'any criminal or *civil*[304] proceedings against any person [....]' It follows that the steps stipulated in *Zulu v The People,*[305] and the observations made in *The People v Banda,*[306] would in principle apply in a civil matter.

4.6 Persons under mental disability as witnesses

At common law, a person of defective intellect was always considered incompetent to give evidence unless they could pass the test set in *R v Hayes.*[307] Known as the 'Hayes test,' it seeks to find out whether the person in question could show appreciation for the solemnity of the occasion and the special duty to tell the truth on oath. The question as to whether the person in question does have appreciation for the solemnity of the occasion and the special duty of telling the truth on oath is for the court to determine.[308] Our discussion here under will be with respect to civil cases on the one hand, and criminal cases on the other.

[300] Act No 12 of 2022.

[301] (CAZ Appeal No 8 of 2016).

[302] Chapter 87 of the Laws of Zambia.

[303] Chapter 53 of the Laws of Zambia as amended by Act No 3 of 2011; by way of comparison see s 53(3) of the YJCEA 1999 of the UK which provides as follows: 'A person is not competent to give evidence in criminal proceedings if it appears to the court that he is not a person who is able to –
  (a) understand questions put to him as a witness and
  (a) give answers to them which can be understood.'

[304] Emphasis added.

[305] [1973] ZR 326 (SC).

[306] [1972] ZR 307 (HC).

[307] [1977] 1 WLR 234.

[308] *R v Hill* (1851) 2 Den 254; *R v Dunning* [1965] Crim LR 372.

4.6.1 *Civil cases*

At common law, a witness with a defective mind is not a competent witness. In the event that questions arise in this regard, same may be investigated in open court. The court may also listen to expert opinion through a *voire dire* on the matter. Competence is dependent on the severity of the defectiveness of mind. It has been shown in *R v Barratt and Sheehan*[309] that to call a witness whose mental condition has given rise to questions regarding his competence, will ordinarily not be necessary.

As noted earlier, the crucial test is the 'Hayes test.' In *R v Hill,*[310] the prosecution wished to call as one of its witnesses, an asylum inmate to give evidence in support of its case. Any asylum attendant indicated in his evidence that the man the prosecution wished to call to the witness stand was deluded and thought that he conversed with spirits. Be that as it may, the attendant indicated that the man in question was capable of relating anything that he had seen. The Court permitted him to give evidence on account of the fact that he could lucidly speak to anything he had perceived except for his delusion.

In *R v Bellamy,*[311] a rape victim/complainant aged 31 had a mental capacity of one aged 10. The EWCA took the view that having satisfied the 'Hayes test' as was clear from her answers to initial questions from the trial court, she ought to have been permitted to give sworn testimony. She realised for example, that if she were to tell a lie, she could be 'put away.' Another important principle to be derived from this case is that want 'of awareness of the divinity was no bar to testimony under oath.'[312]

4.6.2 *Criminal cases*

In England under ss 53-57 of the YJCEA 1999, the law permits a person of majority age of defective intellect to give evidence unsworn with only the requirement for such a person to pass the 'Hayes test,' The rationale has been to allow victims of physical or sexual abuse to bring their abusers where once they were not able to give sworn testimony thanks to their state of mind.[313] As with civil matters, the court may conduct a *voire dire* to determine the competency of the witness in open court. It has been held in *R v Sed,*[314] that the test of competence in s 53(3) of the YJCEA does not inevitably entail 100 per cent common conception of solid interactions giving rise to likely evidence.

The approach to witnesses of defective intellect in this jurisdiction is similar to that in England though there does not appear to be any legislative equivalent

---

[309] [1996] Crim LR 495.

[310] (1851) 2 Den 254.

[311] (1986) 82 Cr App R 222.

[312] Practice and Procedure: *R v Bellamy* (1985) https://www.lccsa.org.uk/r-v-bellamy-1985/ retrieved on 28/2/21.

[313] The Court may take special measures through directions to have the witness in such a situation be examined through an intermediary.

[314] [2004] EWCA Crim 1294, [2005] 1 Cr App R 4 at 42; *R v D* [2002] EWCA Crim 990; [2002] 2 Cr App R 36; *R (on the application of B) v DPP* [2009] EWHC 106 (Admin).

to ss 53-57 for purposes of dealing with competence and capacity to be sworn as witnesses as specifically provided for under s 53(3) of the YJCEA 1999. There is, however, procedure in case of the insanity or other incapacity of an accused person to which we turn next.

4.6.2.1 *Procedure in case of the insanity or other Incapacity of an accused person*

(i) Question whether accused capable of making his defence

In terms of s 160 of the Criminal Procedure Code,[315] [w]here on the trial of a person charged with an offence punishable by[316] imprisonment the question arises, at the instance of the defence or otherwise, whether the accused is, by reason of unsoundness of mind or of any other disability, incapable of making a proper defence, the court shall inquire into and determine such question as soon as it arises.[317]

(ii) Procedure where accused unfit to make his defence

This is provided for under s 161 of the Criminal Procedure Code. [318] According to s 161, '[w]here a court, in accordance with the provisions of section one hundred and sixty, finds an accused incapable of making a proper defence, it shall enter a plea of "not guilty" if it has not already done so and, to the extent that it has not already done so, shall hear the evidence for the prosecution and (if any) for the defence.

In terms of s 161(2), '[a]t the close of such evidence as is mentioned in subsection (1), the court, if it finds that the evidence as it stands-

(a) would not justify a conviction or a special finding under section one hundred and sixty-seven, shall acquit and discharge the accused; or

(b) would, in the absence of further evidence to the contrary, justify a conviction, or a special finding under section one hundred and sixty-seven, shall order the accused to be detained during the President's pleasure.

By s 161(3), '[a]n acquittal and discharge under subsection (2) shall be without prejudice to any implementation of the provisions of the Mental Disorders Act, and the High Court may, if it considers in any case that an inquiry under the provisions of section nine of that Act is desirable, direct that the person acquitted and discharged be detained and taken before a magistrate for the purpose of such inquiry.'

---

[315] Chapter 88 of the Laws of Zambia.

[316] According to s Section 160 of the principal Act is amended by the deletion of the words "death or" immediately after the words "punishable by".

[317] No 76 of 1965 as amended by No 18 of 1966.

[318] Chapter 88 of the Laws of Zambia.

(iii) Procedure following order of detention during President's pleasure

This is provided for under s 162. Section 162(1) provides that '[w]here an order for the detention of an accused during the President's pleasure is made by a Subordinate Court-

(a) the court shall transmit the record or a certified copy thereof to the High Court for confirmation of such order;

(b) the High Court may, and at the request of the prosecution or defence made within fourteen days of the order of the Subordinate Court shall, admit additional evidence or hear the prosecution and defence in relation to the disability of the accused; and

(c) the High Court in dealing with the confirmation of such an order may exercise all or any of the powers which are conferred upon it under Part XI for the purposes of revision.'

It is provided under s 162(2) that '[w]here an order for the detention of an accused during the President's pleasure is made or confirmed by the High Court, the Judge concerned shall submit a written report to the President containing any recommendations or observations on the case which he may think fit to make, together with a certified copy of the record.'

(iv) Detention during President's pleasure

In terms of 163(1), '[w]here under this Code any person is ordered to be detained during the President's pleasure, the order shall be sufficient authority for his detention, until otherwise dealt with under this Code, in any mental institution, prison or other place where facilities exist for the detention of persons, and for his conveyance to that place.' By s 163(2), '[a] person ordered under this Code to be detained during the President's pleasure shall be liable to be detained in such place and under such conditions as the President may by order direct, and while so detained shall be in lawful custody.' In terms of s 163(3), '[t]he officer in charge of the place in which any person is detained during the President's pleasure under this Code shall, at intervals not exceeding six months, submit a report to the President containing the prescribed information in relation to every person so detained in his custody.'[319]

(v) Discharge of persons detained during President's pleasure

According to s 164(1), '[t]he President may at any time by order discharge from detention any person detained during the President's pleasure and such discharge may be absolute or subject to conditions, and if absolute the order under which he has been detained shall cease to be of effect accordingly. In terms of s 164(2), '[t]he President may at any time by order revoke an order of conditional discharge made under subsection (1) and thereupon the person concerned shall be detained during the President's pleasure as though he had never been discharged from detention.'[320]

---

[319] No 76 of 1965.

[320] No 76 of 1965.

(vi) Resumption of trial

In terms of s 165(1), '[i]f on the advice of a medical officer the President, having regard to the requirements of the Constitution, considers that the question of the capacity to make a proper defence of any person detained following an order under section one hundred and sixty-one should be re-examined, he shall by order direct that such person be taken before a court and the court shall inquire into and determine that question.' Section 165(2) provides that '[w]here a court, after inquiry under subsection (1), finds the accused capable of making a proper defence, any order under which the accused has been detained during the President's pleasure shall thereupon cease to have effect and the accused shall be called upon to plead to the charge or information and the trial shall commence de novo.' According to s 165(3), '[w]here a court, after inquiry under subsection (1), finds the accused to be still incapable of making a proper defence, the order under which the accused has been detained during the President's pleasure shall continue to be of force and effect.'

Finally, in terms of s 165(4), '[f]or the purposes of an inquiry under subsection (1), a report concerning the capacity of the accused to conduct his defence by the medical officer in charge of the asylum or other place in which the accused has been detained may be read as evidence but without prejudice to the right of the court to summon and examine such medical officer.'

(vii) Preliminary inquiries

In terms of s 166, the question whether - (a) while before the Subordinate Court an accused person is by reason of unsoundness of mind or of any other disability incapable of making a proper defence; or (b) at the time of the act or omission in respect of which an accused person is charged, such person was by reason of unsoundness of mind incapable of understanding what he was doing, or of knowing that he ought not to do the act or make the omission; shall not be determined in any preliminary inquiry held under Part VII and, for the purposes of any decision whether an accused should be committed for trial, the accused shall be deemed to have been at all material times free from any such disability.'

(viii) Defence of insanity at the time of the offence

This is provided for under s 167. In terms of s 167(1), '[w]here an act or omission is charged against any person as an offence, and it is given in evidence on the trial of such person for that offence that he was insane so as not to be responsible for his actions at the time when the act was done or omission made, then, if it appears to the court before which such person is tried that he did the act or made the omission charged but was insane as aforesaid at the time when he did or made the same, the court shall make a special finding to the effect that the accused was not guilty by reason of insanity. The case of *The People v Banda*[321] came up to the High Court for confirmation of the order made by a magistrate

[321] [1972] ZR 307 (HC).

of the third class detaining the accused during the President's pleasure. It was held *inter alia* that where a question of insanity arises it is essential for a magistrate to decide (a) whether the accused is capable of making his defence at the time he appears before the court, and (b) whether the accused was insane at the time of the commission of the offence.

It was held *inter alia* that it is the duty of the court when faced with a child witness to inquire as to the age of the child and if necessary, assess its age, to investigate whether it understands the meaning of an oath and if it does not understand the meaning of an oath to investigate whether the child understands the difference between truth and falsehood and the need to speak the truth. The court should always show these inquiries and the conclusions reached.

The foregoing is demonstrated in *Joseph Mutapa Tobo v The People.*[322] The particulars of the offence alleged that on 21st September, 1980 at Kasama, in the Kasama District of the Northern Province of the Republic of Zambia, he murdered Salome Safeli Chitabo. It was testified that the appellant was the last person to be seen in the company of the deceased. The following day, one of the villagers and the deceased's father interrogated the appellant on the whereabouts of the deceased whereupon the appellant then led them to an anthill where they found the deceased's half-naked body. The appellant did not offer any testimony in his defence but called a psychiatrist to prove the appellant's defence of insanity. The appellant was tried and convicted for the offence of murder contrary to s 200 of the Penal Code.[323] He was sentenced to death. He appealed against conviction. The crucial evidence of the doctor was that he is a consultant psychiatrist. He talked to and examined the appellant. He made certain observations: "flattening effect and vacant look." The doctor had access to the tests carried on the appellant by other doctors and clinical psychiatrists apart from what he himself carried out. The doctor's evidence was also to the effect that the appellant was likely to have been mentally disturbed at the time of committing the offence. On the material that was before him, the doctor said; "In my opinion Mr. Joseph M. Tobo suffers from "Psychiatric illness [....] It was held that on the balance of probabilities the defence had proved that the appellant was suffering from a disease of the mind at the time of the commission of the offence.

Blagden CJ opined as follows in *Director of Public Prosecutions v Lukwosha* [324]

> By s 13 of the Penal Code,[325] the Legislature limited the application of the defence of insanity to two classes of case-first, insanity which produces in the accused an incapacity to understand what he is doing; and secondly, insanity which produces in the accused an incapacity to

[322] (1991) SJ (SC).

[323] Chapter 88 of the Laws of Zambia.

[324] [1966] ZR 14 (CA); *The People v Kufekisa* [1975] ZR 188 (HC): The law takes no note of the cause of insanity. If actual insanity in fact supervenes, as the result of alcoholic excesses, it furnishes as complete an answer to a criminal charge as insanity induced by any other causes and that insanity, even though temporary is an answer.

[325] Chapter 87 of the Laws of Zambia.

> understand that he ought not to do it. Had the Legislature intended that the defence of insanity should be applicable to a third class of case insanity which produces in the accused an incapacity to know that what he is doing will probably have certain consequences such as the causing of grievous harm to someone- the Legislature would surely have said so.
>
> Where it appears from the evidence that an incapacity to appreciate consequences might reasonably exist although the two types of incapacity referred to in s 13 do not, the defence of insanity would fail, but the position would be that the prosecution, too, would fail - fail, that is, to establish the incidence of malice aforethought beyond reasonable doubt.

Section 167(2) of the Criminal Procedure Code[326] provides that '[f]or the purposes of appeal, whether to the High Court or to the Court of Appeal, a special finding made under subsection (1) shall be deemed to be a conviction. Further to the foregoing, s 167(3) provides that '[w]here a special finding is made under subsection (1), the court so finding shall order the person to whom such finding relates to be detained during the President's pleasure.'

4.7 The President

The starting point as regards a sitting president or a former president who is sued for actions taken while he is/was in office is Article 98 of the Constitution. According to Article 98(1), '[a] person shall not institute or continue civil proceedings against the President or a person performing executive functions, as provided in Article 109, in respect of anything done or omitted to be done by the President or that person in their private capacity during the tenure of office as President.' In terms of Article 98(2), '[t]he President shall not, in the President's private capacity during the tenure of office as President, institute or continue civil proceedings against a person.' However, by Article 98(3), '[f]or purposes of clauses (1) and (2), where a law limits the time within which proceedings may be brought against a person, the term of office shall not be taken into account in calculating the period of time.'[327] It would appear from what we have discussed regarding the competence of witnesses that the president while competent is not a compellable witness.[328] Article 98(5) – (11) provide for procedure for removal of immunity and restoration thereof, where the person in question is a former president or vice president. Article 108 provides for procedure for impeachment of a sitting president. Specifically, Article 108(8)(b), where by a two thirds majority, members of parliament

[326] Chapter 88 of the Laws of Zambia.

[327] Article 98(4)-(11) provide for a detailed procedure of how presidential immunity may be removed for a person who once held the office of president who appears to have committed an offence during his tenure, a subject better suited to a book focused on Constitutional law.

[328] See Article 98(8)(9) and Article 108(9)(b) on this point. For case in which a sitting president appeared freely in his own cause, see *President Sata v Daily Nation* http://www.zambian-economist.com/2014/05/president-sata-vs-daily-nation.html retrieved on 28/2/21.

resolve that the President has committed the violations specified in the motion [of impeachment] and that the President should cease to hold office forthwith; [t]he President shall, on the passing of a resolution in accordance with—[...] (b) clause (7)(b), cease to hold office and be amenable to prosecution without the need to lift the immunity under Article 98.[329]

In *Elias Kundiona v The People*,[330] the Supreme Court observed *obiter*, concerning the compellability of the head of state as a witness, 'that a serving President, while no doubt a competent witness, could not be coerced by criminal process or sanction if he declined to co-operate because the Constitution grants [him/her] immunity.' However, it would appear from a consideration of Article 98 that once the immunity with which he is clothed under that Article is removed, as provided for under the Constitution, the president becomes, not only competent but also compellable. This issue was considered and determined in *Frederick Jacob Titus Chiluba v The Attorney General*.[331] In interpreting what then was Article 43(3) and now is Article 98(8),[332] in the High Court, the learned judge stated:

> The import of this Article is quite plain and straightforward. It simply means what it says – that the National Assembly may, in its absolute discretion, remove from the former Head of State, the veil or the protective shield placed on him by the Article for purposes of facilitating investigations into his activities while he held the office of President and subsequent prosecution for the same if such investigations establish a prima facie case against him. There is simply no other meaning apt enough that can be placed on this Article.'

The Supreme Court agreed but went further in interpreting the predecessor to Article 98 (or 108 as it now stands), Sakala CJ, as he then, reading the judgment of the Court opined as follows:

> We have anxiously considered these authorities. But after looking at the provisions of Article 43(3), we find nothing in these provisions which suggest to us that before lifting the immunity of a former President, the National Assembly should give a former President the opportunity to be heard. The provisions of Article 43(3) should not be read in isolation, but together with the other relevant provisions in the Constitution. The other relevant provisions we find are those in Article 37 dealing with impeachment of the President. Unlike the provisions dealing with removal of immunity of a former President, which do not give the right to be heard, the provisions in Article 37 dealing with impeachment of the President specifically gives the

[329] Article 108(9).

[330] [1993 – 1994] ZR 59 (SC).

[331] (SCZ Appeal No 125 of 2002).

[332] See also procedure under Article 108 for the impeachment of the president with particular reference to Article 108(9)(b).

> President the right to be heard and to be represented by Counsel. Which means that while in Article 37 the President has the right to be heard, it was never the intention of the framers of the Constitution that when the issue of removal of immunity of a former President arises, the former President would have the right to be heard. Of course, one cannot seriously argue that Article 43(3) and Article 37 conflict with each other because Constitutional provisions cannot contradict each other.
>
> The rationale for this arrangement is very easy to find. In impeachment proceedings, the National Assembly has, after going through the whole process, power to finally determine the fate of the President by its own resolution. The National Assembly can either "acquit" the impeached President or remove him from office. In proceedings to remove the immunity of a former President, the National Assembly has no power to call upon a former President to give evidence to rebut allegations against him before removal of his immunity by the National Assembly. What action would the National Assembly take after hearing a former President? The National Assembly cannot acquit or make a finding that there is a prima facie case made out against a former President and should therefore be charged with a criminal offence(s) because the National Assembly has no such powers under the Constitution. The power to determine the guilt or innocence of a person in a criminal matter is assigned to the courts by the Constitution.

It follows from the last bit of the foregoing that once immunity has been lost, prosecution may follow before a court of follow in which proceedings the president becomes a competent and compellable witness.

4.8 Diplomats

By virtue of the Diplomatic Immunities and Privileges Act[333] (DIPA), foreign diplomats enjoy extensive immunity from any court's jurisdiction. According to s 7 of DIPA which provides for 'Immunities and privileges of consulates and persons connected therewith,'

> [s]ubject to the provisions of this Act, a consular officer and a consular employee (other than persons on whom immunities and privileges are conferred by virtue of section three) shall be entitled to immunity from suit and legal process in respect of things done or omitted to be done in the course of the performance of his official duties as such, and to such inviolability of official archives and official correspondence as is necessary to comply with the terms of any treaty or other international agreement applicable to Zambia or as is recognised by the principles of customary international law and usage.

[333] Chapter 20 of the laws of Zambia.

DIPA also provides for the following:

(1) Immunities, privileges and capacities of certain international organisations and persons connected therewith.[334] The matter of immunity as provided for under s 4 of DIPA arose in *Antonio Ventriglia Manuela Ventriglia v Eastern and Southern African Trade and Development Bank.*[335] The plaintiff issued a writ out of the Commercial Registry claiming for:

  (a) A declaration that the defendant having failed to perform its obligations under the loan agreement to declare a dispute and refer the dispute for arbitration should not be seen to benefit out of its own default, and as such the purported appointment of the Receiver under the provisions of the said Agreement be declared a nullity;
  (b) An order that the dispute be declared and that the matter be referred to Arbitration as per clause 16.12 of the Loan Agreement made between the 1st and 2nd defendants;
  (c) An order for an interim and interlocutory injunction restraining the Receiver, his agents, servants, or whosoever from performing duties of a Receiver until the determination of this matter or any further Court order;
  (d) Damages for undue loss of business of the plaintiff's credibility and credit worthiness;
  (e) Damages for loss of business;
  (f) Aggravated damages;
  (g) Costs; and
  (h) Any other relief the Court may deem fit.

  Before hearing the substantive claim, the 1st respondent raised a preliminary issue under Order 14A of the Rules, of the Supreme Court and sought a declaration that the 1st respondent enjoyed absolute immunity and as such was not amenable to any Court proceeding in Zambia. The learned trial judge held that the 1st respondent did not waive its diplomatic immunity and therefore the suit against the 1st respondent was therefore a nullity. Hence the appeal. In answering the questions before the Court, specifically: (1) what was the nature of the immunity accorded to the 1st respondent? (2) what was the extent of that immunity from any suit and legal process? (3) can treaty or international law supersede our Acts of Parliament? the Supreme opined as follows:

> [...] the immunities and privileges enjoyed by treaty bodies are the same as diplomatic immunities accorded to State actors. The immunities granted to State actors in Zambia are the same as the diplomatic immunities granted to treaty

[334] S 4.

[335] SCZ Judgment No 13 of 2010.

> bodies. Hence the title of cap 20 of the Laws of Zambia says: "Diplomatic Immunities Act". Even Statutory Instrument No 123 of 1992, is titled "Diplomatic Immunities and Privileges of COMESA" So, these treaty bodies' immunities do not depend on treaties only; they have to be interpreted against the background of international law (See Article 2 of the COMESA Charter). [...] immunities conferred on treaty bodies in accordance with section 4 of cap 20, are derived from the Vienna Convention. The Vienna Convention, besides being part of statutory law is as much part of the treaty law as it is part of the international customary law. It is binding, as codified international customary law. It is binding also because it has acquired the force of custom through general practice accepted as law [....] the various Statutory Instruments that have been drawn under Section 4 of Cap 20 [...] relating to immunities and privileges cannot have different interpretation form the Vienna Convention or International Customary Law;

On the facts, however, the Supreme Court adopted the approach by Lord Denning in *Trendex,*[336] and *I congreso del Partido,*[337] and other European Courts, the Italian Courts, American Courts and Kenyan Courts and held that the learned trial judge misdirected himself in holding that the 1st respondent was covered by absolute immunity. The facts disclosed, said the Court, established with no doubt that the 1st respondent entered into a commercial transaction with the appellants and as such was not covered by the principle of absolute immunity. The principle of restrictive immunity had to be invoked.

(ii) Immunities and privileges of judges of, and suitors to, the International Court of Justice;[338] and

(iii) Diplomatic immunities of representatives attending international conferences.[339]

In terms of s 15 of that Act, '[i]f in any proceedings any question arises whether or not any person is entitled to immunities or privileges by or under the provisions of this Act, a certificate issued by or under the authority of the Minister stating any fact relevant to that question shall be conclusive evidence of that fact.'

---

[336] *Trendtex Trading Corporation Limited v Central Bank of Nigeria* [1977]1 ALL ER 88.

[337] *I congreso Del Partido* [1981] 2 ALL ER 1064.

[338] S 5.

[339] S 6.

4.9 Persons appearing either in obedience to a summons or by virtue of a warrant, or being present in court and verbally required by the court to give evidence

The position of persons appearing either in obedience to a summons or by virtue of a warrant, or being present in court and verbally required by the court to give evidence is provided for under s 150 of the Criminal Procedure Code[340] which provides under the heading *'Refractory witnesses,'* as follows:

> (1) Whenever any person, appearing either in obedience to a summons or by virtue of a warrant, or being present in court and being verbally required by the court to give evidence-
> (a) refuses to be sworn; or
> (b) having been sworn, refuses to answer any question put to him; or
> (c) refuses or neglects to produce any document or thing which he is required to produce; or
> (d) refuses to sign his deposition;
> without, in any such case, offering any sufficient excuse for such refusal or neglect, the court may adjourn the case for any period not exceeding eight days and may, in the meantime, commit such person to prison, unless he sooner consents to do what is required of him.
> (2) If such person, upon being brought before the court at or before such adjourned hearing, again refuses to do what is required of him, the court may, if it sees fit, again adjourn the case and commit him for the like period, and so again, from time to time, until such person consents to do what is so required of him.
> (3) Nothing herein contained shall affect the liability of any such person to any other punishment or proceeding for refusing or neglecting to do what is so required of him, or shall prevent the court from disposing of the case in the meantime, according to any other sufficient evidence taken before it.

The foregoing section brings within its purview, witnesses called to and present in court who then refuse to be sworn or having been sworn in refuse to answer questions or refuse to produce documents as required nay sign a deposition. Though as alluded to already, there appears to be no judicial imprint on s 150, a similar provision, namely, s 152 of the Kenyan Criminal Procedure Code[341]

[340] Chapter 88 of the Laws of Zambia.
[341] Chapter 75 of the Laws of Zambia.

has been considered in Kenya in *Republic of Kenya v Musyoka Miriti.*[342] Under those circumstances, and in the absence of good and compelling reasons or 'sufficient excuse for refusal or neglect, the court is empowered to not only adjourn the cause in question but to commit such a refractory witness to prison until he changes his mind and decides to cooperate with the proceedings. The crafting of s 150(1) and (2) would appear to suggest that this could in theory go on forever and thereby derail or stop the proceedings simply because of this refractory witness. The power of the court to imprison him may not deter a determined refractory witness from continuing with his intransigence. Under such circumstances, and according to s 150(3), the court may proceed to conduct the trial using other witnesses, documents or otherwise evidence to dispose of the case, even without the participation of the refractory witness. However, the evidence so relied on ought to be sufficient for purposes of disposing such a case. The court ought not to allow itself to proceed on insufficient evidence, and must determine the case on a fair and competent evaluation of the evidence before it and determine all matters with finality.

What may amount to 'sufficient excuse for such refusal or neglect' is not defined in s 150, nor have we had judicial pronouncements on the matter in this jurisdiction. It is however, not too much of a stretch to submit that such sufficient reasons may include a genuine fear of reprisals, and the fact that police have not offered such protection to the witness under the circumstances, as to enable him to freely give evidence given the threats to his life or those of his family members. It may be for religious reasons, though swearing in can also be done through affirmation as discussed elsewhere in this text. It may, as regards a failure to produce documents, be that the witness has had no access or continues not to have access to such documents because they have never been under his custody, control or power. It may well be that the evidence of which it is sought for him to give; is privileged and he has no authority to speak to such matters of which he is asked as they may concern diplomatic business; public policy considerations; or indeed state security or that any evidence given may jeorpadise ongoing investigations. It may well be that the witness while competent is not compellable as in the case of spouses under s 157 of the Criminal Procedure Code; or that he is a child whose evidence is not acceptable because he does not qualify to offer such evidence under s 78(1)(2) of the Children's Code.[343]

---

[342] (2011) eKLR; (Criminal Case 240 of 2008); It has also been shown in that case that a refractory witness is not the same as a hostile witness. Thus, where as in this case the witness ought ordinarily to be considered as a hostile witness, the prosecution ought to apply to cross examine such a witness. '[w]here the prosecution wishes to show that its witness has retracted previous statements made by him to the police, the prosecutor must apply to cross examine his witness as to such previous statements made by him to the police, the prosecutor must apply to cross examine his witness as to such previous statement [....] The witness will then be cross examined by the defence. The purpose of such cross-examination by the prosecution may extend, not only to establishing that the witness retracted his previous statement. The prosecution will be at liberty to cross examine their witness as to his credibility accuracy and veracity among other things. If the prosecution succeeds in shaking the credibility and injuring the character of its witness. The witness will be treated as a hostile witness.'

[343] Act No 12 of 2022.

4.10 Oaths[344] and affirmations

While today a witness may give evidence by oath or affirmation, in years gone by, only witnesses who would give evidence on oath were permitted to do so.[345] The oath was a guarantor of truth and as such could not be made optional if only to protect society and the court system from lies and paganism or atheism.[346] Nor would those with an interest in the outcome of the case, however trifling nor a past criminal conviction. A rather curious consequence of this rule was that litigants were barred from testifying in their own cause.

After 1640 those accused of felonies deserving capital punishment upon their guilt being proved were grudgingly permitted the right to call witnesses as can be seen from the fact that such witnesses could not give evidence on oath which was predicated on the notion, as we have already seen above, that witnesses that contradicted prosecution witnesses were lying.

The 19th century also witnessed the gradual removal of religious based restrictions relating to the competence of witnesses we discussed earlier. The Common Procedure Act 1854 provided for affirmations as an acceptable alternative to taking religious oaths. An amendment to the Act saw the foregoing extended to criminal proceedings in 1861. The Evidence Further Amendment Act 1869 permitted those refused to take an oath other than for religious reasons to do so by way of affirmation.

In this jurisdiction the matter of oaths in proceedings before the High Court is provided for under s 36[347] of the High Court Act[348] in the following terms:

> (1) Whenever an oath is required to be taken under the provisions of this or any other law, or in order to comply with any such law, the following provisions shall apply:
>
> (a) The person taking the oath shall hold, if a Christian, a copy of the Gospels of the Four Evangelists or of the New Testament, or, if a Jew, a copy of the Old Testament, in his uplifted right hand, or, if he be

[344] There exists on our statute books, the Official Oaths Act Chapter 5 of the Laws of Zambia which provides for oaths to be taken and subscribed by various office holders, and to provide for matters connected with or incidental to the foregoing. We are not concerned with that Act here. Quite apart from that, s 37 of the Subordinate Courts Act, chapter 28 of the Laws of Zambia provides for oaths as regards clerks of Court in the following terms: '[e]very clerk of the court shall, before entering upon the duties of his office, take an oath for the faithful performance of his duty in the form following: "I do swear I will truly, faithfully and honestly execute the office of clerk of the court without fear, favour or affection for anyone. So, help me God." This too is not our focus; As to the class of witnesses that need not be sworn in order to give testimony, see *Perry v Gibson* (1834), 1 Ad and El 48; Order 38 Rule 1(6), RSC; *Hickman v Berens* (1895) 2 Ch 638 but see *Pioneer Concrete Gold Coast Pty Ltd v Cassidy* (No 2) (1969) Qd R 290; *R v Secretary of State for India, Ex parte Ezekiel* (1941) 2 KB 169, [1941] 2 All ER 546; *George Bienga v The People* [1978] ZR 32 (HC).

[345] It was thought at the time that only witnesses with a religious affiliation could be considered responsible members of society and as such credible witnesses. The system could not fathom a witness without a religious or theist inclinations to give credible evidence without professing faith in a higher authority who punished wrong doers or liars. Without accountability to a deity and fear of retribution for false testimony, the theory may have gone, how could one be trusted to tell the truth?

[346] See the comment by Taylor, 1872, Vol II, para 1248.

[347] As amended by No 43 of 1961.

[348] Chapter 27 of the Laws of Zambia.

physically incapable of so doing, he may hold such copy otherwise, or, if necessary such copy may be held before him by the officer administering the oath, and shall say or repeat after such officer the words "I swear by Almighty God that . . ." followed by the words of the oath prescribed by law or by the practice of the court, as the case may be:
Provided that if any person desires to take the oath in the form and manner in which an oath is usually administered in Scotland, he shall be permitted to do so.

(b) If the person taking the oath is neither a Christian nor a Jew, he may take the oath in any manner which he declares to be, or accepts as, binding on his conscience or which is lawful according to any law, and in particular he may do so by raising his right hand and saying or repeating after the officer administering the oath the words "I swear by Almighty God that . . ." followed by the words of the oath prescribed by law or by the practice of the court, as the case may be:
Provided that if the person taking the oath is physically incapable of raising his right hand, he may say or repeat the words of the oath without raising his right hand.

(c) If any person shall express any objection to taking an oath or desires to make an affirmation in lieu thereof, he may make such affirmation without being further questioned as to the grounds of such objection or desire, or otherwise, and in such case there shall be substituted for the words "I swear by Almighty God" aforesaid the words "I do solemnly and sincerely affirm" and such consequential variations of form as may be necessary shall thereupon be made.

(2) Notwithstanding any other provision contained in this section, any person may be required to make an affirmation in the form specified in paragraph (c) of subsection (1) if it is not reasonably practicable to administer an oath to him in the manner appropriate to his religious belief, and for the purposes of this subsection "reasonably practicable" means reasonably practicable without inconvenience or delay.

(3) Where any oath has been duly administered and taken, the fact that the person to whom such oath was administered had, at the time of taking such oath, no religious belief, or had a religious belief other than that to which the oath taken normally applies, shall not for any purpose affect the validity of such oath.

(4) For the purposes of this section, "officer" means any person duly authorised by law to administer oaths, and shall include

> any Assistant Registrar, Deputy Assistant Registrar and official interpreter administering an oath in the presence of a Judge or the Registrar or other person authorised by any law to administer oaths.

Under s 109 of the Penal Code:[349]

> [a]ny person who swears falsely or makes a false affirmation or declaration before any person authorised to administer an oath or take a declaration upon a matter of public concern under such circumstances that the false swearing or declaration if committed in a judicial proceeding would have amounted to perjury, is guilty of a misdemeanour.

[349] Chapter 87 of the Laws of Zambia.

5

JUDICIAL DISCRETION AND THE EXCLUSION OF EVIDENCE

5.1 Introduction

The exercise of discretion in so far as the admissibility of evidence is concerned is at the centre of a judge's functions during the course of trial. The exercise of such discretion must be seen within the context of the concept of the court's supervisory function over legal proceedings, and its duty to ensure that any trial before it is fairly conducted. The fact that evidence meets the legal threshold of admissibility does not in and of itself preclude a judge from using his discretion to exclude the evidence in question. While the use of discretion is employed in both civil and criminal trials, it is in the latter that, the contested criminal trial, where at the core will be the conduct of investigations leading to the trial of the accused, that the court's use of discretion is most visible, and its impact mainly felt in real time. During the criminal trial, the court may be called upon to exercise its discretion on grounds that admission of the evidence now impugned, may seriously affect the fairness of the said trial.There are several reasons why a magistrate/judge as the case may be, may be called upon to exercise his discretion. Objections to the admissibility of evidence arise generally as regards items gathered during the investigative process. The items to which this relates may include but are not limited to things like sperm samples or such like fluids resulting from a sexual encounter; covert recordings of the accused; and recordings from a police interview containing incriminating evidence. The objection will thus ordinarily be raised by the defence in criminal proceedings. The reasons for the objections may vary but they ordinarily arise from the conduct of the police during the investigation that led to the charging and eventual trial of the accused during which the objection is raised. Specifically, that the police obtained the evidence in question by employing improper or illegal means. In using his discretion in this context, a judge/magistrate will have to take into account not only the objections in and of themselves, but whether said objections have merit based on the wide-ranging power that is reposed in the police to ably investigate matters.

5.2 The power of the police to investigate

5.2.1 *A common law history*

At common law police were clothed with very few investigatory powers. The said powers were limited to the following:

(i) Preliminary work in gathering evidence through the following means:
   (a) Searching suspects; and
   (b) Searching premises tied to the offence being investigated.
(ii) Power of arrest and detain suspects.

We must state the context in which the foregoing powers were exercised by the police. For starters, the power to search persons and the relevant premises could only be exercised by the police following an arrest. In addition, and curiously, the police had no power to interview suspects (which was deemed to be a job for magistrates only) nor was the suspect under any obligation to answer any questions put to him by the police if no arrest had been effected. The police could not even search suspects or their property where no arrest had been effected. Once arrested, a feature that still remains today in our legal system, the arrested person had to be taken before a magistrate within 24 hours of his arrest. Following the arrest, the police could then proceed to search the suspect as well as premises relevant to their investigations.

During the 20th century changes to the police's investigatory powers began to be made, albeit piecemeal. As a first step the police began interviewing suspects during the subsistence of investigations. From 1912, judges' rules regulated the treatment and questioning of witnesses.

5.2.2 *Relevant provisions in the Criminal Procedure Code*[1]

Such changes as were made to police powers are in this jurisdiction mainly provided for in the Criminal Procedure Code.[2]

5.2.2.1 *Arrest, Escape and Retaking Arrest Generally*

(i) Arrest, how made:

It is provided in 18(1) that [i]n making an arrest, the police officer or other person making the same shall actually touch or confine the body of the person to be arrested, unless there be a submission to the custody by word or action. By s 18(2), [i]f such person forcibly resists the endeavour to arrest him, or attempts to evade the arrest, such police officer or other person may use all means reasonably necessary to effect the arrest. The foregoing must be read together with s 21 wherein it is provided that '[t]he person arrested shall not be subjected to more restraint than is necessary to prevent his escape.'

(ii) Search of place entered by person sought to be arrested

In terms of s 19(1), [i]f any person acting under a warrant of arrest, or any police officer having authority to arrest, has reason to believe that the person to be arrested has entered into or is within any place, the person residing in or being in charge of such place shall, on demand of such person acting as aforesaid

[1] Chapter 88 of the Laws of Zambia.

[2] Chapter 88 of the Laws of Zambia.

or such police officer, allow him free ingress thereto and afford all reasonable facilities for a search therein. By s 19(2), [i]f ingress to such place cannot be obtained under subsection (1), it shall be lawful, in any case, for a person acting under a warrant, and, in any case in which a warrant may issue, but cannot be obtained without affording the person to be arrested an opportunity to escape, for a police officer to enter such place and search therein, and, in order to effect an entrance into such place, to break open any outer or inner door or window of any house or place, whether that of the person to be arrested or of any other person, or otherwise effect entry into such house or place, if, after notification of his authority and purpose, and demand of admittance duly made, he cannot otherwise obtain admittance.

(iii) Power to break out of any house for purposes of liberation

According to s 20, [a]ny police officer or other person authorised to make an arrest may break out of any house or place in order to liberate himself or any other person who, having lawfully entered for the purpose of making an arrest, is detained therein.

(iv) Search of arrested persons

In terms of s 22, [w]henever a person is arrested- (a) by a police officer under a warrant which does not provide for the taking of bail or under a warrant which provides for the taking of bail and the person arrested cannot furnish bail; or (b) without warrant, or by a private person under a warrant, and the person arrested cannot legally be admitted to bail or is unable to furnish bail; the police officer making the arrest or, when the arrest is made by a private person, the police officer to whom he makes over the person arrested may search such person and place in safe custody all articles, other than necessary wearing apparel, found upon him.

(v) Power of police officer to detain and search vehicles and persons in certain circumstances

It is provided in s 23 that [a]ny police officer may stop, search and detain any vessel, aircraft or vehicle in or upon which there shall be reason to suspect that anything stolen or unlawfully obtained may be found and also any person who may be reasonably suspected of having in his possession or conveying in any manner anything stolen or unlawfully obtained, and may seize any such thing.[3]

(vi) Power to seize offensive weapons

According to s 25, [t]he police officer or other person making any arrest may take from the person arrested any offensive weapons which he has about his

[3] As regards the mode of searching women, s 24 provides that whenever it is necessary to cause a woman to be searched, the search shall be made by another woman with strict regard to decency.

person and shall deliver all weapons so taken to the court or officer before which or whom the officer or person making the arrest is required by law to produce the person arrested.

5.2.2.2 Arrest without warrant

(i) Arrest by police officer without warrant

According to s 26, [a]ny police officer may, without an order from a magistrate and without a warrant, arrest-

(a) any person whom he suspects, upon reasonable grounds, of having committed a cognizable offence;
(b) any person who commits a breach of the peace in his presence;
(c) any person who obstructs a police officer while in the execution of his duty, or who has escaped or attempts to escape from lawful custody;
(d) any person in whose possession anything is found which may reasonably be suspected to be stolen property, or who may reasonably be suspected of having committed an offence with reference to such thing;
(e) any person whom he suspects, upon reasonable grounds, of being a deserter from the Defence Force;
(f) any person whom he finds in any highway, yard or other place during the night, and whom he suspects, upon reasonable grounds of having committed or being about to commit a felony;
(g) any person whom he suspects, upon reasonable grounds, of having been concerned in any act committed at any place out of Zambia which, if committed in Zambia, would have been punishable as an offence, and for which he is, under the Extradition Act, or otherwise, liable to be apprehended and detained in Zambia;
(h) any person having in his possession, without lawful excuse, the burden of proving which excuse shall lie on such person, any implement of housebreaking;
(i) any released convict committing a breach of any provision prescribed by section three hundred and eighteen or of any rule made thereunder;
(j) any person for whom he has reasonable cause to believe a warrant of arrest has been issued.

(ii) Arrest of vagabonds, habitual robbers

In terms of s 27, [a]ny officer in charge of a police station may, in like manner, arrest or cause to be arrested-

(a) any person found taking precautions to conceal his presence within the limits of such station, under circumstances which afford reason to believe that he is taking such precautions with a view to committing a cognisable offence;

(b) any person, within the limits of such station, who has no ostensible means of subsistence, or who cannot give a satisfactory account of himself;

(c) any person who is, by repute, a habitual robber, housebreaker or thief, or a habitual receiver of stolen property, knowing it to be stolen, or who, by repute, habitually commits extortion, or, in order to commit extortion, habitually puts or attempts to put persons in fear of injury.

(iii) Procedure when police officer deputes subordinate to arrest without warrant

By s 28, [w]hen any officer in charge of a police station requires any officer subordinate to him to arrest without a warrant (otherwise than in such officer's presence) any person who may lawfully be arrested without a warrant, he shall deliver to the officer required to make the arrest an order in writing, specifying the person to be arrested and the offence or other cause for which the arrest is to be made.

(iv) Refusal to give name and residence

According to s 29(1), when any person who, in the presence of a police officer, has committed or has been accused of committing a non-cognizable offence refuses, on the demand of such officer, to give his name and residence, or gives a name or residence which such officer has reason to believe to be false, he may be arrested by such officer, in order that his name or residence may be ascertained. By s 29(2), when the true name and residence of such person have been ascertained, he shall be released on his executing a bond, with or without sureties, to appear before a magistrate, if so required: Provided that, if such person is not resident in Zambia, the bond shall be secured by a surety or sureties resident in Zambia. In terms of s 29(3), [s]hould the true name and residence of such person not be ascertained within twenty-four hours from the time of arrest, or should he fail to execute the bond, or, if so required, to furnish sufficient sureties, he shall forthwith be taken before the nearest magistrate having jurisdiction. It is provided in s 29(4) that [a]ny police officer may arrest without a warrant any person who in his presence has committed a non-cognizable offence, if reasonable grounds exist for believing that, except by the arrest of the person offending, he could not be found or made answerable to justice.

(v) Disposal of persons arrested by police officer

By s 30, [a] police officer making an arrest without a warrant shall, without unnecessary delay and subject to the provisions herein contained as to bail, take or send the person arrested before a magistrate having jurisdiction in the case or before an officer in charge of a police station.

(vi) Arrest by private persons

According to s 31(1), [a]ny private person may arrest any person who, in his presence, commits a cognizable offence, or whom he reasonably suspects of having committed a felony. It is further provided in s 31(2) that [p]ersons found committing any offence involving injury to property may be arrested without a warrant by the owner of the property or his servants or persons authorised by him.

(vii) Disposal of persons arrested by private person

According to s 32(1), [a]ny private person arresting any other person without a warrant shall, without unnecessary delay, make over the person so arrested to a police officer, or, in the absence of a police officer, shall take such person to the nearest police station. Section 32(2) provides as follows: if there is reason to believe that such person comes under the provisions of section twenty-six, a police officer shall re-arrest him. In terms of s 32(3), [i]f there is reason to believe that he has committed a non-cognisable offence, and he refuses, on the demand of a police officer, to give his name and residence, or gives a name or residence which such officer has reason to believe to be false, he shall be dealt with under the provisions of section twenty-nine. If there is no sufficient reason to believe that he has committed any offence, he shall be at once released.

(viii) Detention of persons arrested without warrant

By s 33(1), [w]hen any person has been taken into custody without a warrant for an offence other than an offence punishable with death, the officer in charge of the police station to which such person shall be brought may, in any case, and shall, if it does not appear practicable to bring such person before an appropriate competent court within twenty-four hours after he was so taken into custody, inquire into the case, and, unless the offence appears to the officer to be of a serious nature, release the person, on his executing a bond, with or without sureties, for a reasonable amount, to appear before a competent court at a time and place to be named in the bond: but, where any person is retained in custody, he shall be brought before a competent court as soon as practicable. Notwithstanding anything contained in this section, an officer in charge of a police station may release a person arrested on suspicion on a charge of committing any offence, when, after due police inquiry, insufficient evidence is, in his opinion, disclosed on which to proceed with the charge.[4]

(ix) Police to report apprehensions

By s 34, [o]fficers in charge of police stations shall report to the nearest magistrate the cases of all persons arrested without warrant within the limits

[4] By s 33(2) in this section, "competent court" means any court having jurisdiction to try or hold a preliminary inquiry into the offence for which the person has been taken into custody.

of their respective stations, whether such persons have been admitted to bail or not.

(x) Offence committed in magistrate's presence

According to s 35 [w]hen any offence is committed in the presence of a magistrate within the local limits of his jurisdiction, he may himself arrest or order any person to arrest the offender, and may, thereupon, subject to the provisions herein contained as to bail, commit the offender to custody.

5.2.2.3 Escape and Retaking Arrest by Magistrate

(i) Escape and retaking arrest by magistrate

According to s 36, [a]ny magistrate may, at any time, arrest or direct the arrest, in his presence, within the local limits of his jurisdiction, of any person for whose arrest he is competent, at the time and in the circumstances, to issue a warrant.

(ii) Recapture of person escaping

The recapture of persons escaping from custody is provided for in s 37 in the following terms: '[i]f a person in lawful custody escapes or is rescued, the person from whose custody he escapes or is rescued may immediately pursue and arrest him in any place in Zambia.'[5]

5.2.3 *The common law and the concept of discretion*

5.2.3.1 The English position

It must be recalled that where questions of admissibility of evidence are raised, the court is called upon to determine the questions in line with the general criteria premised on the two-pronged requirements of relevance and reliability. In addition, the court would have to consider the specific criteria applied to the specific class of evidence in question. In the circumstances and depending on the factual matrix of the scenario the court is faced with, it will be important to note that the mere fact that the particular item of evidence is relevant and reliable ought to generally render it admissible. This is, however, not always the case and just as well. It is quite possible that relevant and reliable evidence is still deemed inadmissible and therefore liable to be excluded for other reasons including, but not limited to a dubious origin, because it has been obtained in a manner that raises questions, were it to be admitted, regarding the fairness of the trial. It has therefore been observed as follows by the Privy Council in *Kuruma Son of Kaniu v R*,[6] that where an illegal search of the accused disclosed

[5] In terms of s 38, [t]he provisions of sections nineteen and twenty shall apply to arrests under the last preceding section, although the person making any such arrest is not acting under a warrant, and is not a police officer having authority to arrest.

[6] [1955] 1 All ER 236.

unlawful possession of ammunition, '[n]o doubt in a criminal case the judge always has a discretion to disallow evidence if the strict rules of admissibility would operate unfairly against the accused.'[7] Even so, at common law, courts generally chose, and to this day still ordinarily choose to concern themselves only with the question of whether the general criteria hereinbefore referenced has been met, and put to the side the origin of the evidence itself (an extraneous issue in this context) so far as doing so does not prejudice the accused. Below, we consider a few authorities that demonstrate the foregoing stance.

In *Kuruma Son of Kaniu v R,*[8] the appellant, a Kenyan, was stopped at a police road block and was searched by two police officers. This was illegal because neither of them was of the rank of inspector or above as required by law. The police alleged that they found a pocket knife and two rounds of ammunition on the appellant. He was convicted of unlawful possession of ammunition, an offence which carried the death sentence. It was held as follows, *Per* Lord Goddard:

> In their Lordships' opinion the test to be applied in considering whether evidence is admissible is whether it is relevant to the matters in issue. If it is, it is admissible and the court is not concerned with how the evidence was obtained. While this proposition may not have been stated in so many words in any English case there are decisions which support it, and in their Lordships' opinion it is plainly right in principle.[9] However, the court retains a wide discretion to exclude evidence, and: There can be no difference in principle for this purpose between a civil and a criminal case. No doubt in a criminal case the judge always has a discretion to disallow evidence if the strict rules of admissibility would operate unfairly against an accused [....] If, for instance, some admission of some piece of evidence, e.g., a document, had been obtained from a defendant by a trick, no doubt the judge might properly rule it out [...] In their Lordships' opinion, when it is a question of the admission of evidence strictly it is not whether the method by which it was obtained is tortious but excusable but whether what has been obtained is irrelevant to the issue being tried.[10]

In *Jeffrey v Black,*[11] the respondent was arrested for the theft of a sandwich from a public house. Before he was charged the police, officers told the respondent that they intended to search his home. The respondent took them to his home and unlocked the door. The police officers then searched his room, finding both cannabis and cannabis resin. The respondent was then charged with unlawful possession of cannabis and cannabis resin. At the hearing the justices

[7] [1955] 1 All ER at 239, [1955] AC at 204 *per* Lord Goddard CJ in giving the reasons for the dismissal of the appeal.

[8] [1955] 1 All ER 236.

[9] See *R v Leatham* [1961] 8 Cox CC 498.

[10] For support, his lordship referred to, among others, the following authorities: *Lloyd v Mostyn* [1842] 10 M&W 478; *Calcraft v Guest* [1898] 1 QB 759; *Elias v Passmore* [1934] 2 KB 164; *Noor Mohammed v The King* [1949] AC 182; *Harris v Director of Public Prosecutions* [1952] AC 694; *HM Advocate v Turnbull* [1951] C 96.

[11] [1978] 1 All ER 555.

found as a fact that the respondent had not given his consent to the search of his room and upheld a defence submission that the evidence so found was inadmissible, and they dismissed the charges. The prosecutor appealed. It was held as follows:

(i) A police officer who arrested a suspect for an offence at one place had no authority without a search warrant or the suspect's consent to search his house at another place when the contents of the house on the face of them bore no relation to the offence charged or the evidence required to support it.[12]

(ii) A judge at a criminal trial had a discretion not to allow evidence to be called by the prosecution which would be unfair or oppressive but the discretion to exclude evidence should be exercised only in exceptional cases. The fact that evidence had been obtained in an irregular manner was not of itself sufficient ground for the exercise of the discretion in favour of the defendant.[13] Accordingly, the justices had exercised their discretion wrongly in excluding the evidence. The appeal would therefore be allowed and the case remitted for rehearing before a different bench.

It appears to follow that there is no automatic discretion at law for automatic exclusion of evidence simply because the police have acted illegally or more specifically, beyond or/and outside their powers.[14] It seems to be the case that under such circumstances, facts permitting, a court ought to consider whether evidence which has been deemed relevant and as such, ordinarily admissible if so admitted, would be prejudicial to the accused and in the main, negatively affect the overall fairness of the trial in question, offend the dignity of the court, taint justice and expose the judicial system to scorn. The discretion to exclude evidence, it is submitted, was one to be deployed sparingly. Lord Widgery CJ[15] observed as follows:

> At this point it would seem that the appellant ought to succeed in his appeal because at this point what he appears to have shown is that the magistrates were wrong in failing to recognise the law as stated in *Kuruma Son of Kaniu v Reginam.*[16] But that is not in fact the end of the matter because the magistrates sitting in this case, like any other criminal tribunal in England sitting under the English law, have a general discretion to decline to allow any evidence to be called by the prosecution if they think that it would be unfair or oppressive to allow that to be done. In getting an assessment of what this discretion means, magistrates ought, I think, to stress to themselves that the discretion is not a discretion which arises only in drug cases. It is not a discretion which arises only in cases where police can enter premises. It is a discretion which every criminal judge has all the time in respect of all the evidence which is tendered by the prosecution. It would probably give magistrates some idea of the extent to which this discretion is used if one asks them whether they are appreciative of the fact that they have the discretion anyway, and it may well be that a number of experienced magistrates would be quite ignorant of

> the possession of this discretion. That gives them, I hope, some idea of how relatively rarely it is exercised in our courts. But if the case is exceptional, if the case is such that not only have the police officers entered without authority, but they have been guilty of trickery or they have misled someone, or they have been oppressive or they have been unfair, or in other respects they have behaved in a manner which is morally reprehensible, then it is open to the justices to apply their discretion and decline to allow the particular evidence to be let in as part of the trial.
>
> I cannot stress the point too strongly that this is a very exceptional situation, and the simple, unvarnished fact that evidence was obtained by police officers who had gone in without bothering to get a search warrant is not enough to justify the magistrates in exercising their discretion to keep the evidence out.

In about a year or so following the decision in *Black*,[17] the extent of the scope of a judge's discretion again arose in *R v Sang*.[18] The appellant was charged with conspiring with others to utter forged United States banknotes. On his arraignment he pleaded not guilty to the charge. Before the case for the Crown was opened, counsel for the appellant applied to the court to hold a trial within a trial in order that it might consider whether the involvement of the appellant in the offence charged arose out of the activities of an agent provocateur.[19] He said that he hoped at such trial to establish, by cross-examination of a police officer and by evidence-in-chief from an alleged police informer, that the appellant had been induced to commit the offence by an informer acting on the instructions of the police and that but for such persuasion the appellant would not have committed the offence. Counsel then hoped to persuade the judge to rule, in the exercise of his discretion, that the Crown should not be allowed to lead any evidence of the commission of the offence thus incited, and to direct that a verdict of not guilty be returned. Without hearing the evidence, the judge ruled that he had no discretion to exclude the evidence. The appellant retracted his plea of not guilty, pleaded guilty and was sentenced to a term of imprisonment. His appeal against the judge's ruling was dismissed by the Court of Appeal. On appeal to the House of Lords, it was held as follows: (i) As part of the judge's function at a criminal trial was to ensure that the accused received a fair trial according to law, the judge always had discretion to refuse to admit evidence if in his opinion its prejudicial effect outweighed its probative value. (ii) Because the court was not concerned with how evidence

[17] [1978] 1 All ER 555.

[18] [1979] 2 All ER 1222 at 1231, *per* Lord Diplock confirming the Court of appeal decision in *R v Sang; R v Mangan* [1979] 2 All ER 46.

[19] The term agent provocateur (French for 'inciting agent') refers to a person who commits a crime or one who acts to lure another to, among other things, commit, an illegal act or indeed deceitfully incriminate them in involvement in an unlawful act, for purposes of ruining the reputation of the person lured or with the clear intention of bringing legal action against, the person or group targeted target, and to which the person lured belongs or is perceived to belong to, such as a political party, a demonstration, a union, a club by whatever name called, and whatever it agenda, or indeed a company. In jurisdictions where conspiracy to commit a crime is a grave offence, it is enough to lure or/and entrap the target into discussing and/or planning of an illegal act. In that context actually preparing for or carrying out the crime is unnecessary: see *Edward Jack Shamwana and 7 Others v The People* (SCZ Judgment No 12 of 1985).

was obtained but merely with how it was used by the prosecution at the trial, a judge had no discretion, except in the case of admissions, confessions and evidence obtained from the accused after the commission of the offence, to refuse to admit relevant admissible evidence merely because it had been obtained by improper or unfair means. If evidence against the accused had been improperly obtained by the police by the use of an agent provocateur or by a policeman and an informer inciting the accused to commit the crime alleged that was not a ground on which the judge could exercise his discretion to exclude the evidence, although it could be a factor in mitigating the sentence imposed on the accused and might also be a matter for civil or disciplinary action against the police or for criminal proceedings against the policeman and the informer as principal offenders. It followed that what was effectively a defence of entrapment (a doctrine which had no place in English law) could not be accepted by the judge by means of the procedural device of exercising his discretion to exclude the prosecution's evidence of the commission of the crime. (iii) There was therefore no justification for the exercise of the discretion to exclude the evidence, whether or not it had been obtained as a result of the activities of an agent provocateur, and it followed that the appeal would be dismissed.[20] Specifically, Lord Diplock opined as follows:[21]

> What it really involves is a claim to a judicial discretion to acquit an accused of any offences in connection with which the conduct of the police incurs the disapproval of the judge. The conduct of the police where it has involved the use of an agent provocateur may well be a matter to be taken into consideration in mitigation of sentence; but under the English system of criminal justice, it does not give rise to any discretion on the part of the judge himself to acquit the accused or to direct the jury to do so, notwithstanding that he is guilty of the offence [....]
>
> Ought your Lordships to go further and to hold that the discretion extends more widely than this, as the comparatively recent dicta to which I have already referred suggest? What has been regarded as the fountain-head of all subsequent dicta on this topic is the statement by Lord Goddard CJ delivering the advice of the Privy Council in *Kuruma Son of Kaniu v R.*[22] That was a case in which the evidence of unlawful possession of ammunition by the accused was obtained as a result of an illegal search of his person. The Board held that this evidence was admissible and had rightly been admitted; but Lord Goddard CJ, although he had earlier said that if evidence is admissible 'the court is not concerned with how the evidence was obtained', nevertheless went on to say:[23]

[20] Editor's notes: For official collaboration in crime, see 11 Halsbury's Laws (4th Edn) para 47, and for cases on the subject, see 14(1) Digest (Reissue) 98, 651–653; For submissions on the admissibility of evidence, see 11 Halsbury's Laws (4th Edn) para 283; For the court's discretion to admit or reject evidence wrongfully obtained, see 17 ibid para 12, and for a case on the subject, see 14(2) Digest (Reissue) 469, 3913.

[21] *R v Sang* [1979] 2 All ER 1222 at 1231, *per* Lord Diplock.

[22] [1955] 1 All ER 236 at 239, [1955] AC 197 at 204.

[23] [1955] 1 All ER 236 at 239, [1955] AC 197 at 204.

> No doubt in a criminal case the judge always has a discretion to disallow evidence if the strict rules of admissibility would operate unfairly against the accused [....][24] If, for instance, some admission of some piece of evidence, e.g., a document, had been obtained from a defendant by a trick, no doubt the judge might properly rule it out.

[...] That statement was not, in my view, ever intended to acknowledge the existence of any wider discretion than to exclude (1) admissible evidence which would probably have a prejudicial influence on the minds of the jury that would be out of proportion to its true evidential value and (2) evidence tantamount to a self-incriminatory admission which was obtained from the defendant, after the offence had been committed, by means which would justify a judge in excluding an actual confession which had the like self-incriminating effect.

Outside this limited field in which for historical reasons the function of the trial judge extended to imposing sanctions for improper conduct on the part of the prosecution before the commencement of the proceedings in inducing the accused by threats, favour or trickery to provide evidence against himself your Lordships should, I think, make it clear that the function of the judge at a criminal trial as respects the admission of evidence is to ensure that the accused has a fair trial according to law. It is no part of a judge's function to exercise disciplinary powers over the police or prosecution as respects the way in which evidence to be used at the trial is obtained by them. If it was obtained illegally there will be a remedy in civil law; if it was obtained legally but in breach of the rules of conduct for the police, this is a matter for the appropriate disciplinary authority to deal with. What the judge at the trial is concerned with is not how the evidence sought to be adduced by the prosecution has been obtained but with how it is used by the prosecution at the trial.

[...] I would accordingly answer the question certified in terms which have been suggested by my noble and learned friend, Viscount Dilhorne, in the course of our deliberations on this case. (1) A trial judge in a criminal trial has always a discretion to refuse to admit evidence if in his opinion its prejudicial effect outweighs its probative value. (2) Save with regard to admissions and confessions and generally with regard to evidence obtained from the accused after commission of the offence, he has no discretion to refuse to admit relevant admissible evidence on the ground that it was obtained by improper or unfair means. The court is not concerned with how it was obtained. It is no ground for the exercise of discretion to exclude that the evidence was obtained as the result of the activities of an agent provocateur.

---

[24] This was emphasised in the case before this *Board of Noor Mohamed v R* [1949] 1 All ER 365 at 370, [1949] AC 182 at 192], and in the recent case in the House of Lords of *Harris v Director of Public Prosecutions* [1952] 1 All ER 1044 at 1048, [1952] AC 694 at 707, *per* Viscount Simon].

Sang[25] is a significant authority in several respects.[26] It makes clear what the job of the judge during trial is and is not. That job is to ensure that the accused person has, so far as this is possible and within the confines of the general law, procedural and judicial discretion, a fair trial. In order to fulfil his judicial functions, the judge need not and is indeed not expected or required to go to the ends of the earth to usurp the administrative responsibilities that properly lie within the police command and more broadly at the Police Complaints Commission.[27] The accused, where impropriety is clear but which impropriety such as illegal searches has occurred does not prejudice him, has as a remedy in civil action against the individual police officer or the Attorney General or both as the case may be. In *Sang*,[28] the House of Lords did however make a distinction between improper conduct by the police to obtain evidence by way of illegal searches away from the police station, and impropriety during an interview at the police station as a result of which the police obtain a confession. The former situation while improper, does not, as does the latter interfere with the constitutional right in criminal cases for an accused person not to incriminate himself. The point worth repeating, quoting Lord Diplock is therefore this: '[h] owever, much the judge may dislike the way in which a particular piece of evidence was obtained before proceedings were commenced, if it is admissible evidence probative of the accused's guilt it is no part of his judicial function to exclude it for this reason.'

What the judge ought to concern himself with is the fairness of the trial and that, according to Lord Diplock is satisfied when the following are present:

> A fair trial according to law involves, in the case of a trial on indictment, that it should take place before a judge [...]; that the case against the accused should be proved to the satisfaction of the [court] beyond all reasonable doubt on evidence that is admissible in law; and, as a corollary to this, that there should be excluded from the [court] information about the accused which is likely to have an influence on [the court's mind] prejudicial to the accused which is out of proportion to the true probative value of admissible evidence conveying that information. If these conditions are fulfilled and the [judge properly applies his mind to] the law applicable to the case, the requirement that the accused should have a fair trial according to law is [...] satisfied [...]

Further, his lordship sought to reiterate what the phraseology 'fair trial' meant which is that those that seek to determine whether a trial fits the bill, should take a holistic approach to the question. According to Lord Diplock:

---

[25] [1979] 2 All ER 1222 at 1231, *per* Lord Diplock confirming the Court of appeal decision in *R v Sang; R v Mangan* [1979] 2 All ER 46.

[26] Though it must now be read within the context of s 78 of the Police and Criminal Evidenced Act (PACE) 1984 which reflects the spirit of Lord Scarman's dissenting judgment in *R v Sang* [1979] 2 All ER 1222 at 1247d-1248c and the now common place application of the doctrine of abuse of process; see also *R v Christou* [1992] 4 All ER 559 at 564e-j *per* Lord Taylor CJ.

[27] See Article 226 of the Constitution.

[28] [1979] 2 All ER 1222.

> [...] the fairness of a trial according to law is not all one-sided: it requires that those who are undoubtedly guilty should be convicted as well as that those about whose guilt there is any reasonable doubt should be acquitted. However much the judge may dislike the way in which a particular piece of evidence was obtained before proceedings were commenced, if it is admissible evidence probative of the accused's guilt it is no part of his judicial function to exclude it for this reason.[29]

At the core of the decision in *Sang*[30] are limits to the use of discretion by trial courts at common law. In *Sang*[31] Lord Diplock only envisaged two scenarios in which evidence, including that which is improperly obtained, may be excluded:

(i) Where the prejudice to the accused person of admitting such evidence will outweigh its probative significance; and

(ii) Where the evidence in question is based on a confession or similar evidence improperly obtained by the police during investigations.

5.2.3.2 *The Zambian position*

The leading authority in this jurisdiction is that of *Liswaniso v The People.*[32] The applicant, an Inspector of Police, was convicted of official corruption, the allegation being that he corruptly received a sum of K80 in cash as consideration for the release of an impounded motor car belonging to the complainant. The evidence on which the applicant was convicted was obtained by means of a trap; the handing over of the currency notes in question by the complainant was pre-arranged with the police, and they were recovered from the complainant's house during a search conducted pursuant to a search warrant. It was common cause that at the time the police officer in question applied for the search warrant to be issued he swore that the money in question was in the applicant's house when in fact it was in that officer's possession. It was argued on behalf of the applicant that the search warrant was invalid and the resultant search illegal, and that anything found as a result of such a search was inadmissible in evidence. It was held as follows:

(i) Apart from the rule of law relating to the admissibility of in voluntary

[32] [1976] ZR 277; see Justice Peter Chitengi, 'Implications of illegally obtained evidence and its effect on human rights of accused persons,' A paper presented to a workshop on human rights law on 15th July, 1998: https://allafrica.com/stories/199807160038.html; Jamil Ddamulira Mujuzi, 'The admissibility of evidence obtained through human rights violations in Zambia: Revisiting *Liswaniso v The People* (1976) Zambia Law Reports 277,' The International Journal of Evidence and Proof, Volume: 23 issue: 3, page(s): 316-329 available at https://journals.sagepub.com/doi/abs/10.1177/1365712719831716?journalCode=epja; For recent criticism of this decision from a Zambian Human rights perspective see J Chirwa, "The Admissibility of Derivative Evidence in Zambia in Light of Human Rights Obligations and the Need to Discard Liswaniso Versus The People (1976) ZR 277": https://www.linkedin.com/pulse/admissibility-derivative-evidence-zambia-light-human-rights-chirwa/ retrieved on 25/09/2021; see also *Karuma, Son of Kania v R* (1955) AC 197; (1955) 1 All ER 236; *Mapp v Ohio* (1961) 367 U.S. 643; *Weeks v United States* (1914) 232 I.S. 383; *State v Reynolds* (1924) 101 Conn. 224; *The People v Defoe* (1926) 242 N.Y. 413; *Cupp v Murphy* (1973) 412 US 29; *King v R* (1968) 2 All ER 610; *R v Doyle* (1 888) 12 Ont. R. 347; *R v Honan* (1912) 26 Ont. L.R. 484; *R v Duroussel* (1933) 2 D.L.R. 446; *Attorney-General for Quebec v Begin* (1955) 5 D.L.R. 394; *Emperor v Alladad Khan* (1913) I.L.R. 350 11-258; *Emperor v Ali Ahmed Khan* (1923) I.L.R. 46 A 11-86; *Chwa Hum Htive v King Emperor* (1926) ILR 11 Rang. 107; *Larrie v Muir* (1950) Scots LT 37; *McGovern v HM Advocate* (1950) Scots LT 133; *Jones v Owen* (1870) 34 JP 759; *The People (AG) v O'Brien* (1965) IR 142.

confessions, evidence illegally obtained, e.g., as a result of an illegal search and seizure or as a result of an in admissible confession is, if relevant, admissible on the ground that such evidence is a fact regardless of whether or not it violates a provision of the Constitution (or some other law).

(ii) The evidence of search and seizure of the currency in the case under consideration, although based upon an irregular search warrant, was rightly admitted by the trial court because that evidence was a relevant fact. (*per curiam*) Any illegal or irregular invasions by the police or anyone else are not to be condoned and anyone guilty of such an invasion may be visited by criminal or civil sanctions.

5.2.3.3 The American position

The American system appears to have taken a different approach to that taken in England and this jurisdiction. Though it itself has seen caveats placed in recent decisions as to the extent of application of the rule 'against unreasonable searches and seizures.' The approach and court decisions are predicated on the 4th amendment to the US Constitution which provides as follows:

> The right of the people to be secure in their persons, houses, papers, and effects, against unreasonable searches and seizures, shall not be violated, and no Warrants shall issue, but upon probable cause, supported by Oath or affirmation, and particularly describing the place to be searched, and the persons or things to be seized.

The leading US case is *Mapp v Ohio*.[33] Police officers broke into Dollree Mapp's boarding house, in search of both gambling paraphernalia and a fugitive. When Ms. Mapp asked to see a warrant (it was clear that a warrantless search was not authorised under the circumstances), one of the officers produced a piece of paper but would not let Ms. Mapp read it; in subsequent proceedings the state all but conceded that the 'warrant' was fraudulent. The police proceeded to ransack the whole house, examining, among other things, all of Ms. Mapp's books and papers. During this process, they found four books that under then governing state law were deemed obscene, though today they would probably be protected by the First Amendment. Ms. Mapp was prosecuted for possession of obscene materials, and offence that the Supreme Court has since invalidated as infringing constitutionally protected freedom of thought (no matter how obscene the material).[34]

The Judicial Conference was held on March 31, 1960, the Saturday following the oral argument. The Justices unanimously agreed that Ohio's anti-obscenity

[33] 367 US 643, (1961); This summary (with only a few stylistic changes) and analysis are taken from *Mapp v. Ohio* - Judicial Conference and Decision: The Cleveland Memory Project: (csuohio.edu)https://web.ulib.csuohio.edu/legallandmarks/mapp/decision.html retrieved on 25/09/2021; for analysis of case, its consequences and relevance today see W. Stuntz 'The American Exclusionary Rule and Defendants' Changing Rights' [1989] Crim LR 117 at 118-119.

[34] *Stanley v Georgia* 394 US 557, (1969).

statute should be overturned; however, the Justices' rationale for overturning the statute varied.

Although Attorneys Kearns and Berkman had mostly cited the Fourth and Fourteenth amendments, the Justices focused on the First and Fourteenth Amendments – noting that the Ohio statute was overly broad; and thus, infringed on Mapp's free speech. The Court reasoned that mere possession of obscene materials, without any evidence that the possessor intended to disseminate those materials, "impermissibly deters freedom of belief and expression, if indeed it is not tantamount to an effort at thought control."[35]

During the conference, Justice Douglas suggested that the Fourth Amendment arguments could be used to overturn *Wolf*.[36] Justices Brennan and Warren agreed, but since there was no majority on that issue, the matter was dropped. (There has been speculation that Justice Frankfurter may have been reluctant to revisit *Wolf*[37] because he authored the majority opinion for that case.) Chief Justice Warren assigned Justice Tom C. Clark to write the majority opinion [....]

Immediately following the Judicial Conference, Justices Clark, Black, and Brennan held an impromptu "rump caucus" in an elevator. They revisited the idea of using *Mapp* to overturn *Wolf*,[38] which would cause the exclusionary rule to apply in all states. If Justice Black agreed, with the support of Justices Clark, Brennan, Warren, and Douglas, they would have the majority required to overturn *Wolf*.[39]

Justice Clark wrote several drafts of his opinion. There is evidence in his personal papers of some wavering about whether or not *Wolf*[40] should be overturned.

A year passed before the final decision was handed down on June 19, 1961. Justice Clark's majority opinion reversed the decision by the Supreme Court of Ohio, with concurrences by Justice Black and, separately, Justice Douglas. Justice Harlan, joined by Justices Frankfurter and Whittaker, dissented. The Court held:

> Having once recognised that the right to privacy embodied in the Fourth Amendment is enforceable against the States, and that the right to be secure against rude invasions of privacy by state officers is, therefore, constitutional in origin, we can no longer permit that right to remain an empty promise. Because it is enforceable in the same manner and to like effect as other basic rights secured by the Due Process Clause, we can no longer permit it to be revocable at the whim of any police officer who, in the name of law enforcement itself, chooses to suspend

[35] Memorandum from U.S. Supreme Court Justice John M. Harlan to U.S. Supreme Court Justice Tom C. Clark (May 1, 1961) (electronically available from the Tarlton Law Library, Jamail Center for Legal Research, at the University of Texas at Austin).

[36] *Wolf v Colorado*, 338 U. S. 25.

[37] *Wolf v Colorado*, 338 U. S. 25.

[38] *Wolf v Colorado*, 338 U. S. 25.

[39] *Wolf v Colorado*, 338 U. S. 25.

[40] *Wolf v Colorado*, 338 U. S. 25.

> its enjoyment. Our decision, founded on reason and truth, gives to the individual no more than that which the Constitution guarantees him, to the police officer no less than that to which honest law enforcement is entitled, and, to the courts, that judicial integrity so necessary in the true administration of justice. The judgment of the Supreme Court of Ohio is reversed and the cause remanded for further proceedings not inconsistent with this opinion.[41]

W. Stuntz[42] makes the following observation on the preceding holding:

> The majority opinion gave a host of reasons for this conclusion, but three stand out as particularly important. The first, and most obvious, is deterrence: exclusion removes the incentive for police to conduct illegal searches. The second is 'the imperative of judicial integrity', the notion being that it is dishonest and hypocritical for courts to admit illegally obtained evidence. The third ground is one that permeates the entire *Mapp* opinion:
>
> > that exclusion of illegally obtained evidence is in some normative sense the defendant's entitlement that it does no more than right the wrong the police have done. Though not framed in these terms, the argument is that the exclusionary rule serves necessary compensatory purpose [....]

Mapp[43] became a landmark case because "in an instant, the Supreme Court imposed the exclusionary rule on half the states in the union.".[44] In addition to changing the way state courts handled evidence in criminal trials, the outcome of *Mapp v Ohio*[45] significantly affected police activities throughout the country. Indeed, "the decision sparked the Warren Court's criminal due process revolution. It was the first in a number of decisions where the Supreme Court nationalized guarantees in the Bill of Rights to regulate police conduct and protect the rights of the criminally accused." [....] The application of the exclusionary rule on the states continues to be a polarizing topic among those who believe *Mapp*[46] limited the investigative power of the police, thereby threatening public safety; and those who think that *Mapp*[47] served to guard the rights of individuals against the unchecked power of law enforcement.

In recent times however, the rather wide-ranging exclusionary rule has seen its application restricted to criminal proceedings. This is exemplified in

---

[41] In October 1961, the Supreme Court of the United States denied a petition submitted by the National District Attorneys Association requesting a retrial.

[42] See W. Stuntz 'The American Exclusionary Rule and Defendants' Changing Rights' [1989] Crim LR 117 at 118-119.

[43] 367 U.S. 643, (1961).

[44] Carolyn N. Long, *Mapp v. Ohio*: Guarding against Unreasonable Searches and Seizures 108 (2006).

[45] 367 U.S. 643, (1961).

[46] 367 U.S. 643, (1961).

[47] 367 U.S. 643, (1961).

US v Janis[48] wherethe rule in *Mapp*[49] was held to be inapplicable in civil tax proceedings.

In *US v Leon,*[50] acting on the basis of information from a confidential informant, officers of the Burbank, Cal., Police Department initiated a drug-trafficking investigation involving surveillance of respondents' activities. Based on an affidavit summarizing the police officers' observations, Officer Rombach prepared an application for a warrant to search three residences and respondents' automobiles for an extensive list of items. The application was reviewed by several Deputy District Attorneys, and a facially valid search warrant was issued by a state-court judge. Ensuing searches produced large quantities of drugs and other evidence. Respondents were indicted for federal drug offenses, and filed motions to suppress the evidence seized pursuant to the warrant. After an evidentiary hearing, the District Court granted the motions in part, concluding that the affidavit was insufficient to establish probable cause. Although recognizing that Officer Rombach had acted in good faith, the court rejected the Government's suggestion that the Fourth Amendment exclusionary rule should not apply where evidence is seized in reasonable, good-faith reliance on a search warrant. The Court of Appeals affirmed, also refusing the Government's invitation to recognize a good-faith exception to the rule. The Government's petition for certiorari presented only the question whether a good-faith exception to the exclusionary rule should be recognized. It was held as follows:

1. The Fourth Amendment exclusionary rule should not be applied so as to bar the use in the prosecution's case in chief of evidence obtained by officers acting in reasonable reliance on a search warrant issued by a detached and neutral magistrate but ultimately found to be invalid.
    (a) An examination of the Fourth Amendment's origin and purposes makes clear that the use of fruits of a past unlawful search or seizure works no new Fourth Amendment wrong. The question whether the exclusionary sanction is appropriately imposed in a particular case as a judicially created remedy to safeguard Fourth Amendment rights through its deterrent effect, must be resolved by weighing the costs and benefits of preventing the use in the prosecution's case in chief of inherently trustworthy tangible evidence. Indiscriminate application of the exclusionary rule—impeding the criminal justice system's truth-finding function and allowing some guilty defendants to go free—may well generate disrespect for the law and the administration of justice.
    (b) Application of the exclusionary rule should continue where a Fourth Amendment violation has been substantial and deliberate, but the balancing approach that has evolved in

[48] 428 U.S. 433, (1976).

[49] 367 U.S. 643, (1961).

[50] 468 U.S. 897, (1984); *United States v Koerth* 312 F.3d 862 (7th Cir. 2002); see also Z. Bray, "Appellate Review and the Exclusionary Rule" [2004] 113 Yale LJ 1143.

determining whether the rule should be applied in a variety of contexts—including criminal trials—suggests that the rule should be modified to permit the introduction of evidence obtained by officers reasonably relying on a warrant issued by a detached and neutral magistrate.

(c) The deference accorded to a magistrate's finding of probable cause for the issuance of a warrant does not preclude inquiry into the knowing or reckless falsity of the affidavit on which that determination was based, and the courts must also insist that the magistrate purport to perform his neutral and detached function and not serve merely as a rubber stamp for the police. Moreover, reviewing courts will not defer to a warrant based on an affidavit that does not provide the magistrate with a substantial basis for determining the existence of probable cause. However, the exclusionary rule is designed to deter police misconduct rather than to punish the errors of judges and magistrates. Admitting evidence obtained pursuant to a warrant while at the same time declaring that the warrant was somehow defective will not reduce judicial officers' professional incentives to comply with the Fourth Amendment, encourage them to repeat their mistakes, or lead to the granting of all colourable warrant requests.

(d) Even assuming that the exclusionary rule effectively deters some police misconduct and provides incentives for the law enforcement profession as a whole to conduct itself in accord with the Fourth Amendment, it cannot be expected, and should not be applied, to deter objectively reasonable law enforcement activity. In the ordinary case, an officer cannot be expected to question the magistrate's probable-cause determination or his judgment that the form of the warrant is technically sufficient. Once the warrant issues, there is literally nothing more the policeman can do in seeking to comply with the law, and penalizing the officer for the magistrate's error, rather than his own, cannot logically contribute to the deterrence of Fourth Amendment violations.

(e) A police officer's reliance on the magistrate's probable-cause determination and on the technical sufficiency of the warrant he issues must be objectively reasonable. Suppression remains an appropriate remedy if the magistrate or judge in issuing a warrant was misled by information in an affidavit that the affiant knew was false or would have known was false except for his reckless disregard of the truth, or if the issuing magistrate wholly abandoned his detached and neutral judicial role. Nor would an officer manifest objective good faith in relying on a warrant based on an affidavit so lacking in indicia of probable cause as to render official belief in its existence entirely unreasonable. Finally, depending on the circumstances of the particular case, a warrant may be so facially deficient—i.e., in failing to particularise the place to be searched or the things to be seized—that the executing officers cannot reasonably presume it to be valid.

2. In view of the modification of the exclusionary rule, the Court of Appeals' judgment cannot stand in this case. Only respondent Leon contended that no reasonably well-trained police officer could have believed that there existed probable cause to search his house. However, the record establishes that the police officers' reliance on the state-court judge's determination of probable cause was objectively reasonable.

The different approaches taken in the treatment of illegally obtained evidence in England and Zambia on the one hand, and the United States on the other, demonstrates what has been described by Justice White in *Leon v US*[51] as:

> the tension between the sometimes-competing goals of, on the one hand, deterring official misconduct and removing inducements to unreasonable invasions of privacy and, on the other, establishing procedures under which criminal defendants are "acquitted or convicted on the basis of all the evidence which exposes the truth."[52]

5.2.3.4 *Growing concerns regarding the criminal justice system and statutory response to the common law doctrine of discretionary exclusion in England*

This part of our discussion is concerned with the changes that happened in England on a statutory front as a challenge to the basis for discretionary exclusion reposed in magistrates/judges in trials under the common law. The importance of considering these developments is partly to demonstrate the many strides that have been made to improve the dispensation of justice during court proceedings especially as regards the criminal trial *vis-a-vis* the admissibility of suspect evidence for reasons other than irrelevance all of which fall within the judge's discretion. It is also partly to persuade our courts to look forward in the treatment of the issue of the judge's discretion based on contemporary decisions in England, Australia, Canada and the European Union which decisions have come about because provisions such as s 78 of the Police and Criminal Evidence Act 1984 (PACE 1984) and Art 8 of the European Convention on Human Rights as same represent best practice in the arena of discretionary exclusion of evidence which, based on police conduct prior to trial may affect the overall fairness of the trial.

This movement towards changes and minimising the scope of discretion had started in the early 1970s but took on more impetus following the *Confait* case in which three boys had been arrested, interrogated and consequent to the confession, convicted of murder and subsequently sent to prison. The

[51] 468 U.S. 897, (1984).

[52] *Alderman v United States*, 394 U.S. 165, 175, 89 S.Ct. 961, 967, 22 L.Ed.2d 176 (1969).

questionable circumstances of their arrest, confession, trial and conviction led to the setting up the Royal Commission on Criminal Procedure for purposes of examining police procedures.[53] One major consequence of that Report was the enactment of PACE 1984. The most important provision in PACE 1984 for our purposes is s 78 headlined *'[e]xclusion of unfair evidence'*which provides as follows:

> (1) In any proceedings the court may refuse to allow evidence on which the prosecution proposes to rely to be given if it appears to the court that, having regard to all the circumstances, including the circumstances in which the evidence was obtained, the admission of the evidence would have such an adverse effect on the fairness of the proceedings that the court ought not to admit it.
>
> (2) Nothing in this section shall prejudice any rule of law requiring a court to exclude evidence.

The provisions under s 78 PACE 1984 are intended, as may be readily apparent on a cursory look, as a protection against wrongful conviction of the accused. To that end s 78 empowers the Court the power to use its discretion in excluding all evidence which if it were to be admitted would have an adverse effect on the fairness of the trial. Examples to which the court must apply its mind include but are not limited to how the evidence in question was acquired by the police/prosecution.

Further to the preceding, it must be noted that s 78 is only applicable to evidence that the prosecution intends to use against the accused person and not the other way round with the discretion to exclude evidence only available to the judge to exercise prior to the admission of the evidence in question. Therefore, once such evidence as is subject of an objection by the defence and to which the discretionary evidence ought to be applied is indeed admitted, the provisions of s 78 PACE 1984 may not be invoked. The only recourse that the defence has is the common law authority the court has to exclude the evidence in question. In this jurisdiction the exclusionary authority is inherent in the courts power to supervise trials within the context of common law. That common law authority remains untouched in England & Wales even with the enactment of s 78.

In *R v Sat-Bhambra*[54] the defendant was accused of importing heroin. He challenged use of his recorded interviews saying he was suffering hypoglycaemia from his diabetes at the time. The judge excluded later interviews for this reason, but the defendant challenged the use of the first few tapes since the doctor said he might be suffering in this way. It was held

[53] Report of an inquiry by the Hon. Sir Fisher into the circumstances leading to the trial of three persons on charges rising out of the death of maxwell Confait and the fire at 27 Doggett Road, London SE 6 (hcp 90 of 1977-78): https://assets.publishing.service.gov.uk/government/uploads/system/uploads/attachment_data/file/228759/0090.pdf retrieved on 21/12/22.

[54] (1988) 88 Cr App Rep 55; https://swarb.co.uk/regina-v-sat-bhambra-cacd-1989/ retrieved on 26/09/21.

as follows: Once the evidence had been heard, the judge had no continuing discretion to exclude under s 76 or s 78. His only remaining discretion was under s 82(3) where he might exclude if the material was more prejudicial than probative. *Per* Lord Lane CJ:

> First, were the answers given by the appellant upon the interviews properly to be described as a confession or confessions? Section 82(1) of the Act defines confession as follows: 'confession' includes any statement wholly or partly adverse to the person who made it, whether made to a person in authority or not and whether made in words or otherwise.' His answers upon the interviews, the tapes of which the jury heard, were, as his counsel described, exculpatory. Their principal damaging effect was to demonstrate that the appellant was evasive and prevaricating and that many of the statements which he made proved eventually to be false. The question therefore arises: can a statement be described as wholly or partly adverse to the person making it, when it is intended by the maker to be wholly exculpatory and appears to be so on its face, but becomes damaging at the trial because, for example, its contents can by then be shown to be evasive or false or inconsistent with the maker's evidence on oath? [...] The words of the section do seem prima facie to be speaking of statements adverse on the face of them. The section is aimed at excluding confessions obtained by words or deeds likely to render them unreliable, i.e., admissions or partial admissions contrary to the interests of the defendant and welcome to the interrogator. They can hardly have been aimed at statements containing nothing which the interrogator wished the defendant to say and nothing apparently adverse to the defendant's interests. If the contentions of the appellant in the present case are correct, it would mean that the statement 'I had nothing to do with it' might in due course become a 'confession', which would be surprising, with or without section 82(1) [....] We are inclined to the view that purely exculpatory statements are not within the meaning of section 82(1). We are supported in this view by the learned author of Cross on Evidence.[55] The same view is taken by Andrews and Hirst on Criminal Evidence, paragraph 19.04. They cite the words of Lord Widgery CJ in *Pearce*,[56] where he says 'A denial does not become an admission because it is inconsistent with another denial' [....] In so far as they express a contrary view we respectfully dissent from the views of the Supreme Court of Canada in *Piche v R*,[57] and of Chief Justice Warren in *Miranda v Arizona*,[58] where he said that such statements 'are incriminating in any meaningful sense of the word' [...] However, in the light of what we have to say hereafter, we do not need to come to any firm conclusion on this aspect of the case [...] and as to the court's powers: 'He may, if he thinks that the matter

[55] 6th edn at 544.

[56] (1979) 69 Cr App R 365.

[57] (1970) 11 DLR 700.

[58] 384 U.S. 436, 477 (1975).

> is not capable of remedy by a direction, discharge the jury; he may direct the jury to disregard the statement; he may by way of direction point out to the jury matters which affect the weight of the confession and leave the matter in their hands.'

One cannot help but see how s 78 appears to address Lord Scarman's concerns as regards the risk of illegalities and irregularities premised on police impropriety if only to get someone arrested, tried and convicted. He indeed had expressed this point of view as a dissentient in *R v Sang*[59] in the following terms:

> My Lords, the certified question, though superficially concerned with the exercise of a criminal judge's discretion as to the admission of evidence, raises profound issues in the administration of criminal justice. What is the role of the judge? How far does his control of the criminal process extend? It is his duty, as we all know, to ensure that an accused has a fair trial; but what does 'fair' mean in this context? And does not the prosecution also have rights which the judge may not by the exercise of his discretion override? These problems lie at the root of the criminal justice of a free society.

Having reviewed prior authorities, Lord Scarman then observed as follows in parts relevant to our discussion:

> If an accused is misled or tricked into providing evidence (whether it be an admission or the provision of fingerprints or medical evidence or some other evidence), the rule against self-incrimination, *nemo tenetur se ipsum prodere*,[60] is likely to be infringed. Each case must, of course, depend on its circumstances. All I would say is that the principle of fairness, though concerned exclusively with the use of evidence at trial, is not susceptible to categorisation or classification, and is wide enough in some circumstances to embrace the way in which, after the crime, evidence has been obtained from the accused [....] In reaching my conclusion that the discretion is a general one designed to ensure the accused a fair trial, I am encouraged by what I understand to be the Scots law. Such research as I have been able to make makes clear that the Scots judges recognise such a discretion. Indeed, I think they go further than the English law, the Scots principle being that evidence illegally or unfairly obtained is inadmissible unless in the exercise of its discretion the court allows it to be given [....][61]
>
> How far the Scots judges have extended 'the discretionary principle

[59] [1979] 2 All ER 1222 at 1247d-1248c *per* Lord Scarman.

[60] Or 'no person shall be compelled in any criminal case to be a witness against himself' is now part of Part III of Our Constitution, the Bill of Rights.

[61] See *Lawrie v Muir* 1950 JC 19 at 27: 'In particular, the case may bring into play the discretionary principle of fairness to the accused which has been developed so fully in our law in relation to the admission in evidence of confessions or admissions by a person suspected or charged 1247 with crime. That principle would obviously require consideration in any case in which the departure from the strict procedure had been adopted deliberately with a view to securing the admission of evidence obtained by an unfair trick.'

> of fairness to the accused' I am not qualified to say. It is, however, plain that by the law of Scotland it may be invoked in a case where, after the commission of the crime, illegal or irregular methods have been used to obtain evidence from the accused.[62] Though differences of emphasis and scope are acceptable, it would be, I think, unfortunate if the 'discretionary principle of fairness to the accused' was not recognised in all the criminal jurisdictions of the United Kingdom. Indeed, it must be a fundamental principle in all British criminal jurisdictions that the court is under the duty to ensure the accused a fair trial, and I do not believe that a judge can effectually discharge his duty without, at the very least, the availability of the discretion I have endeavoured to describe.

What s 78 appears to have done though is to go beyond the foregoing position taken by Lord Scarman in *Sang*.[63] Though s 78 does not explicitly overturned *Sang*,[64] the reality is that its application and the common law doctrine of abuse of process have relegated *Sang*[65] to a less important position as a point of reference in the discretionary exclusion discourse. It is clear from its wording that s 78 permits a judge, in a proper case, to apply his mind to the question of whether the sought of police conduct in question is such that if the evidence to which it relates was admitted, it would affect the overall fairness of the trial. Examples referenced include entrapment, blatant deception, and wiretapping or bugging, as the case may be.

There are instances in which s 78 PACE 1984 has been deployed including the increased use of hearsay where it may be used to temper same or indeed matters relating to the exclusion evidence of bad character as it relates to the accused.

5.2.3.5 *Case law emanating from s 78 PACE 1984*

It is worth repeating here that the discretionary exclusionary authority of the court that is premised on s 78 PACE 1984 while inapplicable to Zambia is all the rage in England & Wales relates to the defence objecting to the prosecution evidence which they contend has been obtained improperly and that if the court admitted same, it would adversely affect the fairness of the trial of the accused. Under the circumstances, the defence bears the evidential burden and it is they that ought to satisfy the court that the circumstances relating to the now impugned evidence are such as do require the court to make a determination . Would it follow that there is also a persuasive burden that falls on any of the contending sides? Authorities are uncertain on the point. However, where the defence raises the relevant objection to the admissibility of evidence in the circumstances envisaged under the common law or more significantly under s 78 PACE 1984, the Courts have premised their decisions on whether the

[62] See also *H M Advocate v Turnbull* 1951 JC 96 at 103 *per* Lord Guthrie.

[63] [1979] 2 All ER 1222 at 1231, *per* Lord Diplock.

[64] [1979] 2 All ER 1222 at 1247d-1248c *per* Lord Scarman.

[65] [1979] 2 All ER 1222 at 1247d-1248c per Lord Scarman.

illegality complained of was significant or/and substantial; and whether there was bad faith by the police during investigations. Having considered these questions, the court may determine the extent of its intervention if any. We discuss the preceding matters below briefly:

(i) Whether the illegality complained of was significant or/and substantial

Based on the fact that the defence, once they raise an objection bear the evidential burden, it behooves them to satisfy the court that the breach or illegality relating to the evidence now impugned was not trivial or insignificant but significant or/and substantial. In *R v Walsh*,[66] W faced a charge of robbery. At the police station on arrest, he was first refused access to a solicitor. The police conceded that the refusal was a breach of s 58, and that the officer had failed to record the interview as required, and to give an opportunity to read and sign the interview record written up later. The judge had nevertheless admitted the evidence obtained. It was held that the failures were a 'significant and substantial' breach both of [s 78] and of the Codes of Practice. Whilst the officer might have acted in good faith that did not constitute an excuse. The court's conclusion that the failures would have made no difference was not supported. As a starting point, breaches of PACE 1984 or/and the relevant Code ought to be, as already stated, 'significant and substantial'[67] to necessitate the exclusion of the confession in question. It was observed further, that 'if there are significant and substantial breaches of s 58 or the provisions of the Code, then *prima facie* at least the standards of fairness set by Parliament have not been met.'[68] The availability of other evidence was not enough to support the conviction and it was quashed.[69]

(ii) Whether there was bad faith by the police during investigations

The question of whether the investigation or portions thereof material to the validity of the evidence now impugned was done in bad faith is an important one to any court called upon to use its discretionary power to exclude evidence. As has been shown in *R v Walsh*,[70] bad faith on the part of the police during investigations may indeed come within the realm of serious and significant breach. It is, however, irrelevant whether the police were acting in good faith, that is, without ill will or favour. In *R v Brine*,[71] the court held that the fact that the police were acting in good faith when they interviewed the accused

[66] (1990) 91 Cr App R 161 see in particular Speech by; summary available at https://swarb.co.uk/regina-v-walsh-gerald-frederick-cacd-1990/ retrieved on 28/9/21.

[67] *R v Keenan* (1989) 90 Cr App Rep 1.

[68] At 163.

[69] See, however, *R v McCarthy* [1996] Crim LR 818, CA (Crim Div) where an opposite decision was reached. The accused was stopped by the police surveillance team which team pretended that the searching of the accused's car was but a routine check and did not involve any investigation into drugs. The failure to tell the accused, later charged with the offence of supplying drugs, was a breach of the relevant Code which required that a person be informed of the real reason for being, as in this case, stopped, and car searched. Be that as it may, an application to exclude huge sums of money recovered from search aforementioned was rejected on the basis that it was neither significant nor substantial.

[70] (1990) Cr App R 161 at 163 *per* Saville J.

[71] [1992] Crim LR 122.

without realising that he was at the material time suffering from a mild form of paranoid psychosis was irrelevant. On that score, the evidence was excluded after medical evidence confirmed that mental state of the accused was defective at the material time.

(iii) Determining the extent of the trial court's intercession

The use of the court's inherent power to exercise discretion as to the admissibility of evidence especially where it is objected to, is crucial in criminal trials and may in some cases determine whether the accused will be convicted or acquitted. For trial defence attorneys, a working knowledge of decided cases on the matter, procedural law, constitutional injunctions under Part III: The Bill of Rights, and how courts in the past have employed the somewhat amorphous concepts of "justice"; "significant"; and/or "fairness" in decided cases may assist in mapping out a defence strategy. At the same time, a prosecutor's knowledge of the foregoing will assist him determine whether the matter before him is one that should be brought to trial at all. It would also follow that the mere fact that there was some impropriety which the prosecutor deems insignificant and insufficient to warrant the exclusion of the evidence in question should not deter him from bringing the case to trial in general and specifically from attempting to introduce the evidence tied to such impropriety unless said illegality or/and breach is significant and substantial. Further still, even if the breach is deemed insignificant and is too trivial to warrant the exclusion of evidence connected to such illegality, it is always worth a try and for defence counsel to make his case premising his arguments on discharging the accused's evidential burden and persuade the court to exclude the evidence. It ought to be one of the many tricks up the sleeves of any defence counsel worth his salt. It is not an exact science but it may well be all that is needed to "kill" the prosecution's case and free one's client. For the prosecution, dissuading the judge from excluding the evidence by contending among other things, that the illegality is trivial, and that the defence have not proved any bad faith on the part of the police may be the difference between securing a conviction and seeing an accused person acquitted.

Ultimately though, what determines whether the court will interfere or not in the use of a trial court's use of discretion has been set out in *Associated Provincial Picture Houses Ltd v Wednesbury Corporation*[72] by Lord Green as follows:

> It is true the discretion must be exercised reasonably. Now what does that mean? Lawyers familiar with the phraseology commonly used in relation to exercise of statutory discretions often use the word "unreasonable" in a rather comprehensive sense. It has frequently been used and is frequently used as a general description of the things that must not be done. For instance, a person entrusted with a

[72] [1948] 1 KB 223 at 229 *per* Greene MR.

> discretion must, so to speak, direct himself properly in law. He must call his own attention to the matters which he is bound to consider. He must exclude from his consideration matters which are irrelevant to what he has to consider. If he does not obey those rules, he may truly be said, and often is said, to be acting "unreasonably." Similarly, there may be something so absurd that no sensible person could ever dream that it lay within the powers of the authority. Warrington LJ in *Short v Poole Corporation*[73] gave the example of the red-haired teacher, dismissed because she had red hair. That is unreasonable in one sense. In another sense it is taking into consideration extraneous matters. It is so unreasonable that it might almost be described as being done in bad faith; and, in fact, all these things run into one another.

According to Lord Diplock in *Council of Civil Service Unions v Minister for the Civil Service*[74] for the Court of Appeal to interfere in the trial Court's use of discretion it must be '[s]o outrageous in its defiance of logic or accepted moral standards that no sensible person who had applied his mind to the question to be decided could have arrived at it.' To be so, the appellate court must draw the conclusion as highlighted in the *Wednesbury case*[75] that in using his discretion:

- The trial judge took into account factors that ought not to have been taken into account, or
- The trial judge failed to take into account factors that ought to have been taken into account, or
- The decision was so unreasonable that no reasonable court would ever consider imposing it.

The foregoing reasoning has been followed cases such as *Nkhata and Others v The Attorney General of Zambia*[76] where it was held in terms similar to those in *Wednesbury*[77]:

> A trial judge sitting alone without a jury can only be reversed on questions of fact if (1) the judge erred in accepting evidence, or (2) the judge erred in assessing and evaluating the evidence by taking into account some matter which he should have ignored or failing to take into account something which he should have considered, or (3) the judge did not take proper advantage of having seen and heard the witnesses, (4) external evidence demonstrates that the judge erred in assessing manner and demeanour of witnesses.

In *Godfrey Miyanda v The High Court*,[78] Ngulube DCJ, as he then was, declined to assume jurisdiction to entertain an original application for mandamus because

---

[73] [1926] Ch 66, 90, 91.

[74] [1984] 3 All ER 935, [1984] 3 WLR 1174, [1985] ICR 14, [1985] AC 374, [1985] IRLR 28 (HL).

[75] *Associated Provincial Picture Houses Ltd. v Wednesbury Corporation* [1948] 1 KB 223.

[76] [1966] ZR 124, 125 (CAZ).

[77] *Associated Provincial Picture Houses Ltd. v Wednesbury Corporation* [1948] 1 KB 223.

[78] [1984] ZR 62 at 64.

the Supreme Court had no jurisdiction to do so noting as follows:

> The original civil jurisdiction of the Supreme Court is very limited indeed,[79] and would appear to cover such matters the granting of injunctions pending appeal, the making of orders to extend time, or for leave to appeal, or as to costs, or security for the costs of appeals. The Supreme Court would also have original jurisdiction, like the Court of Appeal in England, to make orders requiring the fulfilment of an undertaking given to it and an inherent jurisdiction to strike out an incompetent appeal. I would go so far as to assert that the Supreme Court has an inherent jurisdiction to prevent abuses of process and to protect its authority and dignity. What emerges, however, is that this limited original jurisdiction arises either in connection with some matter pending in the courts below or some matter preliminary to, or during, incidental to, some proceedings before the court.

Thus far, it may have become apparent that what is described as a discretion may not in the real sense be a discretion properly so called. The reason for this is predicated on the fact that the magistrate or judge, as the case may be is precluded from using his discretion to include evidence which clearly would have an adverse effect were it to be admitted. In order to prevent being reversed on appeal, what is paramount is for the particular magistrate or judge to apply his mind to significant issues involved in *casu*.[80]

5.2.3.6 *Where evidence is obtained by means of agents provocateurs: device of entrapment*

The criminal law has always maintained that entrapment is no defence. Therefore, even in circumstances where an accused person charged with an offence was led to committing said offence through entrapment, he will not succeed at getting an acquittal on that basis without more.

(i) The position in England & Wales

The position in England is that stated in *R v Sang*:[81]

> I would now refer to what is, I believe, and hope, the unusual case in which a dishonest policeman, anxious to improve his detection record, tries very hard with the help of an agent provocateur to induce a young man with no criminal tendencies to commit a serious crime, and ultimately the young man reluctantly succumbs to the inducement. In such a case, the judge has no discretion to exclude the evidence which proves that the young man has committed the

[79] Halsbury's Laws of England, 65 4th edn, Vol 10 para 899.

[80] For extensive analysis of the foregoing as they relate to calls for rationalisation s 78 of PACE 1984 see D. Ormerod and D. Birch, "The Evolution of the Discretionary Exclusion of Evidence" [2004] Crim LR 767 at 786-787; Lord Justice Auld, *A Review of the Criminal Courts* (2001) Ch 11 para 108.

[81] [1979] 2 All ER 1222.

> offence. He may, however, according to the circumstances of the case, impose a mild punishment on him or even give him an absolute or conditional discharge and refuse to make any order for costs against him. The policeman and the informer who had acted together in inciting him to commit the crime should however both be prosecuted and suitably punished. This would be a far safer and more effective way of preventing such inducements to commit crimes from being made, than a rule that no evidence should be allowed to prove that the crime in fact had been committed.

There are, however, two ways in which control of police participation is controlled in England & Wales: (i) staying of proceedings as an abuse of process at common law: and (ii) Invoking s 78 of PACE and excluding evidence in question.

(ii) The position in the United States

The position in the United States is the complete opposite of that taken in England & Wales. A substantive defence is available to accused persons subjected to entrapment. Three cases demonstrate this.

The first *Sorrells v US.*[82] In 1930, Martin, a Prohibition agent in Haywood County, North Carolina, heard from informers that Vaughno Crawford Sorrells, a factory worker at Champion Fiber Company in Canton, had a reputation as a rumrunner. He arranged to visit Sorrells at his home in Sorrells Cove in Canton, on July 13, accompanied by three acquaintances of Sorrells. He had them introduce him to Sorrells as a fellow veteran of the U.S. Army 30th Infantry Division who had served in World War I and was passing through the area. At several times during an hour and a half of conversation and reminiscing the agent asked Sorrells if he would be so kind as to get a fellow soldier some liquor. Sorrells initially refused, but later wore down and procured him a half-gallon bottle of whiskey for US$5. Martin then arrested him for violating the National Prohibition Act. Sorrells was convicted in federal court largely on the strength of Martin's testimony that he was the only one who had asked about acquiring liquor. Three other witnesses testified on rebuttal as to his general reputation as a rumrunner. In his defence, Sorrells said that he had told Martin that he "did not fool with whiskey" several times before yielding. One of the acquaintances present also testified that he had no idea either that Martin was a government agent or that Sorrells dealt in liquor. His neighbours testified to his character, and the timekeeper at the factory where he worked also testified to his punctuality and good conduct during six years of employment there. In the lower courts, Sorrells's name was entered as CV Sorrells and was never corrected throughout the case. The court did not allow entrapment to be raised, ruling it had not occurred as a matter of law. The appeals court affirmed the conviction,[2] whereupon Sorrells' attorney petitioned for *certiorari*. The court granted it on the condition it was limited to arguing entrapment as a defence.

[82] 287 U.S. 435 (1932).

Ultimately, the United States Supreme Court unanimously took cognizance of the entrapment defence. The majority opinion authored by Chief Justice Charles Evans Hughes, as he then was, regarded as crucial to entrapment the accused's predilection or want thereof to commit the crime in question. A concurring opinion by Owen Josephus Roberts, associate Justice, as he was then, took the view that the entrapment defence ought to be rooted not, as suggested in the majority opinion, in the accused's penchant to commit the offence in question, but rather, the conduct of the law enforcement agents making the arrest when subject to scrutiny by the court. Subsequent decisions have favoured predilection/predisposition view but this has not ended the debate on which one should take precedence as regards entrapment in criminal cases. Calling the investigation, a "gross abuse of authority", Hughes CJ observed as follows:

> It is clear that the evidence was sufficient to warrant a finding that the act for which defendant was prosecuted was instigated by the prohibition agent, that it was the creature of his purpose, that defendant had no previous disposition to commit it but was an industrious, law-abiding citizen, and that the agent lured defendant, otherwise innocent, to its commission by repeated and persistent solicitation in which he succeeded by taking advantage of the sentiment aroused by reminiscences of their experiences as companions in arms in the World War.

He reached his conclusion by construing statutes to mean that Congress wanted to prevent crime, not punish it, therefore entrapment had to be available as a defence. In concurring, Justice Roberts joined by justices Harlan Fiske Stone and Louis Brandeis, took strong issue with this finding:

> This seems a strained and unwarranted construction of the statute; and amounts, in fact, to judicial amendment. It is not merely broad construction, but addition of an element not contained in the legislation ... no guide or rule is announced as to when a statute shall be read as excluding a case of entrapment; and no principle of statutory construction is suggested which would enable us to say that it is excluded by some statutes and not by others. Courts should instead, he said, focus on the conduct of the investigating officers instead of the defendants' predisposition. "Entrapment," he wrote, "is the conception and planning of an offense by an officer, and his procurement of its commission by one who would not have perpetrated it except for the trickery, persuasion, or fraud of the officer."

Justice McReynolds employed a "graveyard dissent," stating only that he "would vote to affirm."

In *US v Russell,*[83] the United States Supreme Court again dealt with the defence of entrapment. At trial, Connolly and Russell both argued that, in their cases,

[83] 411 U.S. 423 (1973).

it was the government agent's assistance in their enterprise — and only that — which had made the specific offenses they were tried for possible. The jury rejected that argument, following instead the subjective entrapment standard, holding that they were predisposed to commit the crime in any event. On appeal Russell had admitted to that during his appeal, but he and his lawyers argued that the entrapment defense should focus entirely on what the federal operatives did and not his state of mind. They asked the Court to overrule two previous cases that had established this "subjective" test in favour of the "objective" one they advocated. It declined to do so. The United States Court of Appeals for the Ninth Circuit agreed that the conduct of the government agents trumped any inclination to make and deal meth and overturned the conviction. Prosecutors petitioned the Supreme Court for *certiorari*.

The Supreme Court accepted to hear the case. In a 5-4 split decision, the Court stuck to the subjective theory first deployed in *Sorrells v United States*.[84] Although an undercover federal agent had helped procure a key ingredient for an illegal methamphetamine manufacturing operation, and assisted in the process, the Court followed its earlier rulings on the subject and found that the defendant had a predisposition to make and sell illegal drugs whether he worked with the government or not.

Writing for the majority, Rehnquist CJ, as he then was, reviewed the case and the appellant's arguments for adopting a new standard for entrapment. He started by pointing out the practical problems in the case at hand in the following terms:

> Even if we were to surmount the difficulties attending the notion that due process of law can be embodied in fixed rules, and those attending respondent's particular formulation, the rule he proposes would not appear to be of significant benefit to him. For, on the record presented, it appears that he cannot fit within the terms of the very rule he proposes. The record discloses that although the propanone was difficult to obtain, it was by no means impossible. The defendants admitted making the drug both before and after those batches made with the propanone supplied by Shapiro. Shapiro testified that he saw an empty bottle labelled phenyl-2-propanone on his first visit to the laboratory on December 7, 1969. And when the laboratory was searched pursuant to a search warrant on January 10, 1970, two additional bottles labelled phenyl-2-propanone were seized. Thus, the facts in the record amply demonstrate that the propanone used in the illicit manufacture of methamphetamine not only could have been obtained without the intervention of Shapiro but was in fact obtained by these defendants.

Chief Justice Rehnquist then authored what has since then, become the most engaging statement as regards the defence in the United States: [...] 'we' he opined, 'may someday be presented with a situation in which the conduct of law enforcement agents is so outrageous that due process principles would absolutely bar the government from invoking judicial processes to obtain a

[84] 287 U.S. 435 (1932).

conviction.' He continued: 'the instant case is distinctly not of that breed.' The foregoing which would clearly be a case in the ultimately extreme, and such intervention by any court of law of the rarest kind, and indeed any instances of entrapment objected to by an accused person would, according to Chief Justice Rehnquist be because of the ever present possibility of 'overzealous law enforcement.'

Justice Rehnquist rejected the notion, as suggested by appellant's counsel, of altering the subjective entrapment standard in favour of an objective one saying that the Court had already reiterated the subjective test in *Sherman* and saw no reason to change now. He then criticised the lower court's attempt to change the test in the following terms:

> We think that the decision of the Court of Appeals in this case quite unnecessarily introduces an unmanageably subjective standard which is contrary to the holdings of this Court in *Sorrells* and *Sherman* ... [T] here are circumstances when the use of deceit is the only practicable law enforcement technique available. It is only when the Government's deception actually implants the criminal design in the mind of the defendant that the defence of entrapment comes into play.

Justice Douglas[85] dissented stating in part:

> Federal agents play a debased role when they become the instigators of the crime, or partners in its commission, or the creative brain behind the illegal scheme. That is what the federal agent did here when he furnished the accused with one of the chemical ingredients needed to manufacture the unlawful drug.

In his dissenting opinion, Justice Potter Stewart[86] made the case for the objective test saying that it was "the only one truly consistent with the underlying rationale of the defence". According to him, the defendant's conduct or state of mind had no bearing, since contending that there had been entrapment was by itself a concession by the accused that he had acted as charged: 'He may not have originated the precise plan or the precise details, but he was "predisposed" in the sense that he has proved to be quite capable of committing the crime.'

The predisposition test had the ability to deter accused persons with a valid case against government agents simply because it permits the prosecution to bring up otherwise prejudicial matters of the accused's previous conduct which would ordinarily be inadmissible.

> Stated another way, this subjective test means that the Government is permitted to entrap a person with a criminal record or bad reputation, and then to prosecute him for the manufactured crime, confident that his record or reputation itself will be enough to show that he

[85] William Brennan signing on.

[86] Joined by Justices Brennan and Thurgood Marshall.

> was predisposed to commit the offense anyway ... In my view, a person's alleged "predisposition" to crime should not expose him to government participation in the criminal transaction that would be otherwise unlawful.

Two subsequent decisions merit our consideration:

The first is *Hampton v. United States.*[87] Defendant's belief that he and government informant were selling legal substance and claiming it to be heroin did not overcome evidence showing predisposition to commit crime. Rehnquist backs away slightly from "outrageous government conduct" here, maintaining that defendants must show a specific violation of constitutional rights or due process.

Finally, in *Jacobson v US,*[88] a narrowly divided Supreme Court of the United States overturned the conviction of a Nebraska man for receiving child pornography through the mail, ruling that postal inspectors had implanted a desire to do so through repeated written entreaties. It was the first time the Court had considered an entrapment case from outside the realm of controlled-substance enforcement, or one involving conduct that had only recently been criminalised. By relying exclusively on whether the defendant had a predisposition to commit the crime, the court appeared to have finally resolved a lingering issue in its previous decisions on the subject.[89] The decision was seen as a rare triumph for defendants before a conservative court that frequently sided with prosecutors.[90] Guidelines for federal law enforcement agents were changed in its wake,[91] and it was described as having brought entrapment "back from the dead."[92] Thus, prior acts by the defendant later made illegal but legal at the time do not demonstrate predisposition *per se*; prosecution must show beyond reasonable doubt that defendant was predisposed to commit crime prior to any contact by government agents.[93]

5.2.3.7 *Criteria relating to the exclusion of evidence obtained by entrapment: case law*

---

[87] 452 U.S. 484 (1976).

[88] 503 U.S. 540 (1992).

[89] Lord, Kenneth; Entrapment and Due Process: Moving Toward A Dual System of Defenses Archived 2007-06-21 at the Wayback Machine, 25 Fl St. U. Law Rev. 473, 1998.

[90] Greenhouse, Linda; April 7, 1992; Justices, in Entrapment Case, Cast a Rare Vote Against Prosecutors; *The New York Times*; retrieved August 15, 2006.

[91] Chin, Id., 30, citing Attorney General's Guidelines on FBI Undercover Operations (Dec. 31, 1980), reprinted in Select Committee to Study Undercover Activities of the Department of Justice, S. Rep. 97-682, at 551 (1982) and The Attorney General's Guidelines on Federal Bureau of Investigation Undercover Operations Archived 2008-03-12 at the Wayback Machine (May 30, 2002).

[92] Paul Marcus, "Presenting, Back from the [Almost] Dead, the Entrapment Defense", 47 Fla L Rev 205 (1995). Cited in Gabriel J. Chin, The Story of *Jacobson v United States*: Catching Criminals or Creating Crime?, Arizona Legal Studies Discussion Paper N. 06-12, February 2006, retrieved August 10, 2006, 31. This draft is described as a chapter in the forthcoming Criminal Law Stories. 31.

[93] Lawrence Stanley, The Child Pornography Myth, 7 Cardozo Arts & Ent L J 295, 324 (1989); cited at Chin, 18n54.

The matter of excluding evidence has been raised and determined in a few leading English cases.

The first case of some relevance was *DPP v Marshall*[94] where it was shown that Police Entrapment is no defence to Criminal Act. The accused complained of his conviction for supplying controlled drugs, saying that the undercover police officer had requested him to make the supply. It was held that it was an abuse of process for the police to go so far as to incite a crime.

The second is *R v Christou and Another.*[95] In 1990, in order to combat a high rate of burglary and robbery in parts of North London, a shop named 'Stardust Jewellers' was set up in the area which purported to conduct the business of buying and selling jewellery on a commercial basis. The shop was in fact a police undercover operation and was staffed solely by two undercover officers who purported to be shady jewellers willing to buy in stolen property. Transactions in the shop were recorded by cameras and sound recording equipment, the object of the operation being to recover stolen property for the owners and to obtain evidence against those who had either stolen or dishonestly handled it. The two appellants were among those charged with burglary and/or handling stolen goods as a result of the operation. At their trial the defence challenged the admissibility of all the evidence resulting from the undercover operation but the trial judge ruled that the evidence was admissible. The appellants then changed their plea to guilty of handling stolen goods and were convicted. They appealed on the ground that the judge had wrongly allowed the evidence resulting from the undercover operation to be admitted, since they had been tricked into expressly or impliedly incriminating themselves, and that a caution under para 10.1 of the Code of Practice for the Detention, Treatment and Questioning of Persons by Police Officers ought to have been administered before the undercover police officers engaged in conversation with the appellants. It was held that the evidence obtained by the police by means of the undercover operation in which criminals were deceived into thinking that they were dealing with a jeweller willing to trade in stolen property was admissible at the appellants' trial since the police operation had not tricked them into committing an offence they would not otherwise have committed and questions asked in the course of such dealings were not questions about an offence which required a caution to be administered. Although the police had engaged in a trick which had produced evidence against the appellants, the trick had not as such been applied to them as they had voluntarily applied themselves to the trick and it had not resulted in unfairness. It followed that the appeals would be dismissed.[96] *Per curiam:* It would be wrong for police

[94] [1988] 3 All ER 683; https://swarb.co.uk/director-of-public-prosecutions-v-marshall-1988/ retrieved on 30/9/21.

[95] [1992] 4 All ER 559.

[96] *R v Payne* [1963] 1 All ER 848 and *R v Mason* [1987] 3 All ER 481 distinguished; *R v Sang* [1979] 2 All ER 1222, dicta of Auld J in *R v Jelen* (1989) 90 Cr App R 456 at 464 and of Hodgson J in *R v Keenan* [1989] 3 All ER 598 at 604 considered; Editor's notes: For the discretion to exclude relevant prosecution evidence, see 11(2) Halsbury's Laws (4th edn reissue) para 1060; For the Police and Criminal Evidence Act 1984, s 78, see 17 Halsbury's Statutes (4th edn) 215.

officers to adopt or use an undercover pose or disguise to enable themselves to ask questions about an offence uninhibited 559 by the requirements of the Code of Practice and with the effect of circumventing it. Were they to do so it would be open to the judge to exclude the questions and answers under s 78 of the Police and Criminal Evidence Act 1984.

The third case was *R v Smurthwaite and Gill.*[97] The appellants in two separate cases, S and G, were each charged with soliciting a person to murder the appellant's spouse. In both cases the person solicited was an undercover police officer posing as a contract killer. It was alleged that S wished to have his wife killed because he could not face continuing with a marriage which he considered a sham and believed that divorce proceedings would expose certain financial dealings known to his wife but unknown to the Inland Revenue. He was alleged to have made arrangements with two men, who were in fact undercover police officers, for his wife to be killed for £20,000, half to be paid before the murder and half later. S paid £10,000 to one of the officers and was then arrested. The Crown's case depended upon secret tape recordings of meetings held between the undercover officers and S. G was alleged to have asked O for help in arranging for the murder of her husband because of his conduct towards her. O informed the police and a meeting was arranged between G, O and an undercover police officer posing as a contract killer. The undercover officer secretly tape recorded the second and subsequent meetings between himself and G. At their trials the appellants' defence was that in neither case had there been any intention that a murder should actually be carried out and that the appellants had been intimidated by the supposed contract killers and had made a pretence of going along with the murder plans out of fear. In addition, G submitted that evidence of the recorded conversations should be excluded under s 78a of the Police and Criminal Evidence Act 1984 but the judge ruled that the evidence was admissible. Under s 78 the court had a discretion to refuse to allow prosecution evidence to be admitted if it appeared that, 'having regard to all the circumstances, including the circumstances in which the evidence was obtained, the admission of the evidence would have such an adverse effect on the fairness of the proceedings that the court ought not to admit it'. The judge in S's trial ruled that the evidence of the recorded conversations should be admitted. Both appellants were convicted. They appealed, contending that any prosecution evidence which included an element of entrapment or which came from an agent provocateur or was obtained by a trick should be excluded by the trial judge under s 78. The appellants submitted that the undercover officers were agent provocateurs because if they had not come on the scene the appellants would not have sought to have their spouses killed and by posing as contract killers, they had obtained the recorded evidence by means of entrapment or a trick. It was

[97] [1994] 1 All ER 898; Editor's notes: For the discretion to exclude relevant prosecution evidence, see 11(2) Halsbury's Laws (4th edn reissue) para 1060, and for cases on the subject, see 15(1) Digest (2nd reissue) 516–517, 520–521, 17086–17087, 17097–17098; For official collaboration in crime, see 15(1) Halsbury's Laws (4th edn reissue) para 48, and for cases on the subject, see 14(1) Digest (2nd reissue) 137–138, 1112–1116; For the Police and Criminal Evidence Act 1984, s 78, see 17 Halsbury's Statutes (4th edn) (1993 reissue) 228.

held that a judge had no discretion to exclude otherwise admissible evidence merely on the ground that it had been obtained improperly or unfairly and the evidential requirement in s 78 of the 1984 Act that prosecution evidence might be excluded having regard to the circumstances in which it was obtained had not altered the substantive rule of law that entrapment or the use of an agent provocateur did not per se afford a defence in law to a criminal charge. However, if the judge considered that in all the circumstances the obtaining of the evidence in that way would have such an adverse effect on the fairness of the proceedings that the court ought not to admit it, he could exclude it. Accordingly, it was not open to the appellants to claim that had it not been for the undercover officers acting as agent provocateurs they would not have solicited the murder of their spouses and on the facts the tape recordings were in each case an accurate and unchallenged record of the actual offence being committed. They had accordingly been properly admitted in evidence. The appeals would therefore be dismissed.[98] According to Lord Taylor CJ,

> In exercising his discretion whether to admit evidence of an undercover officer, some, but not an exhaustive list, of the factors that the judge may take into account are as follows. Was the officer acting as an agent provocateur in the sense that he was enticing the [accused] to commit an offence he would not have otherwise committed? What was the nature of any entrapment? Does the evidence consist of admissions to a completed offence, or does it consist of the actual commission of an offence? How active or passive was the officer's role in obtaining the evidence? Is there an unassailable record of what occurred, or is it strongly corroborated? In *R v Christou* this court held that discussions between suspects and undercover officers, not overtly acting as police officers, were not in the ambit of the codes under the 1984 Act. However, officers should not use their undercover pose to question suspects so as to circumvent the code. In *R v Bryce* the court held that the undercover officer had done just that. Accordingly, a further consideration for the judge in deciding to admit an undercover officer's evidence is whether he has abused his role to ask questions which ought properly to have been asked as a police officer and in accordance with the codes.

The above approach as described in *Smurthwaite*[99] by Lord Taylor CJ is premised on the idea, (at least it so appears from the questions the EWCA asked), of a judge's exclusionary power being predicated on a pre-trial investigative paradigm. It appears to follow that where entrapment has been at play in obtaining evidence, the guidelines laid out in *Smurthwaite* would work to

[98] Bank of *England v Vagliano Bros* [1891–4] All ER Rep 93; *R v Sang* [1979] 2 All ER 1222; *R v Fulling* [1987] 2 All ER 65 considered.

[99] [1994] 1 All ER 898; Editor's notes: For the discretion to exclude relevant prosecution evidence, see 11(2) Halsbury's Laws (4th edn reissue) para 1060, and for cases on the subject, see 15(1) Digest (2nd reissue) 516–517, 520–521, 17086–17087, 17097–17098; For official collaboration in crime, see 15(1) Halsbury's Laws (4th edn reissue) para 48, and for cases on the subject, see 14(1) Digest (2nd reissue) 137–138, 1112–1116; For the Police and Criminal Evidence Act 1984, s 78, see 17 Halsbury's Statutes (4th edn) (1993 reissue) 228.

guide the court as to the evidence in question ought to be admitted. Two things stand out in this regard for the court to admit the evidence: (i) the police ought to show to the satisfaction of the court that they worked within the confines of the law; and (ii) there must be a pellucid chain of dependable evidence so that phone calls are recorded and crucial meetings taped. Uglow suggest that this '[...] is a pragmatic approach, preferable to the "anything goes" approach of *Sang*[100] but one which lacks guiding principle.' It has been said in *Mack v The Queen*[101] as regards the foregoing:

> One reason is that the State does not have unlimited power to intrude into our personal lives or to randomly test the virtue of individuals. Another is the concern that entrapment techniques may result in the commission of crimes by people who would not otherwise become involved in criminal conduct [. . .] Ultimately, we may be saying that there are inherent limits on the power of the State to manipulate people and events for the purpose of attaining the specific objective of obtaining convictions.[46]

Even so, this appears to raise several questions which Uglow[102] relates to the interpretation of s 78[103] but which, it is submitted here, are just as applicable to a common law-based employment of discretionary power by courts in this jurisdiction: "Are the courts excluding improperly obtained evidence because it is not reliable? Is the primary aim disciplining the police? Are they seeking to protect the integrity of the criminal process? Or is the issue the protection of the rights of the accused?" One may add another question to the foregoing: would it not be better to achieve what is intended by device of exclusion of evidence by defence counsel making a stay application on the premise that there was patent abuse of process?

It has been contended that '[a]n entrapment operation must be necessary, its extent proportional and it must be properly managed and supervised.'[104] This is predicated on two cases that were decided on the strength of Art. 6 of the European Convention on Human Rights (ECHR). The first is *Lüdi v Switzerland.*[105] The questions that fell for the court to determine were (i) Whether the applicant had suffered a violation of his right under Article 8 of the Convention for the Protection of Human Rights and Fundamental Freedoms ('European Convention on Human Rights', 'ECHR') to respect for his private life through the use of an undercover agent and the interception of telephone calls in his case; and (ii) Whether the applicant's right to a fair trial

[100] [1980] AC 402.

[101] (1988) 44 C.C.C. 3d 513 at 541.

[102] Uglow S, *Evidence Text and Materials* 140.

[103] He contends that the section lacks rationality hence the questions he raises.

[104] Uglow S, *Evidence Text and Materials* 139.

[105] Merits and Just Satisfaction, App No 12433/86, (1993) 15 EHRR 173, IHRL 2947 (ECHR 1992), 15th June 1992, European Court of Human Rights [ECHR].

under Article 6(1) and Article 6(3)(d) of the ECHR had been infringed when the evidence of an unidentified undercover policeman was relied on by the trial court without calling the agent as a prosecution witness. The operation in question was held by the court to be part of the judicial investigation. In any case, the court observed, the transaction giving rise to the alleged violation(s) was already under way when undercover officers arrived. Therefore, the court concluded, the operation could not be deemed to have been a violation.

A different decision was reached in *Teixeira de Castro v Portugal*[106] despite the fact that the facts were similar to those in *Ludi.*[107] According to the court the facts and circumstances of this case lacked the judicial supervision as regards the undercover operation and unlike the *Ludi case*,[108] there was want of sufficient prior predication or/and evidence implicating the accused. In other words, the validity of a covert operation is premised on answering the question of whether there was a basis for the operation in the first place.

5.2.3.8 *Staying proceedings for abuse of process*

English law has followed the lead of other jurisdictions such as Australia and Canada to, in appropriate cases, exclude evidence obtained as a result of entrapment by the police officers albeit indirectly and less satisfactorily.[109] Though, English law does not, as exemplified in *R v Sang,*[110] offer the defence of entrapment, luring citizens into committing illegal acts and then seeking to prosecute them for so doing is considered an abuse of the court process.[111] Where the foregoing is shown to have been the case, the court will stay proceedings as an abuse of process.[112] The leading authority on the preceding is *R v Loosely.*[113] The case was concerned with the actions of undercover police officers carrying out test purchase operations. Lord Nicholls identified that a useful guide when considering whether the conduct of the police amounted to inciting or instigating crime was to ascertain whether the police did more than present the defendant with an unexceptional opportunity to commit a crime. If the police conduct preceding the commission of the offence was no more than might have been expected by others in the circumstances this would not constitute entrapment. If, however, it went beyond this an abuse of process by

---

[106] App No 25829/94, [1998] 28 EHRR 101; [1998] Crim LR 751.

[107] Merits and Just Satisfaction,App No 12433/86, (1993) 15 EHRR 173, IHRL 2947 (ECHR 1992), 15th June 1992, European Court of Human Rights [ECHR].

[108] Merits and Just Satisfaction,App No 12433/86, (1993) 15 EHRR 173, IHRL 2947 (ECHR 1992), 15th June 1992, European Court of Human Rights [ECHR].

[109] Based on s 78 of PACE 1984.

[110] [1980] AC 402 which is the antithesis of the position taken in the United States where entrapment is a well-established defence: *Sorrells v US* 287 U.S. 435 (1932); *US v Russell,* 411 U.S. 423 (1973); *Jacobson v US,* 503 U.S. 540.

[111] The defence of entrapment is well settled in the United States. Thus, even though, as shown in *Jacobson v US,* 503 U.S. 540, US 'artifice and stratagem may be employed to catch those engaged in criminal enterprises' government and/or its agents and/or servants are proscribed from originating a crime.

[112] See A. Choo, *Abuse of Process and Judicial Stays of Criminal Proceedings* (1993).

[113] [2001] UKHL 53; summary taken from https://www.lawgazette.co.uk/law/the-law-regarding-entrapment/55972.article retrieved on 2/10/21.

the state may well be established.

It is however, unclear what protection is available to those entrapped by undercover journalists into committing criminal offences. In *R v Shannon (aka Alford)*[114] which followed the infamous 'fake-sheikh' sting by the *News of the World*, the former London's Burning actor was filmed supplying drugs to the undercover reporter. Shannon appealed against his conviction on the basis that the evidence was obtained unfairly under s 78 of PACE 1984. In the Court of Appeal, Potter LJ stated that it was insufficient that the unfairness complained of related to the fact that the accused would not have committed the crime but for the incitement of others, unless the behaviour of the police or the prosecuting authority had been such as to justify an abuse of process.

It would seem to follow that the basis for a successful stay of proceedings application on grounds of abuse of process or indeed the exclusion of evidence in cases of entrapment ought to be the conduct of the police or the prosecuting authority by whatever name called.[115] Where the entrapment is predicated on the behaviour of private citizens, the bar is raised, and as such, the chances of an application for exclusion of evidence is likely to be futile. The prosecution will and should argue that they are only presenting evidence obtained from a third party in line with their obligation to prosecute accused persons. There is a basis for such an argument in private cases of entrapment as the prosecution will only get involved once the entrapment has taken place and the offence has been committed. Be that as it may, concerns have been raised in the following terms:[116]

> It appears perverse that, while the law protects against the state causing citizens to commit illegal acts, it does not protect against private parties doing the same thing, where often the participation of the private 'entrapper' goes beyond that which would be deemed appropriate by law enforcement officers. Many newspapers stings involve an expensive and targeted campaign on one individual, based on limited or no intelligence, where the inducement is persistent and the primary incentive is to sell newspapers, not to prevent crime.

Lord Steyn has in *R v Latif*,[117] expressed the need for courts to exercise their jurisdiction to stay proceedings on the grounds of entrapment, where the court takes the view that the prosecution 'amounts to an affront to the public conscience.' This has been exemplified in *Hardwicke* and *Thwaites*[118] where in delivering their verdict the jury stated as follows: 'The jury would like to say that the circumstances surrounding the case have made it very difficult for us

[114] Times 11-Oct-2000, Gazette 19-Oct-2000, [2000] EWCA Crim 1535, [2001] 1 Cr App R 168; Summary taken from https://www.lawgazette.co.uk/law/the-law-regarding-entrapment/55972.article retrieved on 2/10/21.

[115] National Prosecution Authority; Anti-Corruption Commission; Drug Enforcement Commission; Road Traffic and Safety Agency etc.

[116] https://www.lawgazette.co.uk/law/the-law-regarding-entrapment/55972.article retrieved on 2/10/21.

[117] [1996] 1 WLR 104.

[118] [2001] Crim LR 220.

to reach a decision. Had we been allowed to take the extreme provocation into account we would have undoubtedly reached a different verdict.' This should come as no surprise when one considers that:

> In certain circumstances the techniques adopted by undercover reporters to entrap citizens into committing criminal offences must pass this threshold. In any society governed by the rule of law, it is surely undesirable for the press to have an unfettered power to utilise undercover techniques to solicit the commission of criminal offences.[119]

In concluding this part, we return to the decision in *R v Loosely*.[120] The Lords rejected the assertion that entrapment per se should be treated as a substantive defence. It said however, that there were remedies within the common law with respect to entrapment which were as follows:

(i) that the court could stay the proceedings in question for being an abuse of process; and
(ii) the court could, based on its inherent power under the common law, exclude evidence[121] to preserve the fairness of the proceedings *vis-à-vis* the accused person.

Among the things that a magistrates/judge ought to consider include the following:

(i) Whether the accused would, but for the police, have committed the offence;[122]
(ii) Whether the police aided the commission of the offence with which the accused is charged or they just provided an opportunity to do so;[123]
(iii) What is the nature of the offence or of the entrapment in question?
(iv) Did the police have a basis for their suspicion?
(v) Was the police's participation active or passive and/or to be ordinarily expected in their course of work as would be expected from members of the public for example?

5.2.3.9 *Excluding incriminating statements obtained by tricks*

Given the unequal position that the police have as against the suspect with the former having more resources at their disposal including the ability to take away the suspect's liberty, should they be successful at trial, means that the court must ensure that where incriminating evidence is extracted by the device of tricks which in *Sang*,[124] Diplock LJ said amounted to deceitfully persuading

---

[119] https://www.lawgazette.co.uk/law/the-law-regarding-entrapment/55972.article retrieved on 2/10/21.

[120] [2001] UKHL 53; summary taken from https://www.lawgazette.co.uk/law/the-law-regarding-entrapment/55972.article retrieved on 2/10/21.

[121] Under s 78, PACE 1984.

[122] However, the accused's predisposition or criminal record ought not to be at the core of making this determination under normal circumstances.

[123] *R v Moon* [2004] EWCA Crim 2872.

[124] [1979] 2 All ER 1222 at 1222 c-d.

the accused to confess, same is, in a proper case and right circumstances, excluded. In *R v Payne,*[125] the appellant was asked at a police station whether he was willing to be examined by a doctor, and was told that it would be no part of the doctor's duty to examine him in order to give an opinion as to his unfitness to drive. The appellant consented to be, and was, examined by a doctor. At the trial of the appellant on charges of driving, and of being in charge of, a motor vehicle while unfit to drive through drink, the doctor who had examined the appellant gave evidence of the extent to which the appellant was under the influence of drink, testifying that he was under the influence of drink to such an extent as to be unfit to have proper control of a car. The appellant was convicted on both charges, was sentenced and was disqualified from driving for three years. On appeal, it was held that although the doctor's evidence was admissible, the trial court should in its discretion have refused to allow the evidence to be given, since the appellant might have refused to subject himself to examination if he had realised that the doctor would give evidence on that matter; accordingly, the convictions on the two charges, and the order for disqualification, would be quashed.[126]

The position taken in *Sang*[127] and exemplified in *Payne*[128] has not been altered by the enactment of s 78 PACE 1984. This is shown in the post s 78 case of *R v Mason.*[129] The appellant was arrested and questioned regarding an offence of arson. The police had no direct evidence associating the appellant with the crime but they falsely told him and his solicitor that they had found near the scene of the crime a fragment of a bottle which had contained inflammable liquid and that the appellant's fingerprint was on the fragment. The appellant then told the police that he had filled the bottles with the liquid and had asked a friend to commit the offence. At his trial he challenged the admissibility of the confession. The trial judge considered whether, 'having regard to all the circumstances, including the circumstances in which the evidence was obtained', the confession should be excluded under s 78(1)a of the Police and Criminal Evidence Act 1984 and decided that it would not be unfair to admit it. The appellant appealed against the judge's decision to admit the confession. At the hearing of the appeal the Crown contended, inter alia, that s 78 did not apply to confessions since they were expressly dealt with by s 76b which provided that a confession could only be excluded if it had been obtained by oppression or was likely to be unreliable. It was held as follows: For the purpose of s 78

---

[125] [1963] 1 All ER 848.

[126] Editor's notes: The appellant was also convicted on a charge of dangerous driving against which there was no appeal, but the disqualification was stated to have attached to the offences involving the influence of drink and, therefore, fell with those convictions; As to disqualification, see s 104, s 2, of the Road Traffic Act; 1960, and Sch 11 thereto, 40 Halsbury's Statutes (2nd Edn) 808, 712, 947; as to evidence of insobriety on charge of driving while under influence of drink, see 33 Halsbury's Laws (3rd Edn) 628, para 1059, text and note (g); and for a case on the subject, see 14 Digest (Repl) 488, 4697; for the Road Traffic Act, 1960, s 6, see 40 Halsbury's Statutes (2nd Edn) 717.

[127] [1979] 2 All ER 1222 at 1248b-c.

[128] [1963] 1 All ER 848.

[129] Which cited with approval, the decision in *R v Sang* [1979] 2 All ER 1222, [1980] AC 402, [1979] 3 WLR 263, HL.

of the 1984 Act 'evidence' included all evidence, including a confession, that might be introduced by the prosecution at the trial, notwithstanding [the fact] that confessions were expressly dealt with in s 76. Accordingly, the trial judge could exclude a confession under s 78 if it would have an adverse effect on the fairness of the trial, even though it had not been obtained by oppression nor was likely to be unreliable. On the facts, the trial judge had wrongly exercised his discretion because he had failed to consider the deceit practiced on the appellant and his solicitor and if he had done so he would have been bound to exclude the confession. The appeal would be allowed and, there being no other evidence produced by the prosecution, the conviction would be quashed.[130]

R v Bailey and Smith[131] exemplifies a police trick that may lead to self-incrimination by the suspect(s). The appellants were arrested and charged with robbery. When interviewed by the police they exercised their right to silence. The next day they appeared before magistrates and were remanded in police custody so that they could be put up on identification parades. In the meantime, the officer in charge of the case obtained permission to install listening equipment in one of the remand cells at the police station and when they were returned to the police station from the magistrates' court the investigating officers, in order to avoid arousing their suspicions, pretended that they had been forced to place the appellants together in the bugged cell by an unco-operative custody officer. While in the cell together the appellants made damaging admissions in conversation which were recorded. At their trial the appellants submitted that the judge should exercise his discretion under s 78(1)a of the Police and Criminal Evidence Act 1984 to exclude the taped cell conversations but the judge ruled that they were admissible. The appellants were convicted. They appealed on the ground, inter alia, that the evidence of the taped conversations had been wrongly admitted. It was held that the evidence of the secretly taped conversations between the two appellants who had been placed in the same cell while on remand as the result of a police subterfuge was admissible at their trial, since the obtaining of evidence in such a way was not contrary to the Code of Practice for the Detention, Treatment and Questioning of Persons by Police Officers under the 1984 Act, notwithstanding that the police were not entitled to question them further because they had been charged. The police were under no duty to protect them from having the opportunity to speak indiscriminately to each other if they chose to do so and there was nothing in the 1984 Act or the Code of Practice which prohibited the police from bugging a cell, even after an accused person had been charged and had exercised his right to silence. Accordingly, the judge had been entitled in the exercise of his discretion under s 78(1) of the 1984 Act to admit the evidence

[130] Editor's notes: For admissibility of confessions, see 11 Halsbury's Laws (4th edn) para 410, and for cases on the subject, see 14(2) Digest (Reissue) 549–552, 4494–4517; For the Police and Criminal Evidence Act 1984, ss 76, 78, see 17 Halsbury's Statutes (4th edn) 213, 215.

[131] [1993] 3 All ER 513.

of the taped conversations. The appeal would therefore be dismissed.[132]

Wood v UK[133] is authority for the position that it makes no difference whether the deception in question is implied rather than express. In *Allan v UK*,[134]the appellant had been convicted of murder. The police had encouraged an informant to associate with him whilst in prison and to entice admissions from him. They had also recorded conversations whilst he was in the police station cells. It was held as follows: no system regulated such recordings, and accordingly the recordings were not according to law, and were an infringement of his human rights. As to the conversations with the fellow inmate, it was not the function of the Court to adjudicate on matters of fact, nor as to the admissibility of evidence. The question for the court was whether the behaviour was such as to render the proceedings as a whole unfair. This included whether there had been shown due respect for the rights of the defence. The right against self-incrimination includes the right not to incriminate oneself through coercion or oppression, in defiance of the will of the accused. He had here exercised his right of silence on interview. The police had coached the informant to try to extract a confession, and the confessions obtained were not spontaneous or unprompted. The confessions were obtained in defiance of his will, and in breach of his article 6 rights to a fair trial. Art 13 had also been infringed by the use of wrongful surveillance without effective remedy.

Mere police deception which has as its consequence, the extraction of incriminating evidence from the suspect does not, without more, ordinarily lead the court to use its discretion to exclude said evidence. In *Maclean and Kosten*[135] the customs had arrested a drugs courier with a carload of cannabis but wished to implicate the real importer. The police created a story that the courier was in hospital after a car crash and this was used to trap the importer into making arrangements regarding the car in order to recover the cannabis, and into making various tape-recorded statements which were used in evidence against him. He appealed against conviction on the grounds that the evidence should not have been admissible as it had been unfairly obtained by trickery. [It was held inter alia that], unlike Mason and similar cases, outside the police station, there [could] be no expectation of privacy nor that the people with whom [the appellant was] dealing [were] honest, especially if [one was] engaged in illegal activity. Although the police officer became involved in an ongoing offence, his role was relatively passive and an accurate record was provided. It [was therefore] difficult to argue that the fairness of the proceedings [had] been affected.

---

[132] Editor's notes: For the admissibility in evidence of tape and video recordings, see 11(2) Halsbury's Laws (4th edn reissue) para 1157; For the discretion to exclude relevant prosecution evidence, see 11(2) Halsbury's Laws (4th edn reissue) para 1060; For the Police and Criminal Evidence Act 1984, s 78, see 17 Halsbury's Statutes (4th edn) (1993 reissue) 228.

[133] Application No 00023414/02.

[134] Application No 00048539/99, [2003] 36 EHRR 12; As adapted at https://swarb.co.uk/allan-v-the-united-kingdom-echr-5-nov retrieved on 29/12/21.

[135] [1993] Crim LR 687 as adapted in Uglow S *Evidence* 142.

5.2.3.10 Evidence obtained by covert surveillance

The police may undertake covert surveillancein order to acquire evidence relating to offences that have been committed and for which a formal investigation is merited.[136]

5.3 The European Convention on Human Rights and the right to privacy

The relevant provisions in this respect are those under Art 8 of the ECHR. It provides as follows:

> 1. Everyone has the right to respect for his private and family life, his home and his correspondence.
> 2. There shall be no interference by a public authority with the exercise of this right except such as is in accordance with the law and is necessary in a democratic society in the interests of national security, public safety or the economic well-being of the country, for the prevention of disorder or crime, for the protection of health or morals, or for the protection of the rights and freedoms of others.

The article proscribes all interceptions of communications. This includes any surveillance methods which on the face of it would appear to violate the right to one's privacy guaranteed under Art 8. The matter arose and was considered in *Klass and Others v Germany*.[137] The applicants challenged a German law which authorised the state to intercept the correspondence lawyers had with their clients. Moreover, they were surveillant communications between lawyers and their clients. The claimant objected to the disclosure by the police of matters revealed during their investigation. However, the government claimed a legitimate aim of national security interests. As regards the question whether there was a violation of Article 8 ECHR,[138] it was held that this in itself was not a problem. However, this must be done using adequate safeguards and procedures. Furthermore, the court recognised that some operations must be conducted secretly if they are to be conducted effectively. Therefore, the court found no violation of Article 8 ECHR. Specifically, the court noted as follows: '[t]he Court must be satisfied that, whatever system of surveillance is adopted, there exist adequate and effective guarantees against abuse.' The following guidelines were given by the Court:[139]

> (a) the legislation must be designed to ensure that surveillance is not ordered haphazardly, irregularly or without due and proper care;
> (b) surveillance must be reviewed and must be accompanied by procedures which guarantee individual rights;

[136] This part is considered in slightly greater detail in chapter 12.

[137] 5029/71, (1979) 2 EHRR 214, [1978] ECHR 4; summary taken from https://simplestudying.com/klass-and-others-v-germany-1979-2-ehrr-214/ retrieved on 5/10/21.

[138] Right to respect for private and family life.

[139] As summarised in Uglow Steve *Evidence* 143.

(c) it is in principle desirable to entrust the supervisory control to a judge in accordance with the rule of law, but other safeguards might suffice if they are independent and vested with sufficient powers to exercise an effective and continuous control;

(d) if the surveillance is justified under Art.8(2) the failure to inform the individual under surveillance of this fact afterwards is, in principle, justified.

The fact that there is supervision of an investigating judge is not sufficient in obviating the violation of Art.8. The surveillance may well be deemed insufficient where there is want of sufficient safeguards with respect to possible abuses. In *Huvig v France,*[140] the applicants were suspected of, and subsequently convicted of, various offences of tax evasion by the use of forged invoices. In the course of the judicial investigation the investigating judge authorised a senior police officer to have the applicants' business and private telephone lines tapped. The applicants complained of a violation of Article 8 of the Convention. The Court held that telephone tapping undoubtedly amounts to an ' interference by a public authority' with the exercise of an individual's right to privacy in correspondence. In this opinion, the Court referred to its own case law[141] regarding the requirements on the quality of the law, and in particular, the foreseeability of the law. The Court had to assess the relevant domestic 'law' in relation to the requirements of the fundamental principle of the rule of law. The Court then found that the current system in France failed to provide the adequate safeguards against possible abuse.

Kruslin v France[142] was a case concerned with telephone tapping. The applicant was convicted of armed robbery. A decisive piece of evidence against him was a tape recording of his telephone conversation with another person who was tapped in relation to other proceedings. The applicant filed this suit alleging that the recording of his telephone conversations violated Article 8 of the Convention. The court held that Title 8 of the Convention was violated:

> Even though the authorities tapped the telephone of a third party, the tapping amounted to an 'interference by a public authority' with respect to the applicant's right for correspondence and private life. Hence, this tapping violates the Continental system. This Court, however, cannot express an opinion with regards to French law

[140] (Series A No 176-B; Application No 11105/84) European Court of Human Rights (1990) 12 EHRR 528 24 APRIL 1990; Summary taken from http://www.hrcr.org/safrica/privacy/huvig_france.html retrieved on 5/10/21.

[141] *Chappell v United Kingdom,* (1990) 12 EHRR 36; *De Wilde, Ooms and Versyp v Belgium (No 1),* 1 EHRR 373; *Dudgeon v United Kingdom,* (1982) 4 EHRR 149; *Eriksson v Sweden,* judgment of 22 June 1989, Series A, No 156; *Johnston v Ireland,* (1987) 9 EHRR 203; *Klass v Germany,* 2 EHRR 214; *Kostovski v Netherlands,* judgment of 20 November 1989, Series A, No 166; *Malone v United Kingdom,* (1985) 7 EHRR 14; *Markt Intern Verlag Gmbh and Beermann v Germany,* (1990) 12 EHRR 161; *Muller v Switzerland,* judgment of 24 May 1988, Series A, No 133; *Salabiaku v France,* judgment of 7 October 1988, Series A, No 141-A; *Silver v United Kingdom,* (1983) 5 EHRR 347; *The Sunday Times v United Kingdom,* 2 EHRR 245.

[142] [1990] 12 EHRR 547; (Series A No 176-B; Application No 11801/85) European Court of Huma Rights (1990) 12 EHRR 547 24 APRIL 1990; summary taken from http://www.hrcr.org/safrica/privacy/kruslin_france.html retrieved on 5/10/21.

> because that should be settled by the French courts

What appears patent from the preceding cases is the need for the relevant pieces of legislation to make clear classes of persons who are liable to have, among other things, phones tapped. Further, the legislation ought to make clear the nature and character of the offence in question to give sufficient predication for the order of surveillance. In addition, as *Huvig v France*[143] appears to have made clear, the following must be considered as necessary predicates: (i) proper time limits for dealing with the material gathered from surveillance (ii) procedures for dealing with the material gathered from surveillance; and (iii) rules relating to the destruction of recordings from surveillance.

Irrespective of the system in question, the following must be present: (i) lawfulness, (ii) necessity; (iii) proportionality; and (iv) with suitable structures of responsibility. In *Leander v Sweden*,[144] the applicant was a national of Sweden and applied for a high-level position in the Swedish national policy. Secret police files containing information about the applicant's private life were used for the purposes of assessing a person's suitability for the employment. At the time, the applicant's request to access those files was refused. The applicant claimed a violation of his right to private life guaranteed by article 8 of the European Convention. In coming to its judgment, the ECHR did not find a violation of article 8: the use of confidential information in government files was not obstruction of access to information The reasoning behind the court's holding appears to be then fact that there was a breach of article because the use of the secret police files, coupled with a refusal to allow L access to this information, amounted to an interference with the applicant's right to private life. However, the breach of Art. 8(1) was justified by the legitimate aim under 8(2) of protecting national security. Accordingly, there was no violation of Art. 8. Furthermore, Art. 10 does not confer on the individual a right of access to a register containing information on his personal position, nor does it embody an obligation on the Government to impart such information to the individual.

While many jurisdictions such as United States, Canada, France, the Netherlands, Australia, and New Zealand have within their laws statutory provisions relating to the requirement for a judicial warrant prior to listening devices being deployed to intercept private conversations, in this jurisdiction, one would be hard pressed to find equivalent provisions relating to surveillance mechanisms equal to those in the aforementioned jurisdictions. It has been observed that,[145]

> In all these cases, the surveillance is regarded as lawful if there is authorisation from a designated officer and the operation is in the interests of national security, the prevention and detection of crime and disorder, the economic well-being of the state, public safety, public

[143] [1990] 12 EHRR 528.

[144] Summary with a few modifications taken from http://www.hrcr.org/safrica/access_information/ECHR/Leander.html retrieved on 5/10/21.

[145] Uglow S *Evidence* 145.

> health or tax collection.The defendant is not entitled to see the underlying material placed before the surveillance commissioners for the purpose of obtaining approval. [73]

The interplay between Arts 6 and 8 and s 78 of PACE 1984 arose and was considered in *Khan v the appellant.*[146] The appellant, who was suspected by the police of being party to the importation of prohibited drugs, visited the home of another man to which, unknown to both of them, the police had attached a listening device. The police thereby obtained a tape recording of a conversation which clearly showed that the appellant was involved in the importation of prohibited drugs. The appellant was arrested and charged with being knowingly concerned in the fraudulent importation of prohibited drugs. At his trial, the Crown's case rested almost entirely on the contents of the tape recording. The appellant admitted that it was his voice on the tape recording, but contended: (i) that the tape recording was inadmissible as evidence because the installation of the listening device was a civil trespass since the police had no statutory authority to install covert listening devices on private property, (ii) that the admission of the tape recording in evidence would breach the right to respect for private and family life and home protected by art 8a of the European Convention on Human Rights, (iii) that if the evidence had been obtained by means of telephone tapping it would have been inadmissible under the Interception of Communications Act 1985, and (iv) that even if the tape recording were admissible, the judge should exercise his discretion under s 78(1)b of the Police and Criminal Evidence Act 1984 to exclude it because of the breach of art 8 that admissibility would involve. The judge ruled that the tape recording was admissible. The appellant was convicted. He appealed to the Court of Appeal on the grounds that the tape recording had been wrongly admitted in evidence, but the court dismissed his appeal. He appealed to the House of Lords. It was held that the appeal would be dismissed for the following reasons—(1) Under English law, there was in general nothing unlawful about a breach of privacy and the common law rule that relevant evidence obtained by the police by improper or unfair means was admissible in a criminal trial, notwithstanding that it was obtained improperly or even unlawfully, applied to evidence obtained by the use of surveillance devices which invaded a person's 289 privacy. Accordingly, even if the right to privacy for which the appellant contended did exist (which was doubtful) the tape recording was, as a matter of law, admissible in evidence at the trial of the appellant subject, however, to the judge's discretion to exclude it in the exercise of his common law discretion or under s 78 of the 1984 Act. (2) The fact that evidence had been obtained in circumstances which amounted to a breach of the provisions of art 8 of the convention was relevant to, but not determinative of, the judge's

[146] These statutory schemes must be read alongside the requirements of s.78 and Arts 6 and 8; *Taylor Sabori v UK* App No 00047114/99; [2003] 36 EHRR 17; Editor's notes: For admissibility of criminal evidence and discretion to exclude relevant prosecution evidence, see 11(2) Halsbury's Laws (4th edn reissue) paras 1059–1060, and for cases on the subject, see 15(1) Digest (2nd reissue) 516–518, 520, 17086–17088, 17097; For the Police and Criminal Evidence Act 1984, s 78, see 17 Halsbury's Statutes (4th edn) (1993 reissue) 228.

discretion to admit or exclude such evidence under s 78 of the 1984 Act. The judge's discretion had to be exercised according to whether the admission of the evidence would render the trial unfair, and the use at a criminal trial of material obtained in breach of the rights of privacy enshrined in art 8 did not of itself mean that the trial would be unfair. On the facts, the trial judge had been entitled to hold that the circumstances in which the relevant evidence was obtained, even if they constituted a breach of art 8, were not such as to require the exclusion of the evidence.[147]

[147] Decision of the Court of Appeal [1994] 4 All ER 426 affirmed.

6

CORROBORATION

6.1 Introduction

As we have noted in chapters preceding this one, at the core of the adversarial trial is oral testimony. This is, however, not without its limits especially when we consider the many issues and constraints that confront the concept of testimony in general and witnesses in particular, within the greater picture of the adversarial trial. Present in our discussions have been shortcomings of oral testimony, the rather complex, inconsistent, somewhat bewildering nature of rules regarding witness competence, and the invariable need, borne out of the adversarial system's own inanition in places. Given this background, we turn in this chapter, to a discussion concerning the following general themes:

- (i) The treatment of what may be termed suspect or evidence deemed to be unreliable
- (ii) The development of the law and rules regarding when judges/ magistrates ought to warn themselves when they encounter suspect or unreliable evidence
- (iii) Classes of evidence which invite the court to warn itself chief among them, lies by the defendant/accused or identification evidence.

In chapter 1 we encountered the concept of rectitude of decision. It is worth repeating what we noted then which is that a judge who, in adjudicating upon a matter, does so 'with a minimum of foresight, without examination of what they are doing and of probable consequences' of their actions will not last very long in their job or achieve what is termed by Twinning[1] as 'Bentham's rectitude of decision.'[2] The latter is achieved by the accurate application of substantive law to the true facts of the dispute premised on the deployment of rules of evidence in totality. Twinning argues that 'rectitude of decision is seen as the primary end of adjudication, as a necessary means to enforcement of law and vindication of rights (expletive justice); expletive justice is an important, if not necessarily an overriding, social value; the concept of 'rectitude of decision' leads directly to such notions as truth, facts, relevance, evidence, and inference and to a number of assumptions about the possibility of knowledge (or at least of warranted conclusions of fact) and about valid reasoning.'[3] Nor would an adjudicator properly so called and qualified to preside over court proceedings be expected to 'act not upon deliberation but from routine, instinct, the direct pressure of appetite, or a blind 'hunch'.[4]

Be that as it may, history is replete with examples of miscarriages of justice which have gone against the convention we first discussed in chapter 1 which is that where the court believes that the accused is 'probably guilty' or 'likely to be guilty,' the court is admitting of not being 'sure.' Under such circumstances, it must acquit the accused. In Sir William Blackstone's[5] words, '[...] the law holds that it is better that ten guilty persons escape than that one innocent suffer.'[6] It is, as we have noted elsewhere in this text, thus deemed to be better to acquit a guilty party than to convict an innocent one. The concept of burden of proof and the rules thereof are thus designed to minimise the risk of wrong conviction. To quote Lord Denning in *Miller v Minister of Pensions,*[7] '[....] It is true that under our existing jurisprudence in criminal matters, we have to proceed with presumption of innocence, but at the same time, that presumption is to be judged on the basis of conceptions of a reasonable prudent man. Smelling doubts for the sake of giving benefit of doubt is not the law of the land.' In the next portion of this chapter, we turn to the discussion of why miscarriages of justice occur.

6.2 Causes of miscarriage of justice

While the *Adolph Beck case* which we consider in greater detail in chapter 7 provides an extreme case of miscarriage of justice, miscarriages of justice are not rare and happen more often than one may want to admit within the context of the adversarial system of adjudication. Greer[8] has thus postulated as follows:

> A 'mistaken' conviction occurs when he tribunal of fact honestly, and without impropriety, believes the prosecution evidence, either through misunderstanding the issues or because a defence which is in fact true seems to lack credibility. There are various sources of such convictions: vital evidence simply not coming to light, outside interference with vital witnesses resulting in either their failure to testify or perjured evidence at trial, mistaken or misleading directions by otherwise unbiased judges, joint trials in which an innocent defendant may be tarnished with the guilt of a co-defendant, mistaken identity, false confessions volunteered without police pressure, poor defence tactics, mistaken or deliberately false evidence by accomplices or other witnesses, and a failure on the part of [courts] to understand the legal burden of proof or the issue involved in the trial. A [judge] or magistrate may be inclined to convict, for example, if presented with an entirely innocent but unconvincing defendant, who has had the opportunity to commit the offence, has been wrongly identified as the offender by a mistaken or dishonest witness, has no alibi and whose defence may amount to no more than a blank denial of the charge.

---

[5] Blackstone, William, *Commentaries on the Laws of England,* facsimile edition with introductions by Stanley N. Katz.(Univ. Chicago, 1979). 4 vols.

[6] The *Commentaries on the Laws of England* are an influential 18th-century treatise on the common law of England by Sir William Blackstone, originally published by the Clarendon Press at Oxford, 1765–1770.

[7] [1947] 2 ALL ER 272.

[8] S. Greer, "Miscarriage of Criminal Justice Reconsidered" [1994] 57 MLR 58 at 72-73.

It must be noted that different legal systems, some more proactively than others, have recognised the problems highlighted in Greer's comments. This has resulted in the development and crafting of laws, rules and procedures to limit the occurrences of miscarriage of justice. They have included the admissibility *vis-à-vis* reliability tests or/and requirements to be met before confessions can be admitted into evidence; the development of warnings regarding risks inherent in uncorroborated accomplice evidence; the need for care as regards the evaluation of witness oral testimony; and the offence of perjury. The foregoing arrangements are not cast in stone and should be viewed as being amenable to changes and improvements as the needs of society demand from time to time.

Both at common law and by way of statutory law, the quality of evidence has been subjected to scrutiny within the context of the concept of corroboration or independent evidence supportive of evidence of a witness in a material particular. This is with specific reference to accomplice evidence; sexual offences; and the worn evidence of a child. The rationale for the common law and statutory checks may appear to be that determining a dispute or a criminal prosecution must be premised on evidence from multiple sources and at the very least, two sides of the dispute. Thus, testimony by a single witness should always be subjected to scrutiny, and where possible, rejection of uncorroborated evidence.

Criminal proceedings present the most prominent example of the sort of proceedings where single witness testimony ought to be rigorously tested and even question, if not rejected. As noted elsewhere in this text, following the end of the trial, the court is called upon to render a verdict. It is according to Dennis[9], in the verdict that we see whether 'the factual demonstration has or has not been made out.' We further noted Duff's[10] suggestion that 'to indict someone for a criminal offence is to offer a particular criticism of his conduct; to try him is to seek to determine the justice of that criticism; to convict him is to blame him publicly for that offence.' A guilty verdict is thus a moral condemnation of the accused.

Recall that a guilty verdict leads to a sentence, which is society's chosen method of punishing convicts. It therefore falls to reason that only those for whom the evidence shows are guilty of the offence 'beyond a reasonable doubt' must be convicted. Exclusion of doubt would indeed be near impossible if reliance was solely placed on uncorroborated evidence of a single witness. Nor would it be considered fair, save for exceptional cases where justice demands it,[11] for an accused person to be convicted on the uncorroborated evidence of a single witness.[12] If those charged with offences were convicted on insufficient or unreliable evidence inclusive of uncorroborated evidence, society's willingness to accept and respect verdicts handed down as to the accused's guilt when in

---

[9] Dennis I, The Law of Evidence 53.

[10] Duff A, *Trials and Punishments* (1986) 39.

[11] See chapter 14 on the protection of vulnerable witnesses.

[12] See Stephen F, General View of the Criminal Law 1st edn (Macmillan 1863) 249.

fact a vigilant examination of the evidence ought to plausibly have led to an acquittal would be enfeebled.[13]

We must preface the discussion that follows regarding corroboration and supportive evidence with a few observations. There has been a contemporary movement away from the common law rules requiring supporting evidence in more advanced jurisdictions such as England, Canada and Australia. This has led to there being very few instances for the said requirement in English law. The testimony of a single witness is now ordinarily accepted and used as a basis for a criminal conviction or acquittal in criminal cases and civil proceedings. The law in this jurisdiction has not, as is evidenced from many authorities, some of which we consider below and statutory provisions that we will consider shortly, not moved in tandem with changes to English law or indeed other contemporary developments in common law jurisdictions. Why in this day and age the law and our courts should continually insist on there being further evidence from a second source that tends to confirm the fact stated by source is mind boggling and most disconcerting. To ask that the court warns itself if it were to proceed to convict on the basis of uncorroborated evidence is out of sync with modern day legal thinking. It is not in line with best practice, leaves much to be desired and makes our legal system, as in many other instances, seem antiquated, and our Parliament, lethargic for provisions of which we speak and common law rules which we make reference are now of no significance in the contemporary law of evidence.

In this chapter and the next two, we will consider how suspect evidence may be reinforced. Chapter 6 considers corroboration; chapter 7 will discuss identification evidence and chapter 8 confession evidence. First, we turn to a brief historical account of the concept of corroboration.

6.3 A brief historical outline

It has been held *inter alia* in *Machobane v The People,*[14] that while a conviction on the uncorroborated evidence of an accomplice is competent as a strict matter of law, the danger of such conviction is a rule of practice which has become virtually equivalent to a rule of law, and an accused should not be convicted on the uncorroborated testimony of a witness with a possible interest unless there are some special and compelling grounds.The common law recognised the importance of insisting that in certain cases the evidence of one witness be corroborated. Such instances included the following:

(i) The nature of the evidence e.g., identification;
(ii) The gravity of the complaint as in a charge of rape;
(iii) Where there was a motive to lie; and
(iv) Where the witness was mentally incapacitated.

The foregoing position of the common law with respect to the law of evidence in general and corroboration in particular, specifically, the latter's non-

[13] See *L.T. Gen. Geojago Robert Chaswe Musengule, Amon Sibande v The People* HPA /16/2009 and the cases referred to therein.

[14] [1972] ZR 101 (CA).

insistence on a plurality of witnesses may be contrasted with the approach set by civil or canon law which had at its core the application of the maxim *testis unus testis nullus.*[15] English law started off, it must observed here and now, with a requirement for a plurality of witnesses as was the case under Roman law.[16] In a defence concept deployed in medieval times in England referred to as compurgation or wager of law, it was required and expected that there be more than one oath helper. In order to establish his innocence or non-liability, an accused person/defendant as the case may have been, could take an oath. He would also need to get, in aid, an essential number of individuals, characteristically twelve in number to swear oaths that they believed the accused's/defendant's own oath. Employed as a character reference at a time when oaths held more credence than written records, compurgation was a means for giving credibility to the accused's/ defendant's oath initially by the accused's/defendant's kin and in later years, by his neighbours i.e., to say individuals from the same region as the accused/defendant. It was also seen as a means for minimising frolicsome litigation. It was a feature in early Germanic law on the one hand and early French law (*très ancienne coutume de Bretagne*), on the other. It was also a feature of Welsh law, and was employed in the English ecclesiastical courts up until the 17th century.

The Constitutions of Clarendon in 1164 considerably obliterated compurgation as a defence in felonies at common law. It, however, remained in use as a defence in civil actions for debt and remnants of it subsisted until its statutory annulment in England in 1833,[17] and in Queensland sometime time before the enactment of the Queensland Common Practice Act of 1867.[18]

A divergence would occur between English common law and civil/canon law, however, when the English jury started taking on a role familiar in contemporary times from the 17th century. Prior to this period, jurors acted as witnesses. It is therefore easy to appreciate the argument that up until that time, English law required more than one witness. Once the jury ceased acting as witnesses as they had done in times past, legislative efforts were made to impose two or more witnesses.

Be that as it may, it does not appear, from a careful consideration of old common law authorities or such statutory provisions as we refer to above, that there was established a coherent approach to deal with the issue of corroboration. As a consequence, what developed as the law relating to corroboration was more a matter of the courts and the legislature devising ad hoc rules that compelled judges/magistrates to consider whether the evidence

[15] '*Testis Unus, Testis Nullus*' is a legal maxim which means one witness is not a witness. It is a law principle expressing that a single witness is not enough to corroborate a story.' - https://definitions.uslegal.com/t/testis-unus-testis-nullus/ retrieved on 24/7/21; To be sure a court is well within its rights in a proper case, to convict on uncorroborated evidence unless statute specifically mandates it not to do so: *Yuda Nchepeshi v The People* [1978] ZR 362 (SC).

[16] For a more detailed historical account see generally, J H Wigmore, *Evidence in Trials at Common Law*, Chadbourn re, 1978, vol 7, [2032]; J H Langbein, *The Origins of Adversary Criminal Trial*, 2003 203-17; see also *R v Rosemeyer* [1985] VR 945 at 960-966 (FC).

[17] Friedman LM, *The Legal System: A Social Science Perspective* (Russell Sage Foundation, 1975) 272.

[18] Common Law Practice Act 1867, Office of the Queensland Parliamentary Counsel, 24 June 1994, Wager of law abolished – 3. No wager of law shall be allowed.

before them required the support of, and was indeed supported by evidence independent of that already presented before court.

The foregoing was followed by formal rules we now refer to as corroboration. The development of the common law which gave rise to the rules to the evolution of rules relating to corroboration meant, as has been noted elsewhere in this text, the classification of cases which due to their nature or the witness, necessitated the receipt of corroborative evidence. Thus, evidence of accomplices (when called at the behest of the prosecution); complaints in sexual matters; and that of children, all required corroboration. It must be noted though, that all a judge was expected to do under such circumstances and nature of cases calling for it, was simply to warn the jury (in this jurisdiction, warn himself) of the danger of convicting on anyone of the sources covered in the foregoing class of witnesses or cases without corroboration. Be that as it may (and this still remains the case today wherever corroboration is mandated by statute, the common law or rules of practice), the judge was well within his inherent authority that convict on uncorroborated evidence, if having paid heed to the warning, they (jury) or he (the judge as is the case in this jurisdiction) still remained convinced regarding the guilt of the accused.

The progress of rules regarding corroboration continued apace. Unfortunately, instead of simplifying the concept, what followed was technical legalise that confused not only litigants and legal practitioners, but judges too. There were exhaustive rules regarding the meaning of the term "corroboration;" the evidence that could qualify as corroborative; who could be deemed to be an accomplice; the delineation between the functions of the judge on the one hand; and the jury on the other; and the nature of direction a judge could give to the jury.

As a result of the foregoing complexities wrought into the concept by the rules hereinbefore discussed, criticism naturally arose on at least five basic fronts:

(i) The complexity of the rules led Diplock LJ to observe in *R v Hester,*[19]as was commonly believed at the time, that the 'complicated formulae about the concept of corroboration and the respective functions of judge and jury are [...] unintelligible to the ordinary laymen,' a view endorsed by the Law Commission.[20]

(ii) The rules were deemed too inflexible to be of beneficial use to parties, their legal representatives and even the courts in achieving rectitude of decision. The obligatory injunction for a warning to be issued wherever and whenever a witness came within the classes of persons for which a warning was required i.e., say if he was an accomplice called upon by the prosecution, a witness in a sexual offence charge; or a child as the case may have been proved from time to time to be wholly uncalled for, and yes in certain instances, inappropriate: (i) if the proceedings were concerned with a sexual offence having

[19] [1972] AC 296 at 328.

[20] Law Commission para 2.9.

been committed, it may well have been the case that the fact of the offence being committed was common cause- the issue may be determining whether the accused is the person that committed the offence with which he is charged; and (ii) an accomplice called upon by the prosecution in aid of their case may have had no interest to serve except contrition from pangs of conscience, and such nothing to profit from testifying against a co-accused.

(iii) Related to the second point was the criticism that the rules engendered somewhat hilarious incongruities. A specific matter is the one relating to the application of corroborative rules to accomplices and co-accused persons. For purposes of jurisprudential clarity, we discuss the position as it stood in England at the relevant time. Before the enactment of the Criminal Justice and Public Order Act 1994, questions arose as to what warning if any, was needed in instances where one accused person gave incriminating evidence against a co-accused. In the first case on this point, that of *R v Prater*,[21] the EWCA took the view that where such a scenario arose, or where an accomplice was called upon by the prosecution to give evidence in aid of their case, it was appropriate to give a full corroboration warning. This position was not followed in subsequent cases nor was it endorsed in what is now considered the foremost English authority on the subject *R v Knowlden and Knowlden*[22] wherein it was observed thatthe rule in *Prater*[23] was not a rule of law but ultimately in the discretion of the judge: 'in exercising his discretion as to what to say to the jury [or in this jurisdiction, to himself] the judge is at least expected to give a clear warning to a jury [or himself] where [accused persons] have given evidence against one another to examine the evidence of each with care because each has or may have an interest of his own to serve.'[24] The foregoing, the court opined, 'would in most cases suffice to ensure that the jury regarded the evidence in question with proper and adequate caution. 'in exercising his discretion.'[25]

(iv) The direction for corroboration as it specifically related to women in sexual offences was not only seen as sexist and misogynistic but particularly offensive to women. Not only was it expected for a judge/ magistrate to explain the danger of convicting on the uncorroborated evidence of a rape victim for example, but as would ordinarily happen as regards sexual offence, the judge/magistrate had to tell the jury 'that it had been the accumulated experience of the courts that false allegations in such cases were made from time to time.'[26]

---

[21] [1960] 2 QB 464, 44 Cr App R 83 CCA.

[22] 77 Cr App R 94 CA.

[23] [1960] 2 QB 464, 44 Cr App R 83 CCA.

[24] As summarised in Richardson PJ (Ed), *Archbold* (1997 edn Sweet & Maxwell, 1997) para 16-16 at 1497.

[25] https://swarb.co.uk/regina-v-knowlden-and-knowlden-cacd-1983/ retrieved on 25/7/21.

[26] See *Knight v R* 50 Cr App R 122 affirmed in *Zimba v The People* [1980] ZR 259; see also *R v Chauhan* (1981) 73 Cr App R 232; *R v Redpath* (1962) 46 Cr App R 319.

(v) The perception as regards the reliability of evidence given by children saw a positive sea change in England & Wales. We cannot say the same about the antiquated scenario that continues to be perpetuated in this jurisdiction.[27]

The foregoing criticisms led, in England at least, to the abolition of any requirement for a court to issue a warning before it could convict on evidence of a children[28] on the one hand and that of an accomplice or complainant in sexual offences[29] on the other.

R v Baskerville,[30] is authority for the position taken at common law that for the evidence to be considered corroborative, it had to confirm in '[...] some material particular not only the evidence that a crime has been committed, but also that the prisoner committed it.' In other words, not only was corroborative evidence required to verify a material part of the evidence being corroborated, it also needed to implicate the accused as did the evidence in need of corroboration. The case of *R v Sabenzu*[31] demonstrates a scenario in which a conviction on a charge of defilement was quashed for want of corroboration and the failure by the court below to warn itself of the dangers inherent in convicting on uncorroborated evidence.

As noted in our definition above, at common law, corroborative evidence was expected and required to be autonomous or to originate from a source other than the witness whose evidence needed corroboration. In *R v Whitehead*[32] the evidence of recent complaint of a victim in a sexual assault matter was rejected for not being autonomous though evidence an independent observation of the victim's distress after a rape encounter was accepted as corroborative in *R v Chauhan.*[33]

It was also a rule that that corroborative evidence could not come from a witness whose evidence required corroboration nor could a child corroborate another witness.

It was also shown in *R v Hill*[34] that corroboration could be distilled from the cumulative effect of several strands of evidence which when looked at individually could not be considered as meeting the threshold of corroboration but when aggregated amounted to corroboration.

It is submitted that to the extent that any rules concerning corroboration remain, their relevance is limited to specific matters provided for under statutory law. Part of the reason for the foregoing is due to the fact that '[...] complicated formulae about the concept of corroboration and the respective

---

[27] See s 122 of the Juveniles Act chapter 53 as amended by Act No 3 of 2011 and authorities considered under para 4.6.2.2 A child's competence and s 122 in the eyes of Zambian case law.

[28] Ss 16-10 of the Criminal Justice Act 1988.

[29] See ss 16-11 of the Criminal Justice and Public Order Act 1994.

[30] [1916] 2 KB 658 at 667; [1916-17] All ER Rep 38.

[31] (1946) 4 NRLR 45.

[32] [1929] 1 KB 99.

[33] (1981) 73 Cr App R 232; *R v Redpath* (1962) 46 Cr App R.

[34] (1987) 86 Cr App R 232.

functions of [a] judge [...] are [...] unintelligible to the ordinary laymen.'[35] We will thus consider corroboration required by statute (ii) instances where corroboration warning is required namely those involving accomplices, sexual matters and evidence of a child who has attained or is under the age of eighteen.

6.4 Corroboration as a matter of statutory law[36]

Statutory law provides for specific instances in which corroboration is required. In those instances, '[...] the trial judge needs to warn and direct himself that the offence is one for which the statute [concerned] requires corroboration in order to secure a conviction, and that the accused cannot be convicted in the absence of [such] corroboration.'[37] Its absence in those instances is a basis for a court acquitting an accused person. Where the court fails do so, it will be grounds for setting the conviction aside on appeal. We consider these instances below.

6.4.1 *Perjury*

In terms of s 106 of the Penal Code,[38] '[a]ny person who commits perjury or suborns[39] perjury is liable to imprisonment for seven years.' The statutory position as to how evidence leading to conviction ought to be provided is to be found under s 107 of the Penal Code[40] which provides as follows: '[a] person cannot be convicted of committing perjury or of subordination of perjury solely upon the evidence of one witness as to the falsity of any statement alleged to be false.'[41] A literal interpretation of the foregoing provision would at first blush suggest that there must be two witnesses. This indeed would appear to have been the understanding of the provision until the observations made in *R v Threfall:*[42]

> The meaning is this: it used some times to be said that there must be two witnesses; this was a delusion; the evidence of one witness and a confession may be enough, and the section has been drafted so as to make this clear. One witness can prove that the person charged swore to certain statements, but more than the evidence of one witness is required to prove that the statements were false.

It has been shown in *R v Peach*[43] that an accused person's confession as to the falsity of his statement is evidence of its falsity. The appellant gave evidence on oath to a coroner's jury investigating whether valuable ancient Celtic relics

[35] [1972] 2 All ER 1020.

[36] For the nature of corroboration in criminal proceedings, see 11 Halsbury's Laws (4th Edn) para 454, and for cases on the subject, see 15 Digest (Reissue) 962–964, 8320–8342.

[37] Kaluba BC, *Evidence Law* 477.

[38] Chapter 87 of the Laws of Zambia.

[39] Or 'induces.'

[40] Chapter 87 of the Laws of Zambia.

[41] Compare s 13 of the Perjury Act 1911.

[42] (1914) 10 Cr App R 112 at 114.

[43] [1990] 2 All ER 966.

found by him and his brother were treasure trove that the relics had been found under the floorboards of a property owned by his brother. He subsequently admitted to two archaeologists that the relics had in fact been discovered near the remains of a church. He was charged with perjury, contrary to s 1(1)a[44] of the Perjury Act 1911, in respect of the evidence given to the coroner's jury and was convicted on the evidence of the two archaeologists. He appealed, contending that the common law rule, given statutory force in s 13b of the 1911 Act, that a person was not to be convicted of perjury on the evidence of only one witness meant that there had to be at least two witnesses who on separate occasions had heard the defendant admit that he had given false evidence. It was held that the requirement in s 13 of the 1911 Act that a person could not be convicted of perjury solely on the evidence of one witness as to the falsity of the person's statements did not prevent a defendant from being convicted on the evidence of two witnesses who testified to having heard the defendant admit the falsity on the same occasion, since in those circumstances there was evidence of the falsity and two witnesses were able to testify to it. It followed that the appeal would be dismissed.[45]

6.4.2 *Procuration*

The requirement for procuration offences to be predicated on corroborative evidence for a conviction to stand is provided for under ss 140 and 141 of the Penal Code.[46]

(i) It is provided under s 140 that,

> Any person who-
> (a) procures or attempts to procure any child or other person to have unlawful carnal knowledge either in Zambia or elsewhere, with a person or other persons for pornography, bestiality or any other purpose;
> (b) procures or attempts to procure any child or other person to become, either in Zambia or elsewhere, a common prostitute;
> (c) procures or attempts to procure any child or person to leave Zambia, with the intent that the child or person may become an inmate of or frequent a brothel elsewhere; or
> (d) procures or attempts to procure any child or person to leave that child's or other person's usual place of abode in Zambia with intent that the child or other person may, for the purposes of prostitution, become an inmate of or

[44] Section 1(1), so far as material, provides: 'If any person lawfully sworn as a witness [...] in a judicial proceeding wilfully makes a statement material in that proceeding, which he knows to be false or does not believe to be true, he shall be guilty of perjury [....]'

[45] Editor's notes: For perjury, see 11(2) Halsbury's Laws (4th edn reissue) paras 299, 301, and for cases on the subject, see 15 Digest (Reissue) 945, 948, 956–957, 962–964, 8150, 8175–8185, 8260–8273, 8320–8342; For the Perjury Act 1911, ss 1, 13, see 12 Halsbury's Statutes (4th edn) (1989 reissue) 166, 174.

[46] Chapter 87 of the Laws of Zambia; By way of comparison, the requirement for corroboration of offences relating to procuration of women for sex has been removed by s 33 of the Public Order Act 1994.

> frequent a brothel either in Zambia or elsewhere; commits a felony and is liable, upon conviction, to imprisonment for a term of not less than twenty years and may be liable to imprisonment for life:
>
> Provided that no person shall be convicted of an offence under this section upon the evidence of one witness only, unless such witness be corroborated in some material particular by evidence implicating the accused.

(ii) In terms of s 141:[47]

> Any person who-
> (a) by threat or intimidation procures or attempts to procure any child or other person to have any unlawful carnal knowledge, either in Zambia or elsewhere;
> (b) by false pretence or false representation procures any child or other person to have any unlawful carnal knowledge, either in Zambia or elsewhere; or
> (c) applies, administers to, or causes to be taken by any child or other person any drug, matter or thing, with intent to stupefy or overpower so as thereby to enable any third person to have unlawful carnal knowledge with such child or other person; commits a felony and is liable, upon conviction, to imprisonment for a term of not less than twenty years and may be liable to imprisonment for life:
>
> Provided that no person shall be convicted of an offence under this section upon the evidence of one witness only, unless such witness be corroborated in some material particular by evidence implicating the accused.

6.4.3 *Children*[48]

See discussion under 4.6.2 of chapter 4: 'Competence of children as witnesses in criminal matters.'

6.4.4 *Road Traffic Act*[49]

While s 192(3) & (4) under the repealed Roads and Road Traffic Act[50] required corroboration for a conviction to stand, its replacement s 148 of the Road Traffic Act[51] has gotten rid of the requirement for any corroboration to prove the offence of over speeding, nor is the requirement retained under the sister provision of s 170 which provides for road signs. The requirement is also not referenced

[47] As amended by No 9 of 1954, repealed and replaced by Act No 15 of 2005.

[48] This is provided for under s 78(1)(2)(9) of the Children's Code, Act No 12 of 2022; By way of comparison, the Criminal Justice Act 1988 under s 34(1), removed the requirement for corroboration of unsworn evidence of children

[49] No 11 of 2002.

[50] Chapter 464 of the Laws of Zambia (repealed).

[51] No 11 of 2002.

in the global penalty provided for under s 225. One reason for this change is the increased use of speed guns/cameras in detecting such offences as original documentary evidence. As discussed elsewhere in this text,[52] advancements in technology have meant that over the recent past, courts have had to deal with documents which have been produced by mechanical devices without input from human beings. It has thus been held in *R v Wood*,[53] that a computer printout detailing a computer's analysis of evidence was deemed to be original (and not hearsay) evidence of elements constituting the compound in question. It follows from the foregoing that where machines such as radar replace human effort and collect, process and generate data or information such output is original evidence notwithstanding the fact that the programming that allows such a machine to generate such information was done by a human. When looked at this way, the rationale for getting rid of the corroborative requirement in speeding cases becomes clear: the advent of technology makes it unnecessary. The practical difficulty of meeting the corroboration requirement in the traditional sense becomes a superfluous exercise not worth the trouble. In any case, the speed camera would be corroborative of what the arresting officer would present as evidence against the accused person. Vice versa is also true.

It is important to consider the significance of the wording in s 170(1)-(3) of the Road Traffic Act:[54]

> (1) Subject to subsection (3) and unless otherwise directed by a road traffic inspector in uniform or police officer, no person shall fail to comply with any direction conveyed by a road traffic sign displayed in the prescribed manner.
> (2) Any person who fails to comply with any direction conveyed by a road traffic sign commits an offence.
> (3) In any prosecution for an offence under subsection (1), it shall be presumed, in the absence of evidence to the contrary, that the road traffic sign concerned was displayed by the proper authority and in accordance with the provisions of this Act.

In the absence of an express corroborative evidence requirement, it is perhaps important to note the prohibition against non-compliance with any direction conveyed by a road traffic sign, and that such failure, is an offence. The conditions provided for under sub-s (1) are met by police observing the car's speed and a contemporaneous reading of the speed gun. It would appear from the decision in *Brightly v Pearson*[55] that whether the offence with which the accused is charged is overspeeding contrary to s 148 which has done away with the corroboration requirement or indeed s 170 whose import is similar albeit wider than that under s 148, the evidence given by one police officer of excessive speed, estimated by him at a place on the particular road, and even

[52] See chapters 12 and 20 for example.

[53] (1983) 76 Cr App R 23.

[54] No 11 of 2002.

[55] [1938] 4 All ER 127, though decided on the point relating to corroboration.

if the same was 'corroborated' by a second police officer to the same effect on the same road if it can be shown that no reliance had been placed 'on a stop-watch or speedometer, [nor the absence of] any reference to any specified and measured distance for the purpose of calculating the speed of vehicles,' is not enough to have the accused convicted.[56]

The appellant was charged with having unlawfully driven a motor lorry at a speed greater than the maximum speed specified for a vehicle of that class or description in the Road Traffic Act 1934, Sched I, contrary to the Road Traffic Act 1930, s 10(1). Evidence was given by one police officer of excessive speed, estimated by him at a place on the particular road, and by a second police officer to the same effect, estimated by him at a different place on the same road. Neither of the police officers had relied on a stop-watch or speedometer, nor was there any reference to any specified and measured distance for the purpose of calculating the speed of vehicles. The appellant contended that, inasmuch as the opinion of each police officer related to a different place on the road, and to a different time in each case, and inasmuch as the evidence of excessive speed at each place therefore consisted solely of the opinion of one police officer, there could not be a conviction by virtue of the Road Traffic Act 1930, s 10(3), as substituted by the Road Traffic Act 1934, s 2(3), which provided that "the evidence of one witness to the effect that … the person prosecuted was driving the vehicle at a speed exceeding" the speed limit, was by itself not sufficient for a conviction. The justices convicted the appellant, imposed a fine of 20s, and ordered that his licence be indorsed. It was held that as the vehicle had not been observed by the two police officers at the same moment, the justices were wrong in concluding that the evidence was sufficient to comply with the section of the Act with regard to corroboration.[57]

Section 170(3) introduces a presumption which an accused person may rebut if he can provide evidence contrary to the supposition that 'the road traffic sign concerned was displayed by the proper authority and in accordance with the provisions of' the Road Traffic Act.[58] He could show for example that no directional sign had been placed on the material part of the road regarding the speed limit for example, that no speed gun had been relied on or had been shown to him to prove that he had been, at the material time, been 'driving the vehicle at a speed exceeding the speed limit, as provided by the speed limit directional sign or/and contrary to s 170 as read together with s 148 of the Act. Further, that the speed gun employed had not been properly calibrated or had malfunctioned at the material time. The observation by the police officer would have to be supported by a reading taken using a properly calibrated

[56] Editor's Notes: The Road Traffic Act 1934, s 2(3), requires in short that the evidence of one witness that a driver was in his opinion exceeding the speed limit shall be corroborated. In the present case, it is true there is the evidence of two witnesses, but as they do not both speak to the same moment of time, it is held that the evidence of one does not corroborate the other. As to Speed Limit, see Halsbury, Supp, Street and Aerial Traffic, para 682; and for Cases, see Digest, Supp, Street and Aerial Traffic, Nos 199a–207a.

[57] See also *Nicholas v Penny* [1950] 2 KB 46; *Crossland v DPP* [1988] 3 All ER 712.

[58] No 11 of 2002.

and properly working speed gun at the same precise moment failing which the court would acquit. In the event that the court in its discretion directed that there be corroborative evidence, it would call for expert opinion, and when such an expert bases his opinion on speed marks to determine the actual speed of the car for purposes of proving a charge under ss 148 and/or 170, his testimony will be sufficient without more i.e., without corroboration.

In *Crossland v DPP*,[59] the defendant collided with a pedestrian while accelerating across a junction before the traffic lights turned red. She was charged with driving at a speed exceeding 30 mph on a restricted road, contrary to ss 81 and 89(1) of and Sch 7 to the Road Traffic Regulation Act 1984. At the hearing of the information the only witness as to the defendant's speed was a police officer who inspected the scene of the accident shortly after it had occurred and the damage to the defendant's car and the skid marks made by the defendant's braking and who carried out speed and braking tests on the defendant's car, from which he calculated that the defendant had been driving at not less than 41 mph before she started to brake. The defendant was convicted. She appealed by way of case stated, contending that she had been convicted 'solely on the evidence of one witness to the effect that, in the opinion of the witness', she had been driving at excessive speed and therefore her conviction was contrary to s 89(2)a of the 1984 Act. It was held that although the police officer's evidence included a significant element of expert opinion, his evidence did not amount solely to his opinion that the defendant had been driving at excessive speed since he also described in detail the objectively determined phenomena on which his expert opinion was based, namely the inspections and tests he had carried out at the scene of the accident. Accordingly, the defendant had been properly convicted and her appeal would be dismissed.

6.4.5 *Affiliation*

The Children's Code,[60] provides under s 119[61] for what evidence has to be provided at the hearing of an application for an affiliation order in the following terms:

> (1) A court shall, on the hearing of an application for an affiliation order, hear—
>
> (a) the evidence of the mother; and
>
> (b) any evidence tendered by or on behalf of the biological or putative father.
>
> (2) A court shall not make an affiliation order unless the evidence of the mother or any other party is corroborated in some material particular by other evidence.[62]

---

[59] [1988] 3 All ER 712 even though decision was predicated on a provision similar to s 193(3)(4) of the repealed Roads and Road Traffic Act 464 of the Laws of Zambia which mandated corroboration.

[60] Act No 12 of 2022 which in terms of s 297 repeals the Affiliation and Maintenance of Children Act Chapter 64 of the Laws of Zambia. Section 119 ought to be understood within the context of ss 116-118.

[61] Thereby replacing what was s 6 in the now repealed Affiliation and Maintenance of Children Act Chapter 64 of the Laws of Zambia.

[62] By comparison, this requirement has been removed by s 17 of the Family Law Reform Act 1987 in England.

6.5 Corroboration warnings as a matter of law

6.5.1 *General*

As has been noted elsewhere in this text, corroboration as a concept meant (and this jurisdiction and others still means) independent evidence. However, the higher plane requirement was not the norm for all manner of situations. In such situations, a warning would do. It followed that where such a scenario arose, the trier of fact (the jury) was supposed to be warned of the dangers inherent in proceeding to convict on the evidence of a single witness whose evidence was uncorroborated. This need not be construed as meaning that where corroboration was lacking, the jury could not convict. What it meant was that if the jury decided to convict they were doing so on the basis that the single witness was one worthy of reliance and whose testimony could form the basis of a fair conviction even where corroboration was lacking. This they did being fully alive to the inherent risks to such a course of action. The common law covered three areas under these requirements namely; (i) the testimony of complainants in sexual offence;[63] (ii) The testimony of accomplices[64] called upon to testify by the prosecution;[65] and (iii) the sworn testimony of children.[66]

6.6 Corroboration warnings as a matter of practice

6.6.1 *General*

Our starting point here is to state that in this jurisdiction there have been no statutory moves similar to s 32 of the Criminal Justice and Public Order Act 1994 in England which abolished the rules relating to the corroboration of the evidence of children, that of accomplices and complainants in sexual offences. Those rules sadly still remain part and parcel of our jurisprudence partly due to parliamentary reticence and partly due to non-activism by our courts which in any case would be constrained as some common law rules are now, as discussed already, codified. It is the case therefore that in addition to these antiquated rules, our system has, through device of persuasion of English, Commonwealth and foreign authorities and old writings by jurists the rule of practice that in certain instances, the court should warn itself of the special need for caution. As explained elsewhere in this text such scenarios or "analogous cases"[67] have involved on the one hand, the type of evidence involved, and on the other, the type of witness involved. There is no question that given where

[63] Compare s 32(1)(b) of the Criminal Justice and Public Order Act 1994 which removed this requirement in England. It still remains part and parcel of our law in this jurisdiction.

[64] On this point see further, I Dennis "Corroboration Requirements Reconsidered" [1984] Crim LR 316 at 322; but see *Davies v DPP* [1954] 1 All ER 507; The Criminal Law Revision Committee, Eleventh Report para 183.

[65] Compare s 32(1)(a) of the Criminal Justice and Public Order Act 1994 which removed this requirement in England. It still remains part and parcel of our law in this jurisdiction.

[66] Codified in this jurisdiction by s 78(1)(2)(9) of the Children's Code, Act No 12 of 2022; but compare s 34 of the Criminal Justice Act 1988 which removed this requirement in English law.

[67] See *R v Spencer* [1987] AC 128, HL; Archbold 1997 1498 at § 16-18.

we are statutorily speaking and as a matter of practice, "analogous cases" are still part of our law and procedure.

6.6.2 *Cases requiring warning as to special need for caution*

6.6.2.1 *Co-defendants/co-accused persons/accomplices*[68]

Co-defendants/co-accused persons/accomplices have been variously defined by courts and juristic writers alike. In *Davies v Director of Public Prosecutions,*[69] half a dozen youths engaged in a fist fight with another group, but one of their number suddenly produced a knife and stabbed one of their opponents to death. One of the prosecution witnesses was a youth named Lawson. He gave evidence of an oral admission by the appellant after the event. One of the grounds of appeal was that the judge ought to have given the jury a warning that Lawson could be regarded as an accomplice, and therefore was someone whose evidence required to be treated with special caution. Lawson admitted being involved in the fight at some stage, but he denied all knowledge of a knife and there was no evidence that he was present when it was produced. He was initially charged with murder, but no evidence was offered against him. It was held as follows: The others on his side who did not know that he had the knife, were not parties to its use and were not guilty of murder or manslaughter. The House rejected the argument that an accomplice warning was required. Lord Simonds defined what was meant by 'accomplice':[70]

> There is in the authorities no formal definition of the term 'accomplice'; and your Lordships are forced to deduce a meaning for the word from cases in which X, Y and Z have been held to be, or held liable to be treated as accomplices. On the case it would appear that the following persons, if called as witnesses for the prosecution, have been treated as falling within the category: - (1) On any view, persons who are *participes criminis* in respect of the actual crime charged, whether as principals or accessories before or after the fact (in felonies) or persons committing procuring or aiding and abetting (in the case of misdemeanours). This is surely the natural and primary meaning of the term 'accomplice'. But in two cases, persons falling strictly outside the ambit of this category have, in particular decisions, been held to be accomplices for the purpose of the rule: *viz*: (2) Receivers have been held to be accomplices of the thieves from whom they receive goods on a trial of the latter for larceny.[71] (3) When X has been charged with a specific offence on a particular occasion, and evidence is admissible, and has been admitted, of having been committed crimes of this identical type on another occasion, as proving system and intent and negativing accidents; in such cases the court has held that in relation to such other similar offences, if evidence of them were given by parties to them, the evidence of such other parties should not be left to the jury

[68] For corroboration and the evidence of accomplices, see 11 Halsbury's Laws (4th Edn) para 457, and for cases on the subject, see 14(2) Digest (Reissue) 608–621, 4942–5078.

[69] [1954] 1 All ER 507, [1954] AC 378, (1854) 38 Cr App R 11, [1954] 2 WLR 343; This summary is as adapted at https://swarb.co.uk/davies-v-director-of-public-prosecutions-hl-1954/ retrieved on 30/04/2022.

[70] See also *Idahosa v R* (1950) 19 NLR 103.

[71] *Rex v Jennings* (1912) 7 Cr App R 242; *Rex v Dixon* (1925) 19 Cr App R 36.

> without a warning that it is dangerous to accept it without corroboration.[72] In both of these cases (2) and (3) a person not a party or not necessarily a party to the substantive crime charged was treated as an accomplice for the purpose of the requirement of warning. (I say 'not necessarily' to cover the case of receivers. A receiver may on the facts of a particular case have procured the theft, or aided and abetted it, or may have helped to shield the thief from justice. But he can be a receiver without doing any of these things.) The primary meaning of the term 'accomplice,' then, has been extended to embrace these two anomalous cases. In each case there are special circumstances to justify or at least excuse the extension. A receiver is not only committing a crime intimately allied in character with that of theft: he could not commit the crime of receiving at all without the crime of theft having preceded it. The two crimes are in a relationship of 'one-sided dependence.' In the case of 'system,' the requirement of warning within the special field of similar crimes committed is a logical application within that collateral field of the general principle, though it involves a warning as to the evidence of persons not accomplices to the substantive crime charged.

Lord Simonds continued:

> My Lords, I have tried to define the term 'accomplice.' The branch of the definition relevant to this case is that which covers *'participes criminis'* in respect of the actual crime charged, 'whether as principals or accessories before or after the fact.' But, it may reasonably be asked, who is to decide, or how is it to be decided, whether a particular witness was a *'particeps criminis'* in the case in hand? In many or most cases this question answers itself, or, to be more exact, is answered by the witness in question himself, by confessing to participation, by pleading guilty to it, or by being convicted of it. But it is indisputable that there are witnesses outside these straightforward categories, in respect of whom the answer has to be sought elsewhere. The witnesses concerned may never have confessed, or may never have been arraigned or put on trial, in respect of the crime involved. Such cases fall into two classes. In the first, the judge can properly rule that there is no evidence that the witness was, what I will, for short, call a participant. The present case, in my view, happens to fall within this class, and can be decided on that narrow ground. But there are other cases within this field in which there is evidence on which a reasonable jury could find that a witness was a 'participant.' In such a case the issue of *'accomplice vel non'* is for the jury's decision: and a judge should direct them that if they consider on the evidence that the witness was an accomplice, it is dangerous for them to act on his evidence unless corroborated: though it is competent for them to do so if, after that warning, they still think fit to do so.

Unlike the scenario in England whose legal plane has been affected by changes brought about by the Criminal Justice and Public Order Act 1994, the old law and rules still hold sway in this jurisdiction. It is submitted that what amounts to a warning which a judge/magistrate must make, where this is warranted as

[72] *Rex v Farid* 30 Cr App R 168.

matter of practice, should be understood in terms expressed by the EWCA, in *R v Knowlden and Knowlden.*[73] Paraphrased for purposes of practice in this jurisdiction, in exercising his/her discretion as to what to say in instances where one accused person leads evidence incriminating a co-accused upon being called to the stand by the prosecution, the judge/magistrate must at the very least mention in clear terms that because each has or may have an interest of his own to serve, the court has given the evidence of each co-accused due attention.[74] Thus, the view taken in the earlier case of *R v Prater*[75] that a full corroboration warning was desirable is not supported by *Knowlden*[76] or subsequent authorities on the matter.

The Zambian Supreme Court laid down guidelines relating to how courts ought to deal with accomplice evidence in *Emmanuel Phiri and Others v The People.*[77] The appellants were convicted of aggravated robbery; it was alleged that two of them, both wearing women's stockings over their faces, and one armed with a sub-machine gun and the other with a pistol, carried out a robbery in which a cash box was stolen which contained some ZMW20,000.00 in cheques and a sum of money in cash. The third man involved was the driver of the "get-away" car. The prosecution case rested on the evidence of two accomplices, both employees of the firm where the robbery took place. The trial judge warned himself that it would be dangerous to convict on their uncorroborated evidence; he held that there was no corroboration or anything else to support their testimony, but that from their demeanour and the fact that they gave detailed accounts of the offence he was fully convinced that they were speaking the truth. It was argued on behalf of the appellants that a conviction on uncorroborated accomplice evidence and in the absence of any special and compelling grounds was contrary to the decision of the Supreme Court of Zambia in *Machobane*[78] and incompetent. It was submitted by the DPP that, to the extent that *Machobane*[79] laid down the requirement of special and compelling grounds before there can be conviction on uncorroborated accomplice evidence, that case was a departure from settled English law and should be overruled. He argued that once the court has warned itself of the danger of convicting on uncorroborated accomplice evidence it is not necessary for the court to set out precisely what the dangers are or why the

[73] 77 Cr App R 94 CA.

[74] This approach was confirmed in *R v Cheema* 98 Cr App R 195.

[75] [1960] 2 QB 464, 44 Cr App R 83, CCA.

[76] 77 Cr App R 94, CA.

[77] [1978] ZR 79; *Machobane v The People* (1972) ZR 101; As to odd coincidences being corroborative, see *John Mkandawire and Others v The People* (SCZ Judgment No 4 of 1978); As to circumstances in which one accomplice's evidence could corroborate of the other, see *Chimbo and Others v The People* (SCZ Judgment No 23 of 1980) though generally, 'The evidence of suspect witness cannot be corroborated by another suspect witness unless the witnesses are suspect for different reasons;' As to there being no rule of law that accomplice evidence cannot corroborate that of another accomplice provided the risk of fabrication has been considered and eliminated, see: *The People v Edward Jack Shamwana and 12 Others* [1982] ZR 122 (HC); As to accomplice evidence being mutually corroborative see: *Edward Jack Shamwana and 7 Others v The People* (SCZ Judgment No 12 of 1985); As to an opportunity for the accused to commit an offence being corroborative, see: *Gideon Mumba v The People* (SCZ Appeal No 50 of 2017); *Joseph Bwalya v The People* (CAZ Appeal No 174 of 2017); *Mathews Mumba v The People* (CAZ Appeal No 163 of 2017).

[78] [1972] ZR 101.

[79] [1972] ZR 101.

court is satisfied that they have been excluded; he submitted in terms that a court may convict if convinced the accomplice is telling the truth, and that the faith in the truth of the testimony may be based on nothing more than the demeanour of the witness and the plausibility or coherence of his story. The DPP submitted in the alternative that, contrary to the learned judge's finding, there was in fact evidence which constituted special and compelling grounds within the meaning of *Machobane*,[80] and that even if the judge be held to have misdirected himself the proviso should be applied. It was held as follows: (i) A Judge (or magistrate) sitting alone or with assessors must direct himself and the assessors, if any, as to the dangers of convicting on the uncorroborated evidence of an accomplice with the same care as he would direct a jury and his judgment must show that he has done so. No particular form of words is necessary for such a direction. What is necessary is that the judgment show that the judge has applied his mind to the particular dangers raised by the nature and the facts of the particular case before him. (ii) The judge should then examine the evidence and consider whether in the circumstances of the case those dangers have been excluded. The judge should set out the reasons for his conclusions; his "mind upon the matter should be revealed."[81] (iii) As a matter of law those reasons must consist in something more than a belief in the truth of the evidence of the accomplices based simply on their demeanour and the plausibility of their evidence - considerations which apply to any witness. If there be nothing more the court must acquit. (iv) The "something more" must be circumstances which, though not constituting corroboration as a matter of strict law, yet satisfy the court that the danger that the accused is being falsely implicated has been excluded and that it is safe to rely on the evidence of the accomplice implicating the accused. This is what is meant by "special and compelling grounds" as used in *Machobane*.[82] (v) These circumstances do not lend themselves to close description; the nature and sufficiency of the evidence in question will depend on the nature of the facts of the particular case, but as a principle the evidence will be in the nature of corroboration in that it must of necessity support or confirm. (vi) There is a distinction between the rule of practice, which now has the force of a rule of law, that a warning must be given of the dangers of convicting on uncorroborated accomplice evidence, and the law as to the circumstances in which, a proper warning having in fact been given, the dangers may safely be regarded as having been excluded. The rules concerning conviction in the absence of corroboration are rules of law as developed by the decisions of the courts. *Per curiam:* (vii) The modern decisions appear to be adopting a less technical approach to what is corroboration as a matter of law, and to be recognising that identification cases are analogous to, if not virtually indistinguishable from, corroboration cases. The question in all cases is whether the suspect evidence, be it accomplice evidence, evidence of a complainant in a sexual case, or evidence of identification, receives such support from the other evidence or circumstances of the case as to satisfy the trier of fact that the danger inherent in the particular case of relying on that suspect

---

[80] [1972] ZR 101.

[81] *Chiu Nang Hong v Public Prosecutor* [1964] 1 WLR 1279.

[82] [1972] ZR 101.

evidence has been excluded; only then can a conviction be said to be safe and satisfactory. (viii) Because a judge or magistrate sitting alone or with assessors sets out his reasons for his conclusions the test relating to the application of the proviso should not be applied quite its strictly in Zambia as it is supplied in England. (ix) In Zambia the test is; was there corroborative or supporting evidence of such weight that the conclusion is not to be resisted that any court behaving reasonably, moving from the undisputed facts and any findings of fact properly made by the trial court, would, directing itself properly, certainly have arrived at the same conclusion? On the facts, a majority of the members of the court held that the proviso should be applied. On the question whether in a case in which the matter turns on the weight to be attached to, and the inference to be drawn from, a number of items of evidence the proviso can ever be applied by a majority: (x) (Baron DCJ and Gardner JS, dissenting.) There is no cogent or adequate reason in aid of a concept that with regard to the application of the proviso a different approach from the normal one, namely, that the majority view prevails, should be adopted. There is no conflict between the concept of the majority view and the test for the application of the proviso as the two are complementary.[83]

6.6.2.2 *Sexual offences*

We have already discussed this matter above. It is, however, important to just reiterate the law as it stands in this jurisdiction which is the antiquated position that when faced with proceedings relating to sexual offences, the courts are obliged by law to warn themselves of the inherent danger of convicting on the uncorroborated evidence of the complainant in sexual matters. This has been illustrated in several Zambian authorities.

In *R v Sabenzu*,[84] the absence of corroboration and want of warning[85] by the magistrate of the danger of convicting on the basis of a single witness' uncorroborated evidence led to the acquittal of the appellant. In *Ackson Zimba v The People*[86] the appellant was convicted of rape. On appeal the court considered whether the fact that the complainant was crying when she was seen by the

[83] *Per* Baron DCJ and Gardner JS) Once differing views are held as to whether the evidence is of sufficient weight to apply the proviso, to apply it is contrary to the express terms of the test governing such application; Editor's Note: This case, the first in which the Supreme Court has sat as a five-judge bench, raises apparently for the first time the question whether it is competent to apply the proviso by a majority. In *Chibeka v R* 1959 (1) R & N 476 the proviso was so applied; the report does not disclose any discussion as to competence.

[84] (1946) 4 NRLR 45.

[85] But see *Lovemore Musongole v The People* [1978] ZR 171 (SC): It was argued on behalf of the appellant that the trial magistrate had been guilty of certain misdirections, and in particular that no corroboration warning had been given, and that such cases on the authority of *R v Trigg* (1963) 47 Cr App Rep 99 should not be made the subject of the application of the proviso. The court accepted that there had been misdirections and that the conviction could stand only if the proviso could be applied. It was held: as follows: (i) It is settled law that in a proper case notwithstanding that no warning as to corroboration has been given when it should have been given a conviction may be upheld; the question in each case is whether the evidence meets the test for the application of the proviso:*R v Trigg* (1963) 47 Cr App Rep 99 disapproved; *Butembo v The People* (1976) ZR 193, approved (ii) On the facts the evidence was of such weight as to meet the test for the application of the proviso laid down in *Emmanuel Phiri and Others v The People* [1978] ZR 79.

[86] [1980] ZR 259 (SC).

independent witness, could amount to corroboration. It was held that it is necessary for the trial court to warn itself that evidence of distress at the time of the making of the complaint may not be enough to amount to corroboration as it may well be simulated.[87]

Finally, in *Katebe v the People*,[88] the appellant was convicted of indecent assault on a female. The complainant alleged that at 22:35 hours on 1 August 1974, the appellant, who was accompanied by a friend, knocked at the door of her house and when she opened the door, he said that her younger sister wanted to see her. When she went outside the appellant grabbed her, threw her to the ground and attempted to rape her. She shouted for help and the barman of a nearby bar came to her rescue, where upon the appellant and his companion ran away. The complainant said that she had known the appellant for a long time and had seen him clearly in the moonlight. The magistrate warned himself carefully of the danger of convicting on the uncorroborated evidence of the complainant. However, he believed her evidence and convicted in spite of the absence of corroboration. It was held *inter alia:*

(i) The general principle of the cautionary rule as to corroboration applies equally to sexual cases as to accomplice cases.

(ii) If there are "special and compelling grounds" it is competent to convict on the uncorroborated testimony of a prosecutrix.

(iii) Where there can be no motive for a prosecutrix deliberately and dishonestly to make a false allegation against an accused, and the case is in practice no different from any others in which the conviction depends on the reliability of her evidence as to the identity of the culprit, this is a "special and compelling ground" which would justify a conviction on uncorroborated testimony.

As late as 2009, the Supreme Court held on to the general position illustrated in the foregoing cases in *Darius Sinyinza v the People*[89] that '[v]ictims of defilement are suspect witnesses and their evidence should always be corroborated.'

6.6.2.3 *Sworn evidence of children*[90]

The law with respect to sworn evidence of children has as its starting point, s 78(1)(2)(9) of the Children's Code,[91] which we have discussed at length elsewhere in this text.[92] Both this statutory provision and the common law authorities we discuss below are an antiquated approach to the issue of corroboration as regards the evidence of children which has seen remarkable changes to it in England & Wales with specific reference to unsworn evidence

[87] Applying *Knight v R* 50 Cr App Rep 122.

[88] [1975] ZR 13 (SC); see also *Phiri v The People* [1982] ZR 77; J Hatchard, 'Suspect Witnesses in rape cases' ½ *Zimbabwe LawReview*, 252 found in Hatchard J and Ndulo M, *The Law of Evidence in Zambia* 151-153.

[89] SCZ Judgment No 2 of 2009.

[90] See generally Stafford, 'The Child as a Witness' in 7 Mo L Rev 382; Tapper, 'Corroboration from an Independent Source' *36 MLR 541.*

[91] Act No 12 of 2022.

[92] See discussion under 4.6.2 of chapter 4: 'Competence of children as witnesses in criminal matters.'

of children.[93] Nor can the reasons advanced by Hatchard & Ndulo[94] find support here. They posit that there are several reasons why children may be considered suspect. It is contended that their youth lends them to influences from both adults and other children. This must be dismissed as inapplicable to all children. As always, the adults decide without scientific data to apply this reasoning to children and not to adults whom, it has been shown on many occasions, can just as easily be influenced in the same way. They further argue that children do not have the maturity to understand the moral duty to speak the truth. Here again is another blanket approach not verifiable using scientific data. In fact, s 78(1)(2) makes this position untenable at law as *voire dire* must be conducted to determine whether a child is mature enough to underhand the importance of telling the truth. Their testimony cannot just be dismissed out of hand, as any authorities which appear to lend credence to this assertion appear to suggest. Thirdly, Hatchard & Ndulo assert that children may not appreciate the need for accuracy in evidence with important details simply being forgotten. That this point has no legs to stand on can be seen not only from s 78(1)(2) but also the fact that adult witnesses are permitted under certain circumstances to refresh their memory due to the treachery of memory. This is a common challenge that cannot just be simply placed on the door step of children, nor can it logically be gainsaid that, children deliberately tell lies, irrespective. If this were so, perjury would be an offence specifically created for child witnesses, but that is not the case.

The subject has already been discussed at some length in chapter 4 of this text under paragraph 4.6: 'Children as witnesses.' The points thereunder apply with equal force here and as such no further discussion beyond the above rebuttals is merited here.

6.6.2.4 *Evidence of witness tainted by improper motive*

Evidence of a witness tainted by improper motive falls under the class of instances in which a warning by a judge/magistrate is merited. According to Ackner LJ, there exists 'the obligation upon a judge to [...] proceed with caution where there is material to suggest that a witness's evidence may be tainted by an improper motive [....] While not suggesting a one-size fits all approach, he appears to endorse a case-by-case consideration based on a continuum to determine '[t]he strength of that advice' based on the facts of the case.[95] There would appear, it is submitted, to be nothing in the language of the foregoing observation to exclude those whose motive is not tied to the particular offence before court or a related offence with which the witness in question is inextricably linked, and for which he seeks to 'avoid liability or the incrimination of himself or others he might naturally wish to protect, or to shift

[93] The Criminal Justice Act 1988, s 34(1) removed the requirement of corroboration of unsworn evidence of children.

[94] Hatchard J and Ndulo M, *The Law of Evidence in Zambia* 149.

[95] In *R v Beck* 74 Cr App R 221, 228.

the blame elsewhere.'[96] In *Muchabi v The People*,[97] the appellant was convicted of stock theft. The magistrate found certain prosecution witnesses to be persons with a purpose of their own to serve. It was held that a witness with an interest of his own to serve must be treated as an accomplice and his evidence tested to see whether it was corroborated or whether there was a reason for believing it in the absence of corroboration.

Therefore, it ought to be understood that Ackner LJ's judgment, rather than restricting the application of warning rule in the circumstances under discussion extends the application to witnesses with motives ranging from spite, to jealousy, to a hope of profiting financially or indeed to those who seek to derive satisfaction from giving damaging testimony as an avenue of settling old scores as these motives all brought them into the legal aphorism 'witnesses

[96] *Archbold Criminal Pleading, Evidence and Practice*, 1997, para 16-17 at 1498.

[97] [1973] ZR 193; *Muyangwa and Others v The People* [1976] ZR 320 (SC): Where the prosecution puts a witness forward as one who at the very least has an interest to exculpate himself, the court cannot decline to treat him as such without some very positive reasons; *George Musupi v The People* [1978] ZR 271 (SC): At the trial it was urged that the two witnesses had purposes of their own to serve, that the absence of the third man was highly suspicious, that apart from the conflicts in and the unsatisfactory nature of their evidence their behaviour and that of the third man was highly suspicious, and that their evidence should not be relied upon. The trial judge accepted the evidence of these witnesses and convicted on the strength of it. It was held as follows: (i) Although there is a distinction between a witness with a purpose of his own to serve and an accomplice, such distinction is irrelevant so far as the court's approach to their evidence is concerned; the question in every case is whether the danger of relying on the evidence of the suspect witness has been excluded. (ii) The tendency to use the expression "witness with an interest (or purpose) of his own to serve" carries with it the danger of losing sight of the real issue. The critical consideration is not whether the witness does in fact have an interest or a purpose of his own to serve, but whether he is a witness who, because of the category into which he falls or because of the particular circumstances of the case, may have a motive to give false evidence. (iii) Once in the circumstances of the case it is reasonably possible that the witness has motive to give false evidence, the danger of false implication is present and must be excluded before a conviction can be held to be safe; *Yudah Nchepeshi v The People* [1978] ZR 362 (SC): The appellant was convicted of murder, he and the deceased were both fishermen who lived about a mile apart on the banks of a river. The principal evidence for the prosecution was given by two other fishermen who lived in a house about one hundred yards from that of the deceased; they had been away from the district for several weeks, and told the court that when they returned on the 16th July, 1977, they found the appellant apparently burying something with a hoe in the yard outside their house; the witnesses apprehended the appellant and reported the matter to the police. The dismembered body of the deceased was dug up. It was submitted on behalf of the appellant that the two witnesses had a possible interest of their own to serve; and that in any event even if their evidence could be accepted without corroboration the whole of the evidence in the case was circumstantial and was not sufficient to support a conviction. It was held as follows: (i) A court cannot be called upon to address its mind to the question whether or not a witness falls into the category of witnesses whose evidence it is dangerous to accept without corroboration or support unless there is some evidence "fit to be left to a jury" which raises that issue. The mere assertion by the accused that it was the witness and not the accused who was the culprit is not sufficient without more to raise the issue. (ii) Once the issue is properly raised it is incumbent upon the court to consider it and rule upon it; the court should make a positive finding whether or not the witness is one whose evidence it is dangerous to accept without corroboration or support. (iii) The mere raising of the issue does not render the case a corroboration case as distinct from a straightforward issue of credibility; even though the issue has been raised it is still perfectly proper for the court, having considered all the evidence and circumstances of the case, to conclude that the witness is not one who falls into the category of witnesses whose evidence it is dangerous to accept without corroboration or support; *William Muzala Chipango & Others v The People* [1978] ZR 304 (SC): where because of the category into which a witness falls or because of the circumstances of the case he may be a suspect witness that possibility in itself determines how one approaches his evidence. Once a witness may be an accomplice or have an interest, there must be corroboration or support for his evidence before the danger of false implication can be said to be excluded, following *Musupi v The People* SCZ Judgment No 32 of 1978.

with an interest to serve.'[98] In *R v Witts and Witts*,[99] the prosecution called as witnesses persons who had attacked one of the defendants in revenge for the assault which was the subject for the count against the defendants. Those witnesses were to be sentenced for that later attack, which was the subject of a separate count in the same inducements, at the end of the trail. No warning was given to treat their evidence with caution. This was said by the court to be a classic instance of the sort of case where a warning ought to have been given as witnesses, though not accomplices, had a strong incentive to give false evidence against the defendants.

It is perchance good to end with the observations by the Supreme Court in *Yokoniya Mwale v The People*[100] which in many respects were a reiteration of the observations made in earlier cases such as *Muyangwa and Others v The People,*[101] *George Musupi v The People,*[102] and *Yudah Nchepeshi v The People*[103] hereinbefore considered. The Court [...] had occasion to address the evidence of witnesses who were friends and relatives and put the issue in its proper perspective. It concluded that a conviction will [...] be safe if it is based on the uncorroborated evidence of witnesses who are friends and relatives of the deceased or victim provided that on the evidence before it, those witnesses could not be said to have a bias or motive to falsely implicate the accused, or any other interest of their own to serve. That what was key was for the court to satisfy itself that there was no danger for false implication:

> [...] authorities did not establish nor were they intended to cast in stone, a general proposition that friends and relatives of the deceased, or the victim are always to be treated as witnesses with an interest to serve, and whose evidence therefore, routinely required corroboration. Were this to be the case, crime that occurs in family environments where no witness other than the near relatives and friends are present, would go unpunished for want of corroborative evidence. Credible available evidence would be rendered insufficient on the technicality of want of independent corroboration.

6.6.2.5 *Witnesses of bad character*

Witnesses of bad character present another scenario in which a warning is necessary.[104] In *R v Spencer,*[105] the appellants, who were nursing staff at a special hospital, were charged with ill-treating patients, contrary to s 126 of the Mental Health Act 1959. In two separate trials before the same judge, the prosecution relied wholly on the uncorroborated evidence of patients who

[98] *Beck* was quoted with approval in *R v Spencer* [1987] AC 128 at 140.

[99] [1991] Crim L R 562 CA; summarised in Archbold 1997 1498, para 16-17.

[100] SCZ Appeal No 285/2014, as summarised in *Morgan Gipson Mwape v The People* CAZ Appeal No 31 of 2016.

[101] [1976] ZR 320 (SC).

[102] [1978] ZR 271 (SC).

[103] [1978] ZR 362 (SC).

[104] *R v Kilbourne* [1973] AC 729, 740.

[105] [1986] 2 All ER 928.

had criminal convictions or were suffering from mental disorders. At the first trial it became apparent that one of the jurors had formed a definite view of the case and appeared to be biased against the appellants. On the day before the trial ended, during the course of the judge's summing up, the court was informed that the juror's wife worked at another mental hospital which had been referred to in evidence at the trial and that the juror had discussed the case on several occasions with three jurors to whom he gave lifts to and from the court. The judge discharged the juror and the other jurors were directed not to discuss the case with him. The juror was, however, permitted to remain in the precinct of the court and give a lift to the three other jurors at the end of the day's hearing. The judge refused an application by the appellants that the remaining jurors be discharged, on the ground that it had not been shown that there was a high degree of risk that the jury were prejudiced by their discussions with the discharged juror. At both trials the judge directed the jury to approach the evidence of the patients with great caution but did not warn them that it would be dangerous to convict on the patients' uncorroborated evidence. The appellants were all convicted. They appealed to the Court of Appeal which dismissed the appeals, holding (i) that the evidence of patients at a secure hospital did not fall into the category of evidence of witnesses where a full warning of the danger of conviction on their uncorroborated evidence was necessary, and (ii) in relation to the first trial, that, although the judge had applied the wrong test whether there was a real danger that the appellants' position had been prejudiced by the actions of the discharged juror, it had not been shown that their position had in fact been prejudiced or that an injustice had been done. The appellants appealed to the House of Lords.It was held as follows:

(1) Where the evidence for the Crown consisted solely of the evidence of a witness who was not within one of the accepted classes of suspect witnesses but who, by reason of his particular mental condition and criminal connection, fulfilled analogous criteria, the trial judge was required to warn the jury that it would be dangerous to convict on that witness's uncorroborated evidence. In giving the appropriate warning, although it could often be convenient to use the words 'danger' or 'dangerous', the use of such words was not essential to an adequate warning, provided the jury were made fully aware of the dangers of convicting on such evidence. Where a witness did not fall into one of the established categories of suspect witnesses and there existed potential 928 corroborative material, the extent to which the trial judge made reference to that material depended on the facts of the case, subject to the overriding rule that the judge had to put the defence fairly and adequately. Since the judge had told the jury in the clearest possible terms that they must approach the evidence of the patients with great caution and since, having given that warning, he identified the very dangers which justified the exercise of great

caution, it followed that the judge's direction had been adequate and fair. The appeals relating to the judge's direction would therefore be dismissed.[106]

(2) In respect of the appeals on the ground that the discharged juror had prejudiced the jury, it was not possible in the circumstances to discount the likelihood of the possibility that the discharged juror had, after his discharge, expressed to the three jurors to whom he gave lifts his firm view that the defendants were all guilty. In all the circumstances there was a doubt that justice might not have been done and the verdict was therefore unsafe.[107]

Per Lord Hailsham:[108]

> The other point I would like to comment on is the courts Appeal's view on my reference in *R v Kilbourne* [1973] AC 729, 740 when I added witnesses of admittedly bad character' to the number of cases where a warning of some kind was required as to the danger of convicting without corroboration. I was, of course using the phrase in the technical sense of witnesses who have been shown to be not of a character to make them worthy to be believed on their oath. In this connexion I must say that even if they were not authority to support this view (and I believe that there is plenty), I would regard it as a matter of sheer common sense that if a judge did not warn the jury of the possible danger of convicting an innocent man if they convicted solely on the disputed but uncorroborated testimony of such a person, his failure to do so would [....] Make a verdict unsafe and unsatisfactory in the extreme.

6.6.2.6 *Identification*

The inherent dangers of misidentification are recognised in legal circles. The curious case of Alfred Beck which is considered in greater detail in chapter 7 is a case in point. The accused was misidentified by no less than 15 witnesses. It led, we will see in the next chapter, to the establishment of the Court of Criminal Appeal.[109] This therefore enjoins judges/magistrates to the necessity for "special need for caution"[110] before convicting an accused person where the case is almost entirely predicated or substantially predicated on such evidence. We shall discuss the matter of identification in the next chapter.

6.6.2.7 *Form of warning*

The leading authority as regards the form of warning is *R v Makanjuola.*[111] It is apparent from that authority and many that have followed it including *Emmanuel Phiri and Others v The People,*[112] that the particular contents of such warnings as are envisaged in said authorities with respect to suspect evidence (mainly in identification cases), is that they are in the judge's discretion and

[111] [1995] 3 All ER 730 at 731j-733g, *per* Lord Taylor CJ.

[112] [1978] ZR 79 (SC), discussed above.

determined on the basis of the evidence made available to him and surrounding issues as regards the evidence and the witness in question. A few things ought to be borne in mind when discussing the issuance of a warning by the judge in the particular circumstances where one is called for. He ought to warn himself of the special need for caution referenced in *R v Turnbull and Others*.[113] He should support the issuance of such a warning to himself by clearly stating the reasons for it.[114] Thus, May LJ has observed as follows in *R v spencer*:[115]

> [...] indeed, we also agree that the attitude of our courts over the recent years has in fact been to refuse to increase the number of categories in which the full warning, with all the complications it involves, has to be given, but to emphasise the duty of a trial judge in appropriate cases to warn [himself] of a special need for caution in relation to the evidence of certain witnesses, in terms appropriate to the particular case under consideration.[116]

The phraseology employed here is important. It implies that there can be no one size fits all approach to the concept of warning where this is merited. It ought to be 'appropriate to the particular case under consideration.' More to the point:

> [...] in some cases, the potential unreliability of the sole or principal witness for the prosecution is obvious for all to see, whereas in others the potential unreliability of the witness may not be apparent to the [judge/magistrate]. The extent of the obligation to explain the need for caution will vary according to the extent to which the danger of relying on a particular witness is apparent.[117]

6.6.2.8 *Supporting evidence*

As we see below, the complex nature of the rules relating to corroborative evidence invited vigorous criticism leading, in England & Wales at least, to legislative changes with parliament retreating from the obligatory corroboration requirements. The English courts did not seek to nor have they sought to fill in the gaps left by the legislative retreat by employing discretionary warnings where once the mandatory rules stood. The approach followed in the sort of cases requiring a warning to be given is a non-technical one. It comes with what is deemed to constitute supportive evidence as regards any warning that the judge/magistrate concerned might in his choice select to give not being, as in times past, subject to methodological rules. Be that as it may, the approach still requires that the court satisfies itself that the evidence deemed suspect is in fact correct. The foregoing is reflected in Lord Widgery J in *R v Turnbull* that

[113] [1977] QB 224.

[114] *R v Turnbull* [1977] QB 224, 63, Cr App R 132, CA, *ante*, 14-2.

[115] [1985] QB 771.

[116] see *R v Allen* [1965] 2 QB 295; *R v Long* (1973) 57 Cr App R 871 and *R v Turnbull* [....] at 784.

[117] *R v Spencer* [1987] AC 128 at 141-142 per Lord Ackner as paraphrased in Archbold 1997 1500 at Para 16-20.

'[...] the judge should warn [himself] of the special need for caution before convicting the accused n reliance on the correctness of the identification or identifications.

6.7 Corroboration and supportive evidence – a closer look

6.7.1 *General*

The general rule with respect to corroboration is that courts are permitted to, in civil and criminal law, act on the evidence of a single witness.[118] In fact, the Supreme Court has gone so far as to observe as follows in *Katebe v The People*:[119] '[a]lthough the cautionary rule of practice has long since become virtually a rule of law, if as we said in *Machobane v The People*,[120] there are special and compelling grounds for so doing, it is competent to convict on the uncorroborated testimony of a witness with a possible interest to serve.' That notwithstanding, corroboration has traditionally been defined as independent evidence *supportive*[121] of a witness *in a material particular*.[122] It is not a technical term. It connotes and ought to be understood purely as "confirmation."[123] As has been put in *Nsofu v The People*,[124]

> Corroboration must not be equated with independent proof; it is not evidence which needs to be conclusive in itself. Corroboration is independent evidence which tends to confirm that the witness is telling the truth when she says that the offence was committed and that it was the accused who committed it. Where the evidence of a witness requires to be corroborated, it is nonetheless the evidence of the witness on which the conviction is based; the corroborative evidence serves to satisfy the court that it is safe to rely on that of the witness.

There are of course exemptions or occurrences when the need for corroboration must be well-thought-out by the court which, as noted already, are provided for statutorily and have developed at common law and observed as a matter of law and practice. In all such cases, as seen elsewhere in this text and confirmed by other jurists,[125] 'it must take the form of a separate item of admissible[126] evidence

[118] 2 Hawk. c.46, ss 2, 10; Fost. 233; see *DPP v Hester* [1973] AC 296 HL at 324 *per* Lord Diplock.

[119] [1975] ZR 13.

[120] (1972) ZR 101.

[121] But consider Australian authorities such as *R v Apostilides* (1983) 11 A Crim R 381 at 401 (CF) where the use of "support" has been deplored.

[122] See *Credland v Knowler* (1951) 35 Cr App R 48 at 56 *per* Reading CJ.

[123] Australian authorities such as *R v Apostilides* (1983) 11 A Crim R 381 at 401 (CF); *R v Kehagias* [1985] VR 107 at 112 (CF). *CfMcGookin v R* (1986) 20 A Crim R 381 AT 401 (Vic CF) have deplored the use of "support" or "supportive."

[124] [1973] ZR 380; followed in *Michael Bwalya v The People* Appeal No 138/2018.

[125] Heydon JD, *Cross on Evidence* (10th edn Lexis Nexis, 2016) 490.

[126] *Buck v R* [1983] WAR 372 at 376 (CCA).

implicating[127] the person against whom the testimony is given in relation to the matter concerning which corroboration is necessary.'[128] According toViscount Reading CJ in *R v Baskerville*:[129]

> [...] corroboration must be independent testimony which affects the accused by connecting or tending to connect him with the crime. In other words, it must be evidence which implicated him, that is, which confirm in some material particular not only the evidence that a crime has been committed, but also that the prisoner committed it.

There is much to be said about the intractable challenges the requirement that corroborative evidence '[implicate the accused], that is [...] confirm in some material particular not only the evidence that a crime has been committed, but also that the [accused] committed it.' Thus, Isaac J has opined as follows in *Ridley v Whipp:*[130]

> [...] corroboration of whatever statement requires corroboration must be by independent testimony, and [...] if it be required to implicate a person in a given act, the independent testimony must be such as of its own force to connect or tend to connect him with the act [...] In other words, the independent evidence must support the story both as regards the alleged crime and the alleged criminal.

Isaac J's comments should, it is submitted, be construed to mean that what qualifies to be corroborative evidence must be seen within certain confines. This approach to corroborative evidence connotes, by necessary implication, that not everything that may tend to show or even prove that the witness whose evidence requires corroboration is telling the truth will be deemed corroborative. Thus, it has been observed in *Ridley v Whipp*[131] that mere opportunity without more does not amount to corroboration. Further, as demonstrated in *R v Kerim,*[132]it is the case sometimes that corroborative evidence fails to, in terms of *Baskerville,*[133] implicate the accused or connect him to the offence with which he is charged. In *Baskerville,*[134] the letter produced by the prosecution was treated as corroborative on the basis not only that (i) it involved the accused but also that (ii) its contents were consistent with evidence given by the complainants regarding the offence of acts of gross indecency with which the accused was

[127] According to decisions in *R v Kerim* [1988] 1 Qd R 426 at 432 and 453 (CCA); and *R v Dovey* (1988) 37 A Crim R 288, "implicate" in this sense must be construed to mean "involve" and not necessarily "incriminate" or "inculpate". Additionally, it has been construed to, "confirm or tend to confirm the accused's involvement in the events related by the accomplice" in *R v Dovey* (1990) 171 CLR 207 at 211; see also *R v Rayner* [1998] 4 VR 818 (CA); *R v Ferguson* (2009) 24 VR 531.

[128] *R v Berrill* [1982] Qd R 508 at 516 (CCA).

[129] [1916] 2 KB 658 at 667.

[130] (1916) 22 CLR 381 at 392.

[131] (1916) 22 CLR 381; *Eade v R* (1924) 34 CLR 154 *cf.R v King* [1967] 2 QB 338 (CA).

[132] [1988] 1 Qd R 426 (CCA).

[133] [1916] 2 KB 658.

[134] [1916] 2 KB 658.

charged.

A few other points merit our consideration. While, as noted above, corroborative evidence needs to, on the one hand, implicate the accused, and on the other, be consistent with evidence requiring corroboration, it need not, as has been shown in *Eade v R*,[135] demonstrate the guilt of the accused. On this score though, *R v M*[136] is authority for the position that no rule exists to support the assertion that there must be corroboration not only of intercourse but non-consent also. Further to the foregoing, it has been observed in *R v Bryce*,[137] that as regards corroborative consistency, same must be more akin to the accused's guilt than that of any other person. It is to be remembered that the conclusion to which corroborative evidence points is more important as compared to a specific actual account of the witness.[138] There is no requirement that corroboration supports the evidence requiring such corroboration in its entirety. If the evidence requiring corroboration has of its own inanition crumbled and has thus become unreliable and so weakened as not to stand up to scrutiny during cross-examination, any evidence corroborating such evidence will carry very little weight if any.[139] As Lord Hailsham of St Marylebone LC put it in *DPP v Kilbourne*[140] '[c]orroboration can only be afforded to or by a witness who is otherwise to be believed. If a witness's testimony falls of its own inanition the question of his needing, or being capable of giving, corroboration does not arise.' It may indeed, as was shown in *The People v Japau*,[141] invite a successful submission of '[…] no case to answer […] if an essential element of the alleged offence has not been proved, or when the prosecution evidence has been so discredited by cross-examination, or is so manifestly unreliable, that no reasonable tribunal could safely convict on it.'[142] Specifically because corroborative evidence is confirmatory, it need not prove any propositions beyond reasonable doubt.[143]

6.7.2 *Significant issues*

A court may not, in its efforts to determine whether a particular piece of evidence meets the corroboration threshold, discount issues at trial. The point in this is that the corroborative evidence ought to bear upon matters in issue for it, as a necessary predicate of the concept of corroboration, as has been shown in

[135] (1924) 34 CLR 154 at 158; *R v Doney* (1988) 37 A Crim R 288 (NSW CCA).

[136] [1995] 1 Qd R 213.

[137] [1994] 1 Qd R 77 (CA).

[138] *R v Galluzzo* (1986) 23 A Crim R 211 (NSW CCA); *R v Berrill* [1982] Qd R 508 (CCA): where on a charge of rape, evidence that the accused had struck the complainant was corroborated by evidence that she had, had a black eye soon after the material date.

[139] *Re Minister for Immigration and Multicultural Affairs; Ex parte Applicant* S20/2002 (2003) 198 ALR 59 at [49]; compare *WLC v R* (2007) 19 NTLR 136 at [25].

[140] [1973] 1 All ER 440 at 452, [1973] AC 729 at 746.

[141] *The People v Japau* [1967] ZR 95 (HC); see also *The People v Winter Makowela & Another* [1979] ZR 290.

[142] See ss 206 or ss 291 of the Criminal Procedure Code Chapter 88 of the Laws of Zambia; *The People v Winter Makowela & Another* [1979] ZR 290.

[143] *Doney v R* (1990) 171 CLR 207 AT 211; *R v Andrews* (1992) 60 A Crim R 137 at 151-3 and 166-7 (SA CCA).

Peacock v R,[144] to be said to implicate the accused person. Be that as it may, such corroborative evidence as does implicate the accused, need not relate to the incident described by the witness whose evidence requires corroboration. In *R v Beck*,[145] F Ltd, an American-owned company, set up a company in England, C Ltd, to supply money to finance home improvements. M was made its managing director. M arranged with the appellant, who had a double-glazing business, S Ltd, that C Ltd would provide some of the finance for S Ltd. Following a television programme, which was highly critical of the trading activities of S Ltd and C Ltd, the American owners of F Ltd asked the company's auditor to carry out a detailed investigation which revealed that C Ltd was incurring a considerable loss on its business with S Ltd. After speaking to the directors of F Ltd, the auditor made a claim on F Ltd's insurers in respect of the loss. M and the appellant were charged with conspiracy to defraud C Ltd and F Ltd by falsely representing that sums of money were payable by C Ltd to S Ltd and by making false entries in the accounts of C Ltd. Both pleaded not guilty but, unknown to the jury, shortly after the trial began M changed his plea to guilty. He admitted that he and the appellant had been operating a dishonest system but testified that he had been too frightened to tell F Ltd's staff about it. In his defence the appellant contended that F Ltd must have known that the system was being operated because it had been done quite openly. The directors of F Ltd, when called as witnesses, denied any knowledge of it. The auditor, when cross-examined, said that he had understood from the directors of F Ltd at the time of the insurance claim that they did not know about the operation of the dishonest system. The appellant alleged that they had lied to the auditor and were accordingly unreliable witnesses. In his summing up the judge advised the jury that, in view of the appellant's allegation, they should pay particular care and attention to the evidence of the directors and the weight, if any, to be attached to it. He also pointed out to the jury that M was an accomplice and warned them of the danger of acting on his uncorroborated evidence. The judge defined corroboration and pointed out the evidence which he thought was capable of amounting to corroboration. The appellant was convicted. He appealed, contending (i) that although the directors of F Ltd could not be regarded as accomplices or potential accomplices as regards the crime charged, the judge should have warned the jury of the danger of acting on their uncorroborated evidence because they had had a substantial purpose of their own to serve by giving false evidence, namely to cover up false representations made or acceded to by them in the insurance claim, (ii) that evidence was only capable of amounting to corroboration if, and so far as, it directly corroborated the evidence given by an accomplice, so that, if on a particular aspect of the case an accomplice said nothing incriminating the accused, other evidence on that aspect of the case (particularly if it was inconsistent with what the accomplice had said) was incapable of amounting to corroboration however

[144] (1911) 13 CLR 619 at 638-639; *R v Byczzko* (No 1) (1977) 16 SASR 506 (CCA); *BRS v R* (1997) 191 CLR 275; But see *R v Freeman* [1980] VR 1 at 11 (FC); *Forgie v Police* [1969] NZLR 101; *Holman v R* [1970] WAR 2 (CCA); *R v Lindsay* (1977) 18 SASR 103 at 122 (CCA).

[145] [1982] 1 All ER 807 at 815 (CA); *R v Galluzzo* (1986) 23 A Crim R 211 (NSW CCA).

strongly it indicated that the accused was guilty, and (iii) that the judge had misdirected the jury about what could amount to corroboration. It was held that (1) Although a judge was obliged to advise a jury to proceed with caution where there was material to suggest that a witness's evidence might be tainted by an improper motive, he was not bound to give an 'accomplice warning' in respect of that witness's 807 testimony unless there were grounds for believing that he was in some way involved in the crime which was the subject matter of the trial. It followed that, as there was no suggestion that the directors of F Ltd were accomplices of the appellant, the judge's direction in respect of their evidence was correct.[146] (2) Corroborative evidence need not relate to particular incidents spoken to by a 'suspect' witness. It was merely independent testimony which confirmed in some material particular not only the evidence that a crime had been committed but also that the defendant had committed it. Since there were no grounds for criticising the judge's direction as to the matters which were capable of amounting to corroboration, the appeal would be dismissed.[147]

We ought to recall that corroborative evidence need not be absolutely probative of guilt.[148] Gaudron J has opined that evidence is not corroborative if it was 'intractably neutral.'[149] Thus, where evidence has been found to be consistent with the prosecution's case to the same extent that it is with the accused's case; or where it tends to confirm a matter which is common cause, it is not corroborative. In the first as well as the second case, it does not bear upon the matter in issue nor does it, in the least, tend to implicate the accused person. However, where the matter which is common cause does, when seen from the prosecution's standpoint to be capable of implicating the accused or where the matter in question does, on its own, or when combined with other evidence becomes capable of implicating the accused, it will be deemed to amount to corroborative evidence. Thus, in *R v Massey*,[150] the accused who was charged with rape admitted paternity of the victim's child. Even though the admission of paternity lacked probative value of want of consent, it was adjudged corroborative specifically that it increased the probability that the victim's entire oral testimony was truthful.

6.7.3 *Circumstantial evidence as corroboration*

There is no law proscribing the use of circumstantial evidence to corroborate

[146] *Davies v DPP* [1954] 1 All ER 507 and *R v Prater* [1960] 1 All ER 298 explained.

[147] *R v Mullins* (1848) 3 Cox CC 526 and *R v Baskerville* [1916–17] All ER Rep 38 applied; dictum of Lord Hailsham LC in *DPP v Kilbourne* [1973] 1 All ER at 448 considered; editor's notes: For corroboration generally and evidence by accomplice in criminal cases, see 11 Halsbury's Laws (4th edn) paras 453–460, and for cases on the subject, see 14(2) Digest (Reissue) 606–621, 656–661, 4923–5078, 5308–5373.

[148] See for example *R v Kuster* (2008) 21 VR 407 at [14]; *Summer v R* (2010) 29 VR 398 at [42]-[51]; *Bui v R* (2011) 215 A Crim R 93 at [71]-[74].

[149] See *R v Pisano* [1997] 2 VR 342; *R v Kerim* [1988] 1 Qd R 426.

[150] [1997] 1 Qd R 476 at 480; approved in *Doggett v R* (2001) 208 CLR 343 at [68] *per* McHugh J.

evidence given by another person. Authorities[151] point to the fact that in instances where the chain of circumstantial events a combination of which implicate the accused, even when one of them in and of itself would not be corroborative, may still be deemed to be corroborative.

6.7.4 *Inherently credible evidence*

Does the question of corroboration arise in instances where the witness requiring corroboration is not credible? The answer according to several authorities would appear to be that corroboration would only arise if there is necessary predication based on sufficient, believable and/or credible evidence. According to Lord Morris of Both-y-Gest in *Director of Public Prosecutions v Hester*:[152]

> The purpose of corroboration is not to give validity or credence to evidence which is deficient or suspect or incredible but only to confirm and support that which as evidence is sufficient and satisfactory and credible: and corroborative evidence will only fill its role if it itself is completely credible evidence.

In *R v Lim Yong Hong*,[153] a conviction for retaining stolen property was quashed, for it had been arrived at without any independent evidence to corroborate the testimony of an accomplice. 'The whole point of looking for corroboration of "suspect" evidence is to see whether it is to be believed.'[154]

In no way should the foregoing be understood to mean 'that the court must not act upon the evidence of one witness, even if it is unshaken in cross-examination, and in no way discredited by the witness's demeanour.'[155] According to Sir James Fitzjames Stephen:[156]

> The circumstances may be such that there is no check on the willingness and no power to obtain any further evidence on the subject. Under these circumstances [courts] may, and often do, acquit. They may very reasonably say we do not attach such credit to the oath of a single person of whom we know nothing, as to be willing to destroy another person on the strength of it. This case arises where the fact deposed to is a passing occurrence-such as a verbal confession or a sexual crime-leaving no trace behind it, except in the memory of an eye or ear-witness [...] The Justification of this is, that the power of lying is

[151] *R v Tripodi* [1961] VR 186 at 190-191 (CF); *R v Fuhrer* [1961] VR 500 at 509 (CF); *R v Davy* (1964) 84 WN (Pt 1) (NSW) 42 at 47; *R v Colless* (1964) 4 WN (Pt 1) (NSW) 55 at 57; *R v Lindsay* (1977) 18 SASR 103 at 117-120 (CCA); *R v Duke* (1979) 22 SASR 46 at 52 (CCA); *Medcraft v R* [1982] WAR 33 (CCA); *R v Nanette* [1982] VR 81 at 84 (CF); *R v Galluzzo* (1986) 23 A Crim R 211 (NSW CCA), among others.

[152] [1973] AC 296 at 315.

[153] [1919] 14 SSLR 152.

[154] *Phipson on Evidence* 320-17.

[155] Heydon JD, *Cross on Evidence* (10th edn Lexis Nexis, 2016) 465.

[156] Fitzmaurice Stephen, *A General View of the Criminal Law of England* (Macmillan, 1863) 249-50 quoted in Heydon JD, *Cross on Evidence* (10th edn Lexis Nexis, 2016) 465.

> unlimited, the causes of lying and delusion are numerous, and many of them are unknown, and the means of detection are limited.

It has thus been explained by Lord Hailsham in *Boardman v DPP*,[157] that'unless a witness was intrinsically credible, he could neither afford corroboration nor be thought to require it.' In the ordinary course of things, counsel worth his salt or a party appearing in *pro se*[158] will only call a witness whom they trust to tell their story and who possesses the credibility to do so. Thus, when a witness is called to the stand, he is, being presented as a witness who will speak the truth. That a witness lacking in the foregoing qualities would be called either as a principal witness or indeed a corroborative one is quite rare. That it is rare for a witness of a class requiring corroboration whose evidence is placed before court to be the sort who is in want of credibility does not mean that the law should not provide for such an eventuality. Rarity is synonymous with impossibility. Thus, where the evidence is incapable of belief the court will not deem it as prospectively corroborative and in the absence of other corroborative evidence, the prosecution's case must fail of its own inherent weakness where the principal evidence is the kind that calls for corroboration. Where the opposite is true, that is to say, that the evidence is worthy of belief, it then can be used to confirm the principal evidence. No necessity is placed upon a presiding judge or magistrate to satisfy himself of the credibility of corroborative evidence as a basis of determining whether it ought to be used at all. The foregoing is so because in so far as the treatment of this brand of evidence is concerned, its use or non-use is dependent on it being accepted by the court, and if not so accepted, it can play no part in the court's final judgment. Finally, it has been shown in *Director of Public Prosecutions v Kilbourne*,[159] that where the principal witness's evidence is deemed credible, then corroborative evidence may be used to confirm said evidence and indeed dispel any lingering doubts in the mind of the [judge/magistrate].

6.7.5 *Self-corroboration vs physical condition of person who requires corroboration*

6.7.5.1 *The common law rule against self-corroboration*

That to amount to corroboration evidence must be extraneous to the witness who requires corroboration is a fact that has long been settled.[160] Sperling J has however warned that 'for a [judge] to think that evidence of complaint could be treated as corroboration may be an easy mistake in circumstances

[157] [1975] AC 421 at 455; *Director of Public Prosecutions v Kilbourne* [1973] AC 729 at 746.

[158] Latin for self or 'in one's own behalf.'

[159] [1973] AC 729 at 750; *R v Spencer* [1987] AC 128 at 134; *Attorney-General (Hong Kong) v Wong* [1987] AC 501; see also *Turner v Blunden* [1986] Fam 120 at 127 (DC); *R v Doney* (1988) 37 A Crim R 288 at 299-300 (NSW CCA); *R v Panagiotis* (1990) 55 SASR 172 (CCA).

[160] *R v Whitehead* [1929] 1 KB 99 at 102 (CCA) *per* Lord Hewart CJ.

where corroboration is in the air, but it is a monumental mistake.'[161] There is therefore a logical common law objection to self-corroboration if nothing else, the absurdity of the idea. In *R v Whitehead*[162] the accused was charged with the unlawfully carnally knowing a girl under the age of 16. It was contended that the girl's testimony could be said to have been corroborated by the fact that she had talked to her mother about the incident sometime after the material time of its alleged occurrence, after which the mother laid a complaint against the accused. Lord Hewart CJ rejecting this contention somewhat curtly opined as follows: 'a girl cannot corroborate herself, otherwise it is only necessary for her to repeat her story some 25 times in order to get 25 corroborations of it.'

6.7.5.2 *Proscription of self-corroboration under statutory rules*

A consideration of various statutory provisions in relevant pieces of legislation discussed elsewhere in this text reveals that where 'the legislation provides that for the purposes of any rule of law or practice requiring evidence to be corroborated, or regulating the manner in which uncorroborated evidence is to be treated, a statement rendered admissible by the legislation is not to be treated as corroboration of evidence given by the maker.'[163] The effect of statutory provisions such as these is to render inadmissible such statements as the common law would deem admissible within the context of common law rules of evidence. Therefore, evidence relating to police diaries employed to refresh a witness's memory have been held not to corroborate the evidence of the maker.'[164]

6.7.5.3 *Physical condition and distress*

As a general rule, the distressed condition of the victim of a sexual assault, it has been variously suggested, is evidence amenable to corroboration. This position, however, renders itself to several criticisms chief among which is that distress can be simulated. Courts thus take each case on its own facts and set of circumstances and seek to determine whether the distress by the victim in the present case is such as would, 'in light of ordinary experience' be the kind that 'is likely to have been causally related to the alleged incident.'[165] In *Ackson Zimba v The People*[166] the appellant had been charged and following trial, was convicted of rape. Evidence led at trial and accepted as such was that the complainant was seen crying by an independent witness, whom the prosecution used to corroboration the complainant's testimony. It was held on appeal that it is necessary for the trial court to warn itself that evidence

---

[161] *R v Elsworthy* (1996) 39 NSWLR 450 at 460 (CCA).

[162] [1929] 1 KB 99 at 102 (CCA); see also *R v Christie* [1914] AC 545.

[163] Heydon JD, *Cross on Evidence* para 35135 at 1302.

[164] *Senat v Senat* [1965] P 172; *King v Deel, Ex parte Deel* [1932] QWN 4 (FC); *Crutchfield v Lee* [1934] VLR 146; *Moore v Hewitt* [1947] KB 831 (CD of KBD); but see *Jeffrey v Johnson* [1952] 2 QB 8 (CA); *X v Y* [1975] 2 NZLR 524 (CA).

[165] Heydon JD, *Cross on Evidence* para 15195 at 495.

[166] [1980] ZR 259 (SC).

of distress at the time of the making of the complaint may not be enough to amount to corroboration as it may well be simulated.

The decision used as its basis *Knight v R.*[167] In that case, the appellant was convicted of indecently assaulting a girl of seven who gave unsworn evidence of the incident. The complainant's father gave evidence that he came on his daughter when she was walking in the street concerned with the appellant, who walked away, that his daughter seemed frightened and was shaking and that she was holding her hands over her private parts. She also said that, until she saw her father, she was not a bit distressed at all. The appellant's defence was an alibi; that he had never been in the street concerned nor did he even know where it was. He gave no evidence. On appeal against conviction, it was held that although the distress of the girl might have been insufficient corroboration if it had stood alone, yet if the jury believed the father and found that the appellant was lying about not having been in the street concerned, that was very cogent evidence capable of amounting to corroboration.[168] *Per* Curiam: distress shown by a complainant in a sexual case must not be over-emphasised in the sense that juries should be warned that, except in special circumstances, little weight ought to be given to that evidence.[169]

In *R v Flannery*[170] a case that came before Australian Victorian full Court three years following the decision in *Knight v R*,[171] but some eleven years before *Ackson Zimba v The People*,[172] it was observed as follows:

> [...] regard must be had to such factors as the age of the prosecutrix, the time interval between the alleged assault and when she was observed in distress, her conduct and appearance in the interim, and the circumstances existing when she is observed in the distressed condition. Without attempting to enumerate exhaustively the circumstances in which such evidence may amount to corroboration, we are of opinion that if, regard being had to factors of the kind we have mentioned, the reasonable inference from the evidence is that there was a causal connexion between the alleged assault and the distressed condition, evidence of the latter is capable of constituting corroboration. If such inference is not open, evidence is not, in our opinion, capable of amounting to corroboration. We should add that except in special circumstances [...] evidence of distressed condition will carry little weight and juries should be so warned by the trial judge in the course of his charge.

Taking a more cautious tone than that expressed in *R v Flannery*,[173] King CJ

[167] Applying *Knight v R*50 Cr App Rep 122, [1966] 1 All ER 647 (CCA).

[168] *R v Redpath* (1962) 46 Cr App Rep 319 distinguished.

[169] Editor's notes: As to corroboration in sexual offences, see 10 Halsbury's Laws (3rd Edn) 462, para 850; and for cases on the subject, see 14 Digest (Repl) 543, 544, 5271–5279.

[170] [1969] VR 586 at 591; *R v Guilford* (2004) 148 A Crim R 558 at [151].

[171] Applying *Knight v R* 50 Cr App Rep 122; [1966] 1 All ER 647 (CCA).

[172] [1980] ZR 259 (SC).

[173] [1969] VR 586 at 591; *R v Guilford* (2004) 148 A Crim R 558 at [151].

observed thus, in *R v Waye*:[174]

> In order to treat such manifestations as capable in law of amounting to corroboration, it is necessary to be able to exclude, on any reasonable view of the evidence, the possibility that they are concomitants of the relation of a fabricated story or of an account which has its only basis in a disordered imagination.

Following from the preceding, a few more points are deserving of consideration. It may well be that the physical condition and distress of the victim/complainant may have resulted from an assault which does not form the basis of the charge against the accused;[175] or that the physical condition or distress in question may have been observed a long time after the alleged assault.[176] It may also be the case that the victim's physical condition is borderline or equivocal. In any one of the foregoing scenarios the court ought not to view the victim's condition as capable of being corroborative. Whether the trier of fact places weight on the physical condition of the victim/complainant is a matter for the court itself to determine.[177] Further, whether the complainant's physical condition, such as visible injuries are tantamount to corroboration of the testimony given concerning them, and as such implicates the accused, is a matter not of law but of fact to be determined on a case-by-case basis.[178]

6.7.6 *Corroboration and the conduct of the accused or defendant*[179]

The range of conduct with which we are concerned hereunder is with respect to that which would be deemed corroborative evidence. It includes such matters as (i) admissions; (ii) the accused/defendant's evidence; (iii) falsity of evidence; (iv) failure to give evidence; (v) false statements made by the accused/ defendant out of court; (vi) silence upon being charged with a serious offence (vii) conduct on previous occasions; (viii) previous conduct tending to show a particular propensity; and (ix) previous conduct corroborating the accused's statement made to witness. We will discuss these briefly in turn.

6.7.6.1 *Admissions*

An accused or defendant's admission, as the case may be, is capable of constituting corroborative evidence. This is demonstrated in the Australian case of *Hobbs v Davies; Ex parte Davies*.[180] On proceedings for affiliation the complainant gave evidence that the defendant was the father of her child; that when she was about three months advanced in pregnancy she informed him at Dana of her condition; that he thereupon promised to marry her; that Upon

---

[174] (1984) 14 A Crim R 391 at 393 (SA); see also *Grubisic v Western Australia* (2011) 41 WAR 524 at [70].

[175] *R v Richard* [1965] Qd R 54 (CCA).

[176] *R v Moana* [1979] 1 NZLR 181 (CA); *R v Poa* [1979] 2 NZLR 378 (CA); *R v Sailor* [1994] 2 Qd R 342.

[177] *R v Romeo* [2004] 1 Cr App R 30.

[178] *R v Berrill* [1982] Qd R 508 at 527 (CCA); *R v Gallagher* (1986) 41 SASR 73 (CCA); *R v Keast* [1998] Crim LR 748 (CA); *R v Danine* (2004) 145 A Crim R 278 at [14].

[179] See generally, Heydon JD, *Cross on Evidence* para [15200] – [15240] 496-507.

[180] [1943] St R Qd 131 (CCA); see also *R v Mckeon* (1986) 31 A Crim R 357.

her return soon after to her mother's place at Toowoomba she wrote to him from there saying that her mother was very pleased that they were getting married and that it would be all right; that she received no reply either to that letter or to any of four others she wrote to him within a fortnight of it. The only other witness was the complainant's mother, who deposed to having had the following conversation with the defendant alone at his place of employment in Brisbane when the complainant was five months with child. She said to him: "I suppose you know what I am here for, Jaok." He nodded his head and remarked: "It's a bit of a bugger, isn't it?" She said: "Have you received Dulcie's (the complainant's) letters?" He replied: "Yes, I got them all right." Some two months after this conversation the complainant, on visiting the defendant it his home at Bundamba, discovered that he was married. No evidence was given by or on behalf of the defendant. The magistrate adjudged the defendant to be the father of the child and made an order for its maintenance. The defendant appealed by way of quashing order. It was held by a majority that the oath of the complainant was sufficiently corroborated—

Per Webb CJ:

> On the ground that the magistrate had the advantage of seeing and hearing the complainant's mother, who might have conveyed to him that the defendant used the obscene expression in such a manner as to give the impression that the complainant's pregnancy was not merely a regrettable fact from her viewpoint and that of her parents, but also an embarrassing circumstance for the defendant also, the genuine nature of which might have been indicated by the way the expression was used;

Per EA Douglas J:

> On the ground that the construction of the words used by the defendant in his conversation with the complainant's mother was for the magistrate; and that it was open to him, construing the obscene expression in the light of the defendant's knowledge of the complainant's condition, to find that it tended to connect him with the paternity and rendered it probable that he was the father of the child.[181]

Per Maobossan SPJ:

> It is impossible fairly to draw any inference of guilt against the appellant from his conversation with the complainant's mother, since conversations equally consistent with innocence and guilt do not amount to corroboration.[182]

6.7.6.2 *The accused/defendant's evidence*

[181] *R v Pearcy* ([1862] 17 QB 902, note (*a*); 117 ER 1527 followed and applied.

[182] *Ex parte McPherson* ([1932] 32 SBNSW 525) followed and applied.

According to Atkin LJ, '[t]he question of corroboration often assumes an entirely different aspect after the accused person has gone into the witness-box and has been cross-examined.'[183] It must be added though that this does not mean that demeanour will be the determining factor in constituting corroboration. Nor is corroboration to be treated as though it were a question of law. It is a question of fact. Further, though a variance between a witness's testimony and the inference that may be drawn from the tenor of his cross-examination may be factors that may be taken into account, it has been shown in *R v Lander,*[184]the specific contents of the questions paused under cross-examination are incapable of establishing corroboration.

Criminal proceedings that involve the trial of more than one accused raise a different set of issues. A few things may be said about this within the context of our discussion. Firstly, it is that the statement of a co-accused to the police cannot be used to corroborate the evidence against the other accused person.[185] As regards this point, it is important to note that where the statement of a co-accused person tends to show that the co-accused is telling the truth, may be used in the consideration of the case of the other co-accused person only but it will be incapable of corroborating the evidence against the co-accused.[186] Secondly, the unsworn testimony of a co-accused is similarly incapable of corroborating evidence against another accused person.[187]

6.7.6.3 Falsity of evidence

Falsehoods told by the accused person in court are music to the prosecution's ears. They strengthen the prosecution's case and weaken the accused's defence. We have elsewhere in this text discussed such issues as adverse inferences to be drawn from an accused's refusal to answer questions; confessions that incriminate the accused; inability to supply urine samples or the like for purposes of a police investigation; and failure to mount a defence to charges as being actions and/or statements as the case may be which the prosecution may employ as a means of strengthening their case to the detriment of the accused. In this part of our discussion, we focus on scenarios that may involve an accused person lying to the police or that he lied during oral testimony while under oath.

While it is true that an accused's being economical with the truth in or out of court will almost certainly not strengthen an accused's case, it does not quite follow that this in and of itself is suggestive of the accused's guilt. The motive for lying may have nothing to do with avoiding the consequences of an accused's actions and much to do with 'shame or terror.'[188] In *Broadhurst v R*[189]

[183] *R v Dossi* (1918) 13 Cr App R 158; see also *Goguen v Bourgeois* (1957) 6 DLR (2d) 19; *R v McConnon* [1951] SASR 22.

[184] (1989) 52 SASR 424 (CCA).

[185] *R v Smith* [1964] NSWR 537 (CCA).

[186] *R v Jones* (2006) 161 a Crim R 511.

[187] *Montgomery v Counsell* [1956] St R Qd 120 (CCA).

[188] *R v Broadhurst* [1964] AC 441.

[189] [1964] 1 All ER 111.

Lord Devlin observed as follows:

> There is a natural tendency for a [trier of fact] to think that if an accused is lying, it must be because he is guilty and accordingly to convict him without more ado. It is the duty of the judge to make it clear [...] that this is not so. Save in one respect, a case in which an accused gives untruthful evidence is no different from one in which he gives no evidence at all. In either case the burden remains on the prosecution to prove the guilt of the accused. But if on the proved facts two inferences may be drawn about the accused's conduct or state of mind, his untruthfulness is a factor which the jury can properly take into account as strengthening the inference of guilt. What strength it adds depends of course on all the circumstances and especially on whether there are reasons other than guilt that might account for untruthfulness.[190]

In *R v Richens,*[191] the appellant, a 17-year-old student, was charged with the murder of a fellow student who had allegedly raped the appellant's girlfriend. The killing took place a fortnight after the girlfriend complained to the appellant that the victim had raped her. The appellant confronted the victim, who claimed that the girl had been a willing party to all that had taken place. The appellant became enraged and stabbed the deceased to death. His girlfriend assisted in the disposal of the body and she then left the country. When questioned about the victim's disappearance the appellant at first lied to the police, denying any involvement, and when he was arrested 17 days later, he persisted in that denial. Two days later he admitted responsibility for the killing and described where he had buried the body. At his trial the only issue was whether the killing was murder or manslaughter by reason of provocation. The trial judge directed the jury that for provocation to be established the appellant had to have completely lost control to the extent that he really did not know what he was doing. It was the appellant's case that he had lied to the police at first in order to protect his girlfriend, who he said had nothing to do with the killing, and then to protect his parents. In summing up the trial judge invited the jury to consider whether the appellant's admitted lies prior to his admission of the offence were potentially probative of murder. The appellant was convicted of murder. He appealed on the ground, inter alia, that the judge's directions on provocation and the appellant's lies amounted to material misdirections. It was held *inter alia* that in all cases where the jury were invited to regard, or there was a danger that they might regard, lies told by the defendant, or evasive or discreditable conduct by him, as probative of his guilt of the offence in question, the judge ought to direct the jury that before they could treat the lies as tending towards proof of guilt of the offence charged they had to be sure that there was not some possible explanation for the lies which destroyed their potentially probative effect. On the facts, the issue for

[190] See *R v Lucas* [1981] 2 All ER 1008 at 1011 e.g., *per* Lord Lane CJ.

[191] [1993] 4 All ER 877.

the jury had been whether they could be sure that the appellant's attempts to conceal the killing and his lies were inconsistent with his case that he had killed as a result of provocation, and pointed to murder. The trial judge's failure to direct the jury to consider whether there was any explanation for the appellant's lies other than guilt of the offence charged, and his indication that the jury might regard the appellant's lies as probative of murder rather than manslaughter amounted to a material misdirection. Accordingly, the appeal would be allowed, the conviction for murder quashed and a verdict of manslaughter substituted.[192]

As a general rule with respect to all cases where it is required,[193] 'corroboration may well be found in the evidence of an accused person; but that is a different matter, for there confirmation comes, if at all, from what is said, and from the falsity of what is said.'[194] To put it another way, an accused person does not corroborate an accomplice on the basis of his evidence which is deemed unworthy of belief and on the basis that it is false, such corroboration is rejected by the court. The position is, however, subject to many permutations. As a starting point in its consideration, the logical argument as regards false evidence is that the witness who tells it has, as his motivation, the concealment of matters that may lead to his conviction or that of an accomplice. We must hasten repeat, however, that as explained elsewhere in this text, the reasons for falsity of evidence may sometimes be different and may be as a result of shame, terror, panic or motivated by the desire to protect one's own family. Be that as it may, since there is authority to the effect that lies told outside court ought to be deemed corroborative,[195] it logically follows that those told by the accused on the witness stand ought to be treated similarly.[196] Lord Lane CJ in what has come to be known as the Lucas Direction has opined as follows in *R v Lucas:*[197]

> To be capable of amounting to corroboration the lie told out of court must first of all be deliberate. Secondly it must relate to a material issue. Thirdly the motive for the lie must be a realisation of guilt and a fear of the truth. The jury should in appropriate cases be reminded that people sometimes lie, for example, in an attempt to bolster up a just cause, or out of shame or out of a wish to conceal disgraceful behaviour from their family. Fourthly the statement must be clearly shown to be a lie by evidence other than that of the accomplice who is to be corroborated, that is to say by admission or by evidence from an independent witness. As a matter of good sense, it is difficult to see why, subject to the same safeguard, lies proved to have been told in court by a defendant should not equally be capable of providing

---

192 *Broadhurst v R* [1964] 1 All ER 111 considered.

193 *R v Chapman* [1973] QB 774 (CCA).

194 *Tumahole Bereng v R* [1949] AC 253 at 270 *per* Lord MacDermott.

195 *R v Tripodi* [1961] VR 186 at 193 (FC).

196 See *R v Collins* [1976] 2 NZLR 104 (CA); *R v Lucas* [1981] QB 720 (CA); *R v Perera* [1982] VR 901 (FC); but see *R v King* [1967] 2 QB 338 (CA); *Trainer v R* (1906) 4 CLR 126.

197 [1981] 2 All ER 1008 at 1011.

corroboration.

The foregoing is, however, deserving of qualification. The principle cannot, and has not been applied to unembellished denials or denials *simpliciter* by the accused in the witness box without more.[198] The foregoing invariably leads to the circular argument that for the court to disbelieve the accused's testimony on account of its falsity, it inexorably has to accept the prosecution's evidence as true. In Lowe J's words: '[…] there must be evidence *aliunde* to support the petitioner's case, before you can use an untrue denial of the parties charged as affording corroboration of that case.'[199]

However, as has been shown in *Tumahole Bereng v R*,[200]preference of the prosecution's evidence over that of the accused ought not to be treated, in and of itself, as corroborative of the prosecution's evidence. The pronouncement while applicable in proper cases, it is submitted, would appear inapplicable in all cases where the facts and circumstances warrant the treatment of falsity of evidence by an accused person as corroborative of the evidence against him.[201] The foregoing may be explained thus: where the lies in question are responses to specific questions, or a concoction calculated to mislead the court which can only reasonably be deemed to be indicative of the accused's guilt, and as such, tantamount to an admission, albeit impliedly, said lies ought to be treated, as long as they are proved by independent evidence or/and admitted by the accused, to be corroborative of the evidence against him or her as the case may be.

Several authorities illustrate the preceding. In *Corfield v Hodgson*,[202] the appellant's denial in his testimony during evidence in chief that he had taken the respondent home following a dance which was as admitted by him to be false under cross-examination was said to be corroborative of the complainant's mother's evidence.

In the case of *Nsofu v The People*,[203] the Supreme Court observed as follows: '[w]hether evidence of opportunity is sufficient to amount to corroboration must depend on all the circumstances of the particular case.' In *Credland v Knowler*[204] Goddard LJ, quoted with approval the dictum of Lord Dunedin in *Dawson v Mackenzie*[205] that '[m]ere opportunity does not amount to corroboration, but the opportunity may be of such a character as to bring in the element of suspicion. That is the circumstances and locality of the opportunity may be

[198] *Pitman v Byrne* [1926] SASR 207; *R v Mercer* (1993) 67 A Crim R 91 (NSW CCA).

[199] *Edmunds v Edmunds* [1935] VLR 177 at 186; but see *R v Tripodi* [1961] VR 186 at 193 (FC); for examples of errors of this kind see *R v Chapman* [1973] QB 774 (CA).

[200] [1949] AC 253 at 270; *R v Lucas* [1981] QB 720 (CA).

[201] *R v Lucas* [1981] QB 720 (CA); *R v Perera* [1982] VR 901 (FC).

[202] *Corfield v Hodgson* [1966] 1 WLR 590; 2 All ER 205.

[203] [1973] ZR 287 (SC); *Machipisha Kombe v The People* [2009] ZR 282.

[204] (1951) 35 Cr App R 48; *R v Baskerville* [1916] 2 KB 658; *Simon Malambo Choka v The People* [1978] ZR 243; *Emmanuel Phiri v The People* [1978] ZR 79; *Shamwana and Others v The People* (1985) ZR 41; *Mwenya v People* (SCZ Judgment 5 of 1990) [1990] ZMSC 13.

[205] 29 SLR 226.

such as themselves amount to corroboration.' It has been held in *Katebe v The People*,[206] that 'where there can be no motive for a prosecutrix deliberately and dishonestly to make a false allegation against an accused, and the case is in practice no different from any others in which the conviction depends on the reliability of her evidence as to the identity of the culprit, this is a "special and compelling ground" which would justify a conviction on uncorroborated testimony.' The flipside of this position is that a false denial of an opportunity to commit an offence by the accused will be taken to mean that advantage was taken of the opportunity to commit the offence in question.[207] In the South African case of *Poggenpoel v Morris*,[208] a man's denial on a charge of seduction, that he had been with the complainant in an empty building overnight was said to be capable of corroborating the girl's evidence on the premise that the evidence by other witnesses of the two parties having been together in said abandoned building was accepted at trial. This reasoning is similar to that taken by the Zambian Court of Appeal in *Michael Bwalya v The People*.[209] The appellant was convicted of one count of Defilement of a child under the age of sixteen years, contrary to s 138(1) of the Penal Code.[210] The particulars of the offence were that the appellant, on the 27th July, 2017, at Lusaka in the Lusaka District of the Lusaka Province of the Republic of Zambia, had unlawful carnal knowledge of SZ, a girl under the age of sixteen years. Upon conviction, the appellant was committed to the High Court for sentencing. The High Court sentenced him to a prison term of twenty-five years with hard labour. He appealed against conviction and sentence filing two grounds of which one was that the learned trial Magistrate misdirected herself both in law and fact when she convicted the appellant on the uncorroborated evidence of a child witness. Commenting on what the Court deemed, from the tenor of the judgment to be a false denial of opportunity *vis-à-vis* corroboration, the Court observed as follows:

> It is our considered view that the opportunity that existed for the appellant to defile the prosecutrix was of such a character as to bring in the element of suspicion because he was the only person who was with the prosecutrix at his house between 15:00 and 16:00 hours on the material day. We therefore hold that the circumstances and the locality of the opportunity in themselves amount to corroboration of the prosecutrix's evidence of the identity of the defiler.

Given the rather nuanced nature of the subject, it is safe to recognise the complex problems that the issue of fabrications within the context of the concept of corroboration present to a judge/magistrate even when he has before

[206] [1975] ZR 13 (SC).

[207] *Credland v Knowler* (1951) 35 Cr App R 48.

[208] 1938 CPD 90.

[209] Appeal No 138/2018.

[210] Chapter 87 of the Laws of Zambia, as read with Act No 15 of 2005 of the Laws of Zambia.

him competent counsel. It is quite difficult, even at the best of times to, with mathematical, scientific or thematic precision, make an entirely acceptable and sweeping statement as regards the type of falsehood capable of providing corroboration. For this reason, it behooves the judge/ magistrate to ensure utmost care in the consideration of the matter. Heydon[211] observes as follows:

> If the question is whether A's evidence or B's evidence is true, the rejection of B's evidence does not mean that A's evidence or B's evidence is true, the rejection of B's evidence does not mean that A's evidence must be accepted as true, for B might have other reasons for lying. As a matter of logic, the rejection of B's evidence does mean that A's evidence must be accepted if B's evidence is its contradictory. On a charge of rape, the rejection of the accused's assertion that the complainant consented entails acceptance of the assertion of non-consent; the false assertion of consent could not, without more, be corroborative of the complainant's evidence. The conclusion that it did have this effect would amount to holding that mere disbelief in what the accused said amounts to corroboration of the evidence.[212] On the other hand, the accused's assertion of some such specific incident as an invitation by the complainant to take the complainant home and make love there, alleged to be false by another witness, ought, on principle, to be corroborative of the complainant's testimony denying consent if the other witness is believed. The conclusion that the accused invented a particular falsity to support the allegation of consent is more than a mere utilisation of disbelief in that allegation as corroboration, although, as a matter of logic, the rejection of this particular item of the accused's evidence does not entail acceptance of the complainant's statement that the intercourse was nonconsensual.[213]

6.7.6.4 *Failure to give evidence*

The failure of a witness to give evidence cannot without more be said to be corroborative of the evidence of accomplices. In *R v Jackson*,[214] the appellant was convicted of receiving and of being an accessory before the fact to larceny of some tyres. During the trial evidence was given by accomplices, the persons who had been convicted of the larceny of the tyres, that they had arranged the whole transaction with the appellant. He himself did not go into the witness box and give evidence, and the judge directed the jury that they could take that fact as amounting to corroboration of the accomplices' evidence. It was held

[211] Heydon JD, *Cross on Evidence* 498 – 499.

[212] This conclusion is rejected in *Pitman v Byrne* [1926] SASR 207 at 211 (FC).

[213] As to what use the court may make of the fact that the accused's use of an alibi has been rejected, see *R v Turnbull* [1977] QB 224 at 230 (CA); *King v R* (1986) 15 FCR 427 at 438; *R v Pemberton* (1993) 99 Cr App R 228 at 232.

[214] [1953] 1 All ER 872.

that the direction was wrong.[215] *Per* Lord Goddard:[216]

> The difficulty that arises here is on the direction that the learned judge gave, because, having pointed out who might be regarded as accomplices and emphasised the danger of acting on their evidence, in commenting on the fact that the appellant had not gone into the witness box to give evidence he said:
>
> > You, members of the jury, will attach just what weight you think right to that, and if you say: "Well, that, in our view, forms ample corroboration that those thieves were telling the truth. We think he has refrained from going into the witness box because he does not dare, he thinks he will only make matters worse if he does'—if you come to that conclusion—the weight you attach to his silence is entirely a matter for you."
>
> That came just at the end of the learned judge's summing-up and could only have been understood by the jury as meaning that the fact that the appellant had not gone into the witness box might amount to corroboration if they thought fit to treat it as such. That is not correct. One cannot say, because a man has not gone into the witness box to give evidence, that that of itself is corroboration of the evidence of accomplices. It is a matter which the jury could very properly take into account and very probably would, but it is not a right direction to give to a jury, and it should be clearly understood that it is wrong in law.

Lord Goddard's observation appears to suggest that there is a distinction between matters which the trier of fact 'could very properly take into account'

and those which could be deemed corroborative. The rule as expressed by Lord Goddard in *R v Jackson*[217] has found application in affiliation proceedings. In *Cracknell v Smith*[218] a complaint was preferred on 27 October 1959, by the respondent against the appellant that she had been delivered of a male bastard child on 26 December 1958, of which child she alleged the appellant to be the father. At the hearing of the complaint the respondent and her mother gave evidence. The appellant gave no evidence, but called his brother as a witness whose evidence was such that the justices regarded him as a liar and his evidence

[215] Editor's notes: As to Corroboration of Evidence of Accomplices, see Halsbury, Hailsham Edn, Vol 9, p 223, para 311; and for Cases, see Digest, Vol 14, pp 460–462, Nos 4891–4919.

[216] [1953] 1 All ER 872 at 873.

[217] [1953] 1 All ER 872.

[218] [1960] 3 All ER 569 at 571 (DC of QBD).

as being of no account. On the question whether there was corroboration of the respondent's evidence in some material particular as required by s 4(2) of the Affiliation Proceedings Act, 1957, it was held as follows: (i) The evidence of the respondent's mother, being merely evidence of opportunity, could not, of itself, afford corroboration.[219] (ii) the fact that the appellant failed to give evidence, but called his brother who gave untrue evidence, did not amount to corroboration.[220]

According to Parker CJ, '[i]f there is evidence against him, and some corroborative evidence, it may be that the justices are entitled to take into consideration the fact that he gave no evidence in considering the weight to be attached to the corroboration.' The implication of the Lordship's words would appear to be the rather complex distinction that he says exists between corroborative evidence and facts which may add weight to corroborative evidence in another ways.

A question (already alluded to above) that has sometimes arisen in instances where there is failure to give evidence is whether a failure to cross examine a witness would in and of itself constitute corroboration of the witness's evidence. The issue did arise and was dealt with in *Dingwall v F Wharton (Shipping) Ltd.*[221] Lord Keith of Avonholm opined as follows:

> It was said for the pursuer that failure to cross-examine Wemyss on this part of his evidence must of itself be taken as corroboration. The point does not now arise. But apart from admission on record or by joint minute, or by other clear acceptance by Counsel, absence of cross-examination cannot, in my opinion, be treated as the equivalent of corroboration.

The appellate court in *R v Bassett*[222] took the view that the criticism levelled on counsel by the trial court for not cross-examining a co-accused who gave evidence contradicting the first accused was unwarranted.

6.7.6.5 *False statements made by the accused/defendant out of court*

[219] *Moore v Hewitt* [1947] 2 All ER 270 and *Harvey v Anning* (1902) 87 LT 687 distinguished.

[220] Editor's notes: As to corroboration of the mother's evidence, see 3 Halsbury's Laws (3rd Edn) 120, para 184; and for cases on the subject, see 3 Digest 394, 313 *et seq*; For the Affiliation Proceedings Act, 1957, s 4(2), see 37 Halsbury's Statutes (2nd Edn) 40.

[221] [1961] 2 Lloyd's Rep 213 at 213 at 219 (HL).

[222] [1952] VLR 535 (FC). *Cf. R v Tooma* [1981] Qd 720 at 724 (CA).

When then can a lie told out of court amount to corroboration?[223] This question arose in *R v Lucas*.[224] It was, in what is now termed the *Lucas*[225] direction, shown firstly that the fact that a [court] may prefer an accomplice's evidence to that of the defendant does not of itself provide corroboration of the accomplice's otherwise uncorroborated evidence. It is only if the accomplice's evidence is believed that there is any necessity to look for corroboration of it. Secondly, and in parts relevant to our current discussion, that for a lie told by an accused out of court to provide corroboration against him that lie must be deliberate, it must relate to a material issue; the motive for it must be a realisation of guilt and a fear of the truth, and it must be clearly shown to be a lie by evidence other than that of an accomplice to be corroborated, i.e., by admission or by evidence from an independent witness.[226]

If *Lucas*[227] is to be used as a persuasive authority in this jurisdiction it will be with regard to at least three matters that it dealt with:

(i) When and under what circumstances a lie may amount to corroboration whether it was told in or outside court;

(ii) That the prosecution is well within its rights to rely on the accused's lie for purposes of strengthening their case against such accused person; and

(iii) The judge/magistrate must take a cautious approach by being alive to the inherent perils of predicating probative weight on such lies

[223] For corroboration and the evidence of accomplices, see 11 Halsbury's Laws (4th Edn) para 457, and for cases on the subject, see 14(2) Digest (Reissue) 608–621, 4942–5078; *Credland v Knowler* (1951) 35 Cr App R 48, DC, 15 Digest (Reissue) 1234, 10, 540, 1008; *Dawson v M'Kenzie* 1908 SC 648, 45 Sc LR 473, 15 SLT 951, 32 Digest (Reissue) 75, 352; *R v Boardman* [1974] 2 All ER 958, [1975] AC 421, [1974] 3 WLR 673, CA; affd sub nom *Boardman v Director of Public Prosecutions* [1974] 3 All ER 887, [1975] AC 421, [1974] 3 WLR 673, 60 Cr App R 165, HL, 14(2) Digest (Reissue) 527, 4296; *R v Chapman* [1973] 2 All ER 624, [1973] QB 774, [1973] 2 WLR 876, 57 Cr App R 511, 137 JP 525, CA, 14(2) Digest (Reissue) 608, 4947; *R v Knight* [1966] 1 All ER 647, [1966] 1 WLR 23O, 130 JP 187, 50 Cr App R 122, CCA, 15 Digest (Reissue) 1234, 10,541; *Tumahole Bereng v R* [1949] AC 253, [1949] LJR 1603, PC, 14(2) Digest (Reissue) 617, *3967.

[224] [1981] 2 All ER 1008 at 1011 *per* Lord Lane CJ.

[225] [1981] 2 All ER 1008 at 1011.

[226] Dicta of Lord Dunedin in *Dawson v M'Kenzie* 1908 SC at 649 and of Orr LJ in *R v Boardman* [1974] 2 All ER at 963 approved; *R v Chapman* [1973] 2 All ER 624 explained; editor's notes: For the nature of corroboration in criminal proceedings, see 11 Halsbury's Laws (4th Edn) para 454, and for cases on the subject, see 15 Digest (Reissue) 962–964, 8320–8342.

[227] [1981] 2 All ER 1008 at 1011 *per* Lord Lane CJ.

because lies do not necessarily equate to guilt.[228]

The procedure outlined above has been followed in *R v Goodway*.[229] A wedding party, which included the appellant, his wife and a man, C, were involved in a fracas after the wedding reception when their group met a group which had just left a nearby public house. There was evidence that C confronted a man in the other group with a broken bottle and threatened to kill him and that a fight broke out between the appellant's wife and the deceased. In the ensuing mêlée the deceased was stabbed through the heart and another member of the public house party was head-butted and stabbed. When the police arrived, C was lying across the body of the deceased on the ground. He was pulled away and seen to be carrying two metal bars and was described as being 'completely deranged'. A knife found under the deceased's body admittedly belonged to the appellant and there was much blood on the appellant's clothing, most of it being of the same group as that of the deceased and some of it being of the same group as the other victim's. C had no blood on his clothes. The appellant was arrested and charged with murder and wounding with intent. When interviewed by the police the appellant at first denied being anywhere near either victim. At his trial the prosecution relied on the fact that the appellant had lied to the police when interviewed as support for the identification evidence put forward by the Crown. The appellant's defence was that C had taken the appellant's knife from the van which had taken them to the wedding and that C, not the appellant, was responsible for killing the deceased. The defence called a witness, K, who had made a statement after the fracas in which he claimed to have seen C striking the deceased but in evidence he persistently asserted that his statement was untrue. The judge ruled that since the contents of his previous statement had been totally disavowed by K it could not be treated as evidence and in his summing up, he did not give the jury any direction as to how they should approach the fact that the appellant had falsely denied being near the victims when interviewed by the police. The appellant was convicted. He appealed on the grounds that the judge's direction and summing up were wrong. It was held as follows: (1) There was no absolute rule that a hostile witness had to be

[228] Care is necessary when the issue of lies arises: *R v Ray* (2003) 57 NSWLR 616 at [98]; *Healey v R* [2008] NSWCCA 229 at [43]. It is important to distinguish between lies being used to attack the credit of the accused and lies being used as evidence of guilt, and the Crown should make it clear what use it is seeking to make of an allegation that the accused lied: *R v GJH* (2001) 122 A Crim R 361. Where the issue is one of credit, the jury should not usually be directed as to consciousness of guilt: see *Zoneff v The Queen* (2000) 200 CLR 234 at [14]–[17]. It is not always necessary for a judge to give a direction on lies: *Dhanhoa v The Queen* (2003) 217 CLR 1 at [34]; *Ahmed v R* [2012] NSWCCA 260 at [44]–[45]; *KJS v R* [2013] NSWCCA 132 at [56]–[57]. It may be necessary for the judge to warn the jury against using lies as evidence of guilt because of the conduct of the Crown in cross-examination or addresses: *McKey v R* (2012) 219 A Crim R 227 at [26]–[35]. Generally, the Crown will not have to prove the evidence beyond reasonable doubt unless the lie is being relied upon as an implied admission: *Edwards v The Queen* (1993) 178 CLR 193 at 201, 210–211; *R v Adam* (1999) 106 A Crim R 510 at [55]. As to the use of lies to prove a consciousness of guilt: see generally: *Edwards v The Queen* [1993] HCA 63 - [1993] 178 CLR 193 at 210 and *R v Lane* (2011) 221 A Crim R 309 where the lies could be used for that purpose and *R v ST* (1997) 92 A Crim R 390 where they could not. See generally *Criminal Practice and Procedure NSW* at [2-s 161.62]: https://www.judcom.nsw.gov.au/publications/benchbks/criminal/consciousness_of_guilt.html, retrieved on 30/04/2022.

[229] [1993] 4 All ER 894; *R v Burge* [1996] Cr App R 163.

wholly disregarded by the jury. It was a matter for the judge's discretion as to what advice he gave the jury in respect of the evidence of a hostile witness. Thus, for example, if a witness, reminded of his previous statement, adopted it and gave a sensible explanation of his initial evidence at variance with it, he might retain credibility. However, the judge had been justified in directing the jury that K's previous statement could not be treated as evidence because it had been totally disavowed by him and they would probably conclude that K was wholly unreliable and of no value to either side. (2) Since the lies told by the appellant when interviewed by the police were relied upon by the Crown to support the identification evidence the judge should have directed the jury that the appellant's lies had to be deliberate and had to relate to a material issue and that they had to be satisfied that there was no innocent motive for the lies before the lies were relied on to support the identification evidence, and his failure to give such a direction in his summing up was a material misdirection. The appeal would therefore be allowed and a retrial ordered.[230] *Per curiam.*[231] Whenever lies told by a defendant are relied on by the Crown or may be used by the jury to support evidence of guilt as opposed to merely reflecting on the defendant's credibility, and not only when they are relied on as corroboration or support for identification evidence, a direction ought to be given to the jury by the judge, save when it is otiose, to the effect that the lies must be deliberate and must relate to a material issue, that the jury must be satisfied that there was no innocent motive for the lies and that in regard to corroboration the lies had to be established by evidence other than that of the accomplice who was to be corroborated.[232]

The foregoing, by necessary implication, leads to another question, which is when exactly it is appropriate to invoke the *Lucas*[233] direction and in what instances this may be unnecessary. It would appear that the *Lucas*[234] direction and its invocation is only triggered by the existence of lies at trial authored by the accused which the prosecution subsequently rely on. Thus, the *Lucas*[235] direction has been invoked when the prosecution has made much of trivial lies to the extent of relying on such.[236] It has also been invoked when the prosecution has wholly embraced the strategy of relying on, or have substantially or wholly predicated their case on the accused's lies.[237]

Having said that, the *Lucas* direction has been deemed inappropriate for instances where no reliance is substantially or wholly placed on the accused's

---

[230] *R v Lucas* [1981] 2 All ER 1008 applied.

[231] Denoting a decision of an appellate court in unanimous agreement, written anonymously.

[232] *Broadhurst v R* [1964] 1 All ER 111; *R v Dehar* [1969] NZLR 763; *R v Lucas* [1981] 2 All ER 1008 and dictum of Lord Taylor CJ in *R v Richens* [1993] 4 All ER 877 at 886 followed; editor's notes: For the judge's summing up in criminal trials, see 11(2) Halsbury's Laws (4th edn reissue) para 1014, and for cases on the subject, see 15(1) Digest (2nd reissue) 417– 444, 15846 –16147.

[233] [1981] 2 All ER 1008 at 1011.

[234] [1981] 2 All ER 1008 at 1011.

[235] [1981] 2 All ER 1008 at 1011.

[236] *R v Benetto* [2003] UKPC 27.

[237] *R v Nash* [2004] EWCA Crim 164.

lies by the prosecution unless, as has been shown in *R v Rahming*,[238] there is a real chance that the trier of fact will focus on the issue. To reiterate, in the absence of a specific clear lie that the prosecution has relied on, no *Lucas* direction is necessary. Simply because the prosecution alleges that the accused's testimony including but not limited to his pleading not guilty, as does often happen, is a lie, is no reason to invoke the direction to itself. The position has been explained as follows by Potter LJ in *R v Edwards:*[239]

> [...] It seems to us that this is a case where there was essentially no distinction between the issue of guilt and the issue of lies, in the sense that it was a case where evidence of witnesses for the [prosecution] on essential materials had to be established as true in order to justify a finding of guilt, such evidence being in direct and irreconcilable conflict with the evidence for the defence. As made clear in *R v Harron*[240] [...] in such a case the [court], as matter of logic and common sense, have to decide whether the witnesses for the [prosecution] are telling the truth and a conclusion that the accused are lying. Thus, the issue of lies is not a matter which the [court has] taken into account separately from the central issue in the case. This was not a case where, on some collateral matter, there had been some change in evidence or the account of the defendant.

It may also be unnecessary to invoke the direction where the primary purpose of trying to prove an accused's lies is simply to undermine his credibility, essentially that he is not a witness worth[241] believing.[242]

Finally, the judge/magistrate must, in rendering a ruling or indeed a final judgment where the issue of a lie was raised but which he determined, was irrelevant to the issue in the particular case, make this particular point clear. In *R v Gordon*[243] the accused was charged with murder. He raised the defence of self-defence. The prosecution adopted the strategy of trying to undermine the accused's defence by showing that the accused had on a previous occasion not been truthful as regards his possession of the murder weapon. The fact the accused's denial was a lie notwithstanding, same was irrelevant to the accused's subsequent plea of self-defence.

6.7.6.6 *Silence upon being charged with a serious offence*

It has been said by Cave J in *R v Mitchell*[244] that '[...] when persons are speaking on even terms, and a charge is made, and the person charged says nothing, and expresses no indignation, and does nothing to repel the charge, that is some

[238] [2002] UKPC 23.

[239] [2004] EWCA Crim 2102.

[240] [1996] 2 Cr App R 457.

[241] *Ex parte Freeman* (1922) 39 WN (NSW) 73; *Bassela v Stern* (1877) 2 CPD 265 (CA).

[242] See *R v Josephine Smith* [1995] Crim LR 305.

[243] [1995] Crim LR 306.

[244] (1892) 17 Cox CC 503 at 508.

evidence to show that he admits the charged to be true.' The foregoing must, however, be seen within the context of the particular facts and circumstances of each case.[245] Even so, Cave J's sentiments are meant to apply only to persons speaking on even terms. In such cases it may be proper, where the facts permit it, to draw an inference of guilt. However, Cave J's observation does not generally[246] extend to instances where an accused person fails to respond to an allegation by the police or to offer an explanation when charged with an offence.

In *R v Whitehead,*[247] the accused was charged with unlawful carnal knowledge of a girl under the age of sixteen years. It was suggested that her evidence might have been corroborated by the fact that she told her mother about it afterwards. Lord Hewart said: '[i]n order that evidence may amount to corroboration it must be extraneous to the witness who is to be corroborated. A girl cannot corroborate herself, otherwise it is only necessary for her to repeat her story some twenty – five times in order to get twenty – five corroborations of it.'

In *R v Keeling,*[248] the appellant was convicted on a charge of having unlawful carnal knowledge of a girl aged 8 years. On account of her age the girl was not sworn as a witness, and, by reason of the Children and Young Persons Act 1933, s 38(1),[249] it became essential as a matter of law that her evidence should be corroborated.[250] The judge directed the jury that such corroboration could be found in the conduct of the appellant when the accusation in question was made against him. The conduct referred to consisted of the appellant's answers at three stages in the proceedings, preliminary to his trial. When he was cautioned and told of the charge by the police officer who arrested him, he said: "I know what you mean, but not likely [....]" After the warrant had been read over to him, he said: "I have got you—nothing to say." When he had been cautioned by the magistrate, he said: "I am not guilty. I am going to say nothing." It was further said that the fact that, both before the magistrates and at the trial, he elected to give no evidence, should be taken into consideration by the [court] in deciding whether these matters amounted to corroboration: — it was held that the appellant's conduct did not afford the corroboration which was necessary in law. His answer to the committing magistrates could not be

245 *Ex parte Freeman* (1922) 39 WN (NSW) 73.

246 It has, however, been treated as corroboration in *R v Feigenbaum* [1919] 1 KB 431 (CCA); *R v Mckelvey* [1914] St R Q d 42 (FC).

247 [1929] 1 KB 99 at 102; *R v Charavanmuttu* (1930) 22 Cr App R 1; *R v Naylor* [1933] 1 KB 685 (CCA); *R v Littleboy* [1934] 2 KB 408 (CCA); *People (Attorney-General) v Quinn* [1955] IR 57 (CCA).

248 [1942] 1 All ER 507; *R v Feigenbaum* [1919] 1 KB 431; 14 Digest 395, 4151, 88 LJKB 551, 120 LT 572, 26 Cox CC 387, 14 Cr App Rep 1; *R v Christie* [1914] AC 545; 14 Digest 360, 3811, sub nom Public Prosecutions Director v Christie 83 LJKB 1097, 111 LT 220, 24 Cox CC 249, 10 Cr App Rep 141; R *v Whitehead* [1929] 1 KB 99; Digest Supp, 98 LJKB 67, 139 LT 640, 28 Cox CC 547, 21 Cr App Rep 23; *R v Charavanmuttu* (1930) 22 Cr App Rep 1; Digest Supp; *R v Naylor* [1933] 1 KB 685; Digest Supp, 102 LJKB 561, 147 LT 159, 23 Cr App Rep 177, 29 Cox CC 493; *R v Parker* [1933] 1 KB 850; Digest Supp, 102 LJKB 766, 147 LT 502, 24 Cr App Rep 2, 29 Cox CC 550.

249 Compare s 78(1)(2) of the Children's Code, Act No 12 of 2022.

250 Compare s 78(9) of the Children's Code, Act No 12 of 2022.

regarded as constituting corroboration, and, since it was impossible to say whether that part, if any, of the material which was corroboration in law would have been sufficient to satisfy the jury, the conviction must be quashed.[251]

In *Hall v R*,[252] the appellant, Dennis Hall, was charged before the resident magistrate for the parish of St Andrews, jointly with two other defendants, Daphne Thompson and Daisy Gordon, that they unlawfully had in their possession ganja. The evidence against the appellant was that in the early hours of the morning a search was made of a two-roomed building in the parish of St Andrews at which it was said the three defendants lived together. At the time of the search one room was occupied by Daisy Gordon and the other by Daphne Thompson. In Daisy Gordon's room packets of ganja were found in a brown grip and a blue brief case. Daisy Gordon admitted that the grip was hers, but denied all knowledge of the ganja found in it. Packets of ganja were also found in a shopping bag in Daphne Thompson's room. She said that the shopping bag had been brought there by the appellant. The appellant was not on the premises when the search was in progress, but he was brought there shortly afterwards by another police officer. He was told by the officer who had conducted the search that Daphne Thompson had said that the ganja belonged to him. He made no comment on this. He remained silent. All three defendants were then cautioned and none of them said anything. At the conclusion of the prosecution's evidence, it was submitted on behalf of the appellant that the evidence disclosed no case against him. The resident magistrate ruled that there was a case to answer. The defendants gave no evidence and called no witnesses. The appellant and Daphne Thompson made statements from the dock denying all knowledge of the matter and Daisy Gordon said that she wished to say nothing at all. The resident magistrate found all defendants guilty and sentenced the appellant to three years' hard labour. All three defendants appealed to the Court of Appeal. The appeal of Daphne Thompson was allowed on the grounds that it was not established beyond any reasonable doubt that she knew what was in the shopping bag and furthermore she had immediately disclaimed ownership of the bag. The appeals of Daisy Gordon and the appellant were dismissed. From this dismissal the appellant appeals in forma pauperis by special leave of their Lordships' Board. It was held that Although, in very exceptional circumstances, an inference may be drawn from a failure to give an explanation or disclaimer, as a general rule, where a person is informed that an accusation has been made against him, his silence alone cannot give rise to an inference that he accepts the truth of the accusation; furthermore, the fact that he was not informed of his right not to reply to the

---

[251] Editor's notes: The cases on the subject here discussed include the decision in *R v Feigenbaum*, a case a little out of line with later decisions. The court has not seen its way to say definitely that this case is no longer of any authority, but it is clear that *R v Whitehead* must be now treated as stating the better view of the law on the subject, and *R v Parker* must be treated as a decision upon its own facts; As to Evidence of Sexual Offences, see Halsbury (Hailsham Edn), Vol 9, p 224, para 314; and for Cases, see Digest, Vol 14, pp 535–537, Nos 6056–6078.

[252] [1971] 1 All ER 322 (PC).

accusation cannot support an inference that his silence was not in exercise of that right.[253] *Per* Lord Diplock:

> It is a clear and widely-known principle of the common law [...] that a person is entitled to refrain from answering a question put to him for the purpose of discovering whether he has committed a criminal offence. A fortiori he is under no obligation to comment when he is informed that someone else has accused him of an offence. It may be that in very exceptional circumstances an inference may be drawn from a failure to give an explanation or a disclaimer, but in their Lordships' view silence alone on being informed by a police officer that someone else has made an accusation against him cannot give rise to an inference that the person to whom this information is communicated accepts the truth of the accusation.[254]

Commenting on this issue, *Archbold, Pleading Evidence and Practice in Criminal Cases*[255] states:

> A statement made in the presence of an accused person, accusing him of a crime, upon an occasion which may be expected reasonably to call for some explanation or denial from him, is not evidence against him of the facts stated, save in so far as he accepts the statement so as to make it in effect his own. If he accepts the statement in part only, then to that extent alone does it become his statement. He may accept the statement by word or conduct, action or demeanor, and it is the function of the jury which tries the case to determine whether his words, action, conduct or demeanor at the time when the statement was made amount to an acceptance of it in whole or in part.[256]

Finally, a rebuttal to supply samples to a laboratory for purposes of a police investigation when lawfully requested has been held to be capable of being deemed corroborative evidence implicating the accused of the offence with which he is charged.[257]

6.7.6.7 *Conduct on previous occasions*

As a starting point, facts tending to show that the accused committed an offence or civil wrong or otherwise comported himself improperly, on previous occasions may not be deployed in evidence to show that he is the kind of person likely to commit the offence with which he is charged. This is so if said conduct on said previous occasions is only markedly pertinent as to show a disposition to commit offences generally or the kind of offence with

[253] *R v Whitehead* [1928] All ER Rep 186; *R v Keeling* [1942] 1 All ER 507 approved; *R v Feigenbaum* [1918–19] All ER Rep 489 disapproved.

[254] See *R v Whitehead* [1928] All ER Rep 186; *R v Keeling* [1942] 1 All ER 507.

[255] 37th edn, para 1126.

[256] Citing Lord Atkinson in *R v Christie* [1914] AC 545 at 554, [1914–15] All ER Rep 63 at 67.

[257] In *R v Smith* (1985) 81 Cr App R 286; *cf. R v Martin* [1992] 1 NZLR 313.

which the court is seised. Though such evidence may be relevant for another or other reasons, excluded from the preceding is the previous conduct of the party against whom corroboration is sought. Even so it may be admissible under the following scenarios:

(i) It may be admissible to corroborate other evidence against the accused in the following scenarios:
  (a) where it tends to show a more specific propensity to commit an offence in a particular way or with a particular person. In *R v McCann,*[258] evidence of subsequent sexual acts was deemed and admitted as being corroborative of the girl's evidence as they were indicative of a guilty passion.
  (b) where it is capable of corroborating a witness's statement about what was said by a defendant or accused person.[259]

(ii) Conduct on previous occasions may serve as evidence on a circumstantial plane showing aspects of the relationship between the accused and the complainant.[260]

6.7.6.8 *Previous conduct tending to how a particular propensity*

Previous conduct tending to show a certain propensity may be accepted as corroborative evidence against the accused. In *R v Hartley,*[261] the accusedwas convicted of buggery with H on a particular day. H gave evidence of the commission of the offence on the day in question, and he also deposed to the fact that the accused had done the same thing to him on a previous occasion. There was no corroboration of H's evidence so far as the offence mentioned in the indictment was concerned, but his evidence with regard to the previous occasion was corroborated by another witness who saw the accused take H to his office, lock the door and draw the blinds. It was held that H's evidence with regard to the previous occasion was admissible because a person who alleges that an offence such as that which the court was concerned has been committed is entitled to show that the offence was indulged in habitually. It was also held that the corroboration of H's testimony concerning the former crime constituted corroboration of H's testimony concerning the former crime charged.[262]

6.7.6.9 *Previous conduct corroborating statement made to witness by the accused*

[258] [1972] Tas SR (NC 3) 269; see also *R v Massey* [1997] 1 Qd R 404 (CA); *R v H* [1995] 2 AC 596.

[259] It has however been shown in *R v S* (2002) 129 A Crim R 339 at [27] that vidence of similar conduct which forms the basis of counts for which the accused has previously been acquitted may not be deployed to constitute corroborative evidence.

[260] *R v Sakail* [1993] 1 Qd R 312 (CA).

[261] [1941] 1 KB 5 (CCA): This summary is taken from JD Heydon, *Cross on Evidence* para [15235] at 507.

[262] See for comparative purposes, *R v Witham* [1962] Qd R 49 (CCA); *Houston v R* (2007) 170 A Crim R 401 at [94]; *R v Mckeon* (1986) 31 A Crim R 357 at 361 (Qld CCA); *K v R* (1992) 34 FCR 227 (FC); *B v R* (1992) 175 CLR 599; *WLC v R* (2007) 19 NTLR 136 a [24]; for comparative cases in affiliation proceedings that have been decided on the same principle see among others, *Wilcox v Gotfrey* (1872) 26 LT 481 (Exch); *Cole v Manning* (1877) 2 QBD 611 (DC of QBD); *R v Viljoen* 1947 (2) SA 56; *Director of Public Prosecutions v Kilbourne* [1973] AC 729.

Inciting a course of action which leads to the commission of an offence on which the charge in question relates, certainly implicates the accused in the material particular and as such confirms a witness's story as respects such incitement is acceptable as being corroborative. Thus, it has been held in *R v Taylor*[263] that several telephone conversations and visits to a girl's house by a mid-aged man, the accused, to a young girl alone in the house were capable of corroborating the evidence of subsequent molestation. It may well be that the incitement in question relates not to present actions with which the court is concerned but rather, the accused's previous misconduct. In *R v Mitchell*,[264] a man faced the charge of indecently assaulting a girl, S. The girl gave sworn evidence against the accused. Further to the foregoing, S testified that the accused had told her about similar behaviour with respect to J, a girl who lived in another part of the country. It was held that the evidence of J corroborated that of S as S could not have heard of the accused's alleged behaviour from J given the differences in the geography of their residences.

6.8 Functions of a judge/magistrate

6.8.1 *Whether evidence is capable of corroboration and does so*

A judge/magistrate faces a range of difficulties when it comes to dealing with the concept of corroboration. For instance, the question whether evidence is capable of corroboration, and aside from that, whether it does indeed corroborate principal evidence is one for the judge/magistrate to determine, in the first case at law, and in the second, on the facts to which must be added a determination as to whether any weight ought to be attached to such evidence at all.

6.8.2 *Want of corroboration*

It would logically follow from the foregoing that the absence of corroboration, where same is required, ought to lead to an acquittal.[265] There is always the danger that the judge/magistrate may for one reason or other, confuse a corroborative item of evidence with a none-corroborative one.[266] It is therefore important for the trier of fact to, especially for instances where corroboration warning is required as a matter of practice, to warn him/herself of this fact. It has been said in *R v Goddard and Another*,[267] that where there is evidence amounting to corroboration, the duty of the judge in regard to explaining whether particular evidence may or may not amount to corroboration must depend on the exact facts of the case; in general, he should give a broad indication of the

[267] [1962] 3 All ER 582 (CCA); *R v Anslow* [1962] Crim LR 101; *R v O'Reilly* (1967) 51 Cr App R 345; *R v Trotter* (1982) 7 A Crim R 8 at 25 (Vic FC); *Kelleher v R* (1974) 131 CL 534; *R v Jansen* [1970] SASR 531 (CCA); *R v Evans* [1965] 2 QB 295 at 302 (CCA); *Director of Public Prosecutions v Hester* [1973] AC 296 at 328; *R v Matthews* [1972] VR 3 at 19 (FC).

sort of evidence which the jury, if they accept it, may treat as corroboration, but he is not expected to refer in the summing-up to every piece of evidence which is capable of amounting to corroboration.[268] Two appellants, were convicted of being accessories after the fact to store-breaking and were convicted also of receiving. They carried on a garage business; the garage being owned by their father. The main evidence for the prosecution was given by two men who had pleaded guilty to the store-breaking, and was to the effect that they had broken into an office at night and had stolen a safe, which they took to the garage, where the appellants and H worked by day; that at the garage the safe was cut in two at night, using garage equipment, by one of the men who stole it, and that the contents, 10s, were handed to one of the appellants; that one of the appellants was definitely present, but it was more doubtful if the other was. One of the men who stole the safe gave evidence that there had been a prior arrangement with the appellants and H for the garage to be used for cutting the safe. Material had been found in the turn-up of trousers of one of the appellants that corresponded with the ballast and metal of the safe. None had been found on the trousers of the other appellant. Both the appellants denied that they had been present and called evidence to substantiate alibis; they denied any prior arrangement with the two men who stole the safe for the safe to be brought to the garage, and denied that they (the appellants) were to get any part of the proceeds. In the summing-up, the jury were directed, in effect, that if they were satisfied that in pursuance of a prior arrangement the safe was cut up on the premises with the knowledge and permission of the appellants, then they might find them guilty on both charges, even though the appellants were absent. The summing-up included proper warning of the danger of convicting without corroboration and a clear statement of what constituted corroboration, but did not contain any reference to evidence of corroboration, viz, did not indicate what evidence there was which, if the jury accepted it, was capable of amounting to corroboration. On appeal against the convictions, it was held that the convictions must be quashed for the following reasons—(i) the first direction was not good in relation to receiving since, if neither of the appellants was present, neither was shown to have got possession of the stolen safe and its contents, although the premises were in a sense the appellants' premises. (ii) the direction as to corroboration, in relation to the charge of being accessories after the fact to store-breaking, was not good in that, although the fact that the safe had been cut up at the garage might amount to corroboration, yet it was not indicated to the jury that that was as consistent with an arrangement with H as it was with one with the appellants, nor had the direction distinguished between the cases of the two appellants, as to one of whom there was evidence of material on his trousers corresponding with the ballast and metal of the

[268] Dictum of Byrne J in *R v Zielinski* ((1950), 34 Cr App Rep at p 197) qualified.

safe.[269]

6.8.3 *Additional considerations prior to the court rendering a ruling/ judgment*

In our non-jury system, the judge has no jury for which he must sum up the case for the jury. Regardless, at the end of the giving of evidence in a trial, the judge/magistrate must apply the principles employed in a jury system in summing up to him/herself. He must, with specific reference to the issue of corroboration, employ language in the judgment which is tailored to the particular circumstances of the case. He ought to explain what corroboration is (and what it is not), that it is non-dependent evidence of some material particular which implicates the accused and tends to confirm the guilt of the accused as charged.[270] He ought to, in straight forward cases, make reference to the kind of evidence on record that amounts to corroborative evidence.

While the foregoing applies to simple straight forward matters as regards corroboration, more complex cases may require a different approach. A much wider reference to classes of evidence encased with corroborative qualities must be elaborated clearly setting out conditions to be met before the evidence in question can be deemed as sufficiently corroborative as to be accordingly admitted as such. This is not the same thing as saying that for the court to do the foregoing the charge should also have within it each and every item of evidence that the court ought to consider for purposes of corroboration.[271] Be that as it may, it is the judge's sole duty to take into account what evidence is capable of corroboration. He may specifically direct that he be addressed by counsel on these issues through final written submissions following the conclusion of the case.

An overabundance of authorities[272] appear to show that there must be more to answering the question whether a warning ought to be given in instances where an accomplice implicates a co-accused. Such a question ought to be asked within the context of specific circumstances and facts of the case at hand. In *R v Cheema*[273] for example, the appellant was alleged to have entered into a plot with her son, K, and two other men, M and N, to murder her husband for his wealth. The husband was shot by N at his shop but survived. However, he was later murdered by N on the day he was discharged from hospital. M and N were tried separately from and before the appellant and K and either pleaded guilty to or were convicted of both attempted murder and murder.

[269] Editor's notes: As to the need to give warning to a jury in cases where corroboration is required, see 10 Halsbury's Laws (3rd Edn) 461, 462, para 848; and for cases on the subject, see 14 Digest (Repl) 542–545, 5260–5304; As to the offence of being accessory after the fact to felony, see 10 Halsbury's Laws (3rd Edn) 302, 303, para 561; and for cases on the subject, see 14 Digest (Repl) 109, 110, 747–762; *R v Zielinski* [1950] 2 All ER 1114 n; 114 JP 571, 34 Cr App Rep 193, 14 Digest (Repl) 402, 3943.

[270] *R v Clynes* (1961) 44 Cr App R 158.

[271] *R v Goddard* [1962] 3 All ER 582, disproving *R v Zielinski* [1950] 2 All ER 1114.

[272] *Webb v R* (1994) 181 CLR 41; *R v Knowlden* (1981) 77 Cr App R 94 at 100; *R v Jones* [2004] 1 Cr App R; *R v Petkar* [2004] 1 Cr App R 22.

[273] [1994] 1 All ER 639 (CA).

At the trial of the appellant and K the prosecution case depended primarily on M's evidence, while the case against the appellant also depended on the evidence which K gave in his own defence. The appellant was convicted of both attempted murder and murder. She appealed on the grounds that in respect of K's evidence the judge ought to have given the jury the full corroboration warning appropriate to the evidence of an accomplice and that since K was in effect an accomplice, he could not corroborate the evidence of his accomplice M. It was held that the appeal would be dismissed for the following reasons—(1) There was no rule of law which required a full corroboration direction in respect of a co-defendant's evidence. All that was required when one defendant implicated another in evidence was simply a warning to the jury of what might very often be obvious, namely that the defendant witness may have had a purpose of his own to serve. The judge had given just such a direction when he warned the jury that K might have had an axe to grind in giving the evidence he did against the appellant in his own defence.[274] (2) Furthermore, there was no rule of law that one accomplice could not corroborate another. On the facts, K was not to be treated as an accomplice, nor was he to be treated as a witness requiring the judge to give a full corroboration direction because it was not a case of one accomplice called by the prosecution being treated as capable of corroborating another accomplice called by the prosecution. Instead, K and M had had no motive or opportunity to concoct a story together and had different interests to serve. Accordingly, the judge had been entitled to direct the jury that K's evidence was capable of corroborating M's evidence.[275]

It has been said in *Webb v R*[276] that 'it is essential in the interest of the accused who gives the evidence that the warning should be restricted in terms to those parts of the evidence which inculpate any co-accused [....]' It quite logically would follow that a judge/magistrate will not import into the foregoing the idea that the warning he gives to himself is capable of being attached to the accused's evidence in the accused's own case.[277]

The case of *R v Thomas*[278] demonstrates the consequences of a judge erroneously referring to items of evidence as capable of being corroborative when in fact not. The appellant, Anthony Hogarth Thomas, was convicted on 24 January 1959, on three counts of an indictment for child stealing, abduction of and indecent assault on a girl aged thirteen. He appealed against conviction on two main grounds, *viz,* (i) he applied for leave to call additional evidence which, if accepted, would establish that the evidence given by the girl at the trial was false and had been admitted by her to be false, and (ii) that the jury had been wrongly invited to consider as possible corroboration matters which

[274] *R v Barnes, R v Richards* [1940] 2 All ER 229, *R v Knowlden* (1981) 77 Cr App R 94, *R v Loveridge* (1982) 76 Cr App R 125 and *R v Mills* [1983] Crim LR 210 followed; *R v Prater* [1960] 1 All ER 298, *R v Stannard* (1962) [1964] 1 All ER 34 and *R v Russell* (1968) 52 Cr App R 147 considered; *R v Barrow* (1934) 24 Cr App R 141, *R v Garland* (note) (1943) 29 Cr App R 46 and *R v Rudd* (1948) 32 Cr App R 138 doubted.

[275] *DPP v Kilbourne* [1973] 1 All ER 440 applied.

[276] (1994) 181 CLR 41 at 65 quoting *R v Henning* (NSW), 11 May 1990, unreported, BC9002977.

[277] (1994) 181 CLR 41 at 65.

[278] [1959] 3 All ER 522.

could not properly be so regarded. The convictions were quashed on the second ground. The court concluded as regards the question of corroboration, that the jury were invited to regard two matters as capable of constituting corroboration which could not properly be so regarded and that a careful study of the evidence aroused in the mind of the court serious misgivings as to the appellant's guilt.

It would appear from the decision in *People (A-G) v Shaw*[279] that where a situation arises during trial as regards corroboration tending to show that there is corroboration with respect to some and not all counts facing the accused, this must be made plainly clear not only in the judge's mind but in his judgment on this particular issue. The authorities[280] all appear to agree that in warning himself a judge or magistrate ought to make it clear in his judgment that it is dangerous to convict, in a proper case, on the evidence of one witness.[281] To contextualise Salmon LJ, '[…] the rule that the [judge/magistrate must warn himself] does not mean that there has to be some legalistic ritual to be automatically recited by the judge, that some particular form of words or incantation must be used and, if not used, […] the conviction must be quashed.'[282] Nor is it necessary for the judge/magistrate to use the term "corroboration" for this is a term the parties to the proceedings, and for whom the judgment is meant, may not understand.

A surfeit of English authorities[283] appear to suggest the importance of the judge/magistrate inviting counsel to address him *viva voce* or in formal written submissions on the ingredients in the offences in question in respect of which the court should look for corroboration and what evidence, if any, exists which amounts to corroboration. In *R v Ensor*[284] the appellant was accused of two counts of rape alleged to have been committed on two separate occasions against two different complainants. The two counts were quite properly joined in the same indictment but the appellant wanted the two counts severed and made his wishes known to his solicitor and counsel. Since there was no similarity between the two offences an application for severance ought to have succeeded if it had been made. However, counsel appearing for the appellant at his trial decided that there were advantages in the two counts being heard together because in his opinion there was a good chance of an acquittal on one of the

---

279 [1960] IR 168 (CCA).

280 *R v Sabenzu* (1946) 4 NRLR 45; *Katebe v the People* [1975] ZR 13 (SC); *Ackson Zimba v The People* [1980] ZR 259 (SC); see also *Phiri v The People* [1982] ZR 77; *Sinyinza v the People* SCZ Judgment No 2 of 2009; J Hatchard, 'Suspect Witnesses in rape cases' ½ *Zimbabwe Law Review*, 252 found in Hatchard J and Ndulo M, *The Law of Evidence in Zambia* 151-153.

281 *R v Trigg* (1963) 47 Cr App R 94; (1963) 1 WLR 305; *Lovemore Musongole v The People* [1978] ZR 171 (SC).

282 *John Joseph O'Reilly v R* (1967) 51 CAR 345 at 349 quoted with approval in *Ewart Roberts & Eugene Bonell v The Queen* Criminal Appeal Nos 11 and 12 of 1983 (BCA).

283 *R v Ensor*[1989] 2 All ER 586; *R v Nagy* [1990] Crim LR 187 (CA); *R v Royle* [1993] Crim LR 57 (CA).

284 [1989] 2 All ER 586; *R v Nagy* [1990] Crim LR 187 (CA); *R v Royle* [1993] Crim LR 57 (CA). Editor's notes: For the authority of counsel to conduct a case, see 3(1) Halsbury's Laws (4th edn reissue) para 508; For corroboration in rape cases, see 11 Halsbury's Laws (4th edn) para 458, and for cases on the subject, see 15 Digest (Reissue) 1216, 10426–10431; *R v Gautam* (1987) Times, 4 March, CA; *R v Henry and Manning* (1969) 53 Cr App R 150, CCA; *R v Irwin* [1987] 2 All ER 1085, [1987] 1 WLR 902, CA; *R v Lucas* [1981] 2 All ER 1008, [1981] QB 720, [1981] 3 WLR 120, CA; *R v Novac* (1976) 65 Cr App R 107, CA; *R v Stewart* (1986) 83 Cr App R 327, CA; *R v Swain* (12 March 1987, unreported), CA.

charges and that would enhance the possibility of an acquittal on the other. Counsel accordingly decided not to apply for severance of the counts. Counsel did not inform the appellant of his decision or the reasons for it. On the trial of the second count both the fact of intercourse and the absence of consent were in issue but the judge gave a direction as to the need for corroboration only in respect of the lack of consent. The appellant was convicted on both counts. He appealed on the grounds, inter alia, that his counsel's conduct in not applying to sever the counts in the indictment constituted a material irregularity in the conduct of the trial and that the judge should have directed the jury in regard to the second count on the need for corroboration of both the act of intercourse and lack of consent. It was held that except in the case of flagrantly incompetent advocacy on the part of the accused's counsel the court would not set aside a conviction on the ground that counsel had made a decision or pursued a course in the conduct of the trial which later appeared to have been mistaken or unwise, even if that decision or course of conduct was contrary to the accused's wishes. Since the decision of the appellant's counsel not to apply for severance of the counts, even if erroneous, had been carefully considered and could not be described as flagrantly incompetent advocacy the court would not set aside the convictions on the ground that counsel had acted contrary to the appellant's wishes. However, the trial judge had been wrong not to have directed the jury on the need for corroboration of both the act of intercourse and lack of consent in regard in the second count and the conviction on that count would be quashed.[285]

A few more points must be mentioned before concluding this part and this chapter. The first is that a warning given with respect to the dangers of particular evidence e.g., that given by an accomplice or a child or a complainant in sexual matters does not form a basis for disregarding such evidence. As has been shown in *Trade Practices Commission v Vales Wine Co Pty Ltd,*[286] the trier of fact may yet still place reliance on those parts of the evidence which he accepts. Secondly, where the accused admits to the complaint against him this should not be taken to constitute corroboration as it is incapable of doing so.[287] Thirdly, it has been shown in *R v Radford,*[288] that where it is said that a warning is not required in cases where corroboration is found to exist, same may lead to the conclusion that no special care is required in the assessment of the witness's evidence.

---

[285] *R v Irwin* [1987] 2 All ER 1085 doubted.

[286] (1996) 145 ALR 241 a 266-7 (Fed C of A).

[287] *Jones v R* (1997) 191 CLR 439; *R v FP* (2007) 169 A Crim R 318 at [14].

[288] (1993) 66 A Crim R 210 at 238; *R v Lawford* (1993) 61 SASR 42 at 555 (CCA); *R v Baker* (2000) 78 SASR 103 (CCA).

7

IDENTIFICATION EVIDENCE

7.1 Introduction

As we saw in chapter 6, assessing suspect evidence means that judges/ magistrates give careful attention to such evidence when the accused's conviction may well hinge on the evidence of a single witness. The best example in this regard is what is termed eye witness testimony, the most significant part of which is identification of suspects.[1] Identification evidence is premised on the proposition, in each case that it is tendered, that despite the contentions to the contrary by one of the parties, two or more things in question are alike, identical or indistinguishable. As has been observed by Gibbs CJ in *Alexander v R*:[2]

> Normally a person who identifies another will signify by words that the person whom he identifies is the person whom he saw on the occasion connected with the crime - he will use words to the effect, "that is the man" - but even if he does no more than point to the person identified that also expresses his state of mind just as much as words would have done.

In *Chimbini v The People*,[3] the appellant was convicted of robbery. The case against the appellant rested entirely on the evidence of the complainant who said that she had known him before and that she recognised him as one of her assailants. The appellant when called upon to make his defence elected to remain silent. It was held as follows:

(i) Particularly in cases of identification by a single witness the honesty of the witness is not sufficient; the court must be satisfied that he is reliable in his observation.[4]

(ii) Most important among the factors to be taken into account is whether the witness knew accused prior to the incident; there is the greatest difference between recognising someone with whom one is familiar,

[1] This is not the same thing as a witness identifying the accused as the perpetrator of the crime from the witness box for the first time. Courts take a deem view of such identification and consider it suspect: *Roberson Kalonga v The People* [1988 – 1989] ZR 90 (SC).

[2] (1981) 145 CLR 395.

[3] [1973] ZR 191.

[4] See this point restated in *Abdulla Bin Wendo v R* 1953 EACA 166; *Nyambe v The People* [1973] ZR 228; *Love Chimbini v The People* SCZ No 32/73; *Mbundi Nyambe v The People* CAZ No 45/73; *Evaristo Bwalya v The People* [1975] ZR 227 *per* Baron DCJ; *Robert Chate v The People* SCZ No 39/75; *The People v Swillah* [1976] ZR 338.

or at least whom one has seen before, and seeing a person for the first time and attempting to recognise him later from observations made in circumstances which may be charged with stress and emotion.

(iii) Where the evidence against an accused person is purely circumstantial and his guilt entirely a matter of inference, an inference of guilt may not be drawn unless it is the only inference which can reasonably be drawn from the facts. In such cases the fact that an accused person has elected not to give evidence on oath may, in certain circumstances, tend to support the case against him but will certainly not do so unless the inference was one which could properly be drawn in the first place.

(iv) Where there is direct evidence by a complainant that she identified as her assailant a man whom she had known before, and this evidence, if accepted, establishes the guilt of the accused, the fact that he chooses to remain silent may properly be taken into account as part of the totality of the evidence which the court must consider in coming to its conclusion.

Baron JP, as he then was, opined as follows:

> The case against the appellant rests entirely on the evidence of the complainant. It is always competent to convict on the evidence of a single witness if that evidence is clear and satisfactory in every respect; where the evidence in question relates to identification there is the additional risk of an honest mistake, and it is therefore necessary to test the evidence of a single witness with particular care. The honesty of the witness is not sufficient; the court must be satisfied that he is reliable in his observation. Many factors must be taken into account, such as whether it was daytime or night-time and, if the latter, the state of the light, the opportunity of the witness to observe the appellant, the circumstances in which the observation was alleged to have been made (i.e., whether there was a confused fight or scuffle or whether the parties were comparatively stationary). Most importantly it is relevant to consider whether the witness knew the accused prior to the incident, since there is the greatest difference between recognising someone with whom you are familiar, or at least whom you have seen before, and seeing a person for the first time and attempting to recognise and identify him later from observations made in circumstances which are no doubt charged with stress and emotion.

Even so, as Lord Moulton has said in *R v Christie:*[5]

> Identification is an act of the mind, and the primary evidence of what was passing in the mind of a man is his own testimony, where it can be obtained. It would be very dangerous to allow evidence to be given of

[5] (1914) AC 545 at 558 This view was approved by the Judicial Committee in *Teper v The Queen* (1952) AC 480 (1914) AC.

> a man's words and actions, in order to shew by this extrinsic evidence that he identified the prisoner, if he was capable of being called as a witness and was not called to prove by direct evidence that he had thus identified him. Such a mode of proving identification would, in my opinion, be to use secondary evidence where primary evidence was obtainable, and this is contrary to the spirit of the English rules of evidence.[6]

Identification evidence may be categorised as follows:

(i) Visual identification

This is by far the most common form, and which our discussion in this chapter is primarily concerned with.

(ii) Identification by sound

Also referred to as aural identification,[7] this form is pretty standard form of identification evidence albeit not as prominent as visual identification. It may be done by way of identification of voice, distinct coughing or breathing etc. O'Brien CJ Cr Div., has opined in *R v E J Smith*[8] thus:[9]

> [W]hile many features of a person which are visually noticeable are fairly readily capable of description so as to give reasonable reproduction in every day vocabulary, the features of a voice are not by any means as readily capable of verbal description. The Chief [Judge] gave an example of the fact that a person will readily recognise the voice of a political figure heard regularly on the electronic media, but will be quite unable to convey by words the impression of that voice to one who has not heard it.

(iii) Identification by touch

Even rarer than identification by sound but still possible, this may happen by identifying a person through a peculiar feature such as corrugated skin or indeed damaged skin. One cannot, however, overemphasise the difficulties a witness employing this kind of identification evidence is likely to face in much the same way that one using identification by sound may. Continuing with his comments above, O'Brien CJ Cr Div. has opined in *R v E J Smith*[10] thus:[11]

> The same comments apply to the fact that a person may become familiar with a person's touch. On the two occasions when the

[6] See also *per* Lord Reading (1914) AC at 563.

[7] *Bulejcik v R* (1996) 185 CLR 375.

[8] [1984] 1 NSWLR 462 at 478.

[9] *AK v The State of Western Australia* [2006] WASCA 245 at [48].

[10] [1984] 1 NSWLR 462 at 478.

[11] *AK v The State of Western Australia* [2006] WASCA 245 at [48].

> complainant was asked (i.e., by the police in 2003 and then at trial) about who touched her in February 2002 it was after the complainant had experienced other occasions when she had been touched in a sexual way by the appellant.

(iv) Identification by smell or taste

This is an even rarer form of identification still, being more attuned to identifying non-sentient things[12] rather than sentient being such as humans but has still been deemed conceivable.[13]

We will return to the foregoing later. Having said that, it would appear from the preceding scenarios that identification evidence seems possible only through that which is perceived by the witness in question through one of the five senses enumerated and described above. Be that as it may, identification must be more than a product of guesswork. To be deemed worthy of admittance into evidence, it ought to be predicated on an inference from particularised circumstances. Heydon J has observed as follows in *AK v Western Australia:*[14]

> [...] the complainant's evidence cannot be rendered either admissible or of probative value by seeking to explain her inarticulateness on the ground of the inherent difficulty of explaining an intuition, nor on the ground of her claims to be embarrassed or to be experiencing shame, nor by the repeated claim of prosecution counsel, strenuously denied by defence counsel, that she was not "a particularly sophisticated person". Similarly, while Roberts-Smith JA said that the complainant "was familiar with [the appellant's] presence and identified him in that way"[15], she never specified which features of the appellant's "presence" she employed to identify him.

Beyond the foregoing, there are challenges to be noted as regards identification evidence. According to Biggs CJ:[16]

> The problems which afflict identification evidence have their origin in four principal sources: (a) the variable quality of the evidence much of which is inherently fragile; (b) the use by the police of methods of identification which, though well suited to the investigation and detection of crime, are not calculated to yield evidence of high probative value in a criminal trial; (c) the consequential need to balance the interests of the accused in securing a fair trial against the interests of the State in the efficient investigation and detection of crime by the police; and (d) the difficulty of accommodating the reception of certain types of identification testimony to accepted principles of the law of evidence.

---

[12] See for example, the Australian cases of *Union v State* 66 SE 24 (Ga App, 1990); *Sherrand v Jacob* [1965] NILR 151 at 160; *R v Farr* (2001) 118 A Crim R 399.

[13] *AK v Western Australian* (2008) 232 CLR 438 at [66]-[67].

[14] (2008) 232 CLR 438 at [70]-[75].

[15] *AK v The State of Western Australia* [2006] WASCA 245 at [5].

[16] *Alexander v R* (1981) 145 CLR 395 at 426.

We will return to a specific discussion on the above observation a little later. At this point we return to a theme we discussed in chapter 6, that of miscarriage of justice.

7.2 Miscarriage of justice

Identification evidence has much to commend it but also a lot to be concerned about. As regards the former, it is to be noted that identification evidence is direct evidence, and as such, ordinarily more reliable and of greater probative value than circumstantial evidence. Be that as it may, the inherent dangers of misidentification leading to miscarriage of justice are recognised in legal circles. The curious case of Alfred Beck which we discuss in greater detail below is a case in point. It is a classic case of how the probative value said to be inherent in identification evidence may be overestimated. The accused was misidentified by no less than 15 witnesses. It led, like we saw in the previous chapter, to the establishment of the Court of Criminal Appeal.[17] The case highlights the necessity for "special need for caution"[18] before convicting an accused person where the case is almost entirely predicated or substantially predicated on such evidence. *Alfred Beck* case's notoriety is an extreme example of the most egregious miscarriages of justice ever recorded thanks to wrongful eyewitness testimony and erroneous suspect identification.

7.2.1 *The curious case of Adolph Beck*

7.2.1.1 *General*

The case of *Adolf Beck* is occurred towards the end of the 19th and continued on into the early part of the 20th century and considered, rightly so, a *causes célèbres*[19] of its time.[20] It is an extreme example of how eye witness identification evidence coupled with fly-by-night approaches to identification and a court's haste to

[17] Criminal Appeal Act 1907; the Lord Devlin Committee on Evidence of Identification was inspired by similar concerns.

[18] *R v Turnbull and Others* [1977] QB 224 at 228-231, 63 Cr App R 132 at 137 – 140.

[19] A cause célèbre (/ˈkɔːz səˈlɛbrə/,[1] /ˈkɔːz səˈlɛb/,[2] French: [koz selɛbʁ]; pl. causes célèbres (pronounced '*cause*': as in ˈkɔːz səˈlɛbrə) is an issue or incident arousing widespread controversy, outside campaigning, and heated public debate: Hirsch, E. D. Jr.; Kett, Joseph F.; Trefil, James, eds. (2002). "cause célèbre". Telecommunications Essay | Bartleby. The New Dictionary of Cultural Literacy (3rd ed.). Houghton Mifflin Company. Archived from the original on September 21, 2008 – via Bartleby.com; The term is deployed variously in the media. When employed in a positive sense, it is with respect to watershed decisions that set a precedent (i.e., those that become the locus classicus for a particular legal issue or issues). In a negative sense, the term is deployed towards legal cases draped in infamy thanks to the outrage, scandal or conspiracy theories they engender: Homework Help and Textbook Solutions | bartleby. The American Heritage Dictionary of the English Language (4th ed.). Houghton Mifflin Company. 2000. Archived from the original on August 3, 2008 – via Bartleby.com; In French 'cause' means 'legal' (cause) and célèbre means 'famous,' (celebrated) thus simply, 'famous legal case.'

[20] For a critical examination of the circumstances surrounding the case see Dicks, Paula C, "The strange case of Adolf Beck: Press influence and criminal justice reform in Edwardian England" (2007). *Dissertations (1962 - 2010) Access via Proquest Digital Dissertations*. AAI3277080.https://epublications.marquette.edu/dissertations/AAI3277080; "The Sins of our forebears," James Morton (solicitor and former editor of the New Law Journal), 2001, from a seminar given at the Inns of Court School of Law in October 2001" found at http://www.freenetpages.co.uk/hp/peter.hill/nichol.htm retrieved on 15/05/22; See generally, Michael Kurland, MacMillian, *How To Solve A Murder: The Forensic Handbook* (..., 1995) 115-116.

convict the accused may lead to wrongful convictions.[21] The accused,Adolf Beck was, following trial by jury, convicted of misdemeanour and felony offences in 1896. He was again convicted of similar offences by a judge in 1904. The case was a precursor to the *Report of the Committee of Inquiry into the Case of Mr. Adolf Beck (1904),* and therefrom, the formation of the England and Wales Court of Appeal Criminal Division in 1907.[22]

7.2.1.2 Biographical background

Born in Norway in 1841, Adolph Beck[23] trained as a chemist but soon after took to sea and emigrated to England in 1865. Where he worked as a clerk to a shipping broker. He moved to South America in 1868 for a while making a living as a singer. He later turned to ship brokerage and real estate and soon amassed a great deal of savings. On his return to England in 1885, he engaged in numerous financial transactions and schemes which included an investment in a Norwegian Copper mine all which did not pan out leading to his financial ruin and descent into near-poverty. He was indebted to a hotel in Covent Garden for lodging. He was chronically short of cash to the extent that he borrowed from his own secretary. Be that as it may, Adolph Beck kept up appearances by always dressing in a frock coat and top hat whenever he went out, the fact that they had become threadbare notwithstanding.

7.2.1.3 Arrest

The date was 16 December 1895. Adolph Beck was, when he was blocked by a woman, stepping out of the front door of 135 Victoria Street. The woman later identified as Ottilie Meissonier, unmarried and a language teacher, accused Beck of having swindled her out of two-time pieces and a number of rings. Ignoring her, Beck crossed the road but unbeknownst to him, the woman too crossed the street. He remonstrated to a nearby policeman about Ms. Meissonier being a prostitute who had accosted him. Undeterred, Ms. Meissonier demanded Beck's arrest, repeating her accusations concerning Beck to the policeman, specifically, that he had swindled her some three weeks before. The policeman took them to the nearest police station. At the police station Ms. Meissonier alleged that the material time she had been walking down Victoria Street, (the same Street she had, had her encounter with Beck leading to their presence at the police station) when Beck come up to her, tipped his hat and asked if she was Lady Everton. Though she had answered in the negative, she said she was impressed by his gentlemanly manner that the two hit it off, striking up a conversation. She recounted that Beck had introduced

---

[21] Coates T, *The strange story of Adolph Beck* (Stationery Office, 1999).

[22] Criminal Appeal Act, 1907 (U.K.), 7 Edw. VII, c. 23; Less startling in its mistakes as regards identification but with equally similar consequences, this time, for Scotland was the *Oscar Slater case* which led to the creation of the Scottish Court of Criminal Appeals in 1926. Slater was identified as the man leaving the house after a murder. Twelve witnesses maintained that he had kept watch over the house prior to the murder. This evidence was only given after they had seen Slater in custody before identifying him. He was tried and convicted and served eighteen years in prison before his release; More goring than Slater and more recently in the case of *R v Rowland* (1946).

[23] Also, Adolf Beck.

himself as one "Lord Willoughby" and dissuaded her from proceeding to the flower show to which she was headed saying same was not worth the trouble. She stated that Beck spoke of having a working knowledge of horticulture being an owner of gardens on his Lincolnshire a wide-ranging estate requiring six gardeners to which Ms. Meissonier responded by saying that she herself grew chrysanthemums. Requesting to see them, he got an invitation for tea the next day at Ms. Meissonier's house.

He arrived at Ms. Meissonier's house the next day as scheduled and invited her to go to the French Riviera on his yacht in the main insisting upon providing her with elegant clothing for the voyage, bespoke cheque for £40 for his proposed list of purchases. He then proceeded to examine her time pieces and rings, suggesting that he could have them replaced with more expensive pieces, if she let him have them. She did. She soon discovered, after *Lord Willoughby's* departure that her a second watch was missing. As if this was enough and alerted to the possibility that she may have been a victim of fraud, she hurried to the bank to try and have the cheque cashed. It was worthless. She sincerely swore that it was Adolf Beck who had done it. The police arrested Beck in short order.

The inspector assigned to the Beck case learned that in the previous two years twenty-two women had been similarly defrauded by a grey-haired man answering to the names *"Lord Wilton de Willoughby"* in the same manner described by Beck's accuser. An identification parade was arranged upon which the victims were asked to point at the fraudster. Among the ten to fifteen men randomly selected, Beck was the only one with grey hair and a moustache. He was quickly singled out and identified the swindler/fraudster.

Beck was charged with ten misdemeanours and four felonies. The felony charges were based on presumed prior convictions in 1877, when a man named John Smith had been sentenced to five years for swindling unattached women by using the name Lord Willoughby, writing worthless cheques and taking their jewellery. He had disappeared after his release, and it was assumed that Beck and Smith were one and the same. Descriptions of John Smith from prison files were never compared with the current appearance of Adolph Beck. This was the beginning of Beck's many troubles.

At Beck's committal proceedings, a police officer who had arrested a man involved in similar frauds as the ones here involved eighteen years before gave the following account:

> In 1877 I was in the Metropolitan Police Reserve. On 7 May 1877 I was present at the Central Criminal Court where the prisoner in the name of John Smith was convicted of feloniously stealing ear-rings and a ring and eleven shillings of Louisa Leonard and was sentenced to five years' penal servitude. I produce the certificate of that conviction. The prisoner is the man. ... There is no doubt whatever – I know quite well what is at stake on my answer and I say without doubt he is the man.

Beck naturally protested insisting that he had an *alibi* and witnesses to prove it.

7.2.1.4 *Trial*

On 3 March 1896 Beck was brought to trial at the Old Bailey. Interestingly, the judge happened to be Sir Forrest Fulton, who, as a prosecutor, had been responsible for sending John Smith to prison in 1877 and as such, ought to have known better.

For the defence the case was a clear-cut matter of mistaken identity. All that was required was to prove the South American alibi. Once this was done, logically, it would follow that Adolph Beck was not the John Smith who had committed the crimes ascribed to Adolph Beck.

A key witness at trial was a handwriting expert called Thomas Gurrin. Gurrin had compared the lists of clothing Smith had made and given to his victims in 1877 on the one hand to those written in 1894 and 1895 on the other. He had also analysed samples of Beck's handwriting. Gill Defence counsel hoped to prove mistaken identity under cross-examination. Given that Gurrin had previously said that the writing from 1877 was identical to that from 1894 and 1895, defence thought that if this was repeated during oral testimony, Gill would then bring witnesses to court to show that the accused had in fact been in Buenos Aires in 1877. However, the prosecution chose a different path and only asked the witness about the later lists. About those, Gurrin testified that same had been written by Beck in what he termed a "disguised hand." When defence counsel asked for court permission to cross-examine Gurrin as regards the 1877 lists, the court which was under the impression that Beck was Smith, whom the judge had helped prosecute and get convicted years before ruled that past convictions the accused could not be mentioned in court before a verdict had been handed down by the jury.

Even so, there was yet another way in which the defence could achieve their aim. It was by cross-examining a prosecution witness called Elliss Spurrell. The prosecution decided against calling Spurrell to the stand. With this strategy, the prosecution lost the opportunity to prove more serious offences and prove same in court. Be that as it may however, the prosecution could still prosecute Beck for misdemeanours which, unlike felonies, required no proof of prior conviction. Thus, despite the unstated premise on which the prosecution's case was based which was that Adolph Beck and John Smith were the same person, the prosecution chose not to proceed with the felony charges. In doing so, the prosecution dealt a hammer blow to the defence strategy.

The prosecution's strategy having worked thus far, proceeded to call to the witness stand alleged victim after alleged victim of *Lord Wilton de Willoughby"* fraud. One after another, they pointed the finger at Beck as the swindler. The occasional moments of doubt by some witnesses as regards how differently the swindler spoke compared to Beck; or Ottilie Meissonier recollection that the swindler had a scar on the right side of his neck; or that the swindler's moustache was longer and waxed, appeared not to have helped Beck's case as each one of the victims was ultimately convinced that Beck was indeed the swindler.

7.2.1.5 *Conviction and doubts*

On 5 March 1896 Adolf Beck was found guilty of fraud.[24] He was sentenced to seven years of penal servitude at Portland Convict Prison on the Isle of Portland. As if to add salt to injury, in prison Beck was treated as repeat offender John Smith, was give Smith's old prison number, D 523. The letter W was added to indicate the fact that he was a repeat6 convict.

Between 1896 and 1901 Beck's solicitor presented no less than ten petitions for re-examination of his client's case. Nor were his requests to see John Smith's prison description granted. The in fact were denied as often as they were made. Not even the discovery by an official in the Home Office that John Smith whom Beck was presumed to be, would bring anything discernible change to his legal situation except the removal of the letter W from his prison number. However, in May 1898 an official at the Home Office looked at the Smith file and saw that Smith was Jewish and thus had been circumcised, while Beck was not. Asked for his opinion, the judge while conceding that Beck and Smith could not be the same person added that he still believed that Beck was the imposter of 1895 and that the Buenos Aires alibi was one he viewed "with great suspicion."

Beck's cause was taken up by George Robert Sims, a journalist who worked for the *Daily Mail* and who had been acquainted himself with Beck upon his return to England in 1885. Sims contended in an article that Beck had been tried and convicted on the baseless assumption to which the prosecution had provided no evidence substantiating this claim nor had the court given any to justify not only the trial but the conviction. Essentially, an innocent man had, on the basis of mistaken identity and the court's haste to convict been imprisoned. Public opinion followed Sims' lead and came to view the conviction as unjust and a stain on the justice system. When Beck was paroled in July 1901 for good behaviour one would have hoped that this sad episode would not see a repeat. It did however.

7.2.1.6 *Second arrest and conviction*

A little over eight years to the day of his first accusation that led to his erroneous trial and subsequent conviction and incarceration, on 22 March 1904, a servant answering to the names Paulina Scott filed a complaint with the police saying that a grey-haired, distinguished looking man (fitting the description of Adolph Beck) had accosted her on the street, paid compliments, and while at it, stolen her jewellery. The policeman who received the report was familiar with the Adolph Beck case and swiftly concluded it was him. He led the woman to a restaurant that Beck took his breakfast from. Even though the woman could not positively identify him, the policeman was undeterred. He set a trap for Beck.

As arranged, on 15 April 1904, Scott ran up to Beck as he left his flat, and accused him of fleecing her of her jewellery. Horrified, Beck rejected the

[24] "Proceedings of the Old Bailey". *UNLAWFULLY ADOLF\BECK, Deception > fraud, 24th February 1896.* Retrieved 2 February 2014.

accusation. Unrelenting, Scott reiterated her accusations telling Beck that someone was waiting to apprehend him. Panicking, he went for it but was almost immediately arrested by the waiting policeman to whom Beck's response appeared to confirm his guilt as the policeman had strongly suspected.

History would repeat itself. Beck was again put on trial on 27 June, 1904 at the Old Bailey but this time before Sir William Grantham. In similar circumstances as in his first trial eight years before, five women (mis)identified him and, based on this positive (mis)identification, Beck was found guilty by the jury. The judge was however hesitant to pass sentence, expressing doubts about the guilt of the accused. He postponed sentencing. The true culprit with an alias John Smith would confess to the offences ten days later.

7.2.1.7 Truth about John Smith

On 7 July, 1904 Inspector John Kane of the Criminal Investigation Department was on a routine visit to the Tottenham Court Road police station where he was told of the arrest of a man who had tried to swindle a pair of unemployed actresses of some rings that afternoon and who had been apprehended at a pawnshop and was now in detention. Familiar with the Beck case, having been present at Beck's two trials in 1886 and 1904 the inspector and asked for details which he concluded appeared to show a similar pattern to that of the alleged culprit Adolph Beck with one difference. The said Adolph Beck was now in prison awaiting his sentence. He could therefore not have been responsible for the attempted swindle that afternoon.

He went to the new prisoner's cell where, true to form, he found a grey-haired man who looked very similar to Beck but was much older and of a larger build than Beck. He had introduced himself to the police as being William Thomas. The Police inspector was unconvinced. He was sure that the detainee was indeed John Smith. Three of the five women who had been asked to identify Beck at his 1904 trial were called to confront John Smith, and they quickly identified him as the swindler. In addition, other women were brought in and they admitted to having misidentified Beck as the swindler. Finally, when the man who had been John Smith's landlord identified as such, he confessed his crimes.

As it would turn out, "William Thomas" was as much an alias as "John Smith" had been. He also went by the names "William Wyatt" and "William Weiss". His real and legal identity was Wilhelm Meyer. Born in Vienna and graduating from the University of Vienna, he had studied leprosy in the Hawaiian Islands under Father Joseph Damien. He would later serve as surgeon to the Hawaiian king. He also grew coffee, and engaged in various other businesses in the United States including the setting up of a practice as a physician in Adelaide before relocating to London. Having fallen on hard times, he turned to preying on women through fraud. When Beck was tried and convicted in 1896, Meyer fled to the United States and only returned in 1903 and resumed his swindling until he was finally arrested. At trial on 15 September, Wilhelm Meyer pleaded guilty to the offences with which he was charged and those for which Beck had been accused, charged and convicted twice on account of misidentification. He was sentenced to 5 years imprisonment.[25]

7.2.1.8 *Aftermath*

Adolf Beck was pardon by the King on 29 July 1904 and was awarded £2,000, later raised to £5,000 in compensation due to public clamour (about £300,000 in 2020), again due to pressure exerted by people like George Robert Sims. Those at the centre of debacle received public indignation.

The consequences of the Adolph Beck debacle were far reaching. First off, a Committee of Inquiry was established, headed by the noted jurist, Sir Richard Henn Collins MR. It heard evidence from all who had been involved in the two trials which resulted in convictions based on misidentification.[26] They included prosecution and defence counsel and the judges that presided over the infamous trials. The Committee concluded that Adolph Beck should not have been convicted in the first place on account of the numerous errors made by the prosecution in presenting its case. It chastised Judge Fulton as he ought to have known better having been involved in the 1877 case, more so because of his involvement with the 1877 case, prejudiced Beck. Nor was the Home Office spared from criticism for its indifference since it came to their knowledge in 1898 that Beck and Smith were not the same person. Instead of correcting the mistakes which had been made, the Home Office was more interested in preserving the credibility of the judiciary. The omission by the prison authorities mention the fact that Smith was circumcised and as such, Jewish in the records of 1877 and 1881, was the principal root cause of the miscarriage of justice.

As noted earlier, the creation of the England and Wales Court of Criminal Appeal in 1907 was a direct result of the Adolph Beck case. The case still remains one of the most glaring examples of how erroneous eyewitness identification can be. It also shows why there ought to be extreme care in assessing evidence of identification and other suspect evidence.[27] Sadly, Adolf

[25] William Thomas 13th September 1904 Browse - Central Criminal Court (oldbaileyonline.org) retrieved on 12/8/21.

[26] *Report of Committee of Inquiry into the Case of Mr Adolf Beck* (1904) Cd 2315. "The warrant appointing the Committee (Sir Richard Henn Collins MR, Sir Spencer Walpole and Sir John Edge) was dated 9 September 1904. It heard 29 witnesses, some more than once, whose evidence filled over 200 pages, and considered over 100 pages of exhibits. The Committee reported on 14 November 1904: *autre temps, autres moeurs*": Heydon JD *Cross on Evidence* 67 FN 540.

[27] This has been exemplified in *Muvuma Kambanja Situna v The People* [1982] ZR 115 (SC). The appellant was convicted of one count of aggravated robbery and two counts of attempted murder. The trial court considered that the appellant had been properly identified at the parade by the single identifying witness despite allegations by the defence that the parade was improperly conducted and the inherent danger of an honest mistake in the circumstances. Hearsay evidence was admitted supporting the conviction. It was held inter alia: (i) The evidence of a single identifying witness must be tested and evaluated with the greatest care to exclude the dangers of an honest mistake; the witness should be subjected to searching questions and careful note taken of all the prevailing conditions and the basis upon which the witness claims to recognise the accused. (ii) If the opportunity for a positive and reliable identification is poor then it follows that the possibility of an honest mistake has not been ruled out unless there is some other connecting link between the accused and the offence which would render mistaken identification too much of a coincidence.

Beck's exoneration brought him little happiness. He would die on 7 December 1909 a broken man of pleurisy and bronchitis in Middlesex Hospital.

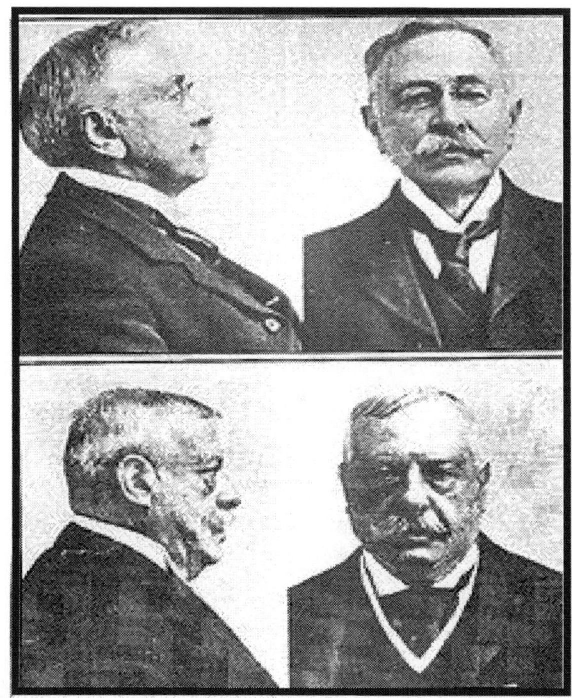

Description:	Police mugshots of Adolf Beck (top), wrongly convicted for the crimes of William Meyer (bottom)
Date:	circa 1907
Author:	Unknown author

7.2.2 *An unwelcome repeat of misidentification in the egregious case of misidentification: R v Rowland*[28]

In a more recent case of alleged mistaken identity no mistake has been admitted. This is *R v Rowland*,[29] where a man was convicted of killing a woman by hitting her on the head with a hammer. The evidence of his connection with the crime was principally the identification by three witnesses who claimed to recognise him after short meetings. One of these witnesses, a second-hand dealer, said he recognised Rowland as a chance customer who had bought the hammer from him with which the murder was committed. When he saw the photograph of the hammer in the newspaper, he recognised it and later picked out Rowland at an identification parade. Before the examining magistrate, and also before the court at the trial, this witness said that the man to whom he sold the hammer was " on the dark side." When he was invited to look at Rowland and invited to agree that Rowland was not on the dark side he did agree, but added: "But he had his hair plastered down with grease that night. That is probably what made him look dark." No reference to this greased hair appeared in the description of his customer which he had previously given the police. It may have been an instance of delayed memory, but it may have been unconscious transference from some other customer. The second witness was a waitress who deposed to seeing the deceased woman with a man at the café where she worked, and picked out Rowland, with some hesitation at first, at an identification parade as being the man. At the trial she said that the reason for her hesitation was that Rowland's hair had fallen over his face, and there was no grease on it, and he did not look as smart as the man she remembered having seen in the café. She had seen this man about twice before the occasion in question. This witness said that the hair of the man in the café was dark or black, but again explained the discrepancy by saying that the hair was greased and that grease makes your hair look black." Whereas the dealer's customer had a thin face, was very pale and looked ill, the waitress's customer had " a fresh complexion."

One fact in particular casts some suspicion on the correctness of the waitress's evidence. Rowland had in fact been in that café on a few occasions, and it is therefore quite possible that when the waitress saw him on the identification parade, she unconsciously effected a transference. It was only after the identification parade that the waitress said she had seen the man before; when she saw him in the café on the occasion in question, she did not recognise him. Does it not appear as if the man she saw was a stranger, and not Rowland whom she had seen before?

The third witness said he had seen a man with the deceased woman on the street at midnight shortly before the murder. He had not seen the man before. He gave a description of the man to the police, and picked out Rowland at an identification parade a fortnight later. There was again the discrepancy over the hair, and this witness again explained it by reference to the grease. Whereas the dealer's customer had a thin face, this witness saw a man with a full round face."

There is much else in the case that cannot be gone into here and it has been fully and admirably studied by Mr. Silverman.[30] The remarkable feature is still to come. After Rowland's conviction, and while he was under sentence of death, a man called Ware purported to confess to the murder for which Rowland had been convicted, and gave a detailed statement to the police which fitted all the known facts. He confessed because he heard of Rowland's conviction, and it worried him a great deal. After making his statement to the police he gave an interview to Rowland's advisers in which he amplified his statement still further. The statement is too long to reproduce here; suffice it to say that it is highly circumstantial and seems to bear the evident stamp of truth.

One might have thought that this statement would have ended the proceedings against Rowland, subject only to the formality of getting his

[30] Paget and Silverman, *Hanged-and Innocent?* (1953) 1 *et seq.*

conviction set aside. I agree with Mr. Silverman in thinking that Ware's confession was true; but whether it was true or not, one cannot believe for a moment that the jury would have convicted Rowland on the evidence given in the case if Ware's confession had also been before them.

What followed can only be described as a stain upon English justice. An appeal was taken by Rowland, but the Court of Criminal Appeal refused to listen to any evidence of the confession by Ware. Undoubtedly it had power to admit the new evidence, but it refused to do so for a series of remarkable reasons, one of which was that there were no exceptional circumstances in the case.[31] The best that can be said of this sorry judgment is that it indicated, and therefore invited, the possibility of Home Office intervention.

The Home Secretary did intervene. He appointed Mr. J. C. Jolly, K.C., to inquire into the whole matter. Mr. Jolly heard Ware, who by this time had decided to withdraw his confession. In his report Mr. Jolly expressed the opinion that there had been no miscarriage of justice. Rowland was accordingly hanged.

It will be seen that, according to this way of managing things, the full case with all the evidence available was considered only by a single person, acting as a one-man jury, and from his decision there could be no further appeal. No opportunity was given to defending counsel to cross-examine the new witnesses who were heard. I do not propose to go through Mr. Jolly's report, because that has already been done by Mr. Silverman in the book referred to, and he has some hard things to say about it. But one point deserves mention, because it is connected with what has gone before: one of the matters that Mr. Jolly thought conclusive against Rowland was that at identification parades arranged by Mr. Jolly, in which NV are consented to take part, the three witnesses who had previously given evidence identifying Rowland failed to identify Ware. To anyone slightly acquainted with the mechanisms of the human mind it will not seem at all surprising that witnesses who have once made what they think is the right identification, telling and retelling their story in private and in public, should refuse to be shaken on it afterwards. It was in just the same way that, in the case of Oscar Slater, Helen Lambie Mistaken Evidence became much more positive of her (mistaken) identification at the trial itself than she had been at the extradition proceedings in America.

Four years after Rowland's execution, namely in 1951, Ware was found guilty but insane of the attempted murder of a woman by raining blows upon her head with a hammer. He had given himself up to the police, telling them: " I don't know what is the matter with me. I keep on having an urge to hit women on the head."

The decision of the Court of Criminal Appeal in *Rowland's case* not to receive the fresh evidence was against common sense and precedent, and the court changed its mind on a later occasion. In 1945 a man had been convicted on the identification of a young woman; in 1954, while he was serving his sentence. another confessed to the crime. This time the Court of Criminal Appeal made no

[31] [1947] KB 460.

difficulty about admitting the new evidence, and the conviction was quashed.[32]

It would be pleasant, but unduly optimistic, to think that the danger inherent in identification evidence by comparative strangers to the accused is now generally recognised. The fact is that juries/judges, as the case may be, do not recognise its unreliable nature, and there is still no practice of cautioning juries upon it. The Court of Criminal Appeal had another opportunity to consider the law in *Williams*[33] but declined to lay down any new rule. It was what one might almost call the usual case of mistaken identity on an identification parade. After the trial, further matters came to light which, with the active assistance of the Crown, caused the conviction to be quashed. On appeal, counsel for the defendant expressly asked the court to give a general direction that in cases where the only evidence against an accused person was identification by one witness the jury should be warned that it would be dangerous to convict without corroboration. For some unstated reason, the Court refused to accede. Even if the rule been accepted, it would still have been stated too narrowly to have saved Rowland, who had the misfortune of being (mis)identified by more than one witness. In the matter of identification there is, unfortunately, no safety in numbers. Perhaps this is most forcefully shown by the celebrated *Tichborne case* of 1874, when one Arthur Orton (as was held) falsely claimed to be Roger Tichborne, the heir to a baronetcy and a fortune. No fewer than 85 witnesses, including Tichborne' s own mother, but against all the other relatives, identified Orton as Tichborne. It is true that there was a special feature to account for the mistake, namely the time that had elapsed since Roger Tichborne was last seen; but there is other evidence to show that a mistake made by one witness is only too often repeated by another.

Commenting on the foregoing case and similar ones such as *Adolph Beck* before it, Professor Williams[34] makes the following useful observations:

> There is reason to suppose that persons are even now in prison who have been falsely convicted as the result of identity parades.[35] Juries are still given no adequate instruction on the limitations of these parades. It is the experience of the police that at the majority of such parades the witness picks out nobody, or the "wrong" man.[36] If a witness fails in this way, he may not be called at the trial, his evidence being useless, or, if no other identification evidence is available either, the prosecution may be dropped. It will be obvious that this fact seriously discounts the probative value of a positive identification.

[32] Ashman, The Times, March 23, 1954; [1954] Crim LR 382. But the CCA continues extremely reluctant to hear new evidence where the Crown opposes it; even where identity is in issue. See Harrigan [1957] Crim LR 52.

[33] The Times, October 4, 1956; [1956] Crim LR 833.

[34] Williams GL, *The Proof of Guilt* (2nd edn, 1963) 100 – 103.

[35] See the case of Gilder, sentenced in 1955 to seven years' preventive detention, which Mr. Victor Collins, M.P., has been unsuccessfully pressing Home Secretary. According to Mr. Collins no witness identified Gilder by his face, though one witness identified him by trousers, his shoes and the clocks on his socks. There is a brief report in The Times, October 17, 1956.

[36] Howe RM, *The Work of the Criminal Investigation Department* (Law Society, London 1952) 20.

Quite apart from this, and even granting a reasonably good memory on the part of the witness, the danger of the identity parade is that the witness expects to find the guilty person present, and therefore points out the man who he thinks is most like the one he remembers. Thus, all that an identification parade can really be said to establish is that the accused resembled the criminal more closely than any other members of the parade did, which is not saying very much. In its evidence to the Royal Commission on Police Powers in 1929 the Howard League for Penal Reform made a valuable suggestion which, if generally adopted, would go some way towards improving the procedure. They urged that the officer in charge of the case should not be present at the parade, and, further, that the witness should be shown blank parades " as well as a parade containing the suspect, the blank parade sometimes preceding, sometimes following, the other. Even at present the officer in charge of the case does not conduct the parade. It is the practice of the police when tracking a professional criminal whose identity is unknown to use the modus operandi index at Scotland Yard, and to show a witness a number of photographs (including photographs of non-criminals) in order to enable him, if possible, to identify the person whom he observed, with a view to an arrest. This practice is regarded as a proper one, and does not render inadmissible evidence of a subsequent identification by the witness at an identification parade.[37] In such circumstances the prosecution should not give evidence that the accused was first picked out from police photographs, because this will lead the jury to infer that the accused has a police record,[38] but the defence may of course elicit this fact if it wishes.[39] If the witness was only shown one photograph before the arrest was made, and identifies the suspect from it, his subsequent identification of the same person at a parade is inadmissible.[40] Also, once a suspect has been arrested, it is most improper for the police to show his photograph to a witness before the identification parade, and if they do so, a conviction may be quashed.[41]

7.2.3 *Artificially constructed experiments*[42]

[37] In *Melany* (1924) 18 CAR 2 it appears to have been held that a judge need not caution a jury on the danger of such an identification. In *Dwyer* [1925] 2 KB at 803, the court appeared to go back on this, saying that afterwards the witness who has so acted in relation to a photograph is not a useful witness for the purpose of identification, or at any rate the evidence of that witness for the purpose of identification is to be taken subject to this, that he has previously seen a photograph. This appears to mean that the trial judge should exclude the evidence or at least caution the jury; but in *Hinds* [1932] 2 KB 644 the court rejected this view and in effect went back to *Melany*. *cf.Chaloner* [1955] Crim LR 110.

[38] *Wainwright* (1925) 19 CAR 52 (even though the defendant is unrepresented); *cf. Dwyer* [1925] 2 KB 799. It seems that *Varley* (1914) 10 CAR 125 would not now be followed. However, where by accident a witness for the prosecution refers to the fact that he saw a photograph of the accused in the rogues' gallery " at Scotland Yard, this will not necessarily invalidate a conviction: Wright (1934) 25 CAR 35.

[39] *Palmer* (1914) 10 CAR 77; *Kingsland* (1919) 14 CAR 8.

[40] *Dwyer* [1925] 2 KB at 799.

[41] *Haslam* (1925) 19 CAR 59.

[42] See generally, Williams GL, *The Proof of Guilt* 2nd edn (1963) 110-10.

Scientific enquiry into the problem of misidentification has led to empirical evidence into the challenge. According to examples given by Professor Williams in his superb but concise text,[43] the experiments were carried out by asking subjects for a description of faces previously seen by them on picture post-cards. According to Bartlett,[44]

> A particular face often at once aroused a more or less convectional attitude appropriate to the given type. Thereupon, the attitude actively affected the detail of representation.... A subject gave the captain [one of the postcards] 'a grave appearance': 'He was a very serious looking young man.' The face was [wrongly] turned into complete profile and assigned a prominent and heavy chin. After a lapse of three weeks the seriousness appeared to have become intensified, and the captain was now referred to as 'the young man in the profile, to the right. He had a square face, and is very serious and determined looking.' Seriousness and decision were emphasized again and again and a fortnight later seemed more striking than ever. This subject had to terminate her experiment at this stage, and so I showed her the card once more. She was amazed, and thought at first that I had substituted a new card. Her captain, she said, was very much more serious; his mouth was firmer, his chin more prominent, his face [squarer] .... It looks very much as if, under the influence of the effective attitude involved, some of the detail given in recall is genuinely being constructed...... Accurate recall is the exception and not the rule.

Gorphe's[45] study shows how scientific research proves all common-sense assessments of a witness's correctness as fabrications.

> Error of recognition breeds an invincible assurance in the witness, highly deceptive for those who are not forewarned of the possibility [....] There is no difference, from the subjective point of view, between true and false recognition, and there are no objective signs to distinguish one from the other [...] the witness's certainty may not be immediate, without this delay being necessarily a sign of error. Nevertheless, error is more frequent when recognition comes sometime after seeing.... The witness cannot always describe the person or object recognised, without this capability being a sign of mistake; the intellectualisation of the feeling is secondary, additional, and it may be more or less lacking; in fact, the greater than familiarity, the feebler the intellectualization. Conversely, a description given correctly by the witness does not prove the correctness of the recognition, and the exact preservation of the memory [...] the act of recognition is very open to suggestion in all its forms. Resemblance is a matter of relativity [...] A person can much better distinguish those of his own age and condition than those of different ages and condition. Uniform is a cause of fallacious

[43] Williams GL, *The Proof of Guilt* 2nd edn (1963) 100-103.

[44] Williams GL, *The Proof of Guilt* 2nd edn (1963) 100-101.

[45] Gorphe, *La critique du témoignage* (1924) 312-318.

> resemblance, above all for those who do not wear it.

Professor Williams[46] points to an experiment carried out by the London School of Economics and Political Sciences (LSE), where nine members of the audience were asked to identify two actors from the play, they had attended a week before in a parade consisting of thirteen people. Only two of the nine were able to correctly identify the Englishmen, and only four, the Welshman. Two innocent men were identified twice. Completely innocent men were identified with varying degrees of assurance.

7.2.4 *Reasons for errors in identification*[47]

Lawyers, judges and scientists have wondered how and why misidentification such as that experienced in *the curious case of Adolph Beck* occur. The question takes on even more impetus when we consider the fact that errors in dentification affect not only those who have defective eyesight or are too young or too old or at the material time suffer from the shock of the moment but curiously, even those who are not affected by any of the preceding limitations. There are indeed various reasons why errors in identification may occur.[48] We will briefly discuss a few here.

7.2.4.1 *Complexity of supporting an assertion of recognition*

Stephen J[49] has taken the view that '[t]he accuracy of any identification of a stranger, seen once only, is likely to be affected by the fallibility of human perception and memory.'[50] This comment was made with respect to visual identification evidence. The statement found support in *Craig v R*[51] where it has been observed as follows:

> An honest witness who says "The prisoner is the man who drove the car," whilst appearing to affirm a simple, clear and impressive proposition, is really asserting: (1) that he observed the driver, (2) that the observation became impressed upon his mind, (3) that he still retains the original impression, (4) that such impression has not been affected, altered or replaced, by published portraits of the prisoner (5) that the resemblance between the original impression of the prisoner is sufficient to base a judgment, not of resemblance, but of identity.

It has also found support in *Nyambe v The People*[52] wherein the Supreme Court

[46] Williams GL, *The Proof of Guilt* (2nd edn 1963) 102-103.

[47] See generally, *Alexander v R* (1981) 145 CLR 395; ALRC 26, Vol 1, Ch 18; JD Jackson, "The Insufficiency of Identification Evidence Based on Personal Impression" [1986] Crim LR 203; *Strauss v Police* (2013) 115 SASR 90 at [12]-[37].

[48] See reasons given especially in *Alexander v R* (1981) 145 CLR 395 *per* Gibbs CJ, Stephen, Mason, Murphy and Aickin JJ.

[49] *Alexander v R* (1981) 145 CLR 395.

[50] *Alexander v R* (1981) 145 CLR 395.

[51] (1933) 49 CLR 429 at 446.

[52] [1973] ZR 228.

opined as follows:[53]

> There is perhaps no area in which there is a greater danger of honest mistake than in the area of identification, particularly where the accused was not known to the witness prior to the occasion on which he is alleged to have been seen. The question is not one of credibility in the sense of truthfulness, but of reliability, and the greatest care should therefore be taken to test the identification. It is not enough for the witness simply to say that the accused is the person who committed the offence; the witness should be asked to specify by what features or unusual marks, if any, he alleges to recognise the accused, what was his build, what clothes he was wearing, and so on; and the circumstances in which the accused was observed - the state of the light, the opportunity for observation, the stress of the moment - should be carefully canvassed. The foregoing considerations are not, of course, exhaustive, but are intended merely to be illustrative; the adequacy of evidence of personal identification will depend on all the surrounding circumstances, and each case must be decided on its own merits.[54]

For the foregoing reasons, it has been held in *Chimbo and Others v The People,*[55] that [a]lthough recognition is accepted to be more reliable than identification of a stranger, it is the duty of the court to warn itself of the need to exclude the possibility of an honest mistake. Additionally, that for purposes of identification, a proper identification parade must be arranged. Identification evidence is for the most part built on a fragile plane.[56] If a system is to be deemed just and fair by the parties concerned, it cannot base the conviction of accused persons on the resemblance with the criminal who committed the offence but on the reasonably unassailable fact that the charge against them has been proved beyond reasonable doubt.[57]

7.2.4.2 Treachery of memory

Also referred to as defective memory, this may arise when the witness had no special reason to remember the accused, or as shown in *R v Turnbull*[58] where too much time has passed between the incident and the report to the police of the incident in question by the witness of the person identified and as such 'he still retains the original impression.'

7.2.4.3 The challenge of a fleeting glimpse

[53] [1973] ZR 228 at 231.

[54] See *Chimbo v The People* [1982] ZR 20 (SC).

[55] [1982] ZR 20 (SC).

[56] *Alexander v R* (1981) 145 CLR 395 at 426 *per* Mason J.

[57] See direction given by Lord Guthrie in the *case of Slater: The trial of Oscar Slater*, 3rd edn 1929 at 239.

[58] [1977] QB 224 at 228 (CA).

The propositions in *Craig v R*,[59] '(1) that he observed the driver, (2) that the observation became impressed upon his mind,' speak to another reason that may lead errors in identification.' Professor Bartlett[60] observes as follows:

> '[f]aces seem peculiarly liable to set up attitudes and consequent reactions which are largely coloured by feeling. They are very rarely, by the ordinary person, discriminated or analysed in detail. We rely rather upon a general impression, obtained at the first glance, and issuing in immediate attitudes of like or dislike, of confidence or suspicion, of amusement or gravity.'

Where, among other scenarios, the witness in question only had a fleeting glance of the criminal's face, made the observation under bad light in the night or under inauspicious weather conditions or indeed in a situation where his view of the criminal was impeded by an object for a time, the strength of the identification will be compromised even in circumstances where the criminal involved was one well known to the witness. In *Love Chipulu v The People*,[61] the appellant was convicted of aggravated robbery contrary to s 294(1) of the Penal Code.[62] It was alleged that he and a person unknown attacked and robbed the sole prosecution witness. The witness who during the attack briefly saw and claimed to have known the appellant previously, searched for and found the appellant at his home and identified him to the police. At the trial the appellant elected to remain silent and called no witness(es). It was held as follows: Where the circumstances of an attack are traumatic and there is only a fleeting glimpse of an assailant, the fact that an appellant had been patronising the same bar as an accused for the past nine months does not render an identification safe.

7.2.4.4 *The likelihood of errors in identifying people who do not look like the witness*

Errors of identification are likely to occur where the person(s) identified are of a different race, age or dress differently from the witness. To an ordinary Zambian witness, there may be no difference between one Chinese person from the next one, nor an Indian from a Lebanese suspect or indeed two individuals who have similar features. They may all look the same. As Gorphe[63] notes,

> '[e]rror of recognition breeds an invincible assurance in the witness, highly deceptive for those who are not forewarned of the possibility [....] Resemblance is a matter of relativity [....] A person can much better distinguish those of his own age and condition than those of different ages and condition. Uniform is a cause of fallacious resemblance, above all for those who do not wear it.'

---

[59] (1933) 49 CLR 429 at 446.

[60] Williams GL, *The Proof of Guilt* 2nd edn 100.

[61] [1986] ZR 73 (SC).

[62] Chapter 87 of the Laws of Zambia.

[63] Quoted in Williams GL, *The Proof of Guilt* 3rd edn 102.

In *The People v Robert Phiri and Tenson Siagutu*[64] the two accused were charged with aggravated robbery contrary to s 294 of the Penal Code Act.[65] It was alleged that in the early hours of the morning of 29th June, in Kafue, they stole property worth ZMW5,906.21 from the plaintiffs. The couple were tied up with wired cords. The two accused unmasked themselves before leaving the room where one of the plaintiffs, the wife was, and she identified accused A1 as their ex-shopkeeper and A2 as the man who was working in the third shop from theirs. The issue before the court was whether the two accused were the participants in the commission of the crime. The defence case was that of honest mistake on the part of the plaintiff who identified the accused persons. The learned judge held that the plaintiff impressed him as a witness of truth and that there was no possibility of an honest mistake on her part. He further held that the prosecution had proved its case beyond reasonable doubt and the two accused were convicted as charged. It was held as follows: (i) The adequacy of evidence of personal identification always depends on all the circumstances surrounding each case which must be decided on its merits. (ii) A person is said to have made an honest mistake when he or she mistakes A for B. both of whom may have similar features. Stress of the moment is the most common cause of persons making honest mistakes. (iii) The prosecution bears the onus of proof as the accused person carries no onus of proving his innocence.

There is, however, authority to the effect that cross-racial misidentification need not be prefaced with the warning generally expected in instances of a court receiving suspect evidence such as identification evidence.

7.2.4.5 Dogmatism and overconfidence

Errors of identification are likely to occur dogmatism and overconfidence score as witnesses are likely to be overconfident of the accuracy of their identification in terms of what they perceived and can recollect despite the fact that their sight may be poor, the weather may have been less than conducive, that they only had a glimpse of the person identified; or their view was somewhat blocked. In *Mackenzie v R*[66] the High Court of Australia commented on the 'dogmatic way in which the appellant dealt with his recollection of events and his unwillingness, almost to the last, to admit the possibility that he might have been mistaken in that recollection.' Even so, said the Court, 'whilst it is true that the appellant appears to have been a dogmatic witness, unwilling to concede mistake, at the very end of his testimony in his own trial he eventually came to face that possibility.' The case is however a perfect illustration of how errors may arise from dogmatism and overconfidence. It takes an alert court and opposing counsel to, as was done in *Mackenzie*,[67] to ensure that such errors do not compromise rectitude of decision.

---

[64] [1980] ZR 249 (HC); *Chimbini v The People* [1973] ZR 191; *Champion Manex Mukwakwa v The People* [1978] ZR 347; *R v Turnbull and Others* [1976] 3 All ER 549.

[65] Chapter 87 of the Laws of Zambia.

[66] (1996) 190 CLR 348 at 373.

[67] (1996) 190 CLR 348 at 373.

7.2.4.6 *Challenges relating to recognition*

This point may be seen as an extension of the foregoing two reasons given as possible reasons for the occurrence of errors in identification. The basis of the conclusion that this is one reason why there may be errors in identification evidence is empirical evidence. According to the Late Professor Glanville L Williams quoting Professor Bartlett,[68] peculiar faces appear to elicit peculiar reactions from observers of occurrences in issue for which identification evidence is called for. Thus, a witness may, on the basis of his feelings about a particular face, draw a certain conclusion which may be adverse without much analysis or deliberation or discrimination. He adds: '[w]e rely rather upon a general impression, obtained at the first glance, and issuing in immediate attitudes of like or dislike, of confidence or suspicion, or amusement or gravity.' Hoffmann[69] has observed that [the witness] may expect people who behave in a particular way or belong to a certain class to have some physical characteristics, which he will scribe to such a person without having verified his belief by observation.' This position is in tandem with that given by professor Williams. Its correctness lies in the fact that witnesses will usually be mistaken as to the correct identity of the criminal on account of similarities of persons especially those that may be known to the witness in question. Further, as has been noted by the Devlin Committee Report,[70] additional obstacles may be encountered by the witness in correctly identifying the criminal like a certain cast of features that elicit certain emotions in the witness likely to disorient them into misidentifying the real criminal behind the offence in question.

7.2.4.7 *Use of unsuitable methods*

As said earlier, one problem that afflicts identification evidence emanates from 'the use by the police of methods of identification which, though well suited to the investigation and detection of crime, are not calculated to yield evidence of high probative value in a criminal trial.'[71] Further, Mason J has observed as follows in *Alexander v R:*[72]

> Identification is notoriously uncertain. It depends upon so many variables. They include the difficulty one has in recognizing on a subsequent occasion a person observed, perhaps fleetingly, on a former occasion; the extent of the opportunity for observation in a variety of circumstances; the vagaries of human perception and recollection; and the tendency of the mind to respond to suggestions, notably the tendency to substitute a photographic image once seen for a hazy recollection of the person initially observed. The use of photographs by

[68] Williams GL, *The Proof of Guilt* 3rd edn 101.

[69] Hoffmann LH, *The South African Law of Evidence* 2nd edn 1970 at 437.

[70] Devlin Committee Report, *(Report of the Committee on Evidence of Identification in Criminal Cases, 1976 Cmnd 338 42)*, [4.13]. See [1390].

[71] JD Heydon, Cross on Evidence para [....].

[72] (1981) 145 CLR 395 at 426; Williams GL, *The Proof of Guilt* 122.

> police, especially photographs of known or suspected criminals, is an essential aid to the detection of persons who have committed crimes. Yet the use of such photographs before a jury may tend to suggest that the accused is known to the police as a criminal who has committed offences of the kind charged. And, as I have said, once a witness has seen a photograph which he links with the person seen, he tends to substitute the photographic image for his recollection. Recognizing these dangers, the English courts have tended to draw a distinction between an identification made in the course of investigating a crime, when the police may request a potential witness to make an identification from photographs, and an identification made after the accused has been taken into custody, when the use of photographs is frowned upon and the arrangement of an identification parade is urged as the course to be preferred. In the second situation the purpose of the identification is purely evidentiary; it is designed to produce evidence for use at the trial.

Can the value of identification evidence be overestimated? To answer this question, we turn to Professor Williams again. He postulates as follows:[73]

> It is he experience of the police that at the majority of such parades the witness picks out nobody, or the "wrong" man. If a witness fails in this way, he may not be called at the trial, his evidence being useless [...] It will be obvious that this fact seriously discounts the probative value of a positive identification. Quite apart from this, and even granting a reasonably good memory on the part of the witness, the danger of the identification parade is that the witness expects to find the guilty person present, and therefore points out the man who he thinks is most like the one he remembers. Thus, all that an identification parade can really be said to establish is that the accused resembled the criminal more closely than any other members if the parade did, which is not saying very much.

The Zambian Courts have just been as cautious as the following decisions demonstrate.

In *Bwalya v The People*[74] Baron, DCJ, as he then was, opined with respect to the question of identification, that '[i]t is not sufficient to be satisfied that a witness is honest; the court must be satisfied that a possibility of an honest mistake has been ruled out.'

It has been held in *Honest Solopi*[75] '[t]hat the question is not one of credibility in the sense of truthfulness but of reliability and that the greatest care should therefore be taken to test the identification because it is not only for the witness simply to say that the accused is the person who committed the offence [....]'

---

[73] Williams GL, *The Proof of Guilt* 120-121.

[74] [1975] ZR 125.

[75] (1974 SCZ Judgment No 11).

The matter was further clarified in *Mbundi Nyambe v The People.*[76] To illustrate the fallibility of single witness identification the court observed as follows:

> There is perhaps no area in which there is a greater danger of honest; mistake than in the area of identification, particularly where the accused was not known to the witness prior to the occasion on which he is alleged to have been seen. The question is not one of credibility in the sense of truthfulness, but of reliability, and the greatest care should therefore be taken to test the identification. It is not enough for the witness simply to say that the accused is the person who committed the offence; the witness should be asked to specify by what features or unusual marks, if any, he alleges to recognise the accused, what was his build, what clothes he was wearing, and so on; and the circumstances in which the accused was observed; the state of the light, the opportunity for observation, the stress of the moment - should be carefully canvassed. The foregoing, considerations are not, of course, exhaustive, but are intended merely to illustrate; the adequacy of evidence of personal identification will depend on all the surrounding circumstances and case must be decided on its merits. The danger of honest mistake in identification is even greater where there is only a single identifying witness.

It has further been observed as follows in the case of *Abdullah Binwendo and Another v R:*[77]

> Subject to certain well-known exceptions it is trite law that a fact may be proved by the testimony of a single witness but this rule does not lessen the need for testing with the greatest care the evidence of a single witness representing identification especially when it is knowing that the conditions favouring a correct identification were difficult. In such circumstances what is needed is other evidence, whether it be circumstantial or direct pointing to guilt from which the judge or jury can reasonably conclude thy the evidence of identification, although based on the testimony of a single witness can safely be accepted as free from the possibility of error.

It has been observed that the danger of an honest mistake in identification is even greater where there is only a single identifying witness. Therefore, before a court can convict, on the testimony of a single witness in so far as identification is concerned, it must, as it was in *The People v Robert Phiri and Tenson Siagutu*[78] be 'satisfied that the possibility of an honest mistake has been ruled out or that it has not been so ruled out.'[79] This has, however, not always been the

[76] [1973] ZR 228.

[77] (1953) 20 EACA 166 at 168.

[78] (1980) ZR 249 (HC).

[79] *Abdallah Bin Wendo and Anor v R* 20 EACA 166; *R v Turnbull and Others* [1976] 3 All ER 549; *Nyambe v The People* (1973) ZR 228; *Chimbini v The People* (1973) ZR 191; *Bwalya v The People* [1975] ZR 227; *Chate v The People* [1975] ZR 232.

case. In *Muvuma Kambanja Situna v The People,*[80] the appellant was convicted of one count of aggravated robbery and two counts of attempted murder. The trial court considered that the appellant had been properly identified at the parade by the single identifying witness despite allegations by the defence that the parade was improperly conducted and the inherent danger of an honest mistake in the circumstances. Hearsay evidence was admitted supporting the conviction.

It was held *inter alia* that the evidence of a single identifying witness must be tested and evaluated with the greatest care to exclude the dangers of an honest mistake; the witness should be subjected to searching questions and careful note taken of all the prevailing conditions and the basis upon which the witness claims to recognise the accused. Delivering the judgment of the Court, Ngulube DCJ, as he then was, observed as follows in part:

> The learned trial commissioner found that PW4 had properly identified the appellant at an identification parade, and dismissed allegations by the defence that the parade had not been properly conducted. It is clear from a reading of the relevant passage in the judgment that the court below considered that, having dismissed the complaint regarding the parade, the identification at the parade alone was sufficient to warrant a conclusion that PW4 had properly identified the appellant. This approach is manifestly unsatisfactory. This was a case where there was in fact only a single identifying witness, a witness who, on his own admission, was frightened and rushed out of the shop together with the customers. PW4 had stated that he had seen the appellant entering the shop as he himself was rushing out for safety. It is quite clear on these facts, therefore, that PW4 could only have had at best a momentary glimpse of the appellant. In these circumstances there is a great deal of merit in the ground appeal which attacks the quality of identification in this case. There is a string of cases which set out the correct116 approach to the evidence of a single identifying witness. Those cases also lay down the requirements that a trial court should show in its judgment that it is alive to the dangers of an honest mistaken identification. The cases [...][81] all establish the need to test and evaluate with greatest care the evidence of a single identifying witness to exclude the dangers of an honest mistake before such evidence can be regarded as reliable. The witness should normally be subjected to searching questions, and careful note taken of all the prevailing conditions as well as the basis upon which the witness claims to be able to recognise the accused. If, in all the circumstances, the opportunity for a positive and reliable identification is poor, then it follows that the possibility of an honest mistake has not been ruled out unless there is some other connecting link between the accused and the offence which would render a mistaken identification too

[80] [1982] ZR 115 (SC).

[81] *Abdallah Bin Wendo and Anor v R* 20 EACA 166; *R v Turnbull and Others* [1976] 3 All ER 549; *Nyambe v The People* (1973) ZR 228; *Chimbini v The People* (1973) ZR 191; *Bwalya v The People* [1975] ZR 227; *Chate v The People* [1975] ZR 232.

> much of coincidence. The evidence in this case showed that out of four possible eye-witnesses only one frightened witness was running out of the shop for safety. Identification in those circumstances could hardly be regarded as reliable and, in any event, the failure on the part of the learned trial commissioner to warn himself with regard to the possibility of an honest mistake on the part of PW4 was misdirection.

Stephen J[82] has pointed out how the methods employed by the police for purposes of identification evidence are fraught with problems. Specifically, when a witness picks a witness by way of photograph, or makes his identification at a pre-arranged identification parade, and at trial identifies the accused by touching him as he sits in the accused's box, he is engaging in a substitution exercise, that is, he is substituting his hazy memory or recollection of the criminal for the clear black and white, two-dimensional, non-sentient, static, well-lit view of the subject. To quote his lordship:

> The accuracy of any identification of a stranger, seen once only, is likely to be affected by the fallibility of human perception and memory. When identification is attempted with the aid of photographs, there are introduced peculiar difficulties, due to the various ways in which photographic representations differ from nature: their two dimensional and static quality, the fact that they are often in black and white and the clear and well-lit picture of the subject which they usually provide. The use of photo-identification in the evidentiary process involves three further factors of a quite different kind which apply only to its use in that process. Unlike the case of an identification parade, an accused whose identity as the offender is sought to be proved at his trial by evidence of previous photo-identification is likely to know nothing at first hand of the way in which the identifying witness earlier identified his photograph as that of the offender. He must rely upon cross-examination of prosecution witnesses for knowledge of the conditions of identification and of what safeguards were taken against error on the part of the identifying witness. Again, by what may be called the "rogues' gallery" effect, evidence that the police had in their possession and showed to the identifying witness photographs of the accused may often strongly suggest to a jury that the accused has a criminal record, perhaps even a propensity to commit a crime of the kind with which he is charged. Their production in evidence, or even reference to their existence, may then be highly prejudicial to an accused. Lastly, there is the "displacement" effect. Having been shown a photograph, the memory of it may be more clearly retained than the memory of the original sighting of the offender and may, accordingly, displace that original memory. Any subsequent face-to-face identification, in court or in an identification parade, may, on the

[82] *Alexander v R* (1981) 145 CLR 395.

> identifying witness's part, in truth involve a matching of the man so identified with the remembered photograph, which has displaced in his memory his recollection of the original sighting.[83]

7.2.4.8 *Rogues gallery effect and cross-examination*

If it were reviewed that the identification of the accused was made possible by a picture that was already in the possession, custody or/and power of the police, this would suggest to the judge/magistrate, prior criminal conduct and possibly prejudice the accused in the mind of the court. This is referred to as the rogue gallery effect. Stephen J[84] explains it thus:

> Once used in the detection process, photo-identification tends inexorably to intrude upon the trial evidence. This occurs most commonly in the following way: the eye-witness who in the detection process has, by the use of photo-identification, put a name to a previously unidentified offender is very likely to be an identifying witness, perhaps the only available one, at the ensuing trial. Yet in that role his earlier association with photo-identification will tend to infect his evidence. Its displacement effect will operate to a greater or lesser extent upon any later identification which he makes in court or of which he gives evidence. To attack his evidence of identification the defence will wish to expose this effect. But cross-examination which reveals the earlier photo-identification will be likely to subject the accused to the rogues' gallery effect. That effect will be introduced even more directly should the prosecution itself be permitted to lead evidence of the photo-identification so as to support the evidence the witness gives of the identity of the accused as the offender. In the evidentiary process, then, photo-identification has serious disadvantages, in addition to that of its inherent unreliability.[85]

7.2.4.9 *The risk of repeated errors*

As demonstrated in the *Adolph Beck case*, it may well be the case that several identification witnesses repeat the same mistake in which case any subsequent witness will not offer any discernible protection.

7.2.4.10 *Where no notice was taken by the identifying witness*

A witness may be called upon to identify persons to whom he did not pay particular attention at the material time. The inevitability of an error of identification under those circumstances is palpable.

---

[83] *Alexander v R* (1981) 145 CLR 395 at 409 *per* Stephen J.

[84] *Alexander v R* (1981) 145 CLR 395 at 410 *per* Stephen J.

[85] See also Devlin Committee Report, [1.24] and [4.25].

7.2.4.11 *Where the witness has an interest to serve*

A witness may seek to identify the person in question because he is motivated by revenge. Here again, the inevitability of erroneous identity is certain.

7.3 Safeguards

The foregoing notwithstanding, the general purpose of the law has always been to ensure rectitude of decision. Therefore, to guard against the foregoing risks of misidentification, sophisticated safeguards have developed over the years in two major spheres (i) at the point of investigation; and (ii) at the point of trial. The former regulates the manner in which the police gather evidence while the latter regulates how courts deal with admissibility of identification evidence. The goal of the safeguards is twofold: (i) to safeguard suspects; and (ii) to provide persuasive evidence on behalf of the prosecution to the court handling the matter in question.

7.3.1 *Safeguards at the point of police investigations*

The importance of safeguards at the point of investigation cannot be overemphasised. This is because miscarriage of justice taints justice, offends the dignity of the court and reduces the chances of society respecting court decisions. The safeguards observed in this jurisdiction are mainly based on the common law. There have, however, been quasi-statutory moves in England where from a plethora of decisions which would be of considerable persuasive value to our courts have been made by English Courts. In 1978 for example, the British Home office sought to buttress already existing safeguards pertaining to investigations in so far as parade identification evidence was concerned. The 1978 Circular was followed by the Report of the Royal Commission[86] which called for the British Home Office procedures and any like them prior to them to be codified. What resulted was called the Code of Practice for the Identification of Persons by Police Officers or simply Code of Practice D promulgated under the Police and Criminal Evidence Act 1984 (PACE). Lacking statutory power has not stopped English Courts from robustly adverting to Code D in order to address Police impropriety as regards their conduct during investigations *vis-à-vis* identification evidence. By way of example, in *R v Quinn*[87] it was emphasised that '[p]olice must follow the published Code of Practice, when conducting identity parades, and may not substitute their own. If the evidence is allowed in despite the breach, the judge should explain the significance of the breach to the jury, as it may go to the weight they attach to the evidence.'[88] The most recent revision of the said Code was brought into being in 2005.

[86] Royal Commission on Criminal Procedure: Report (1981) Cmnd. 8092. Para.3.138.

[87] [1995] Crim LR 56 The EWCA.

[88] *Regina v Quinn*: CACD 15 Mar 1994 https://swarb.co.uk/regina-v-quinn-cacd-15-mar-1994/ retrieved on 16 August 2021.

Generally, it falls to reason that the defence ought to be availed any initial description the police received in so far as identification evidence is concerned prior to any trial to which it will be relevant. It has been shown in *R v Fergus*[89] that a judge should withdraw a case which was based on poor identification evidence, and the prosecution must be sure to disclose all identification evidence.

> In a case dependent on visual identification, and particularly where that is the only evidence, Turnbull makes it clear that it is incumbent on a trial Judge to place before the Jury any specific weaknesses which can arguably be said to have been exposed in the evidence. And it is not sufficient for the Judge to invite the Jury to take into account what counsel for the defence says about the specific weaknesses. Needless to say, the Judge must deal with the specific weaknesses in a coherent manner so that the cumulative impact of those specific weaknesses is fairly placed before the Jury.[90]

The pertinent provisions in Code D discussed here for persuasive purposes only, for use by the courts should they deem them fit for purpose in proper cases cover the following instances:

7.3.1.1 *Suspect's identity is unfamiliar*

Where the identity of the suspect is not known, the police may take the individual witnesses to relevant neighbourhoods in order to enable them identify suspects. This does not, however, include directing such witnesses to any particular individuals or suspects. If there is more than one witness they must be separated during the exercise. It is also permissible for the police to show the witness photographs and/or composites of the suspect(s).[91] However, the police should not engage in this exercise where the suspect in question is known to them.

7.3.1.2 *Suspect is known to witness and accessible*

Where the suspect is known to the witness and is available or the witness asserts that he can identify a suspect, an identification procedure becomes obligatory.[92] This is comparable to the judicial position taken in *R v Forbes*.[93]

---

[89] (1993) 98 Cr App R 313; https://swarb.co.uk/regina-v-fergus-cacd-29-jun-1993/retrieved on 16 August 2021.

[90] *R v Fergus* (1993) 98 Cr App R 313 *per* Steyn LJ.

[91] *R v Gornall* Unreported, March 3, 2005, CA.

[92] *R v Gornall* Unreported, March 3, 2005, CA.

[93] [2001] 1 All ER 686; see 11(1) Halsbury's Laws (4th edn reissue) para 770; *R v Anastasiou* [1998] Crim LR 67, CA; *R v Brizey* (10 March 1994, unreported), CA; *R v Brown* [1991] Crim LR 368, CA; *R v Bush* (27 January 1997, unreported), CA; *R v Conway* (1990) 91 Cr App R 143, CA; *R v Graham* [1994] Crim LR 212, CA; *R v Greaves* (6 May 1994, unreported), CA; *R v Hickin* [1996] Crim LR 584, CA; *R v Macmath* [1997] Crim LR 586, CA; *R v Oscar* [1991] Crim LR 778, CA; *R v Popat* [1998] 2 Cr App R 208, CA; *R v Popat* (No 2) [2000] 1 Cr App R 387, CA; *R v Quinn* [1995] 1 Cr App R 480, CA; *R v Rogers* [1993] Crim LR 386, CA; *R v Togher* (9 November 2000, unreported), CA; *R v Turnbull* [1976] 3 All ER 549, [1977] QB 224, [1976] 3 WLR 445, CA; *R v Vaughan* (30 April 1997, unreported), CA; *R v Wait* [1998] Crim LR 68, CA; *Stott v Brown* (5 December 2000, unreported), PC.

The appellant, F, was identified to the police in the street as the perpetrator of an attempted robbery by the victim shortly after the offence had been committed. He was charged with the offence, which he denied. Three times before his trial he asked for an identification parade to be held, but no such parade was held. At trial, objection was taken to the admission in evidence of the street identification because, inter alia, no identification parade had been held. F contended that that constituted a breach of para 2.3a of the Code of Practice for the Identification of Persons by Police Officers (Code D of the codes of practice made under the Police and Criminal Evidence Act 1984). Paragraph 2.3 provided that, with certain exceptions, an identification parade had to be held whenever a suspect disputed an identification, if the suspect consented. The judge rejected F's submission, holding that a full and complete identification had been made at the scene, and that in those circumstances it was unnecessary for there to be an identification parade. In so concluding, the judge relied on a Court of Appeal authority which held that a distinction was to be drawn between cases where a suspect was produced by a witness to the police rather than the other way round, and that para 2.3 did not apply where there had previously been a 'fully satisfactory' or 'actual and complete' or 'unequivocal' identification of the suspect by the relevant witness. F was convicted, and appealed. The Court of Appeal, declining to follow the earlier authority, held that there had been a breach of para 2.3, but concluded that that breach had not rendered the conviction unsafe. Accordingly, it dismissed the appeal. On F's appeal to the House of Lords, their Lordships were required to determine whether para 2.3 applied even where the suspect had already been positively identified. It was held that on its true construction, para 2.3 of Code D applied even where there had previously been a 'fully satisfactory' or 'actual and complete' or 'unequivocal' identification of the suspect by the relevant witness. A conclusion to the contrary would subvert the clear intention of the code which was intended to be an intensely practical document, giving police officers clear instructions on the approach that they should follow in specified circumstances. It was not old-fashioned literalism but sound interpretation to read it as meaning what it said. Paragraph 2.3 imposed a mandatory obligation on the police. There was no warrant for reading additional conditions into the text and no basis for drawing a distinction between cases where a suspect was produced by the police to a witness rather than by a witness to the police. However, para 2.3 should not be construed to cover all possible situations. It might be futile to mount an identification parade if an eye witness to a crime had made it plain to the police that he could not identify the culprit, or if the case was one of pure recognition of someone well-known to the eye witness. Save, however, in cases such as those, or other exceptional circumstances, the effect of para 2.3 was clear: if the police had sufficient information to justify the arrest of a particular person for suspected involvement in an offence, and an eye witness had identified that person, and the suspect disputed his identification as a person involved in the commission of that offence, an identification parade had to be held if the suspect consented and the exceptions did not apply. It followed that in the instant case there had been a breach of Code D. However, F's conviction could not, in all the circumstances, be regarded as unsafe. Accordingly, the appeal would be dismissed.[94] *Per curiam:* Where a breach of Code D has been established, but the trial judge has rejected an application to exclude evidence to which the defence has objected because of that breach, the judge should in the course of his summing up explain that there has been a breach of the code and how it has arisen, and invite the jury to consider the possible effect of that breach.

The position espoused in *R v Forbes*[95] has been shown to be the case even in instances where there are challenges in arranging a parade or indeed, where the identification is explicit. Logic must lead us to the conclusion that the Police are not at liberty to circumvent this requirement. In *R v Gaynor*[96] the test justice took the position, *inter alia,* that the constabulary could have made a greater attempt to have volunteers of Gaynor's racial group than they did. Whilst *R v Gaynor*[97] may have been an absolutely valid determination on its own facts, the EWCA in *R v Jamel*[98] appears to have taken a softer line, holding that the defence mechanism could not object to the retention of a group designation if the retention of a parade might, in the fortunes, have taken hebdomads[99] to set up; in other words, "impracticable" may entail infeasible with a sensible timescale. All sensible steps must be taken to look into the possibility of one designation option before traveling on to an option.[100]

In this jurisdiction, at least so far as pre-eminence is concerned and case law[101] demonstrates, the identification parade has been all the rage and the dominant source of identification evidence. The advent of technology has, however, spawned and made possible, video identification as a veritable basis for identification evidence. In addition, the police have several methods available to them which include, apart from video identification, identification

---

[94] *R v Popat* [1998] 2 Cr App R 208 disapproved.

[95] [2001] 1 All ER 686; see 11(1) Halsbury's Laws (4th edn reissue) para 770; *R v Anastasiou* [1998] Crim LR 67, CA; *R v Brizey* (10 March 1994, unreported), CA; *R v Brown* [1991] Crim LR 368, CA; *R v Bush* (27 January 1997, unreported), CA; *R v Conway* (1990) 91 Cr App R 143, CA; *R v Graham* [1994] Crim LR 212, CA; *R v Greaves* (6 May 1994, unreported), CA; *R v Hickin* [1996] Crim LR 584, CA; *R v Macmath* [1997] Crim LR 586, CA; *R v Oscar* [1991] Crim LR 778, CA; *R v Popat* [1998] 2 Cr App R 208, CA; *R v Popat* (No 2) [2000] 1 Cr App R 387, CA; *R v Quinn* [1995] 1 Cr App R 480, CA; *R v Rogers* [1993] Crim LR 386, CA; *R v Togher* (9 November 2000, unreported), CA; *R v Turnbull* [1976] 3 All ER 549, [1977] QB 224, [1976] 3 WLR 445, CA; *R v Vaughan* (30 April 1997, unreported), CA; *R v Wait* [1998] Crim LR 68, CA; *Stott v Brown* (5 December 2000, unreported), PC.

[96] [1988] Crim LR 242.

[97] [1988] Crim LR 242.

[98] [1993] Crim LR 52.

[99] (obsolete): A group of seven.

[100] *R v Campbell and Marshall* [1993] Crim LR 47; *R v Ladlow* [1989] Crim LR 21; The foregoing analysis and summary is taken verbatim from Procedures for the pre-trial identification https://tonysplacenanthailand.com/essays/procedures-for-the-pre-trial-identification-5273 retrieved on 16/8/2021.

[101] See *Kamwandi v The People* [1972] ZR 131 (HC); *The People v Chimbala* (1973) ZR 118 (HC); *Toko v The People* [1975] ZR 196; *Bwalya v The People* [1975] ZR 227; *Mwansa Mushala and Others v The People* [1978] ZR 58 (SC); *The People v Swillah* [1978] ZR 338; *Yoani Manongo v The People* (SCZ Judgment No 26 of 1980); *Ilunga Kabala and John Masefu v The People* [1981] ZR 102 (SC); *Kenneth Mtonga and Victor Kaonga v The People* (SCZ Judgment No 5 of 2000); *Simon Mwansa v The People* (SCZ Appeal No 68 of 2004); *Winzy Sakala and Gerald Phiri v The People* (SCZ Judgment No 11 of 2009); *The People v Ronald Musonda and Others* (HW/08/2012).

parade (already referenced above); group identification; and/or confrontation. We will return to these methods below.

There ought to be no requirement for a suspect to submit or consent to any mode of identification. It is neither here nor there to argue and thereby object to a certain form of identification being used at trial by the prosecution simply because the accused would have preferred another form of identification against him. To permit this sort of objection both at investigation level on the one hand, and at trial on the other, would be to impede the smooth running of the criminal justice system and to prejudice the proper and fair prosecution of the accused. Therefore, where a suspect refuses to cooperate with police investigations at this stage of the criminal justice system, he has to be warned that the identification evidence may be used at trial to his detriment.

As with trials, the police have to work within the context of the time and administrative constraints placed upon them while at the same time ensuring not only that they have the right suspects identified but that they have built as strong a case as they can for prosecution counsel to present at trial. To be able to do the foregoing, it is important even when it comes to identification evidence, especially where the suspect is known to the witness that modes of identification that will not profit the police's case or serve any useful purpose are dispensed with. In *R v DPP*,[102] the court used its discretion to permit a witness to testify to the effect that the suspect was well known to him and that he had seen them commit the offence with which they had been charged, despite the fact that there had been no formal identification. The video identification that the police had arranged for in this particular matter was not successful as some of the accused were unable to attend to same prior to the commencement of trial. However, the use of discretion must be seen to have turned on the fact that this was evidence of recognition rather than that of identification. The former issue arose and was tackled in *Chimbo and others v The People*.[103] The appellants were convicted of murder. They were alleged to have taken the deceased and his wife from their home, severely beaten them up and left them in the bush, naked, tied up and gagged. The deceased was rendered unconscious and later died. The prosecution witnesses were the accused's wife, who identified the appellants as the culprits, and the driver of the truck which transported the appellants, a self-confessed accomplice. The appeal was against the admissibility of confessions of the first and second appellants and the identification of the third. As to the latter issue of identification by recognition, Ngulube DCJ, as he then was, who opined as follows:

> The learned trial judge was satisfied that in respect of the third appellant identification by PW2 had been by way of recognition and was, therefore, reliable. While recognition has been accepted to be more reliable than identification of a stranger, the trial judge should nevertheless remind himself that mistakes in recognition even of close relatives or friends are sometimes made, and hence the need to

[102] [2003] EWHC 3074 (Admin).

[103] [1982] ZR 20.

> exclude the possibility of an honest mistake. If PW2's opportunity for observation on the night in question was no better in relation to the third appellant than it was in relation to the co-appellants, it follows that, even if the case fell to be considered as one of recognition., it was the duty of the trial judge to warn himself of the need to exclude the possibility of an honest mistake. The learned trial judge did not so warn himself, and his failure to do so was a misdirection. There is a string of authorities to this effect, such as *Mushala & Others v The People*[104] *Mwasumbe v The People*,[105] and other cases therein referred to.

It has been shown in *R v Davies*[106] that an identification parade was not necessary in circumstances where such identification was predicated on clothing rather than facial features. Should the police dispense with a formal identification procedure such as an identification parade simply because there had been a prior identification by the witness in question? The question arose and was dealt with by the EWCA in *R v Brown.*[107] The Court took the view that once a suspect was in police custody they could not simply dispense with an identification procedure as they were mandated (by Code D) to arrange for one.

7.3.1.3 Suspect is known to witness but inaccessible

Where the case is that the suspect while known is inaccessible, arrangements may be made for still photo or video identification by the witness(es) concerned. Group identification covert operations (kept to a minimum) may all be employed as required in order to determine the witness's ability to identify the suspect as is the device of confrontation.[108]

7.3.1.4 Procedures relating to identification

As said above, the police have available to them, during the investigation stage, several procedures. The importance of strict adherence to these and other procedures *vis-à-vis* the need for fairness has been demonstrated in *The People v Swillah.*[109] The accused was charged on two counts of aggravated robbery arising out of the same transaction. The prosecution case was that the accused with two others assaulted three people and robbed them of ZMW212.00 The accused was identified as one of the robbers by three witnesses. The opportunity to observe the accused was good but the witnesses were terrified and the lighting was poor. It was held as follows: (i) The quality of the identification evidence was poor and it was therefore necessary to seek a connecting link or other supporting evidence to connect the accused with the robbery. In the course of his evidence on oath, the accused told a lie intending to disassociate

[104] [1978] ZR 58.

[105] [1978] ZR 354.

[106] [2004] EWCA Crim 252; *R v Hassan* [2004] EWCA Crim 1478.

[107] [1991] Crim LR 368; *R v Harris* [1992] RTR 270 *per* Potter LJ.

[108] Code D, paras 3.21-23.

[109] [1976] ZR 338 (HC).

himself from a group of charcoal burners who were suspect. (ii) There being no connecting link or supporting evidence, the accused must be acquitted. the following methods in so far as identification evidence is concerned:

(i) Video identification

As said elsewhere in this text, this jurisdiction, for reasons that go beyond availability of resources and competent staff, continues to favour the old and tried method of the identification parade. The video identification method has, however, gained traction in many jurisdictions given advances in technology. It is submitted that this is a route that must receive more attention in this jurisdiction.[110] The usual way to go about it is, as is done in England, for police to propose an identification procedure. Once this is done, a written notice complete with rights, privileges and procedure ought to be served on the suspect's counsel or the suspect himself as the case may be. The practicalities of what follows may be described thus: the officer(s) may select a video image, a still image and/or other computer-generated images plus images (still or motion type) of eight or so images of individuals with similar features to the suspect. These may together be placed on a flash drive or any storage device of similar capabilities. These images must be shown to the suspect and his advocate where one has been appointed before they can be shown to the witnesses. The point of showing these to the suspect or the suspect and his counsel prior to the video identification by the witnesses is for discovery purposes to enable for objections, where any are reasonably raised to be addressed in the spirit of fairness. It has however been held in *R v Middleton*[111] that the right to object is not unfettered. Be that as it may, and as has been shown in the rather curious events in *R v Marcus*,[112] it is imperative that the viewing procedure, images of the witness viewing the images ought to be recorded as should pivotal moments in the identification process such as the date on which the identification was done, whether the witness had seen any news coverage of the suspect and his image as well as service of first descriptions. The police officer had, in breach of Code D, arranged for video identification complete with masked faces on the basis that there were not enough images that resembled the suspect. It was, however, discovered that unbeknownst to the accused, the officer had also arranged another video identification for the witnesses, in what was adjudged to be a cynical way of trying to avoid the requirements of Code D, where those paraded where unmasked.

---

[110] Section 78(5)(b)(6)(a) of the Children's Code, Act No 12 of 2022 permits the receipt of evidence via video link or in lieu of livestream, pre-recorded testimony from a child. In any case, the fact that s 78(4)(d) requires that a child giving testimony 'not interact or be in the same room with a person the child is testifying against by necessary implication demands the use of video-conferencing.

[111] Unreported, March 11, 2005, CA.

[112] [2006] EWCA Crim 3387.

(ii) Identification parades

Identification parades appear to be the default mode of identification in this and many other jurisdictions.[113] While, as already said, and as we soon show several other modes have been developed and have been and continue to be used on their own or in consonance with identification parades, they have not ousted this mode of identification from its perch though reliance on it as a sole criterion for identifying a suspect has been decidedly weakened by more empirically reliable methods such as DNA. The principal use to which an identification parade should be put 'is to test the ability of an identifying witness to pick out a person he claims to have previously seen on a specified occasion.'[114] Other requirements to be met in so far as identification parade is concerned have been outlined in *Ilunga Kabala & John Masefu v The People.*[115] The appellants jointly and whilst acting together and being armed with a firearm were alleged to have robbed one Maganbhai Patel of various specified items of property, including cash, altogether valued at ZMW1,394.00. Whilst together, the appellants visited Twatasha bar less than twenty-four hours after the commission of the robbery at Maganbhai's residence. At the bar the first appellant carried a pistol which resembled that seen by Maganbhai, his wife and his servant. The appellants travelled to and from the bar by means of the Cortina with a black top. The appellant was driving the car which answered the description given by Maganbhai's servant of the get-away car used by two robbers immediately after leaving the scene of the crime. While an identification parade of suspects was held, no identification parade for the firearms was held which came up as a ground of appeal. During the said identification parade suspects of different heights and with visible injuries were placed among persons of comparable heights. The appellants had put up a defence of alibi which their counsel contended had not been disproved. Counsel also contended that the evidence of identification at the parade was of poor quality. It was held as follows:

- (i) To put suspects with visible injuries on their bodies on an identification parade consisting of other persons having no such injuries is tantamount to providing identifying witnesses with a clue.
- (ii) It is enough if suspects of different heights are placed among other persons of comparable heights and that the general standard of dress, let alone general appearance of participants at the parade is more or less similar. The test is always whether a given identification parade is capable of being described as fair to the accused. Emphasis ought to be placed on fairness and not necessarily on the number of parades conducted.

---

[113] See *Kamwandi v The People* [1972] ZR 131 (HC); *The People v Chimbala* (1973) ZR 118 (HC); *Toko v The People* [1975] ZR 196; *Bwalya v The People* [1975] ZR 227; *Mwansa Mushala and Others v The People* [1978] ZR 58 (SC); *The People v Swillah* [1976] ZR 338; *Yoani Manongo v The People* (SCZ Judgment No 26 of 1980); *Ilunga Kabala and John Masefu v The People* [1981] ZR 102 (SC); *Kenneth Mtonga and Victor Kaonga v The People* (SCZ Judgment No 5 of 2000); *Simon Mwansa v The People* (SCZ Appeal No 68 of 2004); *Winzy Sakala and Gerald Phiri v The People* (SCZ Judgment No 11 of 2009); *The People v Ronald Musonda and Others* (HW/08/2012).

[114] *Ilunga Kabala & John Masefu v The People* [1981] ZR 102 (SC).

[115] [1981] ZR 102 (SC).

(iii) The sole object of an identification parade is to test the ability of an identifying witness to pick out a person he claims to have previously seen on a specified occasion. To achieve that object, those charged with the duty of conducting identification parades must ensure that such parades are free from unfairness.
(iv) There is no rule of evidence or practice in Zambia which calls for the holding of a firearm's identification parade.
(v) While it is necessary for an identifying witness to positively pick out a person at a parade, a witness cannot be expected to say any more than that a firearm which he sees on a firearm's identification parade is similar to the one which he saw previously on a specified occasion.
(vi) In any criminal case where an alibi is alleged, the onus is on the prosecution to disprove the alibi. The prosecution takes a serious risk if they do not adduce evidence from witnesses who can discount the alibi unless the remainder of the evidence is itself sufficient to counteract it.
(vii) It is trite law that odd coincidences, if unexplained may be supporting evidence. An explanation which cannot reasonably be true is in this connection no explanation.

Even so, where a dispute arises as regards identification (inclusive of a scenario where the witness claims to be acquainted with the suspect and as such, to recognise instead of identifying the suspect[116]) and where it is practicable, an identification parade may be offered. Even though rare in the grand scheme of things, an identification parade may be the least good mode of identification in certain circumstances such as those where the suspect is endowed with rather unique features or else refuses to participate in the identification parade.

As best practice, the following ought to be noted:

(i) accused persons are to voluntarily participate (a fact they should be made aware of as well as their right to have counsel of their own choice) and as such ought not to be forced to participate[117] in identification parades though a refusal to participate may invite adverse comments from the court an identification.[118]
(ii) A dispassionate uniformed officer ordinarily above the rank of inspector should conduct the parade and not one closely involved with the case.

---

[116] As has been shown in *R v Conway* [1990] Crim L R 402; In *Mwansa Mushala and Others v The People* [1978] ZR 58 (SC) Bruce-Lyle, JS delivering the judgment of the court observed as follows: 'The guidelines in identification cases were laid down in R *v Turnbull* [1976] 3 All ER 549; the Court of Appeal in England stressed that although recognition may be more reliable than identification of a stranger, even when the witness is purporting to recognise someone whom he knows the trial judge should remind himself that mistakes in recognition of close relatives and friends are sometimes made. Even in recognition cases a trial judge should warn himself of the need to exclude the possibility of honest mistake, and the poorer the opportunity for observation the greater that possibility becomes. The momentary glance at the inmates of the Fiat car when the car was in motion cannot be described as good opportunity for observation;' See *Crate v the People* [1975] ZR 232 (SC); *Molley Zulu and Others v The People* (SCZ Judgment No 20 of 1978).

[117] It would appear that in terms of the decision in *US v Wade* (1967) 388 US 218.

[118] See *R v Robert William Smith* (1985) 81 Cr App R 286.

(iii) It is, for purposes of transparency, fairness and propriety necessary to record everything that happens during the identification parade, to ensure that the suspect sees and hears the witness do the identification (though in the event that the witness is behind a screen, the suspect's attorney ought to observe and hear everything said by the police and the witness).

Code D[119] in England & Wales requires that there be at least eight other individuals with similar features on the parade, and where there are two or more suspects, a minimum of twelve other individuals. No names are to be used and only numbered tags are to be used. Therefore, where a witness positively identifies the suspect what is recorded should not be the name of the suspect but rather the number tag. Fairness also requires that suspects choose where they want to stand and indeed, they ought to be allowed to change where they will stand. They are to be permitted to raise objections to the identification parade and such objections as are raised should be noted and as far as is practicable, fair and legal, attended to. The question of fairness of the identification parade is a serious one and one that the judge/magistrate has to pay particular attention to given the inherent weaknesses of identification evidence including wrong procedures employed by the police. An unfairly constituted and erroneously conducted identification parade may be grounds for nullification of said parade, and if same is not done by the trial court, a ground of appeal. In *Kenneth Mtonga and Victor Kaonga v The People,*[120] the first appellant was reported to have escaped from custody and a bench warrant was ordered to issue against him returnable whenever he will have been apprehended. This Judgment is confined to the appeal of the second appellant. The second appellant together with the escapee were tried and convicted on a charge of aggravated robbery. The particulars of the offence alleged that they jointly and whilst acting together and whilst armed with a gun did rob Mable Mandela of her motor vehicle and at the time used or threatened to use actual violence to the complainant. The second appellant and the escapee were each sentenced to undergo twenty-one years imprisonment with hard labour after the learned trial judge convicted them of the non-capital type of aggravated robbery. The second appellant appealed against the conviction and sentence. It was held as follows:

(i) The Police or anyone responsible for conducting an identification parade must do nothing that might directly or indirectly prevent the identification from being proper, fair and independent. Failure to observe this principle may, in a proper case, nullify the identification.

(ii) If, therefore, any irregularity committed in connection with the identification parade can be regarded as having any effect whatsoever on the identification, it would not be to nullify the identification given the ample opportunity available to the witnesses.

[119] Code D, Annex B, para 9.

[120] (SCZ Judgment No 5 of 2000).

(iii) If the identification is weakened then, of course, all it would need is something more, some connecting link in order to remove any possibility of a mistaken identity.

(iv) It is not always necessary that the doctrine of recent possession must be invoked especially where there is evidence of identification which if adequate on its own will be sufficient to sustain a conviction or which if requiring to be supported will then be supported by the possession of stolen goods.

Beyond the foregoing, other matters requiring attention by all involved, especially the police and the trial court, include issues relating to whether the witness, against the requirements of a witness recollecting events from his own memory, was reminded of his initial description of the accused or was shown photos or indeed any other description of the suspect before the identification parade was constituted. In addition to the foregoing courts ought to know whether the police asked the witness if they had had sight of the suspect, where photographs of a suspect have been released to the media prior to the identification parade. Having said that, any requests by the witness for certain types of clothes to be worn or certain gestures to be made by the those on the identification parade must generally be granted. The foregoing is important in that the witnesses' recollection may be triggered and an accurate positive identification made based on the clothes or particular gestures made on the material date. However, no requests in this regard should be acceded to if the intent is only for one of the suspects to make a certain gesture or dressed differently as this will be prejudicial to a particular suspect. To be sure, it is advisable that the witnesses look at the suspects at least twice for purposes of identification. As we have already noted, a failure to constitute and conduct a proper fair parade (even where there may be difficulties to so do[121]) may be grounds for its nullification and exclusion from evidence in order for it not to prejudice the accused or compromise the proceedings. Depending on the circumstances and facts, it may also bring into question the safety and propriety of the conviction itself making it amenable to being quashed on appeal. It is important for rules not to be whimsically changed, and for the rules set in *Turnbull*[122] as well as *Kenneth Mtonga and Victor Kaonga v The People,*[123] to be strictly followed. In *R v Graham,*[124] despite the fact that it was practicable to hold an identification parade, and the fact that the accused had agreed to attend one, none was held. The identification was thus made without the benefit of the identification of the parade. This fact was concealed from the jury (trier of fact). It was held on appeal that due to want of warning to the jury that the identification in question had been held without a parade, the appeal would be allowed. It is however important to remember that not all

[121] See *R v Gaynor* [1988] Crim LR 242; *R v Jamel* [1993] Crim LR 52 considered above: It's the suspect's appearance that should be of prime concern and only that which may raise issues of difficulty and not the challenge of finding volunteers for the parade.

[122] [1976] 3 All ER 549 at 552e *per* Lord Widgery CJ.

[123] (SCZ Judgment No 5 of 2000).

[124] [1994] Crim LR 212; *R v Conway* [1990] Crim LR 402.

defects in an identification warrant nullification of the identification parade itself or the proceedings or conviction therefrom. To warrant nullification, the alleged defects should be first be established and be such that the fairness of the process and therefore the trial itself into question, and making the conviction, if any, unsafe. In *R v Ebanks,*[125] the Privy Council noted that although the trial judge had been in error in suggesting to the jury that an identification parade where there was identification by recognition would have served no useful purpose, the fact was that a parade had been held and the judge had given ample directions on the need to ensure that it had been fairly conducted.

(iii) Group identifications

Group identifications are, in so far as the pecking order of modes of identification are concerned, below video identification and identification parades already discussed above. Group identifications may take place with the suspect in question consenting or, if needed, in covert fashion. In terms of process, this sought of identification entails a witness identifying a suspect while amongst an informal group of persons. As in identification parades, it is expected that for purposes of propriety, the officer charged with the responsibility of the constitution and arrangement of the parade is expected and required to inform the suspect(s) of the following:

(a) the purpose of the group identification;
(b) the exact mechanics of the identification exercise;
(c) the suspect(s)' rights;
(d) that a refusal to participate in the group identification or a substantial change in the appearance of the suspect(s) may be factors used against them by the prosecution and as such, included in evidence at trial;
(e) Whether the witness(es) have had occasion to see any video or photographs supplied by the police to the media. Presumably, this is because this fact may go to the weight of the witnesses' identification evidence making him prejudiced and not using his powers of recollection but rather replacing the deficiencies in his memory with the videos or photographs of the suspect he has seen on the news;
(f) It should be made clear that anything said or observed by the witness should be in the presence of the accused's counsel;
(g) That witnesses are free to point out anything they notice that they noted at the time of the incident in question; and
(h) That witnesses may be asked to take a closer look and to make a positive identification.

Quite apart from the foregoing, the following issues are important to consider and adhere to:

(a) The officer conducting the group identification must ensure that any initial description by any witness in question is recorded.

[125] [2006] UKPC 6.

(b) Officers in the company of the witness are proscribed from discussing the case or in any way indicating that another witness identified the suspect in a prior identification.
(c) It is desirable and recommended that the place for the group identification not be a police station unless there are good and compelling reasons for to so choose it.
(d) What is preferable is a public place such as a mall or market or bus/train station where other people pre-selected for the group identification can freely move around or be stationary, as the case may be, with the suspect joining the group or taking a position with flexibility.
(e) To be sure, the identification scene should, as in identification parades, be videotaped or/and photographed. This acts as a restraint on abuse of the system by the police while at the same time ensures that any questions of propriety can be determined by the court with this evidence presented by the prosecution to counter any allegations of improper conduct by the accused who seeks the nullification of the video identification.

Finally, it would appear that where the mode of identification chosen is one in which the suspect is unaware of its occurrence, and as such without his consent, no lawyer representing the suspect need be present nor do the requirements outlined above need to be adhered to.

(iv) Confrontation[126]

We must start by stating that in the options of modes available for identification, confrontation should only be resorted to when all other modes fail. If this be the case, it is expected that the police will provide the suspect if unrepresented or where he is, to the suspect and his counsel, with details as regards any first description offered by a witness to the police as well as any material such as photographs and videos released to the media. As to venue, it is expected that confrontation take place at a police station[127] where there is a screen is possibly available but with the caveat that it only be done where the suspect's counsel is present or video recording is available for obvious reasons.

(v) Dock identification

It has been shown in *R v Cartwright*[128] that it is unsatisfactory for a witness to first identify the accused in the dock. There are several reasons for this. The Devlin Committee[129] whose report we consider below noted that 'if [...] there is any sort of similarity between the man [the witness in question] saw and the man in the dock, he naturally tends to identify the man in the dock as the criminal.'

---

[126] See the procedures as outlined in Annex D to Code D.

[127] But not within the precincts of the court: *R v Joseph* [1994] Crim LR 48.

[128] (1914) 10 Cr App R 2119; *R v Eatough* [1989] Crim LR 289; *R v Horsham Justices Ex P Bukhari* (1982) 74 Cr App R 291.

[129] Devlin Committee Report, [2.24].

The first is that the admissibility of a witness's out of court statements relating to the identification of an accused person stating that he is the culprit in the dock lends itself to questions of hearsay. Additionally, dock identification will lack any probative value in circumstances where the identifying witness is in want of prior knowledge of the accused person. The preceding is because as has been said by Mason J in *Alexander v R*[130] 'circumstances conspire to compel the witness to identify the accused in the dock.'

For the foregoing reasons, identification solely limited to dock identification has been deemed to be patently unreliable and suspect and as such, insufficient to secure a conviction without more.[131] This is, however, a general rule amenable to several exceptions[132] some of which we discuss here and later in the text. The court has inherent power within its jurisdiction to exclude[133] dock identification or to disregard[134] it with a warning against attaching a lot of weight to the positive identification birthed by dock identification.[135] Thus, dock identification without any prior identification by the witness is generally inadmissible. The foregoing notwithstanding, and as shown in *R v Le*,[136] dock identification may be treated more positively where, in an effort to exclude the accused as the guilty party, defence counsel elicits answers relating to dock identification under cross-examination and same are given by the witness. In this, the propriety of the said dock identification evidence even in the absence of prior identification is enhanced. There is considerable Australian authority[137] to the effect that dock identification evidence must be carried out in every case depending on identification evidence even in circumstances where substantial reliance is placed evidence prior to the trial in which reliance on dock identification is sought. It has been observed[138] that '[t]here may be value in dock identification in a case involving multiple accused since it may assist the [judge/magistrate] in understanding which accused is alleged to have done what.'

As indicated earlier, however, there are several exceptions to the general rule as regards the inadmissibility of dock identification without any prior identification by the witness. Two English authorities demonstrate this. In *R v Lydiate*,[139] the co-accused gave oral testimony to the accused's presence at the scene of the crime. Sir Edwin Jowitt opined in part as follows:[140]

---

[130] (1981) 145 CLR 395 at 427; *Davies v R* (1937) 57 CLR 170 at 181-2.

[131] *Jamal v R* (2000) 182 ALR 307 at [44].

[132] *R v Saxon* [1998] 1 VR 503 at 513 (CA).

[133] *R v Hunter* [1969] Crim LR 262; *R v Howick* [1970] Crim LR 403; *R v John* [1973] Crim LR 113; *R v Haidley and Alford* [1984] VR 229 (FC) at 240-1; *R v Saxon* [1998] 1 VR 503 (Vic CA).

[134] *Cook v R* (1998) 126 NTR 17 at 24 (CCA).

[135] *R v Demeter* [1995] 2 Qd R 626 at 629 (CA); *Tido v R* [2012] 1 WLR 115 (PC) at [21]; *Nelly v R* [2012] 2 Cr App R 20 (PC) at [35]-[36].

[136] (2002) 130A Crim R 256 at [87].

[137] *R v Britten* (1988) 51 SASR 567 at 572; *Grbic v Pitkethly* (1992) 38 FCR 95 at 104 (Fed C of A FC); *R v Gorham* (1997) 68 SASR 505 at 508 (FC); *R v Murdock* (No 1) (2005) 195 FLR 362; aff'd *sub nom Murdock v R* (2007) 167 A Crim R 329 at [110].

[138] JD Heydon Cross on Evidence 1420; see also *R v Clark* (1996) 91 A Crim R 46 at 50 (SA CCA).

[139] [2004] EWCA Crim 245 at [34], [36] [39-40]; http://www.bailii.org/ew/cases/EWCA/Crim/2004/245.html.

[140] [2004] EWCA Crim 245 at [34], [36] [39-40]; http://www.bailii.org/ew/cases/EWCA/Crim/2004/245.html.

> Two things have to be said [....]
>
> Firstly, it was accepted in *Forbes* that if a case is one of pure recognition of someone well known to the eyewitness it may be futile to hold an identification parade. Secondly, it does not follow that a failure to hold an identification parade when one is required by Code D will automatically result in the exclusion of identification evidence under section 78. This point was made in *Forbes* in which, despite the failure to hold a parade, as required by the Code, the conviction was upheld.
>
> In our judgment that was sufficient evidence to establish a case of pure recognition of someone well known to Foster and we take the view that this was not a case, therefore, in which it was necessary to hold an identification parade. This would be sufficient to dispose of the challenge to the admission of Foster's evidence of identification. However, we recognise that in *Forbes* Lord Bingham does not say that in a case of pure recognition an identification parade need never be held. We therefore consider the challenge also on the basis that Foster's evidence about his knowledge of Lydiate did not go sufficiently far to make it appropriate for there to have been no parade.
>
> As we have said already, the fact that an identification parade was not held when there should have been one does not lead automatically to the exclusion of the evidence of identification. The fact that there was evidence of recognition based on a significant number of sightings over a substantial period is an important factor to be taken into account in deciding whether it is established, on the balance of probabilities, that the admission of the evidence had such an adverse effect on the fairness of the proceedings that it ought not to have been admitted.

Thus, where the question is one of recognition of a suspect well known to the witness, dock identification becomes redundant.

In *Holland v HM Advocate*[141] the accused appealed his convictions for robbery. He had been subject to a dock identification, and he complained that the prosecution had failed in its duties of disclosure. It was held as follows: The combination of several failings meant that the defendant had not received a fair trial, and the appeal was allowed. The practice of dock identification was intended often as a protection of the accused, but the court had to look at the particular case. The Convention did not lay down any general rule that certain forms of evidence were inadmissible, but guaranteed the right to a fair trial, and it was against that test that the particular situation had to be judged. It was suggested that a dock identification was in breach of the right against self-incrimination because the defendant's presence was obligatory, and by being present he was picked out for a witness. This was rejected by the Board. As to whether the trial was fair given the admission of such evidence: 'when the advocate depute invites the witness to identify the accused in such a case, the Crown are deliberately introducing an adminicle of evidence which certain

[141] (2005) HRLR 25.

other systems generally exclude – precisely because of the heightened risk that the identification will be mistaken. The issue in any given case is whether, by doing so, the Crown have rendered the accused's trial unfair in terms of article 6.' The court recognised that in Scotland the prosecution has always been reluctant to disclose the criminal records of prosecution witnesses. In this case the defence sought details of impending cases which would be much more difficult to provide. The Board's task was to see whether as a whole the defendant had a fair trial.

Finally, where dock identification falls into anyone of the exceptions discussed above, it will be admitted into evidence. Where this is the case, a witness will normally be asked to identify the accused at the earliest opportunity following the commission of the offence. Evidence emanating from the foregoing is then tendered by the identifying witness and any other persons that may have been witnesses to the prior identification. What ordinarily follows at trial is a leading question in the following terms: 'Do you see the person referred to in Court?' In this jurisdiction, the witness is then asked to point at and touch the accused person as the presiding judge/magistrate looks on and indicates in the record that the witness has identified the accused by touching him.[142]

(vi) Object identification

It has been said that in circumstances where the identification of objects is at the core of major issues in a case, a warning similar to that given in respect of human physiognomy ought to be given.[143] As has been said in *R v Lowe,*[144] '[w]hereas the possibility of mistake plays the greater part in relation to the identification of a person, the lack of distinctiveness will normally play the greater part in relation to the identification of an inanimate object.' The clarity of the acute problem faced in object identification, it would appear from the foregoing, lies in the lack of distinction between many objects which is as a result of a production of many objects which inexorably leads to a lack of distinctiveness common to human beings. Heydon[145] postulates that the warning hereinbefore described ought to bring to the trier of fact the following:

(a) the fallibility of memory;
(b) the risks related to convicting on the basis of identification evidence and the injustices which have occurred in the past from mistakes;
(c) the danger of contamination of memory by facts later discovered;
(d) the high importance of securing an early record of the uncontaminated recall of the witness to prevent later elaboration or distortion in the retelling of the event;

[142] As to the dangers of locating the accused elsewhere in the court rather than the dock, see JD Heydon *Cross on Evidence* 86.

[143] *R v Clout* (1995) 41 NSWLR 312 at 321 (CCA); see also *R v Marijancevic* (1993) 70 A Crim R 272 at 278 (Vic CA); *R v Lowe* (1997) 98 A Crim R 300.

[144] (1997) 98 A Crim R 300 at 317 (NSW CCA).

[145] Heydon JD, Cross on Evidence 90-91 para [1440].

(e) the specific danger that memory ay sometimes become enlarged (even quite innocently) to include matters which the observer expects, or is expected, to recall;
(f) the witness's familiarity or otherwise with the object.[146]

(vii) Voice identification[147]

It has been said that '[t]here can be no doubt that the admission of voice recognition evidence is controversial, perhaps highly controversial.'[148] A full Turnbull warning ought to be given where voice identification is in issue with necessary modifications.[149] A more challenging proposition than conventional identification, voice identification is in terms of reliability, to be preferred than the usual identification especially when those charged with the responsibility of said voice identification are experts who employ such technics as relate to acoustics, spectrographic and related auditory techniques with varying levels of sophistication.[150]

We now turn to the discussion of the matters hereunder under expert evidence on the one hand and lay persons on the other.

(a) Lay persons

For a layperson to accurately identify a voice is dependent on several factors being in place:[151] One will certainly be the quality of the voice. Another would relate to the passage of time since the voice for which identification is sought, was heard. Yet another factor would have to do with the individual witness with respect to their ability to identify a voice correctly, which issue or ability varies from person to person. Additionally, whether the witness is familiar with the voice as well as the nature and duration of the speech may all play a huge role. However, even where all these matters align enabling the witness to confidently identify the voice in question the witness may, as has been shown in *R v Flynn and St. John*[152] still turn out to have been mistaken.

> One study used telephone speech and involved fourteen people representing three generations of the same family being presented with speech recorded over both mobile and land line telephones. The results showed that some listeners produced mis-identifications, failing to identify family members or asserting some recordings

[146] *R v Theos* (1996) 89 A Crim R 486 at 495 (Vic CA); *R v Browning* (1991) 94 Cr App R 109 at 122-3.

[147] The admissibility of voice recognition evidence is treated differently in different jurisdictions: "Sounding Out Expert Voice Identification" by Professor David Ormerod CLR October 2002; *R v Robb* [1991] 93 Cr App R 161; *R v Clare and Peach* [1995] Cr App R 333; *R v O'Doherty* [2003] 1 Cr App R 5 (NI) and A-G's Reference [No 2 of 2002] [2003] 1 CAR 21.

[148] See *R v Flynn and St. John* [2008] 2 Cr App R 20, CA; *R v Roberts* [2000] Crim LR 183, CA.

[149] *R v Hersey* [1998] Crim LR 281, CA.

[150] See *R v Flynn and St. John* [2008] 2 Cr App R 20, CA. It follows that a more stringent warning ought to be given than that given in conventional identification: *R v Roberts* [2000] Crim LR 183, CA.

[151] *R v Flynn and St. John* [2008] 2 Cr App R 20, CA.

[152] [2008] 2 Cr App R

> did not represent any member of the family. The study used clear recordings of people speaking directly into the telephone.[153]

On 7 December 2006 at Reading Crown Court the appellants, Kris Flynn and Joe Phillip St John, were convicted of conspiracy to commit robbery. On 8 December 2006 each was sentenced to 13 years' imprisonment less the appropriate days spent on remand. There were two other co-accused. Mark Bannister pleaded guilty and was sentenced to 12 years' imprisonment. On 4 December the full court quashed his sentence and substituted for it a sentence of 10 years' imprisonment. Frank Sines was acquitted of conspiracy and discharged. The appellants appeal with leave of the full court. These appeals raised issues relating to identification by voice recognition. The evidence was as follows. On 29 April 2006 at about 7.50 am, Samia Taourit, an employee of Elonex Computers plc, arrived for work at the company premises situated at Cricklewood, London. The company acted as a distribution warehouse for IBM computers and stored on its premises expensive computer equipment. The premises had in the past been a target for criminal activity as a result of which a strong room had been placed on the premises as a security measure. It was held as follows:[154]

(i) Identification of a suspect by voice recognition was more difficult than visual identification;
(ii) Identification by voice recognition was likely to be more reliable when carried out by experts using acoustic and spectrographic techniques, as well as sophisticated auditory techniques, than by lay listener identification; and
(iii) The ability of a lay listener to identify voices correctly was subject to a number of variables.

In *R v Robb*[155] the court held that voice recognition evidence given by a phonetician was admissible as expert evidence; and that evidence of police officers who listened to disputed tapes and recognised the voice of the person speaking was admissible as factual evidence. Bingham LJ (as he then was), giving the judgment of the court, accepted that the phonetician was sufficiently qualified to give expert evidence on voice recognition. He said of the expert, Dr Baldwin:

> He was entitled to be regarded as a phonetician well qualified by academic training and practical experience to express an opinion on voice identification. We do not doubt that his judgment, based on close attention to voice quality, voice pitch and the pronunciation of vowels and consonants, would have a value significantly greater than that of

[153] *R v Flynn and St. John* [2008] 2 Cr App R 20, CA *per* Gage J at [16].

[154] Summary taken from Edwards A, https://www.lawgazette.co.uk/law/hearsay-bad-character-and-identification-evidence-/50214.article retrieved on 10/9/2021.

[155] 93 Cr App R 161, CA; The summary is taken from Gage J's speech at [18].

> the ordinary untutored laymen, as the judgment of a hand-writing expert is superior to that of the man in the street.[156]

The question of what ought to happen where police officers are said by the prosecution to have recognised the voice in question has arisen and been considered in *R v Chenia:*[157]

> The police officers were no doubt doing their best to deduce who was speaking when they named a particular speaker on the transcript. None of them was, however, an expert in voice identification. If the prosecution wished to rely upon the evidence of a particular police officer to identify the particular speaker, we are of the view that the basis of that evidence should have been spelled out in a statement so that the defence could see what it was. For example, in the case of the appellant, was the opinion of the particular officer based on recognition of his voice and, if so, how was it that he was sufficiently familiar with the voice to enable him to recognise it? If it was based on some other consideration, the statement should have identified that consideration so that the defence, and indeed the court, could form a view as to whether the evidence was admissible and, if admissible, whether it was reliable. It is not at all clear to us what was the basis for each officer's opinion as to who was speaking.

There are minimum safeguards to observed when the police officers are involved in voice identification. They are set out thus:

(i) the voice recognition routine ought to be undertaken by a disaffected police officer;
(ii) proper records ought to be taken and kept as regards times spent with the suspect, time spent taking the record, the date and time spent by the officer in question in compilation of a transcript of a covert recording including annotations made with regard to his views regarding the identity of the speaker; and
(iii) finally, no transcript bearing the annotations of any other officer is to be provided to any officer attempting voice recognition.

A judge/magistrate is well within his rights to listen to recordings in his efforts to identify who said what. It has, however, been suggested in *R v Flynn and St. John*,[158] that in so doing, a judge/magistrate should not lose sight of the evidence of the expert and non-expert voice recognition witnesses. The test to be applied by a trial judge/magistrate in determining whether to admit voice comparison must be the one as set in *R v Korgbara,*[159] is the quality and quantity of material of such a sufficient nature as to enable and rationalise a suitable comparative

[156] There is a caveat however, which is to the effect that '[...] in any case where police officer's evidence of recognition appears suspect or procured for ulterior motives, or in any case where unfair advantage has been taken of the [accused] to strengthen the case against him:' 93 Cr App R 161, CA *at 168.*

[157] [2003] 2 Cr App R 6; *R v Flynn and St. John* [2008] 2 Cr App R 20, CA.

[158] [2008] 2 Cr App R 20, CA.

[159] Unreported, March 30, 2007 ([2007] NSWCCA 84).

assessment to be made? If it is, then such a comparison should be made by a magistrate or trial judge, as the case may be. If not (even though in the majority of cases the approach in *R v Flynn and St. John*[160] will be appropriate), it would appear to be an exercise in futility and a pervasion of the course of justice for a judge/magistrate to venture into a voice recognition exercise where experts in the field and those who are familiar with the accused's voice are unable to make a proper assessment and draw any conclusions on the matter.[161]

(b) Expert evidence

In instances where an expert has made an identification or more importantly, where the court lacks the requisite knowledge because of its experience, expert evidence is admissible. Thus, on the facts of *R v Flynn and St John*,[162] the poor quality of the covert recording of the voices was such that the expert could not analyse the voices by reference to individual speakers, which was a prerequisite for making a speaker-identification. Recording by means of a telephone device further distorted the voice.[163] Specifically, the court held as follows:[164] (i) Identification of a suspect by voice recognition was more difficult than visual identification; (ii) Identification by voice recognition was likely to be more reliable when carried out by experts using acoustic and spectrographic techniques, as well as sophisticated auditory techniques, than by lay listener identification; and (iii) The ability of a lay listener to identify voices correctly was subject to a number of variables. The following factors were relevant:[165]

- The quality of the recording of the disputed voice or voices;
- The gap in time between the listener hearing the known voice and his attempt to recognise the disputed voice;
- The ability of the individual lay listener to identify voices in general – the ability of an individual to identify voices varied;
- The nature and duration of the speech sought to be identified – some voices were more distinctive than others and the longer the sample of speech the better the prospect of identification; and
- The greater the familiarity of the listener with the known voice the better his or her chance of accurately identifying a disputed voice – research showed that a confident recognition by a lay listener of a familiar voice might nevertheless be wrong.

---

[160] [2008] 2 Cr App R 20, CA.

[161] *R v Chenia* [2003] 2 Cr App R 6 has thus been overruled on this point; see *R v Flynn and St. John* [2008] 2 Cr App R 20, CA.

[162] As adapted at Edwards A, https://www.lawgazette.co.uk/law/hearsay-bad-character-and-identification-evidence-/50214.article retrieved on 30/4/2022.

[163] Edwards A, https://www.lawgazette.co.uk/law/hearsay-bad-character-and-identification-evidence-/50214 .article retrieved on 10/9/2021.

[164] As adapted at Edwards A, https://www.lawgazette.co.uk/law/hearsay-bad-character-and-identification-evidence-/50214.article retrieved on 30/4/2022.

[165] As adapted at Edwards A, https://www.lawgazette.co.uk/law/hearsay-bad-character-and-identification-evidence-/50214.article retrieved on 30/4/2022.

It was further shown in *R v Flynn and St John*,[166] that:

> The crucial difference between a lay listener and expert speech analysis was that the expert was able to draw up an overall profile of the individual's speech patterns. The lay listener's response was fundamentally opaque. The lay listener could not know or explain which aspects of the speaker's speech patterns he was responding to. He also had no way of assessing the significance of individual observed features relative to the overall speech profile (in contrast to a case of visual identification). The opaque nature of the lay listener's voice recognitions would also make it more difficult to challenge the accuracy of the evidence. In this context police officers were lay listeners.[167]

(viii) Fingerprints, palm-prints and footwear imprints

(a) Fingerprints

It has been held in *R v Castleton*[168] that a suspect may be identified by fingerprints without more. According to the decision in *R v Buckley*,[169] identification such as this is a matter solely in the province of fingerprint experts. The EWCA has accordingly pronounced itself thus:

> If there are fewer than eight similar ridge characteristics, it is highly unlikely that a judge will exercise his discretion to admit such evidence and, save in wholly exceptional circumstances, the prosecution should not seek to adduce such evidence. If there are eight or more similar ridge characteristics, a judge may or may not exercise his or her discretion in favour of admitting the evidence. How the discretion is exercised will depend on all the circumstances of the case, including in particular: (i) the experience and expertise of the witness; (ii) the number of similar ridge characteristics; (iii) whether there are dissimilar characteristics; (iv) the size of the print relied on, in that the same number of similar ridge characteristics may be more compelling in fragment of print than in an entire print; and (v) the quality and clarity of the print on the item relied on, which may involve, for example, consideration of possible injury to the person who left the print, as well as factors such as smearing or contamination. In every case where fingerprint evidence is admitted, it will generally be necessary, as in relation to all expert evidence, for the judge to warn the jury that it is evidence opinion [*sic*] only, that the expert's opinion is not conclusive and that it is for the jury to determine whether guilt is proved in the light of all the evidence.[170]

---

[166] Edwards A, https://www.lawgazette.co.uk/law/hearsay-bad-character-and-identification-evidence-/50214.article retrieved on 30/4/2022.

[167] As paraphrased in Edwards A, https://www.lawgazette.co.uk/law/hearsay-bad-character-and-identification-evidence-/50214.article retrieved on 10/9/2021.

[168] 3 Cr App R 74 CCA.

[169] 163 JP 561, CA.

[170] 163 JP 561, CA at 568.

The prosecution has a duty as regards fingerprint identification to show that the fingerprints in question, taken from the scene of the crime, match those on the relevant fingerprint form. It has also been shown in *Chappell v DPP*,[171] that no admission of guilt is to be inferenced from a failure to explain the presence of the accused's finger prints or indeed an inability to deny the fingerprints in question. There must be strict proof.[172]

(a) Palm prints and related matters

It is logically to be expected that standards observed in other forms of identification will apply to palm prints as well as other related forms of identification such as foot prints. There is authority to the effect that the question with respect to what amounts to a palm is a question of fact and degree. Additionally, there is also authority with respect to identification via ear prints. The said authorities appear to suggest a distinction in treatment of *minutiae* such as anatomical features which may include creases, nodules or notches relating to the ear structure on the one hand, and what may be termed gross features such as core cartilaginous folds. The former, have been said to be capable of identifying the person who left the marks in question on a surface. There is doubt as regards the latter, however, as the reliability of evidence in this regard based on the fact that the ear is flexible and that uncertainties will ordinarily surround that pressure that may have applied at the material time of making the mark in question.

(b) Footwear imprints

The leading case as regards footwear imprints is *R v T (Foot wear mark evidence)*.[173] It was held:

(i) in the area footwear mark evidence, there is not a sufficiently reliable statistical basis for an expert to be able to express an evaluative opinion based on the use Of a mathematical formula to arrive at a likelihood ratio (the measure of how likely it is to Obtain a piece of evidence given a proposition compared how likely it is to obtain the same piece of evidence given an alternative proposition);

(ii) the fact that there is no reliable statistical basis does not mean a court cannot admit an evaluative opinion. where there is some other sufficiently reliable basis for its admission; an expert examiner can, in appropriate cases, use his experience to express a more definitive opinion where the conclusion is the mark "could have been made" by the footwear in question, but no likelihood ratios or other mathematical formulae should be used in reaching that judgment; it is essential, if the expert does express a view which goes beyond

[171] 89 Cr App R 82, DC.

[172] But see *R v Smith (Peter)* [2011] 2 Cr App R 6 , CA.

[173] [2011] 1 Cr App R 9, CA.

saying that the footwear could or could not have made the mark, that he makes clear that this is a view which is subjective and based on experience; the word "scientific" should not be used, as it is likely to give an impression of a degree of precision and objectivity that is not present given the current state of this area of expertise; and

(iii) besides being clear and logical, it is also essential that an expert report is transparent; where a mark could have been made by a particular piece of footwear, the factors that enable the expert to express a more definite opinion must be set out, including any data on which reliance is placed; that the use of formulae and statistics might confuse the jury is no justification for not doing so; strict compliance the obligations of transparency should ensure that in each case where a scientific expert seeks to develop a new way of arriving at an opinion, that new way can be examined in open court applying the ordinary principles for the admissibility of expert evidence; but courts cannot apply these principles if they are not made aware of the way in which an expert has reached his opinion.[174]

(ix) Blood, body samples, secretions, scent and odontology[175]

(a) Blood

Blood grouping and the detection and identification of the constituents or characteristics of a blood sample can indicate the degree of probability that the sample emanated from a Proportion of the population which includes or excludes a suspect. The value of any such evidence is according to the circumstances of each case, but it is submitted that evidence of mere probability alone is insufficient to justify a conviction.[176]

(b) DNA[177]

A DNA profile is not unique, it expresses probabilities. (A) Is it a fallacy to confuse the match probability with the DNA profile from the crime sample given that the suspect is innocent? (B) what is the probability that an individual is innocent, if he matches the DNA profile from the crime sample? The "prosecutor's fallacy" consisted of giving the answer to the first question as the answer to the second.[178] In the absence of special features, expert evidence

---

[174] (Considering R *v Doheny; R v Adams and R v Adams (No 2) (post, 14—58)).

[175] "The requirements for taking body samples and impressions, including dental impressions, set out in Code D, para. D:6 (Appendix A-135 et seq.), and the PACE Act 1984, ss.62 and 63.P(Id' 15—181 *et seq*": *Archbold* 2012 at 1552 para 14—56; the entire analysis hereunder including authorities cited and/or quoted is excerpted from Archbold 2012 1552 to 1554 with minor changes for stylistic and structural needs only.

[176] See the observations of Lord Reid in *S v Mcc; VV v AC* 24 at 41E—42B, HL (blood tests in a paternity suit); at 14—57.

[177] For a useful summary of DNA profiling, analysis and low template DNA, see Re *Reed; R v Garmson* [2010] 1 Cr App R 23, CA.

[178] *R v Deen, The Times,* January 10, 1994, CA; and see *R v Gordon* [1995] I Cr App R 290, CA.

should not be admitted to induce juries to attach mathematical values to probabilities arising from non-scientific evidence (i.e., Bayes's theorem) to support or counter DNA evidence or other evidence.[179]

The cogency of DNA evidence makes it particularly important that: (a) DNA testing is rigorously conducted to obviate the risk of laboratory error; (b) the method of DNA analysis and the basis of subsequent statistical calculation should, as far as possible, be transparent to the defence; and (c) the true import of the resultant conclusion is accurately and fairly explained to the jury. To achieve these ends, the following procedural guidelines were laid down:[180]

First, the scientist should adduce the evidence of DNA comparisons together with calculations of the random occurrence ratio. Secondly, the crown should serve on the defence sufficient details of how the calculations were carried out so as to allow the basis of those calculations to be scrutinised. Thirdly, on request, the forensic science service should make available to a defence expert the databases upon which the calculations were based.

When the scientist testifies, it is important that he should not overstep the line that separates his province from that of the jury/court. He should explain the nature of the match between the DNA in the crime stain and the defendant's DNA. He should, on the basis of empirical statistical data, give the jury the random occurrence ratio, the frequency with which the matching DNA characteristics were likely to be found in the population at large. If the necessary data are available, it might be appropriate to state how many people with those matching characteristics were likely to be found within Zambia, or perhaps a more limited sub-group. That would often be the limit of the evidence which could properly be adduced. A scientist should not be asked his opinion on the likelihood that it was the accused who left the crime stain, nor when giving evidence should he use terminology which might lead a jury to believe that he was expressing an opinion.

In summing up, the judge should explain the relevance of the random occurrence ratio; and he should draw attention to the extraneous circumstances that gave its significance; and to any extraneous evidence in conflict with the suggestion that the defendant was responsible for the crime stain.[181]

In *R v Bates*,[182] it was held that partial profile DNA evidence may plainly be relevant in the sense of being probative of a matter in issue between the prosecution and the defence; that there is no reason in principle why such evidence should automatically be excluded on the basis analysis of a fuller profile might have exculpated the accused altogether; but that there may be cases where the probability of a match between the crime scene sample and any given person was so great that the judge would consider the probative value of the DNA evidence to be minimal and that it should, therefore, be

[179] *R v Adams (No 2)* [1998] 1 Cr App R 377, CA.

[180] *R v Doheny; R v Adams* [1997] I Cr App R 369, CA.

[181] For recent confirmation of these principles, see *Pringle v R*, unreported, January 27, 2003, PC ([2003] UKPC 17).

[182] [2006] 9 Archbold News 2, CA.

excluded in the exercise of his discretion. Where such evidence is admitted, however, the court said, the jury should be given sufficient information to enable them to evaluate it properly. As was observed in *R v Doheny, R v Adams, ante,* the significance of DNA evidence depends to a large extent upon other evidence in the case; by itself, particularly if based on a partial profile, it may not take the matter far, but, in conjunction with other evidence, it may be of considerable significance.

In *R v Reed* and *Reed; R v Garmson, ante,* the Court of Appeal observed, *obiter,* that low template DNA can be used to obtain profiles capable of reliable interpretation where the quantity of DNA is above the threshold of randomness (i.e., currently somewhere between 100 and 200 programmes of material). Accordingly, challenges to the validity of low template DNA analysis using the low copy number process should not be permitted as regards samples above that threshold in the absence of new scientific evidence properly placed before the court at a pre-trial healing for detailed consideration by the judge. As to the transferability of DNA from unidentified biological material, whilst scientific knowledge on the subject is incomplete, the underlying science is sufficiently reliable, where the profile is derived from a quantity is above 200 programmes, for a forensic science officer with scenes of Crime experience properly to use knowledge of the scene of the crime and the other agreed circumstances (including the quality of profile) to set out the possible explanations for the presence of DNA at a particular location, and to evaluate possibilities. In such cases, it emphasised, care would need to be taken to avoid such evaluation being tainted the verisimilitude of scientific certainty, but such care had been a clear distinction was drawn between the (challenged) evidence as to the evaluation of those possibilities and the (unchallenged) in relation to DNA match probabilities.

R v Reed and *Reed; R v Garmson* was considered in *R v C.*[183] The court held that the earlier decision had not purported to lay down a rule about the need for a set minimum quantity of material for DNA evidence could be based on it to be admissible. the low It was said that the sole question was whether a reliable profile could be produced despite the low quantity, although the quantity would necessarily affect the consideration that had to be given to the stochastic effects (i.e., the possibility that the results have been produced by chance). One indicator of quality was reproducibility [....]

DNA evidence taken from a crime scene that does not match the accused is powerful evidence which the jury should be invited to consider carefully and weigh in the scales against the prosecution evidence of identification. To raise against a defendant, theoretical or speculative possibilities, that the sample had been contaminated, and to use such speculation to neutralise the significance of the non-matching profile was wrong. Judges should consider with great care the way in which they present scientific evidence to the jury.[184] In our non-jury system, this careful consideration of scientific evidence ought to be part and parcel of the court's final judgment.

[183] [2011] 3 All ER 509.

[184] *R v Mitchell,* The Times, July 8, 2004, CA.

(c) Tracker dogs and scent

Evidence that speaks to the fact that the dog picked up a scent after being taken to the scene of the crime picked up a scent and led investigation officers to the accused has been held to be admissible.[185] Where this scenario arises, it is open for the court to permit enquiry into, among others things, the training of the dog, its skills and habits as well as those of the handler. The court will take judicial notice of the fact that each human being possesses a particular scent which is liable to be picked up by a well-trained dog. There must also be evidence to show that the dog has, over a period of time, shown that it is a reliable pointer to the existence of a particular scent from a certain individual. Be that as it may, the court ought to warn itself that accepting such evidence should be done with a bit of caution as dogs may not always be reliable, and that crucially, they cannot be cross-examined. Evidence as to what the dog was thinking at the material time is inadmissible.[186] The use of tracker dogs and scent came up in *R v Pieterson and Holloway*.[187] The defendants appealed against their convictions for robbery. A dog had been used to follow scents from the scene, picking up items taken in the raid. The defendants objected to admission of evidence of the dog's activities and reliability. It was held that the appeal failed. Evidence discovered after a trace by a dog might be allowed in, subject to stringent conditions, and evidence as to the dog's training. Though the supporting evidence here had not met that standard, the deficiency was peripheral. The item found was found within a short distance from the scene of the crime, and had been identified by the victim. 'In our judgment, if a dog handler can establish that a dog has been properly trained and that over a period of time the dog's reactions indicate that it is a reliable pointer to the existence of a scent from a particular individual, then that evidence should properly be admitted. However, it is important to emphasise two safeguards. First, the proper foundation must be laid by detailed evidence establishing the reliability of the dog in question. Secondly, the learned judge must, in giving his directions to the jury, alert them to the care that they need to take and to look with circumspection at the evidence of tracker dogs, having regard to the fact that the dog may not always be reliable and cannot be cross-examined.'

Ultimately, the judge/magistrates ought to be in a position, by his training, and discretion placed upon him/her by rules of court and evidence, to draw his/her own conclusion based on the overall characteristics of the breed of dogs in general and the dog in question in particular based on scientific study of the breed in question.[188] As noted earlier, however, specific evidence relating to the training, behaviour and abilities of the dog in this specific respect over a period of time, that is, that it has been able to almost consistently pick up scents relating to specific humans in similar circumstances.

---

[185] See *Patterson v Nixon* 1960 SC (J) 42; *R v Lindsay* [1970] NZLR 1002 (CA); *R v McCartney* [1976] 1 NZLR 472 (CA).

[186] *R v TeWhiu & Buckton* [1964] NZLR 784.

[187] [1995] 2 Cr App R I l, CA; As summarised at https://swarb.co.uk/regina-v-pieterson-regina-v-h-cacd-8-nov-1994/ retrieved on 18/04/22; See *R v Sykes* [1997] Cm LR 752, CA.

[188] *R v Pfenning (No 1)* (1992) 57 SASR 507 at 512-513.

(x) Physical marks, features and wounds

As a general principle,[189] police are permitted within certain bounds, to search and examine persons for relevant physical marks, features and wounds. Reasonable force may be employed in the case of those that do not volunteer to be examined. It is also possible to do this kind of identification without the suspect's knowledge. Guidance from general provision relating to arrest under ss 22 and 24 of the Criminal Procedure Code,[190] may be useful. In terms of s 22:

> Whenever a person is arrested-
> (a) by a police officer under a warrant which does not provide for the taking of bail or under a warrant which provides for the taking of bail and the person arrested cannot furnish bail; or
> (b) without warrant, or by a private person under a warrant, and the person arrested cannot legally be admitted to bail or is unable to furnish bail;
> the police officer making the arrest or, when the arrest is made by a private person, the police officer to whom he makes over the person arrested may search such person and place in safe custody all articles, other than necessary wearing apparel, found upon him.

According to s 24, '[w]henever it is necessary to cause a woman to be searched, the search shall be made by another woman with strict regard to decency.'

(xi) Handwriting

Proof of handwriting may occur in several ways which may include but are not limited to the following: (i) admission by the author; and (ii) by any person who may have seen the author write or sign the document subject of identification evidence.[191]

(a) Person with knowledge of handwriting

It has been shown in *Eagleton v Kingston*[192] that proof may be done by means of any witness willing to swear at trial that they believe the handwriting to be that of the party in question. It may also be proved, as has been shown in *R v O'Brien*,[193] that the witness has on a regular basis[194] corresponded with the party

[189] Compare s 54A of *PACE* Act 1984.

[190] Chapter 88 of the Laws of Zambia.

[191] The observation of the act of writing must have been made on several occasions and not just a single occasion: *William v Worall* (1838) 8 C. & P. 380; *Warren v Anderson* (1839) 8 Scott 384 nor will observation of the writing of one's surname only be deemed sufficient for this purpose: *Lewis v Sapio* (1827) M. & M. 39.

[192] (1803) 8 Ves. 438 at 475, *per* Eldon LC.

[193] 7 Cr App R 29 CCA.

[194] This entails acquaintance with handwriting based on regular correspondence, documentation in business transactions availed to the witness, hand written responses by the party whose writing is in question: *Harrington v Fry* (1824) Ry & M 90; *Doe v Suckermore* (1837) 5 A & E 703; *Fitzwalter Peerage Claim* (1843) 10 Cl & F 193; *Carey v Pitt* (1797) Peake Add.Cas 130.

whose handwriting is in question for him to say that the handwriting is similar to that of the party is insufficient for purposes of proof.[195] It is also the case that a witness who has acted on correspondence relating to the handwriting of the party in question may, the fact that he may not have been party to the correspondence notwithstanding, be permitted to identify the handwriting of said correspondence.[196] It is has also been deemed to be a logical conclusion to hold that responses to correspondence sent to a party directly must be taken to have been written by him.[197]

(b) Proof by means of comparison or/and by means of expert evidence

The starting point for this part of our discussion is s 8 of the Criminal Procedure Code 1865. It provides as follows as regards comparison of disputed writing:

> Comparison of a disputed writing with any writing proved to the satisfaction of the judge to be genuine shall be permitted to be made by witnesses; and such writings, and the evidence of witnesses respecting the same, may be submitted to the court and jury as evidence of the genuineness or otherwise of the writing in dispute.

The section mandates the trier of fact with determination of the question of whether the piece of writing in question required for comparison is unaffected. The standard of proof is that in criminal matters, that is, beyond reasonable doubt.[198] As we have said repeatedly in this text, Zambia has no jury system. Therefore, whatever is done by the jury in jury systems such as those that exist in the United Kingdom (in so far as they remain relevant), Australia and the United States, is to be understood as falling under the jurisdiction of a judge/ magistrate at trial, in so far as our system is concerned. The authorities we will encounter, where same are deemed persuasive to our courts, should thus be seen in this light. The magistrate/judge determines the competency of the witness as regards expert evidence pertaining to handwriting. The magistrate/ judge also determines authorship where a dispute arises in this regard with specific reference to forgeries, alterations, erasures etc. It behooves the prosecution to bring to court an expert where a dispute regarding handwriting is anticipated.[199] Further, '[i]t is permissible for an expert to compare genuine and admitted writings with a photocopy[200] of the disputed writing where the latter has been lost and give and opinion as to the authorship of the lost original.'[201] Where a handwriting expert is permitted to give evidence, he is

195 *Drew v Prior* (1843) 5 M & Gr 264.

196 *R v Slaney* (1832) 5 C & P 213.

197 *Carey v Pitt* (1797) Peake Add.Cas 130.

198 *R v Ewing* [1983] QB 1039, 77 Cr App R 47 CA.

199 *R v Tilley and Tilley* 45 Cr App R 360, CCA.

200 Which it must be noted is unable to provide certain qualities unique to the original such as tracings, pressure marks, pen lifts or overwritten words.

201 *Lockheed Arabia v Owen* [1993] QB 806, CA.

required to give good and compelling reasons to the court for the conclusions drawn. Recall that in an adversarial system such as ours, both parties will bring before court their own experts who ordinarily will draw opposite conclusions. It is for the court to determine where the truth lies and to discard evidence of an expert if needs be. Authorities such as *R v Tilley and Tilley*[202] demonstrate the position that a judge should warn himself in very clear terms not to draw a conclusion as regards disputed handwritings and genuine one without the aid of an expert.[203] He cannot thus purport to be an expert when in fact not, by comparing examples of signatures.[204] It is expected that both genuine and disputed handwritings availed to an expert will be made available to both sides on the premise that no objection can be sustained as regards privilege when what is in question are documents availed to an expert for purposes of its case only.

(xii) Evidence of similar facts

See chapter 8 below on evidence of similar facts.

(xiii) Evidence relating to patterns of criminal behaviour

Evidence relating to a pattern of criminal behaviour may tend to, when admitted, support the accuracy of the identification of the accused as the robber. In *R v Wilson*[205] the issue that fell to be determined at trial related to seven counts of robbery committed over four days was that of identity. Evidence to the effect that no crimes similar to those for which the accused, now detained, had been arrested and charged with had been committed for a month following the accused's arrest was deemed relevant, and probative enough as to be admissible.

(xiv) Identification *vis-à-vis* judicial notice of legal proceedings

It has been shown in at least two authorities[206] that a magistrate or a judge as the case may be may take judicial notice of the standard processes prior to trial such as arrest, charge and bail so far as his jurisdiction in the foregoing matters permits.

(xv) Custody, control and power of implicating articles

Whether the custody control and power of implicating articles may be used for purposes of identification, may be determined by considering whether said articles have been used in connection with the offence the accused is charged with. The question is one for the magistrate/judge to determine by

---

[202] 45 Cr App R 360, CCA; R v O'Sullivan, 53 Cr App R 274 CA.

[203] *R v Tilley and Tilley* 45 Cr App R 360, CCA.

[204] *R v Tilley and Tilley* 45 Cr App R 360, CCA; *R v Smith* 3 Cr App R 87; *R v Richard* 13 Cr App R 140.

[205] [2009] Crim LR 193, CA.

[206] *Allan v Ireland,* 79 Cr App R 206 DC; see also *Creed v Scott* [1976] RTR 485, DC.

employing common law reasoning. Where this is the case, the evidence of the items concerned may be adduced as evidence tending to show that the accused is the person who committed the offence in question. Where, however, the article is in no way connected with the offence in question, it logically must be considered and only admitted as evidence of bad character. It can thus be concluded that evidence as regards identification predicated on the custody, control and power of implicating articles is ordinarily admissible based on the following two reasons: (i) that it goes to prove either that the accused is the offender, and (ii) to the extent that it is seen as evidence of transference in no small part because of the thesis that every criminal leaves a trace of his presence at the scene of the crime, and at the same time, 'takes with him some detritus trace of his presence at the scene of the crime,'[207] it proves the identity of the accused as the reprobate.

7.3.2 *Safeguards at the point of trial*

By safeguards at the point of trial is meant the conditions prior to identification evidence being deemed admissible by the court. Our first port of call is the Devlin Report.

7.3.2.1 General – The Devlin report

The Report of the Committee under the chairmanship of Lord Devlin led to drastic changes in the way courts deal with the matter of visual identification in criminal cases. Among other recommendations, the Committee recommended that no convictions should be made based solely or substantially on identification evidence. It was suggested that there be supporting evidence from an independent source linking the accused to the offence with which he was charged. In addition, it was recommended that a warning to the effect that conviction predicated solely or substantially on identification evidence was dangerous. That an effort must be made in looking for independent evidence supportive of a conviction. However, where the identification evidence was so cogent as to support a conviction, the lack of additional independent evidence was not a bar to a conviction. Finally, the Devlin Committee took the view that there be legislation with respect to the foregoing, specifically that there ought to be a special warning statutorily provided for stating that identification in and of itself provided insufficient predication for probable cause for conviction. To be a basis for conviction, the Committee suggested, there ought to be present what it termed 'special circumstances.' These may include but are not limited to familiarity or the failure by the accused to put up a convincing defence against the prosecution's case and evidence even when such evidence consisted solely or substantially of identification evidence.

[207] Archbold 2012 1556 para 14-67.

7.3.2.2 *The decision in R v Turnbull*[208]

What followed the Devlin Report was not legislation as suggested, but the decision of the EWCA in *R v Turnbull*[209] which while rejecting the suggestion that convictions should not be based on identification alone, opined that what was of greater importance was the quality of the identification. The defendants appealed against their convictions which had been based upon evidence of visual identification. It was held that identification evidence can be unreliable, and courts must take steps to reduce injustice. The judge should warn the jury of the special need for caution before convicting the accused in reliance upon the correctness of identification. No special form of words need be used. The court should examine closely the circumstances of the identification. It also has to apply its mind to speak to any relevant item(s) supportive of the identification evidence even though as has been shown in certain decisions, that supporting evidence may itself be identification evidence requiring support of its own.[210] Recognition may be more reliable than identification of a stranger, but mistakes can still be made. Lord Widgery discussed the direction about *alibi* evidence as follows:

> Care should be taken by the judge when directing the jury about the support for an identification which may be derived from the fact that they have rejected an alibi. False alibis may be put forward for many reasons: an accused, for example, who has only his own truthful evidence to rely on may stupidly fabricate an alibi and get lying witnesses to support it out of fear that his own evidence will not be enough. Further, alibi witnesses can make genuine mistakes about dates and occasions like any other witnesses can. It is only when the jury is satisfied that the sole reason for the fabrication was to deceive them and there is no other explanation for its being put forward, that fabrication can provide any support for identification evidence. The jury should be reminded that proving the accused has told lies about where he was at the material time does not by itself prove that he was where the identifying witness says he was.

Lord Widgery continued as follows:

> In our judgment the dangers of miscarriage of justice occurring can be much reduced if trial judges sum up to juries in the way indicated in this judgment. First, whenever the case against an accused depends wholly or substantially on the correctness of one or more identifications of the accused which the defence alleges to be mistaken, the Judge should warn the jury of the special need for caution before convicting the accused in reliance on the correctness of the identification or identifications. In addition, he should instruct

[208] [1976] 3 All ER 549 at 552e *per* Lord Widgery CJ.

[209] [1976] 3 All ER 549 at 552e *per* Lord Widgery CJ.

[210] *Weeder v R* (1980) 71 Cr App R 228; *R v Shelton* [1981] Crim LR 76 (CA); *R v Breslin* (1984) 80 Cr App R 226.

them as to the reason for the need for such a warning and should make some reference to the possibility that a mistaken witness can be a convincing one and that a number of such witnesses can all be mistaken. Provided this is done in clear terms the Judge need not use any particular form of words. Secondly, the judge should direct the jury to examine closely the circumstances in which the identification by each witness came to be made. How long did the witness have the accused under observation? At what distance? In what light? Was the observation impeded in any way, as for example by passing traffic or a press of people? Had the witness ever seen the accused before? How often? If only occasionally, had he any special reason for remembering the accused? How long elapsed between the original observation and the subsequent identification to the police? Was there any material discrepancy between the description of the accused given to the police by the witness when first seen by them and his actual appearance? If in any case, whether it is being dealt with summarily or on indictment, the prosecution have reason to believe that there is such a material discrepancy they should supply the accused or his legal advisers with particulars of the description the police were first given. In all cases if the accused asks to be given particulars of such descriptions, the prosecution should supply them. Finally, he should remind the jury of any specific weaknesses which had appeared in the identification evidence. Recognition may be more reliable than identification of a stranger; but, even when the witness is purporting to recognise someone whom he knows, the jury should be reminded that mistakes in recognition of close relatives and friends are sometimes made.

Recognition may be more reliable than identification of a stranger; but even when the witness is purporting to recognise someone whom he knows, the jury should be reminded that mistakes in recognition of close relatives and friends are sometimes made. All these matters go to the quality of the identification evidence. If the quality is good and remains good at the close of the accused's case, the danger of a mistaken identification is lessened, but the poorer the quality, the greater the danger [...] When, in the judgment of the trial judge, the quality of the identifying evidence is poor, as for example when it depends solely on a fleeting glance or on a longer observation made in difficult conditions, the situation is very different. The judge should then withdraw the case from the jury and direct an acquittal unless there is other evidence which goes to support the correctness of the identification. This may be corroboration in the sense lawyers use that word; but it need not be so if its effect is to make the jury sure that there has been no mistaken identification: for example, X sees the accused snatch a woman's handbag; he gets only a fleeting glance of the thief's face as he runs off but he does see him entering a nearby house. Later he picks out the accused on an identity parade. If there was no more evidence than this, the poor quality of the identification would require the judge to withdraw the case from the jury; but this would not be so if there was evidence that the house into which the accused was alleged by X to have run was his father's [....] In our judgment odd

> coincidences can, if unexplained, be supporting evidence. The trial judge should identify to the jury the evidence which he adjudges is capable of supporting the evidence of identification. If there is any evidence or circumstances which the jury might think was supporting when it did not have this quality, the judge should say so.

One patent consequence of the *Turnbull*[211] decision or *Turnbull*[212] direction as it has been referred to, was that it weakened the need for corroboration in order to convict an accused person. Despite the fact that the hazards of convicting solely or substantially on identification were acknowledged, *Turnbull*[213] took the view that the court was to be allowed to assess the quality of the identification evidence bearing in mind the inherent dangers of doing so. It follows from our perspective that the court ought to seriously consider in detail the circumstances surrounding identification evidence before it can convict based on the court's experience, as discussed above, of the special need for caution[214] to prevent miscarriage of justice.[215] Thus, by circumstances surrounding the identification to be considered is meant the need for a clear appreciation of the strengths and weaknesses of the identification evidence, as well as any aspects of the identification evidence that are open to scrutiny and are likely to weaken or dent it.[216] Even so, it has been shown in *R v I*[217]that the import of being alive to weaknesses in identification evidence does not lie in their identification but rather explaining why the said witnesses are such. As Widgery J saw it, not convicting a suspect in a kidnapping offence would be an 'affront to justice' simply because the evidence of the victim, typically the sole witness to the kidnapping was not corroborated. Lord Ibrahim JA has, in *Fuller v State*,[218] opined as follows:

> We are concerned about the repeated failures of trial judges to instruct juries properly on the Turnbull principles when they deal with the issue of identification. Great care should be taken in identifying [...] all the relevant criteria. Each factor or question should be separately identified and when a factor is identified all the evidence in relation thereto should be drawn to the [court's] attention to enable them not only to understand the evidence properly but also to make a true and proper determination of the issues in question. This must be done before the trial judge goes on to deal with another factor. It is not sufficient merely to read to them the factors set out in Turnbull's case and at a later time to read [...] the evidence of the witnesses [...] What [...] the judge [is required to do is to identify, apply and assess] the

---

[211] [1976] 3 All ER 549.

[212] [1976] 3 All ER 549.

[213] [1976] 3 All ER 549.

[214] *Farquharson v R* (1993) 98 Cr App R (PC); *R v Ley* [2007] Crim LR 642 (CA).

[215] *R v Nash* [2004] EWCA Crim 2696, para 8 *per* Hedley J.

[216] *R v Stanton* [2004] EWCA Crim 490.

[217] [2007] 2 Cr App R 316.

[218] [1995] 52 WIR 424 at 433: Court of Appeal of Trinidad and Tobago.

> evidence in relation to each direction of law [...] and also in relation to the issues that arise for [the judge's] determination.

Several decisions[219] by the EWCA show that a failure to abide by the foregoing directions may be a basis for quashing a conviction on appeal for being unsafe. It is not too much of a stretch to think that our courts would act accordingly on similar facts and circumstances.

7.3.2.3 The ramifications of the decision in R v Turnbull[220]

(i) England & Wales

The implications of the *Turnbull*[221] decision have been far reaching. As already noted above, the failure by English trial courts to observe the direction is grounds for quashing a decision. Even so, it is important to be mindful of a few things:[222] '[...] the *Turnbull*[223] direction is necessary when the witness makes a visual identification of the facial features of a particular person-it is not required for the identification of a car number plate.[224] Nor [...] clothes worn.'[225] It follows from the foregoing that there is no need for a *Turnbull*[226] direction where the identification is non-visual. Visual identification mandates the court to employ the full breadth of the Turnbull direction such as in instances where the issue is recognition rather than identification strictly so defined. Thus, where a police officer gave oral; testimony to the effect that he had known the accused for more than twenty years, it was held that a full *Turnbull*[227] direction was still required[228] as it is even in the face of significant other evidence.[229]

There have been questions as to whether instances in which the issue is concerned with not the accused being present at the scene of the crime but rather whether it is the accused or another person committed the offence ought to be deemed *Turnbull cases*. The issues have arisen in two leading cases. In *R v Oakwell*,[230] the appellant, together with some other young men, was seen fighting by a police officer. The police officer attempted to break up the fight by grabbing hold of the appellant and saying that he was arresting him for a breach of the peace. The appellant continued fighting and struck the officer two blows. The appellant was charged on an indictment (i) with using threatening

[219] See *R v Keane* (1977) 65 Cr App R 247; *R v Hunjan* (1978) 68 Cr App R 99; *Reid v R* [1980] AC 343 (PC).

[220] [1976] 3 All ER 549 at 552e *per* Lord Widgery CJ.

[221] [1976] 3 All ER 549.

[222] Uglow S *Evidence* 427.

[223] [1976] 3 All ER 549.

[224] *R v Hampton* (unreported, July 30, 2004, CA).

[225] *R v Hassan* [2004] EWCA Crim 1478; see also *R v Gayle* [1999] 2 Cr App R 131; *R v Doldur* [2000] Crim LR 178.

[226] [1976] 3 All ER 549.

[227] [1976] 3 All ER 549.

[228] *R v Collins* [2004] 2 Cr App R 11: *R v Aurelio Pop* [2003] UKPC 40.

[229] *R v Andrews* [1993] Crim LR 590.

[230] [1978] 1 All ER 123.

behaviour whereby a breach of the peace was likely to be occasioned, contrary to s 5a of the Public Order Act 1936, and (ii) with assaulting a constable in the execution of his duty. In the presentation of the prosecution case, the Crown drew a distinction between the acts alleged to have taken place before the assault of the police officer and the assault itself. In his summing-up the judge did not distinguish so precisely the pre-assault and post-assault incidents as had counsel for the Crown. The jury were unable to agree on the assault charge but convicted the appellant on the charge of threatening behaviour. On appeal the appellant contended, inter alia, (i) that since the evidence established that, at the time of the alleged offence, he had actually been fighting, and not merely threatening to fight, the proper charge was one of affray and not threatening behaviour; and (ii) that in his summing-up the judge should have followed the procedure adopted by the Crown and, in relation to the charge of threatening behaviour, confined himself to pre-assault incidents. It was held that the appeal would be dismissed for the following reasons—

(i) There were often cases in which there was an overlapping of offences and in which a set of circumstances could amount to one of several offences. There was, however, no principle to the effect that when the facts would fit another offence, that was enough to prevent them being used as a basis for the offence charged if they were the true basis for it. Accordingly, the fact that the appellant had actually been fighting and could have been charged with affray did not preclude a conviction under s 5 of the 1936 Act.

(ii) The obligation of the judge was not to follow precisely and exactly the presentation of the case as put before him by the Crown but to secure a fair and sound conclusion at the end of the case. If the judge had not strictly followed the form of presentation which the Crown had chosen to adopt, it was open to the defence to contend that the verdict had thereby been rendered unsafe or unsatisfactory. In the circumstances it could not be said that the verdict had been rendered unsafe or unsatisfactory by the judge's failure to follow exactly and precisely the method of presentation adopted by the Crown.[231]

In *R v Slater*,[232] the EWCA guided that the *Turnbull*[233] direction ought to be used only in circumstances where there was a possibility of misidentification especially where the issue relates to the presence of the suspect at the scene of crime. Where the foregoing is not in issue a *Turnbull*[234] direction is not necessary. Nor will it be necessary in instances where the accused has admitted to being present at the scene of the crime with only the conduct being in dispute.

---

[231] Editor's notes: For threatening behaviour likely to occasion a breach of the peace, see 11 Halsbury's Laws (4th edn) para 850; For the duty of a judge in summing up, see ibid para 297; For the Public Order Act 1936, s 5, see 8 Halsbury's Statutes (3rd edn) 332.

[232] [1995] Crim LR 244; *R v Chance* [1988] 3 All ER 225.

[233] [1976] 3 All ER 549.

[234] [1976] 3 All ER 549.

(ii) Zambian courts and the *Turnbull*[235] direction

The response to the *Turnbull*[236] direction in this jurisdiction has been the endorsement of the position taken by the EWCA. In *Haamenda v The People,*[237] the appellant and another man were convicted of the theft of a motor vehicle; on appeal to the High Court the conviction of the appellant was upheld but that of his co-appellant was quashed. The two issues relevant to this report were that there was no evidence that the appellant's fingerprints had been found on the stolen motor vehicle, and that the identification of the appellant was unsupported and unsatisfactory. It was held as follows:

(i) Where the nature of a given criminal case necessitates that a relevant matter must be investigated but the Investigating Agency fails to investigate it in circumstances amounting to a dereliction of duty and in consequence of that dereliction of duty the accused is seriously prejudiced because evidence which might have been favourable to him has not been adduced, the dereliction of duty will operate in favour of the accused and result; in an acquittal unless the evidence given on behalf of the prosecution is so overwhelming as to offset the prejudice which might have arisen from the derelictions of duty.

(ii) Where the quality of identification is good and remains so at the close of the defence case the danger of mistaken identification is lessened; the poorer the quality the greater the danger. In the latter event the court should look for supporting evidence which has the effect of buttressing the weak evidence of identification. Odd coincidences can provide corroboration. *Per* Chomba JS:

> The issue of identification which has been mentioned earlier on in the judgment has to be considered at this juncture. Delivering the Judgment of the Court in *R v Turnbull*[238] Lord Widgery CJ, gave useful guidelines as to what duties a trial judge should observe whenever the case against an accused person turns wholly or substantially on the correctness of one or more identifications which the defence alleges to be mistaken. These duties are:
>
> (a) Firstly, that the judge should warn the jury of the special need for caution before convicting the accused in reliance on the correctness of the identifications.
>
> (b) Secondly, the judge should direct the jury to examine closely the circumstances in which the identification by each witness came to be made.
>
> In this country where the Jury System does not exist the warning and direction mentioned in *Turnbull*[239] must be to

[235] [1976] 3 All ER 549.

[236] [1976] 3 All ER 549.

[237] [1977] ZR 184; *Lubinda v The People* [1973] ZR 43; *R v Turnbull* [1976] 3 All ER 549.

[238] [1976] 3 All ER 549.

[239] [1976] 3 All ER 549.

> the trial judge himself. Lord Widgery further said in that same judgment that where the quality of identification is good and remains so at the close of the defence case the danger of mistaken identification is lessened; but that the poorer the quality the greater the danger. In the latter event the judge should direct the jury that they should look for supporting evidence which has the effect of buttressing the weak evidence of identification. In this country this direction should, of course, be to the judge himself.[240]

In *Kateka v The People*,[241] the appellant was convicted of robbery, the allegation being that he had in a bar picked the pocket of the complainant and stolen K25 and that immediately thereafter when the complainant ran after him and caught him, he had punched him in the face four times and then made his escape. The complainant's brother did not see the actual theft but saw the blows, but there was no evidence that he saw the assailant's face. The complainant's opportunity for observing the face of his assailant was only during the second or so while the blows were being delivered; the court described this opportunity as "fleeting only and very poor". The Complainant and his brother searched for the assailant in the vicinity and some two hours later returned to the bar at which the robbery had taken place, where the complainant pointed out the appellant as the man who had robbed him. It was held as follows:

(i) In those cases which rest on the identification of a person who is not previously known to the witnesses it is most important that the features or clothes by which the alleged culprit is identified should be canvassed.
(ii) The question is not one of credibility in the sense of truthfulness, but of reliability, and the greatest care should be taken to test the identification. It is not enough for the witness simply to say that the accused is the person who committed the offence.[242]
(iii) Where, as in this case, none of the right questions to test the identification is asked, the court is left without any information on the basis of which it could satisfy itself that the possibility of honest mistake has been ruled out.
(iv) The magistrate not having considered the possibility of honest mistake, but having simply accepted without question the identification by the complainant and his brother, and the danger of an honest mistake being very real in this case, it would be unsafe and unsatisfactory to allow the conviction to stand.

That the decision in *Turnbull*[243] is now part and parcel of our jurisprudence can be seen from the comments of Baron DCJ in *Kateka v The People*:[244]

---

[240] See also *Situna v The People* [1982] ZR 115.

[241] [1977] ZR 35 (SC).

[242] *Nyambe v The People* (1973) ZR 228 followed.

[243] [1976] 3 All ER 549.

[244] [1977] ZR 35 (SC).

> It might be of assistance to all concerned with the practice of the criminal law to study the recent English case of *R v Turnbull and Another*,[245] an authoritative judgment of a five-judge bench of the Court of Appeal in England, which deals in depth with the question of identification evidence and the proper approach of the courts to such evidence.

(iii) The Australian response - The *Dominican* warning

(a) General

The Dominican warning is comprised of the principles applicable to the identification the accused as well as that of persons other than the accused. It is taken from pronouncements by the High Court of Australia in *Dominican v R*[246] wherein the law has been stated thus:[247]

> Whatever the defence and however the case is conducted, where evidence as to identification represents any significant part of the proof of guilt of an offence, the judge must warn [himself] as to the dangers of convicting on such evidence where its reliability is disputed. The terms of the warning need not follow any particular formula. But it must be cogent and effective. It must be appropriate to the circumstances of the case. Consequently, the [judge] must [apply his mind] "as to the factors which may affect the consideration of [the identification] evidence in the circumstances of the particular case." A warning in general terms is insufficient. The [judge] must have the benefit of a direction which has the authority of the judge's office behind it. It follows that the trial judge should isolate and identify for [his benefit] any matter of significance which may reasonably be regarded as undermining the reliability of the identification evidence.

What appears to be the position of the law as adumbrated in *Dominican v R*[248] is that the warning therein contained ought to be issued in circumstances where the accused or his defence counsel, as the case may be, impugn the identification in question alleging that it is dishonest. The warning ought not to be given where the objection raised is that the identification is mistaken. The rationale behind the foregoing has to do with the court's inherent power to determine whether dishonesty as alleged, poisoned the identification and as such, invalidated it or to draw the conclusion that while dishonesty was absent in the identification process, mistaken identification had occurred for which the accused ought to, where this forms a substantial part or the only basis for the prosecution's case, acquited.

---

[245] [1976] 3 All ER 549.

[246] (1992) 173 CLR 555.

[247] (1992) 173 CLR 555 at 561-2.

[248] (1992) 173 CLR 555 at 570; see *R v Giga* [2007] Crim LR 571.

Trial judges ought to bear in mind the special need to, based on the "Dominican" warning, prevent the accused from being prejudiced by photo-identification.[249] It follows that judges ought to steer clear from making comments during trial which may give the impression of bias against the accused before rendering the final judgment, i.e., before analysing all the evidence from both sides on the merits. Even so, it would be expected that a trial judge will issue a warning to himself/herself as required under the "Dominican" warning when contextualised and applied to the Zambian trial scenario. The warning which a judge/magistrate gives himself should include the danger of permitting, for example, photo board identification to be embellished by dock identification,[250] though it is within his inherent power as overseer of a trial to highlight, in his final judgment, matters from which he drew the conclusion that same were supportive of identification, provided that any feebleness regarding the same which he noted during the trial process are also emphasised.[251]

(b) Contents of the Dominican warning

In the Australian jurisdiction(s) where the "Dominican" warning originates, a failure to warn of the inherent dangers relating to identification evidence have, as shown in *R v Preston and others*,[252] led to the ordering of new trials or the quashing of convictions being set aside. It is not too far a stretch that the same would be the case in this jurisdiction in an appropriate case. As regards what kind of warning ought to be given, it has been observed as follows in *Dominican v R*[253]

> [T]the adequacy of a warning in an identification case must be evaluated in the context of the evidence in the case.[254] But its adequacy is evaluated by reference to the identification evidence and not the other evidence in the case. The adequacy of the warning has to be evaluated by reference to the nature of the relationship between the witness and the person identified, the opportunity to observe the person subsequently identified, the length of time between the incident and the identification, and the nature and circumstances of the first identification - not by reference to other evidence which implicates the accused. A trial judge is not absolved from his or her duty to give general and specific warnings concerning the danger of convicting on identification evidence because there is other evidence, which, if accepted, is sufficient to convict the accused.[255] The judge must direct the jury on the assumption that they may decide to convict solely on the basis of the identification evidence. If a trial judge has failed to

[249] *Alexander v R* (1981) 145 CLR 395 at 413; *R v Clarke* (1993) 71 A Crim R 58 (NSW CCA).

[250] *R v Evans* (2006) 175 A Crim R 1 at [64].

[251] *R v Fox* (No 2) [2000] 1 Qd R 640 at [23].

[252] [1993] 4 All ER 638.

[253] (1992) 173 CLR 555 at 565.

[254] *R v Dickson* (1983) 1 VR at 230; *R v Allen* (1984) 16 A Crim R at 444-445.

[255] See *R v Bartels* (1986) 44 SASR at 270-271; *cf.R v Goode* (1970) SASR 69 at 77.

> give an adequate warning concerning identification, a new trial will ordinarily be ordered even when other evidence makes a very strong case against the accused.[256]

Even so,

> [...] the other evidence in the case may be so compelling that a court of criminal appeal will conclude that the jury must have convicted on that evidence independently of the identification evidence. In such a case, the inadequacy of or lack of a warning concerning the identification evidence, although amounting to legal error, will not constitute a miscarriage of justice. But unless the Court of Criminal Appeal concludes that the jury must inevitably have convicted the accused independently of the identification evidence, the inadequacy of or lack of a warning concerning that evidence constitutes a miscarriage of justice even though the other evidence made a strong case against the accused.

(c) Positive-identification evidence-*vs*-circumstantial identification evidence

Whether there should be a distinction between positive-identification evidence on the one hand and circumstantial identification evidence on the other, is a question that arose in *Festa v R*.[257]As McHugh J saw it, the distinction was an important one. As a starting point, or so his lordship expostulated, the requirement to give a "Dominican" warning was not applicable to all forms of identification evidence. He opined that the discretion pertaining the exclusion of evidence might operate differently as regards the two instances he distinguished because, as he saw it, the dangers of positive-identification evidence were greater than those that relate to circumstantial identification evidence.[258] The rest of the judges on the panel in *Festa v R*[259] did not wholly embrace the approach of erecting different principles based on the distinctions alluded to by McHugh J.[260]

7.3.2.4 *Identification evidence vis-à-vis cumulative evidence and its challenges*

There are two scenarios that may arise here. One is where there are numerous witnesses to an incident to which the accused is linked. Another, is where the accused with several offences. In the former scenario, the problem may arise

---

[256] See *R v Gaunt* (1964) NSWR 864 at 867; for summarised but lucid explanation of the warning see Heydon JD *Cross on Evidence* 83 -5 and the Australian authorities cited thereunder.

[257] (2001) 208 CLR 593.

[258] (2001) 208 CLR 593 at [56]-[67]; for support of this distinction see the following Australian authorities also cited in Heydon JD *Cross on Evidence* 82: *R v King* (1975) 12 SASR 404 (CCA); *R v Benz* (1989) 168 CLR 110 at 119, 12-5, 132-3; *R v Bartels* (1986) 44 SASR 260 at 272-4 (CCA); *R v Marijancevic* (1993) 70 A Crim R 272 at 278 (Vic FC: object identification); *R v Southon* (2003) 85 SASR 436 at [44]-[45] (CCA); *Hirst v Police* (2006) 95 SASR 260 at [62]; *R v Cavkic* (No 2) (2009) 28 VR 341 at [51] – [53] (object identification).

[259] (2001) 208 CLR 593: Kirby J and Hayne J.

[260] Hayne J did however endorse the proposition that in some instances the whole of the *Dominican* warning need not be given: see McHugh J's opinion to the effect that *R v Zullo* [1993] 2 Qd R 572 (CA) followed in *R v Finlay* (2007) 178 A Crim R 373 was wrongly decided in this respect.

because none of the identification evidence by individual witnesses is sufficient predication for a conviction. In that scenario, cumulative evidence may be used to convict. In the latter scenario, there may be a single eye-witness to each of the several offences with which the accused is charged. The challenges here are multifaceted. At first blush, one may be tempted to draw the conclusion that by employing similar facts evidence, the evidence of one witness, insufficient in and of itself to predicate a conviction, may be used to support other identification evidence by another witness to support a conviction. There has, however, been no ringing endorsement for this approach for reasons that become apparent in two EWCA decisions hereinafter discussed. In the first of these, *R v McGranagham,*[261] it was noted that '[...] an identification about which the [court was] not sure cannot support another identification of which [it is] also not sure however similar the facts of the two offences may be.' In the second of these cases, *R v Downey,*[262] the position taken in *R v McGranagham,*[263] was said to forbid the use of doubtful but cumulative identification evidence if only to prove the commission of the many offences by one person. What was proper to do, it was suggested was to use identification evidence cumulatively once it had been shown that all the offences had been committed by the same accused person.[264]

7.4 The rule against hearsay within the context of identification evidence

7.4.1 General

The general position at common law, is that a witness' testimony to the effect that a third person identified the accused as the perpetrator of the offence in question is hearsay and as such inadmissible. Recent common law authorities[265] and statutory provisions[266] in England and the United States[267] appear to suggest that identification evidence which ordinarily ought to be deemed inadmissible should in fact be treated as an exception to the general rule against hearsay at common law. Identification by a third party not called to testify has therefore been treated as analogous to the common law exception of *re gestate*, that is, as an account associated with a relevant act.[268]

---

[261] [1995] 1 Cr App R 559 at 572 *per* Glidewell LJ.

[262] [1995] 1 Cr App R 547.

[263] [1995] 1 Cr App R 559.

[264] *R v Barnes* [1996] Crim LR 39; *R v Black* [1995] Crim LR 640.

[265] *R v McCay* [1991] 1 All ER 232; *R v Osborne and Virtue* [1973] 1 All ER 649; *R v Christie* [1914] AC 545; sub nom *Public Prosecutions Director v Christie* [1914–15] All ER Rep 63, 83 LJKB 1097, 111 LT 220, 78 JP 321, 24 Cox CC 249, 10 Cr App Rep 141, HL, 14 Digest (Repl) 405, 3962; *R v Richardson* [1971] 2 All ER 773, [1971] 2 QB 484, [1971] 2 WLR 889.

[266] See for example, s 120(4) of the Criminal Justice Act 2003 discussed below.

[267] Discussed elsewhere in this text.

[268] See *Howe v Malkin* (1878) 40 LT 196.

7.4.2 *Specific legislation relating to identification evidence and the question of the rule against hearsay*

Some jurisdictions have sought to deal with uncertainties of the status of identification evidence within the context of the hearsay rule by enacting specific provisions to tackle the issue. Thus, in England & Wales, s 120(4) of the Criminal Justice Act 2003 provides as follows regarding *'Other previous statements of witnesses:'*

> (4) A previous statement by the witness is admissible as evidence of any matter stated of which oral evidence by him would be admissible, if—
> (a) any of the following three conditions is satisfied, and
> (b) while giving evidence the witness indicates that to the best of his belief he made the statement, and that to the best of his belief it states the truth.
>
> (5) The first condition is that the statement identifies or describes a person, object or place.

This provision appears to have dealt with residual issues which may have been raised regarding the treatment of 'hearsay identification' as a *res gestae* exception to the general rule in cases such as *R v McCay*[269]which treatment has been said to be inconsistent with respected authorities.[270] It would appear from the foregoing that in handling matters of what may be referred to as 'third party identification' courts, where the police who conducted the investigation is available and willing to testify to the facts of identification which the witnesses themselves have difficulties testifying to, ought to be allowed to testify. This should not be treated as hearsay. Accepting this evidence must however be predicated on the fact that there had been an accurate identification at a prior identification parade. It would also logically follow that in circumstances where doubts regarding the present testimony from an identification witness are raised, the witness's prior statement may be introduced into evidence for two reasons (i) consistency of testimony;[271] and (ii) as evidence of the facts.

7.4.3 *Specific cases relating to the general point on identification evidence and the question of the rule against hearsay*

Decided cases relating to the general point on identification evidence and the question of the rule against hearsay appear to suggest that such identification may operate as an exception to the general rule against hearsay at common law.

[269] [1991] 1 All ER 232.

[270] Comment on *R v McCay* by Birch in [1990] Crim LR 338 at 341.

[271] *Chimbini v The People* [1973] ZR 191.

In *R v Osborne and Virtue,*[272] police officers investigating a robbery arrested the appellants, O and V, and took them to a police station where they were interrogated by a chief inspector. The interrogation took place without any caution being administered to the appellants. At the time of the arrest the chief inspector had reasonable grounds for suspecting that the two appellants had been members of the gang responsible for the robbery, but he had no evidence to justify that suspicion. After the interrogation both the appellants were put up for an identification parade, which was carried out strictly in accordance with police regulations. Both appellants were identified by two female witnesses who had been present when the robbery took place. The appellants were then duly cautioned and charged. Their trial did not take place until some 7 ½ months later. The two witnesses who had identified the appellants gave evidence; one said that she did not remember picking out any one, and the other, who was in a highly nervous and emotional condition, proved in consequence to be a very unsatisfactory witness, first stating that she had picked out the appellant V and then denying that fact. The appellants' defence at the trial was an alibi and a great deal of the evidence against them was provided by what they had said to the chief inspector at their interrogation. The appellants submitted that that evidence was inadmissible since they had not been cautioned in accordance with r 2a of the Judges' Rules (1964) b. The recorder overruled that submission, stating that if there had been a breach of the Judges' Rules, he would have exercised his discretion to exclude the evidence. The trial proceeded and the officer who had conducted the identification parade was asked who it was that the two female witnesses had picked out at the parade. Counsel for the appellant O objected to that question on the ground that the officer's evidence would contradict that of the two witnesses concerned. The recorder rejected the objection and admitted the officer's evidence. The appellants were convicted and appealed. It was held as follows:

(i) Rule 2 of the Judges' Rules did not require a police officer to administer a caution to a suspected person whom he was questioning until he had got some information which could be put before the court as the beginnings of a case. Since at the time when he started to question the appellants, the chief inspector had no information which would have enabled him to put evidence against them before the court, the evidence of the interrogation had been rightly put before the jury.

(ii) The evidence of the officer conducting the identification parade had been properly admitted. Evidence of identification other than identification in the witness box was admissible. The officer's evidence did not contradict the evidence of the two witnesses who attended the identification parade. There was no objection to a witness with a better

[272] [1973] 1 All ER 649; *R v Christie* [1914] AC 545; sub nom *Public Prosecutions Director v Christie* [1914–15] All ER Rep 63, 83 LJKB 1097, 111 LT 220, 78 JP 321, 24 Cox CC 249, 10 Cr App Rep 141, HL, 14 Digest (Repl) 405, 3962; *R v Richardson* [1971] 2 All ER 773, [1971] 2 QB 484, [1971] 2 WLR 889, 135 JP 371, 55 Cr App Rep 244, CA; Editor's notes: For the Judges' Rules, see 10 Halsbury's Laws (3rd Edn) 470–473, para 865.

memory testifying that another witness had identified an accused at an identification parade some months previously even though that witness could not himself remember doing so.[273]

(iii) It followed that the appeals should be dismissed and the convictions affirmed.

In *R v McCay*,[274] the appellant was charged with wounding with intent, the allegation being that he had thrust a beer glass into the face of a man in a public house. A witness to the attack attended an identification parade about three months later. The parade was held in an identification suite where the viewing room for witnesses was soundproofed and separated from the room containing the suspect and volunteers on the parade by a two-way mirror which prevented those on the parade seeing the witnesses. The witness was asked to make his identification verbally by giving the number of the person identified, which he did by saying, 'It is number 8'. When the witness gave his evidence at the trial, some three months after the identification parade, he could not remember the number of the person whom he had identified. Counsel for the Crown asked the police officer who had conducted the parade what the witness had told him when making his identification, but counsel for the appellant objected to the question on the ground that his answer would be hearsay and inadmissible. The judge overruled the objection. There was no other evidence of identification and the appellant was convicted. He appealed on the ground that the admission of the police officer's evidence as to what the witness had said at the identification parade amounted to a material irregularity in the trial. It was held that the words spoken by the witness contemporaneously accompanied, and were necessary to explain, a relevant act, namely the witness's physical and intellectual activity in making the identification, and were thus part of the *res gestae*. Accordingly, the police officer's evidence was admissible either as original evidence or as an exception to the hearsay rule. Furthermore, the admission in evidence of the words used was in accordance with statutory authority since the identification had been conducted in accordance with the requirements of para 15a of Annex A to the Code of Practice for the Identification of Persons by Police Officers issued by the Secretary of State under ss 66 and 67 of the Police and Criminal Evidence Act 1984. The judge had accordingly been right to admit the evidence. The appeal against conviction would therefore be dismissed.[275]

---

[273] *R v Christie* [1914–15] All ER Rep 63 applied.

[274] [1991] 1 All ER 232; *Howe v Malkin* (1878) 40 LT 196; *Myers v DPP* [1964] 2 All ER 881, [1965] AC 1001, [1964] 3 WLR 145, HL.

[275] *Howe v Malkin* (1878) 40 LT 196 applied; Editor's notes: For the hearsay rule generally, see 11(2) Halsbury's Laws (4th edn reissue) paras 1099–1112, and for cases on the subject, see 14(2) Digest (Reissue) 596–598, 4841–4862; For the Police and Criminal Evidence Act 1984, ss 66, 67, see 12 Halsbury's Statutes (4th edn) (1989 reissue) 909, 910; As from 1 April 1991 para 15 of Annex A to the Code of Practice for the Identification of Persons by Police Officers, as brought into force by the Police and Criminal Evidence Act 1984 (Codes of Practice) (No 1) Order 1985, SI 1985/1937, is to be replaced in identical terms by para 15 of Annex A to the Code of Practice for the Identification of Persons by Police Officers, as brought into force by the Police and Criminal Evidence Act 1984 (Codes of Practice) (No 2) Order 1990, SI 1990/2580.

7.4.3 *Specific cases relating to the explicit question of drawings or reconstructions of the likeness of the suspect*

The question of hearsay has also arisen in instances where the question is not, on the one hand, of witnesses basing their testimony on that of third parties not called to testify or those, on the other, who made the identification of the accused at an original identification but cannot do so at trial, in which cases, policemen who were involved in the original identification parade have been permitted to give testimony nonetheless, testimony which has been admitted as an exception to the hearsay rule. It has arisen where the issue concerns drawings or reconstructions of the likeness of a suspect predicated on the instructions of the witness. The issue has arisen and been dealt with in at least two cases which we consider below.

The first is *R v Cook*[276] where Christopher Cook appealed with leave of Roch J against his conviction on 27 March 1986 in the Crown Court at Acton before his Honour Judge Palmer and a jury on one count of robbery and one count of indecent assault for which he was sentenced to concurrent terms of three years' youth custody. He also appealed against the sentences. It was shown that a photofit picture of a defendant is admissible at his trial as part of a witness's evidence and does not constitute a breach of either the hearsay rule or the rule against the admission of earlier consistent statements. *Per* Watkins LJ:[277]

> The rule is said to apply not only to assertions made orally, but to those made in writing or by conduct. Never so far as we know has it been held to apply to this comparatively modern form of evidence, namely the sketch made by the police officer to accord with the witness's recollection of a suspect's physical characteristics and mode of dress and the even more modern photofit compiled from an identical source. Both are manifestations of the seeing eye, translations of vision onto paper through the medium of a police officer's skill of drawing or composing which a witness does not possess. The police officer is merely doing what the witness could do if possessing the requisite skill. When drawing or composing he is akin to a camera without, of course, being able to match in clarity the photograph of a person or scene which a camera automatically produces.
>
> There is no doubt that a photograph taken, for example, of a suspect during the commission of an offence is admissible. In a bigamy case, namely *R v Tolson*,[278] Willes J said:
>
>> The photograph was admissible because it is only a visible representation of the image or impression made upon the minds of the witnesses by the sight of

[276] [1987] 1 All ER 1049; *R v Tolson* (1864) 4 F & F 103 applied; *R v Percy Smith* [1976] Crim LR 511 considered; Editor's notes: For proof of identity, see 11 Halsbury's Laws (4th edn) para 363, and for cases on the subject, see 14(2) Digest (Reissue) 486–490, 4008–4038; For hearsay evidence, see 11 Halsbury's Laws (4th edn) 437–439, and for cases on the subject, see 14(2) Digest (Reissue) 596–598, 4841–4842.

[277] [1987] 1 All ER 1049 at 1054c-j.

[278] (1864) 4 F & F 103 at 104, 176 ER 488.

> the person or the object it represents; and, therefore is, in reality, only another species of the evidence which persons give of identity, when they speak merely from memory.

> That ruling has never since been doubted and is applied with regularity to photographs, including those taken nowadays automatically in banks during a robbery. Such photographs are invaluable aids to identification of criminals. It has never been suggested of them that they are subject to the rule against hearsay.
>
> We regard the production of the sketch or photofit by a police officer making a graphic representation of a witness's memory as another form of the camera at work, albeit imperfectly and not produced contemporaneously with the material incident but soon or fairly soon afterwards. As we perceive it the photofit is not a statement in writing made in the absence of a defendant or anything resembling it in the sense that this very old rule against hearsay has ever been expressed to embrace. It is we think sui generis, that is to say the only one of its kind. It is a thing apart, the admissibility to evidence of which would not be in breach of the hearsay rule.
>
> Seeing that we do not regard the photofit as a statement at all it cannot come within the description of an earlier consistent statement which, save in exceptional circumstances, cannot ever be admissible in evidence. The true position is in our view that the photograph, the sketch and the photofit are in a class of evidence of their own to which neither the rule against hearsay nor the rule against the admission of an earlier consistent statement applies.

The decision in *R v Cook*[279] must now, in England & Wales at least, be seen within the context of s 120 of the Criminal Justice Act 2003 which would suggest that a graphic representation is admissible on account of the very clear fact that it is a previous statement by a witness offering a description of a person. This, it is submitted, would appear to be the logical state of the law for purposes of application where such facts as did arise in *R v Cook*[280] arise in this jurisdiction.

The second is *Taylor v Chief Constable of Cheshire.*[281] The appellant was charged with the theft of a packet of batteries from a shop. The prosecution evidence rested in part on what three police officers had seen in a video recording which allegedly showed the appellant committing the offence. The video recording was mistakenly erased before the trial and was therefore not available to be viewed by the justices, who nevertheless regarded the officers' evidence of what they had seen on the video recording as admissible and convicted the appellant. The appellant appealed, contending that the officers' evidence should have been excluded as hearsay. It was held that there was no effective distinction, for the purpose of admissibility, between a direct view of the actions of an alleged offender by a witness and a view of those actions on

279 [1987] 1 All ER 1049.

280 [1987] 1 All ER 1049.

281 [1987] 1 All ER 225.

a visual display unit of a camera or on a video recording of what the camera recorded, provided that what was seen on the visual display unit or video recording was connected by sufficient evidence to the alleged actions of the accused at the time and place in question. Evidence as to the contents of a film or video recording was not inadmissible because of the hearsay principle, but was direct evidence of what was seen to be happening in a particular place at a particular time. The fact that the video recording was not available at the trial did not of itself render the evidence of the police officers inadmissible, although the court had carefully to assess the weight and reliability of that evidence. Since the evidence of the police officers had been rightly admitted and since the justices had correctly directed themselves as to its weight and reliability, the appeal would be dismissed.[282] *Per* McNeill J:

> Where the identification of an offender depends wholly or largely on the evidence of a witness describing what he saw on a visual display unit contemporaneously with the events which he describes or on a video recording of that display, or on what the tribunal of fact sees from such a recording, that evidence is necessarily subject to the appropriate directions as to identification evidence.[283]

The third is *Attorney-General's Reference (No 2 of 2002)*.[284] The defendants had been seen on video. The prosecution sought to admit, in addition to the video evidence itself, evidence from police officers as to the identity of persons claimed to be shown on the tape. The officer's evidence was offered but not accepted as expert evidence. The defendants said the tapes should have been left to speak for themselves. It was held that the officers' evidence should have been accepted. Photographic evidence could be admitted in four situations, where the image itself was sufficiently clear to allow the jury to make its own direct comparison, where the witness himself knew the defendant, where the witness had spent sufficient time examining images from the scene to have acquired special knowledge, and where an expert with facial mapping skills could use the skills to assist the identification. The officers' evidence could have been admitted. *Per* Rose LJ:[285]

> In our judgment, on the authorities, there are, as it seems to us (at least four circumstances in which, subject to the judicial discretion to exclude, evidence is admissible to show and, subject to appropriate directions in the summing-up) a jury can be invited to conclude, that the defendant committed the offence on the basis of a photographic image from the scene of the crime:

[282] *R v Kajala* (1982) 75 Cr App R 149; *R v Maqsud Ali* [1965] 2 All ER 464; *R v Fowden and White* [1982] Crim LR 588; *and R v Grimer* [1982] Crim LR 674 considered; Editor's notes: For the hearsay rule and exceptions to it, see 11 Halsbury's Laws (4th edn) paras 437–438, and for cases on the subject, see 14(2) Digest (Reissue) 596–598, 4841–4862.

[283] *R v Turnbull* [1976] 3 All ER 549 applied.

[284] Times 17-Oct-2002, [2002] EWCA Crim 2373, [2003] 1 Cr App R 321, [2003] Crim LR 192; https://swarb.co.uk/attorney-generals-reference-no-2-of-2002-CACD-7-Oct-2002/ retrieved on 24/8/21.

[285] 1 Cr App R 21.

(i) where the photographic image is sufficiently clear, the jury can compare it with the defendant sitting in the dock;[286]

(ii) where a witness knows the defendant sufficiently well to recognise him as the offender depicted in the photographic image, he can give evidence of this;[287] and this may be so even if the photographic image is no longer available for the jury;[288]

(iii) where a witness who does not know the defendant spends substantial time viewing and analysing photographic images from the scene, thereby acquiring special knowledge which the jury does not have, he can give evidence of identification based on a comparison between those images and a reasonably contemporary photograph of the defendant, provided that the images and the photograph are available to the jury;[289]

(iv) a suitably qualified expert with facial mapping skills can give opinion evidence of identification based on a comparison between images from the scene, (whether expertly enhanced or not and a reasonably contemporary photograph of the defendant, provided the images and the photograph are available for the jury[290]

7.5 Circumstantial evidence of identity

7.5.1 *Similar fact and other probative circumstances*

In the absence of any doubt as to acts being done and what falls to be resolved relates to the question as to whether said act was one done by a particular person. Any and all evidence relevant to prove that fact is ordinarily admissible. A few examples include physical features of the criminal in question; mental and other physical peculiarities relating to the criminal and any traces from the scene of the crime are all admissible evidence. As we show in chapter 8 where we consider this branch of the law in greater detail, regard must be had to the proscription on evidence whose sole purpose is to merely show, among other things, a disposition to commit a particular crime or crimes or criminal tendencies.

A few matters warrant discussion for purposes of illustrating the foregoing. Under s 166 of the Penal Code:[291]

> Any person who, having a husband or wife living, goes through a ceremony of marriage which is void by reason of its taking place during the life of such husband or wife, is guilty of a felony and is liable to imprisonment for five years:

---

[286] *Dodson & Williams* [1984] 79 Cr App R 220.

[287] *R v Kajala* (1982) 75 Cr App R 149; *R v Fowden and White* [1982] Crim LR 588; *R v Grimer* [1982] Crim LR 674; *R v Blenkinsop* [1995] 1 Cr App R(S) 7.

[288] *Taylor v The Chief Constable of Cheshire* [1987] 1 All ER 225 84 Cr App R 191.

[289] *R v Clare & Peach* [1995] 2 Cr App R 333.

[290] *R v Stockwell* 97 Cr App R 260, *R v Clarke* [1995] 2 Cr App R 425; *R v Hookway* [1999] Crim LR 750.

[291] Chapter 87 of the Laws of Zambia.

> Provided that this section shall not extend to any person whose marriage with such husband or wife has been declared void by a court of competent jurisdiction, nor to any person who contracts a marriage during the life of a former husband or wife, if such husband or wife, at the time of the subsequent marriage, shall have been continually absent from such person for the space of seven years, and shall not have been heard of by such person as being alive within that time.

Under the said provision, a number of factors will go to prove that the accused has been guilty of bigamy. It has been held in *The People v Katongo*[292] that '[t]o constitute the offence of bigamy under s 166 of the Penal Code[293] the second marriage must be one capable of producing a valid marriage known and recognised by the law but for the subsisting first marriage.'[294]

In *The People v Paul Nkhoma,*[295] the accused, who was charged with bigamy, had gone through a ceremony of marriage under the Marriage Act when his first wife, whom he had married under customary law, was still living. In his defence he submitted that he had terminated his first customary marriage by a letter and he believed that the marriage had ended. The first marriage had not been validly dissolved. It was held as follows: (i) Bigamy is committed if a person whose spouse is still living goes through a ceremony of marriage with another which, but for the earlier subsisting marriage, would have resulted in a valid marriage. (ii) A customary marriage is a valid marriage for the purposes of considering a second "Marriage Act" marriage as bigamous.[296] (iii) (Per curiam) Mistake of fact is a defence to bigamy if, at the time of the second marriage, the offending spouse reasonably believed that his earlier marriage had been dissolved.

In *The People v Roxburgh,*[297] the accused was convicted of the offence of bigamy contrary to s 145 (now s 166) of the Penal Code[298] in the Subordinate Court of the First Class, Lusaka. The case came before the High Court on review. It was held *inter alia* that the offence of bigamy is committed by second marriage and the first marriage is not part of the offence, merely creating the necessary status.

However, a necessary predicate to proving the preceding as exemplified in the various authorities considered, is proving that the accused did in fact go through a ceremony of marriage went through a ceremony of marriage with the first spouse. This may be done by calling to the stand the innocent mate. In

[292] [1974] ZR 290.

[293] Chapter 87 of the Laws of Zambia.

[294] The earliest case in this jurisdiction is *The People v Chitambala* [1969] ZR 142 (HC); see also *Moratuoa Hessie Walkerv Jimmy A Walker* 2010/HP/09 *per* Chishimba J.

[295] [1978] ZR 4 (HC).

[296] Editor's note: The court's attention was apparently not drawn to *The People v Katongo* [1974] ZR 290, in which Care J, held that a customary union is not capable of being an "earlier subsisting marriage" which renders a subsequent "Marriage Act" marriage bigamous.

[297] [1972] ZR 31 (HC).

[298] Chapter 87 of the Laws of Zambia.

terms of s 151(1)(b) of the Criminal Procedure Code[299] provides that the spouse will be a competent witness for the prosecution '[…] in any case where such person is charged with an offence under Chapter XV[300] of the Penal Code or with bigamy.' Thus, the innocent spouse may by direct evidence identify the accused.

One may, however, wonder what options are available where such direct evidence is not available either because the wife refuses to give evidence on the basis that while competent, she is not compellable or that there just is want of evidence as regards the celebration of the first marriage. The solution to this predicament for the prosecution is the age-old concept of circumstantial evidence. Recall that in *David Zulu v The People*,[301] it was said that circumstantial evidence '[…] is not direct proof of a matter at issue but rather is proof of facts not in issue but relevant to the fact in issue and from which an inference of the fact in issue may be drawn.'[302] Thus, where direct evidence is not forthcoming, and where there is no other direct proof of a first marriage, such as that of a witness who was present at its celebration, same may be established by circumstantial evidence. It seems logical to submit that the prosecution bringing before court a certificate of marriage on which the accused's name appears together with that of the person it is contended, he/she got married to before the bigamous enterprise will be relevant to the fact in issue and from which an inference of the fact in issue' in this case, the accused having duly gone through an initial marriage ceremony 'may be drawn.' That a conviction would result from such evidence is not far-fetched where 'the circumstantial evidence has taken the case out of the realm of conjecture so that it attains such a degree of cogency which can permit only an inference of guilt.'[303]

The solitary query with respect to the issue of admissibility of circumstantial evidence as it relates to personal characteristics such as the accused's name on the one hand, and such things as one's occupation, their education and their mental or corporeal peculiarities on the other, is whether the specific characteristic in question is of such rarity as to be considered worth the court's time to get evidence which tends to show on the one hand, possession of the characteristic in question and on the other, membership of a class of persons under consideration.[304] According to Wigmore:

> Where a certain circumstance, feature, or mark, may commonly be found associated with a large number of objects, the presence of that feature or mark in two supposed objects is little indication of their identity, because, on the general principle of Relevancy […], other

[299] Chapter 88 of the Laws of Zambia.

[300] CHAPTER XV ss 132 – 164A provides for offences against morality.

[301] [1977] ZR 151 (SCZ).

[302] This, it was said was a peculiar weakness of circumstantial evidence but see *United States v Nelson* [1969] 419 F. 2d 1237.

[303] *David Zulu v The People* [1977] ZR 151 (SCZ); *Saidi Banda v The People* (SCZ Appeal No 144 of 2015); *Maron Sinkala v The People* (SCZ Appeal No 32 of 2017); *Alfred Nyimba v The People* (SCZ Appeal No 258 of 2011); *Chrispin Chuunga and Ernest Choonde v The People* (CAZ Appeal No 183 of 2017).

[304] See the *Lovat Peerage case* (1885) 10 App Cas 763.

conceivable hypotheses are so numerous, i.e., the objects that possess that mark are numerous and therefore any two of them possessing it may well be different. But where the objects possessing the mark are only one or a few, and the mark is found in two Supposed instances, the chances of the two being different are "nil" or are comparatively small. Suppose there existed a parent named John Smith, whose heirs are sought; and there is also a claimant whose parent's name was John Smith. The name John Smith is associated with so many persons that the chances of two supposed persons of that name being different are too numerous to allow us to consider the common mark as having an appreciable probative value. But the chances may be diminished by adding other common Circumstances going to form the common mark. Add, for instance, another name circumstance, as that the name of each supposed person was John Barebones Bonaparte Smith; here the chances of there being two persons of that name, in any district however large, are instantly reduced to minima

8

EVIDENCE OF SIMILAR FACTS

8.1 Introduction

The concept of evidence of similar facts pauses the most intractable challenges to legal students, legal practitioners, and judges alike. Evidence of similar facts is concerned with the admissibility of evidence which does not directly implicate the accused person with the offence with which he is charged. It, however, suggests either directly or indirectly that the accused committed the offence with which he is charged and in addition, one or more offences of a similar kind. It has been held in *Mwiimbe v The people*[1] that' [...] the admission of evidence of similar facts is in the discretion of the trial court which will no doubt, among other things, consider whether its evidential value outweighs its prejudicial effect [....]' The challenges hereinbefore referenced arise from several issues. The first is that individual judgments which were intended only to apply to the particular facts and circumstances specific to them have received pre-eminence as principles of general application as have illustrative expressions. It had also been gainsaid and this received general acceptance, that singular guidelines occur for particular classes of cases e.g., homosexual offences. As we show below though, the notion that there were special categories was rejected by the Lords in *DPP v P.*[2] The House took the view that there were no special rules premised on the nature of the case such as sexual offences for instance. It was, as we show later, the fresh start that the concept of evidence of similar facts craved following the inconsistencies in EWCA decisions that followed *DPP v Boardman.*[3]

Further to the foregoing, it can be argued that the term "evidence of similar facts" is a misnomer. While it may appear to be the case that evidence admitted under the concept of "evidence of similar facts" is indicative of the commission of an offence by the accused, the truth is that in practice, this is not always so. In *Thompson v R*[4] the [accused] was charged with gross indecency against boys. The [accused denied that he was the offender. Evidence was admitted that on arrest the defendant was in possession of powder puffs and that a search of his rooms uncovered indecent photographs of boys. It was held that the evidence

[1] [1986] ZR 15 (SC).

[2] [1991] 2 AC 447.

[3] [1975] AC 421.

[4] [1918] AC 221, HL; summary taken from https://swarb.co.uk/thompson-v-director-of-public-prosecutions-hl-1918/ retrieved on 06/10/21; see also *R v Willis*, unreported, January 29, 1979, CA (transcript no. 2934/B/78).

was admissible on the issue of the identity of the offender. Lord Sumner stated that while proof of guilt of a particular crime does not arise from proof of a general disposition to commit that crime, evidence was admissible to prove guilty knowledge or intent or a system or to rebut an appearance of innocence. However, the prosecution may not credit the accused with fancy defences in order to rebut them at the outset with some damning piece of prejudice. In *R v Butler*,[5] where the accused was charged with rape and the issue of identity arose, the evidence deemed admissible under the concept of "similar fact" as it turned out, was a non-criminal class of evidence given the fact that it was 'committed' with the permission of the person in question.

8.2 General principles

The question of evidence of similar facts is one that is concerned with evidence suggestive of ignominious conduct on the part of the accused, criminal or civil[6] or indeed disreputable evidence of character, and whether such ought to be admissible as evidence of his guilt in the present proceedings, notwithstanding the fact that said evidence has no immediate connection with the present charge the accused faces.[7]

One of the earliest cases on the point was *R v Geering*.[8] This was a trial of the accused on a charge of murder of her husband by administering arsenic. Evidence was tendered with the view of showing that the accused's two sons had died from eating food prepared by the accused under circumstances similar to those that related to the death of her husband. According to Pollock CB, said evidence was admissible in as much as its tendency was to prove that the death of the husband was occasioned by arsenic, and was relevant to the question whether such taking was accidental or not. In *R v Dossett*[9] in which it appeared on a trial for arson, that a rick of wheat-straw had been set on fire thanks to the accused firing a gun next to it, Mauje J admitted evidence whose tendency was to show that the rick in question had been on fire the day before and that the accused was standing near it with his gun. According to the judge, '[a]lthough the evidence offered may be proof of another felony, that circumstance does not render it inadmissible, if the evidence be otherwise receivable. In many cases it is important question whether a thing was done accidentally or wilfully.' Further, in *R v Gray*,[10] where the issue concerned the attempt by the accused to defraud an insurance company for which the accused was on trial for arson in alleged criminal enterprise, evidence that the accused had made similar claims on two other insurance companies previously and in similar circumstances and on similar facts, was admitted for purposes of showing that the fire, subject of the present proceedings was no accident but a product of design.

In the late 19th century, the issue of evidence of similar facts and how it ought to be treated arose in *Makin v Attorney General for New South Wales.*[11] The accused had been charged with the murder of an infant who had been given

[10] 4 F&F 1102.

into their care by the child's mother after payment of a fee. They appealed after admission of evidence that several other infants had been received by the accused persons from other mothers and that their bodies were found buried in gardens of houses occupied by the prisoners. Lord Herschel who read the judgment of the court opined in part:

> It is undoubtedly not competent for the prosecution to adduce evidence tending to show that the accused has been guilty of criminal acts other than those covered in the indictment, for the purpose of leading to the conclusion that the accused is a person likely from his criminal conduct or character to have committed the offence for which he is being tried. On the other hand, the mere fact that the evidence adduced tends to show the commission of other crimes does not render it inadmissible if it is relevant to an issue before the [court] and it may be so relevant if it bears upon the question whether the acts alleged to constitute the crime charged in the indictment were designed or accidental, or to rebut a defence which would otherwise be open to the accused.

His lordship, however, admitted the difficulties that may arise nonetheless opining as follows: 'The statement of these general principles is easy, but it is obvious that it may often be very difficult to draw the line and to decide whether a particular piece of evidence is on the one side or the other.' After considering several authorities,[12] his lordship concluded as follows:

> Under the circumstances their Lordships cannot see that it was irrelevant to the issue to be tried [...] that several other infants had been received from their mothers on like representations, and upon payment of a sum inadequate for the support of the child for more than a very limited period, or that the bodies of infants had been found buried in a similar manner in the gardens of several houses occupied by the prisoners.

Until the decision by the House of Lords in *DPP v P*[13] which we consider shortly, the leading case which still continues to be relevant, the refinement resulting from the decision in *DPP v P*[14] notwithstanding, was *Boardman v DPP*.[15] The

[12] *R v Geering* 18 LJ (NS) (ME) 215; *R v Dossett* 2 C & K 306; *R v Gray* 4 F&F 1102; *R v Winslow* 8 Cox CC, 397 which was deemed irreconcilable with *Geering*.

[13] [1991] 2 AC 447; the decision has been considered as too general and of little assistance. Another point of view is that the decision introduced an unnecessarily stringent test as regards admissibility of similar facts evidence. On that score, those that subscribe to this school of thought contend that *R v Ryder,* 98 Cr App 1e 242, was as part of a backlash to the decision in *DPP v P* [1991] 2 AC 447.

[14] [1991] 2 AC 447.

[15] [1974] 3 All ER 887, [1975] AC 421; Decision of the Court of Appeal, Criminal Division, sub nom *R v Boardman* [1974] 2 All ER 958 affirmed. Editor's notes: For the admissibility of evidence of similar offences and acts of the accused, see 10 Halsbury's Laws (3rd Edn) 442–445, paras 818–820, and for cases on the subject, see 14 Digest (Repl) 416–428, 4061–4159.

appellant was the headmaster of a school which largely catered for boys up to the age of 19 from foreign countries who wished to learn English. He was charged on two counts with offences involving a 16-year-old boy, S, and a 17-year-old boy, H, both of whom were pupils at the school. Count 1 charged the appellant with buggery with S and count 2 charged him with inciting H to commit buggery with him. The counts were tried together and both S and H gave evidence. There was no suggestion that S and H had collaborated together to concoct a similar story. Each boy gave evidence that the appellant had visited the boy's dormitory in the early hours of the morning and invited the boy to go with him to his sitting room and that the appellant had asked each boy to take the active part, while the appellant took the passive part, in acts of buggery. In his summing-up the judge pointed out to the jury that the kind of criminal behaviour alleged against the appellant in the two counts was in each case of a particular, unusual kind; that it was not merely a straightforward case of a schoolmaster indecently assaulting a pupil but that there was an 'unusual feature' in that a grown man had attempted to get an adolescent boy to take the male part while he himself played the passive part in acts of buggery. On that basis the judge directed the jury that it was open to them to find in H's evidence on count 2 corroboration of S's evidence on count 1 and vice versa. The appellant was convicted on both counts. The Court of Appeal[16] dismissed an appeal by the appellant but certified that a question of law of general public importance was involved, i.e., where on a charge involving an allegation of homosexual conduct there was evidence that the accused was a man whose homosexual proclivities took a particular form, whether that evidence was thereby admissible even though it tended to show that the accused had been guilty of criminal acts other than those charged. On appeal, it was held as follows: (i) In exceptional cases evidence that the accused had been guilty of other offences was admissible if it showed that those offences shared with the offence which was the subject of the charge common features of such an unusual nature and striking similarity that it would be an affront to common sense to assert that the similarity was explicable on the basis of coincidence. In such cases the judge had a discretion to admit the evidence if he was satisfied (a) that its probative force in relation to an issue in the trial outweighed its prejudicial effect and (b) that there was no possibility of collaboration between the witnesses.[17] (ii) The general principle relating to the admissibility of 'similar fact' evidence was applicable to all offences. Homosexual offences were not to be treated as forming some separate category distinct from other offences and calling for the application of special rules. In particular the fact that there was evidence that a person accused of a homosexual offence was a man whose homosexual activities took a particular form was not by itself sufficient automatically to render that evidence admissible.[18] (iii) It was doubtful whether

[16] [1974] 2 All ER 958.

[17] *Makin v Attorney General for New South Wales* [1891–94] All ER Rep 24, *R v Sims* [1946] 1 All ER 697 and *Director of Public Prosecutions v Killbourne* [1973] 1 All ER 440 applied.

[18] Dicta of Lord Sumner in *Thompson v R* [1918] AC 221 at 235 and of Lord Goddard CJ in *R v Sims* [1946] 1 All ER at 701 disapproved.

the fact that a grown man had attempted to get an adolescent boy to play the active part, while he played the passive part, in acts of buggery was a sufficiently unusual feature to justify the admission of H's evidence in relation to count 1 and S's evidence in relation to count 2, but since there were other similarities in the two stories, in particular the appellant's nocturnal visits to the dormitories, it could not be said that the similar fact evidence was inadmissible or that the judge had exercised his discretion wrongly in admitting it. Accordingly, the appeal would be dismissed. *Per* Lord Cross of Chelsea:

> Where in cases involving accusations of homosexual offences the prosecution wish to adduce 'similar fact' evidence which the defence says is inadmissible, the question whether it is admissible ought, if possible, to be decided in the absence of the jury at the outset of the trial and if it is decided that the evidence is inadmissible and the accused is being charged in the same indictment with offences against the other men, the charges relating to the different persons ought to be tried separately.

8.3 The foundation of admissibility

The foundation of admissibility in so far as evidence of similar facts is concerned may be seen within the context of, on the one hand, sufficiency of probative value and on the other, the unlikelihood of coincidence. We discuss each instance in turn.

8.3.1 Sufficiency of probative value

The basis for admitting evidence have been carefully crafted through case law over the years purely because it is generally suspect evidence with which the courts must deal with due care to obviate against unjust outcomes. Therefore, to be admissible under the similar facts rule, evidence ought to be of such probative force as to make it supportive of the assertion that the accusation against the person charged is of sufficient gravity as to justify the admissibility of evidence, the fact that such evidence is prejudicial to the accused person as regards its tendency to show that the accused is guilty of having committed another crime, notwithstanding. This may be done by distilling what may be termed striking similarities in the evidence regarding the methods employed to commit the offence in question. A caveat is, however, necessary and it is this: The restriction of circumstances or factual matrix where sufficient probative force is inherent in order to overawe the prejudicial effect of evidence regarding another offence 'to cases where there is some striking similarity between them is to restrict the operation of the principle in a way which gives too much effect to a particular manner of stating it, and is not justified in principle'[19]

[19] *Archbold* 1997 1238.

In the leading case of *DPP v P*,[20] the [accused] faced specimen counts of rape and incest against each of his two daughters. The trial judge refused an application for separate trials in respect of the offences alleged against each daughter. The [accused] was convicted. It was held, allowing the appeal, as follows: The judge had erred in refusing separate trials. Lord Lane CJ said that the court had looked in vain for features of similarity that was striking or that went beyond 'the incestuous father's 'stock in trade' that were considered necessary if the evidence of offences against one daughter was to be admissible in relation to the offences alleged against the other. The prosecution appealed. 'Similar facts' is a shorthand term for identifiable common or related features of probative value going beyond mere coincidence. It is not appropriate to single out striking similarity as an essential element in every case. The essential feature of evidence which is to be admitted is that its probative force is sufficiently great to make it just to admit the evidence, notwithstanding that it is prejudicial to the accused intending to show that he was guilty of another crime.

> Once the principle is recognised, that what has to be assessed is the probative force of the evidence in question, the infinite variety of circumstances in which the question arises, demonstrates that there is no single manner in which this can be achieved. Whether the evidence has sufficient probative value to outweigh its prejudicial effect is a question of degree. Where the identity of the perpetrator is an issue, and evidence of this kind is important in that connection, obviously something in the nature of what has been called in the course of the argument a signature or other special feature will be necessary. To transpose this requirement to other situations where the question is whether a crime has been committed, rather than who did commit it, is to impose an unnecessary and improper restriction upon the application of the principle.[21]

The test for admissibility of evidence of similar facts was set out in *DPP v P*,[22] *per* Lord Mackay LC:[23]

> From all that was said by the House in *DPP v Boardman*[24] I would deduce the essential feature of evidence which is to be admitted is that its probative force in support of the allegation that an accused

[20] [1991] 93 Crim App R 267, [1991] 2 AC 447, [1991] 3 All ER 337, [1991] 3 WLR 161; https://swarb.co.uk/director-of-public-prosecutions-v-p-hl-1991/ retrieved on 10/10/21.

[21] At 447.

[22] [1991] 93 Crim App R 267, [1991] 2 AC 447, [1991] 3 All ER 337, [1991] 3 WLR 161; https://swarb.co.uk/director-of-public-prosecutions-v-p-hl-1991/ retrieved on 10/10/21.

[23] At 447.

[24] [1975] AC 421.

> person committed a crime is sufficiently great to make it just to admit the evidence, notwithstanding that it is prejudicial to the accused in tending to show that he was guilty of another crime.' While probative force may be derived from the striking similarity of the similar fact evidence this was not a precondition of admissibility: 'Once the principle is recognised, that what has to be assessed is the probative force of the evidence in question, the infinite variety of circumstances in which the question arises, demonstrates that there is no single manner in which this can be achieved. Whether the evidence has sufficient probative value to outweigh its prejudicial effect must in each case be a question of degree.

As noted elsewhere in this text following the decision in *DPP v Boardman*,[25] a notion had unfortunately developed that the basis for admissibility was the "striking similarity" test between the similar fact evidence on the one hand and evidence relating to the offence with which the accused was being tried for. *DPP v P*[26] has clarified this position. It now follows that the gradation of likeness mandated will differ based on the issues in the particular case as well as the nature of the other evidence.

Be that as it may, *DPP v P*[27] also raises obvious challenges. The decision appears not to explicitly state what ought to be taken into consideration or what amounts to 'investing evidence' to arm evidence of similar facts with an appropriate degree of probative value. This seeming disadvantage is, however, easily resolved when we make reference to the five speeches in *DPP v Boardman*[28] which Lord Mackay had made reference to in his judgment.

8.3.2 The implausibility of coincidence

Where the explanation of evidence on the basis of coincidence would be an "affront to common sense" or "against all probabilities" or would be an elucidation deemed acceptable to only an "ultra-cautious [court]," such evidence would be admissible under the similar facts rules as it must be taken to have the obligatory probative strength.[29] For any discussion relating to evidence of similar facts we can do no better than to advert to the words of Lord Herschell in *Makin v Att-General for New South Wales:*[30]

> It is undoubtedly not competent for the prosecution to adduce evidence tending to by show the indictment that the accused for the has been guilty of leading of criminal to the acts conclusion other than that those the is a person likely from his conduct or character to have committed the for which he is being tried. mere fact that evidence

[25] [1975] AC 421.

[26] [1991] 93 Crim App R 267, [1991] 2 AC 447, [1991] 3 All ER 337, [1991] 3 WLR 161.

[27] [1991] 93 Crim App R 267, [1991] 2 AC 447, [1991] 3 All ER 337, [1991] 3 WLR 161; Followed in the Canadian cases of *R v C (MH)* (1991) 63 CCC (3d) 385 at 392; *R v B (FF)* (1993) 79 CCC (3d) 112).

[28] [1975] AC 421.

[29] *DPP v Boardman* [1975] AC 421.

[30] [1894] AC 57 PC.

> adduced tends to the commission of other crimes does not render it inadmissible if it be show relevant to an issue before the jury, and it may be so relevant if it bears on the question whether the acts alleged to constitute the crime charged in the indictment were designed to accidental, or to rebut a defence which would be otherwise open to the accused. - The statement of these general principles is easy, but it is obvious that it may often be very difficult to draw the line and to decide whether a particular piece of evidence is on the one side or the other.[31]

In opining as the court did in *Makin*,[32] it is submitted, one may conclude that the justification for the admissibility of evidence of similar facts is the implausibility of coincidence.[33] This conclusion is predicated on the court noting that while there was a possibility of an accidental occurrence, it was inconceivable that the accused may have two or more accidents of a comparable nature. In *DPP v Boardman*[34] the five speeches of which portions are discussed below, made reference to the significance of coincidence in so far as evidence of similar facts was concerned. Lord Morris in particular noted as follows:[35]

> In his speech in *Harris v DPP*[36] Viscount Simon pointed out [...] that it would be an error to attempt to draw up a closed list of the sorts of cases in which the principle operates. Just as a closed list need not be contemplated so also, where what is important is the application of principle, the use of labels or definitive descriptions cannot be either comprehensive or restrictive. While there may be many reasons why what is called 'similar fact' evidence is admissible there are some cases where words used by Hallett J are apt In *R v Robinson*[37] he said, at 'If a jury are precluded by some rule of law from taking the view that something is coincidence which is against all probabilities if the accused person is innocent, then it would seem to be a doctrine of law which prevents a jury from using what looks like ordinary common sense.' But as Viscount Simon pointed out in *Harris v DPP*[38] evidence

[31] *Makin v Att-General for New South Wales* [1894] AC 57 PC at 65; For a New Zealand view see *R v Accused* (1991) 7 CRNZ 604; *R v McIntosh* (1991) 8 CRNZ 514; for an Australian take see as cited and quoted in *Pfenning v R* (1995) 127 ALR 99, *Markby v The Queen* (1978) 140 CLR 108 at 116; *Perry v The Queen* (1982) 150 CLR 580 at 609; *Sutton v The Queen* (1984) 152 CLR at 533, 545-546, 556-557, 562-563) . It was also accepted that, in order to be admissible, propensity evidence must possess "a strong degree of probative force": (35 *Markby v The Queen* (1978) 140 CLR at 117; *Perry v The Queen* (1982) 150 CLR at 586, 589, 604; *Sutton v The Queen* (1984) 152 CLR at 533) or the probative force of the evidence must clearly transcend the prejudicial effect of mere criminality or propensity (36 Perry (1982) 150 CLR at 609; Sutton (1984) 152 CLR at 548-549, 559-560, 565; *Harriman v The Queen* (1989) 167 CLR 590 at 633) . Very often, propensity evidence is received when there is a striking similarity between different offences or between the evidence of different witnesses a (37 *Markby v The Queen* (1978) 140 CLR at 117; *Perry v The Queen* (1982) 150 CLR at 603, 607, 610; *Sutton v The Queen* (1984) 152 CLR at 535, 549, 559, 566-567).

[32] [1894] AC 57 PC.

[33] *DPP v Boardman* [1975] AC 421.

[34] [1975] AC 421.

[35] He was making reference to Lord Herschell's speech in *Makin v Att-General for New South Wales* [1894] AC 57 PC where his lordship mentioned several instances in which similar facts evidence may be admissible.

[36] [1952] AC 694 at 705.

[37] (1953) 37 Cr App R 95.

[38] [1952] AC 694, 708.

> of other occurrences which merely tend to deepen suspicion does not go to prove guilt so evidence of 'similar facts' should be excluded unless such evidence has a really material bearing on the issues to be decided.[39]

It would appear that barring collusion, the probability of innocence of the accused ought to be considered within the context of admissible evidence of similar facts that tends to show that there is considerable similarity between instances of criminal activity in which the accused was involved before to the present charge even if the said instances are not able to show that the accused committed the offence with which he is charged.

Lord Wilberforce for his part anchored the admissibility of evidence on similar facts on in its special nature and profound or/and compelling degree of probative force in the following terms:

> This probative force is derived, if at all, from the circumstance that the facts testified to by the several witnesses bear to each other such a striking similarity that they must when judged by experience and common sense, either all be true or have arisen from a cause common to the witnesses or from pure coincidence.[40]

Lord Hailsham took the view that in all cases without exception, the judge had to, as a matter of law on the one hand, and discretion on the other, apply his mind to the facts and come to the conclusion, once satisfied, that to treat the matter before court as one whose occurrence is attributable to coincidence by way of, among other things, pattern or system or nexus is 'an affront to common sense.'[41] Further, that '[i]n this the ordinary rules of logic and common sense prevail [...] Attempts to codify the rules of common sense are to be resisted'[42]

In his speech[43] Lord Cross opined that when it comes to evidence of similar fact the question ought to be whether the such evidence when it is combined with other evidence would merely strengthen the suspicion that the accused committed the offence with which he is charged without more or whether it would point to the certainty of guilt such that only a radically-vigilant court, if it accepted the account would *prima facie*, convict the accused. He also stated that the question of admissibility of evidence on similar fact rules is one of law and not discretion. Be that as it may, his lordship noted, the question ought to be one of degree.

---

39 [1952] AC 694, 708.

40 At 444.

41 *DPP v Kilbourne* [1973] AC 729 at 759 *per* Lord Simon of Glaisdale.

42 At 453-454.

43 At 457; Compare *R v Sims* [1946] KB. 531, 31 Cr App R 158, CCA, with those arising in cases such as *R v Straffen* [19521 2 QB 911, 36 Cr App R 132, CCA, and *R v Smith* (GJ), 11 Cr App R 229, CCA (the "brides in the bath" case).

The final speech was given by Lord Salmon who opined as follows:[44]

> The test must be—is the evidence capable of tending to persuade a reasonable jury disposition of the accused on some ground other than is charged? In the case of [some] alleged [...] offence, just as in the case of an alleged burglary, evidence which proves merely that the accused has committed crimes in the past and is therefore disposed to commit the crime charged is clearly inadmissible. It has however never been doubted that if the crime charged is committed in a uniquely or strikingly similar manner to other crimes committed by the accused, the manner in which the other crimes were committed may be evidence on which a [court] could reasonably conclude that the accused unique the accused was that guilty of the crime charged. The similarity would have to be so unique or striking that common sense makes it inexplicable on the basis of coincidence [...] the question of whether the evidence is capable of being so regarded by a reasonable [court] is a question of law.

8.3.3 *A divergent view*[45]

In *R v H*,[46] Lord Must took the view, albeit obiter, that the implausibility of coincidence could not predicate a decision that similar fact evidence had the essential probative value. As he saw it, the decision in *DPP v P*,[47] was supportive of his view. Any decisions predicating decision making in so far as similar fact evidence was concerned on implausibility of coincidence were grounded in an erroneous appreciation of the decision in *DPP v Kilbourne*.[48] The position by his lordship is not entirely correct. On one level, Lord Mustill is correct but only to the degree that there indeed was, to some extent as exemplified in several cases following *Kilbourne*,[49] *Boardman*[50] *and Makin*,[51] an elevation of the expression employed in *Kilbourne*[52] specifically, "striking similarity" into a universal

---

[44] At 462.

[45] See generally, Archbold 1997 13-9 1241.

[46] [1995] 2 AC 596, HL; but see Australian decision in *Pfenning v R* (1995) 127 ALR 99 which is more in keeping with decisions in *DPP v Kilbourne* [1973] AC 729, HL; *DPP v Boardman* [1975] AC 421; *DPP v P* [1991] 2 AC 447.

[47] [1991] 2 AC 447.

[48] [1973] AC 729, HL.

[49] [1973] AC 729, HL.

[50] [1975] AC 421.

[51] [1894] AC 57, 65.

[52] [1973] AC 729, HL.

test.[53] What appears to be out of sync with *Kilbourne*[54] itself and *DPP v P*[55] is the supposition by Lord Mustill that any rationalisation of evidence of similar facts on the basis of the implausibility of coincidence is to misunderstand the authorities which he criticises. Nor did *DPP v P*[56] come to his lordship's aid as he supposed. The whole basis of what was said in *Makin*[57] for example is the concept of rationalisation of evidence of similar facts on the implausibility of coincidence. That same concept was at the centre of all the five speeches in *Boardman,*[58] portions of which we have made reference to above. Lord Simon made reference to the implausibility of coincidence in referencing the subject of evidence of similar facts in *Kilbourne*[59] which was cited with approval by the Lord Chancellor in his speech in *R v H.*[60]

That the formulation of Lord Mustill in *R v H*[61] is a rather curious appreciation of the decisions he contends he is basing his opinion is quite clear from what we have said above. His, however, is a formulation that cannot be reconciled with the ultimate import of decisions such as *Kilbourne,*[62] *Boardman*[63] *and Makin.*[64] It is also out of keeping with the Australian decision in *Pfenning v R*[65] whose formulation is considered to be 'of more practical utility than that of Lord Mustill in *H.*'[66] Citing Mason CJ, Wilson and Gaudron JJ in *Hoch v The Queen,*[67] the High Court took the view that the basis for the admission of similar fact

[53] It has been said in *Pfenning v R* (1995) 127 ALR 99 that 'striking similarity, underlying unity and other like descriptions of similar facts are not essential to the admission of such evidence, though usually the evidence will lack the requisite probative force if the evidence does not possess such characteristics [...] that approach conforms with the approach that now exists in the United Kingdom, Canada and New Zealand;' In *Harriman v The Queen* (1989) 167 CLR at 597-598), Dawson J pointed out that '[i]n the past, evidence of a criminal propensity to commit crime in general, or a particular kind of crime, appears to have been regarded as inadmissible because it was thought to be purely prejudicial, and therefore irrelevant, rather than relevant but excluded because of its prejudicial nature. Upon this basis it was said that it became admissible only if some relevance could be shown beyond the propensity itself.'

[54] [1973] AC 729, HL.

[55] [1991] 93 Crim App R 267, [1991] 2 AC 447, [1991] 3 All ER 337, [1991] 3 WLR 161.

[65] (1995) 127 ALR 99; see also *HML v The Queen* (2008) 235 CLR 334; see as cited and quoted in *Pfenning v R* (1995) 127 ALR 99, *Markby v The Queen* (1978) 140 CLR 108 at 116; *Perry v The Queen* (1982) 150 CLR 580 at 609; *Sutton v The Queen* (1984) 152 CLR at 533, 545-546, 556-557, 562-563) . It was also accepted that, in order to be admissible, propensity evidence must possess "a strong degree of probative force"a (*Markby* (1978) 140 CLR at 117; Perry (1982) 150 CLR at 586, 589, 604; *Sutton* (1984) 152 CLR at 533) or the probative force of the evidence must clearly transcend the prejudicial effect of mere criminality or propensity (36 *Perry* (1982) 150 CLR at 609; *Sutton* (1984) 152 CLR at 548-549, 559-560, 565; *Harriman v The Queen* (1989) 167 CLR 590 at 633) . Very often, propensity evidence is received when there is a striking similarity between different offences or between the evidence of different witnesses a (*Markby* (1978) 140 CLR at 117; Perry (1982) 150 CLR at 603, 607, 610; *Sutton* (1984) 152 CLR at 535, 549, 559, 566-567). It is worth noting comments in *Pfenning v R* (1995) 127 ALR 99 [58] about the foregoing authorities which are in keeping with the criticisms of decisions in *DPP v P* [1991] 2 AC 447 which had followed the decision in *DPP v Boardman* which elevated the term "strikingly similar" used in that case into an all-purpose tool: 'The insistence in some of the judgments of this Court on the need to show that propensity evidence was relevant to "some other issue" as one of the prerequisites of its admissibility so as to prove the commission of the offences charged contributed to a misunderstanding of the *Makin* ([1894] AC 57, 65) principles and to statements of principles which lacked a clear and coherent theoretical foundation,' a fact recognised by Mason CJ, Wilson and Gaudron JJ in *Hoch v The Queena* (1988) 165 CLR 292 at 294).

[66] Archbold 1997 1242 13-10.

[67] (1988) 165 CLR 292, at 294-295.

evidence lies in its possessing a particular probative value or cogency such that, if accepted, it bears no reasonable explanation other than the inculpation of the accused in the offence charged. In other words, for propensity or similar fact evidence to be admissible, the objective improbability of it having some innocent explanation is such that there is no reasonable view of it other than as supporting an inference that the accused is guilty of the offence charged. Quoting the preceding passage, Dawson J in *R v Harriman*[68] observed as follows:

> Assuming similar fact evidence to be relevant to some issue in the trial, the criterion of its admissibility is the strength of its probative force [...] That strength lies in the fact that the evidence reveals 'striking similarities', 'unusual features', 'underlying unity', 'system' or 'pattern' such that it raises, as a matter of common sense and experience, the objective improbability of some event having occurred other than as alleged by the prosecution.

Going further, the Court in *Pfeiffer*[69] drew a distinction between cases in which the "similar facts" are not in dispute and cases in which such facts are in dispute. It again premised its reasoning on that of Mason CJ, Wilson and Gaudron JJ in *Hoch v The Queen:*[70]

> Where the happening of the matters said to constitute similar facts is not in dispute and there is evidence to connect the accused person with one or more of the happenings, evidence of those similar facts may render it objectively improbable that a person other than the accused committed the act in question, that the relevant act was unintended, or that it occurred innocently or fortuitously. The similar fact evidence is then admissible as evidence relevant to that issue.

The Court then went to opine as follows:

> Where the propensity or similar fact evidence is in dispute, it is still relevant to prove the commission of the acts charged.[71] The probative value of the evidence lies in the improbability of witnesses giving accounts of happenings having the degree of similarity unless the events occurred. Obviously, the probative value of disputed similar facts is less than the probative value those facts would have if they were not disputed. But the prejudicial effect of those facts may not be significantly reduced because the prejudicial effect that the law is concerned to guard against is the possibility that the jury will treat the similar facts as establishing an inference of guilt where neither logic nor experience would necessitate the conclusion that it clearly points to the guilt of the accused. Because propensity evidence is a special

[68] (1989) 167 CLR at 600.

[69] (1995) HCA 7.

[70] (1988) 165 CLR 292, at 294-295.

[71] *Boardman* (1975) AC at 452, 458-459; *Sutton* (1984) 152 CLR at 556-557; *Hoch* (1988) 165 CLR at 295).

> class of circumstantial evidence, its probative force is to be gauged in the light of its character as such. But because it has a prejudicial capacity of a high order, the trial judge must apply the same test as a jury must apply in dealing with circumstantial evidence and ask whether there is a rational view of the evidence that is consistent with the innocence of the accused.[72]

8.3.4 *Applying the law relating to evidence of similar facts: a real-world approach*

There are at least five instances in which the law relating to evidence of similar facts may find use in practice:

(i) The judge's role
(ii) Issues and evidence
(iii) Where identity is in issue
(iv) Mistake accident or/and innocent association
(v) Assertion relating to a prosecution witness being mistaken or being deceitful

We consider each one in turn.

8.3.4.1 *The judge's role*

Where the prosecution intends and seeks to introduce evidence under the tenets of similar facts evidence, they are calling upon the judge to render a ruling, as a matter of law, on the admissibility of the evidence in question.[73] As has been noted in the Australian High Court decision in *Pfenning v R*:[74]

> Once that criterion of admissibility is accepted, it is apparent that the trial judge is required to discharge an important responsibility. That point was made by the Supreme Court of Canada in *Reg. v B*[75] where it was accepted that the process of balancing the probative value of the evidence against its prejudicial effect was a delicate one. But the trial judge, in making that judgment, must recognize that propensity evidence is circumstantial evidence and that, as such, it should not be used to draw an inference adverse to the accused unless it is the only reasonable inference in the circumstances. More than that, the

---

[72] *Hoch v The Queen* (1988) 165 CLR at 296 (where Mason CJ, Wilson and Gaudron JJ expressed agreement with the remarks of Dawson J in *Sutton* (1984) 152 CLR at 564). See also *Harriman* (1989) 167 CLR at 602). Here "rational" must be taken to mean "reasonable": see *Peacock v The King* (1911) 13 CLR 619 at 634; *Plomp v The Queen* (1963) 110 CLR 234 at 252) and the trial judge must ask himself or herself the question in the context of the prosecution case; that is to say, he or she must regard the evidence as a step in the proof of that case. Only if Only if there is no such view can one safely conclude that the probative force of the evidence outweighs its prejudicial effect. And, unless the tension between probative force and prejudicial effect is governed by such a principle, striking the balance will continue to resemble the exercise of a discretion rather than the application of a principle.

[73] *DPP v Boardman* [1975] AC 421.

[74] (1995) HCA 7; 127 ALR 99; Mason CJ, Deane and Dawson JJ.

[75] (1990) 55 CCC (3d) 1.

> evidence ought not to be admitted if the trial judge concludes that, viewed in the context of the prosecution case, there is a reasonable view of it which is consistent with innocence.[76]

At the core of a judge's considerations are (i) the issues in the case; and (ii) other evidence made available to the court. As a matter of procedure, the judge/magistrate, as the case may be, will call upon the prosecution to state with precision the line of reasoning that the evidence is intended to support. In addition, the judge/magistrate will have to consider whether the nature of the evidence of similar facts of such a species that only an extreme court, within the case when holistically analysed, would not convict upon it or expressed differently, whether explaining the evidence of similar facts on the basis of coincidence would, as Lord Simon has opined in *DPP v Kilbourne,*[77] lead to common sense revolt.

8.3.4.2 *Issues and evidence within the context of criminal proceedings*

The principles relating to evidence of similar facts become clearer when it is considered within the context of the criminal law in general and criminal proceedings in particular. It will be seen how the other evidence available may affect the decision the judge has to make. It seems to be the law as stated in *R v Clarke (Robert Lee)*[78] that prior to any determination regarding the admissibility of evidence of similar facts, whatever the case, the court ought to appreciate what the issue is or is likely to be and further, as regards the charge that the accused faces, what the evidence against him/her is.

A good question to ask then is what issues are likely to rise in instances where the question as regards the admissibility of evidence of similar facts arises. The answer is that there several instances which should be seen not as an exhaustive list but 'useful classes of example:'[79]

(a) The first instance is one where the only issue the court is called upon to determine is whether the accused is the person guilty of an offence subject of the proceedings and with which he is charged. In this case it is common cause that the offence in question has occurred or did indeed occur on a given date or dates and where it is not a victimless offence, that there is a victim.[80] In *R v Lovegrove*[81] the appellant was indicted for unlawfully killing, and for procuring he miscarriage of a Mrs. Purcell. At the trial, evidence was given for the prosecution by the husband of the deceased that, having obtained the appellant's name and address from a Mrs Type, he went to the appellant's house

[76] *R v Sutton* (1984) 152 CLR at 564; *Hochv The Queen*(1988) 165 CLR at 296; *R v Harriman* (1989) 167 CLR at 602.

[77] [1973] AC 729, HL.

[78] [1995] 2 Cr App R 425 at 435, CA.

[79] Which must be seen within the context of speech by Lord Hailsham and especially that of Lord Morris in *DPP v Boardman* [1975] AC 421.

[80] See *R v Straffen* [1952] 2 QB 911, 36 Cr App R 132, CCA.

[81] (1921) 26 Cox CC 683.

and arranged with her for his wife to go there for an abortion. His wife subsequently went to the appellant's house and afterwards had a miscarriage and died of septic abortion. The evidence of Mrs Type was tendered by the prosecution to show that the appellant had performed a similar operation on her some months previously. The evidence was objected to on the ground that the defence was a denial of the husband's evidence and that the appellant had never seen the deceased woman. The evidence was admitted and the appellant convicted. In reading the judgment of the court Earl of Reading CJ observed *inter alia*:

> This Court has said [...] that the question in each case is whether on the facts the evidence is admissible according to the established principles of law [...][82] We do not desire either to extend or to restrict the principle laid down in Makin's Case and in similar cases. But the present case does not depend on the principle there laid down. The evidence of Mrs Type was inadmissible if it was relevant to an issue before the [court], and it was none the less inadmissible though it might prove that the appellant had committed a similar crime on a previous occasion. In our opinion Mrs Type's evidence tended to prove that Purcell's account of what took place at the first interview was true, and that the appellant's version of the interview was untrue; it also tended to prove Purcell did take his wife to the appellant's house in the evening of the same day for the purpose of having an illegal operation performed by the appellant. The evidence was, therefore rightly admitted, and this ground of appeal fails.

(b) The second instance relates to situations which lead to the conclusion that no offence was committed as the physical act (e.g., receipt of stolen goods) necessary to the commission of the offence were predicated on and have an innocent explanation. In such instances there is no doubt as regards the clarity of matters which the accused is alleged to have committed and is thus charged with or that the solitary variation relates to detail only. The real issues to be determined are then narrowed to whether the act(s) were:

(a) By design

In *R v Smith*,[83] the appellant was convicted of the murder of Bessie Munday. Evidence was admitted to show that he murdered two other women at a later date in similar circumstances. This was because the judge concluded that

---

[82] See *Makin v Attorney-General for New South Wales* [1894] AC 57; *R v Ollis* [1900] 2 QB 758, 781; *R v Bond* [1906] 2 KB 389, 414; *R v Shellaker* [1914] 1 KB 414.

[83] (1915) 11 Cr App R 229; portions taken from https://legalhelpdesklawyers.com.au/1915/08/13/1915-brides-in-the-bath-case/ retrieved on 16/10/21.

it was improbable that three different women would have accidentally drowned in the bath given that their deaths occurred not long after entering marriage and financial arrangements under which the accused would stand to benefit if they died. On appeal, the question raised was that the judge was wrong in admitting evidence of the deaths of Alice Burnham and Margaret Lofty. The appeal was unsuccessful.

(b) By accident

Reading LCJ observed as follows in *R v Smith:*[84]

> Now in this case the prosecution tendered the evidence, and it was admitted by the judge on the ground that it tended to show that the act charged had been committed, that is, had been designed. It is sufficient to say that it is not disputed, and could not be disputed, that if as a matter of law there was prima facie evidence that the appellant committed the act charged, evidence of similar acts became admissible, and we have come to the conclusion that there was undoubtedly, as a matter of law, prima facie evidence that the accused committed the act charged, evidence of similar acts became admissible, and we have come to the conclusion that there was undoubtedly, as a matter of law, prima facie evidence that the appellant committed the act charged apart altogether from the other cases [...] In our opinion it was open to the prosecution to give, and the judge was right in admitting, evidence of the facts surrounding the deaths of the two women.

(c) Offence(s) was/were committed by accused under mistake of fact

The starting point is s 10 of the Penal Code[85] which provides as follows:

> [a] person who does or omits to do an act under an honest and reasonable, but mistaken, belief in the existence of any state of things is not

[84] (1915) 11 Cr App R 229; portions taken from https://legalhelpdesklawyers.com.au/1915/08/13/1915-brides-in-the-bath-case/ retrieved on 16/10/21.

[85] Chapter 87 of the Laws of Zambia.

> criminally responsible for the act or omission to any greater extent than if the real state of things had been such as he believed to exist. The operation of this rule may be excluded by the express or implied provisions of the law relating to the subject.

In *R v Francis*,[86] on the trial of an indictment for endeavouring to obtain an advance from a pawnbroker upon a ring by the false pretences that it was a diamond ring, evidence was admitted that two days before the transaction in question the prisoner had obtained an advance from a pawnbroker upon a chain which he represented to be a gold chain, but which was not so, and endeavoured to obtain from' other pawnbrokers advances upon a ring which he represented to be a diamond ring, but which, in the opinion of the witnesses, was not so. This ring was not produced. It was held that the evidence was properly admitted.

(c) The third instance is related to the second because like the second instance, the occurrence of the offence allegedly committed by the accused and with which the accused is charged is denied primarily because the evidence of the witness who speaks to the facts speaking to the commission of the offence is denied. The basis for the foregoing may be an assertion by defence counsel that the evidence is a figment of the witness's imagination, an invention or simply borne of a sincere mistake by the witness in question. As regards the latter point, in *Thompson v R*[87] the accused was charged with gross indecency against boys. The defendant denied that he was the offender. Evidence was admitted that on arrest the defendant was in possession of powder puffs and that a search of his rooms uncovered indecent photographs of boys. It was held that the evidence was admissible on the issue of the identity of the offender. Lord Sumner stated that while proof of guilt of a particular crime does not arise from proof of a general disposition to commit that crime, evidence was admissible to prove guilty knowledge or intent or a system or to rebut an appearance of innocence. However, the prosecution may not credit the accused with fancy defences in order to rebut them at the outset with some damning piece of prejudice.

8.3.4.3 *Where identity is in issue*

Where the issue of identity arises, what the court is concerned with is the degree of similarity required. That aspect will ordinarily vary based on other evidence in the case. In the absence of other evidence, a signature, where one exists or fingerprint, where one was taken or can be found will be required. To

---

[86] (1874) LR 2 CCR 128, (1874) 12 Cox 612.

[87] 1918 AC 221.

illustrate, the foregoing, we must turn to two provisions under Part Chapter XXIX,[88] of the Penal Code.[89] The first is s 300 which defines 'breaking and entering' in the following terms:

> (1) A person who breaks any part, whether external or internal, of a building, or opens by unlocking, pulling, pushing, lifting, or any other means whatever, any door, window, shutter, cellar flap, or other thing, intended to close or cover an opening in a building, or an opening giving passage from one part of a building to another, is deemed to break the building.
> (2) A person is deemed to enter a building as soon as any part of his body or any part of any instrument used by him is within the building.
> (3) A person who obtains entrance into a building by means of any threat or artifice used for that purpose, or by collusion with any person in the building, or who enters any chimney or other aperture of the building permanently left open for any necessary purpose, but not intended to be ordinarily used as a means of entrance, is deemed to have broken and entered the building.

The second is s 301 which is headlined '[h]ouse-breaking and burglary, and provides as follows:

> [a]ny person who-
> (a) breaks and enters any dwelling house with intent to commit a felony therein; or
> (b) having entered any dwelling house with intent to commit a felony therein, or having committed a felony in any such dwelling house, breaks out thereof; is guilty of the felony termed "housebreaking" and is liable to imprisonment for seven years. If the offence is committed in the night, it is termed "burglary" and the offender is liable to imprisonment for ten years.

The importance of the preceding provisions to our discussion is illustrative only. The basic truth is that if a person was charged with committing acts contrary to ss 300 and 301, the prosecution would have to prove their case and prove that the ingredients of the offence as defined in the concerned sections are present. Within the context of our discussion therefore, where housebreaking and/or burglary, as the case may be, has occurred predicated on the accused having pretended to be something he is not e.g., a plumber or telephone technician or electrician from a local utility such as Lusaka Water and Sanitation Company or Zamtel or indeed Zesco, as the case may be, it would not be sufficient for the

[88] Which provides for *Burglary, Housebreaking and Similar Offences* in ss 300 – 307.

[89] Chapter 87 of the Laws of Zambia.

prosecution to predicate their case solely on similar fact evidence to prove or indeed seek to prove that the accused in the present case had, on innumerable occasions been arrested, charged, tried and convicted of committing burglary contrary to ss 300 and 301 by means such as those employed in the present case. The situation would, however, be different if the prosecution could show that in all the burglaries for which the accused in the present case was tried for he, as is the case now, a gold bracelet was stolen, and gold jewellery taken. Would a contention by defence counsel that this was purely coincidental be 'an affront to common sense'?[90] It does not also seem likely that a conviction would follow where the person who pretended to be a plumber or telephone technician or indeed an electrician is identified by the person who was the victim of the deception and burglary a few days or weeks down the line if this was the only evidence following the accused's arrest and eventual trial for burglary. Even so, where the scenario is as described above, that is, that the accused had several run-ins with the law on the premise of pretending that he was anyone of the things he was not, hereinbefore described, for which he was convicted several times, this would constitute admissible evidence, *a fortiori*, because in each case, he only took gold jewellery as in the present case.

The leading case in this regard is *R v Straffen*.[91] The [accused] had been arrested for murders of young girls, but after being found unfit to plead, he was committed to Broadmoor. While he escaped another girl was murdered, and he was charged. The prosecutor sought to bring in evidence of admissions made at Broadmoor and of the earlier allegations. It was held that the Judges' Rules were intended to control the admission of statements made to the police, not statements elsewhere. The statement was admissible. The defendant had denied the murder but in doing so had admitted the earlier murders. The general rule is not to admit such evidence. The similar fact evidence could be described as evidence of pure propensity to commit crimes similar to that with which he was charged.

At every turn the judge/magistrate ought to ask himself/herself whether the disputed evidence as regards identity when identity is in issue would be a proverbial '[...] affront to common sense'[92] or whether it is the kind of evidence that only an 'ultra-cautious [court]' would fail to act on.[93] We, therefore, cannot overemphasise the indispensability to the concept of evidence of similar facts of the consideration of (i) all the relevant evidence; (ii) the question to which the undecided evidence relates; and (iii) how said evidence is said to relate thereto. Inherent in the evidence deemed admissible under the evidence of similar facts is the supposition that the chance that the witness has made a mistake has been excluded. In *Thompson v R*,[94] a case we have already discussed elsewhere in this text, the accused was, as we have already noted, charged with

[90] *DPP v Kilbourne* [1973] AC 729 at 759 *per* Lord Simon of Glaisdale.

[91] [1952] 2 QB 911, 36 Cr App R 132; summary found at https://swarb.co.uk/regina-v-straffen-cca-20-aug-1952/ retrieved on 17/10/21.

[92] *DPP v Kilbourne* [1973] AC 729 at 759 *per* Lord Simon of Glaisdale.

[93] *DPP v Boardman* [1975] AC 421.

[94] [1918] AC 221 HL.

offences of gross indecency committed against two boys in a public commode on a Friday. The defendant denied that he was the offender. Evidence was admitted that on arrest the defendant was in possession of powder puffs and that a search of his rooms uncovered indecent photographs of boys. It was held that the evidence was admissible on the issue of the identity of the offender. Lord Sumner stated that while proof of guilt of a particular crime does not arise from proof of a general disposition to commit that crime, evidence was admissible to prove guilty knowledge or intent or a system or to rebut an appearance of innocence. However, the prosecution may not credit the accused with fancy defences in order to rebut them at the outset with some damning piece of prejudice. For his part, Lord Atkinson appeared to go further than the other lordships had done. While the accused the man on the Friday made an appointment for the Monday, next, he equivocated in his deportment and the contents of his conversation on said Monday. Be that as it may, the articles discovered on his person appeared to disprove the idea of innocent conduct on the Monday. The logical question to ask would then become, according to his lordship, what the chances were that one man 'making an appointment for an obviously immoral purpose and of another man being wrongly identified as that man, yet happening to harbour exactly the same intent as the first man?'[95] There are a few takeaways from the foregoing discussion:

(i) It seems clear that a high degree of cogency is required in matters relating to evidence of similar facts with regard given to the context, facts and circumstances of each case.

(ii) Judges will obviously take great care ,in considering the admissibility of such evidence.

(iii) Care should be taken to analyse any proposition that certain facts cannot be rationally explicated as quirky, for fear that there be an assertion of an element of self-realisation. To illustrate, if a boy complains to the police about being accosted by a man for purposes of having 'carnal knowledge of [him] against the order of nature' contrary to ss 155 and 156 of the Penal Code[96] in an area where such persons are known to frequent, it would be unnecessary to find out whether the person pointed out to the police by the complainant has homosexual convictions, nor would it be necessary to venture on this sort of enquiry if the accused was randomly caught in said area.

8.3.4.4 Mistake accident or/and innocent association

Where what is in issue is mistake, accident or innocent association, the degree of similarity required may not be as stringent as that required when what is in issue is identity. Even so, it only just to expect that for such evidence to be accepted it too must meet a minimum threshold persuasiveness.[97]

---

[95] Archbold 1997 13-14 1244.

[96] Chapter 87 of the Laws of Zambia.

[97] *R v Lewis* (PA), 76 R 33, in 99 LQR 349; *R v Francis* (1874) LR 2 CCR 128.

It is worth remembering that cases in which evidence of similar facts has been held admissible to prove, on the one hand, system or design and on the other, to rebut defences including mistake or accident are legion. Recall what is important in this regard as already discussed above are the following:

(i) The notion that there were special categories has been rejected by the Lords in *DPP v P*[98] with the House taking the view that there were no special rules premised on the nature of the case such as sexual offences for instance.

(ii) Irrespective of the allegation what should concern the judge/magistrate is the question whether the evidence of similar facts proves intent or system so effectively i.e., to say positively on the one hand or negatives the claim of an accident or the accused having operated under a mistake of fact[99] that only an ultra-cautious court would fail to act on it.

(iii) Further and in the alternative, whether the explanation of the evidence predicated on coincidence will be an outrage to communal sense.

(iv) The judge/magistrate ought to bear in mind the evidence in the entire case and the particular issue to which the undecided evidence is germane.

We now proceed to show the application of the above guidelines in decisions made through the years.

In *R v Geering*,[100] a case we came across earlier, the Privy Council held that in order to prove malice on an indictment for the murder of an infant or meet the defence of accident, the prosecution could very properly adduce evidence of similar facts that other infants had been received by the accused persons for a small sum, on a representation that they desired to adopt them, that the payments were insufficient to support the infants long, and that several bodies of infants had been found buried in the accused's garden.[101]

In *R v Gray*[102] the accused was indicted for arson with intent to defraud an insurance company. Evidence of similar facts for the purpose of bringing up issues relating to the accused's intention, and proving that the fire was a product not of an accident but one of design, was deemed admissible and so admitted, as it tended to show that the accused had in fact previously occupied at least two other houses both of which were insured. Further that in both instances, fires had broken out with the accused making a claim in each instance which were paid by the insurance companies based on the supposition that the loss

[98] [1991] 2 AC 447.

[99] See s 10 of the Penal Code Chapter 87 of the Laws of Zambia.

[100] 18 LJ (NS) (ME) 215.

[101] *R v Gray* (1866) 4 F & F 1102; *R v Ollis* [1900] 2 QB 758; *R v Bond* [1906] 2 KB 389; *R v Ball* [1911] AC 47, HL; *R v Shellaker* [1914] 1 KB 414, 9 Cr App R 240; *R v Smith* (1915) 11 Cr App R 229; *R v Starkie* [1922] 2 KB 275, 16 Cr App R 61 CCA; *R v Harrison-Owen*, 35 Cr App R 108, CCA; *Bratty v Att-Gen for Northern Ireland* [1963] AC 386 at 410, HL; *G (an infant) v Coltart* [1967] 1 QB 432, DC; *DPP v Boardman* [1975] AC 421; *cf. R v Davis and Murphy*, 56 Cr App R 249, CA.

[102] (1866) 4 F & F 1102.

was occasioned by accidental fire covered under the respective policies.[103]

In *R v Ollis*[104] the accused was indicted for obtaining money on false pretences specifically that certain cheques given by the accused were not only good but effective orders for the recompense of money. It was held that evidence was admissible that the accused had prior to the present charge but in another case, given another prosecutor another cheque which was dishonoured on presentment. This was notwithstanding the fact that the accused had been acquitted on the charge of fraud in said prior case. According to Channel J:

> In such cases evidence of other transactions is admitted, not for the purpose of showing that the defendant committed other offences, but for the purpose of showing that the transaction the subject of the indictment was done with the intent to defraud, or with guilty knowledge, as the case may be. Such evidence is admitted, not because it tends to show that other offences have been committed, but notwithstanding that, in the particular case, it may happen to do so.[105]

In *R v Bond*[106] the accused was indicted for contrary to s 58 of Offences against the person 1861, for "feloniously and unlawfully using a certain instrumental intent to procure a miscarriage." It was held that in order to prove intent by the accused, the prosecution was at liberty to give evidence that tended to show that at other times the accused was the cause and did in fact cause miscarriages by similar means. Further, that the accused had then employed words inclining to show that he was in the habit of carrying out analogous procedures for the same illegal purpose.

In *R v Ball*[107] [...] a brother and sister were indicted for incest committed in July and 13—19 September, 1910, and it was proved that at these times they were living together and occupying the same bed, evidence was held to have been rightly admitted which showed that they had had a child in 1908, since it went to establish the existence of sexual passion between the parties as an element in proving that they had illicit connection in fact on or between the dates charged, and as negativing the defence of living together innocently.

In *R v Starkie*[108] evidence that the accused administered drugs to one woman of with intent to procure her abortion was deemed admissible in support of having used an instrument with the like intent on another woman, and vice versa in order to refute the contention of the defence that the acts were done innocently.

---

[103] This rule was approved in *Makin v Att-Gen for New South Wales* [1894] AC 57 PC. By parity of reason, proof of malice or intent thereof is provable based on the same principle here espoused.

[104] [1900] 2 QB 758.

[105] At 78; approved and followed in *R v Shellaker* [19141 1 KB 414, 9 Cr App R 240, CCA; *R v Ollis* [1900] 2 QB 758 was however distinguished in *G (an Infant) v Coltart* [19671 1 QB 432 DC where conduct must in another case did not lead to a conviction, it and the evidence thereof ought to be excluded: *cf. P v Davis and Murphy,* 56 Cr App R249 CA.

[106] [1906] 2 KB 389.

[107] [1911] AC 47, HL, as adapted in *Archbold* 1997 at 1246 13-19.

[108] [1922] 2 KB 275, 16 Cr App R 61 CCA, as adapted in *Archbold* 1997 at 1246.

In *R v Harrison-Owen*[109] the accused put up a defence of automatism against a charge of burglary. It was held as impermissible to cross-examine as to convictions for similar offences in order to rebut the accused's defence.

8.3.4.5 *Allegation that a prosecution witness has been mistaken or is being deceitful*

In any criminal proceedings there are three options open to the accused or his counsel as regards what defence to mount put up. The straightest way forward is to admit and plead guilty to the offence as charged; the second and more nuanced involves the accused admitting to most of the facts as regards the charge he faces but doing so while at the same time asserting innocence. The third involves a rejection of the truthfulness of the testimony of the prosecution through its witnesses: essentially pleading 'not guilty' to the charge(s) without nuance or prevarication. This is done through the assertion that the accounts as given by the witnesses are borne of lies, deception or/and that the witness are operating under a mistake of fact.[110] In *R v Sims,*[111] the appellant was charged on an indictment containing ten counts, three of which alleged buggery with three men, three, as an alternative, gross indecency with the same men, one gross indecency with a fourth man, and the remaining three indecent assaults on three boys. An application for separate trials in respect of each separate man or boy involved was refused in so far as the charges against the four men were concerned and they were tried together. The appellant was found guilty of buggery with the three men, but acquitted of gross indecency with the fourth man. The main point involved on appeal was whether the judge ought to have ordered separate trails in respect of each man. The counts were properly included in one indictment by virtue of the Indictments Act, 1915, Sched I, r 3, but sect 5(3) of that Act confers a discretion on the trial judge to order a separate trial on any count or counts, a discretion with which the Court of Appeal will not interfere unless justice has not been done. It was contended that justice had not been done in this case, because, on the trial on the counts

[109] 35 Cr App R 108, CCA; A decision doubted by Lord Denning in *Bratty v Att-Gen for Ireland* [19631 AC 386 at 410, HL.

[110] See *DPP v Boardman* [1975] AC 421.

[111] [1946] KB 531 *per* Lord Goddard CJ at 539-540.

in respect of one man, evidence in respect of the other men was not admissible, and the appellant had, therefore, been improperly prejudiced by the joint trial. A further point raised was in respect of the functions of the judge and jury with regard to corroborative evidence. It was held as follows:

(i) the mere fact that evidence was admissible on one count and inadmissible on another was not, by itself a ground for separate trials, because often the matter could be made clear in the summing up without prejudice to the accused.

(ii) the general principle was that evidence was admissible if it was logically probative, i.e., logically relevant to the issue whether the accused had committed the act charged.

(iii) the exception to that principle—that evidence that the accused had a bad reputation of a bad disposition was not admissible unless the accused himself gave evidence of good character or otherwise under the Criminal Evidence Act, 1898—did not extend further than the interests of justice demanded.

(iv) evidence was not to be excluded merely because it tended to show the accused to be of bad disposition, but only if it showed nothing more; evidence of specific acts or circumstances connecting the accused with specific features of the crime was admissible even though it tended to show him to be of bad disposition.

(v) in regard to the crime of sodomy the repetition of the acts was itself a specific feature connecting the accused with the crime and evidence of that kind was admissible to show the nature of the act done by the accused.

(vi) the correct method of approach to the subject was to start with the general proposition that all evidence that was logically probative was admissible unless excluded; then evidence of this kind did not have to seek a justification, but was admissible irrespective of the issue raised by the defence.

(vii) applying the above principles, on the trial of one of the counts in this case, the evidence on the others was admissible; and although it would be in the interests of the accused that each case should be considered separately without the evidence of the others, the interests of justice required that on each case the evidence on the others should be considered, and, even apart from the defence raised by the accused, the evidence would be admissible.

(viii) in the result, there was nothing in the authorities to compel the court to hold, in the present case, that the counts should have been tried separately, or that the jury should have been directed, when considering each charge, to disregard the evidence on the others.

(ix) on the question of corroboration, it was for the judge to say whether a particular piece of evidence, if accepted, was capable of being corroborative, and then for the jury to act on it or not as they thought right. *Per curium:* Where an indictment contained counts for indecent

> offences against both male and female persons, it would not ordinarily be right to try the counts together, but where the persons assaulted were children, the mere fact that one was a small boy and the other a little girl would not make it improper to try both cases together, because the facts would indicate perverted lust on the part of the accused.

According to the editorial note on this case:[112]

> In this case the court reviews in detail the principles underlying the rule that a judge may order separate trial of different counts charged in the same indictment. The general proposition which provides a starting point is that all evidence which is logically probative is admissible unless it is excluded, and separate trials should in respect of another, without connecting him with the crime. Evidence which shows bad disposition alone is inadmissible, but where it shows something more, e.g., design, intent system, it is admissible. In the case reported, upon those grounds, it is held that there was no duty to order separate trials of counts relating to sodomy with different men, since the repetition shown by such evidence constituted a specific feature connecting the accused with the crime. It was in the interests of justice that this feature should be proved and the question of granting separate trials should be determined on this ground and not on the question of prejudice. Great care is necessary in the application of the principle laid down, and fine distinctions may arise. For example, the court points out that counts for sexual offences against male and female adults should not be tried together prima facie, since the evidence on one count would not be admissible as evidence on the other; on the other hand, where they were children, such evidence would be admissible as evidence of perversion connecting the accused with the crime. The necessity of warning the jury on the question of corroboration is also to be considered where the evidence of accomplices is involved in a joint trial.

What appears patent from *R v Sims*[113] as well as *DPP v Boardman*[114]and allied case law is this simple fact: when what is in question is evidence of similar facts, it is usually reasoned that two or more people cannot fabricate a story or operate under a mistake with regards to their accounts in respect of the accused, unless there has been collusion. As Lord Goddard has opined in *R v Sims:*[115]

> [...] The probative force of all the acts together is much greater than one alone; for, whereas the [court] might think one man might be telling

[112] [1946] 1 All ER 697; 1946 KB 531.

[113] 1946 KB 539-540.

[114] [1975] AC 421.

[115] 1946 KB 539-540.

> an untruth, three or four are hardly likely to tell the same untruth unless they are conspiring. If there is nothing to suggest a conspiracy their evidence would seem to be overwhelming.[116]

The court is of course called upon to critically analyse the evidence of the witnesses to make a determination of mistake or deceit on the part of one of them or so many as may have colluded to do so or were operating under a mistake. The starting point as regards the approach to be taken by the court is set out in *R v H:*[117] assume that the witness(es) is(are) telling the truth. The court must then decide whether predicating the common allegations on the premise of chance or coincidence would, as we have repeatedly said in this chapter, be an affront to common sense. There is no rule as regards the degree of similarity. Even so, as we have noted elsewhere in this text, that two or more people, without collusion, would tell independent stories which are similar to each other against the accused at the same time and in the same trial is highly inconceivable. Lord Mustill has observed in *R v H,*[118] that the '[...] the function of the trial judge is not to decide as an intellectual process whether the evidence satisfies prescribed conditions, but to strike as a matter of individual judgment, in the light of his experience and common sense, a balance between the probative value of the similar fact evidence and its potentially damaging effect.' Thus, applying the court's observation within the context of our jurisdiction, it still remains for the same judge to make a determination on the possibility of collusion in evidence of similar facts.

Be that as it may, the question has always been how to deal with the very real threat of there being collusion or in some cases, what has been termed innocent contamination. For starters, any proof of collusion is a death nail for any arguments predicated on evidence of similar facts. It cannot be used, and if used, will not be sustained. It is in this vein that the decision in *R v H*[119] becomes significant. It had been thought prior to that decision that where it was found that a danger of collusion/conspiracy was real and present or that there was a chance of innocent contamination, the judge/magistrate was not to permit the admission of evidence of similar facts. It was further thought predicated on substantial authority, that a voire dire was necessary in determining the issue of independence of evidence. The foregoing issues came up as they had in cases before it and were determined in *R v H.*[120] The [accused] was charged in 1992 with sexual offences alleged to have been committed against his adopted daughter and stepdaughter between 1987 and 1989. The two girls confided in the defendant's wife, who made the initial complaint to the police, and they also discussed the matter between themselves. At the [accused's] trial the judge

---

[116] See also *DPP v Boardman* [1975] AC 421; *DPP v Kilbourne* [1973] AC 729; see also Scottish cases of *Moorov v HM Advocate* [1930] JC 68 and *HM Advocate v AE* [1937] JC 96.

[117] [1995] 2 AC 596, HL.

[118] [1995] 2 AC 596, HL; as adapted at https://swarb.co.uk/regina-v-h-evidence-corroboration-hl-25-may-1995/ retrieved on 20/10/21.

[119] [1995] 2 AC 596, HL.

[120] [1995] 2 All ER 865, [1995] 2 AC 596, HL.

directed the jury that they had to consider whether the girls had collaborated and concocted a false story against their father and whether they might have fantasised about the assaults, that it was for the prosecution to satisfy the jury that the girls were in fact telling the truth, and that the evidence of one girl could support the evidence of the other only if the jury was sure that the girls had not collaborated to concoct a false story against the defendant. The [accused] was convicted. He appealed on the grounds that, as was accepted by the Crown, there must have existed a risk of collusion between the two girls, having regard to the fact that they both resided in the family home and had complained to their mother long after the offences were alleged to have occurred, and that the judge had misdirected the jury as to that risk. The Court of Appeal dismissed the appeal, holding that except in extreme cases the risk of contamination of a witness's evidence as a result of his contact with other witnesses or complainants affected only the weight and probative value of his evidence and not its admissibility and therefore the judge had properly left to the jury the issue whether one girl's evidence could corroborate the other's evidence. The defendant appealed to the House of Lords. It was held that where similar fact evidence by a witness who was the subject of similar charges against the [accused] was put forward by the Crown as corroboration and there was a risk that such evidence was contaminated by collusion (whether deliberate or by the unconscious influence of one witness by another), the admissibility of such evidence should first be considered, without reference to the issue of collusion, by the judge applying the test of whether, if true, the similar fact evidence was so probative of the crime of which the defendant was accused that it ought to be admitted notwithstanding the prejudicial effect of disclosing that the defendant had committed other crimes. If the evidence was admitted, it was then for the jury to determine its credibility after being directed by the judge that they could not properly rely on the evidence as corroboration unless they were satisfied that it was reliable and true and not tainted by collusion or other defects. However, if in the course of the trial it became apparent that no reasonable [court] could accept the evidence as free from collusion the judge should direct the jury that it could not be relied upon as corroboration or for any other purpose adverse to the defence. Since the credibility of the similar fact evidence was a matter for the jury and not a matter going to the admissibility of such evidence, collusion would only be relevant in considering the admissibility of similar fact evidence in a very exceptional case and therefore a judge should not normally hold a voire dire to determine whether the admissibility of the evidence was affected by possible collusion. Applying those principles, the appeal would be dismissed.[121]

8.4 Further matters for consideration

[121] *R v P* [1991] 3 All ER 337 applied; *R v Ananthanarayanan* [1994] 2 All ER 847, *R v Ryder* [1994] 2 All ER 859 and *R v W* [1994] 2 All ER 872 explained; Decision of the Court of Appeal [1994] 2 All ER 881 affirmed; Editor's notes: For corroboration, see 11(2) Halsbury's Laws (4th edn reissue) paras 1140, 1141, and for evidence of complainants in sexual cases, see ibid para 1142. For cases on the subject, see 15(2) Digest (2nd reissue) 106–107, 19059–19065.

8.4.1 *Is there a discretion beyond the discretion relating to similar facts?*

While it would appear to be the largely held view that beyond the discretion to determine whether evidence is admissible on the evidence of similar facts principle, a judge has inherent power to thereafter, if it appears to him that the prejudicial effect of the evidence now admitted far outweighs its probative value, exclude such evidence. It is not a proposition that received a ringing endorsement in *DPP v Boardman.*[122] In fact, by all accounts, it only received support in two of the five speeches-a minority. It would appear, and this, it is submitted, is the better view, that inherent in a court's decision that evidence of similar facts is admissible is acceptance that its probative value far outweighs its prejudicial effect. It follows from this that there is no second stage at all. TRS Allan in his note to the case of *R v Lewis*[123] observes as follows:

> In all these cases the same test for admissibility applies: does the evidence in question have (in light of all the other evidence) a sufficiently strong probative value to justify the court in departing from the prima facie rule forbidding disclosure to the jury of the defendant's previous conduct or character? Is the evidence so highly relevant that to exclude it would be 'an affront to common sense'? [...] if the general test of high probative value is accepted as governing admissibility, there cannot be any role for a separate discretion to play. The decision that evidence which would be prejudicial to the [accused's] case is, nevertheless, sufficiently probative to require its admission as a matter of justice must itself be reached by an exercise of discretion. It is a discretion given to the trial judge and must be exercised after proper consideration of all the relevant evidence. This is a conclusion that follows, it is suggested, from accepting that application of the test for admissibility is itself a matter of judgment and degree.

We may add to the foregoing by suggesting that what gives evidence of similar facts its probative value is, as demonstrated in *Pfenning v R,*[124] its "devastating" effect on a defence. This would seem to counter positions taken in cases such as *R v Johnson (Kevin)*[125] where the EWCA appeared to suggest the existence of a separate discretion to exclude evidence following its acceptance on the evidence of similar facts principle if it would have a "devastating" effect on a defence of, as was the case in *Pfenning v R*: "not me."[126]

8.4.2 *When should evidence of similar facts be admitted by the court?*

[122] Lord Hailsham and Lord Salmon.

[123] (PA), 76 Cr App R 33, in 99 LQR 349 at 352-353.

[124] (1995) 127 ALR 99.

[125] [19951 2 Cr App R 41.

[126] See also the comments of Lord Nicholls in *R v H*[1995] 2 AC 596 at 627 HL.

The answer to the question as to when evidence of similar facts may be admitted is one that has exercised the minds of many a court as can be clearly seen from decisions of courts in England & Wales. We consider a few below:

The earliest among the cases is *R v Bond*[127] where Darling J observed as follows: 'I do not suppose that Lord Herschell meant that such evidence might be called to rebut any defence possibly open, but of an intention to rely on which there was no probability whatever.'

Lord Summer observed as follows in *Thompson v R*:[128]

> Sometimes, for one reason or another, evidence is admissible, notwithstanding that its general character is to show that the accused had in him the makings of a criminal, for example, in proving guilty knowledge or intent or system or in rebutting an appearance of innocence which, unexplained, the facts might wear. In cases of coining, uttering, procuring abortion, demanding by menaces, false pretences and sundry species of frauds, such evidence is constantly properly admitted. Before an issue can be said to be raised which would permit introduction of such evidence, so obviously prejudicial to the accused, it must have been raised in substance if not in so many words, and the issue so raised one to which the prejudicial evidence is relevant. The mere theory that a plea guilty puts everything material in issue is not enough for this purpose prosecution cannot credit the accused with fancy defences in order to rebut at the outset with some damning piece of evidence."

In *Harris v DPP*,[129] it was laid down that the prosecution may adduce all proper evidence tending to prove the charge against th defendant, including evidence tending to show that the defendant has been guilty of criminal acts other than those covered by the indictment, without waiting for the defendant to set up a specific defence calling for rebuttal. It is submitted, however, that this is subject to the judge being satisfied that such evidence does in fact go to an issue before [court]. If not, he can hardly be satisfied that the evidence has any probative value, let alone such compelling value as is necessary to justify its reception.

It has been said in *R v (Manina)*[130] that if the prosecution knows that a particular defence is going to be advanced, they may call evidence to rebut it as part of their own substantive case even if that tends to show the commission of other crimes. The defendant can be cross-examined about the matter. If the prosecution does not know of the defence in advance, then they may call evidence to rebut it and the defendant can then be recalled, if that is desired, to deal with the rebutting evidence. Alternatively, the procedure may be short-circuited by asking the defendant about the matter in cross-examination. Care should, however, be taken: if potentially damaging matters are put to

[127] [1906] 2 KB 389 at 409.

[128] [1918] AC 221.

[129] [19521 AC 694, HL as adapted in *Archbold* 1997 at 1250 13-29.

[130] [1988] QB 678, 87 Cr App R 349, CA as adapted in *Archbold* 1997 at 1250 13-30.

the defendant in cross-examination and they are denied, the prosecution will have to be able to substantiate an application to call rebuttal evidence. If their application fails, a defence application to discharge the jury may well succeed.

As demonstrated in *R v Downey*,[131] and adapted in *Archbold:*[132]

> Where two or more offences are charged against the defendant and there is evidence not tending to identify the accused but proving that all the offences are the work of the same person, the jury may, for the purpose of deciding whether the defendant is that person, combine evidence tending to incriminate him in respect of one offence with evidence tending to incriminate him in another, or others; it is not necessary that the jury are sure in relation to any one count on the evidence exclusively relating to that count before they take any cognisance of the similar fact evidence.[133]

8.4.3 *Evidence of similar facts within the context of non-criminal conduct*

When it comes to the application of the similar fact principle within the context of non-criminal conduct, our first port of call is *Thompson v R.*[134] It was demonstrated that there is nothing that confines evidence admitted under evidence of similar facts to only that class of evidence which discloses criminal conduct. Further, that evidence does not reveal the commission of an offence nor will evidence which does reveal the commission of another offence be excluded on the basis that any prosecution thereof would be statute barred.[135]

8.4.4 *Possession of incriminating articles*

Hereunder, we consider instances in which a suspect later accused person is arrested and charged with one offence but during a search of his person/his office/ his property such as his car or residence, other items deemed incriminating and suggestive of the accused's participation in, or close connotation with, some form of disgraceful deportment, are found to be in his possession. It would seem to logically follow that where evidence exists to the effect that the articles found in the accused's possession are inextricably linked to the offence with which the accused is currently charged, evidence relating to the finding of such

[131] [1995] 1 Cr App R 547, CA.

[132] 1997 1250 13-31.

[133] See *R v Barnes* [19951 2 Cr App R 491, CA (not following *R v McGranaghan* [1995] 1 Cr App R 559, CA).

[134] [1918] AC 221; *R v Butler* 84 Cr App R 12; *R v Ollis* [1900] 2 QB 758; *R v Sidhu,* 98 Cr App R 59; *R v Downey* [1995] Cr App R 547 CA.

[135] See *R v Shellaker* [1914] 1 KB 414, 9 Cr App R 240, CCA, and *R v Adams*, The Times, April 8, 1993, CA.

articles ought ordinarily to be admissible.[136] In *Thompson v R*,[137] the [accused] was charged with gross indecency against boys. The defendant denied that he was the offender. Evidence was admitted that on arrest the defendant was in possession of powder puffs and that a search of his rooms uncovered indecent photographs of boys. It was held that the evidence was admissible on the issue of the identity of the offender. Lord Sumner stated that while proof of guilt of a particular crime does not arise from proof of a general disposition to commit that crime, evidence was admissible to prove guilty knowledge or intent or a system or to rebut an appearance of innocence. However, the prosecution may not credit the accused with fancy defences in order to rebut them at the outset with some damning piece of prejudice.

With the admission of evidence on the basis of the evidence of similar fact principle, there ought ordinarily, as we have noted elsewhere in this text to be a secondary discretion to determine whether the evidence should be subject to the test of admissibility simply because it would have a devastating effect on the defence's case. Even so, subsidiary issues may still need to be determined by the court where reliance is placed on evidence of similar facts. Where the evidence is relied on under the similar fact principle, there may be a subsidiary issue for the judge to keep in mind: evidence justifying a finding by the court that the articles in question are indeed the accused's as they may well not be. In *R v Wright*,[138] the appellant had been charged with sexual offences against boys who were pupils in the school of which he was headmaster. fie defence was a complete denial. A booklet found in the appellant's study was admitted in evidence: its contents were such that any juror who saw it would recognise that it was aimed at males with homosexual inclinations. The appellant said the booklet had nothing to do with him: his case was that this was no ordinary headmaster's study, being more akin to a social centre with many people having access to it and to his desk. The [EWCA] expressed no view on how this aspect of the admissibility of the booklet should have been dealt with. *Archbold*[139] gives the following comment on the above case:

> On first principles, however, it is submitted that unless the evidence relating to the finding of the booklet was such that the [court] could have concluded that it was the appellant's, it should have been excluded as irrelevant. If admitted, the [court] should be directed not to make any use of it against the defendant for the purpose suggested by the prosecution unless they are sure it was indeed his.[140]

---

[136] *Makin v Att-Gen for New South Wales* [1894] AC 57 PC; *DPP v Boardman* [1975] AC 421; *DPP v P* [1991] 2 AC 447; *R v Clarke (Robert Lee)* [1995] 2 Cr App R 425, CA.

[137] [1918] AC 221 HL; as adapted at https://swarb.co.uk/thompson-v-director-of-public-prosecutions-hl-1918/ retrieved on 22/10/21.

[138] 90 Cr App R 325; as adapted in *Archbold* 1997 1251 13-32.

[139] 1997 1251 13-32.

[140] The other cases normally referred to under this heading are *R v Twiss* [1918] 2 KB 853 13 Cr App R 177, CCA; *R v Taylor* 17 Cr App R 109 CCA; *R v Reading* and others, 50 Cr App R 98, CCA; *R v Mustafa,* 65 Cr App R 26 CA; and *R v Lewis* 76 Cr App R 33 CA; See also note on the case of *Lewis* by TRS Allan at 99 LQR 349; 48 MLR 253.

8.4.5 *The question of motive vis-à-vis evidence of similar facts*

Evidence of motive is ordinarily admissible in criminal proceedings. The point is not that it is indispensable to the prosecution proving its case but rather that the prosecution can through its deployment, show in aid of its case, that not only has an offence been committed but that in all probability, it was committed by the accused person. In his dicta in *R v Ball*[141] which, despite the facts of this case, ought to be considered as being of general application, Lord Atkinson opined as follows:

> Surely in an ordinary prosecution for murder you can prove previous acts or words of the accused to show that he entertained feelings of enmity towards the deceased, and this is evidence not merely of the malicious mind with killed the deceased. but of the fact that he killed him. You can give in enmity of the accused towards the deceased to prove that the accused the deceased's life. Evidence well of motive as his necessarily 'malice afore though goes to prove in as the much fact homicide by the accused, as more probable that men are killed by those that have some motive for than by those who have not.

Similarly, in *R v Buckley*,[142] in which the accused was charged with murder, the deceased's deposition against the accused was deemed admissible though taken on another charge relating to the accused for which he was found guilty to prove malice/motive against the deceased by the accused person.

It would seem to follow from the foregoing authorities, and would not indeed be too much of a stretch to conclude that evidence of motive is admissible, the fact that what may ultimately be proved leads simply to the establishing of the fact that the accused was guilty of committing offences similar to the one he now faces. It ought to be remembered though that the importance of evidence by whatever name called is determined by its probative value. It would logically follow that the more recent the evidence the more valuable and the more remote, the less valuable in so far as probing the issues to which it relates is concerned.[143]

It was held in *R v Bond*[144] that relations of a murdered man to his assailant were properly admitted to proof as integral parts of the history of the alleged crime, so far as they might reasonably be treated as explanatory of the conduct of the accused. Their lordships concluded that those dicta correctly represented the law, and that no further doubt about the matter need be felt.

---

[141] [1911] AC 47 HL.

[142] (1873) 13 Cox 293.

[143] *R v Ball* [1911] AC 47 HL; *R v Dosett* (1846) 3 C & K 306; but see *R v Berry* (DR), 83 Cr App R 7 in which the EWCA called *Ball* a "dubious authority;" However, the conclusions drawn in *R v Berry* were rejected in *R v Williams (Clarence Ivor)* 84 Cr App R 299 *per* Hodgson J.

[144] [1906] 2 KB 389 at 401.

Rejecting the doubts raised in *R v Berry*[145] regarding the decision in *Ball,*[146] the EWCA in *R v Williams (Clarence Ivor)*[147] took the view that the position taken by Lord Atkinson in *Ball*[148] was predicated on a long line of authorities and that there was no need to doubt that position that evidence of motive was admissible to show that it was more probable than not that the accused had committed the offence with which he had been charged. In doing so, the court also approved Purchas LJ's observation in *R v Pettman*:[149]

> Where it is necessary to place before the jury evidence of part of a continual background of history relevant to the offence charged in the indictment and without the totality of which the account placed before the jury would be incomplete or incomprehensible, then the fact that the whole account involves including evidence establishing the commission of an offence with which the accused is not charged is not of itself a ground for excluding the evidence.[150]

The foregoing sentiments were applied in *R v Sidhu.*[151] The [accused] was accused of explosives offences relating to his promotion of the cause of Sikhism through membership of the Khalistan Liberation Force, which promoted an independent Sikh state. The jury considered a video recording of the appellant firing weapons and chanting his support for the Force during the trial of a bomb making conspiracy. During interview, the defendant had said that he was opposed to violence under religious principle, and denied membership of the Force. It was held that the video was admissible 'as evidence of a continual background of history relevant to the appellant's part in the alleged conspiracy. The events recorded were not too distant from the allegations at issue. It was as evidence of a 'continual background of history' relevant to Sidhu's part in the conspiracy, but was not admissible to disprove his assertions that he opposed violence on religious grounds.

8.4.6 *Severance and admissibility within the context of evidence of similar facts*

Within the context of evidence of similar facts, the concept of severance's proximity to the concept of admissibility of evidence is temptingly too close to call.

---

[145] *(DR)* 83 Cr App R 7.

[146] [1911] AC 47 HL.

[147] 84 Cr App R 299.

[148] [1911] AC 47 HL.

[149] Unreported, May 2, 1985, C.A (transcript no. 5048/C/82).

[150] Approved by EWCA as "useful formulation" in *R v Fulcher* [19951 2 Cr App R 251.

[151] (1994) 98 Cr App R 59; As adapted at https://swarb.co.uk/regina-v-sidhu-cacd-22-feb-1993/ retrieved on 22/10/21.

Even so, they do not always move in lockstep. Where there is an application to sever an indictment and the prosecution contend that the evidence supporting the count or counts to be severed is admissible on the remaining count or counts, it will obviously be convenient and desirable for the judge to form at least a preliminary view on admissibility. If his view is that the evidence is admissible under the similar fact rules, severance will be most unlikely. The opposite is not the case.[152]

[152] *Archbold* 1997 1253 13-38; For a more detailed analysis of the general concept of severance see *Archbold* 1997 §§1-162 *et seq.*; see also *R v Christou (George)* [1996] 2 WLR 620 HL.

9

CONFESSIONS AND SUPPORTING EVIDENCE

9.1 Introduction

The question of confession evidence is one that arises both in the criminal law and civil proceedings. A formal confession[1] is considered to be a form of proof in and of itself. It therefore logically follows that it ought not to be, and by necessity, is not considered an item of evidence. The consequence of the foregoing is to then, in so far as the burden of proving a fact in question now confessed, absolve said party as would ordinarily be required to do so, from the necessity to present evidence of any such fact. The reason for this position can logically be said to be predicated on the fact that in so far as presentation of evidence and proof thereof are concerned, the existence of the fact, as confessed, is taken to be irrefutably recognised or established, as the case may be. Further, and as a logical consequence, neither the question of evidence nor that of admissibility of such evidence arises as neither is needed. As has been postulated by some,[2] 'the introduction of a confession makes the other aspects of a trial in court superfluous'[3] Further still, the party who confesses to a fact in issue is bound by such a confession and may not contradict it confession save with leave of court.

In so far as the criminal law is concerned, the first port of call is Article 18(2) of the Constitution which provides as follows: '[e]very person who is charged with a criminal offence - (a) shall be presumed to be innocent until he is proved or has pleaded guilty.' The provision anticipates that where in the general sense, there is no confession, the accused must have his day in court to prove his innocence. It also presupposes that the prosecution will have to discharge its burden of proof. It is also open to the prosecution to admit that the accused has no case to answer and withdraw the charges. Where there is a guilty plea, then the procedure as provided in the Criminal Procedure Code[4] under s 204 on the one hand, and s 279 on the other, as respects criminal proceedings in the Subordinate Court and proceedings in the High Court ought to be followed.

As already indicated, in criminal proceedings, guidance may be gotten from the procedure provided for under s 204 which relates to proceedings before the Subordinate Court which provides as follows:

[1] Or more appropriately a formal admission in civil proceedings.

[2] Emphasis added.

[3] McCormick 1972.

[4] Chapter 88 of the Laws of Zambia.

> (1) The substance of the charge or complaint shall be stated to the accused person by the court, and he shall be asked whether he admits or denies the truth of the charge:
> Provided that where the charge or complaint contains a count charging the accused person with having been previously convicted of any offence, the procedure prescribed by section two hundred and seventy-five shall, mutatis mutandis, be applied.
> (2) If the accused person admits the truth of the charge, his admission shall be recorded, as nearly as possible, in the words used by him, and the court shall convict him and pass sentence upon or make an order against him, unless there shall appear to it sufficient cause to the contrary.
> (3) If the accused person does not admit the truth of the charge, the court shall proceed to hear the case as hereinafter provided.

As regards proceedings before the High Court, the following is provided for under s 279 that '[i]f the accused pleads "guilty", the plea shall be recorded and he may be convicted thereon.'

What is patent from the foregoing provisions, specifically ss 204 and 279 of the Criminal Procedure Code[5] is that a formal admission by an accused person, or as in this case, broadly speaking, a guilty plea 'shall as against that party be conclusive evidence in those proceedings of the fact admitted.' The court is required to record the guilty plea, as it is required to take note of a formal confession on anyone particular fact in issue. To be remembered too is the fact that there is no need to argue over formal confessions which are common cause.

As far as civil proceedings are concerned, the more appropriate phraseology is formal admissions upon which the other party is at liberty to apply for judgment on admission. The limitation of costs is at the centre of admitting to undisputed facts. It follows therefore, that a party whom, without any justifiable reasons, puts an opponent to strict proof of a fact or facts not seriously in dispute is likely to incur costs by order of court even when the party refusing to admit to the fact in question ultimately prevails at trial.

In this chapter, we will proceed to look at confessions within the context of the criminal law i.e., the nature of the confession in general within the context of its historical development; define the concept; and analyse the law regarding admissibility of confessions and attendant risks. We will conclude by specifically considering formal admissions (the civil proceedings equivalent of confessions in the criminal law).

9.2 The common law development

9.2.1 General

Confessions within the context of English law in general and hearsay evidence in particular developed chiefly through the concept of voluntariness on the

[5] Chapter 88 of the Laws of Zambia.

one hand, and the now obsolete (so far as the English jurisdiction is concerned) judges' Rules (1964) on the other. As Lord Sumner observed regarding the test for admissibility of an accused's confession in *Ibrahim v R*:[6]

> It has been long established [...] that no statement [made] by an accused is admissible as evidence against him unless it is shown [...] to have been a voluntary statement [...] that [...] has not been obtained from him [...] by fear of prejudice or hope of advantage exercised or held out by a person in authority.

It is worth noting that the foregoing observation was limited only to admissions relating to incriminating statements made to those in authority. The enactment of s 76 of PACE in England & Wales has brought changes to this area of the law as observed in court decisions which should be of great persuasive value to our courts in so far as the scope of incriminating statements that ought to be admitted into evidence as confession evidence, are concerned. To illustrate, in *R v Elleray*,[7] the accused person confessed to various cases of rape in the course of an interview regarding a different matter with his probation officer. The question that arose was whether the prosecution's reliance on the confession statement depended on the facts of the case. According to Lord Woolf CJ:

> [...] In deciding whether to exclude the evidence it is perfectly appropriate for the court to have in mind the contrast between the position that exists where an offender is interviewed by the police and that which exists hen the offender is interviewed by a probation officer. The court should bear in mind the need for frankness between the offender and the probation officer; the fact that there may not be a reliable record of what was said; that the offender has not been cautioned; and that the offender has not had the benefit of legal representation. The protection which the court can provide under s 78 in the majority of cases should be sufficient to ensure that no unfairness occurs to an offender.
>
> Reference has already been made to the steps which were taken by the probation officers in this particular case. A course which in some cases may be appropriate if an offender starts making a confession is to stop him and ask him whether he would like to see his solicitor before he makes any further remarks.

It has, however, been held in *R v Hasan*,[8] that a neutral exculpatory statement is not tantamount to a confession. The [accused] was charged with aggravated burglary. His defence was duress. He claimed that he had been coerced into committing the burglary by S, who had threatened that if he did not do it, he and his family would be harmed, and that he had had no chance to escape and

[6] [1914] AC 599.

[7] [2003] 2 Cr App R 11; *R v N* [2003] EWCA Crim 3239; *R v Taylor* (unreported March 16, 2000).

[8] [2005] 4 All ER 685 in which the House of Lords relied on *R v Sat-Bhambra* (1989) 88 Cr App R 55 at 61, *per* Lord Lane.

go to the police. S had fortified his reputation for violence by talking about murders he had recently committed. In the course of a separate murder inquiry the defendant had an 'off the record' interview with police officers involved in that inquiry according to the report of which interview the threats by S against the defendant had not been made until after the burglary. The police report of the confidential interview contained nothing adverse to the defendant's interest in respect of the burglary, being either entirely exculpatory or entirely neutral in effect. At the defendant's trial, the Crown relied on the confidential statement first, to assert that the defendant was a dishonest witness, and secondly, as evidence the statement's truth, namely that the [accused] had not become aware of S's claims that he had killed somebody until after the burglary. The questions arose whether the confidential statement was a confession under s 76a of the Police and Criminal Evidence Act 1984 so as to invoke the provisions under that section by which a confession could be excluded or whether it should be excluded under s 78b of the 1984 Act on the basis that its admission would have such an adverse effect on the fairness of the proceedings that the court ought not to admit it. Section 82(1)c of the 1984 Act provided in respect of s 76 that 'confession' included any statement wholly or partly adverse to the person who made it, whether made to a person in authority or not and whether made in words or otherwise. The defence conceded that an exculpatory or neutral statement was not a confession within the meaning of s 76 and the judge ruled that the statement could be admitted in evidence. On the issue of duress, the judge put the following four questions to the jury: 'Question 1: Was the defendant driven or forced to act as he did by threats which, rightly or wrongly, he genuinely believed that if he did not burgle [the] house, his family would be seriously harmed or killed? If you are sure that he was not forced by threats to act as he did, the defence fails and he is guilty. But if you are not sure go on to question 2. Would a reasonable person of the defendant's age and background have been driven or forced to act as the defendant did? If you are sure that a reasonable person would not have been forced to act as the defendant did, then the defence fails and he is guilty. If you are not sure, then go on to question 3. Could the [accused] have avoided acting as he did without harm coming to his family? If you are sure he could, the defence fails and he is guilty. If you are not sure go on to question 4. Did the defendant voluntarily put himself in the position in which he knew he was likely to be subjected to threats? If you are sure he did, the defence fails and he is guilty. If you are not sure, he is not guilty. Those four questions are really tests.' The [accused] was convicted, and his appeal against conviction was allowed by the Court of Appeal, which held, inter alia, (i) that the effect of the requirement in the Human Rights Act 1998 that legislation had to be read and given effect to in a way which was compatible with the rights guaranteed by the European Convention for the Protection of Human Rights and Fundamental Freedoms 1950 (as set out in Sch 1 to the 1998 Act), including the right to a fair trial guaranteed by art 6d of the convention, was that the confidential statement was a confession within the terms of s 76; and (ii) that question 4 in the judge's direction on duress was a misdirection. The Crown appealed to the House of Lords. It was held as follows: (1) A 'confession' in s 76 of the 1984 Act did not include a statement intended by the maker to be exculpatory or neutral and which appeared to be so on its face but which became damaging to him at trial because, for example, its contents could then be shown to be evasive or false or inconsistent with the maker's evidence on oath. There was nothing in the text of art 6 of the convention or in the corpus of European jurisprudence which supported the view that ss 76(1) and 82(1) created any incompatibility with art 6 and given the unrestricted capability of s 78 of the 1984 Act to avoid injustice by excluding any evidence obtained by unfairness, including wholly exculpatory or neutral statements obtained by oppression, ss 76(1) and 82(1) were compatible with art 6.[9] (2) The defence of duress was excluded when as a result of the accused's voluntary association with others engaged in criminal activity he had foreseen or ought reasonably to have foreseen the risk of being subjected to any compulsion by threats of violence. Policy pointed toward an objective test of what the accused, placed as he was and knowing what he did, ought reasonably to have foreseen. (Per Baroness Hale of Richmond) The defence of duress was excluded when as a result of the accused's voluntary association with others he foresaw or should have foreseen the risk of being subjected to compulsion to commit criminal offences. The concept of 'voluntary association with others' was that of a person who exposed himself to the risk of unlawful violence without reasonable excuse.[10]

In *R v Priestly*[11] the term 'in an oppressive manner' was added by Lord Parker. It was defined as follows:

> [...] something which tends to sap, and has sapped [...] [the] free will which must exist before a confession is voluntary [...] the elements [of oppression] include such things as the length of time of any period of individual questioning, whether the accused person had been given refreshment or not, and the characteristics of the person who makes the statement.[12]

9.2.2 *A confession defined*

The contemporary view as reflected in the United Kingdom in s 82(1) of the PACE 1984[13] is that a confession includes '[...] any statement wholly or partly

[9] *R v Sat-Bhambra* (1989) 88 Cr App R 55 approved, *Saunders v UK* (1997) 2 BHRC 358 distinguished.

[10] Accordingly the appeal would be allowed R v Baker [1999] 2 Cr App R 335 disapproved; Editor's notes: For the admissibility of extra-judicial confessions and for confessions; procedure, see 11(2) Halsbury's Laws (4th edn reissue) paras 1124, 1125, for duress, see 11(1) Halsbury's Laws (4th edn reissue) para 24, and for the right to a fair trial, see 8(2) Halsbury's Laws (4th edn reissue) paras 134–138; For the Police and Criminal Evidence Act, ss 76, 78, 82, see 18 Halsbury's Statutes (4th edn) (2005 reissue) 245, 249, 253; For the Human Rights Act 1998, Sch 1, Pt I, art 6, see 7 Halsbury's Statutes (4th edn) (2004 reissue) 706.

[11] (1965) 51 Cr App R 1.

[12] For the current legal position following the enactment of s 67(9) and more relevantly, s 76 Codes C and E of PACE 1984, see *R v Gill* [2004] 1 WLR 469.

[13] Inapplicable to Zambia.

adverse to the person who made it,[14] whether made to a person in authority or not and whether made in words or otherwise.'[15] As exemplified in *Moriarty v London Chatham and Dover Railway,*[16] such statements as are included in the preceding definition may include express or implied representations in word or by conduct. So too a lie may, in a proper case, be deemed as a 'statement adverse to the person who made it. That, however, as we have seen elsewhere in this text is not the same thing as saying that because an accused person has told a lie then he automatically ought to be deemed as guilty. As Lord Devlin has pointed out in *Broadhurst v R:*[17]

> There is a natural tendency for a [trier of fact] to think that if an accused is lying, it must be because he is guilty and accordingly to convict him without more ado. It is the duty of the judge to make it clear [...] that this is not so. Save in one respect, a case in which an accused gives untruthful evidence is no different from one in which he gives no evidence at all. In either case the burden remains on the prosecution to prove the guilt of the accused. But if on the proved facts two inferences may be drawn about the accused's conduct or state of mind, his untruthfulness is a factor which the jury can properly take into account as strengthening the inference of guilt. What strength it adds depends of course on all the circumstances and especially on whether there are reasons other than guilt that might account for untruthfulness.[18]

The House of Lords has admitted a mother's testimony in *R v Christie*[19] where the accused faced the charge of indecent assault of a small boy. In his testimony, the boy identified the accused. The mother's evidence to the effect that she and the boy confronted the accused with the boy saying '[t]hat is the man' and described the assault was admitted at trial while the man denied the allegation protesting his innocence. On appeal, the Lords upheld said evidence as to the allegation by the boy and the accused's response thereto.

---

[14] Thus, it has been held as follows in *Shachikamba and Another v The People* [1973] ZR 185 (CA): (i) A statement must be in the suspect's own words, subject to the rule concerning questions put for the purpose of clarification; and (ii) Where two men sign a single statement, it cannot be in their own words; it is impossible for two men to make a single statement; as to need to translate a vernacular confession, see *Daka v The People* (SCZ Judgment No 5 of 1979); As to effect of a confession by a co-accused incriminating other co-accused persons, and that the court can convict on an uncorroborated confession in a proper case, see *Donald Maketo and Others v The People* [1979] ZR 23 (SC), (applied in *Miyutu & Another v People* (Appeal 23 of 2016), [2017] ZMSC 39) disapproving *Hamainda v The People* [1972] ZR 310 on this point; As to discretion of court not to convict on an uncorroborated confession, see *Pesulani Banda v The People* [1979] ZR 202 (SC): In any particular case it is entirely within the discretion of the court to prefer not to convict on a confession alone unless there is additional evidence which renders it safe to do so; *Alimon Njovu And Felix T. Njovu v The People* [1988 – 1989] ZR 5 (SC): When an accused's confession is used against him, the mitigating factors mentioned in the confession should weigh in his favour unless such factors are specifically disproved.

[15] For resulting interpretation difficulties relating to this definition compare *R v Ward, Andrews and Broadley* [2001] Crim LR 316; *R v Sat-Bhambra* (1988) 88 Cr App R 55; *R v Park* [1993] 99 Cr App R 270; *R v Schofield* (1917) 12 Cr App R 191; *R v Riaz, R v Burke* [1992] Crim LR 366.

[16] (1870) LR 5 [1870] QB 314.

[17] [1964] 1 All ER 111.

[18] See *R v Lucas* [1981] 2 All ER 1008 at 1011 e.g., *per* Lord Lane CJ.

[19] [1914] AC 545 at 554, *per* Lord Atkinson.

9.2.3 *Models of police interviewing*[20]

9.2.3.1 *General*

In terms of s 191 of the Criminal Procedure Code,[21] '[e]xcept as otherwise expressly provided, all evidence taken in any inquiry or trial [...] shall be taken in the presence of the accused, or, when his personal attendance has been dispensed with, in the presence of his advocate (if any).' This in a way underscores the manner in which evidence regarding or against a suspect/ accused person ought to be extracted by the police and at trial, by the courts. In their leading text, *Criminal Interrogations and Confessions*,[22] Inbau *etal* posit that in order to be effective police interviews should take on an interrogative, guilt presumptive, aggressive approach to questioning. They support, as a practical approach to their theory, that such interviews by police officers take place in small rooms with little furniture away from the usual surroundings and sounds familiar to the suspect. By denying the suspect access to known people and surroundings, the technique is calculated to raise the anxiety level of the suspect. Anxiety is further heightened by implementing the following Inbau *etal* technique: The suspect should be made to sit on a hard, armless, non-back support chair, with access to air-conditioning and lighting controls any like them, kept out of reach. The interrogator has to progressively invade the suspect's space during the course of the interview by among other things, maintaining eye contact, touching and by urging him to cooperate with the investigators. If possible, the authors postulate, there ought to be present in the room a one-way mirror that will enable other officers detect signs of anxiety, fatigue, and withdrawal.

Against this backdrop, the Reid technique, a nine step is deployed to great effect.[23] To be sure, the investigator employs an understanding, patient and non-demeaning demeanour during the course of an interrogation. The investigator's goal is to ensure that the suspect gains his trust as he becomes more and more comfortable, and thereby, it is hoped, led to make the suspect acknowledge what they are led to deem to be the presumed truth regarding their alleged offence. The investigator accomplishes this by first conjuring up and then presenting the suspect with various possible psychological constructs as validation for their conduct.

> The first admission of guilt is usually obtained by asking the alternative question "Did you plan this out or did it just happen on the spur of the moment?" This technique uses language that contains the unspoken, implicit assumption of guilt. A famous version of this trick is, "Ma'am, have you stopped embezzling money from the bank yet?" The person under interrogation must catch the hidden assumption and contest it

---

[20] See generally, S Kassin and G Gudjonsson "The Psychology of Confessions: A review of the Literature and Issues" [2004] 5(2) *Psychological Science in the Public Interest* 33-67.

[21] Chapter 88 of the Laws of Zambia.

[22] Inbau FE Reid JE Buckley JP Jayne BC, *Criminal Interrogation and Confessions* 4th edn (2001).

[23] See below.

to avoid the trap. Otherwise, once the subject confesses to the proposed scenario, then active persuasion stops and the interrogator attempts to develop from the subject corroborating information that can be used to shore up the credibility of the confession. Critics regard this strategy as hazardous, arguing that it is subject to confirmation bias (likely to reinforce inaccurate beliefs or assumptions) and may lead to prematurely narrowing an investigation.[24]

9.2.3.2 *Nine steps of interrogation*[25]

The Reid technique's nine steps of interrogation are:

Step 1 – Direct Confrontation. Lead the suspect to understand that the evidence has led the police to the individual as a suspect. Offer the person an early opportunity to explain why the offense took place.

Step 2 – Try to shift the blame away from the suspect to some other person or set of circumstances that prompted the suspect to commit the crime. That is, develop themes containing reasons that will justify or excuse the crime. Themes may be developed or changed to find one to which the accused is most responsive.

Step 3 – Try to discourage the suspect from denying his guilt. Reid training video: "If you've let him talk and say the words 'I didn't do it'[…] the more difficult it is to get a confession."

Step 4 – At this point, the accused will often give a reason why he or she did not or could not commit the crime. Try to use this to move towards the confession.

Step 5 – Reinforce sincerity to ensure that the suspect is receptive.

Step 6 – The suspect will become quieter and listen. Move the theme discussion towards offering alternatives. If the suspect cries at this point, infer guilt.

Step 7 – Pose the "alternative question," giving two choices for what happened; one more socially acceptable than the other. The suspect is expected to choose the easier option but whichever alternative the suspect chooses, guilt is admitted. There is always a third option which is to maintain that they did not commit the crime.

Step 8 – Lead the suspect to repeat the admission of guilt in front of witnesses and develop corroborating information to establish the validity of the confession.

Step 9 – Document the suspect's admission or confession and have him or her prepare a recorded statement (audio, video or written).

---

[24] Second Call Defence, Reid Interrogation https://www.secondcalldefense.org/reid-interrogation/ retrieved on 5/12/21.

[25] As adapted at https://www.secondcalldefense.org/reid-interrogation/ retrieved on 5/12/21.

It is therefore patent from the preceding that the process is more about using psychological manipulation to extract a confession and less about finding truth. Reading the foregoing techniques may not elicit any kind of apprehension given that the reader is not traumatised by a shooting or his arrest and as such in a state of confusion. When the above techniques are employed as discussed above, the suspect is usually in a state of shock. The suspect will experience a swirl of intense emotions and physical effects that will prevent him or her from thinking clearly. The Reid Technique is ordinarily employed in the United States and other jurisdictions because the investigators realise the vulnerabilities of the accused. Using the technique, they are then able, even in the presence of counsel, but more so, when none is available, as the case is for most suspects in this jurisdiction, to take full advantage of this set of facts and circumstances to dispense blame and 'get their man.'

With variations, the same techniques are employed in this jurisdiction not because there is ill-motive on part of the investigators. In fact, as said before, suspects, especially where counsel is present, will usually be amiable. Be that as it may, where the charges are serious, for example homicide (murder/ manslaughter) where the defence is self-defence or provocation, innocent people every so often fall victim to belligerent fact-finding procedures like the Reid Technique. Even in instances where no confession is extracted, the suspect may still find himself so thoroughly manipulated that he gets to say just enough to arm the prosecutor with evidence to get the suspect convicted. The procedure then is one '[...] designed to get suspects to incriminate themselves by increasing the anxiety associated with denial, plunging them into a state of despair, and minimising the perceived consequences of confession.'[26] It is therefore advisable that suspects do not try to outsmart the police. They must assert their rights in the relevant parts of Articles 11, 13,15,16-18 under Part III of the Constitution as read together with the derogations therein, and the general derogation under Article 25. They must remain silent and seek legal counsel before talking to the police.

The scenario as regards police interviews in this jurisdiction may not be very different from the foregoing, but the lackadaisical approach taken with regard to legislation in this space remains a huge problem. Add to that a lack of proper training in interview techniques, what is easily realised is that in many cases you have ineptitude, assumption of guilt of the suspect by the investigators, poor interviewing skills, and a lack of professionalism.

9.2.3.3 PEACE model of interviewing

The PEACE Model was borne out of research and cognitive psychology in the early 1990s. Hewn out of a collective effort between law enforcement on the one hand, and psychologists on the other in England & Wales, it was aimed at stemming the propagation of dishonest confessions that were a direct consequence of an accusatory bravura interviewing techniques employed by the police.

[26] S Kassin and G Gudjonsson "The Psychology of Confessions" 33-67.

The PEACE model, assumes that a stress-free suspect (subject) who develops a rapport with the interviewer is likely to be more cooperative. Further, that it is far more pleasant for all concerned if the atmosphere is bereft of any aggression and intimidation. PEACE stands for:[27]

- *Preparation and Planning:* This is to enable the investigating officer recognise all the relevant details of the suspect and the offence in question.
- *Engage and Explain:* The interviewer engages the interviewee in a non-aggressive and non-intimidatory manner.
- *Account, Clarify and Challenge:* This allows the interviewee (suspect) to give their own account which the officer may seek clarification on and/or challenge
- *Closure:* As the term suggests this signifies the end of the interview at which point the interview ought to ensure that he has relevant documentation relating to the interview as well recordings if any. It also entails that an interview's statement is signed to give it legal teeth. Further, in the event that there is more than one interviewer, the lead interviewer must ensure that all parties to the interview have asked their questions. Finally, it entails the lead interviewer finalising any statements and verbalising the time and date of the interview to signify the end of said interview.
- *Evaluation:* This entails the officer evaluating, and a post-interview to deduce what the officer has learnt.

Given its non-accusatory approach to investigative interviewing, the PEACE model is now largely considered as best practice and deemed suitable for any and all classes of interviewees, victims, witnesses or/and suspects. Even though research by Baldwin[28] found that the quality of interviews had not changed in a discernible way with the use of closed and leading questions still rampant, and as such giving little opportunity for the interviewee to give their own account of events, the PEACE model has gained traction and achieved some success over time in being used successfully throughout the UK and other countries. It has also gained popularity 'across the pond' in North America for what has been viewed as its ethical style to extracting evidence.

9.2.4 *Confessions and the issues of authenticity, legitimacy and reliability*[29]

Confession evidence has the ability to author many challenges to the fair dispensation of justice. Nowhere is this more acutely seen than in cases where there has been a blatant disregard of the law, procedure and more relevantly, the rules of evidence leading to a miscarriage of justice. The issues are readily

[27] See one summary of the model as summarised by T Hutchinson, https://www.iilpm.com/the-peace-investigative-interviewing-model/ retrieved on 5/12/21.

[28] J Baldwin, *Video Taping Police Interviews with Suspects-n Evaluation* (Home Office, Police Research Series, Paper 1) (1992).

[29] See generally, Dennis I *The Law of Evidence* 214-218.

understood when classified into those dealing with (i) authenticity; (ii) legitimacy; and (iii) reliability. We discuss these in turn.

9.2.4.1 *Authenticity*

The question of authenticity in so far as confession evidence is concerned revolves around the issue of whether the confession that the prosecution seeks to have admitted into evidence is one that was given or made at all, and if so, what the exact terms of the said confession were. It logically follows from the foregoing that when a court is dealing with the specific question of a confession it is confronted with determining, on the basis of specific relevance presented to it, whether, as may be claimed by the accused person, the confession in question is a fabrication. That this is possible is demonstrated in one notorious case: *The Birmingham six.*[30] On 21 November, 1974, an IRA bombing campaign in the West Midlands culminated in explosions at two public houses in the centre of Birmingham, 'The Tavern in the Town' and 'The Mulberry Bush'. Twenty-one people died and at least 160 were injured. A few hours later five Irishmen, travelling on a train that had left Birmingham shortly before the explosions, were arrested at the Lancashire port of Heysham, where they had been about to board a ferry for Northern Ireland. A sixth was later arrested in Birmingham. Hugh Callaghan, Paddy Hill, Gerry Hunter, Richard McIlkenny, Billy Power and Johnny Walker were later convicted of planting the bombs and given life sentences. The case against them was based mainly upon confessions signed by Callaghan, McIlkenny, Power and Walker and a forensic test (the 'Greiss Test') carried out by a Home Office scientist, Dr Frank Skuse, which had allegedly found traces of nitro-glycerine on the hands of two of the six. Insisting upon their innocence the six men appealed against conviction and their appeal was rejected in 1976. They then attempted to sue the West Midlands Police for injuries inflicted upon them in police custody following their arrest. This action was thrown out by Lord Denning in 1981. In 1987, following new scientific evidence unearthed by World in Action, the Home Secretary referred the case back to the Court of Appeal which again upheld the convictions. In March,1991, faced with compelling new evidence, including signs that the police notebooks had been extensively re-written, the Appeal Court finally quashed the convictions. Then men were freed and compensated for the 17 years they had spent in prison.[31]

As demonstrated in the foregoing case and others like it, a confession may turn out to be a fabrication after all. This has been shown to occur in at least three forms:

(i) By a practice referred to as, happened in *The Birmingham Six case*, "verballing"[32] in which the police invent a purported oral admission.

[30] The summary is taken from "Birmingham Six Case - Miscarriages of Justice Campaigning - Records of Chris Mullin MP - Archives Hub (jisc.ac.uk)" https://archiveshub.jisc.ac.uk/search/archives/60bbc820-ba84-32cc-bfea-92eb25b48028?component=fbe3b34b-f226-3abf-b5b1-e81bde8005e2 retrieved on 02/12/21.

[31] The other like this case is what is commonly referred to as the Tottenham three case in which words were inserted into a 'confession' which as it turned out was no confession at all.

[32] For a detailed analysis of this abuse, see Dennis "Miscarriage of Justice" [1993] P.L. 291, 295-296.

(ii) A second form of fabrication may occur when, as in the *Birmingham Six case*, the investigation officers tamper with a written statement after it has been signed by the accused by including incriminating material not authored by the accused.

(iii) A third way is by a police officer writing a confession statement purportedly from the accused which allegedly was obtained through coercion, torture, intimidation, sleep deprivation, violence, lengthy periods of interrogation, trickery or improper means such as these.

9.2.4.2 *Legitimacy*

The question of legitimacy within the context of confession evidence is premised on the concept of fairness and legality. In essence it asks whether the means employed to procure the confession in question were legal and fair. The first port of call in determining legitimacy of a confession in this jurisdiction is Article 15[33] of the Constitution which provides in rather unmistakable terms that: '[a] person shall not be subjected to torture, or to inhuman or degrading punishment or other like treatment.'[34] This Article was considered in *The People v Ian Kainda*[35] albeit under a different context from the one under discussion. The accused was found guilty of conduct likely to cause a breach of peace contrary to Section 178(f) of the Penal Code[36] on his own confession and admission of facts by the Subordinate Court of the Third Class for the Livingstone District. He was convicted accordingly. The matter was subsequently referred to the High Court. The accused was charged under a wrong Section and Corporal punishment contravenes the provisions of Article 15 of the Constitution of Zambia. Moving far afield, the following is worthy of consideration:[37]

> During the early 20th century, American police often used "third-degree" methods of interrogation[38] inflicting physical pain and discomfort o extract confessions (e.g., prolonged confinement and isolation; explicit threats of harm or punishment; deprivation of sleep, food, and other needs; extreme sensory discomfort; and physical violence).

In *Brown v Mississippi*,[39] the Petitioners were indicted for a murder that occurred on March 30, 1934. The Petitioners were indicted on April 4, 1934, arraigned thereafter and then pleaded not guilty. The Petitioners were found guilty after a trial solely on the basis of their confessions. During the trial, the Petitioners testified that the confessions were untrue and procured after physical torture. The Petitioners appealed to the Supreme Court of Mississippi arguing that their Fourteenth Amendment rights were violated. The Supreme Court of Mississippi affirmed the trial court's judgment. The Mississippi Supreme Court concluded "(1) that immunity from self- incrimination is not essential to due process of law; and (2) that the failure of the trial court to exclude the

---

[39] 297 U.S. 278, 56 S. Ct. 461, 80 L. Ed. 682 as adapted at https://www.casebriefs.com/blog/law/criminal-procedure/criminal-procedure-keyed-to-weinreb/the-privilege-against-self-incrimination/brown-v-mississippi/ retrieved on 4/12/21.

which resulted in a signed, written confession. At trial, the oral and written confessions were presented to the jury. Miranda was found guilty of kidnapping and rape and was sentenced to 20-30 years imprisonment on each count. On appeal, the Supreme Court of Arizona held that Miranda's constitutional rights were not violated in obtaining the confession.

- *Vignera v New York:* Vignera was picked up by New York police in connection with the robbery of a dress shop that had occurred three days prior. He was first taken to the 17th Detective Squad headquarters. He was then taken to the 66th Detective Squad, where he orally admitted the robbery and was placed under formal arrest. He was then taken to the 70th Precinct for detention, where he was questioned by an assistant district attorney in the presence of a hearing reporter who transcribed the questions and answers. At trial, the oral confession and the transcript were presented to the jury. Vignera was found guilty of first-degree robbery and sentenced to 30-60 years imprisonment. The conviction was affirmed without opinion by the Appellate Division and the Court of Appeals.
- *Westover v United States:* Westover was arrested by local police in Kansas City as a suspect in two Kansas City robberies and taken to a local police station. A report was also received from the FBI that Westover was wanted on a felony charge in California. Westover was interrogated the night of the arrest and the next morning by local police. Then, FBI agents continued the interrogation at the station. After two-and-a-half hours of interrogation by the FBI, Westover signed separate confessions, which had been prepared by one of the agents during the interrogation, to each of the two robberies in California. These statements were introduced at trial. Westover was convicted of the California robberies and sentenced to 15 years' imprisonment on each count. The conviction was affirmed by the Court of Appeals for the Ninth Circuit.
- *California v Stewart*: In the course of investigating a series of purse-snatch robberies in which one of the victims died of injuries inflicted by her assailant, Stewart was identified as the endorser of checks stolen in one of the robberies. Steward was arrested at his home. Police also arrested Stewart's wife and three other people who were visiting him. Stewart was placed in a cell, and, over the next five days, was interrogated on nine different occasions. During the ninth interrogation session, Stewart stated that he had robbed the deceased, but had not meant to hurt her. At that time, police released the four other people arrested with Stewart because there was no evidence to connect any of them with the crime. At trial, Stewart's statements were introduced. Stewart was convicted of robbery and first-degree murder and sentenced to death. The Supreme Court of California reversed, holding that Stewart should have been advised of his right to remain silent and his right to counsel.

Issues: Whether "statements obtained from an individual who is subjected to custodial police interrogation" are admissible against him in a criminal trial and whether "procedures which assure that the individual is accorded his privilege under the Fifth Amendment to the Constitution[76] not to be compelled to incriminate himself" are necessary.

Supreme Court holding: The Court held that "there can be no doubt that the Fifth Amendment privilege is available outside of criminal court proceedings and serves to protect persons in all settings in which their freedom of action is curtailed in any significant way from being compelled to incriminate themselves." As such, "the prosecution may not use statements, whether exculpatory or inculpatory, stemming from custodial interrogation of the defendant unless it demonstrates the use of procedural safeguards effective to secure the privilege against self-incrimination. By custodial interrogation, we mean questioning initiated by law enforcement officers after a person has been taken into custody or otherwise deprived of his freedom of action in any significant way." The Court further held that "without proper safeguards the process of in-custody interrogation of persons suspected or accused of crime contains inherently compelling pressures which work to undermine the individual's will to resist and to compel him to speak where he would otherwise do so freely." Therefore, a defendant "must be warned prior to any questioning that he has the right to remain silent, that anything he says can be used against him in a court of law, that he has the right to the presence of an attorney, and that if he cannot afford an attorney, one will be appointed for him prior to any questioning if he so desires. The Supreme Court reversed the judgment of the Supreme Court of Arizona in *Miranda,* reversed the judgment of the New York Court of Appeals in *Vignera,* reversed the judgment of the Court of Appeals for the Ninth Circuit in *Westover,* and affirmed the judgment of the Supreme Court of California in *Stewart.*

To recapitulate, given the overwhelming power that the prosecution enjoys through state mechanisms such as enacting laws, police power to investigate and arrest, and through the prosecution, to bring charges against individuals and move the courts to accept such charges and the prosecution of individuals in criminal proceedings, the chances of such power being abused through

[76] The Fifth Amendment (Amendment V) to the United States Constitution relates to criminal procedure and related matters of the US Constitution in the following terms: 'No person shall be subject, except in cases of impeachment, to more than one punishment or trial for the same offense; nor shall be compelled to be a witness against himself; nor be deprived of life, liberty, or property, without due process of law; nor be obliged to relinquish his property, where it may be necessary for public use, without just compensation. ... [E]xcept in cases of impeachments, and cases arising in the land or naval forces, or the militia when on actual service, in time of war or public danger [...] in all crimes punishable with loss of life or member, presentment or indictment by a grand jury shall be an essential preliminary [....]'

illegal and even immoral means cannot be overemphasised. It behooves courts therefore to ensure that the constraints in Articles 18 of the Constitution are invoked. Therefore, the important consideration becomes not the relevance of evidence obtained through confessions but that such evidence is only admitted where the conduct of the government through its agents has been above board. Where evidence of improper conduct can be proved, i.e., to say, 'in a case where, after the commission of the crime, illegal or irregular methods have been used to obtain evidence from the accused'[77] as was the case in *Chimba v Attorney-General,*[78] confession evidence ought to be excluded without more. Evidence was led to substantiate the claim [...] It showed that each of the plaintiffs was removed from a lawful place of detention and taken in a closed van to an unknown place where for periods varying between seven and ten days they were each held in very small, empty, completely dark and dirty cells with an earth latrine on the floor. Their clothing was completely removed; they had no clothes and no blankets. They were half-starved, and given little or no water to drink and none to wash. They were each interrogated in a dark office on a number of occasions, under three bright lights, threatened with death, or mutilation, and slapped, punched and kicked. Other than the first plaintiff, they were photographed naked. The first plaintiff reached the stage of mental breakdown. The second and fifth plaintiffs were threatened with electric shock. The fourth plaintiff was subjected to electric shock. Throughout they were under armed guard. Some of the interrogators were recognised to be members of the Criminal Investigation Department and the guards were Constables. The plaintiffs at one time held Ministerial or other high office in the Government but later broke away from the ruling party to join an opposition party, and the interrogation was designed principally to ascertain the source of its funds.

In *The People v Habwacha,*[79] the court pointed out that the courts cannot on a basis of expediency such as this admit confessions which may have been induced [by physical coercion or such like illegal or improper means] lest our whole system of law enforcement degenerated and our whole structure of justice – indeed, of society itself – be imperilled.

Further to the foregoing, the pre-eminence of the autonomy of the individual over the power of the collective does not disappear simply because he has been charged with an offence. After all, in accordance with Article 18(2) of the Constitution, '[e]very person who is charged with a criminal offence - (a) shall be presumed to be innocent until he is proved or has pleaded guilty.' It therefore logically follows that the government ought not to unconstitutionally compel a person to answer questions that will incriminate him. Recall that the Constitution in Article 18(7) provides that '[a] person who is tried for a criminal offence shall not be compelled to give evidence at the trial.' This means that the accused may choose to remain silent. He generally ought not to be treated as being guilty for that reason and that reason alone. Be that as it may, where the confession has been obtained without compulsion and as such

[77] *Per* Lord Scarman citing Lord Guthrie in *H M Advocate v Turnbull* 1951 JC 96 at 103.

[78] [1972] ZR 165 (HC); see also *Miranda v Arizona* 384 U.S. 436.

[79] [1970] HL 77 as adapted in Hatchard J and Ndulo M *The Law of Evidence in Zambia* 273.

given voluntarily, there is nothing to stop the court from admitting same into evidence in order to dispense justice.

Lastly, it is imperative in criminal proceedings that there be an equable autonomous tribunal capable of dispensing justice without fear or favour by observing acceptable standards of fairness and due process.

9.2.7 *The right to silence*

9.2.7.1 *General*

The Constitutional imperative for the right to remain silent even under the discussion relating to police interviews of suspects is, as we have seen elsewhere in this text, to be found under Article 18(2)(a) which provides that '[e]very person who is charged with a criminal offence-shall be presumed to be innocent until he is proved or has pleaded guilty' and Article 18(7) which provides as follows: '[a] person who is tried for a criminal offence shall not be compelled to give evidence at the trial.' While the provisions would, at first blush appear to suggest that their applicability is limited to instances after the suspect has been charged, they must be viewed as a non-derogable guide to the conduct of interviews with suspects by the police. Thus, the fact that a suspect elects to remain silent, is not a factor to be held against them.[80] Further, it need 'not suggest that remaining silent is an indication of guilt.'[81]Even so, as observed in *Chimbini v The People:*[82]

> Where the evidence against an accused person is purely circumstantial and his guilt entirely a matter of inference [...] the fact that an accused person has elected not to give evidence on oath may, in certain circumstances, [may] tend to support the case against him, but will certainly not do so unless the inference was one which could properly be drawn in the first place.

9.2.7.2 *Specific facets of the right to remain silent under the common law*

At common law, the right to silence had several facets which we discuss in turn.

(i) Warn and caution

In this jurisdiction as in many others, the police are required and expected to issue a warn and caution statement which is to the effect that the suspect need not say anything and that, should they choose to say anything, anything said may be used against them in a court of law, i.e., during their prosecution, at trial. The whole basis of this requirement is transparency and fairness to the suspect. The suspect ought to know that he is being investigated and that under

[80] *Dickson Sembauke Changwe and Ifellow Hamuchanje v The People* [1988 – 1989] ZR 144 (SC).

[81] *David Dimuna v The People* [1988 – 1989] ZR 199 (SC).

[82] [1973] ZR 191 (CA).

such circumstances he ought to make an informed decision as to whether he must utter any sentence which if he does, may be used against him. Police are required to observe this requirement at all stages of the criminal justice system. They are to issue a warn and caution statement every time they strongly suspect the 'suspect' to have committed an offense and when the purpose for which they are interviewing such a suspect is to used his responses against him at trial. It has to be issued at the beginning of an interview and after the break, when the interview resumes. It also logically follows that the warn and caution statement has to be issued at the time of arrest.[83] The whole basis of the foregoing is the constitutional injunction that a suspect shall not be compelled to give evidence that incriminates him. The caution has to be repeated once the suspect is formally charged in terms such as these: 'You do not have to say anything. But it may harm your defence if you do not mention when questioned something which you later rely on in Court. Anything you do say may be given in evidence.'

(ii) Burden of proof on the prosecution

The principle espoused in *Woolmington v DPP*[84] as noted elsewhere in this text is that the burden of proof in criminal proceedings lies on the prosecution. In any case, Article 18(7) of the Constitution provides that a '[a] person who is tried for a criminal offence shall not be compelled to give evidence at the trial.' It is the prosecution who must prove the guilt of the accused. It is not for the accused to prove his innocence. Essentially, 'he who accuses must prove.' The general effect of this is that there is no burden on the accused to produce any evidence by whatever name called to answer the police's questions or indeed to disprove the prosecution's claims, assertions or allegations. As we have noted elsewhere in this text though, the general rule in *Woolmington*[85] has seen inroads made into it by specific statutory provisions. As seen from the consideration of *Liato*[86] and *Musengule*[87] elsewhere in this text, there are several statutes that expressly or by implication reverse the burden of proof. They include, as seen earlier, the following: s 49(2) of the Anti-Corruption Commission Act;[88] s 71(2) of the Forfeiture of Proceeds of Crime Act;[89] s 42 of the Forest Act;[90] and s 318(1) of the Penal Code.[91]

[83] The procedure relating to arrest is variously provided for under Part III: 'General Provisions - Arrest, Escape and Retaking Arrest Generally' of the Criminal Procedure Code Chapter 88 of the laws of Zambia or more specifically ss 18-64.

[84] [1935] AC 462.

[85] [1935] AC 462.

[86] [Selected Judgment No 21 of 2015].

[87] [SCZ Selected Judgment No. 19 of 2017].

[88] Chapter 91 of the Laws of Zambia which Act (repealed).

[89] No 19 of 2010 which was construed by the Supreme Court in *Liato* [Selected Judgment No 21 of 2015] as reversing, to a certain extent, the burden of proof in matters involving forfeiture of proceeds of crime.

[90] No 7 of 1999.

[91] Chapter 87 of the Laws of Zambia; see application in *George Nswana v The People* [1988 – 1989] ZR 174 (SC).

(iii) Accused not a compellable witness

This point is a logical extension of the point above. Permitting the prosecution to call the accused as a witness in his own prosecution turns the very essence of not compelling him to incriminate himself once charged with an offence on its head. It would in fact be unconstitutional, explicitly breaching Article 18(7) of the Constitution. It would offend the principle adumbrated in *Woolmington*[92] that the burden of proving a charge lies on the prosecution. It would turn criminal proceedings into farcical travesty which would prejudice the accused at trial, taint justice and offend the dignity of the court.

(iv) Prosecution not to comment on silence

(a) General

At common law the prosecution was not to, at trial, comment on the accused's choice to remain silent at the police station interview. It has been observed in *Hall v R*[93] that although, in very exceptional circumstances, an inference may be drawn from a failure to give an explanation or disclaimer, as a general rule, where a person is informed that an accusation has been made against him, his silence alone cannot give rise to an inference that he accepts the truth of the accusation; furthermore, the fact that he was not informed of his right not to reply to the accusation cannot support an inference that his silence was not in exercise of that right. Nor was it permissible for the prosecution to make (adverse) comments as regards the accused's decision to remain silent at trial. This position has now been codified in proviso (ii) to s 157 of the Criminal Procedure Code[94] which provides that 'the failure of any person charged with an offence or of the wife or husband, as the case may be, of the person so charged, to give evidence shall not be made the subject of any comment by the prosecution,' itself predicated on Article 18(7) of the Constitution.

(b) Exceptions

The prosecution was, however, permitted to adduce evidence of silence in the following instances:

(i) When the accusation had been made by the victim

In *R v Horne*,[95] the victim had been 'glassed' in a restaurant. The [accused] was brought before the victim who immediately identified him as the assailant. He made no answer. It was held that the judge was correct to direct the jury to take

---

[92] [1935] AC 462.

[93] [1971] 1 All ER 322; *R v Whitehead* [1928] All ER Rep 186 and *R v Keeling* [1942] 1 All ER 507 approved; *R v Feigenbaum* [1918–19] All ER Rep 489 disapproved; editor's notes: For statements made in the presence of an accused, see 10 Halsbury's Laws (3rd Edn) 475, 476, para 870, and for cases on the subject, see 14 Digest (Repl) 447, 448, 4342–4356.

[94] Chapter 88 of the Laws of Zambia.

[95] [1990] Crim LR 188; as adapted at https://swarb.co.uk/regina-v-horne-cacd-1990/ retrieved on 6/12/21.

the defendant's silence in the face of an accusation into account. Whether any reply might be expected in the circumstances was one of fact for the jury.

(ii) When the accusation had been made by the parents to the victim

In *Parkes v Queen*[96] the accused was convicted of murdering a young woman, Daphne Graham. He was tried in the Circuit Court for the Parish of Kingston before the Chief Justice and a jury. The evidence against him was circumstantial and given mainly by Mrs. Graham, the mother of the deceased. Leaving home one morning, she noticed the accused on the accused was standing near the veranda to which the deceased's door opened. When she returned home upon receiving some disturbing news, she found that her daughter had been stabbed twice. The daughter told her that the accused had stabbed her. Going into the garden, she confronted the accused who had in his hand a rachet knife in his hand with the words: 'What she do you-why you stab her?' He sought to attack her and upon him opening the knife to do so, she noticed that it had blood stains on it. He slashed one of her fingers when she raised her hands to defend herself which required her to have five stitches. At trial, he elected to give an unsworn statement denying the accusation. He was convicted. On an appeal to the Privy Council, the court considered whether to admit as evidence against the accused his response to an accusation made by the victim's mother when no police officer was present and to which the defendant had reacted by threatening her. In dismissing the appeal, the Court quoted with approval the words of Cave J in *R v Mitchell*:[97]

> Now the whole admissibility of statements of this kind rests upon the consideration that if a charge is made against a person in that person's presence it is reasonable to expect that he or she will immediately deny it, and that the absence of such a denial is some evidence of an admission on the part of the person charged, and of the truth of the charge. Undoubtedly, when persons are speaking on even terms, and a charge is made, and the person charged says nothing, and expresses no indignation, and does nothing to repel the charge, that is some evidence to show that he admits the charge to be true.

The court reasoned that in the instant case, the accused was speaking with Mrs. Graham on even terms. Therefore, so said the Court, 'the Chief Justice was perfectly entitled to instruct the jury that the accused's reactions to the accusations including his silence were matters which they could take into account along with other evidence in deciding whether the accused in fact committed the act with which he was charged.'

(iii) Where the accuse was on 'level terms' with the police

---

[96] [1976] 3 All ER 380.

[97] (1892) 17 Cox CC at 508.

In *R v Chandler*,[98] the appellant was suspected of being one of the members of a gang which had been formed to obtain television sets dishonestly. In the presence of his solicitor, the appellant was questioned by a detective sergeant at a police station. Both before and after being cautioned he answered some questions and remained silent or refused to answer other questions in relation to other alleged members of the gang. He was charged with conspiracy to defraud and at his trial did not give evidence. The only evidence against him was the interview at the police station. The judge directed the jury that it was for them to decide whether the appellant had remained silent before the caution in the exercise of his common law right or had 'remained silent because he might have thought that if he had answered he would in some ways have incriminated himself.' The appellant was convicted and appealed. It was held that some comment by the judge on the appellant's lack of frankness before he was cautioned was justified, provided the jury's attention was directed to the right issue. That issue was whether the appellant's silence amounted to an acceptance by him of what the sergeant had said. If he had accepted what had been said, the jury should then consider whether guilt could reasonably be inferred from what he had accepted. The judge should not have suggested that the appellant's silence could indicate guilt; his comment was not justified and could have led the jury to a wrong conclusion. Furthermore, the unsupported evidence of the interview did not provide a safe foundation for an inference that the appellant had been a member of the conspiracy alleged. The appeal would therefore be allowed and the conviction quashed.

(iv) Judge could only make limited comments on silence of accused

A plethora of authorities, English and those decided in this jurisdiction, have consistently shown that the position at common law is for a judge to limit his comments on the accused's silence. For a court to make adverse comments which imply that an accused's failure to give evidence in his defence when called upon to do so infers that he or she is guilty of the offence charged is unconstitutional and out of touch with a judge's responsibility to be an umpire and fair referee.[99] If it were done, *Waugh v R*[100] shows that this would be a basis for appeal and review by a superior court.[101] *Waugh v R*[102] has been followed in several Supreme Court decisions in this jurisdiction.[103]Lord Parker CJ, as he was then, sought in *R v Bathurst*,[104] has opined as follows on this point:

> the accepted form of comment is to inform the jury that, of course, the

[98] [1976] 3 All ER 105.

[99] Compare Proviso (ii) to s 157 of the Criminal Procedure Code Chapter 88 of the Laws of Zambia.

[100] [1950] AC 203.

[101] But see relevant comments on this point in *David Dimuna v The People* [1988 – 1989] ZR 199 (SC); *Chimbini v The People* [1973] ZR 191 (CA).

[102] [1950] AC 203.

[103] *Dickson Sembauke Changwe and Ifellow Hamuchanje v The People* [1988 – 1989] ZR 144 (SC); *David Dimuna v The People* [1988 – 1989] ZR 199 (SC); *Chimbini v The People* [1973] ZR 191 (CA).

[104] [1968] 2 QB 99 CA.

> accused is not bound to give evidence, that he can sit back and see if the prosecution have proved their case, and that, while the jury had been deprived of the opportunity of hearing his story tested in cross-examination, the one thing they must do is to assume that he is guilty because he has not gone into the witness box.

The accused is not bound to say anything and cannot be compelled to do so.[105] He need not prove anything and cannot, by constitutional guarantee, be forced to incriminate himself.[106] He is after all, presumed innocent.[107] In *David Dumina v The People,*[108] the Supreme Court has held as follows: '[…] a court must not hold the fact that an accused remains silent against him.'[109] Further, in *Dickson Sembauke Changwe and Ifellow Hamuchanje v The People,*[110] it was observed that the fact that the appellants elected to remain silent, was not a factor to be held against them. However, the comments by Lord Parker in *R v Bathurst,*[111] would seem to suggest that if an accused person fails to give evidence in his own defence,[112] the accused person's case is weakened and in such a scenario, said Lawton LJ, a judge was entitled to make a more strident observation or comment, even going beyond *Bathurst*[113] in the interest of justice especially where, as in *Sparrow,*[114] a strong *prima facie* case has been made by the prosecution and the accused has been put on his defence indicating to him that without hearing from him the court would likely convict him.[115]

In 1994, the EWCA in *R v Martinez Tobon,*[116] abridged the relevant principles in the following terms:

> (1) The judge should give the jury a direction along the lines of the Judicial Studies Board specimen direction based on *R v Bathurst*[117]
> (2) The essentials of that direction are that the defendant is under no obligation to testify and the jury should not assume he is guilty

---

[105] Article 18(7) of the Constitution.

[106] Article 18(7) of the Constitution.

[107] Article 18(2)(a) of the Constitution.

[108] [1988 – 1989] ZR 199 (SC).

[109] But See, for academic interests only, *Lt. Gen. Geojago Robert Chaswe Musengule, Amon Sibande v The People* HPA/16/2009 on how, as argued by counsel, but rejected both in this case and on appeal in *Lt. General Geojago Robert Musengule and Amon Sibande v The People* [SCZ Selected Judgment No 19 of 2017], this may be a legal fiction in the light of the provisions of Part VI of the ACC Act, as the Act requires a satisfactory explanation from a person charged with an offence under Part IV; see also for academic reasons only similar arguments by counsel, which were ultimately rejected in *The People v Austin Chisanga Liato* [Selected Judgment No 21 of 2010] regarding a similar provision, s 71(1)&(2) and s 78 of the Forfeiture of Proceeds of Crime Act No 19 of 2010.

[110] [1988 – 1989] ZR 144 (SC).

[111] [1968] 2 QB 99 CA.

[112] An idea seemingly supported by Lawton LJ in *R v Sparrow* (1987) 84 Cr App R 75 CA; see further *R v Squire* [1990] Crim LR 341.

[113] [1968] 2 QB 99 CA.

[114] (1987) 84 Cr App R 75 CA.

[115] *R v Mutch* [1973] 1 All ER 178 at 181, *per* Lawton LJ.

[116] (1994) 98 Cr App R 375 CA.

[117] [1968] 1 All ER 1175 at 1175 [1968] 2 QB 99 at 107.

because he has not given evidence.

(3) Provided those essentials are complied with, the judge may think it appropriate to make a stronger comment where the defence case involves alleged facts which (a) are at variance with prosecution evidence or additional to it and exculpatory, and (b) must, if true, be within the knowledge of the defendant.

(4) The nature and strength of such comment must be a matter for the discretion of the judge and will depend upon the circumstances of the individual case. However, it must not be such as to contradict or nullify the essentials of the conventional direction".

Therefore, as has been said in *David Dumina v The People,*[118] '[...] there is no impropriety in a comment that only the prosecution evidence was available to the court. It is no more than a statement of fact and does not suggest that remaining silent is an indication of guilt.'

(vi) The right not to incriminate oneself

There exists a universal maxim which on the one hand is general and on the other, a technical privilege against self-incrimination.[119] As we have already noted elsewhere in this text, there is a constitutional imperative under Article 18(7) not to compel an accused person to give evidence in his defence.

9.2.7.3 The right to remain silent: a further discussion

(i) General

As we have seen elsewhere in this text, the debate as regards how the choice of the accused to remain silent based on the maxim "he accuses must prove" as adumbrated in *Woolmington v DPP*[120] has seen many twists and turn. That the *Woolmington*[121] position in general is settled is without question. In this jurisdiction it has been elevated to a fundamental right under Article 18(7) which mandates all concerned after a person is charged with an offence not to compel such accused to give evidence. The position in this jurisdiction thus remains that in general terms, except those (an issue that in *Woolmington*[122] had been pointed out as an exception to the general rule), specifically stipulated under statute, that silence by an accused person cannot be used as evidence of his guilt. As we have seen from the second proviso to s 157 of the Criminal Procedure Code[123] and several Supreme Court decisions[124] the prosecution

[118] [1988 – 1989] ZR 199 (SC).

[119] *Dickson Sembauke Changwe and Ifellow Hamuchanje v The People* [1988 – 1989] ZR 144 (SC); *David Dimuna v The People* [1988 – 1989] ZR 199 (SC); *Chimbini v The People* [1973] ZR 191 (CA).

[120] [1935] AC 462.

[121] [1935] AC 462.

[122] [1935] AC 462.

[123] Chapter 88 of the Laws of Zambia.

[124] *Dickson Sembauke Changwe and Ifellow Hamuchanje v The People* [1988 – 1989] ZR 144 (SC); *David Dimuna v The People* [1988 – 1989] ZR 199 (SC); *Chimbini v The People* [1973] ZR 191 (CA).

is not permitted to comment adversely on the accused's election to remain silent. A judge's comments, if any, in this respect, must be limited in scope and gravity.[125]

This principle, as it relates to accused persons, remaining silent following charges being laid against them is logically supposed to apply to investigations at the police station. It leads to what are termed "ambush defences"[126] essentially a scenario in which the defence relies on significant facts which were not disclosed to the police during investigations, and where not made available to the prosecution at trial. The "ambush defence" and by parity of reason, "ambush prosecution" is, as we briefly discuss below, a mainstay of the subordinate court where cases are tried in summary form i.e., via trial by ambush.

Even so, while the "summary defence" has had its criticism,[127] there appears to be no empirical evidence to support the assertion that such defences as are common place and routinely permitted in subordinate court proceedings have led to an unacceptably high number of accused persons being acquitted in England for example. While there appears to be no concrete data on this particular subject, it seems logical to conclude that the ambush defence has not tipped the scale against conviction where cases are properly prosecuted and the evidence weighs heavily against the accused person. In any case, getting rid of the concept of "ambush defences" would not only be unconstitutional, it would lay waste to the whole criminal justice paradigm of the burden of proof lying on the prosecution technically making an accused person a prosecution witness who aids his own prosecution, incriminates himself and makes a mockery of the adversarial system of justice. Be that as it may, a disclosure of aspects of a defence's case would not be wholly out of sync of constitutional guarantees to the right to remain silent. What cannot be entertained is a wholesale removal of this constitutionally guaranteed right.

We may now proceed to ask to what extent a magistrate or judge should use the accused's silence as evidence against him or her. We have shown above that the realm within which a magistrate or judge, as the case may be, may do this is severely circumscribed.[128] There are many good and compelling reasons for this limit placed on a magistrate or judge at common law. The issues raised are not only ethical and policy related, they pertain to the practice of law in general.[129]

(ii) The ethical question

[125] *Dickson Sembauke Changwe and Ifellow Hamuchanje v The People* [1988 – 1989] ZR 144 (SC); *David Dimuna v The People* [1988 – 1989] ZR 199 (SC); *Chimbini v The People* [1973] ZR 191 (CA).

[126] For an analysis of ambush defences in England & Wales see Uglow S *Evidence* 162-166.

[127] See A Zuckerman: "Trial By Unfair Means" [1989] Crim LR 855; R Leng: *The Right to silence in Police Interrogation* (Royal Commission on Criminal Justice Research Study 10 HMSO 1993); M McConville and J Hodgson: Custodial Legal Advice and the Right to Silence (Royal Commission on Criminal Justice Research Study 10 HMSO 1993).

[128] *David Dimuna v The People* [1988 – 1989] ZR 199 (SC).

[129] Ashworth A and Redmayne, *The Criminal Process* (4th edn 2005); D Galligan "The Right to Silence Reconsidered" [1988] CLP 69 at 88.

The ethical question is also a constitutional one in this jurisdiction. It is predicated on Article 18(7) of the Constitution which proscribes compelling an accused person charged with an offence from "self-incrimination:" As Uglow[130] has observed, 'it is unfair to offer [accused persons] a choice between speaking and convicting themselves out of their own mouths, or not speaking and being convicted by default.' The issue has been considered in *Saunders v UK*[131] wherein it was observed by the Grand Chamber that the subsequent use against a defendant in a prosecution, of evidence which had been obtained under compulsion in company insolvency procedures was a convention breach of Art 6. Although not specifically mentioned in Article 6 of the Convention the right to silence and the right not to incriminate oneself are generally recognised international standards which lie at the heart of the notion of a fair procedure under Article 6. The right not to incriminate oneself is primarily concerned, however, with respecting the will of an accused person to remain silent. As commonly understood in the legal systems of the contracting parties to the Convention and elsewhere, it does not extend to the use in criminal proceedings of material which may be obtained from the accused through the use of compulsory powers but which has an existence independent of the will of the suspect such as, *inter alia,* documents acquired pursuant to a warrant, breath, blood and urine samples and bodily tissue for the purpose of DNA testing.

> The Court recalls that, although not specifically mentioned in Article 6 of the Convention, the right to silence and the right not to incriminate oneself, are generally recognised international standards which lie at the heart of the notion of a fair procedure under Article 6. Their rationale lies, *inter alia,* in the protection of the accused against improper compulsion by the authorities thereby contributing to the avoidance of miscarriages of justice and to the fulfilment of the aims of Article 6. The right not to incriminate oneself, in particular [...] that the prosecution in a criminal case seek to prove their case against the accused without resort to evidence obtained through methods of coercion or oppression in defiance of the will of the accused. In this sense the right is closely linked to the presumption of innocence contained in Article 6(2) of the Convention.The right not to incriminate oneself is primarily concerned, however, with respecting the will of an accused person to remain silent. As commonly understood in the legal systems of the contracting parties to the Convention and elsewhere, it does not extend to the use in criminal proceedings of material which may be obtained from the accused through the use of compulsory powers, but which has an existence independent of the will of the suspect, such as, inter alia, documents acquired pursuant to a warrant, breath, blood and urine samples and bodily tissue for the purpose of DNA testing.

[130] Uglow S *Evidence* 161.

[131] Application No 19187/91; [1996], 23 EHRR 313; as adapted at https://swarb.co.uk/saunders-v-the-united-kingdom-echr-17-dec-1996/ retrieved on 8/12/21.

> The court does not accept the Government's premise on this point since some of the Applicant's answers were in fact of an incriminating nature in the sense that they contained admissions to knowledge of information which tended to incriminate him [...] In any event, bearing in mind the concept of fairness in Article 6, the right not to incriminate oneself cannot reasonably be confined to statements of admission of wrongdoing or to remarks which are directly incriminating. Testimony obtained under compulsion which appears on its face to be of a non-incriminating nature – such as exculpatory remarks or mere information on questions of fact – may later be deployed in criminal proceedings in support of the prosecution case, for example to contradict or cast doubt upon other statements of the accused or evidence given by him during the trial or to otherwise undermine his credibility. Where the credibility of an accused must be assessed by a jury, the use of such testimony may be especially harmful. It follows that what is of the essence in this context is the use to which evidence obtained under compulsion is put in the course of the criminal trial.

In *Funke v France*[132] like *Saunders,* the issue that arose related to the use of coercion against the accused in the pre-trial process. M. Funke successfully challenged his conviction for failing to provide documents which the customs authorities had demanded of him, on the grounds that his rights under Article 6 had been infringed: 'The Court observed as follows:

> [...] the customs secured Mr. Funke's conviction in order to obtain certain documents which they believed must exist, although they were not certain of the fact. Being unable or unwilling to procure them by some other means, they attempted to compel the applicant himself to provide the evidence of offences he had allegedly committed. The special features of customs law cannot justify such an infringement of the right of 'anyone charged with a criminal offence' within the autonomous meaning of this expression in Article 6, to remain silent and not to contribute to incriminating itself.

The position taken by the ECHR in the foregoing two authorities was to the effect that where evidence is obtained through coercion, it has the potential to infringe an accused person's right not to self-incriminate. Further, that usage of such evidence by the prosecution would put at risk the impartiality of any consequent trial of the accused person.

(iii) Policy considerations

At the core of the ethical question *vis-à-vis* the right for an accused person to remain silent at all stages of the criminal justice process are public policy considerations. As we have already stated elsewhere in this text, criminal prosecution is essentially a contest between the state and a private individual.

[132] Application No 10828/84; [1993], 16 EHRR 297.

It is quite clear that this is not a contest of equals not only because of the power of the state but its resource availability in so far as investigation and prosecution of a case compared to the accused is concerned. For this reason, it is considered appropriate that the state, and not the accused bears the burden of not only obtaining but discharging such burden beyond reasonable doubt. To redress the overwhelming inequality between the state and the accused, the state is restricted to using only that class of evidence obtained in a legal, fair and ethical manner. Said evidence ought to be heavily scrutinised. Were it not so, more likely than not, it will render even the court itself hopelessly inadequate to counter the power of the state and the conviction of the accused a foregone conclusion. 'Innocent until proven guilty'[133] as constitutionally guaranteed[134] will become 'guilty until proven innocent,'[135] the burden dangerously shifting to the accused, with no safeguards against self-incrimination.[136] In this way, constitutional norms will be desecrated; justice will be tainted; the dignity of the court offended; and the legitimacy of the final outcome deemed highly questionable.As has been observed in *Mack v The Queen:*[137]

> [...] the State does not have unlimited power to intrude into our personal lives or to randomly test the virtue of individuals. Another is the concern that entrapment techniques may result in the commission of crimes by people who would not otherwise become involved in criminal conduct [. . .] Ultimately, we may be saying that there are inherent limits on the power of the State to manipulate people and events for the purpose of attaining the specific objective of obtaining convictions.[46]

We must hasten to add that as with lying, silence by the accused breeds ambiguity and not certainty.[138] It may be motivated by a multiplicity of reasons all of which point away, when discovered, from the guilt of the accused. For silence of an accused person to be used against him in the limited cases that this is permitted the silence must relate to a material issue, the motive for it must be a realisation of guilt and a fear of the truth, and it must be clearly shown to be so by admission or by evidence from an independent source provided by

---

[133] Recall that the burden of proof in criminal trials is always on the prosecution: *Woolmington v DPP* [1935] UKHL 1; [1935] AC 462; 25 Cr App R 72; In *Kalaluka Musole v The People* [1963–1964] & NRLR 173 (CA), the CAZ held, *inter alia*, that it is always for the prosecution to prove that the accused actually had the intent necessary to constitute the crime, and that that proof may emerge from evidence or statements made by the accused about his own state of mind or may be made by way of inference from the totality of the circumstances; In *Maseka v The People* [1972] ZR 9 the High Court was of the view that an explanation which might reasonably be true entitles an accused to an acquittal even if the Court does not believe it, and that *an accused is not required to satisfy the Court as to his innocence but simply to raise a reasonable doubt as to his guilt* (emphasis added).

[134] See Article 18(2)(a).

[135] Recall that Article 18(2)(a) of the Constitution provides that '[e]very person who is charged with a criminal offence- shall be presumed to be innocent until he is proved or has pleaded guilty.'

[136] Recall that Article 18(7) of the Constitution provides that '[a] person who is tried for a criminal offence shall not be compelled to give evidence at the trial.'

[137] (1988) 44 C.C.C. 3d 513 at 541.

[138] Compare *R v Lucas* [1981] QB 720 (CA).

the prosecution.

9.2.7.4 *The right to remain silent: a prognostic view*

Our stated approach in this part of the discussion is to prognosticate the route the law as regards silence of the accused person will, in view of developments in jurisdictions such as England & Wales, is going to take. To do this, we will attempt to analyse the law as it now stands in England & Wales and what lessons, if any, may be taken therefrom.

(i) Developments in England & Wales and lessons for the Zambian jurisdiction

Developments in England & Wales as respects the right to silence have mainly been driven by statutory innovations as respects the following facets of the said right: (a) ambush defences (b) Failure to testify (c) Failure to account for objects, substances or marks (d) Failure to account for presence. We will discuss these in turn.

(a) Ambush defences

(i) Trial by ambush: a Zambian take

In this jurisdiction, the Subordinate Court is popularly known for delays in completion of cases and this usually done by series of adjournments. These adjournments are usually done by both the prosecution and the defence but the common reason behind adjournments by the defence is the fact that trials in the subordinate court are regarded as trial by ambush. That is to say, there is really not disclosure of evidence before the trial. Because of the lack of disclosure of evidence, more often than not counsel for the defence (where the accused is represented) remains with no option but to seek an adjournment so as to study the evidence and obtain instructions from his client. This practice infringes on the rights of an accused person.[139] The rights of the accused person in criminal trials are protected by the constitution of Zambia. Article 18 of the Constitution provides that a person charged with a criminal offence '[...] shall be afforded a fair hearing within a reasonable time by an independent and impartial court established by law.'

A fair hearing as envisaged under Article 18 of the Constitution is achieved through conducting a trial that is in conformity with the principles of justice and equity. This entails, as provided for under Article 18, informing the accused person as regards the case against him before trial for purposes of giving the accused or his counsel an opportunity to sufficiently prepare a defence on time with respect to the charges he faces without going through the process of seeking adjournments when faced with an ambush prosecution.

It has, however, been said in *The People v Kasonkomona*,[140] that 'trial at the

---

[139] Nkonde BS and Ngwira W, *Accused's Right and access to Prosecution information in Subordinate Courts in Zambia.*

[140] CR No 9/04/13 (SubCt).

Subordinate Court is still summary. The prosecution is under no obligation to provide the statements and that is settled law.' In the Namibian case of *S v Lucas,*[141] the court observed as follows:

> There is not a different brand of fairness in the lower courts in comparison to that applicable in any of the superior courts. After all, it is in the magistrates' courts that most members of the public come into contact with the law and, on the strength of their experience there, they form their perceptions of justice and fairness. The same rules of evidence and procedure apply, with certain exceptions, in all courts of law. Where there are distinctions, it concerns practice rather than rules that are designed to ensure fairness and justice to all parties.

Ultimately, the goal of any criminal trial, and the court that presides over such a trial within the broader context of the criminal law, is to avoid prejudice against the accused person.

As regards procedure, where the matter is before the High Court, s 258 of the Criminal Procedure Code[142] provides that the accused person must be provided with a list of all persons the prosecution intends to call as witnesses and a statement of the evidence each of the witnesses will testify to. The rationale here is again to provide the accused or/and his defence team with sufficient opportunity to mount an effective defence prior to trial and to obviate the need for the dreaded adjournments by the defence because it would have prepared its defence well before the prosecution opens its case.

The practice of ambush trials has widely been criticised in other jurisdictions.[143] In the Botswanan case of *Ahmed v Attorney General,*[144] the accused person requested the prosecutor for copies of various documents in the police docket to be released to him so as to enable him to adequately instruct his lawyers to prepare his defence. He made this request while awaiting trial before the Magistrate court. His request was denied and he applied to the High Court wherein he submitted that the refusal by the prosecution to disclose its evidence was in breach of his rights under s 10 of the Constitution of Botswana, which provision assures him of a fair hearing. The court held that the prosecution witness statements are generally privileged, but if that law offends against any of the protective provisions of the constitution, the any aggrieved person is entitled to ask the court to hold on to such law that offends his or her rights.

As discussed elsewhere in this text, it is not the role of the prosecution to conduct criminal proceedings in a manner that ambushes the accused person by withholding cardinal issues until such a time that the accused person or his counsel is not able to prepare a proper defence on time. The mirror compatriot of prosecution by ambush is defence by ambush which, as discussed elsewhere

---

[141] 1997 (9) BCLR 1314.

[142] Chapter 88 of the Laws of Zambia.

[143] See below.

[144] 2002 (2) BLR 431 (HC).

in this text is a scenario where evidence adduced in a court of law by an accused person is evidence which has not been availed in advance to the prosecution thereby constraining the prosecution from rebutting the same. An ambush defence may at times prove fatal to the prosecution's case in that the defence, though not anticipated by the prosecution, may carry so much weight as to negate an accused person's criminal liability. Be that as it may,the prejudicial effect of trial by ambush on the accused person outweighs the prejudicial effect on the prosecution because the prosecution would have already presented its case before the accused person raises an ambush defence. Therefore, the prosecution is required and expected in the two-part system of the criminal trial still used in this jurisdiction, to call any and all the evidence on which it intends to rely before the close of its case. If the prosecution could reasonably have foreseen that a particular piece of evidence was relevant in proving their case, they must tender it before the court as part of their case.[145] Denying the accused access to the evidence against him, which is currently the order of the day for procedures in the Zambian Subordinate Courts, is an affront to the principles of justice and fairness before the law. It not only attracts criticism from the public whom the criminal justice system is supposed to serve, but also greatly contributes to the delay in disposing off criminal cases in the Subordinate Courts. The prosecution cannot wait for the defence to present its case after the defence has closed its case. The rule, however, is subject to some exceptions one of which is evidence in rebuttal.

Evidence in rebuttal also known as case in reply is adduced by the prosecution in situations where the accused person or his witnesses' tender evidence of some new matter which the prosecution could not reasonably have foreseen. Section 210 of the Criminal Procedure Code[146] provides that the court may allow the advocate for the prosecution to adduce evidence in reply to contradict the said matter. In *Joseph Knox Simwanza & The People,*[147] the Court held that evidence in reply is only allowed in cases where in the course of the defence the accused person, as already noted, raises a new issue that the prosecutor could not have anticipated or foreseen.

(ii) The law in England & Wales – Lessons for Zambia

The law with respect to ambush defences in England is mainly predicated on ss 34[148] and 38 of the Criminal Justice and Public Order Act 1994. The aggregate position of these provisions is as follows: a judge may direct the jury to draw "such inference as appears proper" where the accused fails to mention a material fact which he later relies on at trial when it may have reasonably have been brought to the attention of the investigating officers during the relevant police

[145] *Kalebu Banda v The People* [1977] ZR 169.

[146] Chapter 88 of the Laws of Zambia.

[147] 1985 ZR 15.

[148] Section 34(1) has been amended by s 58 of the Youth Justice and Criminal Evidence Act 1999 which precludes a court from drawing adverse inferences when the suspect has not had occasion to consult a solicitor.

interview. This though is only possible in instances where the prosecution has supplied the court with substantial evidence discounting the accused's version of events and on which an equable tribunal would convict.[149] Where this is the case, the court ought to attach less weight to a concealed defence which having only been revealed at trial, is deemed less credible especially where there is little or no evidence to support such. The motivation is to encourage the accused to disclose their defences early in the process. The specific facts to which the court in these circumstances ought to draw its mind are, as shown in *R v Chenia,*[150] those which the accused relies on at trial but which he concealed at the time of the interview.

Suggestions in extant literature appear to point to the motivation for the foregoing changes being to encourage early guilty pleas by the accused or discontinuances by the prosecution. From 1994, the defence in any criminal proceedings have been compelled to disclose the defence prior to trial. The inevitable consequence of this is the infrequent use of 'ambush defence' so much so that the justification of having s 34 on the English law books can, in practice, no longer be sustained.

The question of the legality of s 34 had come up and been considered under Article 6 of the ECHR in *Murray v UK.*[151] The applicant had been denied legal advice for 48 hours after he had been taken into custody. It was held that there had been a violation of article 6(1) read with article 6(3)(c). However, it was not a breach of human rights to draw inferences from the silence of a defendant. The privilege against self-incrimination is not an absolute right. As to the US judgment in Miranda, Walsh J, dissenting in part, pointed out that the US Supreme Court had affirmed that the constitutional protection against self-incrimination contained in the Fifth Amendment: 'guarantees to the individual the 'right to remain silent unless he chooses to speak in the unfettered exercise of his own free will' whether during custodial interrogation or in court.'

In *R v Beckles,*[152] the appellant was tried on an indictment charging robbery, false imprisonment and attempted murder. The prosecution alleged that the victim of the offences had been lured to a fourth floor flat where he was detained, robbed and finally pushed out of a window by the appellant and a co-defendant. On his arrest, the appellant told the police that the victim had jumped out of the window. When he was formally interviewed, however, a solicitor informed the interviewing officer that she had advised the appellant not to answer any questions. During the interview, the appellant duly

[149] *The People v Japau* [1967] ZR 95; *Mwewa Murono v The People* [2004] ZR 207; *The People v Paulo Pupilo* HP/226/2010) [2012] ZMHC.

[150] [2002] EWCA Crim 2345.

[151] (1996) Application No 00018731/91; 22 EHRR 29; as adaptedhttps://swarb.co.uk/murray-v-the-united-kingdom-echr-8-feb-1996/ retrieved on 10/12/21; But see *Condron v UK* Application No 00035718/97; 31 EHRR 1 where Murray was distinguished with the Court holding that the right to silence was not absolute but domestic courts had to exercise particular caution in determining whether to draw adverse inferences. The silence of the accused in this case could be taken into consideration but only on the basis that the court was satisfied that the silence by the accused could not be attributed to him/her having had no answer or the fact that he had none that could stand up to cross-examination.

[152] [2004] EWCA Crim 2766; [2005] 1 All ER 705.

answered 'no comment' to the questions put to him, but in a second interview several months later he again stated that the victim had not been pushed out of the window. At trial, the appellant's evidence did not differ significantly from the account that he had given to the police during his second interview. He added that he had intended to tell the police everything at the first interview, but that the solicitor had advised him to exercise his right to silence and that he had accepted her advice. When the judge summed up, he gave the jury a direction on the adverse inferences that might be drawn, pursuant to s 34a of the Criminal Justice and Public Order Act 1994, from the failure of the various defendants to mention in their first interviews facts upon which they had relied at trial. In particular, he instructed the jury that it was for them to decide what they made of the reasons given for not answering, and that they were not to hold it against the defendants if they thought that the reason given was a good one. The appellant was convicted on all counts, and his subsequent appeal was dismissed. However, the Criminal Cases Review Commission referred the matter back to the Court of Appeal following a decision by the European Court of Human Rights that the judge's direction to the jury had violated the defendant's convention right to a fair trial. On the appeal, the Court of Appeal considered the question the jury had to ask when reliance on legal advice was the reason given by a defendant for not answering questions.

It was held that where a solicitor's advice was relied upon by the defendant, the ultimate question for the jury under s 34 of the 1994 Act remained whether the facts relied on at the trial were facts which the defendant could reasonably have been expected to mention at interview. If they were not, that was the end of the matter. If, however, the jury considered that the defendant genuinely relied on the advice, that was not necessarily the end of the matter. It might still not have been reasonable for him to rely on the advice, or the advice might not have been the true explanation for his silence. If it were possible to say that the defendant genuinely acted upon the advice in a situation where that advice was no more than a convenient way of disguising his true motivation for not mentioning facts, the fact that he did so because it suited his purpose might mean that he was not acting reasonably in not mentioning the facts. His reasonableness in not mentioning the facts remained to be determined by the jury. If they concluded that he was acting unreasonably, they could draw an adverse inference from the failure to mention the facts. In the instant case, the judge had never directed the jury to consider the reasonableness, let alone the genuineness, of the appellant's reliance on his solicitor's advice as the reason why he did not answer questions in interview. The need for a proper direction had been all the more important since the primary adverse inference which the jury could draw was not that the appellant had made up his story later, but that he had not thought that it would stand up to examination. The unfairness caused by the misdirection rendered his convictions unsafe, and accordingly they would be quashed.[153]

The upshot of the foregoing authorities is firstly, that the jury must be

[153] *R v Hoare* (2004) 1 Cr App R 355; [2004] All ER (D) 49 (Apr) considered.

directed [or in a no-jury jurisdiction, the magistrate/judge must apply his/her mind to the fact] that there is on the record, facts which the accused ought to have revealed during the police interview which he/she deliberately concealed but sought to, and did in fact rely on at trial in his defence; following on the preceding, to consider whether the concealment of facts was because of counsel's advice and a genuine reliance on same; or in a situation where the accused was, as noted already, relying on counsel's advice, whether such reliance could be deemed reasonable in the circumstances. If not, an adverse inference ought to be drawn.

The foregoing, it is submitted, is a doubtful approach which raises the question of what having counsel of your own choosing really entails, and what the general right of remaining silent amounts to if in the end, the counsel sought and relied upon is deemed to have been unreasonably been relied on and because of this fact, adverse inferences are drawn against the accused. It is quite unlikely that a constitutional challenge to such an approach if adopted by a court in this jurisdiction would not find favour before the Constitutional Court. This is partly because of the fundamental right for an accused, once charged (and by parity of reason when considered a suspect), not to be compelled to incriminate himself. It is also because unlike the scenario in England & Wales where the prohibition on the prosecution to comment adversely on an accused's election not to testify (or in this case not to answer questions which would incriminate him) as provided for under s 1(b) of the Criminal Evidence Act 1898 has been lifted by virtue of s 168(3) and Sch 11 of th Youth Justice and Criminal Evidence Act 1999, that prohibition still remains in this jurisdiction. As noted elsewhere in this text, proviso (ii) to s 157 of the Criminal Procedure Code[154] provides that 'the failure of any person charged with an offence or of the wife or husband, as the case may be, of the person so charged, to give evidence shall not be made the subject of any comment by the prosecution.' The said proviso (ii) finds support under Article 18(7) of the Constitution which provides that '[a] person who is tried for a criminal offence shall not be compelled to give evidence at the trial.'

A further point to make is that given the misgivings relating to s 34 of the Criminal Justice and Public Order Act 1994 in England & Wales,[155] it is unlikely that the approach adopted above would be adopted by legislative provisions or through our courts. The other point is the nature of the criminal trial which typically has two stages. The first is where the prosecution makes its case. At the close of their case is clear from s 206 as regards subordinate court criminal trials or s 291 with respect to criminal trials in the High Court, the court will have to determine whether a sufficient case has been made against the accused to warrant putting him on his defence. If he is acquitted, that is the end of the matter, and the issues arising out of a provision such as s 34 of the Criminal Justice and Public Order Act 1994 in England & Wales, will not arise.

In the event that he is put on his defence, it would appear that the matters

[154] Chapter 88 of the Laws of Zambia.

[155] See Uglow *Evidence* 163.

envisaged in s 34 of the Criminal Justice and Public Order Act 1994 in England & Wales may well be worthy of consideration. Even so, it may be argued that those issues have been brought about, as seen elsewhere in this text, by statute in this jurisdiction which expressly impose the burden of proof on the prosecution rather than the accused is ordinarily expected given the decision in *Woolmington.*[156] Statutes that provide for special defences abound and include those specifically providing for the defence of diminished responsibility against a charge of murder. Further, as two recent decisions[157] demonstrate, they also include statutes that reverse the burden of proof and those that lower the standard of proof.

(b) Failure to testify

The starting point in this regard is s 35 of the Criminal Justice and Public Order Act 1994 of England & Wales. It is applicable to that stage of the criminal trial where the prosecution has satisfied the court that there is a case to answer necessitating the putting of the accused on his defence. The judge has power to tell the accused at this stage that the time has come for him to give his side of the story, and that if he elects to remain silent, the jury is entitled to draw any inference they deem fit from his silence under the circumstances. This is, however, circumscribed by s 38(3) of the said Act which proscribes convictions solely on an inference drawn from the failure to testify when it would be logical for the accused to do so. The ramifications of s 35 have been considered in *R v Cowan.*[158] The appellants were separately tried in the Crown Court for unrelated offences shortly after s 35a of the Criminal Justice and Public Order Act 1994 came into force on 10 April 1995. That section allowed the court or jury to 'draw such inferences as appear proper from the failure of the accused to give evidence or his refusal, without good cause, to answer any question'. At the trial of the first appellant his counsel put previous convictions to a Crown witness and the appellant decided that he did not wish to give evidence himself because he did not wish to disclose his own previous convictions. At the trial of the second appellant, he did not give evidence because he did not wish to disclose his previous convictions. At the trial of the third appellant, a man of previous good character, he did not give evidence for reasons which he refused to explain. In all three cases the appellants were convicted after the trial judge had directed the jury that they could draw adverse inferences from the appellants' silence. They appealed on the grounds of misdirection, contending that a trial judge should exercise his discretion under s 35 to direct the jury that they could draw adverse inferences from the appellants' silence only in an exceptional case where there was no reasonable possibility of an innocent explanation for the defendant's silence.

---

156 [1935] AC 462.

157 *People v Austin Chisanga Liato* Selected Judgment No 21 of 2015; *Lt Gen Geojago Robert Musengule and Amon Sibanda v The People* [SCZ Selected Judgment No 19 of 2017].

158 [1995] 4 All ER 939; see *R v Becouarm (Darren)* [2005] UKHL 55; [2005] 1 WLR 2589, HL; *Murray v UK* [1994] 18 EHRR CD 1.

It was held as follows: (1) The plain words of s 35 of the 1994 Act did not justify confining its operation to exceptional cases. On the contrary, there had to be either some evidential basis or some exceptional factors in the case before a court could decline to draw an adverse inference from silence at trial, or before the judge could direct or advise a jury against drawing such an inference. In particular, the possibility that the defendant could be cross-examined on his previous criminal record was not a good reason for directing a jury that they should not hold his silence against him. However, the inferences permitted to be made were only such as 'appeared proper', and the trial judge had a broad discretion to decide in all the circumstances whether any proper inference was capable of being drawn by the jury. If not, he should tell them so; otherwise, it was for the jury to decide whether in fact an inference should properly be drawn. (2) In directing the jury the trial judge was required to tell them (i) that the burden of proof remained on the prosecution throughout and what the required standard was, (ii) that the defendant was entitled to remain silent, (iii) that, as expressly provided by s 38(3)b of the 1994 Act, an inference from failure to give evidence could not on its own prove guilt, (iv) that the jury had to be satisfied on the prosecution evidence that the prosecution had established a case to answer before drawing any inferences from the defendant's silence, and (v) that if, despite any evidence relied on to explain his silence or in the absence of any such evidence, the jury concluded the silence could only sensibly be attributed to the defendant's having no answer or none that would stand up to cross-examination, they could then draw an adverse inference. (3) In the circumstances, the first appellant's appeal would be allowed because the judge had failed to tell the jury that they could not infer guilt solely from silence, and did not warn the jury that the condition for holding a defendant's silence at trial against him was that the only sensible explanation for that silence was that he had no answer to the case against him or none that could have stood up to cross-examination. The second appellant's appeal would also be allowed because the judge did not tell the jury that the defendant had the right to remain silent and had given the impression that the right to silence had gone. However, the third appellant's appeal would be dismissed because the appellant had not put forward any reasons to the judge why he should not give an adverse inference direction to the jury, and in those circumstances the judge had been entitled to give such a direction.[159]

To implement a section such as s 35 in this jurisdiction one may face a number of challenges. The very first would be lack of constitutional authority pursuant to Article 18(7). It would also run counter to the proviso (ii) of s 157 of the Criminal Procedure Code[160] unless that particular provision were repealed as has happened in England & Wales where, as we saw above, the prohibition on the prosecution to comment adversely an accused's election not to testify (or in this case not to answer questions which would incriminate him)

[159] Editor's notes: For silence as evidence against the accused at a criminal trial, see 11(2) Halsbury's Laws (4th edn reissue) paras 1123, 1180.

[160] Chapter 88 of the Laws of Zambia.

as provided for under s 1(b) of the Criminal Evidence Act 1898 has been lifted by virtue of s 168(3) and Sch 11 of th Youth Justice and Criminal Evidence Act 1999. Quite apart from the preceding, their additional challenges. They include the following: (i) it would generally run counter to constitutional provisions already alluded to but specifically, the principle that the prosecution bears the burden of proof and having accused, ought to prove. It is not the accused's obligation to prove a charge he has not brought against himself; (ii) It would, as highlighted above, be a breach of the injunction under Article 18(7) of the Constitution against self-incrimination; and (iii) it would run counter to the long-held principle in *R v Sang*[161] which is to the effect that for evidence to be admissible its probative value ought to exceed its prejudicial value. The effect of a section like s 35 is to say that the prejudicial effect of an accused's failure to testify ought to far exceed its probative value, if any.

In any case, as seen elsewhere in this text, the law pertaining to a case to answer or no case to answer stage in criminal proceedings before the High Court is set out in s 291 of the Criminal Procedure Code.[162] In criminal proceedings before the subordinate/magistrates' court, counsel may invoke s 206 of Criminal Procedure Code[163] in aggregation with the authority of *The People v Japau.*[164] In criminal proceedings before the High Court, s 291(1) of the Criminal Procedure Code[165] may be invoked at this stage. As shown earlier in this text, it has been held in *Mwewa Murono v The People*[166] that,

> [t]he finding that a judge has to record under s 291(1) [...] is the same as that under s 206 [....] The judge on considering that there is no evidence that the accused or any one of several accused committed the offence must acquit the accused. The finding must show that there is no evidence that the accused committed the offence followed by an order acquitting the accused.

Section 291(1) is explicit: the prosecution must make a case against the accused sufficiently requiring the accused person or persons to make a defence. Failure to so do is a necessary predicate to the court dismissing the prosecution's case and acquitting the accused proximately. As mentioned elsewhere in this text, the crucial question to invite is whether in the event that the accused elected to remain muted and offered no explanation in view of the evidence so far adduced, an imperturbable tribunal, suitably guiding itself, could convict him. If the answer is yes, then there is a *prima facie* case. If no, there is no case to answer. The prosecution at this point does not need to prove the case beyond reasonable doubt.[167]

[161] [1979] 2 All ER 1222.

[162] Chapter 88 of the Laws of Zambia.

[163] Chapter 88 of the Laws of Zambia.

[164] [1967] ZR 95.

[165] Chapter 88 of the Laws of Zambia.

[166] [2004] ZR 207.

[167] See *The People v Japau* [1967] ZR 95; Consider similar observations by Matibini J (as he then was) in *The People v Paulo Pupilo* HP/226/2010) [2012] ZMHC 54.

(c) Failure to account for objects, substances or marks[168]

Where the suspect is found with objects, substances or/and marks which connects him to the crime under investigation and for which he is a suspect, and he fails to account for them, having been warned and cautioned in ordinary language which the suspect understands, what the consequences of non-disclosure will be, following his arrest, the prosecution will seek to have the court draw an adverse inference. As seen elsewhere in this text, police ordinarily ask persons found in possession of goods suspected to have been stolen. Irrespective of the response from the suspect, witnesses are permitted to give testimony with respect to what the accused's response was following his arrest. According to the holding in *R v Schama and Abramovich,*[169] where the only evidence available is the fact of possession, a failure to offer an explanation entitles the court to draw an inference of guilty knowledge. Be that as it may, '[w]hen a court purports to draw an inference of guilty [knowledge] in a case of recent possession of stolen property it is necessary to consider what other inferences might be drawn.'[170] So too, where a suspect is in possession of items linked to a murder in the absence of an explanation, the court will be entitled to infer guilty knowledge.[171] Further, as shown in *R v Abraham*,[172] any statement made in discovery whether or not same be deemed self-serving, is admissible. Even so, the burden of proof is, as shown in *R v Hepworth,*[173] on the prosecution to prove their case. Failure to discharge such a burden thus raising doubt in the mind, of the court, entitles the accused to an acquittal.

(d) Failure to account for presence

The attendant principles for the failure by an accused person to account for his presence at the scene of the crime[174] is similar to that relating to the failure to account for objects, substances and marks under s 36 of the Criminal Justice and Public Order Act 1994. Like that section, it only comes into play following arrest and the administering the warn and caution statement where the accused would have been warned of the consequences of failure to give an explanation. As with other sections dealt with above from English law, that is, ss 34 & 36 of the Criminal Justice and Public Order Act 1994, s 37 enjoins the police to

[168] The relevant provisions in England & Wales are ss 34, 36 & 37 of the Criminal Justice and Public Order Act 1994; see also *R v Cramp* (1880) 14 Cox 390; *R v Benn* [2004] EWCA Crim 2100; *R v Compton* [2002] EWCA Crim 2835.

[169] (1914) 11 Cr App R 45; *R v Garth* [1949] 1 All ER 773.

[170] *Kape v The People* [1977] ZR 192; *George Chileshe v The People* [1977] ZR 176 (SC).

[171] As was the case in *R v Muller* (1848) 3 Cox 430 where the accused was found in possession of the victim's hat.

[172] (1843) 3 Cox 430.

[173] [1955] 2 All ER 918.

[174] The England & Wales position is to be found under s 37 of the Criminal Justice and Public Order Act 1994; see *Mohammed-Holgate v Duke* [1984] AC 437; J Bentham, *Rationale of Judicial Evidence* (Garland reprint 1978(org 1825).

meet the minimum threshold of 'reasonable grounds' before an arrest (which in this jurisdiction would be in terms of s 18 of the Criminal Procedure Code[175]) is effected. It is within that context that a warn and caution statement may be issued regarding the consequences of a failure to answer. Be that as it may, most of the police work in the early stages is predicated on suspicion. The investigation and employment of the interrogation technique is but meant to confirm their bias to obtain the evidence they seek based on their suspicions, by exerting pressure on the accused person.[176]

It is difficult to imagine how the law in this jurisdiction would follow the lead of English statutory law in this regard. There are several good and compelling reasons for this thesis: (i) the provisions covered only serve to encourage the practice of exerting pressure on the accused to confess simply because there is a suspicion that he committed the offence; (ii) a refusal to answer questions under the said provisions may form part of the prosecution's case against the accused thus strengthening their ability to prove the case against him beyond reasonable doubt; (iii) the said provisions put an accused in an impossible choiceless choice position-in essence, the accused is damned if he answers, and damned if he does not. He is damned irrespective-a rather curious scenario for a system that ought to espouse fairness and rectitude of decision, and the principle that the prosecution must prove their case without the aid of the accused.

It is rather curious that English law on this particular subject has taken this position. It may well be explained to be on the basis of wider public policy considerations to ease the work of the prosecution, and lessen the acquittal of otherwise guilty persons whose crimes may only be proved by them not concealing material facts to the police only for the accused to rely on that which they concealed in their defence. Even so, when it comes to the matter of the accused remaining silent, it is simplistic to gainsay that such silence in the face of an investigation cum interrogation is conclusive as to the guilt of the accused. The law on this aspect of the law follows the reasoning in *R v Lucas*[177] on how lies by an accused person ought to be considered by the trier of fact. It is well to argue that silence, and want of a reasonable explanation,[178] may lend credence to the accused's guilt.

Be that as it may, it is, as already mentioned, not conclusive for several reasons: (i) the silence may be because the accuse is confused; (ii) the silence may be due to the accused falling into the category of witnesses the law deems vulnerable which may include children or persons of unsound mind; (iii) the silence may be because he intends to protect persons he cares for (iv) the

[175] Chapter 88 of the Laws of Zambia: "(1) In making an arrest, the police officer or other person making the same shall actually touch or confine the body of the person to be arrested, unless there be a submission to the custody by word or action. (2) If such person forcibly resists the endeavour to arrest him, or attempts to evade the arrest, such police officer or other person may use all means reasonably necessary to effect the arrest (As amended by No 28 of 1940)."

[176] See *Mohammed-Holgate v Duke* [1984] AC 437.

[177] [1981] 2 All ER 1008 at 1011.

[178] See *L.T. Gen. Geojago Robert Chaswe Musengule, Amon Sibande v The People* HPA /16/2009 and the provisions and cases referred to therein.

silence may be simply down to the accused's unwillingness to co-operate with the police. It is inconceivable that a court should consider the silence in and of itself, without considering the reasons for it, among them, those outlined above, to be sufficient to suppress any reasonable doubt it may entertain about the accused's guilt.

There are broader issues at play here. As Uglow notes, '[t]he controversy surrounding the right to silence encompasses empirical questions and evidential problems but ultimately it should be a decision based on concepts of due process of law and proper constitutional principles.'[179] He further argues that '[i]t is another of those important markers which define the relationship of state and citizen, delineating constraints on the state and underlining our moral choice that prosecution and punishment should not be based on evidence from the accused,'[180] a point we have already stressed elsewhere in this text.

9.3 Police interviews

9.3.1 *Interviews in the police station and the accused's right to access counsel*

Being asked to accompany a police man or receiving a call out to do so or worse still, being arrested on suspicion of having committed an offence can be one of the most traumatic experiences any human can face. The inherent desire for autonomy and liberty, to do as you please, to associate and assemble freely which rights are guaranteed under the constitution[181] may be lost. Therefore, it is required that whenever a person is brought to a police station under arrest, their rights be recognised as by law provided. These rights include the right to be informed of their various rights including, but not limited to the right to counsel of their own choosing, should they be minded to have one; and where they cannot find one, that one be provided through the legal aid scheme.

Our first port of call with respect to interviews in the police station and the accused's access to counsel is Article 18(2) of the Constitution:

> Every person who is charged with a criminal offence-
> (a) shall be presumed to be innocent until he is proved or has pleaded guilty;
> (b) shall be informed as soon as reasonably practicable, in a language that he understands and in detail, of the nature of the offence charged;
> (c) shall be given adequate time and facilities for the preparation of his defence;
> (d) shall unless legal aid is granted to him in accordance with the law enacted by Parliament for such purpose be permitted to defend himself before the court in person, or *at his own expense, by a legal representative of his own*

[179] Uglow S *Evidence* 171-172.

[180] Uglow S *Evidence* 172.

[181] See Article 11-24, but see derogations and claw back clauses as contained in Articles 25-30.

choice (emphasis added);[182]

(e) shall be afforded facilities to examine in person or by his legal representative the witnesses called by the prosecution before the court, and to obtain the attendance and carry out the examination of witnesses to testify on his behalf before the court on the same conditions as those applying to witnesses called by the prosecution; and

(f) shall be permitted to have without payment the assistance of an interpreter if he cannot understand the language used at the trial of the charge; and except with his own consent the trial shall not take place in his absence unless he so conducts himself as to render the continuance of the proceedings in his presence impracticable and the court has ordered him to be removed and the trial to proceed in his absence.

The importance of Article 18(2)(d) cannot be overemphasised. It gives an accused three options which he can take advantage of: (i) he may be provided with legal aid counsel; (ii) he may defend himself (*or appear in prosé*) or (iii) he may be represented by counsel of his own choosing. Indeed, in extremely serious cases such as treason, aggravated robbery, manslaughter, murder and the like, where an accused person is unable to hire counsel of his own choosing, the court will ordinarily order legal aid counsel or indeed any counsel they deem capable, to represent the said accused person.

The scenario envisaged under Articles 18(2)(d) is exemplified in the English case of *R v Chief Constable of South Wales Ex p Merrick.*[183] On 26 April 1993 the applicant was arrested and charged with arson after allegedly setting his estranged wife's car on fire. He was detained in police custody on remand until 12 May. On that day he was represented by a solicitor, who saw the applicant early in the morning in the cells at the court prior to making a further application for bail. The applicant's case was put back until 2.15 pm. At 1.15 pm the solicitor went to the cells to see the applicant but was refused access by a police officer. The application for bail was dismissed and the applicant was remanded until 20 May. At 3.15 pm the solicitor again requested access to the applicant in order to explain the refusal of bail, to obtain instructions concerning the next steps to be taken, and to discuss the contents of papers obtained from the prosecution. Access to the applicant was refused by the police officer in charge of the cells, acting on a standing order by the chief constable prohibiting entry to the cells by solicitors after 10 am. The chief constable, supported by the clerk to the justices, had adopted a policy that it was necessary to regulate access by solicitors to the cells at the court because in his opinion they were not a police custody office but were 'a holding area for the courts' to which the provisions of the Police and Criminal Evidence

[182] Italics added; see *R v Chief Constable of South Wales Ex p Merrick* [1994] 2 All ER 560.

[183] [1994] 2 All ER 560.

Act 1984 did not apply and because of the shortage of police resources and the demands of security. Under that policy, if defendants were produced before 10 am solicitors were expected to interview them before court commenced at 10 am and if solicitors wished to interview clients after 10 am access would be allowed if there was a valid reason for not having seen the client before 10 am and security permitted. The applicant applied for judicial review by way of declarations that the decision of the chief constable and/or the clerk to the justices to refuse him access to his solicitor and the policy of the chief constable and/or the clerk to the justices to refuse access of solicitors to clients in police custody at the magistrates' court after 10 am were unlawful and that it was unlawful to refuse prisoners in custody access to their solicitors at magistrates' courts. The applicant contended that the respondents' policy was contrary to s 58a of the 1984 Act, which provided that 'if a person [in custody] makes such a request he must be permitted to consult a solicitor as soon as is practicable', and that they had acted unlawfully by interfering with the applicant's fundamental right of access to legal advice. It was held that a person held in custody in cells at a courthouse had a common law right, on request, to be permitted to consult a solicitor as soon as was practicable. Although a denial of access to a solicitor was, in some circumstances, unavoidable, and therefore justifiable, if it was not practicable or reasonably practicable for the police to arrange for access, if in the circumstances access was practicable or reasonably practicable there was no justification for refusing access. The chief constable and the clerk to the justices were entitled to impose a policy regulating visits by solicitors to remand prisoners but the particular policy operated by chief constable and the clerk to the justices was unlawful in so far as it authorised or permitted the officers at the cells to refuse access to a solicitor on the sole ground that the request was made after 10 am without reference to whether it was reasonably practicable to allow access at once or within a reasonable period. The failure of the police to allow the applicant's solicitor access to the applicant at 3.15 pm on 12 May 1993 constituted a breach of the applicant's common law right and a declaration would be made to that effect.[184]

The preceding authority must also be seen within the context of the quality of legal representation offered. The assumption in this jurisdiction is that all lawyers have in theory, equal ability. The reality is that this is not an accurate assumption. Lawyers do differ in their strengths and weaknesses; their experience or lack thereof and ability to appreciate the issues at play may all play a part in the quality of representation an accused person gets while at the police station or once trial commences. This may show itself in different ways: a failure to obtain important information from investigative officers; (ii) a failure to obtain material facts from the client. The seriousness of this issue

[184] *Per* curiam. Section 58 of the 1984 Act does not apply to a person who is in custody after being remanded in custody by a magistrates' court except in special circumstances, e.g., where the defendant is the subject of continuing investigations for other offences; For false imprisonment as the result of arrest by a private person, see 45 Halsbury's Laws (th edn) para 1327; For the Police and Criminal Evidence Act 1984, s 58, see 12 Halsbury's Statutes (4th edn) (1994 reissue) 906.

has led the Law Society in England to issue accreditation to those qualified to represent clients at the police station.[185] Not every lawyer can.

We do know the importance of the constitutional imperative for an accused to have the right to counsel of their own choosing. In *R v Vernon*[186] this right was described as "one of the most important and fundamental rights of the citizen." Breach of this obligation by the police may lead to the exclusion of evidence obtained from the accused under those circumstances. In *R v Absalom*[187] the accused person who had been arrested the offence of threatening behaviour was taken to a police station. Having been ordered to empty his pockets to which he obliged, the police knowing that he had been arrested for possession of cannabis told him to 'put the drugs on the table.' He obliged to this command taking a packet from inside his trousers and also admitted selling said drugs. The police, having obtained this vital information then proceeded to warn and caution, reminding him, as they did, of his right to legal representation (which in this jurisdiction is guaranteed under Article 18(2)(b) of our Constitution). As to the application that the answers offered by the accused be excluded from evidence, Lord Bigham opined as follows:

> Everything proceeded unobjectionably until the moment when, in answer to the custody officer's inspired question, the drugs were produced and put on the table. It then became apparent to the officer, as he acknowledged, that an offence had been committed. At that stage the appellant had not been advised of his right to legal advice, but the situation had arisen in which it was plainly necessary that he should not in the light of his apparent guilt be further questioned until he had been offered that opportunity and, if he sought legal advice, had had the opportunity of receiving it.

The question that begs an answer is whether every breach of an accused's right to legal representation by the police ought to lead to, as did happen in *R v Absalom*,[188] the exclusion of evidence obtained under such circumstances. The first point to make was the basis of the exclusion of evidence in *Absalom.*[189] The court took the view that even though the evidence in question had been obtained in circumstances where no oppression had been brought to bear, the questions fit the bill of being a 'serious and substantial breach' and as such fit for exclusion, its reliability notwithstanding. It therefore seems to be the case that not every breach of the right to have counsel may lead to the exclusion of evidence. If the accused has not been prejudiced by such refusal even for a time, and unless it can be shown that such refusal has affected justice to such an extent that the only just thing to do would be to exclude the evidence, the evidence in question will be admissible. This was exemplified in *R v Alladice.*[190]

---

[185] Visit http://lawsociety.org.uk/professional/accreditationpanels/policestation.law (accessed 14/12/21).

[186] [1988] Crim LR 445.

[187] [1988] Crim LR 748; decided on the basis of s 78 of PACE; see also *R v Williams* [1989] Crim LR 66 and *R v Sanusi* [1992] Crim LR 43.

[188] [1988] Crim LR 748; see also *R v Williams* [1989] Crim LR 66 and *R v Sanusi* [1992] Crim LR 43.

[189] [1988] Crim LR 748; see also *R v Williams* [1989] Crim LR 66 and *R v Sanusi* [1992] Crim LR 43.

[190] [1988] Crim LR 608.

Though there had been a breach of the accused's right to counsel, it was held that the admission of the interview statement now impugned, did not unfavourably disturb the general impartiality of the proceedings.[191]

The police have a tall older in satisfying the court that circumstances existed justifying the decision not to permit the accused access to counsel. As has been shown in *R v Samuel,*[192] where an accused person is suspected of having committed an arrestable offence; and access to counsel may lead interference with evidence; or the alerting of accomplices; or hindering of the recovery of property, subject of the investigation, which has led to the arrest of the suspect, the police will be well within their rights to delay access to counsel. According to Hodson J, the basis for the delay by the police ought to a firm and justifiable belief that an individual advocate would, if permitted to access the accused, inadvertently interfere with evidence, alert accomplices or indeed hinder the recovery of evidence material to the case.

On 6 August 1986 the appellant was arrested on suspicion of robbery and taken to a police station. During the course of that day and the next he was interviewed on four occasions about the robbery and two burglaries but he denied the offences. During the second interview he asked for access to a solicitor. Under para 1a of Annex B to the Code of Practice for Detention, Treatment and Questioning of Persons by Police Officers issued by the Secretary of State pursuant to s 66 of the Police and Criminal Evidence Act 1984, a police officer of the rank of superintendent or above was entitled to delay a suspect's right of access to a solicitor if the suspect was being detained in connection with a serious arrestable offence, if he had not yet been charged with an offence and if the officer had reasonable grounds for believing, inter alia, that the granting of access to a solicitor 'will lead' to other suspects being alerted before their arrest. The requirement that the officer should have a reasonable belief that access to a solicitor 'will lead' to the alerting of other suspects was laid down by s 58(8)b of the 1984 Act. The police superintendent to whom the appellant's request was referred decided to refuse him access to a solicitor on the ground that two of the offences being investigated, namely the robbery and one of the burglaries, were serious arrestable offences and there was a likelihood of other suspects involved in the robbery being inadvertently warned. At the fourth interview on the morning of August 7 the appellant confessed to the two offences of burglary and he was charged with those offences at 4.30 pm. At 4.45 pm a solicitor instructed by the appellant's family was informed of the charges but was denied access to the appellant. Shortly thereafter the appellant confessed to the robbery in another interview and was charged with that offence. The solicitor was allowed to see him an hour later. At his trial, the appellant contended that the record of his last interview ought to be excluded under s 78(1)c of the 1984 Act, on the ground that it had taken place in the

[191] See also *R v Dunford* [1988] Crim LR 370; *R v Oliphant* [1992] Crim LR 40; *R v Chalal* [1992] Crim LR 124; *R v Franklin The Times,* June 16, 1994.

[192] [1988] 2 All ER 135 ; the facts appear below.

unjustified absence of a solicitor in breach of para 1 of Annex B to the Code of Practice for Detention because (i) the appellant had already been charged with 'an offence', i.e. the two burglaries, when his access to a solicitor was denied and (ii) the police superintendent did not have reasonable grounds for believing that the granting of access to a solicitor would lead to other suspects being alerted. The trial judge held that there had been no breach of the code, that the police superintendent's belief was reasonable and that if there had been a breach of the code, he would in any event exercise his discretion by allowing the evidence 135 to be admitted. The evidence was admitted, and the appellant was convicted. He appealed. It was held that the appeal would be allowed for the following reasons — (1) On the plain and natural meaning of para 1 of Annex B to the Code of Practice for Detention the right of a person being detained by the police to have access to a solicitor could not be delayed after he had been charged with any offence and certainly not after he had been charged with a serious arrestable offence in connection with which he was in police custody. Since the appellant had already been charged with the two burglaries, one of which was a serious arrestable offence, before his fourth interview, at which he had confessed to the robbery, access to a solicitor had been wrongly denied to him. (2) The right of a person detained by the police to have access to a solicitor was a fundamental right of the citizen and a police officer attempting to justify to the court his decision under s 58 of the 1984 Act to delay access had to do so by reference to the specific circumstances of the case, including evidence as to the person detained or the actual solicitor sought to be consulted. In particular, not only did the officer have to believe that the access 'will', and not merely 'may', lead to the alerting of other suspects but he had also to believe that if a solicitor was allowed access to the detained person the solicitor would thereafter commit the criminal offence of alerting other suspects or would be hoodwinked into doing so inadvertently or unwittingly. Either belief could only rarely be genuinely held by the police officer. (3) In the circumstances the refusal of access to the appellant's solicitor before the last interview took place had been unjustified and the interview should not have taken place. If the trial judge had held that the refusal of access to a solicitor was unjustified and that consequently the final interview was unlawful, he might well have concluded that the admission of evidence of that interview would be so unfair that it ought not to be admitted. It followed therefore that the conviction of robbery would be quashed.[193]

9.3.2 *Interviews at the police station: further considerations*

While, as we have seen above, preventing access to counsel, may be a basis for the exclusion of evidence obtained under such circumstances, there are several

[193] Editor's notes: For admissibility of confessions, see 11 Halsbury's Laws (4th edn) paras 410–415 and 17 ibid para 22, and for cases on the subject, see 14(2) Digest (Reissue) 549–552, 562–575, 4494–517, 4578–4643. For the right of access to a solicitor, see 11 Halsbury's Laws (4th edn) para 419; For the Police and Criminal Evidence Act 1984, ss 58, 78, see 12 Halsbury's Statutes (4th edn) 1011 and 17 *ibid* 215.

other instances under which evidence may be deemed inadmissible. The police have to determine, following investigations and arrests whether there is sufficient evidence to proceed with eventual prosecution.[194] If they determine that more evidence may be required, they may detain the suspect for further interviews. It is at this point of detention that the custody officer ought to ensure that the suspect is aware of their right to counsel of their own choosing or/and notify any person they need to notify of the fact of their arrest. While in theory, the custody officer ought also to ensure that the suspect knows how long the interview is going to take, if medical advice is required and whether proper food and arrangements for sleep have been made, it is unlikely that the foregoing will be done at a police station in this jurisdiction. This is partly because of inadequate facilities, and partly because of inadequately trained officers. Generally, suspects will have to rely on relatives and friends for food, clothing or/and any other assistance they may require while in detention. There are of course requirements for special treatment of the mentally handicapped, the variously vulnerable such as the youth,[195] ill, foreigners, and such other person as may need such special treatment.

The preceding information has to be recorded in a custody book or similar book used for a similar purpose. The importance of the said custody book is brought to the fore when disputes arise as to the validity of a confession for example. This helps both the police and the accused, and at trial, the court as to what was and may not have been said. In addition, s 34 of the Criminal Procedure Code[196] mandates that '[o]fficers in charge of police stations [to] report to the nearest magistrate the cases of all persons arrested without warrant within the limits of their respective stations, whether such persons have been admitted to bail or not.'

9.3.2.1 *Conditions and length of detention*

(i) Under the Criminal Procedure Code[197]

In terms of s 33 of the Criminal Procedure Code[198] which provides for procedure relating to detention of persons arrested without warrant, the following is provided:

> (1) When any person has been taken into custody without a warrant for an offence other than an offence punishable with

[194] Section 33 provides in part, 'Notwithstanding anything contained in this section, an officer in charge of a police station may release a person arrested on suspicion on a charge of committing any offence, when, after due police inquiry, insufficient evidence is, in his opinion, disclosed on which to proceed with the charge.'

[195] See Part 5: ss 45-57 of the Children's Code, Act No 12 of 2022.

[196] Chapter 88 of the Laws of Zambia.

[197] Chapter 88 of the Laws of Zambia, as amended by No 28 of 1940 and No 2 of 1960.

[198] Chapter 88 of the Laws of Zambia, as amended by No 28 of 1940 and No 2 of 1960.

> [life imprisonment],[199] *the officer in charge of the police station to which such person shall be brought may, in any case, and shall, if it does not appear practicable to bring such person before an appropriate competent court within twenty-four hours after he was so taken into custody, inquire into the case, and, unless the offence appears to the officer to be of a serious nature, release the person, on his executing a bond, with or without sureties, for a reasonable amount,* to appear before a competent court at a time and place to be named in the bond: *but, where any person is retained in custody, he shall be brought before a competent court as soon as practicable.* Notwithstanding anything contained in this section, an officer in charge of a police station may release a person arrested on suspicion on a charge of committing any offence, when, after due police inquiry, insufficient evidence is, in his opinion, disclosed on which to proceed with the charge.[200]
>
> (2) In this section, "competent court" means any court having jurisdiction to try or hold a preliminary inquiry into the offence for which the person has been taken into custody.

The foregoing provision has come up and been considered in several cases decided in this jurisdiction. We discuss a few below.

In *In Re Siuluta and Three Others,*[201] the applicants were detained while further inquiries were being made by the police. They had not been charged with any offence. During the application for bail counsel for the applicants submitted that it was improper for the police to detain persons while investigations were being carried out and that it was unreasonable to refuse bail to persons against whom no charge had been preferred. It was held as follows: (i) The police could only arrest for offences and has no power to arrest persons for the purposes of making inquiries. (ii) Having, made an arrest for a specific offence, then the police could hold the arrested person in custody while the inquiries were being made, but if there was enough evidence to prefer a charge, they should do so without delay. (iii) On the evidence available, the reasons for the applicants not having been charged were unjustified and there was a flagrant abuse of the powers contained in s. 33 of the Criminal Procedure Code. (iv) Bail was granted on the ground that the applicants had not been charged with any offence when this should have been done soon after their arrest.

In *Daniel Chizoka Mbandangoma v The Attorney-General*[202] the plaintiff was detained on the 24th December 1973, and released shortly thereafter on police bond. He was however required to and did report to the police and at court on at least four subsequent occasions when he was eventually told that further proceedings were being discontinued. The attendance to the police had been arranged to coincide with the occasions when the police wished to see the

---

[199] In terms of s 3 of Act No 22 of 2022, '[s]ection 33(1) of the principal Act is amended by the deletion of the word "death" and the substitution therefor of the words "life imprisonment".

[200] Emphasis added.

[201] [1979] ZR 14 (HC).

[202] [1979] ZR 45 (HC).

plaintiff for purposes of investigations. It was held as follows: (i) In order to justify the arrest of the plaintiff the defendant must show that at the time of the arrest, the arresting officer had reasonable suspicion that the plaintiff had committed the offence with which he was charged. (ii) The arrest of the plaintiff was unlawful. The police can only arrest persons for offences and have no power to arrest anyone in order to make inquiries about him. (iii) It is improper for the police to detain persons pending further investigations without bringing them before court as soon as practicable, but it is equally improper to require persons released on bond to present themselves at the police station for the same purpose. (iv) An award of ZMW750.00 for unlawful imprisonment would be given.

In *M. Mutemwa v Attorney-General*[203] the plaintiff was arrested without a warrant for having behaved in a disorderly behaviour at police station. She was detained at the police station for three days. She claimed damages for false imprisonment, malicious prosecution and inhuman treatment. The court rejected the last two claims and proceeded to award damages for false imprisonment. It was held as follows: (i) Under s 33 of the Criminal Procedure Code[204] if a person is taken into custody without warrant for an offence other than one punishable with [life imprisonment][205] she must be brought before court within twenty-four hours or else be released on bond. (ii) An award of ZMW450.00 for false imprisonment would be given.

A few more points merit our attention. While s 33 of the Criminal Procedure Code[206] stipulates that if a person is taken into custody without warrant for an offence other than one punishable with death she must be brought before court within twenty-four hours or else be released on bond, where the delay is short, same would not, as did happen in *R v Taylor*,[207] lead to the exclusion of evidence obtained under such circumstances. In addition, prolonged interrogation as was the case in *R v Trussler*;[208] or inhuman and/or degrading treatment such as torture; sleep deprivation; deprivation of food and water; severe beatings, as was the case in *Ireland v UK*,[209] may lead to the exclusion of evidence obtained under such means. So too would evidence obtained under general oppressive conduct, as in *R v Beales*[210] where police officers were found not only to have fabricated evidence, but to have 'hectored and bullied'[211] the suspect. It has been held in *A and Others v Secretary of State for the Home Department*[212] that common law principles mandated the exclusion of any evidence, the obtaining of which was predicated on torture, even when same was perpetrated by a third party

[203] [1979] ZR 251 (HC).

[204] Chapter 88 of the Laws of Zambia.

[205] See s 3 of Act No 22 of 2022.

[206] Chapter 88 of the Laws of Zambia.

[207] [1991] Crim LR 541.

[208] [1988] Crim LR 446.

[209] (1978) 2 EHRR 25.

[210] [1991] Crim LR 118.

[211] See also *Paris v R* (1993) 97 Cr App R 99 at 103 *per* Taylor LCJ.

[212] [2006] 1 All ER 575.

from which such evidence would come, for being not only unreliable and unfair but also for being offensive to generally acceptable standards of humanity and decency. Further, that it was incompatible with a court that sought to dispense justice. The foregoing position is here in this jurisdiction a constitutional imperative. According to Article 15 of the Constitution[213] '[a] person shall not be subjected to torture, or to inhuman or degrading punishment or other like treatment'.

(ii) Under the Constitution[214]

Matters relating to restriction and detention of persons are primarily provided for in Article 26 of the Constitution in the following terms:

> (1) Where a person's freedom of movement is restricted, or he is detained, under the authority of any such law as is referred to in Article 22[215] or 25,[216] as the case may be, the following provisions shall apply-
>
> (a) he shall, as soon as reasonably practicable and in any case not more than fourteen days after the commencement of his detention or restriction, be furnished with a statement in writing in a language that he understands specifying in detail the grounds upon which he is restricted or detained;
>
> (b) not more than fourteen days after the commencement of his restriction or detention a notification shall be published in the Gazette stating that he has been restricted or detained and giving particulars of the place of detention and the provision of law under which his restriction or detention is authorised;
>
> (c) if he so requests at any time during the period of such restriction or detention not earlier than three months after the commencement thereof or after he last made such a request during that period, as the case may be, his case shall be reviewed by an independent and impartial tribunal established by law and presided over by a person, appointed by the Chief Justice who is or is qualified to be a judge of the High Court;
>
> (d) he shall be afforded reasonable facilities to consult a legal representative of his own choice who shall be permitted to make representations to the authority by which the restriction or detention was ordered or to any tribunal established for the review of his case; and
>
> (e) at the hearing of his case by such tribunal he shall be

[213] As amended by Act No 2 of 2016.

[214] As amended by Act No 2 of 2016.

[215] Which provides for the Protection of freedom of movement.

[216] Which provides for derogation from fundamental rights and detention and acts as a general prelude to Article 26.

permitted to appear in person or by a legal representative of his own choice.

(2) On any review by a tribunal under this Article the tribunal shall advise the authority by which it was ordered on the necessity or expediency of continuing his restriction or detention and that authority shall be obliged to act in accordance with any such advice.

(3) The President may at any time refer to the tribunal the case of any person who has been or is being restricted or detained pursuant to any restriction or detention order.

(4) Nothing contained in paragraph (d) or (e) of clause (1) shall be construed as entitling a person to legal representation at the public expense.

(5) Parliament may make or provide for the making of rules to regulate the proceedings of any such tribunal including, but without derogating from the generality of the foregoing, rules as to evidence and the admissibility thereof, the receipt of evidence including written reports in the absence of the restricted or detained person and his legal representative, and the exclusion of the public from the whole or any portion of the proceedings.

(6) Clauses (11) and (12) of Article 18 shall be read and construed subject to the provisions of this Article.

Articles 26 and 27 appear to have been a favourite of the one-party state.[217] They thus led to a lot of legal challenges thereby generating a generous number of authorities on their interpretation. We consider some of those authorities below.

In *Re Puta,*[218] the applicant was detained on 18th October, 1972, by order of [...] the President under the Preservation of Public Security Regulations. The order invoked the powers conferred under regulation 31A. Solicitors for the applicant drew attention to the fact that the relevant regulation had been renumbered 33, under the new edition of the laws which came into effect on 1st June, 1972. Consequently, on the 21st October, 1972, an order was made under regulation 33 (2) revoking the earlier detention order and making a fresh order of detention. On 29th October, 1972, the applicant was served with a written statement, dated the 28th October, 1972, specifying the grounds of his detention. The statement referred to the detention on 11th October. A notice was published in the Gazette on 3rd November, 1972, notifying the detention under regulation 33 (1) without specifying the date of detention. In an application for a writ of habeas corpus, the applicant contended: (i) there was an infringement of his right under s 26A (1) (a) of the Constitution in so far as he was not supplied with two separate statements giving grounds of detention relating to the two orders of detention; (ii) his right under s 26A (1) (b) of the Constitution had been infringed in so far as two separate Gazette notifications had not been

[217] The United National Independence Party (UNIP) led one-party State lasted from 1972-1991.

[218] [1973] ZR 133 (HC); see also *Faustino Lombe v Attorney-General* [1986] ZR 76 (SC); *Mifiboshe Walulya v Attorney-General of Zambia* [1984] ZR 89 (SC); *Mario Satumbu Malyo v The Attorney-General* [1988 – 1989] ZR 36 (SC).

published referring to the two orders of detention. It was held as follows: (1) The procedures laid down in s 26A of the Constitution for the protection of the individual detained must be strictly complied with. (2) The Executive was under no strict constitutional obligation to furnish grounds of detention in respect of a detention revoked within fourteen days. but grounds of detention in relation to an order under which the detainee is being detained must be supplied. (3) It is not an infringement of a person's rights under s 26A(1)(b) of the Constitution if a notification in respect of every order of detention passed in respect of him is not published in the Gazette provided a notification has been published within one month of detention.

Petitioner was detained on 15th May, 1970, under regulation 31A of the Preservation of Public Security Regulations by the order of the President. On 28th May, 1970, she was served with the grounds of detention. By a habeas corpus application the petitioner challenged her detention on the following grounds: (1) Whereas she made a request for the review of her case on 15th May, 1973, pursuant to the provisions of section 26A(l)(c) of the Constitution, the saline had not been reviewed for over three months; (2) the petitioner had been denied the constitutional right of review of her case after one year's detention by "a tribunal established by law" in so far as though the Chairman had been appointed the tribunal was not properly constituted as the other members of the tribunal had not been named; (3) the document served on her stating the grounds of detention was vague in as far as it contained an uninitialed deletion of a date of order of detention and another uninitialed date added thereto; (4) her detention was illegal in so far as she was being detained in a place not authorised by the President under regulation 31A (5) of the Preservation of Public Security Regulations. It was held as follows: (i) It is a detainee's constitutional right to apply for a review of the case at any time after one year's detention and it is the duty of the executive to put the case immediately before the review tribunal. Even though the legislature did not specify any period within which the review must take place it obviously intended that no more than reasonable delay should take place. What is reasonable delay will no doubt depend on the circumstances of each case. (ii) A detainee has a constitutional right under s 26A(1) of the Constitution to a review of the case after one year's detention by a "tribunal established by law". When the Chairman of the tribunal is appointed "the tribunal is established by law" but is not properly constituted and the review cannot take place until other members of the tribunal have been appointed. If other remedies fail to secure the constitution of a tribunal and the review of a detainee's case writ of habeas corpus may be the eventual remedy. (iii) The failure to initial correction of date in the grounds of detention handed to detainee does not affect the validity of the document. (iv) The provisions of sub-regulation (5) of regulation 33 of the Preservation of Security Regulations relating to authorisation of place of detention are mandatory. When mandatory provisions for the benefit of detainee are infringed the test to be applied is not whether the applicant has been prejudiced. The failure to comply with the provisions results in the detainee not being in lawful custody.

In *Fred Petelo Mulenga v The Attorney – General,*[219] the applicant was detained under the Preservation of Public Security Regulations, an allegation being, *inter alia,* that he accommodated an escapee from custody. The applicant argued that the allegation disclosed a criminal offence under a specific Regulation and as such he should be prosecuted under the Regulation and therefore his detention was unreasonable in terms of Article 22 of the Constitution. The applicant alternatively argued that he could not have committed the offence of accommodating an escapee since the escapee was either in detention during the period alleged or was being accommodated by someone else. Therefore, the authorities were furnished with incorrect information and the detention was unreasonable. It was held as follows: (i) it is entirely up to the detaining authority to choose the measures to be taken when the activity also happens to amount to an offence. There has never been an obligation to prosecute recognised by the Courts. (ii) When it is shown on the facts that a detainee could not have done the things alleged so that it is not reasonably necessary to detain such a person, the detainee would discharge the burden on him of showing the measures taken exceeded anything which, having regard to the circumstances prevailing at the time, could have reasonably been thought to be required for the purpose of dealing with the situation.

In *William Musala Chipango v The Attorney-General.*[220] The applicant was detained under an order made by the President under reg. 31A of the Preservation of Public Security Regulations on the 12th February, 1970. Grounds for his detention which were required to be furnished him in accordance with s 26A(1)(a) were furnished on 28th February, 1970, and publication of the detention order required to be published in the Gazette within one month after commencement of the detention took place on 2nd April, 1970. The State admitted contravention of the statutory provisions. Counsel for the applicant submitted that contravention of these provisions made the detention of the applicant void ab initio or the continued detention void. However, the State maintained that this did not invalidate the detention but entitled the applicant to other remedies such as damages. The State further submitted that these were conditions subsequent and not precedent. It was held that these are constitutional conditions subsequent to arrest, they are mandatory and fundamental rights of the individual, and if they are contravened, they render the continued detention of the applicant unconstitutional and unlawful.

In *Re Seegers,*[221] the applicant was arrested by a police officer of the rank of Senior Superintendent on the 6th February, 1976, and detained at Lusaka Remand Prison under the authority of an order signed by that officer under regulation 33(6) of the Preservation of Public Security Regulations. On the 18th February, 1976, the applicant was served with a statement containing the grounds for his detention. On the 3rd March, 1976, he was detained by order of His Excellency the President made on that date under regulation 33(1) of

[219] [1988 – 1989] ZR 26 (SC).

[220] [1970] ZR 31 (HC).

[221] [1976] ZR 117 (HC).

the Preservation of Public Security Regulations, Cap. 106. He was since then in detention. Subsequent to the 3rd March, 1976, he was furnished with the grounds for his detention. An application for leave to issue a writ of *habeas corpus ad subjicendum* was made to the High Court. Counsel for the applicant submitted that in as much as grounds had not been furnished, the provisions of Article 27(1)(a) of the Constitution had not been complied with. It was held as follows: (i) The whole purpose of regulation 33(6) of the Preservation of Public Security Regulations, Cap. 106, is to enable a police officer to arrest and detain temporarily, but immediately, where he has reason to believe that the public security is in danger. (ii) The word "satisfied" in regulation 33(1) of the Preservation of Public Security Regulations,[222] denotes that the making of a detention order is a matter for the President's ultimate subjective satisfaction and detention under regulation 33(1) gives him the opportunity in an emergency to form such satisfaction. (iii) It was obligatory to furnish the applicant with the grounds for his detention under the Presidential order dated 3rd March, 1976, within a period of fourteen days after the commencement of his detention under that order. (iv) The provisions of Article 27(1)(a) of the Constitution have not been complied with and hence the applicant's continued imprisonment after that period of fourteen days was invalid.

In *Babulal Joitram Sharma v Attorney-General,*[223] the appellant was detained on the 9th July, 1977, under reg. 33(6) of the Preservation of Public Security Regulations (the Regulations). On the 5th August, 1977, he was served with a document purporting to revoke that detention and immediately thereafter was served with detention order under reg. 33(1). On the 18th August an ex parte application was made for the issue of a writ of habeas corpus; grounds for the detention as required by Article 27 of the Constitution were served on that day. It was argued on behalf of the appellant that the provisions of Article 27 of the Constitution applied to a detention under reg. 33(6) just as they applied to a detention under reg. 33(1), that the failure to furnish grounds for the former detention within fourteen days of its commencement rendered continued detention thereafter unlawful, that the detentions under the two orders were in fact and must be treated in law as one continuous detention, and that the detention under reg. 33(1) was therefore unlawful. It was argued on behalf of the respondent that there is no requirement to furnish grounds for the detention under reg. 33(6) and that that detention was lawful throughout; it was argued further that in any event the subsequent detention under reg. 33(1) was separate and distinct and not a continuation of the first detention. It was held as follows: (i) Although they relate broadly to the same subject matter, grounds for detention under reg. 33 (6) are not the same as grounds for detention under reg. 33(1); when a person is detained pursuant to reg. 33(6) the provisions of Article 27 of the Constitution must be complied with. (ii) Regulations 33(6) and 33(1) and the resulting detentions thereunder are

[222] Chapter 106.

[223] [1978] ZR 163 (SC); see also *In re Kapwepwe & Kaenga* [1972] ZR 248; *Mike Waluza Kaira v Attorney-General* [1980] ZR 65 (HC); *Godfrey Miyanda v The Attorney-General* [1981] ZR 157 (HC).

quite distinct; the detaining authorities, the purposes of the detention, and the periods of permissible detention are all different. The detention under reg. 33(1) cannot be attacked on the basis of any unlawfulness in the detention under reg. 33(6). (iii) It would not be in the interests of justice that persons detained without trial under exceptional powers should be deterred from raising reasonable legal points as to the validity of their detention by fear of the costs that might be incurred; although the court found no great difficulty in the points of law in issue, one of them was a constitutional point of general importance being raised for the first time.

In *Leonard Mungabangaba v The Attorney-General,*[224] the applicant was detained under a Presidential Detention Order signed on the 9th February, 1977. He was served with the grounds of detention on the 23rd February, 1977. It was contended for the applicant that if one includes the date on which the Presidential Detention Order was signed, and the date on which the grounds for detention were served, then it would appear that the statement for the grounds of detention were served on the applicant on the fifteenth day from the commencement of his detention. It was therefore contended that this was in breach of Article 27(1)(a) of the Constitution which requires the grounds to be served within fourteen days after the commencement of detention. It was held that (i) for purposes of Article 27(1)(a) of the Constitution, the computation of time for furnishing the statement of the grounds for detention should be exclusive of the day on which the actual detention order was signed and the period of 14 days should be calculated thereafter.

In *Valentine Shula Musakanya v The Attorney General,*[225] the applicant was first detained under a police detention order in October, 1980, pursuant to the Preservation of Public Security Regulations. He was a few days later detained under a Presidential Detention Order under reg. 33(1) of the Preservation of Public Security Regulations. His detention was declared unlawful by the High Court on the basis that the grounds for his detention were vague and roving. The applicant was on the same day arrested and charged with the offence of treason. He appeared in the Magistrate's court whereupon the State entered a nolle prosequi and the applicant was discharged. In December, the applicant was again detained under a Presidential Detention Order which is the subject of his application for a writ of habeas corpus ad subjiciendum. He alleged mala fides on the State in ordering his detention on similar grounds and that his detention was punitive in this respect. The applicant further alleged the State's failure to comply with Article 27(1) of the Constitution and that under Article 15 the court should release him conditionally or unconditionally on the ground that he was not tried in proper time. It was held as follows: (i) Vagueness is a relative term. How much detail must be given and what constitutes vagueness will depend upon the circumstances of each case. The detainee or the applicant must be given grounds in such a form as to enable him to make

[224] [1981] ZR 183 (HC); see also *Joyce Banda v Attorney-General* (1978) ZR 233 (SC).

[225] [1981] ZR 188 (HC); see also *Edward Jack Shamwana v The Attorney-General* [1981] ZR 270 (HC).

an adequate representation against his detention on such grounds. (ii) It is trite law that detaining authorities have fourteen days in which to serve grounds of detention. The words "as soon as is reasonably practicable" are intended to impart a sense of urgency but the true limit is the period of fourteen days. (iii) The onus of proving mala fides is on the applicant. The proper approach is to determine whether the order was mala fide. What has got to be made out is not the want of bona fides on the part of the police, but want of bona fides as well as the non-application of mind on the part of the detaining authority *viz.* the President. (iv) The President is empowered by law to detain people for Preservation of Public Security. It cannot be argued that in detaining the applicant the President was being punitive. The court cannot question in any way the discretion of the detaining authority if it is exercised within the power conferred. (v) Persons detained under reg. 33(1) of the Preservation of Public Security Regulations do not come under the provisions of Article 15(3). If they did, the whole purpose of exercising control over the movement of such persons would be defeated.

9.3.2.2 Proper recording

(i) General

The importance of having a proper record of the interview at the police station cannot be overemphasised. Part of the reason why there have been infamous miscarriages of justice such as we have encountered elsewhere in this text was want of a proper record of the interview or contemporaneous notes thereof. A reliable record is not only vital to rectitude of decision, it is indispensable to it.[226] It quite obviously follows that all requisite safeguards be in place when a police interview is taking place to obviate the possibility of having any evidence acquired therefrom from being excluded at trial. A plethora of authorities in this jurisdiction[227] and in jurisdictions such as England & Wales[228] appear to suggest that such safeguards as are required to be observed seem not to be, and have in some cases been admitted into evidence.[229] A curious scenario but one that is all too real for suspects and which may have dire consequences for the suspect when he is later tried.

(ii) Evidence of other prisoners

Where, as in *R v Stone*,[230] a prisoner who while at the police station or because

[226] *Paris v R* (1993) 97 Cr App R 99.

[227] See cases discussed above which came under the province of Articles 26 and 27 of the Constitution.

[228] See the rather fascinating case of *R v Matthews* [1990] Crim LR 190; but see *R v Spark* [1991] Crim LR 128; [1992] Crim LR 582 where statements obtained in informal interviews as was the case in Matthews were excluded.

[229] See the rather fascinating case of *R v Matthews* [1990] Crim LR 190; but see *R v Spark* [1991] Crim LR 128; [1992] Crim LR 582 where statements obtained in informal interviews as was the case in Matthews were excluded.

[230] [2005] EWCA Crim 105.

he shared a prison cell with the accused, claims that he heard the accused confess to an offence with which he is ultimately charged, this may serve to enhance the prosecution's case against the said accused person. This issue has arisen in at least three separate cases the first two of which were determined by the Privy Council, and the last one by the European Court of Human Rights. We consider them in turn.

In *R v Benedetto,*[231] the body of a young woman was found lying in shallow water on the island of Tortola in the British Virgin Islands. The appellants (B and L) and two others (S and G) were charged with her murder. The prosecution case against both B and L was crucially dependent on the evidence which a fellow remand prisoner, P, gave against them. P said that he had overheard conversations between B and L in which B had alleged that L "was more guilty than he was". P also said that L had made a confession to him, whilst they shared the same cell, that he had been responsible for drowning the victim. P was cross-examined at some length about his past conduct to show that he was a liar and a thief and a witness whose word was not to be trusted. The judge upheld a submission of no case to answer by B, S and G, but L was convicted by the jury of the murder. B was granted bail in respect of a charge of conspiracy to pervert the course of justice and returned home to New York. In his absence the Eastern Caribbean Court of Appeal allowed the prosecution's appeal, presented under s 51A(1)(b) of the Criminal Procedure Act, cap 18 of the Laws of the Virgin Islands, against the ruling by the trial judge that there was no case for B to answer on the murder charge, set aside his acquittal and ordered his retrial. L appealed against conviction on the grounds of insufficiency and unreliability of the prosecution evidence, prosecutorial misconduct, errors of the judge in his summing up and in his handling of the jury's deliberations and verdict, non-disclosure and additional evidence. All these grounds of appeal were rejected and his appeal against conviction was dismissed. On appeal to the Privy Council the principal submission on behalf of both B and L *391 was that the failure by the trial judge to give an express warning to the jury to regard P's evidence with caution had resulted in a miscarriage of justice. The Crown contended that B's appeal should be dismissed as he was in the position of an appellant who had escaped or absconded. It was held, allowing the appeals, (1) that in the case of a cell confession, the evidence of a prison informer was inherently unreliable in view of the personal advantage which such witnesses thought they might obtain by providing information to the authorities; that in view of the suspicion that had always to be attached to evidence of a cell confession given by a fellow prisoner, the responsibility of drawing together the various factors indicating that it was a genuine confession lay with the prosecutor; and that in directing the jury, the trial judge had to draw attention to the indications that might justify the inference that the prisoner's evidence was tainted and to advise the jury to be cautious before accepting his evidence. In L's case the judge told the jury that they would have to have careful regard

[231] [2003] 2 Cr App R 25; this summary is as adapted at https://www.studocu.com/en-gb/document/university-of-london/evidence/r-v-benedetto/1601068 retrieved on 16/12/21.

to P's evidence but nowhere did he draw the jury's attention to the various factors which would justify the inference that P's evidence was tainted by self-interest and to their significance. The omission of the necessary steps from the summing up in L's case was in itself such a fundamental defect that on that ground alone L's appeal had to be allowed and his conviction quashed as being unsafe. Since examination of P's evidence and parole history had shown that no value whatever could be attached to his evidence it would be wholly contrary to the interests of justice for L to have to face a new trial based, as it would have to be, wholly on P's evidence.

In *Pringle v R*,[232] the court considered the way in which statistical conclusions drawn from DNA evidence had been presented to the jury. The judge had fallen into the 'Prosecutor's Fallacy.' Also, the court had relied upon evidence of a confession to a cell mate himself awaiting trial. A judge must always be alert to the possibility that the evidence by one prisoner against another is tainted by an improper motive. The appeal succeeded. The case was remitted for a cautious consideration of a retrial.

In *Allan v UK*,[233] the police placed a long-known informer in the same cell as the accused for purposes of extracting a confession. This followed the accused's stand not to answer any questions by the police. The informer's testimony formed the core of the prosecution's case against the accused. The ECHR held that this violated article 6 and contravened the accused's right against self-incrimination.[234]

9.3.2.3 Tricks

It is not unheard of for police in general or investigators in particular to act unethically. When this unethical behaviour is brought to the attention of the court, the court has to consider the seriousness of the offence; the public interest on the one hand; and the police tactics and the position of the accused on the other.[235] In *R v Payne*,[236] the appellant was asked at a police station whether he was willing to be examined by a doctor, and was told that it would be no part of the doctor's duty to examine him in order to give an opinion as to his unfitness to drive. The appellant consented to be, and was, examined by a doctor. At the trial of the appellant on charges of driving, and of being in charge of, a motor vehicle while unfit to drive through drink, the doctor who had examined the appellant gave evidence of the extent to which the appellant was under the influence of drink, testifying that he was under the influence of drink to such an extent as to be unfit to have proper control of a car. The appellant was convicted on both charges, was sentenced and was disqualified from driving for three years. On appeal, it was held that although the doctor's evidence was admissible, the trial court should in its discretion have refused

---

[232] [2003] UKPC 9; as adapted at https://swarb.co.uk/lisc/Commw20032003.php retrieved on 16/12/2021.

[233] Application No.: 00048539/99; [2003] 36 EHRR 12.

[234] Compare Article 18(7) of the Constitution.

[235] *R v Payne* [1963] 1 All ER 848.

[236] [1963] 1 All ER 848.

to allow the evidence to be given, since the appellant might have refused to subject himself to examination if he had realised that the doctor would give evidence on that matter; accordingly, the convictions on the two charges, and the order for disqualification, would be quashed.[237]

It would thus appear to be the case that where, as in *Payne*,[238] there is what appears to be a confession which is obtained by device of tricks, same will be inadmissible. This has been exemplified in cases such as *R v Kirk*.[239] The accused having been arrested for a minor charge of assault and theft of a handbag. He declined legal representation. He was, with the police knowing of the death of the victim following the offence, only interviewed the accused on the basis of the minor charge. They did not reveal that he faced more serious charges of robbery and manslaughter. The record of the interview was held to be inadmissible. However, in *R v Fulling*[240] an accused made a statement which was not excluded at trial as it was deemed not to be oppressive in terms of s 76 of PACE. This followed the police tricking her into believing that her lover had cheated on her with another woman who was being held in a cell next to hers. This decision may be contrasted with that in *R v Mason*.[241] The appellant was arrested and questioned regarding an offence of arson. The police had no direct evidence associating the appellant with the crime but they falsely told him and his solicitor that they had found near the scene of the crime a fragment of a bottle which had contained inflammable liquid and that the appellant's fingerprint was on the fragment. The appellant then told the police that he had filled the bottles with the liquid and had asked a friend to commit the offence. At his trial he challenged the admissibility of the confession. The trial judge considered whether, 'having regard to all the circumstances, including the circumstances in which the evidence was obtained', the confession should be excluded under s 78(1)a of the Police and Criminal Evidence Act 1984 and decided that it would not be unfair to admit it. The appellant appealed against the judge's decision to admit the confession. At the hearing of the appeal the Crown contended, inter alia, that s 78 did not apply to confessions since they were expressly dealt with by s 76b which provided that a confession could only be excluded if it had been obtained by oppression or was likely to be unreliable. It was held that for the purpose of s 78 of the [PACE 1984] 'evidence' included all evidence, including a confession, that might be introduced by the prosecution at the trial, notwithstanding that confessions were expressly dealt with in s 76. Accordingly, the trial judge could exclude a confession under s 78 if it would have an adverse effect on the fairness of the trial, even though

---

[237] Editor's notes: The appellant was also convicted on a charge of dangerous driving against which there was no appeal, but the disqualification was stated to have attached to the offences involving the influence of drink and, therefore, fell with those convictions; As to disqualification, see s 104, s 2, of the Road Traffic Act; 1960, and Sch 11 thereto, 40 Halsbury's Statutes (2nd Edn) 808, 712, 947; As to evidence of insobriety on charge of driving while under influence of drink, see 33 Halsbury's Laws (3rd Edn) 628, para 1059, text and note (g); and for a case on the subject, see 14 Digest (Repl) 488, 4697; For the Road Traffic Act, 1960, s 6, see 40 Halsbury's Statutes (2nd Edn) 717.

[238] [1963] 1 All ER 848.

[239] [2000] 4 All ER 698; [2000] 1 WLR 567.

[240] [1987] 85 Cr App R 136 at 142.

[241] [1987] Crim LR 757; but see *R v Bailey* [1993] Crim LR 681.

it had not been obtained by oppression nor was likely to be unreliable. On the facts, the trial judge had wrongly exercised his discretion because he had failed to consider the deceit practised on the appellant and his solicitor and if he had done so he would have been bound to exclude the confession. The appeal would be allowed and, there being no other evidence produced by the prosecution, the conviction would be quashed.[242]

There appears to be authority to suggest that where the police play act for purposes of deceiving the accused that their cell has not been bugged, which thereby leads the accused to give a confession, same will not ordinarily be excluded. It seems to be the case, it would appear, that matters relating to the question of tricks by the police will be considered on a case-by-case basis. Such consideration will be based on the factual matrix and the surrounding circumstances within the wider context of fairness to the individual and legality of the acts as seen from a constitutional vantage point. The appellants were arrested and charged with robbery. When interviewed by the police they exercised their right to silence. The next day they appeared before magistrates and were remanded in police custody so that they could be put up on identification parades. In the meantime, the officer in charge of the case obtained permission to install listening equipment in one of the remand cells at the police station and when they were returned to the police station from the magistrates' court the investigating officers, in order to avoid arousing their suspicions, pretended that they had been forced to place the appellants together in the bugged cell by an unco-operative custody officer. While in the cell together the appellants made damaging admissions in conversation which were recorded. At their trial the appellants submitted that the judge should exercise his discretion under s 78(1)a[243] of the Police and Criminal Evidence Act

1984 to exclude the taped cell conversations but the judge ruled that they were admissible. The appellants were convicted. They appealed on the ground, inter alia, that the evidence of the taped conversations had been wrongly admitted. The evidence of the secretly taped conversations between the two appellants who had been placed in the same cell while on remand as the result of a police subterfuge was admissible at their trial, since the obtaining of evidence in such a way was not contrary to the Code of Practice for the Detention, Treatment and Questioning of Persons by Police Officers under the 1984 Act, notwithstanding that the police were not entitled to question them further because they had been charged. The police were under no duty to protect them from having the opportunity to speak indiscriminately to each other if they chose to do so and there was nothing in the 1984 Act or the Code of Practice which prohibited the police from bugging a cell, even after an accused person had been charged and

---

[242] Editor's notes: For admissibility of confessions, see 11 Halsbury's Laws (4th edn) para 410, and for cases on the subject, see 14(2) Digest (Reissue) 549–552, 4494–4517; For the Police and Criminal Evidence Act 1984, ss 76, 78, see 17 Halsbury's Statutes (4th edn) 213, 215.

[243] Section 78(1) provides: 'In any proceedings the court may refuse to allow evidence on which the prosecution proposes to rely to be given if it appears to the court that, having regard to all the circumstances, including the circumstances in which the evidence was obtained, the admission of the evidence would have such an adverse effect on the fairness of the proceedings that the court ought not to admit it.'

had exercised his right to silence. Accordingly, the judge had been entitled in the exercise of his discretion under s 78(1) of the 1984 Act to admit the evidence of the taped conversations. The appeal would therefore be dismissed.[244]

9.3.2.4 *Vulnerable suspects*

Vulnerable suspects form that class of suspects for whom specific rules and statutory provisions will apply in determining whether their purported confessions are admissible. They include, among others, the following:

(i) Juveniles[245]: children who have attained or are under the age of 18[246]

(a) A brief history

The law relating to the treatment of juvenile delinquents in this regard be found in the Juveniles Act,[247] specifically s 127(1) which provided as follows:

> Where a juvenile is charged with any offence, or is for any reason brought before a Court, his parent or guardian may in any case, and shall if he can be found and resides within a reasonable distance be required to attend at the Court before which the case is heard or determined during all the stages of the proceedings, unless the Court is satisfied that it would be unreasonable to require his attendance.[248]

The import of this section was that any failure by the police to provide for an adult as required by s 127(1) of the Juveniles Act[249] even where the juvenile had not been charged but was brought to a police station for purposes of interviewing him, any evidence obtained under such circumstances would generally be excluded.[250] In *Tembo v The People*[251] the appellant, a juvenile,

[244] Editor's notes: For the admissibility in evidence of tape and video recordings, see 11(2) Halsbury's Laws (4th edn reissue) para 1157.

[245] The Children's Code, Act No 12 of 2022 appears to have discarded the term 'juvenile' in favour of child whose definition is that found under Article 266 of the Constitution, that is, a child who has attained or is under the age of eighteen. Interestingly though the term Juvenile Court is still retained: "juvenile court" means a Subordinate Court, sitting for the purposes of hearing a charge or matter involving a child,—(a) of the First Class or Second Class; or (b) in the case of a Subordinate Court of the Third Class, a Subordinate Court presided over by a Magistrate of not less than one year experience.' Thus, "Children's Court" means the division of the High Court established under the Constitution.

[246] See generally, the Children's Code, Act No 12 of 2022 which repealed the Juveniles Act Chapter 53 of the Laws of Zambia; Center for Law and Justice (Zambia), Cornell Law School. Avon Global Center for Women and Justice, and Cornell Law School. International Human Rights Clinic, "Handbook on Juvenile Law in Zambia" (2014). Avon Global Center for Women and Justice and Dorothea S. Clarke Program in Feminist Jurisprudence. Paper 7 https://scholarship.law.cornell.edu/avon_clarke/?utm_source=scholarship.law.cornell.edu%2Favon_clarke%2F7&utm_medium=PDF&utm_campaign=PDFCoverPages retrieved on 19/12/2021.

[247] Chapter 53 of the Laws of Zambia.

[248] See application in *The People v Felix Chibanda* HPC/41/2011.

[249] Chapter 53 of the Laws of Zambia (repealed).

[250] See the logical application of this provision to pre-trial procedures which the section does not specifically relate to in *The People v Nephat Dimeni* [1980] ZR 234 (HC).

[251] [1974] ZR 286.

appealed against a finding of guilty and a reformatory order made against him by the juvenile court following a plea of guilty. The record disclosed that the resident magistrate made no inquiry concerning the whereabouts of the appellant's parents until after the plea had been taken and the finding of guilt recorded. Further, the appellant was charged with attempted rape, which is a specified offence by virtue of the Specification of Offences Order made under the Legal Aid Act, Cap 546. No legal aid certificate was issued until after the plea had been taken. There was nothing to indicate on the record that any inquiry was made as to the reason for the non-attendance of a legal aid representative and the facts were read out and put to the appellant and a finding of guilt entered before any further reference to legal aid representation was made. It was held as follows in part: (i) Section 127 of the Juveniles Act,[252] stresses the importance which the legislature attaches to the attendance wherever possible, during all stages of the proceedings, of the parent or guardian of a juvenile, and sets out in detail the procedure to be adopted and the circumstances in which such attendance may be dispensed with. In all cases the record should disclose that these provisions have in fact been complied with and, where the parent or guardian is not required to be present, the reasons why his attendance has been dispensed with should be stated. In *Clever Chalimbana v The People*,[253] the appellant, a juvenile, was found guilty of the offence of entry and theft, the particulars being that he broke into a dwelling house and stole a camera and a radio, valued together at K500. At his trial the appellant first pleaded not guilty, then changed his plea to one of guilty. He informed the court that his parents lived at Magoye (only some ten to fifteen kilometres from the Mazabuka court where he was tried) but no arrangements were made by the authorities for a parent or guardian to be present during the trial. At one stage the record indicated that the attendance of a parent or guardian was dispensed with but no reason was given for this. Gardner JS delivered the judgment of the court:

> Section 127 of the Juveniles Act provides that at any trial of a juvenile a parent or guardian should be present during all stages of the proceedings and this provision was not complied with in this case. In the case of *Tembo v The People*[254] we pointed out that the Juveniles Act[255] stresses the importance which the legislature attaches to the attendance wherever possible, during all stages of the proceedings, of the parent or guardian, and sets out in detail the procedure to be adopted and the circumstances in which attendance may be dispensed with. In that case we went on to say: "We cannot over-emphasise that provisions such as these, which are designed for the protection of juveniles, are there to be complied with and not ignored." We reiterate those observations in this case. The important consideration is that if these provisions are

[252] Chapter 53 of the Laws of Zambia (repealed).

[253] [1977] ZR 282 (SC).

[254] [1974] ZR 286.

[255] Chapter 53 of the Laws of Zambia (repealed).

> not complied with they may prejudice juveniles. In this case, having once indicated his wish to plead not guilty, the juvenile changed his plea. We do not know whether this was the fairest course for him to take without the advantage of advice from a parent or guardian. In the circumstances we are of the opinion that, because of the possibility of prejudice, it would be proper to allow this appeal which we do. We set aside the finding of guilty and the Reformatory Order. This is an appropriate case for a retrial and we make an order accordingly. No doubt the attention of the court of retrial will be drawn to the fact that the appellant has already spent over a year in custody.

In *Mbewe v The People*,[256] the Supreme Court observed as follows:

> Mr Osakwe further drew the attention of the court to the absence of a parent or guardian of the appellant at the police station when the statement of the appellant was recorded and has asked this court to lay down a general rule for the guidance of the police in the taking of statements from juveniles. We feel reluctant to lay down any Judges' rule in this regard. Section 127 of the Juveniles Act[257] stresses the importance which the legislature attaches to the attendance whenever possible, during all stages of the proceedings in court, of a parent or guardian of a juvenile but there is no such provision in the Act for the attendance of a parent or guardian at a police station during the taking down of a statement of a juvenile. We would however urge that it is desirable in the interests of both the police and the juvenile to have a parent or guardian whenever possible to be present at the police station when a statement is being taken from a juvenile and no doubt the legislature would view the importance of such a procedural provision in the Act in the same light as obtains in section 127 of the Juveniles Act.[258]

In *The People v Nephat Dimeni*,[259] the juvenile was charged with murder and the prosecution sought to produce a statement recorded from him by a Police constable under warn and caution. The defence counsel objected to the production of the statement on the ground that it was not signed freely and voluntarily. The statement was recorded in the presence of two Police officers. It was held that it is desirable to have the parent or guardian present when a statement is being taken from a juvenile and in cases where the juvenile has no parent or guardian, it would be desirable in the interest of justice to have some other person other than a Police officer. *Per* Sakala J (as he then was):

> In the case before me although the juvenile has no parents in Zambia

[256] [1976] ZR 317 at 319 to 320.

[257] Chapter 53 of the Laws of Zambia (repealed).

[258] Chapter 53 of the Laws of Zambia.

[259] [1980] ZR 234 (HC); see also *DPP v Stratford Youth Court* [2001] EWHC Admin 615.

(as per his evidence) in the absence also of a guardian it would have been desirable in the interest of justice to have some other person not a police officer, to have been present when recording the statement. Although the Supreme Court has accepted the desirability to have a parent or guardian at the police station when a statement is being taken from a juvenile it is perhaps unfortunate that Zambia still operates under the pre-1964 English Judges' Rules.[260] The pre - 1964 Judges' Rules' have no provisions for the presence of a parent or guardian at the Police station during the interrogation of children and young persons which is specifically provided for in the revised English Judges' Rules.[261] For reasons outlined above, I am satisfied that this is "a proper case" in which I should exercise my discretion to exclude the confession, notwithstanding that it was voluntary and therefore strictly admissible, because in all the circumstances, the strict application of the rules as to admissibility would operate unfairly against the juvenile offender. Accordingly, I refuse to accept the introduction of the confession into the evidence.[262]

(b) The Children's Code: a new and more robust approach to child protections

The relevant parts of the Children's Code[263] that provide for the protection of children when they become suspects are to be found under Part V: ss 45 -57 headlined: ARREST, BAIL AND DEPRIVATION OF CHILD'S LIBERTY; and Part VII: ss 65-83: COURT PROCEEDINGS.

(i) Information of arrest of child

What appears to have replaced s 127 of the now repealed Juveniles Act,[264] now repealed, atleast in terms of pre-trial procedures relating to the interests of the child as regards arrest is s 50(1) of the Children's Code[265] which provides as follows:

> (1) A child welfare inspector shall, within forty-eight hours, where an arrest of a child is made in the presence of a child welfare inspector as provided under section 49 (3) and the child's parent, guardian, close relative of the child or person having parental

---

[260] *Chinyama and Others v The People* [1977] ZR 426.

[261] See Rule 4 at 763, *para* 1391a of Archbold, 39th edn.

[262] It has been said inter alia in *Shamwana and 7 Others v The People* [1985] ZR 41 that Although statement made in breach of the Judges' Rules is admissible the breach raises rebuttable presumption of involuntariness and unfairness. Where a breach of the Judges' Rules has been admitted or established, it is for the prosecution to advance an explanation acceptable to the court for such breach explaining *Chilufya v The People* [1975] ZR 138.

[263] Act No 12 of 2022.

[264] Chapter 53 of the Laws of Zambia (repealed).

[265] Act No 12 of 2022.

responsibility for the child cannot be found, trace the parent, guardian or close relative of the child or the person having parental responsibility for the child.

(2) A child welfare inspector shall, where a child welfare inspector cannot trace the parent, guardian, close relative of the child or the person having parental responsibility for the child, take responsibility of the child and place the child in a place of safety.

(ii) Evidence of child

The recent changes to the law in this space means that what was s 122 of the now repealed Juveniles Act has been replaced by a more expansive s 78 which not only expands on the specific issue of receipt of evidence from a child, now defined, in terms of Article 266 as '[...] a person who has attained, or is below, the age of eighteen years,' but in terms of s 78(3)-(9), makes additional provisions as to conditions to be met at trial if evidence received from a child is to be admissible. This is discussed in greater detail in chapter 14.

It ought to logically follow that the authorities covered above which were decided in terms of the now repealed Juveniles Act[266] ought now, ordinarily to be seen within the confines of the relevant parts of s 78 of the Children's Code.[267]

(ii) Those with mental or physical disorders or impairment

It goes without saying that an officer having custody of any vulnerable persons must ensure that he is aware of the needs of the vulnerable person, in this regard, one with a mental disorder or impairment. In *R v Lamont*,[268] the EWCA excluded (based on PACE s 77)[269] confession evidence which was the only evidence of attempted murder because the interrogation birthing said confession had been that an accused had an IQ of 73.[270] Similarly evidence a confession was excluded in *R v Brine*[271] despite the fact that the police were acting in good faith when they interviewed the accused without realising that he was, at the material time, suffering from a mild form of paranoid psychosis was irrelevant.[272]

(iii) Those in fear such as victims of rape

---

[266] Chapter 53 of the Laws of Zambia (repealed).

[267] Act No 12 of 2022.

[268] [1989] Crim LR 813.

[269] Which provides for the law as regards Confessions by mentally handicapped persons in England & Wales.

[270] IQ stands for Intelligence Quotient. According to the Stanford-Binet IQ Scale (1986), IQ of 132 and above is classed as 'Very superior;' that between 121–131 is classed as 'Superior;' that between 111–120 is classed as 'High average;' that between 89–110 is classed as 'Average;' that between 79–88 is classed as 'Low average;' that between 68–78 is classed as 'Slow learner;' and that rated at 67 or lower is classed as 'Mentally retarded.'

[271] [1992] Crim LR 122.

[272] But see *R v Clark* [1989] Crim LR 892.

Rape victims present the most intractable challenges to the criminal justice system. In the face of a patriarchal society such as ours, it is difficult for such persons who may be in fear because of their traumatic experience and as a consequence, susceptibility to intimidation, to manage the stress associated with being a witness at the police station or even more so, at trial. Without the assistance of certain shielding actions, it is unlikely that they will give the best evidence required for the case the police intend to take to court. The AGBVA 2010 goes some way to address these issues as we show elsewhere in this text in the chapter dealing with vulnerable witnesses.

9.3.2.5 *Inadmissible statement followed by appropriate interview*

There is a plethora of authorities[273] to the effect that the exclusion of one statement because of a breach of the law does not automatically negateeverything that follows including interviews that are properly conducted.

9.3.3 *Interviews outside the police station*

Though it is ordinarily expected that interviews will take place at the police station, the same standards observed at the police station in terms of the pre-1964 Judge's Rules have to be observed. However, the English position appears far removed from the foregoing as demonstrated in several authorities[274] which are liberally discussed in English text books on the law of Evidence. The England and Wales Police Code of Practice designates the police station as the place suitable for an interview. This is because safeguards are likely to be observed including recording of any interview with a suspect, among other things.

9.4 Evidence discovered as a result of a confession deemed inadmissible

The common law never considered evidence discovered as a result of a confession inadmissible as fruits of a poisonous tree. Thus, in *R v Warickshall*[275] where the accused was charged as an accessory for receiving goods reasonably expected to have been stolen. Evidence (predicated on the accused's confession) that stolen goods were found under the bed of the accused was admitted notwithstanding that the discovery was made in consequence of her inadmissible confession obtained on the basis of inducements. On the question whether evidence obtained by oppression should be admitted to court, it was held that involuntary statements are inherently unreliable, that is to say, 'a confession forced from the mind by the flattery of hope, or by the torture of fear

[273] *Y v DPP* [1991] Crim LR 917; *R v Canale* [1990] Crim LR 329; *R v Conway* [1994] Crim LR 838; *R v McGovern* [1991] Crim LR 124.

[274] See s 30(1) of the PACE 1984; *R v Pattinson* (1973) 58 Cr App R 417; *R v Parchment* [1989] Crim LR 290; *R v Maguire* [1989] Crim LR 815; *R v Hunt* [1992] Crim LR 582; [1994] Crim LR 46; *R v Cox* [1993] Crim LR 382; *R v Marsh* [1991] Crim LR 45; *R v Langiert* [1991] Crim LR 777; *R v White* [1991] Crim LR 779; *R v Chung* [1991] Crim LR 622; *R v Park* [1994] Crim LR 285.

[275] (1783) 1 Leach 263; summary is adapted from summary at https://swarb.co.uk/rex-v-warickshall-1783/ retrieved on 18/12/21; see also *Chalmers v HM Advocate* 1954 SLT 177.

comes in so questionable a shape when it is to be considered as the evidence of guilt, that no credit ought to be given to it; and therefore, it is rejected.' As regards the admissibility of evidence relating to the finding of the property, which as shown was a s a result of inadmissible evidence, Nares J observed as follows:[276]

> A free and voluntary confession is deserving of the highest credit, because it is presumed to flow from the strongest sense of guilt, and therefore it is admitted as proof of the crime to which it refers; but a confession forced from the mind by the flattery of hope, or by the torture of fear, comes in so questionable a shape when it is to be considered as evidence of guilt, that no credit ought to be given to it; and therefore, it is rejected. This principle respecting confessions has no application whatever as to the admission or rejection of facts, whether the knowledge of them be obtained in consequence of an extorted confession, or whether it arises from some other source; for a fact, if it exists at all, must exist invariably in the same manner, whether the confession from which it is derived be in other respects true or false. Facts thus obtained, however, must be fully and satisfactorily proved, without calling in aid of any part of the confession from which they have been derived.

It is safe to conclude that the common law rule notwithstanding, it was possible to link the accused to the stolen goods discovered in her bedroom without reference to her inadmissible confession.

In *R v Voisin*,[277] the [accused] stood charged with the murder of a woman, part of whose body was found in a parcel along with a handwritten note bearing the words 'Bladie Belgiam'. The defendant, who had not yet been cautioned, was asked by the police to write the words 'Bloody Belgian', which he did. He made exactly the same misspelling as had the writer of the note. The handwriting was admitted in evidence. It was held that the accused's appeal failed. It did not make any difference to the admissibility of the handwriting whether it was written voluntarily or under compulsion. Where it is alleged that a statement has been obtained in breach of the Judges' Rules, the court has a discretion to admit or reject such evidence. Lawrence J spoke of the Judges' Rules:

> These Rules have not the force of law; they are administrative directions the observance of which the police authorities should enforce upon their subordinates as tending to the fair administration of justice. It is important that they should do so, for statements obtained from prisoners contrary to the spirit of these Rules may be rejected as evidence by the judge presiding at the trial.

---

[276] (1783) 1 Leach 263 at 264.

[277] [1918] 1 KB 531, [1918-19] All ER 491; this summary is taken from https://swarb.co.uk/rex-v-voisin-1918/ retrieved on 18/12/21.

9.5 Civil proceedings and the concept of formal/informal admissions

9.5.1 General

At its very basic, the concept of formal admissions entails a scenario in which a party (usually but not always the defendant) to civil proceedings admits in whole in part the plaintiff's case with the useful and positive consequence being that the court's time is saved, and may then be used to attend to more urgent matters in dispute. It is irrelevant when the admissions may be made as same can be done prior to commencement of proceedings following the commencement thereof. Admissions then serve the purpose of having all matters in controversy being determined in the sense of a volcanic eruption as opposed to the otherwise glacial pace that may ensue in their absence. Dealing with the term in *Muyuni Estate Limited v MPH Chartered Accountants,*[278] Chisanga J, as she then was, observed that '[…] the word is not technical and bears the ordinary meaning in the English language. According to the Oxford Compact Thesaurus, the word "admission" means, "acknowledge, acceptance, concession, disclosure or divulgence." The law regarding admissions is found in the following, as the case may be:

- Order XVI of the Subordinate Court Rules, Chapter 28 of the Laws of Zambia
- Order XXI of the High Court Rules (HCR), Chapter 27 of the Laws of Zambia
- Order 27 of the Supreme Court Rules (SCR), Chapter 25 of the Laws of Zambia

9.5.2 *Effect of admissions*[279]

An admission, whether made in response to a notice to admit facts or not, is not necessarily binding for all purposes. It is only binding as against the party making it, and if made under [Order 27/2/2, RSC] is only binding in the action (including an appeal) and *semble* at a new trial. An admission of facts made without a notice under the rule can expressly be made for the purposes of the action only, or for the purposes of the trial only, and in the latter case would not be effective at a new trial of the same action.[280]An admission in an action was held not binding on an application to attach under the Debtors Act 1869, s 4(3).[281] An admission in a pleading is not binding in a subsequent action.[282]

9.5.3 *Formal or/and informal admissions*

[278] [2013] 2 ZR 120 at 124.

[279] Everything hereunder together with authorities is excerpted from Order 27/2/2, RSC.

[280] *Dawson v GC Ry* (1919) 121 LT 263.

[281] *Harper v McIntyre* (1908) 99 LT 191.

[282] *British Thomson-Houston Co v British Insulated & Helsby Cables* [1924] 1 Ch 203 at 210; affirmed [1924] 2 Ch 160, CA.

Admissions may be formal or informal. This is exemplified by Order 27 r 3 of the Rules of the Supreme Court, 1965, The (White Book) 1999 Edition (RSC), 'admissions of fact or of part of a case are made by a party to a cause or matter by his pleadings or otherwise.' We explore the two themes in turn below.

9.5.3.1 *Formal admissions*

As seen in Order 27 r 3, RSC, formal admissions may be formally made during proceedings by means of 'pleadings' such as a statement of claim or indeed through a non-*salvo jure* dispatch. Such admissions may be '[...] of fact or of part of a case' implying that formal admissions may be made of the other party's entire case or indeed of some relevant facts constituting the other party's case. It is also possible to admit to facts by omitting to deal with allegations raised by the other party in his pleadings.

As has been postulated by some, 'the introduction of [an admission] makes the other aspects of a trial in court superfluous.'[283] Further still, the party who [admits] to a fact in issue is bound by such a confession and may not contradict such a confession save with leave of court. The preceding thus assist in achieving the goal of formal admissions which is, as McCormick[284] notes, to get speedy judgment to the extent that there is an admission. This is exemplified in the following authorities.

It has been shown in *Pioneer Plastic Containers Limited v Commissioners of Customs and Excise*[285] that it is the law that the effect of the defendant's admission of the fact pleaded in the statement of claim is that there is no issue between the parties on that point of the case which is concerned with those matters of fact; and therefore, no evidence is admissible in reference to those facts.

In *AJ Trading Company Limited v Chilombo,*[286] the plaintiff sold and delivered goods to the proprietor of a shop which subsequently came under the control of the defendant when the proprietor left the country after unsuccessfully negotiating with the defendant for the sale of the shop to the defendant. The proprietor failed to pay off the plaintiff in full before leaving and attempts were made by the plaintiff to secure payment for the goods from the defendant during the time of the negotiations between the proprietor and the defendant and after the departure of the proprietor. The defendant made attempts to settle during the period of negotiations but never settled in full. The plaintiff brought an action against the defendant, alleging on his Statement of Claim that the defendant was the proprietor of the shop - an allegation which was not formally denied by the defendant until after the trial started. The defendant then alleged that she was not the proprietor and no objection was made by the plaintiff's advocates to the admission of this evidence. It was held as follows: (i) The efforts of the defendant to settle with the plaintiff did not amount to an

---

[283] McCormick 1972.

[284] McCormick 1972.

[285] (1967) Ch D 597.

[286] 1973 ZR 55 (HC).

admission of liability but were merely designed to aid the negotiations then going on. (ii) An admission by the defendant of an allegation in the plaintiff's Statement of Claim means that there is no issue between the parties on that joint and no further evidence is admissible in reference to that point. (iii) The plaintiff's advocate did not object to admission of evidence of the defendant that she was never the proprietor of the shop. Therefore, the evidence, once admitted, could not be ignored by the court. (iv) The court was bound to consider the probative value and effect of this evidence and as it was not challenged, the defendant was to be deemed not to have been the proprietor of the shop when the goods were delivered.

In the recent case of *Chazya Silwamba v Lamba Simpito*,[287] the action was commenced by way of writ of summons accompanied by a statement of claim. Subsequently, the plaintiff took out summons or leave to enter judgment on admission. The summons was taken out pursuant to Order 21 r 2, HCR. It was held as follows: (i) a party may admit the truth of the whole or any part of another party's case. When a fact is admitted, it is unnecessary for a party to advance evidence in relation to the admitted fact(s) at trial. (ii) when a fact is admitted, it ceases to be an issue, and neither [party] is required or permitted to advance evidence about it at trial. (iii) An admission may be made expressly in a defence, or in a defence to a counterclaim. (iv) An admission may also arise by virtue of the rules. For instance, where a defendant fails to traverse an allegation of fact.

Where there is a formal admission either of a relevant fact or the plaintiff's case in its entirety, a party need not wait until the conclusion of the entire matter to take positive steps in securing its interests. Order XXI of the High Court Rules (HCR) provides as follows:[288]

(i) Notice of admissions, r 1

Any party to a suit may give notice, by his own statement or otherwise, that he admits the truth of the whole or any part of the case stated or referred to in the writ of summons, statement of claim, defence or other statement of any other party.

(ii) Notice to admit, r 2

Any party may call upon any other party to admit, saving just exceptions, any document or fact.

(iii) Costs on refusal to make reasonable admissions, r 3

In case of refusal or neglect to admit after notice, the costs of proof of the document or fact shall be paid by the party refusing or neglecting to admit, whatever be the result of the suit, unless the Court or a Judge is of opinion that the refusal or neglect to admit was reasonable.

[287] [2010] 1 ZR 475.

[288] Chapter 27 of the Laws of Zambia as amended by SI No 71 of 1997.

(iv) Judgment by consent, r 4

If the plaintiff and defendant shall agree as to the terms and conditions on which judgment shall be entered, the Court or a Judge, unless it or he sees good reason to the contrary, shall enter judgment on such terms and conditions.

(v) Admission by defendants, r 5

If any defendant shall sign a statement admitting the amount claimed in the summons or any part of such amount, the Court or a Judge, on being satisfied as to the genuineness of the signature of the person before whom such statement was signed, and unless it or he sees good reason to the contrary, shall, in case the whole amount is admitted, or in case the plaintiff consents to a judgment for the part admitted, enter judgment for the plaintiff for the whole amount or the part admitted, as the case may be, and, in case the plaintiff shall not consent to judgment for the part admitted, shall receive such statement in evidence as an admission without further proof.[289]

(vi) Application on admissions, r 6

A party may apply, on motion or summons, for cancelled judgment on admissions where admissions of facts or part of a case are made by a party to the cause or matter either by his pleadings or otherwise.

Order XXI r 6 is worthy of further consideration. The import of the Order appears to be that the judgment in admission is not granted as a matter of right and ought to be applied for. Once a formal application is made and a response if any filed into court, the court is then empowered under Order 27 r 2, RSC, to give judgment to the extent of the admission without waiting for the determination of other outstanding matters between the parties. In *Finance Bank Zambia Ltd v Lamasat International Ltd*,[290] the Supreme Court opined that the court has discretion to enter judgment where the admission is clear and unequivocal. Further, that an admission has to be plain and obvious on the face of it. Additionally, that a court cannot refuse to enter judgment on admission on the face of the admission. Thus, where the admission is unclear and equivocal; uncertain and requiring further investigation; or it appears to the court that the issue in the proceedings is one not fit for a judgment on admission to be issued; or where there is a bonafide counterclaim, as opposed to a vexatious and frivolous one, the court may refuse to issue the judgment on admission.

Ray[291] has outlined the following conditions as being necessary before a court may use its discretion to issue a judgment on admission:

- The admission must have been made either in pleadings or otherwise.
- The admission must have been made orally or in writing.

[289] See Orders 21, 22, 23, HCR.

[290] Appeal No 175 of 2017.

[291] Ray Textbook on the Code of Civil Procedure 138 as quoted in Matibini P, *Zambian Civil Procedure* at 609.

- The admission must be clear and unequivocal.
- The admission must be taken as a whole and it is not permissible to rely on a part of the admission, ignoring the other part.

Further, Order LIII Rule 6(2), (3), (4) and (5) of the High Court Rules (HCR) provides as follows:

> (1) ....
> (2) The defence shall specifically traverse every allegation of fact made in the statement of claim or counter-claim, as the case may be.
> (3) A general or bare denial of allegations of fact or a general statement of non-admission of the allegations of fact shall not be a traverse thereof.
> (4) A defence that fails to meet the requirements of this rule shall be deemed to have admitted the allegations not specifically traversed.
> (5) Where a defence fails under sub-rule (4), the plaintiff or defendant, or the court on its own motion, may in an appropriate case, enter judgement on admission.

Therefore, where the defendant's defence, only states a denial of the plaintiff's statement of claim the same will, in terms of Order LIII r 3, HCR, amount to a bare denial of the allegation of fact falling short of the requirement as set out in the said rule.[292] Where the fact and circumstances bring an admission within the province of the law and rules providing for it, it makes such a case a proper one in which the court can exercise its power and order for Judgment on Admission to be entered for the Plaintiff in regards to his/her/its claim.[293] According to Chisanga J, as she then was, in *Muyuni Estate Limited v MPH Chartered Accountants*,[294]

> [Order XL r 11] was framed for the express purpose that if there was no dispute between the parties and if there was in the pleadings such an admission as to make it plain that the plaintiff was entitled to a particular order, he should be able to obtain that order at once upon motion. It must however be such an admission of facts as would show that the plaintiff is clearly entitled to the order asked for, whether to be in the nature of a decree or judgment or anything else[295] [...] In my judgment it applies whenever there is a clear admission of facts in the face of which it is impossible for the party making it to succeed.

The foregoing matters and the attendant law and procedure arose and were determined in the earliest decision relating to Order LIII, HCR, that of *China*

---

[292] *China Henan International Economic Technical Cooperation v Mwange Contractors Limited* SCZ Judgment No 7 of 2002 discussed below.

[293] See *Kawambwa Tea Company 1996 Limited v Zygo Bonsai Limited* SCZ Appeal No 11 of 2003 and *China Henan International Economic Technical Corporation v Mwange Contractors Ltd* [2002] ZR 28.

[294] [2013] 2 ZR 120 at 124.

[295] Citing and quoting with approval *Gilbert v Smith* [19751976] Ch 686; *Ellis v Allen* [1914] 1 Ch 904 at 909 *per* Sargant J.

Henan International Economic Technical Cooperation v Mwange Contractors Limited.[296] Mambilima AJS, delivered the judgment of the Court:

> [....] This is an appeal against the ruling of the Court below given on 3rd October, 2001, in which the Court entered Judgment on Admission at a scheduling conference on the ground that the defence which was filed by the appellant did not rebut in full allegations contained in the Statement of Claim. The appellant has advanced six grounds of appeal namely:
>
> '1. The Court below misdirected itself in not considering a judgment given or obtained in the absence of the other party as equivalent to a default Judgment and therefore liable to be set aside, or alternatively that such Judgment is liable to be set aside in its own right.
>
> '2. The learned Judge in the Court below did not act judiciously when he failed to consider that a Scheduling Conference afforded the defendant's Counsel opportunity to make an application including an indication to amend the defence and therefore that it is improper to enter Judgment on admission in the absence of such party.
>
> '3. That the Court below acted contrary to established practice in proceeding in the absence of Counsel for the defendant without in the first place satisfying himself that there was proper service of the Notice of Hearing on the defendant or its Counsel.
>
> '4. The Court below misdirected itself in law when it considered the general traverse contained in paragraph 3 of the defendant's defence as an admission of the plaintiff's claim.
>
> '5. The Court below misdirected itself in proceeding with the Scheduling Conference in view of the plaintiff Counsel's expressed reluctance to proceed in the absence of the defence.
>
> '6. The Court below misapprehended the provisions of the law and the relevant Practice Direction when it held that Judgment on admission need not be applied for by the plaintiff. He further erred on a point of fact when he held that in this particular for Judgment.
>
> At the hearing of the appeal, it was evident that the main grievance by the appellant was that the Judgment on Admission was entered at the Scheduling Conference in the absence of its Counsel and that had Counsel been present, he could have had an opportunity to apply to amend the defence for it to comply with the Practice Directions which govern commercial matters. Mr. Kasonde, for the respondent conceded that had the learned Counsel for the appellant been present at the Scheduling Conference, he would have had an opportunity to amend the defence. He argued however that whether such an amendment if made could have introduced a viable defence on merits, is another issue. Rule 2 of the Practice Directions which govern commercial matters states:

[296] SCZ Judgment No 7 of 2002.

"The defence shall specifically traverse allegation of fact made in the statement of claim or counter-claim as the case may be. A general or bare denial of such allegation or a general statement of non-admission of them shall not be a traverse thereof. A defence that fails to meet requirements of this direction shall be deemed to have admitted the allegations not traversed and in an appropriate case the plaintiff may be entitled to enter Judgment on Admission."

The statement of claim which was filed by the respondent is very detailed. It explains the facts on which the plaintiff relies and claims damages for breach of contract. The defence filed by the appellant contains three paragraphs:

'1. The defendant admits paragraphs 1 and 2.

'2. The contents of paragraphs 3,4,5,6,7,8,9 and 10 are denied and the defendant shall put the plaintiff to strict proof thereof.

'3. SAVE as hereinafter expressly admitted the defendant denies each and every allegation contained in the statement of claim as though seriatim."

This defence clearly falls far short of the standard required in commercial cases as provided by Practice Direction 2. It does not traverse specific allegations of fact contained in the Statement of claim. It is a general statement of non-admission, containing bare denials. The new dispensation in commercial matters is that Parties must place their cards on the table early in the litigation to assist in narrowing issues of contention and for the real issues in the dispute to surface. It is not prudent for a party to wait for trial before exposing their side of the story. At the Scheduling Conference, the nature of directions given to chart the course of events in the case depends in the main, on the issues raised in the pleadings before the Court. At that stage, these pleadings are contained in the statement of claim and defence. When issues are well defined in the statement of claim and the defence, the Court is in a position to properly direct the parties or indeed decide whether or refer the matter to Mediation or Arbitration. In keeping with the Practice Directions, where a defence in a commercial matter does not satisfy the requirements of rule 2, the court is entitled to enter Judgment on Admission in an appropriate case.

Mr. Malila argues further that the Court can only enter Judgment on Admission upon application by either motion or summons. For this proposition, he referred us to order 27 of rule 3 of the Supreme Court Rules and Order 21 Rule 6 of the High Court Act.

Order 27 Rule 3 of the Rules of the Supreme Court, [RSC], ([The] White Book) [1999 Edition] provides: - "Where admission of fact or of part of a case are made by a party to a cause or matter either by his pleading or otherwise any other party may apply to the Court for such judgment or order as upon those admissions he may be entitled to, without waiting for the determination of any other question between the parties and the Court may give such Judgment or make such Order, on the application as it thinks just.

An application for an Order under this rule may be made by Motion or Summons".

Order 21 Rule 6 of the High Court Rules states that:

"a Party may apply on Motion or Summons, for Judgment on admission where admissions of fact or part of a case are made by a Party to the cause or matter whether by his pleadings or otherwise."

In the context of commercial matters, however, Order 53 of the High Court Act provides for a Scheduling Conference to be held after filing of a Memorandum of Appearance and a defence. If a defence fails to meet the requirements of Practice Direction 2, "the plaintiff may be entitled to enter Judgment on Admission". This, in our view, does not entail a party going back to take out summons or a motion to enter Judgment on Admission. The Judgment can be entered at the Scheduling Conference because this is the time when the Court is considering the pleadings; what directions to give and decide whether the matter should proceed further. The case flow management techniques at play requires the Court to be in control of the pace of litigation and properly direct the course of events. It would be absurd to expect a Court which is in control, to pause and wait for an application where clearly the defence is deemed to have admitted the claim. This is without prejudice to Order 27 Rule 3 of the Rules of the Supreme Court and Order 21 Rule 6 of the High Court Act where a plaintiff "may" apply by Motion or Summons to enter Judgment on admission.

We allowed this appeal for the reason that the Judgment on Admission in this case was entered in the absence of Counsel and the reason given for the absence of Counsel at the Scheduling conference was that the Counsel was not aware of the return date of the Scheduling Conference since she was not served with the notice for the Scheduling Conference. The record shows that there was no affidavit of service filed by the plaintiff to counteract this position. The Court below ought to have been satisfied with the service of the Notice of Scheduling Conference before entering judgment on Admission. It is our view that had the defendant's Counsel been present at the Scheduling Conference, he would have an opportunity to make an appropriate application to amend the defence. To this effect, procedural justice was compromised. For these reasons, we allowed the appeal and referred the matter back to the Court below to proceed with the Scheduling Conference.

9.5.3.2 Informal admissions

Informal admissions may be said to be statements made by a party to the proceedings (usually the defendant or the plaintiff where there is a counter-claim by the defendant) entitling the court to, but not obligating it to find facts or otherwise draw adverse inferences against the party making the informal admissions. Informal admissions such as out of court statements in writing or those orally made by a party are but items of evidence to be taken into considerations with respect to the determination of the specific question of there being an admission necessitating a judgment or the judgment in the matter in its entirety.[297]

9.5.3.3 *Admissions vis-à-vis document production as per list of documents*

Zambian civil procedure permits for no ambush evidence. As a logical consequence therefore, it is expected and required material documents are produced at the same time or at such a time as the rulers of court demand. These documents will be in addition to each party's pleadings which may include the Writ of summons, Statement of Claim, Defence, Reply or Counterclaim. So necessary are these documents that no civil proceedings will take place without them being lodged in the form of bundles, and produced in form of a list of documents. It is thus logically permissible for a party to use as circumstantial evidence against a party producing the documents in question in whose custody, power and/or possession they have been, as respects such a party to show that he has knowledge of the transaction to which the documents relate, has knowledge of their contents, has connection with or is otherwise complicit in the transaction in question. Further to the preceding, receipt of the said documents, as admissions i.e., to say as an exception to the hearsay rule, is permissible, against the party producing them where he has in any way, shape or form, adopted, is familiar with them or otherwise acted upon them, in order to prove the truthfulness of their contents.

The first port of call in this regard is Order 27 r 4, RSC which provides as follows:

> (1) Subject to paragraph (2) and without prejudice to the right of a party to object to the admission in evidence of any document, a party on whom a list of documents is served in pursuance of any provision of Order 24 shall, unless the Court otherwise orders, be deemed to admit - (a) that any document described in the list as an original document is such a document and was printed, written, signed or executed as it purports respectively to have been, and (b) that any document described therein as a copy is a true copy. This paragraph does not apply to a document the authenticity of which the party has denied in his pleading.
>
> (2) If before the expiration of 21 days after inspection of the documents specified in a list of documents or after the time limited for inspection of those documents expires, whichever is the later, the party on whom the list is served serves on the party whose list it is a notice stating, in relation to any document specified therein, that he does not admit the authenticity of that document and requires it to be proved at the trial, he shall not be deemed to make any admission in relation to that document under paragraph (1).
>
> (3) A party to a cause or matter by whom a list of documents is served on any other party in pursuance of any provision of

[297] Sime *A Practical Approach to Civil Procedure* 455.

Order 24 shall be deemed to have been served by that other party with a notice requiring him to produce at the trial of the cause or matter such of the documents specified in the list as are in his possession, custody or power.

(4) The foregoing provisions of this rule apply in relation to an affidavit made in compliance with an order under Order 24, rule 7, as they apply in relation to a list of documents served in pursuance of any provision of that Order.

The goal of Order 27 r 4 is to, so far as is possible, secure a just, speedy and fair trial for the parties concerned. It also serves to lessen or prevent the production of manufactured evidence, and the delayed production of documents likely to prejudice the other side. As has been noted by some,[298] '[t]he object of Order [27 r 4], is to achieve wherever possible the effect of a notice to produce and notice to admit documents without putting the parties to the trouble and expense of serving them and also to encourage admissions.'

9.5.3.4 *Notice to admit*

The rules relating to the service of a notice to admit facts are to be found in Order 27 r 2(1)(2), RSC[299] which provides as follows:

(1) A party to a cause or matter may not later than 21 days after the cause or matter is set down for trial serve on any other party a notice requiring him to admit, for the purpose of that cause or matter only, such facts or such part of his case as may be specified in the notice.

(2) An admission made in compliance with a notice under this rule shall not be used against the party by whom it was made in any cause or matter other than the cause or matter for the purpose of which it was made or in favour of any person other than the person by whom the notice was given, and the Court may at any time allow a party to amend or withdraw an admission so made by him on such terms as may be just.

9.5.3.5 *Notices to admit or produce documents*

The rules relating to *Notices to admit or produce documents* is to be found in Order 27 r 5, RSC[300] which provides as follows:

(1) Except where rule 4 (1) applies, a party to a cause or matter may within 21 days after the cause or matter is set down for trial serve on any other party a notice requiring him to admit the authenticity of the documents specified in the notice.

(2) If a party on whom a notice under paragraph (1) is served desires

[298] Matibini P, *Zambian Civil Procedure: Commentary and Cases* vol 1 (Lexis Nexis, 2017) 604.

[299] See also 27/3/7, RSC; *Showell Bouron* [1883] 52 LJ QB 284.

[300] See also 27/3/7, RSC; *Showell Bouron* [1883] 52 LJ QB 284.

to challenge the authenticity of any document therein specified he must, within 21 days after service of the notice, serve on the party by whom it was given a notice stating that he does not admit the authenticity of the document and requires it to be proved at the trial.

(3) A party who fails to give a notice of non-admission in accordance with paragraph (2) in relation to any document shall be deemed to have admitted the authenticity of that document unless the Court otherwise orders.

(4) Except where rule 4 (3) applies, a party to a cause or matter may serve on any other party a notice requiring him to produce the documents specified in the notice at the trial of the cause or matter.

9.5.3.6 *Amendment or withdrawal of an admission*

The court may, upon an appropriate application by the party who has made an admission, permit same to be amended or withdrawn. This is in keeping with Order 27 r (2), RSC which provides as follows:

> An admission made in compliance with a notice under this rule shall not be used against the party by whom it was made in any cause or matter other than the cause or matter for the purpose of which it was made or in favour of any person other than the person by whom the notice was given, and *the Court may at any time allow a party to amend or withdraw an admission so made by him on such terms as may be just.*[301]

In a commentary on a similar Indian provision, it is observed as follows:[302]

> "As a general rule, leave to amend will be granted so as to enable the real question in issue between the parties to be raised on the pleadings, where the amendment will occasion no injury to the opposite party except such as can be sufficiently compensated for by costs or other terms to be imposed by the order. It does not matter whether the original omission arose from negligence or carelessness [...] Broadly stating it, there is no injustice in granting the amendment if the opposite side can be compensated in costs. It is only when costs would not be adequate compensation that amendment will be refused. It is immaterial whether the error sought to be amended was accidental or not. There is no rule limiting amendments to accidental errors [...] The court can allow the plaintiff to amend the plaint by permitting him to substitute one ground or exemption from limitation for another. There is no kind of error or mistake which, if not fraudulent or intended to overreach, the court ought not to correct if it can be done without injustice to the other party. Thus, a plaintiff, in a suit for debt, may be allowed to amend the plaint by setting out an acknowledgement, but is not good ground for refusing the application. Even an admission made by mistake may be allowed to

[301] Italics added.

[302] Mulla, *Code of Civil Procedure,* 13th edn, vol 1, at 726.

be withdrawn, and the pleading amended accordingly.[303]

In *Kenya Cold Storage (1964) Ltd v Overseas Food Services (Africa) Ltd,*[304] the defendant made an application to amend its defence which was filed on September 5, 1975 "to the extent that the amount admitted be reduced to Nil", based on Order VIA rule 3[305] of the Civil Procedure Rules, which provided that the court may at any stage of the proceedings, on such terms as to costs or otherwise as may be just allow each party to amend his pleadings notwithstanding that such an application is made after the expiry of a period of limitation upon which the other party might be entitled to rely, or substitute a party, or alter the capacity in which a party sues or even add or substitute a new cause of action. The Court granted the application, allowing the defence to be amended in all particulars as applied for. The Court further ordered that the defendant pays the costs of the application to the plaintiff and that such costs be taxed and payable forthwith. The Court further considered the case to be a fit and proper one in which to order, as it did, the defendant to deposit in court the amount represented by the retracted admission. The foregoing notwithstanding, the application to withdraw or amend an admission may still not be granted. In *Gale v Superdrug Stores Plc,*[306] Waite U, observed as regards the use of the court's discretion in the face of an application to withdraw an admission:'I prefer Mr Vineall's submission that the discretion is a general one in which all the circumstances have to be taken into account, and a balance struck between the prejudice suffered by each side if the admission is allowed to be withdrawn (or made to stand as the case may be).' Thus, it has been observed in *International Life Insurance Co (UK) Ltd v Chimanbhai Jethabhai Amin,*[307] that '[a] party will not normally be allowed to retract a pleaded admission unless it was made under a genuine mistake of fact, and then leave will normally only be granted on terms.'[308] O'Hare and Browne[309] observe that any judge faced with an application for withdrawal or/and amendment of an admission ought to, in considering whether to grant such an application, the following matters:[310]

- The grounds upon which the applicant seeks to withdraw the admission including whether or not new evidence has come to light which was not available at the time the admission was made.
- The conduct of the parties, including any conduct which led the party making the admission to do so.
- The prejudice that may be caused to any person if the admission is withdrawn

[303] See *Hollis v Burton* (1892) 8 Ch 226 at 236.

[304] Civil Case No 414 of 1975.

[305] As cited in *Kenya Cold Storage (1964) Ltd v Overseas Food Services (Africa) Ltd* Civil Case No 414 of 1975.

[306] [1996] 1 WLR 1089 at 1097H.

[307] Civil Application No NBI 12 of 1968 (unreported), The Court of Appeal for East Africa *per* Law J A (as he then was).

[308] See also *Hollis v Burton* [1892] 3 Ch 226.

[309] O'Hare and Browne, *Civil Litigation* 276; See also English Practice Direction No 14 para 7.2

[310] As adapted in Matibini P, *Zambian Civil Procedure* 606-607.

- The prejudice that may be caused to any person if the application is refused.
- The stage in the proceedings at which the application to withdraw is made, in particular in relation to the date or period fixed for trial.
- The prospect of success (if the admission is withdrawn) of the claim or part of the claim in relation to which the offer was made.
- The interests of the administration of justice.

In *Wooland v Stopford and others,*[311] the [plaintiff] appealed against a decision allowing a defendant to withdraw an admission of liability. As a child she had got into difficulties during a class swimming lesson, and had ceased to breathe leaving her with catastrophic hypoxic brain injury. There had been confusion about the involvement of the Swimming Teachers' Association. The claimant said that there had been no new evidence to justify the court allowing the withdrawal. It was held as follows: The appeal failed. The judge had impeccably applied the law, and carefully exercised his discretion. He was entitled to the conclusion he had reached, and the court could not disturb it.

In *Keith Thomas Sollit v DJ Broady Limited and TD Broady Investments Ltd*[312] the question at the heart of [the] appeal [...] was whether the Recorder was right in a judgment handed down on 18 May 1999 to refuse permission to the first defendant to withdraw pleaded admissions of fact and an admission of liability. On that decision, on the unusual facts of this case, depended the injured claimant's chance of recovering any of the damages to which he was in principle entitled. On 1 June 1994 Mr Sollitt was employed by a company named Tolent Construction Limited. He was working on a site at Hull when he was hit and injured by the bucket of an excavator operated by an employee of another company. On 3 June 1994, just two days after the accident, Mr Sollitt's employers, Tolent, wrote to DJ Broady Limited at 122, Stoneferry Road, Hull, complaining that this accident had been caused by the negligence of a Mr Neylon, an employee of D J Broady Limited, who had been driving the excavator at the time, and Tolent gave notice of a claim [...] It is necessary to diverge from the chronology to explain the confusion in company names which lies at the heart of this case. On 28 January 1963 a company was incorporated by the name DJ Broady Limited. It was a substantial company. This is the company for which the driver of the excavator worked on 1 June 1994. On 15 September 1995 this company did two things. First, it sold its assets for a very substantial consideration to another company, Deamcrest Limited, to whom it did not transfer its liabilities. Secondly, it changed its name to TD Broady Investments Limited ("Investments"), although before 15 September 1995 it was not known by that name. Deamcrest Limited was incorporated on 18 August 1995. On 15 September 1995 it changed its name to DJ Broady Limited ("DJB"). On that date it acquired the assets of Investments. The employees of

[311] [2011] EWCA Civ. 266 as adapted at https://swarb.co.uk/*woodland-v-stopford-and-others*-ca-16-mar-2011/ retrieved on 02/01/22.

[312] February 23, 2000 CAhttps://www.bailii.org/ew/cases/EWCA/Civ/2000/450.html retrieved on 02/01/2022; see also in *Floviis v Pouley* [2002] EWHC 2886.

Investments were transferred to it and Mr Wakefield, who had formerly been a director of Investments, became the general manager of DJB. Thus, by the time the proceedings were issued on 17 May 1996 the name of the company for which the negligent excavator driver had worked at the time of the accident was borne by a different corporate entity. In law of course the liability to Mr Sollitt (if there was such a liability) lay with Investments. DJB was not at that date in existence. But DJB had admitted that the excavator driver had worked for it at the material time and that he had been negligent. In the event, the confusion over names having been realised, the new company applied to withdraw its earlier admission, and to have the claimant's employer joined to the proceedings. As it turned out however, the claimant's employer was by this time a company in name only bereft of any assets and in want of insurance. The court declined to grant the application to withdraw the admission but granted the application to add the co-defendant as sought. Ultimately, judgment for a sum of £10,000.00 was entered against the two companies, and the appeal dismissed.

9.5.3.7 *Consequences of refusal or neglect to make an admission*

There are cost implications to a party of refusing to admit or neglect to so do consequent to being served with a notice to admit. This is set out in the rules of procedure as follows:

According to Order 62 r 6(7), RSC:

> If a party on whom a notice to admit facts is served under Order 27, rule 2, refuses or neglects to admit the facts within 14 days after the service on him of the notice or such longer time as may be allowed by the Court, the costs of proving the facts and the costs occasioned by and thrown away as a result of his failure to admit the facts shall be borne by him.

According to Order XXI r 3, HCR:

> In case of refusal or neglect to admit after notice, the costs of proof of the document or fact shall be paid by the party refusing or neglecting to admit, whatever be the result of the suit, unless the Court or a Judge is of opinion that the refusal or neglect to admit was reasonable.

According to Order XVI r 3, SCR:

> In case of refusal or neglect to admit after notice, the costs of proof of the document or fact shall be paid by the party refusing or neglecting to admit, whatever be the result of the suit, unless the court is of opinion that the refusal or neglect to admit was reasonable.

In *Lipkin Gorman v Karpnale Limited,*[313] the plaintiff firm of solicitors sought to recover money which had been stolen from them by a partner, and then gambled away with the defendant. He had purchased their gaming chips, and the plaintiff argued that these, being gambling debts, were worthless, and that therefore no consideration had been given. It was held that the casino's defence succeeded. The defence against a restitutionary claim that the defendant had altered his position was available to a person who had changed his position acting in good faith so that it would be inequitable to require him to make restitution [for facts not admitted].

In *Baden v Société Générale Pour Favoiser le Development du commerce et de Industrie enFrance SA*[314] Mr Georges Baden, Jacques Delvaux and Ernest Lecuit were liquidators of the Luxembourg Mutual Investment Fund (FOF Proprietary Funds Ltd, along with a fund of funds, Venture Fund (International) NV, and IOS Growth Fund Ltd, all mutual 'dollar funds'). They claimed that Société Générale owed it $4,009,697.91, which it held for its customer, the Bahamas Commonwealth Bank Ltd in a trust account. On 10 May 1973, it followed BCB's instructions, in arrangement with Algemene Bank, Amsterdam, transferred the money to Banco Nacional de Panama, to a non-trust account in BCB's name. This, claimed Baden, made Société Générale a constructive trustee, and so had a duty to account. Alternatively, Société Générale was claimed to owe a duty of care, and to be liable in damages for the loss suffered. It was held in parts relevant to our discussion that the court had inherent jurisdiction to determine the reasonableness of a party contesting some of the facts stated in the Notice to Admit but not others and to apply the rule as regards costs as respects facts which ought to have been admitted but were not.

[313] [1989] 1 WLR 1340; excerpted from https://swarb.co.uk/lipkin-gorman-a-firm-v-karpnale-ltd-hl-6-jun-1991/ retrieved on 02/01/22.

[314] [1993] 1 WLR 501.

10

ILLEGALLY OR UNFAIRLY OBTAINED EVIDENCE

10.1 Introduction

Conventional wisdom tells us that adjudication, however, performed, that is, whether inquisitorial as in the civil law jurisdictions or adversarial as in all common law jurisdictions, is done by courts of law. By their very nature, courts are required and expected to be fair and just; to ensure that justice is not only done but seen to be done. This is exemplified in the Latin maxim, *Fīat jūstitia ruat cælum*: "Let justice be done though the heavens fall." It is indicative of the belief that justice ought to be realised irrespective of consequences thereof. It therefore falls to reason that courts will not preside over resolving disputes borne of illegal transactions. They will not enforce illegality simply because if they did, justice would be tainted, the dignity of the courts offended and illegality condoned with cataclysmic consequences for the entire edifice of the justice system as we know it.

Thus, when it comes to a specific area of the law such as the adjectival law of evidence, one can rightfully ask whether, based on the preceding, there is, and if not, there ought to be a rule providing for the exclusion of evidence on the basis that said evidence was obtained illegally. Examples of illegality may include, but are not limited to misrepresentation, fraud, undue influence, duress, a criminal enterprise, tortious action or contravention of rules regulating police conduct in interviews.

That the question should be asked at all is indicative of the intestinal struggle within the law of evidence. On the one hand, is the general rule relating to relevance and admissibility: all evidence that is relevant is admissible irrespective of the manner it was obtained as such a consideration, even where the manner of obtaining such evidence is illegal, is immaterial so far as the case before court is concerned. This argument can be stretched thus: illegality predicating the manner in which evidence is obtained in no way justifies setting the accused at liberty.[1] What it may warrant is remedial action against the perpetrators of such illegality. On the other hand, is the school of thought that prizes adherence to legality at every stage of the criminal justice system

[1] See *Liswaniso v The People*[1976] ZR 277; See also *Karuma, Son of Kania v R* (1955) AC 197; (1955) 1 All ER 236.

based on what are recognised as fundamental rights.[2] The basis of this position is that even the slightest toleration of illegality in general and in particular the encouragement of deployment of illegal methods by the police to extract evidence is a sliding scale which, in the grand scheme of things, is a greater evil than the escape of the occasional criminal.

10.2 The American response

The American system predicates its approach, as we have seen elsewhere in this text, on the 4th amendment to the US Constitution which provides as follows:

> The right of the people to be secure in their persons, houses, papers, and effects, against unreasonable searches and seizures, shall not be violated, and no Warrants shall issue, but upon probable cause, supported by Oath or affirmation, and particularly describing the place to be searched, and the persons or things to be seized.

US courts have taken a strict adherence or rigid approach to, where same is apparent, the exclusion of the 'fruits of the poisonous tree.' As stressed in *Mapp v Ohio,*[3] '[...] the purpose of the exclusionary rule 'is to deter – to compel respect for the constitutional [guarantee] [against illegal searches] in the only effectively available way-by removing the incentive to disregard it.' The US position demonstrates what has been described in *Leon v US*[4]as:

> [t]he tension between the sometimes-competing goals of, on the one hand, deterring official misconduct and removing inducements to unreasonable invasions of privacy and, on the other, establishing procedures under which criminal defendants are "acquitted or convicted on the basis of all the evidence which exposes the truth.[5]

---

[2] *Mapp v Ohio* (1961) 367 U.S. 643; *Weeks v United States* (1914) 232 I.S. 383; *State v Reynolds* (1924) 101 Conn. 224; *The People v Defoe* (1926) 242 N.Y. 413; *Cupp v Murphy* (1973) 412 US 29; *King v R* (1968) 2 All ER 610; *R v Doyle* (1 888) 12 Ont. R. 347; *R v Honan* (1912) 26 Ont. L.R. 484; *R v Duroussel* (1933) 2 D.L.R. 446; *Attorney-General for Quebec v Begin* (1955) 5 D.L.R. 394; *Emperor v Alladad Khan* (1913) I.L.R. 350 11-258; *Emperor v Ali Ahmed Khan* (1923) I.L.R. 46 A 11-86; *Chwa Hum Htive v King Emperor* (1926) ILR 11 Rang. 107; *Larrie v Muir* (1950) Scots LT 37; *McGovern v HM Advocate* (1950) Scots LT 133; *Jones v Owen* (1870) 34 JP 759; *The People (AG) v O'Brien* (1965) IR 142; see Justice Peter Chitengi, 'Implications of illegally obtained evidence and its effect on human rights of accused persons,' A paper presented to a workshop on human rights law on 15th July, 1998: https://allafrica.com/stories/199807160038.html; Jamil Ddamulira Mujuzi, 'The admissibility of evidence obtained through human rights violations in Zambia: Revisiting *Liswaniso v The People* (1976) Zambia Law Reports 277,' The International Journal of Evidence and Proof, Volume: 23 issue: 3, page(s): 316-329 available at https://journals.sagepub.com/doi/abs/10.1177/1365712719831716?journalCode=epja; For recent criticism of this decision from a Zambian Human rights perspective see J Chirwa, "The Admissibility of Derivative Evidence in Zambia in Light of Human Rights Obligations and the Need to Discard Liswaniso Versus The People (1976) ZR 277": https://www.linkedin.com/pulse/admissibility-derivative-evidence-zambia-light-human-rights-chirwa/ retrieved on 25/09/2021; see also *Karuma, Son of Kania v R* (1955) AC 197; (1955) 1 All ER 236.

[3] 67 U.S. 643 (1961) at 656 which quoted with approval, *Elikins v US* 364 US 206 (1960) at 217.

[4] 468 U.S. 897, (1984) *per*Justice White.

[5] *Alderman v United States,* 394 U.S. 165, 175, 89 S.Ct. 961, 967, 22 L.Ed.2d 176 (1969).

10.3 The English position

10.3.1 General

The English position with respect to the treatment of illegally obtained evidence has been to admit all relevant evidence. The task of implementing the competing policy relating to the protection of the accused from unfair and unlawful methods by the police is left to the individual judges in individual cases. As we see later, the discretion to exclude evidence was recognised in *R v Christie,*[6] by the House of Lords, and said dicta has been followed in different commonwealth jurisdictions.[7] These decisions have all but focused on the judge's power to exclude otherwise admissible evidence where there is a basis, specifically, that admittance of such evidence would prejudice the accused or otherwise result in an unfair trial. In the leading authority of *R v Sang*[8]which we consider in greater detail below, the House of Lords accepted the existence of the judge's general discretion to control the deployment of evidence for purposes of ensuring fairness. It further noted that the much narrower discretion, as it had existed at common law, had been placed on a statutory footing by a much wider discretion in s 78 of the Police and Criminal Evidence Act 1984 (PACE).[9] As regards, civil proceedings, the question of an explicit exclusionary discretion is now to be found in r 32.1 which was introduced as part of the new Civil Procedure Rules (CPR) in the year 1997.

We must turn to briefly discussing the nature of the discretion in general before discussing the discretion to exclude otherwise relevant evidence in criminal proceedings; the discretion to exclude otherwise relevant evidence in civil proceedings; and appeals.

10.3.1.1 Nature of the discretion

As with almost every aspect of the law evidence discussed above and below, there always lies the danger, real and present, of a loose employment of terminology which leads to confusion in the appreciation and application of terms be they of art or law. The term 'discretion' is in this respect not different, and as such, not immune to this tendency, that is, it being used in different contexts or senses[10] thus breeding confusion, as we demonstrate shortly. First off, there ought to be a recognition of the fine distinction, on the one hand, of the thinking that the judge has the power to decide on the facts brought before him of a term that to all intents and purposes is vague, and on the other, the

[6] (1914) 10 Cr App Rep 141, 149.

[7] See similar dicta in *Festa v R* [2001] HCA 72, 208 CLR 593 *per* Gleeson CJ; *R v Juric* [2002] VSCA 77, 129 ACR 408.

[8] [1980] AC 402.

[9] This has been followed in the criminal law, by the enactment of the Criminal Justice Act 2003 which has in s 114(1)(d), enacted explicit inclusionary discretion with respect to hearsay; see also pronouncements by the EWCA in *R v Renda* [2005] EWCA Crim 2826, [2006] 2 All ER 553 of its willingness to admit evidence of bad character of the accused on similar principles.

[10] See Pattenden *Judicial Discretion and Criminal Litigation* (1990).

postulation that the judge is at liberty to decide as he sees fit on the facts before him. In the former case, the judge is expected and required to act in a particular way once he finds the relevant facts. In the latter, he is free to act as he sees fit based on the facts before him. The indiscriminate use of the term has been all the rage. In *R v Renda*[11] the EWCA has observed in part that it '[...] will adopt the same general approach to appeals from the judgment of a trial judge in the specific factual context of an individual case as apply to appeals from the exercise of a judicial discretion. The trial judge's 'feel' for the case is usually the critical ingredient of the decision at first instance so that context is therefore vital [....]' The importance of the dichotomy and the irritation its indiscriminate use has wrought is not only limited to views expressed by academics[12] but courts. In the latter instance, two authorities are worthy of consideration. The first is *R v Viola.*[13] The appellant was charged with rape. The alleged rape occurred in the complainant's flat shortly before midnight after the appellant, who was acquainted with the complainant, had sought refuge in her flat because he was having trouble with the police over the driving of a car. The only issue at the trial was whether the complainant had consented to sexual intercourse with the appellant. After the complainant had given evidence-in-chief the appellant applied to the trial judge, under s 2a of the Sexual Offences (Amendment) Act 1976, for leave to cross-examine her regarding two incidents concerning her sexual relations with other men shortly before and shortly after the alleged rape. The judge refused leave to cross-examine the complainant about those incidents because he was not 'satisfied that it would be unfair to [the] defendant to refuse to allow' the cross-examination, within s 2(2) of the 1976 Act. The appellant was convicted. He appealed against the conviction on the ground that the judge erred in law in refusing to allow the cross-examination. It was held as follows: (1) The test whether a trial judge should give a defendant leave under s 2(2) of the 1976 Act to cross-examine a complainant about her sexual experience with other men was whether the proposed cross-examination was relevant to the defendant's case according to the common law rules of evidence, and if so whether the judge was satisfied that it was more likely than not that the cross-examination, if allowed, might reasonably lead the jury to take a different view of the complainant's evidence. However, since the purpose of s 2 was to protect a complainant from questions which went merely to her credit, as a general rule a judge ought not to allow cross-examination which merely sought to establish that because the complainant had had sexual experience with other men she ought not to be believed under oath. If, on the other hand, the cross-examination was relevant to an issue in the trial such as consent, it ought usually to be allowed.[14] (2) A trial judge's decision to exclude or allow the proposed cross-examination under s 2 was an exercise of his

[11] [2006] 2 All ER 553, [2006] 1 WLR 2948, [2006] 1 Cr App R 380.

[12] See Cross (1979) 30 NILQ 289, 294 in his criticism of the use of the term "discretion" by Lord Edmund Davies in *D v National Society for the prevention of cruelty to Children* [1978] AC 171, [1977] 1 All ER 589; 246, 618 to describe the judge's duty to perform the expected balancing act.

[13] [1982] 3 All ER 73, [1982] 1 WLR 1138, 75Cr App Rep 125, [1982] Crim LR 515.

[14] *R v Mills* (1978) 68 Cr App R 327 followed; *R v Lawrence* [1977] Crim LR 492 approved.

judgment, and not of his discretion, and therefore the Court of Appeal, which was in as good a position as the trial judge to reach a conclusion on the matter, could substitute its own conclusion for that of the trial judge if it thought that he had been wrong.[15] (3) In all the circumstances the incidents regarding the complainant's sexual relations with other men were relevant to the issue of consent and could not be regarded as so trivial or of so little relevance to that issue that the judge was entitled to conclude that no injustice would be done to the appellant if cross-examination about them was excluded. It followed that the judge had been wrong to exclude the cross-examination, and the appeal would accordingly be allowed and the conviction quashed.

The holding at (2) is of particular importance as regards our current discussion. Concerning the question of discretion, Lord Lane CJ observed as follows:

> We would further like to say this about the judgment in *R v Mills*[16] and say it with the greatest possible deference to that court. It has been agreed on all hands, not only by the appellant and by the Crown but also by counsel who has assisted us as amicus curiae, that it is wrong to speak of a judge's 'discretion' in this context. The judge has to make a judgment whether he is satisfied or not in the terms of s 2. But once having reached his judgment on the particular facts, he has no discretion. If he comes to the conclusion that he is satisfied it would be unfair to exclude the evidence, then the evidence has to be admitted and the questions have to be allowed.

The second authority is that of *R v Hasan.*[17] Hasan was charged with the crime of aggravated burglary. He was associated with a gang and relied on the defence of duress, pleading that he was blackmailed into committing the burglary to prevent his family from being harmed. The issue for determination was whether the defence of duress was available to Hasan and whether his statement to the police when arrested was admissible evidence under s 76 of the Police and Criminal Evidence Act 1984 (the Act) and deemed to be a confession. The court held that the defence of duress was unavailable for Hasan because of his voluntary gang association and as such, he should have foreseen or ought to have foreseen the risk of being subjected to compulsion to commit criminal offences. While he may not have foreseen that he would be compelled to commit a burglary, his association with the gang and other persons with a tendency to commit unlawful acts was enough to exclude the defence. Further, the court found that his confession (argued by the defence to be inadmissible evidence contrary to s 76 of the Act, was initially intended to be neutral on the face of it. However, its contents became damaging at trial

[15] Dictum of Roskill LJ in *R v Mills* (1978) 68 Cr App R at 330 considered.

[16] (1978) 68 Cr App R 327.

[17] [2005] UKHL 22, [2005] 2 AC 467, [53]; summary with a few modifications, taken from https://www.lawteacher.net/cases/r-v-hasan.php retrieved on 21/12/21; see also *R v Chalkley* [1998] QB 848, [1998] 2 All ER 155; 874D, 178d.

when it was clear that it was inconsistent with the defence of duress Hasan was relying on. Therefore, it was admissible evidence under s 76(1) of the Act. The appeal was allowed and the conviction upheld. As regards the operation of s 78,[18] the Court observed in similar terms to those in *R v Viola*[19]as follows:

> [a]lthough it is formally cast in the form of a discretion ('the court may') the objective criterion whether 'the evidence would have such an adverse effect on the fairness of the proceedings' in truth imports a judgment whether in the light of the statutory criterion of fairness the court ought to admit the evidence.

There are several consequences that arise from the preceding authorities and the distinction that they intimated, ought to be made therein. In *Evans v Bartland*,[20] the appellant owed to the respondent (a bookmaker) a certain sum in respect of unsuccessful bets on horse races, and was alleged to have agreed with the respondent's agent that, in consideration of the respondent not pressing his claim for a short period, and refraining from causing the appellant to be declared a defaulter at Tattersalls, the appellant would pay the debt within a reasonable time. The respondent later brought an action against the appellant upon his promise to pay. The writ was served personally upon the appellant, who did not enter an appearance, and judgment was signed against him in default of appearance. In response to a request by the respondent's solicitor for payment of the sum due under the judgment, the appellant asked for time to pay, which was granted. Thereafter, the appellant made an application to have the judgment set aside, and for leave to defend the action. The application was dismissed by the master; on appeal the judge in chambers granted the application and gave leave to defend upon terms. The Court of Appeal, by a majority,[21] directed that the order of the master be restored:—holding that there was no reason to interfere with the discretion of the judge in chambers, who thought it proper to set aside the judgment and, unless it was clear that the judge's discretion was wrongly exercised, his order should be affirmed.[22]

---

[18] Which provides for 'Exclusion of unfair evidence' in the following terms: (1) In any proceedings the court may refuse to allow evidence on which the prosecution proposes to rely to be given if it appears to the court that, having regard to all the circumstances, including the circumstances in which the evidence was obtained, the admission of the evidence would have such an adverse effect on the fairness of the proceedings that the court ought not to admit it. (2) Nothing in this section shall prejudice any rule of law requiring a court to exclude evidence.

[19] [1982] 3 All ER 73, [1982] 1 WLR 1138, 75Cr App Rep 125, [1982] Crim LR 515.

[20] [1937] AC 473, [1937] 2 All ER 646.

[21] Greer LJ dissenting.

[22] Order of Court of Appeal [1936] 1 KB 202 set aside, and an order of Greaves-Lord J restored; Editor's notes: The foundation of the doctrine of approbation and reprobation is that the person against whom it is applied has accepted a benefit from the matter he reprobates. Similarly, the foundation of estoppel by representation is that by the conduct of one party the other has altered his position to his disadvantage. To ask for a stay of execution is not a process by which the person asking obtains a benefit from the judgment nor does the opposing party if the stay is granted alter his position to his detriment. Therefore, asking for time to pay the amount due under a judgment in default of defence does not prevent a party from applying to have the judgment set aside; As to Setting Aside Judgment by Default, see Halsbury (Hailsham Edn), Vol 19, pp 263, 264, para 562; and for Cases, see Digest, Practice, pp 391–393, Nos 948–970.

That said, the extensive powers that an appellate court has to review a lower court's discretion pale in comparison to those that it is clothed with when dealing with the incorrect application of a rule by a lower court. Thus, in *Charles Osenton & Co v Johnson,*[23] the plaintiff entrusted the defendants, the appellants in this appeal, with the development of certain land as a housing estate. He subsequently brought an action against them for breach of contract and for negligence in the performance of the obligations thus undertaken. Negligence was alleged in many matters in connection with the lay-out of the estate, more especially in respect of the system of drainage recommended by them and the density of houses on the estate. The plaintiff applied for an order under the Supreme Court of Judicature (Consolidation) Act 1925, s 89(b) that the action be referred to an official referee, on the ground that it could not be conveniently tried by a judge. It was contended that, having regard to the number of plans to be examined, the technical nature of the questions involved, and the need for local investigation, the matter was a proper one for trial by an official referee. On the other hand it was contended that, as, under the Administration of Justice Act 1932, s 1, the official referee's decision on a question of fact would be final, it was not a proper exercise of the court's discretion to refer a case where charges of negligence were alleged against professional persons:—holding that an action in which the character or professional ability of a person is attacked, should not be referred to an official referee unless a prolonged examination of accounts or scientific or local investigation renders such a course necessary. The facts here did not show such an investigation to be necessary, and the exercise of the discretion of the court by which the action had been referred to an official referee was a wrongful exercise of that discretion which an appellate court ought to correct.[24]

Giving his view in *Cookson v Knowles,*[25] Lord Diplock made an explicit distinction between the role of an appellate court as regards a rule on the one hand, and discretion on the other in the following terms:

---

[23] [1942] AC 130, [1941] 2 All ER 245; see also *Cookson v Knowles* [1979] AC 556, [1978] 2 All ER 604; 566, 607; *R v Chung* (1991) 92 Cr App Rep 314, 323.

[24] Decision of the Court of Appeal (Slesser LJ and Singleton J, Clauson LJ dissenting) ([1940] 2 All ER 503) reversed; Editor's notes: The Administration of Justice Act 1932, restricted the right of appeal from the decision of an official referee, making his finding upon any question of fact final. The House of Lords have here held that, where a charge of fraud or a charge of negligence is made against professional persons, this restriction on the right of appeal makes it a case which, prima facie should not be referred to an official referee. The serious nature of such a charge makes it desirable that the person charged should have the right to have the matter tried by a High Court judge with the opportunity of appeal on any question of fact which would then be available. Although the court has a discretion to refer such a case, the exercise of that discretion in the circumstances of the present case, was a wrongful exercise thereof and one which the appellate court ought to correct; The House has expressed its views upon many matters arising under the Supreme Court of Judicature (Consolidation) Act 1925, s 89(b) which are probably not necessary for the decision in this case. Though these matters are, therefore, strictly obiter, they are of considerable importance in a matter of practice, as this is, and among them the distinction between matters of account and the prolonged examination of documents or scientific or local investigation should be specially noted;' As to Referring Action to Official Referee, see Halsbury (Hailsham Edn), Vol 26, p 87, para 158; and for Cases, see Digest, Practice, pp 567, 568, 245Nos 2250–2253. See Yearly Practice of The Supreme Court 1940, pp 622–625.

[25] [1979] AC 556, [1978] 2 All ER 604; 566, 607; *R v Chung* (1991) 92 Cr App Rep 314, 323.

> It is therefore appropriate for an appellate court to lay down guidelines as to what matters it is proper for the judge to take into account in deciding how to exercise the discretion conferred on him by the statute. In exercising this appellate function, the court is not expounding a rule of law from which a judge is precluded from departing where special circumstances exist in a particular case; nor indeed, even in cases where there are no special circumstances, is an appellate court justified in giving effect to the preference of its members for exercising the discretion in a different way from that adopted by the judge if the choice between the alternative ways of exercising it is one on which judicial opinion might reasonably differ.

Additionally, an appellate court is unlikely to consider on appeal, exercising an exclusionary initial discretion on a matter not put to trial in the court below.[26] As a general rule, where the trial judge has '[...] not [erred] in law, [taken] into account all relevant matters and [excluded] consideration of irrelevant matters'[27] the discretion he exercises at trial will still stand. In order to persuade an appellate court to interfere with the exercise of discretion by a court of first instance,[28] it will have to be proved that the court below failed to exercise discretion;[29] exercised discretion in disregard of a principle;[30] exercised its discretion under mistake of law;[31] took into consideration irrelevant matters;[32] or that as shown in *G v G*,[33] the conclusion drawn by the court of first instance in its exercise of jurisdiction was 'outside the generous ambit within which a reasonable disagreement is possible.' According to Charles J in *Diamond v The Standard Bank of South Africa Limited (Executor) and Others*:[34]

> It follows that, if there is a distinction between appeals in respect of discretionary judgments or orders and appeals in respect of non-discretionary judgments or orders, the concern of an appellate court on an appeal relating to an order under the Act is that which arises on appeals in respect of any non-discretionary judgment or order. That concern is whether the judgment or order of the court below was wrong in principle or application of the relevant law, whether its findings of primary facts were supported by the evidence and by a proper approach to the evidence, and whether its conclusions from the primary facts were correct. It may be noted in passing that if there

[26] See *R v Goldenberg* (1988) 88 Cr App Rep 285, 289; *R v Kempster* [1989] 1 WLR 1125, 90 Cr App Rep 14; *Braham v DPP* (1994) 159 JP 527; *R v Mullen* [2000] QB 520, [1999] 2 Cr App Rep 143.

[27] *R v Scarrott* [1978] QB 1016, [1978] 1 All ER 672; 1028, 681; applied to the s 78 discretion hereinbefore considered and considered in *R v Rankin* (1995) The Times, 5 September; *R v Webster* (12 December 2000, unreported) CA, [20].

[28] See Order 59 r 1 (142), RSC.

[29] *Growther v Eglood* [1887] 34 Ch D 691.

[30] *Young v Thomas* [1892] 2 Ch D 691.

[31] *Evans v Bartland* [1937] AC 473.

[32] *Egrerton v Jones* [1939] 3 All ER 889.

[33] [1985] 1 WLR 647.

[34] [1965] ZR 61 at 66; Blagden CJ and Pickett J concurred.

> is a distinction between the two classes of approach it is not as to the concern of the appellate court but only in the scope afforded to the appellate court to manifest its concern: with either class the appellate court will allow the appeal if it is satisfied that the trial judge was wrong.[35]

Special mention must be made of the approach as respects criminal proceedings which we consider shortly below. The appellate court will only interfere if the discretion exercised by the judge is one that no reasonable judge properly applying his mind to the facts before him would have so exercised.[36] Whether the appeal relating to discretion succeeds is dependent on several factors which we have already touched on above. To state with some specificity, however, where a judge duly notes specific factors enumerated for his consideration, he reduces the prospects of being overturned on appeal.[37] The opposite is also true.[38] Further to the preceding, it is more likely that an appellate court will overturn an inclusionary rule predicated on statutory provisions.[39] It would logically follow from the preceding that while the exercise of appellate jurisdiction with respect to the exercise of discretion by the court below would be to exclude otherwise admissible evidence, it cannot, as has been shown in *Myers v DPP*,[40] be deployed to admit evidence which, in and of itself, would ordinarily be inadmissible. The appellant was convicted together with another accused on counts of conspiracy, and he was convicted on several counts of receiving stolen property. The case for the prosecution was that he would buy wrecked motor cars with their log books, and then would disguise stolen cars, which were as nearly identical as possible to the wrecked cars, so that they conformed with the details of the log books of the wrecked cars. In so doing he removed from the wrecked cars the small plates which contained the engine and chassis numbers and transferred them to the stolen cars. To prove their case the prosecution called, among their witnesses, persons who had owned the stolen cars and who were able to identify them by peculiar marks and also insurance assessors who had, after accidents, examined some of the wrecked cars and who testified that such cars were not those that the appellant had sold. The appellant's defence was that he had repaired the wrecked cars and sold them. At the trial the learned judge permitted the prosecution to adduce evidence of a witness in charge of the records that were kept of every car built at a manufacturer's works. At the works when each car was being completed a workman filled in a card which contained the engine and chassis

[35] See *Ward v James* [1965] 1 All ER 56 at 570 *per* Lord Denning MR pro Cur.

[36] *R v Quinn* [1995] 1 Cr App Rep 480, 489C; *R v Miller* [1998] Crim LR 209; but see *R v Duffy* [1998] Crim LR 650 which espouses a relatively less stringent requirement of it having been 'incumbent' on the judge to exercise his jurisdiction.

[37] *Yates v Thakeham Tiles Ltd* [1995] PIQR P135.

[38] See *Stanoevsky v R* [2001] HCA 4, (2001) 202 CLR 115; *DPP v Clarkson* [1996] CLTY 1124.

[39] Compare ss 114(1)(d) or 116(2)(e) of the Criminal Justice Act 2003: *CfR v Radak* [1999] 1 Cr App Rep 187; for rules that are rigidly drafted, requiring the construction of guidelines for the exercise of a discretion designed to avoid injustice, see *R v Britzman* [1983] 1 All ER 369, [1983] 1 WLR 350; 373, 355.

[40] [1965] AC 1001, [1964] 2 All ER 881; 1024, 887; but see *R v Greasby* [1984] Crim LR 488.

number of the car and also the cylinder block number. This block number was indelibly stamped on the engine and could not be removed. The cards were microfilmed and then destroyed. The relevant microfilms were extracted and the numbers were scheduled for the purpose of the trial. The schedules and films were produced on oath by the witness; these schedules showed that the cylinder block numbers of the cars in question belonged to the stolen cars. On appeal on the ground that the production of these records was inadmissible as hearsay, it was held as follows: (i)[41] the records of the cylinder block numbers were tendered in evidence in order to prove the truth of the facts recorded, viz, that the cylinder block of a particular car when manufactured bore a particular number, and this evidence was hearsay evidence which could not be brought within any established exception to the rule that hearsay evidence was inadmissible, for the records were not public records and, although they had been made in the course of duty and contemporaneously, it was not shown that the persons who made them had died; therefore (Lord Pearce and Lord Donovan dissenting) the evidence ought not to have been admitted, since its reception would involve an alteration of the existing law, which, despite the technicalities of this branch of the common law, at the present day required the intervention of the legislature, and was not for the court to effect.[42] (ii) since, however, a reasonable jury, properly directed, would without doubt have convicted the appellant, the proviso to s 4(1) of the Criminal Appeal Act, 1907, should be applied and the appeal would be dismissed.[43] Lord Reid observed as follows in his speech:

> In argument the Solicitor General maintained that, although the general rule may be against the admission of private records to prove the truth of entries in them, the trial judge has a discretion to admit a record in a particular case if satisfied that it is trustworthy, and that justice requires its admission. That appears to me to be contrary to the whole framework of the existing law. *It is true that a judge has a discretion to exclude legally admissible evidence if justice so requires, but it is a very different thing to say that he has a discretion to admit legally inadmissible evidence.* The whole development of the exceptions to the hearsay rule is based on the determination of certain classes of evidence as admissible or inadmissible and not on the apparent credibility of particular evidence tendered.[44] No matter how cogent

---

[41] *Per* Lord Reid, Lord Morris Of Borth-Y-Gest and Lord Hodson.

[42] *Sturla v Freccia* ((1880), 5 App Cas 623) considered; Dictum of Lord Herschell LC in *Woodward v Goulstone* ([1886–90] All ER Rep at p 239) applied; Reasoning of the Court of Criminal Appeal in *R v Myers* [1964] 1 All ER 877 disapproved.

[43] Dictum of Viscount Simon LC in *Stirland v Director of Public Prosecutions* ([1944] 2 All ER at p 15) applied; Editor's notes: It was not in dispute that the log books of the cars were admissible in evidence as public documents, but they did not record the cylinder block numbers; As to hearsay evidence, see 10 Halsbury's Laws (3rd Edn) 467, para 857; 15 Halsbury's Laws (3rd Edn) 294, para 533; and for cases on the subject, see 14 Digest (Repl) 507, 508, 4909–4926; 22 Digest (Repl) 71–74, 463–485, 307, 3179–3186.

[44] See a further discussion of the inclusionary or/and exclusionary rule as respects discretion with specific reference to statutory provisions such as s 78 of the Police and Criminal Evidence Act 1984; s 6(2)(a) of the Civil Evidence Act 1995; ss 114(1)(d) and 116(2)(e) of the Criminal Justice Act 2003 in Tapper C, *Cross & Tapper on Evidence* 10th edn (OUP, 2004) 212-213.

> particular evidence may seem to be, unless it comes within a class which is admissible it is excluded. Half a dozen witnesses may offer to prove that they heard two men of high character, who cannot now be found, discuss in detail the fact now in issue and agree on a credible account of it, but that evidence would not be admitted although it might be by far the best evidence available (emphasis added).

A few more points are worthy of note as we end this portion of our discussion. The first is that there is no place for an exclusionary discretion in proceedings where exclusionary rules of evidence are inapplicable. The second is that where the range of material available has been extended by statutory provisions, the tribunal has no power to cut same down by way of discretion.[45] The third which may be seen as an extension of the second point, is one encased in this jurisdiction, in provisions such as s 206[46] and 291[47] of the Criminal Procedure Code[48] that there is not much room for the exercise of an exclusionary rule where the situation involves the court merely determining whether there is a case to answer.[49]

Extradition proceedings appear to be, on authority, treated differently. In *R v Governor of Brixton Prison, ex P Levin,*[50] the appellant was alleged to have used a computer terminal in St Petersburg, Russia, to gain unauthorised access to the computerised fund transfer service of a bank in New Jersey, USA, and make fraudulent transfers of funds from the bank to accounts which he or his associates controlled. He was charged before a Federal District Court in the United States with the Federal offences of wire fraud, bank fraud and misuse of computers and arrested in the United Kingdom on a provisional warrant issued at the request of the United States government. Following his arrest, the Secretary of State issued an order to proceed and at the committal proceedings before the metropolitan stipendiary magistrate the United States government submitted evidence of an accomplice and computer print-outs to identify the means of the fraud and the appellant's part in it. The magistrate held that a prima facie case had been made out against the appellant and ordered that he be detained with a view to his extradition to the United States. The appellant applied for a writ of habeas corpus on the grounds that the evidence submitted to the magistrate did not justify his committal to await extradition but the Divisional Court dismissed his application. He appealed to the House of Lords, contending that the computer print-outs were hearsay and inadmissible in extradition proceedings because such proceedings were not criminal proceedings and therefore s 69(1) of the Police and Criminal Evidence Act 1984 permitting the admissibility in criminal proceedings of statements produced by computers did not apply, alternatively, that if extradition proceedings were criminal proceedings the magistrate should have exercised his discretion under s 78(1)a of the 1984 Act to refuse to allow the computer evidence and the evidence of the accomplice on which the prosecution proposed to rely to be admitted because the admission of the evidence had an adverse effect on

[50] [1997] AC 741, [1997] 3 All ER 289; 748, 295; *Re Proulx* [2001] 1 All ER 57.

the fairness of the proceedings. It was held as follows: For the purposes of the 1984 Act extradition proceedings were criminal proceedings since s 9(2) of and para 6(1) of Sch 1 to the Extradition Act 1989 required that extradition proceedings should be conducted 'as nearly as may be' as if they were committal proceedings before magistrates; since such committal proceedings were criminal proceedings it followed that the normal rules of criminal evidence and procedure applied to extradition proceedings. However, the computer print-outs were not hearsay, and so admissible in any event, because they were tendered to prove the transfers of funds which they recorded 289 and did not assert that such transfers had taken place. Moreover, under s 78(1) of the 1984 Act, which applied to extradition proceedings, the issue was whether the admission of the disputed evidence would have an adverse effect on the fairness of the extradition proceedings themselves, not whether it would have an adverse effect on the fairness of the trial, and magistrates should ordinarily assume that the powers available to the judge at the trial would ensure that the trial was fair. Accordingly, a magistrate hearing extradition proceeding could properly exercise his discretion under s 78 of the 1984 Act to exclude evidence only in very unusual circumstances, e.g., if evidence which was technically admissible had been obtained in a way which outraged civilised values. On the facts, it would have been unreasonable for the magistrate to have refused to admit the computer evidence and the evidence of the accomplice as the admissibility of such evidence was a matter to be raised at the trial of the appellant in the United States. The appeal would therefore be dismissed.[51]

The decision in *R v Governor of Brixton Prison, ex P Levin,*[52] was followed in *R v Bow Street Magistrates' Court and another, ex parte Proulx,*[53] the Canadian police suspected P, who was living in England, of having committed a murder in Canada. In order to obtain evidence, they launched an undercover operation in England with the co-operation of the local police. During the course of that operation, P made statements to a Canadian police officer, confessing to the killing. In subsequent proceedings for P's extradition, the stipendiary magistrate concluded that those confessions satisfied the evidential requirements of s 9(8)a of the Extradition Act 1989, and made an order for P's committal to custody pending the Secretary of State's decision on his return to Canada. P applied for habeas corpus and judicial review, contending that the

---

[51] *Ex p Woodhall* (1888) 20 QBD 832 and *Amand v Secretary of State for Home Affairs* [1942] 2 All ER 381 applied; Dictum of *Beldam LJ in R v King's Lynn Magistrates' Court, ex p Holland* [1993] 2 All ER 377 at 380–381 approved; Dictum of McCowan LJ in *R v Governor of Belmarsh Prison, ex p Francis* [1995] 3 All ER 634 at 639 disapproved; Per curiam. As ordinary committal proceedings have been excluded from the application of s 78 of the 1984 Act by para 26 of Sch 1 to the Criminal Procedure and Investigations Act 1996 it seems likely that the effect of s 9(2) of and para 6(1) of Sch 1 to the 1989 Act is also to exclude extradition proceedings from the application of s 78 of the 1984 Act (see p 291 e f, p 295 a and p 296 c, post); Decision of the Divisional Court [1996] 4 All ER 350 affirmed; Editors notes: For evidence in committal proceedings for extradition, see 18 Halsbury's Laws (4th edn) paras 224–228, and for cases on the subject, see 25 Digest (2nd reissue) 47–50, 229–263; For the Police and Criminal Evidence Act 1984, ss 69, 78, see 17 Halsbury's Statutes (4th edn) (1993 reissue) 222, 228; For the Extradition Act 1989, s 9, Sch 1, para 6, see 17 Halsbury's Statutes (4th edn) (1993 reissue) 572, 609.

[52] [1997] AC 741, [1997] 3 All ER 289; 748, 295; *Re Proulx* [2001] 1 All ER 57.

[53] [2001] 1 All ER 57.

confessions ought to have been excluded under s 76(2)(b)b of the Police and Criminal Evidence Act 1984. That provision required the court to exclude from evidence a confession which was or might have been obtained in consequence of anything said or done which was likely, in the circumstances, to render unreliable 'any confession' which the accused might make 'in consequence thereof'. Alternatively, he contended that the confessions ought to have been excluded under s 78c of the 1984 Act which gave the court a discretion to exclude evidence if, having regard to all the circumstances, including the circumstances in which the evidence was obtained, its admission 'would have such an adverse effect on the fairness of the proceedings that the court ought not to admit it'. In determining those issues, the Divisional Court considered the approach to be adopted on a review of a magistrate's decision on the admissibility of evidence in extradition proceedings. It also considered, inter alia, the meaning of the term 'any confession' in s 76(2)(b) of the 1984 Act. It was held as follows: (1) Provided that a magistrate had correctly directed himself on the law, the Divisional Court would only interfere with his findings of fact and assessment of their significance when ruling on the admissibility of evidence in the extradition context if they were outside the range of conclusions open to a reasonable magistrate. Thus, a magistrate's decision on the admissibility of evidence under s 76 of the 1984 Act, in such a context, would only be reviewed on those grounds. Such an approach was justified by the context of extradition, when any issue of admissibility would be revisited at trial, and by the fact that the statute made the magistrate the primary decision maker.[54] (2) The reference to 'any confession' in s 76(2)(b) of the 1984 Act was to be understood as indicating 'any such' or 'such a' confession as the accused had made. Thus, in the instant case, the relevant confessions were those made by P, and the test in s 76 could not be satisfied by postulating some entirely different confession. Moreover, the magistrate had been entitled to conclude that P's confessions were not obtained as a result of things said or done which were likely in the circumstances to render them unreliable within the meaning of s 76.[55] (3) Where a magistrate was concerned, in extradition proceedings, with the fairness of admitting evidence, he was entitled and bound to have regard to the extradition context in which the issue arose. His decision whether or not to admit the evidence was solely in and for the purpose of his determination on the issue of extradition. The trial judge in the proposed country of trial remained the person who should and would determine the critical issue of the admission of such evidence at trial. Thus, in the instant case, the question for the magistrate had not been whether the confessions would fall to be excluded in a purely English context. Rather, it was whether, bearing in mind that the ultimate issue was whether P should be extradited to stand trial in Canada, the magistrate should under s 78 of the 1984 Act exclude the confessions from consideration as part of the evidence. A magistrate ought only to exclude evidence where to admit it would outrage civilised values. The circumstances of the instant case did not fall within that exceptional class, and the magistrate

[54] *R v Governor of Pentonville Prison, ex p Osman* [1989] 3 All ER 701 applied.

[55] *R v Barry* (1992) Cr App R 384 considered.

had been right to refuse to exclude the confessions under s 78. Accordingly, the applications would be dismissed.[56]

10.3.1.2 Discretion to exclude otherwise relevant evidence in criminal proceedings

The leading authority in this regard is *Kuruma Son of Kaniu v R.*[57] The appellant, a Kenyan, was stopped at a police road block and was searched by two police officers. This was illegal because neither of them was of the rank of inspector or above as required by law. The police alleged that they found a pocket knife and two rounds of ammunition on the appellant. He was convicted of unlawful possession of ammunition, an offence which carried the death sentence. Rejecting the submission that the evidence in question, having been illegally obtained ought to be inadmissible, Lord Goddard opined as follows:

> In their Lordships' opinion the test to be applied in considering whether evidence is admissible is whether it is relevant to the matters in issue. If it is, it is admissible and the court is not concerned with how the evidence was obtained. While this proposition may not have been stated in so many words in any English case there are decisions which support it, and in their Lordships' opinion it is plainly right in principle.[58] However, the court retains a wide discretion to exclude evidence, and: There can be no difference in principle for this purpose between a civil and a criminal case. No doubt in a criminal case the judge always has a discretion to disallow evidence if the strict rules of admissibility would operate unfairly against an accused [....] If, for instance, some admission of some piece of evidence, e.g., a document, had been obtained from a defendant by a trick, no doubt the judge might properly rule it out.[59] In their Lordships' opinion, when it is question of the admission of evidence strictly it is not whether the method by which it was obtained is tortious but excusable but whether what has been obtained is irrelevant to the issue being tried.

The question of dealing with the competing policies which prize the autonomy of the individual and the fundamental need to protect him from the overwhelming power of the state by ensuring that he is not subjected to unfair and illegal practices by the police is left to the judges concerned, to deal with on a case-by-case basis. The exercise of such discretion was once considered ill-disposed to the function of a judge.[60] The discretion had, as discussed above,

[56] Dicta of Lord Hoffmann in *R v Governor of Brixton Prison, ex p Levin* [1997] 3 All ER 289 at 295 applied.

[57] [1955] 1 All ER 236.

[58] See *R v Leatham* [1961] 8 Cox CC 498.

[59] For support, his lordship referred to, among others, the following authorities: *Lloyd v Mostyn* [1842] 10 M&W 478; *Calcraft v Guest* [1898] 1 QB 759; *Noor Mohammed v The King* [1949] AC 182; *Harris v Director of Public Prosecutions* [1952] AC 694; *HM Advocate v Turnbull* [1951] C 96.

[60] See for example, *R v Inhabitants of Eriswell* (1790) 3 Term Rep 707, 711; *R v Cargill* (1913) 8 Cr App Rep 224, 229; *R v Funderburk* [1990] 2 All ER 482, [1990] 1 WLR 587; Wigmore (1942) 28 *ABA Jo* 23.

however, been earlier recognised in *R v Christie*,[61] by the House of Lords.[62] Thus, in *Jeffrey v Black*,[63] the respondent was arrested for the theft of a sandwich from a public house. Before he was charged, the police officers told the respondent that they intended to search his home. The respondent took them to his home and unlocked the door. The police officers then searched his room, finding both cannabis and cannabis resin. The respondent was then charged with unlawful possession of cannabis and cannabis resin. At the hearing the justices found as a fact that the respondent had not given his consent to the search of his room and upheld a defence submission that the evidence so found was inadmissible, and they dismissed the charges. The prosecutor appealed. It was held as follows: (i) A police officer who arrested a suspect for an offence at one place had no authority without a search warrant or the suspect's consent to search his house at another place when the contents of the house on the face of them bore no relation to the offence charged or the evidence required to support it.[64] (ii) A judge at a criminal trial had a discretion not to allow evidence to be called by the prosecution which would be unfair or oppressive but the discretion to exclude evidence should be exercised only in exceptional cases. The fact that evidence had been obtained in an irregular manner was not of itself sufficient ground for the exercise of the discretion in favour of the defendant.[65] Accordingly, the justices had exercised their discretion wrongly in excluding the evidence. The appeal would therefore be allowed and the case remitted for rehearing before a different bench. The discretion to exclude evidence was one to be deployed sparingly. Lord Widgery CJ[66] observed as follows:

> [...] magistrates sitting in this case, like any other criminal tribunal in England sitting under the English law, have a general discretion to decline to allow any evidence to be called by the prosecution if they think that it would be unfair or oppressive to allow that to be done [...] magistrates ought, I think, to stress to themselves that the discretion is not a discretion which arises only in drug cases. It is not a discretion which arises only in cases where police can enter premises. It is a discretion which every criminal judge has all the time in respect of all the evidence which is tendered by the prosecution [....] But if the case is exceptional, if the case is such that not only have the police officers entered without authority, but they have been guilty of trickery or they have misled someone, or they have been oppressive or they have been unfair, or in other respects they have behaved in a manner which is morally reprehensible, then it is open to the justices to apply their discretion and decline to allow the particular evidence to be let in as part of the trial.

[61] (1914) 10 Cr App Rep 141, 149.

[62] See similar dicta in *Festa v R* [2001] HCA 72, 208 CLR 593 *per* Gleeson CJ; *R v Juric* [2002] VSCA 77, 129 ACR 408.

[63] [1978] 1 All ER 555.

[64] Dictum of Lord Denning MR in *Ghani v Jones* [1969] 3 All ER at 1703 explained.

[65] *Kuruma Son of Kaniu v R* [1955] 1 All ER 236 at 239 *per* Lord Goddard CJ.

[66] *Jeffrey v Black* [1978] 1 All ER 555 at 558j-559g.

The extent of the scope of a judge's discretion again arose in a key and much celebrated later decision on the question made in *R v Sang*.[67] Therein, the House of Lords was faced with the following question:

> Does a trial judge have a discretion to refuse to allow evidence, being evidence other than evidence of admission, to be given in any circumstances in which such evidence is relevant and of more than minimal probative value.

With unanimity their lordships opined as follows:

> (1) A trial judge in a criminal trial has always a discretion to refuse to admit evidence if in his opinion its prejudicial effect outweights its probative value.
>
> (2) Save with regard to admissions and confessions and generally with regard to evidence obtained from the accused after commission of the offence, he has no discretion to refuse to admit relevant admissible evidence on the ground that it was obtained by improper or unfair means. The Court is not concerned with how it was obtained. It is no ground for the exercise of discretion to exclude that the evidence was obtained as the result of the activities of an agent provocateur.

Lord Diplock opined as follows:[68]

> What it really involves is a claim to a judicial discretion to acquit an accused of any offences in connection with which the conduct of the police incurs the disapproval of the judge. The conduct of the police where it has involved the use of an agent provocateur may well be a matter to be taken into consideration in mitigation of sentence; but under the English system of criminal justice, it does not give rise to any discretion on the part of the judge himself to acquit the accused or to direct the jury to do so, notwithstanding that he is guilty of the offence [....] Ought your Lordships to go further and to hold that the discretion extends more widely than this, as the comparatively recent dicta to which I have already referred suggest? What has been regarded as the fountain-head of all subsequent dicta on this topic is the statement by Lord Goddard CJ delivering the advice of the Privy Council in *Kuruma Son of Kaniu v R.*[69] That was a case in which the evidence of unlawful possession of ammunition by the accused was obtained as a result of an illegal search of his person. The Board held that this evidence was admissible and had rightly been admitted; but Lord Goddard CJ, although he had earlier said that if evidence is admissible 'the court is not concerned with how the evidence was obtained', nevertheless went on to say:[70]

[70] [1955] 1 All ER 236 at 239, [1955] AC 197 at 204.

> No doubt in a criminal case the judge always has a discretion to disallow evidence if the strict rules of admissibility would operate unfairly against the accused [....][71] If, for instance, some admission of some piece of evidence, e.g., a document, had been obtained from a defendant by a trick, no doubt the judge might properly rule it out.

> [...] That statement was not, in my view, ever intended to acknowledge the existence of any wider discretion than to exclude (1) admissible evidence which would probably have a prejudicial influence on the minds of the jury that would be out of proportion to its true evidential value and (2) evidence tantamount to a self-incriminatory admission which was obtained from the defendant, after the offence had been committed, by means which would justify a judge in excluding an actual confession which had the like self-incriminating effect.
>
> Outside this limited field in which for historical reasons the function of the trial judge extended to imposing sanctions for improper conduct on the part of the prosecution before the commencement of the proceedings in inducing the accused by threats, favour or trickery to provide evidence against himself your Lordships should, I think, make it clear that the function of the judge at a criminal trial as respects the admission of evidence is to ensure that the accused has a fair trial according to law. It is no part of a judge's function to exercise disciplinary powers over the police or prosecution as respects the way in which evidence to be used at the trial is obtained by them. If it was obtained illegally there will be a remedy in civil law; if it was obtained legally but in breach of the rules of conduct for the police, this is a matter for the appropriate disciplinary authority to deal with. What the judge at the trial is concerned with is not how the evidence sought to be adduced by the prosecution has been obtained but with how it is used by the prosecution at the trial.
>
> [...] I would accordingly answer the question certified in terms which have been suggested by my noble and learned friend, Viscount Dilhorne, in the course of our deliberations on this case. (1) A trial judge in a criminal trial has always a discretion to refuse to admit evidence if in his opinion its prejudicial effect outweighs its probative value. (2) Save with regard to admissions and confessions and generally with regard to evidence obtained from the accused after commission of the offence, he has no discretion to refuse to admit relevant admissible evidence on the ground that it was obtained by improper or unfair means. The court is not concerned with how it was obtained. It is no ground for the exercise of discretion to exclude that the evidence was obtained as the result of the activities of an agent provocateur.

While the *ratio* in *Sang*[72] is to be found in the statement '[i]t is no ground for the

[71] This was emphasised in the case before this *Board of Noor Mohamed v R* [1949] 1 All ER 365 at 370, [1949] AC 182 at 192], and in the recent case in the House of Lords of *Harris v Director of Public Prosecutions* [1952] 1 All ER 1044 at 1048, [1952] AC 694 at 707, *per* Viscount Simon].

[72] [1980] AC 402.

exercise of discretion to exclude that the evidence was obtained as the result of the activities of an agent provocateur,' the persuasive effect of the rest of the holding cannot be discounted. In *Morris v Beardmore*[73] for example,an accident occurred involving a car driven by the appellant. Police officers in uniform, who knew about the accident, went to the appellant's home to interview him about it. They were let into the house by the appellant's son. The appellant refused five requests by the senior police officer to come down from his bedroom and discuss the accident. He then passed on a message through his son to the police officers that they were trespassers and requested them to leave his house. The officers then went upstairs to the appellant's bedroom and requested him to provide a specimen for a breath test. The appellant refused, was arrested and taken to a police station. There he refused to supply a specimen of breath for a breath test and subsequently a specimen of blood or urine for a laboratory test. He was then charged with contravening ss 8(3)a and 9(3)b of the Road Traffic Act 1972. The justices dismissed the information, being of opinion that in the circumstances the requirement for a breath test specimen had been made not by a constable but by a trespasser, that the appellant's arrest was accordingly unlawful and that all evidence of matters following that arrest was inadmissible. On appeal by the prosecutor, the Divisional Court of the Queen's Bench Division[74] held that, provided the statutory conditions for the request of a breath test had been complied with by the constable, the fact that he was a trespasser at the time of the request did not affect the validity of the police actions, since if the action of the constable was found to be oppressive the court could exercise its discretion to exclude the evidence, and, in any event, the person requested to undergo the test would have a civil remedy. It was held that because a constable's power under s 8(2) of the 1972 Act to require a person to provide a specimen of breath was a serious erosion of the citizen's common law rights, it was to be presumed that, in the absence of express provision to the contrary, Parliament did not intend any further encroachment on those rights by a constable acting unlawfully, whether in breach of the criminal law or the civil law. In order to be able validly to require a person to take a breath test a constable not only had to be in uniform but had to be acting in the execution of his duty, which he was not if at the time of making the request he was a trespasser on the premises of the person to whom he had made the request; and evidence of an accused's failure to comply with a request in such circumstances was not admissible under the rule that all relevant evidence ought to be admitted at trial no matter how it was obtained but subject to judicial discretion to exclude it, because evidence of an accused's failure to comply with a requirement to provide a specimen of breath was not evidence of an offence that the accused had already committed but direct evidence of the ingredients of the offence itself. Since it was not disputed that the police officers were trespassing at the time they required the appellant to provide

[73] [1981] AC 446, [1980] 2 All ER 753.

[74] [1979] 3 All ER 290.

a specimen for a breath test it followed that the appeal would be allowed.[75] According to Lord Roskill, *Sang*[76] settled any existing doubts with respect to the exercise of discretion but added that it would be regressive to, as he put it, to 'enlarge the now narrow limits of that discretion or to engraft an exception.'

It appears to follow that there is no automatic discretion at law for automatic exclusion of evidence simply because the police have acted illegally or more specifically, beyond or/and outside their powers.[77] It seems to be the case that under such circumstances, facts permitting, a court ought to consider whether evidence which has been deemed relevant, and as such, ordinarily admissible, if so admitted, would be prejudicial to the accused and in the main, negatively affect the overall fairness of the trial in question, offend the dignity of the court, taint justice and expose the judicial system to scorn.

The import of *Sang*[78] is all too obvious.[79] It makes clear that the magistrate/ judge's job is to ensure that the accused person has a fair trial. The accused, where impropriety is clear but which impropriety such as an illegal search has occurred but does not prejudice him, has as a remedy in civil action against the individual police officer or the Attorney General or both as the case may be. In *Sang*,[80] the House of Lords did, however, make a distinction between improper conduct by the police to obtain evidence by way of illegal searches away from the police station, and impropriety during an interview at the police station as a result of which the police obtain a confession. The former situation while improper, did not, as did the latter, interfere with the constitutional right in criminal cases for an accused person not to incriminate himself. We quote Diplock LJ again: 'However, much the judge may dislike the way in which a particular piece of evidence was obtained before proceedings were commenced, if it is admissible evidence probative of the accused's guilt it is no part of his judicial function to exclude it for this reason.' What the judge ought to concern himself with is the fairness of the trial and that, according to Lord Diplock, is satisfied when the following are present:

> A fair trial according to law involves, in the case of a trial on indictment, that it should take place before a judge [...]; that the case against the accused should be proved to the satisfaction of the

---

[75] *R v Sang* [1979] 2 All ER 1222 distinguished; Decision of the Divisional Court of the Queen's Bench Division [1979] 3 All ER 290 reversed; Editor's notes: For the power to require a specimen of breath for a breath test and the power of arrest following refusal to provide a specimen, see Supplement to 33 Halsbury's Laws (3rd Edn) para 1061 A.3,6; For the Road Traffic Act 1972, ss 8, 9, see 42 Halsbury's Statutes (3rd Edn) 1651, 1655.

[76] [1980] AC 402.

[77] The leading Zambian case on this point is *Liswaniso v The People* [1976] ZR 272 discussed below.

[78] [1979] 2 All ER 1222 at 1231, *per* Lord Diplock confirming the Court of appeal decision in *R v Sang; R v Mangan* [1979] 2 All ER 46

[79] Though it must now be read within the context of s 78 of the Police and Criminal Evidenced Act (PACE) 1984 which reflects the spirit of Lord Scarman's dissenting judgment in *R v Sang* [1979] 2 All ER 1222 at 1247d-1248c and the now common place application of the doctrine of abuse of process; see also *R v Christou* [1992] 4 All ER 559 at 564e-j *per* Lord Taylor CJ.

[80] [1979] 2 All ER 1222 at 1231, *per* Lord Diplock confirming the Court of appeal decision in *R v Sang; R v Mangan* [1979] 2 All ER 46.

> [court] beyond all reasonable doubt on evidence that is admissible in law; and, as a corollary to this, that there should be excluded from the [court] information about the accused which is likely to have an influence on [the court's mind] prejudicial to the accused which is out of proportion to the true probative value of admissible evidence conveying that information. If these conditions are fulfilled and the [judge properly applies his mind to] the law applicable to the case, the requirement that the accused should have a fair trial according to law is [...] satisfied [...]

Further, his lordship suggested taking a holistic approach to the question of what amounts to a 'fair trial:'

> [...] the fairness of a trial according to law is not all one-sided: it requires that those who are undoubtedly guilty should be convicted as well as that those about whose guilt there is any reasonable doubt should be acquitted. However much the judge may dislike the way in which a particular piece of evidence was obtained before proceedings were commenced, if it is admissible evidence probative of the accused's guilt it is no part of his judicial function to exclude it for this reason.[81]

At the core of the decision in *Sang*[82] are limits to the use of discretion by trial courts at common law. In *Sang*,[83] Lord Diplock only envisaged two scenarios in which evidence, including that which is improperly obtained, may be excluded: (i) Where the prejudice to the accused person of admitting such evidence will outweigh its probative significance; and (ii) Where the evidence in question is based on a confession or similar evidence improperly obtained by the police during investigations.

10.3.1.3 Discretion to exclude otherwise relevant evidence in civil proceedings

The discretion to exclude otherwise relevant evidence in civil proceedings under English law is now set out under r 32.1.2 of the Civil Procedure Rules.[84] It provides as follows: 'The court may use its power under this rule to exclude evidence that would otherwise be admissible.' If there has been anything

[81] Diplock LJ concluded as he had in this particular case they would be reverting to the law as it was laid down by Lord Moulton in *R v Christie*, [1914-15] All ER Rep 63; *R v McEvilly; R v Lee* (1974) 60 Cr App R 150. Lord du Parcq in *Noor Mohamed v R* [1949] 1 All ER 365, [1949] AC 182, PC 14(2) Digest (Reissue) 510, 4177 and Viscount Simon in *Harris v Director of Public Prosecutions* [1952] 1 All ER 1044, [1952] AC 694, 116 JP 248, 36 Cr App R 39, HL, 14(2) Digest (Reissue) 513, 4198 before the growth of what I believe to have been a misunderstanding of Lord Goddard CJ's dictum in *Kuruma Son of Kaniu v R* [1955] 1 All ER 236 at 239, [1955] AC 197 at 204.

[82] [1979] 2 All ER 1222 at 1231, *per* Lord Diplock; *R v Mangan* [1979] 2 All ER 46 confirmed.

[83] [1979] 2 All ER 1222 at 1231, *per* Lord Diplock.

[84] By way of comparison, our rules of civil procedure are mainly set out in the Subordinate Court and High Court Rules found in the Subordinate Courts Act Chapter 28 of the Laws of Zambia and the High Court Act Chapter 27 of the Laws of Zambia respectively. Appellate Courts such as the Court of Appeal, Constitutional Court and the Supreme Court Act also provide for rules of civil procedure pursuant to the individual Acts creating them namely, Act No 9 of 2016; Act No 8 of 2016; and Chapter 25 of the Laws of Zambia, as discussed elsewhere in this text.

that has been lacking in the use of this power coupled with the wide-ranging inherent power of the judge to use his discretion correctly, as discussed elsewhere in this text, it is clarity. It has, on the one hand been proclaimed[85] in what may be described as indistinct terms, that the discretion hereinbefore mentioned ought to be exercised with the goal of a just dealing with the case[86] in question in order to achieve the superseding objective. On the other hand, the reasoning has tended to support the thesis that a refusal by a witness to testify should lead to the use of the discretion to exclude prepared hearsay statement. This has been exemplified in *Polanski v Condé Nast Publications Ltd.*[87] The defendant edited and published an American magazine in New York. The magazine had a substantially larger circulation in the United States than in England. It was also published in France. The claimant, who had dual Polish and French nationality, began a libel action in England against the defendant over an article in the magazine published in 2002. He had pleaded guilty in 1977 before a Californian court to unlawful sexual intercourse with a 13-year-old girl, but had left the United States before being sentenced and was living in France, a country from which he could not be extradited to the United States. He did not wish to give his evidence in the libel case in England, fearing that he would be arrested and extradited, and successfully applied to the court for an order under CPR 32.3, which provided that the court might allow a witness to give evidence by means of a video conference link. The defendant appealed. It was held as follows: There could be no absolute rule as to the proper application of CPR 32.3 where a witness wished to give his evidence by video conference link abroad so as to avoid the risk of being arrested in England. The general policy of the court should be to discourage litigants from escaping the normal processes of the law rather than facilitating it. The relevant considerations in deciding whether to make a video conference link order included: (i) the nature of the offence for which the witness risked arrest and whether he had already been convicted of it; (ii) the nature of any civil claim in which the witness sought to give his evidence by video conference link and any relationship between the claim and the offence; (iii) the witness's role in the proceedings; (iv) the importance of the claim to the witness and the possibilities of litigating it elsewhere; and (v) the likely disadvantages of video conference link evidence compared to live evidence. In the instant case, it had been wrong to make an order. The claimant was a fugitive offender, convicted of a serious offence for which he had yet to be sentenced; his libel action was a volunteer action and, moreover, one which could more appropriately have been brought in the United States of America or in France. He was invoking the court's jurisdiction for his own benefit, not defending a claim brought against

[85] See *Grobbelaar v Sun Newspapers Ltd* (1999) The Times, 2 August; *Great Future International Ltd Sealand Housing Corp* [2002] EWCA Civ 1183, [24].

[86] Less so with jury enthused proceedings: *Watson v Chief Constable of Cleveland* [2001] EWCA Civ 1547, [23]-[24].

[87] [2003] EWCA Civ 1573, [2004] 1 All ER 1220, [23].

him. Accordingly, the appeal would be allowed.[88]

Another case of importance is that of *Jones v University of Warwick*.[89] The claimant commenced proceedings against the defendant employer, claiming damages for personal injury to her right hand, as a result of which she alleged that she was suffering continuing disability. The defendant admitted liability but disputed that the claimant was suffering continuing disability. An inquiry agent, acting for the defendant's insurers, obtained access to the claimant's home on two occasions by posing as a market researcher, and recorded the claimant, without her knowledge, using a hidden video camera. The defendant's expert, having viewed the video recordings, was of the opinion that the claimant had an entirely satisfactory function in her right hand. The defendant applied for directions as to whether the video recordings were admissible in evidence. The claimant, relying on the court's discretion under CPR 32.1(2)a and on the right to privacy in art 8(1)b of the European Convention for the Protection of Human Rights and Fundamental Freedoms 1950 (as set out in Sch 1 to the Human Rights Act 1998), contended that the recordings should not be admitted. The district judge concluded that the evidence should be excluded, because the court should not give approval to the methods used by the defendant's agent. The defendant appealed, and the judge held that the evidence was admissible, the primary question for the court being not whether or not to give approval to the method whereby evidence had been obtained, but rather whether justice and fairness required its admission. The claimant appealed. It was held as follows: The judge's approach to the question whether the evidence was admissible was consistent with that which would have been adopted prior to the coming into force of the CPR and the 1998 Act, when the achieving of justice in the particular case before the court was the paramount consideration. That approach, however, did nothing to promote the observance of the law by those engaged or about to be engaged in legal proceedings, which was also a matter of real public concern. If the conduct of the insurers went uncensured, there would be a significant risk that practices of the type which they had adopted would be encouraged, and that would be highly undesirable. Proactive management of civil proceedings, which was at the heart of the CPR, was not only concerned with an individual piece of litigation which was before the court, but was concerned with litigation as a whole. Where, therefore, as in the instant case, a defendant's insurers had been responsible for trespass and for contravention of a claimant's privacy, in violation of art 8 of the convention, that was a relevant consideration for the court in the exercise of its discretion in making orders as to the management of the proceedings. In the instant case, the conduct of the insurers had not been

[88] *Rowland v Bock* [2002] 4 All ER 370 distinguished; Editor's notes: For the court's power to allow use of video links and general guidance to video conferencing, see 17(1) Halsbury's Laws (4th edn reissue) paras 1013, 1014.

[89] [2003] EWCA Civ 151, [2003] 3 All ER 760.

so outrageous that the defence should be struck out, and it would be artificial and undesirable for evidence which was relevant and admissible not to be before the judge who had the task of trying the case. Accordingly, it would not be right to interfere with the decision of the judge below. The court could, however, reflect its disapproval of the insurers' conduct by ordering that the defendant pays the costs of the proceedings relating to the admissibility of the evidence before the district judge, the judge, and on the appeal.[90]

A line of authorities[91] appear to suggest the non-existence of a discretionary exclusionary rule or set of rules predicated on the more prejudicial/less probative value paradigm *vis-à-vis* revealing evidence relating to peripheral disreputable actions in English law.[92] In *Ibrahim v R*,[93]it was said that there was no such thing as a discretion to exclude improperly obtained evidence in civil matters.the [accused] was an Afghan subject with the British Army in Hong Kong. He was accused of murder. Having accepted the protection of the British Armed forces, he became subject to their laws. In custody, he was asked about the offence by a senior officer, and admitted the act. He appealed on the basis that the admission was not voluntary, having being made to an officer with authority over him, and should not have been admitted. It was held as follows: The committee was not inclined to enunciate a general rule for admissibility of evidence in such circumstances, this is a matter for the Court of Criminal Appeal. It could only say that any defect must be such as to deprive the accused of a fair trial, before a decision could be set aside. The appellate court should ask whether the summing up contains 'Something which [...] deprives the accused of the substance of a fair trial and the protection of the law, or which, in general, tends to divert the due and orderly administration of the law into a new course, which may be drawn into an evil precedent in future.'

> It has long been established as a positive rule of English criminal law, that no statement by an accused is admissible in evidence against him unless it is shewn by the prosecution to have been a voluntary statement, in the sense that it has not been obtained from him either by fear of prejudice or hope of advantage exercised or held out by a person in authority. The principle is as old as Lord Hale.

[90] Editor's notes: For the court's power to control evidence, see 17(1) Halsbury's Laws (4th edn reissue) para 427; For the Human Rights Act 1998, Sch 1, Pt I, art 8, see 7 Halsbury's Statutes (4th edn) (2002 reissue) 555.

[91] *Bradford City Metropolitan Council v K* [1990] Fam 140; *Re C (Minors)* [1993] 4 All ER 690, 694; *Vernon v Bosley* [1994] PIQR P337.

[92] See *Polycarpou v Australian Wire Industries Pty Ltd* (1995) 36 NSWLR 49; *Berger v Raymond & Son Ltd* [1984] 1 WLR 625; *Al-Hawaz v Thomas Cook Group Ltd* LEXIS 27 October 2000.

[93] [1914] AC 599; [1914-15] All ER Rep 874; 610, 878; summary taken from https://swarb.co.uk/ibrahim-v-the-king-pc-6-mar-1914/ retrieved on 24/12/21.

It has been observed in *Helliwell v Piggott-Sims*[94] that,

> [...] in criminal cases the judge may have a discretion have a discretion. That is shown by *Kuruma v R.*[95] But so far as civil cases are concerned, it seems to me that the judge has no discretion. The evidence is relevant and admissible. The judge cannot refuse it on the ground that it may have been unlawfully obtained in the beginning.

One last matter to turn our attention to is the application of the discretion within the context of claims of privilege which matter is considered in greater detail in the following two chapters. It appears to be settled that where a privilege exists no question of discretion arises. In *Rank Film Distributors Ltd v Video Information Centre*,[96] the appellants, who were film companies owning the copyright to films produced and made by them, believed that certain unauthorised persons were engaged in pirating copies of their films and recording and selling unauthorised video cassettes of them. The respondents were suspected of selling the cassettes. The appellants accordingly issued a writ against the suspected unauthorised persons seeking an injunction restraining them from infringing the appellants' copyright. The appellants also sought and were granted Anton Piller orders which, *inter alia*, required the respondents to disclose (i) the names and addresses of persons who supplied the cassettes and customers who bought them, (ii) all invoices, letters and other documents relating to the cassettes, and (iii) the whereabouts of all pirate cassettes and master copies known to the respondents. The respondents applied to the court to have the orders varied by expunging the requirements as to disclosure, on the grounds that by disclosing the information they might incriminate themselves and the orders therefore infringed the privilege against self-incrimination. The respondents contended that if they were compelled to disclose the information they would incriminate themselves by providing evidence on which they could be prosecuted and convicted of (i) contravention of s 21 of the Copyright Act 1956, (ii) contravention of s 18 of the Theft Act 1968 and (iii) conspiracy to defraud at common law. A person associated with the respondents in the pirating of the films was in the course of being prosecuted on charges of conspiracy to defraud. The judge dismissed the respondents' application but on appeal the Court of Appeal[97] held that the orders requiring disclosure should be expunged because they were contrary to the principle of privilege against self-incrimination. The appellants appealed to the House of Lords seeking reinstatement of the orders. The appellants, while recognising the existence of privilege against self-incrimination by discovery, contended that the court ought to compel the respondents to disclose the information sought while imposing a restriction on the information being used in a criminal prosecution of the respondents. It was

[94] [1980] FSR 356, 357; *R v Christie* [1914] AC 545, [1914-15] All ER Rep 63; see also *ITC Film Distributors v Video Exchange Ltd* [1982] Ch 431, [1982] 2 All ER 241.

[95] [1955] AC 197.

[96] [1982] AC 380, [1981] 2 All ER 76; 442, 81.

[97] [1980] 2 All ER 273.

held as follows: Since a charge against the respondents of conspiracy to defraud would not be a contrived, fanciful or remote possibility but an appropriate and exact description of what the respondents and the other persons involved had done, it was clear that disclosure by the respondents of the information sought would tend to expose them to such a charge, which would be a serious charge and would, if proved, attract heavy penalties. It followed that the claim of privilege against self-incrimination should be upheld. Moreover, there was no way in which the court could compel disclosure while at the same time protecting the respondents from the consequences of self-incrimination, since an express restriction imposed by the court on the use of any information disclosed would be binding only on the appellants and not on anyone else who brought a criminal prosecution and, in any event, would not bind a criminal court to exclude the information as inadmissible evidence. The appeal would accordingly be dismissed.[98]

It appears that the guiding principle as to the applicability of discretion with respect to the question of privilege is as stated in *Science Research Council v Nassé*:[99] 'to consider fairly the strength and value of the interest in preserving confidentiality and the damage which may be caused by breaking it; then to consider hether the objective, to dispose fairly of the case, can be achieved without doing so.' It has been held in *Savings and Investment Bank Ltd v Gasco Investments (Netherlands) BV (No 2)*[100] that the exclusion of hearsay evidence was to not to be predicated on the court's discretion but rather, the fact that it was unlikely to be bestowed with weight of such sufficiency as to discharge the heavy burden of proof required.

[98] *Riddick v Thames Board Mills Ltd* [1977] 3 All ER 677 distinguished; *Per Curiam*. In cases involving large scale and systematic infringements of copyright, offences against s 21 of the 1956 Act are probably too trivial, having regard to the maximum penalty of a £50 fine, to be taken into account when considering whether a claim for privilege against self-incrimination should succeed. Furthermore, the risk of a successful prosecution under s 18 of the 1968 Act, which applies to theft of 'property', is too remote to be considered because copyright is not 'property' for the purposes of s 18; *Per* Lord Russell: Because the privilege against incrimination could largely deprive the owner of a copyright of his just rights to the protection of his property, legislation similar to s 31 of the 1968 Act would be welcome; the aim of such legislation should be to remove the privilege while at the same time preventing the use in criminal proceedings of statements which would otherwise be privileged; *Per* Lord Wilberforce: '[...] to substitute for the privilege a dependence on the court's discretion would substantially be to the defendant's detriment;' As to when the discretion arises see *D v National Society for the Prevention of Cruelty to Children* [1977] 1 All ER 589; 239, 613 *per* Lord Simon; as to whether the discretion's application to discovery also applies to prevent evidence from being adduced, see *Mc Guinness v A-G of Victoria* (1940) 63 CLR 73, 104 *per* Sir Owen Dixon whom in rejecting that the rules limiting discovery applied to evidence opined that '[...] it is not a rule of evidence but a practice of refusing in an action for libel [...] to compel discovery of the name of [...] the informants.' Decision of the Court of Appeal [1980] 2 All ER 273 affirmed; Editor's notes: For privilege from production of documents exposing a party to penalties, see 13 Halsbury's Laws (4th Edn) para 92, and for cases on the subject, see 18 Digest (Reissue) 19, 149–152, 97–102, 1195–1246 and 22 Digest (Reissue) 433–437, 4310–4346; For the Copyright Act 1956, s 21, see 7 Halsbury's Statutes (3rd Edn) 171; For the Theft Act 1968, ss 18, 31, see 8 ibid 794, 802.

[99] [1980] AC 1028, [1979] 3 All ER 673; 1067, 681; see also *A-G v Mulholland* [1963] 2 QB 477, [1963] 1 All ER 767; *A-G v Clough* [1963] 1 QB 773, [1963] 1 All ER 420.

[100] [1988] Ch 422, [1988] 1 All ER 975; but see suggestions for reform *per* Butler Sloss LJ in *Re M and R* (Minors) [1996] 4 All ER 239, 255.

10.3.1.4 *Appeals*

English law in this regard as it pertains to criminal cases, is to be found under the provisions of the Criminal Appeal Act 1995. The Civil Procedure Rules as amended in 2000. The changes have been described in *Tanfern Ltd v Cameron-MacDonald*[101] as 'the most significant changes in the arrangements for civil appeals in this country for over 125 years.'[102] Of particular importance is CPR 52.11 which changes the focus of the appeal from a rehearing to review.[103] Still, as has been shown in *HK v Secretary of State for Home Department,*[104] where the lower court erroneously rejects evidence, the question is whether on the basis of the remnant of the evidence, the lower court's decision can be sustained. An important point to note is the guidance given by Goff LJ in *Armagas Ltd v Mundogas SA*[105] as regards the basis for accepting a decision from a court of first instance.[106]

10.3.2 *The Scottish position*

The Scottish position as exemplified in *Lawrie v Muir*[107] is that evidence obtained as a result of an illegal search at an accused's premises is inadmissible for want of legal excuse. Therefore, where illegality and/or unfairness are shown to have occurred in obtaining evidence now impugned by the defence, the prosecution must obtain leave of court to introduce it. As has been shown in *HM Advocates v Turnbull,*[108] when faced with such an application the court will have to consider whether the particular scenario that played out birthing the objection by the defence, and the application for said excuse by the prosecution was a one off or an unhurried course of behaviour by the police, in effect giving the police an opportunity to explain or justify their lapse.[109]

As regards civil matters, it is perhaps worth mentioning that the Scottish system provides for no common law discretion for the exclusion of evidence which is otherwise admissible.[110]

---

[101] [2000] 2 All ER 801, [2000] 1 WLR 1311, [50] *per* Brooke LJ.

[102] That is, since the Judicature Act.

[103] But see *Assicurazioni Generali Spa v Arab Insurance Group (BSC)* [2002] EWCA Civ 1642, [2003] 1 All ER (Comm) 140, [2003] 1 WLR 77; *R (Sivasubramaniam) v Wandsworth County Court* [2002] EWCA Civ 1738, [2003] 2 All ER 160, [2003] 1 WLR 475; as to discretion to receive fresh evidence, see *Madarassy v Nomura International* [2006] EWHC 748 (QB); *Ladd v Marshall* [1954] 3 All ER 745, [1954] 1 WLR 1489; *Prentice v Hereward Housing Association* [2001] EWCA Civ 437, [2001] 2 All ER (Comm) 900, [25].

[104] [2006] EWCA Civ 107, [46].

[105] [1985] Lloyd's Rep 1, 57.

[106] See *G v G (minors: custody appeal)* [1985] 2 All ER 225, 1 WLR 647, HL; 229, 652; *Rowland v Bock* [2002] EWHC 692 (QB), [2002] EWHC 692 (QB), [2002] 4 All ER 370.

[107] 1950 SC (J) 19.

[108] 1951 SC (J) 96.

[109] Compare the operation of this discretion in New Zealand: *R v Capner* [1975] 1 NZLR 411 (CA); *R v Pethig* [1977] 1 NZLR 448; *R v Loughlin* [1982] 1 NZLR 236 at 238 (CA); and in Northern Ireland: *R v Murphy* [1965] NI 138; but see *R v Sang* [1980] AC 402 which has now overruled the position taken therein; For a lucid analysis of the Australian position see Heydon JD *Cross on Evidence* 992 [27240] to 995 [27270] and the cases quoted and cited thereunder.

[110] Therefore, in *McVinnie v McVinnie* 1995 SLT 81; approved in *Glaser v Glaser* 1997 SLT 456; but see *Lobban v Phillip* 1995 SCLR 1104.

10.3.3 The Australian position

10.3.3.1 General

The position taken in Australia is similar to that taken under Scottish law. The public policy prescription upon which this position is predicated has been stated in the following terms:[111]

> [...] the courts should not be seen to be acquiescent in the face of the unlawful conduct of those whose task it is to enforce the law. On the other hand, it may be quite inappropriate to treat isolated and merely accidental non-compliance with statutory safeguards as leading to inadmissibility of the resultant evidence when of their very nature they involve no overt defiance of the will of the legislature or calculated disregard of the common law and when the reception of the evidence thus provided does not demean the court as a tribunal whose concern is in upholding the law.

In *R v Ireland*,[112] Barwick CJ in a passage quoted as representing the law in Australia[113] opined as follows:

> Evidence of relevant facts or things ascertained or procured by means of unlawful or unfair acts is not, for that reason alone, inadmissible. This is so, in my opinion, whether the unlawfulness derives from the common law or from statute. But it may be that acts in breach of a statute would more readily warrant the rejection of the evidence as a matter of discretion : or the statute may on its proper construction itself impliedly forbid the use of facts or things obtained or procured in breach of its terms. On the other hand, evidence of facts or things so ascertained or procured is not necessarily to be admitted, ignoring the unlawful or unfair quality of the acts by which the facts sought to be evidenced were ascertained or procured. Whenever such unlawfulness or unfairness appears, the judge has a discretion to reject the evidence. He must consider its exercise. In the exercise of it, the competing public requirements must be considered and weighed against each other. On the one hand there is the public need to bring to conviction those who commit criminal offences. On the other hand, there is the public interest in the protection of the individual from unlawful and unfair treatment. Convictions obtained by the aid of unlawful or unfair acts may be obtained at too high a price. Hence the judicial discretion.[114]

R v Ireland[115] was concerned with real evidence, that is photographs taken against the wish of the accused. However, the discretion has been identified in wide ranging matters including those concerned with the administration

[115] (1970) 126 CLR 321; see also *Cleland v R* (1982) 151 CLR 1 at 8 and 34; *Wendo v R* (1963) 109 CLR 559; *Bunning v Cross* (1978) 141 CLR 54 at 74 and 75 *per* Stephen and Aickin JJ.

of a breathalyser in contravention of statutory requirements as in *Bunning v Cross;*[116] and those, as in *Cleland v R*,[117] relating to confessional evidence extracted thanks to the employment by the police of illegal methods or their impropriety. The general premise for exclusion of evidence are cases, as shown in *R v Lobban,*[118] in which it can be shown that evidence in question was improperly or/and unlawfully extracted. By implication this excludes any behaviour subsequent to the improper/unlawful conduct. Thus, where the police tell falsities about the method in which the evidence was obtained but the actual manner of obtaining such evidence was neither improper nor illegal, the discretion will not be applicable.[119] It has been shown in *French v Scarman*[120] that for subsequent behaviour to come within the purview of the discretion, it would have to be closely connected to the initial improper or/and illegal behaviour. It has therefore been held in *Director of Public Prosecutions (Vic) v Moore*,[121] in parts relevant to our discussion, that the conduct complained of ought to be 'the means by which the evidence was obtained or where the obtaining of the evidence involved [the] conduct [about which a complaint has been made].' The absence of a '[...] strict causal link' between the improper or illegal act on the one hand and obtaining of the evidence now impugned on the other, may yet lead to the discretion being exercised. Even so, the significance of there being a 'relevant connection' cannot be discounted. As has been held in *Bunning v Cross,*[122]the conduct must birth the evidence now impugned.

The basis of the discretion in Australia has been explained in as follows[123]:

> The contrast between these statements of principle and that enunciated in *Ireland's Case*[124] becomes apparent as soon as the objects sought to be attained by the exercise of the discretion, as stated in the judgment of Barwick CJ in *Ireland's Case*,[125] are examined. What *Ireland*[126] involves is no simple question of ensuring fairness to an accused but instead the weighting against each other of two competing requirements of public policy, thereby seeking to resolve the apparent conflict between the desirable goal of bringing to conviction the wrongdoer and the undesirable effect of curial approval, or even encouragement, being given to the unlawful conduct of those whose task it is to enforce the law. This being the aim of the discretionary process called for by Ireland it follows that it by no means takes as its central point the question of unfairness to the accused. It is, on the contrary, concerned

[116] (1978) 141 CLR 54.

[117] (1982) 151 CLR 1.

[118] (2000) 77 SASR 24 (CCA); *Question of Law Reserved (No 1 of 1998)* (1998) 70 SASR 281 (FC); *Police v Hall* (2006) 95 SASR 482.

[119] *Question of Law Reserved (No 1 of 1998)* (1998) 70 SASR 281 at 288-9 (FC).

[120] (1979) 20 SASR 333 (FC); see also *DPP v Moore* (2003) 6 VR 430 and [93].

[121] (2003) 6 VR 430; see also *Terry v Johnson* (2009) 198 A Crim R 128.

[122] (1978) 141 CLR 54 at 75.

[123] *Bunning v Cross* (1978) 141 CLR 54 at 75.

[124] (1970) 126 CLR 321.

[125] (1970) 126 CLR at 335.

[126] (1970) 126 CLR at 335.

> with broader questions of high public policy, unfairness to the accused being only one factor which, if present, will play its part in the whole process of consideration. Since it is with these matters of public policy that the discretionary process called for in Ireland is concerned it follows that it will have a more limited sphere of application than has that general discretion to which Lord Widgery refers, which applies in all criminal cases. It applies only when the evidence is the product of unfair or unlawful conduct on the part of the authorities (or, as Dixon CJ put it in *Wendo's Case*,[127] unlawful or improper conduct). Moreover, it does not entrench upon the quite special rules which apply to the case of confessional evidence. Its principal area of operation will be in relation to what might loosely be called "real evidence," such as articles found by search, recordings of conversations, the result of breathalyser tests, fingerprint evidence and so on.

One cannot help but draw the conclusion from the preceding that while the alacrity to exercise discretion by using the notions of fairness or unfairness in cases of involuntary confessions, there is little appetite in the Australian jurisdiction for enforcing the notions of fairness or the lack therefore in instances where the issue in question is the use of discretion to reject real evidence that has been obtained inappropriately or illegally.[128] As Heydon[129] observed,

> In the case of real evidence which has substantial probative value, fingerprints or possession of a bloodstained knife, it is difficult to say that its reception into evidence produces an unfair trial, by whatever means those objects came into the hands of the police.[130] That evidence may operate unfortunately for the accused, but not unfairly.[131]

10.3.3.2 Relevant considerations

The relevant considerations will vary based on the factual matrix and circumstances of each case; the ones highlighted in *Collins v R*[132] are a useful starting point:

- Whether the unlawfulness act is attributable to something other than the result of a mistaken belief on the part of police officers or a thoughtful disdain of the law[133] in which case infringement of the provisions of the

[127] (1963) 109 CLR at 562.

[128] See *Collins v R* (1980) 31 ALR 257 (Fed C of A FC).

[129] JD Heydon, *Cross on Evidence* 994.

[130] *Bunning Cross* (1978) 141 CLR 54 at 75.

[131] *R v Wray* [1971] SCR 272 at 293. The actual decision in this case has been "eroded"; AW Bryant, SN Lederman and MK Fuerst, *The Law of Evidence in Canada* 3rd edn 2009 [8.174].

[132] (1978) 141 CLR 54 at 78-80 *per* Stephhen and Aickin JJ.

[133] *O'Neil v Wratten* (1986) 11 FCR 404; *R v Edelsten* (1990) 21 NSWLR 542 at 557 (CCA); *Pacillo v Hentschke* (1988) 47 SASR 261 (FC); *Coleman v Zanker* (1991) 58 SASR 7 at 15; *R v Smith* (1996) 16 WAR 205 at 216-17 (WA CCA); *R v Tang* [1998] 3 VR 508 at 518-21; *R v Nicholas* (2000) 1 VR 356 at [95] (CA); *R v Chapman* (2001) 79 SASR 342 at [33]; *R v Ng* (2002) 5 VR 257 at [60]; *R v Theophanous* (2003) 141 A Crim R 216 at [117]; *Sims v Thomas* (2007) 179 A Crim R 412.

law by the same police officer may be led.[134]

- Whether the nature of the illegality in question affects the cogency of the evidence so obtained.[135]
- Whether the case at hand is one in which the law might have been complied with in procuring the evidence in question.
- Whether the illegal act or acts was/were a deliberate "cutting of corners" to ease the work of the police and as such, would tend against the admissibility of evidence illegally obtained.[136]
- Whether the nature of the offence charged would militate against any illegality brought to the fore.[137]
- Whether upon examination of the legislation concerned there was a quite deliberate intent on the part of the legislature narrowly to restrict the police in their power.[138]

There are several factors which may favour the admission of evidence otherwise obtained illegally:

- Were, as in *C Cockerill & Sons (Vic) Pty Ltd v County Court of Victoria*,[139] such acceptance will not be unfair to the accused.
- Where, as in *R v Tilev*,[140] a serious delay in the seizure of the evidence in question may lead it to being removed by the accused, his agents or servants.
- Where, as in *R v Edeslsten*,[141] the evidence illegally obtained is the only evidence pointing to the guilt of the accused.

The foregoing reasons notwithstanding, where there had been an egregious but non-deliberate disregard of the law the evidence obtained against the applicant in the search of his premises albeit in good faith, will be excluded. Thus, where, as in *R v Christensen*,[142] a warrant to enter and search premises was issued pursuant to s 68(1) of the Police Powers and Responsibilities Act 2000 (Qld) which was for the purpose of obtaining evidence in relation to an offence; where an offence was stated on the warrant for which no name or details were stated and evidence showed that no specific offence was contemplated by police seeking the warrant; where police intelligence had shown, generally, that offences may occur on the premises subject to the warrant; where the warrant did not comply with the Police Powers and Responsibilities Act 2000 (Qld) in various other respects; whether the warrant was invalid and whether the evidence obtained pursuant to its purported execution was admissible.

---

[134] *Milner v Anderson* (1982) 42 ACTR 23.

[135] *Tregenza v Bryson* (1989) 8 MVR 529 (SA SC); *Police v Astley* (1997) 69 SASR 319 at 329.

[136] *R v Jamieson* (2003) 9 VR 119 at [53] where there was an inadvertent omission to have the senior officer append his signature.

[137] It has been shown in cases such as *R v Addabbo* (1982) 33 SASR 84 at 98 on the one hand, and *King v R* (1996) 16 WAR 540 (FC), that the seriousness of the offence will determine whether the court excludes the probative evidence. The likelihood of exclusion reduces the graver the offence in question.

[138] *R v Padman* [1979] Tas R 37 (Tas SC).

[139] (2007) 18 VR 222 at [52].

[140] (1983) 33 SASR 344 at 354.

[141] (1990) 21 NSWLR 542 AT 557 (CCA).

[142] (2005) 156 A Crim R 397.

Holmes J observed as follows:

> I should say at once I accept the contention that the police officers acted in good faith. Constable Jones was entirely frank in explaining the basis on which the warrant was obtained; the warrant on its face strongly suggests the misapprehension as to its possible ambit which underlay its issue. But while I am satisfied that there was no deliberate disregard of the law, this can only be regarded as a reckless disregard: no proper attention can have been paid to the requirements or purpose of the relevant provisions. The importance of strict adherence to statutory requirements in the context of search warrants has repeatedly been emphasised.[143] This was not some mere technical defect in the warrant; the entire basis on which it was sought and issued was misconceived and wrong. The offences, if made out, are undoubtedly serious. Assuming that the tablets seized are proved to be ecstasy, a large quantity is involved. However, the purported use of a power which entailed the invasion of the privacy of citizens to such an extent, with so little regard for what was actually permitted by the statutory provisions, is an error of such proportions as to tilt the balance of public interest against the receipt of the evidence so obtained.

A further point to note regarding the position taken in Australia is explained in *Brain v Froude.*[144] A reading resulting from a breath analysis unlawfully required by police was held not to be a matter going to admissibility but rather to be excluded in exercise of the *Bunning v Cross*[145] discretion. Therefore, though there appears to be some alacrity for courts to exclude evidence obtained because of a contravention of a statutory provision, mere non-compliance with statutory requirements is not fatal. Thus, where, as in *Edelsten v Investigating Committee of New South Wales*,[146] there has been a deliberate effort to illegally wire-tap suspects, evidence has been admitted in a case against them at trial.

10.3.3.3 Incapacity in the suspect

Incapacity in suspects is not considered a factor in the question of illegality of manner of obtaining evidence. The logical reason for this position has to do with the fact that the question of exercising jurisdiction has nothing to do with the suspect, whatever his capacity or lack thereof, but everything to do with the conduct of the police. Be that as it may, the court may not so easily discard the impact of the conduct on the accused and thus ultimately, on the evidence in question. Thus, such things as age, limited intellect, ill-health or the fact that the suspect is a minor have all been taken into consideration when the courts

[143] *George v Rocket* (1990) 170 CLR 104 at 110-111; *Ousley v The Queen* (1997) 192 CLR 69 at 106-107.

[144] (1992) SASR 65.

[145] (1978) 141 CLR 54.

[146] (1986) 7 NSWLR 222; see also *R v Padman* [1979] Tas R 37 (Tas SC); but see *Reichelt v Lewis* (1986) 23 A Crim R 284 (QSC).

have exercised the discretion to exclude evidence.[147]

10.3.3.4 *Civil cases*

Though there is little authority on the use of discretion in civil proceedings, the logical conclusion to draw under the circumstances is that the principle as espoused in several criminal cases considered above is one of general application. Thus, as has been shown in several Australian authorities[148] there is nothing to stop a judge from exercising such discretion in a civil matter.

10.4 The Zambian position

The leading authority in this jurisdiction is that of *Liswaniso v The People.*[149] The applicant, an Inspector of Police, was convicted of official corruption, the allegation being that he corruptly received a sum of ZMW80.00 in cash as consideration for the release of an impounded motor car belonging to the complainant. The evidence on which the applicant was convicted was obtained by means of a trap; the handing over of the currency notes in question by the complainant was pre-arranged with the police, and they were recovered from the complainant's house during a search conducted pursuant to a search warrant. It was common cause that at the time the police officer in question applied for the search warrant to be issued he swore that the money in question was in the applicant's house when in fact it was in that officer's possession. It was argued on behalf of the applicant that the search warrant was invalid and the resultant search illegal, and that anything found as a result of such a search was inadmissible in evidence. It was held as follows: (i) Apart from the rule of law relating to the admissibility of involuntary confessions, evidence illegally obtained, e.g., as a result of an illegal search and seizure or as a result

[147] *R v Larson* [1984] VR 559; *T v Waye* (1983) 35 SASR 247 (CCA): the case of a 14 year old suspect; *R v Gillespie* (1988) 36 A Crim R 235 (NSW CCA);

[148] *Miller v Miller* (1978) 141 CLR 269; see also *Mazinski v Bakka* (1979) 20 SASR 350 at 361 and 381 (FC); *Pearce v Button* (1985) 8 FCR 388 at 401-3; *Sheldon v Sun Alliance Ltd* (1988) 50 SASR 236 at 247: *Duke Group Ltd (In Liq) v Pilmer* (1994) 63 SASR 364 at 377-8; *Southern Equities Corp Ltd (In Liq) v Bond (No2)* (2001) 78 SASR 554 at [101] -[113]; *Jones v University of Warwick* [2003] 3 All ER 760 (CA).

[149] [1976] ZR 277; see Justice Peter Chitengi, 'Implications of illegally obtained evidence and its effect on human rights of accused persons,' A paper presented to a workshop on human rights law on 15th July, 1998: https://allafrica.com/stories/199807160038.html; Jamil Ddamulira Mujuzi, 'The admissibility of evidence obtained through human rights violations in Zambia: Revisiting Liswaniso v The People (1976) Zambia Law Reports 277,' The International Journal of Evidence and Proof, Volume: 23 issue: 3, page(s): 316-329 available at https://journals.sagepub.com/doi/abs/10.1177/1365712719831716?journalCode=epja; For recent criticism of this decision from a Zambian Human rights perspective see J Chirwa, "The Admissibility ofDerivative Evidence in Zambia in Light of Human Rights Obligations and the Need to Discard Liswaniso Versus The People (1976) ZR 277": https://www.linkedin.com/pulse/admissibility-derivative-evidence-zambia-light-human-rights-chirwa/ retrieved on 25/09/2021; see also *Karuma, Son of Kania v R* (1955) AC 197; (1955) 1 All ER 236; *Mapp v Ohio* (1961) 367 U.S. 643; *Weeks v United States* (1914) 232 I.S. 383; *State v Reynolds* (1924) 101 Conn. 224; *The People v Defoe* (1926) 242 N.Y. 413; *Cupp v Murphy* (1973) 412 US 29; *King v R* (1968) 2 All ER 610; *R v Doyle* (1 888) 12 Ont. R. 347; *R v Honan* (1912) 26 Ont. L.R. 484; *R v Duroussel* (1933) 2 D.L.R. 446; *Attorney-General for Quebec v Begin* (1955) 5 D.L.R. 394; *Emperor v Alladad Khan* (1913) I.L.R. 350 11-258; *Emperor v Ali Ahmed Khan* (1923) I.L.R. 46 A 11-86; *Chwa Hum Htive v King Emperor* (1926) ILR 11 Rang. 107; *Larrie v Muir* (1950) Scots LT 37; *McGovern v HM Advocate* (1950) Scots LT 133; *Jones v Owen* (1870) 34 JP 759; *The People (AG) v O'Brien* (1965) IR 142.

of an in admissible confession is, if relevant, admissible on the ground that such evidence is a fact regardless of whether or not it violates a provision of the Constitution (or some other law). (ii) The evidence of search and seizure of the currency in the case under consideration, although based upon an irregular search warrant, was rightly admitted by the trial court because that evidence was a relevant fact. (*per curiam*) Any illegal or irregular invasions by the police or anyone else are not to be condoned and anyone guilty of such an invasion may be visited by criminal or civil sanctions.

10.5 Facts that come to light as a result of inadmissible confessions

Under this head we revisit a discussion we had considered in the preceding paragraph. Here though, we will attempt to go a little further by asking questions and seeking answers to those questions through the lens of several decided cases. We will also attempt to add a few more dimensions to the subject of facts that come to light as a result of inadmissible confessions. It is worth remembering that unlike voluntary confessions whose receipt is prized and shorten the trial process: '[a] free and voluntary confession is deserving of the highest credit, because it is presumed to flow from the strongest sense of guilt, and therefore it is admitted as proof of the crime to which it refers [....]'[150] The situation regarding involuntary confessions is entirely different. Involuntary confessions raise all manner of issues whose very likely outcome is the exclusion of such evidence as is obtained by illegal means leading to such confessions: '[...] a confession forced from the mind by the flattery of hope, or by the torture of fear, comes in so questionable a shape when it is to be considered as evidence of guilt, that no credit ought to be given to it; and therefore, it is rejected.'[151]

As Gibbs CJ has noted in *Cleland v R.*[152] '[d]isputed confessions are probably the most controversial problem in the administration of criminal justice.'[153] In the earlier English decision of *R v Thompson*,[154] Cave J observed as follows:[155]

> [...] I always suspect these confessions, which are supposed to be the offspring of penitence and remorse, and which nevertheless are repudiated by the prisoner at the trial. It is remarkable that it is of very rare occurrence for evidence of a confession to be given when the proof of the prisoner's guilt is otherwise clear and satisfactory; but, when it is not clear and satisfactory, the prisoner is not infrequently alleged to have been seized with the desire born of penitence and remorse to supplement it with a confession; - a desire which vanishes as soon as he appears in a court of justice.

The common law never considered evidence discovered as a result of a confession inadmissible as fruits of a poisonous tree. Be that as it may, we ought to, as a logical consequence of the preceding position taken by the common law ask and answer a few questions arising therefrom. The questions include but are not limited to the following: whether incriminating evidence which is borne out of inadmissible confessions ought to be admitted; whether the "confirmation by subsequent facts" renders confession which was inadmissible, subsequently admissible following the discovery of incriminating evidence. Thus, in *R v Warickshall*[156] where the accused was charged as an accessory for receiving goods reasonably expected to have been stolen. Evidence (predicated on the accused's confession) that stolen goods were found under the bed of the accused was admitted notwithstanding that the discovery was made in consequence of her inadmissible confession obtained on the basis of inducements. On the question whether evidence obtained by oppression should be admitted to court, it was held that involuntary statements are inherently unreliable, that is to say, 'a confession forced from the mind by the flattery of hope, or by the torture of fear comes in so questionable a shape when it is to be considered as the evidence of guilt, that no credit ought to be given to it; and therefore, it is rejected.' As regards the admissibility of evidence relating to the finding of the property, which as shown was a s a result of inadmissible evidence, Nares J observed as follows:[157]

> This principle respecting confessions has no application whatever as to the admission or rejection of facts, whether the knowledge of them be obtained in consequence of an extorted confession, or whether it arises from some other source; for a fact, if it exists at all, must exist invariably in the same manner, whether the confession from which it is derived be in other respects true or false. Facts thus obtained, however, must be fully and satisfactorily proved, without calling in aid of any part of the confession from which they have been derived.

It is safe to conclude that the common rule notwithstanding, it was possible to link the accused to the stolen goods discovered in her bedroom without reference to her inadmissible confession. Put another way, since the decision on this point in *R v Warickshall,*[158] the law that facts that come to light as a result of inadmissible confessions is now settled. For example, in *R v Barker,*[159] in the course of investigating the defendant for tax fraud, he was interviewed by the Inland Revenue. Relying upon a standard statement by the Revenue, the appellant produced two ledgers which had been fraudulently prepared in order to induce the Revenue to believe that the irregularities amounted to only £7,000.00. The statement by the Revenue, which reflected a statement in Parliament, was partly a promise or an inducement and that it was not admissible on a charge of conspiring to cheat the Revenue by producing false statements of account. It was held, that 'those documents stand on precisely the

[156] (1783) 1 Leach 263; summary is adapted from summary at https://swarb.co.uk/rex-v-warickshall-1783/ retrieved on 18/12/21; see also *Chalmers v HM Advocate* 1954 SLT 177.

[157] (1783) 1 Leach 263 at 264.

[158] (1783) 1 Leach 263; summary is adapted from summary at https://swarb.co.uk/rex-v-warickshall-1783/ retrieved on 18/12/21; see also *Chalmers v HM Advocate* 1954 SLT 177.

[159] [1941] 2 KB 381, [1941] 3 All ER 33; *Cleland v R* (1982) 151 CLR 1 at 17.

same footing as an oral or written confession which is brought into existence as the result of such a promise, inducement or threat.'

In *R v Voisin*,[160] the [accused] stood charged with the murder of a woman, part of whose body was found in a parcel along with a handwritten note bearing the words 'Bladie Belgiam'. The defendant, who had not yet been cautioned, was asked by the police to write the words 'Bloody Belgian', which he did. He made exactly the same misspelling as had the writer of the note. The handwriting was admitted in evidence. It was held that the accused's appeal failed. It did not make any difference to the admissibility of the handwriting whether it was written voluntarily or under compulsion. Where it is alleged that a statement has been obtained in breach of the Judges' Rules, the court has a discretion to admit or reject such evidence. Lawrence J spoke of the Judges' Rules in the following terms:

> These Rules have not the force of law; they are administrative directions the observance of which the police authorities should enforce upon their subordinates as tending to the fair administration of justice. It is important that they should do so, for statements obtained from prisoners contrary to the spirit of these Rules may be rejected as evidence by the judge presiding at the trial.

The foregoing authorities are indeed the correct exposition of the law as we know it. Even so, the mere proof of facts as was the case in *R v Warickshall*,[161] *R v Barker*,[162] and *R v Voisin*,[163] considered above may not in and of itself be sufficient for the prosecution to prove its case against the accused in the absence of any reference to the accused's confession. By way of illustration, where an accused person confesses to having stolen a mobile phone, proof of its finding in a park without the accused having expressed knowledge of its whereabouts will be of little assistance unless the prosecution can show that it bore/bears his fingerprints. For the preceding reasons, efforts were made, as the following authorities demonstrate, as early as the 19th century to prove, at the very least, that part of the confession which the accused made was provable by the subsequent discovery of the facts thus connecting him to the offence with which he is charged.

In *R v Griffin*,[164] the accused made an inadmissible confession stating that he had stolen money from the prosecutor. Further, that he later handed the prosecutor a note the contents of were that said money was part of the property the accused had taken. It was held by the majority that the prosecution could

---

[160] [1918] 1 KB 531, [1918-19] All ER 491; this summary is taken from https://swarb.co.uk/rex-v-voisin-1918/ retrieved on 18/12/21.

[161] (1783) 1 Leach 263; summary is adapted from summary at https://swarb.co.uk/rex-v-warickshall-1783/ retrieved on 18/12/21; see also *Chalmers v HM Advocate* 1954 SLT 177.

[162] [1941] 2 KB 381, [1941] 3 All ER 33; *Cleland v R* (1982) 151 CLR 1 at 17.

[163] [1918] 1 KB 531, [1918-19] All ER 491; this summary is taken from https://swarb.co.uk/rex-v-voisin-1918/ retrieved on 18/12/21.

[164] (1809) Russ & Ry 151 (CCCR).

not only the production of the money in question but also the prisoner's statement that made reference to it.

In *R v Gould,*[165] the accused who had been charged with burglary made a statement to a policeman in circumstances that led the prosecution not to introduce it into evidence. Be that as it may, the accused's statement alluded to a lantern which was later found in a particular location. The policeman was subsequently asked whether based on the accused's statement, he searched for the said lantern. It seems certain that the location of the lantern by the policeman would have been irrelevant to the accused's guilt had the accused not stated that he had knowledge about its whereabouts.

Wigmore[166] has postulated as follows on this matter:

> [C]onfirmation on material points produces ample persuasion of the trustworthiness of the whole. It can hardly be supposed that at certain parts the possible fiction stopped and the truth began, and that by a marvellous coincidence the truthful parts are exactly those which a subsequent search (more or less controlled by chance) happened to confirm.

This view has been supported by Denman LJ whom, in *R v Garbett*[167] who took the view that the discovery of property as a direct result of an inadmissible confession inexorably ought to lead to justifies the reception of the accused's statement in its entirety. Erle J, however, took the traditional view in *R v Berriman*[168] that no part of the accused's otherwise inadmissible confession is rendered admissible by facts discovered in consequence of said inadmissible confession.[169] It seems patent from the preceding English authorities that,[170]

> The only statement that can confidently be made [...] is that facts discovered in consequence of inadmissible confessions may certainly be proved in evidence if their relevance can be established without resorting to any part of the confession, and the cases conflict so far as the admissibility of the part of the confession showing the accused's knowledge of those facts is concerned.[171]

In *Lam Chi-ming v R,*[172] the sister of the first and second appellants told them

[165] (1840) 9 Car & P 364.

[166] JH Wigmore, *Evidence in Trials at Common Law*, Chadburn rev, 1970, vol 3, [857].

[167] (1847) 2 Car & Kir 474 at 490.

[168] (1854) 6 Cox CC 388; *R v Beere* [1965] Qd R 370 at 372.

[169] See also *R v Barker* [1941] 2 KB 381 (CCA).

[170] JD Heydon *Cross on Evidence* at 998.

[171] 'It seems clear that, in Scotland, no part of an inadmissible confession can be received however much of it is confirmed: *Chalmers v HM Advocate* 1954 SC (J) 66 (FB). The same is now true in Canada: *R v Black* [1989] 2 SCR 138. Subsequent discovered facts, and parts of the confession which relate "distinctly" to them, were admissible under the Indian Evidence Act 1872 s 27 and the Ceylon Evidence Ordinance s 27: *R v Ramasamy* [1965] AC 1 (PC) and *Lam Chi-ming v R* [1991] 2 AC 212 (PC):' JD Heydon *Cross on Evidence* at 998 fn 337.

[172] [1991] 2 AC 212 (PC), [1991] 3 All ER 172, (1991) 93 Cr App R 358, [1991] 2 WLR 1082.

and the third appellant, who was her boyfriend, that she had been raped by the deceased on a number of occasions. Shortly afterwards, the deceased was found stabbed to death. The appellants were arrested for his murder. They all made confession statements to the police and the next day re-enacted the actions described in their statements. The re-enactment was video-taped with a sound track. The appellants then directed the police to the waterfront and each in turn pointed to the place where the knife which they said they had used to kill the deceased had been thrown into the sea. That episode was also video-taped with sound. A knife recovered at the place indicated by the appellants was later identified as the murder weapon. At their trial the appellants objected to the admission of both their statements and the video recordings on the grounds that they had been extracted by police brutality and were not voluntary and were therefore inadmissible. The judge ruled that the appellants' statements were inadmissible but he admitted in evidence the second video recording without sound in which the appellants had indicated the location of the murder weapon. Without that evidence there was nothing to link the appellants to the murder weapon. The appellants were convicted of murder. They applied for leave to appeal against their convictions on the ground that the second video recording should not have been admitted. The Court of Appeal of Hong Kong refused their applications and they appealed to the Privy Council. It was held as follows: the rule of law applicable in Hong Kong as well as England that a confession was not admissible in evidence unless the prosecution established that it had been obtained voluntarily was based not only on the possible unreliability of the statement but also on the principle that a man could not be compelled to incriminate himself and on the importance attached to proper behaviour by the police towards those in their custody. Accordingly, where a confession statement was not made voluntarily, the fact that part of the confession was later shown to be reliable by the discovery of the evidence to which it related was not sufficient to render the statement admissible. Accordingly, the evidence of the police and the silent video recording relating to the conduct of the appellants leading to the discovery of the murder weapon should not have been admitted since it was evidence of an inadmissible confession. The appeal would therefore be allowed.[173] Lord Griffiths said: -

> [...] the question raised by this appeal is whether that part of a confession which is shown to be reliable by the discovery of the evidence to which it relates may be given in evidence despite the fact that the admission may have been obtained by police brutality which renders inadmissible all other parts of the confession.' and held: 'the more recent English cases established that the rejection of an improperly obtained confession is not dependent only upon possible unreliability but also upon the principle that a man cannot be compelled to incriminate himself and upon the

[173] *Ng Wai-ming v R* [1980] HKLR 228 overruled; Editor's notes: For facts discovered as a result of inadmissible confessions, see 11(2) Halsbury's Laws (4th edn reissue) para 1130, and for cases on the subject, see 14(2) Digest (Reissue) 596, 4831–4840.

> importance that attaches in a civilised society to proper behaviour by the police towards those in their custody. But it is surely just as reprehensible to use improper means to force a man to give information that will reveal he has knowledge that will ensure his conviction as it is to force him to make a full confession. In either case a man is being forced into a course of action that will result in his conviction: he is being forced to incriminate himself. The privilege against self-incrimination is deep rooted in English law and it would make a grave inroad upon it if the police were to believe that if they improperly extracted admissions from an accused which were subsequently shown to be true they could use those admissions against the accused for the purpose of obtaining a conviction. Without this evidence there was nothing to link the defendants to the murder weapon and the prosecution do not seek to uphold the convictions in the absence of such evidence.

A last point to consider is the question of confessions and the concept of real evidence. A confession's value may not only be limited to it containing assertions of the guilt of the accused but may extend to the fact that it may lead to the identity of the accused as the culprit on the basis that the confession shows that he writes or speaks in a particular way. A leading authority is the Australian case of *Mclean v Cahill.*[174] The accused was charged with a gaming offence. Following this, he wrote out, without prior warning, a police officer dictated bail bond. The bail bond document was produced at trial by the prosecution for purposes of comparing the now known handwriting with another document implicated in the offence with which the accused was charged. On appeal against conviction on the ground of inadmissibility of the bail bond document, the court drew the conclusion that the document was rightly admitted into evidence [because it was of evidential value showing that the make of the confession wrote in a particular way]. In the court's view, this was a case similar to the scenario in *R v Voisin*[175] in which the handwriting was characterised as being tantamount to real evidence. Short of the evidence whose true importance is the specimen of the handwriting and not the contents of the document in question, being prejudicial, which again is left to the court to determine using its discretion, it is unlikely that any objection to its receipt would be sustained.

10.6 Evidence obtained as a result of illegal searches and other illegal acts

Our discussion as respects evidence obtained as a result of illegal searches and other illegal acts will be discussed under two heads, that is, (i) illegal searches; and (ii) Illegalities other than illegal searches. We discuss each in turn briefly.

10.6.1 Illegal searches

[174] [1932] SASR 359.

[175] [1918] 1 KB 531 (CCA) considered above.

There is a plethora of authorities[176] that suggest that evidence procured in consequence of an unlawful act or illegal search ought to be admissible.[177] In *Jones v Owen*,[178] the accused was searched illegally by constable and twenty-five young salmon found in his pocket. This evidence was held by Justices to be admissible upon a charge of unlawful fishing. On appeal to the Divisional Court of the Kings Bench Division, Mellor, J, said '[i]t would be a dangerous obstacle to the administration of justice if we were to hold, because evidence was obtained by illegal means, it could not be used against a party charged with an offence.'[179] In *Elias v Pasmore,*[180] in order to effect the arrest of H., the defendants, police officers, entered the plaintiffs' premises. While there they seized and carried away documents found on the premises, being (a) documents which were afterwards used on the trial, and (c) documents which did not constitute evidence on these trials. At the conclusion of the trials the documents under (a) and (b) were not returned; those under (c) were returned soon after seizure. It was held as follows: (i) that although the original seizure of the documents was unlawful it was excused as regards documents under (a) and (b), it being to the interest of the State that material evidence should be preserved. (ii) that the police have a right to search H. on his arrest, and also to seize any documents in his possession which would form material evidence against him or anybody else on a criminal charge. Any property so taken might be retained by the police until the conclusion of proceedings under any such charge. The police, having lawfully entered the premises to arrest H. did not by reason of the subsequent unlawful seizure of the documents under (c) become trespassers ab initio as to the land, but only as to the documents. What the authorities appear to suggest is not an automatic exclusion of evidence illegally seized or procured through an illegal act but rather that under such circumstances, the courts ought to consider a basis, if any, to exclude such evidence to guard against creating 'a dangerous obstacle to the administration of justice'[181] by taking the route of least resistance without any consideration and dismissing such evidence, out of hand. The foregoing is, however, not the same thing as saying that courts will admit evidence where its tender amounts to a crime, which courts will not do,[182] it is simply a consideration of evidence whose tender is not a criminal offence but whose extraction is done through illegal means.

Questions have arisen as to how privileged documents seized by a warrant which lacked the authority to seize such documents. The issue arose and was

[176] *Jones v Owen* (1870) 34 JP 759; *Elias v Pasmore* [1934] 2 KB 164; *R v Conley* (1979) 21 SASR 166 (CCA); *See v Milner* (1979) 25 ACTR 21; *Milner v Anderson* (1982) 42 ACTR 23.

[177] *Jones v Owen* (1870) 34 JP 759; *Elias v Pasmore* [1934] 2 KB 164; *R v Conley* (1979) 21 SASR 166 (CCA); *See v Milner* (1979) 25 ACTR 21; *Milner v Anderson* (1982) 42 ACTR 23.

[178] (1870) 34 JP 759 as cited and quoted in *Liswaniso v People* [1976] ZR 277.

[179] At 760, Lush J concurring.

[180] [1934] 2 KB 164.

[181] *Jones v Owen* (1870) 34 JP 759.

[182] *Thomas v Nash* (2010) 107 SASR 309.

considered in *Allitt v Sullivan.*[183] In May 2018, while investigating whether the Respondent had committed an unspecified offence, the Police obtained a search warrant in support of their investigation, authorising the search of a specified Gold Coast residency. The warrant extended to the search and seizure of the Respondents' mobile phone. Seizure in this context includes the ability of officers to obtain 'access information' as necessary to access the content of a seized item. Any refusal to comply with an officers' enforcement of a valid warrant constitutes an offence where such refusal is *'without reasonable excuse'.*[184] [In] the Magistrates Court Proceedings: [r]elevantly, in this case, the Respondent was asked to unlock his phone, pursuant to the authorising warrant. The Respondent refused to comply with the request and consequently was charged with an offence.[185] The Respondent claimed that he was regularly in contact with his solicitor through various texting apps and for this reason, had refused the police access to his phone. The Magistrates court, at first instance rejected this defence and found the respondent guilty of disobeying the Officers' lawful order. On appeal to the District Court: the District Court upheld the Respondents' appeal in recognising his entitlement to maintain privilege against the disclosure of certain information present on his phone, notwithstanding the fact that not all such information was of a privileged nature. Namely, the Court here considered the protection and maintenance of legal privilege to be a *reasonable excuse* for refusing the Officers' request to access his device. The conviction was set aside. In theSupreme Court of Victoria: The Police Commissioner subsequently applied for leave to appeal the District Courts' decision, suggesting that it had failed to account for the information on the device which did not attract legal privilege. It was argued that, in the absence of the Respondent demonstrating the applicability of legal privilege to all of the information on the device, the *dominant purpose*[186] test could not be satisfied and consequently, privilege could not be relied on. The court rejected the Officers' submission that legal privilege could not be relied on as a result of the Respondents' failure to meet the dominant purpose test.[187] This test, as established in *Esso Australia Resources Ltd v Federal Commissioner of Taxation,*[188] is specifically concerned with discerning whether legal privilege attaches, at first instance, to a particular piece of information. Accordingly, the court considered it irrelevant in light of the non-disputed finding that legal privilege had attached to some of the documents on the phone. In rejecting the Commissions submissions, the Court referenced the established nature of legal professional privilege being a rule of substantive law which may be relied on by persons to resist the giving of information or provision of documents that would reveal client – lawyer communications. Importantly, this right extends

[183] [1988] VR 621, as adapted in article at https://www.corneyandlind.com.au/criminal-law/legal-privilege-trumps-police-search-warrant/ retrieved on 28/12/21.

[184] Disobedience to a lawful order issued by statutory authority; Criminal Code 1899 (Qld) s205A.

[185] Criminal Code 1899 (Qld) s154(1).

[186] Emphasis added.

[187] *Esso Australia Resources Ltd v Federal Commissioner of Taxation* (1999) 201 CLR 49 [61].

[188] (1999) 201 CLR 49 at [61].

to the right to refuse to comply with a search warrant. The court proceeded to consider the question of *'reasonable excuse'* and whether, in this instance, the Respondents refusal to comply on the basis of the protection of his legal privilege would constitute a reasonable excuse and consequently absolve him of a criminal charge. Three factors were emphasised in this respect:

1. The term *'reasonable'* necessitates an objective consideration of the reasonableness of an excuse in question
2. In determining whether something is *reasonable,* both the surrounding circumstances of the case, and the statutory context wherein the word appears will be relevant
3. The asserted *reasonable excuse* need not be the only reason, but must be an actual reason behind the persons' withholding of access to information.

In application, the term *reasonable* was framed by its inclusion in the search warrant, through which, the Police were seeking to obtain evidence that may prove the commission of an offence by the Respondent. Accordingly, the police officers' exercise of search powers under the warrant in requesting the Respondents' access code demonstrated a clear and unmistakable intention to read the information contained on the phone. Importantly, it was interpreted by the court as an intention to read every document on the phone, without limitation despite the relevant existence of legal privilege over a number of solicitors – client correspondence. The court emphasised the purpose of the warrant in assessing whether the Respondent's legal privilege was a *reasonable excuse.* Namely, it was noted that the search warrant authorised a process which sought, and intended to reveal evidence which would implicate a person and could be subsequently relied on by the prosecution in obtaining a conviction. The information on the Respondents' phone, including correspondence between himself and his solicitor was the precise kind of evidence the officers were seeking despite its in inadmissible nature. The Respondents' refusal was found to be the only avenue open to him in protecting the confidentiality of the privileged information and accordingly the Court considered such refusal to be on the basis of a *reasonable excuse.* Notably however, the court emphasised the Officers' authority under the warrant, to validly seize the phone for the purposes of preserving evidence, despite the privileged information it contained. The appeal was dismissed.

To say, based on the foregoing decision in *Sullivan,*[189] that legal privilege would always trump a search warrant would be too optimistic and too wide a conclusion to draw. It is important to remember that what the court did in *Sullivan,*[190] even as it dismissed the appeal was to carefully draw a distinction between those circumstances which involve the authorised seizure of a contraption and those relating to the examination the contraption in question. Therefore, nowhere was the court saying that legal privilege would prevent a police officer seised with a matter from seizing any item in circumstances in which there was no question of delay in handing over the said item to a

[189] [1988] VR 621.

[190] [1988] VR 621.

judicial officer.[191] What was of concern in this particular matter was the real and present danger of the police reading privileged material. Nor can it be said that *Sullivan,*[192] would be a basis for exercising discretion to exclude, in this case,privileged material. There is a logical argument to be made in this respect which ought not to be taken as a contradiction in terms. The operation of the discretion such as we have discussed at length in this chapter and elsewhere in this text in general and with specific reference to privileged material is predicated on a perception that the otherwise illegal or wrongful act or acts were not only wilful and egregious but were such that they warranted criminal sanctions. Various authorities[193] have thus shown that where a genuine mistake is made, and one that is neither wilful nor egregious, the evidence obtained as a result will still be admissible.

Sullivan[194] then is authority for the position that legal privilege within the justice system is fundamental. It also shows that courts will go to great lengths to ensure its observance even if that means destroying the prosecution's case and, in some cases, the staying of criminal proceedings.[195]

10.6.2 *Illegalities other than illegal searches*

The issue of illegalities other than illegal searches suffers even more from the dearth of authority than that relating to illegal searches considered above. The starting point for the position of the law in this regard is generally said to be Crompton J's robust dictum in *R v Leatham:*[196] '[i]t matters not how you get it; if you steal it even, it would be admissible.' This position was supported byLord Goddard in *Kuruma Son of Kaniu v R:*[197]

> In their Lordships' opinion the test to be applied in considering whether evidence is admissible is whether it is relevant to the matters in issue. If it is, it is admissible and the court is not concerned with how the evidence was obtained. While this proposition may not have been stated in so many words in any English case there are decisions which support it, and in their Lordships' opinion it is plainly right in principle.[198]

Crompton J's dictum should be taken to be of general application but one that is subject to justifiable exceptions. It will not apply, for example, in instances where a party to the proceedings steals documents from another party in the

[191] *Allitt v Sullivan* [1988] VR 621.

[192] [1988] VR 621.

[193] *Zanet v Hentschke* (1988) 33 A Crim R 51 (SA SC); *Roswell v Larter* (1986) 6 NSWLR 21; but see *R v Mcleod* [1991] Tas R 144.

[194] [1988] VR 621.

[195] *R v Leach* [2019] 1 QD R 459.

[196] (1861) 8 Cox CC 498 at 501.

[197] [1955] 1 All ER 236.

[198] See *R v Leatham* [1961] 8 Cox CC 498.

same proceedings or surreptitiously obtains such documents furtively or/and by deceit.[199]

10.7 Evidence obtained improperly though not illegally

The approach taken by courts at least in commonwealth/common law jurisdictions such as Australia with respect to evidence obtained improperly though not illegally is similar to that taken with respect to evidence obtained in contravention of a statutory requirement.[200] What appears to be best practice has been to employ the test of whether the confession now impugned was one extracted in breach of the accused's right of choice as to whether to speak or not. Thus, the Australian High Court in *R v Swaffield*[201] has by majority '[...] upheld a discretionary decision to exclude admissions elicited by an undercover police officer, but also upheld a discretionary decision not to exclude the reception of admissions made to a friend of the suspect equipped by the police with a recording device on the basis that they were "volunteered" – "made in the course of the conversation" – rather than being "elicited" by "interrogation."'[202]

10.8 Evidence obtained by means of agents provocateurs

The use of undercover agents by the police in order to uncover perpetrators of crimes is commonplace and part of the *modus oparandi*, and when done within the confines of the law, an acceptable means of extracting evidence from suspects. Be that as it may, the system is prone to abuse and, on some levels, may be considered unethical as it is predicated on deceit for the undercover agent to gain and maintain the confidence of the suspect. Though as we have seen elsewhere in this text, the United States recognises the defence of entrapment,[203] English law has rejected an outright acceptance of the concept

---

[199] *ITC Film Distributors v Video Exchange Ltd* [1982] Ch 431; but see *R v Tompkins* (1977) 67 Cr App R 181; *Baker v Campbell* (1983) 153 CLR 52 at 66-7; *Roswell v Larter* (1986) 6 NSWLR 21; *Director of Public Prosecutions Reference (No 1 of 1984)* [1984] VR 727 at 732 (FC); *Bercove v Hermes* (No 3) (1983) 51 ALR 109 (Fed C of A); *R v Stead* [1994] 1 Qd R 665 (CA); *R v D 'Arrigo* [1994] 1 Qd R 603 (CA); for use of discretion in matters relating to privilege see: *Hammond v Commonwealth* (1982) 152 CLR 188; *R v McDonald* (1983) 50 ALR 471 at 483; *R v Clyne* (1985) 2 NSWLR 740 (CCA).

[200] See *R v Ireland* (1970) 126 CLR 321; *Callis v Gunn* [1964] 1 QB 495 (DC or QBD); *R v Masquid Ali* [1966] 1 QB 688 at 702 (CCA); *Sneddon v Stevenson* [1967] 2 All ER 1277 (DC of QBD); see *Bunning v Cross* (1978) 141 CLR 54 at 75; *R v Pfenning (No 1)* (1992) 57 SASR 507; *R v Smith, Turner & Altintas* (1994) 63 SASR 123; *R v Giaccio* (1997) 68 SASR 484 at 497-8 (CCA); see also *R v Geesing* (1985) 38 SASR 226 (CCA); *cf. R v O'Neill* [1996] 2 Qd R 326 *(CA)*; *R v Davidson; Ex parte A-G* [1996] 2 Qd R 505 (CA); On decisions to exclude evidence based on the accused's loss of the right to silence by trickery, see *R v Swaffield* (1998) 192 CLR 159 (preferring the dissenting approach in *R v O'Neill* [1996] 2 Qd R 326 *(CA)*; and *R v Davidson; Ex parte A-G* [1996] 2 Qd R 505 (CA); *R v Hebert* [1990] 2 SCR 151; *R v Broyles* [1991] 3 SCR 595; *R v Davidson* (1996) 92 A Crim R 1 (QCA).

[201] [1998] HCA 1; 192 CLR 159; 151 ALR 98; 72 ALJR 339.

[202] As summarised in Heydon JD *Cross on Evidence* 1002; see also *R v Cavalli* (2010) 206 A Crim R 306; *Robinett v Police* (2000) 78 SASR 85.

[203] *Sorrells v US* 287 U.S. 435 (1932); *US v Russell*, 411 U.S. 423 (1973); *Jacobson v US*, 503 U.S. 540.

of entrapment as a defence. Thus, in *R v Sang*,[204] the House of Lords took the view that the court has no general discretion to exclude evidence where the accused has been, among other things, incited, tricked or otherwise procured to commit a crime.[205]

[204] [1980] AC 402; but for the possibility of exclusion under s 78 of PACE 1984, see *Nottingham City Council v Amin* [2000] 2 All ER 946 (DC or QBD); *R v Loosely* [2001] 4 All ER 897 at [54] – [56] (HL).

[205] For an Australian take on the issue see the leading case of *Ridgeway v R* (1995) 184 CLR 19 at 35-6, 37 50 and 64; but see legislative changes that have affected this leading authority in Heydon JD *Cross on Evidence* 1005 n 381.

SELECT BIBLIOGRAPHY

Anderson T, Schum D and Twining W, *Analysis of Evidence* (2nd edn CUP, 2005)

Ashworth, A. and Blake, M. 'The presumption of innocence in English criminal law' [1998] Crim LR 306

Baki, N. and Agate, J. 'Too much, too little, too late? Draft CPS guidance on speaking to witnesses' [2015] Ent LR 155

Bennion, F. 'Statutory exceptions: a third knot in the golden thread' [1988] Crim LR 31

Birch, D. 'A better deal for vulnerable witnesses?' [2000] Crim LR 223

Birch, D. 'Children's evidence' [1992] Crim LR 262

Birch, D. 'Corroboration: Goodbye to All That?' [1995] Crim LR 524

Birch, D. 'Criminal Justice Act 2003: (4) Hearsay – same old story, same old song?' (2004) Crim LR, Jul, 556–573

Birch, D. 'Hunting the snark: the elusive statutory exception' [1988] Crim LR 221

Blom-Cooper QC, Sir L. 'Witness immunity: the argument against' (2006) 156 (7232) NLJ 1088–1089

Brabyn, J. 'A criminal defendant's spouse as a prosecution witness' [2011] Criminal Law Review 613

Branston, G. 'A reprehensible use of cautions as bad character evidence' [2015] Crim LR 594

Brennan, G. 'Sexual history evidence: The Youth Justice and Criminal Evidence Act 1999' (2002) 8 Queen Mary Law Journal 7

Brevis, B., Jackson, A. and Stockdale, M. 'Bad character evidence and potential satellite litigation' [2013] J Crim L 110

Brewis, B. and Stockdale, M. 'False allegations: the limitations of the "evidential basis" test' [2014] J Crim L 453

Bridge, C. 'Care Proceedings: burden of proof' [2012] Family Law 1074

Brown, S. 'Public interest immunity' (1994) PL, Win, 579–595

Buxton, R. 'Victims as witnesses in trials of sexual offences: towards equality of arms' [2015] Crim LR 679

Chippindall, A. 'Expert advice and legal professional privilege' (2003) JPI Law, Jan, 61–70

Chippindall, A.C. 'Expert evidence and legal professional privilege' (2003) JPI Law, Jan, 61–70

Choo, A. L. T. and Nash, S. 'Evidence law in England and Wales: the impact of the Human Rights Act 1998' (2003) 7(1) International Journal of Evidence and Proof 31–61

Civil Procedure Rules 1998: www.justice.gov.uk/courts/procedure-rules/civil/rules/part01

Coe, P. 'Justifying reverse burdens of proof: a tale of diminished responsibility and a tangled knot of authorities' [2013] J Crim L 360

Cooper, D. 'Pigot unfulfi lled: video recorded evidence under section 28 of the YJCEA 1999' [2005] Crim LR 456

Cooper, P., Backen, P., and Marchant, R. 'Getting to grips with ground rules hearings: a checklist for judges, advocates and intermediaries to promote the fair treatment of vulnerable people in court' [2015] Crim LR 420

Cornish, W.R. and Sealy, A.P. 'Juries and the rules of evidence' [1973] Crim LR 208

Creaton, J. 'Competence to give evidence' [2007] Police Journal 356

Creighton, P. 'Spouse competence and compellability' [1990] Crim LR 34

Daniele, M. 'Testimony through a live link in the perspective of the right to confront witnesses' [2014] Crim LR 189

Dein, A. 'Police misconduct revisited' [2000] Crim LR 801

Dennis, I. 'Reverse onuses and the presumption of innocence: in search of principle' [2005] Crim

LR 901
Dennis, I. 'Sexual history evidence: evaluating Section 41' [2006] Crim LR 869
Dennis I, *The Law of Evidence* (5th edn Sweet & Maxwell, 2013)
Dingwall, G. 'Statutory exceptions, burdens of proof and the Human Rights Act 1998' (2002) 65 MLR 450
Doak, J. and Huxley-Binns, R. 'Anonymous witnesses in England and Wales: charting a course from Strasbourg?' [2009] 73(6) 508
Douglas, G. 'Care Proceedings: medical evidence – burden and standard of proof' [2012] Family Law 936
Durston, G. 'Previous (in)consistent statements after the Criminal Justice Act 2003' [2005] Crim LR 206
Ellison, L. 'Cross-examination in rape trials' [1998] Crim LR 605
Ettinger, C. 'Case comment' (2005) JPI Law 3, C114–117
European Convention on Human Rights: www.echr.coe.int/Documents/Convention_ENG.pdf
Federal Rules of Evidence (2015) rules 801-807 at https://www.rulesofevidence.org/article-viii/ (accessed 1 July 2015)
Fitzpatrick, B. 'Reverse burden and Art 6(2) of the European Convention on Human Rights: official secrets' [2008] J Crim L 190
Gallanis, T.P. 'The rise of modern evidence law' (1999) 84 Iowa L Rev 499
Gillespie, A. 'Compellability of a child victim' (2000) (64)1 J Crim L 98
Gillespie, A. and Bettinson, V. 'Preventing secondary victimisation through anonymity' [2007] 70 MLR 114
Gooderham, P. 'Witness immunity: the argument in favour' (2006) 156 (7232), NLJ 1086–1087
Government Actuary's Department. Compensation for injury and death (Ogden tables): http://www.gad.gov.uk/services/Other%20Services/Compensation_for_injury_and_death.html
Hamer, D. 'Presumptions, standards and burdens: managing the cost of error' [2014] LP&R 221
Hamer, D. 'The presumption of innocence and reverse burdens: a balancing act' (2007) 66 CLJ 142
Hartshorne, J. 'Corroboration and care warnings after Makanjuola' (1998) 2 E & P (1) 1–12
Healey, P. 'Proof and policy: no golden threads' [1987] Crim LR 355
Henderson, E (2014) All the proper protections—the Court of Appeal rewrites the rules for the cross-examination of vulnerable witnesses. Crim LR 93–108.
Henderson, E. 'Bigger fish to fry: should the reform of cross-examination be expanded beyond vulnerable witnesses?' [2015] E&P 83
Henderson, E. 'Communicative competence? Judges, advocates and intermediaries discuss communication issues in the cross-examination of vulnerable witnesses' [2015] Crim LR 659
Henderson, E. 'Root or branch? Reforming the cross-examination of children' [2010] CLJ 460
Heydon JD, *Cross on Evidence* (10th edn Lexis Nexis, 2016)
Hjalmarsson, J. 'The standard of proof in civil cases: an insurance fraud perspective' [2013] E&P 47
Ho, H. 'Similar facts in civil cases' (2006) 26 Oxford Journal of Legal Studies 131
Hoffmann, L. 'Similar facts after Boardman' (1975) 91 LQR 193
Hoyano, L. 'Coroners and Justice Act 2009: special measures directions take two: entrenching unequal access to justice' [2010] Criminal Law Review 345
Hoyano, L. 'Reforming the adversarial trial for vulnerable witnesses and defendants' [2015] Crim LR 107
Hoyano, L. 'Striking a balance between the rights of defendants and vulnerable witnesses: will special measures directions contravene guarantees of a fair trial?' [2001] Crim LR 948
Hoyano, L. 'Variations on a theme by Pigot: special measures directions for child witnesses' [2000] Crim LR 250
Hoyano, L. 'Vulnerable witnesses: manner of cross-examination – witnesses young, female complainants' [2012] Crim LR 565
Jackson, J. 'Insufficiency of identification evidence based on personal impression' [1986] Crim

LR 203

Jackson, J.D. 'The ultimate issue rule – one rule too many' [1984] Crim LR 75

James, J. 'Good character directions and blemished defendants' [1996] 2 Web JCLI

Jones, D. 'The evidence of a three-year-old child' [1987] Crim LR 677

Jones, I. 'A problem of the past? The politics of "relevance" in evidential reform' [2012] Contemporary Issues of Law 277

Justice website – Achieving Best Evidencewww.cps.gov.uk/publications/docs/best_evidence_in_criminal_proceedings.pdf

Kaluba BC, *Evidence Law: Practice and Procedure in Zambia* (Chribwa Publishers, 2022)

Keane, A. 'The collateral evidence rule: a sad forensic fable involving a circus, its sideshow, confusion, vanishing tricks and alchemy' [2015] E&P 100

Keane, A. 'Towards a principled approach to cross-examination of vulnerable witnesses' [2012] Crim LR 407

Keane, A. and Fortson, R. 'Leading questions – a critical analysis' [2011] Crim LR 280

Keane, A. and McKeown, P. (2012) The Modern Law of Evidence. Ninth edition.Oxford: Oxford University Press

Kibble, N. 'Judicial discretion and the admissibility of prior sexual history evidence' [2005] Crim LR 263

Kibble, N. 'Judicial perspectives on the operation of Section 41' [2005] Crim LR 190

Kibble, N. 'Sexual offences: whether a rape complainant's false complaint "misconduct" is the result of personality problems?' [2011] Crim LR 818

Law Commission (1997) Evidence in Criminal Proceedings: Hearsay and Related Topics, Law Com No 245

Law Commission Report, Law Com No 273 (2001) 'Evidence in criminal proceedings: previous misconduct of a defendant'

Lewis, P. 'The Human Rights Act 1998: shifting the burden' [2000] Crim LR 667

Lippke, R. 'Justifying the proof structure of criminal trials' [2013] E&P 323

Lloyd Bostock, S. 'The effects on juries of hearing about the defendant's previous criminal record: a simulation study' [2000] Crim LR 734

Mackie, J. 'A question of character' [2012] SJ 156(6), 7

Malek HM (Ed), *Phipson on Evidence* (16th edn Sweet & Maxwell, 2016)

Matibini, P (2017) Zambian Civil Procedure. London: Lexis Nexis

May, R and Powles, S. (2004) Criminal Evidence. Fifth edition. London: Sweet & Maxwell

Mirfi eld, P. (1998) Silence, Confessions and Improperly Obtained Evidence, Oxford Monographs on Criminal Law and Justice, Oxford University Press

Mirfi eld, P. 'Corroboration after the 1994 Act' [1995] Crim LR 448

Mirfield, P. 'Bad character and the Law Commission' (2002) 6 E&P 141

Mirfield, P. 'Character and credibility' [2009] Crim LR 135

Mirfield, P. 'Character, credibility and truthfulness' [2008] LQR 1

Mirfield, P. 'Human wrongs?' (2002) 118 LQR 20

Mirfield, P. 'The legacy of Hunt' [1988] Crim LR 19

Monaghan, N. 'Reconceptualising good character' [2015] E&P 190

Munday, R. (2011) The Law of Evidence. Sixth edition. Oxford: Oxford University Press

Munday, R. 'Adverse denial and purposive confession' (2003) Crim LR, Dec, 850–864

Munday, R. 'Athwal and all that: previous statements, narratives and the taxonomy of hearsay' (2010) 74 Crim JC L 415

Munday, R. 'Calling a hostile witness' [1989] Crim LR 866

Munday, R. 'Case management, similar fact evidence in civil cases, and a divided law of evidence' (2006) 10 International Journal of Evidence and Proof 81

Munday, R. 'Convicting on confessional evidence in the complete absence of a corpus delicti' (1993) 157 JPJo 275

Munday, R. 'Cut-throat defences and the "propensity to be untruthful" under Section 104 of the Criminal Justice Act 2003' [2005] Crim LR 624

Munday, R. 'Misconduct that "has to do with the alleged facts of the offence with which the defendant is charged" . . . more or less' [2008] Crim L 214
Munday, R. 'Refreshing memory: previous statements that fail to revive witnesses' memories' [2012] CL&J 213
Munday, R. 'Sham marriages and spousal compellability' [2001] 65(4) J Crim L 336
Munday, R. 'Single-act propensity' [2010] J Crim L 128
Munday, R. 'The purposes of Gateway (g)' [2006] Crim LR 300
Munday, R. 'What constitutes "other reprehensible behaviour" under the bad character provisions of the Criminal Justice Act 2003?' [2005] Crim LR 24
Munday, R. 'What constitutes a good character?' [1997] Crim LR 247
Murphy P, *Murphy on Evidence* (12th edn OUP, 2005)
Mwanza BJ, *Passing The Bar Made Easy: Evidence and Procedure* (Brian J Mwanza, 2020).
Ormerod, D. 'Case Comment Evidence: hearsay - Criminal Justice Act 2003 s.116 - D C... Ali v Revenue and Customs Prosecutions Office [2008] EWCA Crim 1466.
Ormerod, D. 'Evidence: previous inconsistent statements – admissibility' [2007] Crim LR 887
Ormerod, D. 'Hostile witness maintaining contents of prior statement not true' [2009] Crim LR 197
Ormerod, D. 'Previous inconsistent statements: directing juries in relation to
Ormerod, D. 'R v Athwal: evidence – hearsay – previous consistent statement –admissibility – rebutting fabrication' [2009] Crim LR 726
Ormerod, D. 'Sounds familiar? Voice identifi cation evidence' [2001] Crim LR 595
Ormerod, D. and Birch, D. 'The evolution of the discretionary exclusion of evidence' [2004] Crim LR 767
Ormerod, D., Choo, A. and Easter, R. 'Coroners and Justice Act 2009: the witness anonymity and investigation anonymity provisions' [2010] Criminal Law Review 368
PACE 1984 Codes of Practice: www.homeoffi ce.gov.uk/police/powers/pace-codes
Padfield, N. 'The burden of proof unresolved' (2005) 64 CLJ 17
Pattenden, R. 'Evidence of previous malpractice by police witnesses and R v Edwards' [1992] Crim LR 549
Pattenden, R. 'The hostile witness' (1992) 56 J C L 414
Pattenden, R. 'The submission of no case – some recent developments' [1982] Crim LR 558
Picinali, F. 'The threshold lies in the method: instructing jurors about reasoning beyond reasonable doubt' [2015] E&P 139
Practice Direction 33 – Civil Evidence Act 1995 and Part 33 of the Civil Procedure Rules (Miscellaneous Rules About Evidence): http://www.justice.gov.uk/courts/procedure-rules/civil/rules/part33).
previous inconsistent statements in view of effect and application of s 119 of the Criminal Justice Act 2003' [2009] Crim LR 529
R v Delaney (1989) 88 Cr App R 338 – 'Case comment: evidence and the admissibility of a confession' (1989) Crim LR, Feb, 139–140
R v Goldenberg (1989) 88 Cr App R 285 – 'Case comment: admissions and confessions: words or acts of person making confession not included in matters affecting reliability'(1988) Crim LR, Oct, 678–679
Ragavan, S. 'The compellability rule in England and Wales: support for the spouse of the defendant' [2013] J Crim L 310
Redmayne, M. 'Recognising propensity' [2011] Crim LR 117
Redmayne, M. 'Rethinking the privilege against self-incrimination' (2007) 27(2) OJLS 209–232
Redmayne, M. 'The relevance of bad character' (2002) CLJ 684
Reforming the European Convention on Human Rights: Interlaken, Izmir, Brighton and beyond: http://www.coe.int/t/dghl/standardsetting/cddh/reformechr/Publications/Compilation%20ReformECHR2014_en.pdf
Roberts, A. 'Evidence – non-defendant's bad character' [2011] Crim LR 58
Roberts, A. 'Evidence: bad character of defendant – attack on prosecution witness – Criminal

Justice Act 2003 s 101(1)(g) – test for admissibility' [2011] Crim LR 642
Roberts, P. 'Modernising police powers – again?' (2007) Crim LR, Dec, 934–948
Roberts, P. 'Taking the burden of proof seriously' [1995] Crim LR 783
Roberts, P. 'The presumption of innocence brought home/Kebilene deconstructed' (2002) 118 LQR 41
rules for the cross-examination of vulnerable witnesses' [2014] Crim LR 93
Rogers WVM, *Winfield & Jolowicz Tort* (18th edn Sweet & Maxwell, 2010).
Seabrooke, S. 'Current topic: the vanishing trick – blurring the line between credit and issue' [1999] Crim LR 387
Singh C and Ramjohn M, *Unlocking Evidence* (3rd edn Routledge, 2016).
Singh C, *Evidence: Question and Answers 2015–2016* (11th edn Routledge, 2015)
Singh, C. (2015). Quis custodiet ipsos custodies? Should Justice Beware: a review of the debate surrounding the reliability of voice identification evidence in light of advances in biometric voice identification technology. International Commentary on Evidence. Volume 11: 1–28. Germany and the USA: De Grutyer.
Smaller, E. 'Giving the vulnerable a voice' [2012] Counsel 25
Smith, E, and Stockdale, M. 'Bad character evidence as evidence of identity' [2015] J Crim L 12
Smith, J.C. 'The presumption of innocence' (1987) 38 NILQ 223
Spencer, J. 'Cautions as character evidence: a reply to Judge Branston' [2015] Crim LR 611
Spencer, J. 'Evidence of bad character – where we are today' [2014] Arch Rev 5
Spencer, J. 'Rape shields and the right to a fair trial' [2001] Cambridge Law Journal 452
Stapleton, J. 'Factual causation of mesothelioma and statistical validity' [2012] LQR 221
Stone, J. 'The rule of exclusion of similar fact evidence: England' (1932) 46 Harvard LR 954
Tapper C, *Cross & Tapper on Evidence* (11th edn, 2007)
Tapper, C. 'The Criminal Evidence Act 2003: evidence of bad character' [2004] Crim LR 533
Tavros, V. and Tierney, S. 'Presumption of innocence and the Human Rights Act' (2004) 67 MLR 402
The Crown Prosecution Service Website provides a useful summary of the law on hearsay at: www.cps.gov.uk/legal/h_to_k/hearsay/ (accessed 17 December 2012)
Twining W, *Rethinking Evidence: Exploratory Essays* (NUP, 1994)
Uglow S, *Evidence: Cases and Materials* (2nd edn Sweet & Maxwell, 1997)
Walchover, D. and Heaton-Armstrong, A. 'Reasonable doubt' (2010) 174 Criminal Law and Justice Weekly 484
Waterman, A. and Dempster, T. 'Bad character: feeling our way one year on' [2006] Crim LR 614
Williams, G. 'Evidential burdens on the defence' (1977) 127 NLJ 182
Williams, G. 'The evidential burden: some common misapprehensions' (1977) 127 NLJ 156
Worthern, T. 'Legislative comment: the hearsay provisions of the Criminal Justice Act 2003: so far, not so good?' (2008) 6 Crim LR 431–442
Wurtzel, D. 'The youngest witness in a murder trial: making it possible for very young children to give evidence' [2014] Crim LR 893
Zuckerman, A. 'The third exception to the Woolmington Rule' (1976) 92 LQR 402

INDEX

D

E

L

M

O

P

R